CENTURY 21
Accounting

CENTURY 21
Accounting

FIRST-YEAR COURSE

SIXTH EDITION

Kenton E. Ross, CPA
Professor of Accounting
East Texas State University
Commerce, Texas

Robert D. Hanson
Associate Dean
College of Business Administration
Central Michigan University
Mount Pleasant, Michigan

Claudia Bienias Gilbertson, CPA
Teaching Professor
Anoka-Ramsey Community College
Coon Rapids, Minnesota

Mark W. Lehman, CPA
Instructor
School of Accountancy
Mississippi State University
Starkville, Mississippi

Robert M. Swanson
Professor Emeritus of Business Education
and Office Administration
Ball State University
Muncie, Indiana

South-Western Publishing Co.
BA20FA

Vice-President/Editor-in-Chief: Dennis M. Kokoruda
Senior Developmental Editor: Carol Volz
Art Director: John Robb
Design Coordinator: Darren Wright
Marketing Manager: Larry Qualls
Coordinating Editor: Mark Beck
Production Manager: Carol Sturzenberger
Senior Production Editor: Mark Cheatham
Production Editor: Kimberlee Kusnerak
Production Editor I: Denise Wheeler
Associate Director/Photo Editing: Devore Nixon
Photo Editor: Kimberly A. Larson

Cover Design: The Optimum Group
Internal Design: Lesiak/Crampton Design

Preface

This preface is addressed primarily to the student. A complete examination guide for the CENTURY 21 ACCOUNTING, First-Year Course, learning package is included in the wraparound teacher's edition of this text.

This first-year accounting text will give you a thorough background in the basic accounting procedures used to operate a business. The accounting procedures presented will also serve as a sound background for employment in office jobs and preparation for studying business courses in college. Because the complete accounting cycle is covered, it is easy to see how each employee's job fits into the cycle for a business, an important qualification to employers. After this textbook is mastered, an advanced, or second-year, text is also available for learning more complex accounting concepts.

How to Use This Text

This textbook is carefully designed to function as a learning tool. The overall organization is in five parts, with one or more chapters in each part. Parts 1 and 5 are special parts that have only one chapter each. Parts 2, 3, and 4 each consist of several chapters that present a complete accounting cycle. For each part, a business is identified and described and that business is used to illustrate all the concepts for the rest of that part. In addition, each of these parts begins with a chart of accounts that is used throughout the part; it is an excellent preview for the part and serves as a convenient reference as you study each chapter.

Each chapter begins with a set of enabling performance tasks, or learning objectives, that describe what you will be able to do after studying the chapter. The task statements preview the chapter. A list of new terms that are defined and used within the chapter is also printed at the start of the chapter. Begin your study of each chapter with reading the enabling performance tasks and new accounting terms.

Each chapter has a number of headings that should be previewed to help understand the chapter. These headings can also function as a topical outline for a chapter if your studying method includes taking notes in outline format. Abundant illustrations highlight concepts in the chapter narrative. Note that each illustration has both an illustration number that is referenced within the narrative of the chapter and a descriptive caption that describes what is being illustrated. A summary illustration at the end of each chapter ties the main points of the chapter together in graphic terms. All new accounting vocabulary terms are printed in bold type within the sentence that defines the term so these definitions can be easily found.

Special Features

The following special features appear throughout the textbook:

Multicultural Awareness: This feature describes the contributions of a variety of cultures to accounting and business. Some of these features focus on historical contributions while others describe a situation in the United States today. This feature will help strengthen your awareness of the value of diversity in the work force and society.

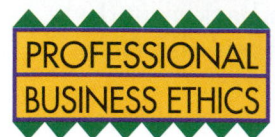

Professional Business Ethics: The news media are full of stories about unethical behavior in business and the effect of this unethical behavior on businesses and individuals. Boxed features throughout the text present ethical dilemmas that employees and business owners encounter in real life. Chapter 1 discusses ethical behavior in general and presents a 3-step checklist as a model for analyzing ethical decisions.

Global Perspective: Global business topics provide information and activities to enhance preparation for working in the global economy. These topics provide practical real-life information about trading across national boundaries and furnish activities to demonstrate how this information is applied.

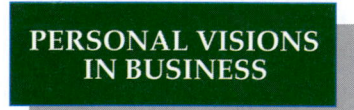

Personal Visions in Business: These personality profiles describe individuals in the business world today from a variety of occupations and cultural backgrounds. The individuals portrayed describe how an accounting background can be useful when starting and maintaining your own business and what they have learned about business from their own experiences.

Careers in Accounting: This feature presents a list of job duties for different job titles. This feature can help you select the kinds of jobs you might want to pursue based on the responsibilities of each job.

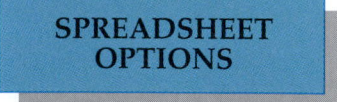

Spreadsheet Options: Features of spreadsheet software can help streamline business practices. The Spreadsheet Options feature describes some of the techniques used by businesses to make their financial reporting and analysis more efficient.

Applied Mathematics: If accounting is the language of business, then numbers are probably the words of the language. Many different mathematical calculations are involved in accounting for a business. Within a chapter, each time a new mathematical calculation is presented, the formula is highlighted by a color box and the Applied Math Icon appears beside it. The Applied Math Icon is repeated next to end-of-chapter activities that first apply each calculation.

Audit Your Understanding Questions: At the end of each short section of a chapter, a list of questions are given for assessing your grasp of the concepts covered. Self-check answers are provided in Appendix D.

FYI ("For Your Information"): Boxes in the margins emphasize important points from the chapter and sometimes present additional interesting information about accounting and business.

End-of-Chapter Activities

The end of each chapter provides questions, cases, drills, and problems for practicing the new skills learned in the chapter and demonstrating your grasp of the concepts. Each section identifies the enabling performance tasks to be performed. The identifying letters of the tasks are placed in parentheses next to the heading of each activity.

The first section at the end of each chapter presents a list of all the new accounting terms defined in the chapter. You should be sure you know the meaning of each of these terms. This activity is followed by questions that help you review the concepts in the chapter. The next section, called Cases for Critical Thinking, describes case scenarios based on chapter concepts for which you are required to stretch your knowledge to provide the best answer or select the best alternative from those presented. Frequent Applied Communications sections furnish opportunities for honing your communication skills in the context of topics that are related to accounting.

The remaining end-of-chapter activities are drills and problems. The drills require you to analyze procedures from the chapter in a short-answer format. Application Problems apply your new accounting skills as you complete a problem for each section of the chapter. The Mastery Problem is a further application of all the new skills from the chapter in one single problem. The Challenge Problem concludes the chapter by stretching your knowledge to cover new applications. A Recycling Problem is available at the end of the textbook, in Appendix C, to use for additional practice or review. Reinforcement Activities and simulations for each of the three accounting cycles are milestone activities that synthesize all the activities from the chapters in the part.

Software

There are four pieces of software that may be used to complete end-of-chapter activities. Each piece of software is represented by an icon. These icons are placed on the appropriate drills and problems that may be completed using the computer.

Automated Accounting: This icon identifies a problem that is appropriate for solving using the *Automated Accounting 6.0* or higher software. A template for this problem is available that contains the chart of accounts and opening balances for selected problems.

Application Program: This icon identifies a problem that is available on the Application Program Disk software.

Accounting Tutorial: This icon identifies a section for which learning can be enhanced using the Accounting Tutorial software.

Spreadsheet Template: This icon identifies a problem for which a template file is available that can be used with commercial spreadsheet software for solving the problem.

All problems that are identified as being appropriate for solving with the use of software can also be completed manually with pencil and paper.

Reference Material

Reference material at the end of the book includes four appendices, a glossary of terms, and an index. Appendix A briefly describes each of the major accounting concepts described in more detail within the text narrative. Appendix B includes information about using a 10-key calculator and computer keypad. Appendix C presents a recycling problem for each chapter in the textbook for additional practice, or review. Appendix D provides the answers to the Audit Your Understanding questions in each chapter so that the questions can be used for self-review. The glossary of terms lists all the terms defined in the text and their definitions for easy reference. The index shows the page location for each topic in the text. This can be useful if you need to look up a topic but do not know where to find it.

ACKNOWLEDGMENTS

We thank the following individuals who contributed to the review process for this edition:

Mrs. Pam Caldwell
Godwin High School
Richmond, Virginia

Ms. Carolyn Francis
Robert E. Lee High School
Baytown, Texas

Mr. Neil Yeager
Cordova High School
Rancho Cordova, California

Dr. Arvella Jones
Commerce High School
Commerce, Texas

Mr. Robert Greer
John Jay High School
San Antonio, Texas

Dr. De Lois Gibson
Cass Technical High School
Detroit, Michigan

Mr. Peter Eisen
Murry Bergtraum High School
New York, New York

Mrs. Linda Songer
Orange Park High School
Orange Park, Florida

Mr. Joe McFarland
Shasta High School
Redding, California

We also appreciate the ongoing feedback provided by the classroom professionals who use CENTURY 21 ACCOUNTING every day.

Contents

PART 3

Accounting for a Merchandising Business Organized as a Partnership

PART 4

Accounting for a Merchandising Business Organized as a Corporation

PART 5

The Legal Environment of Business

PHOTO CREDITS

## PART 1

Accounting as a Career

GENERAL GOALS

1. Know accounting terminology related to accounting careers.

2. Understand entry-level positions, educational requirements, and career opportunities in accounting.

3. Understand that success in the accounting profession depends on the ability to communicate and make ethical decisions.

1

Accounting Careers: Communication and Ethics in the Workplace

ENABLING PERFORMANCE TASKS

After studying Chapter 1, you will be able to:

a Define accounting terms related to accounting careers.

b Identify how accounting serves as a basis for careers.

c Identify the tasks of various accounting occupations.

d Describe how communication skills are important in reporting accounting information.

e Describe how individuals make ethical business decisions.

TERMS PREVIEW

accounting • accounting system • accounting records • accountant • public accounting firm • private accountant • bookkeeper • accounting clerk • general office clerk • ethics • business ethics

A successful business is involved in numerous financial activities. Summary reports of these financial activities are needed by several people. Owners and managers must understand financial reports to make good business decisions. *How much should be charged for the product or service? Are profits sufficient? Should new products be sold? Should new services be provided? Can costs be decreased?*

Individuals outside the business also use summary reports to make decisions that affect the business. The business' banker uses these summary reports to make loan decisions. *How much should the bank allow the business to borrow? Is the business likely to be able to repay the loan?*

A business must also submit summary reports to certain government agencies. The government requires that the business report financial information when it pays taxes. Other government agencies examine the financial activities of the business to assure that it follows various federal and state laws.

Persons responsible for nonprofit organizations also need accounting information as the basis for making financial decisions. The mayor of a community uses summary reports to determine how taxpayers' money should be spent. *How efficient is the community's water department? Can the community afford to purchase a new fire truck? Must taxes be raised to pay for a new high school building?* Nonprofit organizations, such as churches, public service organizations, and city governments, must keep spending within available financial resources.

Career opportunities exist for individuals to provide businesses, government, and nonprofit organizations with necessary financial information. Many young people choose to prepare for a career in the field of accounting.

WHAT IS ACCOUNTING?

To create useful reports, financial information must be maintained in an organized way. Planning, recording, analyzing, and interpreting financial information is called **accounting**. A planned process for providing financial information that will be useful to management is called an **accounting system**. Organized summaries of a business' financial activities are called **accounting records**.

Inaccurate accounting records often contribute to business failure and bankruptcy. Failure to understand accounting information can result in poor business decisions for both businesses and nonprofit organizations. Accounting education helps managers and owners make better business decisions.

Accounting is the language of business. Many individuals in a business complete accounting forms and prepare accounting reports. Owners, managers, and accounting personnel use their knowledge of accounting to understand the information provided in the accounting reports. Regardless of their responsibilities within an organization, individuals can perform their jobs more efficiently if they know the language of business—accounting.

Accounting is used by most individuals in everyday life. Nearly everyone in the United States earns money and must submit income tax reports to the federal and state governments. Everyone, personally or for a business, must plan ways to keep spending within available income. Individuals having accounting skills are better prepared to keep personal financial records.

JOB OPPORTUNITIES IN ACCOUNTING

Accounting positions fit into several classifications that include accountants, bookkeepers, accounting clerks, and other general office workers. An increasing amount of accounting work is done using computers. However, the increase in the use of computers does not appear to be decreasing the need for all kinds of accounting personnel.

FYI

According to a survey by the Gallup organization, approximately 1 in 20 high school and college students expects to be an accountant by age 30.

Accountants

A person who plans, summarizes, analyzes, and interprets accounting information is called an **accountant**. Accountants prepare various accounting reports and assist owners and managers in making financial decisions. Accountants also supervise the work of other accounting personnel and check the accuracy of financial statements.

CONTROLLER

Accountant needed to maintain accounting system and supervise accounting personnel. Five or more years experience, professional certification, and computer skills required.

ACCOUNTANT

Local business needs an accountant to supervise all accounting functions. Good interpersonal and communications skills are required.

Some accountants work as members of accounting firms that sell accounting services to other businesses. A business selling accounting services to the general public is called a **public accounting firm**. Public accounting firms provide a variety of accounting services to businesses and individuals. These accounting services may include planning an accounting system, preparing accounting reports, and submitting income tax reports to the government. For example, a medical clinic may not need a full-time accountant. The doctor, a nurse, or another office employee may do the day-to-day accounting tasks. The doctor may hire a public accounting firm to help plan the accounting system and analyze, report, and interpret the accounting information.

An accountant who is employed by a single business is called a **private accountant**. The work of private accountants is similar to that done by public accounting firms. However, a private accountant works for only one business.

Bookkeepers

A person who does general accounting work plus some summarizing and analyzing of accounting information is called a **bookkeeper**. In some businesses bookkeepers may supervise the work of other accounting personnel. In small to medium-size businesses, bookkeepers may also help owners and managers interpret accounting information.

BOOKKEEPER

Work without supervision. Experience in general ledger and payroll required. Experience in supervising accounting clerks desirable. Electronic spreadsheet and word processing skills required.

BOOKKEEPER-CLERICAL

Bookkeeper required to supervise accounts receivable and general ledger. Computer and keyboarding skills a must.

Bookkeepers in small businesses may do additional general office work. Many businesses require that bookkeepers have filing and keyboarding skills. Filing skills are needed for storing accounting records. Keyboarding skills are necessary to efficiently use computers to prepare accounting records and reports.

Accounting Clerks

A person who records, sorts, and files accounting information is often called an **accounting clerk**. Some businesses have large amounts of routine accounting tasks that are assigned to accounting clerks.

PAYROLL CLERK

Opening for responsible payroll clerk. Coordination of all payroll activities. Salary depends on training and experience.

ACCOUNTS PAYABLE CLERK

Retail store. Automated system. Will train person with general accounting background.

PROFESSIONAL BUSINESS ETHICS

Can I Say This In My Resume?

Kenneth Reed just graduated from high school with one year of high school accounting. Not sure of his long-term career goal, Kenneth decided to apply for a position as bookkeeper with Jackson Industries. In an effort to improve his chances to get the job, Kenneth overstated the leadership experience he had acquired in several part-time jobs. For example, Kenneth's experience as a janitor was exaggerated on his resume as ''Asset Maintenance Engineer—accountable for the acquisition and maintenance of productive assets.'' In the same way, Kenneth's job as a lifeguard was exaggerated as ''Recreational Director—responsible for coordinating customers' recreational activities.''

Based on the impressive nature of his resume, Kenneth was hired for the bookkeeping position. After one year of employment, Kenneth received above average ratings on his annual employment evaluation. Shortly thereafter, the accountant met Kenneth's former employers and learned the truth of Kenneth's work experience.

The three-step checklist presented in this chapter is useful in determining whether Kenneth demonstrated ethical behavior in preparing his resume.

INSTRUCTIONS Use the following three-step checklist for making ethical decisions. The first activity has been completed for you as follows.

1. Is the action illegal? No. Overstating qualifications is not illegal, but it does provide the employer the opportunity to terminate employment.
2. Does the action violate company or professional standards? No. Since Kenneth was neither an employee of the company nor a member of any profession, this question does not apply.

FYI

Analyzing ethical behavior is discussed in more detail on pages 12–14.

Accounting clerks are often given a title, such as payroll clerk or accounts payable clerk, to describe the specific accounting activities they perform. These clerks usually work with only a small part of the total accounting system. However, accounting clerks who understand the total accounting system will understand the importance of the work being done. With accounting knowledge and some experience, accounting clerks may earn promotions to more responsible accounting positions.

General Office Clerks

A person who does general kinds of office tasks, including some accounting tasks, is called a **general office clerk**. Many office personnel and computer operators perform some accounting tasks. For example, a secretary may be in charge of a small cash fund. A telephone operator may key-enter sales order information directly into a computer. A computer operator may key-enter data from special accounting documents. Regardless of who completes the accounting activities, the work must be done according to established

3. Who is affected, and how, by the action?

People Affected	Negative	Positive
Kenneth Reed	Could be terminated since management can no longer rely on his honesty. If retained, he could lose any chance of promotion.	Obtains employment.
Other Job Applicants	More highly qualified applicants lost an opportunity for employment.	
Company	Managers may lose trust and may delegate important tasks to other employees.	

As a bookkeeper, Kenneth has been placed in a position of trust. Management must be able to have faith in the accounting records and reports prepared by a bookkeeper. Knowing that Kenneth has the capacity to misrepresent the facts, management may lose faith in Kenneth's honesty.

Kenneth's success in performing the functions of bookkeeper may affect management's decisions. Management may forgive Kenneth for his previous actions since he has proved to be a loyal employee. Although Kenneth may not be terminated, his relationship with management has been damaged.

accounting concepts and procedures. General office clerks with some knowledge of accounting will be able to understand the importance of the accounting tasks they complete.

SECRETARY

Requires 3 years secretarial experience, word processing, communication skills, and bookkeeping experience or accounting education.

SALES REPRESENTATIVE

Direct merchandising company. Key phone orders into automated sales/inventory system. Keyboarding and communications skills required. Knowledge of accounting a plus.

A CAREER IN ACCOUNTING

The career ladder shown in Illustration 1-1 represents the educational requirements and promotional possibilities in accounting careers.

Career Ladder

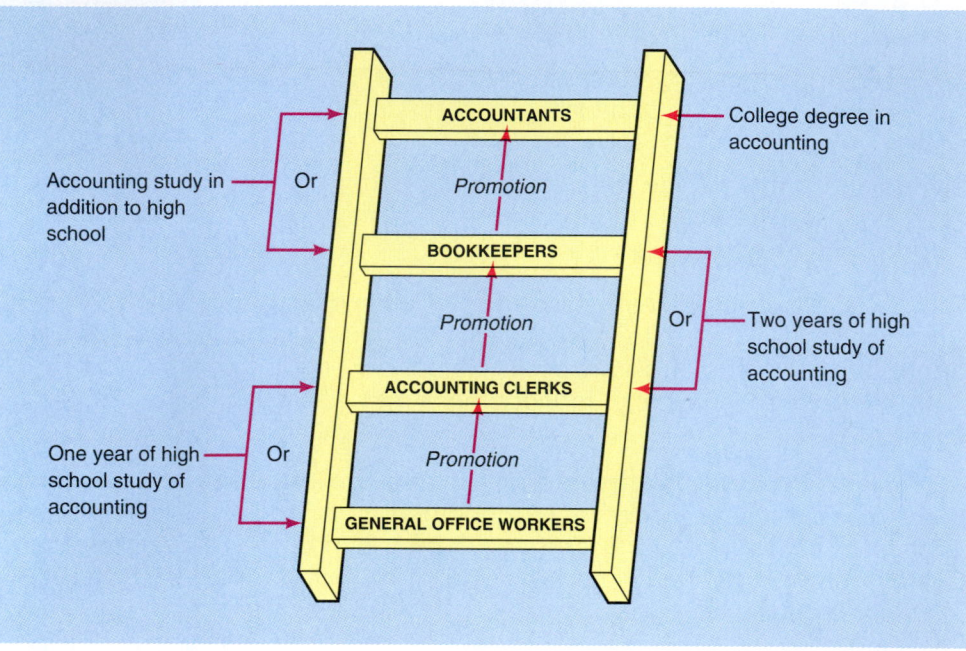

Immediately after high school graduation, individuals may start an accounting career as accounting clerks or general office clerks. A few of the better students may start as bookkeepers. High school study in accounting is useful as preparation for these accounting positions. The study of high school accounting is also good preparation for the study of accounting in college. With experience and additional accounting study, accounting personnel can earn a promotion to a higher position on the career ladder.

Professional Certification

FYI

All states require that a candidate pass an examination prepared by the AICPA to be certified as a CPA. The examination is administered twice a year, in May and November.

Almost all persons seeking positions as accountants must complete some study of accounting beyond high school and must gain accounting experience. Most public accountants also earn the Certified Public Accountant (CPA) designation. Each state sets the standards for earning a CPA certificate. Usually, the requirements include the study of college accounting, some accounting experience, and a passing score on a professional test covering all aspects of the accounting field.

Many private accountants often earn certification from a variety of professional accounting organizations. Private accountants can demonstrate their expertise in specific fields of accounting by earning certification such as the Certified Management Accountant (CMA) or the Certified Internal Auditor (CIA).

Professional Organizations

During the past one hundred years accountants have joined to form many professional organizations. The oldest and largest of these organizations is the American Institute of Certified Public Accountants (AICPA). The AICPA has a diverse membership of both public and private accountants. Other organizations, such as the American Woman's Society of Certified Public Accountants, the National Association of Black Accountants, and the International Federation of Accountants provide unique services to meet the needs of their members. Together, these organizations strive to promote job opportunities in accounting, to support and develop the professional skills of their members, and to improve the usefulness of accounting information.

Audit Your Understanding

1. What is accounting?
2. List several classifications of accounting positions.
3. What is the full name of the AICPA?

THE IMPORTANCE OF COMMUNICATION AND ETHICS IN ACCOUNTING

Your knowledge of accounting will provide you with an important skill necessary for success in any profession or business. Yet, accounting knowledge alone will not assure success. Your ability to communicate and make ethical decisions will increase your chances of achieving professional success.

Communication

FYI

Examples of other professional associations are: Institute of Management Accountants, American Accounting Association, Work in America Institute, and Families and Work Institute.

Effective accounting records can provide individuals with accurate and timely information regarding the financial activities of a business. Yet this information is of little value unless it can be communicated effectively to individuals responsible for making business decisions. Effective communication is essential because managers and accountants must often communicate accounting information to individuals with little or no accounting knowledge. Business leaders emphasize that communication skills are as important as technical skills in achieving career success.

Communication is the transfer of information between two or more individuals. Communication can be either oral or written. Oral communication includes phone conversations, one-on-one meetings, and group meetings. Written communication includes memorandums, letters, and reports.

Effective communication requires both a knowledge of good communication skills and regular practice using those skills. You have learned communication skills in a variety of language and communication classes. This textbook provides you the opportunity to practice your communication and language arts skills. Throughout the textbook you will be presented with a variety of business situations that require you to prepare an oral or written message.

Business Ethics

In your personal life you are faced daily with making decisions between right and wrong. The principles of right and wrong that guide an individual in making decisions are called **ethics**. Your personal ethics enable you to make decisions that consider the impact of your actions on others as well as yourself. Personal ethics are developed throughout your life from your relationships with family, friends, teachers, and other individuals that influence your life.

The use of personal ethics in making business decisions is called **business ethics**. Regardless of your position in an organization, you will be challenged to apply business ethics in making business decisions. The increasing complexity of today's business environment is also increasing the number of difficult business decisions that must be made.

Causes of Unethical Behavior. Unethical behavior occurs when an individual disregards his or her principles of right and wrong by choosing the wrong action. An understanding of the causes of unethical behavior is critical to preventing unethical behavior. Effective managers can identify and correct situations that would allow their employees to make decisions that may be unethical.

Six different factors may cause an individual to make an unethical decision.

1. Excessive emphasis on profits. Business managers are often judged on their ability to increase business profits. The salaries of business managers are often based on the amount of profits earned.
2. Misplaced business loyalty. Business managers often develop a misplaced dedication to their company. Disregarding their business ethics, managers may make decisions that appear to benefit the business without considering the negative impact on others.
3. Personal advancement. Some individuals have a "whatever it takes" attitude toward their personal careers. Their decisions are based solely on the degree that an action will advance their personal careers.
4. Expectation of not getting caught. An individual can recognize that an action is ethically wrong yet select that action because the chance of getting caught is small.
5. Unethical business environment. Individuals working in a business are less likely to apply business ethics if their managers are also making unethical decisions. The ethical environment set by business managers influences the ethical behavior of everyone in the business.

6. Unwillingness to take a stand. How often have you seen something wrong but not taken any action to correct it? Individuals can be unwilling to take a stand against unethical behavior because they fear losing their jobs, missing a deserved promotion, or alienating other employees.

Competition and the pursuit of success are the foundation of the free enterprise system. However, these factors are also common elements of unethical behavior. The desire to gain a competitive edge can motivate some individuals and businesses to make unethical decisions. The pursuit of success can motivate some individuals to overlook their principles of right and wrong. Fortunately, most business leaders now recognize that ethical behavior is the only way to attain long-term success.

Making Ethical Decisions. The increasing complexity of today's business environment requires that you be able to apply ethics in making business decisions. Determining whether an action is ethical can be difficult. In many business situations the line between right and wrong is not clear.

Analyzing a situation is the first step in deciding whether an action is ethical. The following three-step checklist will serve as a guide in collecting all relevant information regarding an action.

1 *Is the action illegal?* Does the action violate international, federal, state, or local laws? You should not consider an action if it is illegal. Obeying the law is in your best interest and the best interest of your business. Individuals will often encourage you to violate laws when the chance of being caught is small or the fine is minimal. Such an approach is shortsighted and does not consider all people who may be effected by the action.

2 *Does the action violate company or professional standards?* Public laws often set only minimum standards of behavior. Many businesses and professions set even higher standards of behavior. Thus, an action may be legal, yet still violate standards of the business or profession. Violating these standards may affect your job security and professional certification. The action may also have a negative effect on your business.

Several professional accounting organizations have adopted codes of professional conduct to assist their members in making ethical decisions. These codes have been written by the organizations' members to encourage their members to act and uphold the professional image of the accounting profession.

3 *Who is affected, and how, by the action?* If an action is legal and complies with business and professional standards, you must rely on your principles of right and wrong to determine if the action is ethical. Determine

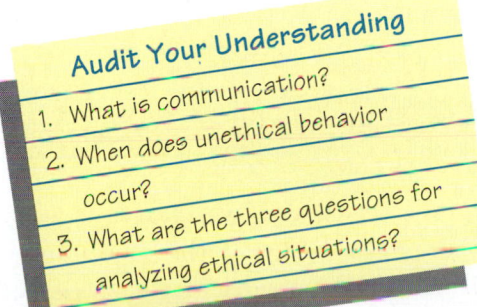

Audit Your Understanding

1. What is communication?
2. When does unethical behavior occur?
3. What are the three questions for analyzing ethical situations?

how the action affects a variety of people or groups, including the business employees and owners, customers, the local community, and society. In evaluating ethical situations, individuals often fail to consider how their actions affect a wide range of people.

Throughout this textbook you will have the opportunity to analyze common business situations. Use this three-step checklist to help determine whether each action demonstrates ethical behavior.

ACCOUNTING TERMS

What is the meaning of each of the following?

1. accounting
2. accounting system
3. accounting records
4. accountant
5. public accounting firm
6. private accountant
7. bookkeeper
8. accounting clerk
9. general office clerk
10. ethics
11. business ethics

QUESTIONS FOR INDIVIDUAL STUDY

1. Who uses summary reports of the financial activities of a business?
2. Why do persons responsible for nonprofit organizations need accounting information?
3. What personal reasons do individuals have for learning accounting facts and procedures?
4. What are the responsibilities of accountants?
5. What accounting services do public accounting firms offer?
6. What is the difference between a private accountant and a public accountant?
7. What does a bookkeeper do?
8. Why do general office clerks need to study accounting?
9. What entry-level accounting jobs might be obtained by persons who have studied high school accounting?
10. How can a person earn a designation as a CPA?
11. Why must managers and accountants have effective communication skills?
12. How are personal ethics developed?
13. What are the causes of unethical behavior?
14. What do most business leaders now recognize about ethical behavior?
15. What is the three-step checklist for collecting information for making an ethical decision?

CASES FOR CRITICAL THINKING

CASE 1 Cynthia's career goal is to be the accountant responsible for her community's accounting system. After completing one year of high school accounting, she hopes to obtain an accounting clerk job in city government. She believes that several years of hard work in city government will provide her with the experience necessary to assume the accountant's job. Do you think Cynthia can reach her goal? Explain.

CASE 2 When planning his high school course selections, Duane selects accounting as a career field. He plans to complete two years of high school accounting study. Duane is not planning to complete any other high school business courses. Duane's school counselor suggests that he also complete at least one year of keyboarding. Should Duane take the counselor's advice? Explain.

APPLIED COMMUNICATIONS

A resume provides a statement of your education, experience, and qualifications for a prospective employer. Your resume should be accurate, honest, and perfect in every respect.

Your resume should include all work experience along with the companies and dates of employment. Education, activities, and interests are all important items that should be included. It is preferable to keep the resume to one typed page.

INSTRUCTIONS:

1. Go to the library and research how to prepare an appropriate resume.
2. Prepare a personal resume that you could send to a prospective employer.

## PART 2

Accounting for a Service Business Organized as a Proprietorship

GENERAL GOALS

1. Know accounting terminology related to an accounting system for a service business organized as a proprietorship.

2. Understand accounting concepts and practices related to an accounting system for a service business organized as a proprietorship.

3. Demonstrate accounting procedures used in an accounting system for a service business organized as a proprietorship.

RUGCARE

CHART OF ACCOUNTS

Balance Sheet Accounts

(100) ASSETS
110	Cash
120	Petty Cash
130	Supplies
140	Prepaid Insurance

(200) LIABILITIES
210	Butler Cleaning Supplies
220	Dale Office Supplies

(300) OWNER'S EQUITY
310	Ben Furman, Capital
320	Ben Furman, Drawing
330	Income Summary

Income Statement Accounts

(400) REVENUE
410	Sales

(500) EXPENSES
510	Advertising Expense
520	Insurance Expense
530	Miscellaneous Expense
540	Rent Expense
550	Repair Expense
560	Supplies Expense
570	Utilities Expense

The chart of accounts for Rugcare is illustrated above for ready reference as you study Part 2 of this textbook.

2

Starting a Proprietorship

ENABLING PERFORMANCE TASKS

After studying Chapter 2, you will be able to:

a Define accounting terms related to starting a service business organized as a proprietorship.

b Identify accounting concepts and practices related to starting a service business organized as a proprietorship.

c Classify accounts as assets, liabilities, or owner's equity.

d Analyze how transactions related to starting a service business organized as a proprietorship affect accounts in an accounting equation.

e Prepare a balance sheet for a service business organized as a proprietorship from information in an accounting equation.

TERMS PREVIEW

service business • proprietorship • asset • equities • liability • owner's equity • accounting equation • transaction • account • account title • account balance • capital • balance sheet

A person who chooses to start a business must make many decisions. To make these decisions, a businessperson needs financial information about the business. To provide the information, many records and reports relating to the business must be kept. In order to create useful records and reports, financial information must be kept in an organized way. Planning, recording, analyzing, and interpreting financial information is known as accounting. A planned process for providing financial information that will be useful to management is known as an accounting system.

THE BUSINESS

A business that performs an activity for a fee is called a **service business.** Ben Furman worked for a service business that cleans carpets for a fee. Mr. Furman wants to be in control of his hours and his earnings. Therefore, he decided to start his own carpet-cleaning business. A business owned by one person is called a **proprietorship.** A proprietorship is also referred to as a sole proprietorship. Mr. Furman has named his new proprietorship *Rugcare*. Rugcare will rent office space and the equipment used to operate the business.

Since a new business is being started, Mr. Furman must design the accounting system that will be used to keep Rugcare's accounting records. In the accounting system, Mr. Furman must be careful to keep Rugcare's accounting records separate from his own personal financial records. For example, Mr. Furman owns a house and a personal car. Rugcare's financial records must *not* include information about Mr. Furman's house, car, or other personal belongings. For example, Mr. Furman must use one checking account for his personal expenses and another checking account for Rugcare. The financial records for Rugcare and Mr. Furman's personal belongings must be kept separate. The accounting concept, *Business Entity*, is applied when a business' financial information is recorded and reported separately from the owner's personal financial information. (CONCEPT: *Business Entity*)

Accounting concepts are described throughout this textbook when an application of a concept first occurs. When additional applications occur, a concept reference, such as (CONCEPT: *Business Entity*), indicates an application of a specific accounting concept. A brief description of each accounting concept used in this text is also provided in Appendix A.

THE ACCOUNTING EQUATION

A business has many items that have value. Rugcare will own items such as cash and supplies that will be used to conduct daily operations. Anything of value that is owned is called an **asset.** Assets have value because they can be used to acquire other assets or be used to operate a business. For example, Rugcare will use cash to buy supplies for the business. Rugcare will then use the asset, supplies, in the operation of the rug-cleaning business.

Financial rights to the assets of a business are called **equities**. A business has two types of equities. (1) Equity of those to whom money is owed. For example, Rugcare may buy some supplies and agree to pay for the supplies at a later date. The business from whom supplies are bought will have a right to some of Rugcare's assets until Rugcare pays for the supplies. An amount owed by a business is called a **liability**. (2) Equity of the owner. Mr. Furman will own Rugcare and invest in the assets of the business. Therefore, he will have a right to decide how the assets will be used. The amount remaining after the value of all liabilities is subtracted from the value of all assets is called **owner's equity**.

The relationship among assets, liabilities, and owner's equity can be written as an equation. An equation showing the relationship among assets, liabilities, and owner's equity is called the **accounting equation**. The accounting equation is most often stated as:

$$\text{Assets} = \text{Liabilities} + \text{Owner's Equity}$$

The accounting equation must be in balance to be correct. Thus, the total of the amounts on the left side of the equation must always equal the total of the amounts on the right side. Before Mr. Furman actually starts the business, Rugcare's accounting equation would show the following amounts.

Assets	=	Liabilities + Owner's Equity
Left side amount		Right side amounts
$0	=	$0 + $0

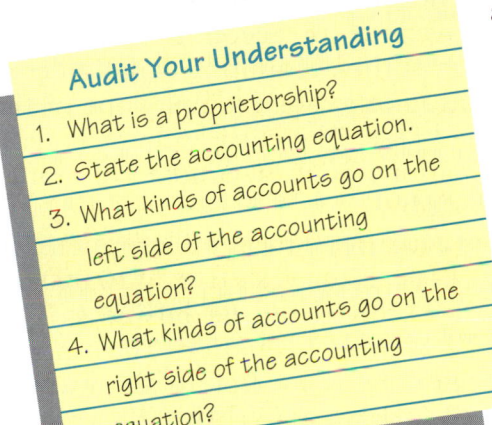
HOW BUSINESS ACTIVITIES CHANGE THE ACCOUNTING EQUATION

Business activities change the amounts in the accounting equation. A business activity that changes assets, liabilities, or owner's equity is called a **transaction**. For example, a business that pays cash for supplies is engaging in a transaction. After each transaction, the accounting equation must remain in balance.

The accounting concept, *Unit of Measurement*, is applied when business transactions are stated in numbers that have common values—that is, using a common unit of measurement. *(CONCEPT: Unit of Measurement)* For example, in the United States, business transactions are recorded in dollars. In Switzerland, business transactions are recorded in Swiss francs. The unit of measurement concept is followed so that the financial reports of businesses can be clearly stated and understood in numbers that have comparable values. For example, reports would not be clear if some information was reported in United States dollars and some in Swiss francs.

FYI

The left side of the accounting equation must always equal the right side.

Received Cash from Owner as an Investment

Mr. Furman uses $10,000.00 of his own money to invest in Rugcare. Rugcare should only be concerned with the effect of this transaction on Rugcare's records. The business should *not* be concerned about Mr. Furman's personal records. (CONCEPT: Business Entity)

> *Transaction 1   August 1, 19--. Received cash from owner as an investment, $10,000.00.*

A record summarizing all the information pertaining to a single item in the accounting equation is called an **account.** The name given to an account is called an **account title.** Each part of the accounting equation consists of one or more accounts. For example, one of the asset accounts is titled Cash. The cash account is used to summarize information about the amount of money the business has available.

In the accounting equation shown in Illustration 2-1, the asset account, Cash, is increased by $10,000.00, the amount of cash received by the business. This increase is on the left side of the accounting equation. The amount in an account is called the **account balance.** Before the owner's investment, the account balance of Cash was zero. After the owner's investment, the account balance of Cash is $10,000.00.

ILLUSTRATION 2-1	Receiving cash from owner as an investment changes one asset and owner's equity

	Assets	=	Liabilities	+	Owner's Equity
	Cash	=			Ben Furman, Capital
Beg. Balances	$0		$0		$0
Transaction 1	+10,000				+10,000 (investment)
New Balances	$10,000		$0		$10,000

The account used to summarize the owner's equity in business is called **capital.** The capital account is an owner's equity account. Rugcare's capital account is titled Ben Furman, Capital. In the accounting equation shown in Illustration 2-1, the owner's equity account, Ben Furman, Capital, is increased by $10,000.00. This increase is on the right side of the accounting equation. Before the owner's investment, the account balance of Ben Furman, Capital was zero. After the owner's investment, the account balance of Ben Furman, Capital is $10,000.00.

The accounting equation has changed as a result of the receipt of cash as the owner's investment. However, both sides of the equation are changed by the same amount, $10,000.00. The $10,000.00 increase on the left side of the equation equals the $10,000.00

increase on the right side of the equation. Therefore, the accounting equation is still in balance.

Paid Cash for Supplies

Rugcare needs supplies to operate the business. Ben Furman uses some of Rugcare's cash to buy supplies.

Transaction 2   August 3, 19--. Paid cash for supplies, $1,577.00.

The effect of this transaction on the accounting equation is shown in Illustration 2-2. In this transaction, two asset accounts are changed. One asset, cash, has been exchanged for another asset, supplies. The asset account, Cash, is decreased by $1,577.00, the amount of cash paid out. This decrease is on the left side of the accounting equation. The asset account, Supplies, is increased by $1,577.00, the amount of supplies bought. This increase is also on the left side of the accounting equation.

ILLUSTRATION 2-2   Paying cash for supplies changes two assets

	Assets		=	Liabilities	+	Owner's Equity
	Cash	+ Supplies	=			Ben Furman, Capital
Balances	$10,000	$0		$0		$10,000
Transaction 2	−1,577	+1,577				
New Balances	$8,423	$1,577		$0		$10,000

Total of left side:
$8,423 + $1,577 = $10,000

Total of right side:
$10,000

For this transaction, two assets are changed. Therefore, the two changes are both on the left side of the accounting equation. When changes are made on only one side of the accounting equation, the equation must still be in balance. Therefore, if one account is increased, another account on the same side of the equation must be decreased. After this transaction, the new account balance of Cash is $8,423.00. The new account balance of Supplies is $1,577.00. The sum of the amounts on the left side is $10,000.00 (Cash, $8,423.00 + Supplies, $1,577.00). The amount on the right side is also $10,000.00. Therefore, the accounting equation is still in balance.

Paid Cash for Insurance

Insurance premiums must be paid in advance. For example, Rugcare pays a $1,200.00 insurance premium for future insurance coverage.

Transaction 3   August 4, 19--. Paid cash for insurance, $1,200.00.

In return for this payment, Rugcare is entitled to insurance coverage for the length of the policy. The insurance coverage is something of value owned by Rugcare. Therefore, the insurance coverage is an asset. Because insurance premiums are paid in advance, or *prepaid*, the premiums are recorded in an asset account titled Prepaid Insurance.

The effect of this transaction on the accounting equation is shown in Illustration 2-3. In this transaction, two assets are changed. One asset, cash, has been exchanged for another asset, prepaid insurance. The asset account, Cash, is decreased by $1,200.00, the amount of cash paid out. This decrease is on the left side of the accounting equation. The asset account, Prepaid Insurance, is increased by $1,200.00, the amount of insurance bought. This increase is also on the left side of the accounting equation.

ILLUSTRATION 2-3

Paying cash for insurance changes two assets

	Assets			=	Liabilities	+ Owner's Equity
	Cash	+ Supplies	+ Prepaid Insurance =			Ben Furman, Capital
Balances	$8,423	$1,577	$0		$0	$10,000
Transaction 3	−1,200		+1,200			
New Balances	$7,223	$1,577	$1,200		$0	$10,000

Total of left side: $7,223 + $1,577 + $1,200 = $10,000

Total of right side: $10,000

Since two assets are changed by this transaction, both changes are on the left side of the accounting equation. Since one account is increased, the other account on the same side of the equation must be decreased. After this transaction, the new account balance of Cash is $7,223.00. The new account balance of Prepaid Insurance is $1,200.00. The sum of the amounts on the left side is $10,000.00 (Cash, $7,223.00 + Supplies, $1,577.00 + Prepaid Insurance, $1,200.00). The amount on the right side is also $10,000.00. Therefore, the accounting equation is still in balance.

Bought Supplies on Account

Rugcare needs to buy additional supplies. The supplies are obtained from Butler Cleaning Supplies, which is located in a different city. It is a common business practice to buy items and pay for them at a future date. Another way to state this activity is to say that these items are bought *on account*.

Transaction 4   August 7, 19--. Bought supplies on account from Butler Cleaning Supplies, $2,720.00.

The effect of this transaction on the accounting equation is shown in Illustration 2-4. In this transaction, one asset and one liability are changed. The asset account, Supplies, is increased by $2,720.00, the amount of supplies bought. This increase is on the left side of the accounting equation. Butler Cleaning Supplies will have a claim against some of Rugcare's assets until Rugcare pays for the supplies bought. Therefore, Butler Cleaning Supplies is a liability account. The liability account, Butler Cleaning Supplies, is increased by $2,720.00, the amount owed for the supplies. This increase is on the right side of the accounting equation.

ILLUSTRATION 2-4   Buying supplies on account changes one asset and one liability

	Assets			**= Liabilities +**	**Owner's Equity**
	Cash	+ Supplies	+ Prepaid Insurance =	Butler Cleaning Supplies +	Ben Furman, Capital
Balances	$7,223	$1,577	$1,200	$0	$10,000
Transaction 4		+2,720		+2,720	
New Balances	$7,223	$4,297	$1,200	$2,720	$10,000

Total of left side: $7,223 + $4,297 + $1,200 = $12,720	Total of right side: $2,720 + $10,000 = $12,720

This transaction changes both sides of the accounting equation. When changes are made on both sides of the equation, the change on the left side must equal the change on the right side. After this transaction, the new account balance of Supplies is $4,297.00. The new account balance of Butler Cleaning Supplies is $2,720.00. The sum of the amounts on the left side is $12,720.00 (Cash, $7,223.00 + Supplies, $4,297.00 + Prepaid Insurance, $1,200.00). The sum of the amounts on the right side is also $12,720.00 (Butler Cleaning Supplies, $2,720.00 + Ben Furman, Capital, $10,000.00). Therefore, the accounting equation is still in balance.

Paid Cash on Account

Since Rugcare is a new business, Butler Cleaning Supplies has not done business with Rugcare before. Butler Cleaning Supplies allows Rugcare to buy supplies on account but requires Rugcare to send a check for one-half of the amount immediately. Rugcare will pay the remaining liability at a later date.

Transaction 5   August 11, 19--. Paid cash on account to Butler Cleaning Supplies, $1,360.00.

The effect of this transaction on the accounting equation is shown in Illustration 2-5. In this transaction, one asset and one lia-

ILLUSTRATION 2-5   Paying cash on account changes one asset and one liability

	Assets			= Liabilities + Owner's Equity		
	Cash	+ Supplies +	Prepaid Insurance =	Butler Cleaning Supplies	+	Ben Furman, Capital
Balances	$7,223	$4,297	$1,200	$2,720		$10,000
Transaction 5	−1,360			−1,360		
New Balances	$5,863	$4,297	$1,200	$1,360		$10,000

Total of left side:
$5,863 + $4,297 + $1,200 = $11,360

Total of right side:
$1,360 + $10,000 = $11,360

bility are changed. The asset account, Cash, is decreased by $1,360.00, the amount of cash paid out. This decrease is on the left side of the accounting equation. After this payment, Rugcare owes less money to Butler Cleaning Supplies. Therefore, the liability account, Butler Cleaning Supplies, is decreased by $1,360.00, the amount paid on account. This decrease is on the right side of the accounting equation.

This transaction changes both sides of the accounting equation. When changes are made on both sides of the equation, the change on the left side must equal the change on the right side. After this transaction, the new account balance of Cash is $5,863.00. The new account balance of Butler Cleaning Supplies is $1,360.00. The sum of the amounts on the left side is $11,360.00 (Cash, $5,863.00 + Supplies, $4,297.00 + Prepaid Insurance, $1,200.00). The sum of the amounts on the right side is also $11,360.00 (Butler Cleaning Supplies, $1,360.00 + Ben Furman, Capital, $10,000.00). Therefore, the accounting equation is still in balance.

Audit Your Understanding

1. What does it mean if the accounting equation is "in balance?"

2. What must be done if a transaction increases the left side of the accounting equation?

3. How can a transaction affect only one side of the accounting equation?

REPORTING FINANCIAL INFORMATION ON A BALANCE SHEET

FYI

Every financial statement has a three-line heading that consists of the name of the company, the name of the statement, and the date.

Periodically a business reports details about its assets, liabilities, and owner's equity. The financial details about assets, liabilities, and owner's equity could be found on the last line of the accounting equation. However, most businesses prepare more formal financial statements that may be copied and sent to interested persons. A financial statement that reports assets, liabilities, and owner's equity on a specific date is called a **balance sheet.**

When a business is started, it is expected that the business will continue to operate indefinitely. For example, Ben Furman assumes that he will own and operate Rugcare for many years. When he retires, he expects to sell Rugcare to someone else who will continue its operation. The accounting concept, *Going Concern*, is applied when financial statements are prepared with the expectation that a business will remain in operation indefinitely. *(CONCEPT: Going Concern)*

Body of a Balance Sheet

A balance sheet has three major sections. (1) *Assets* are on the left side of the accounting equation. Therefore, Rugcare lists its assets on the left side of the balance sheet. (2) *Liabilities* are on the right side of the accounting equation. Therefore, Rugcare lists its liabilities on the right side of the balance sheet. (3) *Owner's equity* is also on the right side of the accounting equation. Therefore, Rugcare lists its owner's equity on the right side of the balance sheet.

Rugcare's balance sheet, prepared after the transaction on August 11, is shown in Illustration 2-6.

ILLUSTRATION 2-6 Balance sheet for a service business organized as a proprietorship

	Assets		= Liabilities + Owner's Equity	
	Cash + Supplies +	Prepaid Insurance =	Butler Cleaning Supplies +	Ben Furman, Capital
Balances	$5,863 $4,297	$1,200	$1,360	$10,000

Rugcare				
Balance Sheet				
August 11, 19--				
Assets		**Liabilities**		
Cash	5863 00	Butler Cleaning Supplies	1360 00	
Supplies	4297 00	**Owner's Equity**		
Prepaid Insurance	1200 00	Ben Furman, Capital	10000 00	
Total Assets	11360 00	Total Liab. and Owner's Eq.	11360 00	

Preparing a Balance Sheet

Rugcare's balance sheet is prepared in six steps.

1 Write the *heading* on three lines at the top of the balance sheet. Center each line. The heading for Rugcare's balance sheet is:

> Name of the business: Rugcare
> Name of the report: Balance Sheet
> Date of the report: August 11, 19--

2 Prepare the *assets section* on the LEFT side. Center the word *Assets* on the first line of the wide column on the left side. Under this heading, write each asset account title and

FOREIGN CURRENCY

As our world becomes smaller and global trade increases, more and more United States businesses will get involved in business transactions with companies in foreign countries. Transactions with foreign businesses may be stated in terms of U.S. dollars or the currency of the other country. If the transaction involves foreign currency, the U.S. business must convert the foreign currency into U.S. dollars before the transaction can be re-

corded. *(CONCEPT: Unit of Measurement)*

The value of foreign currency can change daily. The **exchange rate** is the value of foreign currency in relation to the U.S. dollar. Current exchange rates can be found in many daily newspapers or by contacting a bank. The above list of exchange rates is taken from a newspaper. Because the

COUNTRY	CURRENCY	U.S. $ EQUIVALENT
Australia	Dollar	.7303
Canada	Dollar	.7908
Germany	Mark	.6757
Hong Kong	Dollar	.12935
Mexico	New Peso	.323154
Peru	New Sol	.7931
South Africa	Rand	.2519

rates change daily, the current exchange rates could be quite different than these rates which were current when this book was published.

The exchange rate is stated in terms of one unit of foreign currency. Using Germany as an example, the rate means that one German mark is worth .6757 U.S. dollars (or 68

U.S. cents). This rate would be used when exchanging German marks for U.S. dollars.

A **conversion formula** can be used to find out how many foreign currency units can be purchased with one U.S. dollar. The formula is:

---

1 ÷ exchange rate = foreign currency per U.S. dollar

1 dollar ÷ .6757 = 1.4799 marks per dollar

Applying the conversion formula to Germany, one U.S. dollar would buy 1.48 German marks. The formula could be applied to each rate stated above to determine how many foreign currency units can be purchased with one U.S. dollar.

---

amount. The asset accounts are: Cash, $5,863.00; Supplies, $4,297.00; and Prepaid Insurance, $1,200.00.

3 Prepare the *liabilities section* on the RIGHT side. Center the word *Liabilities* on the first line of the wide column on the right side. Under this heading, write each liability account title and amount. Rugcare has only one liability account to be listed, Butler Cleaning Supplies, $1,360.00.

4 Prepare the *owner's equity section* on the RIGHT side. Center the words *Owner's Equity* on the next blank line of the wide column on the right side. Under this heading, write the owner's equity account title and amount. Rugcare's owner's equity account is Ben Furman, Capital, $10,000.00.

5 Determine if the balance sheet is *in balance*. Use a calculator, if available, or a sheet of scratch paper. Add all the asset amounts on the LEFT side. The total on the left side of Rugcare's balance sheet is $11,360.00 ($5,863.00 + $4,297.00 + $1,200.00). Add the liabilities and owner's equity amounts on the RIGHT side. The total on the right side of Rugcare's balance sheet is $11,360.00 ($1,360.00 + $10,000.00). The total of the LEFT side is the same as the total of the RIGHT side, $11,360.00. Therefore, Rugcare's balance sheet is in balance.

Audit Your Understanding

1. List the three sections of a balance sheet.

2. What kinds of accounts are listed on the left side of a balance sheet?

3. What kinds of accounts are listed on the right side of a balance sheet?

4. What should be done if a balance sheet is not in balance?

If the balance sheet is NOT in balance, find the errors before completing any more work.

6 Complete the balance sheet. Rule a single line across both amount columns. A single line means that amounts are to be added or subtracted. On the next line, write *Total Assets* in the wide column on the left side. On the same line, write the total asset amount, $11,360.00, in the left amount column. On the same line, write *Total Liabilities and Owner's Equity* in the wide column on the right side. On the same line, write the total liabilities and owner's equity amount, $11,360.00, in the right amount column. Rule double lines below the amount column totals. Double lines mean that the totals have been verified as correct.

When possible, words are spelled in full so there can be no doubt about what word was intended. However, in a few situations, where there is insufficient room to spell the words in full, words may be abbreviated. On Rugcare's balance sheet, it is necessary to abbreviate the words *Total Liab. and Owner's Eq.*

SUMMARY OF HOW TRANSACTIONS CHANGE THE ACCOUNTING EQUATION

Changes in the accounting equation caused by Transactions 1 to 5 are summarized in Illustration 2-7 on the following page.

Four basic rules relate to how transactions affect the accounting equation

1 Each transaction changes at least two accounts in the accounting equation.

2 When all the changes occur on one side of the accounting equation, increases on that side must be matched by decreases on the same side. Transactions 2 and 3 are examples of this rule.

3 When a transaction increases one side of the accounting equation, the other side of the equation must also be increased by the same amount. Transactions 1 and 4 are examples of this rule.

4 When a transaction decreases one side of the accounting equation, the other side of the equation must also be decreased by the same amount. Transaction 5 is an example of this rule.

Summary of how transactions change the accounting equation

Four basic rules relate to how transactions affect the accounting equation.

1 Each transaction changes at least two accounts in the accounting equation.

2 When all the changes occur on one side of the accounting equation, increases on that side must be matched by decreases on the same side. Transactions 2 and 3 are examples of this rule.

3 When a transaction increases one side of the accounting equation, the other side of the equation must also be increased by the same amount. Transactions 1 and 4 are examples of this rule.

4 When a transaction decreases one side of the accounting equation, the other side of the equation must also be decreased by the same amount. Transaction 5 is an example of this rule.

Transaction	Assets			= Liabilities +	Owner's Equity
	Cash	+ Supplies +	Prepaid Insurance	= Butler Cleaning Supplies	+ Ben Furman, Capital
Beginning Balance	$0	$0	$0	$0	$0
1. Received cash from owner as an investment	+10,000				+10,000 (investment)
New Balances	$10,000	$0	$0	$0	$10,000
2. Paid cash for supplies	−1,577	+1,577			
New Balances	$8,423	$1,577	$0	$0	$10,000
3. Paid cash for insurance	−1,200		+1,200		
New Balances	$7,223	$1,577	$1,200	$0	$10,000
4. Bought supplies on account		+2,720		+2,720	
5. New Balances	$7,223	$4,297	$1,200	$2,720	$10,000
Paid cash on account	−1,360			−1,360	
New Balances	$5,863	$4,297	$1,200	$1,360	$10,000

Total of left side:
$5,863 + $4,297 + $1,200 = $11,360

Total of right side:
$1,360 + $10,000 = $11,360

ACCOUNTING TERMS

What is the meaning of each of the following?

1. service business
2. proprietorship
3. asset
4. equities
5. liability
6. owner's equity
7. accounting equation
8. transaction
9. account
10. account title
11. account balance
12. capital
13. balance sheet

1. Which accounting concept is being applied when a business records and reports financial information separate from the owner's personal financial information?
2. What are the two types of equities of a business?
3. What must be true about the accounting equation after each transaction?
4. Which accounting concept is being applied when a business in the United States reports financial information in dollars?
5. What accounts are affected, and how, when the owner invests cash in a business?
6. What accounts are affected, and how, when a business pays cash for supplies?
7. Why is Prepaid Insurance an asset?
8. How are liabilities affected when a business buys supplies on account?
9. How are liabilities affected when a business pays cash for a liability?
10. Which accounting concept is being applied when financial statements are prepared with the expectation that a business will remain in operation indefinitely?
11. What three items are included in the heading of a balance sheet?
12. What six steps are followed in preparing a balance sheet?
13. What do double lines below a column total mean?
14. What are the four basic rules relating to how transactions affect the accounting equation?

CASE 1 James Patton starts a new business. Mr. Patton uses his personal car in the business with the expectation that later the business can buy a car. All expenses for operating the car, including license plates, gasoline, oil, tune-ups, and new tires, are paid for out of business funds. Is this an acceptable procedure? Explain.

CASE 2 At the end of the first day of business, Quick Clean Laundry has the following assets and liabilities:

Assets	
Cash	$3,500.00
Supplies	950.00
Prepaid Insurance	1,200.00
Liabilities	
Smith Office Supplies	$ 750.00
Super Supplies Company	1,500.00

The owner, Susan Whiteford, wants to know the amount of her equity in Quick Clean Laundry. Determine this amount and explain what this amount represents.

DRILL 2-D1 Classifying assets, liabilities, and owner's equity

Use a form similar to the following.

Item	Asset	Liability	Owner's Equity
1. Cash	√		

INSTRUCTIONS:

Classify each item listed below as an asset, liability, or owner's equity. Place a check mark in the appropriate column. Item 1 is given as an example.

1. Cash
2. Alice Jones, Capital
3. Prepaid Insurance
4. Steward Supply Company
5. Supplies
6. Any amount owed
7. Owner's capital account
8. Anything owned

DRILL 2-D2 Determining how transactions change an accounting equation

Use a form similar to the following.

Trans. No.	Assets	=	Liabilities	+ Owner's Equity
1.	+		+	

Transactions
1. Bought supplies on account.
2. Paid cash for insurance.
3. Received cash from owner as an investment.
4. Paid cash for supplies.
5. Paid cash on account to Konroy Company.

INSTRUCTIONS:

Decide which classification(s) are changed by each transaction. Place a plus (+) in the appropriate column if the classification is increased. Place a minus (−) in the appropriate column if the classification is decreased. Transaction 1 is given as an example.

DRILL 2-D3 Determining where items are listed on a balance sheet

Use a form similar to the following.

1	2	3
	Balance Sheet	
Items	**Left Side**	**Right Side**
1. Cash	*Asset*	

INSTRUCTIONS:

Classify each item as an asset, liability, or owner's equity. Write the classification in Column 2 or 3 to show where each item is listed on a balance sheet. Item 1 is given as an example.

1. Cash
2. Gretchen Murphy, Capital
3. Supplies
4. Prepaid Insurance
5. Action Laundry
6. Anything owned
7. Any amount owed
8. Owner's capital account

APPLICATION PROBLEMS

EPT(d,e)

PROBLEM 2-1 Determining how transactions change an accounting equation

Frank Mori is starting Mori Repair Shop, a small service business. Mori Repair Shop uses the accounts shown in the following accounting equation. Use a form similar to the following to complete this problem.

Trans. No.	Assets			=	Liabilities			+	Owner's Equity
	Cash +	Supplies +	Prepaid Insurance	=	Swan's Supply Company +	York Company	+		Frank Mori, Capital
Beg. Bal.	0	0	0		0	0			0
1.	+2,000								+2,000 (investment)
New Bal.	2,000	0	0		0	0			2,000
2.									

Transactions
1. Received cash from owner as an investment, $2,000.00.
2. Paid cash for insurance, $600.00.
3. Bought supplies on account from Swan's Supply Company, $100.00.
4. Bought supplies on account from York Company, $500.00.
5. Paid cash on account to Swan's Supply Company, $100.00.
6. Paid cash on account to York Company, $300.00.
7. Paid cash for supplies, $500.00.
8. Received cash from owner as an investment, $500.00.

INSTRUCTIONS:

For each transaction, complete the following. Transaction 1 is given as an example.

a. Analyze the transaction to determine which accounts in the accounting equation are affected.

b. Write the amount in the appropriate columns using a plus (+) if the account increases or a minus (−) if the account decreases.

c. For transactions that change owner's equity, write in parentheses a description of the transaction to the right of the amount.

d. Calculate the new balance for each account in the accounting equation.

e. Before going on to the next transaction, determine that the accounting equation is still in balance.

PROBLEM 2-2 Preparing a balance sheet from information in an accounting equation

On September 30 the Steffens Company's accounting equation indicated the following account balances.

| Trans. No. | Assets | | | = Liabilities | + Owner's Equity |
	Cash +	Supplies +	Prepaid Insurance	= Morton Company	+ Steve Steffens, Capital
New Bal.	1,200	150	300	250	1,400

INSTRUCTIONS:

Using the September 30 balance in the accounting equation, prepare a balance sheet for the Steffens Company.

PROBLEM 2-3 Determining how transactions change an accounting equation and preparing a balance sheet

Nancy Dirks is starting Dirks Company, a small service business. Dirks Company uses the accounts shown in the following accounting equation. Use a form similar to the following to complete this problem.

| Trans. No. | Assets | | | = Liabilities | + Owner's Equity |
	Cash +	Supplies +	Prepaid Insurance	= Helfrey Company	+ Nancy Dirks, Capital
Beg. Bal.	0	0	0	0	0
1.	+350				+350 (investment)
New Bal.	350	0	0	0	350
2.					

Transactions
1. Received cash from owner as an investment, $350.00.
2. Bought supplies on account from Helfrey Company, $100.00.
3. Paid cash for insurance, $150.00.
4. Paid cash for supplies, $50.00.
5. Received cash from owner as an investment, $300.00.
6. Paid cash on account to Helfrey Company, $75.00.

INSTRUCTIONS:

1. For each transaction, complete the following. Transaction 1 is given as an example.
   a. Analyze the transaction to determine which accounts in the accounting equation are affected.
   b. Write the amount in the appropriate columns, using a plus (+) if the account increases or a minus (−) if the account decreases.
   c. For transactions that change owner's equity, write in parentheses a description of the transaction to the right of the amount.
   d. Calculate the new balance for each account in the accounting equation.
   e. Before going on to the next transaction, determine that the accounting equation is still in balance.
2. Using the final balances in the accounting equation, prepare a balance sheet for Dirks Company. Use July 31 of the current year as the date of the balance sheet.

ENRICHMENT PROBLEMS EPT(d,e)

MASTERY PROBLEM 2-M Determining how transactions change an accounting equation and preparing a balance sheet

Gregory Morgan is starting a limousine service called Luxury Limo. Luxury Limo uses the accounts shown in the following accounting equation. Use a form similar to the following to complete this problem.

Trans. No.	Assets					=	Liabilities	+	Owner's Equity
	Cash	+	Supplies	+	Prepaid Insurance	=	Limo Supply Company	+	Gregory Morgan, Capital
Beg. Bal.	0		0		0		0		0
1.	+2,000								+2,000 (investment)
New Bal.	2,000		0		0		0		2,000
2.									

Transactions
1. Received cash from owner as an investment, $2,000.00.
2. Paid cash for supplies, $250.00.
3. Bought supplies on account from Limo Supply Company, $300.00.
4. Paid cash for insurance, $600.00.
5. Paid cash on account to Limo Supply Company, $150.00.

INSTRUCTIONS:

1. For each transaction, complete the following. Transaction 1 is given as an example.
   a. Analyze the transaction to determine which accounts in the accounting equation are affected.
   b. Write the amount in the appropriate columns, using a plus (+) if the account increases or a minus (−) if the account decreases.

   c. For transactions that change owner's equity, write in parentheses a description of the transaction to the right of the amount.

   d. Calculate the new balance for each account in the accounting equation.

   e. Before going on to the next transaction, determine that the accounting equation is still in balance.

2. Using the final balances in the accounting equation, prepare a balance sheet for Luxury Limo. Use February 5 of the current year as the date of the balance sheet.

CHALLENGE PROBLEM 2-C Applying accounting concepts to determine how transactions change the accounting equation

Olson Delivery Service, a new business owned by Jerome Olson, uses the accounts shown in the following accounting equation. Use a form similar to the following to complete this problem.

Trans. No.	Assets			=	Liabilities		+	Owner's Equity
	Cash +	Supplies +	Prepaid Insurance	=	Mutual Savings Bank	+	Nelson Supply Co. +	Jerome Olson, Capital
Beg. Bal.	0	0	0		0		0	0
1.	+1,500							+1,500 (investment)
New Bal.	1,500	0	0		0		0	1,500
2.								

Transactions

1. Owner invested cash, $1,500.00.
2. Bought supplies for cash, $400.00.
3. Paid cash for insurance, $240.00.
4. Supplies were bought on account from Nelson Supply Company, $80.00.
5. The owner, Jerome Olson, paid $1,000.00 of his personal cash to Mutual Savings Bank for the car payment on his personal car.
6. Wrote a check for supplies. The supplies were bought from a Canadian company. The supplies cost $120.00 in Canadian dollars, which is equivalent to $100.00 in United States dollars.

INSTRUCTIONS:

For each transaction, complete the following. Transaction 1 is given as an example.

   a. Analyze the transaction to determine which business accounts in the accounting equation, if any, are affected. You will need to apply the Business Entity and Unit of Measurement concepts in this problem.

   b. If business accounts are affected, determine the appropriate amount of the change. Write the amount in the appropriate columns, using a plus (+) if the account increases or a minus (−) if the account decreases.

   c. For transactions that change owner's equity, write in parentheses a description of the transaction to the right of the amount.

   d. Calculate the new balance for each account in the accounting equation.

   e. Before going on to the next transaction, determine that the accounting equation is still in balance.

3

Starting a Proprietorship: Changes That Affect Owner's Equity

ENABLING PERFORMANCE TASKS

After studying Chapter 3, you will be able to:

a Define accounting terms related to changes that affect owner's equity for a service business organized as a proprietorship.

b Identify accounting practices related to changes that affect owner's equity for a service business organized as a proprietorship.

c Analyze changes that affect owner's equity for a service business organized as a proprietorship in an accounting equation.

d Prepare a balance sheet for a service business organized as a proprietorship from information in the accounting equation.

TERMS PREVIEW

revenue • expense • withdrawals

A business activity that changes assets, liabilities, or owner's equity is known as a transaction. Chapter 2 describes five transactions involved in starting Rugcare, a proprietorship. Rugcare is now ready to open for business. This chapter presents the transactions that commonly occur during the daily operations of a business. Each of these transactions changes Ben Furman's equity in Rugcare.

HOW TRANSACTIONS CHANGE OWNER'S EQUITY IN AN ACCOUNTING EQUATION

The accounting equation for Rugcare as of August 11, showing the effect of transactions for starting a business, is shown in Illustration 3-1.

The sum of the balances on the left side of the accounting equation, $11,360.00, equals the sum of the balances on the right side of the equation, $11,360.00. The equation is in balance.

Many transactions involved in the daily operations of a business increase or decrease owner's equity. Detailed information about these changes in owner's equity is needed by owners and managers to make sound business decisions.

ILLUSTRATION 3-1   Accounting equation after transactions for starting a proprietorship

	Assets			= Liabilities	+ Owner's Equity
	Cash	+ Supplies	+ Prepaid Insurance =	Butler Cleaning Supplies +	Ben Furman, Capital
Balances	$5,863	$4,297	$1,200	$1,360	$10,000
	Total of left side: $5,863 + $4,297 + $1,200 = $11,360			Total of right side: $1,360 + $10,000 = $11,360	

Received Cash from Sales

A transaction for the sale of goods or services results in an increase in owner's equity. An increase in owner's equity resulting from the operation of a business is called **revenue.** When cash is received from a sale, the total amount of assets and owner's equity is increased.

When Rugcare receives cash for services performed, two accounts in the accounting equation are affected. The asset account, Cash, is increased by the amount of cash received. The owner's equity account, Ben Furman, Capital, is increased by the same amount.

Transaction 6   August 12, 19--. Received cash from sales, $525.00.

The effect of this transaction on the accounting equation is shown in Illustration 3-2. The asset account, Cash, is increased by $525.00, the amount of cash received. This increase is on the left side of the equation. The owner's equity account, Ben Furman, Capital, is also increased by $525.00. This increase is on the right side of the equation.

ILLUSTRATION 3-2   Receiving cash from sales increases assets and owner's equity

	Assets			= Liabilities +	Owner's Equity
	Cash	+ Supplies	+ Prepaid Insurance =	Butler Cleaning Supplies +	Ben Furman, Capital
Balances	$5,863	$4,297	$1,200	$1,360	$10,000
Transaction 6	+525				+525 (revenue)
New Balances	$6,388	$4,297	$1,200	$1,360	$10,525

Total of left side: $6,388 + $4,297 + $1,200 = $11,885   Total of right side: $1,360 + $10,525 = $11,885

FYI

When all the changes occur on one side of the accounting equation, increases on that side must be matched by decreases on the same side.

After this transaction is recorded, the sum of the balances on the left side of the equation equals the sum of the balances on the right side, $11,885.00. The equation is still in balance.

In this chapter, three different kinds of transactions that affect owner's equity are described. Therefore, a description of the transaction is shown in parentheses to the right of the amount in the accounting equation. Transaction 6 is a revenue transaction. Therefore, *(revenue)* is shown beside the $525.00 change in owner's equity in Illustration 3-2.

Paid Cash for Expenses

A transaction to pay for goods or services needed to operate a business results in a decrease in owner's equity. A decrease in owner's equity resulting from the operation of a business is called an **expense.** When cash is paid for expenses, the business has less cash. Therefore, the asset account, Cash, is decreased. The owner's equity account, Ben Furman, Capital, is also decreased by the same amount.

> *Transaction 7   August 12, 19--. Paid cash for rent, $250.00.*

The effect of this transaction on the accounting equation is shown in Illustration 3-3. The asset account, Cash, is decreased by $250.00, the amount of cash paid out. This decrease is on the left side of the equation. The owner's equity account, Ben Furman, Capital, is also

ILLUSTRATION 3-3 Paying cash for an expense decreases assets and owner's equity

	Assets			**= Liabilities + Owner's Equity**	
	Cash	+ Supplies	+ Prepaid Insurance =	Butler Cleaning Supplies +	Ben Furman, Capital
Balances	$6,388	$4,297	$1,200	$1,360	$10,525
Transaction 7	−250				−250 (expense)
New Balances	$6,138	$4,297	$1,200	$1,360	$10,275

Total of left side:
$6,138 + $4,297 + $1,200 = $11,635

Total of right side:
$1,360 + $10,275 = $11,635

decreased by $250.00. This decrease is on the right side of the equation.

After this transaction is recorded, the sum of the balances on the left side of the equation equals the sum of the balances on the right side, $11,635.00. The equation is still in balance.

Transaction 8   August 12, 19--. Paid cash for telephone bill, $45.00.

Most businesses must make payments for goods and services provided by public utilities, such as telephone companies. These goods and services are often referred to as utilities. In addition to telephone services, electricity, gas, water, and sanitation are also considered to be utilities.

The effect of this transaction on the accounting equation is shown in Illustration 3-4. The asset account, Cash, is decreased by $45.00, the amount of cash paid out. This decrease is on the left side of the equation. The owner's equity account, Ben Furman, Capital, is also decreased by $45.00. This decrease is on the right side of the equation.

> **FYI**
>
> Accounting is not just for accountants. For example, a doctor starting a new practice needs to consider the investment needed to acquire office space, furnishings, and equipment. A doctor must also consider what additional employees must be hired to run the practice.

ILLUSTRATION 3-4 Paying cash for an expense decreases assets and owner's equity

	Assets			**= Liabilities + Owner's Equity**	
	Cash	+ Supplies	+ Prepaid Insurance =	Butler Cleaning Supplies +	Ben Furman, Capital
Balances	$6,138	$4,297	$1,200	$1,360	$10,275
Transaction 8	−45				−45 (expense)
New Balances	$6,093	$4,297	$1,200	$1,360	$10,230

Total of left side:
$6,093 + $4,297 + $1,200 = $11,590

Total of right side:
$1,360 + $10,230 = $11,590

After this transaction is recorded, the sum of the balances on the left side of the equation equals the sum of the balances on the right side, $11,590.00. The equation is still in balance.

Other expense transactions might be for advertising, equipment rental or repairs, charitable contributions, and other miscellaneous items. All expense transactions affect the accounting equation in the same way as Transactions 7 and 8.

Paid Cash to Owner for Personal Use

Assets taken out of a business for the owner's personal use are called **withdrawals.** A withdrawal decreases owner's equity. Although an owner may withdraw any kind of asset, usually an owner withdraws cash. The withdrawal decreases the account balance of the withdrawn asset, such as Cash.

Transaction 9   August 12, 19--. Paid cash to owner for personal use, $100.00.

The effect of this transaction on the accounting equation is shown in Illustration 3-5 on the next page. The asset account, Cash, is decreased by $100.00, the amount of cash paid out. This decrease is on the left side of the accounting equation. The owner's equity account, Ben Furman, Capital, is also decreased by $100.00. This decrease is on the right side of the equation.

After this transaction is recorded, the sum of the balances on the left side of the equation equals the sum of the balances on the right side, $11,490.00. The equation is still in balance.

A decrease in owner's equity because of a withdrawal is not a result of the normal operations of a business. Therefore, a withdrawal is not an expense.

Summary of Changes in Owner's Equity

After recording the transactions for starting Rugcare as a proprietorship, the total owner's equity was $10,000.00. Five transactions

FYI

Some organizations were formed to support the interest of professional women. Examples of these organizations are American Society of Women Accountants, National Association for Female Executives, and National Association of Women Business Owners.

ILLUSTRATION 3-5   Paying cash to owner for personal use decreases assets and owner's equity

						Assets		=	Liabilities	+	Owner's Equity
	Cash	+	Supplies	+	Prepaid Insurance	=	Butler Cleaning Supplies	+	Ben Furman, Capital
Balances	$6,093		$4,297		$1,200		$1,360		$10,230
Transaction 9	−100								−100 (withdrawal)
New Balances	$5,993		$4,297		$1,200		$1,360		$10,130

Total of left side: $5,993 + $4,297 + $1,200 = $11,490

Total of right side: $1,360 + $10,130 = $11,490

have affected owner's equity. In Chapter 2, Ben Furman made a $10,000.00 investment. In this chapter, four transactions that changed owner's equity were recorded in the accounting equation.

Transaction Number	Kind of Transaction	Change in Owner's Equity
6	Revenue	+525.00
7	Expense (rent)	−250.00
8	Expense (telephone)	−45.00
9	Withdrawal	−100.00
	Net change in owner's equity	+130.00

A revenue transaction increased owner's equity. Expense and withdrawal transactions decreased owner's equity. These transactions together increased total owner's equity by $130.00, from $10,000.00 to $10,130.00.

For a business to succeed, revenues must be greater than expenses during most periods of time. An established business should rarely experience a decrease in its owner's equity.

REPORTING A CHANGED ACCOUNTING EQUATION ON A BALANCE SHEET

A balance sheet may be prepared on any date to report information about the assets, liabilities, and owner's equity of a business. The balance sheet prepared in Chapter 2, Illustration 2-6, reports Rugcare's financial condition at the end of business on August 11. The transactions recorded in Chapter 3 have changed the account balances of Cash and Ben Furman, Capital in the accounting equation. A revised balance sheet is prepared to report Rugcare's financial condition after recording these transactions.

The last transaction on August 12 is recorded in the accounting equation as shown in Illustration 3-5. The new account balances in the accounting equation after Transaction 9 are used to prepare the balance sheet. Rugcare's balance sheet as of August 12 is shown in Illustration 3-6.

The August 12 balance sheet is prepared using the same steps as described in Chapter 2.

ILLUSTRATION 3-6   Balance sheet

	Assets			= Liabilities	+ Owner's Equity
	Cash	+ Supplies	+ Prepaid Insurance =	Butler Cleaning Supplies +	Ben Furman, Capital
New Balances	$5,993	$4,297	$1,200	$1,360	$10,130

Rugcare
Balance Sheet
August 12, 19--

Assets		Liabilities	
Cash	5 9 9 3 00	Butler Cleaning Supplies	1 3 6 0 00
Supplies	4 2 9 7 00	Owner's Equity	
Prepaid Insurance	1 2 0 0 00	Ben Furman, Capital	10 1 3 0 00
Total Assets	11 4 9 0 00	Total Liab. and Owner's Eq.	11 4 9 0 00

The accounts on the left side of the accounting equation are reported on the left side of Rugcare's balance sheet. The accounts on the right side of the accounting equation are shown on the right side of the balance sheet. The total of the left side of the balance sheet, $11,490.00, is equal to the total of the right side of the balance sheet. The balance sheet is in balance.

A comparison of the August 11 and August 12 balance sheet totals is shown in Illustration 3-7.

The balance sheet has an increase of $130.00 on the left side (Assets) and an increase of $130.00 on the right side (Liabilities + Owner's Equity).

ILLUSTRATION 3-7 Comparison of balance sheet totals

	Assets			= Liabilities + Owner's Equity		
	Cash	+ Supplies	+ Prepaid Insurance =	Butler Cleaning Supplies	+	Ben Furman, Capital
August 11	$5,863	$4,297	$1,200	$1,360		$10,000
August 12	$5,993	$4,297	$1,200	$1,360		$10,130
	+$130	$0	$0	$0		+$130

Few businesses need to prepare a balance sheet every day. Many businesses prepare a balance sheet only on the last day of each month. Monthly balance sheets provide business owners and managers with frequent and regular information for making business decisions.

SUMMARY OF TRANSACTIONS THAT AFFECT OWNER'S EQUITY

Revenue, expense, and withdrawal transactions affect owner's equity. A revenue transaction increases owner's equity. Expense and withdrawal transactions decrease owner's equity.

The accounting equation has two sides. The left side of the equation shows assets. The right side of the equation shows liabilities and owner's equity. A transaction changes the account balances of two or more accounts. After each transaction, the total of accounts on the left side must equal the total of accounts on the right side. The effects of the transactions analyzed in Chapters 2 and 3 on the accounting equation are shown in Illustration 3-8 on the following page. After these transactions are recorded, the total of the balances on the left side equals the total of the balances on the right side, $11,490.00. Therefore, the accounting equation is in balance.

The new balances of the accounting equation are used to prepare a balance sheet. The left side of the balance sheet contains asset accounts. The right side contains liability and owner's equity accounts.

Audit Your Understanding

1. What is the heading on the left side of the balance sheet?

2. What are the headings on the right side of the balance sheet?

3. What is the total on the left side of the balance sheet?

4. What is the total on the right side of the balance sheet?

SUMMARY ILLUSTRATION 3-8

Summary of how transactions affect the accounting equation

Transaction	Assets			= Liabilities +	Owner's Equity
	Cash +	Supplies +	Prepaid Insurance	= Butler Cleaning Supplies +	Ben Furman, Capital
Beginning Balance	$0	$0	$0	$0	$0
1. Received cash from owner as an investment	+10,000				+10,000 (investment)
New Balances	$10,000	$0	$0	$0	$10,000
2. Paid cash for supplies	−1,577	+1,577			
New Balances	$ 8,423	$1,577	$0	$0	$10,000
3. Paid cash for insurance	−1,200		+1,200		
New Balances	$ 7,223	$1,577	$1,200	$0	$10,000
4. Bought supplies on account		+2,720		+2,720	
New Balances	$ 7,223	$4,297	$1,200	$2,720	$10,000
5. Paid cash on account	−1,360			−1,360	
New Balances	$ 5,863	$4,297	$1,200	$1,360	$10,000
6. Received cash from sales	+525				+525 (revenue)
New Balances	$ 6,388	$4,297	$1,200	$1,360	$10,525
7. Paid cash for rent	−250				−250 (expense)
New Balances	$ 6,138	$4,297	$1,200	$1,360	$10,275
8. Paid cash for telephone bill	−45				−45 (expense)
New Balances	$ 6,093	$4,297	$1,200	$1,360	$10,230
9. Paid cash to owner for personal use	−100				−100 (withdrawal)
New Balances	$ 5,993	$4,297	$1,200	$1,360	$10,130

Total of left side:
$5,993 + $4,297 + $1,200 = $11,490

Total of right side:
$1,360 + $10,130 = $11,490

What is the meaning of each of the following?

1. **revenue**
2. **expense**
3. **withdrawals**

1. Why do owners and managers need information about changes in owner's equity?

2. What accounts are affected, and how, when cash is received from sales?

3. How does a cash payment for goods or services needed to operate a business affect owner's equity?

4. What accounts are affected, and how, by a cash payment for an expense?

5. What must be true of the accounting equation after each transaction is recorded?

6. What are four expense transactions other than rent and utilities?

7. Which asset is normally withdrawn by an owner for personal use?

8. What accounts are affected, and how, when an owner withdraws $200.00 for personal use?

9. What transactions decrease owner's equity?

10. What must be true of changes in owner's equity if a business is to be successful?

11. What are three accounts that might be found on the left side of a balance sheet?

12. How often might a business be expected to prepare a balance sheet?

CASE 1 Garcia Books received an investment from its owner, Mrs. Juanita Garcia. This transaction is recorded in the following accounting equation. Is the analysis correct? Explain.

	Assets			=	Liabilities	+	Owner's Equity
Cash	+	Supplies	+	Prepaid Insurance =	Panther Supply Company	+	Juanita Garcia, Capital
$1,000		$3,000		$2,000	$2,500		$3,500
+750							
$1,750		$3,000		$2,000	$2,500		$3,500

CASE 2 The manager of Phillip's Department Store prepares a balance sheet at the end of each business day. Is this a satisfactory procedure? Explain.

DRILL 3-D1 Determining how revenue, expense, and withdrawal transactions change an accounting equation

TUTORIAL

Use a form similar to the following.

Trans. No.	Assets						= Liabilities + Owner's Equity		
	Cash	+	Supplies	+	Prepaid Insurance	=	Maxwell Company	+	Susan Sanders, Capital
1.	+								+

Transactions

1. Received cash from owner as an investment.
2. Received cash from sales.
3. Paid cash for telephone bill.
4. Paid cash for advertising.
5. Paid cash to owner for personal use.
6. Paid cash for rent.
7. Received cash from sales.
8. Paid cash for equipment repairs.

INSTRUCTIONS:

Decide which accounts in the accounting equation are changed by each transaction. Place a plus (+) in the appropriate column if the account is increased. Place a minus (−) in the appropriate column if the account is decreased. Transaction 1 is given as an example.

DRILL 3-D2 Determining how transactions change an accounting equation

Use a form similar to the following.

Trans. No.	Assets						= Liabilities + Owner's Equity		
	Cash	+	Supplies	+	Prepaid Insurance	=	Barrett Company	+	Sue Marist, Capital
1.			+				+		

Transactions

1. Bought supplies on account from Barrett Company.
2. Paid cash for electric bill.
3. Received cash from owner as an investment.
4. Paid cash for insurance.

5. Received cash from sales.
6. Paid cash for rent.
7. Paid cash for supplies.
8. Paid cash for advertising.
9. Paid cash on account to Barrett Company.
10. Paid cash to owner for personal use.

INSTRUCTIONS:

Decide which accounts in the accounting equation are changed by each transaction. Place a plus (+) in the appropriate column if the account is increased. Place a minus (−) in the appropriate column if the account is decreased. Transaction 1 is given as an example.

APPLICATION PROBLEMS   EPT(c,d)

PROBLEM 3-1 Determining how revenue, expense, and withdrawal transactions change an accounting equation

Peter Smith operates a service business called Peter's Service Company. Peter's Service Company uses the accounts shown in the following accounting equation. Use a form similar to the following to complete this problem.

Trans. No.	Assets					= Liabilities + Owner's Equity		
	Cash	+	Supplies	+	Prepaid Insurance	= Kline Company	+	Peter Smith, Capital
Beg. Bal.	625		375		300	200		1,100
1.	−300							−300 (expense)
New Bal.	325		375		300	200		800
2.								

Transactions

1. Paid cash for rent, $300.00.
2. Paid cash to owner for personal use, $150.00.
3. Received cash from sales, $800.00.
4. Paid cash for equipment repairs, $100.00.
5. Paid cash for telephone bill, $60.00.
6. Received cash from sales, $650.00.
7. Paid cash for charitable contributions, $35.00.
8. Paid cash for miscellaneous expenses, $25.00.

INSTRUCTIONS:

For each transaction, complete the following. Transaction 1 is given as an example.

a. Analyze the transaction to determine which accounts in the accounting equation are affected.

b. Write the amount in the appropriate columns, using a plus (+) if the account increases or a minus (−) if the account decreases.

c. For transactions that change owner's equity, write in parentheses a description of the transaction to the right of the amount.

d. Calculate the new balance for each account in the accounting equation.

e. Before going on to the next transaction, determine that the accounting equation is still in balance.

PROBLEM 3-2 Determining how transactions change an accounting equation and preparing a balance sheet

Doris Becker operates a typing business called QuickType. QuickType uses the accounts shown in the following accounting equation. Use a form similar to the following to complete this problem.

| Trans. No. | Assets | | | | | | = Liabilities | + Owner's Equity |
	Cash	+	Supplies	+	Prepaid Insurance	=	Teale Company	+	Doris Becker, Capital
Beg. Bal.	500		260		300		100		960
1.	−50								−50 (expense)
New Bal.	450		260		300		100		910
2.									

Transactions
1. Paid cash for equipment repair, $50.00.
2. Received cash from sales, $325.00.
3. Paid cash for supplies, $200.00.
4. Bought supplies on account from Teale Company, $1,200.00.
5. Paid cash for advertising, $200.00.
6. Received cash from sales, $280.00.
7. Paid cash for water bill, $60.00.
8. Paid cash for insurance, $400.00.
9. Paid cash to owner for personal use, $125.00.
10. Received cash from sales, $260.00.
11. Paid cash for equipment rental, $45.00.
12. Paid cash for charitable contributions, $25.00.
13. Received cash from sales, $300.00.
14. Paid cash on account to Teale Company, $100.00.
15. Received cash from owner as an investment, $1,000.00.
16. Paid cash for rent, $600.00.
17. Received cash from sales, $430.00.
18. Paid cash on account to Teale Company, $750.00.

INSTRUCTIONS:

1. For each transaction, complete the following. Transaction 1 is given as an example.
   a. Analyze the transaction to determine which accounts in the accounting equation are affected.
   b. Write the amount in the appropriate columns, using a plus (+) if the account increases or a minus (−) if the account decreases.
   c. For transactions that change owner's equity, write in parentheses a description of the transaction to the right of the amount.

d. Calculate the new balance for each account in the accounting equation.

e. Before going on to the next transaction, determine that the accounting equation is still in balance.

2. Using the final balances in the accounting equation, prepare a balance sheet for Quick-Type. Use the date July 17 of the current year.

ENRICHMENT PROBLEMS   EPT(c,d)

MASTERY PROBLEM 3-M Determining how transactions change an accounting equation and preparing a balance sheet

Fred Nance operates a service business called Nance Company. Nance Company uses the accounts shown in the following accounting equation. Use a form similar to the following to complete this problem.

Trans. No.	Assets				= Liabilities	+ Owner's Equity
	Cash	+	Supplies	+ Prepaid Insurance	= Sickle Company	+ Fred Nance, Capital
Beg. Bal. 1.	1,400 −100		300	400	1,500	600 −100 (expense)
New Bal. 2.	1,300		300	400	1,500	500

Transactions
1. Paid cash for telephone bill, $100.00.
2. Received cash from owner as an investment, $200.00.
3. Paid cash for rent, $500.00.
4. Paid cash for equipment rental, $100.00.
5. Received cash from sales, $895.00.
6. Bought supplies on account from Sickle Company, $600.00.
7. Paid cash for equipment repair, $15.00.
8. Paid cash for miscellaneous expense, $30.00.
9. Received cash from sales, $920.00.
10. Paid cash for advertising, $50.00.
11. Paid cash for charitable contribution, $10.00.
12. Paid cash for supplies, $400.00.
13. Paid cash for advertising, $250.00.
14. Received cash from sales, $795.00.
15. Paid cash on account to Sickle Company, $1,500.00.
16. Paid cash for insurance, $250.00.
17. Received cash from sales, $960.00.
18. Paid cash to owner for personal use, $1,000.00.

INSTRUCTIONS:
1. For each transaction, complete the following. Transaction 1 is given as an example.
 a. Analyze the transaction to determine which accounts in the accounting equation are affected.

b. Write the amount in the appropriate columns, using a plus (+) if the account increases or a minus (−) if the account decreases.

c. For transactions that change owner's equity, write in parentheses a description of the transaction to the right of the amount.

d. Calculate the new balance for each account in the accounting equation.

e. Before going on to the next transaction, determine that the accounting equation is still in balance.

2. Using the final balances in the accounting equation, prepare a balance sheet for Nance Company. Use the date April 30 of the current year.

CHALLENGE PROBLEM 3-C Calculating the missing amounts in an accounting equation

Each of the following statements includes four of the five amounts needed to complete an accounting equation.

Statements

1. Cash, $400.00; Supplies, $300.00; Prepaid Insurance, $800.00; Dexter Company, $500.00.
2. Cash, $200.00; Prepaid Insurance, $400.00; Dexter Company, $250.00; Pat Bouwman, Capital, $900.00.
3. Cash, $300.00; Supplies, $1,000.00; Prepaid Insurance, $750.00; Pat Bouwman, Capital, $1,200.00.
4. Supplies, $2,000.00; Prepaid Insurance, $1,200.00; Dexter Company, $2,400.00; Pat Bouwman, Capital, $3,500.00.
5. Cash, $100.00; Supplies, $2,700.00; Dexter Company, $1,100.00; Pat Bouwman, Capital, $2,500.00.
6. Cash, $250.00; Supplies, $400.00; Prepaid Insurance, $300.00; Pat Bouwman, Capital, $500.00.
7. Cash, $600.00; Supplies, $2,200.00; Prepaid Insurance, $900.00; Dexter Company, $500.00.
8. Supplies, $100.00; Prepaid Insurance, $400.00; Dexter Company, $150.00; Pat Bouwman, Capital, $500.00.

INSTRUCTIONS:

1. Use a form similar to the following. Record the information from each of the statements. Statement 1 is given as an example.

| State-ment | Assets | | | = Liabilities | + Owner's Equity |
	Cash +	Supplies +	Prepaid Insurance =	Dexter Company +	Pat Bouwman, Capital
1.	400	300	800	500	_____
	Total: _____			Total: _____	

2. Use a form similar to the one shown on page 51. Calculate the sum of the balances on the side of the accounting equation that is complete. The totals of the balances on the left and right sides must be equal for the accounting equation to be in balance.

3. For each line of the form, calculate the amount of the missing item in the accounting equation. Statement 1 is given as an example.

| State-ment | Assets | | | | | = | Liabilities | + | Owner's Equity |
	Cash	+	Supplies	+	Prepaid Insurance	=	Dexter Company	+	Pat Bouwman, Capital
1.	400		300		800		500		1,000
	Total: 1,500						Total: 1,500		

Analyzing Transactions into Debit and Credit Parts

ENABLING PERFORMANCE TASKS

After studying Chapter 4, you will be able to:

a Define accounting terms related to analyzing transactions into debit and credit parts.

b Identify accounting practices related to analyzing transactions into debit and credit parts.

c Use T accounts to analyze transactions showing which accounts are debited or credited for each transaction.

d Verify the equality of debits and credits for each transaction.

TERMS PREVIEW

T account • debit • credit • chart of accounts • contra account

How business transactions affect accounts in an accounting equation is described in Chapters 2 and 3. Even though the effects of transactions *can* be recorded in an accounting equation, the procedure is not practical in an actual accounting system. Accountants need more detail about the changes affecting each account than will appear in an accounting equation. Also, the number of accounts used by most businesses would make the accounting equation cumbersome to use as a major financial record. Therefore, a separate record is commonly used for each account.

ACCOUNTS

The accounting equation can be represented as a *T*, as shown in Illustration 4-1.

ILLUSTRATION 4-1 Sides of an accounting equation

The values of all things owned (assets) are on the left side of the accounting equation. The values of all equities or claims against the assets (liabilities and owner's equity) are on the right side of the accounting equation.

The total of amounts on the left side of the accounting equation must always equal the total of amounts on the right side. Therefore, the total of all assets on the left side of the accounting equation must always equal the total of all liabilities and owner's equity on the right side.

A record summarizing all the information pertaining to a single item in the accounting equation is known as an account. Transactions change the balances of accounts in the accounting equation. Accounting transactions must be analyzed to determine how account balances are changed. An accounting device used to analyze transactions is called a **T account**. The relationship of a T account to the accounts in the accounting equation is shown in Illustration 4-2.

> **FYI**
>
> Always draw T accounts when analyzing transactions so that you can see the debit and credit sides.

ILLUSTRATION 4-2 Relationship of a T account to the accounting equation

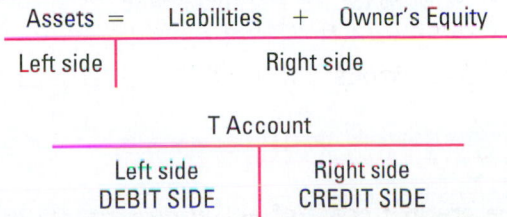

Accountants have special names for amounts recorded on the left and right sides of a T account. An amount recorded on the left side of a T account is called a **debit**. An amount recorded on the right side of a T account is called a **credit**. The T account is the basic device used to analyze the effect of transactions on accounts.

The normal balance side of an asset, liability, or capital account is based on the location of the account in the accounting equation, as shown in Illustration 4-3.

ILLUSTRATION 4-3

Relationship of asset, liability, and capital accounts to the accounting equation

Assets	=	Liabilities	+	Owner's Equity

Left side		Right side
ASSETS		LIABILITIES

Left side	Right side		Left side	Right side
Debit side	Credit side		Debit side	Credit side
NORMAL BALANCE				NORMAL BALANCE

	OWNER'S CAPITAL ACCOUNT

		Left side	Right side
		Debit side	Credit side
			NORMAL BALANCE

Asset accounts have normal debit balances (left side) because assets are on the left side of the accounting equation. Liability accounts have normal credit balances (right side) because liabilities appear on the right side of the accounting equation. The owner's capital account has a normal credit balance (right side) because the capital account appears on the right side of the accounting equation.

The sides of a T account are also used to show increases and decreases in account balances, as shown in Illustration 4-4.

ILLUSTRATION 4-4

Increase and decrease sides of asset, liability, and capital accounts

Assets	=	Liabilities	+	Owner's Equity

Left side		Right side
ASSETS		LIABILITIES

Left side	Right side		Left side	Right side
Debit side	Credit side		Debit side	Credit side
Normal balance				Normal balance
INCREASE	DECREASE		DECREASE	INCREASE

	OWNER'S CAPITAL

		Left side	Right side
		Debit side	Credit side
			Normal balance
		DECREASE	INCREASE

Two basic accounting rules regulate increases and decreases of account balances. (1) Account balances increase on the normal balance side of an account. (2) Account balances decrease on the side opposite the normal balance side of an account.

Asset accounts have normal debit balances; therefore, asset accounts increase on the debit side and decrease on the credit side. Liability accounts have normal credit balances; therefore, liability accounts increase on the credit side and decrease on the debit side. The owner's capital account has a normal credit balance; therefore, the capital account increases on the credit side and decreases on the debit side.

ANALYZING HOW TRANSACTIONS AFFECT ACCOUNTS

Before a transaction is recorded in the records of a business, the information is analyzed to determine which accounts are changed and how. Each transaction changes the balances of at least two accounts. In addition, debits equal credits for each transaction, as shown in Illustration 4-5.

ILLUSTRATION 4-5

Debits equal credits for each transaction

Supplies		Cash	
Left side	Right side	Left side	Right side
Debit side	Credit side	Debit side	Credit side
Normal balance		Normal balance	
Increase 1,577.00	Decrease	Increase	1,577.00 Decrease

DEBITS ------------------------------ equal ---------------------------- CREDITS

The total debits, $1,577.00, equal the total credits, $1,577.00, for this transaction.

Four questions are used in analyzing a transaction into its debit and credit parts.

1 What accounts are affected? A list of accounts used by a business is called a **chart of accounts**. The account titles used by Rugcare are found on the chart of accounts on page 18.

2 How is each account classified? Rugcare's accounts are classified as assets, liabilities, owner's equity, revenue, and expenses.

3 How is each account balance changed? Is each account increased or decreased?

4 How is each amount entered in the accounts? The amount is either debited or credited to the account.

Received Cash from Owner as an Investment

August 1, 19--. Received cash from owner as an investment, $10,000.00.

The effect of this transaction in the accounting equation is shown in Illustration 4-6.

ILLUSTRATION 4-6

How debits and credits affect accounts when receiving cash from owner as an investment

Assets	=	Liabilities	+	Owner's Equity
Left side				Right side
Cash				Ben Furman, Capital
+10,000.00				+10,000.00 (investment)

Any Asset		Owner's Capital	
Left side	Right side	Left side	Right side
Debit side	Credit side	Debit side	Credit side
Normal balance			Normal balance
Increase	Decrease	Decrease	Increase

Cash		Ben Furman, Capital	
Left side	Right side	Left side	Right side
Debit side	Credit side	Debit side	Credit side
Normal balance			Normal balance
Increase 10,000.00	Decrease	Decrease	Increase 10,000.00

DEBITS ------------------------------ equal ------------------------------ CREDITS

Four questions are used to analyze this transaction.

1 What accounts are affected? Cash and Ben Furman, Capital.

2 How is each account classified? Cash is an asset account with a normal debit balance. Ben Furman, Capital is an owner's equity account with a normal credit balance.

3 How is each account balance changed? Cash is increased. Ben Furman, Capital is increased.

4 How is each amount entered in the accounts? The asset account, Cash, has a normal debit balance and is increased by a debit, $10,000.00. The owner's equity account, Ben Furman, Capital, has a normal credit balance and is increased by a credit, $10,000.00.

For this transaction, the total debits, $10,000.00, equal the total credits, $10,000.00.

Paid Cash for Supplies

August 3, 19--. Paid cash for supplies, $1,577.00.

The effect of this transaction is shown in Illustration 4-7.

Assets		=	Liabilities	+	Owner's Equity
Cash	Supplies				
−1,577.00	+1,577.00				

Any Asset

Left side	Right side
Debit side	Credit side
Normal balance	
Increase	Decrease

Supplies

Left side	Right side
Debit side	Credit side
Normal balance	
Increase 1,577.00	Decrease

Cash

Left side	Right side
Debit side	Credit side
Normal balance	
Increase	Decrease 1,577.00

DEBITS ------------ equal ------------ CREDITS

Four questions are used to analyze this transaction.

1 What accounts are affected? Cash and Supplies.

2 How is each account classified? Cash is an asset account with a normal debit balance. Supplies is an asset account with a normal debit balance.

3 How is each account balance changed? Cash is decreased. Supplies is increased.

4 How is each amount entered in the accounts? The asset account, Supplies, has a normal debit balance and is increased by a debit, $1,577.00. The asset account, Cash, has a normal debit balance and is decreased by a credit, $1,577.00.

For this transaction, the total debits, $1,577.00, equal the total credits, $1,577.00.

Paid Cash for Insurance

August 4, 19--. Paid cash for insurance, $1,200.00.

The effect of this transaction is shown in Illustration 4-8.
Four questions are used to analyze this transaction.

1 What accounts are affected? Cash and Prepaid Insurance.

2 How is each account classified? Cash is an asset account with a normal debit balance. Prepaid Insurance is an asset account with a normal debit balance.

MULTICULTURAL AWARENESS

Fra Luca Pacioli

Fra Luca Pacioli, an Italian mathematician, is the "Father of Accounting." He is called this because he was the first person to explain an accounting system in writing. His book, The Method Of Venice, which first described the double-entry accounting system, was published in 1494.

ILLUSTRATION 4-8

How debits and credits affect accounts when paying cash for insurance

Assets		=	Liabilities	+	Owner's Equity

Cash	Prepaid Insurance
−1,200.00	+1,200.00

Any Asset

Left side	Right side
Debit side	Credit side
Normal balance	
Increase	Decrease

Prepaid Insurance

Left side	Right side
Debit side	Credit side
Normal balance	
Increase 1,200.00	Decrease

Cash

Left side	Right side
Debit side	Credit side
Normal balance	
Increase	Decrease 1,200.00

DEBITS ------------ equal ------------ CREDITS

3 How is each account balance changed? Cash is decreased. Prepaid Insurance is increased.

4 How is each amount entered in the accounts? The asset account, Prepaid Insurance, has a normal debit balance and is increased by a debit, $1,200.00. The asset account, Cash, has a normal debit balance and is decreased by a credit, $1,200.00.

For this transaction, the total debits, $1,200.00, equal the total credits, $1,200.00.

Bought Supplies on Account

August 7, 19--. Bought supplies on account from Butler Cleaning Supplies, $2,720.00.

The effect of this transaction is shown in Illustration 4-9.
Four questions are used to analyze this transaction.

FYI

Always use the four steps of analyzing transactions. This will make the analyzing process easier.

1 What accounts are affected? Supplies and Butler Cleaning Supplies.

2 How is each account classified? Supplies is an asset account with a normal debit balance. Butler Cleaning Supplies is a liability account with a normal credit balance.

3 How is each account balance changed? Supplies is increased. Butler Cleaning Supplies is increased.

4 How is each amount entered in the accounts? The asset account, Supplies, has a normal debit balance and is increased

ILLUSTRATION 4-9   How debits and credits affect accounts when buying supplies on account

Assets	=	Liabilities	+	Owner's Equity
Supplies +2,720.00		Butler Cleaning Supplies +2,720.00		

Any Asset		Any Liability	
Left side Debit side Normal balance Increase	Right side Credit side Decrease	Left side Debit side Decrease	Right side Credit side Normal balance Increase

Supplies		Butler Cleaning Supplies	
Left side Debit side Normal balance Increase 2,720.00	Right side Credit side Decrease	Left side Debit side Decrease	Right side Credit side Normal balance Increase 2,720.00

DEBITS ---------------------------- equal ---------------------------- CREDITS

by a debit, $2,720.00. The liability account, Butler Cleaning Supplies, has a normal credit balance and is increased by a credit, $2,720.00.

For this transaction, the total debits, $2,720.00, equal the total credits, $2,720.00.

Paid Cash on Account

August 11, 19--. Paid cash on account to Butler Cleaning Supplies, $1,360.00.

The effect of this transaction is shown in Illustration 4-10.

ILLUSTRATION 4-10   How debits and credits affect accounts when paying cash on account

Assets	=	Liabilities	+	Owner's Equity
Cash −1,360.00		Butler Cleaning Supplies −1,360.00		

Any Asset		Any Liability	
Left side Debit side Normal balance Increase	Right side Credit side Decrease	Left side Debit side Decrease	Right side Credit side Normal balance Increase

Cash		Butler Cleaning Supplies	
Left side Debit side Normal balance Increase	Right side Credit side Decrease 1,360.00	Left side Debit side Decrease 1,360.00	Right side Credit side Normal balance Increase

CREDITS ----- equal ------ DEBITS

Four questions are used to analyze this transaction.

1 *What accounts are affected?* Cash and Butler Cleaning Supplies.

2 *How is each account classified?* Cash is an asset account with a normal debit balance. Butler Cleaning Supplies is a liability account with a normal credit balance.

3 *How is each account balance changed?* Cash is decreased. Butler Cleaning Supplies is decreased.

4 *How is each amount entered in the accounts?* The liability account, Butler Cleaning Supplies, has a normal credit balance and is decreased by a debit, $1,360.00. The asset account, Cash, has a normal debit balance and is decreased by a credit, $1,360.00.

For this transaction, the total debits, $1,360.00, equal the total credits, $1,360.00.

Received Cash from Sales

Revenue increases the owner's capital. The increases from revenue could be recorded directly in the owner's capital account. However, to avoid a capital account with a large number of entries and to

■ **Joe Arriola** ■

AVANTI PRESS, MIAMI, FLORIDA

Cuban-born Joe Arriola is the chairperson and chief executive officer of Avanti Press in Miami, Florida. Avanti Press prints high-quality catalogs and brochures. Clients include Walt Disney Company, Avon, Royal Caribbean Cruise Line, J.C. Penney, and many others. Avanti has sales of over $65 million a year. Winning the Minority Supplier of the Year Award has also attracted national attention and resulted in new business for the firm.

When he was 25 years old Arriola joined his father's printing business, which he began to expand when his father retired. A high school friend, Gene Martinez, helped in the expansion and is now president of the firm. Together, the two friends expanded the firm from 12 employees to over 425. In the process, the small offset printing company expanded into a full-service business offering different kinds of printing, design, photography, copy writing, and graphics. New areas for the

business are telemarketing and fulfillment services for their customers.

Arriola admits that when he and Martinez began the expansion they thought they knew a lot more than they really did about how to run a business. However, with hard work and some luck they prospered. Arriola says, "Back then we worked a lot of twenty-hour days. Now that we've been very successful, we've cut back to 16-hour workdays."

Arriola also maintains that the two best courses he has ever taken were the two years of accounting courses he took in high school in Miami. The accounting courses gave him the background to be able to read and understand financial statements and to communicate with bankers and financial institutions in the language of business, accounting.

Looking back on the early days of his business, Arriola said that the biggest surprise was that he thought "you open your doors, work hard, sell a lot, and make a lot of money. But it's not as easy as that. You have to plan for cash flows so that you can pay your accounts payable, and so many other things that you never thought of."

Personal Visions in Business

summarize revenue information separately from the other records, Rugcare uses a separate revenue account.

August 12, 19--. Received cash from sales, $525.00.

The effect of this transaction is shown in Illustration 4-11.

ILLUSTRATION 4-11 How debits and credits affect accounts when receiving cash from sales

Assets	=	Liabilities	+	Owner's Equity

Cash
+525.00

Owner's Capital
+525.00 (revenue)

Owner's Capital

Left side	Right side
Debit side	Credit side
	Normal balance
Decrease	Increase

Any Revenue Account

Left side	Right side
Debit side	Credit side
	Normal balance
Decrease	Increase

Cash

Left side	Right side
Debit side	Credit side
Normal balance	
Increase 525.00	Decrease

Sales

Left side	Right side
Debit side	Credit side
	Normal balance
Decrease	Increase 525.00

DEBITS ----------------------------- equal ----------------------------- CREDITS

The owner's capital account has a normal credit balance. A revenue account shows increases in capital. Therefore, a revenue account also has a normal credit balance. Revenue accounts increase on the credit side and decrease on the debit side. Rugcare's revenue account is titled Sales.

Four questions are used to analyze this revenue transaction.

1 *What accounts are affected?*   Cash and Sales.

2 *How is each account classified?*   Cash is an asset account with a normal debit balance. Sales is a revenue account with a normal credit balance.

3 *How is each account balance changed?*   Cash is increased. Sales is increased.

4 *How is each amount entered in the accounts?*   The asset account, Cash, has a normal debit balance and is increased by a debit, $525.00. The revenue account, Sales, has a normal credit balance and is increased by a credit, $525.00.

For this transaction, the total debits, $525.00, equal the total credits, $525.00.

Paid Cash for an Expense

Expenses decrease the owner's capital. Expenses could be recorded directly in the owner's capital account. However, to avoid a capital account with a large number of entries and to summarize expense information separately from the other records, Rugcare uses separate expense accounts.

The titles of Rugcare's expense accounts are shown on the chart of accounts, page 18. The expense account, Utilities Expense, is used to record all payments of utility bills. These include payments made for electricity, telephone, gas, water, and sanitation.

August 12, 19--. Paid cash for rent, $250.00.

The effect of this transaction is shown in Illustration 4-12.

ILLUSTRATION 4-12	How debits and credits affect accounts when paying cash for an expense

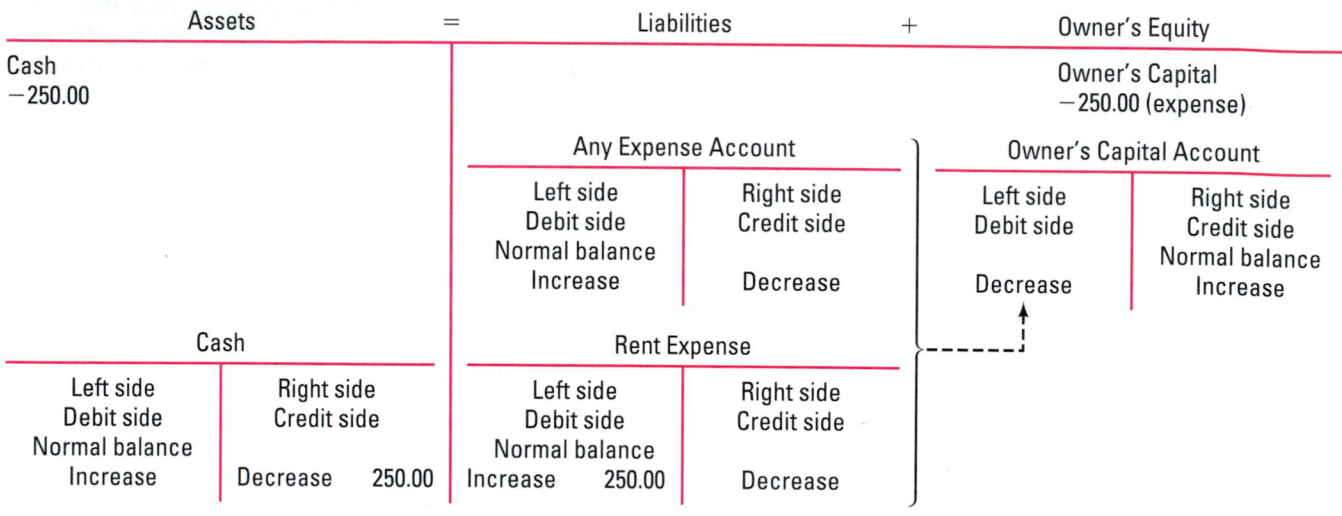

The owner's capital account has a normal credit balance. Decreases in the owner's capital account are shown as debits. An expense account shows decreases in owner's equity. Therefore, an expense account has a normal debit balance. An expense account increases on the debit side and decreases on the credit side.

Four questions are used to analyze this expense transaction.

1 *What accounts are affected?* Cash and Rent Expense.

2 *How is each account classified?* Cash is an asset account with a normal debit balance. Rent Expense is an expense account with a normal debit balance.

3 *How is each account balance changed?* Cash is decreased. Rent Expense is increased.

FYI

Do not confuse the word credit with increase or decrease. Credit only means the right side of an account.

4 *How is each amount entered in the accounts?* The expense account, Rent Expense, has a normal debit balance and is increased by a debit, $250.00. The asset account, Cash, has a normal debit balance and is decreased by a credit, $250.00.

For this transaction, the total debits, $250.00, equal the total credits, $250.00.

Paid Cash to Owner for Personal Use

Assets taken out of a business for the personal use of the owner are known as withdrawals. Withdrawals are considered to be part of the owner's equity taken out of a business. Therefore, withdrawals decrease the owner's equity. Withdrawals could be recorded as decreases directly in the owner's capital account. However, common accounting practice is to record withdrawals in a separate account to provide a separate record of the withdrawals for each fiscal period. In this way, the owner knows how much has been withdrawn from the business each fiscal period.

An account that reduces a related account on a financial statement is called a **contra account.** The drawing account is a contra capital account because the account shows decreases in capital.

August 12, 19--. Paid cash to owner for personal use, $100.00.

The effect of this transaction is shown in Illustration 4-13.

| ILLUSTRATION 4-13 | How debits and credits affect accounts when paying cash to owner for personal use |

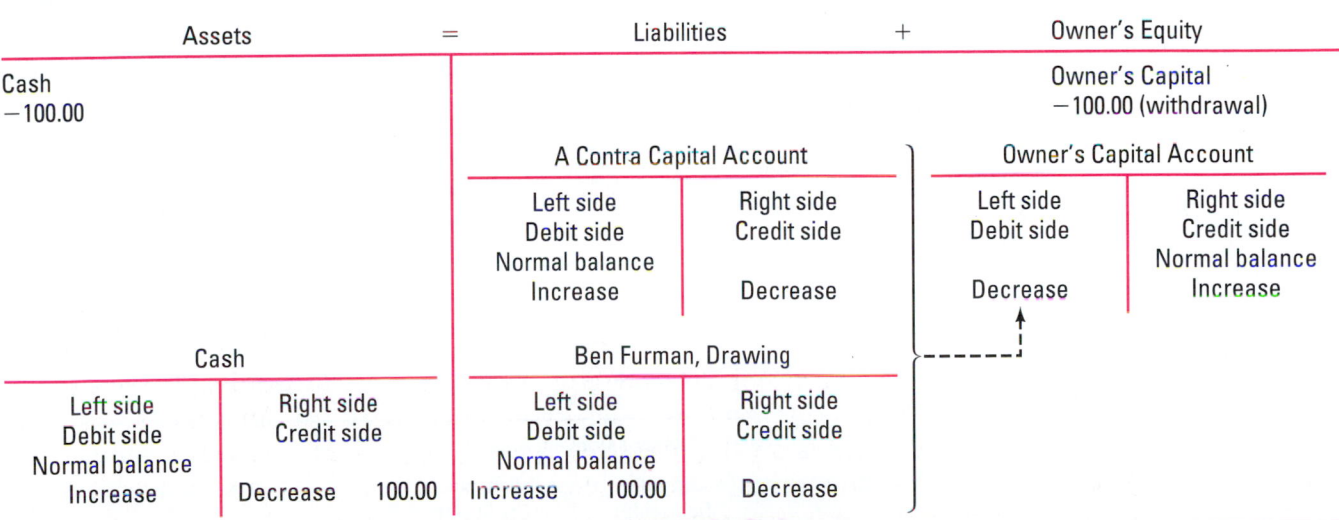

The owner's capital account has a normal credit balance. Decreases in the owner's capital account are shown as debits. Because a drawing account shows decreases in capital, a drawing account has a normal debit balance. A drawing account increases on the debit side and decreases on the credit side.

<table>
<tr><td>

Audit Your Understanding

1. State the four questions to analyze a transaction.

2. Are asset accounts increased on the debit side or credit side?

3. Are liability accounts increased on the debit side or credit side?

4. Is the owner's drawing account increased on the debit side or credit side?

5. Are revenue accounts increased on the debit side or credit side?

6. Are expense accounts increased on the debit side or credit side?

</td></tr>
</table>

Four questions are used to analyze this transaction.

1 What accounts are affected? Cash and Ben Furman, Drawing.

2 How is each account classified? Cash is an asset account with a normal debit balance. Ben Furman, Drawing is a contra capital account with a normal debit balance.

3 How is each account balance changed? Cash is decreased. Ben Furman, Drawing is increased.

4 How is each amount entered in the accounts? The contra capital account, Ben Furman, Drawing, has a normal debit balance and is increased by a debit, $100.00. The asset account, Cash, has a normal debit balance and is decreased by a credit, $100.00.

For this transaction, the total debits, $100.00, equal the total credits, $100.00.

SUMMARY OF ANALYZING TRANSACTIONS INTO DEBIT AND CREDIT PARTS

The total debits and total credits for a transaction must be equal, as shown in the following T accounts.

Supplies			Cash	
Debits 1,577.00	Credits		Debits	Credits 1,577.00

DEBITS -------------------- equal ------------------- CREDITS

Debits and credits affect account balances as shown in the following.

Assets	=	Liabilities	+	Owner's Equity

| Equation's left side | | | | | Equation's right side |

Asset Accounts		Liability Accounts		Owner's Capital Account	
Left side Debit side Normal balance Increases	Right side Credit side Decreases	Left side Debit side Decreases	Right side Credit side Normal balance Increases	Left side Debit side Decreases	Right side Credit side Normal balance Increases

Owner's Drawing Account	
Left side Debit side Normal balance Increases	Right side Credit side Decreases

Expense Accounts		Sales	
Left side Debit side Normal balance Increases	Right side Credit side Decreases	Left side Debit side Decreases	Right side Credit side Normal balance Increases

A summary analysis of transactions is shown in Illustration 4-14.

SUMMARY ILLUSTRATION 4-14
Summary analysis of transactions into debit and credit parts

Transaction	Accounts Affected	Account Classification	How is Account Affected?		Entered in Account as a	
			Increase	Decrease	Debit	Credit
Received cash from owner as an investment	Cash Ben Furman, Capital	Asset Owner's Equity	X X		X	 X
Paid cash for supplies	Supplies Cash	Asset Asset	X	 X	X	 X
Paid cash for insurance	Prepaid Insurance Cash	Asset Asset	X	 X	X	 X
Bought supplies on account	Supplies Butler Cleaning Supplies	Asset Liability	X X		X	 X
Paid cash on account	Butler Cleaning Supplies Cash	Liability Asset		X X	X	 X
Received cash from sales	Cash Sales	Asset Revenue	X X		X	 X
Paid cash for rent	Rent Expense Cash	Expense Asset	X	 X	X	 X
Paid cash to owner for personal use	Ben Furman, Drawing Cash	Contra Capital Asset	X	 X	X	 X

What is the meaning of each of the following?

1. **T account**
2. **debit**
3. **credit**
4. **chart of accounts**
5. **contra account**

QUESTIONS FOR INDIVIDUAL STUDY

EPT(b)

1. What basic accounting device is used to help analyze transactions?

2. What determines which side of a T account will be the normal balance side?

3. What is the normal balance side of an asset account? Of a liability account? Of a capital account?

4. What two basic accounting rules regulate the increases and decreases of an account?

5. On which sides of a T account are increases and decreases recorded for asset accounts? For liability accounts? For the capital account?

6. What is the relationship between total debits and total credits in accounting records?

7. What accounts are affected, and how, when cash is received from an owner as an investment?

8. What accounts are affected, and how, when cash is paid for supplies?

9. What accounts are affected, and how, when cash is paid for insurance?

10. What accounts are affected, and how, when supplies are bought on account?

11. What accounts are affected, and how, when cash is paid on account?

12. What is the normal balance side of a revenue account?

13. What accounts are affected, and how, when cash is received from sales?

14. What is the normal balance side of an expense account?

15. What accounts are affected, and how, when cash is paid for rent?

16. What is the normal balance side of a drawing account?

17. What accounts are affected, and how, when cash is paid to an owner for personal use?

CASES FOR CRITICAL THINKING

EPT(b)

CASE 1 Sharon Morris records *all* cash receipts as revenue and *all* cash payments as expenses. Is Miss Morris recording her cash receipts and cash payments correctly? Explain your answer.

CASE 2 Thomas Bueler records all investments, revenue, expenses, and withdrawals in his capital account. At the end of each month, Mr. Bueler sorts the information to prepare a summary of what has caused the changes in his capital account balance. To help Mr. Bueler prepare this summary in the future, what changes would you suggest he make in his records?

DRILL 4-D1 **Determining the normal balance, increase, and decrease sides for accounts**

TUTORIAL

Jeff Dixon owns a service business called HouseClean. HouseClean uses the following accounts.

Cash	Sales
Supplies	Advertising Expense
Prepaid Insurance	Miscellaneous Expense
Miller Supplies	Rent Expense
Wayne Office Supplies	Repair Expense
Jeff Dixon, Capital	Utilities Expense
Jeff Dixon, Drawing	

INSTRUCTIONS:

1. Prepare a T account for each account. Label the debit and credit sides of each account. The T account for Cash is given as an example.
2. For each account, label the side of the T account that is used for each of the following. The T account for Cash is given as an example.
   a. Normal balance
   b. Increase side
   c. Decrease side

Cash

Debit Side	Credit Side

Cash

Debit Side	Credit Side
Normal balance	
Increase	Decrease

DRILL 4-D2 **Analyzing how transactions affect accounts**

Use a form similar to the following. Transaction 1 is given as an example.

1	2	3	4	5	6	7	8	9
Trans. No.	Accounts Affected	Account Classification	Account's Normal Balance		How is Account Affected?		Entered in Account as a	
			Debit	Credit	(+)	(−)	Debit	Credit
1.	Cash	Asset	√		√		√	
	Jeff Dixon, Capital	Owner's Equity		√	√			√

Transactions
1. Received cash from owner as an investment.
2. Paid cash for supplies.
3. Paid cash for insurance.
4. Bought supplies on account from Miller Supplies.
5. Received cash from sales.
6. Paid cash on account to Miller Supplies.
7. Paid cash for rent.
8. Paid cash for repairs.
9. Paid cash for miscellaneous expense.
10. Paid cash for telephone bill (utilities expense).
11. Paid cash to owner for personal use.

INSTRUCTIONS:

1. Use the account titles given in Drill 4-D1. In Column 2, write the accounts affected by each transaction.
2. For each account title, write the account classification in Column 3.
3. For each account title, place a check mark in either Column 4 or 5 to indicate the normal balance.
4. For each account title, place a check mark in either Column 6 or 7 to indicate if the account is increased (+) or decreased (−) by this transaction.
5. For each account title, place a check mark in either Column 8 or 9 to indicate if the account is changed by a debit or a credit.

APPLICATION PROBLEMS   EPT(c,d)

PROBLEM 4-1   Analyzing transactions into debit and credit parts

Dixie Conastar owns a business called Conastar Company. Conastar Company uses the following accounts.

Cash	Sales
Supplies	Advertising Expense
Prepaid Insurance	Miscellaneous Expense
Bales Office Supplies	Rent Expense
Dixie Conastar, Capital	Utilities Expense
Dixie Conastar, Drawing	

Transactions

Apr. 1. Received cash from owner as an investment, $5,000.00.
   2. Paid cash for supplies, $50.00.
   3. Paid cash for insurance, $75.00.
   6. Bought supplies on account from Bales Office Supplies, $100.00.
   7. Received cash from sales, $400.00.
   8. Paid cash for water bill (utilities expense), $25.00.
   9. Paid cash for advertising, $40.00.
   13. Paid cash on account to Bales Office Supplies, $50.00.
   14. Received cash from sales, $400.00.
   15. Paid cash for miscellaneous expense, $5.00.
   16. Paid cash to owner for personal use, $50.00.
   18. Paid cash for rent, $250.00.

INSTRUCTIONS:

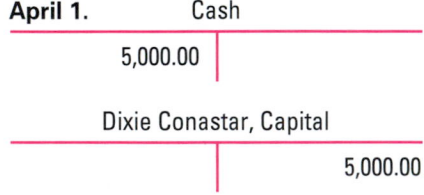

April 1.	Cash
5,000.00	

Dixie Conastar, Capital	
	5,000.00

1. Prepare two T accounts for each transaction. On each T account, write the account title of one of the accounts affected by the transaction.
2. Write the debit or credit amount in each T account to show how the transaction affected that account. T accounts for the first transaction are given as an example.

PROBLEM 4-2   Analyzing transactions into debit and credit parts

Buelah VanBorne owns a business called VanBorne Services. VanBorne Services uses the following accounts.

Cash	Sales
Supplies	Advertising Expense
Prepaid Insurance	Miscellaneous Expense
Fortune Supplies	Rent Expense
Herdle Office Supplies	Repair Expense
Buelah VanBorne, Capital	Utilities Expense
Buelah VanBorne, Drawing	

Transactions

May 1. Received cash from owner as an investment, $2,000.00.
     4. Bought supplies on account from Herdle Office Supplies, $500.00.
     6. Paid cash for rent, $500.00.
     7. Received cash from sales, $400.00.
    11. Paid cash on account to Herdle Office Supplies, $250.00.
    13. Paid cash for repairs, $80.00.
    14. Received cash from sales, $500.00.
    15. Paid cash for supplies, $600.00.
    19. Paid cash for insurance, $240.00.
    20. Bought supplies on account from Fortune Supplies, $50.00.
    21. Paid cash for supplies, $500.00.
    21. Received cash from sales, $750.00.
    25. Paid cash for telephone bill (utilities expense), $90.00.
    26. Paid cash for advertising, $130.00.
    28. Paid cash for miscellaneous expense, $15.00.
    28. Received cash from sales, $520.00.
    29. Paid cash to owner for personal use, $600.00.
    31. Received cash from sales, $400.00.

INSTRUCTIONS:

1. Prepare a T account for each account.
2. Analyze each transaction into its debit and credit parts. Write the debit and credit amounts in the proper T accounts to show how each transaction changes account balances. Write the date of the transaction in parentheses before each amount. The amounts for Transaction 1 are given in T accounts as an example.

Cash	
(1) 2,000.00	

Buelah VanBorne, Capital	
	(1) 2,000.00

MASTERY PROBLEM 4-M Analyzing transactions into debit and credit parts

James Lands owns a business called LandScape. LandScape uses the following accounts.

Cash	Sales
Supplies	Advertising Expense
Prepaid Insurance	Miscellaneous Expense
Derner Office Supplies	Rent Expense
Janitor Supplies	Repair Expense
James Lands, Capital	Utilities Expense
James Lands, Drawing	

Transactions

June 1. Received cash from owner as an investment, $3,000.00.
      2. Paid cash for supplies, $60.00.
      4. Paid cash for rent, $200.00.
      4. Received cash from sales, $350.00.
      5. Paid cash for repairs, $10.00.
      9. Bought supplies on account from Janitor Supplies, $500.00.
     10. Paid cash for insurance, $100.00.
     11. Received cash from owner as an investment, $900.00.
     11. Received cash from sales, $300.00.
     12. Bought supplies on account from Derner Office Supplies, $50.00.
     15. Paid cash for miscellaneous expense, $5.00.
     16. Paid cash on account to Janitor Supplies, $50.00.

18. Received cash from sales, $400.00.
22. Paid cash for electric bill (utilities expense), $35.00.
23. Paid cash for advertising, $30.00.
25. Received cash from sales, $220.00.
26. Paid cash to owner for personal use, $600.00.
30. Received cash from sales, $100.00.

INSTRUCTIONS:

1. Prepare a T account for each account.
2. Analyze each transaction into its debit and credit parts. Write the debit and credit amounts in the proper T accounts to show how each transaction changes account balances. Write the date of the transaction in parentheses before each amount.

CHALLENGE PROBLEM 4-C Analyzing transactions recorded in T accounts

Edward Burns owns a business for which the following T accounts show the current financial situation.

Cash					Sales		
(1)	5,000.00	(2)	80.00			(6)	475.00
(6)	475.00	(4)	15.00			(8)	350.00
(8)	350.00	(5)	16.00			(9)	400.00
(9)	400.00	(7)	900.00				
		(10)	150.00				
		(11)	95.00				
		(12)	50.00				

Supplies				Advertising Expense		
(3)	300.00			(5)	16.00	
(11)	95.00					

Midwest Supplies				Miscellaneous Expense		
(10)	150.00	(3)	300.00	(4)	15.00	

Edward Burns, Capital				Rent Expense		
		(1)	5,000.00	(7)	900.00	

Edward Burns, Drawing				Utilities Expense		
(2)	80.00			(12)	50.00	

INSTRUCTIONS:

1. Use a form similar to the following.

1	2	3	4	5	6
Trans. No.	Accounts Affected	Account Classification	Entered in Account as a		Description of Transaction
			Debit	Credit	
1.	Cash Edward Burns, Capital	Asset Owner's Equity	√	√	Received cash from owner as an investment

2. Analyze each numbered transaction in the T accounts. Write the titles of accounts affected in Column 2. For each account, write the classification of the account in Column 3.

3. For each account, place a check mark in either Column 4 or 5 to indicate if the account is affected by a debit or a credit.

4. For each transaction, write a brief statement in Column 6 describing the transaction. Information for Transaction 1 is given as an example.

5

Journalizing Transactions

As described in Chapter 4, transactions are analyzed into debit and credit parts before information is recorded. A form for recording transactions in chronological order is called a **journal**. Recording transactions in a journal is called **journalizing.**

Transactions could be recorded in the accounting equation. However, generally accepted accounting practice is to make a more permanent record by recording transactions in a journal.

A JOURNAL

Each business uses the kind of journal that best fits the needs of that business. The nature of a business and the number of transactions to be recorded determine the kind of journal to be used.

Journal Form

Rugcare uses a journal that has five amount columns, as shown in Illustration 5-1.

ILLUSTRATION 5-1   Five-column journal

					JOURNAL				PAGE	
					1	2	3	4	5	
	DATE	ACCOUNT TITLE	DOC. NO.	POST. REF.	GENERAL		SALES CREDIT	CASH		
					DEBIT	CREDIT		DEBIT	CREDIT	
1										1
2										2
3										3

The five amount columns in Rugcare's journal are General Debit, General Credit, Sales Credit, Cash Debit, and Cash Credit. A journal amount column headed with an account title is called a **special amount column.** Special amount columns are used for frequently occurring transactions. For example, most of Rugcare's transactions involve receipt or payment of cash. A large number of the transactions involve receipt of cash from sales. Therefore, Rugcare uses three special amount columns in its journal: Sales Credit, Cash Debit, and Cash Credit.

Using special amount columns eliminates writing an account title in the Account Title column. Therefore, recording transactions in a journal with special amount columns saves time.

A journal amount column that is not headed with an account title is called a **general amount column.** In Rugcare's journal, the General Debit and General Credit columns are general amount columns.

Accuracy

Information recorded in a journal includes the debit and credit parts of each transaction recorded in one place. The information can be verified by comparing the data in the journal with the source document data to assure that all information is correct.

Chronological Record

Transactions are recorded in a journal by date in the order in which the transactions occur. All the information about each transaction is recorded in one place making the information for a specific transaction easy to locate.

Double-Entry Accounting

Information for each transaction recorded in a journal is called an **entry.** The recording of debit and credit parts of a transaction is called **double-entry accounting.** In double-entry accounting, each transaction affects at least two accounts. Both the debit part and the credit part are recorded for each transaction. This procedure reflects the dual effect of each transaction on the business' records. For example, cash paid for advertising causes (1) a decrease in cash and (2) an increase in expenses. Double-entry accounting assures that debits equal credits.

SOURCE DOCUMENTS

A business paper from which information is obtained for a journal entry is called a **source document.** Each transaction is described by a source document that proves that the transaction did occur. For example, Rugcare prepares a check stub for each cash payment made. The check stub describes information about the cash payment transaction for which the check is prepared. The accounting concept, *Objective Evidence,* is applied when a source document is prepared for each transaction. *(CONCEPT: Objective Evidence)*

A transaction should be journalized only if it actually occurs. The amounts recorded must be accurate and true. Nearly all transactions result in the preparation of a source document. One way to verify the accuracy of a specific journal entry is to compare the entry with the source document. Rugcare uses four source documents: checks, calculator tapes, receipts, and memorandums.

Checks

A business form ordering a bank to pay cash from a bank account is called a **check.** The source document for cash payments is a check. Rugcare makes all cash payments by check. The checks are prenumbered to help Rugcare account for all checks. Rugcare's record of information on a check is the check stub prepared at the same time as the check. A check and check stub prepared by Rugcare are shown in Illustration 5-2.

ILLUSTRATION 5-2   Check and check stub

NO. 1	$ *1,577.00*		
Date *August 3*			19 --
To *Janitorial Supplies Co.*			
For *Supplies*			
BAL. BRO'T. FOR'D.		*0*	*00*
AMT. DEPOSITED ... *8 1 --* Date		*10,000*	*00*
SUBTOTAL		*10,000*	*00*
OTHER:			
SUBTOTAL		*10,000*	*00*
AMT. THIS CHECK		*1,577*	*00*
BAL. CAR'D. FOR'D.		*8,423*	*00*

RugCare 623 Walnut Street Billings, MT 59101-1946

NO. 1   93-109 / 929

August 3, _____ 19 ___

PAY TO THE ORDER OF *Janitorial Supplies Co.* _____ $ *1,577.00*

One thousand five hundred seventy-seven and $^{no}/_{100}$ ____ DOLLARS

For Classroom Use Only

Peoples national bank Billings, MT 59101-2320

FOR *Supplies*   *Ben Furman*

⑈0929010941⑈ 43⑈452119⑈

Procedures for preparing checks and check stubs are described in Chapter 7.

Calculator Tapes

Rugcare collects cash at the time services are rendered to customers. At the end of each day, Rugcare uses a printing electronic calculator to total the amount of cash received from sales for that day. By totaling all the individual sales, a single source document is produced for the total sales of the day. Thus, time and space are saved by recording only one entry for all of a day's sales. The calculator tape is the source document for daily sales. *(CONCEPT: Objective Evidence)* A calculator tape used as a source document is shown in Illustration 5-3.

ILLUSTRATION 5-3   Calculator tape used as a source document

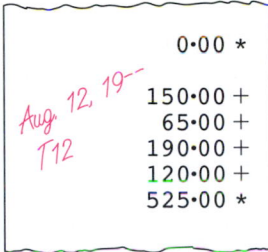

```
        0·00 *
Aug. 12, 19--  150·00 +
         65·00 +
T12     190·00 +
        120·00 +
        525·00 *
```

Rugcare dates and numbers each calculator tape. For example, in Illustration 5-3, the number, *T12*, indicates that the tape is for the twelfth day of the month.

Receipts

A business form giving written acknowledgement for cash received is called a **receipt**. When cash is received from sources other than sales, Rugcare prepares a receipt. The receipts are prenumbered to help account for all the receipts. A receipt is the source document for cash received from transactions other than sales. *(CONCEPT: Objective Evidence)* Rugcare's receipt is shown in Illustration 5-4.

ILLUSTRATION 5-4

Receipt used as a source document

No. **1**	Receipt No. **1**
Date _August 1,_ 19 _--_	_August 1,_ 19 _--_
From _Ben Furman_	Rec'd from _Ben Furman_
For _Investment_	For _Investment_
	Ten thousand and no/100 ———— Dollars
$ 10,000 00	Amount $ 10,000 00

RUGCARE
623 Walnut Street
Billings, MT 59101-1946

Ben Furman
Received By

Memorandums

A form on which a brief message is written describing a transaction is called a **memorandum**. When no other source document is prepared for a transaction, or when additional explanation is needed about a transaction, Rugcare prepares a memorandum. *(CONCEPT: Objective Evidence)* Rugcare's memorandums are prenumbered to help account for all the memorandums. A brief note is written on the memorandum to describe the transaction. The memorandum used by Rugcare is shown in Illustration 5-5.

ILLUSTRATION 5-5

Memorandum used as a source document

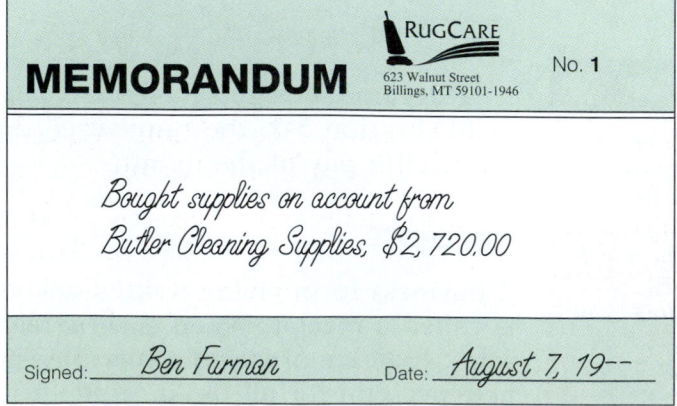

MEMORANDUM **RUGCARE** 623 Walnut Street Billings, MT 59101-1946 No. **1**

Bought supplies on account from
Butler Cleaning Supplies, $2,720.00

Signed: _Ben Furman_   Date: _August 7, 19--_

RECORDING TRANSACTIONS IN A FIVE-COLUMN JOURNAL

Information for each transaction recorded in a journal is known as an entry. An entry consists of four parts: (1) date, (2) debit, (3) credit, and (4) source document. Before a transaction is recorded in a journal, the transaction is analyzed into its debit and credit parts.

Received Cash from Owner as an Investment

August 1, 19--. Received cash from owner as an investment, $10,000.00. Receipt No. 1.

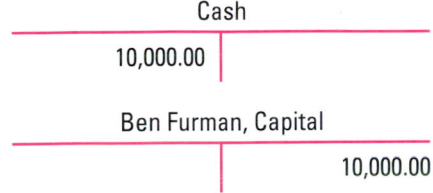

Cash

10,000.00

Ben Furman, Capital

10,000.00

The source document for this transaction is Receipt No. 1. *(CONCEPT: Objective Evidence)* The analysis of this transaction is shown in the T accounts.

All T account analysis in Chapter 5 is described in detail in Chapter 4.

The asset account, Cash, is increased by a debit, $10,000.00. The owner's capital account, Ben Furman, Capital, is increased by a credit, $10,000.00. The journal entry for this transaction is shown in Illustration 5-6.

ILLUSTRATION 5-6   Journal entry to record receiving cash from owner as an investment

					1	2	3	4	5
					GENERAL		SALES CREDIT	CASH	
	DATE	ACCOUNT TITLE	DOC. NO.	POST. REF.	DEBIT	CREDIT		DEBIT	CREDIT
1	*Aug.* 19-- *1*	*Ben Furman, Capital*	*R1*			10000 00		10000 00		1

JOURNAL   PAGE **1**

---

1 *Date.* Write the date, *19--, Aug. 1,* in the Date column. This entry is the first one on this journal page. Therefore, the year and month are both written for this entry. Neither the year nor the month are written again on the same page.

2 *Debit.* The journal has a special amount column for debits to Cash. The title of the account is in the column heading. Therefore, the account title does not need to be written in the Account Title column. Write the debit amount, *$10,000.00,* in the Cash Debit column.

3 *Credit.* Write the title of the account credited, *Ben Furman, Capital,* in the Account Title column. There is no special amount column with the title of the account credited, Ben Furman, Capital, in its heading. Therefore, the credit amount is recorded in the General Credit column. Write the credit amount, *$10,000.00,* in the General Credit column.

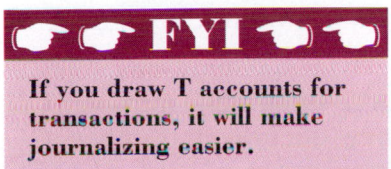

FYI

If you draw T accounts for transactions, it will make journalizing easier.

All amounts recorded in the General Debit or General Credit amount columns must have an account title written in the Account Title column.

4 *Source document.* Write the source document number, *R1*, in the Doc. No. column. The source document number, *R1*, indicates that this is Receipt No. 1.

The source document number is a cross reference from the journal to the source document. If more details are needed about this transaction, a person can refer to Receipt No. 1.

Paid Cash for Supplies

August 3, 19--. Paid cash for supplies, $1,577.00. Check No. 1.

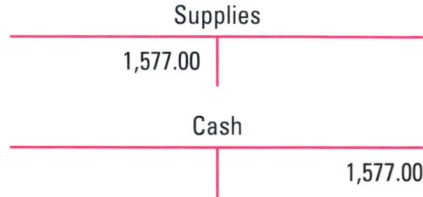

The source document for this transaction is Check No. 1. *(CONCEPT: Objective Evidence)* The analysis of this transaction is shown in the T accounts.

The asset account, Supplies, is increased by a debit, $1,577.00. The asset account, Cash, is decreased by a credit, $1,577.00. The journal entry for this transaction is shown in Illustration 5-7.

ILLUSTRATION 5-7   Journal entry to record paying cash for supplies

					GENERAL		SALES	CASH		
	DATE	ACCOUNT TITLE	DOC. NO.	POST. REF.	DEBIT	CREDIT	CREDIT	DEBIT	CREDIT	
2	3	Supplies	C1		1 5 7 7 00				1 5 7 7 00	2

1 *Date.* Write the date, *3*, in the Date column. This is not the first entry on the journal page. Therefore, the year and month are not written for this entry.

2 *Debit.* Write the title of the account debited, Supplies, in the Account Title column. There is no special amount column with the title of the account debited, Supplies, in its heading. Therefore, the debit amount is recorded in the General Debit column. Write the debit amount, *$1,577.00*, in the General Debit column.

3 *Credit.* The journal has a special amount column for credits to Cash. The title of the account is in the column heading. Therefore, the account title does not need to be written in the Account Title column. Write the credit amount, *$1,577.00*, in the Cash Credit column.

4 *Source document.* Write the source document number, *C1*, in the Doc. No. column. The source document number, *C1*, indicates that this is Check No. 1.

FYI

Dollars and cents signs and decimal points are not used when writing amounts on ruled accounting paper. Sometimes a color tint or a heavy vertical rule is used on printed accounting paper to separate the dollars and cents columns.

Paid Cash for Insurance

August 4, 19--. Paid cash for insurance, $1,200.00. Check No. 2.

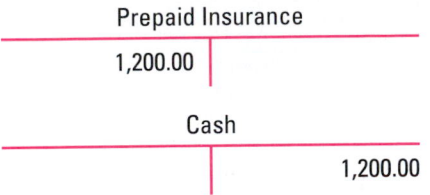

Prepaid Insurance	
1,200.00	

Cash	
	1,200.00

The source document for this transaction is Check No. 2. *(CONCEPT: Objective Evidence)* The analysis of this transaction is shown in the T accounts.

The asset account, Prepaid Insurance, is increased by a debit, $1,200.00. The asset account, Cash, is decreased by a credit, $1,200.00. The journal entry for this transaction is shown in Illustration 5-8.

ILLUSTRATION 5-8   Journal entry to record paying cash for insurance

					GENERAL		SALES	CASH	
	DATE	ACCOUNT TITLE	DOC. NO.	POST. REF.	DEBIT	CREDIT	CREDIT	DEBIT	CREDIT
3	4	*Prepaid Insurance*	C2		1 2 0 0 00				1 2 0 0 00

1 Date. Write the date, *4*, in the Date column.

2 Debit. Write the title of the account debited, *Prepaid Insurance*, in the Account Title column. There is no special amount column with the title of the account debited, Prepaid Insurance, in its heading. Therefore, the debit amount is recorded in the General Debit column. Write the debit amount, *$1,200.00*, in the General Debit column.

3 Credit. The journal has a special amount column for credits to Cash. The title of the account is in the column heading. Therefore, the account title does not need to be written in the Account Title column. Write the credit amount, *$1,200.00*, in the Cash Credit column.

4 Source document. Write the source document number, *C2*, in the Doc. No. column.

Bought Supplies on Account

August 7, 19--. Bought supplies on account from Butler Cleaning Supplies, $2,720.00. Memorandum No. 1.

Supplies	
2,720.00	

Butler Cleaning Supplies	
	2,720.00

Rugcare ordered these supplies by telephone. Rugcare wishes to record this transaction immediately. Therefore, a memorandum is prepared that shows supplies were received on account.

The source document for this transaction is Memorandum No. 1. *(CONCEPT: Objective Evidence)* The analysis of this transaction is shown in the T accounts.

The asset account, Supplies, is increased by a debit, $2,720.00. The liability account, Butler Cleaning Supplies, is increased by a credit, $2,720.00. The journal entry for this transaction is shown in Illustration 5-9.

ILLUSTRATION 5-9   Journal entry to record buying supplies on account

	DATE	ACCOUNT TITLE	DOC. NO.	POST. REF.	GENERAL DEBIT	GENERAL CREDIT	SALES CREDIT	CASH DEBIT	CASH CREDIT	
4	7	*Supplies*	M1		2 7 2 0 00					4
5		*Butler Cleaning Supplies*				2 7 2 0 00				5

JOURNAL   PAGE *1*

1 Date.   Write the date, 7, in the Date column.

2 Debit.   The journal does not have a special amount column for either the debit to Supplies or credits to Butler Cleaning Supplies. Therefore, both account titles need to be written in the Account Title column. The debit and credit amounts are recorded in the General Debit and General Credit columns. Write the title of the account debited, *Supplies*, in the Account Title column. Write the debit amount, *$2,720.00*, in the General Debit column.

3 Credit.   On the next line, write the title of the account credited, *Butler Cleaning Supplies*, in the Account Title column. Write the credit amount, *$2,720.00*, in the General Credit column on the same line as the account title.

This entry requires two lines in the journal because account titles for both the debit and credit amounts must be written in the Account Title column.

4 Source document.   Write the source document number, *M1*, in the Doc. No. column on the first line of the entry.

Paid Cash on Account

August 11, 19--. Paid cash on account to Butler Cleaning Supplies, $1,360.00. Check No. 3.

The source document for this transaction is Check No. 3. *(CONCEPT: Objective Evidence)* The analysis of this transaction is shown in the T accounts.

The liability account, Butler Cleaning Supplies, is decreased by a debit, $1,360.00. The asset account, Cash, is decreased by a credit, $1,360.00. The journal entry for this transaction is shown in Illustration 5-10.

Butler Cleaning Supplies
| 1,360.00 | |

Cash
| | 1,360.00 |

ILLUSTRATION 5-10   Journal entry to record paying cash on account

	DATE	ACCOUNT TITLE	DOC. NO.	POST. REF.	GENERAL DEBIT	GENERAL CREDIT	SALES CREDIT	CASH DEBIT	CASH CREDIT	
6	11	*Butler Cleaning Supplies*	C3		1 3 6 0 00				1 3 6 0 00	6

JOURNAL   PAGE *1*

1 Date. Write the date, *11*, in the Date column.

2 Debit. Write the title of the account debited, *Butler Cleaning Supplies*, in the Account Title column. There is no special amount column with the title of the account debited, Butler Cleaning Supplies, in its heading. Therefore, the debit amount is recorded in the General Debit column. Write the debit amount, *$1,360.00*, in the General Debit column.

3 Credit. The journal has a special amount column for credits to Cash. The title of the account is in the column heading. Therefore, the account title does not need to be written in the Account Title column. Write the credit amount, *$1,360.00*, in the Cash Credit column.

4 Source document. Write the source document number, *C3*, in the Doc. No. column.

Received Cash from Sales

August 12, 19--. Received cash from sales, $525.00. Tape No. 12.

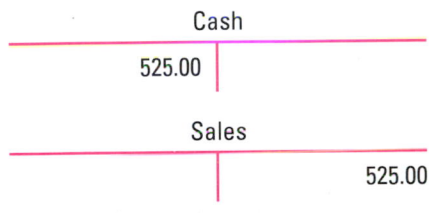

The source document for this transaction is Calculator Tape No. 12. *(CONCEPT: Objective Evidence)* The analysis of this transaction is shown in the T accounts.

The asset account, Cash, is increased by a debit, $525.00. The revenue account, Sales, is increased by a credit, $525.00. The journal entry for this transaction is shown in Illustration 5-11.

| **ILLUSTRATION 5-11** | Journal entry to record receiving cash from sales |

| | | | | | GENERAL | | SALES | CASH | |
| | | | | | | | CREDIT | | |
DATE	ACCOUNT TITLE	DOC. NO.	POST. REF.		DEBIT	CREDIT		DEBIT	CREDIT
				1	2	3	4	5	
7	12 ✓	T12 ✓					525 00	525 00		7

1 Date. Write the date, *12*, in the Date column.

2 Debit. The journal has a special amount column for debits to Cash. The title of the account is in the column heading. Therefore, the account title does not need to be written in the Account Title column. Write the debit amount, *$525.00*, in the Cash Debit column.

3 Credit. The journal also has a special amount column for credits to Sales. The title of the account is in the column heading. Therefore, the account title does not need to be written in the Account Title column. Write the credit amount, *$525.00*, in the Sales Credit column.

Because both amounts for this entry are recorded in special amount columns, no account titles are written in the

Account Title column. Therefore, a check mark is placed in the Account Title column to show that no account titles need to be written for this transaction. A check mark is also placed in the Post. Ref. column to show that no separate amounts on this line are to be posted individually.

Posting procedures are described in Chapter 6.

4 *Source document.* Write the source document number, *T12*, in the Doc. No. column.

Paid Cash for an Expense

August 12, 19--. Paid cash for rent, $250.00. Check No. 4.

The source document for this transaction is Check No. 4. *(CONCEPT: Objective Evidence)* The analysis of this transaction is shown in the T accounts.

The expense account, Rent Expense, is increased by a debit, $250.00. The asset account, Cash, is decreased by a credit, $250.00. The journal entry for this transaction is shown on line 8 in Illustration 5-12.

ILLUSTRATION 5-12   Journal entries to record paying cash for expenses

	DATE	ACCOUNT TITLE	DOC. NO.	POST. REF.	GENERAL DEBIT	GENERAL CREDIT	SALES CREDIT	CASH DEBIT	CASH CREDIT	
8	12	Rent Expense	C4		250 00				250 00	8
9	12	Utilities Expense	C5		45 00				45 00	9

1 *Date.* Write the date, *12*, in the Date column.

2 *Debit.* Write the title of the account debited, *Rent Expense*, in the Account Title column. There is no special amount column with the title of the account debited, Rent Expense, in its heading. Therefore, the debit amount is recorded in the General Debit column. Write the debit amount, *$250.00*, in the General Debit column.

3 *Credit.* The journal has a special amount column for credits to Cash. The title of the account is in the column heading. Therefore, the account title does not need to be written in the Account Title column. Write the credit amount, *$250.00*, in the Cash Credit column.

4 *Source document.* Write the source document number, *C4*, in the Doc. No. column.

The journal entry shown in Illustration 5-12 includes a cash payment for another expense, Utilities Expense. This transaction is journalized in the same way as the cash payment for rent.

Paid Cash to Owner for Personal Use

August 12, 19--. Paid cash to owner for personal use, $100.00. Check No. 6.

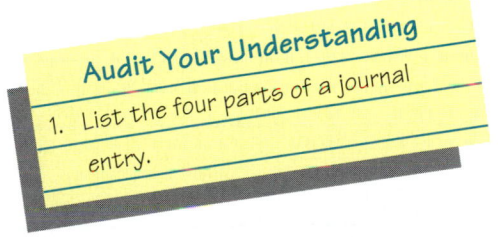

Ben Furman, Drawing

| 100.00 | |

Cash

| | 100.00 |

The source document for this transaction is Check No. 6. (CONCEPT: *Objective Evidence*) The analysis of this transaction is shown in the T accounts.

The contra capital account, Ben Furman, Drawing, is increased by a debit, $100.00. The asset account, Cash, is decreased by a credit, $100.00. The journal entry for this transaction is shown in Illustration 5-13.

| **ILLUSTRATION 5-13** | Journal entry to record paying cash to owner for personal use |

JOURNAL   PAGE 1

| | | | | | 1 | 2 | 3 | 4 | 5 |
| | | DOC. | POST. | GENERAL | | SALES | CASH | |
DATE	ACCOUNT TITLE	NO.	REF.	DEBIT	CREDIT	CREDIT	DEBIT	CREDIT
12	Ben Furman, Drawing	C6		100 00				100 00

1 **Date.** Write the date, *12*, in the Date column.

2 **Debit.** Write the title of the account debited, *Ben Furman, Drawing*, in the Account Title column. There is no special amount column with the title of the account debited, Ben Furman, Drawing, in its heading. Therefore, the debit amount is recorded in the General Debit column. Write the debit amount, *$100.00*, in the General Debit column.

3 **Credit.** The journal has a special amount column for credits to Cash. The title of the account is in the column heading. Therefore, the account title does not need to be written in the Account Title column. Write the credit amount, *$100.00*, in the Cash Credit column.

4 **Source document.** Write the source document number, *C6*, in the Doc. No. column.

Audit Your Understanding

1. List the four parts of a journal entry.

PROVING AND RULING A JOURNAL

After Rugcare uses all but the last line on a journal page, columns are proved and ruled before totals are carried forward to the next page. At the end of each month, Rugcare also proves and rules the journal.

After all entries on August 20 are recorded, page 1 of Rugcare's journal is filled, as shown in Illustration 5-14 on the next page.

Page 1 is proved and ruled before totals are carried forward to page 2.

Proving a Journal Page

To prove a journal page, Rugcare verifies that the total debits on the page equal the total credits. Three steps are followed in proving a journal page.

1 *Add each of the amount columns.* Use a calculator if one is available. If a calculator is not available, total the columns on a sheet of paper.

2 *Add the debit column totals, and then add the credit column totals.* The figures from page 1 of Rugcare's journal are below.

Column	Debit Column Totals	Credit Column Totals
General	$ 7,920.00	$12,920.00
Sales		2,319.00
Cash	12,319.00	5,000.00
Totals	$20,239.00	$20,239.00

3 *Verify that the total debits and total credits are equal.* The total debits and the total credits on page 1 of Rugcare's journal are $20,239.00. Because the total debits equal the total credits, page 1 of Rugcare's journal is proved.

ILLUSTRATION 5-14   Completed page 1 of a journal

JOURNAL   PAGE 1

	DATE	ACCOUNT TITLE	DOC. NO.	POST. REF.	GENERAL DEBIT (1)	GENERAL CREDIT (2)	SALES CREDIT (3)	CASH DEBIT (4)	CASH CREDIT (5)	
1	Aug. 1	Ben Furman, Capital	R1			1000 00		1000 00		1
2	3	Supplies	C1		157 700				157 700	2
3	4	Prepaid Insurance	C2		120 000				120 000	3
4	7	Supplies	M1		272 000					4
5		Butler Cleaning Supplies				272 000				5
6	11	Butler Cleaning Supplies	C3		136 000				136 000	6
7	12 √		T12	√			525 00	525 00		7
8	12	Rent Expense	C4		250 00				250 00	8
9	12	Utilities Expense	C5		45 00				45 00	9
10	12	Ben Furman, Drawing	C6		100 00				100 00	10
11	13	Repair Expense	C7		20 00				20 00	11
12	13	Miscellaneous Expense	C8		25 00				25 00	12
13	13 √		T13	√			229 00	229 00		13
14	14	Advertising Expense	C9		68 00				68 00	14
15	14 √		T14	√			360 00	360 00		15
16	17	Petty Cash	C10		200 00				200 00	16
17	17 √		T17	√			350 00	350 00		17
18	18	Miscellaneous Expense	C11		70 00				70 00	18
19	18 √		T18	√			320 00	320 00		19
20	19 √		T19	√			290 00	290 00		20
21	20	Repair Expense	C12		85 00				85 00	21
22	20 √		T20	√			245 00	245 00		22
23	20	Supplies	M2		200 00					23
24		Dale Office Supplies				200 00				24
25	20	Carried Forward		√	7920 00	12920 00	2319 00	12319 00	5000 00	25

If the total debits do not equal the total credits, the errors must be found and corrected before any more work is completed.

Ruling a Journal Page

After a journal page is proved, the page is ruled as shown in Illustration 5-14.

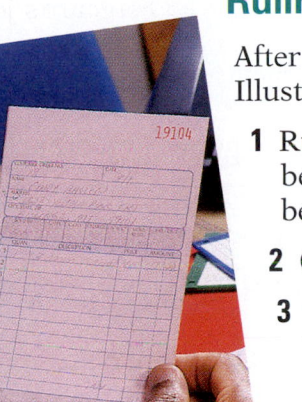

1 Rule a single line across all amount columns directly below the last entry to indicate that the columns are to be added.

2 On the next line, write the date, *20*, in the Date column.

3 Write the words, *Carried Forward*, in the Account Title column. A check mark is also placed in the Post. Ref. column to show that nothing on this line needs to be posted.

4 Write each column total below the single line.

5 Rule double lines below the column totals across all amount columns. The double lines mean that the totals have been verified as correct.

Starting a New Journal Page

The column totals from the previous page are carried forward to a new page. The totals are recorded on the first line of the new page as shown in Illustration 5-15.

ILLUSTRATION 5-15	Starting a new journal page

JOURNAL   PAGE 2

	DATE	ACCOUNT TITLE	DOC. NO.	POST. REF.	GENERAL DEBIT (1)	GENERAL CREDIT (2)	SALES CREDIT (3)	CASH DEBIT (4)	CASH CREDIT (5)	
1	Aug. 20	Brought Forward		✓	7 9 2 0 00	12 9 2 0 00	2 3 1 9 00	12 3 1 9 00	5 0 0 0 00	1
2										2

1 Write the page number, *2*, at the top of the journal.

2 Write the date, *19--, Aug. 20*, in the Date column. Because this is the first time that a date is written on page 2, the year, month, and day are all written in the Date column.

3 Write the words, *Brought Forward*, in the Account Title column. A check mark is also placed in the Post. Ref. column to show that nothing on this line needs to be posted.

4 Record the column totals brought forward from the previous page.

Completing a Journal at the End of a Month

Rugcare always proves and rules a journal at the end of each month even if the last page for the month is not full. Page 2 of Rugcare's journal on August 31 is shown in Illustration 5-16.

ILLUSTRATION 5-16 Ruling a journal at the end of a month

	DATE		ACCOUNT TITLE	DOC. NO.	POST. REF.	1 GENERAL DEBIT	2 GENERAL CREDIT	3 SALES CREDIT	4 CASH DEBIT	5 CASH CREDIT	
1	Aug.	20	Brought Forward		✓	7 9 2 0 00	12 9 2 0 00	2 3 1 9 00	12 3 1 9 00	5 0 0 0 00	1
2		21	✓	T21	✓			2 7 0 00	2 7 0 00		2
3		24	✓	T24	✓			3 0 0 00	3 0 0 00		3
4		25	✓	T25	✓			3 1 0 00	3 1 0 00		4
5		26	✓	T26	✓			2 4 5 00	2 4 5 00		5
6		27	Utilities Expense	C13		7 0 00				7 0 00	6
7		27	✓	T27	✓			2 9 0 00	2 9 0 00		7
8		28	Supplies	C14		4 3 4 00				4 3 4 00	8
9		28	✓	T28	✓			2 6 7 00	2 6 7 00		9
10		28	Miscellaneous Expense	M3			3 00			3 00	10
11		31	Miscellaneous Expense	C15		7 00				1 2 00	11
12			Repair Expense			5 00					12
13		31	Ben Furman, Drawing	C16		5 0 0 00				5 0 0 00	13
14		31	✓	T31	✓			2 9 0 00	2 9 0 00		14
15		31	Totals			8 9 3 9 00	12 9 2 0 00	4 2 9 1 00	14 2 9 1 00	6 0 1 9 00	15

The entries on lines 10, 11, and 12, Illustration 5-16, are described in Chapter 7.

Double lines ruled below totals mean the totals have been verified as correct.

Proving Page 2 of a Journal. The last page of a journal for a month is proved using the same steps previously described. Then, cash is proved and the journal is ruled. The proof of page 2 of Rugcare's journal is shown below.

Column	Debit Column Totals	Credit Column Totals
General	$ 8,939.00	$12,920.00
Sales		4,291.00
Cash	14,291.00	6,019.00
Totals	$23,230.00	$23,230.00

Page 2 of Rugcare's journal is proved because the total debits are equal to the total credits, $23,230.00.

Proving Cash. Determining that the amount of cash agrees with the accounting records is called **proving cash**. Cash can be proved at any time Rugcare wishes to verify the accuracy of the cash records. However, Rugcare *always* proves cash at the end of a month when the journal is proved. Rugcare uses two steps to prove cash.

1 *Calculate the cash balance.*

Cash on hand at the beginning of the month. . .	$0.00

Rugcare began the month with no cash balance. Mr. Furman invested the initial cash on August 1.

Plus total cash received during the month	+14,291.00

This amount is the total of the journal's Cash Debit column.

Equals total	$14,291.00
Less total cash paid during the month	− 6,019.00

This amount is the total of the journal's Cash Credit column.

Equals cash balance at the end of the month. . .	$ 8,272.00
Checkbook balance on the next unused check stub	$ 8,272.00

2 *Verify that the cash balance equals the checkbook balance on the next unused check stub in the checkbook.* Because the cash balance calculated using the journal and the checkbook balance are the same, *$8,272.00,* cash is proved.

Ruling a Journal at the End of a Month. A journal is ruled at the end of each month even if the last journal page is not full. Rugcare's journal is ruled as shown in Illustration 5-16.

The procedures for ruling a journal at the end of a month are similar to those for ruling a journal page to carry the totals forward.

Rugcare uses five steps in ruling a journal at the end of each month.

1 Rule a single line across all amount columns directly below the last entry to indicate that the columns are to be added.

2 On the next line, write the date, *31*, in the Date column.

Audit Your Understanding

1. List the formula for proving cash.

2. List the 5 steps to rule a journal at the end of a month.

3 Write the word, *Totals,* in the Account Title column.

Some of the column totals will be posted as described in Chapter 6. Therefore, a check mark is not placed in the Post. Ref. column for this line.

4 Write each column total below the single line.

5 Rule double lines below the column totals across all amount columns. The double lines mean that the totals have been verified as correct.

PROFESSIONAL ACCOUNTING ASSOCIATIONS

Accounting for financial activities of businesses around the world has many similarities as well as differences. In many countries, accounting associations grant a title to designate accountants as professionals in their field.

Qualification requirements for a title designation are generally established by a professional accounting organization. The requirements normally consist of a stated amount of education and experience in accounting. Upon meeting these requirements, individuals are designated with a special ti-

tle. Some countries also have special requirements and title designations for individuals who perform tax

accounting work.

The following is a selected list of countries and their professional account-

ing title designation and the organization that grants that title.

COUNTRY	TITLE	ORGANIZATION
Australia	Chartered Accountant	Institute of Chartered Accountants in Australia
Bangladesh	Chartered Accountant	Institute of Chartered Accountants of Bangladesh
Canada	Chartered Accountant	Canadian Institute of Chartered Accountants
India	Chartered Accountant	Institute of Chartered Accountants of India
Japan	Certified Public Accountant	Japanese Institute of Certified Public Accountants
Mexico	Contador Público (Public Accountant)	Mexican Institute of Public Accountants Federation of Societies of Public Accountants
Nigeria	Chartered Accountant	Institute of Chartered Accountants of Nigeria
Pakistan	Chartered Accountant	Institute of Chartered Accountants of Pakistan
Republic of China (Taiwan)	Certified Public Accountant	National Federation of Certified Public Accountants Associations of the Republic of China Chartered Accountants
South Africa	Chartered Accountant	South African Institute of Chartered Accountants

The Summary Illustration on page 90 analyzes the procedure for journalizing transactions.

GENERALLY ACCEPTED ACCOUNTING PRACTICES

In completing accounting work, Rugcare is guided by generally accepted accounting practices, including those shown in Illustration 5-17.

1. Errors are corrected in a way that does not cause doubts about what the correct information is. If an error is recorded, cancel the error by neatly drawing a line through the incorrect item. Write the correct item immediately above the canceled item, as

shown in the Cash Debit column on line 17 of Illustration 5-17.

2. Sometimes an entire entry is incorrect and is discovered before the next entry is journalized. Draw neat lines through all parts of the incorrect entry. Journalize the entry correctly on the next blank line, as shown on lines 18 and 19, Illustration 5-17.

ILLUSTRATION 5-17 Some generally accepted accounting practices

	DATE	ACCOUNT TITLE	DOC. NO.	POST. REF.	GENERAL DEBIT	GENERAL CREDIT	SALES CREDIT	CASH DEBIT	CASH CREDIT	
17	28	√ **4**	T28		**5**		3 5 0 00	~~3 5 0 0 00~~ 3 5 0 00 ← **1**		17
18	**2**→ ~~29~~	~~Rent Expense~~	~~C22~~		~~5 00~~				~~5 00~~	18
19	29	Repair Expense	C22		5 0 00			**7**	5 0 00	19
20	**3**→ 29	*Supplies* ~~Miscellaneous Expense~~	C21		1 0 0 00			↓	1 0 0 00	20
21	30	Don Better, Drawing	C24		5 0 0 00 ← **6**				5 0 0 00	21
22	30	Totals			8 7 5 0 00	9 2 0 0 00	4 0 0 0 00	12 3 0 0 00	7 8 5 0 00	22
23			**8**→	**9**→						23

3. Sometimes several correct entries are recorded after an incorrect entry is made. The next blank lines are several entries later. Draw neat lines through all incorrect parts of the entry. Record the correct items on the same lines as the incorrect items, directly above the canceled parts. This procedure is shown on line 20 of Illustration 5-17.

4. Words in accounting records are written in full when space permits. Words may be abbreviated only when space is limited. All items are written legibly.

5. Dollars and cents signs and decimal points are not used when writing amounts on ruled accounting paper. Sometimes a color tint or a heavy vertical rule is used on printed accounting paper to separate the dollars and cents columns.

6. Two zeros are written in the cents column when an amount is in even dollars, such as $500.00. If the cents column is left blank, doubts may arise later about the correct amount.

7. A single line is ruled across amount columns to indicate addition or subtraction as shown on line 21, Illustration 5-17.

8. A double line is ruled across amount columns to indicate that the totals have been verified as correct.

9. Neatness is very important in accounting records so that there is never any doubt about what information has been recorded. A ruler is used to make single and double lines.

Summary of journalizing transactions

1 Analyze transactions

a. From source document information

Receipts	Calculator Tapes	Checks	Memorandums

Rent Expense   Cash

b. Using T accounts

50.00   50.00

Debits ⟶ equal ⟶ Credits

c. Verify for each entry that:

2 Record entries in a journal

Transactions	Written in Account Title Column	Journal Amount Columns Used				
		General		Sales	Cash	
		Debit	Credit	Credit	Debit	Credit
Received cash from owner as an investment	Capital Account Title		✓		✓	
Paid cash for supplies	Supplies	✓				✓
Paid cash for insurance	Prepaid Insurance	✓				✓
Bought supplies on account	Supplies Liability Account Title	✓	✓			
Paid cash on account	Liability Account Title	✓				✓
Received cash from sales	✓			✓	✓	
Paid cash for an expense	Expense Account Title	✓				✓
Paid cash to owner for personal use	Drawing Account Title	✓				✓

3 Prove the journal

a. Rule a single line across amount columns.

b. Add amount columns.

c. Add all debit totals and add all credit totals.

d. Verify that total debits equal total credits.

4 Prove cash

a. Cash at beginning + Total cash received = Total
Total − Total cash paid = Ending cash balance

b. Verify that the cash balance is the same as the amount shown on the next unused check stub.

5 Complete the journal by ruling double lines across all amount columns.

What is the meaning of each of the following?

1. journal
2. journalizing
3. special amount column
4. general amount column
5. entry
6. double-entry accounting
7. source document
8. check
9. receipt
10. memorandum
11. proving cash

QUESTIONS FOR INDIVIDUAL STUDY   EPT(b)

1. What are the five amount columns in the journal used by Rugcare?
2. Which of the columns in Rugcare's journal are special amount columns?
3. What is the source document for a cash payment transaction?
4. What is the source document for a sales transaction?
5. What is the source document for cash received from transactions other than sales?
6. What is the source document for a transaction when no other source document is prepared or when additional explanation is needed?
7. What are the four parts of a journal entry?
8. What two journal amount columns are used to record cash received from the owner as an investment?
9. What two journal amount columns are used to record cash paid for supplies?
10. What two journal amount columns are used to record cash paid for insurance?
11. What two journal amount columns are used to record supplies bought on account?
12. What two journal amount columns are used to record cash paid on account?
13. What two journal amount columns are used to record cash received from sales?
14. What two journal amount columns are used to record cash paid for an expense?
15. What two journal amount columns are used to record cash paid to the owner for personal use?
16. What is the procedure for proving a journal page?
17. What are the two steps that Rugcare uses in proving cash?

CASES FOR CRITICAL THINKING   EPT(b)

CASE 1 During the summer, Willard Kelly does odd jobs to earn money. Mr. Kelly keeps all his money in a single checking account. He writes checks to pay for personal items and for business expenses. These payments include personal clothing, school supplies, gasoline for his car, and recreation. Mr. Kelly uses his check stubs as his accounting records. Are Mr. Kelly's accounting procedures and records correct? Explain your answer.

CASE 2 In his business, Michael Rock uses a journal with the following columns: Date, Account Title, Check No., Cash Debit, and Cash Credit. Mr. Rock's wife, Jennifer, suggests that he needs three additional amount columns: General Debit, General Credit, and Sales Credit. Mr. Rock states that all his business transactions are for cash, and he never buys on account. Therefore, he does not see the need for more than the Cash Debit and Cash Credit special amount columns. Who is correct, Mr. or Mrs. Rock? Explain your answer.

DRILL 5-D1 Analyzing transactions

This drill provides continuing practice in analyzing transactions into debit and credit parts. Use Rugcare's chart of accounts, page 18.

Transactions
1. Paid cash for supplies, $100.00.
2. Bought supplies on account from Butler Cleaning Supplies, $500.00.
3. Paid cash to owner for personal use, $50.00.
4. Received cash from sales, $300.00.
5. Paid cash for rent, $200.00.
6. Paid cash for insurance, $250.00.
7. Received cash from owner as an investment, $1,000.00.
8. Paid cash for repairs, $25.00.
9. Paid cash for telephone bill, $30.00.
10. Paid cash for advertising, $40.00.
11. Paid cash on account to Butler Cleaning Supplies, $300.00.
12. Paid cash for miscellaneous expense, $3.00.

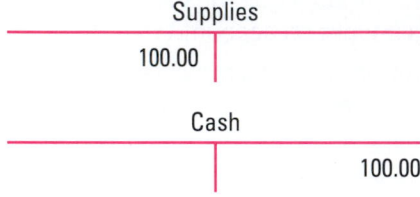

INSTRUCTIONS:

1. For each transaction, prepare two T accounts. On the T accounts, write the account titles affected by the transaction.
2. Write the debit or credit amount in each T account to show how the transaction affected that account. T accounts for Transaction 1 are given as an example.

DRILL 5-D2 Analyzing transactions

This drill continues the practice in analyzing transactions. Mark Jacobs owns a service business called Jacobs Secretarial Services. Jacobs Secretarial Services uses the following accounts.

Cash	Sales
Supplies	Advertising Expense
Prepaid Insurance	Miscellaneous Expense
Gable Supplies	Rent Expense
Mark Jacobs, Capital	Repair Expense
Mark Jacobs, Drawing	Utilities Expense

Use a form similar to the following. Transaction 1 is given as an example.

1	2	3	4	5	6	7
Trans. No.	Accounts Affected	Account Classification	How is Account Affected?		Entered in Account as a	
			(+)	(−)	Debit	Credit
1.	Advertising Expense	Expense	✓		✓	
	Cash	Asset		✓		✓

Transactions
1. Paid cash for advertising.
2. Paid cash for repairs.
3. Received cash from owner as an investment.
4. Paid cash for miscellaneous expense.
5. Bought supplies on account from Gable Supplies.

6. Paid cash on account to Gable Supplies.
7. Paid cash for water bill.
8. Paid cash for supplies.
9. Paid cash for rent.
10. Paid cash to owner for personal use.
11. Received cash from sales.
12. Paid cash for insurance.

INSTRUCTIONS:

1. In Column 2, write the titles of the accounts affected by each transaction.
2. For each account title, write the account classification in Column 3.
3. For each account title, place a check mark in either Column 4 or 5 to indicate if each account is increased (+) or decreased (−) by this transaction.
4. For each account title, place a check mark in either Column 6 or 7 to indicate if the amount is entered in the account as a debit or a credit.

APPLICATION PROBLEMS   EPT(c,d,e,f,g)

PROBLEM 5-1 Journalizing transactions

Dorothy Gilbert owns a service business called Lane Company. Lane Company uses the following accounts.

Cash	Sales
Supplies	Advertising Expense
Prepaid Insurance	Miscellaneous Expense
Mertz Supplies	Rent Expense
Dorothy Gilbert, Capital	Repair Expense
Dorothy Gilbert, Drawing	Utilities Expense

INSTRUCTIONS:

1. Journalize the following transactions completed during February of the current year. Use page 1 of a journal similar to the one described in this chapter for Rugcare. Source documents are abbreviated as follows: check, C; memorandum, M; receipt, R; calculator tape, T.

Transactions

Feb. 1. Received cash from owner as an investment, $12,000.00. R1.
 3. Paid cash for rent, $600.00. C1.
 4. Paid cash for insurance, $1,200.00. C2.
 5. Bought supplies on account from Mertz Supplies, $1,500.00. M1.
 6. Paid cash for supplies, $1,000.00. C3.
 7. Paid cash on account to Mertz Supplies, $750.00. C4.
 10. Paid cash for miscellaneous expense, $5.00. C5.
 12. Received cash from sales, $500.00. T12.
 14. Received cash from sales, $450.00. T14.
 17. Paid cash for repairs, $75.00. C6.
 17. Received cash from sales, $300.00. T17.
 20. Received cash from sales, $370.00. T20.
 21. Received cash from sales, $470.00. T21.
 24. Received cash from sales, $400.00. T24.
 25. Paid cash for electric bill, $50.00. C7.
 25. Received cash from sales, $450.00. T25.
 26. Paid cash for advertising, $90.00. C8.
 26. Received cash from sales, $300.00. T26.
 27. Received cash from sales, $350.00. T27.
 28. Paid cash to owner for personal use, $250.00. C9.
 28. Received cash from sales, $500.00. T28.

2. Prove the journal. Rule a single line across all amount columns. Write the amount column totals below the single line.

3. Prove cash. The beginning cash balance on February 1 is zero. The ending cash balance on the next unused check stub is $12,070.00.

4. Rule the journal.

PROBLEM 5-2 Journalizing transactions

Rona Dowling owns a service business called LawnCare. LawnCare uses the following accounts.

Cash	Sales
Supplies	Advertising Expense
Prepaid Insurance	Miscellaneous Expense
Main Office Supplies	Rent Expense
Westley Supplies	Repair Expense
Rona Dowling, Capital	Utilities Expense
Rona Dowling, Drawing	

INSTRUCTIONS:

1. Journalize the following transactions completed during April of the current year. Use page 1 of a journal similar to the one described in this chapter for Rugcare. Source documents are abbreviated as follows: check, C; memorandum, M; receipt, R; calculator tape, T.

Transactions

Apr. 1. Received cash from owner as an investment, $10,000.00. R1.
   2. Paid cash for rent, $800.00. C1.
   3. Paid cash for insurance, $3,000.00. C2.
   6. Bought supplies on account from Westley Supplies, $2,000.00. M1.
   7. Paid cash for supplies, $700.00. C3.
   8. Paid cash on account to Westley Supplies, $1,000.00. C4.
   8. Received cash from sales, $500.00. T8.
   9. Paid cash for telephone bill, $60.00. C5.
   9. Received cash from sales, $650.00. T9.
   10. Paid cash for repairs, $85.00. C6.
   10. Received cash from sales, $600.00. T10.
   13. Paid cash for miscellaneous expense, $15.00. C7.
   13. Received cash from sales, $700.00. T13.
   14. Received cash from sales, $650.00. T14.
   15. Paid cash to owner for personal use, $350.00. C8.
   15. Received cash from sales, $500.00. T15.
   16. Paid cash for supplies, $1,000.00. C9.
   16. Received cash from sales, $600.00. T16.
   17. Received cash from sales, $650.00. T17.
   20. Bought supplies on account from Main Office Supplies, $500.00. M2.
   20. Received cash from sales, $570.00. T20.
   21. Received cash from sales, $670.00. T21.

2. Prove and rule page 1 of the journal. Carry the column totals forward to page 2 of the journal.

3. Use page 2 of the journal. Journalize the following transactions completed during April of the current year.

Apr. 22. Paid cash for electric bill, $55.00. C10.
   22. Received cash from sales, $600.00. T22.
   23. Bought supplies on account from Main Office Supplies, $50.00. M3.
   23. Received cash from sales, $650.00. T23.
   24. Paid cash for advertising, $100.00. C11.

24. Received cash from sales, $500.00. T24.
27. Received cash from sales, $550.00. T27.
28. Received cash from sales, $500.00. T28.
29. Paid cash for supplies, $150.00. C12.
29. Received cash from sales, $650.00. T29.
30. Paid cash to owner for personal use, $350.00. C13.
30. Received cash from sales, $500.00. T30.

4. Prove page 2 of the journal.

5. Prove cash. The beginning cash balance on April 1 is zero. The balance on the next unused check stub is $12,375.00.

6. Rule page 2 of the journal.

ENRICHMENT PROBLEMS

MASTERY PROBLEM 5-M Journalizing transactions

APPLICATION

Rachel Frank owns a service business called Frank's Car Wash. Frank's Car Wash uses the following accounts.

Cash	Sales
Supplies	Advertising Expense
Prepaid Insurance	Miscellaneous Expense
Delancy Supplies	Rent Expense
Long Supplies	Repair Expense
Rachel Frank, Capital	Utilities Expense
Rachel Frank, Drawing	

INSTRUCTIONS:

1. Journalize the following transactions completed during June of the current year. Use page 1 of a journal similar to the one described in this chapter for Rugcare. Source documents are abbreviated as follows: check, C; memorandum, M; receipt, R; calculator tape, T.

Transactions

June 1. Received cash from owner as an investment, $18,000.00. R1.
2. Paid cash for rent, $900.00. C1.
3. Paid cash for supplies, $1,500.00. C2.
4. Bought supplies on account from Delancy Supplies, $3,000.00. M1.
5. Paid cash for insurance, $4,500.00. C3.
8. Paid cash on account to Delancy Supplies, $1,500.00. C4.
8. Received cash from sales, $750.00. T8.
9. Paid cash for electric bill, $75.00. C5.
9. Received cash from sales, $700.00. T9.
10. Paid cash for miscellaneous expense, $7.00. C6.
10. Received cash from sales, $750.00. T10.
11. Paid cash for repairs, $100.00. C7.
11. Received cash from sales, $850.00. T11.
12. Received cash from sales, $700.00. T12.
15. Paid cash to owner for personal use, $350.00. C8.
15. Received cash from sales, $750.00. T15.
16. Paid cash for supplies, $1,500.00. C9.
16. Received cash from sales, $650.00. T16.
17. Bought supplies on account from Long Supplies, $750.00. M2.
17. Received cash from sales, $600.00. T17.
18. Received cash from sales, $800.00. T18.
19. Received cash from sales, $750.00. T19.

2. Prove and rule page 1 of the journal. Carry the column totals forward to page 2 of the journal.

3. Use page 2 of the journal. Journalize the following transactions completed during June of the current year.

Transactions

June 22. Bought supplies on account from Long Supplies, $80.00. M3.
22. Received cash from sales, $700.00. T22.
23. Paid cash for advertising, $130.00. C10.
23. Received cash from sales, $650.00. T23.
24. Paid cash for telephone bill, $60.00. C11.
24. Received cash from sales, $600.00. T24.
25. Received cash from sales, $550.00. T25.
26. Paid cash for supplies, $70.00. C12.
26. Received cash from sales, $600.00. T26.
29. Received cash from sales, $750.00. T29.
30. Paid cash to owner for personal use, $375.00. C13.
30. Received cash from sales, $800.00. T30.

4. Prove page 2 of the journal.

5. Prove cash. The beginning cash balance on June 1 is zero. The balance on the next unused check stub is $18,883.00.

6. Rule page 2 of the journal.

CHALLENGE PROBLEM 5-C Journalizing transactions

APPLICATION

Wilbur Moore owns a service business called Moore's Tailors. Moore's Tailors uses the following accounts.

Cash	Sales
Supplies	Advertising Expense
Prepaid Insurance	Miscellaneous Expense
Marker Supplies	Rent Expense
O'Brien Supplies	Repair Expense
Wilbur Moore, Capital	Utilities Expense
Wilbur Moore, Drawing	

INSTRUCTIONS:

1. Use page 1 of a journal similar to the following.

Journal									Page 1
Cash		Date	Account Title	Doc. No.	Post Ref.	General		Sales Credit	
Debit	Credit					Debit	Credit		

Journalize the following transactions completed during June of the current year. Source documents are abbreviated as follows: check, C; memorandum, M; receipt, R; calculator tape, T.

Transactions

June 1. Owner invested money, $17,000.00. R1.
2. Wrote a check for supplies, $1,400.00. C1.
3. Paid June rent, $800.00. C2.
4. Wrote a check for insurance, $3,000.00. C3.
5. Bought supplies on account from Marker Supplies, $2,500.00. M1.
7. Received cash from sales, $550.00. T7.

June 9. Paid monthly telephone bill, $70.00. C4.
9. Wrote a check to Marker Supplies on account, $1,300.00. C5.
10. Received cash from sales, $550.00. T10.
11. Paid for miscellaneous expense, $6.00. C6.
11. Received cash from sales, $550.00. T11.
12. Wrote a check for repairs, $90.00. C7.
12. Cash was received from sales, $600.00. T12.
15. Paid for supplies, $1,300.00. C8.
15. Total cash sales, $540.00. T15.
16. Owner withdrew money for personal use, $300.00. C9.
16. Cash was received from sales, $400.00. T16.
17. Total cash sales, $780.00. T17.
18. Bought supplies on account from O'Brien Supplies, $900.00. M2.
18. Received cash from sales, $600.00. T18.
19. Wrote a check for supplies, $85.00. C10.
19. Cash was received from sales, $850.00. T19.

2. Prove and rule page 1 of the journal. Carry the column totals forward to page 2 of the journal.

3. Use page 2 of the journal. Journalize the following transactions completed during June of the current year.

Transactions
June 22. Received cash from sales, $700.00. T22.
23. Bought supplies on account from Marker Supplies, $95.00. M3.
23. Received cash from sales, $720.00. T23.
24. Paid for July advertising, $100.00. C11.
24. Received cash from sales, $550.00. T24.
25. Paid water bill, $75.00. C12.
25. Received cash from sales, $600.00. T25.
26. Received cash from sales, $450.00. T26.
29. Wrote a check to O'Brien Supplies on account, $900.00. C13.
29. Received cash from sales, $630.00. T29.
30. Owner withdrew cash for personal use, $450.00. C14.
30. Received cash from sales, $360.00. T30.

4. Prove page 2 of the journal.

5. Prove cash. The cash balance on June 1 is zero. The balance on the next unused check stub is $16,554.00.

6. Rule page 2 of the journal.

6

Posting to a General Ledger

ENABLING PERFORMANCE TASKS

After studying Chapter 6, you will be able to:

a Define accounting terms related to posting from a journal to a general ledger.

b Identify accounting concepts and practices related to posting from a journal to a general ledger.

c Prepare a chart of accounts for a service business organized as a proprietorship.

d Post amounts from a journal to a general ledger.

TERMS PREVIEW

ledger • general ledger • account number • file maintenance • opening an account • posting

Rugcare records transactions in a journal as described in Chapter 5. A journal is a permanent record of the debit and credit parts of each transaction with transactions recorded in chronological order. A journal does not show in one place all the changes in a single account. If only a journal is used, a business must search through all journal pages to find items affecting a single account balance. For this reason, a form is used to summarize in one place all the changes to a single account. A separate form is used for each account.

An account form is based on and includes the debit and credit sides of a T account as shown in Illustration 6-1.

ILLUSTRATION 6-1

Relationship of a T account to an account form

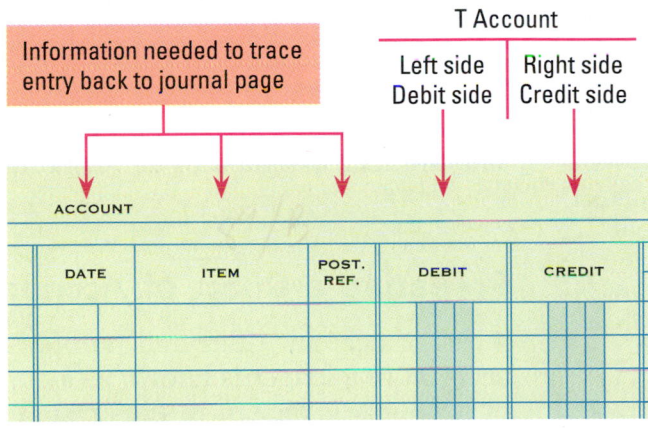

In addition to debit and credit columns, space is provided in the account form for recording the transaction date and journal page number. This information can be used to trace a specific entry back to where a transaction is recorded in a journal.

The major disadvantage of the account form shown in Illustration 6-1 is that no current, up-to-date account balance is shown. If the form in Illustration 6-1 is used, an up-to-date balance must be calculated each time the account is examined. Also, the balance is difficult and time consuming to calculate when an account has a large number of entries. Therefore, a more commonly used account form has Debit and Credit Balance columns as shown in Illustration 6-2. Because the form has columns for the debit and credit balance, it is often referred to as the balance-ruled account form.

ILLUSTRATION 6-2

Account form

ACCOUNT					ACCOUNT NO.	
DATE	ITEM	POST. REF.	DEBIT	CREDIT	BALANCE	
					DEBIT	CREDIT

Balance columns

The account balance is calculated and recorded as each entry is recorded in the account. Recording information in an account is described later in this chapter. The T account is a useful device for analyzing transactions into debit and credit parts. However, the balance-ruled account form is more useful as a permanent record of changes to account balances than is the T account. Rugcare uses the balance-ruled account form.

ARRANGING ACCOUNTS IN A GENERAL LEDGER

A group of accounts is called a **ledger**. A ledger that contains all accounts needed to prepare financial statements is called a **general ledger**. The name given to an account is known as an account title. The number assigned to an account is called an **account number**.

Preparing a Chart of Accounts

A list of account titles and numbers showing the location of each account in a ledger is known as a chart of accounts. Rugcare's chart of accounts is shown in Illustration 6-3.

ILLUSTRATION 6-3   Chart of accounts

RUGCARE

CHART OF ACCOUNTS

Balance Sheet Accounts	Income Statement Accounts
(100) ASSETS	**(400) REVENUE**
110 Cash	410 Sales
120 Petty Cash	
130 Supplies	**(500) EXPENSES**
140 Prepaid Insurance	510 Advertising Expense
	520 Insurance Expense
(200) LIABILITIES	530 Miscellaneous Expense
210 Butler Cleaning Supplies	540 Rent Expense
220 Dale Office Supplies	550 Repair Expense
	560 Supplies Expense
(300) OWNER'S EQUITY	570 Utilities Expense
310 Ben Furman, Capital	
320 Ben Furman, Drawing	
330 Income Summary	

ILLUSTRATION 6-4

For ease of use while studying Part 2, Rugcare's chart of accounts is also shown on page 100.

Accounts in a general ledger are arranged in the same order as they appear on financial statements. Rugcare's chart of accounts, Illustration 6-3, shows five general ledger divisions. (1) Assets, (2) Liabilities, (3) Owner's Equity, (4) Revenue, and (5) Expenses.

Numbering General Ledger Accounts

Rugcare assigns a three-digit account number to each account. For example, Supplies is assigned the number *130* as shown in Illustration 6-4.

Account numbers

```
1   3   0   Supplies
↓   └─┬─┘
General ledger division    Location within general ledger division
```

The first digit of each account number shows the general ledger division in which the account is located. For example, the asset division accounts are numbered in the 100s. Therefore, the number for the asset account, Supplies, begins with a *1*.

The second two digits indicate the location of each account within a general ledger division. The *1* in the account number 130, Supplies, indicates that the account is located in the asset division. The *30* in the account number for Supplies indicates that the account is located between account number 120 and account number 140.

Rugcare initially assigns account numbers by 10s so that new accounts can be added easily. Nine numbers are unused between each account on Rugcare's chart of accounts, Illustration 6-3. For example, numbers 111 to 119 are unused between accounts numbered 110 and 120. New numbers can be assigned between existing account numbers without renumbering all existing accounts. The procedure for arranging accounts in a general ledger, assigning account numbers, and keeping records current is called **file maintenance.**

Unused account numbers are assigned to new accounts. Rugcare records payments for gasoline in Miscellaneous Expense. If Mr. Furman found that the amount paid each month for gasoline had become a major expense, he might decide to use a separate account. The account might be titled Gasoline Expense. Rugcare arranges expense accounts in alphabetic order in its general ledger. Therefore, the new account would be inserted between Advertising Expense and Insurance Expense.

510	Advertising Expense	(Existing account)
	GASOLINE EXPENSE	(NEW ACCOUNT)
520	Insurance Expense	(Existing account)

The number selected for the new account should leave some unused numbers on either side of it for other accounts that might need to be added. The middle, unused account number between existing numbers 510 and 520 is 515. Therefore, 515 is assigned as the account number for the new account.

510	Advertising Expense	(Existing account)
515	GASOLINE EXPENSE	(NEW ACCOUNT)
520	Insurance Expense	(Existing account)

When an account is no longer needed, it is removed from the general ledger and the chart of accounts. For example, if Rugcare were to buy its own equipment and building, there would be no need for the rent expense account. The account numbered 540 would be removed, and that number would become unused and available to assign to another account if the need should arise.

When a new account is added at the end of a ledger division, the next number in a sequence of 10s is used. For example, suppose Rugcare needs to add another expense account, Water Expense, to show more detail about one of the utility expenses. The expense accounts are arranged in alphabetic order. Therefore, the new account would be added at the end of the expense section of the chart of accounts. The last used expense account number is 570, as shown on the chart of accounts, Illustration 6-3. The next number in the sequence of 10s is 580, which is assigned as the number of the new account.

560	Supplies Expense	(Existing account)
570	Utilities Expense	(Existing account)
580	WATER EXPENSE	(NEW ACCOUNT)

Rugcare has relatively few accounts in its general ledger and does not anticipate adding many new accounts in the future. Therefore, a three-digit account number adequately provides for the few account numbers that might be added. However, as the number of general ledger accounts increases, a business may change to four or more digits.

Charts of accounts with more than three digits are described in later chapters.

Opening General Ledger Accounts

Writing an account title and number on the heading of an account is called **opening an account**. A general ledger account is opened for each account listed on a chart of accounts. Accounts are opened and arranged in a general ledger in the same order as on the chart of accounts.

Cash, account number 110, is the first account on Rugcare's chart of accounts. The cash account is opened as shown in Illustration 6-5.

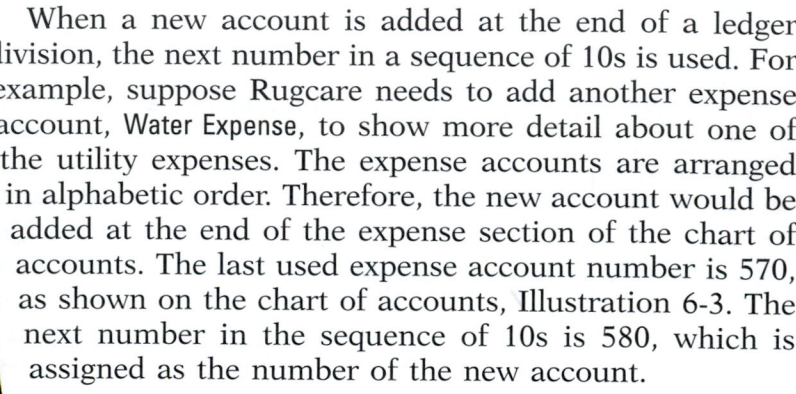

FYI

There are two steps to opening an account: Write the account title and account number on the heading of the account.

ILLUSTRATION 6-5   Opening an account in a general ledger

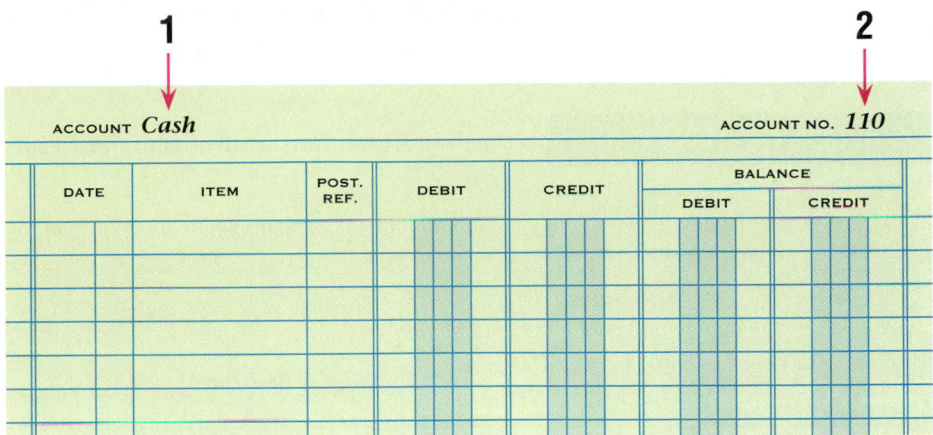

1 Write the account title, *Cash*, after the word *Account* in the heading.

2 Write the account number, *110*, after the words *Account No.* in the heading.

The same procedure is used to open all accounts listed on Rugcare's chart of accounts.

POSTING FROM A JOURNAL TO A GENERAL LEDGER

Transferring information from a journal entry to a ledger account is called **posting.** Posting sorts journal entries so that all debits and credits affecting each account are brought together in one place. For example, all changes to Cash are brought together in the cash account.

Amounts in journal entries are recorded in either general amount columns or special amount columns. There are two rules for posting amounts from a journal. (1) Separate amounts in a journal's general amount columns are posted individually to the account written in the Account Title column. (2) Separate amounts in a journal's special amount columns are not posted individually. Instead, the special amount column totals are posted to the account named in the heading of the special amount column.

Posting Separate Amounts

For most, but not all journal entries, at least one separate amount is posted individually to a general ledger account. When an entry in a journal includes an amount in a general amount column and an account title in the Account Title column, the amount is posted individually.

Posting a Separate Amount from a General Debit Column. Each separate amount in the General Debit and General Credit columns of a journal is posted to the account written in the Account Title column. Posting an amount from the General Debit column is shown in Illustration 6-6.

ILLUSTRATION 6-6   Posting an amount from a General Debit column

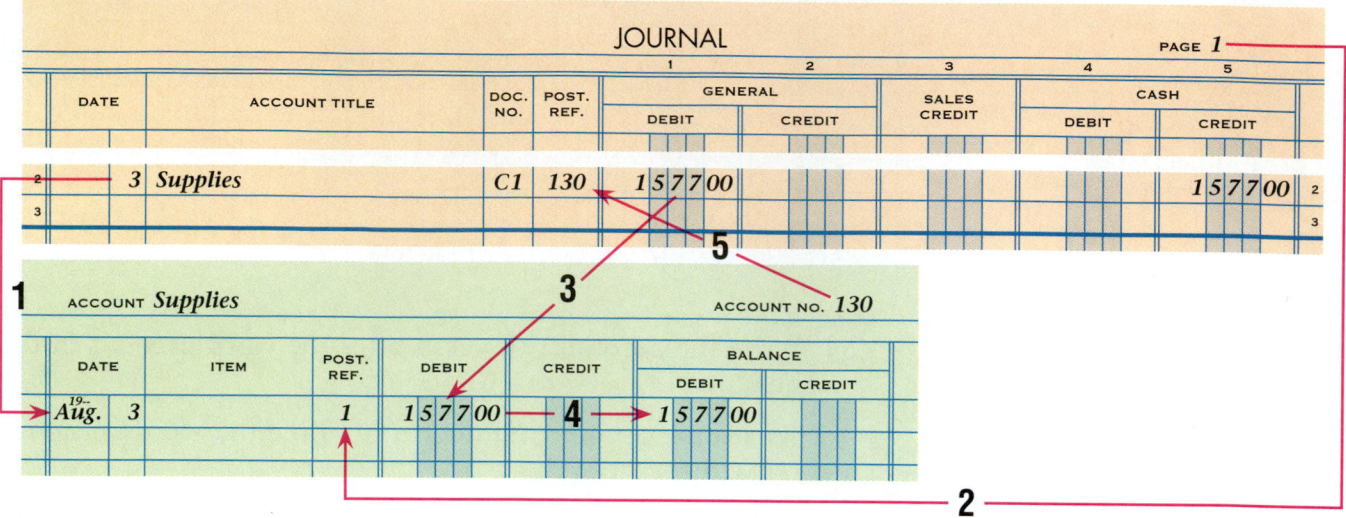

1 Write the date, *19--, Aug. 3,* in the Date column of the account, Supplies.

2 Write the journal page number, *1,* in the Post. Ref. column of the account. Post. Ref. is an abbreviation for Posting Reference.

3 Write the debit amount, *$1,577.00,* in the Debit amount column.

4 Write the new account balance, *$1,577.00,* in the Balance Debit column. Because this entry is the first in the supplies account, the previous balance is zero. The new account balance is calculated as shown below.

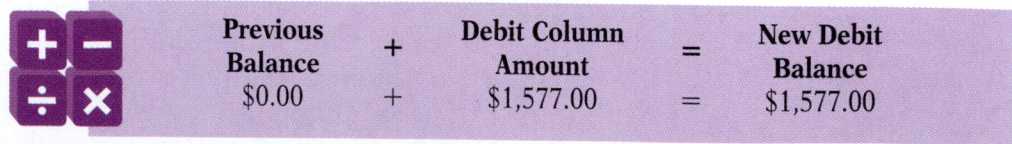

	Previous Balance	+	Debit Column Amount	=	New Debit Balance
	$0.00	+	$1,577.00	=	$1,577.00

5 Return to the journal and write the account number, *130,* in the Post. Ref. column of the journal.

The numbers in the Post. Ref. columns of the general ledger account and the journal serve three purposes. (1) An entry in an account can be traced to its source in a journal. (2) An entry in a journal can be traced to where it was posted in an account. (3) If posting is interrupted, the accounting personnel can easily see which entries in the journal still need to be posted. A blank in the Post. Ref. column of the journal indicates that posting for that line still needs to be completed. *Therefore, the posting reference is always recorded in the journal as the last step in the posting procedure.*

A second amount is posted to the supplies account from Rugcare's journal, line 4, as shown in Illustration 6-7.

ILLUSTRATION 6-7   Posting a second amount to an account

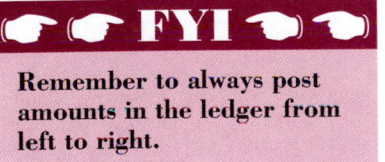

1 Write the date, 7, in the Date column of the account. The month and year are written only once on a page of a ledger account unless the month or year changes.

2 Write the journal page number, *1*, in the Post. Ref. column of the account.

3 Write the debit amount, *$2,720.00*, in the Debit amount column.

4 Write the new account balance, *$4,297.00*, in the Balance Debit column. The new account balance is calculated as shown below.

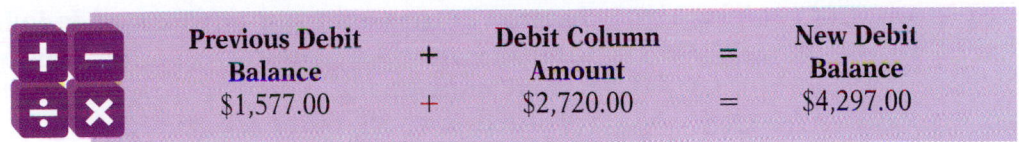

	Previous Debit Balance	+	Debit Column Amount	=	New Debit Balance
	$1,577.00	+	$2,720.00	=	$4,297.00

5 Return to the journal and write the account number, *130*, in the Post. Ref. column of the journal.

Posting a Separate Amount from a General Credit Column. An amount in the General Credit column of a journal is posted as shown in Illustration 6-8.

ILLUSTRATION 6-8   Posting an amount from a General Credit column

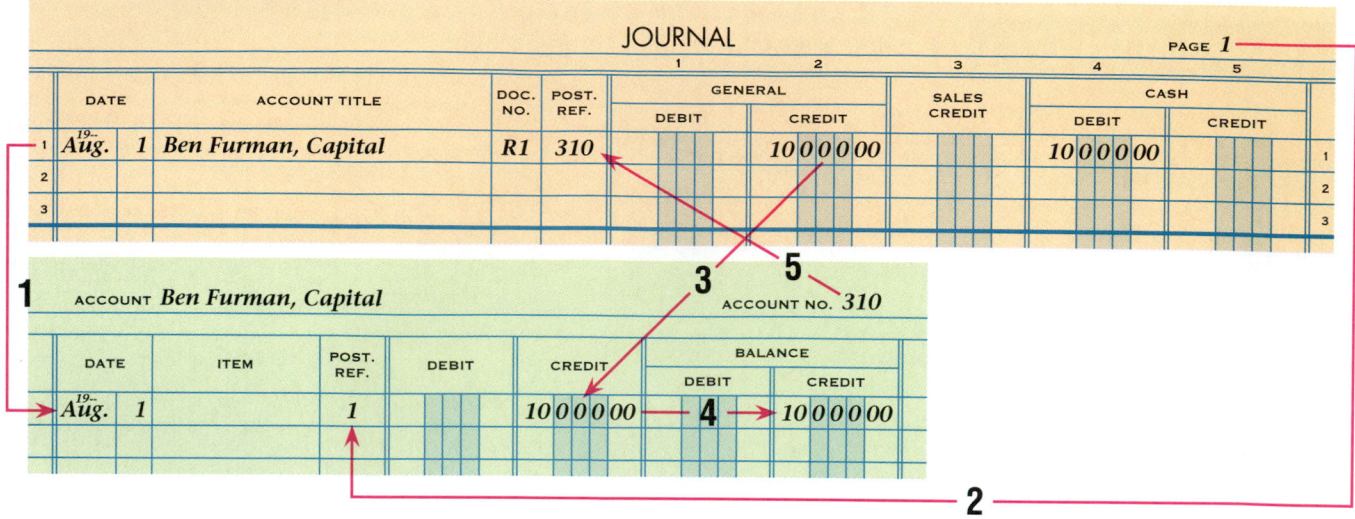

1 Write the date, *19--, Aug. 1,* in the Date column of the account.

2 Write the journal page number, *1,* in the Post. Ref. column of the account.

3 Write the credit amount, *$10,000.00,* in the Credit amount column.

4 Write the new account balance, *$10,000.00,* in the Balance Credit column. The new account balance is calculated as shown below.

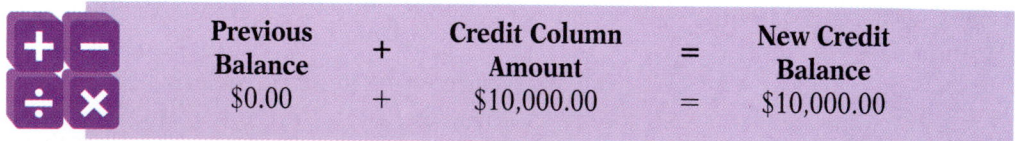

Previous Balance	+	Credit Column Amount	=	New Credit Balance
$0.00	+	$10,000.00	=	$10,000.00

5 Return to the journal and write the account number, *310,* in the Post. Ref. column of the journal.

Journal Entries that are not Posted Individually.   Several lines in Rugcare's journal contain separate amounts that are not to be posted individually. These include forwarding totals and amounts recorded in special amount columns.

The totals brought forward from page 1 are shown on line 1 of the journal in Illustration 6-9. None of these separate total amounts on line 1 are posted individually to general ledger accounts. To assure that no postings are overlooked, no blank posting reference spaces should be left in the Post. Ref. column of the journal. Therefore, when the totals were forwarded to page 2 of the journal, a check mark was placed in the Post. Ref. column of line 1 to show that no separate amounts are posted individually.

ILLUSTRATION 6-9   Check marks show that amounts are not posted

	DATE	ACCOUNT TITLE	DOC. NO.	POST. REF.	GENERAL DEBIT 1	GENERAL CREDIT 2	SALES CREDIT 3	CASH DEBIT 4	CASH CREDIT 5	
1	Aug. 20	Brought Forward		✓	7 9 2 0 00	12 9 2 0 00	2 3 1 9 00	12 3 1 9 00	5 0 0 0 00	1
11	31	Miscellaneous Expense	C15	530	7 00				1 2 00	11
12		Repair Expense		550	5 00					12
13	31	Ben Furman, Drawing	C16	320	5 0 0 00				5 0 0 00	13
14	31 ✓		T31	✓			2 9 0 00	2 9 0 00		14
15	31	Totals		↑	8 9 3 9 00	12 9 2 0 00	4 2 9 1 00	14 2 9 1 00	6 0 1 9 00	15
16					(✓)	(✓)				16
17										17

JOURNAL   PAGE 2

Check mark indicates that amounts ARE NOT posted individually

Check marks indicate that general amount column totals ARE NOT posted

Separate amounts in the special amount columns, Sales Credit, Cash Debit, and Cash Credit, are not posted individually. For example, on line 14 of the journal, Illustration 6-9, two separate $290.00 amounts are recorded in two special amount columns, Sales Credit and Cash Debit.

A check mark was placed in the Post. Ref. column on line 14 when the entry was journalized. The check mark indicates that no separate amounts are posted individually from this line. Instead, the totals of the special amount columns are posted.

Posting the Totals of Amount Columns

Separate amounts in special amount columns *are not* posted individually. The separate amounts are part of the special amount column totals. Only the totals of special amount columns *are* posted.

Totals of General Debit and General Credit Amount Columns. The General Debit and General Credit columns are not special amount columns because the column headings do not contain the name of an account. All of the separate amounts in the General Debit and General Credit amount columns are posted individually.

Therefore, the column totals *are not* posted. A check mark in parentheses is placed below each general amount column total as shown in Illustration 6-9. The check mark indicates that the totals of the General Debit and General Credit columns are not posted.

A check mark in the Post. Ref. column indicates that amounts are not to be posted individually. On the totals line, the amounts in the special amount columns are posted. Therefore, a check mark is not placed in the Post. Ref. column for the totals line.

Posting the Totals of Special Amount Columns. Rugcare's journal has three special amount columns for which only totals are posted: Sales Credit, Cash Debit, and Cash Credit.

Posting the Total of the Sales Credit Column. The Sales Credit column of a journal is a special amount column with the account title Sales in the heading. Each separate amount in a special amount column could be posted individually. However, all of the separate amounts are debits or credits to the same account. Therefore, an advantage of a special amount column is that only the column total needs to be posted. For example, 14 separate sales transactions are recorded in the Sales Credit column of Rugcare's August journal. Instead of making 14 separate credit postings to Sales, only the column total is posted. As a result, only one posting is needed, which saves 13 postings. The smaller number of postings means 13 fewer opportunities to make a posting error. Posting special amount column totals saves time and results in greater accuracy.

The total of Rugcare's Sales Credit column is posted as shown in Illustration 6-10.

ILLUSTRATION 6-10   Posting the total of the Sales Credit column

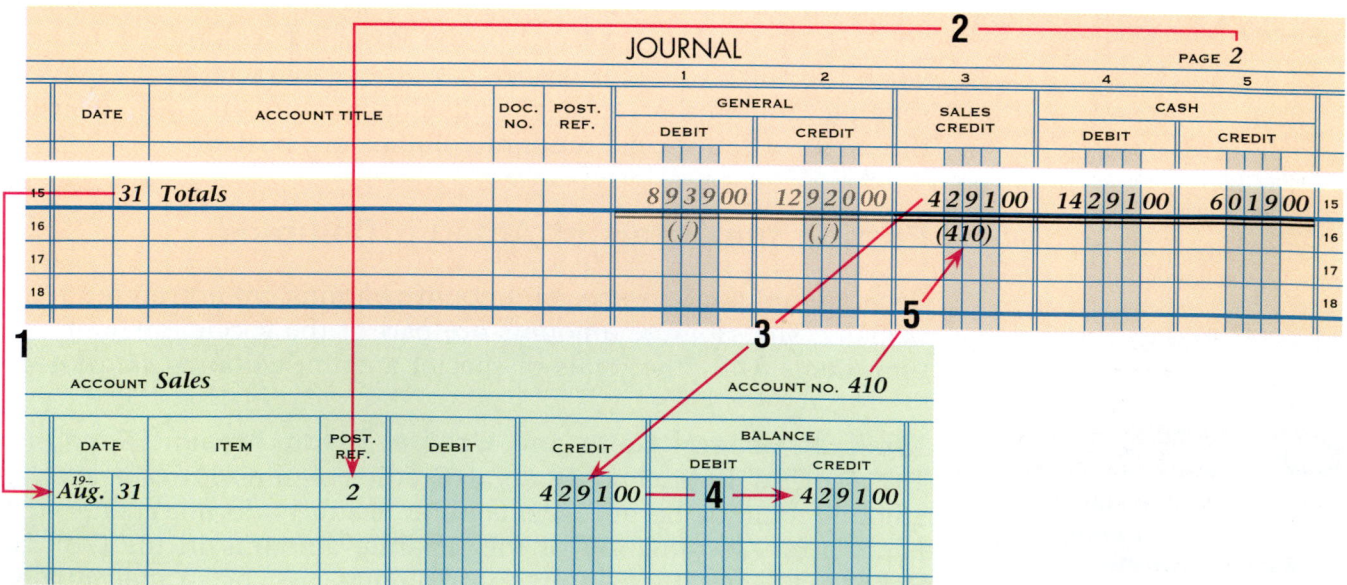

1 Write the date, *19--, Aug. 31*, in the Date column of the account, **Sales.**

2 Write the journal page number, *2*, in the Post. Ref. column of the account.

3 Write the column total, *$4,291.00*, in the Credit amount column.

4 Write the new account balance, *$4,291.00*, in the Balance Credit column. The new account balance is calculated as shown below.

	Previous Balance	+	Credit Column Amount	=	New Credit Balance
	$0.00	+	$4,291.00	=	$4,291.00

5 Return to the journal and write the account number in parentheses, *(410)*, below the Sales Credit column total.

■ Belinda Hughes ■

BOO-BOO-BABY, INC., NEW YORK, NEW YORK

Belinda Hughes is looking for investors with $250,000 to help turn her company into a large corporation. Her business, Boo-Boo-Baby, Inc., based in New York, makes a designer line of children's coats and accessories. It all started for Hughes, formerly head designer of women's coats in a New York company, when she became an aunt and made her first children's coat in 1986. Then she turned an interest into an opportunity by starting her own company designing children's outerwear.

Hughes started her business with an investment of $15,000 from her personal savings. By 1991 she had sold $240,000 of children's wear and expects solid future growth. Five years after the start of her Boo-Boo-Baby line, her children's coats were carried in over 100 stores across the country, including major department stores such as Macy's, Bloomingdale's, Sak's, and Nordstrom's.

Hughes uses bold colors, unusual fabrics, and her own creative designs to distinguish her products in the large children's apparel market. She describes her coats as "funky" and says, "I design coats so that when people see them, they absolutely must have them."

She has a plan for the future of her business which includes the continued distribution of her coats to major department stores. Her ambitions also include a moderately priced line for chain stores.

Hughes is a graduate of the Parsons School of Design and has strong opinions about the value of education. When asked what she would recommend to students who would like to be successful business owners, she said "a good education is very important." She also believes that a course in accounting is crucial for business success because "you have to know the numbers to succeed." Although her degree is in design, her degree program included business courses. Drawing from personal experience, she emphasized that students should pay attention in school because you can't know today what will be important in real life later.

Personal Visions in Business

Posting the Total of the Cash Debit Column. The Cash Debit column of a journal is posted as shown in Illustration 6-11.

ILLUSTRATION 6-11 Posting the total of the Cash Debit column

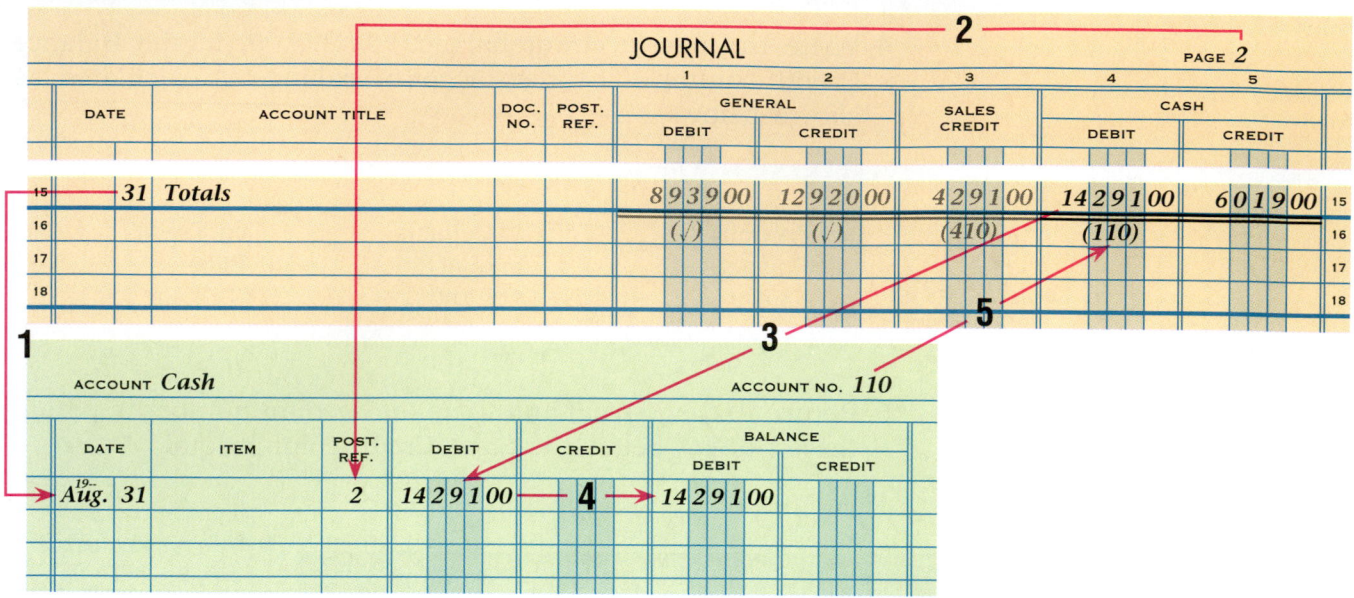

FYI

Two zeros are written in the cents column when an amount is in even dollars, such as $500.00. If the cents column is left blank, doubts may arise later about the correct amount.

1 Write the date, *19--, Aug. 31*, in the Date column of the account, Cash.

2 Write the journal page number, *2*, in the Post. Ref. column of the account.

3 Write the column total, *$14,291.00*, in the Debit amount column.

4 Write the new account balance, *$14,291.00*, in the Balance Debit column. The new account balance is calculated as shown below.

Previous Balance	+	Debit Column Amount	=	New Debit Balance
$0.00	+	$14,291.00	=	$14,291.00

5 Return to the journal and write the account number in parentheses, *(110)*, below the Cash Debit column total.

Posting the Total of the Cash Credit Column. Posting the total of a journal's Cash Credit column is shown in Illustration 6-12.

ILLUSTRATION 6-12   Posting the total of the Cash Credit column

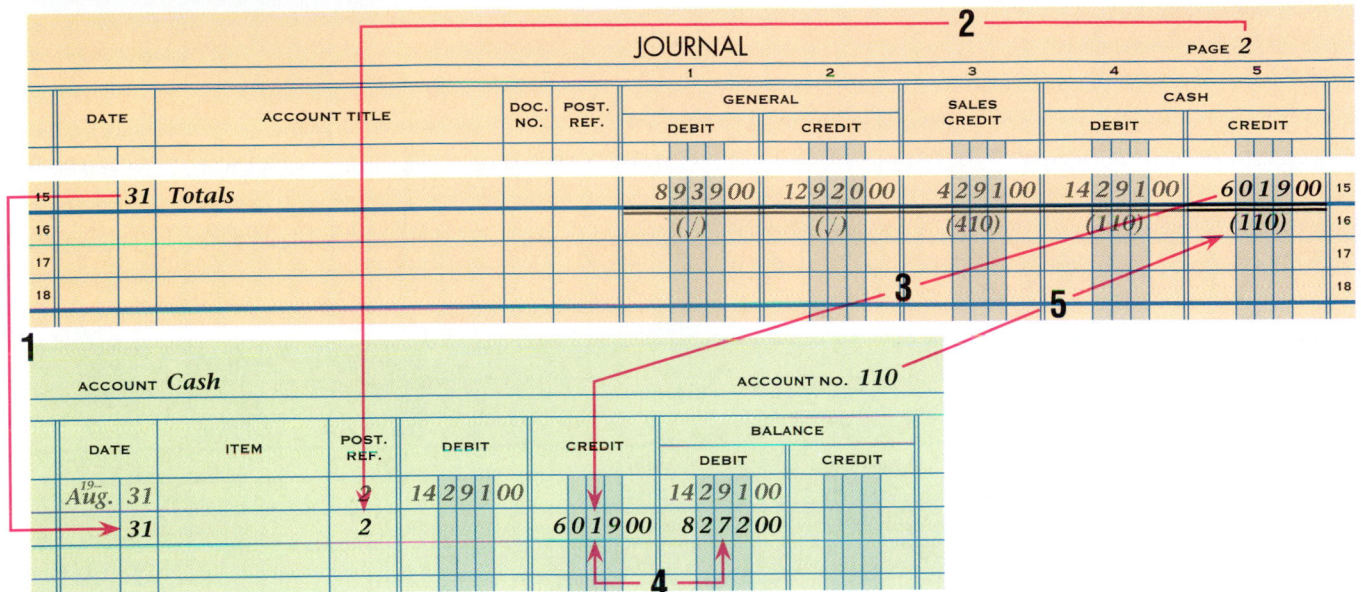

1. Write the date, *31*, in the Date column of the account, Cash.

2. Write the journal page number, *2*, in the Post. Ref. column of the account.

3. Write the column total, *$6,019.00*, in the Credit amount column.

4. Write the new account balance, *$8,272.00*, in the Balance Debit column. The new account balance is calculated as shown below.

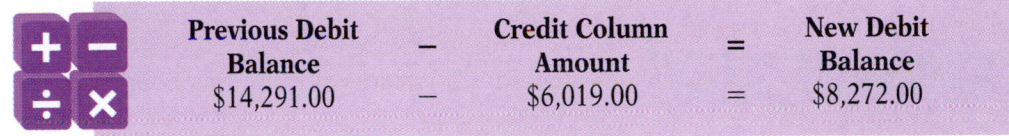

	Previous Debit Balance	−	Credit Column Amount	=	New Debit Balance
	$14,291.00	−	$6,019.00	=	$8,272.00

Whenever the debits in an account exceed the credits, the account balance is a debit. Whenever the credits in an account exceed the debits, the account balance is a credit.

5. Return to the journal and write the account number in parentheses, *(110)*, below the Cash Credit column total.

Journal Page with Posting Completed

Page 2 of Rugcare's August journal, after all posting has been completed, is shown in Illustration 6-13.

ILLUSTRATION 6-13   A journal page after posting has been completed

JOURNAL

PAGE 2

	DATE	ACCOUNT TITLE	DOC. NO.	POST. REF.	GENERAL DEBIT	GENERAL CREDIT	SALES CREDIT	CASH DEBIT	CASH CREDIT	
1	Aug. 20	Brought Forward		✓	7 9 2 0 00	12 9 2 0 00	2 3 1 9 00	12 3 1 9 00	5 0 0 0 00	1
2	21	✓	T21	✓			2 7 0 00	2 7 0 00		2
3	24	✓	T24	✓			3 0 0 00	3 0 0 00		3
4	25	✓	T25	✓			3 1 0 00	3 1 0 00		4
5	26	✓	T26	✓			2 4 5 00	2 4 5 00		5
6	27	Utilities Expense	C13	570	7 0 00				7 0 00	6
7	27	✓	T27	✓			2 9 0 00	2 9 0 00		7
8	28	Supplies	C14	130	4 3 4 00				4 3 4 00	8
9	28	✓	T28	✓			2 6 7 00	2 6 7 00		9
10	28	Miscellaneous Expense	M3	530	3 00				3 00	10
11	31	Miscellaneous Expense	C15	530	7 00				1 2 00	11
12		Repair Expense		550	5 00					12
13	31	Ben Furman, Drawing	C16	320	5 0 0 00				5 0 0 00	13
14	31	✓	T31	✓			2 9 0 00	2 9 0 00		14
15	31	Totals			8 9 3 9 00	12 9 2 0 00	4 2 9 1 00	14 2 9 1 00	6 0 1 9 00	15
16					(✓)	(✓)	(410)	(110)	(110)	16
17										17

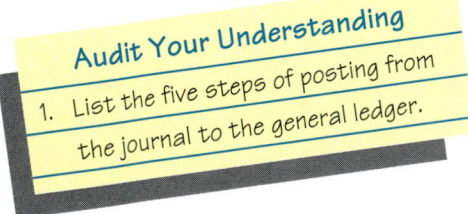
General Ledger with Posting Completed

Rugcare's general ledger, after all posting from the August journal is completed, is shown in Illustration 6-14.

The use of the accounts, Income Summary, Insurance Expense, and Supplies Expense, is described in Chapter 8.

ILLUSTRATION 6-14   A general ledger after posting has been completed

ACCOUNT **Cash**   ACCOUNT NO. 110

DATE	ITEM	POST. REF.	DEBIT	CREDIT	BALANCE DEBIT	BALANCE CREDIT
Aug. 31		2	14 2 9 1 00		14 2 9 1 00	
31		2		6 0 1 9 00	8 2 7 2 00	

ACCOUNT **Petty Cash**   ACCOUNT NO. 120

DATE	ITEM	POST. REF.	DEBIT	CREDIT	BALANCE DEBIT	BALANCE CREDIT
Aug. 17		1	2 0 0 00		2 0 0 00	

ACCOUNT *Supplies*   ACCOUNT NO. *130*

DATE	ITEM	POST. REF.	DEBIT	CREDIT	BALANCE DEBIT	BALANCE CREDIT
Aug. 3		1	1 5 7 7 00		1 5 7 7 00	
7		1	2 7 2 0 00		4 2 9 7 00	
20		1	2 0 0 00		4 4 9 7 00	
28		2	4 3 4 00		4 9 3 1 00	

ACCOUNT *Prepaid Insurance*   ACCOUNT NO. *140*

DATE	ITEM	POST. REF.	DEBIT	CREDIT	BALANCE DEBIT	BALANCE CREDIT
Aug. 4		1	1 2 0 0 00		1 2 0 0 00	

ACCOUNT *Butler Cleaning Supplies*   ACCOUNT NO. *210*

DATE	ITEM	POST. REF.	DEBIT	CREDIT	BALANCE DEBIT	BALANCE CREDIT
Aug. 7		1		2 7 2 0 00		2 7 2 0 00
11		1	1 3 6 0 00			1 3 6 0 00

ACCOUNT *Dale Office Supplies*   ACCOUNT NO. *220*

DATE	ITEM	POST. REF.	DEBIT	CREDIT	BALANCE DEBIT	BALANCE CREDIT
Aug. 20		1		2 0 0 00		2 0 0 00

ACCOUNT *Ben Furman, Capital*   ACCOUNT NO. *310*

DATE	ITEM	POST. REF.	DEBIT	CREDIT	BALANCE DEBIT	BALANCE CREDIT
Aug. 1		1		1 0 0 0 0 00		1 0 0 0 0 00

ACCOUNT _Ben Furman, Drawing_   ACCOUNT NO. _320_

DATE	ITEM	POST. REF.	DEBIT	CREDIT	BALANCE DEBIT	BALANCE CREDIT
Aug. 12		1	100 00		100 00	
31		2	500 00		600 00	

ACCOUNT _Income Summary_   ACCOUNT NO. _330_

DATE	ITEM	POST. REF.	DEBIT	CREDIT	BALANCE DEBIT	BALANCE CREDIT

ACCOUNT _Sales_   ACCOUNT NO. _410_

DATE	ITEM	POST. REF.	DEBIT	CREDIT	BALANCE DEBIT	BALANCE CREDIT
Aug. 31		2		4291 00		4291 00

ACCOUNT _Advertising Expense_   ACCOUNT NO. _510_

DATE	ITEM	POST. REF.	DEBIT	CREDIT	BALANCE DEBIT	BALANCE CREDIT
Aug. 14		1	68 00		68 00	

ACCOUNT _Insurance Expense_   ACCOUNT NO. _520_

DATE	ITEM	POST. REF.	DEBIT	CREDIT	BALANCE DEBIT	BALANCE CREDIT

ACCOUNT **Miscellaneous Expense**   ACCOUNT NO. **530**

DATE	ITEM	POST. REF.	DEBIT	CREDIT	BALANCE DEBIT	BALANCE CREDIT
Aug. 13		1	25 00		25 00	
18		1	70 00		95 00	
28		2	3 00		98 00	
31		2	7 00		105 00	

ACCOUNT **Rent Expense**   ACCOUNT NO. **540**

DATE	ITEM	POST. REF.	DEBIT	CREDIT	BALANCE DEBIT	BALANCE CREDIT
Aug. 12		1	250 00		250 00	

ACCOUNT **Repair Expense**   ACCOUNT NO. **550**

DATE	ITEM	POST. REF.	DEBIT	CREDIT	BALANCE DEBIT	BALANCE CREDIT
Aug. 13		1	20 00		20 00	
20		1	85 00		105 00	
31		2	5 00		110 00	

ACCOUNT **Supplies Expense**   ACCOUNT NO. **560**

DATE	ITEM	POST. REF.	DEBIT	CREDIT	BALANCE DEBIT	BALANCE CREDIT

ACCOUNT **Utilities Expense**   ACCOUNT NO. **570**

DATE	ITEM	POST. REF.	DEBIT	CREDIT	BALANCE DEBIT	BALANCE CREDIT
Aug. 12		1	45 00		45 00	
27		2	70 00		115 00	

The procedures for posting from Rugcare's journal are summarized in Illustration 6-15.

SUMMARY ILLUSTRATION 6-15

Summary of posting to a general ledger

Seven steps are followed in posting amounts from a journal to a general ledger.

1 The date is written in the Date column of the account.

2 The journal page number is written in the Post. Ref. column of the account.

3 The amount is written in the Debit or Credit amount column of the account.

4 A new account balance is calculated and recorded in the Balance Debit or Balance Credit column of the account.

5 An account number is placed in the Post. Ref. column of the journal to show to which account a separate amount on that line has been posted. The account number is written in the journal *as the last step* in the posting procedure.

6 Check marks are placed in parentheses below general amount columns of a journal to show that the totals of these columns *are not* posted.

7 Account numbers are placed in parentheses below special amount column totals of a journal to show that these column totals have been posted.

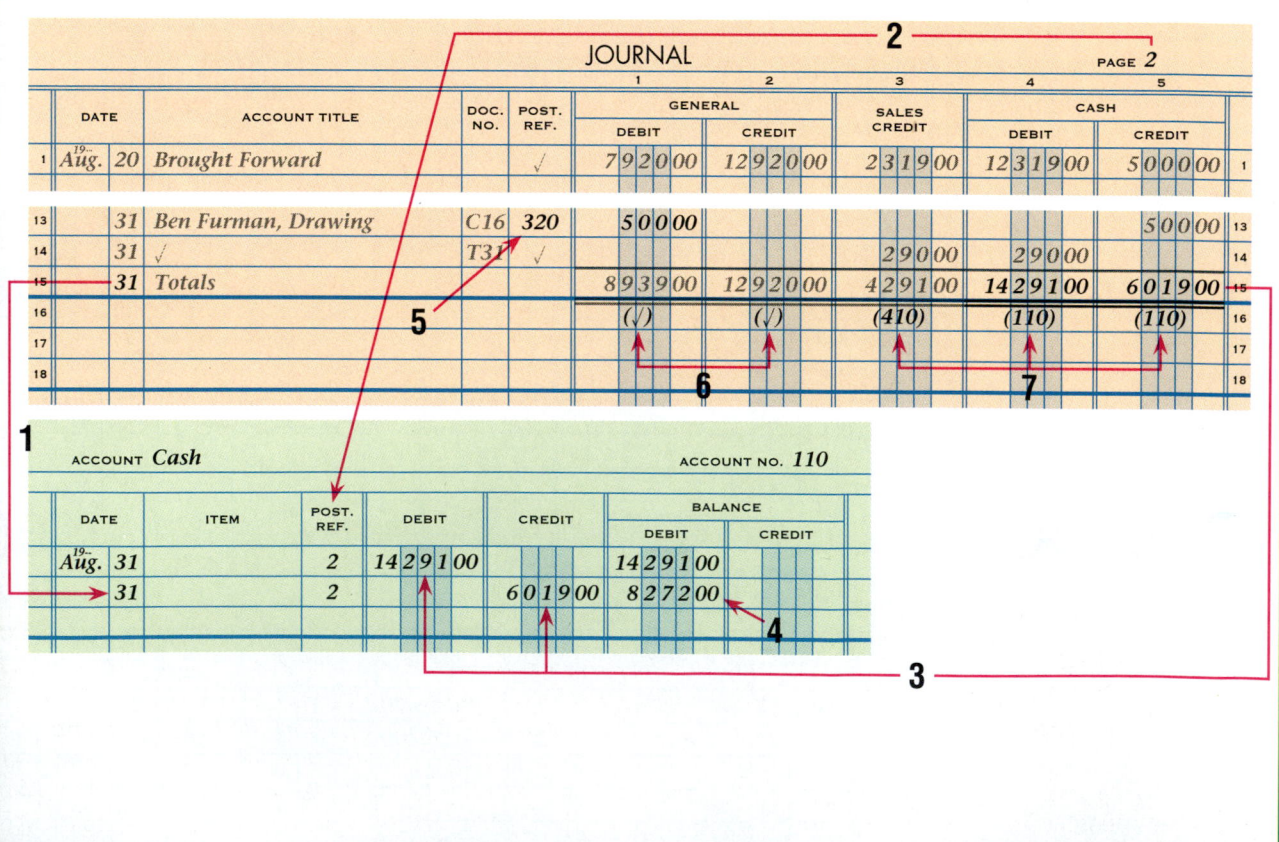

What is the meaning of each of the following?

1. **ledger**
2. **general ledger**
3. **account number**
4. **file maintenance**
5. **opening an account**
6. **posting**

1. Why are general ledger accounts used in an accounting system?
2. In what order are accounts arranged in a general ledger?
3. On Rugcare's chart of accounts, what is indicated by each digit in an account number?
4. Why are unused numbers usually left between account numbers on a chart of accounts?
5. What number is assigned to a new account inserted in a chart of accounts between accounts numbered 530 and 540?
6. What number is assigned to a new account added at the end of a division in which the last account is numbered 550?
7. What are the two steps in opening a new account?
8. Why are amounts posted from a journal to general ledger accounts?
9. What three purposes are served by recording posting reference numbers in journals and accounts?
10. How is a new account balance calculated when the previous balance is a debit and a debit entry is posted?
11. Why are separate amounts in special amount columns of a journal not posted individually?
12. Why are totals of a journal's general amount columns not posted?
13. What is done to indicate that the general amount column totals are not posted?
14. What is done to indicate that a special amount column total in a journal has been posted?
15. How is a new account balance calculated when the previous balance is a debit, a credit entry is posted, and the previous debit balance is larger than the credit entry?

CASE 1 Angela Silva does not use a journal in her business records. She records the debits and credits for each transaction directly in the general ledger accounts. Is Ms. Silva using the correct procedure? Explain your answer.

CASE 2 Philip Westing does the accounting work for his business. When posting, he first transfers all of the information to the general ledger accounts. Then he returns to the journal and, all at one time, writes the account numbers in the Post. Ref. column of the journal. Diana Young also does the accounting work for her business. When posting, she writes all the account numbers in the Post. Ref. column of the journal before she transfers any information to the accounts. Is Mr. Westing or Miss Young following the correct procedure? Explain your answer.

APPLIED COMMUNICATIONS

A fax machine allows a business to send documents anywhere in a matter of minutes using a telephone line. Business managers no longer have to wait days to obtain the information needed to make timely business decisions. Some businesses use fax machines to increase sales, allowing customers to order items without leaving their offices or homes.

Most fax machines in offices are located in one or more central locations and used by a number of different workers for both sending and receiving documents. To facilitate directing the document to the intended receiver, it is usual practice to include a cover sheet in the fax transmission. The cover sheet should include the information below.

1. Name of the person sending the message.
2. Name of the person to receive the message.
3. Phone number of both sending and receiving fax machines.

4. Total number of pages being transmitted, including the cover sheet.

INSTRUCTIONS:

1. Write a memorandum responding to the following scenario: Ben Furman is at the bank applying for a business loan. The bank's loan officer has asked for a list of Rugcare's asset, liability, owner's equity, sales, and expense accounts, and their current balances. Mr. Furman has just called you and asked that you fax him at the bank with this information. In your memorandum include an introductory sentence or paragraph and end with a concluding statement.

2. Prepare a cover sheet for transmitting a fax message. The bank's fax machine telephone number is 800-555-3333. Use your own name and personal telephone number or school telephone number.

DRILLS FOR UNDERSTANDING   EPT(b,c,d)

DRILL 6-D1   Preparing a chart of accounts

The following account descriptions refer to the location of accounts in a chart of accounts similar to the one for Rugcare, page 100.

1. The first asset account
2. The first liability account
3. The first owner's equity account
4. The first revenue account
5. The first expense account
6. The third asset account
7. The fourth expense account
8. The owner's drawing account
9. The cash account
10. The sales account
11. The owner's capital account

Use a form similar to the following. Account description 1 is given as an example.

1	2
Account Description	**Account Number**
1. The first asset account	*110*

INSTRUCTIONS:

1. In Column 1, write the account description.
2. In Column 2, write the account number. Account numbers are assigned by 10s.
3. Check your answers with Rugcare's chart of accounts, page 100. Determine if your answers are the same for each account as shown on the chart of accounts.
4. Cover your answers in Column 2. Practice rapidly recalling the account numbers for each account.

DRILL 6-D2 Analyzing posting from a journal

INSTRUCTIONS:

1. Use completed page 2 of the journal shown in Illustration 6-13. For each of the following lines in that illustration, write the separate amount, if any, that is posted individually. Also, write the account title to which the amount is posted.

   a. Line 6   **c.** Line 10   **e.** Line 12

   b. Line 9   **d.** Line 11   **f.** Line 13

2. Use the general ledger accounts shown in Illustration 6-14. Answer the following questions.

   a. What item or transaction is represented by the amount in the cash account's Credit column?

   b. What item or transaction is represented by the amount in the prepaid insurance account's Debit Balance column?

   c. What item or transaction is represented by the amount in the sales account's Credit column?

   d. Where in the journal is the information found about the item or transaction recorded in the advertising expense account's Debit column?

APPLICATION PROBLEMS   EPT(c,d)

PROBLEM 6-1 Preparing a chart of accounts

Marie Wilson owns a service business called Wilson's Services. Wilson's Services uses the following accounts.

Automobile Expense	Miscellaneous Expense
Bartel Supplies	Novack Office Supplies
Cash	Prepaid Insurance
Insurance Expense	Sales
Marie Wilson, Capital	Supplies
Marie Wilson, Drawing	Supplies Expense

INSTRUCTIONS:

1. Prepare a chart of accounts similar to the one described in this chapter. Arrange expense accounts in alphabetic order. Use 3-digit account numbers and number the accounts within a division by 10s.

2. Two new accounts, Gasoline Expense and Utilities Expense, are to be added to the chart of accounts prepared in Instruction 1. Assign account numbers to the two new accounts.

PROBLEM 6-2 Posting to a general ledger

MATHEMATICS

Don Ley owns a service business called AquaCare. AquaCare's journal, which is needed to complete this problem, is in the working papers that accompany this textbook.

INSTRUCTIONS:

1. Open a general ledger account for each of the following accounts.

Assets	Revenue
110 Cash	410 Sales
120 Supplies	**Expenses**
130 Prepaid Insurance	510 Advertising Expense
Liabilities	520 Miscellaneous Expense
210 Donard Supplies	530 Rent Expense
220 Fell Office Supplies	540 Utilities Expense
Owner's Equity	
310 Don Ley, Capital	
320 Don Ley, Drawing	

2. Post the separate amounts on each line of the journal that need to be posted individually.

3. Post the journal's special amount column totals.

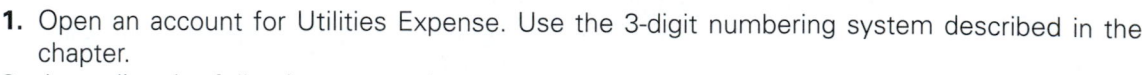

ENRICHMENT PROBLEMS

EPT(d)

MASTERY PROBLEM 6-M Journalizing and posting to a general ledger

AUTOMATED

APPLICATION

Al Hiatt owns a service business called Hiatt Cleaning. Hiatt Cleaning's general ledger accounts are given in the working papers that accompany this textbook.

INSTRUCTIONS:

1. Open an account for Utilities Expense. Use the 3-digit numbering system described in the chapter.

2. Journalize the following transactions completed during November of the current year. Use page 1 of a journal. Source documents are abbreviated as follows: check, C; memorandum, M; receipt, R; calculator tape, T.

Nov. 1. Received cash from owner as an investment, $7,000.00. R1.

    3. Paid cash for rent, $300.00. C1.

    5. Paid cash for insurance, $200.00. C2.

    6. Received cash from sales, $750.00. T6.

    9. Paid cash for miscellaneous expense, $5.00. C3.

    11. Paid cash for supplies, $500.00. C4.

    13. Bought supplies on account from Major Supplies, $600.00. M1.

    13. Received cash from sales, $700.00. T13.

    16. Paid cash for electric bill, $40.00. C5.

    18. Paid cash on account to Major Supplies, $300.00. C6.

    20. Paid cash for advertising, $30.00. C7.

    20. Received cash from sales, $770.00. T20.

    25. Paid cash for supplies, $150.00. C8.

    27. Paid cash for supplies, $100.00. C9.

    27. Received cash from sales, $1,150.00. T27.

    30. Paid cash to owner for personal use, $300.00. C10.

    30. Received cash from sales, $410.00. T30.

3. Prove the journal.

4. Prove cash. The beginning cash balance on November 1 is zero. The balance on the next unused check stub is $8,855.00.

5. Rule the journal.

6. Post from the journal to the general ledger.

CHALLENGE PROBLEM 6-C Journalizing and posting to a general ledger

AUTOMATED

Dee Worthy owns a service business called HouseCare. HouseCare's general ledger accounts are given in the working papers that accompany this textbook.

HouseCare uses the following journal.

JOURNAL							Page	
Debit		Date	Account Title	Doc. No.	Post Ref.	**Credit**		
Cash	General					General	Sales	Cash
1								

INSTRUCTIONS:

1. Journalize the following transactions completed during March of the current year. Use page 5 of a journal. Source documents are abbreviated as follows: check, C; memorandum, M; receipt, R; calculator tape, T.

Mar. 1. Owner invested money, $8,000.00. R1.
  3. Paid March rent, $350.00. C1.
  5. Wrote a check for miscellaneous expense, $5.00. C2.
  9. Paid for quarterly insurance, $250.00. C3.
 11. Paid for supplies, $400.00. C4.
 13. Cash sales, $450.00. T13.
 16. Supplies were bought on account from Hartwood Supplies, $700.00. M1.
 18. Hartwood Supplies was paid on account, $350.00. C5.
 19. Paid telephone bill, $60.00. C6.
 20. Cash was received from sales, $1,100.00. T20.
 23. Wrote a check for June advertising, $50.00. C7.
 23. Paid for supplies, $150.00. C8.
 27. Paid for supplies, $150.00. C9.
 27. Received cash from sales, $1,830.00. T27.
 30. Owner withdrew cash for personal use, $400.00. C10.
 31. Received cash from sales, $410.00. T31.

2. Prove the journal.
3. Prove cash. The beginning cash balance on March 1 is zero. The balance on the next unused check stub is $9,625.00.
4. Rule the journal.
5. Post from the journal to the general ledger.

Safety and Health Considerations

ELECTRICAL EQUIPMENT

The following rules protect the operator of the equipment, other persons in the environment, and the equipment itself.

1. Do not unplug equipment by pulling on the electrical cord. Instead, grasp the plug at the outlet and remove it.
2. Do not stretch electrical cords across an aisle where someone might trip over them.
3. Avoid food and beverages near equipment where a spill might result in an electrical short.
4. Do not attempt to remove the cover of equipment for any reason while the power is turned on.
5. Do not attempt to repair equipment while it is plugged in. To avoid damage most repairs should be done by an authorized service technician.
6. Always turn the power off when finished using equipment.
7. Do not overload extension cords.
8. Follow manufacturer recommendations for safe use.
9. Replace frayed electrical cords immediately.

MICROCOMPUTERS

1. To avoid damage to the drives, do not insert pencils or other implements in floppy disk drives.
2. To prevent overheating, avoid blocking air vents.
3. Position keyboards to prevent bumping or dropping them off the work surface.

MONITORS

1. Most manufacturers advise repair by authorized service technicians only.

2. Adjust brightness and focus for comfortable viewing.
3. Avoid glare on the monitor screen.
4. Do not leave fingerprints on the screen. Keep the screen clear of dust. Only use a soft cloth for cleaning the screen.

PRINTERS

1. Do not let jewelry, ties, scarves, loose sleeves, or other clothing get caught in the machinery. This could result in damage to the machinery and could cause personal injury.
2. Exercise caution when using toxic chemicals such as toner in order to avoid spills.

DISKETTES

1. Write/protect all program software to avoid accidental erasure.
2. Do not bend or fold diskettes.
3. Do not write on a diskette with a hard or sharp-pointed pen or pencil; use a felt-tip marker.
4. Do not touch exposed surfaces of diskettes.
5. Be sure the disk drive is not running when you insert or remove a diskette.
6. Keep diskettes away from extreme hot or cold temperatures. Do not leave diskettes in a car during very hot or cold weather.
7. Keep diskettes away from magnetic fields such as transformers and magnets.
8. Store diskettes in the storage envelopes.
9. Keep diskettes away from smoke, ashes, and dust, including chalk dust.
10. Do not leave diskettes in the disk drive for prolonged periods, such as overnight.

Recording Transactions for a Proprietorship

Financial data may be recorded and reported by hand or by machine. An accounting system in which data are recorded and reported mostly by hand is referred to as **manual accounting**. Some businesses use automated machines to speed the recording and reporting process. An accounting system in which data are recorded and reported mostly by using automated machines is **automated accounting**. However, even in automated accounting, some procedures are done by hand.

Rugcare, the service business described in Part 2, uses a manual accounting system. Rugcare's manual journalizing and posting procedures are described in Chapters 5 and 6. Integrating Automated Accounting Topic 1 describes procedures for using automated accounting software to journalize and post Rugcare's transactions. The Automated Accounting Problems contain instructions for using automated accounting software to solve Mastery Problem 6-M and Challenge Problem 6-C, Chapter 6.

COMPUTER PROGRAMMING

A **computer program** is a set of instructions followed by a computer to process data. The programs used to direct the operations of a computer are **software**. An **automated accounting system** is a collection of computer programs designed to automate accounting procedures.

A person needs special training to be a **computer programmer**. Understanding accounting concepts and procedures is helpful to a computer programmer. Just as important, an accountant needs to know basic computer concepts and procedures in order to assist a computer programmer and to use a computer.

AUTOMATED GENERAL LEDGER ACCOUNTING

Automated general ledger accounting is based on the same accounting concepts as a manual accounting system. The only differences are equipment and procedures.

General Ledger Data Base

A pre-arranged file in which data can be entered and retrieved is a **data base**. In automated accounting the general ledger is a data base. A general ledger data base contains general information about the business, the chart of accounts, and financial activity for each account. A model of a computer application stored on a computer disk for repeated use is a **template**. Rugcare stores its general ledger data base as a template.

To perform accounting procedures, the general ledger data base is retrieved from the template. The file is saved as a new file using another file name, which allows the template to remain in its original format. Changes to the original template should be made only when necessary to update the file for future repeated use.

The new file is then used to complete accounting activities. Transaction data may then be recorded in the general ledger accounts. At the end of a fiscal period, financial data are retrieved and financial reports are prepared.

Chart of Accounts Numbering Systems

Chart of accounts numbering systems are similar for both automated and manual accounting. Rugcare's three-digit numbering system is described in Chapter 6. The procedures for arranging accounts in a general ledger, assigning account numbers, and keeping records current are **file maintenance**.

File Maintenance

File maintenance procedures are similar for both automated and manual accounting. In automated accounting the chart of accounts is part of the general ledger data base. The chart of accounts requires maintenance periodically to add and change accounts. File maintenance requires five steps. (1) A chart of accounts input form is prepared. (2) The general ledger data base is retrieved. (3) Data

To save a file under another name, pull down the File menu and choose the Save As menu command. Key the path to the drive and directory that contains the data files. Save your data base with a file name of XXX1A (where XXX are your initials).

from the chart of accounts input form are keyed into the computer to change the chart of accounts. (4) A revised chart of accounts report is prepared to verify the accuracy of the data that was keyed. (5) The revised chart of accounts is stored as part of the general ledger data base.

Adding an Account Within a Ledger Division. Rugcare decided to add a new account titled Gasoline Expense within the expenses division of the chart of accounts. The entry on the chart of accounts input form to add Gasoline Expense is shown on line 1 of Illustration T1-1.

ILLUSTRATION T1-1

Entry for file maintenance

RUN DATE 08/12/-- MM DD YY	CHART OF ACCOUNTS Input Form	
1		**2**
ACCOUNT NUMBER	ACCOUNT TITLE	
1 515	Gasoline Expense	1
2		2
3		3
4		4

A new account number added within a ledger division is determined using procedures described in Chapter 6. Using the unused middle number, the new account number for Gasoline Expense is 515.

510	Advertising Expense	(Existing Account)
515	Gasoline Expense	(NEW ACCOUNT)
520	Insurance Expense	(Existing Account)

Three steps are followed to complete a chart of accounts input form.

1 The run date, *08/12/--*, is written in the space provided at the top of the form. The **run date** is the date to be printed on reports prepared by a computer.

2 Each account number is written in the Account Number column.

3 Each account title is written in the Account Title column just as it will appear on the output. The automated accounting software specifies the maximum number of spaces that can be used for account numbers and account titles. Any account title that contains more than 25 characters must be abbreviated when recorded on the chart of accounts input form. All of Rugcare's account titles fit the 25-character space allowed, so none have to be abbreviated.

FYI

Automated Accounting 6.0 software limits account titles to 25 characters. Therefore, abbreviations may be necessary.

Adding an Account at the End of a Ledger Division. A new account number added at the end of a ledger division is determined following procedures described in Chapter 6. The next number in a sequence of 10 is used for a new account added at the end of a chart of accounts division.

Processing File Maintenance Data

In automated accounting the activities are arranged so that each activity may be selected using a keyboard or some other input device such as a mouse. A list of options from which an activity may be selected is a **menu**. Rugcare's software has a menu bar and a series of pull-down menus. When a menu is selected from the menu bar, a pull-down list of commands will appear. The menu bar shown in Illustration T1-2 contains six different menus. (1) File. (2) Options. (3) Journals. (4) Ledgers. (5) Reports. (6) Help.

ILLUSTRATION T1-2   Menu bar and pull-down file menu

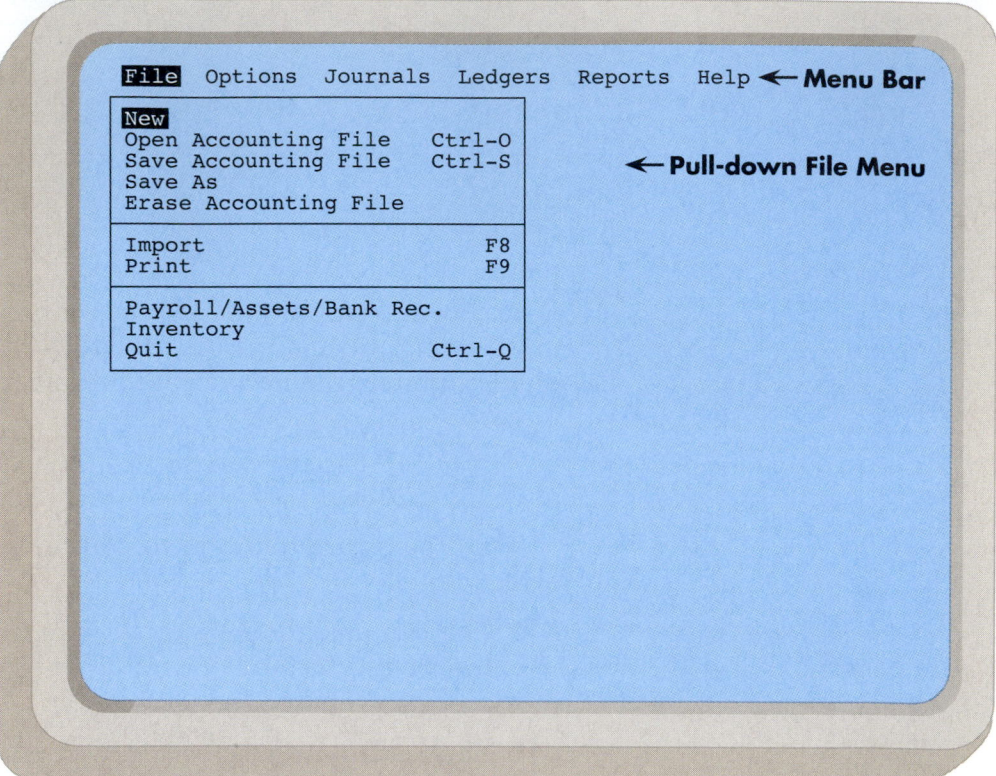

The general ledger data base is retrieved from the template disk by first selecting File from the menu bar. The Open Accounting File command is then chosen from the File menu, as shown in Illustration T1-2, to retrieve a specific general ledger data base from the template disk.

To process file maintenance data, select the Ledgers menu from the menu bar. The Maintain Accounts command is then chosen from the Ledgers menu to display the data entry window for entering file maintenance data. File maintenance data are keyed from the chart of accounts input form. The entry for Gasoline Expense is shown in Illustration T1-3.

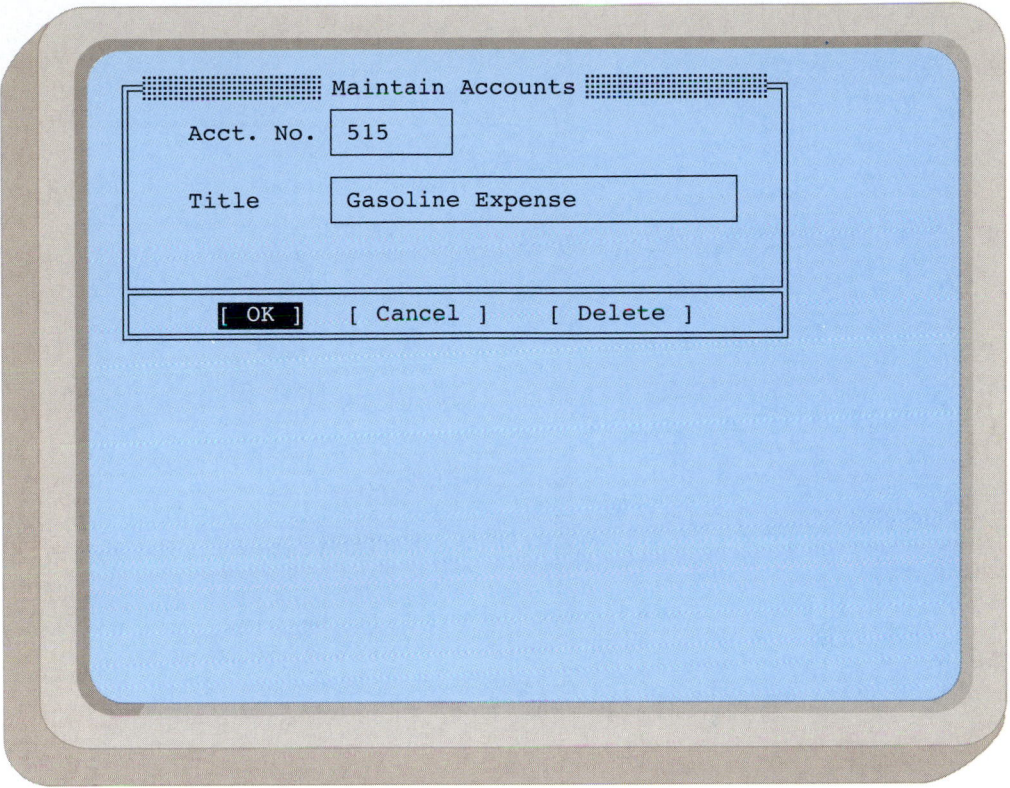

After all file maintenance data have been keyed, the Reports menu is selected from the menu bar. The Accounts command is chosen from the Reports menu to display the Report Selection window. When the Report Selection window appears, select the Chart of Accounts option to display the revised chart of accounts report. The revised chart of accounts report is checked for accuracy by comparing the report with the chart of accounts input form. The revised chart of accounts report, as shown in Illustration T1-4 on the next page, is printed and filed for future reference.

RECORDING TRANSACTIONS

In manual accounting, transactions are analyzed into debit and credit parts as described in Chapter 4 and recorded in a journal as described in Chapter 5. Transaction data are then periodically posted from a journal to a general ledger as described in Chapter 6.

In automated accounting, transactions are also analyzed into debit and credit parts. A general journal input form is used to journalize transactions. After each transaction has been keyed, the software is directed to post to the general ledger accounts.

```
                    Rugcare
              Chart of Accounts
                 08/12/--
-----------------------------------------
Account    Account
Number     Title
-----------------------------------------
110        Cash
120        Petty Cash
130        Supplies
140        Prepaid Insurance
210        Butler Cleaning Supplies
220        Dale Office Supplies
310        Ben Furman, Capital
320        Ben Furman, Drawing
410        Sales
510        Advertising Expense
515        Gasoline Expense
520        Insurance Expense
530        Miscellaneous Expense
540        Rent Expense
550        Repair Expense
560        Supplies Expense
570        Utilities Expense
```

The following transactions completed by Rugcare are analyzed into debit and credit parts in Chapter 4.

Received Cash from Owner as an Investment

August 1, 19--. Received cash from owner as an investment, $10,000.00. Receipt No. 1.

Dollar and cent signs are not entered on input forms.

The journal entry to record this transaction is on lines 1 and 2 of the general journal input form shown in Illustration T1-5.

The run date, *08/12/--*, is written in the space provided at the top of the input form. The run date indicates the date to be printed on the report.

On line 1, the date, *08/01*, is written in the Date column. The source document number, *R1*, is entered in the Reference column. The cash account number, *110*, is recorded in the Account No. column. The Customer/Vendor No. column is left blank. Entries requiring the use of this column are described in Part 3, Integrating Automated Accounting Topic 4. The amount debited to Cash, *$10,000.00*, is written in the Debit column.

On line 2, the account number for Ben Furman, Capital, *310*, is written in the Account No. column. The Date and Reference numbers are entered only once for each complete transaction. Therefore, the Date and Reference columns are left blank starting with the second line of an entry. The amount credited to Ben Furman, Capital, *$10,000.00*, is recorded in the Credit column.

RUN DATE 08/12/-- MM DD YY		GENERAL JOURNAL Input Form				
DATE MM/DD	REFERENCE	ACCOUNT NO.	CUSTOMER/ VENDOR NO.	DEBIT	CREDIT	
1	08/01	R1	110		10000 00		1
2	/		310			10000 00	2
3	/03	C1	130		1577 00		3
4	/		110			1577 00	4
5	/04	C2	140		1200 00		5
6	/		110			1200 00	6
7	/07	M1	130		2720 00		7
8	/		210			2720 00	8
9	/11	C3	210		1360 00		9
10	/		110			1360 00	10
11	/12	T12	110		525 00		11
12	/		410			525 00	12
13	/12	C4	540		250 00		13
14	/		110			250 00	14
15	/12	C5	570		45 00		15
16	/		110			45 00	16
17	/12	C6	320		100 00		17
18	/		110			100 00	18
19	/						19
25	/						25
			PAGE TOTALS	17777 00	17777 00	
			FINAL TOTALS	17777 00	17777 00	

Paid Cash for Supplies

August 3, 19--. Paid cash for supplies, $1,577.00. Check No. 1.

The journal entry to record this transaction is on lines 3 and 4 of Illustration T1-5. Supplies is debited and Cash is credited for $1,577.00.

Paid Cash for Insurance

August 4, 19--. Paid cash for insurance, $1,200.00. Check No. 2.

The journal entry to record this transaction is on lines 5 and 6 of Illustration T1-5. Prepaid Insurance is debited and Cash is credited for $1,200.00.

Bought Supplies on Account

August 7, 19--. Bought supplies on account from Butler Cleaning Supplies, $2,720.00. Memorandum No. 1.

The journal entry to record this transaction is on lines 7 and 8 of Illustration T1-5. Supplies is debited and Butler Cleaning Supplies is credited for $2,720.00.

FYI

Dollar signs and cent signs are not keyed when using Automated Accounting 6.0 software. When the cents are zero (.00), key only the dollar amount. For example, if the amount is 15.00, key 15. The software automatically assigns the .00.

Paid Cash on Account

August 11, 19--. Paid cash on account to Butler Cleaning Supplies, $1,360.00. Check No. 3.

The journal entry to record this transaction is on lines 9 and 10 of Illustration T1-5. Butler Cleaning Supplies is debited and Cash is credited for $1,360.00.

Received Cash from Sales

August 12, 19--. Received cash from sales, $525.00. Tape No. 12.

The journal entry to record this transaction is on lines 11 and 12 of Illustration T1-5. Cash is debited and Sales is credited for $525.00.

Paid Cash for an Expense

August 12, 19--. Paid cash for rent, $250.00. Check No. 4.

The journal entry to record this transaction is on lines 13 and 14 of Illustration T1-5. Rent Expense is debited and Cash is credited for $250.00.

Illustration T1-5 includes a journal entry, lines 15 and 16, for Utilities Expense. This transaction is journalized in the same way as the cash payment for rent.

Paid Cash to Owner for Personal Use

August 12, 19--. Paid cash to owner for personal use, $100.00. Check No. 6.

The journal entry to record this transaction is on lines 17 and 18 of Illustration T1-5. Ben Furman, Drawing is debited and Cash is credited for $100.00.

Completing a General Journal Input Form

After all transactions have been journalized, Rugcare totals the Debit and Credit amount columns. The totals are recorded on the Page Totals line provided at the bottom of the input form.

A journal entry should not be split on two different general journal input forms. Therefore, if a complete journal entry cannot be entered on an input form, a new input form is started. The totals for all pages are then entered *only* on the last page on the Final Totals line. The two totals are compared to assure that debits equal credits. If only one general journal input form is required then the totals are recorded on the Page Totals line and the Final Totals line.

A journal entry should not be split on two different general journal input forms.

Processing Journal Entries

To process journal entries, the Journals menu is selected from the menu bar. The General Journal command is chosen from the Journals menu to display the data entry window for entering transaction data from the general journal input form. Rugcare keys the transaction data from the general journal input form one line at a time. Lines 1 and 2 are shown entered in Illustration T1-6.

Data entry window with a general journal entry recorded

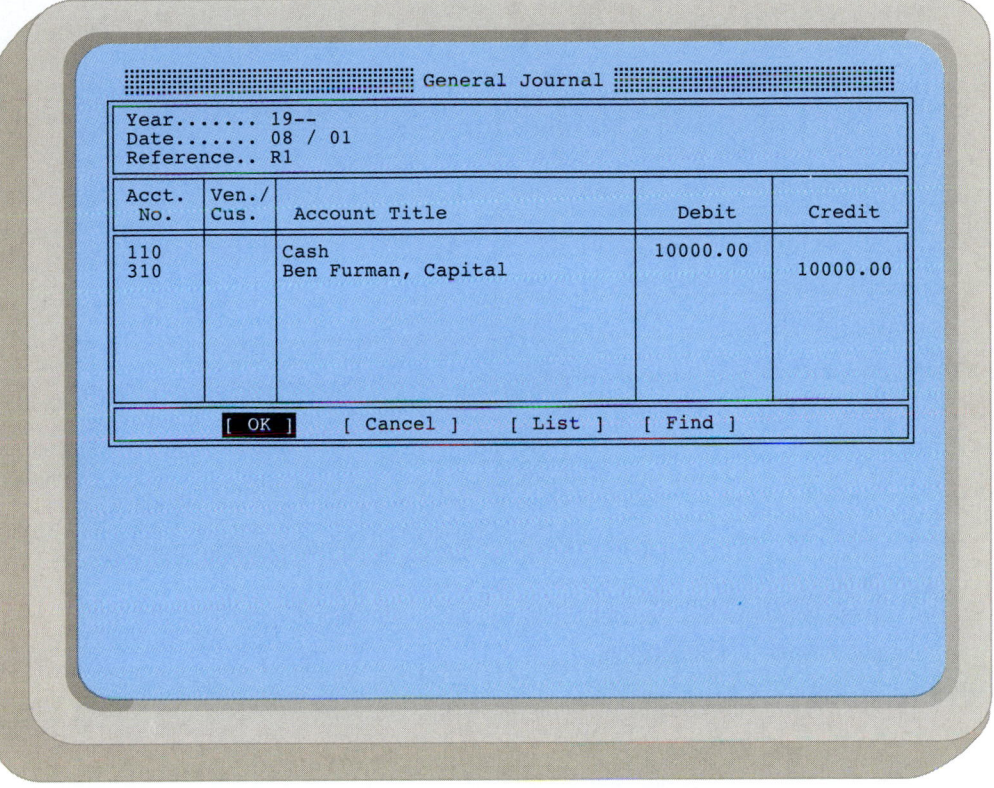

After all lines on the input form have been keyed and posted, the Reports menu is selected from the menu bar. The Journals command is chosen from the Reports menu. The General Journal report is chosen from the Report Selection window. This selection displays the Selection Options screen shown in Illustration T1-7.

The data to be printed on reports can be restricted by specifying the date range or reference numbers as shown on Illustration T1-7. As Rugcare wants to print all transactions recorded on the general journal input form, pushing the *Ok* box directs the software to display a general journal report. The displayed general journal report is checked for accuracy by comparing the report totals, $17,777.00, with the totals on the general journal input form. Because the totals are the same, the general journal report is assumed to be correct. The general journal report is printed, as shown in Illustration T1-8, and is filed for future reference.

FYI

To avoid damage to disk drives on the computer, do not insert any implements such as pencils in the disk drive.

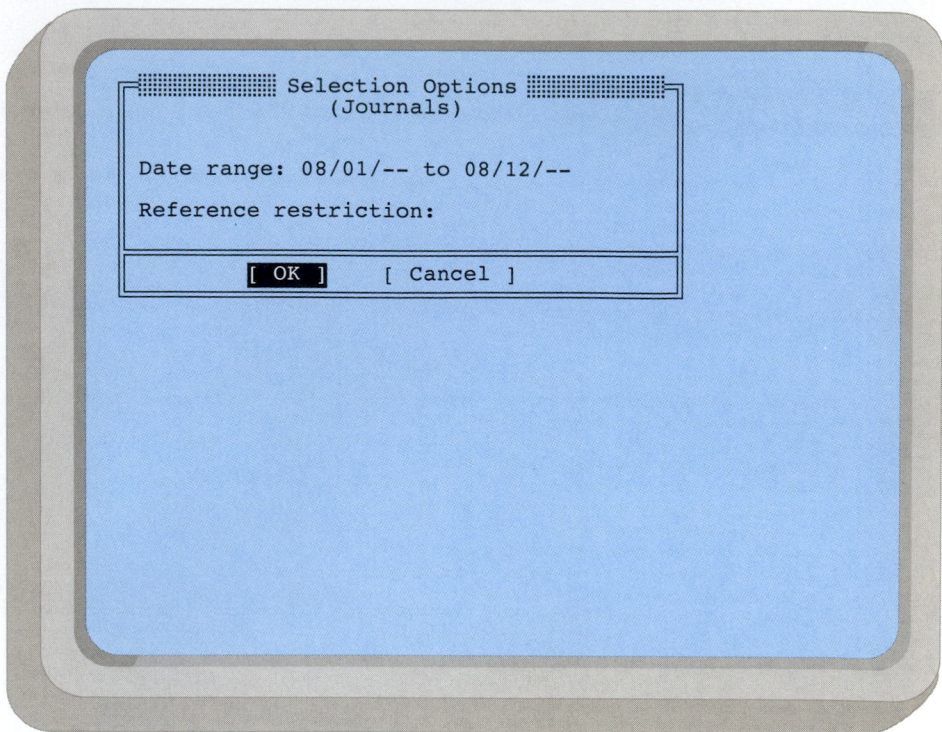

```
┌┄┄┄┄┄┄┄┄┄┄┄ Selection Options ┄┄┄┄┄┄┄┄┄┄┄┐
│                  (Journals)                │
│                                            │
│  Date range: 08/01/-- to 08/12/--          │
│                                            │
│  Reference restriction:                    │
│                                            │
│         [ OK ]       [ Cancel ]            │
└────────────────────────────────────────────┘
```

ILLUSTRATION T1-8   General journal report

```
                            Rugcare
                        General Journal
                          08/12/--
--------------------------------------------------------------------
Date    Refer.  V/C  Acct.  Title                    Debit     Credit
--------------------------------------------------------------------
08/01   R1           110    Cash                   10000.00
08/01   R1           310    Ben Furman, Capital                10000.00

08/03   C1           130    Supplies                1577.00
08/03   C1           110    Cash                                1577.00

08/04   C2           140    Prepaid Insurance       1200.00
08/04   C2           110    Cash                                1200.00

08/07   M1           130    Supplies                2720.00
08/07   M1           210    Butler Cleaning Supplies            2720.00

08/11   C3           210    Butler Cleaning Supplies 1360.00
08/11   C3           110    Cash                                1360.00

08/12   T12          110    Cash                     525.00
08/12   T12          410    Sales                                525.00

08/12   C4           540    Rent Expense             250.00
08/12   C4           110    Cash                                 250.00

08/12   C5           570    Utilities Expense         45.00
08/12   C5           110    Cash                                  45.00

08/12   C6           320    Ben Furman, Drawing      100.00
08/12   C6           110    Cash                                 100.00

                                                  ----------  ----------
                            Totals               17777.00    17777.00
                                                  ==========  ==========
```

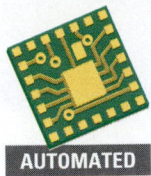

OPTIONAL PROBLEM DB-1A

Rugcare's general ledger data base is on the accounting textbook template. If you wish to complete these file maintenance activities and record transactions using automated accounting software, load the *Automated Accounting 6.0* or higher software. Select Data Base 1A (DB-1A) from the template disk. Read the Problem Instructions screen. Use the completed input forms in Illustrations T1-1 and T1-5, and follow the procedures described to process Rugcare's file maintenance activities and to record transactions.

AUTOMATED ACCOUNTING PROBLEMS

AUTOMATING MASTERY PROBLEM 6-M Journalizing and posting to a general ledger

INSTRUCTIONS:

1. Prepare input forms for Mastery Problem 6-M, Chapter 6.
   a. Prepare a chart of accounts input form to add Utilities Expense to the general ledger chart of accounts using the 3-digit numbering system described in Chapter 6. Use November 30 of the current year as the run date. Hiatt Cleaning uses the following chart of accounts.

   Assets
   110 Cash
   120 Supplies
   130 Prepaid Insurance

   Liabilities
   210 Major Supplies

   Owner's Equity
   310 Al Hiatt, Capital
   320 Al Hiatt, Drawing

   Revenue
   410 Sales

   Expenses
   510 Advertising Expense
   520 Miscellaneous Expense
   530 Rent Expense

   b. Record Hiatt Cleaning's transactions on a general journal input form. Use November 30 of the current year as the run date.
2. Load the *Automated Accounting 6.0* or higher software. Select data base *F6-M (First-Year Course Problem 6-M)* from the accounting textbook template. Read the Problem Instructions screen.
3. Select File from the menu bar and choose the Save As menu command. Key the path to the drive and directory that contains your data files. Save the data base with a file name of XXX6M (where XXX are your initials).
4. Key the data from the completed chart of accounts input form.
5. Display/print the revised chart of accounts report. Check the report for accuracy.
6. Key the transactions from the completed general journal input form.
7. Display/print the general journal report. Check the report for accuracy by comparing the report totals with the totals on the input form.

AUTOMATING CHALLENGE PROBLEM 6-C Journalizing and posting to a general ledger

INSTRUCTIONS:

1. Prepare input forms for Challenge Problem 6-C, Chapter 6.
2. Load the *Automated Accounting 6.0* or higher software. Select data base *F6-C (First-Year Course Problem 6-C)* from the accounting textbook template. Read the Problem Instructions screen.
3. Select File from the menu bar and choose the Save As menu command. Key the path to the drive and directory that contains your data files. Save the data base with a file name of XXX6C (where XXX are your initials).
4. Key the transactions from the completed general journal input form.
5. Display/print the general journal report. Check the report for accuracy by comparing the report totals with the totals on the input form.

7

Cash Control Systems

ENABLING PERFORMANCE TASKS

After studying Chapter 7, you will be able to:

a Define accounting terms related to using a checking account and a petty cash fund.

b Identify accounting concepts and practices related to using a checking account.

c Prepare business papers related to using a checking account.

d Reconcile a bank statement.

e Establish and replenish a petty cash fund.

f Record selected transactions related to using a checking account and a petty cash fund.

TERMS PREVIEW

checking account • endorsement • blank endorsement • special endorsement • restrictive endorsement • postdated check • bank statement • dishonored check • electronic funds transfer • petty cash • petty cash slip

In accounting, money is usually referred to as cash. Most businesses make major cash payments by check. However, small cash payments for items such as postage and some supplies may be made from a cash fund kept at the place of business.

Because cash transactions occur more frequently than other types of transactions, more chances occur to make recording errors affecting cash. Cash can be transferred from one person to another without any question about ownership. Also, cash may be lost as it is moved from one place to another.

As a safety measure, Rugcare keeps most of its cash in a bank. Because all cash receipts are placed in a bank, Rugcare has written evidence to support its accounting records. Rugcare can compare its record of checks written with the bank's record of checks paid. Greater control of Rugcare's cash and greater accuracy of its cash records result from these procedures.

CHECKING ACCOUNTS

A business form ordering a bank to pay cash from a bank account is known as a check. A bank account from which payments can be ordered by a depositor is called a **checking account**.

Authorizing Signatures

When a checking account is opened, the bank customer must provide a signature on a signature card for the bank records. If several persons are authorized to sign checks, each person's signature must be on the signature card. Checks should always be signed with the same signature as on the signature card. Only Ben Furman is authorized to sign checks for Rugcare.

Depositing Cash

A bank customer prepares a deposit slip each time cash or checks are placed in a bank account. Deposit slips may differ slightly from one bank to another. Each bank designs its own deposit slips to fit the bank's recording machines. However, all deposit slips contain the same basic information as the slip shown in Illustration 7-1.

Checks are listed on a deposit slip according to the bank number on each check. For example, in Illustration 7-1, the number *93-108* identifies the bank on which the $10,000.00 check is written.

When a deposit is made, a bank gives the depositor a receipt. Many banks use a copy of the deposit slip with a printed or stamped verification as the receipt. The printed verification, *AUG 1 19-- D10000.00 RDS*, is shown along the top left edge of the deposit slip in Illustration 7-1. This printed verification means that a total of $10,000.00 was deposited on August 1. The initials *RDS* next to the amount are those of the bank employee who accepted the deposit.

ILLUSTRATION 7-1

Deposit slip

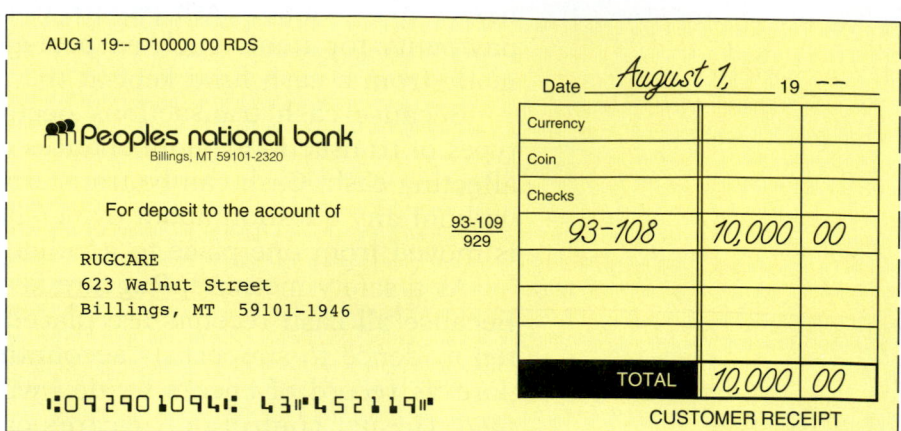

Rugcare records the August 1 deposit on the next unused check stub, as shown in Illustration 7-2.

ILLUSTRATION 7-2

Deposit recorded on a check stub

After the deposit is recorded on the check stub, a checkbook subtotal is calculated. The balance brought forward on Check Stub No. 1 is zero. The previous balance, $0.00, *plus* the deposit, $10,000.00, *equals* the subtotal, $10,000.00.

Cash receipts are journalized at the time cash is received. Later, the cash receipts are deposited in the checking account. Therefore, no journal entry is needed for deposits because the cash receipts have already been journalized.

Endorsing Checks

Ownership of a check can be transferred. The name of the first owner is stated on a check following the words *Pay to the order of*. Therefore, the person to whom payment is to be made must indi-

cate that ownership of the check is being transferred. One person transfers ownership to another person by signing on the back of a check. A signature or stamp on the back of a check transferring ownership is called an **endorsement.**

An endorsement should be signed exactly as the person's name appears on the front of the check. For example, a check made payable to B.E. Furman is endorsed on the back as *B.E. Furman.* Immediately below that endorsement, Mr. Furman writes his official signature, *Ben Furman.*

Ownership of a check might be transferred several times, resulting in several endorsements. Each endorser guarantees payment of the check. If a bank does not receive payment from the person who signed the check, each endorser is individually liable for payment.

Three types of endorsements are commonly used, each having a specific use in transferring ownership.

Blank Endorsement. An endorsement consisting only of the endorser's signature is called a **blank endorsement.** A blank endorsement indicates that the subsequent owner is whoever has the check. A blank endorsement is shown in Illustration 7-3.

ILLUSTRATION 7-3   Blank endorsement

Federal regulations require that an endorsement be confined to a limited amount of space that is indicated on the back of a check.

If a check with a blank endorsement is lost or stolen, the check can be cashed by anyone who has it. Ownership may be transferred without further endorsement. A blank endorsement should be used *only* when a person is at the bank ready to cash or deposit a check.

Special Endorsement. An endorsement indicating a new owner of a check is called a **special endorsement.** Special endorsements are sometimes known as endorsements in full. A special endorsement is shown in Illustration 7-4.

ILLUSTRATION 7-4   Special endorsement

Special endorsements include the words *Pay to the order of* and the name of the new check owner. Only the person or business named in a special endorsement can cash, deposit, or further transfer ownership of the check.

Restrictive Endorsement. An endorsement restricting further transfer of a check's ownership is called a **restrictive endorsement**. A restrictive endorsement limits use of the check to whatever purpose is stated in the endorsement. A restrictive endorsement is shown in Illustration 7-5.

ILLUSTRATION 7-5

Restrictive endorsement

On all checks received, Rugcare stamps a restrictive endorsement which states that the check is for deposit only. This restrictive endorsement prevents unauthorized persons from cashing a check if it is lost or stolen.

Writing Checks

FYI

Checks should be written in ink so that no one can alter them.

Rugcare uses printed checks with check stubs attached. Consecutive numbers are preprinted on Rugcare's checks. Consecutive numbers on checks provide an easy way of identifying each check. Also, the numbers help keep track of all checks to assure that none are lost or misplaced.

Preparing Check Stubs. A check stub is a business' record of each check written for a cash payment transaction. *(CONCEPT: Objective Evidence)* To avoid forgetting to prepare a check stub, the check stub is prepared before the check is written. Rugcare's check stub and check are shown in Illustration 7-6.

ILLUSTRATION 7-6

Completed check stub and check

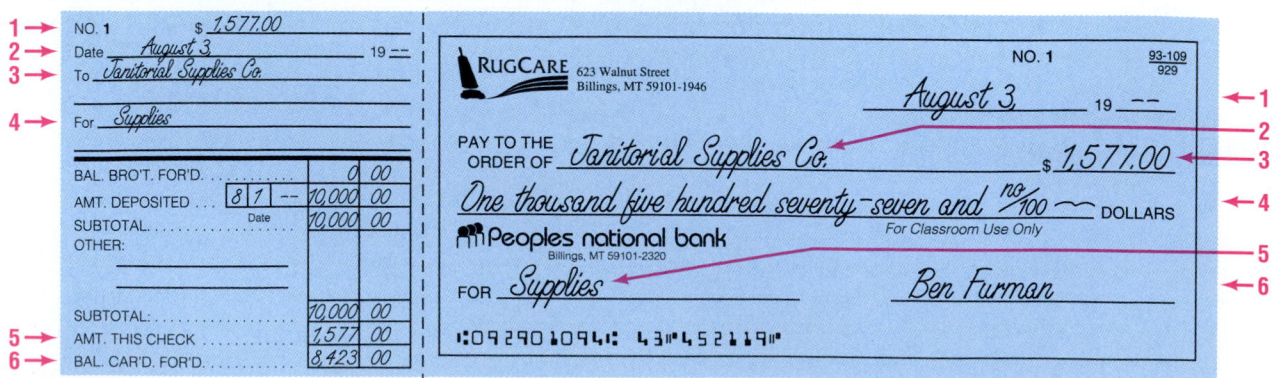

Six steps are used to complete Rugcare's Check Stub No. 1.

1 Write the amount of the check, *$1,577.00*, in the space after the dollar sign at the top of the stub.

2 Write the date of the check, *August 3, 19--*, on the Date line at the top of the stub.

3 Write to whom the check is to be paid, *Janitorial Supplies Co.*, on the To line at the top of the stub.

4 Record the purpose of the check, *Supplies*, on the For line.

5 Write the amount of the check, *$1,577.00*, in the amount column at the bottom of the stub on the line with the words "Amt. this Check."

6 Calculate the new checking account balance, *$8,423.00*, and record the new balance in the amount column on the last line of the stub. The new balance is calculated as shown below.

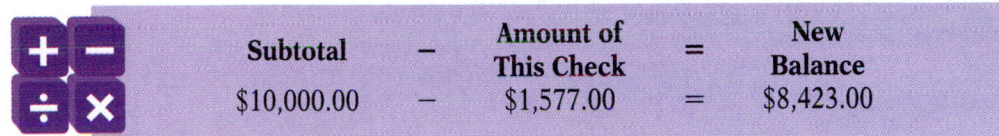

	Subtotal	–	Amount of This Check	=	New Balance
	$10,000.00	–	$1,577.00	=	$8,423.00

Preparing Checks. After the check stub is completed, the check is written. The check shown in Illustration 7-6 is prepared as follows.

1 Write the date, *August 3, 19--*, in the space provided.

The date should be the month, day, and year on which the check is issued. A check with a future date on it is called a **postdated check.** Most banks will not accept postdated checks because money cannot be withdrawn from a depositor's account until the date on the check.

2 Write to whom the check is to be paid, *Janitorial Supplies Co.*, following the words "Pay to the order of."

If the person to whom a check is to be paid is a business, use the business' name rather than the owner's name. *(CONCEPT: Business Entity)* If the person to whom the check is to be paid is an individual, use that person's name.

3 Write the amount in figures, *$1,577.00*, following the dollar sign.

Write the figures close to the printed dollar sign. This practice prevents anyone from writing another digit in front of the amount to change the amount of the check.

4 Write the amount in words, *One thousand five hundred seventy-seven and no/100*, on the line with the word "Dollars."

This written amount verifies the amount written in figures after the dollar sign. Begin the words at the extreme left. Draw a line through the unused space up to the word "Dollars." This line prevents anyone from writing in additional words to change the amount.

If the amounts in words and in figures are not the same, a bank may pay only the amount in words. Often, when the amounts do not agree, a bank will refuse to pay the check.

5 Write the purpose of the check, *Supplies*, on the line labeled "For."

> On some checks this space is labeled "Memo." Some checks do not have a line for writing the purpose of the check.

6 Sign the check.

> A check should not be signed until each item on the check and its stub has been verified for accuracy.

Voiding Checks. Banks usually refuse to accept altered checks. If any kind of error is made in preparing a check, a new check should be prepared. Because checks are prenumbered, all checks not used should be retained for the records. This practice helps account for all checks and assures that no checks have been lost or stolen.

A check that contains errors must be marked so that others will know that it is not to be used. The word *VOID* is written in large letters across both the check and its stub.

When Rugcare records a check in its journal, the check number is placed in the journal's Doc. No. column. If a check number is missing from the Doc. No. column, there is a question whether all checks have been journalized. To assure that all check numbers are listed in the journal, Rugcare records voided checks in the journal. The date is recorded in the journal's Date column. The word *VOID* is written in the Account Title column. The check number is recorded in the Doc. No. column. A check mark is entered in the Post. Ref. column. A dash is placed in the Cash Credit column.

Audit Your Understanding

1. List the three types of endorsements.

2. List the six steps for preparing a check stub.

BANK STATEMENT

Banks keep separate records for each depositor. Information from deposit slips and checks is recorded daily in depositors' accounts. A report of deposits, withdrawals, and bank balance sent to a depositor by a bank is called a **bank statement.** Rugcare's bank statement for August 27 is shown in Illustration 7-7.

The balance for Rugcare's checking account on August 27, according to the bank's records, is $8,731.00.

When a bank receives checks, the amount of each check is deducted from the depositor's account. Then, the bank stamps the checks to indicate that the check is canceled and is not to be transferred further. Canceled checks are returned to a depositor with a bank statement. Outstanding checks are those checks issued by a depositor but not yet reported on a bank statement. Outstanding deposits are those deposits made at a bank but not yet shown on a bank statement. A bank may assess a charge for maintaining a checking account. Account service charges are also listed on a bank statement.

Banks may have different kinds of checking accounts to fit special needs of depositors. Each bank has its own regulations for its services, and fees are not charged for some checking accounts.

ILLUSTRATION 7-7   Bank statement

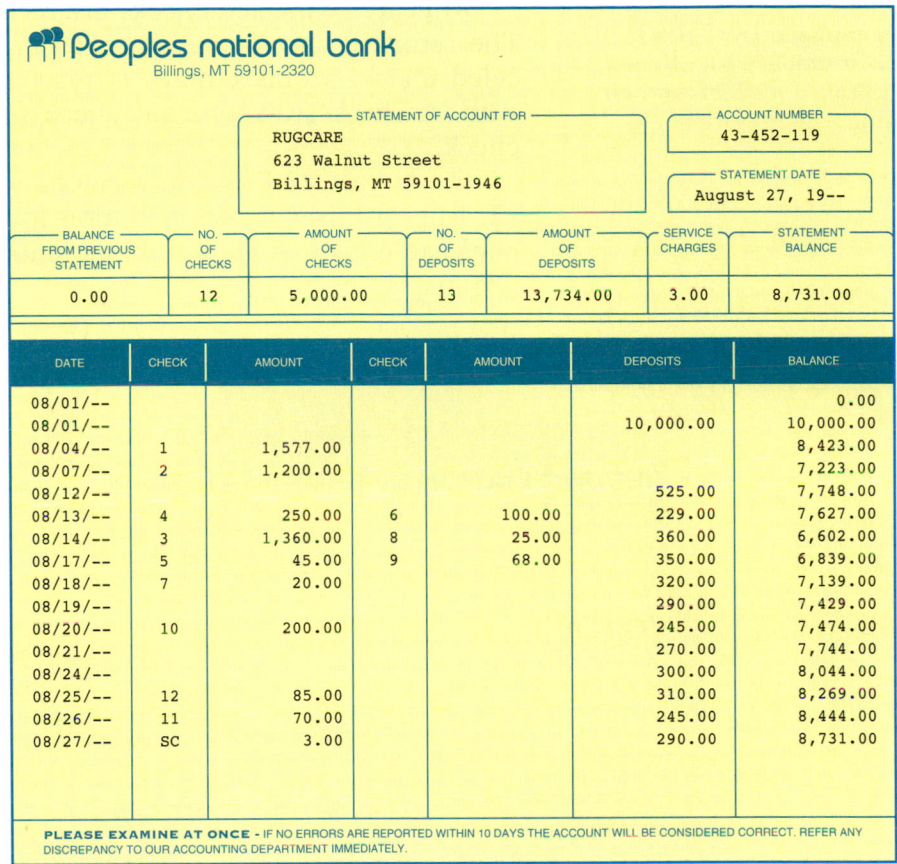

Peoples national bank
Billings, MT 59101-2320

STATEMENT OF ACCOUNT FOR	ACCOUNT NUMBER
RUGCARE 623 Walnut Street Billings, MT 59101-1946	43-452-119
	STATEMENT DATE August 27, 19--

BALANCE FROM PREVIOUS STATEMENT	NO. OF CHECKS	AMOUNT OF CHECKS	NO. OF DEPOSITS	AMOUNT OF DEPOSITS	SERVICE CHARGES	STATEMENT BALANCE
0.00	12	5,000.00	13	13,734.00	3.00	8,731.00

DATE	CHECK	AMOUNT	CHECK	AMOUNT	DEPOSITS	BALANCE
08/01/--						0.00
08/01/--					10,000.00	10,000.00
08/04/--	1	1,577.00				8,423.00
08/07/--	2	1,200.00				7,223.00
08/12/--					525.00	7,748.00
08/13/--	4	250.00	6	100.00	229.00	7,627.00
08/14/--	3	1,360.00	8	25.00	360.00	6,602.00
08/17/--	5	45.00	9	68.00	350.00	6,839.00
08/18/--	7	20.00			320.00	7,139.00
08/19/--					290.00	7,429.00
08/20/--	10	200.00			245.00	7,474.00
08/21/--					270.00	7,744.00
08/24/--					300.00	8,044.00
08/25/--	12	85.00			310.00	8,269.00
08/26/--	11	70.00			245.00	8,444.00
08/27/--	SC	3.00			290.00	8,731.00

PLEASE EXAMINE AT ONCE - IF NO ERRORS ARE REPORTED WITHIN 10 DAYS THE ACCOUNT WILL BE CONSIDERED CORRECT. REFER ANY DISCREPANCY TO OUR ACCOUNTING DEPARTMENT IMMEDIATELY.

Verifying a Bank Statement

Although banks seldom make mistakes, occasionally a check or deposit might be recorded in a wrong account. When a bank statement is received, a depositor should verify its accuracy. If errors are discovered, the bank should be notified at once. However, a bank's records and a depositor's records may differ and still be correct. The difference may exist for several reasons.

1. A service charge may not have been recorded in the depositor's business records.
2. Outstanding deposits may be recorded in the depositor's records but not yet reported on a bank statement.
3. Outstanding checks may be recorded in the depositor's records but not yet reported on a bank statement.
4. A depositor may have made errors in doing arithmetic or in recording information in the business records. The most common mistakes made by depositors are arithmetic errors.
5. The bank may have made an error.

Reconciling a Bank Statement

A bank statement is reconciled by verifying that information on a bank statement and a checkbook are in agreement. Rugcare reconciles a bank statement on the same day that the statement is received. Reconciling immediately is an important aspect of cash control.

Rugcare's canceled checks are received with the bank statement. The returned checks are arranged in numeric order. For each canceled check, a check mark is placed on the corresponding check stub. A check stub with no check mark indicates an outstanding check.

On August 28 Rugcare receives a bank statement dated August 27. Rugcare uses a reconciliation form printed on the back of the bank statement. Rugcare's bank statement reconciliation is shown in Illustration 7-8.

| **ILLUSTRATION 7-8** | Bank statement reconciliation |

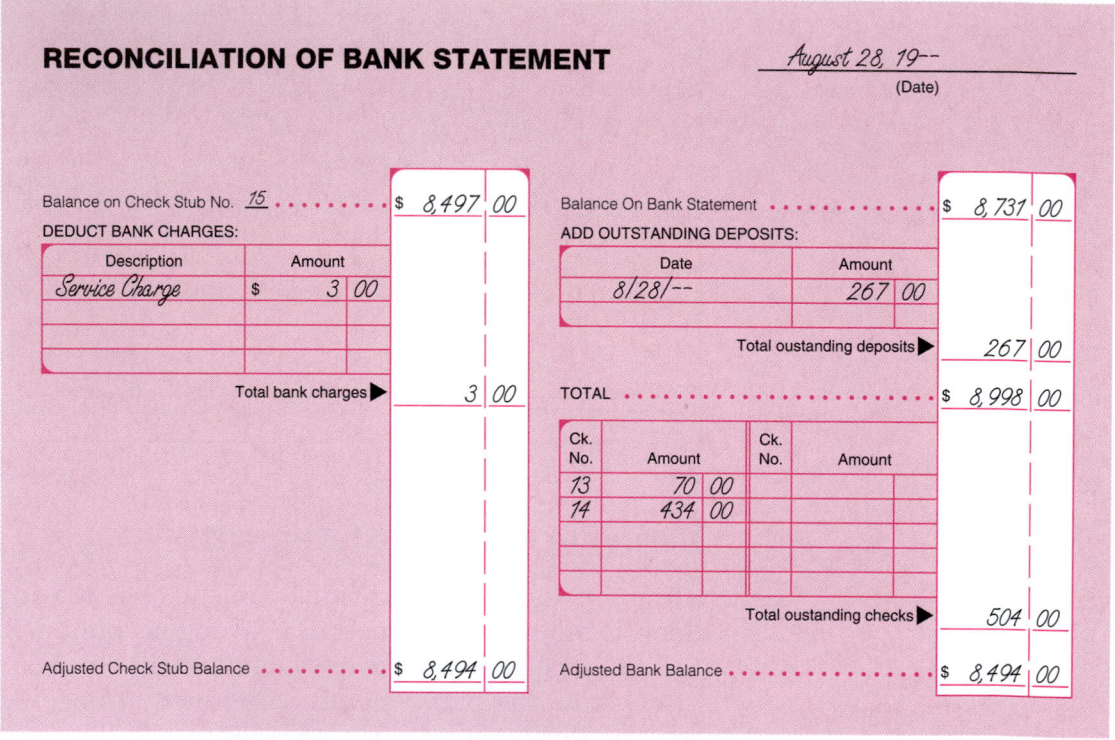

Rugcare uses three steps to reconcile a bank statement.

1 Calculate the adjusted check stub balance.

- Write the date on which the reconciliation is prepared, *August 28, 19--*.

- In the left amount column, list the balance brought forward on Check Stub No. 15, the next unused check stub, *$8,497.00*.

- In the space for bank charges, list any charges. The only such charge for Rugcare is the bank service charge, *$3.00*.

The bank service charge is labeled *SC* on the bank statement.

- Write the adjusted checkbook balance, *$8,494.00*, in the space provided at the bottom of the left amount column. The balance on the check stub, $8,497.00, *minus* the bank's service charge, $3.00, *equals* the adjusted check stub balance, $8,494.00.

2 Calculate the adjusted bank balance.

- Write the ending balance shown on the bank statement, *$8,731.00*, in the right amount column.
- Write the date, *8/28/--* and the amount, *$267.00*, of any outstanding deposits in the space provided. Add the outstanding deposits. Write the total outstanding deposits, *$267.00*, in the right amount column.
- Add the ending bank statement balance to the total outstanding deposits. Write the total, *$8,998.00*, in the space for the Total.
- List the outstanding checks, *Nos. 13 and 14*, and their amounts, *$70.00 and $434.00*, in the space provided. Add the amounts of the outstanding checks, and write the total, *$504.00*, in the right amount column.
- Calculate the adjusted bank balance, and write the amount, *$8,494.00*, in the space provided at the bottom of the right amount column. The total, *$8,998.00*, *minus* the total outstanding checks, *$504.00*, *equals* the adjusted bank balance, *$8,494.00*.

3 Compare adjusted balances.

- The adjusted balances must be the same. The adjusted check stub balance is the same as the adjusted bank balance, *$8,494.00*. Because the two amounts are the same, the bank statement is reconciled. The completed reconciliation form is filed for future reference.
- If the two adjusted balances are not the same, the errors must be found and corrected before any more work is done.

Recording a Bank Service Charge on a Check Stub

The bank deducts the service charge from Rugcare's checking account each month. Although Rugcare did not write a check for the bank service charge, this cash payment must be recorded in Rugcare's accounting records as a cash payment. Rugcare makes a record of a bank service charge on a check stub as shown in Illustration 7-9.

Three steps are used to record a bank service charge on a check stub.

1 Write the words, *Service charge, $3.00*, on the check stub under the heading "Other."

2 Write the amount, *$3.00*, in the check stub's amount column.

FYI

If you study classified advertisements, you will find that many listings for various office workers require the ability to use spreadsheets.

3 Calculate and record the new balance, *$8,494.00*, on the Subtotal line.

ILLUSTRATION 7-9

Bank service charge recorded on a check stub

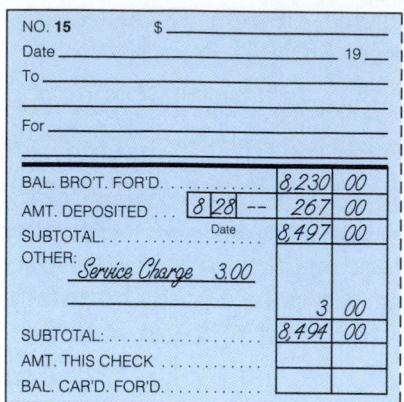

Journalizing a Bank Service Charge

Because the bank service charge is a cash payment for which no check is written, Rugcare prepares a memorandum as the source document. Rugcare's bank service charges are relatively small and occur only once a month. Therefore, a separate ledger account for the expense is not used. Instead, Rugcare records the bank service charge as a miscellaneous expense.

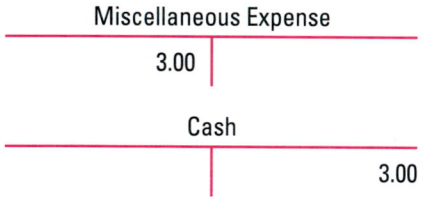

August 28, 19--. Received bank statement showing August bank service charge, $3.00. Memorandum No. 3.

A memorandum is the source document for a bank service charge transaction. *(CONCEPT: Objective Evidence)* The analysis of this transaction is shown in the T accounts.

Miscellaneous Expense is debited for $3.00 to show the increase in this expense account balance. Cash is credited for $3.00 to show the decrease in this asset account balance. The journal entry to record Rugcare's bank service charge is shown in Illustration 7-10.

ILLUSTRATION 7-10

Journal entry to record a bank service charge

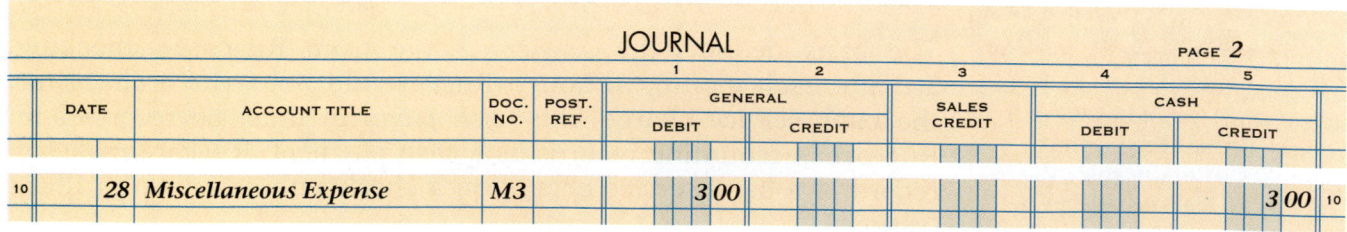

This entry is journalized using four steps.

1 Date. Write the date, *28*, in the Date column.

2 Debit. Write the title of the account to be debited, Miscellaneous Expense, in the Account Title column. Record the amount

USING AN ELECTRONIC SPREADSHEET TO PREPARE A BANK RECONCILIATION

Businesses often use forms to prepare accounting reports. The bank reconciliation form in Illustration 7-8 increases the efficiency of verifying a bank statement. Electronic spreadsheet software is another useful tool for preparing accounting reports. Unlike paper forms, however, electronic spreadsheets contain formulas that automatically perform calculations.

An **electronic spreadsheet** displayed on a computer monitor is a group of rows and columns. The space where a column intersects with a row is a **cell**. Cell A17 is located at the intersection of column A and row 17. This is known as the **cell address**.

A spreadsheet prepared for reconciling a bank statement would look like the one in the following illustration. Electronic spreadsheets can be extremely large, having hundreds of columns and thousands of rows.

The power of the electronic spreadsheet comes from the ability to let the software make calculations. This is accomplished by attaching formulas to different cells. This spread-

sheet was created with all the formulas necessary to complete a bank reconciliation. For example, the formula at cell I15, +H12+H13, calculates the total outstanding deposits. The spreadsheet adds the values in cells H12 and H13, and displays the value, $1,131.00, in cell I15.

After the bank reconciliation is printed, the same spreadsheet can be used to reconcile other bank statements. Preparing a bank reconciliation using an electronic spreadsheet assures the preparer that the calculations are accurate.

```
        A          B        C     D    E     F      G     H        I
 1  General Ledger: 110                          Date: March 31, 19--
 2  Account Number: 34-2353-26
 3
 4  RECONCILIATION OF BANK STATEMENT
 5
 6  Balance on Check Stub.. 6,234.00    Balance on Bank Statement.. 6,247.00
 7
 8  DEDUCT BANK CHARGES:                 ADD OUTSTANDING DEPOSITS:
 9
10    Description   Amount               Date                 Amount
11    ------------------------           ----------------------------
12  Service Charge     8.00              3/30/--               436.00
13                                       3/31/--               695.00
14                                       ----------------------------
15  ------------------------             Total outstanding deposits. 1,131.00
16  ------------------------
17  Total bank charges.....     8.00     TOTAL.................... 7,378.00
18                           ----------
19                                       DEDUCT OUTSTANDING CHECKS:
20
21                                       Ck.          Ck.
22                                       No.  Amount  No.  Amount
23                                       ----------------------------
24                                       423   85.00  458   54.00
25                                       455  343.00  459  147.00
26                                       457  523.00
27                                       ----------------------------
28                                       Total outstanding checks... 1,152.00
29                           ----------                      ----------
30  Adjusted Check Stub
31    Balance.............. 6,226.00     Adjusted Bank Balance...... 6,226.00
32                          ==========                      ==========
33
34
35
```

debited to Miscellaneous Expense, *$3.00*, in the General Debit column.

3 Credit. Record the amount credited to Cash, *$3.00*, in the Cash Credit column.

4 Source document. Write the source document number, *M3*, in the Doc. No. column.

Rugcare reconciled its bank statement on August 28. The entry for the bank service charge is journalized on the same date. Rugcare continues to record entries in the journal until the end of the month as shown in Illustration 6-10, Chapter 6.

DISHONORED CHECKS

A check that a bank refuses to pay is called a **dishonored check.** Banks may dishonor a check for a number of reasons. (1) The check appears to be altered. (2) The signature of the person who signed the check does not match the one on the signature card at the bank. (3) The amounts written in figures and in words do not agree. (4) The check is postdated. (5) The person who wrote the check has stopped payment on the check. (6) The account of the person who wrote the check has insufficient funds to pay the check.

Issuing a check on an account with insufficient funds is illegal in most states. Altering or forging a check is illegal in all states. A dishonored check may affect the credit rating of the person or business who issued the check. Checking accounts and records should be maintained in such a way that all checks will be honored when presented to the bank.

Sometimes money for a dishonored check can be collected directly from the person or business who wrote the check. Often, however, the value of a dishonored check cannot be recovered and becomes an expense to the business.

Most banks charge a fee for handling dishonored checks that have been previously accepted for deposit. This fee is an expense of the business receiving a dishonored check. Rugcare's bank charges a $5.00 fee for handling dishonored checks. Rugcare attempts to collect the $5.00 fee in addition to the amount of the dishonored check.

Rugcare records a check as a cash debit and deposits the check. When a check is dishonored, the bank deducts the amount of the check plus the fee, $5.00, from Rugcare's checking account. Therefore, Rugcare records a dishonored check in its journal as a cash payment transaction.

Recording a Dishonored Check on a Check Stub

A dishonored check recorded on a check stub is shown in Illustration 7-11.

| ILLUSTRATION 7-11 | Dishonored check recorded on a check stub |

NO. **41**	$			
Date			19	
To				
For				
BAL. BRO'T. FOR'D.		6,128	00	
AMT. DEPOSITED ...				
SUBTOTAL. .... Date		6,128	00	
OTHER: *Service Charge 3.00*				
Dis. Check 15.00		18	00	
SUBTOTAL:		6,110	00	
AMT. THIS CHECK				
BAL. CAR'D. FOR'D.				

The words, *Dishonored check*, are written on the line below the words "Other." The total amount of the dishonored check plus the fee, *$15.00*, is written in the amount column on the same line. A new subtotal is calculated by subtracting the total, $18.00 ($3.00 service charge *plus* $15.00 dishonored check), from the balance brought forward, $6,128.00. The new subtotal, *$6,110.00*, is written on the Subtotal line. A new Balance Carried Forward is not calculated until after Check No. 41 is written.

Journalizing a Dishonored Check

During August, Rugcare received no checks that were subsequently dishonored. However, in November Rugcare did receive a check that was dishonored.

November 29, 19--. Received notice from the bank of a dishonored check, $10.00, plus $5.00 fee; total, $15.00. Memorandum No. 6.

Because Rugcare did not write a check for this cash payment, a memorandum is prepared as the source document. *(CONCEPT: Objective Evidence)*

All checks received are deposited in Rugcare's checking account. The entry for each cash receipts transaction includes a debit to Cash. If a check is subsequently returned as dishonored, the previous cash debit for the amount of the check must be offset by a cash credit. The analysis of this transaction is shown in the T accounts.

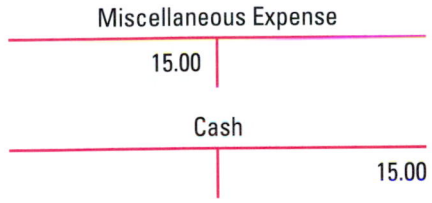

Miscellaneous Expense is debited for $15.00 to show the increase in this expense account balance. Cash is credited for $15.00 to show the decrease in this asset account balance. The journal entry to record this transaction is shown in Illustration 7-12.

This entry is journalized using four steps.

1 Date. Write the date, *29*, in the Date column.

2 Debit. Write the title of the account to be debited, Miscellaneous Expense, in the Account Title column. Record the amount debited to Miscellaneous Expense, *$15.00*, in the General Debit column.

3 Credit. Record the amount credited to Cash, *$15.00*, in the Cash Credit column.

4 Source document. Write the source document number, *M6*, in the Doc. No. column.

ILLUSTRATION 7-12 Journal entry to record a dishonored check

	DATE	ACCOUNT TITLE	DOC. NO.	POST. REF.	GENERAL DEBIT	GENERAL CREDIT	SALES CREDIT	CASH DEBIT	CASH CREDIT	
19	29	Miscellaneous Expense	M6		1 5 00				1 5 00	19

JOURNAL — PAGE 10

ELECTRONIC FUNDS TRANSFER

A computerized cash payments system that uses electronic impulses to transfer funds is called **electronic funds transfer.** Many businesses use electronic funds transfer to pay vendors. To use electronic funds transfer (EFT), a business makes arrangements with its bank to process EFT transactions. Arrangements are also made with vendors to accept EFT on account. After arranging for EFT payments on account, a telephone call is all that is needed to transfer funds from the business' account to the vendor's account.

To control cash payments through EFT, the person responsible for requesting transfers should be given a password. The bank should be instructed to not accept EFT requests from any person unable to provide an established password.

Superior Cleaning Service uses electronic funds transfer to make payments on account to vendors. The journal entry for making payments on account through electronic funds transfer is the same as when a check is written. The only change is the source document used to prove that the transaction did occur. Superior Cleaning Service uses a memorandum as the source document for an electronic funds transfer. A note is written on the memorandum to describe the transaction.

September 2. Paid cash on account to Kelson Enterprises, $350.00, using EFT. Memorandum No. 10.

The source document for this transaction is Memorandum No. 10. (CONCEPT: Objective Evidence) The analysis of this transaction is shown in the T accounts.

The liability account, Kelson Enterprises, is decreased by a debit, $350.00. The asset account, Cash, is decreased by a credit, $350.00.

A cash payment made by EFT is recorded on the check stub as "Other." This procedure keeps the checkbook in balance during the time lag from when the EFT is made until receipt of the bank statement. The EFT payments are verified as part of the regular bank statement reconciliation process. EFT payments are identified in the Check column of the bank statement by the notation *EFT* rather than by a check number.

A summary of procedures for using checking accounts is shown in Illustration 7-13.

Kelson Enterprises

350.00 |

Cash

| 350.00

FYI

Individuals can also use a form of electronic funds transfer. Personal accounts can be accessed through Automated Teller Machines (ATMs) to make inquiries, withdraw money, deposit money, and transfer funds from one account to another.

FYI

Financial Management Service of the Department of the Treasury issues over 250 million Electronic Funds Transfer (EFT) payments annually.

Summary of checking account procedures

1 A deposit slip is prepared to deposit cash and checks in a checking account.

2 Checks are written to make payments from the checking account.

3 Cash payments transactions are journalized from check stubs.

4 A bank statement showing details of deposits, checks, and service charges.

5 The bank statement is reconciled to assure that the bank statement and checkbook information agree.

6 Bank service changes are journalized and recorded in the checkbook.

7 Dishonored checks are recorded in the checkbook and in the journal.

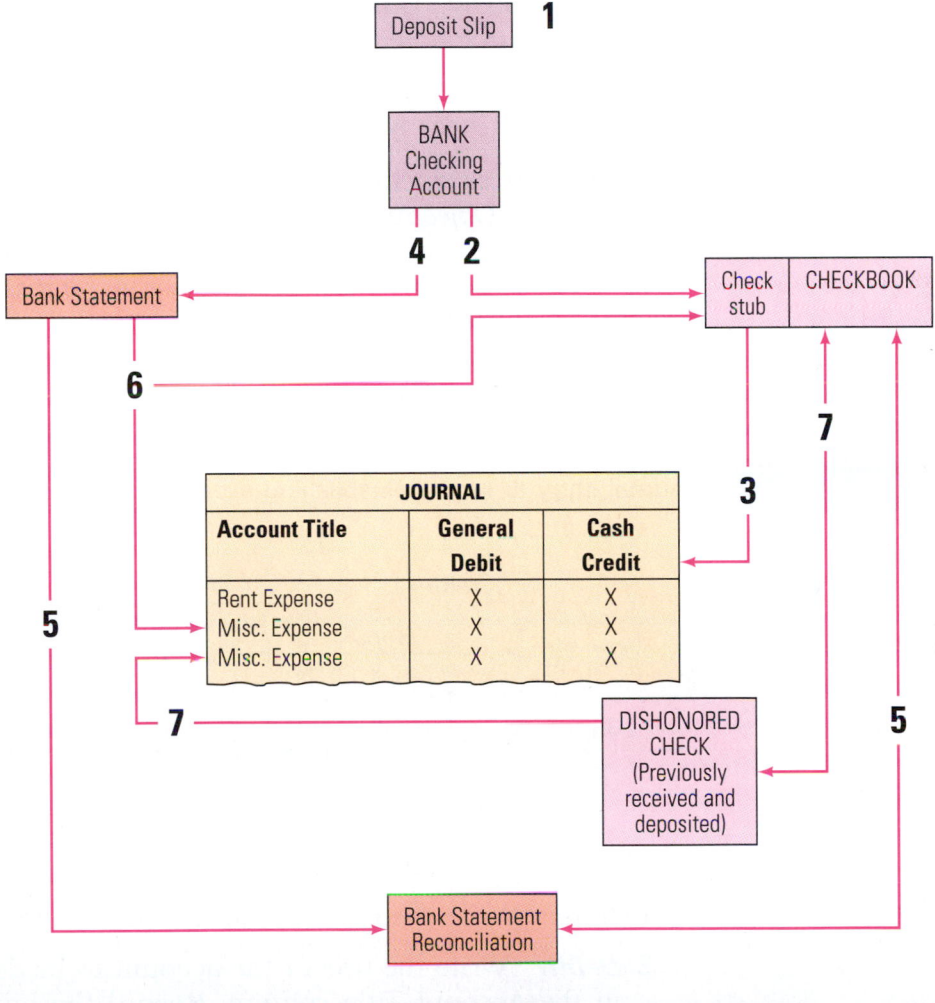

PETTY CASH

An amount of cash kept on hand and used for making small payments is called **petty cash.** Cash control is effective if all cash payments are made by check and cash receipts are deposited in the bank. However, a business usually has some small payments for which writing a check is not time or cost effective. Therefore, a business may maintain a separate cash fund for making small cash payments. The actual dollar amount considered to be a small payment differs from one business to another. Mr. Furman has set $5.00 as the maximum amount to be paid at any one time from the petty cash fund.

The petty cash account is an asset with a normal debit balance. The balance of the petty cash account increases on the debit side and decreases on the credit side.

Petty Cash	
Debit side NORMAL BALANCE Increases	Credit side Decreases

Establishing a Petty Cash Fund

On August 17 Mr. Furman decided that Rugcare needed a petty cash fund of $200.00. This amount should provide for the small cash payments anticipated during a month.

> *August 17, 19--. Paid cash to establish a petty cash fund, $200.00. Check No. 10.*

The source document for this transaction is Check No. 10. (CONCEPT: *Objective Evidence*) The analysis of this transaction is shown in the T accounts.

Petty Cash is debited for $200.00 to show the increase in this asset account balance. Cash is credited for $200.00 to show the decrease in this asset account balance. The journal entry to record this transaction is shown in Illustration 7-14.

Petty Cash	
200.00	

Cash	
	200.00

ILLUSTRATION 7-14   Journal entry to record establishing a petty cash fund

					GENERAL		SALES	CASH	
	DATE	ACCOUNT TITLE	DOC. NO.	POST. REF.	DEBIT	CREDIT	CREDIT	DEBIT	CREDIT
16	17	Petty Cash	C10		200 00				200 00

JOURNAL — PAGE 1

This entry is journalized using four steps.

1 Date.   Write the date, *17*, in the Date column.

2 Debit.   Write the title of the account to be debited, *Petty Cash*, in the Account Title column. Record the amount debited to Petty Cash, *$200.00*, in the General Debit column.

3 Credit.   Record the amount credited to Cash, *$200.00*, in the Cash Credit column.

4 Source document.   Write the source document number, *C10*, in the Doc. No. column.

Mr. Furman cashed the check and placed the $200.00 in a locked petty cash box kept at Rugcare's place of business. Only Mr. Furman is authorized to make payments from the petty cash fund.

Making Payments from a Petty Cash Fund

Each time a small payment is made from the petty cash fund, Mr. Furman prepares a form showing the purpose and amount of the payment. A form showing proof of a petty cash payment is called a **petty cash slip**.

A petty cash slip used by Rugcare is shown in Illustration 7-15.

Petty cash slip

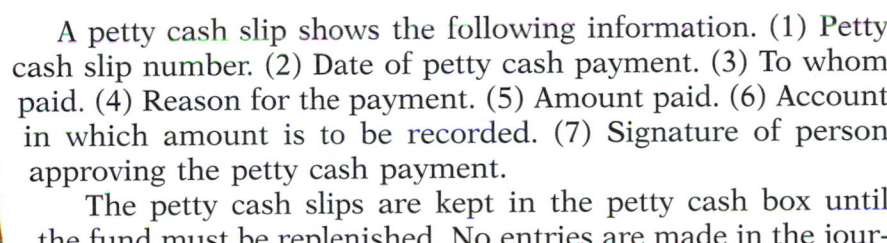

PETTY CASH SLIP	No. 1
Date: *August 18, 19--*	
Paid to: *Bernie's Repair Shop*	
For: *Hose Repair*	$ *5.00*
Account: *Repair Expense*	
Approved: *Ben Furman*	

A petty cash slip shows the following information. (1) Petty cash slip number. (2) Date of petty cash payment. (3) To whom paid. (4) Reason for the payment. (5) Amount paid. (6) Account in which amount is to be recorded. (7) Signature of person approving the petty cash payment.

The petty cash slips are kept in the petty cash box until the fund must be replenished. No entries are made in the journal for the individual petty cash payments.

Replenishing a Petty Cash Fund

As petty cash is paid out, the amount in the petty cash box decreases. Eventually, the petty cash fund must be replenished and the petty cash payments recorded. Rugcare replenishes its petty cash fund whenever the amount on hand is reduced to $75.00. Also, the petty cash fund is always replenished at the end of each month so that all of the expenses are recorded in the month they are incurred.

Rugcare completes four steps in replenishing the petty cash fund.

1 *Prove the petty cash fund.* On August 31 Mr. Furman proves petty cash as shown below.

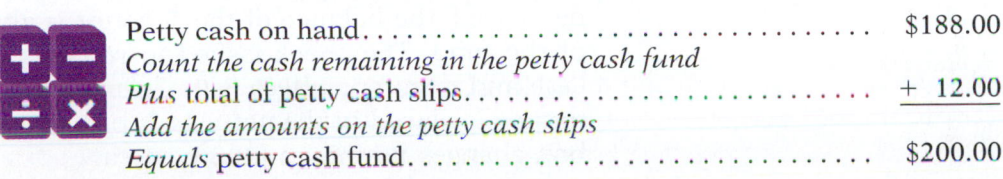

Petty cash on hand....................................	$188.00
Count the cash remaining in the petty cash fund	
Plus total of petty cash slips...........................	+ 12.00
Add the amounts on the petty cash slips	
Equals petty cash fund...............................	$200.00

The last line of the proof must show the same total as the original balance of the petty cash fund, $200.00. If petty cash does not prove, the errors must be found and corrected before any more work is done.

2 *Prepare a petty cash report.* At the end of August, Mr. Furman totals the petty cash slips and prepares a report. Rugcare's August petty cash report is shown in Illustration 7-16.

ILLUSTRATION 7-16 Petty cash report

PETTY CASH REPORT	Date: August 31, 19--		
Explanation	Amounts		
Fund total			200 00
Payments:			
Miscellaneous Expense	7 00		
Repair Expense	5 00		
Less total payments			12 00
Equals recorded amount on hand			188 00
Actual amount on hand			188 00

The report shows that a total of $12.00 has been paid out of petty cash for repairs and miscellaneous expenses. Thus, $12.00 needs to be added to the remaining $188.00 to bring the petty cash fund back to its normal size, $200.00.

3 *Write a check to replenish the petty cash fund.*

4 *Journalize the entry to replenish petty cash.*

Miscellaneous Expense	
7.00	

Repair Expense	
5.00	

Cash	
	12.00

August 31, 19--. Paid cash to replenish the petty cash fund, $12.00: miscellaneous expense, $7.00; repairs, $5.00. Check No. 15.

The source document for this transaction is Check No. 15. (CONCEPT: *Objective Evidence*) The analysis of this transaction is shown in the T accounts.

Miscellaneous Expense is debited for $7.00 and Repair Expense is debited for $5.00 to show the increases in these expense account balances. Cash is credited for $12.00 to show a decrease in this asset account balance.

Unless the petty cash fund is permanently increased or decreased, the balance of the account is always the original amount of the fund. The check issued to replenish petty cash is a credit to Cash and does not affect Petty Cash. When the check is cashed, the money is placed in the petty cash box. The amount in the petty cash box changes as shown below.

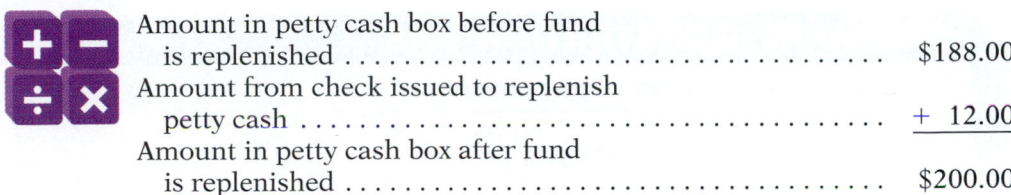

	Amount in petty cash box before fund is replenished	$188.00
	Amount from check issued to replenish petty cash	+ 12.00
	Amount in petty cash box after fund is replenished	$200.00

The total amount in the petty cash box, $200.00, is again the same as the balance of the petty cash account. The journal entry to record the transaction to replenish petty cash is shown in Illustration 7-17.

ILLUSTRATION 7-17   Journal entry to record replenishing of petty cash

						GENERAL		SALES	CASH	
	DATE	ACCOUNT TITLE	DOC. NO.	POST. REF.	DEBIT	CREDIT	CREDIT	DEBIT	CREDIT	
11	31	*Miscellaneous Expense*	C15		7 00				12 00	11
12		*Repair Expense*			5 00					12

JOURNAL   PAGE 2

This entry is journalized using four steps.

1 Date. Write the date, *31*, in the Date column.

2 Debit. Write the title of the first account to be debited, Miscellaneous Expense, in the Account Title column. Write the amount to be debited to Miscellaneous Expense, *$7.00*, in the General Debit column on the same line as the account title. Write the title of the second account to be debited, Repair Expense, on the next line in the Account Title column. Record the amount to be debited to Repair Expense, *$5.00*, in the General Debit column on the same line as the account title.

3 Credit. Record the amount to be credited to Cash, *$12.00*, in the Cash Credit column on the first line of this entry.

4 Source document. Write the source document number, *C15*, in the Doc. No. column.

The check is cashed, and the money is placed in the petty cash box. The amount in the petty cash box is now the original amount of the petty cash fund, $200.00. Petty cash on hand, $188.00, *plus* the cash to replenish, $12.00, *equals* the original amount of the petty cash fund, $200.00. The amount in the petty cash fund is now the same as the balance of the petty cash account, $200.00.

A summary of procedures for using a petty cash fund is shown in Illustration 7-18.

Audit Your Understanding

Draw T accounts to analyze the following transactions:

1. An EFT transaction to pay cash on account to Kelson Enterprises.
2. Establishment of a petty cash fund.
3. Replenishment of a petty cash fund with payments for miscellaneous and repair expenses.

SUMMARY ILLUSTRATION 7-18

Summary of petty cash fund procedures

1 A check is issued to establish a petty cash fund.

2 The cash payment to establish a petty cash fund is journalized.

3 A petty cash slip is prepared for each payment from the petty cash fund.

4 When the petty cash fund needs to be replenished, a petty cash report is prepared summarizing the petty cash slips.

5 A check is issued to replenish the petty cash fund.

6 The cash payment to replenish petty cash is journalized.

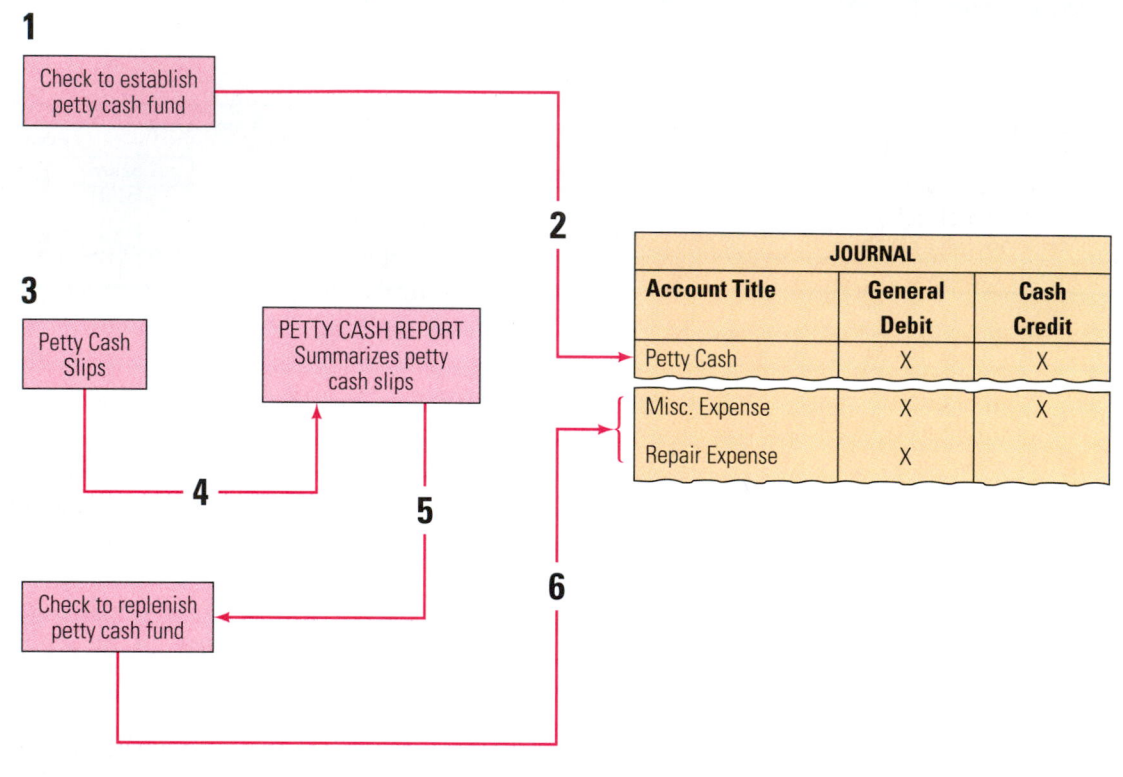

What is the meaning of each of the following?

1. checking account
2. endorsement
3. blank endorsement
4. special endorsement
5. restrictive endorsement
6. postdated check
7. bank statement
8. dishonored check
9. electronic funds transfer
10. petty cash
11. petty cash slip

QUESTIONS FOR INDIVIDUAL STUDY

EPT(b)

1. What evidence does a depositor have that money has been deposited in a checking account?
2. Why is no journal entry made by a business for a deposit in a checking account?
3. Why is the amount written in both numbers and words on a check?
4. What is the most common way of voiding a check?
5. Under what circumstances can a depositor assume that a bank statement reconciliation is correct?
6. Which accounting concept is being applied when a memorandum is prepared for the service charges deducted from a checking account?
7. What accounts are affected, and how, by an entry to record a bank service charge for a checking account?
8. What accounts are affected, and how, when Rugcare is notified that a deposited check has been dishonored?
9. What is the source document for an electronic funds transfer (EFT) transaction?
10. What is the purpose of a petty cash fund?
11. What accounts are affected, and how, when a petty cash fund is established?
12. What is Rugcare's initial record of amounts that have been paid from the petty cash fund?
13. How is the petty cash fund proved?
14. What accounts are affected, and how, by an entry to replenish petty cash when the petty cash slips show payments for miscellaneous expense and repair expense?
15. When is a journal entry made to record payments from the petty cash fund?

CASES FOR CRITICAL THINKING

EPT(d,e)

CASE 1 Iris Velez has a personal checking account in which she maintains a small balance. She receives a bank statement every three months. She files the statement and does not prepare a reconciliation. Sueanne Merker also has a personal checking account in which she maintains a balance of several hundred dollars. She receives bank statements once a month. She prepares a bank statement reconciliation for each bank statement received. Is Mrs. Velez or Ms. Merker following the better procedure? Explain your answer.

CASE 2 Dorset Company decides to establish a petty cash fund. The owner, Edna Dorset, wants to establish a $100.00 petty cash fund and limit payments to $5.00 or less. The manager, Roy Evans, suggests a petty cash fund of $3,000.00 limited to payments of $50.00 or less. Mr. Evans claims this limit will help him avoid writing so many checks. Do you agree with Ms. Dorset or Mr. Evans? Explain your answer.

DRILL 7-D1 Reconciling a bank statement

TUTORIAL

SPREADSHEET

On July 29 of the current year, DeepClean received a bank statement dated July 28. The following information is obtained from the bank statement and from the records of the business.

Bank statement balance	$1,528.00
Bank service charge	2.00
Outstanding deposit, July 28	150.00
Outstanding checks:	
No. 103	70.00
No. 105	35.00
Checkbook balance on Check Stub No. 106	1,575.00

MATHEMATICS

INSTRUCTIONS:

Prepare a bank statement reconciliation. Use July 29 of the current year as the date.

DRILL 7-D2 Reconciling a bank statement

On September 30 of the current year, Ajax Service Co. received a bank statement dated September 29. The following information is obtained from the bank statement and from the records of the business.

Bank statement balance	$3,208.00
Bank service charge	5.00
Outstanding deposits:	
September 29	310.00
September 30	330.00
Outstanding checks:	
No. 214	90.00
No. 215	135.00
No. 217	50.00
Checkbook balance on Check Stub No. 218	3,578.00

INSTRUCTIONS:

Prepare a bank statement reconciliation. Use September 30 of the current year as the date.

DRILL 7-D3 Replenishing a petty cash fund

MATHEMATICS

KeepClean replenished petty cash on the dates shown in Column 2 of the following table. The information in Columns 3 to 5 is obtained from the petty cash reports.

1	2	3	4	5
Trans.	Replenished on	Summary of Petty Cash Slips		
		Supplies	Advertising	Miscellaneous
A	July 31	32.00	25.00	
B	August 31	21.00	20.00	5.00
C	September 30	40.00	20.00	15.00
D	October 31	10.00		20.00

INSTRUCTIONS:

Prepare T accounts for Cash, Supplies, Advertising Expense, and Miscellaneous Expense. Use the T accounts to analyze each transaction given in the table. Label each amount in the T accounts with the corresponding transaction letter.

APPLICATION PROBLEMS

PROBLEM 7-1 Endorsing checks

For each of the following situations, prepare the appropriate endorsement.

INSTRUCTIONS:

1. Write a blank endorsement. Use your own signature.
2. Write a special endorsement to transfer a check to Delbert Richardson. Use your own signature.
3. Write a restrictive endorsement to deposit a check in the account of OddJobs. Use your own signature.

PROBLEM 7-2 Writing checks

You are authorized to sign checks for OddJobs.

INSTRUCTIONS:

1. Record the balance brought forward on Check Stub No. 50, $1,396.35.
2. Record a deposit of $390.00 made on October 30 of the current year on Check Stub No. 50.
3. Prepare check stubs and write the following checks. Use October 30 of the current year as the date.

Check No. 50. To Corner Garage for repairs, $138.00.
Check No. 51. To OfficeWorld for supplies, $50.00.
Check No. 52. To Dixon Papers for supplies, $15.00.

PROBLEM 7-3 Reconciling a bank statement and recording a bank service charge

Use the bank statement, canceled checks, and check stubs given in the working papers accompanying this textbook.

INSTRUCTIONS:

1. Compare the canceled checks with the check stubs. For each canceled check, place a check mark next to the appropriate check stub number.
2. For each deposit shown on the bank statement, place a check mark next to the deposit amount on the appropriate check stub.
3. Prepare a bank statement reconciliation. Use August 29 of the current year as the date.
4. Record the following transactions on page 8 of a journal. The abbreviation for memorandum is M.

Sept. 1. Received bank statement showing August bank service charge, $5.00. M25.
     1. Received notice from the bank of a dishonored check, $170.00, plus $5.00 fee; total, $175.00. M26.

5. Record the bank service charge and dishonored check on Check Stub No. 165.

PROBLEM 7-4 Paying cash on account using electronic funds transfer

Century Service uses electronic funds transfer to make payments on account.

INSTRUCTIONS:

Journalize the following transactions completed during July of the current year. Use page 8 of a journal. The abbreviation for memo is M.

July 8. Paid cash on account to Central Supply, $268.00, using EFT. M32.
12. Paid cash on account to Lapham Enterprises, $420.00, using EFT. M33.
16. Paid cash on account to Miller Sales, $355.00, using EFT. M34.

PROBLEM 7-5 Establishing and replenishing a petty cash fund

SweepUp established a petty cash fund on August 3 of the current year. At the end of August, the business replenished the petty cash fund.

INSTRUCTIONS:

Journalize the following transactions completed during August of the current year. Use page 10 of a journal. The abbreviation for check is C.

Aug. 3. Paid cash to establish a petty cash fund, $100.00. C57.
31. Paid cash to replenish the petty cash fund, $78.00: supplies, $25.00; miscellaneous expense, $8.00; repairs, $45.00. C97.

ENRICHMENT PROBLEMS   EPT(c,d,e,f)

MASTERY PROBLEM 7-M File maintenance; reconciling a bank statement; journalizing a bank service charge, a dishonored check, and petty cash transactions

Joseph Cruz owns a business called LawnMow. Selected general ledger accounts are given below.

110	Cash	520	Miscellaneous Expense
115	Petty Cash	530	Rent Expense
120	Supplies	535	Repair Expense
130	Prepaid Insurance	540	Supplies Expense
320	Joseph Cruz, Drawing	550	Utilities Expense

INSTRUCTIONS:

1. Journalize the following transactions completed during August of the current year. Use page 20 of a journal. Source documents are abbreviated as follows: check, C; memorandum, M.

Aug. 21. Paid cash to establish a petty cash fund, $100.00. C61.
24. Paid cash for repairs, $135.00. C62.
26. Paid cash for supplies, $40.00. C63.
27. Received notice from the bank of a dishonored check, $35.00, plus $5.00 fee; total, $40.00. M22.
28. Paid cash for miscellaneous expense, $12.00. C64.
31. Paid cash to owner for personal use, $300.00. C65.
31. Paid cash to replenish the petty cash fund, $55.00: supplies, $35.00; miscellaneous expense, $20.00. C66.

2. On August 31 of the current year, LawnMow received a bank statement dated August 30. Prepare a bank statement reconciliation. Use August 31 of the current year as the

date. The following information is obtained from the August 30 bank statement and from the records of the business.

Bank statement balance	$1,521.00
Bank service charge...................................	5.00
Outstanding deposit, August 31.......................	430.00
Outstanding checks, Nos. 65 and 66.	
Checkbook balance on Check Stub No. 67..............	1,601.00

3. Continue using the journal and journalize the following transaction.

Aug. 31. Received bank statement showing August bank service charge, $5.00. M23.

CHALLENGE PROBLEM 7-C Reconciling a bank statement

AUTOMATED

On November 30 of the current year, Johnson Company received a bank statement dated November 29. Miss Johnson placed a check mark beside the amount on each check stub for which a canceled check was received. She also placed a check mark on the check stub beside the amount of each deposit shown on the bank statement. She then prepared a bank statement reconciliation.

The last eight check stubs for the month of November and the bank statement reconciliation are given in the working papers accompanying this textbook. Both the check stubs and reconciliation contain errors.

INSTRUCTIONS:

1. Verify the amounts on the check stubs. Assume that the check amounts in the upper right corner of each stub are correct. Also assume that all deposits have been entered correctly on the check stubs.

2. Draw a line through all incorrect amounts on the check stubs. Write the correct amounts either above or below the incorrect amounts, depending on where space is available.

3. Prepare a correct bank statement reconciliation. Assume that the check marks written beside check and deposit amounts on the check stubs are correct. Therefore, the outstanding deposits and checks are those that are not checked.

Automated Cash Control Systems

Rugcare's manual cash control systems are described in Chapter 7. Integrating Automated Accounting Topic 2 describes procedures for using automated accounting software to reconcile a bank statement. Topic 2 also describes procedures to record selected transactions for using a checking account and petty cash fund. The Automated Accounting Problems contain instructions for using automated accounting software to solve Mastery Problem 7-M and Challenge Problem 7-C, Chapter 7.

RECONCILING A BANK STATEMENT

To reconcile a bank statement using automated accounting software, File is selected from the menu bar. The Payroll/Assets/Bank

Rec. command is selected from the File menu. File is again selected from the menu bar. The Open Data File command is then chosen to retrieve the bank reconciliation data base from the template disk.

System is selected from the menu bar and the Bank Reconciliation option is chosen. Reconciliation is selected from the menu bar. The Reconciliation Data command is then chosen to display the data entry window for keying bank reconciliation data. The following information is obtained from the August 28 bank statement and from the records of Rugcare.

Bank statement balance	$7,586.00
Checkbook balance	8,497.00
Bank service charge	3.00
Outstanding deposit	1,412.00
Outstanding checks:	
No. 13	70.00
No. 14	434.00

The bank statement reconciliation data are keyed as shown in Illustration T2-1.

ILLUSTRATION T2-1   Completed bank reconciliation data entry window

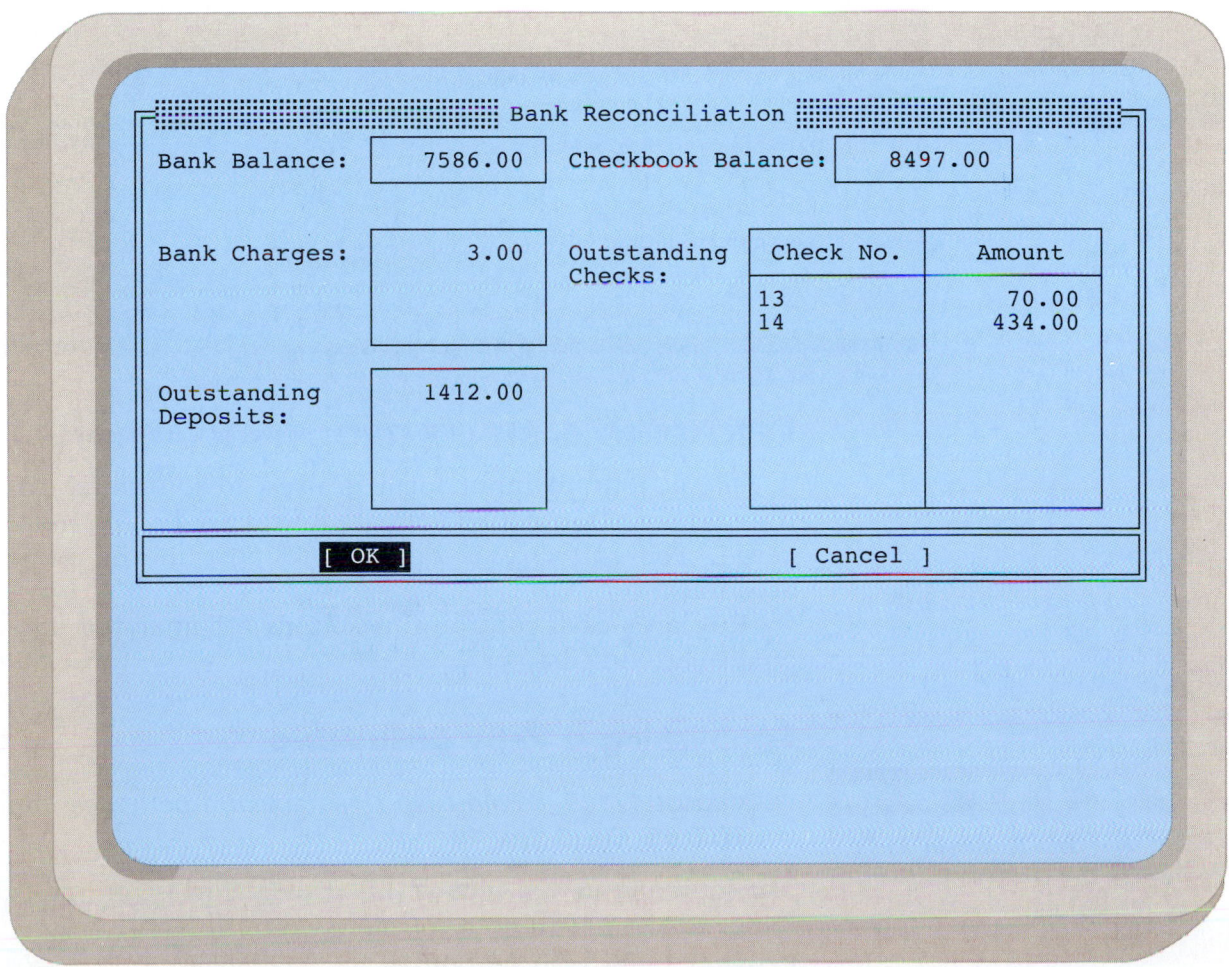

After the bank reconciliation data are keyed, Reports is selected from the menu bar. The Bank Reconciliation command is chosen from the Reports menu to display the bank reconciliation report. The report is checked for accuracy by comparing the Adjusted Checkbook Balance with the Adjusted Bank Balance. As these two totals are the same, the bank statement reconciliation is assumed to be correct. The bank statement reconciliation report is printed, as shown in Illustration T2-2, and filed for future reference.

ILLUSTRATION T2-2   Bank statement reconciliation report

```
                              Rugcare
                        Bank Reconciliation
                           08/28/--

Checkbook Balance                                          8497.00
                                              3.00
                                          -----------
Less Bank Charges                                             3.00
                                          -----------
Adjusted Checkbook Balance                                 8494.00
                                          ===========


Bank Balance                                               7586.00
                                           1412.00
                                          -----------
Plus Outstanding Deposits                                  1412.00
                               13            70.00
                               14           434.00
                                          -----------
Less Outstanding Checks                                     504.00
                                          -----------
Adjusted Bank Balance                                      8494.00
                                          ===========
```

RECORDING CASH CONTROL TRANSACTIONS

A general journal input form is used to journalize cash control transactions. Transaction data are journalized on an input form and keyed. The software is directed to post to the general ledger accounts.

Rugcare's cash control transactions are analyzed into debit and credit parts in Chapter 7.

Establishing a Petty Cash Fund

August 17, 19--. Paid cash to establish a petty cash fund, $200.00. Check No. 10.

The journal entry to record this transaction is on lines 1 and 2 of the general journal input form shown in Illustration T2-3. Petty Cash is debited and Cash is credited for $200.00.

General journal input form with transactions recorded

RUN DATE 08,31,-- MM DD YY		GENERAL JOURNAL Input Form				
DATE MM/DD	REFERENCE	ACCOUNT NO.	CUSTOMER/ VENDOR NO.	DEBIT	CREDIT	
1 08,17	C10	120		200 00		1
2 /		110			200 00	2
3 ,28	M3	530		3 00		3
4 /		110			3 00	4
5 ,29	M6	530		15 00		5
6 /		110			15 00	6
7 ,31	C15	530		7 00		7
8 /		550		5 00		8
9 /		110			12 00	9
10 /						10
11 /						11
12 /						12
25						25
			PAGE TOTALS	230 00	230 00	
			FINAL TOTALS	230 00	230 00	

Recording a Bank Service Charge

August 28, 19--. Received bank statement showing August bank service charge, $3.00. Memorandum No. 3.

The journal entry to record this transaction is on lines 3 and 4 of Illustration T2-3. Miscellaneous Expense is debited and Cash is credited for $3.00.

Recording a Dishonored Check

August 29, 19--. Received notice from the bank of a dishonored check, $10.00, plus $5.00 fee; total, $15.00. Memorandum No. 6.

The journal entry to record this transaction is on lines 5 and 6 of Illustration T2-3. Miscellaneous Expense is debited and Cash is credited for $15.00.

Replenishing a Petty Cash Fund

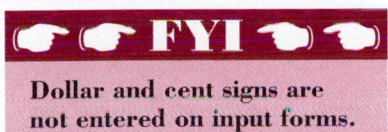

FYI

Dollar and cent signs are not entered on input forms.

August 31, 19--. Paid cash to replenish the petty cash fund, $12.00: miscellaneous expense, $7.00; repairs, $5.00. Check No. 15.

The journal entry to record this transaction is on lines 7 through 9 of Illustration T2-3. Miscellaneous Expense is debited for $7.00. Repair Expense is debited for $5.00. Cash is credited for $12.00.

After all transactions have been journalized, Rugcare totals the Debit and Credit amount columns. The totals are recorded on the Page Totals and Final Totals lines provided at the bottom of the input form. The totals are compared to assure that debits equal credits.

Processing Cash Control Journal Entries

To process cash control journal entries, File is selected from the menu bar. The Open Accounting File command is chosen from the File menu to retrieve the general ledger data base from the template disk. The Journals menu is selected from the menu bar. The General Journal command is chosen from the Journals menu to key the cash control transaction data.

After all lines on the input form have been keyed and posted, the Reports menu is selected from the menu bar. The Journals command is chosen from the Reports menu. The General Journal report is selected from the Reports Selection menu. This selection displays the Selection Options screen. As Rugcare wants to print all transactions journalized on Illustration T2-3, pushing the *Ok* button directs the software to display a general journal report. The displayed general journal report is checked for accuracy by comparing the report totals, $230.00, with the totals on the general journal input form. Because the totals are the same, the general journal report is assumed to be correct. The general journal report is printed, as shown in Illustration T2-4, and filed for future reference.

ILLUSTRATION T2-4   General journal report

```
                            Rugcare
                       General Journal
                         08/31/--
-----------------------------------------------------------------------
Date   Refer.   V/C Acct.   Title                     Debit      Credit
-----------------------------------------------------------------------
08/17  C10          120     Petty Cash               200.00
08/17  C10          110     Cash                                 200.00

08/28  M3           530     Miscellaneous Expense      3.00
08/28  M3           110     Cash                                   3.00

08/29  M6           530     Miscellaneous Expense     15.00
08/29  M6           110     Cash                                  15.00

08/31  C15          530     Miscellaneous Expense      7.00
08/31  C15          550     Repair Expense             5.00
08/31  C15          110     Cash                                  12.00
                                                     --------   --------
                            Totals                   230.00     230.00
                                                     ========   ========
```

OPTIONAL PROBLEM DB-2A

Rugcare's general ledger data base is on the accounting textbook template. If you wish to reconcile Rugcare's bank statement using automated accounting software, load the *Automated Accounting 6.0* or higher software. Pull down the File menu from the menu bar and choose the Payroll/Assets/Bank Rec. command. Pull down the File menu and choose the Open Data File command to retrieve Data Base 2A (DB-2A) from the template disk. Read the Problem Instructions screen. Use Illustration T2-1 and follow the procedures described to reconcile Rugcare's bank statement.

OPTIONAL PROBLEM DB-2B

Rugcare's general ledger data base is on the accounting textbook template. If you wish to process Rugcare's cash control transactions using automated accounting software, load the *Automated Accounting 6.0* or higher software. If you just completed Optional Problem DB-2A, you must first load the Accounting System module before you begin. Pull down the File menu and choose the Accounting System command. Pull down the File menu and choose the Open File menu command to retrieve Data Base 2B (DB-2B) from the template disk. Read the Problem Instructions screen. Use Illustration T2-3 and follow the procedures described to process Rugcare's cash control journal entries.

AUTOMATED ACCOUNTING PROBLEMS

AUTOMATING MASTERY PROBLEM 7-M Reconciling a bank statement; journalizing a bank service charge, a dishonored check, and petty cash transactions

INSTRUCTIONS:

1. Journalize transactions from Mastery Problem 7-M, Chapter 7 on a general journal input form. Use August 31 of the current year as the run date.
2. Load the *Automated Accounting 6.0* or higher software. Select data base F7-M (First-Year Course Problem 7-M) from the accounting textbook template. Read the Problem Instructions screen.
3. Select File from the menu bar and choose the Save As menu command. Key the path to the drive and directory that contains your data files. Save the data base with a file name of XXX7M (where XXX are your initials).
4. Key the transactions from the completed general journal input form.
5. Display/print the general journal report. Check the report for accuracy by comparing the report totals with the totals on the input form.
6. Save your file.
7. To complete the bank reconciliation, select File from the menu bar and select the Payroll/Assets/Bank Rec. command. Select File and then the Open Data File command to retrieve data base F7-M from the template disk. The following information is obtained from the bank statement and from the records of the business.

Bank statement balance	$1,521.00
Checkbook balance	1,601.00
Bank service charge	5.00
Outstanding deposit	430.00
Outstanding checks:	
No. 65	300.00
No. 66	55.00

8. Key the bank statement reconciliation data.
9. Display/print the bank statement reconciliation.

AUTOMATED

AUTOMATING CHALLENGE PROBLEM 7-C Reconciling a bank statement

INSTRUCTIONS:

1. Load the *Automated Accounting 6.0* or higher software. Select File from the menu bar and select the Payroll/Assets/Bank Rec. command. Select File and then the Open Data File command to retrieve data base F7-C from the template disk.
2. Use the manual solution prepared for Challenge Problem 7-C. Key the bank statement reconciliation data.
3. Display/print the bank statement reconciliation.

An Accounting Cycle for a Proprietorship: Journalizing and Posting Transactions

AUTOMATED

Reinforcement activities strengthen the learning of accounting concepts and procedures. Reinforcement Activity 1 is a single problem divided into two parts. Part A includes learnings from Chapters 2 through 7. Part B includes learnings from Chapters 8 through 10. An accounting cycle is completed in Parts A and B for a single business—The Fitness Center.

THE FITNESS CENTER

In May of the current year, Gail Davis starts a service business called The Fitness Center. The business provides exercise facilities for its clients. In addition, Miss Davis, a professional dietician, offers diet and exercise counseling for clients who request her assistance. The business rents the facilities with which it operates, pays the utilities, and is responsible for maintenance. The Fitness Center charges clients for each visit.

CHART OF ACCOUNTS

The Fitness Center uses the following chart of accounts.

CHART OF ACCOUNTS

Balance Sheet Accounts	Income Statement Accounts
(100) ASSETS	**(400) REVENUE**
110 Cash	410 Sales
120 Petty Cash	
130 Supplies	**(500) EXPENSES**
140 Prepaid Insurance	510 Advertising Expense
	520 Insurance Expense
(200) LIABILITIES	530 Miscellaneous Expense
210 Dunnel Supplies	540 Rent Expense
220 Morgan Office Supplies	550 Repair Expense
	560 Supplies Expense
(300) OWNER'S EQUITY	570 Utilities Expense
310 Gail Davis, Capital	
320 Gail Davis, Drawing	
330 Income Summary	

RECORDING TRANSACTIONS

INSTRUCTIONS:

1. Journalize the following transactions completed during May of the current year. Use page 1 of the journal. Source documents are abbreviated as follows: check stub, C; memorandum, M; receipt, R; calculator tape, T.

May 1. Received cash from owner as an investment, $15,000.00. R1.

     1. Paid cash for rent, $1,000.00. C1.

     2. Paid cash for electric bill, $45.00. C2.

     4. Paid cash for supplies, $500.00. C3.

     4. Paid cash for insurance, $960.00. C4.

     7. Bought supplies on account from Dunnel Supplies, $800.00. M1.

   11. Paid cash to establish a petty cash fund, $200.00. C5.

   12. Received cash from sales, $550.00. T12.

   13. Paid cash for repairs, $25.00. C6.

   13. Paid cash for miscellaneous expense, $35.00. C7.

   13. Received cash from sales, $185.00. T13.

   14. Paid cash for advertising, $100.00. C8.

   14. Received cash from sales, $335.00. T14.

   15. Paid cash to owner for personal use, $250.00. C9.

   15. Paid cash on account to Dunnel Supplies, $300.00. C10.

   15. Received cash from sales, $325.00. T15.

   18. Paid cash for miscellaneous expense, $100.00. C11.

   18. Received cash from sales, $295.00. T18.

   19. Received cash from sales, $155.00. T19.

   20. Paid cash for repairs, $125.00. C12.

   20. Bought supplies on account from Morgan Office Supplies, $150.00. M2.

   20. Received cash from sales, $195.00. T20.

2. Prove and rule page 1 of the journal. Carry the column totals forward to page 2 of the journal.

3. Post the separate amounts on each line of page 1 of the journal that need to be posted individually.

4. Use page 2 of the journal. Journalize the following transactions.

May 21. Paid cash for water bill, $110.00. C13.

   21. Received cash from sales, $235.00. T21.

   25. Paid cash for supplies, $50.00. C14.

   25. Received cash from sales, $295.00. T25.

   26. Paid cash for miscellaneous expense, $25.00. C15.

   26. Received cash from sales, $300.00. T26.

   27. Received cash from sales, $195.00. T27.

   28. Paid cash for telephone bill, $210.00. C16.

   28. Received cash from sales, $275.00. T28.

5. The Fitness Center received a bank statement dated May 27. The following information is obtained from the bank statement and from the records of the business. Prepare a bank statement reconciliation. Use May 29 as the date.

Bank statement balance.	$14,312.00
Bank service charge	3.00
Outstanding deposit, May 28	275.00
Outstanding checks:	
No. 14	50.00
No. 15	25.00
No. 16	210.00
Checkbook balance on Check Stub No. 17	14,305.00

6. Continue using page 2 of the journal, and journalize the following transactions.

May 29. Received bank statement showing May bank service charge, $3.00. M3.
    29. Paid cash for supplies, $60.00. C17.
    29. Received cash from sales, $240.00. T29.
    31. Paid cash to replenish the petty cash fund, $17.00: miscellaneous expense, $10.00; repairs, $7.00. C18.
    31. Paid cash to owner for personal use, $250.00. C19.
    31. Received cash from sales, $280.00. T31.

7. Prove page 2 of the journal.
8. Prove cash. The beginning cash balance on May 1 is zero. The balance on the next unused check stub is $14,495.00.
9. Rule page 2 of the journal.
10. Post the separate amounts on each line of page 2 of the journal that need to be posted individually.
11. Post the column totals on page 2 of the journal.

The general ledger prepared in Reinforcement Activity 1, Part A, is needed to complete Reinforcement Activity 1, Part B.

Work Sheet for a Service Business

ENABLING PERFORMANCE TASKS

After studying Chapter 8, you will be able to:

a Define accounting terms related to a work sheet for a service business organized as a proprietorship.

b Identify accounting concepts and practices related to a work sheet for a service business organized as a proprietorship.

c Plan adjustments for supplies and prepaid insurance.

d Complete a work sheet for a service business organized as a proprietorship.

e Identify selected procedures for finding and correcting errors in accounting records.

TERMS PREVIEW

fiscal period • work sheet • trial balance • adjustments • income statement • net income • net loss

General ledger accounts contain information needed by managers and owners. Before the information can be used, however, it must be analyzed, summarized, and reported in a meaningful way. The accounting concept, *Consistent Reporting*, is applied when the same accounting procedures are followed in the same way in each accounting period. *(CONCEPT: Consistent Reporting)* For example, in one year a delivery business might report the number of deliveries made. The next year the same business reports the amount of revenue received for the deliveries made. The information for the two years cannot be compared because the business has not been consistent in reporting information about deliveries.

FISCAL PERIODS

The length of time for which a business summarizes and reports financial information is called a **fiscal period**. A fiscal period is also known as an accounting period. Businesses usually select a period of time, such as a month, six months, or a year, for which to summarize and report financial information. The accounting concept, *Accounting Period Cycle*, is applied when changes in financial information are reported for a specific period of time in the form of financial statements. *(CONCEPT: Accounting Period Cycle)* Each business chooses a fiscal period length that meets its needs. Because federal and state tax reports are based on one year, most businesses use a one-year fiscal period. However, because Rugcare is a new business, Mr. Furman wishes to have financial information reported frequently to help him make decisions. For this reason, Rugcare uses a one-month fiscal period.

A fiscal period can begin on any date. However, most businesses begin their fiscal periods on the first day of a month. Rugcare started business on August 1. Therefore, Rugcare's monthly fiscal period is for the period from August 1 through August 31, inclusive. Another business might use a one-year fiscal period from August 1 of one year through July 31 of the next year. Many businesses use a calendar year starting on January 1 and ending on December 31. Businesses often choose a one-year fiscal period that ends during a period of low business activity. In this way, the end-of-year accounting work comes at a time when other business activities are the lightest. For example, a store with a large volume of Christmas holiday sales might prefer to begin its fiscal period on February 1 or March 1.

> Most individuals use a one-year fiscal period that begins on January 1 and ends on December 31. This fiscal period corresponds to the period for which they must file income tax returns for the federal and state governments. However, individuals may use a different fiscal period if approved by the Internal Revenue Service.

Financial information may be analyzed, summarized, and reported on any date a business needs the information. However, financial information is always summarized and reported at the end of a fiscal period.

A summary of preparing a work sheet is shown on the Work Sheet Overlay on pages 176A through 176C.

WORK SHEET

A columnar accounting form used to summarize the general ledger information needed to prepare financial statements is called a **work sheet.**

Accountants use a work sheet for four reasons. (1) To summarize general ledger account balances to prove that debits equal credits. (2) To plan needed changes to general ledger accounts to bring account balances up to date. (3) To separate general ledger account balances according to the financial statements to be prepared. (4) To calculate the amount of net income or net loss for a fiscal period.

Journals and ledgers are permanent records of a business and are usually prepared in ink. However, a work sheet is a planning tool and is not considered a permanent accounting record. Therefore, a work sheet is prepared in pencil.

☞ ☞ FYI ☞ ☞

The work sheet has a three-line heading which includes the name of the company, the name of the form, and the time period the work sheet covers.

Preparing the Heading of a Work Sheet

The heading on a work sheet consists of three lines. (1) Name of the business. (2) Name of the report. (3) Date of the report. The heading for Rugcare's work sheet is shown in Illustration 8-1.

ILLUSTRATION 8-1

Heading on a work sheet

> *Rugcare*
> *Work Sheet*
> *For Month Ended August 31, 19--*

The date on Rugcare's work sheet indicates that the work sheet covers the 31 days from August 1 through and including August 31. If the work sheet were for a calendar year fiscal period, it might have a date stated as *For Year Ended December 31, 19--. (CONCEPT: Accounting Period Cycle)*

Preparing a Trial Balance on a Work Sheet

The equality of debits and credits in the general ledger must be proved. The total of all debit account balances must equal the total of all credit account balances. A proof of the equality of debits and credits in a general ledger is called a **trial balance.** Rugcare prepares a trial balance on a work sheet. Rugcare's August 31 trial balance on a work sheet is shown in Illustration 8-2.

Information for the trial balance is taken from the general ledger. General ledger account titles are listed on a trial balance in the same order as listed on the chart of accounts. All the account titles are listed, even if some accounts do not have balances. The accounts that do not have balances in the Trial Balance columns will be needed in other parts of the work sheet.

ILLUSTRATION 8-2   Trial balance on a work sheet

		TRIAL BALANCE	
	ACCOUNT TITLE	DEBIT	CREDIT

Rugcare
Work Sheet
For Month Ended August 31, 19--

#	ACCOUNT TITLE	DEBIT	CREDIT
1	Cash	8 2 7 2 00	
2	Petty Cash	2 0 0 00	
3	Supplies	4 9 3 1 00	
4	Prepaid Insurance	1 2 0 0 00	
5	Butler Cleaning Supplies		1 3 6 0 00
6	Dale Office Supplies		2 0 0 00
7	Ben Furman, Capital		10 0 0 0 00
8	Ben Furman, Drawing	6 0 0 00	
9	Income Summary		
10	Sales		4 2 9 1 00
11	Advertising Expense	6 8 00	
12	Insurance Expense		
13	Miscellaneous Expense	1 0 5 00	
14	Rent Expense	2 5 0 00	
15	Repair Expense	1 1 0 00	
16	Supplies Expense		
17	Utilities Expense	1 1 5 00	
18		15 8 5 1 00	15 8 5 1 00
19			
20			
21			
22			
23			
24			
25			
26			

Seven steps are used in preparing a trial balance on a work sheet.

1 Write the general ledger account titles in the work sheet's Account Title column.

2 Write the general ledger account debit balances in the Trial Balance Debit column. Write the general ledger account credit balances in the Trial Balance Credit column. If an account does not have a balance, the space in the Trial Balance columns is left blank.

3 Rule a single line across the two Trial Balance columns below the last line on which an account title is written. This single line shows that the two columns are to be added.

4 Add both the Trial Balance Debit and Credit columns. Use a calculator if one is available. For Rugcare's work sheet, the totals are Debit, $15,851.00 and Credit, $15,851.00.

5 Check the equality of the two amount column totals. If the two column totals are the same, then debits equal credits in the general ledger accounts. Because the totals, $15,851.00, are the same, the Trial Balance columns on Rugcare's work sheet are in balance.

> If the two column totals are not the same and the trial balance is not in balance, recheck the Trial Balance columns to find the error. Other parts of a work sheet are not completed until the Trial Balance columns are proved. Suggestions for locating errors are described later in this chapter.

6 Write each column's total, *$15,851.00*, below the single line.

7 Rule double lines across both Trial Balance columns. The double lines mean that the Trial Balance column totals have been verified as correct.

Complete the Trial Balance columns of the work sheet before going on to the other columns. If the Trial Balance columns are not correct, the remaining columns will also be incorrect.

Planning Adjustments on a Work Sheet

Sometimes a business will pay cash for an expense in one fiscal period, but the expense is not used until a later period. The expense should be reported in the same fiscal period that it is used to produce revenue. The accounting concept, *Matching Expenses with Revenue*, is applied when revenue from business activities and expenses associated with earning that revenue are recorded in the same accounting period. For example, Rugcare buys supplies in quantity in August, but some of the supplies are not used until September. Only the value of the supplies used in August should be reported as expenses in August. In this way, August revenue and the supplies expense associated with earning the August revenue are recorded in the same accounting period. *(CONCEPT: Matching Expenses with Revenue)*

In order to give accurate information on financial statements, some general ledger accounts must be brought up to date at the end of a fiscal period. For example, Rugcare debits an asset account, Supplies, each time supplies are bought. Supplies on hand are items of value owned by a business until the supplies are used. The value of supplies that are used becomes an expense to the business. However, recording an expense each time an individual supply, such as a pencil, is used would be impractical. Therefore, on August 31 the balance of the asset account, Supplies, is the value of all supplies bought rather than the value of only the supplies that

have not been used. The amount of supplies that have been used must be deducted from the asset account, Supplies, and recorded in the expense account, Supplies Expense.

Likewise, the amount of insurance that has been used during the fiscal period is also an expense of the business. When the insurance premium for a year of insurance coverage is paid, the entire amount is debited to an asset account, Prepaid Insurance. Each day during August a portion of the insurance coverage is used. The value of the insurance used is an expense of the business. However, recording each day's amount of insurance used is impractical. Therefore, at the end of a fiscal period, the balance of Prepaid Insurance is the value of all insurance coverage bought, rather than the value of only the insurance coverage that still remains. The amount of the insurance coverage used must be deducted from the asset account, Prepaid Insurance, and recorded in the expense account, Insurance Expense.

Changes recorded on a work sheet to update general ledger accounts at the end of a fiscal period are called **adjustments**. The assets of a business, such as supplies and prepaid insurance, are used to earn revenue. The portion of the assets consumed in order to earn revenue become expenses of the business. The portions consumed are no longer assets but are now expenses. Therefore, adjustments must be made to both the asset and expense accounts for supplies and insurance. After the adjustments are made, the expenses incurred to earn revenue are reported in the same fiscal period as the revenue is earned and reported. *(CONCEPT: Matching Expenses with Revenue)*

A work sheet is used to plan adjustments. Changes are not made in general ledger accounts until adjustments are journalized and posted. The accuracy of the planning for adjustments is checked on a work sheet before adjustments are actually journalized.

Procedures for journalizing Rugcare's adjustments are described in Chapter 10.

Supplies Adjustment. On August 31, before adjustments, the balance of Supplies is $4,931.00, and the balance of Supplies Expense is zero, as shown in the T accounts.

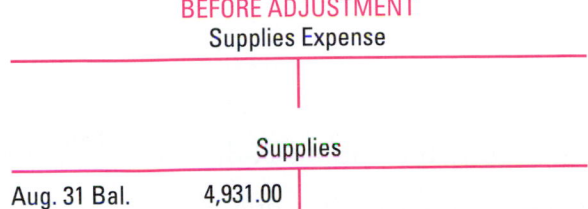

On August 31 Mr. Furman counted the supplies on hand and found that the value of supplies still unused on that date was $2,284.00. The value of the supplies used is calculated as shown below.

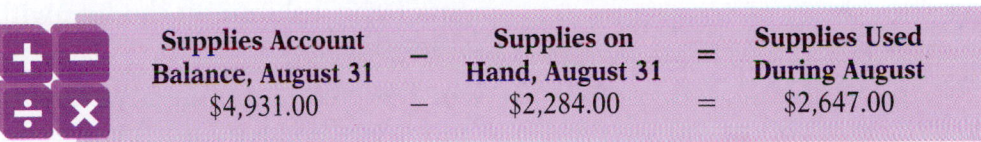

Supplies Account Balance, August 31	−	Supplies on Hand, August 31	=	Supplies Used During August
$4,931.00	−	$2,284.00	=	$2,647.00

Four questions are asked in analyzing the adjustment for the asset account, Supplies.

1.	What is the balance of Supplies?................	$4,931.00
2.	What should the balance be for this account?....	$2,284.00
3.	What must be done to correct the account balance?	
	Decrease	$2,647.00
4.	What adjustment is made?	
	Debit Supplies Expense	$2,647.00
	Credit Supplies..............................	$2,647.00

AFTER ADJUSTMENT

Supplies Expense

Adj. (a)	2,647.00

Supplies

Aug. 31 Bal.	4,931.00	Adj. (a)	2,647.00
(New Bal.	*2,284.00)*		

The expense account, Supplies Expense, is increased by a debit, $2,647.00, the value of supplies used. The balance of Supplies Expense, $2,647.00, is the value of supplies used during the fiscal period from August 1 to August 31. *(CONCEPT: Matching Expenses with Revenue)*

The asset account, Supplies, is decreased by a credit, $2,647.00, the value of supplies used. The debit balance, $4,931.00, *less* the credit adjustment, $2,647.00, *equals* the new balance, $2,284.00. The new balance of Supplies is the same as the value of supplies on hand on August 31.

Rugcare's supplies adjustment is shown on lines 3 and 16 of the work sheet in Illustration 8-3.

ILLUSTRATION 8-3   Supplies adjustment on a work sheet

		1	2	3	4	
	ACCOUNT TITLE	TRIAL BALANCE		ADJUSTMENTS		
		DEBIT	CREDIT	DEBIT	CREDIT	
3	*Supplies*	4 9 3 1 00			(a) 2 6 4 7 00	3
16	*Supplies Expense*			(a) 2 6 4 7 00		16
17						17
18						18
19						19
20						20

Three steps are used to record the supplies adjustment on the work sheet.

1 Write the debit amount, *$2,647.00*, in the work sheet's Adjustments Debit column on the line with the account title Supplies Expense (line 16).

2 Write the credit amount, *$2,647.00*, in the Adjustments Credit column on the line with the account title Supplies (line 3).

3 Label the two parts of this adjustment with a small letter *a* in parentheses *(a)*. The letter *a* identifies the debit and credit amounts as part of the same adjustment.

SUMMARY OF PREPARATION OF A WORK SHEET FOR A SERVICE BUSINESS

The following overlay summarizes the preparation of a work sheet. Follow the directions below in using the overlay.

1. Before using the overlay, be sure the pages and transparent overlays are arranged correctly. The correct arrangement is shown below.

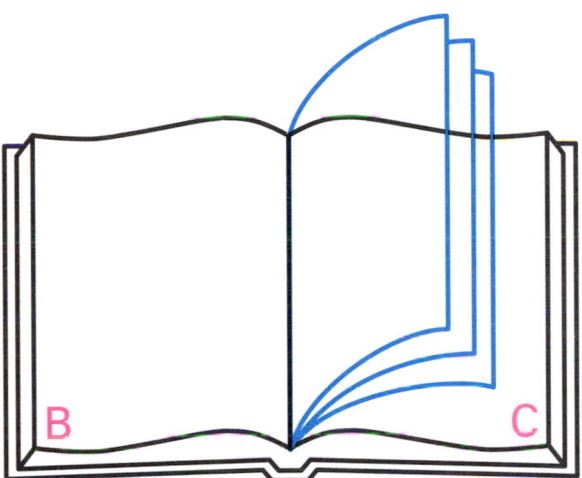

2. Place your book in a horizontal position. Study the steps on page C in preparing the work sheet. You will be able to read the text through the transparent overlays. When directed, carefully lift the transparent overlays and lay them over the work sheet as shown below.

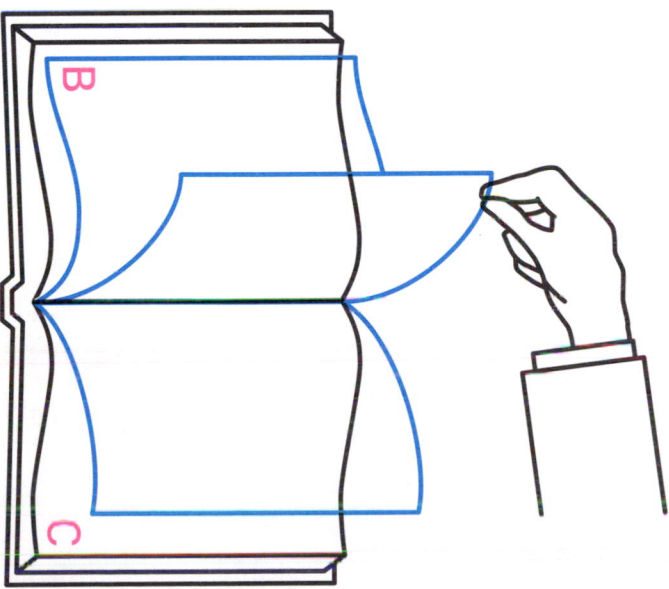

PREPARING A WORK SHEET

To correctly use the insert, read the steps below. Apply the transparent overlays when directed to do so in the steps.

Rugcare

Work Sheet

For Month Ended August 31, 19---

	ACCOUNT TITLE	TRIAL BALANCE DEBIT	TRIAL BALANCE CREDIT	ADJUSTMENTS DEBIT	ADJUSTMENTS CREDIT	INCOME STATEMENT DEBIT	INCOME STATEMENT CREDIT	BALANCE SHEET DEBIT	BALANCE SHEET CREDIT	
1	Cash	8 2 7 2 00								1
2	Petty Cash	2 0 0 00								2
3	Supplies	4 9 3 1 00								3
4	Prepaid Insurance	1 2 0 0 00								4
5	Butler Cleaning Supplies		1 3 6 0 00							5
6	Dale Office Supplies		2 0 0 00							6
7	Ben Furman, Capital		1 0 0 0 0 00							7
8	Ben Furman, Drawing	6 0 0 00								8
9	Income Summary									9
10	Sales		4 2 9 1 00							10
11	Advertising Expense	6 8 00								11
12	Insurance Expense									12
13	Miscellaneous Expense	1 0 5 00								13
14	Rent Expense	2 5 0 00								14
15	Repair Expense	1 1 0 00								15
16	Supplies Expense									16
17	Utilities Expense	1 1 5 00								17
18		1 5 8 5 1 00	1 5 8 5 1 00							18
19										19
20										20
21										21
22										22
23										23
24										24
25										25

PREPARING A WORK SHEET

1 Write the heading.

2 Record the trial balance.
- Write the general ledger account titles in the Account Title column.
- Write the account balances in either the Trial Balance Debit or Credit column.
- Rule a single line across the Trial Balance columns.
- Add the Trial Balance columns, and compare the totals.
- Rule double lines across both Trial Balance columns. *Carefully apply the first overlay.*

3 Record the supplies adjustment.
- Write the debit amount in the Adjustments Debit column on the line with the account title Supplies Expense.
- Write the credit amount in the Adjustments Credit column on the line with the account title Supplies.
- Label this adjustment (a).

4 Record the prepaid insurance adjustment.
- Write the debit amount in the Adjustments Debit column on the line with the account title Insurance Expense.
- Write the credit amount in the Adjustments Credit column on the line with the account title Prepaid Insurance.
- Label this adjustment (b).

5 Prove the Adjustments columns.
- Rule a single line across the Adjustments columns.
- Add the Adjustments columns, and compare the totals to assure that they are equal.
- Write the proving totals below the single line.
- Rule double lines across both Adjustments columns. *Carefully apply the second overlay.*

6 Extend all balance sheet account balances.
- Extend the up-to-date asset account balances to the Balance Sheet Debit column.
- Extend the up-to-date liability account balances to the Balance Sheet Credit column.
- Extend the owner's capital and drawing account balances to the Balance Sheet columns.

7 Extend all income statement account balances.
- Extend the up-to-date revenue account balance to the Income Statement Credit column.
- Extend the up-to-date expense account balances to the Income Statement Debit column. *Carefully apply the third overlay.*

8 Calculate and record the net income (or net loss).
- Rule a single line across the Income Statement and Balance Sheet columns.
- Add the columns, and write the totals below the single line.
- Calculate the net income or net loss amount.
- Write the amount of net income (or net loss) below the smaller of the two Income Statement column totals. Write the words *Net Income* or *Net Loss* in the Account Title column.
- Extend the amount of net income (or net loss) to the Balance Sheet columns. Write the amount under the smaller of the two column totals. Write the amount on the same line as the words *Net Income* (or *Net Loss*).

9 Total and rule the Income Statement and Balance Sheet columns.
- Rule a single line across the Income Statement and Balance Sheet columns immediately below the net income (or net loss) amounts.
- Add the net income (or net loss) to the previous column totals. Compare the column totals to assure that totals for each pair of columns are in balance.
- Write the proving totals for each column below the single line.
- Rule double lines across the Income Statement and Balance Sheet columns immediately below the proving totals.

176C

Prepaid Insurance Adjustment. When Rugcare pays for insurance, the amount is debited to the asset account, Prepaid Insurance. However, to debit Insurance Expense daily for the amount of that day's insurance premium used is impractical. Therefore, at the end of a fiscal period, Rugcare's prepaid insurance account does not show the actual value of the remaining prepaid insurance.

On August 31, before adjustments, the balance of Prepaid Insurance is $1,200.00, and the balance of Insurance Expense is zero, as shown in the T accounts.

On August 31 Mr. Furman checked the insurance records and found that the value of insurance coverage remaining was $1,100.00. The value of insurance coverage used during the fiscal period is calculated as shown below.

BEFORE ADJUSTMENT

Insurance Expense

Prepaid Insurance

Aug. 31 Bal.	1,200.00

	Prepaid Insurance Balance, August 31	–	Insurance Coverage Remaining Unused, August 31	=	Insurance Coverage Used During August
	$1,200.00	–	$1,100.00	=	$100.00

Four questions are asked in analyzing the adjustment for the asset account, Prepaid Insurance.

1. What is the balance of Prepaid Insurance? $1,200.00
2. What should the balance be for this account? $1,100.00
3. What must be done to correct the account balance?
   Decrease . . . . $ 100.00
4. What adjustment is made?
   Debit Insurance Expense . . . . $ 100.00
   Credit Prepaid Insurance . . . . $ 100.00

AFTER ADJUSTMENT

Insurance Expense

Adj. (b)	100.00

Prepaid Insurance

Aug. 31 Bal.	1,200.00	Adj. (b)	100.00
(New Bal.	1,100.00)		

The expense account, Insurance Expense, is increased by a debit, $100.00, the value of insurance used. The balance of Insurance Expense, $100.00, is the value of insurance coverage used from August 1 to August 31. (*CONCEPT: Matching Expenses with Revenue*)

The asset account, Prepaid Insurance, is decreased by a credit, $100.00, the value of insurance used. The debit balance, $1,200.00, *less* the credit adjustment, $100.00, *equals* the new balance, $1,100.00. The new balance of Prepaid Insurance is the same as the amount of insurance coverage unused on August 31.

Rugcare's prepaid insurance adjustment is shown on lines 4 and 12 of the work sheet in Illustration 8-4.

ILLUSTRATION 8-4   Prepaid insurance adjustment on a work sheet

	ACCOUNT TITLE	TRIAL BALANCE		ADJUSTMENTS	
		DEBIT	CREDIT	DEBIT	CREDIT
1	Cash	8 2 7 2 00				1
2	Petty Cash	2 0 0 00				2
3	Supplies	4 9 3 1 00			(a) 2 6 4 7 00	3
4	Prepaid Insurance	1 2 0 0 00			(b) 1 0 0 00	4
12	Insurance Expense			(b) 1 0 0 00		12
13	Miscellaneous Expense	1 0 5 00				13
14	Rent Expense	2 5 0 00				14
15	Repair Expense	1 1 0 00				15
16	Supplies Expense			(a) 2 6 4 7 00		16
17	Utilities Expense	1 1 5 00				17
18		15 8 5 1 00	15 8 5 1 00	2 7 4 7 00	2 7 4 7 00	18
19						19

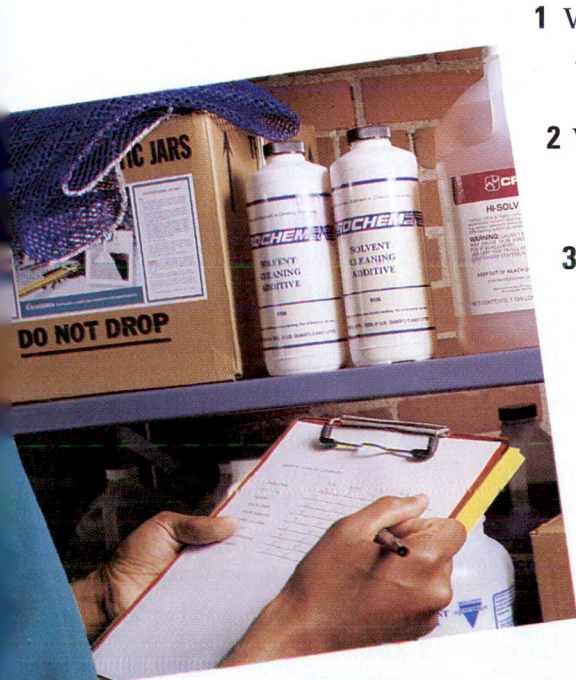

Three steps are used to record the prepaid insurance adjustment on a work sheet.

1 Write the debit amount, *$100.00*, in the work sheet's Adjustments Debit column on the line with the account title Insurance Expense (line 12).

2 Write the credit amount, *$100.00*, in the Adjustments Credit column on the line with the account title Prepaid Insurance (line 4).

3 Label the two parts of this adjustment with a small letter *b* in parentheses *(b)*. The letter *b* identifies the debit and credit amounts as part of the same adjustment.

Proving the Adjustments Columns of a Work Sheet. After all adjustments are recorded in a work sheet's Adjustments columns, the equality of debits and credits for the two columns is proved. Rugcare's completed Adjustments columns are shown in Illustration 8-4.

Three steps are used in proving a work sheet's Adjustments columns.

1 Rule a single line across the two Adjustments columns on the same line as the single line for the Trial Balance columns.

2 Add both the Adjustments Debit and Credit columns. If the two column totals are the same, then debits equal credits for these two columns, and the work sheet's Adjustments columns are in balance. On Rugcare's work sheet, the Adjustments Debit and Credit column totals are $2,747.00. Therefore, the

Adjustments columns on Rugcare's work sheet are in balance. Write each column's total below the single line.

> If the two Adjustments column totals are not the same, the Adjustments columns are rechecked and errors corrected before completing the work sheet.

3 Rule double lines across both Adjustments columns. The double lines mean that the totals have been verified as correct.

Extending Financial Statement Information on a Work Sheet

At the end of each fiscal period, Rugcare prepares two financial statements from information on a work sheet. *(CONCEPT: Accounting Period Cycle)* A financial statement that reports assets, liabilities, and owner's equity on a specific date is known as a balance sheet. A financial statement showing the revenue and expenses for a fiscal period is called an **income statement**. The up-to-date account balances on a work sheet are extended to columns for the two financial statements.

Extending Balance Sheet Account Balances on a Work Sheet.
The balance sheet accounts are the asset, liability, and owner's equity accounts. Up-to-date balance sheet account balances are extended to the Balance Sheet Debit and Credit columns of the work sheet. The extension of Rugcare's balance sheet account balances is shown on lines 1 through 9 of the work sheet in Illustration 8-5.

Three steps are used in extending balance sheet items on a work sheet.

1 Extend the up-to-date balance of each asset account.

- The balance of Cash in the Trial Balance Debit column is up to date because no adjustment affects this account. Extend the balance of Cash, *$8,272.00*, to the Balance Sheet Debit column. Balances of all asset accounts not affected by adjustments are extended in the same way.

- The balance of Supplies in the Trial Balance Debit column is not up to date because it is affected by an adjustment. Calculate the up-to-date adjusted balance. The debit balance, $4,931.00, *minus* the credit adjustment, $2,647.00, *equals* the up-to-date adjusted balance, $2,284.00. Extend the up-to-date balance, *$2,284.00*, to the Balance Sheet Debit column. The same procedure is used to calculate and extend the up-to-date adjusted balance of the other asset account affected by an adjustment, Prepaid Insurance.

2 Extend the up-to-date balance of each liability account.

- The balance of Butler Cleaning Supplies is the up-to-date balance because no adjustment affects this account. Extend the up-to-date balance, *$1,360.00*, to the Balance Sheet Credit column. The balance of the other liability account is extended in the same way.

FYI

A work sheet is prepared in manual accounting to adjust the accounts and sort amounts needed to prepare financial statements. However, in automated accounting adjustments are prepared from the trial balance and the software automatically generates the financial statements with no need for a work sheet.

ILLUSTRATION 8-5   Balance sheet account balances extended on a work sheet

ACCOUNT TITLE	TRIAL BALANCE		ADJUSTMENTS		INCOME STATEMENT		BALANCE SHEET	
	DEBIT	CREDIT	DEBIT	CREDIT	DEBIT	CREDIT	DEBIT	CREDIT
1 Cash	8272 00						8272 00	
2 Petty Cash	200 00						200 00	
3 Supplies	4931 00			(a) 2647 00			2284 00	
4 Prepaid Insurance	1200 00			(b) 100 00			1100 00	
5 Butler Cleaning Supplies		1360 00						1360 00
6 Dale Office Supplies		200 00						200 00
7 Ben Furman, Capital		10000 00						10000 00
8 Ben Furman, Drawing	600 00						600 00	
9 Income Summary								
10								

Rugcare
Work Sheet
For Month Ended August 31, 19--

3 Extend the up-to-date balances of the owner's equity accounts.

- The balance of Ben Furman, Capital in the Trial Balance Credit column is the up-to-date balance because no adjustment affects this account. Extend the balance, *$10,000.00*, to the Balance Sheet Credit column.

- The balance of Ben Furman, Drawing in the Trial Balance Debit column is the up-to-date balance because no adjustment affects this account. Extend the balance, *$600.00*, to the Balance Sheet Debit column.

- Income Summary has no balance in the Trial Balance columns. Therefore, no amount needs to be extended for this account.

Extending Income Statement Account Balances on a Work Sheet.

Rugcare's income statement accounts are the revenue and expense accounts. The extension of income statement account balances is shown on lines 10 through 17 of the work sheet in Illustration 8-6.

Two steps are used in extending income statement accounts on a work sheet.

1 Extend the up-to-date balance of the revenue account.

- The balance of Sales in the Trial Balance Credit column is the up-to-date balance because no adjustment affects this account. Extend the balance, *$4,291.00*, to the Income Statement Credit column.

2 Extend the up-to-date balance of each expense account.

- The balance of Advertising Expense in the Trial Balance Debit column is the up-to-date balance because no adjustment affects this account. Extend the balance, *$68.00*, to the Income Statement Debit column. Balances of all expense

FYI

Use a ruler when extending amounts on a work sheet to keep track of the line you are on.

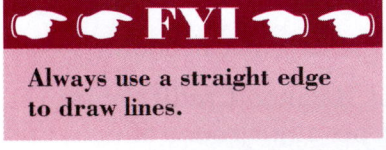

ILLUSTRATION 8-6 Income statement account balances extended on a work sheet

Rugcare

Work Sheet

For Month Ended August 31, 19--

	ACCOUNT TITLE	TRIAL BALANCE DEBIT	TRIAL BALANCE CREDIT	ADJUSTMENTS DEBIT	ADJUSTMENTS CREDIT	INCOME STATEMENT DEBIT	INCOME STATEMENT CREDIT	BALANCE SHEET DEBIT	BALANCE SHEET CREDIT	
		1	2	3	4	5	6	7	8	
10	Sales		4 2 9 1 00				4 2 9 1 00			10
11	Advertising Expense	6 8 00				6 8 00				11
12	Insurance Expense			(b) 1 0 0 00		1 0 0 00				12
13	Miscellaneous Expense	1 0 5 00				1 0 5 00				13
14	Rent Expense	2 5 0 00				2 5 0 00				14
15	Repair Expense	1 1 0 00				1 1 0 00				15
16	Supplies Expense			(a) 2 6 4 7 00		2 6 4 7 00				16
17	Utilities Expense	1 1 5 00				1 1 5 00				17
18		15 8 5 1 00	15 8 5 1 00	2 7 4 7 00	2 7 4 7 00					18
19										19

accounts not affected by adjustments are extended in the same way.

- The balance of **Insurance Expense** in the Trial Balance columns is zero. This zero balance is not the up-to-date balance because this account is affected by an adjustment. Calculate the up-to-date adjusted balance. The debit balance, $0.00, *plus* the debit adjustment, $100.00, *equals* the adjusted balance, $100.00. Extend the up-to-date adjusted debit balance, *$100.00*, to the Income Statement Debit column. The same procedure is used to calculate and extend the up-to-date adjusted balance of each expense account affected by an adjustment.

Calculating and Recording Net Income on a Work Sheet. The difference between total revenue and total expenses when total revenue is greater is called **net income**. Rugcare's August net income is shown on line 19 of the work sheet in Illustration 8-7.

Five steps are used in calculating net income on a work sheet.

1 Rule a single line across the four Income Statement and Balance Sheet columns.

2 Add both the Income Statement and Balance Sheet columns. Write the totals below the single line.

3 Calculate the net income. Rugcare's net income is calculated as shown below.

> **FYI**
> Always use a straight edge to draw lines.

	Income Statement Credit Column Total	−	Income Statement Debit Column Total	=	Net Income
	$4,291.00	−	$3,395.00	=	$896.00

ILLUSTRATION 8-7

Completed work sheet

Rugcare

Work Sheet

For Month Ended August 31, 19--

	1	2	3	4	5	6	7	8	
ACCOUNT TITLE	TRIAL BALANCE		ADJUSTMENTS		INCOME STATEMENT		BALANCE SHEET		
	DEBIT	CREDIT	DEBIT	CREDIT	DEBIT	CREDIT	DEBIT	CREDIT	
1 Cash	8 2 7 2 00						8 2 7 2 00		1
2 Petty Cash	2 0 0 00						2 0 0 00		2
3 Supplies	4 9 3 1 00			(a) 2 6 4 7 00			2 2 8 4 00		3
4 Prepaid Insurance	1 2 0 0 00			(b) 1 0 0 00			1 1 0 0 00		4
5 Butler Cleaning Supplies		1 3 6 0 00						1 3 6 0 00	5
6 Dale Office Supplies		2 0 0 00						2 0 0 00	6
7 Ben Furman, Capital		10 0 0 0 00						10 0 0 0 00	7
8 Ben Furman, Drawing	6 0 0 00						6 0 0 00		8
9 Income Summary									9
10 Sales		4 2 9 1 00				4 2 9 1 00			10
11 Advertising Expense	6 8 00				6 8 00				11
12 Insurance Expense			(b) 1 0 0 00		1 0 0 00				12
13 Miscellaneous Expense	1 0 5 00				1 0 5 00				13
14 Rent Expense	2 5 0 00				2 5 0 00				14
15 Repair Expense	1 1 0 00				1 1 0 00				15
16 Supplies Expense			(a) 2 6 4 7 00		2 6 4 7 00				16
17 Utilities Expense	1 1 5 00				1 1 5 00				17
18	15 8 5 1 00	15 8 5 1 00	2 7 4 7 00	2 7 4 7 00	3 3 9 5 00	4 2 9 1 00	12 4 5 6 00	11 5 6 0 00	18
19 Net Income					8 9 6 00			8 9 6 00	19
20					4 2 9 1 00	4 2 9 1 00	12 4 5 6 00	12 4 5 6 00	20
21									21

Rugcare's August work sheet shows a net income because the Income Statement Credit column (revenue) exceeds the Income Statement Debit column (expenses).

4 Write the amount of net income, *$896.00*, below the Income Statement Debit column total. Write the words, *Net Income*, on the same line in the Account Title column.

5 Extend the amount of net income, *$896.00*, to the Balance Sheet Credit column on the same line as the words *Net Income*. The owner's equity account, Ben Furman, Capital, is increased by a credit. Therefore, the net income amount is extended to the Balance Sheet Credit column.

◖◖FYI◗◗

A single line is ruled across amount columns to indicate addition or subtraction. A double line is ruled across amount columns to indicate that the totals have been verified as correct.

Totaling and Ruling a Work Sheet. Four steps are used in totaling and ruling a work sheet.

1 Rule a single line across the four Income Statement and Balance Sheet columns just below the net income amounts.

2 Add the subtotal and net income amount for each column to get proving totals for the Income Statement and Balance Sheet columns. Write the proving totals below the single line.

Proving totals are used to determine that the debits equal credits for each pair of column totals.

3 Check the equality of the proving totals for each pair of columns. A summary of preparing a work sheet is shown on the Work Sheet Overlay on pages 176A through 176C.

- As shown on line 20 of the work sheet in Illustration 8-7, the proving totals for the Income Statement columns, $4,291.00, are the same.

- As shown on line 20 of the work sheet in Illustration 8-7, the proving totals for the Balance Sheet columns, $12,456.00, are the same.

4 Rule double lines across the Income Statement and Balance Sheet columns. The double lines mean that the totals have been verified as correct.

Calculating and Recording a Net Loss on a Work Sheet. Rugcare's completed work sheet shows a net income. However, a business might have a net loss to report. The difference between total revenue and total expenses when total expenses is greater is called a **net loss**. A net loss on a work sheet is shown in Illustration 8-8.

ILLUSTRATION 8-8   Net loss shown on a work sheet

	ACCOUNT TITLE		5 INCOME STATEMENT DEBIT	6 INCOME STATEMENT CREDIT	7 BALANCE SHEET DEBIT	8 BALANCE SHEET CREDIT	
19			2 0 0 0 00	1 9 0 0 00	5 4 0 0 00	5 5 0 0 00	19
20	Net Loss			1 0 0 00	1 0 0 00		20
21			2 0 0 0 00	2 0 0 0 00	5 5 0 0 00	5 5 0 0 00	21
22							22
23							23

Six steps are used in completing a work sheet with a net loss.

1 Rule a single line across the four Income Statement and Balance Sheet columns.

2 Add both the Income Statement and Balance Sheet columns. Write the totals below the single line.

3 The net loss is calculated as shown below.

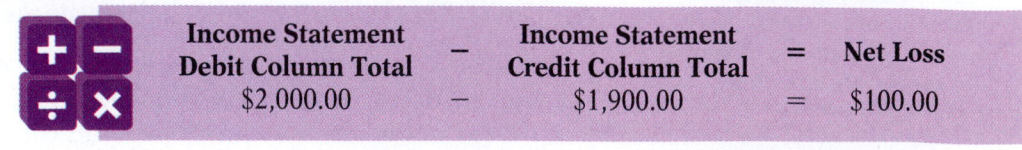

	Income Statement Debit Column Total	−	Income Statement Credit Column Total	=	Net Loss
	$2,000.00	−	$1,900.00	=	$100.00

Audit Your Understanding

1. What is the length of the fiscal period for most businesses?

2. What is written on the three-line heading on a work sheet?

3. List the four questions to analyze an adjustment on a work sheet.

4. Which accounts are extended into the Balance Sheet columns of the work sheet?

5. Which accounts are extended into the Income Statement columns of the work sheet?

The Income Statement Debit column total (expenses) is greater than the Income Statement Credit column total (revenue). Therefore, because expenses exceed revenue, there is a net loss.

4 Write the amount of net loss, *$100.00*, below the Income Statement Credit column total. Write the words, *Net Loss*, on the same line in the Account Title column.

5 Extend the amount of net loss, *$100.00*, to the Balance Sheet Debit column on the same line as the words *Net Loss*. The owner's capital account is decreased by a debit. Therefore, a net loss is extended to the Balance Sheet Debit column.

6 Total and rule the work sheet using the same steps as when there is net income.

FINDING AND CORRECTING ERRORS

Some errors in accounting records are not discovered until a work sheet is prepared. For example, a debit to the supplies account may not have been posted from a journal to the general ledger supplies account. The omission may not be discovered until the work sheet's trial balance does not balance. Also, information may be transferred incorrectly from general ledger accounts to the work sheet's trial balance. Additional errors may be made on a work sheet, such as recording adjustment information incorrectly or adding columns incorrectly. In addition, errors may be made in extending amounts to the Income Statement and Balance Sheet columns.

Any errors found on a work sheet must be corrected before any further work is completed. If an incorrect amount is found on a work sheet, erase the error and replace it with the correct amount. If an amount is written in an incorrect column, erase the amount and record it in the correct column. If column totals do not balance, add the columns again.

FYI

Use the Work Sheet Overlay to review the steps for preparing a work sheet.

Checking for Typical Arithmetic Errors

When two column totals are not in balance, subtract the smaller total from the larger total to find the difference. Check the difference between the two amounts against the following guides.

1 *The difference is 1, such as $.01, $.10, $1.00, or $10.00.* For example, if the totals of the two columns are Debit, $12,542.00 and Credit, $12,543.00, the difference between the two columns is $1.00. The error is most likely in addition. Add the columns again.

2 *The difference can be divided evenly by 2.* For example, the difference between two column totals is $48.00. The differ-

ence, $48.00, *divided* by 2 *equals* $24.00 with no remainder. Look for a $24.00 amount in the Trial Balance columns of the work sheet. If the amount is found, check to make sure it has been recorded in the correct Trial Balance Debit or Credit column. A $24.00 debit amount recorded in a credit column results in a difference between column totals of $48.00. If the error is not found on the work sheet, check the general ledger accounts and journal entries. An entry for $24.00 may have been recorded in an incorrect column in the journal or in an account.

3 ***The difference can be divided evenly by 9.*** For example, the difference between two columns is $45.00. The difference, $45.00, *divided* by 9 *equals* $5.00 with no remainder. When the difference can be divided equally by 9, look for transposed numbers such as 54 written as 45 or 19 written as 91. Also, check for a "slide." A "slide" occurs when numbers are moved to the right or left in an amount column. For example, $12.00 is recorded as $120.00 or $350.00 is recorded as $35.00.

4 ***The difference is an omitted amount.*** Look for an amount equal to the difference. If the difference is $50.00, look for an account balance of $50.00 that has not been extended. Look for any $50.00 amount on the work sheet and determine if it has been handled correctly. Look in the accounts and journals for a $50.00 amount, and check if that amount has been handled correctly. Failure to record a $50.00 account balance will make a work sheet's Trial Balance column totals differ by $50.00.

the individual is instructed to send the author a registration fee if the individual uses the software. Some shareware authors request a specific dollar amount while other authors ask users to pay whatever they consider to be a fair amount.

INSTRUCTIONS Use the three-step checklist to analyze whether each of the following situations demonstrates ethical behavior.

Situation 1. A large company purchased one copy of a copyrighted software program and made numerous copies for use on other computers.

Situation 2. An individual used a shareware program extensively but did not send the shareware author the requested registration fee.

Situation 3. A public university, lacking adequate funds to purchase the required number of copies of a copyrighted electronic spreadsheet program, purchased a single copy and made numerous copies. A label stating "For educational purposes only" was attached to each copy of the software. Students regularly copy the software for personal use.

Checking for Errors in the Trial Balance Columns

1 Have all general ledger account balances been copied in the Trial Balance columns correctly?

2 Have all general ledger account balances been recorded in the correct Trial Balance column?

Correct any errors found and add the columns again.

Checking for Errors in the Adjustments Columns

1 Do the debits equal the credits for each adjustment? Use the small letters that label each part of an adjustment to help check accuracy and equality of debits and credits.

2 Is the amount for each adjustment correct?

Correct any errors found and add the columns again.

Checking for Errors in the Income Statement and Balance Sheet Columns

1 Has each amount been copied correctly when extended to the Income Statement or Balance Sheet column?

2 Has each account balance been extended to the correct Income Statement or Balance Sheet column?

3 Has the net income or net loss been calculated correctly?

4 Has the net income or net loss been recorded in the correct Income Statement or Balance Sheet column?

Correct any errors found and add the columns again.

Between 1960 and 1990 the number of accountants more than doubled.

Checking for Errors in Posting to General Ledger Accounts

Sometimes a pair of work sheet columns do not balance, and an error cannot be found on the work sheet. If this is the situation, check the posting from the journal to the general ledger accounts. As each item in an account or a journal entry is verified, a check mark should be placed next to it. The check mark indicates that the item has been checked for accuracy.

1 Have all amounts that need to be posted actually been posted from the journal?

- For an amount that has not been posted, complete the posting to the correct account.

- In all cases where posting is corrected, recalculate the account balance and correct it on the work sheet.

    When an omitted posting is recorded as described above, the dates in the general ledger accounts may be out of order.

2 Have all amounts been posted to the correct accounts?

- For an amount posted to the wrong account, draw a line through the entire incorrect entry. Recalculate the account balance.

- Record the posting in the correct account. Recalculate the account balance, and correct the work sheet. Make the correction in the general ledger accounts, as shown in Illustration 8-9.

When correcting errors in the ledger, draw a line through the error using a straight edge. Write the correct number above the correction.

ILLUSTRATION 8-9   Correcting an error in posting to the wrong account

ACCOUNT **Supplies**   ACCOUNT NO. **130**

DATE		ITEM	POST. REF.	DEBIT	CREDIT	BALANCE DEBIT	BALANCE CREDIT
Feb.	1		1	4 0 0 00		4 0 0 00	
	25		2	9 0 00		4 9 0 00	
	12		1	5 0 00		5 4 0 00	

ACCOUNT **Prepaid Insurance**   ACCOUNT NO. **140**

DATE		ITEM	POST. REF.	DEBIT	CREDIT	BALANCE DEBIT	BALANCE CREDIT
Feb.	9		1	6 0 0 00		6 0 0 00	
	~~12~~		~~1~~	~~5 0 00~~		~~6 5 0 00~~	

Errors in permanent records should *never* be erased. Erasures in permanent records raise questions about whether important financial information has been altered.

3 Have all amounts been written correctly? Have all amounts been posted to the correct Debit or Credit columns of an account?

- If an amount has been written incorrectly, draw a line through the incorrect amount. Write the correct amount just above the correction in the same space. Recalculate the account balance, and correct the account balance on the work sheet. Correcting an error in writing an amount incorrectly is shown on the first line of the utilities expense account in Illustration 8-10.

ILLUSTRATION 8-10

Correcting an amount written incorrectly and an error in posting to the wrong column of an account

ACCOUNT	*Utilities Expense*					ACCOUNT NO. *570*	
						BALANCE	
DATE	ITEM	POST. REF.	DEBIT	CREDIT		DEBIT	CREDIT
Sept. 8		1	70 00			~~70 0 00~~ 7 0 00	
17		1	27 00	~~27 00~~		~~67 3 00~~ 9 7 00	

- For an amount posted to the wrong amount column, draw a line through the incorrect item in the account. Record the posting in the correct amount column. Recalculate the account balance, and correct the work sheet. Correcting an error in posting to a wrong amount column is shown on the second line of the utilities expense account in Illustration 8-10.

Checking for Errors in Journal Entries

1 Do debits equal credits in each journal entry?

2 Is each journal entry amount recorded in the correct journal column?

3 Is information in the Account Title column correct for each journal entry?

4 Are all of the journal amount column totals correct?

5 Does the sum of debit column totals equal the sum of credit column totals in the journal?

6 Have all transactions been recorded?

Some suggestions for correcting errors in journal entries are described in Chapter 5.

Preventing Errors

The best way to prevent errors is to work carefully at all times. Check the work at each step in an accounting procedure. Most errors occur in doing the required arithmetic, especially in adding columns. When possible, use a calculator to add columns. When an error is discovered, do no more work until the cause of the error is found and corrections are made.

FYI

Never erase ink or it will look as if the numbers were altered. Altered numbers arouse suspicion of wrongdoing.

Audit Your Understanding

1. What is the first step in checking for arithmetic errors when two column totals are not in balance?

2. What is one way to check for an error caused by transposed numbers?

3. What term is used to describe an error that occurs when numbers are moved to the right or left in an amount column?

ACCOUNTING TERMS

What is the meaning of each of the following?

1. fiscal period
2. work sheet
3. trial balance
4. adjustments

5. income statement
6. net income
7. net loss

QUESTIONS FOR INDIVIDUAL STUDY

1. What are typical lengths of fiscal periods?
2. Which accounting concept is being applied when a business summarizes and reports financial information for a fiscal period?
3. What are four reasons for preparing a work sheet?
4. Why is a work sheet prepared in pencil?
5. How is the equality of debits and credits proved in a general ledger?
6. Why is an adjustment for supplies planned at the end of a fiscal period?
7. What accounts are affected, and how, by the adjustment for supplies?
8. After a supplies adjustment, what does the supplies account balance represent?
9. What accounts are affected, and how, by the adjustment for prepaid insurance?

10. Why are the Adjustments columns on a work sheet totaled?
11. What two financial statements are prepared from information on a work sheet?
12. If a work sheet shows a net income, in which two columns will the net income be recorded?
13. How are the amounts in the Income Statement and Balance Sheet columns of a work sheet proved?
14. If two work sheet column totals are not equal and the difference between the totals is one, what is the most likely error?
15. If two work sheet column totals are not equal and the difference between the totals is evenly divisible by nine, what is the most likely error?

CASES FOR CRITICAL THINKING

CASE 1   Peter Dowther owns a small business. At the end of a fiscal period, he does not make an adjustment for supplies. Are Mr. Dowther's accounting procedures correct? What effect will Mr. Dowther's procedures have on the business' financial reporting? Explain your answer.

CASE 2   When posting amounts from a journal to general ledger accounts, a $10.00 debit to Supplies is mistakenly posted as a credit to Utilities Expense. Will this error be discovered when the work sheet is prepared? Explain.

DRILLS FOR UNDERSTANDING

DRILL 8-D1   Extending account balances on a work sheet

TUTORIAL

A partial work sheet form with account titles is given in the working papers that accompany this textbook.

INSTRUCTIONS:

1. Place a check mark in either Column 1 or 2 to indicate the Trial Balance column in which each account's balance will appear. The first account is given as an example.
2. Place a check mark in Columns 5, 6, 7, or 8 to indicate the column to which each up-to-date account balance will be extended.

DRILL 8-D2 Calculating net income or net loss on a work sheet

The column totals from the work sheets of five different businesses are given in the working papers that accompany this textbook.

INSTRUCTIONS:

Complete the following for each company. The amounts for Company A are given as an example.

1. Calculate the amount of net income or net loss. Write the amount on line 2 in the correct columns. Label the amount as *Net Income* or *Net Loss*.
2. Add the amounts in each column. Write the totals on line 3.
3. Verify the accuracy of your proving totals.

APPLICATION PROBLEMS   EPT(c,d,e)

PROBLEM 8-1 Completing a work sheet

On September 30 of the current year, CleanLawn has the following general ledger accounts and balances. The business uses a monthly fiscal period.

Account Titles	Account Balances Debit	Credit
Cash.	$3,000.00	
Petty Cash	100.00	
Supplies.	2,000.00	
Prepaid Insurance	900.00	
Bix Supplies		$ 600.00
OfficeWorld.		100.00
Dorothy Daily, Capital		4,100.00
Dorothy Daily, Drawing	200.00	
Income Summary.	—	—
Sales		2,505.00
Advertising Expense	75.00	
Insurance Expense.	—	
Miscellaneous Expense.	110.00	
Rent Expense.	600.00	
Repair Expense	180.00	
Supplies Expense.	—	
Utilities Expense	140.00	

INSTRUCTIONS:

1. Prepare the heading and trial balance on a work sheet. Total and rule the Trial Balance columns.
2. Analyze the following adjustment information into debit and credit parts. Record the adjustments on the work sheet.

Adjustment Information, September 30

Supplies on hand	$1,100.00
Value of prepaid insurance	600.00

3. Total and rule the Adjustments columns.
4. Extend the up-to-date balances to the Balance Sheet or Income Statement columns.
5. Rule a single line across the Income Statement and Balance Sheet columns. Total each column. Calculate and record the net income or net loss. Label the amount in the Account Title column.
6. Total and rule the Income Statement and Balance Sheet columns.

PROBLEM 8-2 Completing a work sheet

On October 31 of the current year, Village Service Co. has the following general ledger accounts and balances. The business uses a monthly fiscal period.

Account Titles	Account Balances Debit	Credit
Cash..	$4,900.00	
Petty Cash	300.00	
Supplies......................................	2,500.00	
Prepaid Insurance	2,100.00	
National Supplies		$ 1,400.00
Office Distributors		1,200.00
Wensk Movies................................		800.00
Susan Haile, Capital...........................		6,000.00
Susan Haile, Drawing	1,200.00	
Income Summary..............................	—	—
Sales		20,100.00
Advertising Expense	4,200.00	
Insurance Expense............................	—	
Miscellaneous Expense........................	600.00	
Rent Expense.................................	8,000.00	
Repair Expense	2,400.00	
Supplies Expense.............................	—	
Utilities Expense	3,300.00	

INSTRUCTIONS:

1. Prepare the heading and trial balance on a work sheet. Total and rule the Trial Balance columns.
2. Analyze the following adjustment information into debit and credit parts. Record the adjustments on the work sheet.

Adjustment Information, October 31

Supplies on hand.................................	$1,500.00
Value of prepaid insurance.........................	900.00

3. Total and rule the Adjustments columns.
4. Extend the up-to-date balances to the Balance Sheet or Income Statement columns.
5. Rule a single line across the Income Statement and Balance Sheet columns. Total each column. Calculate and record the net income or net loss. Label the amount in the Account Title column.
6. Total and rule the Income Statement and Balance Sheet columns.

PROBLEM 8-3 Finding and correcting errors in accounting records

Paul Coty has completed the September monthly work sheet for his business, LeafyLift. The work sheet and general ledger accounts are given in the working papers accompanying this textbook.

Mr. Coty believes that he has made one or more errors in preparing the work sheet. He asks you to help him verify the work sheet.

INSTRUCTIONS:

1. Examine the work sheet and the general ledger accounts. Make a list of the errors you find.
2. Correct any errors you find in the general ledger accounts.
3. Prepare a corrected work sheet.

ENRICHMENT PROBLEMS   EPT(c,d)

MASTERY PROBLEM 8-M Completing a work sheet

On April 30 of the current year, FastGrow has the following general ledger accounts and balances. The business uses a monthly fiscal period.

Account Titles	Account Balances Debit	Credit
Cash..	$5,800.00	
Petty Cash	200.00	

Supplies.	4,000.00	
Prepaid Insurance	1,000.00	
Wheaton Supplies		$ 200.00
Norton Company		115.00
Roger Bently, Capital.		7,200.00
Roger Bently, Drawing	400.00	
Income Summary.	—	—
Sales		5,300.00
Advertising Expense	325.00	
Insurance Expense.	—	
Miscellaneous Expense.	140.00	
Rent Expense.	500.00	
Supplies Expense.	—	
Utilities Expense	450.00	

INSTRUCTIONS:

1. Prepare the heading and trial balance on a work sheet. Total and rule the Trial Balance columns.
2. Analyze the following adjustment information into debit and credit parts. Record the adjustments on the work sheet.

Adjustment Information, April 30

Supplies inventory.	$2,050.00
Value of prepaid insurance.	450.00

3. Extend the up-to-date account balances to the Balance Sheet or Income Statement columns.
4. Complete the work sheet.

CHALLENGE PROBLEM 8-C   Completing a work sheet

APPLICATION

Clean and Mow had a small fire in its office. The fire destroyed some of the accounting records. On November 30 of the current year, the end of a monthly fiscal period, the following information was constructed from the remaining records and other sources.

Remains of the general ledger:

Account Titles	Account Balances
Supplies.	$1,800.00
Donna Edwards, Drawing.	150.00
Sales	4,000.00
Advertising Expense	420.00
Rent Expense.	700.00
Utilities Expense	490.00

Information from the business' checkbook:
Cash balance on last unused check stub, $3,400.00
Total payments for miscellaneous expense, $60.00
Total payments for insurance, $325.00

Information obtained through inquiries to other businesses:
Owed to Outdoor Supplies, $2,000.00
Value of prepaid insurance, November 30, $250.00

Information obtained by counting supplies on hand after the fire:
Supplies on hand, $1,100.00

INSTRUCTIONS:

1. From the information given, prepare a heading and reconstruct a trial balance on a work sheet. The owner's capital account balance is the difference between the total of all debit account balances minus the total of all credit account balances.
2. Complete the work sheet.

9

Financial Statements for a Proprietorship

ENABLING PERFORMANCE TASKS

After studying Chapter 9, you will be able to:

a Define the accounting term related to financial statements for a service business organized as a proprietorship.

b Identify accounting concepts and practices related to preparation of financial statements for a service business organized as a proprietorship.

c Prepare an income statement for a service business organized as a proprietorship.

d Analyze an income statement using component percentages.

e Prepare a balance sheet for a service business organized as a proprietorship.

TERMS PREVIEW

component percentage

The financial information needed by managers and owners to make good business decisions can be found in the general ledger accounts. However, the information in the general ledger is very detailed. Therefore, to make this general ledger information more usable, the information is summarized, organized, and reported to the owners and managers.

Also, *all* financial information *must* be reported if good business decisions are to be made. A financial statement with incomplete information is similar to a book with missing pages. The complete story is not told. If a business has both rent and utilities expenses but reports only the rent expense, managers will have incomplete information on which to base decisions. The accounting concept, *Adequate Disclosure*, is applied when financial statements contain all information necessary to understand a business' financial condition. *(CONCEPT: Adequate Disclosure)*

Rugcare prepares two financial statements: an income statement and a balance sheet. Rugcare always prepares financial statements at the end of each monthly fiscal period. *(CONCEPT: Accounting Period Cycle)* The time periods covered by Rugcare's financial statements are shown in Illustration 9-1.

ILLUSTRATION 9-1   Time periods for financial statements

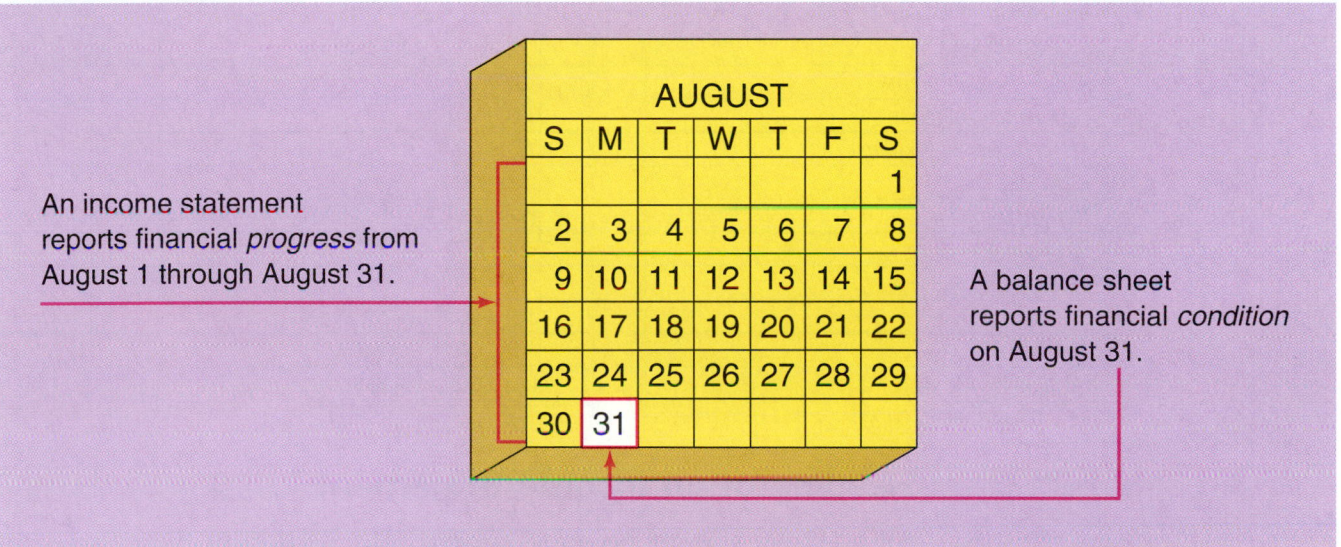

An income statement reports financial *progress* from August 1 through August 31.

A balance sheet reports financial *condition* on August 31.

An income statement reports financial information over a *specific period of time*, indicating the financial *progress* of a business in earning a net income or net loss.

A balance sheet reports financial information on a *specific date*, indicating the financial *condition* of a business. The financial condition of a business refers to its financial strength. If a business has adequate available assets and few liabilities, that business is financially strong. If the business' financial condition is not strong, adverse changes in the economy might cause the business to fail.

INCOME STATEMENT

Revenue is the earnings of a business from business activities. Expenses are the amounts a business pays to operate the business and earn the revenue. The revenue earned and the expenses incurred to earn that revenue are reported in the same fiscal period. *(CONCEPT: Matching Expenses with Revenue)*

Information needed to prepare financial statements could be obtained from the general ledger accounts. However, a work sheet is prepared to assist in planning the financial statements. Rugcare's income statement information on a work sheet is shown in Illustration 9-2.

Information needed to prepare Rugcare's income statement is obtained from two places on the work sheet. Account titles are obtained from the work sheet's Account Title column. Account balances are obtained from the work sheet's Income Statement columns.

The income statement for a service business has four sections: (1) heading, (2) revenue, (3) expenses, and (4) net income or net loss.

ILLUSTRATION 9-2   Income statement information on a work sheet

	ACCOUNT TITLE	INCOME STATEMENT DEBIT	INCOME STATEMENT CREDIT	BALANCE SHEET DEBIT	BALANCE SHEET CREDIT	
10	Sales		4 2 9 1 00			10
11	Advertising Expense	6 8 00				11
12	Insurance Expense	1 0 0 00				12
13	Miscellaneous Expense	1 0 5 00				13
14	Rent Expense	2 5 0 00				14
15	Repair Expense	1 1 0 00				15
16	Supplies Expense	2 6 4 7 00				16
17	Utilities Expense	1 1 5 00				17
18		3 3 9 5 00	4 2 9 1 00			18
19	Net Income	8 9 6 00				19
20		4 2 9 1 00	4 2 9 1 00			20

Heading of an Income Statement

All financial statements have similar information in their three-line headings. (1) The name of the business. (2) The name of the statement. (3) The date of the statement. The three-line heading for Rugcare's income statement is shown in Illustration 9-3.

ILLUSTRATION 9-3   Heading of an income statement

Rugcare
Income Statement
For Month Ended August 31, 19--

The income statement's date shows that this income statement reports information for the one-month fiscal period from August 1 through August 31.

Revenue Section of an Income Statement

Information from the work sheet's Account Title column and Income Statement Credit column is used to prepare the revenue section. The revenue section of an income statement is shown in Illustration 9-4.

ILLUSTRATION 9-4

Revenue section of an income statement

Revenue:			
Sales			4 2 9 1 00

Write the name of this section, *Revenue:*, at the extreme left of the wide column on the first line. Write the title of the revenue account, *Sales*, on the next line indented about one centimeter. Record the balance of the account, *$4,291.00*, on the same line in the second amount column.

Expenses Section of an Income Statement

Information from the work sheet's Account Title column and Income Statement Debit column is used to prepare the expenses section. The expenses section of Rugcare's income statement is shown in Illustration 9-5.

ILLUSTRATION 9-5

Expenses section of an income statement

Expenses:			
Advertising Expense	6 8 00		
Insurance Expense	1 0 0 00		
Miscellaneous Expense	1 0 5 00		
Rent Expense	2 5 0 00		
Repair Expense	1 1 0 00		
Supplies Expense	2 6 4 7 00		
Utilities Expense	1 1 5 00		
Total Expenses		3 3 9 5 00	

Write the name of this section, *Expenses:*, at the extreme left of the wide column on the next blank line. Write the title of each expense account in the wide column indented about one centimeter. Record the balance of each expense account in the first amount column on the same line as the account title.

To indicate addition, rule a single line across the first amount column under the last expense account balance. Write the words, *Total Expenses*, on the next blank line in the wide column. Record the amount of total expenses, $3,395.00, on the same line in the second amount column.

Net Income Section of an Income Statement

The amount of net income is calculated and verified using two steps.

1 The net income is calculated from information on the income statement as shown below.

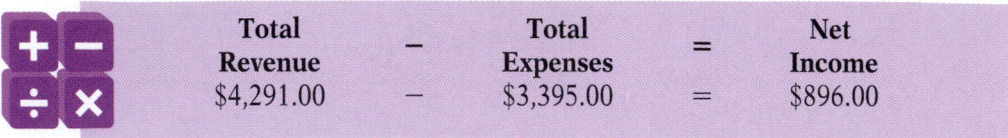

	Total Revenue	–	Total Expenses	=	Net Income
	$4,291.00	–	$3,395.00	=	$896.00

2 The amount of net income, *$896.00*, is compared with the net income shown on the work sheet, Illustration 9-2. The net income calculated for the income statement and the net income shown on the work sheet must be the same. The net income calculated for Rugcare's income statement, $896.00, is the same as that on the work sheet.

> If the net income calculated for the income statement is not the same as that shown on the work sheet, an error has been made. No more work on the income statement should be completed until the error is found and corrected.

A single line is drawn across the second amount column just below the amount of total expenses, as shown in Illustration 9-6.

Write the words, *Net Income*, on the next line at the extreme left of the wide column. On the same line, record the amount of net income, *$896.00*, in the second amount column. Rule double lines across both amount columns below the amount of net income to show that the amount has been verified as correct. Rugcare's completed income statement is shown in Illustration 9-6.

> If total expenses exceed total revenue, a net loss is reported on an income statement. When a net loss is reported, write the words, *Net Loss*, in the wide column. Subtract the total expenses from the revenue to calculate the net loss. Record the amount of net loss in the second amount column in parentheses. An amount written in parentheses on a financial statement indicates a negative amount.

Component Percentage Analysis of an Income Statement

For a service business, the revenue reported on an income statement includes two components: (1) total expenses and (2) net income. To make decisions about future operations, Mr. Furman

ILLUSTRATION 9-6   An income statement

Rugcare Income Statement For Month Ended August 31, 19--			% OF SALES
Revenue:			
Sales		4 2 9 1 00	100.0
Expenses:			
Advertising Expense	6 8 00		
Insurance Expense	1 0 0 00		
Miscellaneous Expense	1 0 5 00		
Rent Expense	2 5 0 00		
Repair Expense	1 1 0 00		
Supplies Expense	2 6 4 7 00		
Utilities Expense	1 1 5 00		
Total Expenses		3 3 9 5 00	79.1
Net Income		8 9 6 00	20.9

analyzes relationships between these two income statement components and the total sales. The percentage relationship between one financial statement item and the total that includes that item is called a **component percentage.** On an income statement, component percentages are calculated by dividing the amount of each component by the total amount of sales. Rugcare calculates a component percentage for total expenses and net income. The relationship between each component and total sales is shown in a separate column on the income statement at the right of the amount columns.

Acceptable Component Percentages. For a component percentage to be useful, Mr. Furman needs to know what component percentages are acceptable for businesses similar to Rugcare. Various industry organizations publish average percentages for similar businesses. In the future Mr. Furman could also compare Rugcare's component percentages from one fiscal period with the percentages of previous fiscal periods.

Total Expenses Component Percentage. The total expenses component percentage, based on information from the August income statement shown in Illustration 9-6, is calculated as shown below.

Total Expenses	÷	Total Sales	=	Total Expenses Component Percentage
$3,395.00	÷	$4,291.00	=	79.1%

For businesses similar to Rugcare, an acceptable total expenses component percentage is not more than 80.0%. Therefore, Rugcare's percentage, 79.1%, is less than 80.0% and is acceptable.

Net Income Component Percentage. The net income component percentage, based on information from the August income statement, is calculated as shown below.

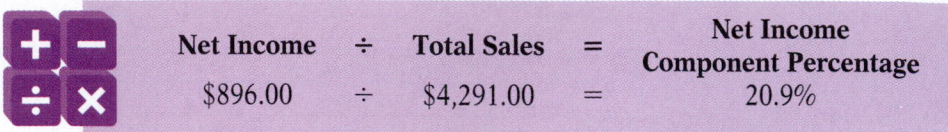

	Net Income	÷	Total Sales	=	Net Income Component Percentage
	$896.00	÷	$4,291.00	=	20.9%

For businesses similar to Rugcare, an acceptable net income component percentage is not less than 20.0%. Therefore, Rugcare's percentage, 20.9%, is greater than 20.0% and is acceptable. The net income component percentage will improve if Rugcare can reduce total expenses in future months. Also, the net income component percentage will improve if Rugcare can increase the amount of revenue in future months.

When there is a net loss, the component percentage for net loss is written in parentheses. A net loss is considered unacceptable.

Income Statement with Two Sources of Revenue

Rugcare receives revenue from only one source, the sale of services for rug and carpet cleaning. Milton Lawn Service receives revenue from two sources, the sale of services to fertilize lawns and the sale of services to trim and care for trees. The business' owner wants to know how much revenue is earned from each source. Therefore, the business uses two revenue accounts: Sales—Lawns and Sales—Tree Care.

When an income statement is prepared for Milton Lawn Service, both revenue accounts are listed, as shown in Illustration 9-7.

ILLUSTRATION 9-7   Revenue section of an income statement showing two sources of revenue

Milton Lawn Service					% OF SALES
Income Statement					
For Month Ended August 31, 19--					
Revenue:					
Sales—Lawns			3 3 6 0 00		
Sales—Tree Care			2 2 5 0 00		
Total Sales				5 6 1 0 00	100.0
Expenses:					

Audit Your Understanding

1. List the four sections of an income statement.

2. What is the formula for calculating the total expenses component percentage?

3. What is the formula for calculating the net income component percentage?

Only the revenue section of Milton Lawn Service's income statement differs from the income statement prepared by Rugcare. Write the section heading, *Revenue:*, at the left of the wide column. Write the titles of both revenue accounts in the wide column indented about one centimeter. Record the balance of each account in the first amount column on the same line as the account title. Total the two revenue account balances. Write the total amount on the next line in the second amount column. Write the words, *Total Sales*, in the wide column indented about one centimeter on the same line as the total revenue amount.

BALANCE SHEET

Information about assets, liabilities, and owner's equity might be obtained from the general ledger accounts or from a work sheet. However, the information is easier to use if reported in an organized manner such as on a balance sheet. Rugcare's balance sheet information on a work sheet is shown in Illustration 9-8.

ILLUSTRATION 9-8

Balance sheet information on a work sheet

	ACCOUNT TITLE	BALANCE SHEET	
		DEBIT	CREDIT
1	Cash	8 2 7 2 00	
2	Petty Cash	2 0 0 00	
3	Supplies	2 2 8 4 00	
4	Prepaid Insurance	1 1 0 0 00	
5	Butler Cleaning Supplies		1 3 6 0 00
6	Dale Office Supplies		2 0 0 00
7	Ben Furman, Capital		10 0 0 0 00
8	Ben Furman, Drawing	6 0 0 00	
17			
18		12 4 5 6 00	11 5 6 0 00
19	Net Income		8 9 6 00
20		12 4 5 6 00	12 4 5 6 00

FYI

Information needed to prepare the balance sheet is obtained from two places on the work sheet. Account titles are obtained from the work sheet's Account Title column. Account balances are obtained from the work sheet's Balance Sheet columns.

Information needed to prepare Rugcare's balance sheet is obtained from two places on the work sheet. Account titles are obtained from the work sheet's Account Title column. Account balances are obtained from the work sheet's Balance Sheet columns.

A balance sheet has four sections: (1) heading, (2) assets, (3) liabilities, and (4) owner's equity.

Heading of a Balance Sheet

The heading of a balance sheet consists of three lines. (1) The name of the business. (2) The name of the statement. (3) The date of the statement. Rugcare's balance sheet heading is shown in Illustration 9-9.

ILLUSTRATION 9-9

Heading of a balance sheet

| *Rugcare* |
| *Balance Sheet* |
| *August 31, 19--* |

Assets, liabilities, and owner's equity are reported on Rugcare's balance sheet as of a specific date, August 31.

Assets Section of a Balance Sheet

A balance sheet reports information about the elements of the accounting equation.

Assets = Liabilities + Owner's Equity

The assets are on the LEFT side of the accounting equation and on the LEFT side of Rugcare's balance sheet.

The information needed to prepare the assets section is obtained from the work sheet's Account Title column and the Balance Sheet Debit column. The assets section of Rugcare's balance sheet is shown in Illustration 9-10.

ILLUSTRATION 9-10

Assets section of a balance sheet

Assets		
Cash	8 2 7 2	00
Petty Cash	2 0 0	00
Supplies	2 2 8 4	00
Prepaid Insurance	1 1 0 0	00

Write the title of the section, *Assets*, in the middle of the left wide column. Under the heading write the titles of all asset accounts. Record the balance of each asset account in the left amount column on the same line as the account title.

Equities Section of a Balance Sheet

Two kinds of equities are reported on a balance sheet: (1) liabilities and (2) owner's equity. Liabilities and owner's equity are on the RIGHT side of the accounting equation and on the RIGHT side of Rugcare's balance sheet.

FYI

The word Liabilities can be abbreviated as "Liab."

Liabilities Section of a Balance Sheet. The information needed to prepare the liabilities section is obtained from the work sheet's Account Title column and the Balance Sheet Credit column. The liabilities are reported on a balance sheet as shown in Illustration 9-11.

ILLUSTRATION 9-11 Liabilities section of a balance sheet

		Liabilities		
		Butler Cleaning Supplies	1 3 6 0	00
		Dale Office Supplies	2 0 0	00
		Total Liabilities	1 5 6 0	00

Write the title of the section, *Liabilities*, in the middle of the right wide column. Under this heading write the titles of all liability accounts. Record the balance of each liability account in the right amount column on the same line as the account title. To indicate addition, rule a single line across the right amount column under the last amount. Write the words, *Total Liabilities*, in the right wide column on the next blank line. Record the total of all liabilities, *$1,560.00*, in the right amount column.

Remember that there are two kinds of equity: Liabilities and Owner's Equity.

Owner's Equity Section of a Balance Sheet. Only the amount of current capital is reported on Rugcare's balance sheet. The amounts needed to calculate the current capital are found in the work sheet's Balance Sheet Debit and Credit columns. The amount of current capital is calculated as shown below.

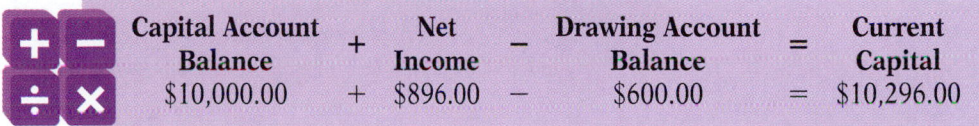

Capital Account Balance	+	Net Income	−	Drawing Account Balance	=	Current Capital
$10,000.00	+	$896.00	−	$600.00	=	$10,296.00

The title of the owner's capital account is obtained from the work sheet's Account Title column. Owner's equity is reported on a balance sheet as shown in Illustration 9-12.

Write the title of the section, *Owner's Equity*, in the middle of the right wide column on the next line. On the next line, write the title of the owner's capital account, *Ben Furman, Capital*. Record the current amount of owner's equity, *$10,296.00*, in the right amount column.

Rugcare's balance sheet prepared on August 31 is shown in Illustration 9-12. Rule a single line across both amount columns under the last amount in the amount column that is the longest. For Rugcare's balance sheet, the longest column is the right amount

The word Equity can be abbreviated as "Eq."

ILLUSTRATION 9-12   A balance sheet

Rugcare				
Balance Sheet				
August 31, 19--				
Assets		**Liabilities**		
Cash	8 2 7 2 00	Butler Cleaning Supplies	1 3 6 0 00
Petty Cash	2 0 0 00	Dale Office Supplies	2 0 0 00
Supplies	2 2 8 4 00	Total Liabilities	1 5 6 0 00
Prepaid Insurance	1 1 0 0 00	*Owner's Equity*	
		Ben Furman, Capital	10 2 9 6 00
Total Assets	11 8 5 6 00	Total Liab. and Owner's Eq.	11 8 5 6 00

FYI

Capital is not copied from the work sheet to the balance sheet. Capital is calculated using beginning capital, minus drawing, plus net income or minus net loss.

column. The line is ruled under the amount of Ben Furman's capital, $10,296.00. On the next line, in the right wide column, write the words, *Total Liab. and Owner's Eq.* Record the amount of total liabilities and owner's equity, *$11,856.00*, in the right amount column.

The total assets amount is not recorded at the time the rest of the assets section is prepared. The placement of the total assets line is determined after the equities section is prepared so that the two final totals are on the same line.

Write the words, *Total Assets*, in the left wide column on the same line as the words *Total Liab. and Owner's Eq.* Record the amount of total assets, *$11,856.00*, in the left amount column.

Compare the totals of the two amount columns. Because the totals are the same on both sides of Rugcare's balance sheet, $11,856.00, the balance sheet is in balance. The accounting equation being reported is also in balance.

	Assets	=	Liabilities	+	Owner's Equity
	$11,856.00	=	$1,560.00	+	$10,296.00

If the total assets do not equal the total liabilities and owner's equity, the error or errors must be found and corrected before the balance sheet is completed.

Rule double lines across both the left and right amount columns just below the column totals to show that the totals have been verified as correct.

When a business has a net loss, current capital is calculated as shown below.

	Capital Account Balance	–	Net Loss	–	Drawing Account Balance	=	Current Capital
	$15,000.00	–	$200.00	–	$500.00	=	$14,300.00

SPREADSHEET OPTIONS

ELECTRONIC SPREADSHEETS HELP ANSWER "WHAT IF?" QUESTIONS

Ben Furman analyzes the income statement in Illustration 9-6 to make decisions about Rugcare's future operations. Mr. Furman may analyze several "what if?" questions to determine what action might improve net income and the net income component percentage. What if the amount spent on advertising was increased to $300.00? Mr. Furman estimated that this would increase sales to $5,000.00. However, if sales increase, Rugcare will also need additional supplies to clean more rugs. Therefore, Mr. Furman estimates that supplies expense will increase to $2,900.00.

Electronic spreadsheets eliminate the need to manually erase data and recalculate totals each time a change is made. When data is keyed on the spreadsheet, formulas use the new data to recalculate other values. Formulas may consist of a combination of values, mathematical operations, and cell addresses. The electronic spreadsheet uses the standard mathematical operations of addition (+), subtraction (−), multiplication (*), and division (/). For example,

the formula to calculate the net income component percentage, +E19/E7, divides the value currently displayed at E19 by the value currently displayed at E7.

The analysis indicates that spending $300.00 on advertising would improve net income and the net income component percentage. Mr. Furman will save the spreadsheet on a computer disk for use in answering other "what if?" questions. In the future, Mr. Furman can retrieve the spreadsheet, key new data, and instantly analyze the revised net income and net income component percentage.

```
F7      (P1) +E7/E7
     A       B              C            D          E        F        G
 1                              Rugcare
 2                          Income Statement
 3                        Projection of Net Income
 4                                                          % of
 5                                                          Sales
 6        Revenue:                                         -------
 7          Sales                                 5,000.00  100.0%
 8        Expenses:
 9          Advertising Expense       300.00
10          Insurance Expense         100.00
11          Miscellaneous Expense     105.00
12          Rent Expense              250.00
13          Repair Expense            110.00
14          Supplies Expense        2,900.00
15          Utilities Expense         115.00
16                                 ----------
17        Total Expenses                         3,880.00   77.6%
18                                               ----------
19     Net Income                                1,120.00   22.4%
20                                               ==================
```

The current capital, $14,300.00, is reported on the balance sheet in the same way as shown in Illustration 9-12.

Owner's Equity Reported in Detail on a Balance Sheet

Rugcare's balance sheet reports the current capital on August 31 but does not show how this amount was calculated. Rugcare is a small business with relatively few changes in owner's equity to report. Therefore, Ben Furman decided that the business does not need to report all the details in the owner's equity section. However, some businesses prefer to report the details about how owner's equity is calculated.

If Rugcare were to report details about owner's equity, the balance sheet would be prepared as shown in Illustration 9-13.

FYI

The General Accounting Office is the investigative arm of Congress and examines all matters relating to the receipt and disbursement of public funds.

ILLUSTRATION 9-13   Owner's equity reported in detail on a balance sheet

Total Liabilities			1 5 6 0 00	
Owner's Equity				
Ben Furman, Capital, August 1		10,000.00		
Net Income	896.00			
Less Ben Furman, Drawing	600.00	296.00		
Ben Furman, Capital, August 31			10 2 9 6 00	
Total Liabilities and Owner's Equity			11 8 5 6 00	

Audit Your Understanding

1. List the four sections of a balance sheet.

2. What is the formula for calculating current capital?

First, the owner's capital account balance, $10,000.00, is reported. Second, the balance of the drawing account, $600.00, is subtracted from the net income for the fiscal period, $896.00. The difference, $296.00, is added to the previous capital account balance. The current capital, $10,296.00, is recorded as the amount of Ben Furman, Capital on August 31.

A summary of financial statements for a service business organized as a proprietorship is shown in Illustration 9-14.

SUMMARY OF FINANCIAL STATEMENTS FOR A PROPRIETORSHIP

1 An income statement is prepared using information from the Account Title column and Income Statement columns of a work sheet.

2 Component percentages for total expenses and net income are calculated as shown below.

Total Expenses ÷ Total Sales = Total Expenses Component Percentage

Net Income ÷ Total Sales = Net Income Component Percentage

3 A balance sheet is prepared using information obtained from the work sheet's Account Title column and Balance Sheet columns. Current capital to be reported on the balance sheet is calculated as shown below:

$$\text{Capital Account Balance} + \text{Net Income} - \text{Drawing Account Balance} = \text{Current Capital}$$

1 An income statement is prepared using information from the Account Title column and Income Statement columns of a work sheet.

2 Component percentages for total expenses and net income are calculated as shown below.

Total Expenses ÷ Total Sales = Total Expenses Component Percentage
Net Income ÷ Total Sales = Net Income Component Percentage

3 A balance sheet is prepared using information obtained from the work sheet's Account Title column and Balance Sheet columns. Current capital to be reported on the balance sheet is calculated as shown below.

$$\text{Capital Account Balance} + \text{Net Income} - \text{Drawing Account Balance} = \text{Current Capital}$$

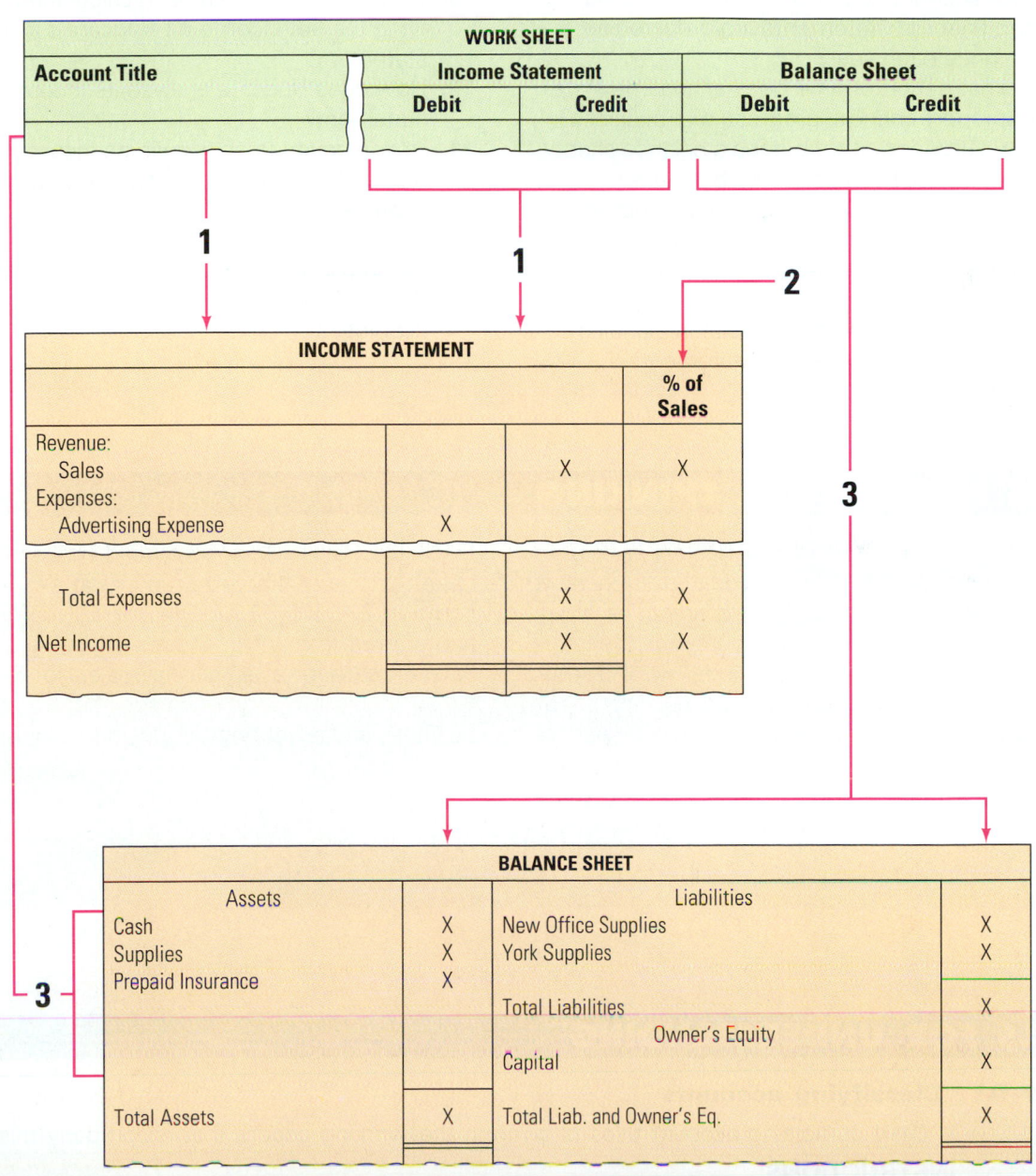

What is the meaning of the following?

1. component percentage

1. Which accounting concept is being applied when all the information about a business' financial condition is reported on financial statements?
2. Which accounting concept is being applied when financial statements are prepared at least once each year?
3. For what period of time does an income statement report financial progress of a business?
4. For what period of time does a balance sheet report financial condition of a business?
5. Which accounting concept is being applied when revenue earned and the expenses incurred to earn that revenue are recorded in the same fiscal period?
6. What does Rugcare do to assist in planning the preparation of financial statements?
7. Where does Rugcare obtain the information for preparing an income statement?
8. What information is found in an income statement heading?
9. What are the two steps in calculating and verifying the net income on Rugcare's income statement?
10. How does Rugcare analyze its income statement?
11. How is revenue shown on an income statement when a business has two sources of revenue?
12. Where does Rugcare obtain the information for preparing a balance sheet?
13. What information is found in a balance sheet heading?

CASE 1 James Worth and Mary Derner each own small businesses. Mr. Worth prepares an income statement and balance sheet at the end of each day for his business. He claims that he needs the information to make business decisions. Mrs. Derner prepares an income statement and balance sheet for her business only at the end of each one-year fiscal period. She claims that she needs the information only at the end of the year when preparing tax reports. Which owner is using the better procedure? Explain your answer.

CASE 2 Ralph Macy owns and manages a business that has produced an average annual net income of $21,600.00 for five years. George Wayne has offered to buy Mr. Macy's business and retain him as manager at a monthly salary of $2,000.00. What should Mr. Macy consider before selling his business and accepting the position as manager?

DRILL 9-D1 Classifying accounts

A chart containing account titles is given in the working papers that accompany this textbook.

INSTRUCTIONS:

1. For each account title on the chart, place a check mark in either Column 2, 3, 4, 5, or 6 to indicate the classification of each account.

2. Place a check mark in either Column 7 or 8 to indicate on which financial statement each account will be reported.

DRILL 9-D2 Calculating net income or net loss and owner's current capital

MATHEMATICS

A chart containing information for 8 companies is given in the working papers that accompany this textbook.

INSTRUCTIONS:

Complete the following for each company given in the chart.

1. Use the information in Columns 5 and 6. Calculate the amount of net income or net loss for each company. For example, Company A: Revenue, $2,300, − expenses, $900, = net income, $1,400.
2. Calculate the amount of current capital for each company using the net income or net loss from Instruction 1 and the information in Columns 3 and 4. For example, Company A: Capital account balance, $2,320, + net income, $1,400, − drawing, $120, = current capital, $3,600.
3. Use the accounting equation to check the accuracy of your answers in Instructions 1 and 2. For example, Company A: Assets, $5,600, = liabilities, $2,000, + owner's equity, $3,600. If the equation is not in balance, recalculate and correct your answers to Instructions 1 and 2.

APPLICATION PROBLEMS   EPT(c,d,e)

PROBLEM 9-1 Preparing an income statement

MATHEMATICS

The following information is obtained from the work sheet of LawnMow for the month ended June 30 of the current year.

	ACCOUNT TITLE	5 INCOME STATEMENT DEBIT	6 INCOME STATEMENT CREDIT	7 BALANCE SHEET DEBIT	8 BALANCE SHEET CREDIT	
10	Sales		3 1 0 0 00			10
11	Advertising Expense	3 0 00				11
12	Insurance Expense	1 4 0 00				12
13	Miscellaneous Expense	6 5 00				13
14	Rent Expense	8 0 0 00				14
15	Supplies Expense	4 0 0 00				15
16	Utilities Expense	7 5 00				16
17		1 5 1 0 00	3 1 0 0 00			17
18	Net Income	1 5 9 0 00				18
19		3 1 0 0 00	3 1 0 0 00			19
20						20

INSTRUCTIONS:

Prepare an income statement for the month ended June 30 of the current year. Calculate and record the component percentages for total expenses and net income. Round percentage calculations to the nearest 0.1%.

PROBLEM 9-2 Preparing a balance sheet

The information on page 208 is obtained from the work sheet of LawnMow for the month ended June 30 of the current year.

INSTRUCTIONS:

Prepare a balance sheet for June 30 of the current year.

ACCOUNT TITLE	BALANCE SHEET 7 DEBIT	8 CREDIT	
1	Cash	7 5 3 0 00		1
2	Petty Cash	2 0 0 00		2
3	Supplies	6 8 6 0 00		3
4	Prepaid Insurance	2 5 0 0 00		4
5	Barker Supplies		4 4 0 0 00	5
6	Richmond Office Supplies		1 3 0 0 00	6
7	Clem Sutter, Capital		11 0 0 0 00	7
8	Clem Sutter, Drawing	1 2 0 0 00		8
9	Income Summary			9
16				16
17		18 2 9 0 00	16 7 0 0 00	17
18	Net Income		1 5 9 0 00	18
19		18 2 9 0 00	18 2 9 0 00	19

ENRICHMENT PROBLEMS

EPT(c,d,e)

MASTERY PROBLEM 9-M Preparing financial statements

SPREADSHEET

The following information is obtained from the work sheet of Ace Delivery Service for the month ended July 31 of the current year.

	ACCOUNT TITLE	INCOME STATEMENT 5 DEBIT	6 CREDIT	BALANCE SHEET 7 DEBIT	8 CREDIT	
1	Cash			7 5 0 0 00		1
2	Petty Cash			2 0 0 00		2
3	Supplies			7 8 0 0 00		3
4	Prepaid Insurance			2 6 0 0 00		4
5	Down Supplies				4 7 0 0 00	5
6	Melton Office Supplies				1 2 0 0 00	6
7	Clark Smith, Capital				12 0 0 0 00	7
8	Clark Smith, Drawing			1 4 0 0 00		8
9	Income Summary					9
10	Sales		5 6 7 0 00			10
11	Advertising Expense	3 9 0 00				11
12	Insurance Expense	1 9 0 00				12
13	Miscellaneous Expense	1 5 0 00				13
14	Rent Expense	3 0 0 0 00				14
15	Supplies Expense	2 0 0 00				15
16	Utilities Expense	1 4 0 00				16
17		4 0 7 0 00	5 6 7 0 00	19 5 0 0 00	17 9 0 0 00	17
18	Net Income	1 6 0 0 00			1 6 0 0 00	18
19		5 6 7 0 00	5 6 7 0 00	19 5 0 0 00	19 5 0 0 00	19

INSTRUCTIONS:

1. Prepare an income statement for the month ended July 31 of the current year. Calculate and record the component percentages for total expenses and net income. Round percentage calculations to the nearest 0.1%.

2. Prepare a balance sheet for July 31 of the current year.

CHALLENGE PROBLEM 9-C Preparing financial statements with two sources of revenue and a net loss

SPREADSHEET

The following information is obtained from the work sheet of Mercer Lawn Service for the month ended August 31 of the current year.

		5	6	7	8	
	ACCOUNT TITLE	INCOME STATEMENT		BALANCE SHEET		
		DEBIT	CREDIT	DEBIT	CREDIT	
1	Cash			6 0 2 0 00		1
2	Petty Cash			2 0 0 00		2
3	Supplies			6 0 0 00		3
4	Prepaid Insurance			2 5 0 00		4
5	Choice Supplies				3 0 0 00	5
6	Poll Office Supplies				2 0 0 00	6
7	Lydia Roland, Capital				13 0 0 0 00	7
8	Lydia Roland, Drawing			1 3 0 0 00		8
9	Income Summary					9
10	Sales—Lawn Care		4 7 0 0 00			10
11	Sales—Shrub Care		2 6 0 0 00			11
12	Advertising Expense	3 9 0 00				12
13	Insurance Expense	3 0 0 00				13
14	Miscellaneous Expense	4 5 0 00				14
15	Rent Expense	3 0 0 0 00				15
16	Supplies Expense	3 1 0 0 00				16
17	Utilities Expense	2 4 0 00				17
18		7 4 8 0 00	7 3 0 0 00	16 0 2 0 00	16 2 0 0 00	18
19	Net Loss		1 8 0 00	1 8 0 00		19
20		7 4 8 0 00	7 4 8 0 00	16 2 0 0 00	16 2 0 0 00	20

INSTRUCTIONS:

1. Prepare an income statement for the month ended August 31 of the current year. Calculate and record the component percentages for total expenses and net loss. Place the percentage for net loss in parentheses to show that it is for a net loss. Round percentage calculations to the nearest 0.1%.
2. Prepare a balance sheet for August 31 of the current year.

10

Recording Adjusting and Closing Entries for a Service Business

ENABLING PERFORMANCE TASKS

After studying Chapter 10, you will be able to:

a Define accounting terms related to adjusting and closing entries for a service business organized as a proprietorship.

b Identify accounting concepts and practices related to adjusting and closing entries for a service business organized as a proprietorship.

c Record adjusting entries for a service business organized as a proprietorship.

d Record closing entries for a service business organized as a proprietorship.

e Prepare a post-closing trial balance for a service business organized as a proprietorship.

TERMS PREVIEW

adjusting entries • permanent accounts • temporary accounts • closing entries • post-closing trial balance • accounting cycle

Rugcare prepares a work sheet at the end of each fiscal period to summarize the general ledger information needed to prepare financial statements. *(CONCEPT: Accounting Period Cycle)* Financial statements are prepared from information on the work sheet. *(CONCEPT: Adequate Disclosure)*

RECORDING ADJUSTING ENTRIES

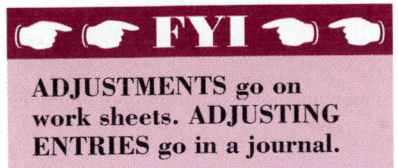

ADJUSTMENTS go on work sheets. ADJUSTING ENTRIES go in a journal.

Rugcare's adjustments are analyzed and planned on a work sheet. However, these adjustments must be journalized so that they can be posted to the general ledger accounts. Journal entries recorded to update general ledger accounts at the end of a fiscal period are called **adjusting entries.**

Adjusting entries are recorded on the next journal page following the page on which the last daily transactions for the month are recorded. The adjusting entries are entered in the General Debit and General Credit columns of a journal.

Rugcare records two adjusting entries. (1) An adjusting entry to bring the supplies account up to date. (2) An adjusting entry to bring the prepaid insurance account up to date.

Adjusting Entry for Supplies

The information needed to journalize the adjusting entry for supplies is obtained from lines 3 and 16 of Rugcare's work sheet. A partial work sheet and the adjusting entry for supplies are shown in Illustration 10-1.

ILLUSTRATION 10-1   Adjusting entry for supplies recorded in a journal

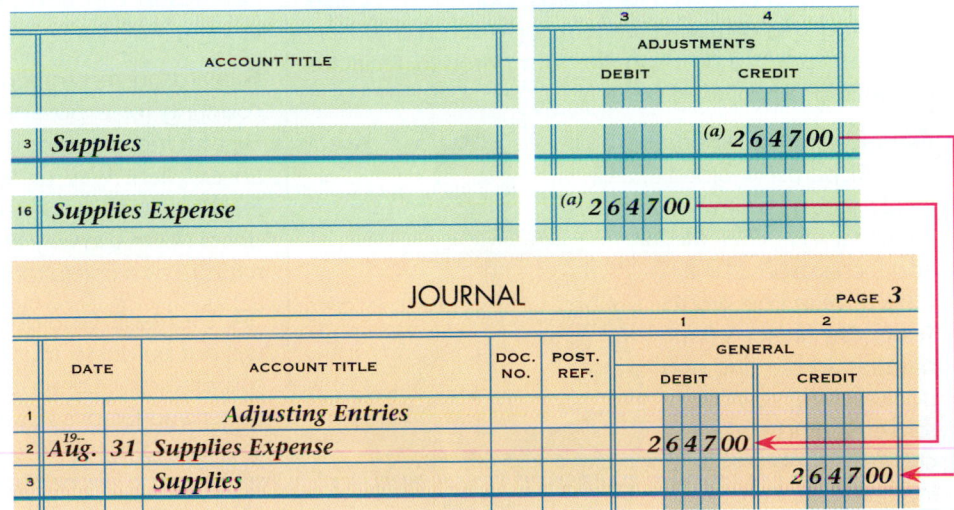

The heading, *Adjusting Entries*, is written in the middle of the Account Title column of the journal. Because no source document is prepared for adjusting entries, the entries are identified with a

heading in the journal. This heading explains all of the adjusting entries that follow. Therefore, the heading is written only once for all adjusting entries.

The date, *19--, Aug. 31*, is written in the Date column. The title of the account debited, *Supplies Expense*, is written in the Account Title column. The debit amount, *$2,647.00*, is recorded in the General Debit column on the same line as the account title. The title of the account credited, *Supplies*, is written on the next line. The credit amount, *$2,647.00*, is recorded in the General Credit column on the same line as the account title.

The effect of posting the adjusting entry for supplies to the general ledger accounts is shown in the T accounts.

Supplies Expense has an up-to-date balance of $2,647.00, which is the value of the supplies used during the fiscal period. Supplies has a new balance of $2,284.00, which is the value of the supplies on hand at the end of the fiscal period.

Supplies Expense			
Adj. (a)	2,647.00		

Supplies			
Bal.	4,931.00	Adj. (a)	2,647.00
(New Bal.	*2,284.00)*		

Adjusting Entry for Prepaid Insurance

The information needed to journalize the adjusting entry for prepaid insurance is obtained from lines 4 and 12 of Rugcare's work sheet. A partial work sheet and the adjusting entry for prepaid insurance are shown in Illustration 10-2.

ILLUSTRATION 10-2 Adjusting entry for prepaid insurance recorded in a journal

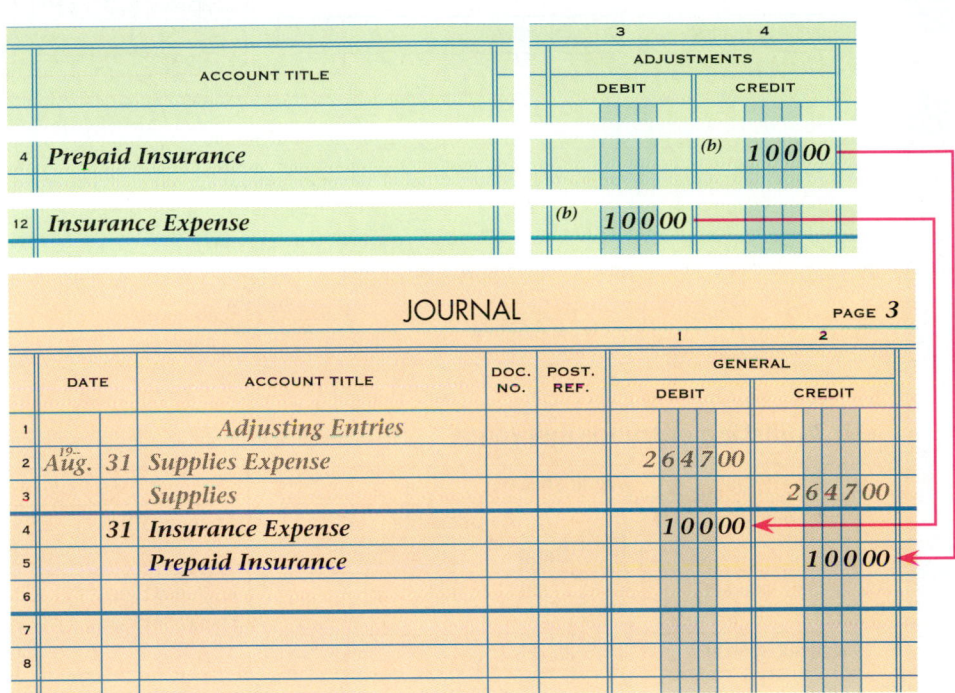

The date, *31*, is written in the Date column. The title of the account debited, *Insurance Expense*, is written in the Account Title column. The debit amount, *$100.00*, is recorded in the General Debit column on the same line as the account title. The title of the account credited, *Prepaid Insurance*, is written on the next line in the Account Title column. The credit amount, *$100.00*, is recorded in the General Credit column on the same line as the account title.

The effect of posting the adjusting entry for insurance to the general ledger accounts is shown in the T accounts.

Insurance Expense has an up-to-date balance of $100.00, which is the value of insurance premiums used during the fiscal period. Prepaid Insurance has a new balance of $1,100.00, which is the value of insurance premiums that remain unused at the end of the fiscal period. (*CONCEPT: Matching Expenses with Revenue*)

The two adjusting entries for a service business organized as a proprietorship are summarized in Illustration 10-3.

Insurance Expense	
Adj. (b) 100.00	

Prepaid Insurance	
Bal. 1,200.00	Adj. (b) 100.00
(New Bal. 1,100.00)	

Summary of adjusting entries for a service business organized as a proprietorship

1. Adjusting entry for supplies

WORK SHEET				JOURNAL		
Account Title		**Adjustments**		**Account Title**		**General**
		Debit	**Credit**		**Debit**	**Credit**
Supplies			(a) X	Supplies Expense	X	
				Supplies		X
Supplies Expense		(a) X				

```
              Supplies Expense
         Adjusting  |

                Supplies
        Balance  |  Adjusting
```

2. Adjusting entry for insurance

WORK SHEET				JOURNAL		
Account Title		**Adjustments**		**Account Title**		**General**
		Debit	**Credit**		**Debit**	**Credit**
Prepaid Insurance			(b) X	Insurance Expense	X	
				Prepaid Insurance		X
Insurance Expense		(b) X				

```
              Insurance Expense
         Adjusting  |

              Prepaid Insurance
        Balance  |  Adjusting
```

RECORDING CLOSING ENTRIES

Permanent accounts are sometimes referred to as real accounts.

Accounts used to accumulate information from one fiscal period to the next are called **permanent accounts**. Permanent accounts are also referred to as real accounts. Permanent accounts include the asset and liability accounts and the owner's capital account. The ending account balances of permanent accounts for one fiscal period are the beginning account balances for the next fiscal period.

Accounts used to accumulate information until it is transferred to the owner's capital account are called **temporary accounts**. Temporary accounts are also referred to as nominal accounts. Temporary accounts include the revenue, expense, and owner's drawing accounts plus the income summary account. Temporary accounts show changes in the owner's capital for a single fiscal period. Therefore, at the end of a fiscal period, the balances of temporary accounts are summarized and transferred to the owner's capital account. The temporary accounts begin a new fiscal period with zero balances.

Need for Closing Temporary Accounts

Journal entries used to prepare temporary accounts for a new fiscal period are called **closing entries**. The temporary account balances must be reduced to zero at the end of each fiscal period. This procedure prepares the temporary accounts for recording information about the next fiscal period. Otherwise, the amounts for the next fiscal period would be added to amounts for previous fiscal periods. (CONCEPT: Matching Expenses with Revenue) The net income for the next fiscal period would be difficult to calculate because amounts from several fiscal periods remain in the accounts. Therefore, the temporary accounts must start each new fiscal period with zero balances.

To close a temporary account, an amount equal to its balance is recorded in the account on the side opposite to its balance. For example, if an account has a credit balance of $4,291.00, a debit of $4,291.00 is recorded to close the account.

Need for the Income Summary Account

Whenever a temporary account is closed, the closing entry must have equal debits and credits. If an account is debited for $3,000.00 to close the account, some other account must be credited for the same amount. A temporary account titled *Income Summary* is used to summarize the closing entries for the revenue and expense accounts.

The income summary account is unique because it does not have a normal balance side. The balance of this account is determined by the amounts posted to the account at the end of a fiscal period. When revenue is greater than total expenses, resulting in a net income, the income summary account has a credit balance, as shown in the T account.

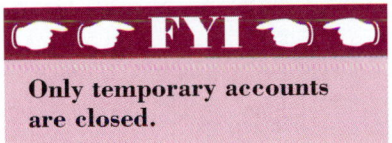

FYI

Only temporary accounts are closed.

Income Summary	
Debit side	Credit side
Total expenses	Revenue (greater than expenses)
	(Credit balance is the net income.)

When total expenses are greater than revenue, resulting in a net loss, the income summary account has a debit balance, as shown in the T account on the following page.

	Income Summary	
Debit side		**Credit side**
Total expenses (greater than revenue)		Revenue
(Debit balance is the net loss.)		

Thus, whether the balance of the income summary account is a debit or a credit depends upon whether the business earns a net income or incurs a net loss. Because Income Summary is a temporary account, the account is also closed at the end of a fiscal period when the net income or net loss is recorded.

Rugcare records four closing entries. (1) An entry to close income statement accounts with credit balances. (2) An entry to close income statement accounts with debit balances. (3) An entry to record net income or net loss and close Income Summary. (4) An entry to close the owner's drawing account.

Information needed to record the four closing entries is found in the Income Statement and Balance Sheet columns of the work sheet.

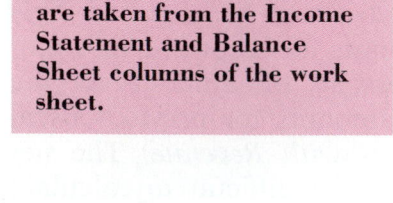

FYI

Amounts for closing entries are taken from the Income Statement and Balance Sheet columns of the work sheet.

Closing Entry for an Income Statement Account with a Credit Balance

Rugcare has one income statement account with a credit balance, Sales, as shown on the partial work sheet in Illustration 10-4. This credit balance must be reduced to zero to prepare the account for the next fiscal period. To reduce the balance to zero, Sales is debited for the amount of the balance. Because debits must equal credits for each journal entry, some other account must be credited. The account used for the credit part of this closing entry is Income Summary. The closing entry for Sales is journalized as shown in Illustration 10-4.

ILLUSTRATION 10-4   Closing entry for an income statement account with a credit balance

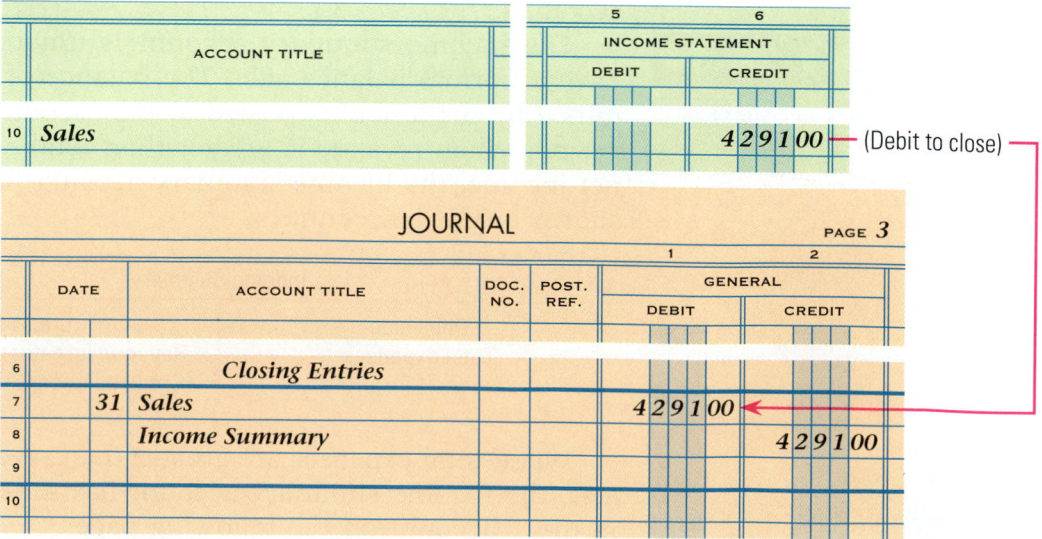

No source document is used for closing entries. Therefore, the heading, *Closing Entries*, is written in the Account Title column of the journal. For Rugcare, this heading is placed in the journal on the first blank line after the last adjusting entry.

The date, *31*, is written on the next line in the Date column. The title of the account debited, *Sales*, is written in the Account Title column. The debit amount, *$4,291.00*, is recorded in the General Debit column on the same line as the account title. The title of the account credited, *Income Summary*, is written in the Account Title column on the next journal line. The credit amount, *$4,291.00*, is recorded in the General Credit amount column on the same line as the account title.

The effect of this closing entry on the general ledger accounts is shown in the T accounts.

The balance of **Sales** is now zero, and the account is ready for the next fiscal period. The credit balance of **Sales** is transferred to Income Summary.

	Sales		
Closing	4,291.00	Bal. *(New Bal. zero)*	4,291.00

	Income Summary	
	Closing (revenue)	4,291.00

Closing Entry for Income Statement Accounts with Debit Balances

Rugcare has several income statement accounts with debit balances. The seven expense accounts have normal debit balances at the end of a fiscal period, as shown on the partial work sheet in Illustration 10-5, on page 218. The balances of the expense accounts must be reduced to zero to prepare the accounts for the next fiscal period. Each expense account is credited for an amount equal to its balance, and Income Summary is debited for the total of all the expense account balances. The closing entry for the expense accounts is journalized as shown in Illustration 10-5.

The heading for closing entries is written only once. Therefore, the closing entry for expenses starts on the next blank line in the journal.

The date, *31*, is written in the Date column. The title of the account debited, *Income Summary*, is written in the Account Title column. The amount debited to Income Summary is not entered in the amount column until all expenses have been journalized and the total amount calculated. The account title and balance of each expense account is recorded in the Account Title and General Credit columns. After all expense accounts and their balances have been written in the journal, the credit amounts for this entry are added. The total of all expenses, *$3,395.00*, is recorded in the General Debit column on the same line as the account title, Income Summary.

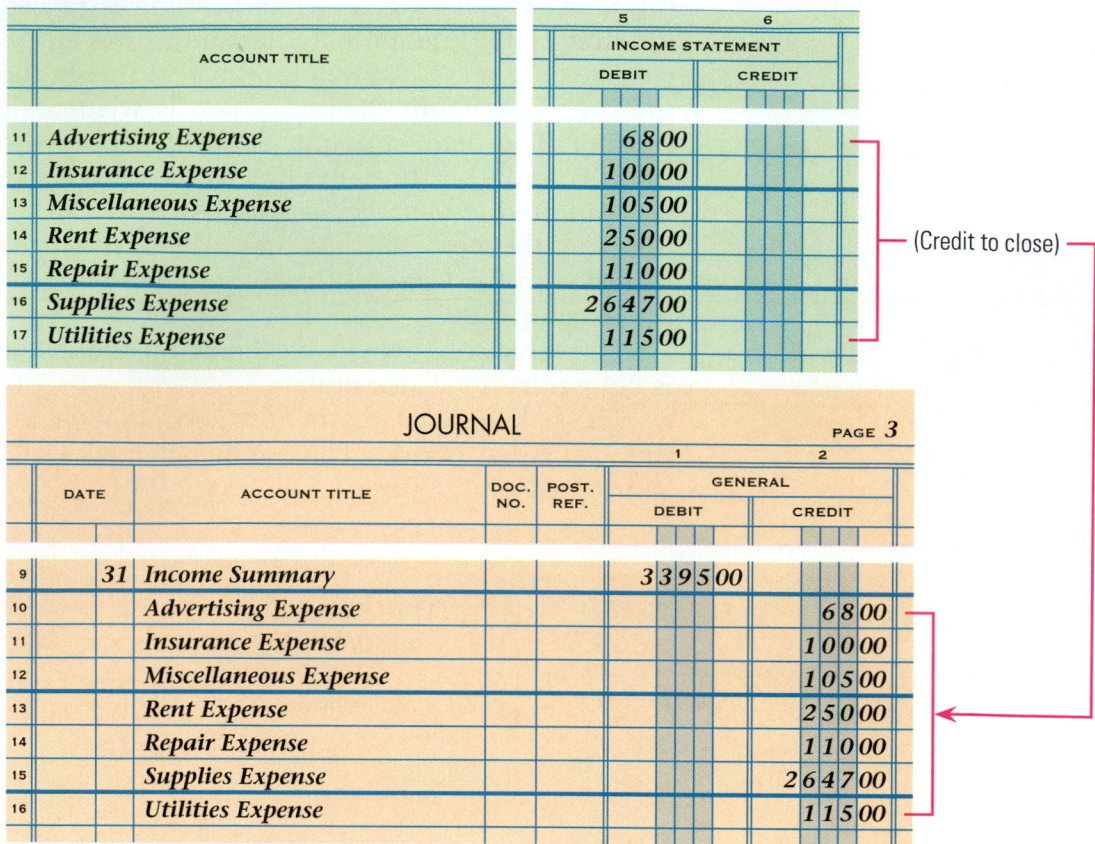

	ACCOUNT TITLE	INCOME STATEMENT	
		5 DEBIT	**6** CREDIT
11	*Advertising Expense*	6 8 00	
12	*Insurance Expense*	1 0 0 00	
13	*Miscellaneous Expense*	1 0 5 00	
14	*Rent Expense*	2 5 0 00	
15	*Repair Expense*	1 1 0 00	
16	*Supplies Expense*	2 6 4 7 00	
17	*Utilities Expense*	1 1 5 00	

(Credit to close)

JOURNAL   PAGE 3

	DATE	ACCOUNT TITLE	DOC. NO.	POST. REF.	**1** GENERAL DEBIT	**2** GENERAL CREDIT
9	31	*Income Summary*			3 3 9 5 00	
10		*Advertising Expense*				6 8 00
11		*Insurance Expense*				1 0 0 00
12		*Miscellaneous Expense*				1 0 5 00
13		*Rent Expense*				2 5 0 00
14		*Repair Expense*				1 1 0 00
15		*Supplies Expense*				2 6 4 7 00
16		*Utilities Expense*				1 1 5 00

The effect of the closing entry for Rugcare's expense accounts is shown in the T accounts.

Income Summary			
Closing (expenses)	3,395.00	Closing (revenue)	4,291.00
		(New Bal.	*896.00)*

Advertising Expense					Repair Expense			
Bal.	68.00	Closing	68.00		Bal.	110.00	Closing	110.00
(New Bal. zero)					*(New Bal. zero)*			

Insurance Expense					Supplies Expense			
Bal.	100.00	Closing	100.00		Bal.	2,647.00	Closing	2,647.00
(New Bal. zero)					*(New Bal. zero)*			

Miscellaneous Expense					Utilities Expense			
Bal.	105.00	Closing	105.00		Bal.	115.00	Closing	115.00
(New Bal. zero)					*(New Bal. zero)*			

Rent Expense			
Bal.	250.00	Closing	250.00
(New Bal. zero)			

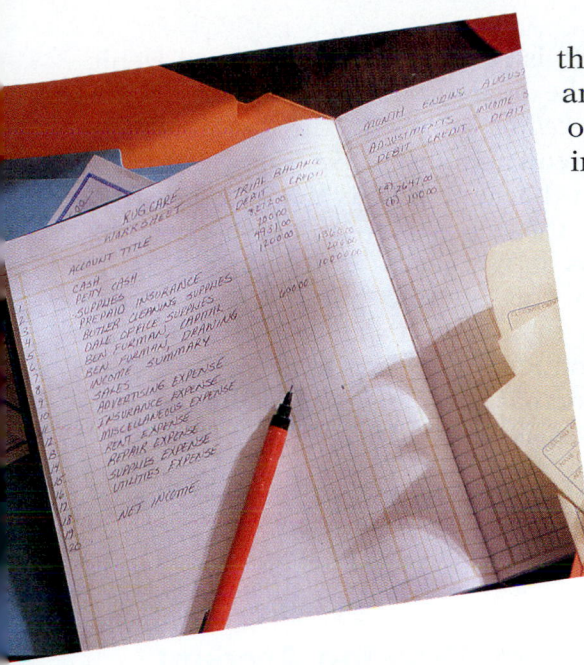

The balance of each expense account is returned to zero, and the accounts are ready for the next fiscal period. The debit balances of the expense accounts are recorded in Income Summary as one debit amount. The balance of Income Summary is the net income for the fiscal period, $896.00.

Closing Entry to Record Net Income or Loss and Close the Income Summary Account

Rugcare's net income is on the partial work sheet shown in Illustration 10-6. The amount of net income increases the owner's capital and, therefore, must be credited to the owner's capital account. The balance of the temporary account, Income Summary, must be reduced to zero to prepare the account for the next fiscal period. The closing entry to record net income and close the income summary account is journalized as shown in Illustration 10-6.

ILLUSTRATION 10-6 Closing entry to record net income and close the income summary account

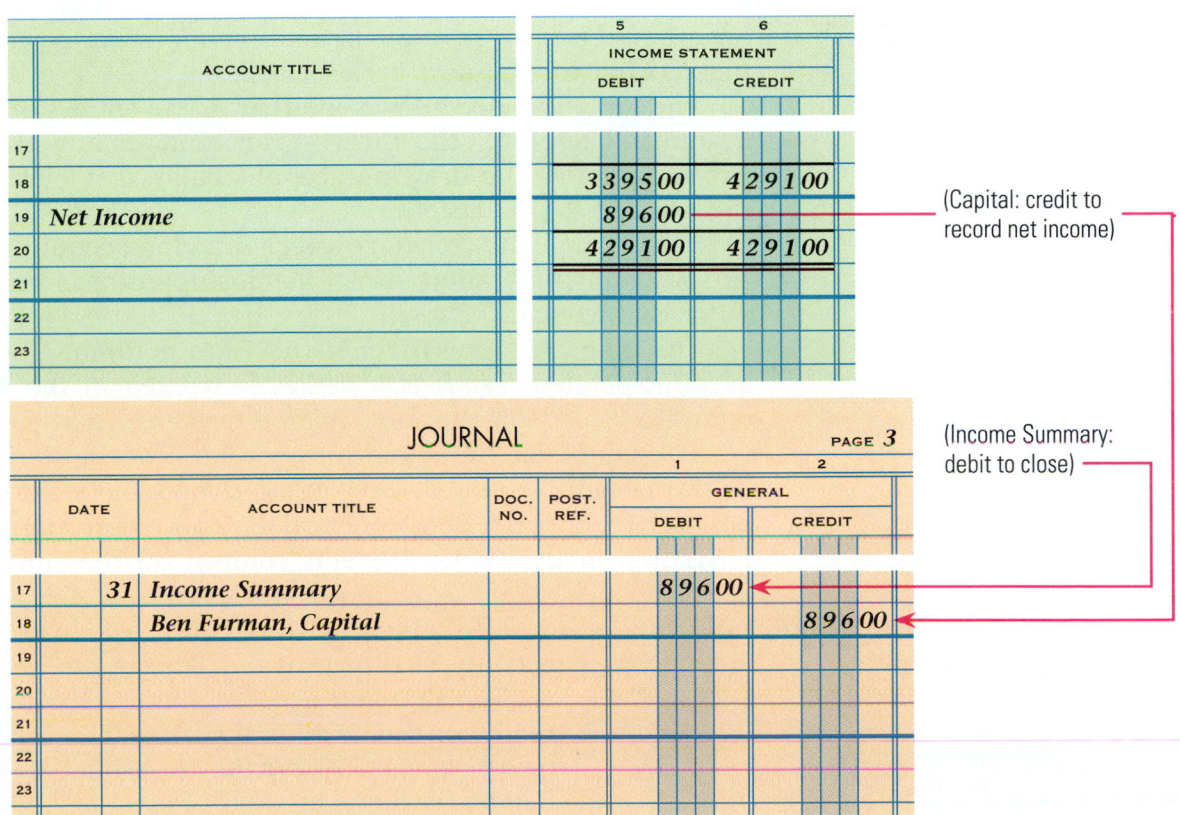

The date, *31*, is written in the Date column. The title of the account debited, *Income Summary*, is written in the Account Title column. The debit amount, *$896.00*, is recorded in the General Debit column on the same line as the account title. The title of the account credited, *Ben Furman, Capital*, is written in the Account Title column on the next line. The credit amount, *$896.00*, is recorded in the General Credit column on the same line as the account title.

The effect of this closing entry on the general ledger accounts is shown in the T accounts.

The debit to the income summary account, $896.00, reduces the account balance to zero and prepares the account for the next fiscal period. The credit, $896.00, increases the balance of the owner's capital account, Ben Furman, Capital.

If the business incurs a net loss, the closing entry is a debit to the owner's capital account and a credit to the income summary account.

Income Summary		
Closing (expenses) 3,395.00	Closing (revenue) 4,291.00	
Closing 896.00	*(New Bal. zero)*	

Ben Furman, Capital	
	Bal. 10,000.00
	Closing (net income) 896.00
	(New Bal. 10,896.00)

Closing Entry for the Owner's Drawing Account

Withdrawals are assets that the owner takes out of a business and which decrease the amount of the owner's equity. The drawing account is a temporary account that accumulates information separately for each fiscal period. Therefore, the drawing account balance is reduced to zero at the end of one fiscal period to prepare the account for the next fiscal period.

The drawing account is neither a revenue nor an expense account. Therefore, the drawing account is not closed through Income Summary. The drawing account balance is closed directly to the owner's capital account.

The closing entry for the owner's drawing account is journalized as shown in Illustration 10-7. The closing entry is on lines 19 and 20 of the journal.

The date, *31*, is written in the Date column. The title of the account debited, *Ben Furman, Capital*, is written in the Account Title column. The debit amount, *$600.00*, is recorded in the General Debit column on the same line with the account title. The title of the account credited, *Ben Furman, Drawing*, is written in the Account Title column on the next line. The credit amount, *$600.00*, is written in the General Credit column on the same line as the account title.

The effect of the entry to close the drawing account is shown in the T accounts.

The drawing account has a zero balance and is ready for the next fiscal period. The capital account's new balance, $10,296.00, is verified by checking the balance with the amount of capital shown on the balance sheet prepared at the end of the fiscal period. The capital account balance shown on Rugcare's balance sheet in Chapter 9, Illustration 9-12, is $10,296.00. The two amounts are the same, and the capital account balance is verified.

Ben Furman, Capital	
Closing 600.00	Bal. 10,000.00
	Net Income 896.00
	(New Bal. 10,296.00)

Ben Furman, Drawing	
Bal. 600.00	Closing 600.00
(New Bal. zero)	

ILLUSTRATION 10-7   Closing entry for the drawing account recorded in a journal

	ACCOUNT TITLE		BALANCE SHEET	
			7 DEBIT	**8** CREDIT
7	*Ben Furman, Capital*			1 0 0 0 00	7
8	*Ben Furman, Drawing*		6 0 0 00		8 — (Credit to close)
9					9
10					10
11					11

JOURNAL   PAGE *3*

	DATE	ACCOUNT TITLE	DOC. NO.	POST. REF.	DEBIT	CREDIT	
6		*Closing Entries*					6
7	31	Sales			4 2 9 1 00		7
8		Income Summary				4 2 9 1 00	8
9	31	Income Summary			3 3 9 5 00		9
10		Advertising Expense				6 8 00	10
11		Insurance Expense				1 0 0 00	11
12		Miscellaneous Expense				1 0 5 00	12
13		Rent Expense				2 5 0 00	13
14		Repair Expense				1 1 0 00	14
15		Supplies Expense				2 6 4 7 00	15
16		Utilities Expense				1 1 5 00	16
17	31	Income Summary			8 9 6 00		17
18		Ben Furman, Capital				8 9 6 00	18
19	31	Ben Furman, Capital			6 0 0 00		19
20		Ben Furman, Drawing				6 0 0 00	20
21							21
22							22
23							23

Closing entries are journalized and posted to prepare temporary accounts for the next fiscal period. The income summary account is used to summarize all revenue and expense accounts before recording net income or net loss in the owner's capital account. A summary of closing entries is shown in Illustration 10-8.

To complete a fiscal period, Rugcare records four journal entries to close temporary accounts.

1 Close income statement accounts with credit balances.

2 Close income statement accounts with debit balances.

3 Record the net income or net loss in the owner's capital account and close Income Summary.

4 Close the owner's drawing account.

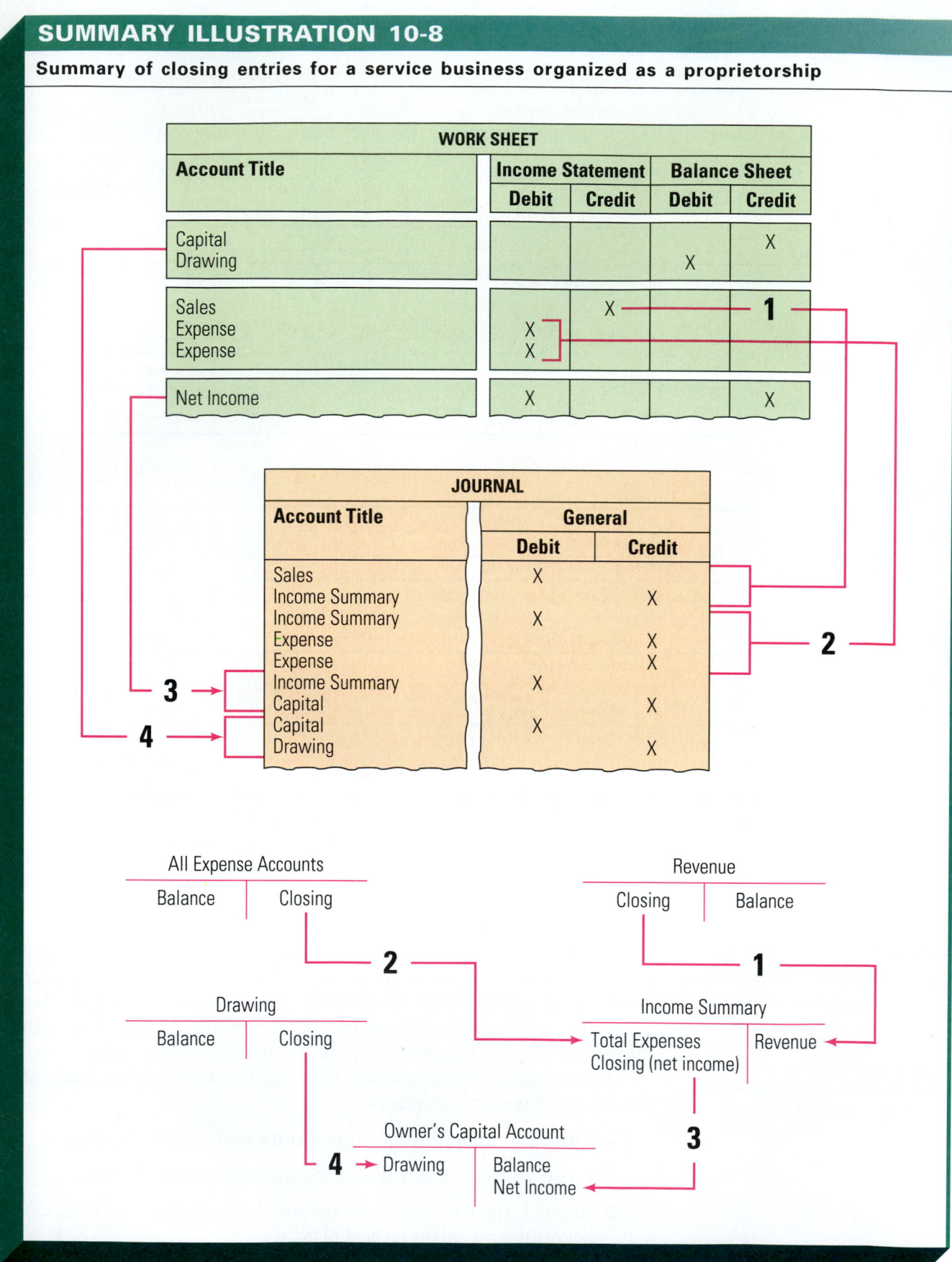

GENERAL LEDGER AFTER ADJUSTING AND CLOSING ENTRIES ARE POSTED

Rugcare's general ledger after the adjusting and closing entries are posted is shown in Illustration 10-9. When an account has a zero balance, lines are drawn in both the Balance Debit and Balance Credit columns. The lines assure a reader that a balance has not been omitted.

Audit Your Understanding

1. What do the ending balances of permanent accounts for one fiscal period represent at the beginning of the next fiscal period?

2. What do the balances of temporary accounts show?

3. List the four closing entries.

ILLUSTRATION 10-9   General ledger accounts after adjusting and closing entries are posted

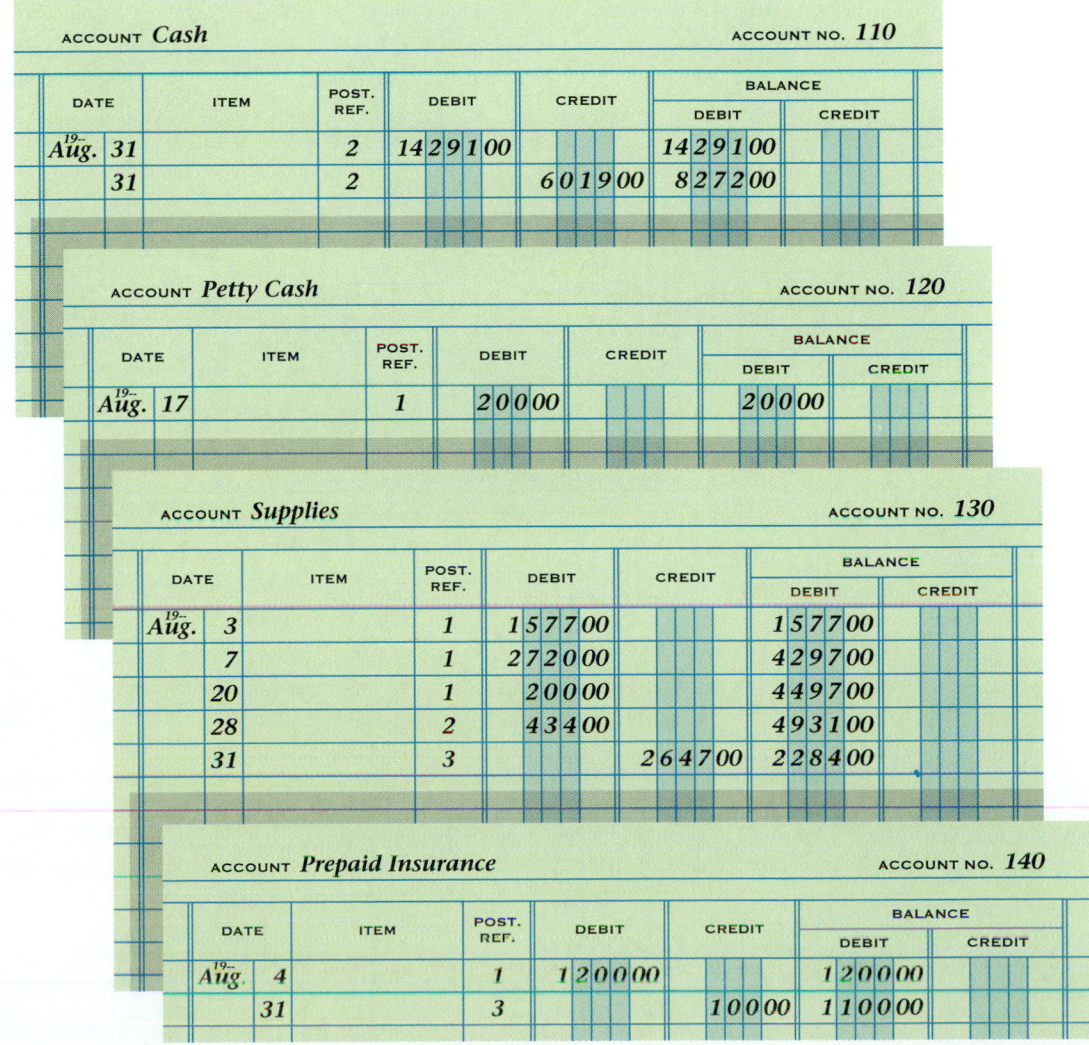

ACCOUNT **Cash**   ACCOUNT NO. **110**

DATE	ITEM	POST. REF.	DEBIT	CREDIT	BALANCE DEBIT	BALANCE CREDIT
Aug. 31		2	14 29 1 00		14 29 1 00	
31		2		6 01 9 00	8 27 2 00	

ACCOUNT **Petty Cash**   ACCOUNT NO. **120**

DATE	ITEM	POST. REF.	DEBIT	CREDIT	BALANCE DEBIT	BALANCE CREDIT
Aug. 17		1	20 0 00		20 0 00	

ACCOUNT **Supplies**   ACCOUNT NO. **130**

DATE	ITEM	POST. REF.	DEBIT	CREDIT	BALANCE DEBIT	BALANCE CREDIT
Aug. 3		1	1 57 7 00		1 57 7 00	
7		1	2 72 0 00		4 29 7 00	
20		1	20 0 00		4 49 7 00	
28		2	43 4 00		4 93 1 00	
31		3		2 64 7 00	2 28 4 00	

ACCOUNT **Prepaid Insurance**   ACCOUNT NO. **140**

DATE	ITEM	POST. REF.	DEBIT	CREDIT	BALANCE DEBIT	BALANCE CREDIT
Aug. 4		1	1 20 0 00		1 20 0 00	
31		3		10 0 00	1 10 0 00	

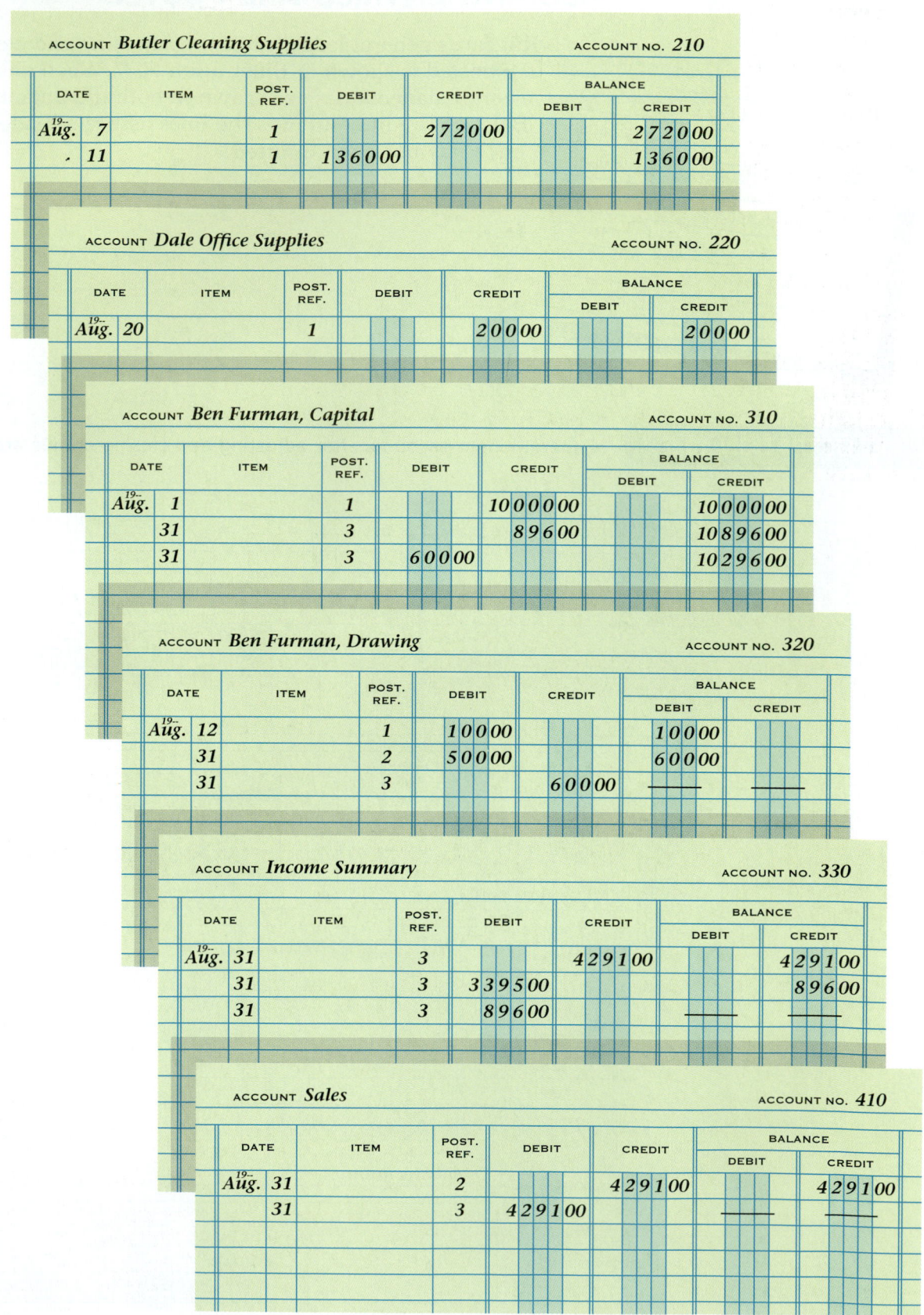

ACCOUNT *Butler Cleaning Supplies*   ACCOUNT NO. *210*

DATE	ITEM	POST. REF.	DEBIT	CREDIT	BALANCE DEBIT	BALANCE CREDIT
Aug. 7		1		2 7 2 0 00		2 7 2 0 00
11		1	1 3 6 0 00			1 3 6 0 00

ACCOUNT *Dale Office Supplies*   ACCOUNT NO. *220*

DATE	ITEM	POST. REF.	DEBIT	CREDIT	BALANCE DEBIT	BALANCE CREDIT
Aug. 20		1		2 0 0 00		2 0 0 00

ACCOUNT *Ben Furman, Capital*   ACCOUNT NO. *310*

DATE	ITEM	POST. REF.	DEBIT	CREDIT	BALANCE DEBIT	BALANCE CREDIT
Aug. 1		1		10 0 0 0 00		10 0 0 0 00
31		3		8 9 6 00		10 8 9 6 00
31		3	6 0 0 00			10 2 9 6 00

ACCOUNT *Ben Furman, Drawing*   ACCOUNT NO. *320*

DATE	ITEM	POST. REF.	DEBIT	CREDIT	BALANCE DEBIT	BALANCE CREDIT
Aug. 12		1	1 0 0 00		1 0 0 00	
31		2	5 0 0 00		6 0 0 00	
31		3		6 0 0 00	—	—

ACCOUNT *Income Summary*   ACCOUNT NO. *330*

DATE	ITEM	POST. REF.	DEBIT	CREDIT	BALANCE DEBIT	BALANCE CREDIT
Aug. 31		3		4 2 9 1 00		4 2 9 1 00
31		3	3 3 9 5 00			8 9 6 00
31		3	8 9 6 00		—	—

ACCOUNT *Sales*   ACCOUNT NO. *410*

DATE	ITEM	POST. REF.	DEBIT	CREDIT	BALANCE DEBIT	BALANCE CREDIT
Aug. 31		2		4 2 9 1 00		4 2 9 1 00
31		3	4 2 9 1 00		—	—

ACCOUNT **Advertising Expense**   ACCOUNT NO. *510*

DATE	ITEM	POST. REF.	DEBIT	CREDIT	BALANCE DEBIT	BALANCE CREDIT
Aug. 14		1	6 8 00		6 8 00	
31		3		6 8 00	—	—

ACCOUNT **Insurance Expense**   ACCOUNT NO. *520*

DATE	ITEM	POST. REF.	DEBIT	CREDIT	BALANCE DEBIT	BALANCE CREDIT
Aug. 31		3	1 0 0 00		1 0 0 00	
31		3		1 0 0 00	—	—

ACCOUNT **Miscellaneous Expense**   ACCOUNT NO. *530*

DATE	ITEM	POST. REF.	DEBIT	CREDIT	BALANCE DEBIT	BALANCE CREDIT
Aug. 13		1	2 5 00		2 5 00	
18		1	7 0 00		9 5 00	
28		2	3 00		9 8 00	
31		2	7 00		1 0 5 00	
31		3		1 0 5 00	—	—

ACCOUNT **Rent Expense**   ACCOUNT NO. *540*

DATE	ITEM	POST. REF.	DEBIT	CREDIT	BALANCE DEBIT	BALANCE CREDIT
Aug. 12		1	2 5 0 00		2 5 0 00	
31		3		2 5 0 00	—	—

ACCOUNT **Repair Expense**   ACCOUNT NO. *550*

DATE	ITEM	POST. REF.	DEBIT	CREDIT	BALANCE DEBIT	BALANCE CREDIT
Aug. 13		1	2 0 00		2 0 00	
20		1	8 5 00		1 0 5 00	
31		2	5 00		1 1 0 00	
31		3		1 1 0 00	—	—

ACCOUNT **Supplies Expense**   ACCOUNT NO. *560*

DATE	ITEM	POST. REF.	DEBIT	CREDIT	BALANCE DEBIT	BALANCE CREDIT
Aug. 31		3	2 6 4 7 00		2 6 4 7 00	
31		3		2 6 4 7 00	—	—

ACCOUNT **Utilities Expense**   ACCOUNT NO. *570*

DATE		ITEM	POST. REF.	DEBIT	CREDIT	BALANCE DEBIT	BALANCE CREDIT
Aug.	12		1	4 5 00		4 5 00	
	27		2	7 0 00		1 1 5 00	
	31		3		1 1 5 00	———	———

POST-CLOSING TRIAL BALANCE

The word "Post" means "after." The *Post*-Closing Trial Balance is prepared *after* closing entries.

After the closing entries are posted, Rugcare verifies that debits equal credits in the general ledger accounts by preparing a trial balance. A trial balance prepared after the closing entries are posted is called a **post-closing trial balance**.

Only general ledger accounts with balances are included on a post-closing trial balance. The permanent accounts (assets, liabilities, and owner's capital) have balances and do appear on a post-closing trial balance. Because the temporary accounts (income summary, revenue, expense, and drawing) are closed and have zero balances, they do not appear on a post-closing trial balance. Rugcare's post-closing trial balance is shown in Illustration 10-10.

ILLUSTRATION 10-10 Post-closing trial balance

	Rugcare	
	Post-Closing Trial Balance	
	August 31, 19--	
ACCOUNT TITLE	DEBIT	CREDIT
Cash	8 2 7 2 00	
Petty Cash	2 0 0 00	
Supplies	2 2 8 4 00	
Prepaid Insurance	1 1 0 0 00	
Butler Cleaning Supplies		1 3 6 0 00
Dale Office Supplies		2 0 0 00
Ben Furman, Capital		10 2 9 6 00
Totals	11 8 5 6 00	11 8 5 6 00

If you have misspelled words in your written communication, people may also mistrust the quality of your accounting skills. The word trial can be a difficult word to spell. Note that it is "ia" not "ai."

Audit Your Understanding

1. Why are lines drawn in both the Balance Debit and Balance Credit columns when an account has a zero balance?

2. Which accounts go on the post-closing trial balance?

3. Why are temporary accounts omitted from a post-closing trial balance?

Rugcare uses eight steps to prepare a post-closing trial balance.

1 Write the heading on three lines.

2 Write the titles of all general ledger accounts with balances in the Account Title column.

3 On the same line with each account title, write each account's balance in either the Debit or Credit column.

4 Rule a single line across both amount columns below the last amount, and add each amount column.

5 Compare the two column totals. The two column totals must be the same. The total of all debits must equal the total of all credits in a general ledger. The totals of both columns on Rugcare's post-closing trial balance are the same, $11,856.00. Rugcare's post-closing trial balance shows that the general ledger account balances are in balance and ready for the new fiscal period. If the two column totals are not the same, the errors must be found and corrected before any more work is completed.

6 Write the word, *Totals*, on the line below the last account title.

7 Write the column totals, *$11,856.00*, below the single line.

8 Rule double lines across both amount columns to show that the totals have been verified as correct.

After adjusting entries are journalized and posted and the post-closing trial balance has been prepared, the accounting cycle is complete and ready to begin a new cycle.

THE ACCOUNTING CYCLE FOR A SERVICE BUSINESS

Chapters 2 through 10 describe Rugcare's accounting activities for a one-month fiscal period. The series of accounting activities included in recording financial information for a fiscal period is called an **accounting cycle**. *(CONCEPT: Accounting Period Cycle)* Rugcare's accounting cycle is summarized in Illustration 10-11.

For the next fiscal period, the cycle begins again at Step 1.

SUMMARY ILLUSTRATION 10-11

Summary of an accounting cycle for a service business

1 Source documents are checked for accuracy, and transactions are analyzed into debit and credit parts.

2 Transactions, from information on source documents, are recorded in a journal.

3 Journal entries are posted to the general ledger.

4 A work sheet, including a trial balance, is prepared from the general ledger.

5 Financial statements are prepared from the work sheet.

6 Adjusting and closing entries are journalized from the work sheet.

7 Adjusting and closing entries are posted to the general ledger.

8 Post-closing trial balance of the general ledger is prepared.

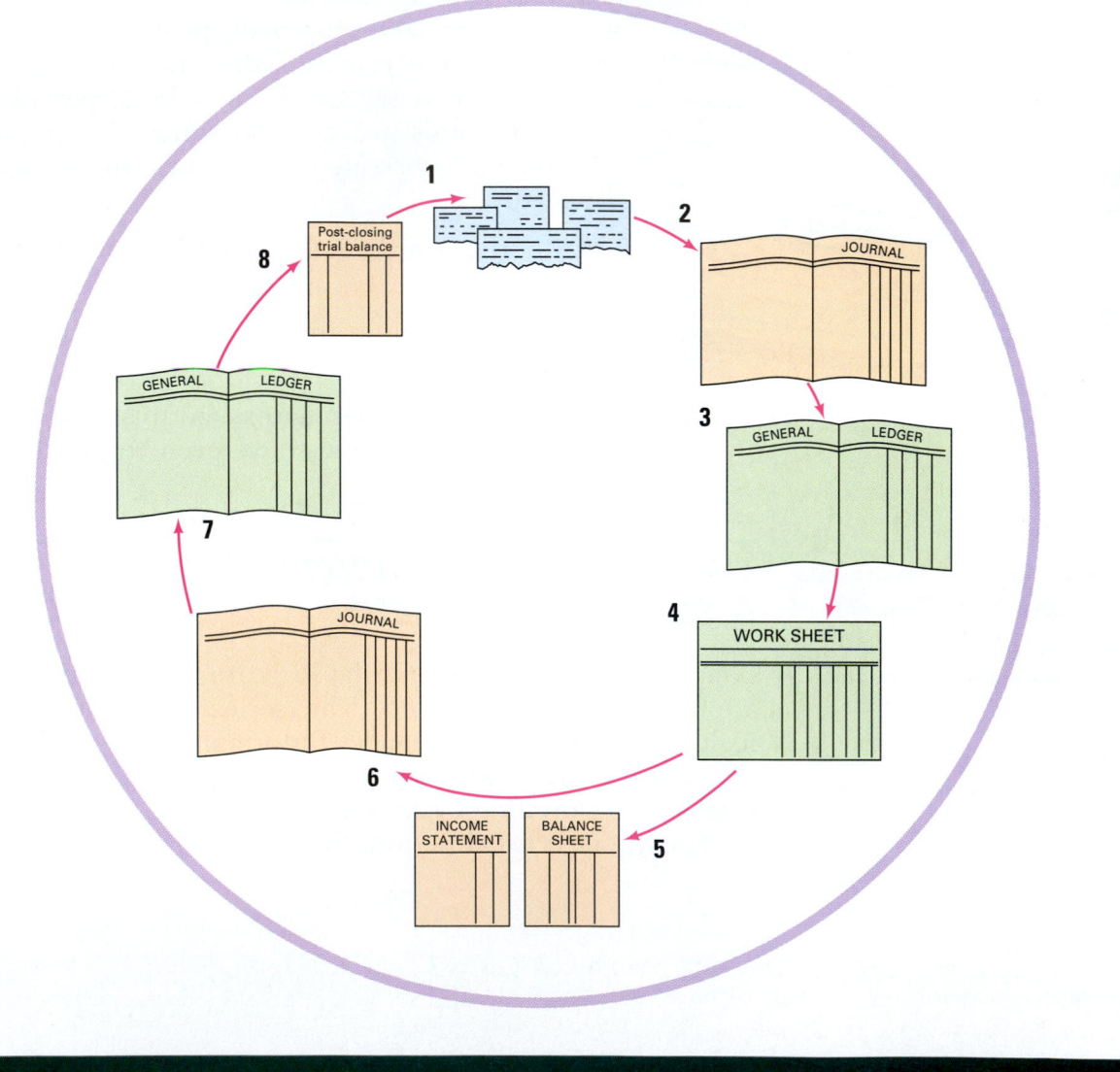

ACCOUNTING TERMS

What is the meaning of each of the following?

1. **adjusting entries**
2. **permanent accounts**
3. **temporary accounts**
4. **closing entries**
5. **post-closing trial balance**
6. **accounting cycle**

QUESTIONS FOR INDIVIDUAL STUDY

1. Which accounting concept is being applied when information in a general ledger is summarized on a work sheet at the end of each fiscal period?
2. How are adjusting entries identified in a journal?
3. What accounts are affected, and how, by the adjusting entry for supplies?
4. What accounts are affected, and how, by the adjusting entry for prepaid insurance?
5. Why are closing entries journalized and posted at the end of a fiscal period?
6. How is the income summary account used?
7. Why is the income summary account considered unique?
8. What kind of balance will the income summary account have if a business has a net income?
9. What four closing entries are recorded by Rugcare?
10. What effect do withdrawals have on the owner's equity?
11. After the closing entries are posted, how is the balance of the capital account verified?
12. Why is a post-closing trial balance prepared after the closing entries have been posted?
13. What are the eight steps of an accounting cycle?

CASES FOR CRITICAL THINKING

CASE 1 Thomas Westcott forgot to journalize and post the adjusting entry for prepaid insurance at the end of the June fiscal period. What effect will this omission have on the records of Mr. Westcott's business as of June 30? Explain your answer.

CASE 2 Jason Fields states that his business is so small that he just records supplies and insurance as expenses when he pays for them. Thus, at the end of a fiscal period, Mr. Fields does not record adjusting and closing entries for his business. Do you agree with his accounting procedures? Explain your answer.

APPLIED COMMUNICATIONS

You have learned that accounting information is used by managers to make business decisions. But exactly what kind of decisions does the owner of a local business make? How does accounting information enable the manager to make better decisions?

INSTRUCTIONS:

Identify a local business of personal interest to you. Write five questions you would ask the manager to learn how accounting information is used to make decisions.

DRILL 10-D1   Determining accounts affected by adjusting and closing entries

TUTORIAL

Rapid Service Company uses the general ledger accounts that appear on the chart in the working papers that accompany this textbook.

INSTRUCTIONS:

1. For each account title, place a check mark in either Column 2 or 3 to indicate whether the account is affected by an adjusting entry.
2. For each account title, place a check mark in either Column 4 or 5 to indicate whether the account is affected by a closing entry.
3. For each account title, place a check mark in either Column 6 or 7 to indicate whether the account has a balance after the closing entries are posted.

APPLICATION PROBLEM

EPT(c,d,e)

PROBLEM 10-1   Journalizing and posting adjusting and closing entries; preparing a post-closing trial balance

Eiler Company's partial work sheet for the month ended October 31 of the current year is given below. The general ledger accounts are given in the working papers that accompany this textbook. (The general ledger accounts do not show all details for the fiscal period. The "Balance" shown in each account is the account's balance before adjusting and closing entries are posted.)

	ACCOUNT TITLE	3 ADJUSTMENTS DEBIT	4 ADJUSTMENTS CREDIT	5 INCOME STATEMENT DEBIT	6 INCOME STATEMENT CREDIT	7 BALANCE SHEET DEBIT	8 BALANCE SHEET CREDIT	
1	Cash					2 6 0 0 00		1
2	Supplies		(a) 1 4 5 00			5 6 0 00		2
3	Prepaid Insurance		(b) 1 9 0 00			2 1 0 00		3
4	Kurtz Supplies						3 0 0 00	4
5	Wiley Supplies						9 0 00	5
6	Norma Delk, Capital						2 8 5 0 00	6
7	Norma Delk, Drawing					2 5 0 00		7
8	Income Summary							8
9	Sales				1 1 0 0 00			9
10	Insurance Expense	(b) 1 9 0 00		1 9 0 00				10
11	Miscellaneous Expense			6 5 00				11
12	Rent Expense			3 2 0 00				12
13	Supplies Expense	(a) 1 4 5 00		1 4 5 00				13
14		3 3 5 00	3 3 5 00	7 2 0 00	1 1 0 0 00	3 6 2 0 00	3 2 4 0 00	14
15	Net Income			3 8 0 00			3 8 0 00	15
16				1 1 0 0 00	1 1 0 0 00	3 6 2 0 00	3 6 2 0 00	16
17								17
18								18
19								19

INSTRUCTIONS:

1. Use page 3 of a journal. Journalize and post the adjusting entries.
2. Continue to use page 3 of the journal. Journalize and post the closing entries.
3. Prepare a post-closing trial balance.

MASTERY PROBLEM 10-M Journalizing and posting adjusting and closing entries; preparing a post-closing trial balance

Kellerman Services' partial work sheet for the month ended November 30 of the current year is given below. The general ledger accounts are given in the working papers that accompany this textbook. (The general ledger accounts do not show all details for the fiscal period. The "Balance" shown in each account is the account's balance before adjusting and closing entries are posted.)

INSTRUCTIONS:

1. Use page 3 of a journal. Journalize and post the adjusting entries.
2. Continue to use page 3 of the journal. Journalize and post the closing entries.
3. Prepare a post-closing trial balance.

	ACCOUNT TITLE	ADJUSTMENTS		INCOME STATEMENT		BALANCE SHEET		
		3 DEBIT	4 CREDIT	5 DEBIT	6 CREDIT	7 DEBIT	8 CREDIT	
1	Cash					3 5 0 00		1
2	Supplies		(a) 1 9 5 00			7 5 0 00		2
3	Prepaid Insurance		(b) 2 6 0 00			2 8 0 00		3
4	Kern Supplies						5 0 0 00	4
5	Waite Supplies						1 2 0 00	5
6	A. Kellerman, Capital						3 7 2 5 00	6
7	A. Kellerman, Drawing					3 5 0 00		7
8	Income Summary							8
9	Sales				1 5 0 0 00			9
10	Insurance Expense	(b) 2 6 0 00		2 6 0 00				10
11	Miscellaneous Expense			8 5 00				11
12	Rent Expense			4 2 5 00				12
13	Supplies Expense	(a) 1 9 5 00		1 9 5 00				13
14		4 5 5 00	4 5 5 00	9 6 5 00	1 5 0 0 00	4 8 8 0 00	4 3 4 5 00	14
15	Net Income			5 3 5 00			5 3 5 00	15
16				1 5 0 0 00	1 5 0 0 00	4 8 8 0 00	4 8 8 0 00	16

CHALLENGE PROBLEM 10-C Completing end-of-fiscal-period work

A trial balance on a work sheet for Reed Company is given in the working papers that accompany this textbook.

INSTRUCTIONS:

1. Complete the work sheet.

Adjustment Information, December 31

Supplies on hand	$980.00
Value of prepaid insurance	700.00

2. Use page 3 of a journal. Journalize the adjusting entries.
3. Continue to use page 3 of the journal. Journalize the closing entries.

End-of-Fiscal-Period Work
for a Proprietorship

Chapters 8 through 10 describe Rugcare's manual accounting procedures for completing end-of-fiscal-period work. Integrating Automated Accounting Topic 3 describes procedures for using automated accounting software to complete Rugcare's end-of-fiscal-period work. The Automated Accounting Problems contain instructions for using automated accounting software to solve Mastery Problem 10-M and Challenge Problem 10-C, Chapter 10.

COMPLETING END-OF-FISCAL-PERIOD WORK

In automated accounting end-of-fiscal-period reports are generated by the software. The run date used for all end-of-fiscal-period reports is the ending date of the accounting period. Before printing financial statements, the software is directed to prepare a trial balance. The trial balance is prepared to prove equality of general ledger debits and credits. The trial balance is also used to plan adjustments to general ledger accounts.

Preparing a Trial Balance

To prepare a trial balance, the File menu is selected from the menu bar. The Open Accounting File command is then chosen to retrieve the general ledger data base from the template disk.

The Reports menu is selected from the menu bar. The Ledgers command is then chosen from the Reports menu. The Trial Balance is then selected from the Report Selection menu to display the trial balance as shown in Illustration T3-1.

ILLUSTRATION T3-1   Trial balance

```
                           Rugcare
                        Trial Balance
                          08/31/--
------------------------------------------------------------------
Acct.   Account
Number  Title                              Debit           Credit
------------------------------------------------------------------
110     Cash                             8272.00
120     Petty Cash                        200.00
130     Supplies                         4931.00
140     Prepaid Insurance                1200.00
210     Butler Cleaning Supplies                         1360.00
220     Dale Office Supplies                              200.00
310     Ben Furman, Capital                             10000.00
320     Ben Furman, Drawing               600.00
410     Sales                                            4291.00
510     Advertising Expense                68.00
530     Miscellaneous Expense             105.00
540     Rent Expense                      250.00
550     Repair Expense                    110.00
570     Utilities Expense                 115.00
                                        ---------        ---------
        Totals                          15851.00         15851.00
                                        =========        =========
```

Recording Adjusting Entries

Adjusting entries are recorded on a general journal input form. Rugcare records two adjusting entries. (1) An adjusting entry to bring the supplies account up to date. (2) An adjusting entry to bring the prepaid insurance account up to date.

Rugcare has the following adjustment data on August 31.

Adjustment Information, August 31

Supplies on hand...............................	$2,284.00
Value of prepaid insurance	1,100.00

The information needed to journalize the adjusting entries is obtained from the trial balance. The expense account, Supplies

FYI

Dollar signs and cent signs are not keyed when using Automated Accounting 6.0 software. When the cents are zero (.00), key only the dollar amount. The software automatically assigns the .00.

Expense, is increased by a debit, $2,647.00, the value of supplies used. The asset account, Supplies, is decreased by a credit, $2,647.00, the value of the supplies used. The journal entry to record this adjustment is on lines 1 and 2 of the general journal input form shown in Illustration T3-2. The abbreviation for adjusting entries, *Adj. Ent.*, is written in the Reference column for each entry.

The expense account, Insurance Expense, is increased by a debit, $100.00, the value of insurance used. The asset account, Prepaid Insurance, is decreased by a credit, $100.00, the value of insurance used. The journal entry to record this adjustment is shown on lines 3 and 4 of Illustration T3-2.

| ILLUSTRATION T3-2 | General journal report for adjusting entries |

RUN DATE 08,31,-- (MM DD YY)

GENERAL JOURNAL
Input Form

	DATE MM/DD	REFERENCE	ACCOUNT NO.	CUSTOMER/ VENDOR NO.	DEBIT	CREDIT	
1	08,31	Adj. Ent.	560		2647,00		1
2	/		130			2647,00	2
3	31	Adj. Ent.	520		100,00		3
4	/		140			100,00	4
21	/						21
22	/						22
23	/						23
24	/						24
25	/						25
				PAGE TOTALS	2747,00	2747,00	
				FINAL TOTALS	2747,00	2747,00	

CAREERS IN ACCOUNTING

DATA ENTRY CLERK

- *Compiles, sorts, and verifies accuracy of source documents*
- *Prepares computer input forms*
- *Enters data from input forms into computer*
- *Verifies accuracy of data entered with computer printouts*

Processing Adjusting Entries

To process adjusting entries, the Journals menu is selected from the menu bar. The General Journal command is chosen to display the data entry window for keying adjustment data.

After all lines on the input form have been keyed and posted, the Reports menu is selected from the menu bar. The Journals command is selected from the Reports menu. The General Journal report is chosen from the Report Selection menu. This selection displays the Selection Options screen. The *Ok* button is pushed to display the general journal report. The general journal report is checked for accuracy by comparing the report totals, $2,747.00, with the totals on the general journal input form. Because the totals are the same, the general journal report is assumed to be correct. The general journal report is printed, as shown in Illustration T3-3, and filed for future reference.

```
                              Rugcare
                         General Journal
                            08/31/--
------------------------------------------------------------------------
Date   Refer.    V/C Acct.  Title                       Debit     Credit
------------------------------------------------------------------------
08/31  Adj.Ent.  560        Supplies Expense           2647.00
08/31  Adj.Ent.  130        Supplies                              2647.00

08/31  Adj.Ent.  520        Insurance Expense           100.00
08/31  Adj.Ent.  140        Prepaid Insurance                      100.00

                                                       ---------- ----------
                           Totals                       2747.00   2747.00
                                                       ========== ==========
```

FYI

To save a file under another name, pull down the File menu and choose the Save As menu command. Key the path to the drive and directory that contains the data files. Save your data base under another file name.

PROCESSING FINANCIAL STATEMENTS

To process the income statement, the Reports menu is selected from the menu bar. The Financial Statements command is then selected from the menu. The Income Statement option is chosen from the Report Selection window to display the income statement. The income statement is printed, as shown in Illustration T3-4, and filed for future reference.

ILLUSTRATION T3-4   Income statement

```
                              Rugcare
                         Income Statement
                     For Period Ended 08/31/--
------------------------------------------------------------------------
                          *****Monthly*****      *****Yearly******
                          Amount    Percent      Amount    Percent
------------------------------------------------------------------------
Operating   Revenue
------------------------
Sales                     4291.00    100.00      4291.00    100.00
                         ---------- ----------   ---------- ----------
Total Operating Revenue   4291.00    100.00      4291.00    100.00

Operating   Expenses
------------------------
Advertising Expense         68.00      1.58        68.00      1.58
Insurance Expense          100.00      2.33       100.00      2.33
Miscellaneous Expense      105.00      2.45       105.00      2.45
Rent Expense               250.00      5.83       250.00      5.83
Repair Expense             110.00      2.56       110.00      2.56
Supplies Expense          2647.00     61.69      2647.00     61.69
Utilities Expense          115.00      2.68       115.00      2.68
                         ---------- ----------   ---------- ----------
Total Operating Expenses  3395.00     79.12      3395.00     79.12
                         ---------- ----------   ---------- ----------
Net Income                 896.00     20.88       896.00     20.88
                         ========== ==========   ========== ==========
```

The income statement prepared by Rugcare's automated accounting software provides both current month and yearly amounts and percentages. This additional data allows Mr. Furman to analyze both monthly and yearly performance. As the month of August was Rugcare's first month of operation, monthly and yearly amounts are the same.

To process the balance sheet, the Reports menu is selected from the menu bar. The Financial Statements command is then selected from the Reports menu. The Balance Sheet option is selected from the Report Selection window to display the balance sheet. The balance sheet is printed, as shown in Illustration T3-5, and filed for future reference.

A balance sheet may be prepared in one of two forms: (1) account form or (2) report form. An account form of balance sheet lists assets on the left and equities on the right. Rugcare's manual accounting system uses the account form of balance sheet. A report form of balance sheet lists the assets, liabilities, and owner's equity vertically. Illustration T3-5 is a report form of balance sheet.

FYI

To prevent the computer from overheating, avoid blocking air vents.

ILLUSTRATION T3-5   Balance sheet

```
                                    Rugcare
                                 Balance Sheet
                                   08/31/--

Assets
----------
Cash                                 8272.00
Petty Cash                            200.00
Supplies                             2284.00
Prepaid Insurance                    1100.00
                                   ----------
Total Assets                                      11856.00
                                                  ==========
Liabilities
--------------------
Butler Cleaning Supplies             1360.00
Dale Office Supplies                  200.00
                                   ----------
Total Liabilities                                  1560.00

Owner's Equity
---------------------------
Ben Furman, Capital                 10000.00
Ben Furman, Drawing                  -600.00
Net Income                            896.00
                                   ----------
Total Owner's Equity                              10296.00
                                                  ----------
Total Liabilities & Equity                        11856.00
                                                  ==========
```

Closing Temporary Accounts

In automated accounting the software contains instructions for closing temporary accounts. The Options menu is selected from the menu bar. The Period-End Closing command is selected from the Options menu to close all temporary accounts.

Processing a Post-Closing Trial Balance

After the financial statements have been prepared and closing entries have been posted, a post-closing trial balance is prepared. A **post-closing trial balance** is a trial balance that is prepared after closing entries have been posted.

To process a post-closing trial balance, the Reports menu is selected from the menu bar. The Ledgers menu command is selected and the Trial Balance is then chosen from the Report Selection menu. The post-closing trial balance is printed, as shown in Illustration T3-6, and is filed for future reference.

| **ILLUSTRATION T3-6** | Post-closing trial balance |

```
                            Rugcare
                         Trial Balance
                          08/31/--
------------------------------------------------------------------------
Acct.   Account
Number  Title                                    Debit           Credit
------------------------------------------------------------------------
110     Cash                                   8272.00
120     Petty Cash                              200.00
130     Supplies                               2284.00
140     Prepaid Insurance                      1100.00
210     Butler Cleaning Supplies                               1360.00
220     Dale Office Supplies                                    200.00
310     Ben Furman, Capital                                   10296.00
                                             ----------      ----------
        Totals                                11856.00       11856.00
                                             ==========      ==========
```

COMPARISON OF MANUAL AND AUTOMATED ACCOUNTING CYCLE

The accounting cycle is the same for both manual and automated accounting, only the procedures change. A comparison is shown in Illustration T3-7.

Manual Accounting Cycle	Automated Accounting Cycle
Analyze source documents	Analyze source documents
Record transactions in a journal	Record transactions on an input form and key
Post journal entries	Select posting command
Prepare a work sheet	Print a trial balance
(Adjustments are planned on the work sheet)	Analyze adjusting entries using the trial balance; record adjusting entries on input form, key, and post
Prepare financial statements	Print financial statements
Journalize and post adjusting entries	(Adjusting entries already recorded)
Record closing entries	Select closing command
Prepare a post-closing trial balance	Print a post-closing trial balance

OPTIONAL PROBLEM DB-3A

Rugcare's general ledger data base is on the accounting textbook template. If you wish to process Rugcare's end-of-fiscal-period work using automated accounting software, load the *Automated Accounting 6.0* or higher software. Select Data Base 3A (DB-3A) from the template disk. Read the Problem Instructions screen. Use Illustration T3-2 and follow the procedures described to process Rugcare's end-of-fiscal-period work.

AUTOMATED ACCOUNTING PROBLEMS

AUTOMATING MASTERY PROBLEM 10-M Journalizing and posting adjusting entries; end-of-fiscal-period work for a proprietorship

INSTRUCTIONS:

1. Use the end-of-fiscal period work for Mastery Problem 10-M, Chapter 10. Use November 30 of the current year as the run date.

2. Load the *Automated Accounting 6.0* or higher software. Select data base F10-M (First-Year Course Problem 10-M) from the accounting textbook template. Read the Problem Instructions screen.

3. Select File from the menu bar and choose the Save As menu command. Key the path to the drive and directory that contains your data files. Save the data base with a file name of XXX10M (where XXX are your initials).

4. Display/print a trial balance.

5. Record the adjusting entries on a general journal input form using the following information. Use the account numbers from the trial balance that was printed in Instruction 4.

Adjustment Information, November 30

Supplies on hand.	$750.00
Value of prepaid insurance.	280.00

6. Key the adjusting entries from the general journal input form.

7. Display/print the general journal report.
8. Display/print the income statement.
9. Display/print the balance sheet.
10. Perform period-end closing.
11. Display/print the post-closing trial balance.

AUTOMATED

AUTOMATING CHALLENGE PROBLEM 10-C Completing end-of-fiscal period work

INSTRUCTIONS:

1. Load the *Automated Accounting 6.0* or higher software. Select data base F10-C from the accounting textbook template. Read the Problem Instructions screen.
2. Select File from the menu bar and choose the Save As menu command. Key the path to the drive and directory that contains your data files. Save the data base with a file name of XXX10C (where XXX are your initials).
3. Display/print a trial balance.
4. Record the adjusting entries on a general journal input form using the following information. Use the account numbers from the trial balance that was printed in Instruction 3.

Adjustment Information, December 31

Supplies on hand.	$980.00
Value of prepaid insurance.	700.00

5. Key the adjusting entries from the general journal input form.
6. Display/print the general journal report.
7. Display/print the income statement.
8. Display/print the balance sheet.
9. Perform period-end closing.
10. Display/print the post-closing trial balance.

An Accounting Cycle for a Proprietorship: End-of-Fiscal-Period Work

AUTOMATED

The general ledger prepared in Reinforcement Activity 1, Part A, is needed to complete Reinforcement Activity 1, Part B.

Reinforcement Activity 1, Part B, includes end-of-fiscal-period activities studied in Chapters 8 through 10.

WORK SHEET

INSTRUCTIONS:

12. Prepare a trial balance on a work sheet. Use a one-month fiscal period ended May 31 of the current year.
13. Analyze the following adjustment information into debit and credit parts. Record the adjustments on the work sheet.

Adjustment Information, May 31

Supplies on hand	$515.00
Value of prepaid insurance	800.00

14. Total and rule the Adjustments columns.
15. Extend the up-to-date account balances to the Balance Sheet and Income Statement columns.
16. Complete the work sheet.

FINANCIAL STATEMENTS

17. Prepare an income statement. Figure and record the component percentages for sales, total expenses, and net income. Round percentage calculations to the nearest 0.1%.
18. Prepare a balance sheet.

ADJUSTING ENTRIES

19. Use page 3 of the journal. Journalize and post the adjusting entries.

CLOSING ENTRIES

20. Continue using page 3 of the journal. Journalize and post the closing entries.

POST-CLOSING TRIAL BALANCE

21. Prepare a post-closing trial balance.

This simulation covers the transactions completed by Video Transfer, a service business organized as a proprietorship. Video Transfer begins business on September 1 of the current year. The business produces personal videos for such events as weddings and family reunions. In addition, the business also transfers home movies and slides to video tape.

The activities included in the accounting cycle for Video Transfer are listed below. The company uses a journal and a general ledger similar to those described for Rugcare in Part 2.

This simulation is available from the publisher in either manual or automated versions.

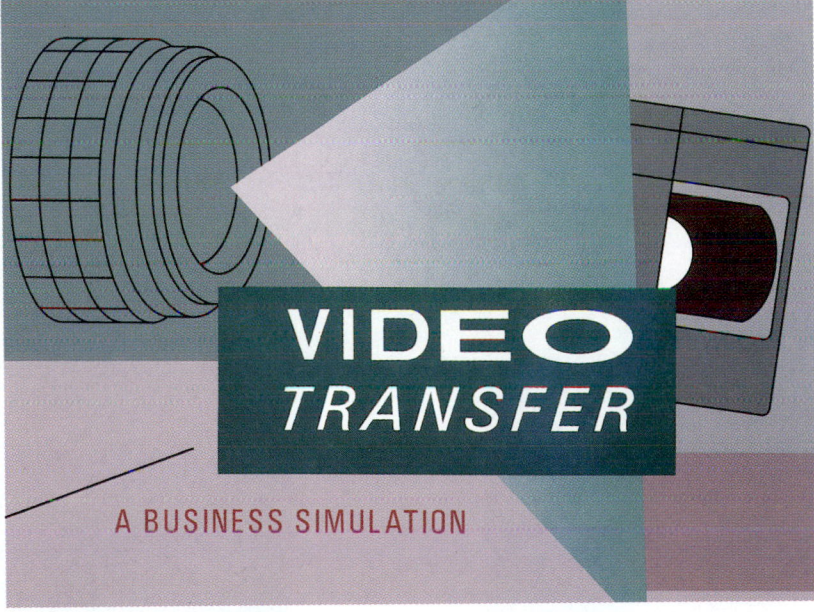

VIDEO TRANSFER

A BUSINESS SIMULATION

The following activities are included in this simulation.

1. Journalizing transactions in a journal.
2. Forwarding column totals to a new journal page.
3. Preparing a bank statement reconciliation and recording a bank service charge.
4. Proving cash.
5. Proving and ruling a journal.
6. Posting from a journal to a general ledger.
7. Preparing a trial balance on a work sheet.
8. Recording adjustments on a work sheet.
9. Completing a work sheet.
10. Preparing financial statements (income statement and balance sheet).
11. Journalizing and posting adjusting entries.
12. Journalizing and posting closing entries.
13. Preparing a post-closing trial balance.

Accounting for a Merchandising Business Organized as a Partnership

Access to Capital
Management Talent
Ease of Formation
Benefits

GENERAL GOALS

1. Know accounting terminology related to an accounting system for a merchandising business organized as a partnership.

2. Understand accounting concepts and practices related to an accounting system for a merchandising business organized as a partnership.

3. Demonstrate accounting procedures used in an accounting system for a merchandising business organized as a partnership.

CHART OF ACCOUNTS
GENERAL LEDGER

Balance Sheet Accounts

(1000) ASSETS
1110 Cash
1120 Petty Cash
1130 Accounts Receivable
1140 Merchandise Inventory
1145 Supplies—Office
1150 Supplies—Store
1160 Prepaid Insurance

(2000) LIABILITIES
2110 Accounts Payable
2120 Employee Income Tax Payable
2130 FICA Tax Payable
2140 Sales Tax Payable
2150 Unemployment Tax Payable—Federal
2160 Unemployment Tax Payable—State
2170 Health Insurance Premiums Payable
2180 U.S. Savings Bonds Payable
2190 United Way Donations Payable

(3000) OWNERS' EQUITY
3110 Amy Kramer, Capital
3120 Amy Kramer, Drawing
3130 Dario Mesa, Capital
3140 Dario Mesa, Drawing
3150 Income Summary

Income Statement Accounts

(4000) OPERATING REVENUE
4110 Sales

(5000) COST OF MERCHANDISE
5110 Purchases

(6000) OPERATING EXPENSES
6110 Advertising Expense
6120 Credit Card Fee Expense
6130 Insurance Expense
6140 Miscellaneous Expense
6150 Payroll Taxes Expense
6160 Rent Expense
6170 Salary Expense
6175 Supplies Expense—Office
6180 Supplies Expense—Store
6190 Utilities Expense

SUBSIDIARY LEDGERS

Accounts Receivable Ledger

110 Ashley Delivery
120 Autohaus Service
130 Friendly Auto Service
140 Keystone Delivery
150 Powell Rent-A-Car
160 Wood Sales & Service

Accounts Payable Ledger

210 Antelo Supply
220 Bell Office Products
230 Filtrex Tires
240 Nilon Motor Parts
250 Q-Ban Distributors
260 Veloz Automotive

The charts of accounts for CarLand are illustrated above for ready reference as you study Part 3 of this textbook.

11

Journalizing Purchases and Cash Payments

ENABLING PERFORMANCE TASKS

After studying Chapter 11, you will be able to:

a Define accounting terms related to purchases and cash payments for a merchandising business.

b Identify accounting concepts and practices related to purchases and cash payments for a merchandising business.

c Analyze purchases and cash payments transactions for a merchandising business.

d Journalize purchases and cash payments transactions for a merchandising business.

TERMS PREVIEW

partnership • partner • merchandising business • merchandise • cost of merchandise • markup • vendor • purchase on account • invoice • purchase invoice • terms of sale • correcting entry

Rugcare, the business described in Part 2, is owned by one person. A business owned by one person is known as a proprietorship.

Businesses often require the skills of more than one person. Many businesses also need more capital than one owner can provide. Therefore, some businesses are owned by two or more persons. A business in which two or more persons combine their assets and skills is called a **partnership.** Each member of a partnership is called a **partner.** Partners must agree on how each partner will share the business' profit or loss. As in proprietorships, reports and financial records of the business are kept separate from the personal records of the partners. *(CONCEPT: Business Entity)*

Rugcare, the business described in Part 2, sells services for a fee. A business that sells a service for a fee is known as a service business. However, many other businesses purchase goods to sell. A business that purchases and sells goods is called a **merchandising business.** Goods that a merchandising business purchases to sell are called **merchandise.** The selling of merchandise rather than a service is what makes the activities of a merchandising business different from those of a service business.

CarLand, the business described in this part, is a merchandising business organized as a partnership. The business is owned by Amy Kramer and Dario Mesa. The business purchases and sells automotive supplies. CarLand rents the building in which the business is located as well as the equipment used for operation. CarLand expects to make money and continue in business indefinitely. *(CONCEPT: Going Concern)*

USING AN EXPANDED JOURNAL

A service business generally has a large number of cash transactions and a limited number of noncash transactions. Noncash transactions are those that do not involve either the receipt or payment of cash. Rugcare uses a 5-column journal to record all cash and noncash transactions.

Need for Expanded Journal

The number and arrangement of columns in a journal is determined by the type and frequency of transactions.

CarLand, a merchandising business, has many noncash and other frequently occurring transactions that affect single accounts. CarLand could use the same journal as the one used by Rugcare. However, without adding more special amount columns to the journal, the large number of transactions would require many entries in the General Debit and Credit columns.

Form of Expanded Journal

To save time and space in journalizing transactions, CarLand uses an 11-column journal. The journal includes additional special amount columns for recording frequently occurring transactions that affect single accounts. A journal expanded to provide for the recording of frequently occurring transactions that affect single accounts is shown in Illustration 11-1.

ILLUSTRATION 11-1   Amount columns of an expanded journal

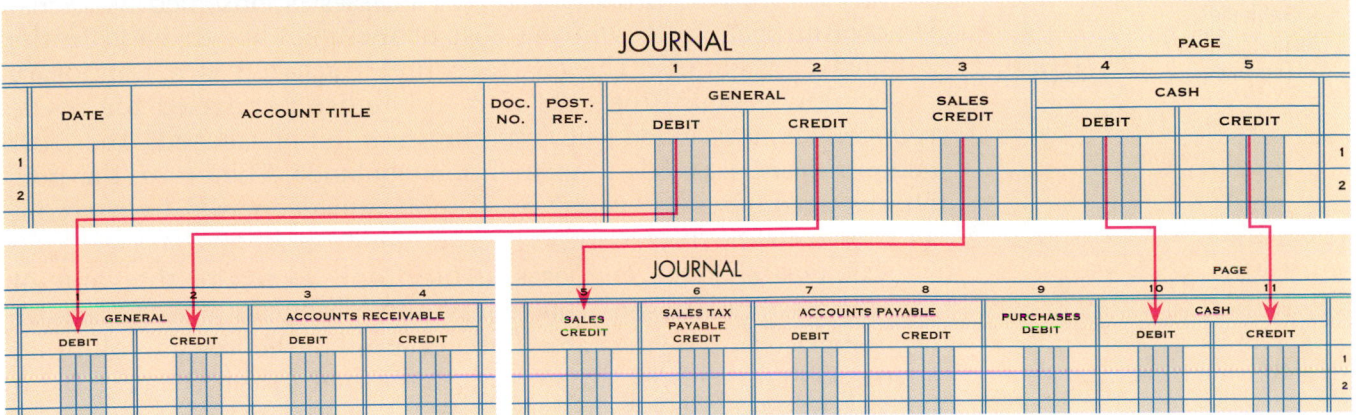

An expanded journal is commonly used by small merchandising businesses in which only one person records transactions. Amy Kramer records all transactions for CarLand.

CarLand's journal, Illustration 11-1, has special amount columns for the recording of frequently occurring transactions related to the purchasing and selling of merchandise. The columns are arranged to make accurate journalizing and posting easier. Debit and credit columns for Cash, Accounts Receivable, and Accounts Payable are arranged in pairs. This arrangement helps avoid errors in recording amounts in the wrong columns. All columns are placed to the right of the Account Title column. The General Debit and Credit amount columns are placed first so that amounts in these columns will be close to the titles in the Account Title column.

The number and arrangement of columns in a journal is determined by the type and frequency of transactions. CarLand determined that the journal described above would best meet the needs of the business.

JOURNALIZING PURCHASES OF MERCHANDISE

The price a business pays for goods it purchases to sell is called **cost of merchandise.** The selling price of merchandise must be greater than the cost of merchandise for a business to make a profit. The amount added to the cost of merchandise to establish the selling price is called **markup.** Revenue earned from the sale of merchandise includes both the cost of merchandise and markup. Only the markup increases capital. Accounts for the cost of merchandise are kept in a separate division of the general ledger. The cost of merchandise division is shown in CarLand's chart of accounts, page 244.

> **FYI**
>
> The cost account, Purchases, is only used to record the value of merchandise purchased. All other items bought, such as supplies, are recorded in the appropriate asset account.

Purchases

Debit side	Credit side
Normal balance	
Increase	Decrease

In addition to purchasing merchandise to sell, a merchandising business also buys supplies and other assets for use in the business. A business from which merchandise is purchased or supplies or other assets are bought is called a **vendor**.

The account used for recording the cost of merchandise purchased to sell is titled Purchases. Purchases is classified as a cost account because it is in the cost of merchandise division in the chart of accounts. The cost account, Purchases, is a temporary account. Because the cost of merchandise purchased for resale reduces capital when the merchandise is purchased, the cost account, Purchases, has a normal debit balance. Therefore, the purchases account is increased by a debit and decreased by a credit, as shown in the T account.

The cost account, Purchases, is used only to record the value of merchandise purchased. Therefore, only purchases of merchandise are recorded in the Purchases Debit column of the journal. All other items bought, such as supplies, are recorded in the General Debit column of the journal. Merchandise and other items bought are recorded and reported at the price agreed upon at the time the transactions occur. The price agreed upon at the time the transaction occurs may be lower than the given price. The accounting concept, *Historical Cost*, is applied when the actual amount paid for merchandise or other items bought is recorded. *(CONCEPT: Historical Cost)*

Purchase of Merchandise for Cash

CarLand pays cash for some purchases. All cash payments are made by check.

November 2, 19--. Purchased merchandise for cash, $483.00. Check No. 259.

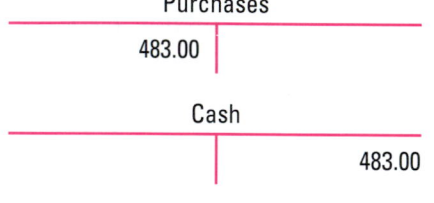

A cash purchase transaction increases the purchases account balance and decreases the cash account balance.

Because the purchases account has a normal debit balance, Purchases is debited for $483.00 to show the increase in this cost account. The cash account also has a normal debit balance. Therefore, Cash is credited for $483.00 to show the decrease in this asset account.

The journal entry to record this transaction is shown in Illustration 11-2.

ILLUSTRATION 11-2   Journal entry to record a purchase of merchandise for cash

	DATE	ACCOUNT TITLE	DOC. NO.	POST. REF.		PURCHASES DEBIT	CASH DEBIT	CASH CREDIT	
						9	10	11	
1	Nov. 2 ✓		C259	✓		483 00		483 00	1
2									2

PAGE 21   JOURNAL   PAGE 21

A check mark in the Account Title column means that all account titles have their own column. A check mark in the Post. Ref. column means don't post.

The date, *19--, Nov. 2*, is recorded in the Date column. Both the debit and credit amounts will be recorded in special amount columns. Therefore, a check mark is placed in the Account Title column to show that no account title needs to be written. The check number, *C259*, is recorded in the Doc. No. column. Both the debit and credit amounts will be posted as part of special amount column totals. Therefore, a check mark is placed in the Post. Ref. column to show that amounts on this line are not to be posted individually. The debit to Purchases, *$483.00*, is entered in the Purchases Debit column. The credit to Cash, *$483.00*, is entered in the Cash Credit column.

Purchase of Merchandise on Account

A transaction in which the merchandise purchased is to be paid for later is called a **purchase on account**. Some businesses that purchase on account from only a few vendors keep a separate general ledger account for each vendor to whom money is owed. Businesses that purchase on account from many vendors will have many accounts for vendors. To avoid a bulky general ledger, the total amount owed to all vendors can be summarized in a single general ledger account. A liability account that summarizes the amounts owed to all vendors is titled Accounts Payable. CarLand uses an accounts payable account.

The liability account, Accounts Payable, has a normal credit balance. Therefore, the accounts payable account is increased by a credit and decreased by a debit, as shown in the T account.

Accounts Payable	
Debit side	Credit side
	Normal balance
Decrease	Increase

When a vendor sells merchandise to a buyer, the vendor prepares a form showing what has been sold. A form describing the goods sold, the quantity, and the price is called an **invoice**. An invoice used as a source document for recording a purchase on account transaction is called a **purchase invoice**. *(CONCEPT: Objective Evidence)* A purchase invoice received by CarLand is shown in Illustration 11-3.

ILLUSTRATION 11-3   Purchase invoice

veloz automotive
2611 Industrial
Fremont, NH 03044-2672

REC'D 11/02/-- P74

TO: CarLand
1374 Parklane
Rockville, RI 02873-4121

DATE: 10/26/--
INV. NO.: 2768
TERMS: 30 days
ACCT. NO.: 260

QUANTITY	CAT. NO.	DESCRIPTION	UNIT PRICE	TOTAL
8	4422	All-season tires	73.00	584.00 ✓
6	4424	All-season tires	73.00	438.00 ✓
12	6620	Floor mats	16.00	192.00 ✓
12	7715	Seat covers	45.00	540.00 ✓
		Total		1,754.00

Pst

A purchase invoice lists the quantity, the description, the price of each item, and the total amount of the invoice. A purchase invoice provides the information needed for recording a purchase on account.

When CarLand receives a purchase invoice, a date and a number are stamped in the upper right-hand corner. The date stamped is the date the invoice is received. CarLand received the invoice in Illustration 11-3 on 11/02/--. This date should not be confused with the vendor's date on the invoice, 10/26/--. CarLand assigns numbers in sequence to easily identify all purchase invoices. The number stamped on the invoice, *P74*, is the number assigned by CarLand to this purchase invoice. This number should not be confused with the invoice number, *2768*, assigned by the vendor. Each vendor uses a different numbering system. Therefore, vendor invoice numbers could not be recorded in sequence, which would make it impossible to detect a missing invoice.

A buyer needs to know that all items ordered have been received and that the prices are correct. The check marks on the invoice show that the items have been received and that amounts have been checked and are correct. The initials near the total are those of the person at CarLand who checked the invoice.

An agreement between a buyer and a seller about payment for merchandise is called the **terms of sale**. The terms of sale on the invoice, Illustration 11-3, are 30 days. These terms mean that payment is due within 30 days from the date of the invoice. The invoice is dated October 26. Therefore, payment must be made by November 25.

November 2, 19--. Purchased merchandise on account from Veloz Automotive, $1,754.00. Purchase Invoice No. 74.

A purchase on account transaction increases the amount owed to a vendor. This transaction increases the purchases account balance and increases the accounts payable account balance.

Because the purchases account has a normal debit balance, Purchases is debited for $1,754.00 to show the increase in this cost account. The accounts payable account has a normal credit balance. Therefore, Accounts Payable is credited for $1,754.00 to show the increase in this liability account.

The journal entry to record this purchase on account transaction is shown in Illustration 11-4.

Purchases	
1,754.00	

Accounts Payable	
	1,754.00

ILLUSTRATION 11-4   Journal entry to record a purchase of merchandise on account

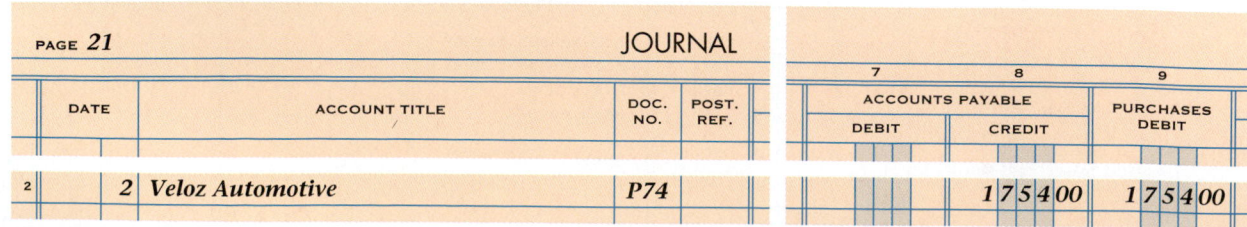

PAGE *21*   JOURNAL

	DATE	ACCOUNT TITLE	DOC. NO.	POST. REF.	ACCOUNTS PAYABLE DEBIT	ACCOUNTS PAYABLE CREDIT	PURCHASES DEBIT
2	2	*Veloz Automotive*	P74			1 7 5 4 00	1 7 5 4 00

The date, *2*, is written in the Date column. No special amount column is provided for Veloz Automotive Therefore, the vendor name, *Veloz Automotive*, is recorded in the Account Title column. CarLand's purchase invoice number, *P74*, is entered in the Doc. No. column. The credit to Accounts Payable, *$1,754.00*, is recorded in the Accounts Payable Credit column. The debit to Purchases, *$1,754.00*, is recorded in the Purchases Debit column.

The debit to Purchases and the credit to Accounts Payable are recorded in special amount columns. Therefore, writing the titles of either general ledger account in the Account Title column is not necessary. However, the name of the vendor is written in the Account Title column to show to whom the amount is owed. The way CarLand keeps records of the amount owed to each vendor is described in Chapter 13.

JOURNALIZING BUYING SUPPLIES

CarLand buys supplies for use in the business. Supplies are not recorded in the purchases account because supplies are not intended for sale. Cash register tapes and price tags are examples of supplies used in a merchandising business.

Buying Supplies for Cash

CarLand buys most of its supplies for cash.

November 5, 19--. Paid cash for office supplies, $87.00. Check No. 261.

Supplies—Office	
87.00	

Cash	
	87.00

This transaction increases the office supplies account balance and decreases the cash account balance.

Because the office supplies account has a normal debit balance, Supplies—Office is debited for $87.00 to show the increase in this asset account. The cash account also has a normal debit balance. Therefore, Cash is credited for $87.00 to show the decrease in this asset account.

The journal entry to record this buying supplies for cash transaction is shown in Illustration 11-5, page 252.

The date, *5*, is recorded in the Date column. No special amount column is provided for Supplies—Office. Therefore, the account title, *Supplies—Office*, is written in the Account Title column. The check number, *C261*, is entered in the Doc. No. column. The debit to Supplies—Office, *$87.00*, is recorded in the General Debit column. The credit to Cash, *$87.00*, is recorded in the Cash Credit column.

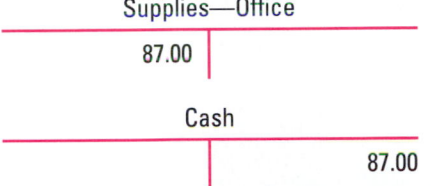

FYI

Supplies are not recorded in the Purchases account because supplies are not intended for sale.

ILLUSTRATION 11-5

Journal entry to record buying supplies for cash

	DATE	ACCOUNT TITLE	DOC. NO.	POST. REF.	GENERAL DEBIT	GENERAL CREDIT	CASH DEBIT	CASH CREDIT	
6	5	Supplies—Office	C261		8 7 00			8 7 00	6
7									7
8									8

PAGE 21 — JOURNAL — PAGE 21

Buying Supplies on Account

CarLand usually buys supplies for cash. Occasionally, however, CarLand buys some supplies on account.

November 6, 19--. Bought store supplies on account from Antelo Supply, $160.00. Memorandum No. 43.

When CarLand buys supplies on account, an invoice is received from the vendor. This invoice is similar to the purchase invoice received when merchandise is purchased. To assure that no mistake is made, a memorandum is attached to the invoice noting that the invoice is for supplies and not for purchases. Memorandum 43 is shown in Illustration 11-6.

ILLUSTRATION 11-6

Memorandum for buying supplies on account

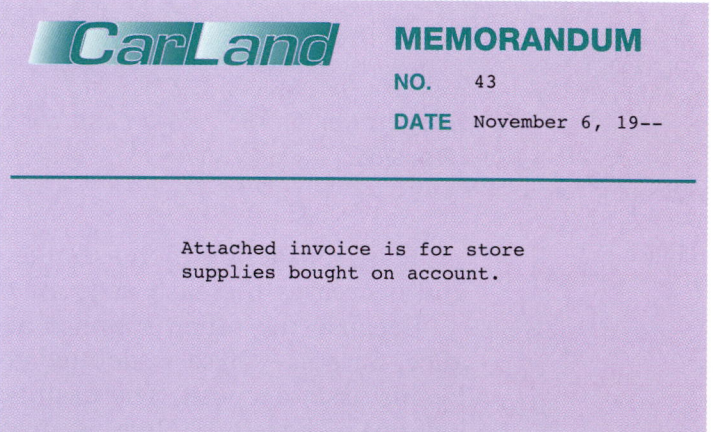

CarLand

MEMORANDUM

NO. 43

DATE November 6, 19--

Attached invoice is for store supplies bought on account.

Supplies—Store

160.00

Accounts Payable

160.00

This transaction increases the store supplies account balance and increases the accounts payable account balance.

Because the store supplies account has a normal debit balance, Supplies—Store is debited for $160.00 to show the increase in this asset account. The accounts payable account has a normal credit balance. Therefore, Accounts Payable is credited for $160.00 to show the increase in this liability account.

The journal entry to record this buying supplies on account transaction is shown in Illustration 11-7.

ILLUSTRATION 11-7 Journal entry to record buying supplies on account

	DATE	ACCOUNT TITLE	DOC. NO.	POST. REF.	GENERAL DEBIT	GENERAL CREDIT	ACCOUNTS PAYABLE DEBIT	ACCOUNTS PAYABLE CREDIT
					1	2	7	8
9	6	Supplies—Store	M43		160 00			
10		Antelo Supply						160 00

PAGE 21 — JOURNAL

The date, 6, is written in the Date column. No special amount column is provided for Supplies—Store Therefore, the account title, *Supplies—Store*, is recorded in the Account Title column. The memorandum number, *M43*, is entered in the Doc. No. column. The debit to Supplies—Store, *$160.00*, is written in the General Debit column on the same line. An account title is also required for the credit part of the entry. Therefore, the vendor name, *Antelo Supply*, is recorded in the Account Title column on the next line. The credit to Accounts Payable, *$160.00*, is entered in the Accounts Payable Credit column on the same line.

JOURNALIZING CASH PAYMENTS

Most of CarLand's cash payments are to vendors or for expenses. Payment to vendors is made according to the terms of sale on the purchase invoices. Payment for an expense is usually made at the time the expense occurs.

Cash Payment on Account

CarLand pays by check for all cash purchases and for payments on account.

November 7, 19--. Paid cash on account to Filtrex Tires, $970.00, covering Purchase Invoice No. 72. Check No. 263.

This cash payment on account transaction decreases the amount owed to vendors. This transaction decreases the accounts payable account balance and decreases the cash account balance.

Because the accounts payable account has a normal credit balance, Accounts Payable is debited for $970.00 to show the decrease in this liability account. The cash account has a normal debit balance. Therefore, Cash is credited for $970.00 to show the decrease in this asset account.

Accounts Payable
970.00 |

Cash
| 970.00

PROFESSIONAL BUSINESS ETHICS

Am I Cheating the Company?

Frances Phillips and Stella Rushing are partners in a frozen food market named The Fishing Net. The partners continually monitor the expiration dates of their inventory to assure that only fresh products are stored in the freezers.

Rather than discarding the inventory, the partners agreed to donate the inventory to an orphanage just prior to its expiration date. After several months, Ms. Rushing began to take some expiring items home for personal use. Lately, Ms. Rushing has even taken home new items.

INSTRUCTIONS:

1. Use the three-step checklist to analyze whether Stella Rushing's latest actions demonstrate ethical behavior.
2. What actions should Ms. Phillips take?

The journal entry to record this cash payment on account transaction is shown in Illustration 11-8.

ILLUSTRATION 11-8 Journal entry to record a cash payment on account

PAGE *21* JOURNAL PAGE *21*

	DATE		ACCOUNT TITLE	DOC. NO.	POST. REF.	7 ACCOUNTS PAYABLE DEBIT	8 ACCOUNTS PAYABLE CREDIT	10 CASH DEBIT	11 CASH CREDIT	
13		*7*	*Filtrex Tires*	*C263*		*970 00*			*970 00*	13
14										14
15										15
16										16

The date, *7,* is written in the Date column. No special amount column is provided for Filtrex Tires. Therefore, the vendor name, *Filtrex Tires,* is recorded in the Account Title column. The check number, *C263,* is entered in the Doc. No. column. The debit to Accounts Payable, *$970.00,* is written in the Accounts Payable Debit column. The credit to Cash, *$970.00,* is written in the Cash Credit column.

Cash Payment of an Expense

CarLand usually pays for an expense at the time the transaction occurs.

November 9, 19--. Paid cash for advertising, $125.00. Check No. 265.

This cash payment increases the advertising expense account balance and decreases the cash account balance.

Advertising Expense

| 125.00 | |

Cash

| | 125.00 |

Because the advertising expense account has a normal debit balance, Advertising Expense is debited for $125.00 to show the increase in this expense account. The cash account also has a normal debit balance. Therefore, Cash is credited for $125.00 to show the decrease in this asset account.

The journal entry to record this cash payment of an expense transaction is shown in Illustration 11-9.

ILLUSTRATION 11-9   Journal entry to record a cash payment of an expense

						GENERAL		CASH	
PAGE 21	JOURNAL					1	2	10	11 PAGE 21
DATE	ACCOUNT TITLE	DOC. NO.	POST. REF.			DEBIT	CREDIT	DEBIT	CREDIT
17	9 Advertising Expense	C265				125 00			125 00	17

The date, *9*, is written in the Date column. No special amount column is provided for Advertising Expense. Therefore, the account title, *Advertising Expense*, is recorded in the Account Title column. The check number, *C265*, is entered in the Doc. No. column. The debit to Advertising Expense, *$125.00*, is written in the General Debit column. The credit to Cash, *$125.00*, is written in the Cash Credit column.

Cash Payment to Replenish Petty Cash

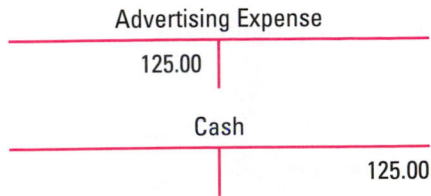

The account title Petty Cash is used only when establishing the petty cash account.

CarLand deposits all cash in a bank. Some cash, however, is kept in a petty cash fund for making change at the cash register and for making small cash payments. CarLand has a petty cash fund of $500.00, which is replenished whenever the petty cash on hand drops below $200.00.

November 9, 19--. Paid cash to replenish the petty cash fund, $301.00: office supplies, $58.00; store supplies, $65.00; advertising, $92.00; miscellaneous, $86.00. Check No. 266.

This cash payment increases the balances of the supplies accounts and several expense accounts and decreases the cash account balance.

The supplies accounts have normal debit balances. Therefore, Supplies—Office is debited for $58.00 and Supplies—Store is debited for $65.00 to show the increases in these two asset accounts. The expense accounts also have normal debit balances. Therefore, Advertising Expense is debited for $92.00 and Miscellaneous Expense is debited for $86.00 to show the increases in these expense accounts. The cash account has a normal debit balance. Therefore, Cash is credited for $301.00, the total amount needed to replenish the petty cash fund, to show the decrease in this asset account.

The journal entry to record this cash payment to replenish petty cash transaction is shown in Illustration 11-10.

Supplies—Office

| 58.00 | |

Supplies—Store

| 65.00 | |

Advertising Expense

| 92.00 | |

Miscellaneous Expense

| 86.00 | |

Cash

| | 301.00 |

	DATE	ACCOUNT TITLE	DOC. NO.	POST. REF.	GENERAL DEBIT	GENERAL CREDIT	CASH DEBIT	CASH CREDIT	
18	9	Supplies—Office	C266		5 8 00			3 0 1 00	18
19		Supplies—Store			6 5 00				19
20		Advertising Expense			9 2 00				20
21		Miscellaneous Expense			8 6 00				21

PAGE 21   JOURNAL   PAGE 21

The date, 9, is written once in the Date column, line 18. No special amount columns are provided for any of the accounts for which the petty cash fund was used. Therefore, the account titles are recorded in the Account Title column. The check number, C266, is entered once in the Doc. No. column, line 18. The debit amounts are written in the General Debit column. The credit amount is recorded in the Cash Credit column.

JOURNALIZING OTHER TRANSACTIONS

Most transactions of merchandising businesses are related to purchasing and selling merchandise. A merchandising business, however, has other transactions that must be recorded. CarLand records these other transactions in its journal.

Withdrawals by Partners

Amy Kramer, Drawing

Debit side Normal balance Increase	Credit side Decrease

Dario Mesa, Drawing

Debit side Normal balance Increase	Credit side Decrease

The two assets generally taken out of a merchandising business by owners are cash and merchandise.

Assets taken out of a business for the personal use of an owner are known as withdrawals. The two assets generally taken out of a merchandising business are cash and merchandise. Withdrawals reduce the amount of a business' capital. The account titles of the partners' drawing accounts are Amy Kramer, Drawing and Dario Mesa, Drawing. The drawing accounts are classified as contra capital accounts. Since capital accounts have credit balances, partners' drawing accounts have normal debit balances. Therefore, the drawing accounts are increased by a debit and decreased by a credit, as shown in the T accounts.

Withdrawals could be recorded as debits directly to the partners' capital accounts. However, withdrawals are normally recorded in separate accounts so that the total amounts are easily determined for each accounting period.

Cash Withdrawal.   When either Amy Kramer or Dario Mesa withdraws cash from CarLand, a check is written for the payment.

November 10, 19--. Dario Mesa, partner, withdrew cash for personal use, $1,500.00. Check No. 267.

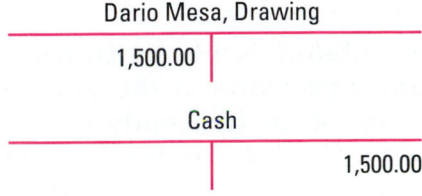

This cash withdrawal increases Dario Mesa's drawing account balance and decreases the cash account balance.

Because the drawing account has a normal debit balance, Dario Mesa, Drawing is debited for $1,500.00 to show the increase in this contra capital account. The cash account also has a normal debit balance. Therefore, Cash is credited for $1,500.00 to show the decrease in this asset account.

The journal entry to record this cash withdrawal is shown in Illustration 11-11.

ILLUSTRATION 11-11   Journal entry to record a cash withdrawal by a partner

PAGE 21	JOURNAL				1	2		10	11 PAGE 21
			DOC. NO.	POST. REF.	GENERAL			CASH	
DATE	ACCOUNT TITLE				DEBIT	CREDIT		DEBIT	CREDIT
22	10	Dario Mesa, Drawing	C267		1500 00				1500 00	22

The date, *10*, is written in the Date column. No special amount column is provided for Dario Mesa, Drawing. Therefore, the contra capital account title, *Dario Mesa, Drawing*, is recorded in the Account Title column. The check number, C267, is entered in the Doc. No. column. The debit to Dario Mesa, Drawing, *$1,500.00*, is written in the General Debit column. The credit to Cash, *$1,500.00*, is written in the Cash Credit column.

Merchandise Withdrawal. A partner may also withdraw merchandise for personal use.

> *November 12, 19--. Dario Mesa, partner, withdrew merchandise for personal use, $200.00. Memorandum No. 44.*

This merchandise withdrawal increases Dario Mesa's drawing account balance and decreases the purchases account balance.

Because the drawing account has a normal debit balance, Dario Mesa, Drawing is debited for $200.00 to show the increase in this contra capital account. The purchases account also has a normal debit balance. Therefore, Purchases is credited for $200.00 to show the decrease in this cost account.

The journal entry to record this merchandise withdrawal is shown in Illustration 11-12.

ILLUSTRATION 11-12   Journal entry to record a merchandise withdrawal by a partner

PAGE 21	JOURNAL				1	2
			DOC. NO.	POST. REF.	GENERAL	
DATE	ACCOUNT TITLE				DEBIT	CREDIT
26	12	Dario Mesa, Drawing	M44		200 00	
27		Purchases				200 00

The date, *12,* is written in the Date column. Neither a Drawing Debit nor a Purchases Credit column is provided in the journal because merchandise withdrawals do not occur frequently. Therefore, the account title, *Dario Mesa, Drawing,* is recorded in the Account Title column. The memorandum number, *M44,* is entered in the Doc. No. column. The debit to Dario Mesa, Drawing, *$200.00,* is written in the General Debit column. The account title, *Purchases,* is recorded in the Account Title column on the next line. The credit to Purchases, *$200.00,* is entered in the General Credit column.

Correcting Entry

Errors may be made even though care is taken in recording transactions. Simple errors may be corrected by ruling through the incorrect item, as described in Chapter 5. However, a transaction may have been improperly journalized and posted to the ledger. When an error in a journal entry has already been posted, the incorrect journal entry should be corrected with an additional journal entry. A journal entry made to correct an error in the ledger is called a **correcting entry.**

> *November 13, 19--. Discovered that a payment of cash for advertising in October was journalized and posted in error as a debit to* Miscellaneous Expense *instead of* Advertising Expense, *$120.00. Memorandum No. 45.*

If an accounting error is discovered, a memorandum is prepared describing the correction to be made. The source document for a correcting entry is the memorandum. *(CONCEPT: Objective Evidence)* A memorandum for this correcting entry is shown in Illustration 11-13.

ILLUSTRATION 11-13   Memorandum for a correcting entry

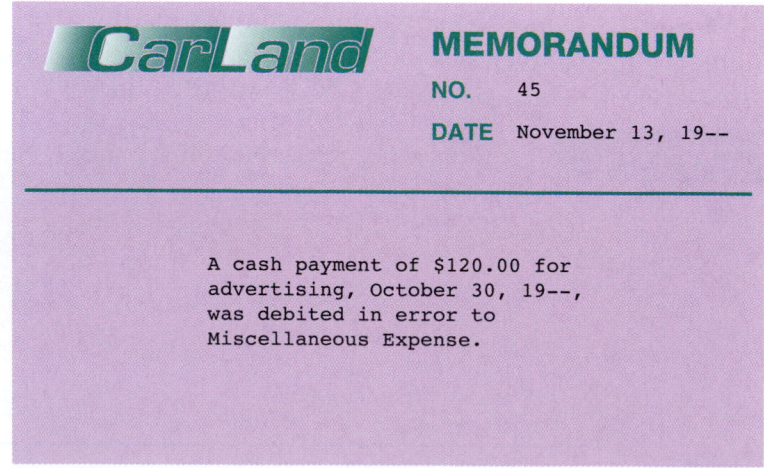

To correct the error, an entry is made to add $120.00 to the advertising expense account. The entry must also deduct $120.00 from the miscellaneous expense account. The correcting entry increases the advertising expense account balance and decreases the miscellaneous expense account balance.

Because the advertising expense account has a normal debit balance, Advertising Expense is debited for $120.00 to show the increase in this expense account. The miscellaneous expense account also has a normal debit balance. Therefore, Miscellaneous Expense is credited for $120.00 to show the decrease in this expense account.

The journal entry to record this correcting entry is shown in Illustration 11-14.

Advertising Expense	
120.00	

Miscellaneous Expense	
	120.00

ILLUSTRATION 11-14   Journal entry to record a correcting entry

PAGE 21   JOURNAL

	DATE		ACCOUNT TITLE	DOC. NO.	POST. REF.	GENERAL DEBIT	GENERAL CREDIT
28		13	Advertising Expense	M45		1 2 0 00	
29			Miscellaneous Expense				1 2 0 00
30							
31							
32							
33							
34							

The date, *13*, is written in the Date column. The account title, *Advertising Expense*, is recorded in the Account Title column. The memorandum number, *M45*, is entered in the Doc. No. column. The debit to Advertising Expense, *$120.00*, is entered in the General Debit column. The account title, *Miscellaneous Expense*, is written in the Account Title column on the next line. The credit to Miscellaneous Expense, *$120.00*, is recorded in the General Credit column.

The chart shown in Illustration 11-15 summarizes the entries for purchases, cash payments, and other transactions in an expanded journal.

Summary of entries for purchases, cash payments, and other transactions in an expanded journal

TRANSACTION	JOURNAL										
	1 GENERAL	2	3 ACCOUNTS RECEIVABLE	4	5 SALES CREDIT	6 SALES TAX PAYABLE CREDIT	7 ACCOUNTS PAYABLE	8	9 PURCHASES DEBIT	10 CASH	11
	DEBIT	CREDIT	DEBIT	CREDIT			DEBIT	CREDIT		DEBIT	CREDIT
Purchase merchandise for cash									X		X
Purchase merchandise on account								X	X		
Buying supplies for cash	X										X
Buying supplies on account	X							X			
Cash payment on account							X				X
Cash payment of an expense	X										X
Cash payment to replenish petty cash	X										X
Cash withdrawal	X										X
Merchandise withdrawal	X	X									

What is the meaning of each of the following?

1. **partnership**
2. **partner**
3. **merchandising business**
4. **merchandise**
5. **cost of merchandise**
6. **markup**
7. **vendor**
8. **purchase on account**
9. **invoice**
10. **purchase invoice**
11. **terms of sale**
12. **correcting entry**

QUESTIONS FOR INDIVIDUAL STUDY   EPT(b)

1. Why would two or more persons want to own a single business?

2. What makes the activities of a merchandising business different from those of a service business?

3. What are noncash transactions?

4. Why does CarLand use an 11-column journal rather than a 5-column journal like the one used by Rugcare?

5. What is the title of the account that shows the cost of merchandise purchased for sale?

6. What is the account classification of Purchases?

7. Which accounting concept is being applied when merchandise and other items bought are recorded and reported at the price agreed upon at the time the transactions occur?

8. What accounts are affected, and how, when merchandise is purchased for cash?

9. Why is a check mark placed in the Account Title column of an expanded journal for a cash purchase transaction?

10. Why would a business use a single general ledger account to summarize the amount owed to all vendors?

11. What is the name of the liability account that summarizes the amounts owed to all vendors?

12. Why does CarLand use its own set of sequential purchase invoice numbers rather than using the numbers assigned by vendors?

13. What accounts are affected, and how, when merchandise is purchased on account?

14. Why are the account titles (Purchases and Accounts Payable) for a purchase on account entry not written in the Account Title column in the expanded journal?

15. Why are supplies bought recorded in a separate supplies account rather than in the purchases account?

16. What accounts are affected, and how, when store supplies are bought on account?

17. What accounts are affected, and how, when a cash payment on account is made?

18. How does CarLand use a petty cash fund?

19. What accounts are affected, and how, when a withdrawal of merchandise is made?

20. When should a journal entry be made to correct errors in recording transactions?

CASE 1 Deborah Butler owns and operates a gift shop in a downtown shopping area. Because of a shopping mall that has opened in one of the suburbs, the gift shop's business has been declining. Ms. Butler has an opportunity to move the business to the shopping mall. Additional capital, however, is required to move and operate the business in a new location. The local bank has agreed to lend the money needed. The business hours would be extended at the new location. The business would also be open seven days a week. The extended hours plus the expected increase in business would require the hiring of one additional employee. Ms. Butler has been contacted by Fred Chaney, a person with similar merchandising experience, who would like to become a partner. As an alternative to borrowing cash, Mr. Chaney would provide the capital necessary to move the business to the new location. For the capital provided, Mr. Chaney would share equally in the net income or loss of the business. Mr. Chaney would also share equally in the operation of the business. Should Ms. Butler (1) borrow the money from the bank or (2) bring in a partner? Explain your answer.

CASE 2 Daryl Hodges is a high school student who works part-time in a local clothing store. As part of his duties, he records daily transactions in a journal. One day he asks the owner: "You use the purchase invoice as your source document for recording purchases of merchandise on account. You use a memorandum as your source document for recording the entry when supplies are bought on account. Why don't you use the invoice for both entries?" How would you respond to this question?

DRILL 11-D1   Analyzing transactions into debit and credit parts

INSTRUCTIONS:

Prepare two T accounts for each of the following transactions. Use the T accounts to analyze each transaction. Use account titles similar to CarLand's, as shown in the chart of accounts, page 244. The partners' names are Irma Gilbert and Alex Jensen. The first transaction is given as an example.

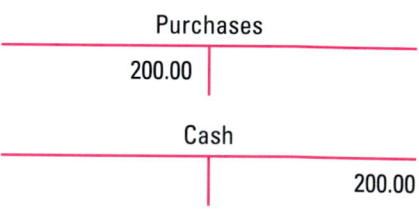

1. Purchased merchandise for cash, $200.00.
2. Purchased merchandise on account from Klein Co., $900.00.
3. Paid cash for office supplies, $75.00.
4. Bought store supplies on account from Central Supply, $240.00.
5. Bought office supplies on account from Cratin Supply, $125.00.
6. Purchased merchandise for cash, $175.00.
7. Paid cash for office supplies, $70.00.
8. Paid cash on account to Matson Company, $750.00.
9. Purchased merchandise on account from Garber Company, $1,200.00.
10. Paid cash for advertising, $85.00.
11. Irma Gilbert, partner, withdrew cash for personal use, $1,000.00.
12. Alex Jensen, partner, withdrew cash for personal use, $1,000.00.
13. Irma Gilbert, partner, withdrew merchandise for personal use, $130.00.
14. Paid cash on account to Butler Enterprises, $360.00.

15. Discovered that a transaction for office supplies bought last month was journalized and posted in error as a debit to Prepaid Insurance instead of Supplies—Office, $60.00.

16. Alex Jensen, partner, withdrew merchandise for personal use, $95.00.

The solution to Drill 11-D1 is needed to complete Drill 11-D2.

DRILL 11-D2 Analyzing journal entries

The solution to Drill 11-D1 is needed to complete Drill 11-D2.

INSTRUCTIONS:

A form for analyzing transactions is given in the working papers that accompany this textbook. Based on the answers in Drill 11-D1, write the amounts in the amount columns to be used to journalize each transaction. Transaction 1 is given as an example in the working papers.

APPLICATION PROBLEM   EPT(c,d)

PROBLEM 11-1 Journalizing purchases, cash payments, and other transactions

Mary Demski and Eileen Ivan, partners, own a gift shop.

INSTRUCTIONS:

Journalize the following transactions completed during September of the current year. Use page 21 of a journal similar to the one described in this chapter for CarLand. Source documents are abbreviated as follows: check, C; memorandum, M; purchase invoice, P.

Sept. 1. Purchased merchandise for cash, $150.00. C220.
1. Purchased merchandise on account from Kemp Fashions, $1,350.00. P60.
2. Paid cash for office supplies, $75.00. C221.
2. Purchased merchandise on account from Bonner & Co., $740.00. P61.
3. Purchased merchandise on account from Burton Fabrics, $585.00. P62.
4. Paid cash for office supplies, $55.00. C222.
7. Bought store supplies on account from Pulver Supply, $135.00. M42.
7. Purchased merchandise for cash, $120.00. C223.
8. Paid cash for telephone bill, $120.00. C224.
9. Bought office supplies on account from Lorand Supply, $85.00. M43.
11. Purchased merchandise for cash, $110.00. C225.
12. Paid cash for store supplies, $60.00. C226.
14. Mary Demski, partner, withdrew cash for personal use, $1,200.00. C227.
14. Eileen Ivan, partner, withdrew cash for personal use, $1,200.00. C228.
18. Paid cash on account to Kemp Fashions, $1,350.00, covering P60. C229.
21. Paid cash for advertising, $87.00. C230.
22. Paid cash on account to Bonner & Co., $740.00, covering P61. C231.
24. Mary Demski, partner, withdrew merchandise for personal use, $160.00. M44.
25. Discovered that a transaction for office supplies bought in August was journalized and posted in error as a debit to Purchases instead of Supplies—Office, $88.00. M45.
26. Paid cash on account to Burton Fabrics, $585.00, covering P62. C232.
29. Eileen Ivan, partner, withdrew merchandise for personal use, $120.00. M46.
30. Paid cash to replenish the petty cash fund, $305.00: office supplies, $63.00; store supplies, $51.00; advertising, $88.00; miscellaneous, $103.00. C233.
30. Paid cash on account to Pulver Supply, $135.00, covering M42. C234.

MASTERY PROBLEM 11-M Journalizing purchases, cash payments, and other transactions

APPLICATION

Sylvia Prior and Julia Steger, partners, own a bookstore.

INSTRUCTIONS:

Journalize the following transactions completed during November of the current year. Use page 23 of a journal similar to the one described in this chapter for CarLand. Source documents are abbreviated as follows: check, C; memorandum, M; purchase invoice, P.

Nov. 2. Paid cash for rent, $1,250.00. C261.
    2. Sylvia Prior, partner, withdrew cash for personal use, $1,500.00. C262.
    2. Julia Steger, partner, withdrew cash for personal use, $1,500.00. C263.
    3. Purchased merchandise for cash, $130.00. C264.
    4. Paid cash on account to BFL Publishing, $920.00, covering P71. C265.
    4. Purchased merchandise on account from Quality Books, $1,450.00. P74.
    5. Paid cash for office supplies, $48.00. C266.
    7. Julia Steger, partner, withdrew merchandise for personal use, $42.00. M32.
    9. Paid cash for electric bill, $154.00. C267.
    9. Paid cash on account to Quality Books, $1,235.00, covering P72. C268.
   10. Bought store supplies on account from Carson Supply Co., $106.00. M33.
   11. Paid cash on account to Matson Book Service, $975.00, covering P73. C269.
   14. Purchased merchandise on account from Falk Book Co., $1,525.00. P75.
   16. Paid cash for store supplies, $62.00. C270.
   16. Sylvia Prior, partner, withdrew merchandise for personal use, $64.00. M34.
   17. Bought store supplies on account from Gray Supplies, $214.00. M35.
   18. Purchased merchandise for cash, $145.00. C271.
   18. Paid cash to replenish the petty cash fund, $302.00: office supplies, $73.00; store supplies, $47.00; advertising, $92.00; miscellaneous, $90.00. C272.
   19. Paid cash on account to Quality Books, $1,450.00, covering P74. C273.
   21. Purchased merchandise on account from Voss Publishing, $925.00. P76.
   24. Paid cash on account to Falk Book Co., $1,525.00, covering P75. C274.
   26. Discovered that a transaction for office supplies bought in October was journalized and posted in error as a debit to Purchases instead of Supplies—Office, $94.00. M36.
   28. Bought store supplies on account from Carson Supply, $118.00. M37.
   30. Purchased merchandise for cash, $68.00. C275.

CHALLENGE PROBLEM 11-C Journalizing correcting entries

A review of Meir Decorating's accounting records for last month revealed the following errors.

INSTRUCTIONS:

Journalize the needed correcting entries on page 8 of a journal similar to the one described in this chapter for CarLand. Use December 2 of the current year.

Dec. 2. Merchandise withdrawn by Alice Reyes, partner, was journalized and posted in error as a credit to Cash instead of Purchases, $116.00. M35.
    2. Office supplies bought for cash were journalized and posted in error as a debit to Purchases instead of Supplies—Office, $95.00. M36.
    2. A check written for advertising was journalized and posted in error as a debit to Miscellaneous Expense instead of Advertising Expense, $125.00. M37.
    2. Store supplies bought on account were journalized and posted in error as a debit to Utilities Expense instead of Supplies—Store, $52.00. M38.
    2. Merchandise purchased on account was journalized and posted in error as a debit to Supplies—Office instead of Purchases, $850.00. M39.

Dec. 2. A check written for rent was journalized and posted in error as a debit to Salary Expense instead of Rent Expense, $1,200.00. M40.

2. A cash withdrawal by Harold Atkins, partner, was journalized and posted in error as a credit to Purchases instead of Cash, $200.00. M41.

2. A check written for miscellaneous expense was journalized and posted in error as a debit to Supplies Expense—Store instead of Miscellaneous Expense, $89.00. M42.

2. Office supplies bought for cash were journalized and posted in error as a debit to Prepaid Insurance instead of Supplies—Office, $160.00. M43.

2. A check written for store supplies was journalized and posted in error as a debit to Supplies—Office instead of Supplies—Store, $151.00. M44.

12

Journalizing Sales and Cash Receipts

ENABLING PERFORMANCE TASKS

After studying Chapter 12, you will be able to:

a Define accounting terms related to sales and cash receipts for a merchandising business.

b Identify accounting concepts and practices related to sales and cash receipts for a merchandising business.

c Analyze sales and cash receipts transactions for a merchandising business.

d Journalize sales and cash receipts transactions for a merchandising business.

e Prove and rule a journal.

TERMS PREVIEW

customer • sales tax • cash sale • credit card sale • sale on account • sales invoice

Purchases and sales of merchandise are the two major activities of a merchandising business. A person or business to whom merchandise or services are sold is called a **customer.** Rugcare, described in Part 2, sells services. CarLand, described in this part, sells merchandise. Other businesses may sell both services and merchandise.

SALES TAX

Laws of most states and some cities require that a tax be collected from customers for each sale made. A tax on a sale of merchandise or services is called a **sales tax.** Sales tax rates are usually stated as a percentage of sales. Regardless of the tax rates used, accounting procedures are the same.

Every business collecting a sales tax needs accurate records of the amount of tax collected. Businesses must file reports with the proper government unit and pay the amount of sales tax collected. Records need to show (1) total sales and (2) total sales tax. The amount of sales tax collected by CarLand is a business liability until paid to the state government. Therefore, the sales tax amount is recorded in a separate liability account titled *Sales Tax Payable*. The liability account, Sales Tax Payable, has a normal credit balance. This account is increased by a credit and decreased by a debit, as shown in the T account.

CarLand operates in a state with a 6% sales tax rate. A customer must pay for the price of the goods plus the sales tax. The total amount of a sale of merchandise priced at $200.00 is calculated as shown below.

Sales Tax Payable	
Debit side	Credit side
	Normal balance
Decrease	Increase

Price of Goods	×	Sales Tax Rate	=	Sales Tax
$200.00	×	6%	=	$12.00

Price of Goods	+	Sales Tax	=	Total Amount Received
$200.00	+	$12.00	=	$212.00

A customer must pay $212.00 for the merchandise ($200.00 for the goods plus $12.00 for the sales tax). CarLand records the price of goods sold, the sales tax, and the total amount received.

JOURNALIZING SALES AND CASH RECEIPTS FOR SALES

A sale of merchandise may be (1) for cash or (2) on account. A sale of merchandise increases the revenue of a business. Regardless of when payment is made, the revenue should be recorded at the time of a sale, not on the date cash is received. For example, on June 15 CarLand sells merchandise on account to a customer. The customer pays CarLand for the merchandise on July 12. CarLand records the revenue on June 15, the date of the sale. The accounting concept, *Realization of Revenue*, is applied when revenue is recorded at the time goods or services are sold. *(CONCEPT: Realization of Revenue)*

Cash and Credit Card Sales

CarLand sells most of its merchandise for cash. A sale in which cash is received for the total amount of the sale at the time of the transaction is called a **cash sale.** CarLand also sells merchandise to customers who have a bank approved credit card. A sale in which a credit card is used for the total amount of the sale at the time of the transaction is called a **credit card sale.** Major bank approved credit cards include VISA, MasterCard, Discover Card, and Carte Blanche. CarLand accepts all major bank approved credit cards from customers. A customer who uses a credit card promises to pay the amount due for the credit card transaction to the bank issuing the credit card.

CarLand prepares a credit card slip for each credit card sale. At the end of each week, these credit card slips are included with Car-Land's bank deposit. CarLand's bank accepts the credit card slips the same way it accepts checks and cash for deposit. The bank increases CarLand's bank account by the total amount of the credit card sales deposited. If a credit card was issued by another bank, CarLand's bank sends the credit card slips to the issuing bank. The bank that issues the credit card then bills the customer and collects the amount owed. The bank that accepts and processes the credit card slips for a business charges a fee for this service. This fee is included on CarLand's monthly bank statement.

Cash and credit card sales are both revenue items that increase the revenue account, Sales. Because the bank accepts credit card slips the same way it accepts cash, CarLand's bank account increases after each deposit as though cash had been deposited. Therefore, CarLand combines all cash and credit card sales and records the two revenue items as a single cash sales transaction.

> *November 7, 19--. Recorded cash and credit card sales, $6,450.00, plus sales tax, $387.00; total, $6,837.00. Cash Register Tape No. 7.*

CarLand uses a cash register to list all cash and credit card sales. When a transaction is entered on the cash register, a paper tape is printed as a receipt for the customer. The cash register also internally accumulates data about total cash and credit card sales.

At the end of each week, a cash register tape is printed showing total cash and credit card sales. The tape is removed from the cash register and marked with a *T* and the date (T7). The cash register tape is used by CarLand as the source document for weekly cash and credit card sales transactions. *(CONCEPT: Objective Evidence)*

A cash and credit card sales transaction increases the balances of the cash account, the sales account, and the sales tax payable account.

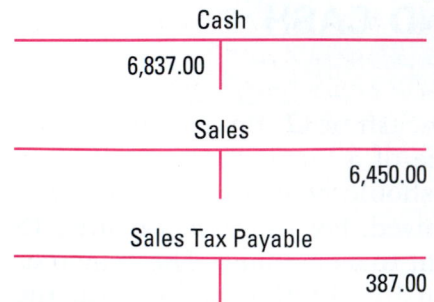

Cash	
6,837.00	

Sales	
	6,450.00

Sales Tax Payable	
	387.00

Because the asset account, Cash, has a normal debit balance, Cash is debited for the total sales and sales tax, $6,837.00, to show the increase in this asset account. The sales account has a normal credit balance. Therefore, Sales is credited for the total price of all goods sold, $6,450.00, to show the increase in this revenue account. The sales tax payable account also has a normal credit balance. Therefore, Sales Tax Payable is credited for the total sales tax, $387.00, to show the increase in this liability account.

The journal entry to record this cash and credit card sales transaction is shown in Illustration 12-1.

ILLUSTRATION 12-1   Journal entry to record cash and credit card sales

PAGE 21													PAGE 21	
				JOURNAL				5	6			10	11	
												CASH		
	DATE	ACCOUNT TITLE		DOC. NO.	POST. REF.		SALES CREDIT	SALES TAX PAYABLE CREDIT			DEBIT	CREDIT	
14	7 ✓			T7	✓		6 4 5 0 00	3 8 7 00			6 8 3 7 00			14

The date, 7, is written in the Date column. Special amount columns are provided for all accounts in this transaction. Therefore, a check mark is placed in the Account Title column to show that no account title needs to be written. The cash register tape number, *T7*, is recorded in the Doc. No. column. A check mark is also placed in the Post. Ref. column to show that amounts on this line do not need to be posted individually. The credit to Sales, *$6,450.00*, is written in the Sales Credit column. The credit to Sales Tax Payable, *$387.00*, is recorded in the Sales Tax Payable Credit column. The debit to Cash, *$6,837.00*, is entered in the Cash Debit column.

Sales on Account

A sale for which cash will be received at a later date is called a **sale on account.** A sale on account is also referred to as a charge sale. CarLand sells on account only to businesses. Other customers must either pay cash or use a credit card.

CarLand summarizes the total due from all charge customers in a general ledger account titled *Accounts Receivable.* Accounts Receivable is an asset account with a normal debit balance. Therefore, the accounts receivable account is increased by a debit and decreased by a credit, as shown in the T account.

Accounts Receivable	
Debit side Normal balance Increase	Credit side Decrease

When merchandise is sold on account, the seller prepares a form showing what has been sold. A form describing the goods sold, the quantity, and the price is known as an invoice. An invoice used as a source document for recording a sale on account is called a **sales invoice.** *(CONCEPT: Objective Evidence)* A sales invoice is also referred to as a sales ticket or a sales slip. The sales invoice used by CarLand is shown in Illustration 12-2.

ILLUSTRATION 12-2   Sales invoice

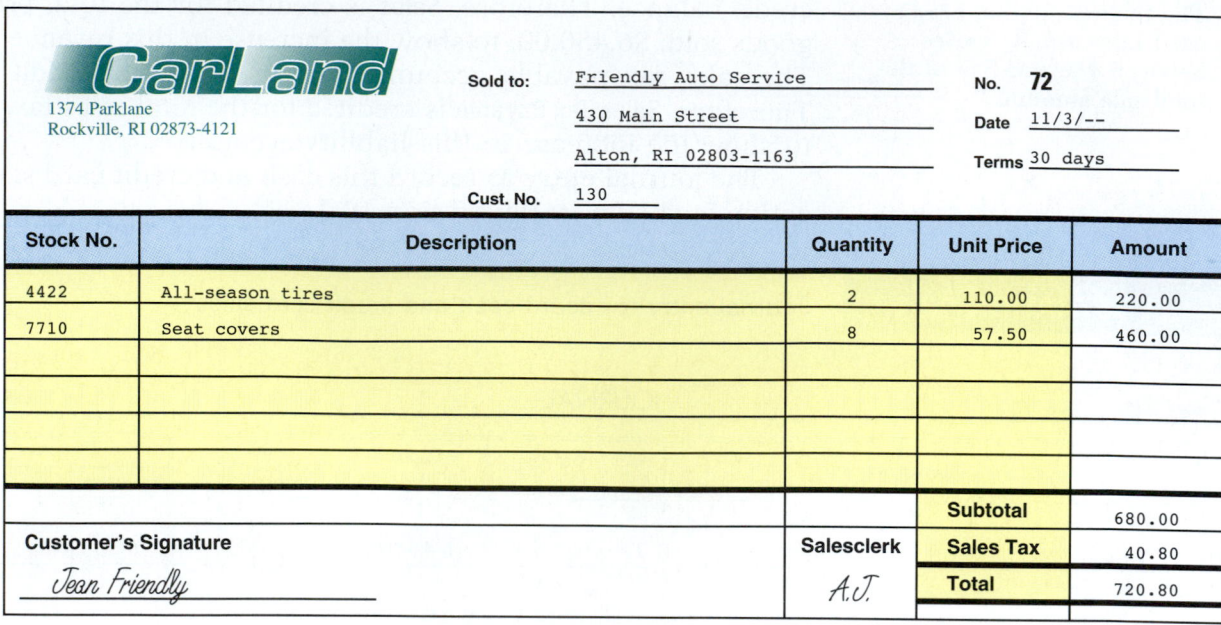

The seller considers an invoice for a sale on account to be a sales invoice. The same invoice is considered by the customer to be a purchase invoice.

A sales invoice is prepared in duplicate. The original copy is given to the customer. The carbon copy is used as the source document for the sale on account transaction. *(CONCEPT: Objective Evidence)* Sales invoices are numbered in sequence. The number 72 is the number of the sales invoice issued to Friendly Auto Service.

November 3, 19--. Sold merchandise on account to Friendly Auto Service, $680.00, plus sales tax, $40.80; total, $720.80. Sales Invoice No. 72.

A sale on account transaction increases the amount to be collected later from a customer. Payment for this sale will be received at a later date. However, the sale is recorded at the time the sale is made because the sale has taken place and payment is due to CarLand. *(CONCEPT: Realization of Revenue)*

Because the accounts receivable account has a normal debit balance, Accounts Receivable is debited for the total sales and sales tax, $720.80, to show the increase in this asset account. The sales account has a normal credit balance. Therefore, Sales is credited for the price of the goods, $680.00, to show the increase in this revenue account. The sales tax payable account also has a normal credit balance. Therefore, Sales Tax Payable is credited for the amount of sales tax, $40.80, to show the increase in this liability account.

The journal entry to record this sale on account transaction is shown in Illustration 12-3.

Accounts Receivable	
720.80	

Sales	
	680.00

Sales Tax Payable	
	40.80

INTERNATIONAL WORK WEEK

American business offices normally operate Monday through Friday, eight hours a day, with a 30 to 45 minute lunch break. However, that is not necessarily true in other countries. When doing business internationally, the business day must be taken into consideration when telephone communication is made.

For example, in Spain, many businesses close at 2:00 p.m. so that employees may eat lunch with their families. The office reopens at 5:00 p.m. and stays open until about 8:00 p.m.

In the People's Republic of China, employees usually work Monday through Saturday, eight hours a day, with lunch from 1:00 p.m. to 2:00 p.m.

Before attempting to telephone or fax communication to foreign countries, the time differences and working hours must be taken into consideration. The following chart shows the time zones around the world.

World Time Zone Map

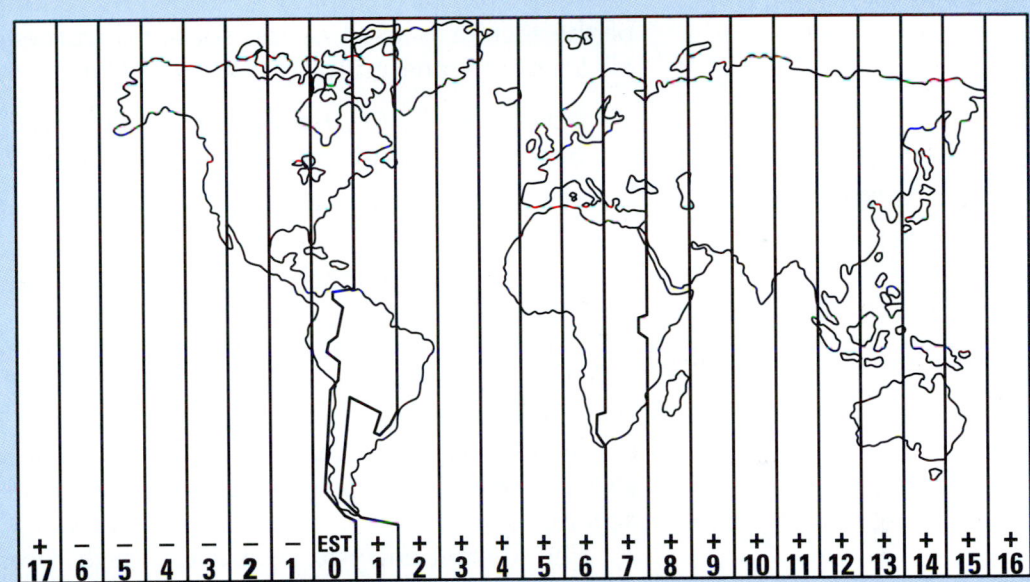

| ILLUSTRATION 12-3 | Journal entry to record a sale on account |

PAGE 21	JOURNAL						
				ACCOUNTS RECEIVABLE		**SALES CREDIT**	**SALES TAX PAYABLE CREDIT**
DATE	ACCOUNT TITLE	DOC. NO.	POST. REF.	DEBIT	CREDIT		
3	*Friendly Auto Service*	S72		7 20 80		6 80 00	4 08 0

The date, *3*, is written in the Date column. The customer name, *Friendly Auto Service*, is recorded in the Account Title column. The sales invoice number, *S72*, is entered in the Doc. No. column. The debit to Accounts Receivable $720.80, is written in the Accounts Receivable Debit column. The credit to Sales, $680.00, is recorded in the Sales Credit column. The credit to Sales Tax Payable, $40.80, is entered in the Sales Tax Payable Credit column.

The debit and credit amounts are recorded in special amount columns. Therefore, writing the titles of the ledger accounts in the Account Title column is not necessary. However, the name of the customer is written in the Account Title column to show from whom the amount is due. CarLand's procedures for keeping records of the amounts to be collected from each customer are described in Chapter 13.

Cash Receipts on Account

When cash is received on account from a customer, CarLand prepares a receipt. The receipts are prenumbered so that all receipts can be accounted for. Receipts are prepared in duplicate. The original copy of the receipt is given to the customer. The carbon copy of the receipt is used as the source document for the cash receipt on account transaction. (CONCEPT: Objective Evidence)

November 6, 19--. Received cash on account from Autohaus Service, $1,802.00, covering S65. Receipt No. 86.

A cash receipt on account transaction decreases the amount to be collected from a customer. This transaction increases the cash account balance and decreases the accounts receivable account balance.

Because the cash account has a normal debit balance, Cash is debited for the amount of cash received, $1,802.00, to show the increase in this asset account. The accounts receivable account also has a normal debit balance. Therefore, Accounts Receivable is credited for $1,802.00 to show the decrease in this asset account.

The journal entry to record this cash receipt on account transaction is shown in Illustration 12-4.

	Cash
1,802.00	

	Accounts Receivable
	1,802.00

ILLUSTRATION 12-4   Journal entry to record a cash receipt on account

PAGE 21		JOURNAL			ACCOUNTS RECEIVABLE		CASH PAGE 21	
					3	4	10	11
DATE	ACCOUNT TITLE		DOC. NO.	POST. REF.	DEBIT	CREDIT	DEBIT	CREDIT
11	6	Autohaus Service	R86			1 8 0 2 00	1 8 0 2 00		11
12									12

The date, 6, is written in the Date column. The customer name, *Autohaus Service*, is recorded in the Account Title column. The receipt number, *R86,* is entered in the Doc. No. column. The credit to Accounts Receivable, *$1,802.00,* is written in the Accounts Receivable Credit column. The debit to Cash, *$1,802.00,* is recorded in the Cash Debit column.

The Summary Illustration on page 277 summarizes the entries for sales and cash receipts transactions in an expanded journal.

PROVING AND RULING AN EXPANDED JOURNAL

A journal is proved and ruled whenever a journal page is filled and always at the end of a month.

Totaling and Proving an Expanded Journal Page

After all November 14 entries are recorded, page 21 of CarLand's journal is filled. Page 21 is totaled and proved before column totals are forwarded to page 22. To prove a journal page, CarLand uses a calculator to verify that the total debit amounts equal the total credit amounts. CarLand's debit totals equal the credit totals on page 21 of the journal. Therefore, the equality of debits and credits has been proved.

Ruling an Expanded Journal Page to Carry Totals Forward

After a journal page has been proved, the journal must be prepared for forwarding. CarLand's journal column totals prepared for forwarding are shown on line 34, Illustration 12-5 on pages 274 and 275.

Five steps are followed to rule CarLand's journal.

1 Rule a single line across all amount columns directly below the last entry to indicate that the columns are to be added.

2 On the next line write the date, *14,* in the Date column.

3 Write the words, *Carried Forward,* in the Account Title column. A check mark is also placed in the Post. Ref. column to show that nothing on this line needs to be posted.

4 Write each column total below the single line.

5 Rule double lines below the column totals across all amount columns to show that the totals have been verified as correct.

Starting a New Expanded Journal Page

The totals from the previous journal page are carried forward to the next journal page. The totals are recorded on the first line of the new page. Column totals brought forward to a new page are shown on line 1, Illustration 12-6 on pages 274 and 275.

ILLUSTRATION 12-5   Journal prepared for forwarding (left page)

	DATE		ACCOUNT TITLE	DOC. NO.	POST. REF.	GENERAL		ACCOUNTS RECEIVABLE		
						DEBIT	CREDIT	DEBIT	CREDIT	
1	Nov.	2	✓	C259	✓					1
2		2	Veloz Automotive	P74						2
32		14	Powell Rent-A-Car	R89					3 1 8 00	32
33		14	✓	T14	✓					33
34		14	Carried Forward		✓	4 2 9 3 00	3 2 0 00	3 3 9 2 00	3 9 7 5 00	34

PAGE 21 · JOURNAL

ILLUSTRATION 12-6   Journal totals brought forward to a new page (left page)

PAGE 22 · JOURNAL

	DATE	ACCOUNT TITLE	DOC. NO.	POST. REF.	GENERAL		ACCOUNTS RECEIVABLE		
					DEBIT	CREDIT	DEBIT	CREDIT	
1	Nov. 14	Brought Forward		✓	4 2 9 3 00	3 2 0 00	3 3 9 2 00	3 9 7 5 00	1
2									2
3									3
4									4

Four steps are followed for forwarding totals.

1 Write the page number, *22,* at the top of the journal.

2 Write the date, *19--, Nov. 14,* in the Date column.

3 Write the words, *Brought Forward,* in the Account Title column. A check mark is also placed in the Post. Ref. column to show that nothing on this line needs to be posted.

4 Record the column totals brought forward from page 21 of the journal.

Proving an Expanded Journal at the End of a Month

Equality of debits and credits in a journal is proved at the end of each month. The proof for CarLand's journal, Illustration 12-7 on pages 276 and 277, is calculated as follows.

ILLUSTRATION 12-5

Journal prepared for forwarding (right page)

	5 SALES CREDIT	6 SALES TAX PAYABLE CREDIT	7 ACCOUNTS PAYABLE DEBIT	8 ACCOUNTS PAYABLE CREDIT	9 PURCHASES DEBIT	10 CASH DEBIT	11 CASH CREDIT	
1					4 8 3 00		4 8 3 00	1
2				1 7 5 4 00	1 7 5 4 00			2
32						3 1 8 00		32
33	5 1 0 0 00	3 0 6 00				5 4 0 6 00		33
34	14 7 5 0 00	8 8 5 00	5 3 6 0 00	11 6 9 0 00	12 0 1 3 00	16 2 1 8 00	9 6 5 6 00	34

PAGE *21*

ILLUSTRATION 12-6

Journal totals brought forward to a new page (right page)

	5 SALES CREDIT	6 SALES TAX PAYABLE CREDIT	7 ACCOUNTS PAYABLE DEBIT	8 ACCOUNTS PAYABLE CREDIT	9 PURCHASES DEBIT	10 CASH DEBIT	11 CASH CREDIT	
1	14 7 5 0 00	8 8 5 00	5 3 6 0 00	11 6 9 0 00	12 0 1 3 00	16 2 1 8 00	9 6 5 6 00	1
2								2
3								3
4								4

PAGE *22*

Col. No.	Column Title	Debit Totals	Credit Totals
1	General Debit	$15,686.22	
2	General Credit		$ 2,029.02
3	Accounts Receivable Debit	9,222.00	
4	Accounts Receivable Credit		7,950.00
5	Sales Credit		31,600.00
6	Sales Tax Payable Credit		1,896.00
7	Accounts Payable Debit	10,820.00	
8	Accounts Payable Credit		15,870.00
9	Purchases Debit	14,773.00	
10	Cash Debit	32,224.00	
11	Cash Credit		23,380.20
	Totals	$82,725.22	$82,725.22

FYI

Double lines below totals show that the totals have been verified as correct.

The two totals, *$82,725.22,* are equal. Equality of debits and credits in CarLand's journal for November is proved.

	DATE	ACCOUNT TITLE	DOC. NO.	POST. REF.	GENERAL DEBIT	GENERAL CREDIT	ACCOUNTS RECEIVABLE DEBIT	ACCOUNTS RECEIVABLE CREDIT	
15	30 ✓			T30 ✓					15
16	30	Totals			15 686 22	20 290 2	9 222 00	7 950 00	16
17									17
18									18
19									19
20									20

PAGE 23   JOURNAL

Proving Cash at the End of a Month

CarLand's cash proof at the end of November is calculated as shown below.

Cash on hand at the beginning of the month . . . . (November 1 balance of cash account in general ledger)	$14,706.20
Plus total cash received during the month . . . . (Cash Debit column total, line 16, Illustration 12-7)	32,224.00
Equals total	$46,930.20
Less total cash paid during the month . . . . (Cash Credit column total, line 16, Illustration 12-7)	23,380.20
Equals cash balance on hand at end of the month . . .	$23,550.00
Checkbook balance on the next unused check stub . .	$23,550.00

Since the balance on the next unused check stub is the same as the cash proof, cash is proved.

Ruling an Expanded Journal at the End of a Month

CarLand's journal is ruled at the end of each month. CarLand's expanded journal totaled and ruled at the end of November is shown on line 16, Illustration 12-7. Five steps are followed to rule a journal.

1 Rule a single line across all amount columns directly below the last entry to indicate that the columns are to be added.

FYI

When cash is proved, it must always equal the amount on the next unused check stub.

ILLUSTRATION 12-7 Journal page totaled and ruled at the end of a month (right page)

PAGE *23*

	5	6	7	8	9	10	11	
	SALES CREDIT	SALES TAX PAYABLE CREDIT	ACCOUNTS PAYABLE		PURCHASES DEBIT	CASH		
			DEBIT	CREDIT		DEBIT	CREDIT	
15	1 150 00	69 00				1 219 00		15
16	31 600 00	1 896 00	10 820 00	15 870 00	14 773 00	32 224 00	23 380 20	16
17								17
18								18
19								19
20								20

Audit Your Understanding

1. How is a journal proved before column totals are forwarded to a new page?
2. List the four steps for starting a new expanded journal page.
3. How is cash proved for an expanded journal?

2 On the next line write the date, *30,* in the Date column.

3 Write the word, *Totals,* in the Account Title column.

4 Write each column total below the single line.

5 Rule double lines across all amount columns to show that the totals have been verified as correct.

Some of the column totals will be posted as described in Chapter 13. Therefore, a check mark is not placed in the Post. Ref. column for this line.

The chart shown in Illustration 12-8 summarizes the entries for sales and cash receipts transactions in an expanded journal.

SUMMARY ILLUSTRATION 12-8

Summary of entries for sales and cash receipts transactions in an expanded journal

TRANSACTION	JOURNAL 1 GENERAL DEBIT	2 GENERAL CREDIT	3 ACCOUNTS RECEIVABLE DEBIT	4 ACCOUNTS RECEIVABLE CREDIT	5 SALES CREDIT	6 SALES TAX PAYABLE CREDIT	7 ACCOUNTS PAYABLE DEBIT	8 ACCOUNTS PAYABLE CREDIT	9 PURCHASES DEBIT	10 CASH DEBIT	11 CASH CREDIT
Cash and credit card sale					X	X				X	
Sale on account			X		X	X					
Cash receipt on account				X						X	

What is the meaning of each of the following?

1. customer
2. sales tax
3. cash sale
4. credit card sale
5. sale on account
6. sales invoice

1. What are the two major activities of a merchandising business?
2. How are sales tax rates usually stated?
3. Why must every business that collects a sales tax keep accurate records of the amount of tax collected?
4. What two amounts must sales tax records show?
5. Why is sales tax collected considered a liability?
6. What is the normal balance of the sales tax payable account, and how is the account increased and decreased?
7. Which accounting concept is being applied when revenue is recorded at the time a sale is made, regardless of when payment is made?
8. Which accounting concept is being applied when a cash register tape is used as the source document for cash and credit card sales?
9. How often does CarLand journalize cash sales?
10. What accounts are affected, and how, for a cash and credit card sales transaction?
11. Why is a check mark placed in the Account Title column of an expanded journal when journalizing cash and credit card sales?
12. What is another name used for a sale on account?
13. What is the title of the general ledger account used to summarize the total amount due from all charge customers?
14. What is the source document for a sale on account transaction?
15. What are other names used for a sales invoice?
16. What accounts are affected, and how, for a sale on account transaction?
17. Which amount columns in a journal are used to record a sale on account transaction?
18. What accounts are affected, and how, for a cash receipt on account transaction?
19. How often is the equality of debits and credits in a journal proved?
20. How often is a journal page ruled?

CASE 1 Carrie and Karl Lott, partners, operate a shoe store. A 5-column journal similar to the one described in Chapter 5 is used to record all transactions. The business sells merchandise for cash and on account. The business also purchases most of its merchandise on account. Mrs. Lott asked an accountant to check the accounting system and recommend changes. The accountant suggests that an expanded journal similar to the one described in Chapters 11 and 12 be used. Which journal would be better? Why?

CASE 2 Amy Pryor, an accountant for a sporting goods store, has noted a major increase in overdue amounts from charge customers. All invoice amounts from sales on account are due within 30 days. The amounts due have reduced the amount of cash available for the day-to-day operation of the business. Miss Pryor recommends that the business (1) stop all sales on account and (2) begin accepting bank credit cards. The owner is reluctant to accept the recommendations because the business might lose some reliable customers who do not have credit cards. Also, the business will have increased expenses because of the credit card fee. How would you respond to Miss Pryor's recommendations? What alternatives might the owner consider?

How often have you heard people complain about the rising costs of products? The tendency for prices to increase over time is referred to as inflation. Increasing prices reduce what an individual or company can purchase with the same amount of money.

INSTRUCTIONS:

The following table represents the prices for selected consumer goods in 1980. Copy the table and add a column for the current year and a column for the percent of change. Use the newspaper and identify current prices for the products listed. Determine the percentage change in the price of each item. If an item decreased in price, can you explain the reason for the decrease?

COMPARISON OF PRICES FOR SELECTED CONSUMER ITEMS 1980 AND 19--

Item	1980 Price
19-inch color television	$439.00
Cassette tape	6.95
Milk (gallon)	1.99
Ground beef (pound)	1.69
Eggs, medium (dozen)	.69
Raisin bran	1.39
Film, 12 exposures	1.13
Theater ticket	3.50
Motor oil (quart)	.84
Refrigerator (19.1 cu. ft.)	679.00

DRILLS FOR UNDERSTANDING

EPT(c,d)

DRILL 12-D1 Analyzing transactions into debit and credit parts

TUTORIAL

INSTRUCTIONS:

Prepare T accounts for each of the following transactions. Use the T accounts to analyze each transaction. A 5% sales tax has been added to each sale. The first transaction is given as an example.

Cash	
1,575.00	

Sales	
	1,500.00

Sales Tax Payable	
	75.00

1. Recorded cash and credit card sales, $1,500.00, plus sales tax, $75.00; total, $1,575.00.

2. Sold merchandise on account to Steven Kramer, $300.00, plus sales tax, $15.00; total, $315.00.

3. Sold merchandise on account to Mark Fields, $360.00, plus sales tax, $18.00; total, $378.00.

4. Received cash on account from Jackson White, $157.50.

5. Received cash on account from Gloria Burton, $68.25.

6. Recorded cash and credit card sales, $1,750.00, plus sales tax, $87.50; total, $1,837.50.

The solution to Drill 12-D1 is needed to complete Drill 12-D3.

DRILL 12-D2 Analyzing sales transactions

MATHEMATICS

INSTRUCTIONS:

1. Prepare a T account for each of the following accounts: Cash, Accounts Receivable, Sales, and Sales Tax Payable.

2. Using the T accounts, analyze the following transactions. Add a 6% sales tax to each sale. Write the transaction number in parentheses to the left of each amount. The first transaction is given as an example.

1. Recorded cash and credit card sales, $2,700.00.
2. Sold merchandise on account to Melissa Bedo, $180.00.
3. Sold merchandise on account to Kim Lea, $170.00.
4. Received cash on account from Maria Jones, $148.40.
5. Received cash on account from Jack Mumford, $79.50.
6. Recorded cash and credit card sales, $2,375.00.

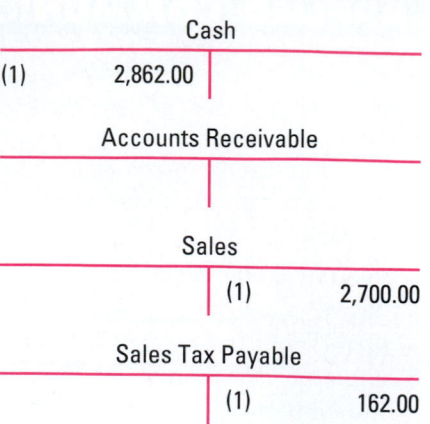

Cash	
(1) 2,862.00	

Accounts Receivable	

Sales	
	(1) 2,700.00

Sales Tax Payable	
	(1) 162.00

DRILL 12-D3 Analyzing journal entries

The solution to Drill 12-D1 is needed to complete Drill 12-D3.

INSTRUCTIONS:

A form for analyzing journal entries is given in the working papers that accompany this textbook. Based on the answers in Drill 12-D1, write the amounts in the amount columns to be used to journalize each transaction. Transaction 1 is given as an example in the working papers.

APPLICATION PROBLEM

EPT(c,d,e)

PROBLEM 12-1 Journalizing sales and cash receipts

Mark Butler and Betty Rivers, partners, own a tennis equipment and clothing store.

INSTRUCTIONS:

1. Journalize the following transactions completed during September of the current year. Use page 16 of a journal similar to the one described in this chapter. A 4% sales tax has been added to each sale. Source documents are abbreviated as follows: receipt, R; sales invoice, S; cash register tape, T.

Sept. 1. Sold merchandise on account to Valerie Seeley, $50.00, plus sales tax, $2.00; total, $52.00. S66.

2. Sold merchandise on account to Jill Folker, $125.00, plus sales tax, $5.00; total, $130.00. S67.

4. Sold merchandise on account to Jerome Hodges, $85.00, plus sales tax, $3.40; total, $88.40. S68.

5. Received cash on account from Rita Picken, $140.40, covering S62. R93.

5. Recorded cash and credit card sales, $2,360.00, plus sales tax, $94.40; total, $2,454.40. T5.

7. Received cash on account from Karla Doyle, $182.00, covering S63. R94.

9. Sold merchandise on account to Anthony Zolte, $115.00, plus sales tax, $4.60; total, $119.60. S69.

12. Recorded cash and credit card sales, $2,890.00, plus sales tax, $115.60; total, $3,005.60. T12.

12. Received cash on account from Jonathan Ames, $50.40, covering S64. R95.

14. Received cash on account from Robert Hall, $67.60, covering S65. R96.

15. Sold merchandise on account to Beth Klein, $115.00, plus sales tax, $4.60; total, $119.60. S70.

Sept. 17. Received cash on account from Valerie Seeley, $52.00, covering S66. R97.

19. Recorded cash and credit card sales, $2,810.00, plus sales tax, $112.40; total, $2,922.40. T19.

25. Received cash on account from Jill Folker, $130.00, covering S67. R98.

26. Sold merchandise on account to Jill Folker, $75.00, plus sales tax, $3.00; total, $78.00. S71.

26. Recorded cash and credit card sales, $2,650.00, plus sales tax, $106.00; total, $2,756.00. T26.

28. Received cash on account from Jerome Hodges, $88.40, covering S68. R99.

29. Sold merchandise on account to Karla Doyle, $95.00, plus sales tax, $3.80; total, $98.80. S72.

30. Recorded cash and credit card sales, $1,540.00, plus sales tax, $61.60; total, $1,601.60. T30.

2. Total the journal. Prove the equality of debits and credits.

3. Rule the journal.

MASTERY PROBLEM 12-M   Journalizing transactions

Kevin Sykes and David Webb, partners, own a bicycle and motorcycle store.

INSTRUCTIONS:

1. Journalize the following transactions completed during November of the current year. Use page 18 of a journal similar to the one described in this chapter. A 6% sales tax has been added to each sale. Source documents are abbreviated as follows: check, C; memorandum, M; purchase invoice, P; receipt, R; sales invoice, S; cash register tape, T.

Nov. 2. Paid cash for rent, $1,250.00. C244.

2. Kevin Sykes, partner, withdrew cash for personal use, $600.00. C245.

2. David Webb, partner, withdrew cash for personal use, $600.00. C246.

3. Paid cash for electric bill, $130.00. C247.

3. Purchased merchandise on account from Vista Cycle Co., $2,275.00. P58.

4. Paid cash on account to Daley Motorcycles, $1,360.00, covering P56. C248.

5. Sold merchandise on account to Loree Adams, $1,130.00, plus sales tax, $67.80; total, $1,197.80. S61.

5. Paid cash for office supplies, $62.00. C249.

6. Purchased merchandise for cash, $165.00. C250.

7. Recorded cash and credit card sales, $5,850.00, plus sales tax, $351.00; total, $6,201.00. T7.

9. Sold merchandise on account to Victor Droste, $358.00, plus sales tax, $21.48; total, $379.48. S62.

9. Received cash on account from Wayne Ivory, $1,775.50, covering S57. R112.

11. Bought office supplies on account from Walden Supply, $68.00. M43.

12. Purchased merchandise for cash, $180.00. C251.

12. Received cash on account from Robert Melvin, $996.40, covering S58. R113.

13. Paid cash on account to Action Cycles, $1,365.00, covering P57. C252.

14. David Webb, partner, withdrew merchandise for personal use, $385.00. M44.

Nov. 14. Recorded cash and credit card sales, $2,680.00, plus sales tax, $160.80; total, $2,840.80. T14.

16. Kevin Sykes, partner, withdrew cash for personal use, $600.00. C253.

16. David Webb, partner, withdrew cash for personal use, $600.00. C254.

17. Purchased merchandise on account from United Bicycle Co., $825.00. P59.

18. Purchased merchandise for cash, $196.00. C255.

18. Bought store supplies on account from Baker Supply, $92.00. M45.

19. Paid cash on account to Walden Supply, $68.00, covering M43. C256.

21. Recorded cash and credit card sales, $2,430.00, plus sales tax, $145.80; total, $2,575.80. T21.

23. Discovered that a payment of cash for advertising in October was journalized and posted in error as a debit to Miscellaneous Expense instead of Advertising Expense, $125.00. M46.

23. Paid cash for office supplies, $44.00. C257.

2. Prepare page 18 of the journal for forwarding. Total the amount columns. Prove the equality of debits and credits, and record the totals to be carried forward on line 32.

3. Record the totals brought forward on line 1 of page 19 of the journal. Prove the equality of debits and credits again.

4. Journalize the following transactions on page 19 of the journal.

Nov. 23. Received cash on account from Esther Lorand, $630.70, covering S59. R114.

24. Sold merchandise on account to Celia Sotelo, $325.00, plus sales tax, $19.50; total, $344.50. S63.

27. Purchased merchandise on account from Cycle World, $1,240.00. P60.

27. Paid cash for advertising, $85.00. C258.

28. Recorded cash and credit card sales, $2,680.00, plus sales tax, $160.80; total, $2,840.80. T28.

28. Received cash on account from Leonard Kane, $1,147.00, covering S60. R115.

30. Sold merchandise on account to Jonathan Hunt, $45.00, plus sales tax, $2.70; total, $47.70. S64.

30. Paid cash to replenish the petty cash fund, $301.00: office supplies, $62.00; store supplies, $71.00; advertising, $88.00; miscellaneous, $80.00. C259.

30. Recorded cash and credit card sales, $640.00, plus sales tax, $38.40; total, $678.40. T30.

5. Total page 19 of the journal. Prove the equality of debits and credits.

6. Prove cash. The November 1 cash account balance in the general ledger was $9,431.00. On November 30 the balance on the next unused check stub was $21,511.40.

7. Rule page 19 of the journal.

CHALLENGE PROBLEM 12-C Journalizing transactions

The columns of a journal may be arranged in different ways. For example, the journal used in this chapter is referred to as an expanded journal. All of the amount columns are to the right of the Account Title column. However, another arrangement is to have the amount columns divided by the Account Title column. Some of the amount columns are to the left and some are to the right of the Account Title column.

INSTRUCTIONS:

1. Use a journal with the columns arranged as follows.

Cash		Date	Account Title	Doc. No.	Post Ref.	General		Accts. Rec.		Sales Cr.	Sales Tax Pay. Cr.	Accts. Payable		Purchases Dr.
Dr.	Cr.					Dr.	Cr.	Dr.	Cr.			Dr.	Cr.	

2. Use the transactions and instructions for Mastery Problem 12-M. Complete all of the instructions using the journal above.

13

Posting to General and Subsidiary Ledgers

ENABLING PERFORMANCE TASKS

After studying Chapter 13, you will be able to:

a Define accounting terms related to posting to ledgers.

b Identify accounting practices related to posting to ledgers.

c Post to a general ledger from a journal.

d Open accounts in ledgers.

e Post to subsidiary ledgers from a journal.

f Prepare subsidiary schedules.

TERMS PREVIEW

subsidiary ledger • accounts payable ledger • accounts receivable ledger • controlling account • schedule of accounts payable • schedule of accounts receivable

A journal provides a permanent record of transactions listed in chronological order. Journal entries are sorted and summarized by transferring information to ledger accounts. Transferring information from journal entries to ledger accounts is known as posting. Posting information from a journal to ledger accounts summarizes in one place transactions affecting each account.

LEDGERS AND CONTROLLING ACCOUNTS

A business' size, number of transactions, and type of transactions determine the number of ledgers used in an accounting system.

General Ledger

A business with transactions affecting mostly the receipt and payment of cash may use only a general ledger.

A ledger that contains all accounts needed to prepare financial statements is known as a general ledger. A general ledger sorts and summarizes all information affecting income statement and balance sheet accounts. A business with transactions involving mostly the receipt and payment of cash may use only a general ledger. Rugcare, described in Part 2, uses only a general ledger. CarLand also uses a general ledger. CarLand's general ledger chart of accounts is on page 244. However, because of the business' size and the number and type of transactions, CarLand also uses additional ledgers in its accounting system.

Subsidiary Ledgers

A business needs to know the amount owed each vendor as well as the amount to be collected from each charge customer. Therefore, a separate account is needed for each vendor and each customer. A general ledger could contain an account for each vendor and for each customer. However, a business with many vendors and customers would have a bulky general ledger and a long trial balance. CarLand eliminates these problems by keeping a separate ledger for vendors and a separate ledger for customers. Each separate ledger is summarized in a single general ledger account. A ledger that is summarized in a single general ledger account is called a **subsidiary ledger.** A subsidiary ledger containing only accounts for vendors from whom items are purchased or bought on account is called an **accounts payable ledger.** A subsidiary ledger containing only accounts for charge customers is called an **accounts receivable ledger.**

The total amount owed to all vendors is summarized in a single general ledger account, Accounts Payable. The total amount to be collected from all charge customers is summarized in a single general ledger account, Accounts Receivable.

Controlling Accounts

The total amount owed to all vendors is summarized in a single general ledger account, Accounts Payable. The total amount to be collected from all charge customers is summarized in a single general ledger account, Accounts Receivable.

An account in a general ledger that summarizes all accounts in a subsidiary ledger is called a **controlling account.** The balance of a controlling account equals the total of all account balances in its related subsidiary ledger. Thus, the balance of the controlling account, Accounts Payable, equals the total of all vendor account balances in the accounts payable subsidiary ledger. The balance of the controlling account, Accounts Receivable, equals the total of all charge customer account balances in the accounts receivable subsidiary ledger.

POSTING TO A GENERAL LEDGER

Daily general ledger account balances are usually not necessary. Balances of general ledger accounts are needed only when financial statements are prepared. Posting from a journal to a general ledger can be done periodically throughout a month. The number of transactions determines how often to post to a general ledger. A business with many transactions would normally post more often than a business with few transactions. Posting often helps keep the work load evenly distributed throughout a month. However, posting must always be done at the end of a month. CarLand uses the same 4-column general ledger account form and posting procedures as described for Rugcare in Chapter 6.

Posting a Journal's General Amount Columns

Amounts recorded in a journal's general amount columns are amounts for which no special amount columns are provided. Therefore, separate amounts in a journal's General Debit and General Credit columns *ARE* posted individually to the accounts written in the journal's Account Title column. The posting of the General Debit entry on line 6 of CarLand's journal is shown in Illustration 13-1.

ILLUSTRATION 13-1   Posting from a journal's General Debit column

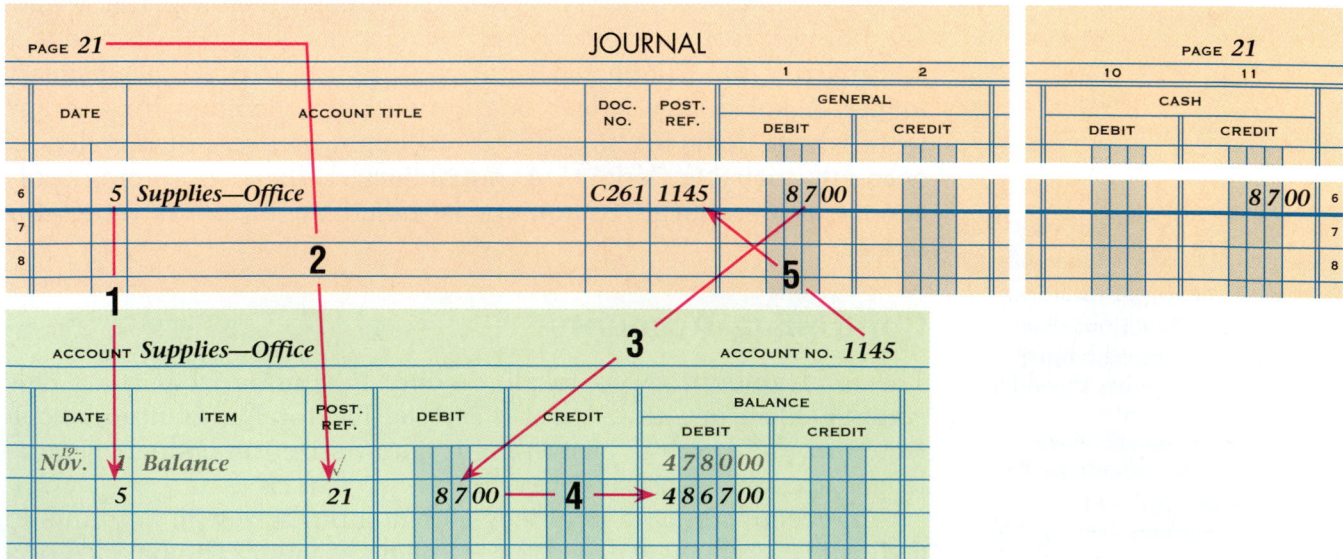

Five steps are followed to post the debit entry to the general ledger.

1 Write the date, *5*, in the Date column of the account.

2 Write the journal page number, *21*, in the Post. Ref. column of the account.

3 Write the debit amount, *$87.00*, in the account's Debit amount column.

4 Add the amount in the Debit amount column to the previous balance in the Balance Debit column ($4,780.00 + $87.00 = $4,867.00). Write the new account balance, *$4,867.00*, in the Balance Debit column.

5 Write the general ledger account number, *1145*, in the Post. Ref. column of the journal.

Posting a Journal's Special Amount Columns

CarLand's journal has nine special amount columns. Separate amounts written in these special amount columns *ARE NOT* posted individually to the general ledger. Separate amounts in a special

■ **Jan Robbins** ■

NAS, INC.

Jan Robbins owns NAS, Inc., a systems engineering company that specializes in government contracting. NAS, Inc. employs approximately 200 workers. Robbins is of Cherokee Indian heritage and wondered when she started her business whether she would encounter any discrimination. She was surprised to find that there was discrimination, not because she is a Native American, but because she is a woman. The industry she had entered, systems engineering for government contracts, was dominated by males who considered it to be an industry just for men. However, Robbins has worked hard and succeeded. She also finds that attitudes toward women in business are changing so that women starting out today should not face as much discrimination as she did.

Robbins worked as a sales representative for an adver-

tising agency before starting NAS, Inc. She also did some copywriting for an advertising agency. When she started her business, she started small because she had only a small amount of savings to invest. She began by being willing to work on even the smallest government contracts, usually as a subcontractor to the contractor who had won the contract.

Robbins attributes her ability to set up her business to the year of accounting she studied in high school. She says that it helped her set up her expenses and to understand the language that businesses use every day. Robbins strongly believes in the value of business courses for success and especially favors courses in accounting and banking as preparation for entrepreneurship.

Asked about her basic philosophy of business, Robbins replied, "No one plans to fail, they just fail to plan. A day doesn't pass that I don't think of that statement."

Personal Visions in Business

amount column all affect the same general ledger account. Therefore, only the totals of special amount columns *ARE* posted to the general ledger. Each special amount column total is posted to the general ledger account listed in the column heading. Posting of the Cash Credit amount column total is shown in Illustration 13-2.

ILLUSTRATION 13-2 Posting the Cash Credit column total

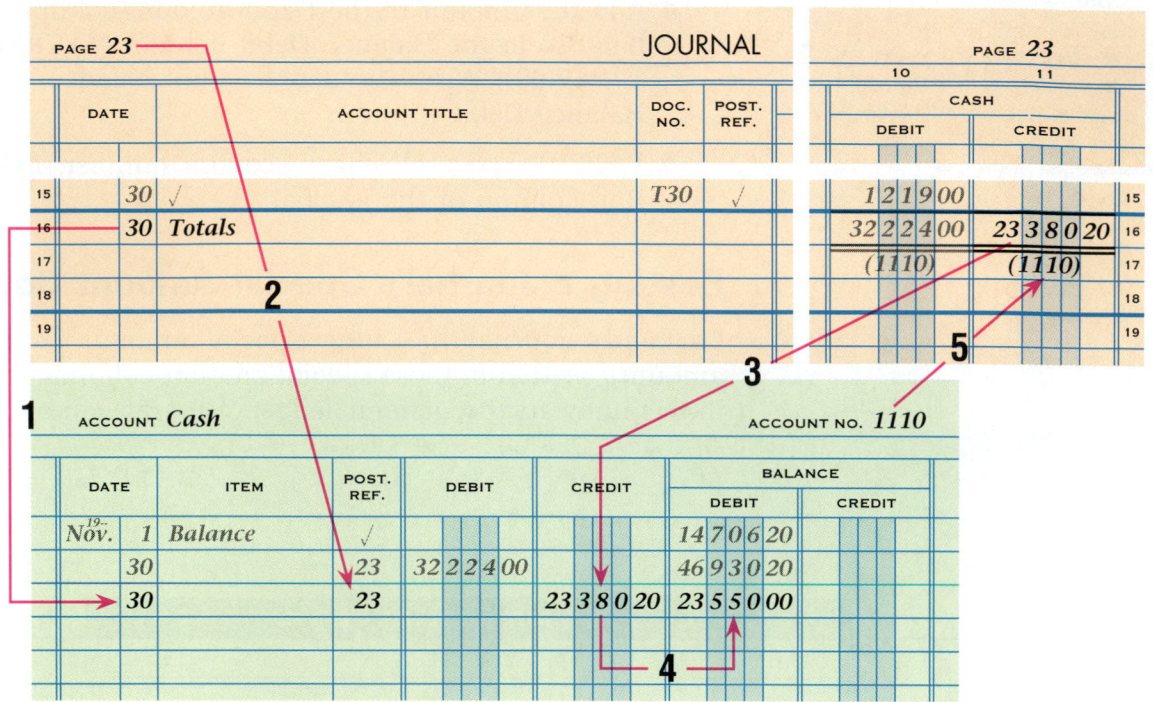

Five steps are followed to post the Cash Credit column total.

1 Write the date, *30*, in the Date column of the account.

2 Write the journal page number, *23*, in the Post. Ref. column of the account.

3 Write the Cash Credit column total, *$23,380.20*, in the account's Credit amount column.

4 Subtract the amount in the Credit amount column from the previous balance in the Balance Debit column ($46,930.20 − $23,380.20 = $23,550.00). Write the new account balance, *$23,550.00*, in the Balance Debit column.

5 Return to the journal and write the general ledger account number, *1110*, in parentheses below the Cash Credit column total.

Rules for Posting a Journal's Column Totals

Rules for posting a journal's column totals are shown in Illustration 13-3.

FYI

Posting must always be done at the end of the month.

ILLUSTRATION 13-3   Rules for posting a journal's column totals

						1	2	3	4	
PAGE 23			JOURNAL							
	DATE	ACCOUNT TITLE	DOC. NO.	POST. REF.		GENERAL		ACCOUNTS RECEIVABLE		
						DEBIT	CREDIT	DEBIT	CREDIT	
16	30	Totals				1568622	202902	922200	795000	16
17						(√)	(√)	(1130)	(1130)	17
18										18
19										19

General amount column totals ARE NOT posted

Special amount column totals ARE posted

A check mark is placed in parentheses below the General Debit and General Credit column totals to indicate that the two amount column totals *ARE NOT* posted. The general ledger account number of the account listed in the column heading is written in parentheses below the special amount column totals to show that the totals *ARE* posted.

OPENING A NEW PAGE FOR AN ACCOUNT IN A GENERAL LEDGER

The number of entries that may be recorded on each general ledger account form depends on the number of lines provided. When all lines have been used, a new page is prepared. The account title, account number, and account balance are recorded on the new page.

On November 1 CarLand prepared a new page for Cash in the general ledger because the existing page was full. On that day, the account balance was $14,706.20. The new page for Cash in the general ledger is shown in Illustration 13-4.

ILLUSTRATION 13-4   Opening a new page for an account in a general ledger

ACCOUNT Cash					ACCOUNT NO. 1110		
DATE	ITEM	POST. REF.	DEBIT	CREDIT	BALANCE		
					DEBIT	CREDIT	
Nov. 1	Balance	√			1470620		

Audit Your Understanding

1. What is a controlling account?

2. What is the relationship between a controlling account and a subsidiary ledger?

3. What are the four amount columns of the general ledger account form?

4. What accounts does an accounts payable ledger contain?

5. What accounts does an accounts receivable ledger contain?

The account title and account number are written on the heading at the top of the new page. The date, *19--, Nov. 1,* is recorded in the Date column. The word *Balance* is written in the Item column. A check mark is placed in the Post. Ref. column to show that the entry has been carried forward from a previous page rather than posted from a journal. The account balance, *$14,706.20,* is written in the Balance Debit column.

ASSIGNING ACCOUNT NUMBERS TO SUBSIDIARY LEDGER ACCOUNTS

CarLand assigns a vendor number to each account in the accounts payable ledger. A customer number is also assigned to each account in the accounts receivable ledger. A three-digit number is used. The first digit identifies the division in which the controlling account appears in the general ledger. The second two digits show each account's location within a subsidiary ledger. Accounts are assigned by 10s beginning with the second digit. Accounts in the subsidiary ledgers can be located by either number or name.

The vendor number for Antelo Supply is 210. The first digit, *2,* shows that the controlling account is a liability, Accounts Payable. The second and third digits, *10,* show the vendor number assigned to Antelo Supply.

The customer number for Ashley Delivery is 110. The first digit, *1,* shows that the controlling account is an asset, Accounts Receivable. The second and third digits, *10,* show the customer number assigned to Ashley Delivery.

The procedure for adding new accounts to subsidiary ledgers is the same as described for Rugcare's general ledger in Chapter 6. Accounts are arranged in alphabetic order within the subsidiary ledgers. New accounts are assigned the unused middle number. If the proper alphabetic order places a new account as the last account, the next number in the sequence of 10s is assigned. CarLand's chart of accounts for the subsidiary ledgers is on page 244.

FYI

Account numbers are assigned by 10s. A new account is assigned the unused middle number which places it in the correct alphabetic order.

POSTING TO AN ACCOUNTS PAYABLE LEDGER

When the balance of a vendor account in an accounts payable ledger is changed, the balance of the controlling account, Accounts Payable, is also changed. The total of all vendor account balances in the accounts payable ledger equals the balance of the controlling account, Accounts Payable. The relationship between the accounts payable ledger and the general ledger controlling account, Accounts Payable, is shown in Illustration 13-5.

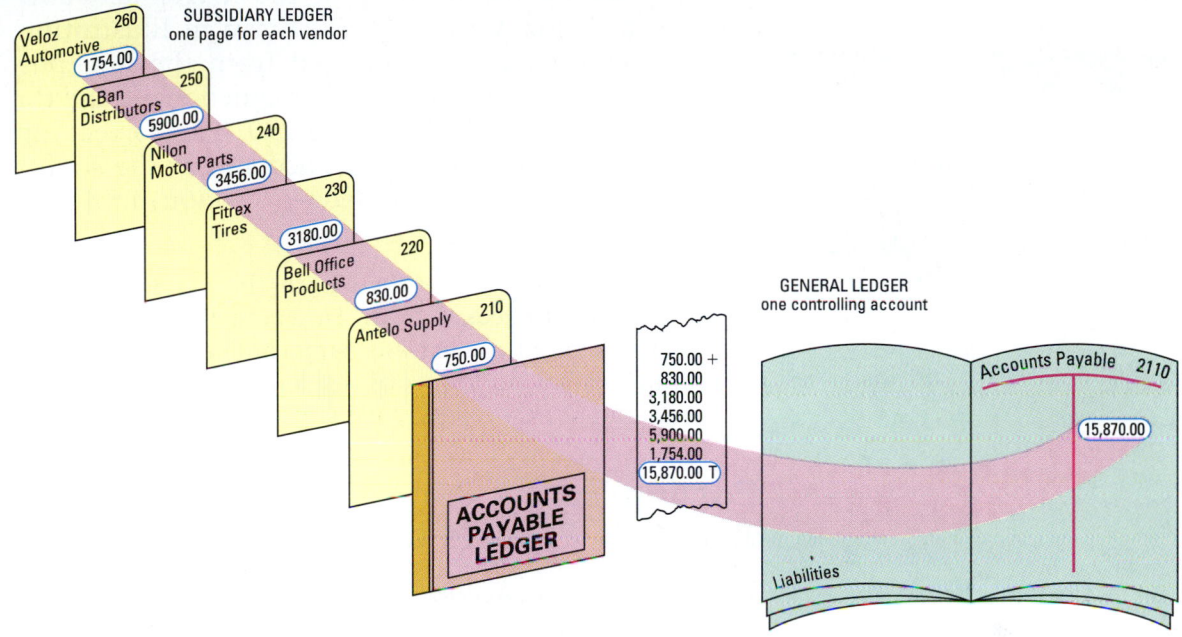

Accounts Payable Ledger Form

CarLand uses the 3-column accounts payable subsidiary account form shown in Illustration 13-6.

ILLUSTRATION 13-6   Three-column account form used in an accounts payable ledger

VENDOR *Veloz Automotive*						VENDOR NO. *260*
DATE	ITEM	POST. REF.	DEBIT	CREDIT	CREDIT BALANCE	

Information to be recorded in the accounts payable ledger is essentially the same as that recorded in the 4-column general ledger account. The information includes the date, posting reference, debit or credit amount, and new account balance. Accounts payable are liabilities, and liabilities have normal credit balances. Therefore, the Debit Balance column is usually not needed for the accounts payable ledger accounts. The accounts payable account form is the same as the general ledger account form except that there is no Debit Balance column.

Accounts in CarLand's accounts payable ledger are arranged in alphabetic order and kept in a loose-leaf binder. Periodically, accounts for new vendors are added and accounts no longer used are removed from the accounts payable ledger. If the number of accounts becomes large enough to make a loose-leaf binder inappropriate, ledger pages may be kept in a file cabinet.

Opening Vendor Accounts

Each new account is opened by writing the vendor name and vendor number on the heading of the ledger account. The account opened for Veloz Automotive is shown in Illustration 13-6.

The vendor name is obtained from the first purchase invoice received. The vendor number is assigned using the three-digit numbering system described on page 290. The correct alphabetic order for Veloz Automotive places the account as the sixth account in the accounts payable subsidiary ledger. Vendor number 260 is assigned to Veloz Automotive.

Some businesses record both the vendor name and vendor address on the ledger form. However, the address information is usually kept in a separate name and address file. This practice eliminates having to record the vendor address on the ledger form each time a new ledger page is opened or the address changes.

Posting from a Journal to an Accounts Payable Ledger

Each entry in the Accounts Payable columns of a journal affects the vendor named in the Account Title column. CarLand posts each amount in these two columns often. Posting often keeps each vendor account balance up to date. Totals of Accounts Payable special amount columns are posted to the general ledger at the end of each month.

Posting a Credit to an Accounts Payable Ledger. Posting a credit for a purchase on account from the journal to the accounts payable ledger is shown in Illustration 13-7.

| ILLUSTRATION 13-7 | Posting a credit to an accounts payable ledger |

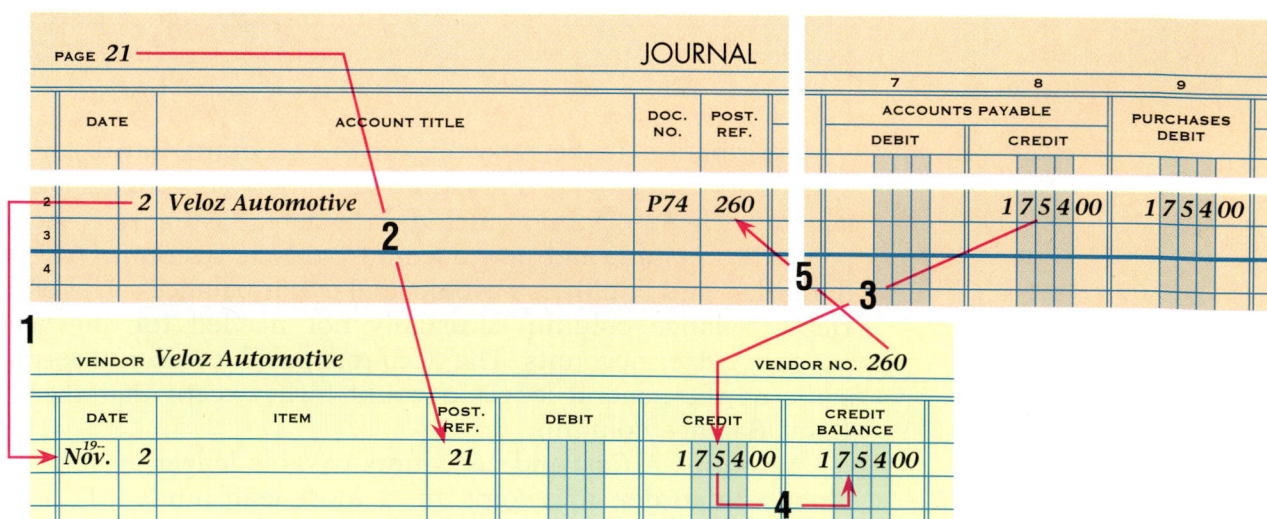

Five steps are followed to post the entry on line 2 of the journal to the accounts payable ledger.

1 Write the date, *19--, Nov. 2,* in the Date column of the account.

2 Write the journal page number, *21,* in the Post. Ref. column of the account.

3 Write the credit amount, *$1,754.00,* in the Credit amount column of the account for Veloz Automotive.

4 Add the amount in the Credit amount column to the previous balance in the Credit Balance column. (Veloz Automotive has no previous balance; therefore, $0 + $1,754.00 = $1,754.00.) Write the new account balance, *$1,754.00,* in the Credit Balance column.

5 Write the vendor number, *260,* in the Post. Ref. column of the journal. The vendor number shows that the posting for this entry is complete.

The controlling account in the general ledger, Accounts Payable, is also increased by this entry. At the end of the month, the journal's Accounts Payable Credit column total is posted to the controlling account, Accounts Payable.

Posting a Debit to an Accounts Payable Ledger. The same steps are followed to post a debit to a vendor account as are used to post a credit. However, the debit amount is entered in the Debit amount column of the vendor account. The debit amount is subtracted from the previous credit balance. Posting a cash payment on account from the journal to the accounts payable ledger is shown in Illustration 13-8.

The controlling account in the general ledger, Accounts Payable, is decreased by this entry. At the end of the month, the journal's

ILLUSTRATION 13-8   Posting a debit to an accounts payable ledger

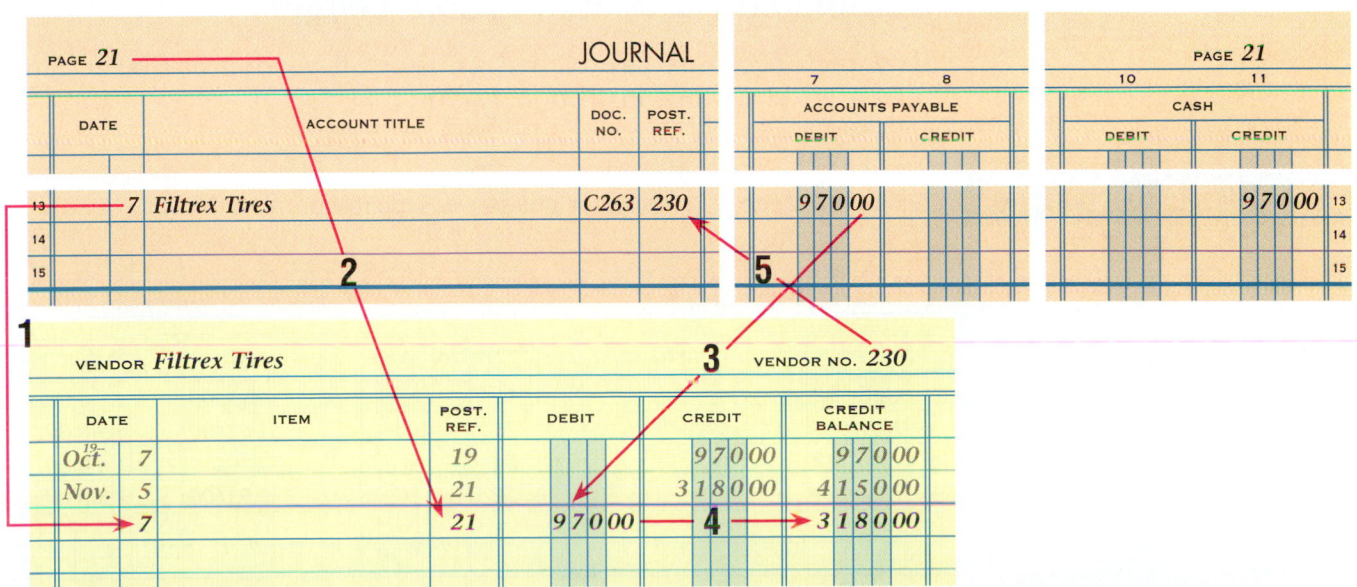

Accounts Payable Debit column total is posted to the controlling account, Accounts Payable.

Opening a New Page for a Vendor in an Accounts Payable Ledger

The number of entries that may be recorded on each account form depends on the number of lines provided. When all lines have been used, a new page is prepared. The vendor name, vendor number, and account balance are recorded on the new page.

On November 1 CarLand prepared a new page for Nilon Motor Parts in the accounts payable ledger because the existing page was full. On that day, the account balance was $4,840.00. The new page for Nilon Motor Parts in the accounts payable ledger is shown in Illustration 13-9.

ILLUSTRATION 13-9

Opening a new page for a vendor in the accounts payable ledger

VENDOR Nilon Motor Parts						VENDOR NO. 240
DATE	ITEM	POST. REF.	DEBIT	CREDIT	CREDIT BALANCE	
19-- Nov. 1	Balance	✓			4 8 4 0 00	

The vendor name and vendor number are written at the top of the account page. The date, *19--, Nov. 1,* is recorded in the Date column. The word *Balance* is written in the Item column. A check mark is placed in the Post. Ref. column to show that the amount has been carried forward from a previous page rather than posted from a journal. The account balance, *$4,840.00,* is written in the Credit Balance column.

Completed Accounts Payable Ledger

CarLand's accounts payable ledger after all posting has been completed is shown in Illustration 13-10.

ILLUSTRATION 13-10

Accounts payable ledger after posting has been completed

VENDOR Antelo Supply						VENDOR NO. 210
DATE	ITEM	POST. REF.	DEBIT	CREDIT	CREDIT BALANCE	
19-- Oct. 12		19		4 3 0 00	4 3 0 00	
Nov. 6		21		1 6 0 00	5 9 0 00	
12		21	4 3 0 00		1 6 0 00	
23		22		5 9 0 00	7 5 0 00	

VENDOR **Bell Office Products**   VENDOR NO. **220**

DATE	ITEM	POST. REF.	DEBIT	CREDIT	CREDIT BALANCE
Oct. 23		20		62000	62000
Nov. 23		22	62000		—
24		22		83000	83000

VENDOR **Filtrex Tires**   VENDOR NO. **230**

DATE	ITEM	POST. REF.	DEBIT	CREDIT	CREDIT BALANCE
Oct. 7		19		97000	97000
Nov. 5		21		318000	415000
7		21	97000		318000

VENDOR **Nilon Motor Parts**   VENDOR NO. **240**

DATE	ITEM	POST. REF.	DEBIT	CREDIT	CREDIT BALANCE
Nov. 1	Balance	✓			484000
4		21		345600	829600
20		22	484000		345600

VENDOR **Q-Ban Distributors**   VENDOR NO. **250**

DATE	ITEM	POST. REF.	DEBIT	CREDIT	CREDIT BALANCE
Nov. 1	Balance	✓			396000
6		21	396000		—
13		21		314000	314000
20		22		276000	590000

VENDOR **Veloz Automotive**   VENDOR NO. **260**

DATE	ITEM	POST. REF.	DEBIT	CREDIT	CREDIT BALANCE
Nov. 2		21		175400	175400

FYI

An error in posting may cause a business to overpay or underpay its vendors.

POSTING TO AN ACCOUNTS RECEIVABLE LEDGER

When the balance of a customer account in an accounts receivable ledger is changed, the balance of the controlling account, Accounts Receivable, is also changed. The total of all customer account balances in the accounts receivable ledger equals the balance of the controlling account, Accounts Receivable. The relationship between the accounts receivable ledger and the general ledger controlling account, Accounts Receivable, is shown in Illustration 13-11.

ILLUSTRATION 13-11 Relationship of accounts receivable ledger and general ledger controlling account

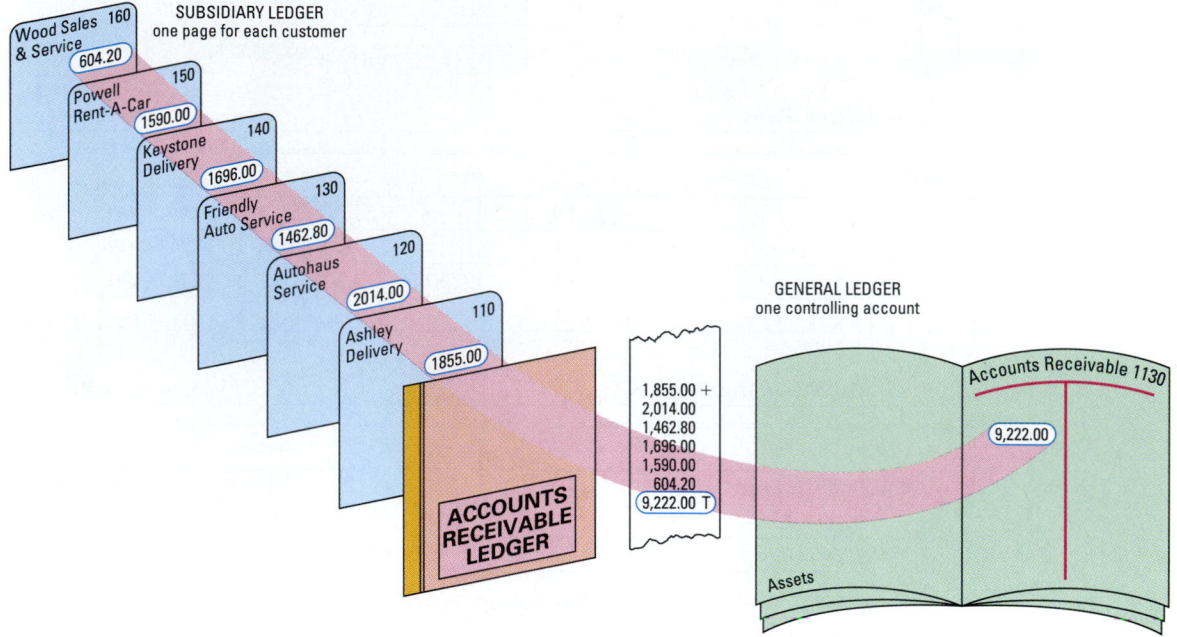

Accounts Receivable Ledger Form

CarLand uses the 3-column accounts receivable subsidiary account form shown in Illustration 13-12.

ILLUSTRATION 13-12 Three-column account form used in an accounts receivable ledger

CUSTOMER *Friendly Auto Service*					CUSTOMER NO. *130*
DATE	ITEM	POST. REF.	DEBIT	CREDIT	DEBIT BALANCE

The accounts receivable account form is similar to the one used for the accounts payable ledger. Accounts receivable are assets, and assets have normal debit balances. Therefore, the form used in the accounts receivable ledger has a Debit Balance column instead of a Credit Balance column.

Accounts in CarLand's accounts receivable ledger are arranged in alphabetic order and kept in a loose-leaf binder. Periodically, accounts for new customers are added and accounts no longer used are removed from the accounts receivable ledger. The customer number 130 had been assigned to a former customer. That account, however, had been removed from the ledger. Therefore, customer number 130 is available for assignment to Friendly Auto Service.

Some businesses record both the customer name and customer address on the ledger form. However, the address information is usually kept in a separate name and address file. This practice eliminates having to record the customer address on the ledger form each time a new ledger page is opened or the address changes.

Opening Customer Accounts

Procedures for opening customer accounts are similar to those used for opening vendor accounts. The customer name is obtained from the first sales invoice prepared for a customer. The customer number is assigned using the three-digit numbering system described on page 290. The customer name and customer number are written on the heading of the ledger account. The account opened for Friendly Auto Service is shown in Illustration 13-12.

Posting from a Journal to an Accounts Receivable Ledger

Separate amounts in a journal's general amount columns are posted individually.

Each entry in the Accounts Receivable columns of a journal affects the customer named in the Account Title column. Each amount listed in these two columns is posted to a customer account in the accounts receivable ledger often. Posting often keeps each customer account balance up to date. Totals of Accounts Receivable special amount columns are posted to the general ledger at the end of each month.

Posting a Debit to an Accounts Receivable Ledger. Posting a debit for a sale on account from the journal to the accounts receivable ledger is shown in Illustration 13-13.

Five steps are followed to post the entry on line 4 of the journal to the accounts receivable ledger.

1 Write the date, *3*, in the Date column of the account.

2 Write the journal page number, *21*, in the Post. Ref. column of the account.

3 Write the debit amount, *$720.80*, in the Debit amount column of the account for Friendly Auto Service.

4 Add the amount in the Debit amount column to the previous balance in the Debit Balance column ($265.00 + $720.80 = $985.80). Write the new account balance, *$985.80*, in the Debit Balance column.

5 Write the customer number, *130*, in the Post. Ref. column of the journal. The customer number shows that the posting for this entry is completed.

ILLUSTRATION 13-13   Posting a debit to an accounts receivable ledger

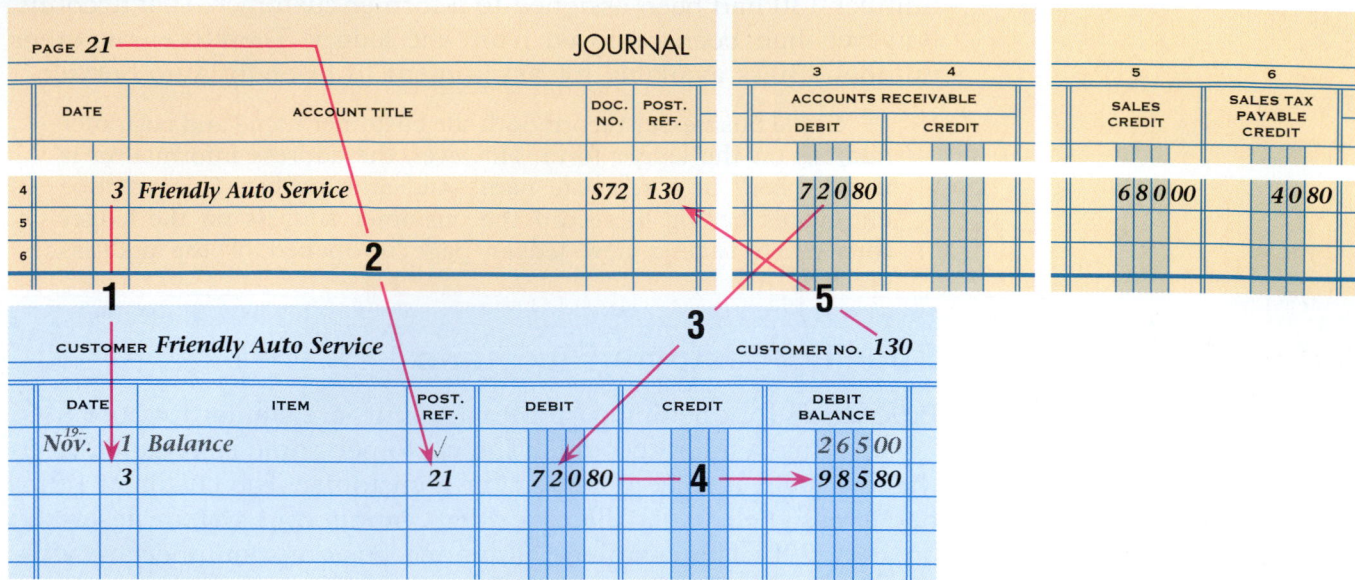

The controlling account in the general ledger, Accounts Receivable, is also increased by this entry. At the end of the month, the journal's Accounts Receivable Debit column total is posted to the controlling account, Accounts Receivable.

Posting a Credit to an Accounts Receivable Ledger. The same steps are followed to post a credit to a customer account as are used to post a debit. However, the credit amount is written in the Credit amount column of the customer account. The credit amount is subtracted from the previous debit balance. Posting a cash receipt on account from the journal to the accounts receivable ledger is shown in Illustration 13-14.

The controlling account in the general ledger, Accounts Receivable, is decreased by this entry. However, the amount is not posted individually to the accounts receivable account. At the end of the month, the amount, $318.00, is posted as part of the special amount column total to Accounts Receivable.

Opening a New Page for a Customer in an Accounts Receivable Ledger

Procedures for opening a new page in an accounts receivable ledger are similar to those for an accounts payable ledger. The customer name and customer number are written at the top of the new account page. The date is recorded in the Date column. The word *Balance* is written in the Item column. A check mark is placed in the Post. Ref. column to show that the amount has been carried forward from a previous page rather than posted from a journal. The account balance is recorded in the Debit Balance column.

Audit Your Understanding

1. What is the title of the balance amount column of the accounts payable ledger form? Why?

2. How is a new vendor account opened?

3. List the five steps for posting to the accounts payable ledger.

4. What is the title of the balance amount column of the accounts receivable ledger form? Why?

ILLUSTRATION 13-14

Posting a credit to an accounts receivable ledger

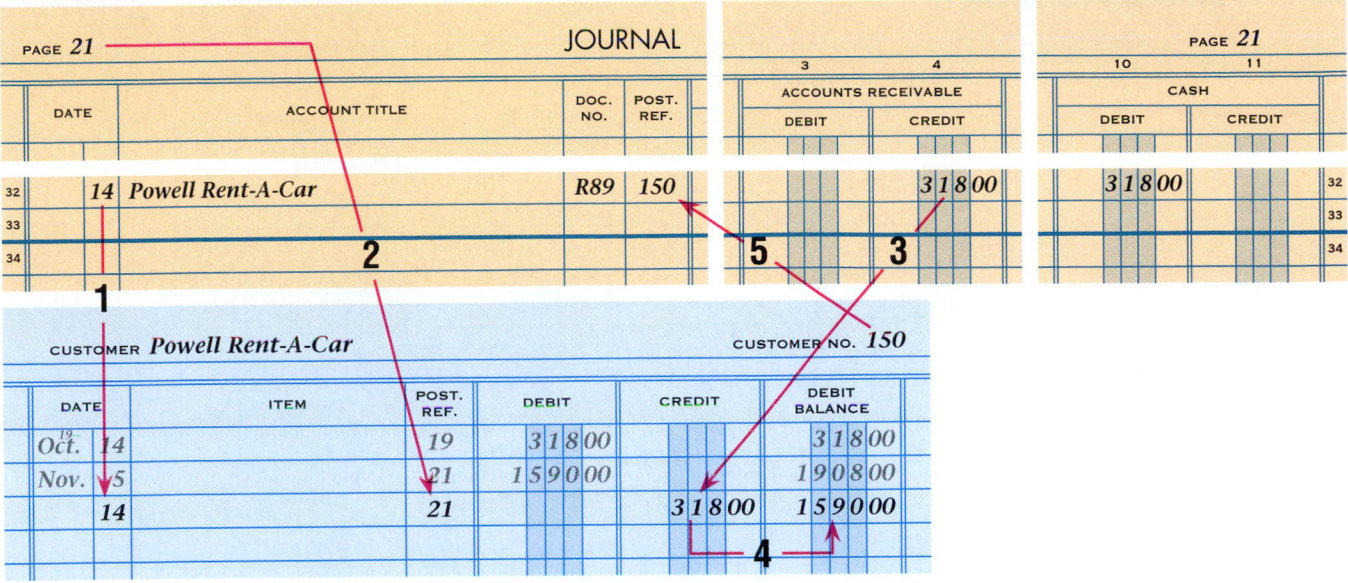

Completed Accounts Receivable Ledger

CarLand's accounts receivable ledger after all posting has been completed is shown in Illustration 13-15.

ILLUSTRATION 13-15

Accounts receivable ledger after posting has been completed

CUSTOMER *Ashley Delivery*　　　CUSTOMER NO. *110*

DATE	ITEM	POST. REF.	DEBIT	CREDIT	DEBIT BALANCE
Nov. 1	Balance	√			2 4 9 1 00
9		21	4 7 7 00		2 9 6 8 00
16		22	1 3 7 8 00		4 3 4 6 00
17		22		2 4 9 1 00	1 8 5 5 00

CUSTOMER *Autohaus Service*　　　CUSTOMER NO. *120*

DATE	ITEM	POST. REF.	DEBIT	CREDIT	DEBIT BALANCE
Nov. 1	Balance	√			1 8 0 2 00
6		21		1 8 0 2 00	—
18		22	2 0 1 4 00		2 0 1 4 00

CUSTOMER *Friendly Auto Service*   CUSTOMER NO. *130*

DATE		ITEM	POST. REF.	DEBIT	CREDIT	DEBIT BALANCE
Nov.	1	Balance	✓			2 6 5 00
	3		21	7 2 0 80		9 8 5 80
	24		22	7 4 2 00		1 7 2 7 80
	25		22		2 6 5 00	1 4 6 2 80

CUSTOMER *Keystone Delivery*   CUSTOMER NO. *140*

DATE		ITEM	POST. REF.	DEBIT	CREDIT	DEBIT BALANCE
Oct.	10		19	9 5 4 00		9 5 4 00
Nov.	10		21		9 5 4 00	—
	24		22	3 1 8 00		3 1 8 00
	29		22	1 3 7 8 00		1 6 9 6 00

CUSTOMER *Powell Rent-A-Car*   CUSTOMER NO. *150*

DATE		ITEM	POST. REF.	DEBIT	CREDIT	DEBIT BALANCE
Oct.	14		19	3 1 8 00		3 1 8 00
Nov.	5		21	1 5 9 0 00		1 9 0 8 00
	14		21		3 1 8 00	1 5 9 0 00

CUSTOMER *Wood Sales & Service*   CUSTOMER NO. *160*

DATE		ITEM	POST. REF.	DEBIT	CREDIT	DEBIT BALANCE
Nov.	1	Balance	✓			2 1 2 0 00
	11		21	6 0 4 20		2 7 2 4 20
	13		21		9 0 1 00	1 8 2 3 20
	20		22		1 2 1 9 00	6 0 4 20

PROVING THE ACCURACY OF POSTING

A single error in posting to a ledger account may cause the trial balance to be out of balance. An error in posting may cause the cash account balance to disagree with the actual cash on hand. An error in posting may also cause the income to be understated or overstated on an income statement. An error in posting may also cause a business to overpay or underpay its vendors. Posting must be accurate to assure correct account balances. Therefore, to prove the accuracy of posting, three things are done. (1) Cash is proved. (2) Subsidiary schedules are prepared to prove that the total of the balances in the subsidiary ledgers equals the balance of the controlling account in the general ledger. (3) A trial balance is prepared to prove that debits equal credits in the general ledger.

Preparation of a trial balance is described in Chapter 16.

Proving Cash

The method used to prove cash is described in Chapter 12. The cash proof total is compared with the balance on the next unused check stub in the checkbook.

Proving the Subsidiary Ledgers

A controlling account balance in a general ledger must equal the sum of all account balances in a subsidiary ledger. CarLand proves the accounts payable and accounts receivable subsidiary ledgers at the end of each month.

Proving Accounts Payable. A listing of vendor accounts, account balances, and total amount due all vendors is called a **schedule of accounts payable.** A schedule of accounts payable is prepared after all entries in a journal are posted. CarLand's schedule of accounts payable, prepared on November 30, is shown in Illustration 13-16.

ILLUSTRATION 13-16   Schedule of accounts payable

CarLand	
Schedule of Accounts Payable	
November 30, 19--	
Antelo Supply	750 00
Bell Office Products	830 00
Filtrex Tires	3180 00
Nilon Motor Parts	3456 00
Q-Ban Distributors	5900 00
Veloz Automotive	1754 00
Total Accounts Payable	15870 00

The balance of Accounts Payable in the general ledger is $15,870.00. The total of the schedule of accounts payable is $15,870.00. Because the two amounts are the same, the accounts payable ledger is proved.

Proving Accounts Receivable. A listing of customer accounts, account balances, and total amount due from all customers is called a **schedule of accounts receivable.** A schedule of accounts receivable is prepared after all entries in a journal are posted. CarLand's schedule of accounts receivable, prepared on November 30, is shown in Illustration 13-17.

ILLUSTRATION 13-17

Schedule of accounts receivable

CarLand	
Schedule of Accounts Receivable	
November 30, 19--	
Ashley Delivery	1 8 5 5 00
Autohaus Service	2 0 1 4 00
Friendly Auto Service	1 4 6 2 80
Keystone Delivery	1 6 9 6 00
Powell Rent-A-Car	1 5 9 0 00
Wood Sales & Service	6 0 4 20
Total Accounts Receivable	9 2 2 2 00

The balance of Accounts Receivable in the general ledger is $9,222.00. The total of the schedule of accounts receivable is $9,222.00. Because the two amounts are the same, the accounts receivable ledger is proved.

A summary of the posting steps from Rugcare's journal is in Chapter 6. The steps described for Rugcare also apply to posting from an expanded journal. However, special amount columns and controlling accounts require an additional set of posting steps.

Audit Your Understanding

1. How are the accounts payable and accounts receivable subsidiary ledgers proved at the end of the month?

2. What accounts are listed on a schedule of accounts payable?

3. How does a schedule of accounts receivable prove the accounts receivable ledger?

SUMMARY ILLUSTRATION 13-18

Summary of posting

Separate amounts in General columns *ARE* posted individually. Totals of General Debit and Credit columns *ARE NOT* posted.

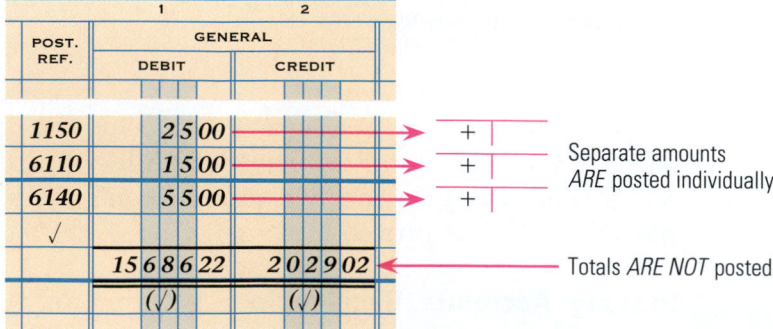

Summary of posting

Totals of special amount columns *ARE* posted to the account named in the column heading. Separate amounts in special columns *ARE NOT* posted individually unless the columns affect a controlling account.

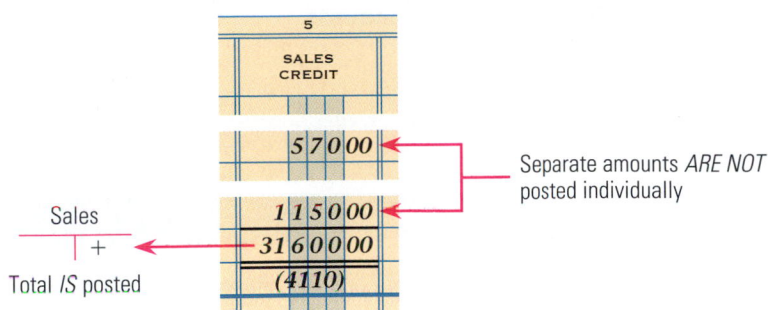

Separate amounts and total amounts are posted from special columns for controlling accounts. Separate amounts in the Accounts Receivable Debit and Credit columns *ARE* posted individually to customer accounts. As the last posting step, a customer number is written in the Post. Ref. column of the journal.

Totals of special columns *ARE* posted to the controlling accounts named in the column headings. The total of an Accounts Receivable Debit column is posted as a debit to **Accounts Receivable** in the general ledger. The total of an Accounts Receivable Credit column is posted as a credit to **Accounts Receivable** in the general ledger. As a last posting step, an account number is placed in parentheses under the total of a special amount column.

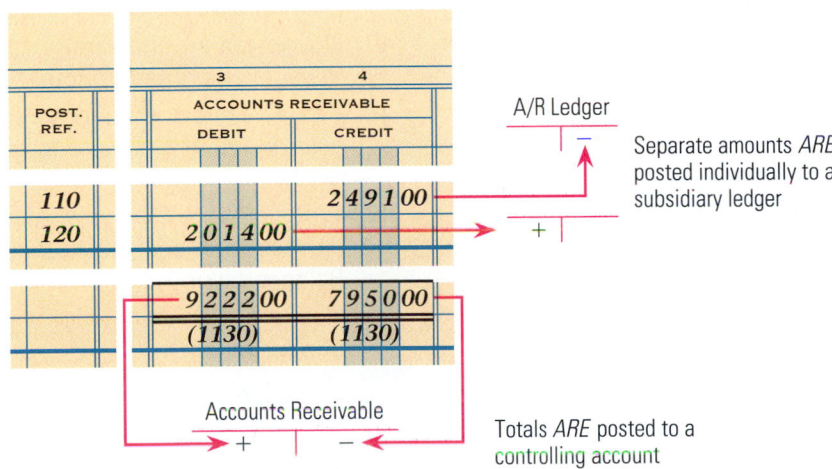

The same principles used for Accounts Receivable amount columns also apply to Accounts Payable amount columns in a journal.

What is the meaning of each of the following?

1. subsidiary ledger
2. accounts payable ledger
3. accounts receivable ledger
4. controlling account
5. schedule of accounts payable
6. schedule of accounts receivable

QUESTIONS FOR INDIVIDUAL STUDY

EPT(b)

1. How is journal entry information sorted and summarized?
2. What determines the number of ledgers used in an accounting system?
3. What ledger contains all accounts needed to prepare an income statement and a balance sheet?
4. What type of business would generally use a single ledger?
5. Why would a business keep a separate account for each vendor and each customer?
6. Why would a business keep a separate ledger for vendors and a separate ledger for customers?
7. What is the title of the general ledger controlling account for vendors?
8. What is the title of the general ledger controlling account for customers?
9. Why is posting to a general ledger done only periodically throughout the month?
10. What determines the frequency of posting to a general ledger?
11. Why are amounts recorded in a journal's general amount columns posted individually?
12. Why are separate amounts in special amount columns not posted individually to the general ledger?
13. Why is a check mark placed in parentheses below the General Debit and General Credit column totals?
14. What does the first digit in a vendor or customer number identify?
15. Why does the 3-column account form used in an accounts payable ledger have a Credit Balance column?
16. Why is posting of separate amounts in the Accounts Payable columns done often?
17. How often are the totals of the Accounts Payable columns of a journal posted?
18. Why is a check mark entered in the Post. Ref. column when a new page is opened for a vendor?
19. Why does the 3-column account form used in an accounts receivable ledger have a Debit Balance column?
20. How are subsidiary ledgers proved at the end of a month?

CASES FOR CRITICAL THINKING

EPT(b)

CASE 1 Automart purchased merchandise on account six weeks ago for $400.00 from Belview Supply. A check for $400.00 was sent three weeks ago in payment of the account. Although no additional purchases have been made, Automart recently received a bill from Belview Supply that listed the balance due as $800.00. What probably caused this error? When would the error probably be discovered?

CASE 2 Leon Reyes observes his accountant at work and says, "You post each individual accounts receivable entry in the journal. Then you post the totals of the Accounts Receivable columns. You are posting these entries twice, which will make the records wrong." The accountant does not agree that the posting procedure is incorrect. Is Mr. Reyes or his accountant correct? Why?

DRILL 13-D1   Analyzing transactions of a merchandising business

INSTRUCTIONS:

Prepare T accounts for each of the following transactions. Use the T accounts to analyze each transaction. A 6% sales tax has been added to each sale. The first transaction is given as an example.

Accounts Receivable	
127.20	

Sales	
	120.00

Sales Tax Payable	
	7.20

1. Sold merchandise on account to Sarah Burke, $120.00, plus sales tax, $7.20; total, $127.20.
2. Paid cash on account to Casa Enterprises, $950.00.
3. Paid cash for rent, $1,250.00.
4. Discovered that a payment for advertising was journalized and posted in error as a debit to Miscellaneous Expense instead of Advertising Expense, $125.00.
5. Paid cash for office supplies, $80.00.
6. Recorded cash and credit card sales, $1,850.00, plus sales tax, $111.00; total, $1,961.00.
7. Joyce Berling, partner, withdrew merchandise for personal use, $90.00.
8. Purchased merchandise on account from Irvine Products, $1,640.00.
9. Received cash on account from Carl Downing, $227.90.
10. Purchased merchandise for cash, $130.00.
11. Michael Zolty, partner, withdrew cash for personal use, $700.00.
12. Bought store supplies on account from Carter Supply, $315.00.

The solution to Drill 13-D1 is needed to complete Drill 13-D2.

DRILL 13-D2   Analyzing, journalizing, and posting transactions of a merchandising business

The solution to Drill 13-D1 is needed to complete Drill 13-D2.

INSTRUCTIONS:

A form for analyzing transactions is provided in the working papers that accompany the textbook.

1. Based on the answers in Drill 13-D1, place a check mark in the amount columns to be used to journalize each transaction.

A form for analyzing posting is provided in the working papers that accompany this textbook.

2. Based on the answers to Instruction 1, place a check mark in the proper column to indicate whether the amount will or will not be posted individually to the ledgers.

APPLICATION PROBLEM

EPT(c,d,e,f)

PROBLEM 13-1   Opening accounts and posting to ledgers from a journal

The journal for Carpet Magic is given in the working papers accompanying this textbook.

INSTRUCTIONS:

1. Open new pages for the following accounts in the general ledger. Record the balances as of September 1 of the current year.

Account No.	Account Title	Account Balance
1110	Cash	$ 18,300.00
1130	Accounts Receivable.................	8,470.00
1150	Supplies—Office	3,680.00
1160	Supplies—Store.................	4,260.00
1170	Prepaid Insurance	1,560.00
2110	Accounts Payable	10,555.00
2120	Sales Tax Payable	1,235.00
3120	Diane Engler, Drawing	8,000.00
3140	Paul Sisco, Drawing	8,340.00
4110	Sales	172,420.00
5110	Purchases......................	96,500.00
6110	Advertising Expense	1,860.00
6140	Miscellaneous Expense	1,310.00
6160	Rent Expense......................	8,000.00

2. Open new pages for the following vendor accounts in the accounts payable ledger. Record the balances as of September 1 of the current year.

Vendor No.	Vendor Name	Purchase Invoice No.	Account Balance
210	Crown Carpet Co..................	52	$2,575.00
220	Marlow Industries...............	53	4,220.00
230	Superior Carpeting	—	—
240	V & P Carpet Co.	51	3,760.00

3. Open new pages for the following customer accounts in the accounts receivable ledger. Record the balances as of September 1 of the current year.

Customer No.	Customer Name	Sales Invoice No.	Account Balance
110	Cameo Shoe Store................	44	$3,680.00
120	Paula Hughs	42	1,850.00
130	Elsa Leyba......................	43	2,940.00
140	Scott Ward	—	—

4. Post the separate items recorded in the following columns of the journal. (a) General Debit and Credit. (b) Accounts Receivable Debit and Credit. (c) Accounts Payable Debit and Credit.

5. Post the totals of the special columns of the journal.

6. Prepare a schedule of accounts payable. Compare the total of the schedule with the balance of the controlling account, Accounts Payable, in the general ledger. If the totals are not the same, find and correct the errors.

7. Prepare a schedule of accounts receivable. Compare the total of the schedule with the balance of the controlling account, Accounts Receivable, in the general ledger. If the totals are not the same, find and correct the errors.

ENRICHMENT PROBLEMS

EPT(c,e,f)

MASTERY PROBLEM 13-M Posting to ledgers from a journal

The journal and ledgers for Anton Leather Goods are given in the working papers accompanying this textbook.

INSTRUCTIONS:

1. Post the separate items recorded in the following columns of the journal. (a) General Debit and Credit. (b) Accounts Receivable Debit and Credit. (c) Accounts Payable Debit and Credit.

2. Post the totals of the special columns of the journal.

3. Prepare a schedule of accounts payable and a schedule of accounts receivable. Prove the accuracy of the subsidiary ledgers by comparing the schedule totals with the balances of the controlling accounts in the general ledger. If the totals are not the same, find and correct the errors.

CHALLENGE PROBLEM 13-C Journalizing and posting business transactions

AUTOMATED

The general, accounts payable, and accounts receivable ledgers for Par Golf Products are given in the working papers accompanying this textbook. Use the following account titles.

GENERAL LEDGER

Account No.	Account Title	Account No.	Account Title
1110	Cash	3140	Lawrence Phipps, Drawing
1130	Accounts Receivable	3150	Income Summary
1140	Merchandise Inventory	4110	Sales
1150	Supplies—Office	5110	Purchases
1160	Supplies—Store	6110	Advertising Expenses
2110	Accounts Payable	6140	Miscellaneous Expenses
2120	Sales Tax Payable	6160	Rent Expense
3120	Maria Adolpho, Drawing	6190	Utilities Expense

ACCOUNTS PAYABLE LEDGER

Vendor No.	Vendor Name
210	Artex Golf Products
220	Ecola Golf Equipment
230	Garcia Supply
240	Patton Golf Co.
250	Valiant Golf Co.

ACCOUNTS RECEIVABLE LEDGER

Customer No.	Customer Name
110	William Backus
120	Linda Boge
130	Jonathan Dunbar
140	James Patco
150	Bertha Welsh

INSTRUCTIONS:

1. Journalize the following transactions completed during November of the current year. Use page 18 of a journal similar to the one described in this chapter. Add a 6% sales tax to all sales transactions. Source documents are abbreviated as follows: check, C; memorandum, M; purchase invoice, P; receipt, R; sales invoice, S; cash register tape, T.

Nov. 2. Wrote a check for rent, $950.00. C275.

3. Received an invoice from Valiant Golf Co. for merchandise purchased on account, $1,625.00. P76.

4. Paid for merchandise, $119.00. C276.

5. A check was received in payment on account from Linda Boge, $678.40, covering S50. R45.

7. Ecola Golf Equipment was paid on account, $1,965.00, covering P72. C277.

7. Cash and credit card sales, $4,730.00. T7.

   Posting. Post the items that are to be posted individually.

9. Maria Adolfo, partner, withdrew merchandise for personal use, $165.00. M35.

11. Merchandise was sold on account to James Patco, $255.00. S54.

12. Discovered that a transaction for store supplies bought for cash was journalized and posted in error as a debit to Advertising Expense instead of Supplies—Store, $93.00. M36.

14. Store supplies were bought on account from Garcia Supply, $215.00. M37.

14. Cash and credit card sales, $4,840.00. T14.

   Posting. Post the items that are to be posted individually.

16. Cash was withdrawn by Maria Adolfo, partner, for personal use, $1,200.00. C278.

Nov. 16. Cash was withdrawn by Lawrence Phipps, partner, for personal use, $1,200.00. C279.
17. Wrote a check for electric bill, $183.50. C280.
20. Wrote a check to Valiant Golf Co. on account, $2,680.00, covering P73. C281.
21. Recorded cash and credit card sales, $4,480.00. T21.
   Posting. Post the items that are to be posted individually.
23. Artex Golf Products was paid on account, $2,430.00, covering P74. C282.
24. Jonathan Dunbar bought merchandise on account, $1,095.00. S55.
26. Received payment on account from Bertha Welsh, $233.20, covering S51. R46.
26. Merchandise was purchased on account from Patton Golf Co., $1,285.00. P77.
27. A check was received in payment on account from William Backus, $795.00, covering S52. R47.
28. Received an invoice on account from Artex Golf Products for merchandise purchased on account, $2,325.00. P78.
28. Merchandise was sold on account to Bertha Welsh, $1,095.00. S56.
28. Recorded cash and credit card sales, $4,630.00. T28.
   Posting. Post the items that are to be posted individually.
30. Replenish the petty cash fund, $302.00: office supplies, $48.00; store supplies, $62.00; advertising, $74.00; miscellaneous, $118.00. C283.
30. Recorded cash and credit card sales, $840.00. T30.
   Posting. Post the items that are to be posted individually.

2. Total the journal. Prove the equality of debits and credits.
3. Prove cash. The balance on the next unused check stub is $28,218.30.
4. Rule the journal.
5. Post the totals of the special columns of the journal.
6. Prepare a schedule of accounts payable and a schedule of accounts receivable. Prove the accuracy of the subsidiary ledgers by comparing the schedule totals with the balances of the controlling accounts in the general ledger. If the totals are not the same, find and correct the errors.

Recording Transactions for a Partnership

CarLand, the merchandising business described in Part 3, uses a manual accounting system. CarLand's manual journalizing procedures for purchases, cash payments, sales, and cash receipts are described in Chapters 11 and 12. Manual posting procedures are described in Chapter 13. Integrating Automated Accounting Topic 4 describes procedures for using automated accounting software to journalize and post CarLand's transactions. The Automated Accounting Problem contains instructions for using automated accounting software to solve Challenge Problem 13-C, Chapter 13.

AUTOMATED ACCOUNTING PROCEDURES FOR CARLAND

A group of journal entries is a **batch**. CarLand uses five input forms to batch transaction data for automated accounting.

1. Purchases journal input form for purchases on account.
2. Cash payments journal input form for cash payments.
3. Sales journal input form for sales on account.
4. Cash receipts journal input form for cash receipts.
5. General journal input form for all other transactions.

FILE MAINTENANCE

CarLand's chart of accounts for the general and subsidiary ledgers is on page 244. CarLand uses the same procedures as described for Rugcare in Part 2 to maintain its general ledger chart of accounts. The subsidiary ledgers are also a part of the general ledger data base on the template disk. Procedures for adding or changing a subsidiary account are the same as for a general ledger account. (1) An input form is prepared. (2) The data base is retrieved. (3) Data from the input form are keyed. (4) A revised chart of accounts, vendor list, or customer list is displayed to verify the accuracy of the data keyed. (5) The revised chart of accounts or subsidiary ledger lists are stored as part of the general ledger data base on the template disk.

RECORDING PURCHASES

CarLand batches purchases on account transactions and records them on a purchases journal input form.

Purchase of Merchandise on Account

November 2, 19--. Purchased merchandise on account from Veloz Automotive, $1,754.00. Purchase Invoice No. 74.

The journal entry to record this transaction is on line 1 of the purchases journal input form shown in Illustration T4-1.

ILLUSTRATION T4-1   Purchases journal input form with transactions recorded

	DATE MM/DD	VENDOR NO.	INVOICE NO.	INVOICE AMOUNT	ACCOUNT NO.	DEBIT	CREDIT	
1	11 02	260	P74	1754 00	5110	1754 00		1
2	05	240	P75	3456 00	5110	3456 00		2
3	05	230	P76	3180 00	5110	3180 00		3
4	13	250	P77	3140 00	5110	3140 00		4
5	20	250	P78	2760 00	5110	2760 00		5
25								25

RUN DATE 11/30/-- MM DD YY — PURCHASES JOURNAL Input Form

NOTE: A credit to Accounts Payable is made automatically by the software.

The run date, *11/30/--*, is written in the space provided at the top of the input form.

On line 1, the date of the transaction, *11/02*, is recorded in the Date column. The vendor number, *260*, is entered in the Vendor No. column. The source document number, *P74*, is written in the

Invoice No. column. The invoice amount, *$1,754.00*, is recorded in the Invoice Amount column. The general ledger account number for Purchases, *5110*, is entered in the Account No. column. The debit amount, *$1,754.00*, is written in the Debit column. The Credit column is left blank. The software automatically records the credit to Accounts Payable for a purchases on account transaction.

RECORDING CASH PAYMENTS

CarLand batches cash payments and records them on a cash payments journal input form. CarLand has two types of cash payments. (1) Direct payments. (2) Payments on account. A direct payment transaction does not affect Accounts Payable. Whereas, a payment on account transaction does affect Accounts Payable.

Purchase of Merchandise for Cash

A purchase of merchandise for cash transaction is a direct payment not affecting Accounts Payable.

> *November 2, 19--. Purchased merchandise for cash, $483.00. Check No. 259.*

The journal entry to record this transaction is on line 1 of the cash payments journal input form shown in Illustration T4-2.

| ILLUSTRATION T4-2 | Cash payments journal input form with transactions recorded |

RUN DATE 11/30/-- (MM DD YY)

CASH PAYMENTS JOURNAL
Input Form

	DATE MM/DD	VENDOR NO.	CHECK NO.	ACCOUNTS PAY. DEBIT	ACCOUNT NO.	DEBIT	CREDIT	
1	11/02		C259		5110	483 00		1
2	02		C260		6160	1500 00		2
3	05		C261		1145	87 00		3
4	06	250	C262	3960 00				4
5	07	230	C263	970 00				5
6	09		C264		6190	300 00		6
7	09		C265		6110	125 00		7
8	09		C266		1145	58 00		8
9					1150	65 00		9
10					6110	92 00		10
11					6140	86 00		11
12	10		C267		3140	1500 00		12
13	12	210	C268	430 00				13
14	15		C272		3120	1500 00		14
15	20	240	C273	4840 00				15
16	23	220	C274	620 00				16
25								25

NOTE: A credit to Cash is made automatically by the software.

The run date, *11/30/--*, is written in the space provided at the top of the form.

On line 1, the date of the transaction, *11/02*, is entered in the Date column. The Vendor No. column is left blank because a purchase of merchandise for cash transaction does not affect a vendor account. The source document number, *C259*, is recorded in the Check No. column. The Accounts Pay. Debit column is left blank. The general ledger account number for Purchases, *5110*, is written in the Account No. column. The amount, *$483.00*, is entered in the Debit column. The software automatically makes the credit to Cash, *$483.00*. Therefore, the Credit column is left blank.

Buying Supplies for Cash

A buying supplies for cash transaction is a direct payment not affecting accounts payable.

> *November 5, 19--. Paid cash for office supplies, $87.00. Check No. 261.*

The journal entry to record this transaction is on line 3 of Illustration T4-2. The entry is similar to other direct payment transactions.

Cash Payment on Account

A cash payment on account transaction affects both the controlling account Accounts Payable and a vendor account in an accounts payable subsidiary ledger.

> *November 6, 19--. Paid cash on account to Q-Ban Distributors, $3,960.00. Check No. 262.*

The journal entry to record this transaction is on line 4 of Illustration T4-2.

The date of the transaction, *06*, is written in the Date column. The vendor number, *250*, is entered in the Vendor No. column. The check number, *C262*, is written in the Check No. column. The amount, *$3,960.00*, is recorded in the Accounts Pay. Debit column. The Account No., Debit, and Credit columns are left blank.

Cash Payment of an Expense

A cash payment of an expense transaction is a direct cash payment not affecting Accounts Payable.

> *November 9, 19--. Paid cash for advertising, $125.00. Check No. 265.*

The journal entry to record this transaction is on line 7 of Illustration T4-2. This journal entry is similar to other direct payments.

Cash Payment to Replenish Petty Cash

A cash payment to replenish petty cash transaction is a direct payment not affecting Accounts Payable.

FYI

The run date is usually the date of the last transaction or the last day of a fiscal period.

November 9, 19--. Paid cash to replenish the petty cash fund, $301.00: office supplies, $58.00; store supplies, $65.00; advertising, $92.00; miscellaneous, $86.00. Check No. 266.

The journal entry to record this transaction is on lines 8 through 11 of Illustration T4-2. This journal entry is similar to other direct payments.

RECORDING OTHER TRANSACTIONS

CarLand batches transactions that are not recorded on any of the other input forms and records them on a general journal input form.

Buying Supplies on Account

November 6, 19--. Bought store supplies on account from Antelo Supply, $160.00. Memorandum No. 43.

The run date, 11/30/--, is written in the space provided at the top of the form.

The journal entry to record this transaction is on lines 1 and 2 of the general journal input form shown in Illustration T4-3. Supplies—Store is debited and Accounts Payable is credited for $160.00.

ILLUSTRATION T4-3

General journal input form with transactions recorded

RUN DATE 11/30/-- MM DD YY

GENERAL JOURNAL
Input Form

	DATE MM/DD	REFERENCE	ACCOUNT NO.	CUSTOMER/ VENDOR NO.	DEBIT	CREDIT	
1	11/06	M43	1150		160 00		1
2	/		2110	210		160 00	2
3	12	M44	3140		200 00		3
4	/		5110			200 00	4
5	13	M45	6110		120 00		5
6	/		6140			120 00	6
7	20	M46	3120		250 00		7
8	/		5110			250 00	8
9	23	M47	1150		590 00		9
10	/		2110	210		590 00	10
11	24	M48	1145		830 00		11
12	/		2110	220		830 00	12
25	/						25
				PAGE TOTALS	2150 00	2150 00	
				FINAL TOTALS	2150 00	2150 00	

Withdrawal of Merchandise by a Partner

November 12, 19--. Dario Mesa, partner, withdrew merchandise for personal use, $200.00. Memorandum No. 44.

The journal entry to record this transaction is on lines 3 and 4 of the general journal input form shown in Illustration T4-3. Dario Mesa, Drawing is debited and Purchases is credited for $200.00.

Correcting Entry

November 13, 19--. Discovered that a payment of cash for advertising in October was journalized and posted in error as a debit to Miscellaneous Expense instead of Advertising Expense, $120.00. Memorandum No. 45.

The journal entry to record this transaction is on lines 5 and 6 of the general journal input form shown in Illustration T4-3. Advertising Expense is debited and Miscellaneous Expense is credited for $120.00.

PROCESSING PURCHASES, CASH PAYMENTS, AND OTHER TRANSACTIONS

The general ledger data base is retrieved from the template disk. To process purchases, the Journals menu is selected from the menu bar. The Purchases Journal command is chosen from the Journals menu to display the data entry window for keying transaction data.

After all transaction data have been keyed and posted, the Reports menu is selected from the menu bar. The Journals command is chosen to display the Report Selection window. The Purchases Journal report is selected from the Report Selection window. As CarLand wants to print all transactions from 11/01/-- to 11/30/--, the *Ok* button is pushed to display the purchases journal report. The displayed report is checked for accuracy by comparing the report with the purchases journal input form. The purchases journal report is printed, as shown in Illustration T4-4, and filed for future reference.

	FYI
The petty cash account is only used when establishing petty cash.	

ILLUSTRATION T4-4	Purchases journal report

```
                        CarLand
                    Purchases Journal
                        11/30/--
-------------------------------------------------------------------------
Date    Refer.    V/C Acct.   Title                      Debit      Credit
-------------------------------------------------------------------------
11/02   P74           5110    Purchases               1754.00
11/02   P74       260 2110    AP/Veloz Automotive                  1754.00

11/05   P75           5110    Purchases               3456.00
11/05   P75       240 2110    AP/Nilon Motor Parts                 3456.00

11/05   P76           5110    Purchases               3180.00
11/05   P76       230 2110    AP/Filtrex Tires                     3180.00

11/13   P77           5110    Purchases               3140.00
11/13   P77       250 2110    AP/Q-Ban Distributors                3140.00

11/20   P78           5110    Purchases               2760.00
11/20   P78       250 2110    AP/Q-Ban Distributors                2760.00
                                                    ----------  ----------
                Totals                               14290.00    14290.00
                                                    ==========  ==========
```

To process cash payments, the Journals menu is selected from the menu bar. The Cash Payments command is chosen from the Journals menu to display the data entry window for keying transaction data.

After all transactions have been keyed and posted, a cash payments journal report is displayed. The same steps are followed as for displaying the purchases journal report. However, Cash Payments Journal is selected from the Report Selection window. The displayed report is checked for accuracy by comparing the report with the cash payments journal input form. The cash payments report is printed, as shown in Illustration T4-5, and filed for future reference.

ILLUSTRATION T4-5   Cash payments journal report

```
                               CarLand
                       Cash Payments Journal
                             11/30/--
-----------------------------------------------------------------------
Date   Refer.   V/C Acct.   Title                   Debit      Credit
-----------------------------------------------------------------------
11/02 C259        5110   Purchases                 483.00
11/02 C259        1110   Cash                                   483.00

11/02 C260        6160   Rent Expense             1500.00
11/02 C260        1110   Cash                                  1500.00

11/05 C261        1145   Supplies--Office            87.00
11/05 C261        1110   Cash                                    87.00

11/06 C262    250 2110   AP/Q-Ban Distributors    3960.00
11/06 C262        1110   Cash                                  3960.00

11/07 C263    230 2110   AP/Filtrex Tires          970.00
11/07 C263        1110   Cash                                   970.00

11/09 C264        6190   Utilities Expense         300.00
11/09 C264        1110   Cash                                   300.00

11/09 C265        6110   Advertising Expense       125.00
11/09 C265        1110   Cash                                   125.00

11/09 C266        1145   Supplies--Office           58.00
11/09 C266        1150   Supplies--Store            65.00
11/09 C266        6110   Advertising Expense        92.00
11/09 C266        6140   Miscellaneous Expense      86.00
11/09 C266        1110   Cash                                   301.00

11/10 C267        3140   Dario Mesa, Drawing      1500.00
11/10 C267        1110   Cash                                  1500.00

11/12 C268    210 2110   AP/Antelo Supply          430.00
11/12 C268        1110   Cash                                   430.00

11/15 C272        3120   Amy Kramer, Drawing      1500.00
11/15 C272        1110   Cash                                  1500.00

11/20 C273    240 2110   AP/Nilon Motor Parts     4840.00
11/20 C273        1110   Cash                                  4840.00

11/23 C274    220 2110   AP/Bell Office Products   620.00
11/23 C274        1110   Cash                                   620.00

                         --------- ---------
                 Totals                          16616.00    16616.00
                         ========= =========
```

To process other transactions, the Journals menu is selected from the menu bar. The General Journal command is chosen from the Journals menu to display the data entry window for keying transactions.

After all transactions have been keyed and posted, a general journal report is displayed. The same steps are followed as for displaying the purchases journal report. However, General Journal is selected from the Report Selection window. The displayed general journal report is checked for accuracy by comparing the report totals, *$2,150.00*, with the totals on the general journal input form. Because the totals are the same, the general journal report is assumed to be correct. The general journal report is printed, as shown in Illustration T4-6, and filed for future reference.

| ILLUSTRATION T4-6 | General journal report |

```
                              CarLand
                          General Journal
                             11/30/--
-------------------------------------------------------------------------
Date   Refer.   V/C Acct.   Title                        Debit      Credit
-------------------------------------------------------------------------
11/06 M43            1150   Supplies--Store             160.00
11/06 M43        210 2110   AP/Antelo Supply                       160.00

11/12 M44            3140   Dario Mesa, Drawing         200.00
11/12 M44            5110   Purchases                              200.00

11/13 M45            6110   Advertising Expense         120.00
11/13 M45            6140   Miscellaneous Expense                  120.00

11/20 M46            3120   Amy Kramer, Drawing         250.00
11/20 M46            5110   Purchases                              250.00

11/23 M47            1150   Supplies--Store             590.00
11/23 M47        210 2110   AP/Antelo Supply                       590.00

11/24 M48            1145   Supplies--Office            830.00
11/24 M48        220 2110   AP/Bell Office Products                830.00
                                                      ---------- ----------
                            Totals                     2150.00    2150.00
                                                      ========== ==========
```

PROVING THE ACCOUNTS PAYABLE SUBSIDIARY LEDGER

A general ledger controlling account balance must equal the sum of all account balances in a subsidiary ledger. CarLand proves the accounts payable subsidiary ledger at the end of each month.

To prove the accounts payable ledger, the Reports menu is selected from the menu bar. The Ledgers command is chosen to display the Report Selection window. General Ledger and Schedule of Accounts Payable are selected from the Report Selection window. As CarLand wants to print the transaction activity in only the general ledger controlling account, Accounts Payable, Account No. 2110 to 2110 is keyed as the account number range. After keying the account number range, the *Ok* button is pushed to display the general ledger account, Accounts Payable. The accounts payable account is printed as shown in Illustration T4-7. The schedule of accounts payable is then displayed. The total of the schedule of accounts payable is compared to the balance of the accounts payable account. As the two amounts are the same, *$15,870.00*, the accounts payable ledger is proved. The schedule of accounts payable is printed, as shown in Illustration T4-8, and filed for future reference.

ILLUSTRATION T4-7   Accounts payable account

```
                        CarLand
                     General Ledger
                        11/30/--
-------------------------------------------------------------------
Account          Journal  Date   Refer.    Debit    Credit   Balance
-------------------------------------------------------------------
2110-Accounts Payable
                 Bal. Fwd.                                   10820.00
                 Purchases 11/02 P74                1754.00  12574.00
                 Purchases 11/05 P75                3456.00  16030.00
                 Purchases 11/05 P76                3180.00  19210.00
                 Cash Pymt 11/06 C262    3960.00             15250.00
                 General   11/06 M43                 160.00  15410.00
                 Cash Pymt 11/07 C263     970.00             14440.00
                 Cash Pymt 11/12 C268     430.00             14010.00
                 Purchases 11/13 P77                3140.00  17150.00
                 Purchases 11/20 P78                2760.00  19910.00
                 Cash Pymt 11/20 C273    4840.00             15070.00
                 Cash Pymt 11/23 C274     620.00             14450.00
                 General   11/23 M47                 590.00  15040.00
                 General   11/24 M48                 830.00  15870.00
```

ILLUSTRATION T4-8   Schedule of accounts payable

```
                     CarLand
             Schedule of Accounts Payable
                     11/30/--
-------------------------------------------------------
Account
Number    Name                          Balance
-------------------------------------------------------
210       Antelo Supply                   750.00
220       Bell Office Products            830.00
230       Filtrex Tires                  3180.00
240       Nilon Motor Parts              3456.00
250       Q-Ban Distributors             5900.00
260       Veloz Automotive               1754.00
                                      ----------
          Total                         15870.00
                                      ==========
```

RECORDING SALES ON ACCOUNT

CarLand batches sales on account transactions and records them on a sales journal input form.

November 3, 19--. Sold merchandise on account to Friendly Auto Service, $680.00, plus sales tax, $40.80; total, $720.80. Sales Invoice No. 72.

The journal entry to record this transaction is on lines 1 and 2 of the sales journal input form shown in Illustration T4-9.

ILLUSTRATION T4-9   Sales journal input form with transactions recorded

	DATE MM/DD	CUSTOMER NO.	INVOICE NO.	INVOICE AMOUNT	ACCOUNT NO.	DEBIT	CREDIT	
1	11 03	130	S72	720 80	4110		680 00	1
2	/				2140		40 80	2
3	05	150	S73	1590 00	4110		1500 00	3
4	/				2140		90 00	4
5	09	110	S74	477 00	4110		450 00	5
6	/				2140		27 00	6
7	11	160	S75	604 20	4110		570 00	7
8	/				2140		34 20	8
9	16	110	S76	1378 00	4110		1300 00	9
10	/				2140		78 00	10
11	18	120	S77	2014 00	4110		1900 00	11
12	/				2140		114 00	12
13	24	130	S78	742 00	4110		700 00	13
14	/				2140		42 00	14
15	24	140	S79	318 00	4110		300 00	15
16	/				2140		18 00	16
17	29	140	S80	1378 00	4110		1300 00	17
18	/				2140		78 00	18
25	/							25

RUN DATE 11/30/-- (MM DD YY) — SALES JOURNAL Input Form

NOTE: A debit to Accounts Receivable is made automatically by the software.

The run date, *11/30/--*, is written in the space provided at the top of the form.

On line 1, the date of the transaction, *11/03*, is entered in the Date column. The customer number, *130*, is recorded in the Customer No. column. The source document number, *S72*, is written in the Invoice No. column. The invoice amount, *$720.80*, is written in the Invoice Amount column. The general ledger account number for Sales, *4110*, is entered in the Account No. column. The Debit column is left blank. The software automatically makes the debit to the accounts receivable account. The sale on account amount, $680.00, is recorded in the Credit column.

On line 2 for a sales on account transaction, the Date, Customer No., and Invoice Amount columns are left blank. The general ledger account number for Sales Tax Payable, 2140, is written in the Account No. column. The sales tax amount, $40.80, is entered in the Credit column.

Always remember to record the run date before beginning a problem.

RECORDING CASH RECEIPTS

CarLand batches cash receipts and records them on a cash receipts journal input form. Two types of cash receipts are recorded. (1) Receipts on account. (2) Direct receipts. A receipt on account transaction affects Accounts Receivable. Whereas, a direct receipt transaction does not affect Accounts Receivable.

Cash Receipt on Account

> November 6, 19--. Received cash on account from Autohaus Service, $1,802.00. Receipt No. 86.

The journal entry to record this transaction is on line 1 of the cash receipts journal input form shown in Illustration T4-10.

ILLUSTRATION T4-10   Cash receipts journal input form with transactions recorded

RUN DATE 11/30/-- MM DD YY

CASH RECEIPTS JOURNAL
Input Form

	DATE MM/DD	CUSTOMER NO.	REFERENCE	ACCOUNTS REC. CREDIT	ACCOUNT NO.	DEBIT	CREDIT	
1	11 06	120	R86	1802 00				1
2	07		T7		4110		6450 00	2
3					2140		387 00	3
4	10	140	R87	954 00				4
5	13	160	R88	901 00				5
6	14	150	R89	318 00				6
7	14		T14		4110		5100 00	7
8					2140		306 00	8
9	17	110	R90	2491 00				9
10	20	160	R91	1219 00				10
11	21		T21		4110		5100 00	11
12					2140		306 00	12
13	25	130	R92	265 00				13
14	28		T28		4110		5100 00	14
15					2140		306 00	15
16	30		T30		4110		1150 00	16
17					2140		69 00	17
25								25

NOTE: A debit to Cash is made automatically by the software.

The run date, *11/30/--*, is written in the space provided at the top of the form.

On line 1, the date of the transaction, *11/06*, is entered in the Date column. The customer number, *120*, is recorded in the Customer No. column. The source document number, *R86*, is written in the Reference column. The amount of the cash receipt on account, *$1,802.00*, is entered in the Accounts Rec. Credit column. The software automatically makes the debit to *Cash*. Therefore, the Account No. and Debit columns are left blank.

Cash and Credit Card Sales

A cash or credit card sales transaction is a direct receipt not affecting Accounts Receivable.

> *November 7, 19--. Recorded cash and credit card sales, $6,450.00 plus sales tax, $387.00; total, $6,837.00. Cash Register Tape No. 7.*

The journal entry to record this transaction is on lines 2 and 3 of Illustration T4-10.

On line 2, the date of the transaction, *07*, is written in the Date column. The source document number, *T7*, is entered in the Reference column. The software automatically makes the debit to Cash. Therefore, the Debit column is left blank. The general ledger account number for Sales, *4110*, is recorded in the Account No. column. The amount of the sale, *$6,450.00*, is written in the Credit column.

On line 3, the general ledger account number for Sales Tax Payable, *2140*, is entered in the Account No. column. The sales tax payable amount, *$387.00*, is recorded in the Credit column.

PROCESSING SALES AND CASH RECEIPTS

To process sales on account, the Journals menu is selected from the menu bar. The Sales Journal command is chosen from the Journals menu to display the data entry window for keying transaction data.

After all sales on account transactions have been keyed and posted, the Reports menu is selected from the menu bar. The Journals command is chosen to display the Report Selection window. The Sales Journal report is selected from the Report Selection window. As CarLand wants to prints all transactions from 11/01/-- to 11/30/--, the *Ok* button is pushed to display the Sales Journal report. The displayed report is checked for accuracy by comparing the report with the sales journal input form. The sales journal report is printed, as shown in Illustration T4-11, and filed for future reference.

Display your work before printing to make sure the information is correct. This will save you time and paper.

```
                                CarLand
                              Sales Journal
                                11/30/--
-------------------------------------------------------------------------
Date    Refer.  V/C  Acct.  Title                       Debit      Credit
-------------------------------------------------------------------------
11/03   S72     130  1130   AR/Friendly Auto Service    720.80
11/03   S72          4110   Sales                                   680.00
11/03   S72          2140   Sales Tax Payable                        40.80

11/05   S73     150  1130   AR/Powell Rent-A-Car       1590.00
11/05   S73          4110   Sales                                  1500.00
11/05   S73          2140   Sales Tax Payable                        90.00

11/09   S74     110  1130   AR/Ashley Delivery          477.00
11/09   S74          4110   Sales                                   450.00
11/09   S74          2140   Sales Tax Payable                        27.00

11/11   S75     160  1130   AR/Wood Sales & Service     604.20
11/11   S75          4110   Sales                                   570.00
11/11   S75          2140   Sales Tax Payable                        34.20

11/16   S76     110  1130   AR/Ashley Delivery         1378.00
11/16   S76          4110   Sales                                  1300.00
11/16   S76          2140   Sales Tax Payable                        78.00

11/18   S77     120  1130   AR/Autohaus Service        2014.00
11/18   S77          4110   Sales                                  1900.00
11/18   S77          2140   Sales Tax Payable                       114.00

11/24   S78     130  1130   AR/Friendly Auto Service    742.00
11/24   S78          4110   Sales                                   700.00
11/24   S78          2140   Sales Tax Payable                        42.00

11/24   S79     140  1130   AR/Keystone Delivery        318.00
11/24   S79          4110   Sales                                   300.00
11/24   S79          2140   Sales Tax Payable                        18.00

11/29   S80     140  1130   AR/Keystone Delivery       1378.00
11/29   S80          4110   Sales                                  1300.00
11/29   S80          2140   Sales Tax Payable                        78.00

                                                      ----------  ----------
                            Totals                      9222.00     9222.00
                                                      ==========  ==========
```

To process cash receipts, the Journals menu is selected from the menu bar. The Cash Receipts command is chosen from the Journals menu to display the data entry window for keying transaction data.

After all transactions have been keyed and posted, the Reports menu is selected from the menu bar. The Journals command is chosen to display the Report Selection window. The Cash Receipts Journal report is selected from the Report Selection window. As CarLand wants to print all transactions from 11/01/-- to 11/30/--, the *Ok* button is pushed to display the Cash Receipts report. The displayed report is checked for accuracy by comparing the report to the cash receipts journal input form. The cash receipts journal report is printed, as shown in Illustration T4-12, and is filed for future reference.

ILLUSTRATION T4-12 Cash receipts journal report

```
                            CarLand
                     Cash Receipts Journal
                           11/30/--
---------------------------------------------------------------------
Date   Refer.   V/C Acct.   Title                      Debit     Credit
---------------------------------------------------------------------
11/06  R86          1110    Cash                      1802.00
11/06  R86      120 1130    AR/Autohaus Service                  1802.00

11/07  T7           1110    Cash                      6837.00
11/07  T7           4110    Sales                                6450.00
11/07  T7           2140    Sales Tax Payable                     387.00

11/10  R87          1110    Cash                       954.00
11/10  R87      140 1130    AR/Keystone Delivery                  954.00

11/13  R88          1110    Cash                       901.00
11/13  R88      160 1130    AR/Wood Sales & Service               901.00

11/14  R89          1110    Cash                       318.00
11/14  R89      150 1130    AR/Powell Rent-A-Car                  318.00

11/14  T14          1110    Cash                      5406.00
11/14  T14          4110    Sales                                5100.00
11/14  T14          2140    Sales Tax Payable                     306.00

11/17  R90          1110    Cash                      2491.00
11/17  R90      110 1130    AR/Ashley Delivery                   2491.00

11/20  R91          1110    Cash                      1219.00
11/20  R91      160 1130    AR/Wood Sales & Service              1219.00

11/21  T21          1110    Cash                      5406.00
11/21  T21          4110    Sales                                5100.00
11/21  T21          2140    Sales Tax Payable                     306.00

11/25  R92          1110    Cash                       265.00
11/25  R92      130 1130    AR/Friendly Auto Service              265.00

11/28  T28          1110    Cash                      5406.00
11/28  T28          4110    Sales                                5100.00
11/28  T28          2140    Sales Tax Payable                     306.00

11/30  T30          1110    Cash                      1219.00
11/30  T30          4110    Sales                                1150.00
11/30  T30          2140    Sales Tax Payable                      69.00

                                                      ---------- ----------
                            Totals                    32224.00   32224.00
                                                      ========== ==========
```

PROVING THE ACCOUNTS RECEIVABLE SUBSIDIARY LEDGER

CarLand proves the accounts receivable subsidiary ledger at the end of each month.

To prove the accounts receivable ledger, the Reports menu is selected from the menu bar. The Ledgers command is chosen to display the Report Selection window. General Ledger and Schedule of Accounts Receivable are selected from the Report Selection window. As CarLand wants to print the transaction activity only in the general ledger controlling account, Accounts Receivable, Account No. 1130 to 1130 is keyed as the account number range. After keying the account number range, the *Ok* button is pushed to display the general ledger account, Accounts Receivable. The accounts receivable account is printed as shown in Illustration T4-13. The schedule of accounts receivable is then displayed. The total of the schedule of accounts receivable is compared to the accounts receivable account balance. As the two amounts are the same, *$9,222.00*, the accounts receivable ledger is proved. The schedule of accounts receivable is printed, as shown in Illustration T4-14 on page 324, and is filed for future reference.

ILLUSTRATION T4-13   Accounts receivable account

```
                              CarLand
                          General Ledger
                             11/30/--
-----------------------------------------------------------------------
Account             Journal   Date  Refer.     Debit    Credit   Balance
-----------------------------------------------------------------------
1130-Accounts Receivable
         Bal. Fwd.                                               7950.00
         Sales      11/03 S72            720.80                  8670.80
         Sales      11/05 S73           1590.00                 10260.80
         Cash Rcpt  11/06 R86                     1802.00        8458.80
         Sales      11/09 S74            477.00                  8935.80
         Cash Rcpt  11/10 R87                      954.00        7981.80
         Sales      11/11 S75            604.20                  8586.00
         Cash Rcpt  11/13 R88                      901.00        7685.00
         Cash Rcpt  11/14 R89                      318.00        7367.00
         Sales      11/16 S76           1378.00                  8745.00
         Cash Rcpt  11/17 R90                     2491.00        6254.00
         Sales      11/18 S77           2014.00                  8268.00
         Cash Rcpt  11/20 R91                     1219.00        7049.00
         Sales      11/24 S78            742.00                  7791.00
         Sales      11/24 S79            318.00                  8109.00
         Cash Rcpt  11/25 R92                      265.00        7844.00
         Sales      11/29 S80           1378.00                  9222.00
```

```
                        CarLand
             Schedule of Accounts Receivable
                       11/30/--
---------------------------------------------------------
Account
Number        Name                             Balance
---------------------------------------------------------
110           Ashley Delivery                  1855.00
120           Autohaus Service                 2014.00
130           Friendly Auto Service            1462.80
140           Keystone Delivery                1696.00
150           Powell Rent-A-Car                1590.00
160           Wood Sales & Service              604.20
                                              ----------
              Total                            9222.00
                                              ==========
```

OPTIONAL PROBLEM DB-4A

CarLand's general ledger data base is on the accounting textbook template. If you wish to process CarLand's purchases, cash payments, and other transactions using automated accounting software, load the *Automated Accounting 6.0* or higher software. Select Data Base 4A (DB-4A) from the template disk. Read the Problem Instructions screen. Use the completed purchases, cash payments, general journal input forms, Illustrations T4-1, T4-2, and T4-3, and follow the procedures described to process CarLand's purchases, cash payments, and other transactions.

OPTIONAL PROBLEM DB-4A

CarLand's general ledger data base is on the accounting textbook template. If you wish to process CarLand's sales and cash receipts transactions using automated accounting software, load the *Automated Accounting 6.0* or higher software. Continue using Data Base 4A (DB-4A) from the template disk. Use the completed sales and cash receipts journal input forms, Illustrations T4-9 and T4-10, and follow the procedures described to process CarLand's sales and cash receipts.

AUTOMATED ACCOUNTING PROBLEM

AUTOMATING CHALLENGE PROBLEM 13-C Recording transactions for a partnership

INSTRUCTIONS:

1. Journalize the transactions from Challenge Problem 13-C, Chapter 13 on the appropriate input forms. Use November 30 of the current year as the run date.
2. Load the *Automated Accounting 6.0* or higher software. Select data base F13-C (First-Year Course Problem 13-C) from the accounting textbook template. Read the Problem Instructions screen.
3. Select File from the menu bar and choose the Save As menu command. Key the path to the drive and directory that contains your data files. Save the data base with a file name of XXX13C (where XXX are your initials).
4. Key the data from the completed purchases journal input form.
5. Display/print the purchases journal report.
6. Key the data from the completed cash payments journal input form.
7. Display/print the cash payments journal report.
8. Key the data from the completed general journal input form.

9. Display/print the general journal report.
10. Display/print the accounts payable account.
11. Display/print the schedule of accounts payable.
12. Key the data from the completed sales journal input form.
13. Display/print the sales journal report.
14. Key the data from the cash receipts journal input form.
15. Display/print the cash receipts journal report.
16. Display/print the accounts receivable account.
17. Display/print the schedule of accounts receivable.

Preparing Payroll Records

ENABLING PERFORMANCE TASKS

After studying Chapter 14, you will be able to:

a Define accounting terms related to payroll records.

b Identify accounting practices related to payroll records.

c Calculate employee earnings and deductions.

d Complete payroll records.

e Prepare payroll checks.

TERMS PREVIEW

salary • pay period • payroll • total earnings • payroll taxes • withholding allowance • Medicare • FICA tax • federal unemployment tax • state unemployment tax • payroll register • tax base • net pay • automatic check deposit • employee earnings record • pegboard

CarLand employs several people to work in the business. These employees record the time they work for CarLand each day. Periodically CarLand pays its employees for the number of hours each employee has worked. The money paid for employee services is called a **salary**. The period covered by a salary payment is called a **pay period**. A business may decide to pay employee salaries every week, every two weeks, twice a month, or once a month. CarLand uses a semimonthly pay period. Employees are paid twice a month, on the 15th and last day of each month.

The total amount earned by all employees for a pay period is called a **payroll**. The payroll is reduced by state and federal taxes and other deductions, such as health insurance, to determine the amount paid to all employees. Special payroll records support the recording of payroll transactions in a journal. The business also uses these records to inform employees of their annual earnings and to prepare payroll reports for the government.

PAYROLL TIME CARDS

A payroll system must include an accurate record of the time each employee has worked. Several methods are used for keeping time records. One of the more frequently used methods is a time card. Time cards are used as the basic source of information to prepare a payroll.

Some time cards only require employees to record the total hours worked each day. Employees who record the total hours worked each day usually complete time cards by hand.

A business may use a time card that requires employees to record their arrival and departure times. CarLand uses a time clock to record the daily arrival and departure times of its employees. The time card for Patrick S. Turner for the pay period December 1–15 is shown in Illustration 14-1.

ILLUSTRATION 14-1

Payroll time card

CarLand

EMPLOYEE NO. _____4_____
NAME _Patrick S. Turner_
PERIOD ENDING _December 15, 19--_

MORNING		AFTERNOON		OVERTIME		HOURS	
IN	OUT	IN	OUT	IN	OUT	REG	OT
758	12⁰²	12⁵⁹	5⁰⁶			8	
759	12⁰⁰	12⁵⁷	5⁰¹			8	
755	12⁰¹	12⁵⁶	5⁰²	7⁰¹	9³³	8	2½
756	12⁰²					8	
754	12⁰⁴	12⁵⁹	5⁰¹			8	
755	12⁰⁰	12⁵⁸	5⁰¹	6²⁸	8³¹	8	2

	HOURS	RATE	AMOUNT
REGULAR	88	8.00	704.00
OVERTIME	4½	12.00	54.00
TOTAL HOURS	92½	TOTAL EARNINGS	758.00

TIMEKEEPER

- Reviews timecards
- Calculates total time worked by employees
- Calculates time worked and units produced by piecework employees
- Posts time worked to master records

Analyzing a Payroll Time Card

Mr. Turner's employee number is at the top of the card. Below the employee number are the employee name and the ending date of the pay period.

CarLand's time cards have three sections, Morning, Afternoon, and Overtime, with In and Out columns under each section. When Mr. Turner reported for work on December 1, he inserted the card in the time clock. The clock recorded his time of arrival, 7:58, on the first line of the time card. The other entries on this line indicate that he left for lunch at 12:02. He returned at 12:59 and left for the day at 5:06. On December 3 he worked overtime, starting at 7:01 and leaving at 9:33.

CarLand calculates overtime pay for each employee who works more than 8 hours in one day. No employee works more than 5 days in any one week.

Calculating Hours Worked

The first task in preparing a payroll is to calculate the number of hours worked by each employee. Four steps are followed to calculate employee hours worked.

1 Calculate the number of regular hours for each day and enter the amounts in the Hours Reg column.

> Mr. Turner works 8 hours during a normal day. The hours worked on December 3, the third line of the time card, are calculated using the arrival and departure times imprinted on the time card. Times are rounded to the nearest quarter hour to calculate the hours worked.

	Departure Time	−	Arrival Time	=	Hours Worked
Morning:					
Time card	12:01		7:55		
Nearest quarter hour	12:00	−	8:00	=	4:00
Afternoon:					
Time card	5:02		12:56		
Nearest quarter hour	5:00	−	1:00	=	4:00
Total regular hours worked on December 3					8:00

> The hours worked in the morning and afternoon are calculated separately. The morning departure time of 12:01 is rounded to the nearest quarter hour, 12:00. The rounded arrival time, 8:00, *subtracted* from the departure time, 12:00, *equals* the morning hours worked. Hours worked of 4:00 means that Mr. Turner worked 4 hours and no (00) minutes. The total regular hours worked, *8*, is recorded in the Hours Reg column on line 3 of the time card.

2 Calculate the number of overtime hours for each day and enter the amounts in the Hours OT column.

Overtime hours for December 3 are calculated using the same procedure as for regular hours.

	Departure Time	−	Arrival Time	=	Hours Worked
Time card	9:33		7:01		
Nearest quarter hour	9:30	−	7:00	=	2:30

The hours worked of 2:30 means that Mr. Turner worked 2 hours and 30 minutes (½ hour) of overtime. Therefore, 2½ is recorded in the Hours OT column.

3 Add the hours worked in the Hours Reg and OT columns. Enter the totals in the spaces provided at the bottom of the time card.

Mr. Turner worked 88 regular hours (8 hours × 11 days) and 4½ overtime hours during the semimonthly pay period. Therefore, *88* is recorded in the Regular Hours space at the bottom of the card and *4½* is recorded in the Overtime Hours space.

4 Add the Hours column to calculate the total hours. Enter the total in the Hours column at the bottom of the time card.

Mr. Turner worked 88 regular hours and 4½ overtime hours for a total of 92½ hours. Total hours, *92½*, are entered in the Total Hours space.

Calculating Employee Total Earnings

Once the total regular and overtime hours are determined, employee earnings can be calculated. The total pay due for a pay period before deductions is called **total earnings**. Total earnings are sometimes referred to as gross pay or gross earnings. Four steps are followed to calculate employee total earnings.

1 Enter the rate for regular time in the Rate column. Calculate the regular earnings by multiplying regular hours times the regular rate.

Mr. Turner's regular hourly rate, *$8.00*, is entered in the Regular Rate space. The regular earnings are calculated as shown below.

	Regular Hours	×	Regular Rate	=	Regular Earnings
	88	×	$8.00	=	$704.00

The amount of regular earnings, *$704.00*, is entered in the Regular Amount space.

2 Enter the rate for overtime in the Rate column.

Mr. Turner is paid 1½ times his regular rate for overtime work. The overtime rate for Mr. Turner is calculated as shown below.

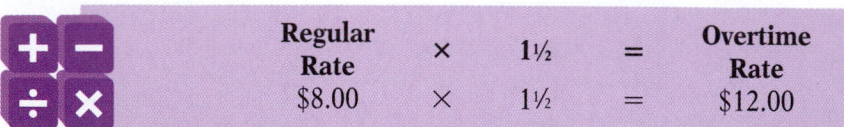

	Regular Rate	×	1½	=	Overtime Rate
	$8.00	×	1½	=	$12.00

The overtime rate, *$12.00,* is entered in the Overtime Rate space.

3 Calculate the overtime earnings by multiplying overtime hours times the overtime rate.

The overtime earnings for Mr. Turner are calculated as shown below.

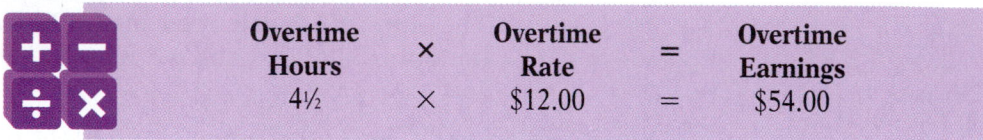

	Overtime Hours	×	Overtime Rate	=	Overtime Earnings
	4½	×	$12.00	=	$54.00

The amount of overtime earnings, $54.00, is entered in the Overtime Amount space.

4 Add the Amount column to calculate the total earnings.

The total earnings for Mr. Turner are calculated as shown below.

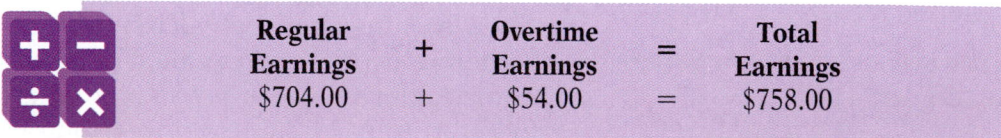

	Regular Earnings	+	Overtime Earnings	=	Total Earnings
	$704.00	+	$54.00	=	$758.00

The amount of total earnings, $758.00, is entered in the Total Earnings space.

CarLand owes Mr. Turner $758.00 for his work during the pay period ending December 15. However, taxes and other deductions must be subtracted from total earnings to determine the actual amount CarLand will pay Mr. Turner. Therefore, CarLand will not pay Mr. Turner the entire $758.00.

FYI

Total earnings are sometimes referred to as gross pay or gross earnings.

Audit Your Understanding

1. What is a payroll?

2. How does CarLand calculate overtime earnings?

3. How many hours were worked by an employee who arrived at 8:29 and departed at 12:02?

4. What are the total earnings of an employee who worked 40 hours and earns $10.00 per hour?

PAYROLL TAXES

Taxes based on the payroll of a business are called **payroll taxes.** A business is required by law to withhold certain payroll taxes from employee salaries. A business is

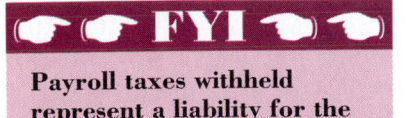
also required to pay additional payroll taxes. All payroll taxes are based on employee total earnings. Therefore, accurate and detailed payroll records must be maintained. Errors in payroll records could cause incorrect payroll tax payments. Federal and state governments may charge a business a penalty for failure to pay correct payroll taxes when they are due.

Payroll taxes withheld represent a liability for the employer until payment is made. Federal payroll taxes may be paid to a Federal Reserve Bank. The taxes may also be paid to a bank authorized to receive such funds for the government. Local and state governments that assess payroll taxes also designate how, when, and where a business will pay the liability for employee taxes withheld.

Employee Income Tax

A business must withhold federal income taxes from employee total earnings. Federal income taxes withheld must be forwarded periodically to the federal government. Federal income tax is withheld from employee earnings in all 50 states. Employers in many states also are required to withhold state, city, or county income taxes from employee earnings.

The information used to determine the amount of income tax withheld is identified on Form W-4, Employee's Withholding Allowance Certificate. The completed Form W-4 for Mr. Turner is shown in Illustration 14-2.

ILLUSTRATION 14-2   Form W-4, Employee's Withholding Allowance Certificate

Form **W-4**	**Employee's Withholding Allowance Certificate**	OMB No. 1545-0010
Department of the Treasury Internal Revenue Service	▶ For Privacy Act and Paperwork Reduction Act Notice, see reverse.	**19** --

1 Type or print your first name and middle initial Last name	**2** Your social security number
Patrick S. Turner	450-70-6432

Home address (number and street or rural route)	**3** ☐ Single ☒ Married ☐ Married, but withhold at higher Single rate.
1625 Northland Drive	**Note:** *If married, but legally separated, or spouse is a nonresident alien, check the Single box.*
City or town, state, and ZIP code	**4** If your last name differs from that on your social security card,
Rockville, RI 02873	check here and call 1-800-772-1213 for more information . ▶ ☐

5	Total number of allowances you are claiming (from line G above or from the Worksheets on back if they apply)	**5**	4
6	Additional amount, if any, you want deducted from each paycheck	**6** $	–0–

7 I claim exemption from withholding and I certify that I meet **ALL** of the following conditions for exemption:
- Last year I had a right to a refund of **ALL** Federal income tax withheld because I had **NO** tax liability; **AND**
- This year I expect a refund of **ALL** Federal income tax withheld because I expect to have **NO** tax liability; **AND**
- This year if my income exceeds $600 and includes nonwage income, another person cannot claim me as a dependent.

If you meet all of the above conditions, enter the year effective and "Exempt" here . . . . ▶ | **7** 19

8 Are you a full-time student? (**Note:** *Full-time students are not automatically exempt.*) . . . . | **8** ☒ Yes ☐ No

Under penalties of perjury, I certify that I am entitled to the number of withholding allowances claimed on this certificate or entitled to claim exempt status.

Employee's signature ▶ *Patrick S. Turner*   Date ▶ *June 27*   ,19 --

9 Employer's name and address (Employer: Complete 9 and 11 only if sending to the IRS)	**10** Office code (optional)	**11** Employer identification number

Information from the completed Form W-4 is used when a business calculates the amount of federal income taxes to be withheld. Employers are required to have on file a current Form W-4 for all employees. The amount of income tax withheld is based on employee marital status and withholding allowances.

Marital Status. Employees identify on Form W-4 whether they are married or single. A married employee will have less income tax withheld than a single employee with the same total earnings.

Mr. Turner checked the married box for item 3 of the Form W-4 shown in Illustration 14-2.

Withholding Allowance. A deduction from total earnings for each person legally supported by a taxpayer is called a **withholding allowance.** The larger the number of the withholding allowances claimed, the smaller the income tax withheld from employee salaries.

Mr. Turner claimed four withholding allowances, one each for himself, his wife, and his two children. The number of withholding allowances was recorded in item 5 of the Form W-4.

Most employees are required to have federal income taxes withheld from their salaries. An exemption from withholding is available for certain low-income and part-time employees. The employee must meet the requirements listed in the instructions which accompany Form W-4. The requirements are very restrictive. Most students with part-time jobs who live with their parents do *not* qualify for the exemption. Students who earn over $500 in salary or any interest from a savings or checking account are not eligible to claim the exemption.

The federal government occasionally changes the way income taxes are withheld from employee total earnings. The Form W-4 shown in Illustration 14-2 was the form in use when the materials for this textbook were prepared. Employers must be aware of changes in tax laws and forms. If Form W-4 is changed, an employer must obtain a new W-4 from each employee.

Employee and Employer Social Security Tax

The federal social security law includes three programs.

1. Old-age, survivors, and disability insurance benefits for qualified employees and their spouses, widows or widowers, dependent children, and parents.
2. Payments to senior citizens for the cost of certain hospital and related services. The federal health insurance program for people who have reached retirement age is called **Medicare.**
3. Grants to states that provide benefits for persons temporarily unemployed and for certain relief and welfare purposes.

Each employee must have a social security number. Current law requires that most infants who are at least one year old by the

USING FUNCTIONS TO PREPARE A PAYROLL REGISTER

Many computations are required to prepare a payroll register. When computations require many values, formulas with individual cell references can become burdensome. For example, the formula to compute the total regular wages at G17 would be +G10+G11+G12+G13+G14+G15. A lengthy formula can sometimes by replaced with a function which is a short-cut formula. Functions make keying easier and more efficient.

A typical function begins with the @ sign, followed by the function name, and ending with cell references. The name of the function describes what calculation will be performed. The cell references identify the location of values to be used in the computation. The most common function, @SUM, computes the sum of the values in a range of cells. The function @SUM(G10..G15) would add the amounts in cells G10 through G15 to compute total regular wages.

In subsequent payroll periods, Ms. Bauch may have different earnings or change her number of withholding allowances. The electronic spreadsheet will use these new values to determine the correct income tax withholding from the data base. The electronic spreadsheet can perform this task instantly and accurately.

```
        A      B          C       D    E  F    G        H         I    J    K
 1                                                            PAYROLL REGISTER
 2   Semimonthly Period Ended:    December 15, 19--
 3
 4                                                 Earnings
 5                                        ------------------------    ---------
 6                           No.                                      Federal
 7   Empl.            Mar.   of                                       Income
 8   No.   Employee's Name   St.   All.  Regular Overtime  Total      Tax
 9        ----------------------------------------------------------  ---------
10      2  Bauch, Mary R.     2    2      660.00            660.00      57.00
11      5  Clay, Richard P.   1    1       80.00             80.00        .00
12      1  Javorski, Adam B.  2    2      384.00   18.00    402.00      17.00
13      6  Maggio, Brenda A.  1    1       40.00             40.00        .00
14      4  Turner, Patrick S. 2    4      704.00   54.00    758.00      45.00
15      3  Wilkes, Samuel R.  1    1      616.00            616.00      73.00
16                                     ------------------------    ---------
17                                      2,484.00   72.00  2,556.00     192.00
18                                     ========================    =========
19
20
   G17     (,2)  @SUM(G10..G15)
```

end of a tax year have a social security number. Therefore, most employees will have received their social security number as a child. Employees without social security numbers can apply for a number at the nearest Social Security office.

FICA Tax. A federal tax paid by employees and employers for old-age, survivors, disability, and hospitalization insurance is called **FICA tax.** FICA is the abbreviation for the Federal Insurance Contributions Act. FICA tax is based on the total earnings of the employees. Employers are required to withhold FICA tax from a specified amount of employee salary paid in a calendar year. In addition, employers must pay the same amount of FICA tax as withheld from employee salaries.

Federal Unemployment Tax. A federal tax used for state and federal administrative expenses of the unemployment program is

FYI

FICA is an acronym for Federal Insurance Contributions Act.

called **federal unemployment tax**. This tax is paid entirely by employers.

State Unemployment Tax. A state tax used to pay benefits to unemployed workers is called **state unemployment tax**. This tax is usually paid by employers. The Social Security Act specifies certain standards for unemployment compensation laws. Therefore, a high degree of uniformity exists in state unemployment laws. However, details of state unemployment laws do differ. Because of these differences, employers must know the requirements of the states in which they operate.

Retention of Records. Employers are required to retain all payroll records showing payments and deductions. Some records must be retained longer than others. Records pertaining to social security tax payments and deductions must be retained for four years. The length of time state unemployment tax payment records must be retained varies from state to state.

PAYROLL REGISTER

A business form used to record payroll information is called a **payroll register**. A payroll register summarizes the total earnings and payroll withholdings of all employees. CarLand's payroll register for the semimonthly period ended December 15 is shown in Illustration 14-3.

Regular, overtime, and total earnings are recorded in a payroll register from information on time cards. Amounts deducted for payroll taxes, health insurance, and charitable contributions are calculated and recorded in a payroll register. Also, the total amount

ILLUSTRATION 14-3   Payroll register

EMPL. NO.	EMPLOYEE'S NAME	MARITAL STATUS	NO. OF ALLOWANCES	REGULAR	OVERTIME	TOTAL	FEDERAL INCOME TAX	FICA TAX	HEALTH INSURANCE	OTHER	TOTAL	NET PAY	CHECK NO.
2	Bauch, Mary R.	M	2	660 00		660 00	57 00	52 80	38 00	B 5 00	152 80	507 20	419
5	Clay, Richard P.	S	1	80 00		80 00	00	6 40			6 40	73 60	420
1	Javorski, Adam B.	M	2	384 00	18 00	402 00	17 00	32 16	38 00		87 16	314 84	421
6	Maggio, Brenda A.	S	1	40 00		40 00	00	3 20			3 20	36 80	422
4	Turner, Patrick S.	M	4	704 00	54 00	758 00	45 00	60 64	50 00	B 10 00 uw 10 00	175 64	582 36	423
3	Wilkes, Samuel R.	S	1	616 00		616 00	73 00	49 28	32 00		154 28	461 72	424
	Totals			2484 00	72 00	2556 00	192 00	204 48	158 00	B 15 00 uw 10 00	579 48	1976 52	

SEMIMONTHLY PERIOD ENDED *December 15, 19--*   PAYROLL REGISTER   DATE OF PAYMENT *December 15, 19--*

EARNINGS   DEDUCTIONS

to be paid to each employee and the check number of each payroll check are recorded in a payroll register.

The two partners of CarLand, Amy Kramer and Dario Mesa, are not listed on the payroll register. Owners of partnerships are not employees of the company. Cash payments to partners are recorded as withdrawals rather than as salaries.

Recording Earnings in a Payroll Register

The employee number, name, marital status, and withholding allowances are listed in a payroll register. Employee earnings for a pay period are written in the appropriate columns of a payroll register.

Recorded on line 5 of the payroll register are Mr. Turner's employee number, *4*, and name, *Turner, Patrick S.* Also recorded are Mr. Turner's marital status, *M* for married; the number of withholding allowances, *4*; regular earnings, *$704.00*; overtime earnings, *$54.00*; and total earnings, *$758.00*. This information is obtained from Mr. Turner's Form W-4 and time card.

Businesses must withhold federal income tax from employee total earnings in all fifty states.

Recording Deductions in a Payroll Register

The deductions section of a payroll register is used to record the payroll taxes and other deductions withheld from employee earnings. Also, some companies deduct amounts for retirement plans. These deductions will vary from one company to another depending on policies established between management and employees.

Five steps are followed to calculate and record deductions.

1 The Federal Income Tax column is used to record the amount of federal income tax withheld from employee earnings. This amount is determined from tables furnished by the federal government. Portions of the tables showing the tax to be withheld are shown in Illustration 14-4.

Mr. Turner's federal income tax on total earnings of $758.00 is found in the table for married persons. Since CarLand pays its payroll twice a month, the table for a semimonthly pay period is used. The proper wage bracket is from $740.00 to $760.00. The income tax to be withheld is the amount shown on this line under the column for four allowances, $45.00.

No federal income tax was withheld from the earnings of Richard Clay and Brenda Maggio. Although they are students who work part-time, they are not exempt from federal income tax withholding. They did not, however, have enough total earnings *in this pay period* to require any income tax to be withheld. Federal income tax withholding tables are also available for daily, weekly, biweekly, and monthly pay periods. The tables in Illustration 14-4 are those available when materials for this textbook were prepared.

2 The FICA Tax column is used to record the amount deducted for social security tax. FICA tax is calculated by multiplying

SEMIMONTHLY PAYROLL PERIOD — MARRIED PERSONS

And the wages are—		And the number of withholding allowances claimed is—										
At least	But less than	0	1	2	3	4	5	6	7	8	9	10
		The amount of income tax to be withheld shall be—										
$0	$130											
130	135	1										
135	140	2										
140	145	2										
145	150	3										
400	410	42	30	17	5							
410	420	43	31	19	7							
420	430	45	33	20	8							
430	440	46	34	22	10							
440	450	48	36	23	11							
450	460	49	37	25	13							
460	470	51	39	26	14	2						
470	480	52	40	28	16	3						
480	490	54	42	29	17	5						
490	500	55	43	31	19	6						
500	520	57	45	33	21	9						
520	540	60	48	36	24	12						
540	560	63	51	39	27	15	3					
560	580	66	54	42	30	18	6					
580	600	69	57	45	33	21	9					
600	620	72	60	48	36	24	12					
620	640	75	63	51	39	27	15	2				
640	660	78	66	54	42	30	18	5				
660	680	81	69	57	45	33	21	8				
680	700	84	72	60	48	36	24	11				
700	720	87	75	63	51	39	27	14	2			
720	740	90	78	66	54	42	30	17	5			
740	760	93	81	69	57	45	33	20	8			
760	780	96	84	72	60	48	36	23	11			
780	800	99	87	75	63	51	39	26	14	2		
800	820	102	90	78	66	54	42	29	17	5		
820	840	105	93	81	69	57	45	32	20	8		
840	860	108	96	84	72	60	48	35	23	11		
860	880	111	99	87	75	63	51	38	26	14	2	
880	900	114	102	90	78	66	54	41	29	17	5	
900	920	117	105	93	81	69	57	44	32	20	8	
920	940	120	108	96	84	72	60	47	35	23	11	
940	960	123	111	99	87	75	63	50	38	26	14	2
960	980	126	114	102	90	78	66	53	41	29	17	5
980	1,000	129	117	105	93	81	69	56	44	32	20	8
1,000	1,020	132	120	108	96	84	72	59	47	35	23	11
1,020	1,040	135	123	111	99	87	75	62	50	38	26	14
1,040	1,060	138	126	114	102	90	78	65	53	41	29	17
1,060	1,080	141	129	117	105	93	81	68	56	44	32	20
1,080	1,100	144	132	120	108	96	84	71	59	47	35	23
1,100	1,120	147	135	123	111	99	87	74	62	50	38	26
1,120	1,140	150	138	126	114	102	90	77	65	53	41	29
1,140	1,160	153	141	129	117	105	93	80	68	56	44	32
1,160	1,180	156	144	132	120	108	96	83	71	59	47	35
1,180	1,200	159	147	135	123	111	99	86	74	62	50	38
1,200	1,220	162	150	138	126	114	102	89	77	65	53	41
1,220	1,240	165	153	141	129	117	105	92	80	68	56	44
1,240	1,260	168	156	144	132	120	108	95	83	71	59	47
1,260	1,280	171	159	147	135	123	111	98	86	74	62	50
1,280	1,300	174	162	150	138	126	114	101	89	77	65	53
1,300	1,320	177	165	153	141	129	117	104	92	80	68	56
1,320	1,340	180	168	156	144	132	120	107	95	83	71	59
1,340	1,360	183	171	159	147	135	123	110	98	86	74	62
1,360	1,380	187	174	162	150	138	126	113	101	89	77	65
1,380	1,400	192	177	165	153	141	129	116	104	92	80	68

SEMIMONTHLY MARRIED PERSONS

total earnings by the tax rate. From time to time, Congress changes the tax rate used to calculate FICA taxes. A FICA tax rate of 8% is used to illustrate the FICA tax calculations in this textbook. The FICA tax for Mr. Turner is calculated as shown below.

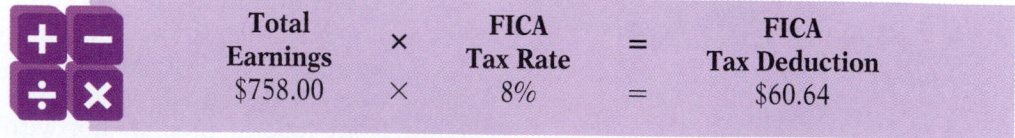

Total Earnings	×	FICA Tax Rate	=	FICA Tax Deduction
$758.00	×	8%	=	$60.64

Congress has limited the amount of FICA tax that each individual must pay. The FICA tax is not calculated on total earnings over a specific maximum amount. The maximum amount of earnings on which a tax is calculated is called a **tax base.**

The FICA tax rate is a combination of two different tax rates: (1) a tax for old-age, survivors, and disability and (2) a

SEMIMONTHLY PAYROLL PERIOD — SINGLE PERSONS

And the wages are—		And the number of withholding allowances claimed is—										
At least	But less than	0	1	2	3	4	5	6	7	8	9	10
		The amount of income tax to be withheld shall be—										
$0	$45											
45	50	1										
50	55	1										
55	60	2										
60	65	3										
65	70	4										
70	75	4										
75	80	5										
80	85	6										
85	90	7										
380	390	51	39	27	15	2						
390	400	53	41	28	16	4						
400	410	54	42	30	18	5						
410	420	56	44	31	19	7						
420	430	57	45	33	21	8						
430	440	59	47	34	22	10						
440	450	60	48	36	24	11						
450	460	62	50	37	25	13	1					
460	470	63	51	39	27	14	2					
470	480	65	53	40	28	16	4					
480	490	66	54	42	30	17	5					
490	500	68	56	43	31	19	7					
500	520	70	58	46	33	21	9					
520	540	73	61	49	36	24	12					
540	560	76	64	52	39	27	15	3				
560	580	79	67	55	42	30	18	6				
580	600	82	70	58	45	33	21	9				
600	620	85	73	61	48	36	24	12				
620	640	88	76	64	51	39	27	15	3			
640	660	91	79	67	54	42	30	18	6			
660	680	94	82	70	57	45	33	21	9			
680	700	97	85	73	60	48	36	24	12			
700	720	100	88	76	63	51	39	27	15	2		
720	740	103	91	79	66	54	42	30	18	5		
740	760	106	94	82	69	57	45	33	21	8		
760	780	109	97	85	72	60	48	36	24	11		
780	800	112	100	88	75	63	51	39	27	14	2	
800	820	118	103	91	78	66	54	42	30	17	5	
820	840	123	106	94	81	69	57	45	33	20	8	
840	860	129	109	97	84	72	60	48	36	23	11	
860	880	135	112	100	87	75	63	51	39	26	14	2
880	900	140	118	103	90	78	66	54	42	29	17	5
900	920	146	123	106	93	81	69	57	45	32	20	8
920	940	151	129	109	96	84	72	60	48	35	23	11
940	960	157	134	112	99	87	75	63	51	38	26	14
960	980	163	140	117	102	90	78	66	54	41	29	17
980	1,000	168	146	123	105	93	81	69	57	44	32	20
1,000	1,020	174	151	128	108	96	84	72	60	47	35	23
1,020	1,040	179	157	134	111	99	87	75	63	50	38	26
1,040	1,060	185	162	140	117	102	90	78	66	53	41	29
1,060	1,080	191	168	145	122	105	93	81	69	56	44	32
1,080	1,100	196	174	151	128	108	96	84	72	59	47	35
1,100	1,120	202	179	156	134	111	99	87	75	62	50	38
1,120	1,140	207	185	162	139	116	102	90	78	65	53	41
1,140	1,160	213	190	168	145	122	105	93	81	68	56	44
1,160	1,180	219	196	173	150	128	108	96	84	71	59	47
1,180	1,200	224	202	179	156	133	111	99	87	74	62	50
1,200	1,220	230	207	184	162	139	116	102	90	77	65	53
1,220	1,240	235	213	190	167	144	122	105	93	80	68	56
1,240	1,260	241	218	196	173	150	127	108	96	83	71	59

SEMIMONTHLY SINGLE PERSONS

tax for Medicare. The two taxes also have different tax bases. The FICA tax rates and bases used in this text are shown below.

	Tax Rate	Tax Base
Old-age, survivors, and disability	6.5%	earnings up to $55,500
Medicare	1.5%	earnings up to $130,200
Total	8.0%	

Therefore, the effective FICA tax rate for earnings up to the tax base of $55,500 is 8.0% (6.5% + 1.5%). The additional FICA tax rate for earnings from $55,500 to $130,200 is 1.5%.

Before calculating Mr. Turner's FICA tax, his accumulated earnings are compared to the tax base. Between January 1 and December 1, Mr. Turner has earned $16,794.00. Since his earnings are less than either tax base, the total FICA tax of 8.0%

of earnings ($758.00 × 8% = $60.64) is recorded in the payroll register. If Mr. Turner had accumulated earnings over $55,500.00 but not yet $130,200.00, only the Medicare portion of FICA tax (1.5% of earnings) would be owed. If Mr. Turner had accumulated earnings over $130,200.00, no FICA tax would be owed and no amount would have been recorded in the payroll register.

3 The Health Insurance column is used to record health insurance premiums. Full-time employees of CarLand participate in a group health insurance plan to take advantage of lower group rates.

Mr. Turner's semimonthly health insurance premium is $50.00. Premiums are set by the insurance company and are usually based on the employee marital status and whether coverage is for an individual or a family. Some health insurance premiums may be based on the number of individuals covered.

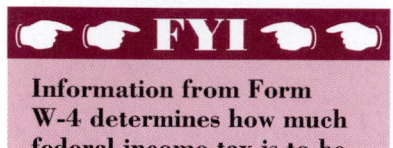
4 The Other column is used to record voluntary deductions requested by an employee. Entries are identified by code letters. CarLand uses the letter *B* to identify amounts withheld for buying U.S. Savings Bonds. *UW* is used to identify amounts withheld for employee contributions to United Way.

Mr. Turner has authorized CarLand to withhold $10.00 each pay period to buy U.S. Savings Bonds for him. Mr. Turner has also authorized that $10.00 be withheld as a contribution to the United Way.

5 The Total column is used to record total deductions. All deductions on a line for each employee are added. The total deductions for Mr. Turner are calculated as shown below.

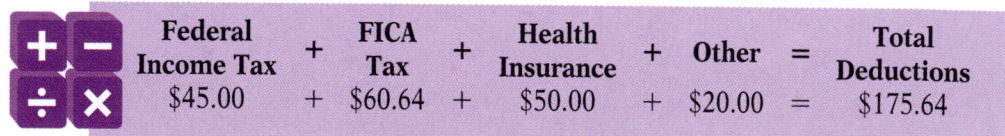

	Federal Income Tax	+	FICA Tax	+	Health Insurance	+	Other	=	Total Deductions
	$45.00	+	$60.64	+	$50.00	+	$20.00	=	$175.64

Calculating Net Pay in a Payroll Register

The total earnings paid to an employee after payroll taxes and other deductions is called **net pay**. Net pay is calculated by subtracting total deductions from total earnings. The Net Pay column is used to record the amount. The net pay for Mr. Turner is calculated as shown below.

	Total Earnings	−	Total Deductions	=	Net Pay
	$758.00	−	$175.64	=	$582.36

Completing a Payroll Register

After the net pay has been recorded for each employee, the word *Totals* is written in the Employee name column and each amount column is totaled. A separate total is shown for each different type of deduction in the Other column. Accuracy of these totals is verified by subtracting the Total Deductions column total from the Total Earnings column total as shown below.

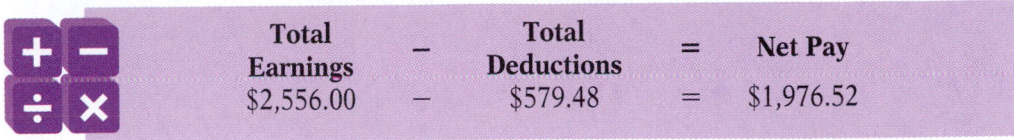

	Total Earnings	−	Total Deductions	=	Net Pay
	$2,556.00	−	$579.48	=	$1,976.52

The net pay calculated above, $1,976.52, is compared to the total of the Net Pay column. The payroll register is proved because these amounts are equal. After the payroll register is proved, a double rule is drawn below the totals, and the register is given to a partner of the company for approval.

Before checks are written for employee net pay, the payroll calculations are checked for accuracy. A partner approves the payroll after the accuracy is verified. After each check is written, the check number is recorded in the Ck. No. column.

PAYROLL CHECKS

CarLand pays its employees with checks written on a special payroll checking account. A check for the total net pay is written on CarLand's general checking account. The check is deposited in the payroll checking account. Illustration 14-5 shows the check written for the December 1-15 pay period. The check amount, $1,976.52, is the total of the Net Pay column of the payroll register in Illustration 14-3.

Check for total net pay

No. 287
Date 12/15 19 -- $ 1,976.52
To Payroll Account
005972165
For Payroll for December 1-15

Bal. Bro't For'd	3,261	94
Amt. Deposited		
Total	3,261	94
Amt. This Check	1,976	52
Bal. Car'd For'd	1,285	42

GENERAL ACCOUNT   No. 287   57-63 / 115

CarLand   December 15,   19 --

Pay to the
order of   Payroll Account 005972165 $ 1,976.52

One thousand nine hundred seventy-six and 52/100 _____ Dollars

FOR CLASSROOM USE ONLY

FIRST SECURITY BANK OF ROCKVILLE

Dario Mesa

⑈011500638⑈ 005972164⑈

The information used to prepare payroll checks is taken from a payroll register. The payroll check for Mr. Turner is shown in Illustration 14-6. A special payroll check form is used that has a detachable stub for recording earnings and amounts deducted. Employees keep the stubs for a record of deductions and cash received.

ILLUSTRATION 14-6   Payroll check with detachable stub

Check No. **423**			PAYROLL ACCOUNT	57-63 / 115

PERIOD ENDING	12	15	--
EARNINGS	$	758|00	
REG.	$	704.00	
O.T.	$	54.00	
DEDUCTIONS	$	175|64	
INC. TAX	$	45.00	
FICA TAX	$	60.64	
HEALTH INS.	$	50.00	
OTHER	$	B 10.00 / UW 10.00	
NET PAY	$	582|36	

December 15, 19 --

No. **423**

Pay to the order of _Patrick S. Turner_ $ _582.36_

Five hundred eighty-two and ³⁶/₁₀₀ —————————— Dollars

FOR CLASSROOM USE ONLY

FIRST SECURITY BANK OF ROCKVILLE

CarLand

Dario Mesa

⑆011500638⑆ 005972165⑈

The two deductions for FICA tax would normally be shown separately on a payroll check stub. For simplicity, illustrations in this textbook will show the FICA tax as a single amount on payroll check stubs.

Payroll Bank Account

A separate checking account for payroll checks helps to protect and control payroll payments. The exact amount needed to pay the payroll is deposited in the special payroll account. If amounts on checks are altered or unauthorized payroll checks are prepared, the amount in the special payroll account would be insufficient to cover all the checks. Thus, the bank and CarLand would be alerted quickly to an unauthorized payroll check. Also, since payroll checks are drawn on the separate account, any balance in this account will correspond to the sum of outstanding payroll checks.

Automatic Check Deposit

FYI

Using a separate checking account for payroll checks provides internal control and helps to prevent fraud.

Employees may authorize an employer to deposit payroll checks directly in their checking account at a specific bank. Depositing payroll checks directly to an employee's checking or savings account in a specific bank is called **automatic check deposit**. When automatic check deposit is used, the employer sends the check to the employee's bank for deposit.

Electronic Funds Transfer

A computerized cash payments system that uses electronic impulses to transfer funds is known as electronic funds transfer (EFT). Some businesses deposit employee net pay directly to each employee bank

Audit Your Understanding

1. What does the payroll register summarize?
2. How is federal income tax determined?
3. How is net pay calculated?

account through EFT. When EFT is used, the bank's computer deducts the amount of net pay from the business' bank account and adds the amount to each employee bank account. The payroll must still be calculated, but individual checks are not written and do not have to be distributed. Under this system, each employee receives a statement of earnings and deductions similar to the detachable stub on a payroll check.

EMPLOYEE EARNINGS RECORDS

A business form used to record details affecting payments made to an employee is called an **employee earnings record.** This information is recorded each pay period. The record includes earnings, deductions, net pay, and accumulated earnings for the calendar year. Employee earnings records enable the company to complete required tax forms at the end of the year.

Recording Information in an Employee Earnings Record

CarLand keeps all employee earnings records on cards. One card for each employee is used for each quarter in the calendar year. After a payroll register has been prepared, the payroll data for each employee are recorded on each employee earnings record. The December 15 payroll register data for Patrick S. Turner are recorded on his fourth quarter employee earnings record shown in Illustration 14-7, page 342.

Quarterly totals are used in the preparation of payroll reports required by the government. The accumulated earnings are also used to determine if the employee has earned more than the FICA tax base.

Analyzing an Employee Earnings Record

Accumulated earnings are also called year-to-date earnings.

Mr. Turner's employee number, name, social security number, and other payroll data are entered at the top of his fourth quarter employee earnings record.

Amount columns of an employee earnings record are the same as amount columns of a payroll register. Amounts opposite an employee name in a payroll register are recorded in the corresponding columns of the employee earnings record. The pay period ending December 15 is the fifth pay period in the fourth quarter. Therefore, Mr. Turner's earnings and deductions for that pay period are entered on line 5 of his employee earnings record.

The earnings record also has an Accumulated Earnings column. The first entry in this column is the accumulated earnings at the end of the previous quarter. Accumulated earnings of $13,918.00 were carried forward from the third quarter earnings record to the fourth quarter earnings record, as shown in Illustration 14-7.

ILLUSTRATION 14-7 Employee earnings record

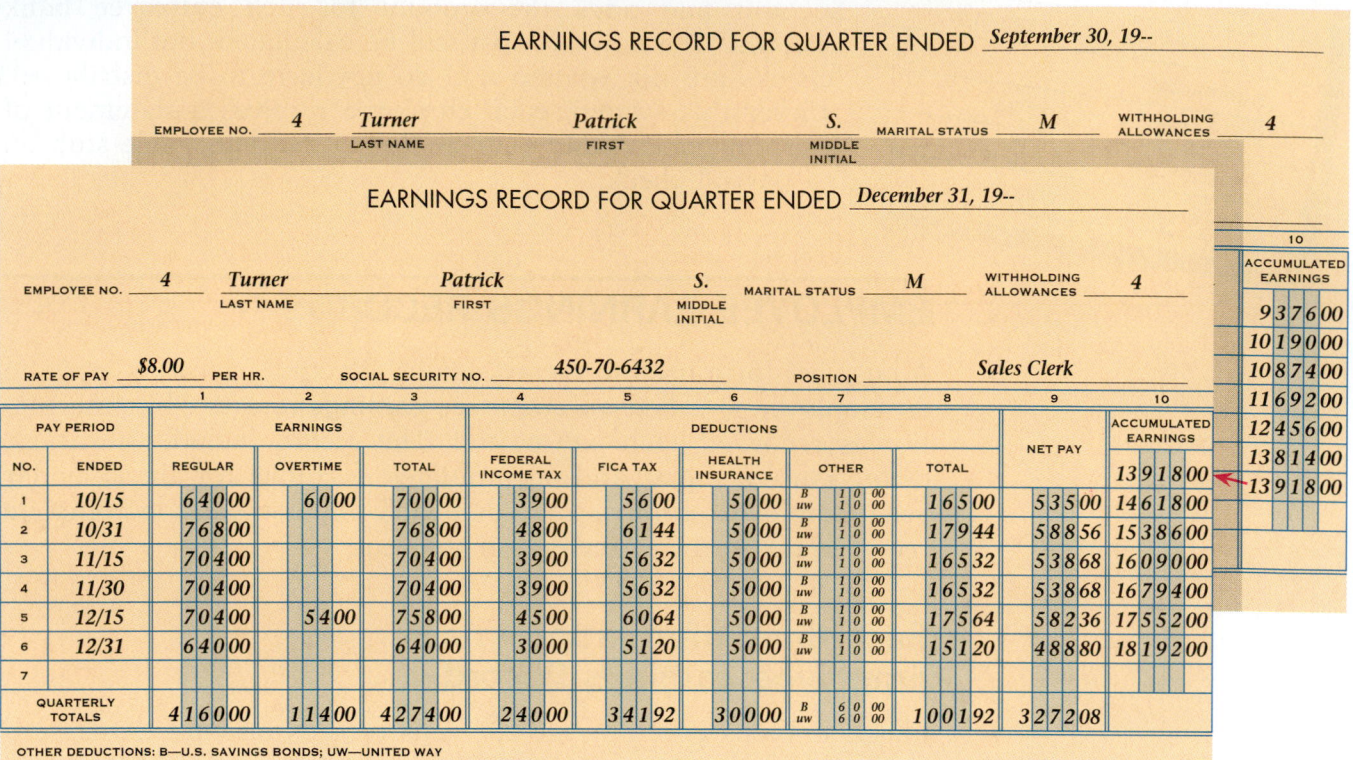

EARNINGS RECORD FOR QUARTER ENDED September 30, 19--

EMPLOYEE NO. 4 Turner (LAST NAME) Patrick (FIRST) S. (MIDDLE INITIAL) MARITAL STATUS M WITHHOLDING ALLOWANCES 4

EARNINGS RECORD FOR QUARTER ENDED December 31, 19--

EMPLOYEE NO. 4 Turner (LAST NAME) Patrick (FIRST) S. (MIDDLE INITIAL) MARITAL STATUS M WITHHOLDING ALLOWANCES 4

RATE OF PAY $8.00 PER HR. SOCIAL SECURITY NO. 450-70-6432 POSITION Sales Clerk

PAY PERIOD NO.	ENDED	REGULAR (1)	OVERTIME (2)	TOTAL (3)	FEDERAL INCOME TAX (4)	FICA TAX (5)	HEALTH INSURANCE (6)	OTHER (7)	TOTAL (8)	NET PAY (9)	ACCUMULATED EARNINGS (10)
1	10/15	640 00	60 00	700 00	39 00	56 00	50 00	B 10 00 / UW 10 00	165 00	535 00	14618 00
2	10/31	768 00		768 00	48 00	61 44	50 00	B 10 00 / UW 10 00	179 44	588 56	15386 00
3	11/15	704 00		704 00	39 00	56 32	50 00	B 10 00 / UW 10 00	165 32	538 68	16090 00
4	11/30	704 00		704 00	39 00	56 32	50 00	B 10 00 / UW 10 00	165 32	538 68	16794 00
5	12/15	704 00	54 00	758 00	45 00	60 64	50 00	B 10 00 / UW 10 00	175 64	582 36	17552 00
6	12/31	640 00		640 00	30 00	51 20	50 00	B 10 00 / UW 10 00	151 20	488 80	18192 00
7											
QUARTERLY TOTALS		4160 00	114 00	4274 00	240 00	341 92	300 00	B 60 00 / UW 60 00	1001 92	3272 08	

OTHER DEDUCTIONS: B—U.S. SAVINGS BONDS; UW—UNITED WAY

(September 30 quarter, Accumulated Earnings column 10)

ACCUMULATED EARNINGS
9376 00
10190 00
10874 00
11692 00
12456 00
13814 00
13918 00
13918 00

Total earnings for a pay period are added to the accumulated earnings in the previous line to calculate the new total accumulated earnings. Accumulated earnings are sometimes referred to as year-to-date earnings. Mr. Turner's accumulated earnings as of December 15 are calculated as shown below.

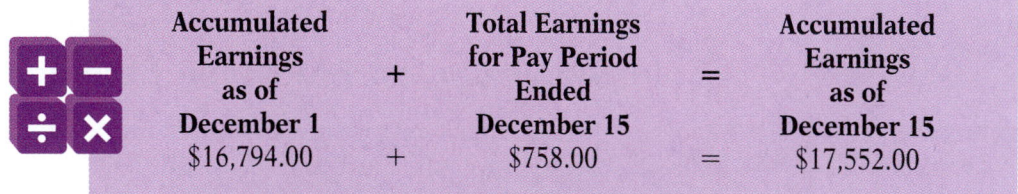

Accumulated Earnings as of December 1	+	Total Earnings for Pay Period Ended December 15	=	Accumulated Earnings as of December 15
$16,794.00	+	$758.00	=	$17,552.00

The Accumulated Earnings column shows the total earnings for Mr. Turner since the first of the year. The amounts in the Accumulated Earnings column supply an up-to-date reference for an employee's year-to-date earnings. When employee earnings reach the tax base, certain payroll taxes do not apply. For example, employers pay state and federal unemployment taxes only on a specified amount of each employee earnings. FICA taxes are also paid only on a specified amount of earnings.

Quarterly totals will be calculated on Mr. Turner's employee earnings record after the payroll for the pay period ended December 31 is recorded. The Quarterly Totals line provides space for the totals for the quarter. The accuracy of the quarterly totals is verified with the same steps used to verify payroll register totals. The Total Deductions column total is subtracted from the Total Earnings column total as shown below.

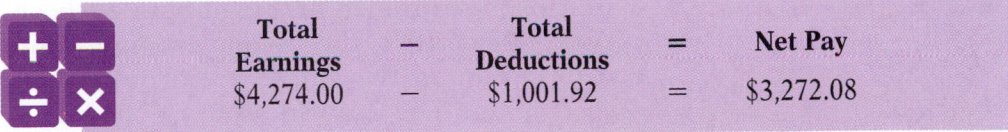

	Total Earnings	−	Total Deductions	=	Net Pay
	$4,274.00	−	$1,001.92	=	$3,272.08

The net pay calculated above, $3,272.08, is compared to the total of the Net Pay column. The earnings record is proved because these amounts are equal. These totals are needed to prepare required government reports.

PROCESSING A PAYROLL USING A PEGBOARD

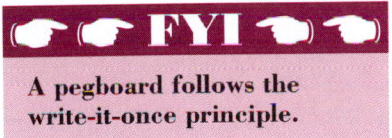
Preparing a payroll requires calculating, recording, and reporting payroll information. Each business selects a system for processing the payroll that results in adequate control for the least amount of cost.

A special device used to write the same information at one time on several forms is called a **pegboard.** One type of pegboard is shown in Illustration 14-8.

ILLUSTRATION 14-8   A pegboard

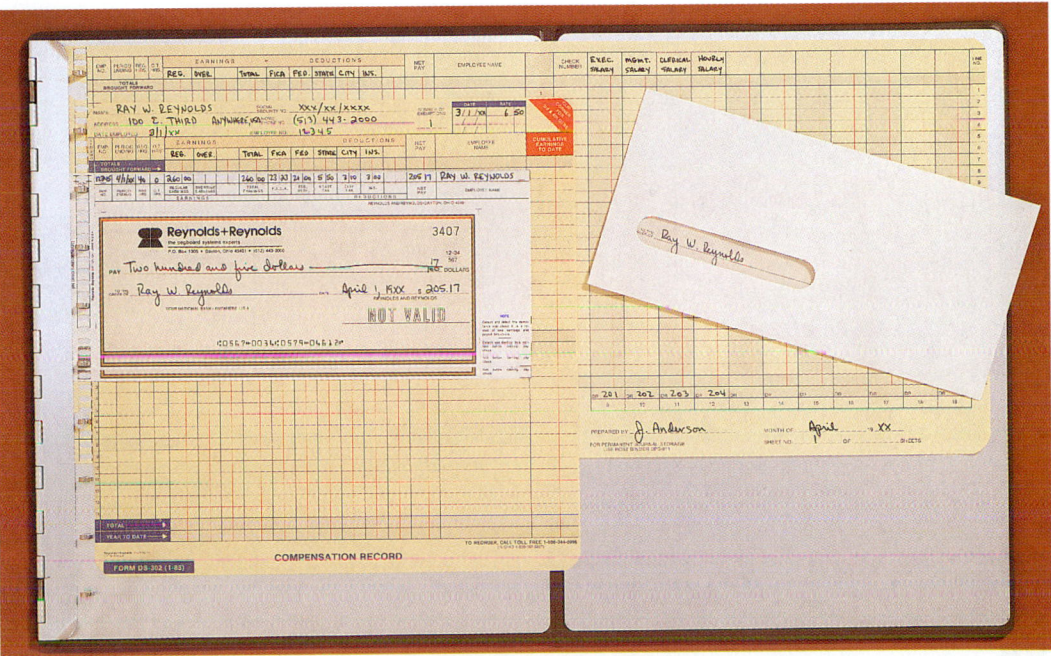

The name pegboard comes from the pegs along one side of the board. The forms used with this device have holes punched along one side. Each of the forms is placed on the pegs. Thus, the line on each form on which information is to be written is aligned one below the other.

When a payroll is recorded, a page of the payroll register is attached to the pegboard. Next, the employee earnings record is properly positioned on top of the payroll register page. Then the check is positioned on top of both of these sheets. As the check stub is written, the carbonless paper imprints the same information on the employee earnings record and the payroll register. The information is written only once. However, the information is recorded on three different records at the same time. Recording information on several forms with one writing is referred to as the write-it-once principle.

The pegboard has two major purposes. First, the pegboard provides a solid writing base for writing on the forms by hand. Second, information is recorded on several forms with one writing, thus saving time and reducing the chance of error.

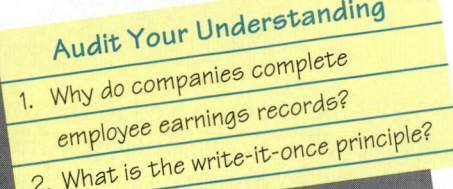

Audit Your Understanding

1. Why do companies complete employee earnings records?

2. What is the write-it-once principle?

SUMMARY ILLUSTRATION 14-9

Summary of preparing payroll records

1 A time card is used to record employee hours worked and to calculate regular, overtime, and total earnings. Payroll taxes are calculated using tax tables and information on the Form W-4. This information is recorded for each employee in a payroll register.

2 A check is written on a general checking account for the total of the Net Pay column on the payroll register. The check is deposited in a special payroll checking account.

3 Payroll checks are written on the special payroll checking account for the net pay of each employee.

4 Information from the payroll register is recorded on each employee earnings record.

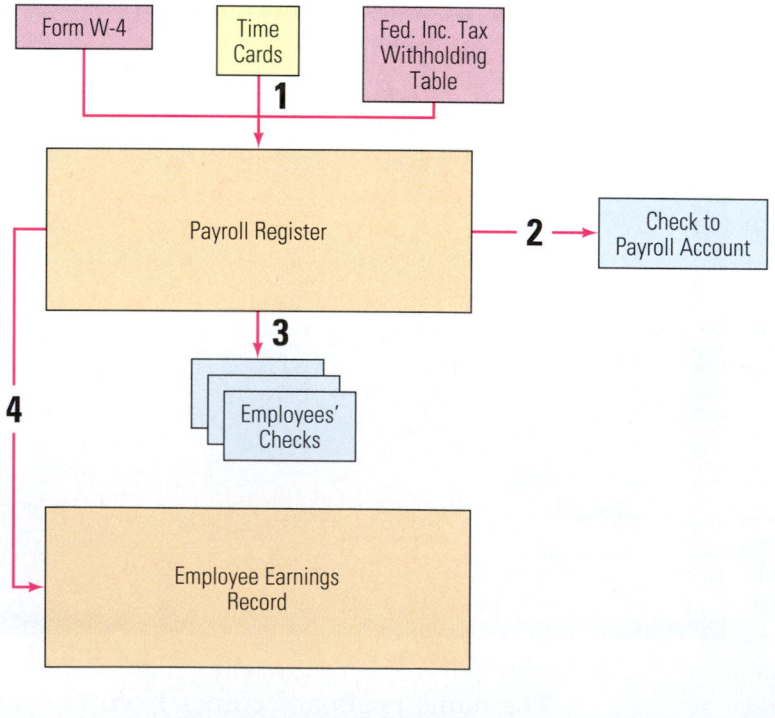

What is the meaning of each of the following?

1. salary
2. pay period
3. payroll
4. total earnings
5. payroll taxes
6. withholding allowance
7. Medicare
8. FICA tax
9. federal unemployment tax
10. state unemployment tax
11. payroll register
12. tax base
13. net pay
14. automatic check deposit
15. employee earnings record
16. pegboard

1. How often may a business decide to pay its employees?
2. What information is presented at the top of a time card?
3. To calculate hours worked to the nearest quarter hour, how would an arrival time of 7:54 be rounded?
4. On what amount are employee payroll taxes based?
5. What factors determine the amount of federal income tax withheld from an employee?
6. How does the number of withholding allowances affect the amount of federal income tax withheld?
7. Who pays FICA tax?
8. How long must records pertaining to social security tax payments and deductions be retained?
9. What is the source of the earnings amounts reported in a payroll register?
10. Why are partners of a company not listed in the company's payroll register?
11. How is the amount of federal income tax withheld from employee salaries determined?
12. Under what circumstances can an employee who is not exempt from federal income tax withholding have no tax withheld on a payroll register?
13. What must an employer know to be able to calculate the amount of FICA tax to be withheld from the salary of an employee?
14. How is a payroll register proved?
15. What amount is deposited into a payroll checking account?
16. Where is the information obtained to prepare a payroll check?
17. What is the major purpose of the Accumulated Earnings column of an employee earnings record?
18. What are two major purposes for using a pegboard for processing a payroll?

CASE 1 Kilton Hardware currently requires each employee to inform the accounting clerk of the total hours worked each day during the pay period. The total number of hours worked by all employees has been steadily increasing during the prior pay periods. The new store manager has suggested that a time clock be installed to record arrival and departure times. The accounting clerk believes the current system is satisfactory. Do you agree with the new manager or the accounting clerk? Explain your response.

CASE 2 A banker has recommended that Tillman Construction Company open a second checking account. The company would write payroll checks on the new checking account. The company's 50 employees are currently paid with checks written on its general checking account. Do you agree with the banker's recommendation? Explain the reason for your decision.

APPLIED COMMUNICATIONS

The employees of Ritter Company currently use time cards and a time clock to record their arrival and departure times. Management plans to replace the time clock with a device that reads a magnetic strip on the back of each employee's name badge. The name badge is scanned by the badge reader in the same manner that credit cards are scanned. Since the badge reader is connected to a computer, the information is recorded directly to a computer file. Thus, the new system will enable management to make daily analyses of employee hours and pro-

ductivity. Management expects this information will allow its managers to make more timely decisions and increase profits.

INSTRUCTIONS:

Assume you are the payroll clerk for Ritter Company. Write a memo to the employees informing them of the new system. Because some employees may not be happy with this new system, be sure to include reasons why the policy is being implemented.

DRILLS FOR UNDERSTANDING

EPT(c)

DRILL 14-D1 Calculating employee total earnings

MATHEMATICS

Information taken from employee time cards is given in the working papers accompanying this textbook.

INSTRUCTIONS:

For each employee, calculate the amount of regular, overtime, and total earnings. Overtime hours are paid at one and one-half times the regular rate.

DRILL 14-D2 Determining payroll taxes withholding

MATHEMATICS

Information taken from a semimonthly payroll register is given in the working papers accompanying this textbook.

INSTRUCTIONS:

1. Determine the federal income tax that must be withheld for each of the eight employees. Use the tax withholding tables shown in Illustration 14-4.

2. Calculate the amount of FICA tax that must be withheld for each employee using an 8% tax rate. None of the eight employees has accumulated earnings greater than the tax base.

APPLICATION PROBLEMS

EPT(c,d,e)

PROBLEM 14-1 Completing payroll time cards

MATHEMATICS

Employee time cards are given in the working papers accompanying this textbook.

INSTRUCTIONS:

1. Calculate the regular, overtime, and total hours worked by each employee. Any hours over the regular 8-hour day are considered overtime. Record the hours on the time cards.

2. Determine the regular, overtime, and total earnings for each employee. The overtime rate is 1½ times the regular rate. Complete the time cards.

PROBLEM 14-2 Preparing a semimonthly payroll

SPREADSHEET

MATHEMATICS

The information for the semimonthly pay period April 1–15 of the current year is given in the working papers accompanying this textbook.

INSTRUCTIONS:

1. Prepare a payroll register. The date of payment is April 15. Use the federal income tax withholding tables in Illustration 14-4 to find the income tax withholding for each employee. Calculate FICA tax withholding using an 8% tax rate. None of the employee accumulated earnings has exceeded the FICA tax base.
2. Prepare a check for the total amount of the net pay. Make the check payable to Payroll Account, and sign your name as partner of City Hardware Company. The beginning check stub balance is $8,365.79.
3. Prepare payroll checks for Jill V. Gunter, Check No. 765, and Ronald E. Webb, Check No. 769. Sign your name as a partner of City Hardware Company. Record the two payroll check numbers in the payroll register.

PROBLEM 14-3 Preparing an employee earnings record

SPREADSHEET

MATHEMATICS

Derrick M. Hammond's earnings for the six semimonthly pay periods in April, May, and June of the current year are given in the working papers accompanying this textbook.

The following additional data about Derrick Hammond are needed to complete the employee earnings record.

1. Employee number: 32
2. Marital status: married
3. Withholding Allowances: 2
4. Rate of pay: regular, $14.00
5. Social security number: 218-78-2164
6. Position: service manager
7. Accumulated earnings for the first quarter: $7,928.00
8. Deductions from total earnings:
   a. Health insurance: $40.00 each semimonthly pay period
   b. U.S. Savings Bonds: $10.00 each semimonthly pay period
   c. Federal income tax: determined each pay period by using the withholding tables in Illustration 14-4
   d. FICA taxes: 8% of total earnings each pay period

INSTRUCTIONS:

1. Prepare an employee earnings record for Derrick Hammond for the second quarter of the year.
2. Verify the accuracy of the completed employee earnings record. The Quarter Total for Regular and Overtime Earnings should equal the Quarter Total for Net Pay plus Total Deductions. The Quarter Total for Total Earnings should equal the end-of-quarter Accumulated Earnings minus the beginning-of-quarter Accumulated Earnings.

ENRICHMENT PROBLEMS   EPT(c,d,e)

MASTERY PROBLEM 14-M Preparing a semimonthly payroll

The following information is for the semimonthly pay period May 15–31 of the current year.

Employee		Marital Status	No. of Allow- ances	Earnings		Deductions	
No.	Name			Regular	Overtime	Health Insurance	Savings Bonds
3	Abney, Patricia D.	M	2	$512.00	$12.80	$30.00	$10.00
6	Blanks, Wilma E.	S	1	576.00	21.60		
8	Fitts, Deborah S.	M	3	624.00	11.70	38.00	5.00
1	Greer, Daniel J.	M	2	399.00	34.20	30.00	5.00
5	Habig, Vincent W.	S	1	672.00			
9	Jones, Phyllis M.	M	2	608.00	79.80	30.00	10.00
10	Malloy, Timothy R.	S	2	544.00	10.20	30.00	10.00
2	Paxton, Alice Y.	M	4	496.00		44.00	
4	Tait, Michelle D.	S	1	640.00	36.00		
7	Walzak, Thomas T.	S	1	472.00			15.00

INSTRUCTIONS:

1. Prepare a payroll register. The date of payment is May 31. Use the income tax withholding tables in Illustration 14-4 to find the income tax withholding for each employee. Calculate FICA tax withholding using an 8% tax rate. None of the employee accumulated earnings has exceeded the FICA tax base.

2. Prepare a check for the total amount of the net pay. Make the check payable to Payroll Account, and sign your name as a partner of Mercer Company. The beginning check stub balance is $10,287.20.

3. Prepare payroll checks for Daniel Greer, Check No. 426, and Michelle Tait, Check No. 431. Sign your name as a partner of Mercer Company. Record the two payroll check numbers in the payroll register.

CHALLENGE PROBLEM 14-C Calculating piecework wages

Production workers in factories are frequently paid on the basis of the number of units they produce. This payroll method is referred to as the piecework incentive wage plan. Most piecework incentive wage plans include a guaranteed hourly rate to employees regardless of the number of units they produce. This guaranteed hourly rate is referred to as the base rate.

Time and motion study engineers usually determine the standard time required for producing a single unit. Assume, for example, that time studies determine that one-third of an hour is the standard time required to produce a unit. Then the standard rate for an 8-hour day would be 24 units (8 hours divided by 1/3 hour = 24 units per day). If a worker's daily base pay is $66.00, the incentive rate per unit is $2.75 ($66.00 divided by 24 units = $2.75 per unit). Therefore, the worker who produces 24 or fewer units per day is paid the base pay, $66.00. However, each worker is paid an additional $2.75 for each unit over 24 produced each day.

Southern Woodworks Company has eight employees in production departments that are paid on a piecework incentive wage plan. The following standard and incentive wage rates are listed by department.

Department	Standard Production per Employee	Incentive Rate per Unit
Cutting	30 units per day	$2.30
Assembly	20 units per day	$4.10
Finishing	40 units per day	$1.80

Each employee worked eight hours a day during the semimonthly pay period, August 1–15. Payroll records for August 1–15 are summarized in the following table.

Employee		Marital Status	No. of Allow-ances	Guaranteed Daily Rate	Units Produced per Day									
No.	Name				Pay Period August 1–15									
					2	3	4	5	6	9	10	11	12	13
	Cutting Department													
C2	Simpson, Alan J.	S	1	$69.00	29	32	31	34	28	27	30	32	36	26
C4	Creek, Janice A.	M	1	$69.00	32	31	28	29	27	29	31	32	27	28
C8	Pate, Marie S.	M	2	$69.00	31	28	27	24	31	33	32	29	30	29
	Assembly Department													
A1	Meese, Frank K.	S	1	$82.00	20	21	19	19	18	18	19	21	20	21
A6	Harris, Kevin E.	M	3	$82.00	25	21	17	18	19	21	20	20	21	18
A7	Martin, Angela M.	S	1	$82.00	22	24	25	21	20	19	23	21	18	17
	Finishing Department													
F5	Quinn, Karen A.	M	2	$72.00	41	40	38	39	42	43	41	40	38	37
F3	Raines, Jon S.	M	2	$72.00	37	37	38	38	39	38	40	41	41	42

INSTRUCTIONS:

Prepare a payroll register. The earnings column headed *Incentive* is used instead of Overtime. The date of payment is August 16. Use the income tax withholding tables in Illustration 14-4. Calculate the employee FICA tax withholding using an 8% tax rate. None of the employees has health insurance or other deductions.

15

Payroll Accounting, Taxes, and Reports

ENABLING PERFORMANCE TASKS

After studying Chapter 15, you will be able to:

a Identify accounting concepts and practices related to payroll accounts, taxes, and reports.

b Analyze payroll transactions.

c Journalize and post payroll transactions.

d Prepare selected payroll tax reports.

Payroll information for each pay period is recorded in a payroll register. Each pay period the payroll information for each employee is also recorded on each employee earnings record. Separate payroll accounts for each employee are not kept in the general ledger. Instead, accounts are kept in the general ledger to summarize total earnings and deductions for all employees.

The payroll register and employee earnings records provide all the payroll information needed to prepare a payroll and payroll tax reports. Journal entries are made to record the payment of the payroll and the employer payroll taxes. In addition, various quarterly and annual payroll tax reports are required to report the payment of payroll taxes.

RECORDING A PAYROLL

The payroll register for CarLand's semimonthly pay period ended December 15 is shown in Illustration 15-1, on page 352.

Analyzing Payment of a Payroll

The column totals of a payroll register provide the debit and credit amounts needed to journalize a payroll. CarLand's December 15 payroll is summarized in the following T accounts.

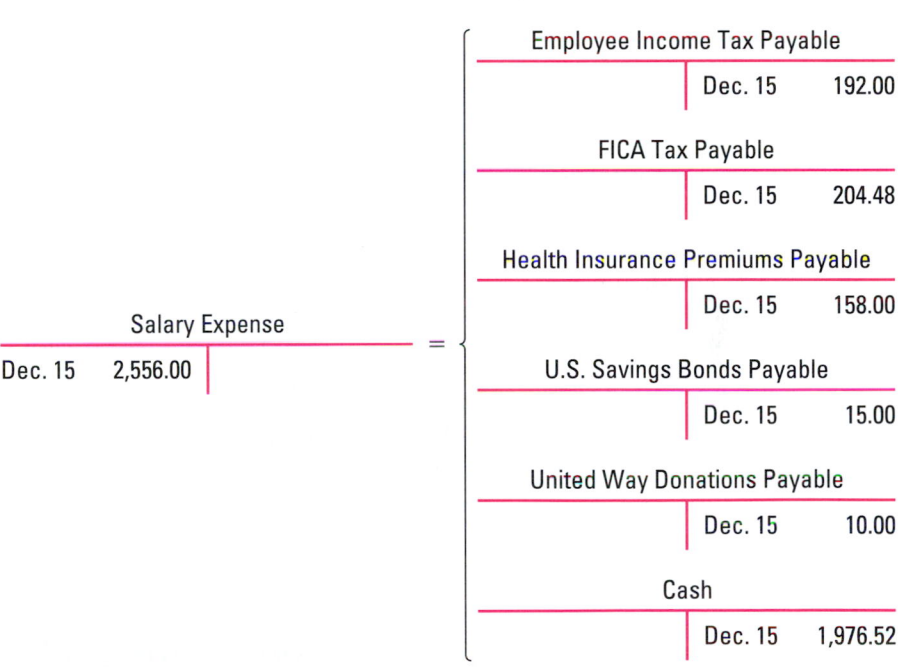

The Total Earnings column total, $2,556.00, is the salary expense for the period. Salary Expense is debited for this amount.

The Federal Income Tax column total, $192.00, is the amount withheld from employee salaries for federal income tax. The amount withheld is a liability of the business until the taxes are sent to the federal government. Employee Income Tax Payable is credited for $192.00 to record this liability.

The FICA Tax column total, $204.48, is the amount withheld from salaries of all employees for FICA tax. The amount withheld

ILLUSTRATION 15-1   Payroll register

	EMPL. NO.	EMPLOYEE'S NAME	MARITAL STATUS	NO. OF ALLOWANCES	EARNINGS			DEDUCTIONS					NET PAY	CHECK NO.	
					1 REGULAR	2 OVERTIME	3 TOTAL	4 FEDERAL INCOME TAX	5 FICA TAX	6 HEALTH INSURANCE	7 OTHER	8 TOTAL	9 NET PAY	CHECK NO.	
1	2	Bauch, Mary R.	M	2	660 00		660 00	57 00	52 80	38 00	B 5 00	152 80	507 20	419	1
2	5	Clay, Richard P.	S	1	80 00		80 00	00	6 40			6 40	73 60	420	2
3	1	Javorski, Adam B.	M	2	384 00	18 00	402 00	17 00	32 16	38 00		87 16	314 84	421	3
4	6	Maggio, Brenda A.	S	1	40 00		40 00	00	3 20			3 20	36 80	422	4
5	4	Turner, Patrick S.	M	4	704 00	54 00	758 00	45 00	60 64	50 00	B 10 00 / UW 10 00	175 64	582 36	423	5
6	3	Wilkes, Samuel R.	S	1	616 00		616 00	73 00	49 28	32 00		154 28	461 72	424	6
7		Totals			2484 00	72 00	2556 00	192 00	204 48	158 00	B 15 00 / UW 10 00	579 48	1976 52		7

SEMIMONTHLY PERIOD ENDED December 15, 19--   PAYROLL REGISTER   DATE OF PAYMENT December 15, 19--

FYI

Other payroll deductions may include a deduction for savings bonds and United Way contributions.

is a liability of the business until the tax is paid to the government. FICA Tax Payable is credited for $204.48.

The Health Insurance column total, $158.00, is the amount withheld from salaries for health insurance premiums. The amount withheld is a liability of the business until the premiums are paid to the insurance company. Health Insurance Premiums Payable is credited for $158.00 to record this liability.

The Other column of the deductions section may contain more than one total. Two types of *Other* deductions are recorded in CarLand's payroll register. The $15.00 Other column total identified with the letter B is withheld to buy savings bonds for employees. The $10.00 total identified with the letters *UW* is withheld for employee United Way pledges. Until these amounts have been paid by the employer, they are liabilities of the business. U.S. Savings Bonds Payable is credited for $15.00. United Way Donations Payable is credited for $10.00.

The Net Pay column total, $1,976.52, is the net amount paid to employees. Cash is credited for $1,976.52. A check for the total net pay amount, $1,976.52, is written on CarLand's general checking account. This amount is deposited in a special payroll checking account used only for employee payroll checks. Individual payroll checks are then written on the special payroll checking account.

Journalizing Payment of a Payroll

December 15, 19--. Paid cash for semimonthly payroll, $1,976.52 (total payroll, $2,556.00, less deductions: employee income tax, $192.00; FICA tax, $204.48; health insurance premiums, $158.00; U.S. Savings Bonds, $15.00; United Way donations, $10.00). Check No. 287.

The journal entry to record payment of CarLand's December 15 payroll is shown in Illustration 15-2.

The date, *15*, is written in the Date column. The title of the account debited, *Salary Expense*, is recorded in the Account Title col-

ILLUSTRATION 15-2 — Journal entry to record a payroll

PAGE 24

JOURNAL

PAGE 24

	DATE	ACCOUNT TITLE	DOC. NO.	POST. REF.	GENERAL DEBIT	GENERAL CREDIT	CASH DEBIT	CASH CREDIT	
21	15	Salary Expense	C287		2 5 5 6 00			1 9 7 6 52	21
22		Employee Income Tax Payable				1 9 2 00			22
23		FICA Tax Payable				2 0 4 48			23
24		Health Insurance Premiums Payable				1 5 8 00			24
25		U.S. Savings Bonds Payable				1 5 00			25
26		United Way Donations Payable				1 0 00			26

FYI

Total Earnings is the debit amount for Salary Expense. Net pay is the credit amount for cash.

umn. The check number, *C287*, is entered in the Doc. No. column. The amount debited to Salary Expense, *$2,556.00*, is written in the General Debit column. On the same line, the net amount paid to employees, *$1,976.52*, is written in the Cash Credit column. Five liability accounts are credited for the amounts deducted from employee salaries. The five account titles are written in the Account Title column. The five credit amounts are written in the General Credit column.

Posting the Journal Entry for Payment of a Payroll

Amounts recorded in the General columns of a journal are posted individually to general ledger accounts. After the December 15 payroll entry is posted, the liability and salary expense accounts appear as shown in Illustration 15-3.

ILLUSTRATION 15-3 — General ledger accounts after journal entry for payment of a payroll is posted

ACCOUNT *Employee Income Tax Payable*   **ACCOUNT NO.** *2120*

DATE	ITEM	POST. REF.	DEBIT	CREDIT	BALANCE DEBIT	BALANCE CREDIT
15		24		1 9 2 00		1 9 2 00

ACCOUNT *FICA Tax Payable*   **ACCOUNT NO.** *2130*

DATE	ITEM	POST. REF.	DEBIT	CREDIT	BALANCE DEBIT	BALANCE CREDIT
15		24		2 0 4 48		2 0 4 48

ACCOUNT *Health Insurance Premiums Payable*   ACCOUNT NO. *2170*

DATE		ITEM	POST. REF.	DEBIT	CREDIT	BALANCE	
						DEBIT	CREDIT
Dec.	1	Balance	√				5 2 4 00
	15		24		1 5 8 00		6 8 2 00

ACCOUNT *U.S. Savings Bonds Payable*   ACCOUNT NO. *2180*

DATE		ITEM	POST. REF.	DEBIT	CREDIT	BALANCE	
						DEBIT	CREDIT
Dec.	1	Balance	√				1 0 00
	15		24		1 5 00		2 5 00

ACCOUNT *United Way Donations Payable*   ACCOUNT NO. *2190*

DATE		ITEM	POST. REF.	DEBIT	CREDIT	BALANCE	
						DEBIT	CREDIT
Dec.	1	Balance	√				4 0 00
	15		24		1 0 00		5 0 00

ACCOUNT *Salary Expense*   ACCOUNT NO. *6170*

DATE		ITEM	POST. REF.	DEBIT	CREDIT	BALANCE	
						DEBIT	CREDIT
Dec.	1	Balance	√			54 9 5 2 00	
	15		24	2 5 5 6 00		57 5 0 8 00	

The credit to Cash, $1,976.52, is not posted separately to the cash account. The amount is included in the journal's Cash Credit column total that is posted at the end of the month.

RECORDING EMPLOYER PAYROLL TAXES

Employers must pay to the government the taxes withheld from employee earnings. CarLand has withheld federal income tax and FICA tax from employee salaries. The amounts withheld are liabil-

ities to the business until they are actually paid to the government. In addition, employers must pay several of their own payroll taxes. Employer payroll taxes are business expenses.

Calculating Employer Payroll Taxes

Most employers must pay three separate payroll taxes. These taxes are (1) employer FICA tax, (2) federal unemployment tax, and (3) state unemployment tax. Employer payroll taxes expense is based on a percentage of employee earnings.

Employer FICA Tax. CarLand withheld $204.48 in FICA tax from employee wages for the pay period ended December 15. CarLand owes the same amount of FICA taxes as the amount withheld from employees. Therefore, CarLand's FICA tax for the pay period ended December 15 is also $204.48.

Congress sets the FICA tax rate for employees and employers. Periodically, Congress may change the tax rate and tax base. The FICA tax rate is a combination of two different tax rates: (1) a tax for old-age, survivors, and disability and (2) a tax for Medicare. The two taxes also have different tax bases. The FICA tax rates and bases used in this text are shown below.

	Tax Rate	Tax Base
Old-age, survivors, and disability	6.5%	earnings up to $55,500
Medicare	1.5%	earnings up to $130,200
Total	8.0%	

Therefore, the effective FICA tax rate for earnings up to the tax base of $55,500 is 8.0% (6.5% + 1.5%). The additional FICA tax rate for earnings from $55,500 to $130,200 is 1.5%.

The FICA tax is the only payroll tax paid by *both* the employees and the employer. Employees pay 8% of their total earnings up to a tax base of $55,500.00 and 1.5% of their total earnings up to $130,200.00 as a FICA tax. Employers also pay FICA tax on each employee's earnings using the same tax rates and tax bases.

Federal Unemployment Tax. Federal unemployment insurance laws require that employers pay taxes for unemployment compensation. These tax funds are used to pay workers benefits for limited periods of unemployment and to administer the unemployment compensation program. All of the federal unemployment tax is paid by the employer.

The federal unemployment tax for most businesses is 0.8% of total earnings of each employee up to a tax base of $7,000.00 during a calendar year. The total earnings of CarLand's December 1-15 pay period subject to the federal unemployment tax is referred to

as unemployment taxable earnings. The amount of unemployment taxable earnings is calculated as shown in Illustration 15-4.

Accumulated earnings are calculated on each employee earnings record. Patrick S. Turner's accumulated earnings as of November 30, $16,794.00, are recorded in the first column. Total earnings for Mr. Turner for the December 15 pay period, $758.00, are recorded

ILLUSTRATION 15-4

Total earnings subject to federal unemployment tax

CarLand Taxable Earnings for December 15, 19-- Pay Period			
	Accumulated Earnings as of Nov. 30, 19--	Total Earnings for Dec. 15, 19-- Pay Period	Unemployment Taxable Earnings
Bauch, Mary R.	$14,520.00	$660.00	$ —
Clay, Richard P.	2,160.00	80.00	80.00
Javorski, Adam B.	5,792.50	402.00	402.00
Maggio, Brenda A.	1,680.00	40.00	40.00
Turner, Patrick S.	16,794.00	758.00	—
Wilkes, Samuel R.	4,976.50	616.00	616.00
			$1,138.00

in the second column. Since the accumulated earnings for Mr. Turner are greater than $7,000.00, none of his current earnings are subject to federal unemployment tax. Thus, the amount of unemployment taxable earnings recorded in the third column is zero, which is represented by a dash.

The accumulated earnings for Samuel R. Wilkes, $4,976.50, are less than $7,000.00. Therefore, his total earnings for the December 15 pay period are subject to federal unemployment tax. Total earnings for Mr. Wilkes for the December 15 pay period, $616.00, are recorded in the Unemployment Taxable Earnings column.

The total earnings for the pay period are entered in the Unemployment Taxable Earnings column for employees whose accumulated earnings are less than $7,000.00. The sum of the Unemployment Taxable Earnings Column, $1,138.00, is the amount used to calculate federal unemployment tax.

CarLand's federal unemployment tax is calculated as shown below.

FYI

Seniority is the amount of time an employee has been employed by a company.

Unemployment Taxable Earnings	×	Federal Unemployment Tax Rate	=	Federal Unemployment Tax
$1,138.00	×	0.8%	=	$9.10

State Unemployment Tax. Most states require that employers pay unemployment tax of 5.4% on the first $7,000.00 earned by each employee. The unemployment taxable earnings used to calculate the federal unemployment tax are also used to calculate the state unemployment tax. The unemployment taxable earnings subject to the state unemployment tax are calculated in Illustration 15-4. Thus, the state employment tax to be paid by CarLand is calculated as shown below.

	Unemployment Taxable Earnings	×	State Unemployment Tax Rate	=	State Unemployment Tax
	$1,138.00	×	5.4%	=	$61.45

Journalizing Employer Payroll Taxes

Employer payroll taxes are paid to the government at a later date. However, the liability is incurred when salaries are paid. Therefore, the transaction to record employer payroll taxes expense is journalized on the same date the payroll is journalized. The salary expense and the employer payroll taxes expense are, therefore, both recorded in the same accounting period.

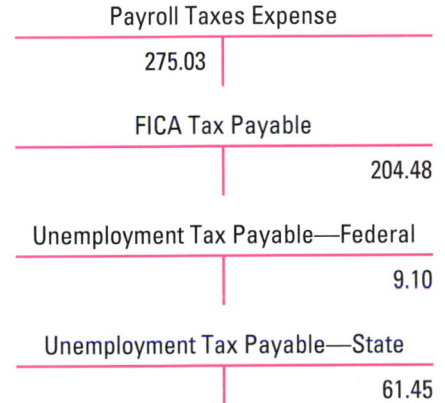

Payroll Taxes Expense
275.03

FICA Tax Payable
204.48

Unemployment Tax Payable—Federal
9.10

Unemployment Tax Payable—State
61.45

December 15, 19--. Recorded employer payroll taxes expense, $275.03, for the semimonthly pay period ended December 15. Taxes owed are: FICA tax, $204.48; federal unemployment tax, $9.10; state unemployment tax, $61.45. Memorandum No. 54.

Payroll Taxes Expense is debited for $275.03 to show the increase in the balance of this expense account. Three liability accounts are credited to show the increase in payroll tax liabilities. FICA Tax Payable is credited for $204.48. Unemployment Tax Payable—Federal is credited for $9.10. Unemployment Tax Payable—State is credited for $61.45.

CarLand's journal entry to record the employer payroll taxes expense is shown in Illustration 15-5.

ILLUSTRATION 15-5   Journal entry to record employer payroll taxes

					GENERAL			CASH		
PAGE 24				JOURNAL					PAGE 24	
					1	2		10	11	
	DATE	ACCOUNT TITLE	DOC. NO.	POST. REF.	DEBIT	CREDIT		DEBIT	CREDIT	
27	15	Payroll Taxes Expense	M54		275 03					27
28		FICA Tax Payable				204 48				28
29		Unemployment Tax Payable—Federal				9 10				29
30		Unemployment Tax Payable—State				61 45				30
31										31

The date, *15*, is written in the Date column. The title of the account debited, *Payroll Taxes Expense*, is written in the Account Title column. The memorandum number, *M54*, is entered in the Doc. No. column. The debit amount, *$275.03*, is entered in the General Debit column. The titles of the liability accounts are entered in the Account Title column. The amounts credited to the liability accounts are entered in the General Credit column.

Posting an Employer Payroll Taxes Entry

After the entry for the employer payroll taxes is posted, the accounts involved appear as shown in Illustration 15-6.

ILLUSTRATION 15-6

General ledger accounts after journal entry for employer payroll taxes expense is posted

ACCOUNT **FICA Tax Payable**   ACCOUNT NO. **2130**

DATE	ITEM	POST. REF.	DEBIT	CREDIT	BALANCE DEBIT	BALANCE CREDIT
15		24		2 04 48		2 04 48
15		24		2 04 48		4 08 96

ACCOUNT **Unemployment Tax Payable—Federal**   ACCOUNT NO. **2150**

DATE	ITEM	POST. REF.	DEBIT	CREDIT	BALANCE DEBIT	BALANCE CREDIT
Dec. 1	Balance	✓				40 48
15		24		9 10		49 58

tionist busy. Thus, the receptionist frequently reads magazines and completes crossword puzzles to occupy the extra time.

Situation 2. Sandi's Hamburger Hut limits most of its employees to 32 hours per week. Only full-time employees who work 40 or more hours per week are eligible for the company's health insurance program.

Situation 3. Accountants of Adams and Associates, a CPA firm, receive a monthly salary. Although the accountants can work 60-70 hours per week during busy seasons, they do not receive overtime wages. Instead, they are able to take extra vacation after the busy season is over.

INSTRUCTIONS Use the three-step checklist to analyze whether the employment practices above demonstrate ethical behavior.

ILLUSTRATION 15-6   General ledger accounts after journal entry for employer payroll taxes expense is posted (concluded)

ACCOUNT **Unemployment Tax Payable—State**   ACCOUNT NO. **2160**

DATE	ITEM	POST. REF.	DEBIT	CREDIT	BALANCE DEBIT	BALANCE CREDIT
Dec. 1	Balance	√				2 7 3 22
15		24		6 1 45		3 3 4 67

ACCOUNT **Payroll Taxes Expense**   ACCOUNT NO. **6150**

DATE	ITEM	POST. REF.	DEBIT	CREDIT	BALANCE DEBIT	BALANCE CREDIT
Dec. 1	Balance	√			6 7 3 8 96	
15		24	2 7 5 03		7 0 1 3 99	

A job description is a list of basic responsibilities and tasks for a particular job.

The FICA Tax Payable account has two credits. The first credit, $204.48, is the FICA tax withheld from *employee* wages for the semimonthly period ended December 15. This amount was posted from the journal entry that recorded payment of the payroll, Illustration 15-2. The second credit, $204.48, is the *employer* liability for FICA tax. This amount was posted from the journal entry that recorded the employer payroll taxes, Illustration 15-5.

Summary of Amounts Posted to the General Ledger

Both the employees and employer owe payroll taxes. Federal income tax and FICA tax are withheld from employee salaries. An equal amount of FICA tax is owed by the employer. The employer must also record federal and state unemployment taxes. The payroll taxes resulting from CarLand's December 1–15 pay period are summarized on page 360.

Only the employer payroll taxes, $275.03, are recorded as payroll taxes expense in CarLand's general ledger accounts. The payroll taxes of both the employees and the employer create liabilities to the business which must be paid at times specified by the government.

REPORTING WITHHOLDING AND PAYROLL TAXES

Each employer is required by law to periodically report the payroll taxes withheld from employee salaries and the employer payroll taxes due the government. Some reports are submitted quarterly and others are submitted annually.

Employer Quarterly Federal Tax Return

Each employer must file a quarterly federal tax return showing the federal income tax and FICA taxes due the government. This information is submitted every three months on Form 941, Employer's Quarterly Federal Tax Return. Form 941 is filed before the last day of the month following the end of a calendar quarter. CarLand's Form 941 for the calendar quarter ended December 31 is shown in Illustration 15-7, page 361. The information needed to prepare Form 941 is obtained from employee earnings records.

Total earnings, *$15,192.85*, are recorded on line 2 of Form 941. This amount is the sum of the fourth quarter total earnings of all CarLand employees. The amount of total earnings, *$15,192.85*, is also recorded on the line to the left of line 6a and 7. The income tax withheld, *$1,168.00*, is recorded on line 3 of Form 941. The amount is the total of the fourth quarter federal income tax withheld from CarLand's employees.

The social security (FICA) taxes due are calculated as shown below.

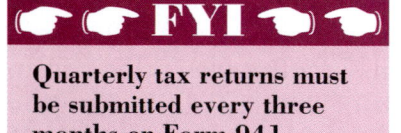

	Total Earnings	×	FICA Tax Rate	=	Social Security (FICA) Tax
Old-age, survivors, and disability	$15,192.85	×	13%	=	$1,975.07
Medicare	$15,192.85	×	3%	=	$ 455.79
TOTAL					$2,430.86

ILLUSTRATION 15-7   Form 941, Employer's Quarterly Federal Tax Return

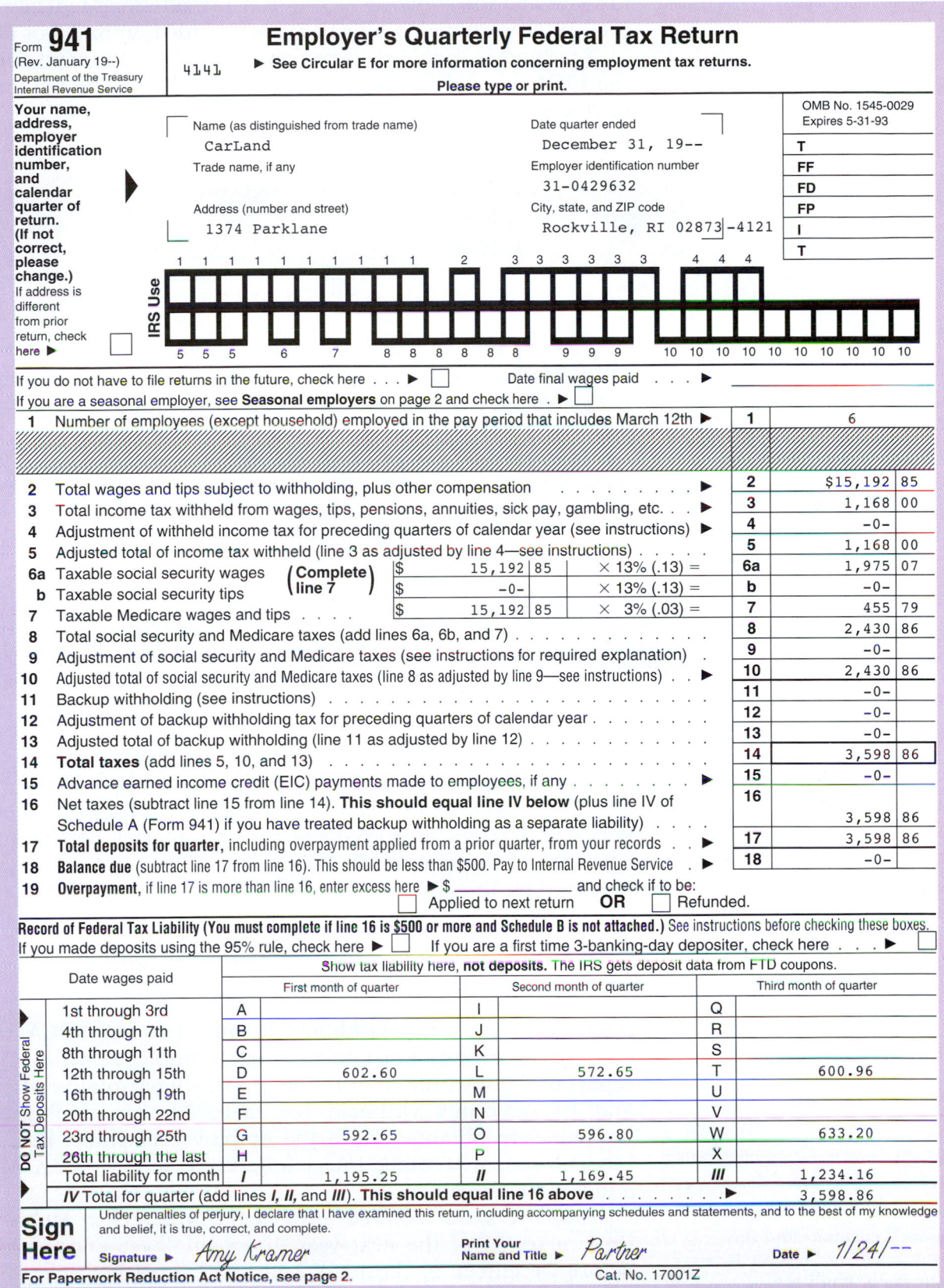

The 13% tax rate is the sum of the *employee* 6.5% FICA tax rate and the employer 6.5% FICA tax rate for old-age, survivors, and disability tax. The 3% tax rate is the sum of the *employee* 1.5% FICA tax rate and the *employer* 1.5% FICA tax rate for Medicare tax. The total FICA tax amount, $2,430.86, is recorded on line 8 of Form 941.

CarLand is required to pay the federal government the sum of the FICA tax and federal income tax withheld. The amount of the payment is calculated as shown below.

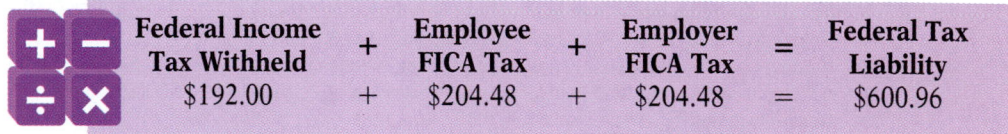

Federal Income Tax Withheld	+	FICA Tax	=	Total Payment
$1,168.00	+	$2,430.86	=	$3,598.86

Federal Income Tax withheld is copied from line 3 to line 5. FICA Tax is copied from line 8 to line 10. The total payment owed to the federal government, *$3,598.86,* is recorded on line 14 of Form 941.

The lower section of Form 941 lists the amounts and dates when payroll taxes were withheld from employees and are owed by the employer. For the pay period ended December 15, the amount of taxes owed is calculated as shown below.

Federal Income Tax Withheld	+	Employee FICA Tax	+	Employer FICA Tax	=	Federal Tax Liability
$192.00	+	$204.48	+	$204.48	=	$600.96

The federal tax liability for the December 15 pay period, *$600.96,* is recorded on line T of Form 941. The December 15 pay period ended in the third month of the quarter between the 12th and 15th of the month. The December 15 pay period is, therefore, recorded on line T.

Employer Annual Report to Employees of Taxes Withheld

Each employer who withholds income tax and FICA tax from employee earnings must furnish each employee with an annual report of these withholdings. The report shows total year's earnings and the amounts withheld for taxes for an employee. These amounts are obtained from the employee earnings records. The report is prepared on the Internal Revenue Service Form W-2, Wage and Tax Statement.

Employers are required to furnish Form W-2 to each employee by January 31 of the next year. If an employee ends employment before December 31, Form W-2 must be furnished within 30 days of the last date of employment.

FYI

Form W-2 shows the total year's earnings and the amounts withheld for taxes for each employee.

The Form W-2 prepared by CarLand for Patrick S. Turner is shown in Illustration 15-8.

ILLUSTRATION 15-8 Form W-2, Wage and Tax Statement

1 Control number	22222	For Official Use Only ▶ OMB No. 1545-0008		
2 Employer's name, address, and ZIP code CarLand 1374 Parklane Rockville, RI 02873-4121		6 Statutory employee ☐ Deceased ☐ Pension plan ☐ Legal rep. ☐ 942 emp. ☐ Subtotal ☐ Deferred compensation ☐ Void ☐		
		7 Allocated tips	8 Advance EIC payment	
		9 Federal income tax withheld 1,032.00	10 Wages, tips, other compensation 18,192.00	
3 Employer's identification number 31-0429632	4 Employer's state I.D. number	11 Social security tax withheld 1,182.48	12 Social security wages 18,192.00	
5 Employee's social security number 450-70-6432		13 Social security tips	14 Medicare wages and tips 18,192.00	
19a Employee's name (first, middle initial, last) Patrick S. Turner		15 Medicare tax withheld 272.88	16 Nonqualified plans	
		17 See Instrs. for Form W-2	18 Other	
1625 Northland Drive Rockville, RI 02873-5073				
19b Employee's address and ZIP code				
20 /////	21 /////	22 Dependent care benefits	23 Benefits included in Box 10	
24 State income tax	25 State wages, tips, etc.	26 Name of state	27 Local income tax	28 Local wages, tips, etc.	29 Name of locality

Copy A For Social Security Administration   Department of the Treasury—Internal Revenue Service

Form **W-2 Wage and Tax Statement 19--**

Four copies (A to D) of Form W-2 are prepared for each employee. Copies B and C are given to the employee. The employee attaches Copy B to a personal federal income tax return and keeps Copy C for a personal record. The employer sends Copy A to the Social Security Administration and keeps Copy D for the business' records.

Businesses in states with state income tax must prepare additional copies of Form W-2. The employee attaches the additional copy to the personal state income tax return.

Employer Annual Reporting of Payroll Taxes

Form W-3, Transmittal of Income and Tax Statements, is sent to the Social Security Administration by February 28 each year. Form W-3 reports the previous year's earnings and payroll taxes withheld for all employees. Attached to Form W-3 is Copy A of each employee Form W-2. A Form W-3 prepared by CarLand is shown in Illustration 15-9 on the next page.

ILLUSTRATION 15-9   Form W-3, Transmittal of Income and Tax Statements

DO NOT STAPLE

1 Control number	33333	For Official Use Only ▶ OMB No. 1545-0008		

☐ **Kind of Payer** ▶	2 941/941E [X] Military ☐ 943 ☐ CT-1 ☐ 942 ☐ Medicare govt. emp. ☐	3 Employer's state I.D. number	5 Total number of statements
		4	6

6 Establishment number	7 Allocated tips	8 Advance EIC payments

9 Federal income tax withheld 4,612.00	10 Wages, tips, and other compensation 60,153.00	11 Social security tax withheld 3,909.95
12 Social security wages 60,153.00	13 Social security tips	14 Medicare wages and tips 60,153.00
15 Medicare tax withheld 902.29	16 Nonqualified plans	17 Deferred compensation

18 Employer's identification number 31-0429632	19 Other EIN used this year
20 Employer's name CarLand	21 Dependent care benefits
1374 Parklane Rockville, RI 02873-4121	23 Adjusted total social security wages and tips 60,153.00
	24 Adjusted total Medicare wages and tips 60,153.00
	25 Income tax withheld by third-party payer
22 Employer's address and ZIP code (If available, place label over Boxes 18 and 20.)	

Under penalties of perjury, I declare that I have examined this return and accompanying documents, and, to the best of my knowledge and belief, they are true, correct, and complete.

Signature ▶ *Amy Kramer*   Title ▶ *Partner*   Date ▶ 2/27/--

Telephone number ___(401) 555-9368___

Form **W-3 Transmittal of Income and Tax Statements 19--**   Department of the Treasury Internal Revenue Service

---

At the end of a calendar year, employers must also report to the federal and state governments a summary of all earnings paid to employees during the twelve months.

Employers with more than 250 employees have different procedures for reporting withholding tax information. The information is sent to the Internal Revenue Service in computer files rather than the actual Forms W-2 and W-3.

PAYING WITHHOLDING AND PAYROLL TAXES

At least quarterly, employers must pay to the federal government the federal income taxes and FICA taxes withheld from employee salaries. The payment also includes the amount of employer FICA taxes.

Paying the Liability for Employee Income Tax and FICA Tax

Employee withheld income tax, employee FICA tax, and employer FICA tax are paid periodically in a combined payment. Tax payments are made to banks authorized by the Internal Revenue Service to accept these payments or to a Federal Reserve bank. The timing of these tax payments is based on the amount of taxes owed. A payment is accompanied by a Form 8109, Federal Tax Deposit Coupon, which shows the amount and purpose of the payment.

In December, CarLand withheld $402.00 from employee salaries for federal income taxes. The liability for FICA tax for December is $832.16. This amount includes both the employer share and the amounts withheld from employees. CarLand's federal tax payment is sent January 15 to an authorized bank with Form 8109 as shown in Illustration 15-10.

ILLUSTRATION 15-10   Form 8109, Federal Tax Deposit Coupon for withheld income tax and FICA taxes

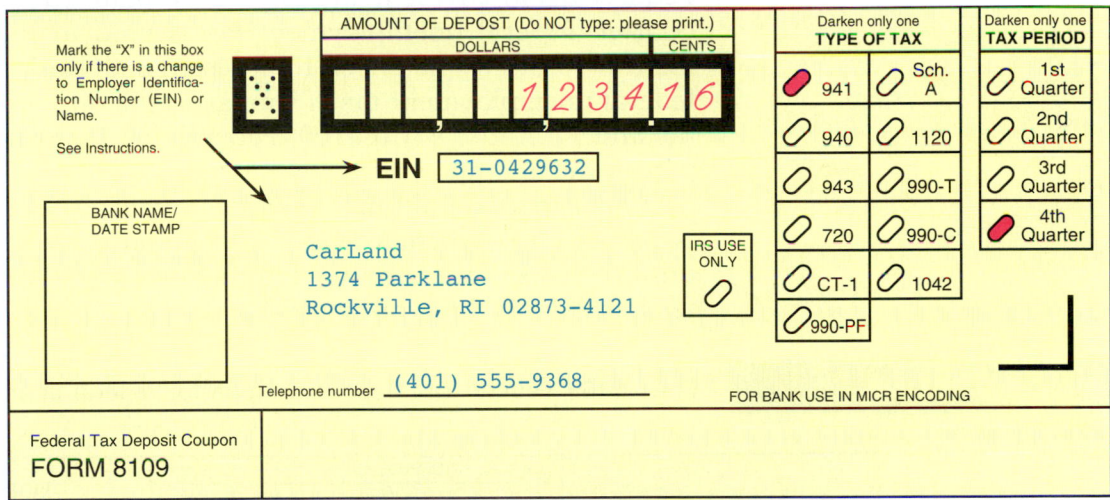

The type of tax, federal income and FICA taxes, is identified by marking the 941 circle. These taxes are reported to the government using Form 941. The calendar quarter is identified on the right side of the form.

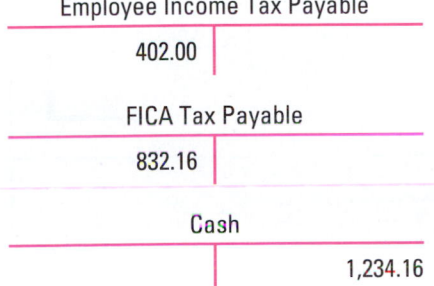

January 15, 19--. Paid cash for liability for employee income tax, $402.00, and for FICA tax, $832.16; total, $1,234.16. Check No. 305.

The balances of the liability accounts are reduced by this transaction. Therefore, Employee Income Tax Payable is debited for $402.00. FICA Tax Payable is debited for $832.16. The balance of the Cash account is decreased by a credit for the total payment, $1,234.16.

The journal entry to record payment of these liabilities is shown in Illustration 15-11 on the next page.

The date, *15*, is written in the Date column. The titles of the two accounts debited, *Employee Income Tax Payable* and *FICA Tax Payable*, are written in the Account Title column. The check number, *C305*, is entered in the Doc. No. column. The two debit amounts are entered in the General Debit column. The amount of the credit to Cash, *$1,234.16*, is recorded in the Cash Credit column.

| ILLUSTRATION 15-11 | Journal entry to record payment of liability for employee income tax and FICA tax |

JOURNAL

PAGE *27*   PAGE *27*

	DATE	ACCOUNT TITLE	DOC. NO.	POST. REF.	GENERAL DEBIT	GENERAL CREDIT	CASH DEBIT	CASH CREDIT	
25	15	Employee Income Tax Payable	C305		4 0 2 00			1 2 3 4 16	25
26		FICA Tax Payable			8 3 2 16				26
27									27

Paying the Liability for Federal Unemployment Tax

Federal unemployment tax is usually paid after the end of each quarter. Federal unemployment tax is paid to the federal government by sending the check to a designated bank. The payment for federal unemployment tax is similar to the one required for income tax and FICA tax. Form 8109, Federal Tax Deposit Coupon, accompanies the unemployment tax payment.

CarLand's federal unemployment tax at the end of December 31 is $59.15. A payment is made each quarter but no report is due until the end of the year. CarLand's Form 8109 for the fourth quarter is shown in Illustration 15-12.

| ILLUSTRATION 15-12 | Form 8109, Federal Tax Deposit Coupon for federal unemployment tax |

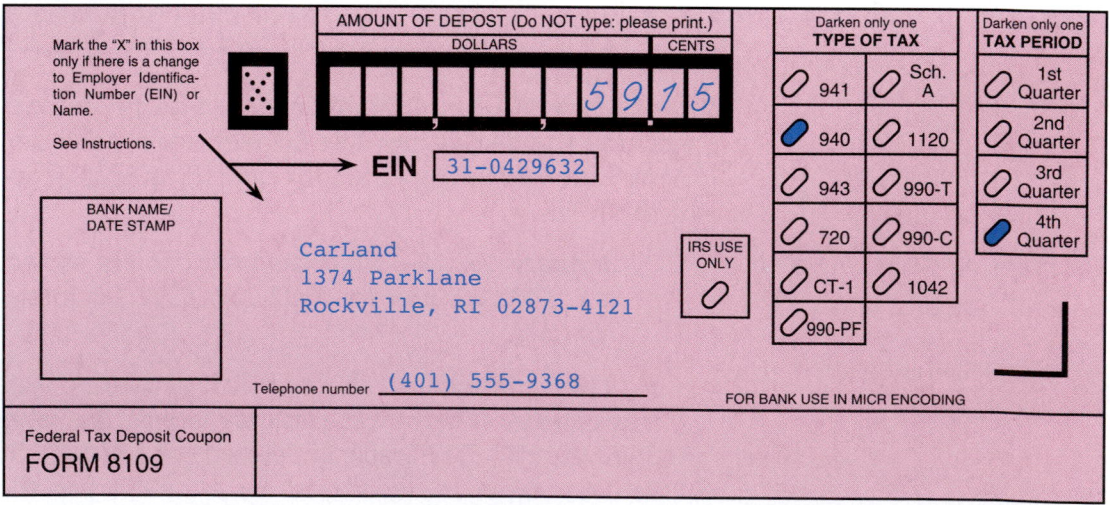

The type of tax, federal unemployment tax, is identified by marking the 940 circle since this tax is reported to the government using Form 940. The calendar quarter is identified on the right side of the form.

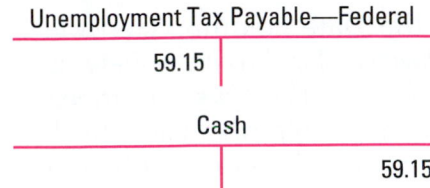

Unemployment Tax Payable—Federal

| 59.15 | |

Cash

| | 59.15 |

January 31, 19--. Paid cash for federal unemployment tax liability for quarter ended December 31, $59.15. Check No. 318.

The balance of the liability account is reduced by this transaction. Therefore, Unemployment Tax Payable—Federal is debited for $59.15. The balance of the asset account, Cash, is decreased by a credit for the payment, $59.15.

The journal entry to record payment of the liability for federal unemployment taxes is shown in Illustration 15-13.

The date, *31*, is written in the Date column. The title of the account debited, *Unemployment Tax Payable—Federal*, is written in the Account Title column. The check number, *C318*, is entered in the Doc. No. column. The check amount, *$59.15*, is entered in the General Debit and Cash Credit columns.

ILLUSTRATION 15-13   Journal entry to record payment of liability for federal unemployment tax

PAGE *28*   JOURNAL   PAGE *28*

					1	2		10	11
	DATE	ACCOUNT TITLE	DOC. NO.	POST. REF.	GENERAL DEBIT	GENERAL CREDIT		CASH DEBIT	CASH CREDIT
27	31	Unemployment Tax Payable—Federal	C318		59 15				59 15	27
28										28

Paying the Liability for State Unemployment Tax

State requirements for reporting and paying state unemployment taxes vary. In general, employers are required to pay the state unemployment tax during the month following each calendar quarter.

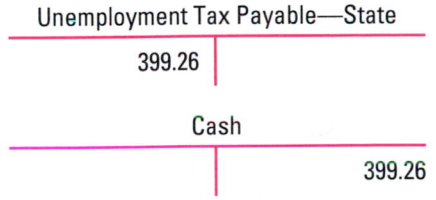

Unemployment Tax Payable—State

| 399.26 | |

Cash

| | 399.26 |

January 31, 19--. Paid cash for state unemployment tax liability for quarter ended December 31, $399.26. Check No. 319.

The liability account is reduced by this transaction. Therefore, Unemployment Tax Payable—State is debited for $399.26. The balance of the asset account, Cash, is decreased by a credit, $399.26.

The journal entry to record payment of the liability for state unemployment tax is shown in Illustration 15-14.

ILLUSTRATION 15-14   Journal entry to record payment of liability for state unemployment tax

PAGE *28*   JOURNAL   PAGE *28*

					1	2		10	11
	DATE	ACCOUNT TITLE	DOC. NO.	POST. REF.	GENERAL DEBIT	GENERAL CREDIT		CASH DEBIT	CASH CREDIT
28	31	Unemployment Tax Payable—State	C319		399 26				399 26	28

The date, *31*, is written in the Date column. The title of the account debited, *Unemployment Tax Payable—State*, is written in the Account Title column. The check number, *C319*, is entered in the Doc. No. column. The check amount, *$399.26*, is entered in the General Debit and Cash Credit columns.

The entries to journalize a payroll and payroll taxes are summarized in Illustration 15-15.

SUMMARY ILLUSTRATION 15-15

Summary of payroll accounting, taxes, and reports

The payroll register provides the amounts required to journalize the payroll. Employer payroll taxes are calculated and recorded in the journal. Later, the employee and employer payroll taxes are paid to the federal and state governments.

ACCOUNT TITLE	1 GENERAL DEBIT	2 GENERAL CREDIT	10 CASH DEBIT	11 CASH CREDIT
Pay the Payroll:				
Salary Expense	X			X
Employee Income Tax Payable		X		
FICA Tax Payable		X		
Health Insurance Premiums Payable		X		
U.S. Savings Bonds Payable		X		
United Way Donations Payable		X		
Record Employer Payroll Taxes:				
Payroll Taxes Expense	X			
FICA Tax Payable		X		
Unemployment Tax Payable—Federal		X		
Unemployment Tax Payable—State		X		
Pay Employee and Employer Taxes:				
Employee Income Tax Payable	X			X
FICA Tax Payable	X			X
Unemployment Tax Payable—Federal	X			X
Unemployment Tax Payable—State	X			X

Tax	Who Pays the Tax	
	Employee	Employer
Federal Income Tax	X	
FICA Tax	X	X
Federal Unemployment Tax		X
State Unemployment Tax		X

1. Why does a business need to keep payroll information about individual employees?
2. What two business forms provide the payroll information needed about individual employees?
3. What accounts are affected, and how, by an entry to record a payroll?
4. Where is the amount obtained that is used to write a payroll check?
5. What are the three payroll taxes paid by most employers?
6. What is the only payroll tax paid by both the employee and the employer?
7. What amount is used to calculate federal unemployment tax?
8. When is the transaction to record employer payroll taxes expense journalized?
9. What accounts are affected, and how, by an entry to record employer payroll taxes?
10. Where is the information obtained that is needed to prepare a quarterly federal tax return, Form 941?

11. What amounts are used to calculate the tax liability for a pay period as reported on the quarterly federal tax return, Form 941?
12. What information is reported on a Form W-2, Wage and Tax Statement?
13. Who receives a completed Form W-2, Wage and Tax Statement?
14. What should an employee do with Copies B and C of Form W-2, Wage and Tax Statement, received from an employer?
15. What is the purpose of Form W-3, Transmittal of Income and Tax Statements?
16. What payroll taxes are deposited using Form 8109, Federal Tax Deposit Coupon?
17. What accounts are affected, and how, by an entry to record payment of an employer liability for federal unemployment tax?

CASE 1 The partners of Smith and Tyson have decided to hire a sales manager. They agree that the business can only afford to pay the manager a salary of $30,000.00. The accounting clerk informs the partners that hiring the manager will cost the business more than the $30,000.00 salary. Do you agree with the accounting clerk? Explain your response.

CASE 2 Miller Manufacturing had total salary expense for the month of November of $40,000.00. Sandra Peterson, accounting clerk, calculated the November employer FICA tax as $3,200.00 ($40,000.00 × 8%). Samuel Grissom, accountant, stated that the FICA taxes withheld from employee earnings were $2,850.00. What is the most likely reason for the difference between Ms. Peterson's and Mr. Grissom's calculations for FICA taxes? Explain.

DRILL 15-D1 Analyzing payroll transactions

INSTRUCTIONS:

1. Prepare the following T accounts for four different businesses: Cash, Employee Income Tax Payable, FICA Tax Payable, Unemployment Tax Payable—Federal, Unemployment Tax Payable—State, Payroll Taxes Expense, and Salary Expense.

Business	Total Earnings	Federal Income Tax Withheld	Employee FICA Tax	Employer FICA Tax	Federal Unemployment Tax	State Unemployment Tax
A	$ 9,000.00	$1,350.00	$ 720.00	$ 720.00	$ 72.00	$486.00
B	4,200.00	590.00	336.00	336.00	33.60	226.80
C	12,600.00	2,016.00	1,008.00	1,008.00	100.80	680.40
D	7,800.00	1,140.00	624.00	624.00	62.40	421.20

2. Use T accounts to analyze the following payroll entries for each business. (a) Entry to record payment of a payroll. (b) Entry to record employer payroll taxes.

DRILL 15-D2 Calculating employer payroll taxes

MATHEMATICS

Payroll information taken from a payroll register and employee earnings records is given in the working papers accompanying this textbook.

INSTRUCTIONS:

1. Calculate the amount of earnings subject to unemployment taxes. Unemployment taxes are owed on the first $7,000.00 of earnings for each employee.
2. Calculate the amount of employer payroll taxes owed for the May 1–15 pay period. Employer payroll tax rates are as follows: FICA, 8%; federal unemployment, 0.8%; state unemployment, 5.4%.

APPLICATION PROBLEMS   EPT(b,c,d)

PROBLEM 15-1   Journalizing and posting payment of semimonthly payrolls

Lambert's payroll register has the following totals for two semimonthly pay periods, August 1–15 and August 16–31 of the current year.

| Period | Total Earnings | Deductions | | | | Net Pay |
		Federal Income Tax	FICA Tax	Other	Total	
Aug. 1–15.	$3,670.00	$514.00	$293.60	B $90.00	$897.60	$2,772.40
Aug. 16–31.	$3,180.00	$437.00	$254.40	B $75.00	$766.40	$2,413.60

Other Deductions: B—U.S. Savings Bonds

INSTRUCTIONS:

1. Journalize payment of the two payrolls on page 17 of a journal. The first payroll was paid by Check No. 756 on August 15 of the current year. The second payroll was paid by Check No. 768 on August 31 of the current year.
2. Post the items that are to be posted individually. The balances in the general ledger as of August 1 of the current year are recorded in the accounts.

The general ledger accounts used in Problem 15-1 are needed to complete Problem 15-2.

PROBLEM 15-2   Calculating, journalizing, and posting employer payroll taxes

SPREADSHEET

The general ledger accounts used in Problem 15-1 are needed to complete Problem 15-2.

Lambert's semimonthly payroll register totals are shown in Problem 15-1. Employer payroll tax rates are as follows: FICA, 8%; federal unemployment, 0.8%; state unemployment, 5.4%. Unemployment taxes are owed on the first $7,000.00 of earnings for each employee.

Information about accumulated earnings and total earnings for the August 1–15 pay period is given in the working papers accompanying this textbook.

INSTRUCTIONS:

1. Calculate the amount of earnings subject to unemployment taxes for the August 1–15 pay period.
2. Calculate the employer payroll tax amounts for the August 1–15 pay period.
3. Journalize the employer payroll taxes on page 18 of a journal. Use the date of August 15 of the current year. The source document is Memorandum No. 75.
4. Post the items that are to be posted individually.
5. Total earnings for the August 16–31 pay period are given in the working papers. Calculate the employer payroll taxes for the August 16–31 pay period. Calculate August 15 accumulated earnings by adding total earnings for the August 1–15 pay period to the July 31 accumulated earnings.
6. Journalize the employer payroll taxes on page 18 of a journal. Use the date of August 31 of the current year. The source document is Memorandum No. 82.
7. Post the items that are to be posted individually.

PROBLEM 15-3   Reporting employer quarterly withholding and payroll taxes

The following payroll data is for Jenson Clothing Company for the second quarter of the current year.

Date Paid	Total Earnings	Federal Income Tax Withheld	Employee FICA Tax Withheld
April 15	$2,825.00	$416.00	$226.00
April 30	2,987.00	438.00	238.96
May 15	3,142.00	468.00	251.36
May 31	2,936.00	428.00	234.88
June 15	3,212.00	489.00	256.96
June 30	2,849.00	422.00	227.92

Additional Data

1. Company address: 669 Eagle Street, Warrenville, IL 62325-4600
2. Employer identification number: 60-8909267
3. Number of employees: 5
4. Federal tax payments have been made on May 15, June 15, and July 15.

INSTRUCTIONS:

Prepare a Form 941, Employer's Quarterly Federal Tax Return, for Jenson Clothing Company. The return is for the second quarter of the current year. Use the date July 21. Sign your name as a partner of the company.

PROBLEM 15-4   Calculating and journalizing withholding and payroll taxes

The following payroll data is for Hawbecker Company for the first quarter of the current year.

Period	Total Earnings	Federal Income Tax Withheld
March	$12,537.00	$2,138.00
First Quarter	37,293.00	—

In addition, total earnings are subject to 8% employee and 8% employer FICA tax. The federal unemployment tax rate is 0.8% and the state unemployment tax rate is 5.4% of total earnings. No total earnings have exceeded the tax base for calculating unemployment taxes.

INSTRUCTIONS:

1. Calculate the appropriate liability amount of FICA tax for March. Journalize the payment of the federal income tax and FICA tax liabilities on page 7 of a journal. The taxes were paid by Check No. 785 on April 3 of the current year.

2. Calculate the appropriate federal unemployment tax liability for the first quarter. Journalize payment of this liability in the journal. The tax was paid by Check No. 802 on April 30 of the current year.

3. Calculate the appropriate state unemployment tax liability for the first quarter. Journalize payment of this liability in the journal. The tax was paid by Check No. 803 on April 30 of the current year.

ENRICHMENT PROBLEMS

MASTERY PROBLEM 15-M Journalizing and posting payroll transactions

AUTOMATED

APPLICATION

Star Equipment completed payroll transactions during the period April 1 to May 15 of the current year. Payroll tax rates are as follows: FICA, 8%; federal unemployment, 0.8%; state unemployment, 5.4%. The company buys savings bonds for employees as accumulated withholdings reach the necessary amount to purchase a bond. No total earnings have exceeded the tax base for calculating unemployment taxes.

The balances in the general ledger as of April 1 of the current year are recorded in the working papers accompanying this textbook.

CHART OF ACCOUNTS

Account Number	Account Title	Account Number	Account Title
1110	Cash	2150	Unemployment Tax Pay.—Fed.
1130	Accounts Receivable	2160	Unemployment Tax Pay.—St.
1140	Merchandise Inventory	2180	U.S. Savings Bonds Pay.
2110	Accounts Payable	3150	Income Summary
2120	Employee Income Tax Pay.	6150	Payroll Taxes Expense
2130	FICA Tax Payable	6170	Salary Expense

INSTRUCTIONS:

1. Journalize the following transactions on page 14 of a journal. Source documents are abbreviated as follows: check, C, and memorandum, M.

Apr. 15. Paid cash for liability for employee income tax, $945.00, and for FICA tax, $984.99; total, $1,929.99. C356.

15. Paid cash for semimonthly payroll, $2,463.52 (total payroll, $3,256.00, less deductions: employee income tax, $482.00; FICA tax, $260.48; U.S. Savings Bonds, $50.00). C357.

15. Recorded employer payroll taxes expense. M25.

15. Paid cash for U.S. Savings Bonds for employees, $250.00. C358.

30. Paid cash for semimonthly payroll, $2,527.36, (total payroll, $3,358.00, less deductions: employee income tax, $512.00; FICA tax, $268.64; U.S. Savings Bonds, $50.00). C376.

30. Recorded employer payroll taxes expense. M29.

30. Paid cash for federal unemployment tax liability for quarter ended March 31, $147.75. C377.

30. Paid cash for state unemployment tax liability for quarter ended March 31, $997.30. C378.

   Posting. Post the items that are to be posted individually.

May 15. Paid cash for liability for employee income tax, $994.00, and for FICA tax, $1,058.24; total, $2,052.24. C405.

15. Paid cash for semimonthly payroll, $2,373.40 (total payroll, $3,145.00, less deductions: employee income tax, $470.00; FICA tax, $251.60; U.S. Savings Bonds, $50.00). C406.

May 15. Recorded employer payroll taxes expense. M36.

Posting. Post the items that are to be posted individually.

2. Prove and rule the journal.

CHALLENGE PROBLEM 15-C Journalizing and posting payroll transactions

Danner Hardware completed payroll transactions during the period January 1 to April 30 of the current year. Payroll tax rates are as follows: FICA, 8%; federal unemployment, 0.8%; and state unemployment, 5.4%. The company buys savings bonds for employees as the accumulated withholdings reach the necessary amount to purchase a bond. No total earnings have exceeded the tax base for calculating unemployment taxes.

The balances in the general ledger as of January 1 of the current year are recorded in the working papers accompanying this textbook.

CHART OF ACCOUNTS

Account Number	Account Title	Account Number	Account Title
1110	Cash	2150	Unemployment Tax Pay.—Fed.
1130	Accounts Receivable	2160	Unemployment Tax Pay.—St.
1140	Merchandise Inventory	2180	U.S. Savings Bonds Pay.
2110	Accounts Payable	3150	Income Summary
2120	Employee Income Tax Pay.	6150	Payroll Taxes Expense
2130	FICA Tax Payable	6170	Salary Expense

INSTRUCTIONS:

1. Journalize the following transactions on page 1 of a journal. Source documents are abbreviated as follows: check, C, and memorandum, M.

Jan. 2. Wrote a check for 12 U.S. Savings Bonds at $25.00 each for employees. C143.
15. Paid the December liability for employee income tax and for FICA tax. C152.
31. Wrote a check for federal unemployment tax liability for quarter ended December 31. C158.
31. Wrote a check for state unemployment tax liability for quarter ended December 31. C159.
31. Paid January payroll, $6,283.04 (total payroll, $8,487.00, less deductions: employee income tax, $1,425.00; FICA tax, $678.96; U.S. Savings Bonds, $100.00). C164.
31. Recorded employer payroll taxes expense. M95.
Posting. Post the items that are to be posted individually.
Feb. 15. Wrote a check for January liability for employee income tax and for FICA tax. C170.
28. Paid February payroll, $6,348.16 (total payroll, $8,598.00, less deductions: employee income tax, $1,462.00; FICA tax, $687.84; U.S. Savings Bonds, $100.00). C180.
28. Recorded employer payroll taxes expense. M104.
Posting. Post the items that are to be posted individually.
Mar. 15. Wrote a check for February liability for employee income tax and for FICA tax. C195.
31. Paid March payroll, $6,660.76 (total payroll, $9,028.00, less deductions: employee income tax, $1,545.00; FICA tax, $722.24; U.S. Savings Bonds, $100.00). C206.
31. Recorded employer payroll taxes expense. M113.
Posting. Post the items that are to be posted individually.
Apr. 1. Paid cash for 12 U.S. Savings Bonds at $25.00 each for employees. C207.
15. Wrote a check for March liability for employee income tax and for FICA tax. C218.
30. Wrote a check for federal unemployment tax liability for quarter ended March 31. C224.
30. Wrote a check for state unemployment tax liability for quarter ended March 31. C225.
Posting. Post the items that are to be posted individually.

2. Prove and rule the journal.

Recording Payroll Transactions

CarLand's manual journalizing and posting procedures for payroll transactions are described in Chapter 15. Integrating Automated Accounting Topic 5 describes procedures for using automated accounting software to journalize and post CarLand's payroll transactions. The Automated Accounting Problems contain instructions for using automated accounting software to solve the April payroll transactions from Mastery Problem 15-M and Challenge Problem 15-C, Chapter 15.

AUTOMATED PAYROLL ACCOUNTING PROCEDURES FOR CARLAND

CarLand uses two input forms to batch payroll transaction data for automated accounting.

1. Cash payments journal input form for all cash payments.
2. General journal input form for all other transactions.

Recording Payment of a Payroll

CarLand uses a cash payments journal input form to journalize payment of a payroll.

> *December 15, 19--. Paid cash for semimonthly payroll, $1,976.52 (total payroll, $2,556.00, less deductions: employee income tax, $192.00; FICA tax, $204.48; health insurance premiums, $158.00; U.S. Savings Bonds, $15.00; United Way donations, $10.00). Check No. 287.*

The journal entry to record this transaction is on lines 1 through 6 of the cash payments journal input form shown in Illustration T5-1.

ILLUSTRATION T5-1   Cash payments journal input form with payroll transactions recorded

	DATE MM/DD	VENDOR NO.	CHECK NO.	ACCOUNTS PAY. DEBIT	ACCOUNT NO.	DEBIT	CREDIT	
1	12 15		C287		6170	2556 00		1
2					2120		192 00	2
3					2130		204 48	3
4					2170		158 00	4
5					2180		15 00	5
6					2190		10 00	6
25								25

RUN DATE 12/15/-- MM DD YY

CASH PAYMENTS JOURNAL Input Form

NOTE: A credit to Cash is made automatically by the software.

The run date, *12/15/--*, is written in the space provided at the top of the form.

On line 1, the date of the transaction, *12/15*, is entered in the Date column. The source document number, *C287*, is recorded in the Check No. column. The general ledger account number for Salary Expense, *6170*, is written in the Account No. column. The debit amount, *$2,556.00*, is written in the Debit column.

On lines 2 through 6, the account numbers for the payroll liabilities are written in the Account No. column. The credit amounts are entered in the Credit column. The software automatically makes the credit to **Cash**, *$1,976.52*.

Recording Employer Payroll Taxes

CarLand journalizes employer payroll taxes on a general journal input form.

> December 15, 19--. Recorded employer payroll taxes expense, $275.03, for the semimonthly pay period ended December 15. Taxes owed are: FICA tax, $204.48; federal unemployment tax, $9.10; state unemployment tax, $61.45. Memorandum No. 54.

The journal entry to record this transaction is on lines 1 through 4 of the general journal input form shown in Illustration T5-2.

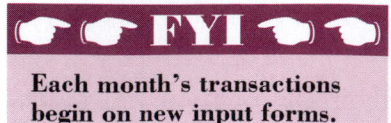

Each month's transactions begin on new input forms.

ILLUSTRATION T5-2

General journal input form with employer taxes recorded

	DATE MM/DD	REFERENCE	ACCOUNT NO.	CUSTOMER/ VENDOR NO.	DEBIT	CREDIT	
RUN DATE *12/15/--* MM DD YY			GENERAL JOURNAL Input Form				
1	12/15	M54	6150		275 03		1
2	/		2130			204 48	2
3	/		2150			9 10	3
4	/		2160			61 45	4
25	/						25
				PAGE TOTALS	275 03	275 03	
				FINAL TOTALS	275 03	275 03	

The run date, *12/15/--*, is written in the space provided at the top of the input form.

On line 1, the date of the transaction, *12/15*, is entered in the Date column. The source document number, *M54*, is recorded in the Reference column. The general ledger account number for **Payroll Taxes Expense**, *6150*, is written in the Account No. column. The debit amount, *$275.03*, is entered in the Debit column.

On lines 2 through 4, the account numbers for the payroll taxes are recorded in the Account No. column. The credit amounts are written in the Credit column.

After the employer payroll taxes transaction has been journalized, CarLand totals the Debit and Credit columns. The totals are recorded on the Page Totals and Final Totals lines provided at the bottom of the input form.

Processing a Payroll Payment and Employer Payroll Taxes

To process a cash payment, the Journals menu is selected from the menu bar. The Cash Payments Journal command is selected from

Always compare the computer printout to the input forms to assure accuracy.

the Journals menu to display the data entry window for keying payroll data.

After the payroll payment has been keyed and posted, the Reports menu is selected from the menu bar. The Journals command is chosen to display the Report Selection window. The Cash Payments Journal is selected from the Report Selection window. As CarLand wants to print all transactions from 12/01/-- to 12/15/--, the *Ok* button is pushed to display the cash payments report. The report is checked for accuracy by comparing the report with the cash payments journal input form. The cash payments journal report is printed, as shown in Illustration T5-3, and filed for future reference.

ILLUSTRATION T5-3   Cash payments journal report with a payroll payment recorded

```
                              CarLand
                       Cash Payments Journal
                             12/15/--
------------------------------------------------------------------------
Date    Refer.   V/C Acct.   Title                      Debit      Credit
------------------------------------------------------------------------
12/15   C287         6170    Salary Expense            2556.00
12/15   C287         2120    Employee Income Tax Pay.               192.00
12/15   C287         2130    FICA Tax Payable                       204.48
12/15   C287         2170    Health Ins. Premiums Pay.              158.00
12/15   C287         2180    U.S. Savings Bonds Pay.                 15.00
12/15   C287         2190    United Way Donations Pay.              10.00
12/15   C287         1110    Cash                                  1976.52

                                                      ----------  ----------
                             Totals                     2556.00    2556.00
                                                      ==========  ==========
```

To process general journal entries, the Journals menu is selected from the menu bar. The General Journal command is chosen from the Journals menu to display the data entry window for keying transaction data.

After all lines on the input form have been keyed and posted, the general journal report is displayed. The same steps are followed as for displaying the cash payments journal report. However, the General Journal is selected from the Report Selection window. The report is checked for accuracy by comparing the report totals, *$275.03*, with the totals on the general journal input form. Because the totals are the same, the general journal report is assumed to be correct. The general journal report is printed, as shown in Illustration T5-4, and is filed for future reference.

PAYING WITHHOLDING AND PAYROLL TAXES

CarLand journalizes the payment of withholding and payroll taxes on a cash payments journal input form.

INTEGRATING AUTOMATED ACCOUNTING — TOPIC 5 **377**

```
                              CarLand
                          General Journal
                             12/15/--
-----------------------------------------------------------------------
Date   Refer.   V/C  Acct.  Title                        Debit    Credit
-----------------------------------------------------------------------
12/15  M54           6150   Payroll Taxes Expense        275.03
12/15  M54           2130   FICA Tax Payable                      204.48
12/15  M54           2150   Unemployment Tax Pay--Fed                9.10
12/15  M54           2160   Unemployment Tax Pay--St.               61.45

                                                        ---------- ----------
                            Totals                        275.03    275.03
                                                        ========== ==========
```

Recording Payment of Employee Income Tax and FICA Tax

January 15, 19--. Paid cash for liability for employee income tax, $402.00, and for FICA tax, $832.16; total, $1,234.16. Check No. 305.

The journal entry to record this transaction is on lines 1 and 2 of the cash payments journal input form shown in Illustration T5-5.

ILLUSTRATION T5-5

Cash payments journal input form with withholding and payroll taxes recorded

	DATE MM/DD	VENDOR NO.	CHECK NO.	ACCOUNTS PAY. DEBIT	ACCOUNT NO.	DEBIT	CREDIT	
RUN DATE 01/31/--			CASH PAYMENTS JOURNAL					
MM DD YY			Input Form					
1	01/15		C305		2120	402 00		1
2	/				2130	832 16		2
3	/31		C318		2150	59 15		3
4	/31		C319		2160	399 26		4
25	/							25

NOTE: A credit to Cash is made automatically by the software.

FYI

For the purpose of this illustration, check numbers 306–317 have been omitted.

Paying the Liability for Federal Unemployment Tax

January 31, 19--. Paid cash for federal unemployment tax liability for quarter ended December 31, $59.15. Check No. 318.

The journal entry to record this transaction is on line 3 of Illustration T5-5.

Paying the Liability for State Unemployment Tax

January 31, 19--. Paid cash for state unemployment tax liability for quarter ended December 31, $399.26. Check No. 319.

The journal entry to record this transaction is on line 4 of Illustration T5-5.

Processing the Payment of Withholding and Payroll Taxes

To process the cash payment for withholding and payroll taxes, the transaction data are keyed from the cash payments journal input form. After all lines have been keyed and posted, a cash payments report is displayed. The displayed cash payments report is checked for accuracy by comparing the report with the cash payments journal input form. After accuracy has been verified, the cash payments report is printed, as shown in Illustration T5-6, and is filed for future reference.

ILLUSTRATION T5-6   Cash payments journal report with withholding and payroll taxes recorded

```
                            CarLand
                      Cash Payments Journal
                           01/31/--
-------------------------------------------------------------------------
Date    Refer.    V/C Acct.   Title                    Debit      Credit
-------------------------------------------------------------------------
01/15 C305         2120      Employee Income Tax Pay.   402.00
01/15 C305         2130      FICA Tax Payable           832.16
01/15 C305         1110      Cash                                 1234.16

01/31 C318         2150      Unemployment Tax Pay--Fed   59.15
01/31 C318         1110      Cash                                   59.15

01/31 C319         2160      Unemployment Tax Pay--St.  399.26
01/31 C319         1110      Cash                                  399.26
                                                       ---------  ---------
                             Totals                     1692.57   1692.57
                                                       =========  =========
```

OPTIONAL PROBLEM DB-5A

CarLand's general ledger data base is on the accounting textbook template. If you wish to process CarLand's December payroll transactions using automated accounting software, load the *Automated Accounting 6.0* or higher software. Select Data Base 5A (DB-5A) from the template disk. Read the Problem Instructions screen. Using the completed cash payments and general journal input forms, Illustrations T5-1, T5-2, and T5-5, follow the procedures described to process CarLand's payroll transactions.

AUTOMATED ACCOUNTING PROBLEMS

AUTOMATING MASTERY PROBLEM 15-M Journalizing and posting payroll transactions

INSTRUCTIONS:

1. Journalize transactions for the month of April *only* from Mastery Problem 15-M, Chapter 15, on the appropriate input forms. Use April 30 of the current year as the run date.
2. Load the *Automated Accounting 6.0* or higher software. Select data base F15-M (First-Year Course Problem 15-M) from the accounting textbook template. Read the Problem Instructions screen.
3. Select File from the menu bar and choose the Save As menu command. Key the path to the drive and directory that contains your data files. Save the data base with a file name of XXX15M (where XXX are your initials).
4. Key the data from the completed cash payments journal input form.
5. Display/print the cash payments journal report.
6. Key the data from the completed general journal input form.
7. Display/print the general journal report.

AUTOMATING CHALLENGE PROBLEM 15-C Journalizing and posting payroll transactions

INSTRUCTIONS:

1. Journalize transactions for the month of January *only* from Challenge Problem 15-C, on the appropriate input forms. Use January 31 of the current year as the run date.
2. Load the *Automated Accounting 6.0* or higher software. Select data base F15-C from the accounting textbook template. Read the Problem Instructions screen.
3. Select File from the menu bar and choose the Save As menu command. Key the path to the drive and directory that contains your data files. Save the data base with a file name of XXX15C (where XXX are your initials).
4. Key the data from the completed cash payments journal input form.
5. Display/print the cash payments journal report.
6. Key the data from the completed general journal input form.
7. Display/print the general journal report.

An Accounting Cycle for a Partnership: Journalizing and Posting Transactions

AUTOMATED

Reinforcement Activity 2 reinforces learnings from Part 3, Chapters 11 through 18. Activities cover a complete accounting cycle for a merchandising business organized as a partnership. Reinforcement Activity 2 is a single problem divided into two parts. Part A includes learnings from Chapters 11 through 15. Part B includes learnings from Chapters 16 through 18.

The accounting work of a single merchandising business for the last month of a yearly fiscal period is used in this reinforcement activity. The records kept and reports prepared, however, illustrate the application of accounting concepts for all merchandising businesses.

CLEARVIEW OPTICAL

Tara Bruski and James Myler, partners, own and operate ClearView Optical, a merchandising business. The business sells a complete line of fashion, sun, and sport eyewear. ClearView is located in a downtown shopping area and is open for business Monday through Saturday. A monthly rent is paid for the building and fixtures. ClearView accepts credit cards from customers.

CHART OF ACCOUNTS

ClearView Optical uses the chart of accounts shown on the next page.

JOURNAL AND LEDGERS

The journal and ledgers used by ClearView Optical are listed in the following chart. Models of the journal and ledgers are shown in the textbook illustrations given in the chart.

Journal and Ledgers	Chapter	Illustration Number
Expanded journal............	12	12-5
Accounts payable ledger......	13	13-10
Accounts receivable ledger....	13	13-15
General ledger..............	16	16-1

CLEARVIEW OPTICAL
CHART OF ACCOUNTS

Balance Sheet Accounts

(1000) ASSETS

1110	Cash
1120	Petty Cash
1130	Accounts Receivable
1140	Merchandise Inventory
1145	Supplies—Office
1150	Supplies—Store
1160	Prepaid Insurance

(2000) LIABILITIES

2110	Accounts Payable
2120	Employee Income Tax Payable
2130	FICA Tax Payable
2140	Sales Tax Payable
2150	Unemployment Tax Payable—Federal
2160	Unemployment Tax Payable—State
2170	Health Insurance Premiums Payable
2180	U.S. Savings Bonds Payable
2190	United Way Donations Payable

(3000) OWNERS' EQUITY

3110	Tara Bruski, Capital
3120	Tara Bruski, Drawing
3130	James Myler, Capital
3140	James Myler, Drawing
3150	Income Summary

Income Statement Accounts

(4000) OPERATING REVENUE

4110	Sales

(5000) COST OF MERCHANDISE

5110	Purchases

(6000) OPERATING EXPENSES

6110	Advertising Expense
6120	Credit Card Fee Expense
6130	Insurance Expense
6140	Miscellaneous Expense
6150	Payroll Taxes Expense
6160	Rent Expense
6170	Salary Expense
6175	Supplies Expense—Office
6180	Supplies Expense—Store
6190	Utilities Expense

SUBSIDIARY LEDGERS

Accounts Receivable Ledger

110	Theresa Abbey
120	Nancy Bonner
130	Jonathan Doran
140	Irma Iznaga
150	Brian Patco
160	Norman Witte

Accounts Payable Ledger

210	A & B Optical Co.
220	Central Office Supply
230	Kosh Optical Lab
240	Optical Imports
250	Trend Optics Co.
260	Weaver Supply

RECORDING TRANSACTIONS

The December 1 account balances for the general and subsidiary ledgers are given in the working papers accompanying this textbook.

INSTRUCTIONS:

1. Journalize the following transactions on page 23 of a journal. A 6% sales tax has been added to each sale. Source documents are abbreviated as follows: check, C; memorandum, M; purchase invoice, P; receipt, R; sales invoice, S; cash register tape, T.

Dec. 1. Paid cash for rent, $1,000.00. C272.
1. Tara Bruski, partner, withdrew cash for personal use, $1,200.00. C273.
1. James Myler, partner, withdrew cash for personal use, $1,200.00. C274.
2. Paid cash for electric bill, $288.50. C275.
2. Received cash on account from Nancy Bonner, $344.50, covering S64. R82.
3. Paid cash for miscellaneous expense, $60.00. C276.
3. Paid cash on account to Trend Optics Co., $483.80, covering P73. C277.
4. Sold merchandise on account to Theresa Abbey, $375.00, plus sales tax, $22.50; total, $397.50. S67.
5. Recorded cash and credit card sales, $4,830.00, plus sales tax, $289.80; total, $5,119.80. T5.
   Posting. Post the items that are to be posted individually.
7. Sold merchandise on account to Jonathan Doran, $385.00, plus sales tax, $23.10; total, $408.10. S68.
7. Received cash on account from Norman Witte, $360.40, covering S65. R83.
8. Bought office supplies on account from Central Office Supply, $293.00. M43.
9. Purchased merchandise on account from Optical Imports, $1,125.00. P77.
9. Bought store supplies on account from Weaver Supply, $275.00. M44.
10. Tara Bruski, partner, withdrew merchandise for personal use, $250.00. M45.
10. Paid cash for office supplies, $145.00. C278.
10. Discovered that a payment of cash for advertising in November was journalized and posted in error as a debit to Miscellaneous Expense instead of Advertising Expense, $125.00. M46.
11. Paid cash on account to Kosh Optical Lab, $975.80, covering P74. C279.
11. Purchased merchandise on account from Trend Optics Co., $860.00. P78.
12. Paid cash for store supplies, $220.00. C280.
12. Recorded cash and credit card sales, $5,940.00, plus sales tax, $356.40; total, $6,296.40. T12.
    Posting. Post the items that are to be posted individually.
14. James Myler, partner, withdrew merchandise for personal use, $325.00. M47.
14. Purchased merchandise on account from Kosh Optical Lab, $2,730.00. P79.
14. Sold merchandise on account to Brian Patco, $140.00, plus sales tax, $8.40; total, $148.40. S69.
14. Paid cash for advertising, $345.00. C281.
15. Paid cash on account to A & B Optical Co., $1,060.40, covering P75. C282.
15. Received cash on account from Irma Iznaga, $683.70, covering S66. R84.
15. Sold merchandise on account to Nancy Bonner, $410.00, plus sales tax, $24.60; total, $434.60. S70.
    Posting. Post the items that are to be posted individually.

2. Prove and rule page 23 of the journal.

3. Carry the column totals forward to page 24 of the journal.

4. Journalize the following transactions on page 24 of the journal.

Dec. 15. Paid cash for semimonthly payroll, $1,751.80 (total payroll, $2,315.00, less deductions: employee income tax, $181.00; FICA tax, $185.20; health insurance, $142.00; U.S. Savings Bonds, $25.00; United Way donations, $30.00). C283.

Dec. 15. Recorded employer payroll taxes, $250.30, for the semimonthly pay period ended December 15. Taxes owed are: FICA tax, $185.20; federal unemployment tax, $8.40; and state unemployment tax, $56.70. M48.

19. Recorded cash and credit card sales, $5,760.00, plus sales tax, $345.60; total, $6,105.60. T19.

23. Paid cash on account to Optical Imports, $1,840.00, covering P76. C284.

26. Recorded cash and credit card sales, $5,820.00, plus sales tax, $349.20; total, $6,169.20. T26.

Posting. Post the items that are to be posted individually.

ClearView Optical's bank charges a fee for handling the collection of credit card sales deposited during the month. The credit card fee is deducted from ClearView Optical's bank account. The amount is then shown on the bank statement. The credit card fee is recorded in the journal as a reduction in cash.

Dec. 28. Recorded credit card fee expense, $285.20. M49. (Debit Credit Card Fee Expense; credit Cash.)

30. Purchased merchandise on account from A & B Optical Co., $1,620.00. P80.

31. Paid cash to replenish the petty cash fund, $304.00: office supplies, $62.00; store supplies, $59.00; advertising, $87.00; miscellaneous, $96.00. C285.

31. Paid cash for semimonthly payroll, $1,882.00 (total payroll, $2,460.00, less deductions: employee income tax, $184.20; FICA tax, $196.80; health insurance, $142.00; U.S. Savings Bonds, $25.00; United Way donations, $30.00). C286.

31. Recorded employer payroll taxes, $263.92, for the semimonthly pay period ended December 31. Taxes owed are: FICA tax, $196.80; federal unemployment tax, $8.66; and state unemployment tax, $58.46. M50.

31. Received bank statement showing December bank service charge, $4.50. M51.

31. Recorded cash and credit card sales, $3,240.00, plus sales tax, $194.40; total, $3,434.40. T31.

Posting. Post the items that are to be posted individually.

5. Total page 24 of the journal. Prove the equality of debits and credits.

6. Prove cash. The balance on the next unused check stub was $34,918.00.

7. Rule the journal.

8. Post the totals of the special columns of the journal.

9. Prepare a schedule of accounts payable and a schedule of accounts receivable. Prove the accuracy of the subsidiary ledgers by comparing the schedule totals with the balances of the controlling accounts in the general ledger. If the totals are not the same, find and correct the errors.

The ledgers used in Reinforcement Activity 2, Part A, are needed to complete Reinforcement Activity 2, Part B.

Stellar Attractions Pegboard Payroll System provides experience in preparing records using a pegboard and no-carbon-required forms. When data are entered on the statement of earnings and deductions stub on the check, the employee earnings record and the payroll register are simultaneously prepared. Posting is eliminated. The following activities are included in the accounting cycle for Stellar Attractions. This business simulation is available from the publisher.

Activities in Stellar Attractions:

1. Preparing necessary forms for new employees.

2. Completing time cards by entering summary data.

3. Assembling forms on a pegboard: checks with earnings and deductions stubs, employee earnings records, and payroll register. All records are completed with one writing.

4. Recording time card summary data on the statement of earnings and deductions stubs of checks on the pegboard.

5. Determining appropriate deductions using tax tables and figuring net pay.

6. Recording deductions and net pay on the statement of earnings and deductions stubs.

7. Totaling, proving, ruling, and filing the payroll register. Filing employee earnings records.

8. Separating, writing, and signing payroll checks.

9. Totaling and proving employee earnings records for the end of the quarter and year to date.

10. Preparing quarterly and annual reports.

16

Work Sheet for a Merchandising Business

ENABLING PERFORMANCE TASKS

After studying Chapter 16, you will be able to:

a Define accounting terms related to a work sheet for a merchandising business.

b Identify accounting concepts and practices related to a work sheet for a merchandising business.

c Plan adjustments on a work sheet for a merchandising business.

d Complete a work sheet for a merchandising business.

TERMS PREVIEW

inventory • merchandise inventory

Management decisions about future business operations are often based on financial information. Financial information shows whether a profit is being made or a loss is being incurred. Profit or loss information helps an owner or manager determine future changes. Financial information is also needed to prepare required tax reports. A business summarizes financial information at least once each fiscal period. CarLand uses a one-year fiscal period that begins on January 1 and ends on December 31. Therefore, CarLand summarizes its financial information on December 31 of each year.

GENERAL LEDGER WITH POSTING COMPLETED

CarLand's completed general ledger on December 31, after all transactions have been posted, is shown in Illustration 16-1, pages 388 through 393. No entries have been posted in the following accounts: Income Summary, Insurance Expense, Supplies Expense—Office, and Supplies Expense—Store. Transactions during the year did not affect these accounts.

AN 8-COLUMN WORK SHEET FOR A MERCHANDISING BUSINESS

A columnar accounting form on which the financial information needed to prepare financial statements is summarized is known as a work sheet. A work sheet is used to plan adjustments and sort financial statement information. A work sheet may be prepared whenever a business wishes to summarize and report financial information. A work sheet is always prepared at the end of each fiscal period because financial statements are prepared at the end of each fiscal period. (CONCEPT: Accounting Period Cycle) CarLand prepares a work sheet and financial statements annually.

Work sheets for service and merchandising businesses are similar. CarLand's work sheet is similar to the one used by Rugcare described in Chapter 8. CarLand's work sheet, however, also includes accounts for accounts receivable, merchandise inventory, accounts payable, sales tax, and purchases.

RECORDING A TRIAL BALANCE ON A WORK SHEET

To prove the equality of debits and credits in the general ledger, a trial balance is prepared. CarLand prepares a trial balance in the Trial Balance columns of a work sheet. CarLand's trial balance on December 31 is shown in Illustration 16-2, page 394.

ILLUSTRATION 16-1 General ledger with posting completed

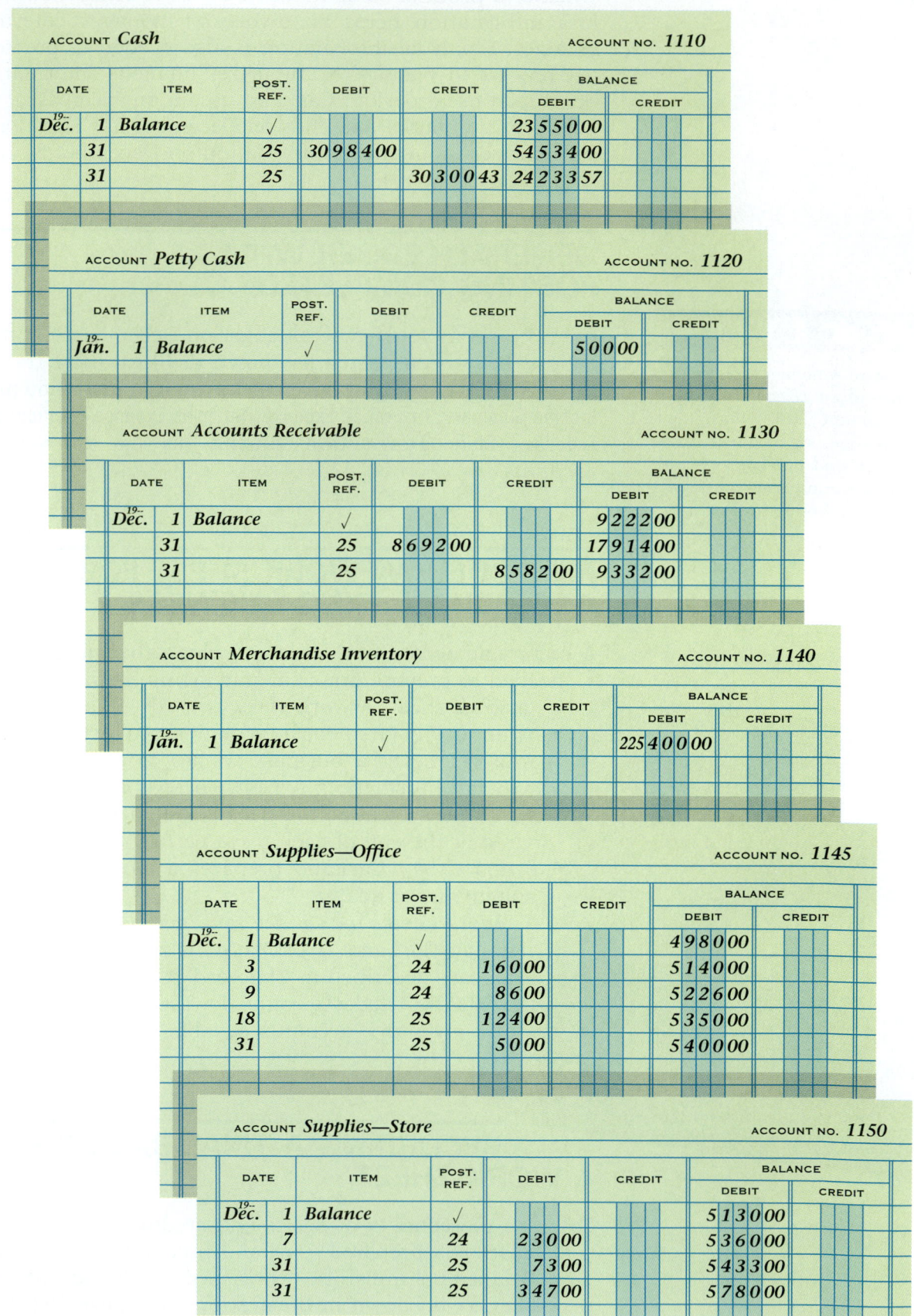

ACCOUNT *Cash*   ACCOUNT NO. *1110*

DATE		ITEM	POST. REF.	DEBIT	CREDIT	BALANCE DEBIT	BALANCE CREDIT
Dec.	1	Balance	✓			23 5 5 0 00	
	31		25	30 9 8 4 00		54 5 3 4 00	
	31		25		30 3 0 0 43	24 2 3 3 57	

ACCOUNT *Petty Cash*   ACCOUNT NO. *1120*

DATE		ITEM	POST. REF.	DEBIT	CREDIT	BALANCE DEBIT	BALANCE CREDIT
Jan.	1	Balance	✓			5 0 0 00	

ACCOUNT *Accounts Receivable*   ACCOUNT NO. *1130*

DATE		ITEM	POST. REF.	DEBIT	CREDIT	BALANCE DEBIT	BALANCE CREDIT
Dec.	1	Balance	✓			9 2 2 2 00	
	31		25	8 6 9 2 00		17 9 1 4 00	
	31		25		8 5 8 2 00	9 3 3 2 00	

ACCOUNT *Merchandise Inventory*   ACCOUNT NO. *1140*

DATE		ITEM	POST. REF.	DEBIT	CREDIT	BALANCE DEBIT	BALANCE CREDIT
Jan.	1	Balance	✓			225 4 0 0 00	

ACCOUNT *Supplies—Office*   ACCOUNT NO. *1145*

DATE		ITEM	POST. REF.	DEBIT	CREDIT	BALANCE DEBIT	BALANCE CREDIT
Dec.	1	Balance	✓			4 9 8 0 00	
	3		24	1 6 0 00		5 1 4 0 00	
	9		24	8 6 00		5 2 2 6 00	
	18		25	1 2 4 00		5 3 5 0 00	
	31		25	5 0 00		5 4 0 0 00	

ACCOUNT *Supplies—Store*   ACCOUNT NO. *1150*

DATE		ITEM	POST. REF.	DEBIT	CREDIT	BALANCE DEBIT	BALANCE CREDIT
Dec.	1	Balance	✓			5 1 3 0 00	
	7		24	2 3 0 00		5 3 6 0 00	
	31		25	7 3 00		5 4 3 3 00	
	31		25	3 4 7 00		5 7 8 0 00	

ILLUSTRATION 16-1   General ledger with posting completed (continued)

ACCOUNT *Prepaid Insurance*   ACCOUNT NO. *1160*

DATE	ITEM	POST. REF.	DEBIT	CREDIT	BALANCE DEBIT	BALANCE CREDIT
Dec. 1	Balance	✓			4 8 4 0 00	

ACCOUNT *Accounts Payable*   ACCOUNT NO. *2110*

DATE	ITEM	POST. REF.	DEBIT	CREDIT	BALANCE DEBIT	BALANCE CREDIT
Dec. 1	Balance	✓				15 8 7 0 00
31		25	15 5 4 5 59			3 2 4 41
31		25		10 1 2 7 49		10 4 5 1 90

ACCOUNT *Employee Income Tax Payable*   ACCOUNT NO. *2120*

DATE	ITEM	POST. REF.	DEBIT	CREDIT	BALANCE DEBIT	BALANCE CREDIT
Dec. 1	Balance	✓				3 8 4 00
15		24	3 8 4 00		———	
15		24		1 9 2 00		1 9 2 00
31		25		2 1 0 00		4 0 2 00

ACCOUNT *FICA Tax Payable*   ACCOUNT NO. *2130*

DATE	ITEM	POST. REF.	DEBIT	CREDIT	BALANCE DEBIT	BALANCE CREDIT
Dec. 1	Balance	✓				8 1 7 92
15		24	8 1 7 92		———	
15		24		2 0 4 48		2 0 4 48
15		24		2 0 4 48		4 0 8 96
31		25		2 1 1 60		6 2 0 56
31		25		2 1 1 60		8 3 2 16

ACCOUNT *Sales Tax Payable*   ACCOUNT NO. *2140*

DATE	ITEM	POST. REF.	DEBIT	CREDIT	BALANCE DEBIT	BALANCE CREDIT
Dec. 1	Balance	✓				1 8 9 6 00
15		24	1 8 9 6 00		———	
31		25		1 7 6 0 00		1 7 6 0 00

ILLUSTRATION 16-1   General ledger with posting completed (continued)

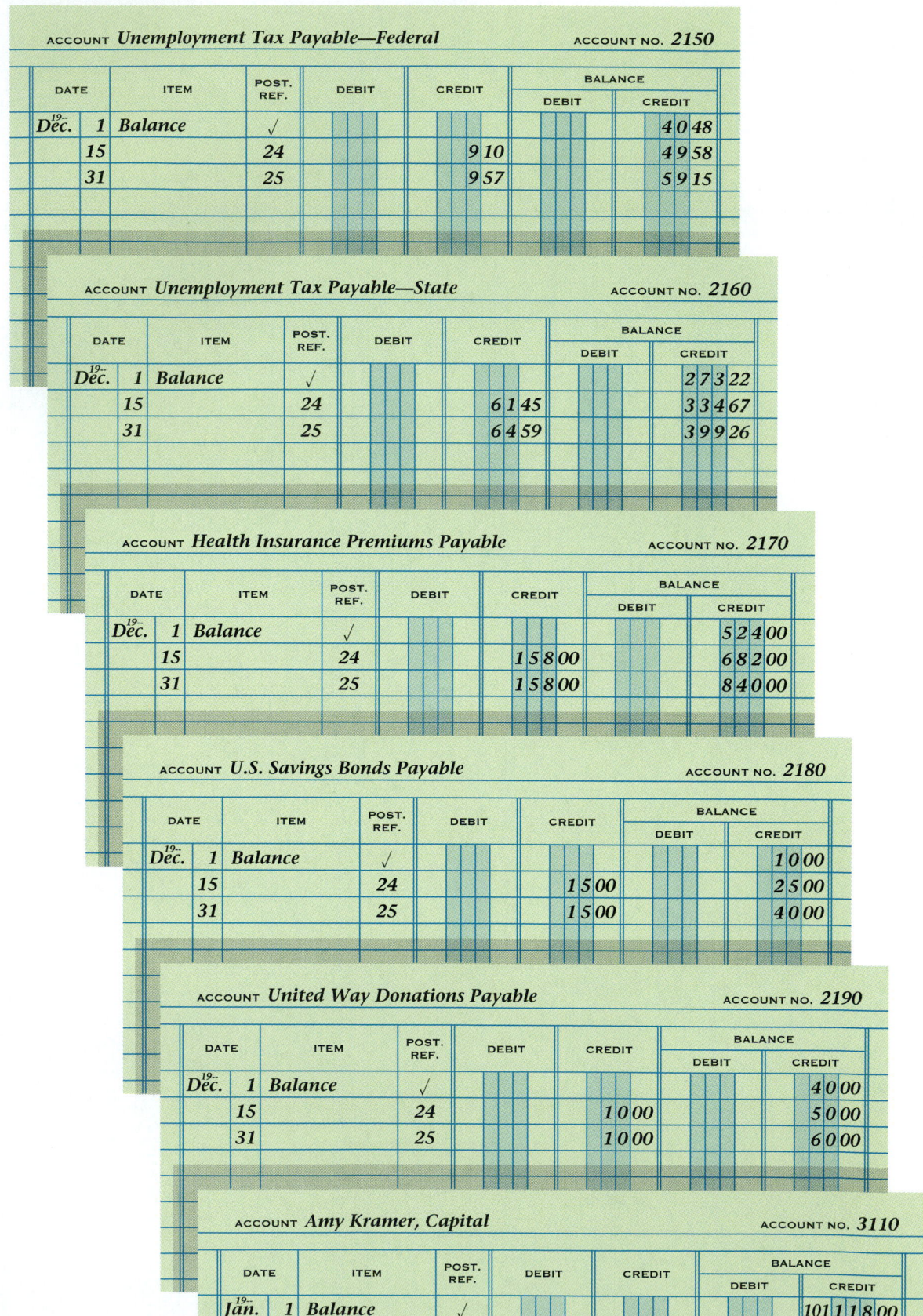

ACCOUNT Unemployment Tax Payable—Federal   ACCOUNT NO. 2150

DATE	ITEM	POST. REF.	DEBIT	CREDIT	BALANCE DEBIT	BALANCE CREDIT
Dec. 19-- 1	Balance	✓				40 48
15		24		9 10		49 58
31		25		9 57		59 15

ACCOUNT Unemployment Tax Payable—State   ACCOUNT NO. 2160

DATE	ITEM	POST. REF.	DEBIT	CREDIT	BALANCE DEBIT	BALANCE CREDIT
Dec. 19-- 1	Balance	✓				273 22
15		24		61 45		334 67
31		25		64 59		399 26

ACCOUNT Health Insurance Premiums Payable   ACCOUNT NO. 2170

DATE	ITEM	POST. REF.	DEBIT	CREDIT	BALANCE DEBIT	BALANCE CREDIT
Dec. 19-- 1	Balance	✓				524 00
15		24		158 00		682 00
31		25		158 00		840 00

ACCOUNT U.S. Savings Bonds Payable   ACCOUNT NO. 2180

DATE	ITEM	POST. REF.	DEBIT	CREDIT	BALANCE DEBIT	BALANCE CREDIT
Dec. 19-- 1	Balance	✓				10 00
15		24		15 00		25 00
31		25		15 00		40 00

ACCOUNT United Way Donations Payable   ACCOUNT NO. 2190

DATE	ITEM	POST. REF.	DEBIT	CREDIT	BALANCE DEBIT	BALANCE CREDIT
Dec. 19-- 1	Balance	✓				40 00
15		24		10 00		50 00
31		25		10 00		60 00

ACCOUNT Amy Kramer, Capital   ACCOUNT NO. 3110

DATE	ITEM	POST. REF.	DEBIT	CREDIT	BALANCE DEBIT	BALANCE CREDIT
Jan. 19-- 1	Balance	✓				101 118 00

ILLUSTRATION 16-1 General ledger with posting completed (continued)

ACCOUNT **Amy Kramer, Drawing**   ACCOUNT NO. **3120**

DATE		ITEM	POST. REF.	DEBIT	CREDIT	BALANCE DEBIT	BALANCE CREDIT
Dec.¹⁹⁻⁻	1	Balance	✓			16 7 0 0 00	
	15		24	1 5 0 0 00		18 2 0 0 00	

ACCOUNT **Dario Mesa, Capital**   ACCOUNT NO. **3130**

DATE		ITEM	POST. REF.	DEBIT	CREDIT	BALANCE DEBIT	BALANCE CREDIT
Jan.¹⁹⁻⁻	1	Balance	✓				101 2 2 8 00

ACCOUNT **Dario Mesa, Drawing**   ACCOUNT NO. **3140**

DATE		ITEM	POST. REF.	DEBIT	CREDIT	BALANCE DEBIT	BALANCE CREDIT
Dec.¹⁹⁻⁻	1	Balance	✓			17 1 0 0 00	
	15		24	1 5 0 0 00		18 6 0 0 00	

ACCOUNT **Income Summary**   ACCOUNT NO. **3150**

DATE	ITEM	POST. REF.	DEBIT	CREDIT	BALANCE DEBIT	BALANCE CREDIT

ACCOUNT **Sales**   ACCOUNT NO. **4110**

DATE		ITEM	POST. REF.	DEBIT	CREDIT	BALANCE DEBIT	BALANCE CREDIT
Dec.¹⁹⁻⁻	1	Balance	✓				323 2 6 6 00
	31		25		29 3 3 4 00		352 6 0 0 00

ACCOUNT **Purchases**   ACCOUNT NO. **5110**

DATE		ITEM	POST. REF.	DEBIT	CREDIT	BALANCE DEBIT	BALANCE CREDIT
Dec.¹⁹⁻⁻	1	Balance	✓			148 1 7 2 51	
	31		25	10 1 2 7 49		158 3 0 0 00	

ACCOUNT **Advertising Expense**   ACCOUNT NO. **6110**

DATE		ITEM	POST. REF.	DEBIT	CREDIT	BALANCE DEBIT	BALANCE CREDIT
Dec.¹⁹⁻⁻	1	Balance	✓			4 8 6 0 00	
	4		24	1 6 5 00		5 0 2 5 00	
	16		25	8 3 00		5 1 0 8 00	
	22		25	3 9 2 00		5 5 0 0 00	

ILLUSTRATION 16-1   General ledger with posting completed (continued)

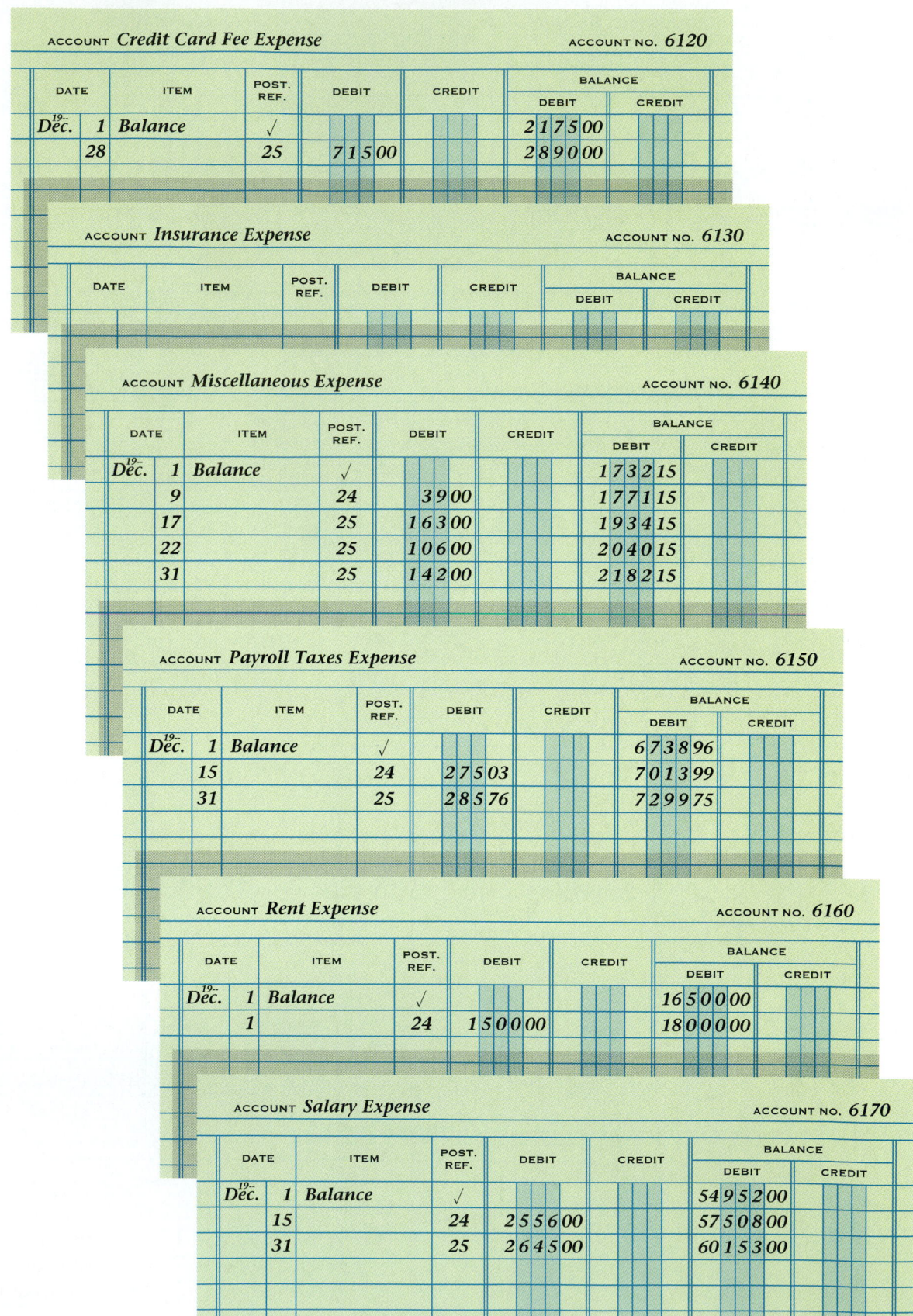

ACCOUNT **Credit Card Fee Expense**   ACCOUNT NO. **6120**

DATE		ITEM	POST. REF.	DEBIT	CREDIT	BALANCE DEBIT	BALANCE CREDIT
Dec.	1	Balance	✓			2 1 7 5 00	
	28		25	7 1 5 00		2 8 9 0 00	

ACCOUNT **Insurance Expense**   ACCOUNT NO. **6130**

DATE	ITEM	POST. REF.	DEBIT	CREDIT	BALANCE DEBIT	BALANCE CREDIT

ACCOUNT **Miscellaneous Expense**   ACCOUNT NO. **6140**

DATE		ITEM	POST. REF.	DEBIT	CREDIT	BALANCE DEBIT	BALANCE CREDIT
Dec.	1	Balance	✓			1 7 3 2 15	
	9		24	3 9 00		1 7 7 1 15	
	17		25	1 6 3 00		1 9 3 4 15	
	22		25	1 0 6 00		2 0 4 0 15	
	31		25	1 4 2 00		2 1 8 2 15	

ACCOUNT **Payroll Taxes Expense**   ACCOUNT NO. **6150**

DATE		ITEM	POST. REF.	DEBIT	CREDIT	BALANCE DEBIT	BALANCE CREDIT
Dec.	1	Balance	✓			6 7 3 8 96	
	15		24	2 7 5 03		7 0 1 3 99	
	31		25	2 8 5 76		7 2 9 9 75	

ACCOUNT **Rent Expense**   ACCOUNT NO. **6160**

DATE		ITEM	POST. REF.	DEBIT	CREDIT	BALANCE DEBIT	BALANCE CREDIT
Dec.	1	Balance	✓			16 5 0 0 00	
	1		24	1 5 0 0 00		18 0 0 0 00	

ACCOUNT **Salary Expense**   ACCOUNT NO. **6170**

DATE		ITEM	POST. REF.	DEBIT	CREDIT	BALANCE DEBIT	BALANCE CREDIT
Dec.	1	Balance	✓			54 9 5 2 00	
	15		24	2 5 5 6 00		57 5 0 8 00	
	31		25	2 6 4 5 00		60 1 5 3 00	

ILLUSTRATION 16-1 General ledger with posting completed (concluded)

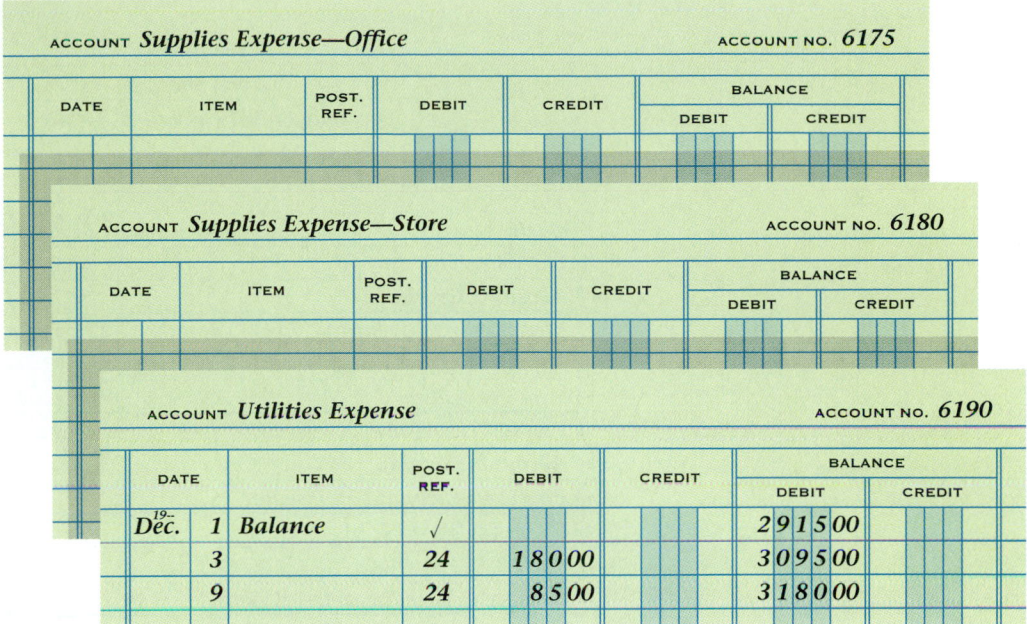

ACCOUNT Supplies Expense—Office					ACCOUNT NO. 6175	
DATE	ITEM	POST. REF.	DEBIT	CREDIT	BALANCE DEBIT	BALANCE CREDIT

ACCOUNT Supplies Expense—Store					ACCOUNT NO. 6180	
DATE	ITEM	POST. REF.	DEBIT	CREDIT	BALANCE DEBIT	BALANCE CREDIT

ACCOUNT Utilities Expense					ACCOUNT NO. 6190	
DATE	ITEM	POST. REF.	DEBIT	CREDIT	BALANCE DEBIT	BALANCE CREDIT
Dec. 1	Balance	✓			2 9 1 5 00	
3		24	1 8 0 00		3 0 9 5 00	
9		24	8 5 00		3 1 8 0 00	

General ledger accounts are listed in the work sheet's Account Title column in the same order in which they appear in the general ledger. All accounts are listed regardless of whether there is a balance or not. Listing all accounts reduces the possibility of overlooking an account that needs to be brought up to date.

PLANNING ADJUSTMENTS ON A WORK SHEET

After posting is completed at the end of a fiscal period, some general ledger accounts, such as the two supplies accounts and the prepaid insurance account, are not up to date. Adjustments for supplies and prepaid insurance are described in Chapter 8. In addition to supplies and prepaid insurance, CarLand needs to adjust the merchandise inventory account. Changes recorded on a work sheet to update general ledger accounts at the end of a fiscal period are known as adjustments.

Adjustments are planned in the Adjustments columns of a work sheet. Adjustments recorded on a work sheet are for planning purposes only. The general ledger account balances are not changed until entries are journalized and posted. Journal entries made to bring general ledger accounts up to date are known as adjusting entries.

Merchandise Inventory Adjustment

The amount of goods on hand is called an **inventory**. The amount of goods on hand for sale to customers is called **merchandise inventory**. The general ledger account in which merchandise inventory is

ILLUSTRATION 16-2   Trial balance on a work sheet

		CarLand Work Sheet For Year Ended December 31, 19--	
		1	**2**
	ACCOUNT TITLE	TRIAL BALANCE	
		DEBIT	CREDIT
1	Cash	24 23 3 57	
2	Petty Cash	5 0 0 00	
3	Accounts Receivable	9 3 3 2 00	
4	Merchandise Inventory	225 40 0 00	
5	Supplies—Office	5 4 0 0 00	
6	Supplies—Store	5 7 8 0 00	
7	Prepaid Insurance	4 8 4 0 00	
8	Accounts Payable		10 4 5 1 90
9	Employee Income Tax Payable		4 0 2 00
10	FICA Tax Payable		8 3 2 16
11	Sales Tax Payable		1 7 6 0 00
12	Unemploy. Tax Payable—Federal		5 9 15
13	Unemploy. Tax Payable—State		3 9 9 26
14	Health Insurance Premiums Payable		8 4 0 00
15	U.S. Savings Bonds Payable		4 0 00
16	United Way Donations Payable		6 0 00
17	Amy Kramer, Capital		101 1 1 8 00
18	Amy Kramer, Drawing	18 2 0 0 00	
19	Dario Mesa, Capital		101 2 2 8 00
20	Dario Mesa, Drawing	18 6 0 0 00	
21	Income Summary		
22	Sales		352 6 0 0 00
23	Purchases	158 3 0 0 00	
24	Advertising Expense	5 5 0 0 00	
25	Credit Card Fee Expense	2 8 9 0 00	
26	Insurance Expense		
27	Miscellaneous Expense	2 1 8 2 15	
28	Payroll Taxes Expense	7 2 9 9 75	
29	Rent Expense	18 0 0 0 00	
30	Salary Expense	60 1 5 3 00	
31	Supplies Expense—Office		
32	Supplies Expense—Store		
33	Utilities Expense	3 1 8 0 00	
34		569 7 9 0 47	569 7 9 0 47
35			

recorded is titled *Merchandise Inventory*. Merchandise Inventory is an asset account with a normal debit balance, as shown in the T account.

Merchandise Inventory	
Debit side Normal balance Increase	Credit side Decrease

Analyzing a Merchandise Inventory Adjustment. CarLand's merchandise inventory account on January 1, the beginning of the fiscal year, has a debit balance of $225,400.00, as shown in the T account.

Merchandise Inventory

Jan. 1 Bal.	225,400.00

The balance of the merchandise inventory account on December 31, the end of the fiscal year, is the same amount, $225,400.00. The January 1 and December 31 balances are the same because no entries have been made in the account during the fiscal year. The changes in inventory resulting from purchases and sales transactions have not been recorded in the merchandise inventory account.

During a fiscal period, the amount of merchandise on hand increases each time merchandise is purchased. However, all purchases are recorded in the purchases account. The amount of merchandise on hand decreases each time merchandise is sold. However, all sales are recorded in the sales account. This procedure makes it easier to quickly determine the total purchases and sales during a fiscal period. The merchandise inventory account balance, therefore, must be adjusted to reflect the changes resulting from purchases and sales during a fiscal period.

The two accounts used to adjust the merchandise inventory are Merchandise Inventory and Income Summary. The T accounts show the merchandise inventory and income summary accounts before the merchandise inventory adjustment is made.

BEFORE ADJUSTMENT

Income Summary

Merchandise Inventory

Jan. 1 Bal.	225,400.00

Before the adjustment, the merchandise inventory account has a January 1 debit balance of $225,400.00. The merchandise inventory account balance, however, is not up to date. The actual count of merchandise on December 31 shows that the inventory is valued at $212,200.00. Therefore, the merchandise inventory account balance must be adjusted to show the current value of merchandise on hand.

Most accounts needing adjustment at the end of a fiscal period have a related temporary account. For example, when the account Supplies is adjusted, Supplies Expense is the related expense account, a temporary account. Merchandise Inventory, however, does not have a related expense account. Therefore, Income Summary, a temporary account, is used to adjust the merchandise inventory account at the end of a fiscal period.

Four questions are asked in analyzing the adjustment for merchandise inventory.

1. What is the balance of Merchandise Inventory?... $225,400.00
2. What should the balance be for this account? .. $212,200.00
3. What must be done to correct the account balance? Decrease .... $ 13,200.00
4. What adjustment is made?
   Debit Income Summary .... $ 13,200.00
   Credit Merchandise Inventory................ $ 13,200.00

The merchandise inventory adjustment is shown in the T accounts.

Income Summary is debited and Merchandise Inventory is credited for $13,200.00. The beginning debit balance of Merchandise Inventory, $225,400.00, *minus* the adjustment credit amount, $13,200.00, *equals* the ending debit balance of Merchandise Inventory, $212,200.00.

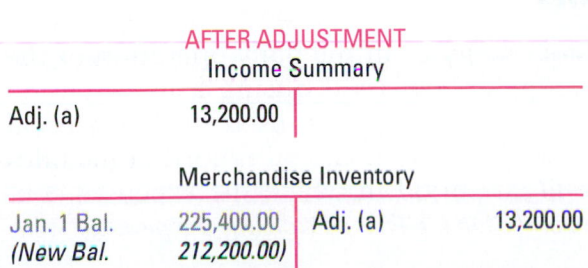

AFTER ADJUSTMENT

Income Summary

Adj. (a)	13,200.00

Merchandise Inventory

Jan. 1 Bal.	225,400.00	Adj. (a)	13,200.00
(New Bal.	212,200.00)		

Recording a Merchandise Inventory Adjustment on a Work Sheet.

The merchandise inventory adjustment is shown on lines 4 and 21 in the work sheet's Adjustments columns in Illustration 16-3.

ILLUSTRATION 16-3   Merchandise inventory adjustment on a work sheet

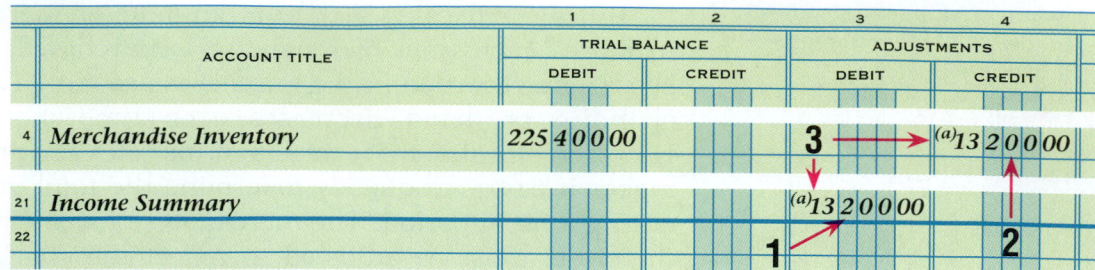

Three steps are used to record CarLand's adjustment for merchandise inventory on a work sheet.

1 Write the debit amount, *$13,200.00*, in the Adjustments Debit column on the line with the account title Income Summary (line 21).

2 Write the credit amount, *$13,200.00*, in the Adjustments Credit column on the line with the account title Merchandise Inventory (line 4).

3 Label the two parts of this adjustment with the small letter a in parentheses, *(a)*.

AFTER ADJUSTMENT

Merchandise Inventory

Jan. 1 Bal.	245,600.00
Adj. (a)	5,200.00
(New Bal.	250,800.00)

Income Summary

	Adj. (a) 5,200.00

If the amount of merchandise inventory on hand is greater than the balance of Merchandise Inventory, opposite entries would be made—debit Merchandise Inventory and credit Income Summary. For example, Kobrin Company's merchandise inventory account on January 1 has a debit balance of $245,600.00. The count of merchandise on December 31 shows that the inventory is valued at $250,800.00. The merchandise on hand is $5,200.00 *greater* than the balance of Merchandise Inventory. This merchandise inventory adjustment is shown in the T accounts.

Merchandise Inventory is debited and Income Summary is credited for $5,200.00.

Supplies Adjustments

CarLand uses office and store supplies in the daily operation of the business. The amount of supplies *not used* during a fiscal period represents an asset. The amount of supplies used during a fiscal period represents an expense. Accurate financial reporting includes recording expenses in the fiscal period in which the expenses contribute to earning revenue. (*CONCEPT: Matching Expenses with Revenue*)

Supplies—Office

Dec. 31 Bal.	5,400.00

BEFORE ADJUSTMENT

Supplies Expense—Office

Supplies—Office

Dec. 31 Bal.	5,400.00

AFTER ADJUSTMENT

Supplies Expense—Office

Adj. (b)	3,940.00

Supplies—Office

Dec. 31 Bal.	5,400.00	Adj. (b)	3,940.00
(New Bal.	1,460.00)		

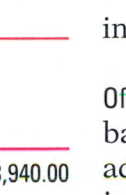

Analyzing an Office Supplies Inventory Adjustment.

CarLand's office supplies account on December 31, the end of the fiscal period, has a debit balance of $5,400.00, as shown in the T account.

The account balance for Supplies—Office, $5,400.00, includes two items. (1) The account balance on January 1. (2) The cost of office supplies bought during the year. The account balance does not reflect the value of any office supplies *used* during the year (an expense). Therefore, the office supplies account balance must be adjusted to show the value of office supplies on hand on December 31. The amount of supplies on hand on December 31 is determined by counting the supplies on hand and calculating the value.

The two accounts used to adjust office supplies are Supplies—Office and Supplies Expense—Office. The T accounts show the two accounts before the adjustment is made.

Before the adjustment, the office supplies account has a December 31 debit balance of $5,400.00. However, office supplies have been used throughout the fiscal period. These changes in office supplies were not recorded in the office supplies account. Therefore, the office supplies account balance is not up to date. The actual count of office supplies on December 31 shows that the value of the office supplies inventory is $1,460.00. The office supplies account balance must be adjusted to show the current value of the office supplies inventory.

Four questions are asked in analyzing the adjustment for office supplies inventory.

1. What is the balance of Supplies—Office? $5,400.00
2. What should the balance be for this account? $1,460.00
3. What must be done to correct the account balance? Decrease $3,940.00
4. What adjustment is made?
   Debit Supplies Expense—Office................. $3,940.00
   Credit Supplies—Office $3,940.00

The office supplies inventory adjustment is shown in the T accounts.

Supplies Expense—Office is debited and Supplies—Office is credited for $3,940.00. The beginning debit balance of Supplies—Office, $5,400.00, *minus* the adjustment credit amount, $3,940.00, *equals* the ending debit balance of Supplies—Office, $1,460.00.

Recording Supplies Inventory Adjustments on a Work Sheet.

CarLand makes a similar adjustment for store supplies. The steps in recording the *two* supplies inventory adjustments are the same as those described for Rugcare in Chapter 8. The *two* supplies inventory adjustments are shown in the Adjustments columns of the work sheet in Illustration 16-4 on page 398. The adjustment for Supplies—Office is labeled *(b)* and is shown on lines 5 and 31. The adjustment for Supplies—Store is labeled *(c)* and is shown on lines 6 and 32.

ILLUSTRATION 16-4 Supplies inventory adjustments on a work sheet

ACCOUNT TITLE	TRIAL BALANCE		ADJUSTMENTS	
	DEBIT	CREDIT	DEBIT	CREDIT
5 Supplies—Office	5 4 0 0 00			(b) 3 9 4 0 00
6 Supplies—Store	5 7 8 0 00			(c) 3 2 6 0 00
31 Supplies Expense—Office			(b) 3 9 4 0 00	
32 Supplies Expense—Store			(c) 3 2 6 0 00	
33				
34				

Prepaid Insurance Adjustment

FYI

The adjustment for prepaid insurance is the amount of insurance used or expired.

Payment for insurance protection is paid in advance. The value of prepaid insurance *not expired* during a fiscal period is an asset. The value of prepaid insurance *expired* during a fiscal period is an expense.

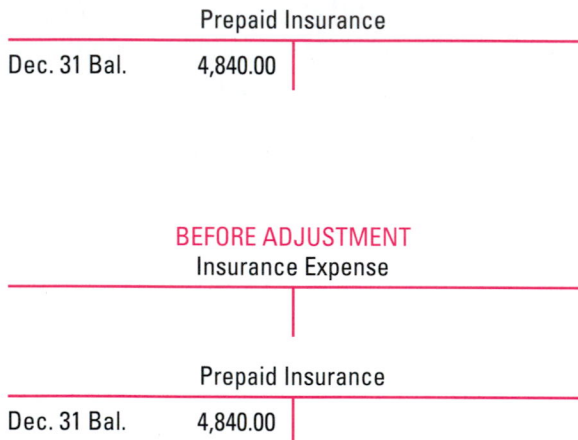

Prepaid Insurance

Dec. 31 Bal.   4,840.00

BEFORE ADJUSTMENT

Insurance Expense

Prepaid Insurance

Dec. 31 Bal.   4,840.00

Analyzing a Prepaid Insurance Adjustment. CarLand's prepaid insurance account on December 31, the end of the fiscal period, has a debit balance of $4,840.00, as shown in the T account.

The account balance for Prepaid Insurance, $4,840.00, includes two items. (1) The account balance on January 1. (2) The cost of insurance premiums paid during the year. The account balance does not reflect the value of the insurance expired during the year (an expense). Therefore, the prepaid insurance account balance must be adjusted to bring the balance up to date. *(CONCEPT: Matching Expenses with Revenue)*

The two accounts used to adjust the prepaid insurance account are Prepaid Insurance and Insurance Expense. The T accounts show the two accounts before the adjustment is made.

Before the adjustment, the prepaid insurance account has a December 31 debit balance of $4,840.00. The account balance, however, is not up to date. The value of the prepaid insurance *not expired* is determined to be $2,200.00. The prepaid insurance account balance must be adjusted to show its current value.

Four questions are asked in analyzing the adjustment for prepaid insurance.

1. What is the balance of Prepaid Insurance?............$4,840.00
2. What should the balance be for this account?.....$2,200.00
3. What must be done to correct the account
    balance? Decrease $2,640.00
4. What adjustment is made?
    Debit Insurance Expense......................................$2,640.00
    Credit Prepaid Insurance.....................................$2,640.00

Audit Your Understanding

1. What is a work sheet?
2. Why is a trial balance prepared?
3. What account must a merchandising business adjust that a service business does not?
4. What accounts are used for the adjustment for merchandise inventory?

AFTER ADJUSTMENT

Insurance Expense

Adj. (d)	2,640.00

Prepaid Insurance

Dec. 31 Bal. (New Bal.	4,840.00 2,200.00)	Adj. (d)	2,640.00

The prepaid insurance adjustment is shown in the T accounts.

Insurance Expense is debited and Prepaid Insurance is credited for $2,640.00. The beginning debit balance of Prepaid Insurance, $4,840.00, *minus* the adjustment credit amount, $2,640.00, *equals* the ending debit balance of Prepaid Insurance, $2,200.00.

Recording a Prepaid Insurance Adjustment on a Work Sheet. The steps in recording the prepaid insurance adjustment on a work sheet are the same as those followed by Rugcare in Chapter 8. The adjustment for Prepaid Insurance is labeled *(d)* and is shown in the Adjustments columns on lines 7 and 26 of the work sheet in Illustration 16-5.

ILLUSTRATION 16-5   Prepaid insurance adjustment on a work sheet

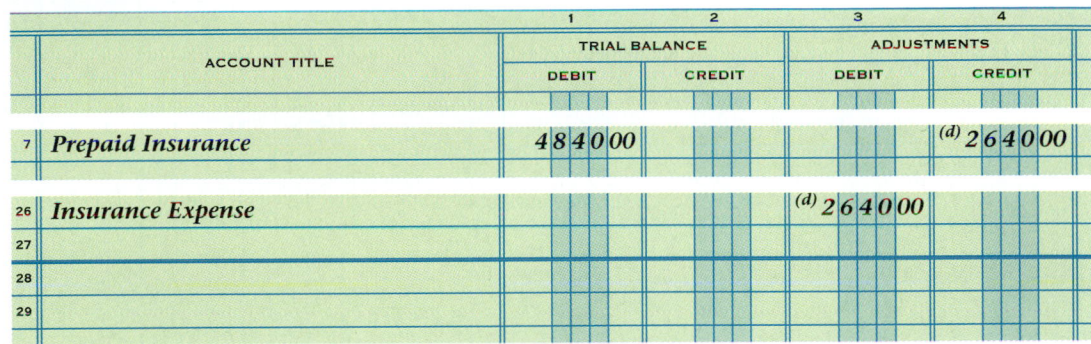

	ACCOUNT TITLE	TRIAL BALANCE		ADJUSTMENTS	
		1 DEBIT	**2** CREDIT	**3** DEBIT	**4** CREDIT
7	*Prepaid Insurance*	4 84 0 00			(d) 2 64 0 00
26	*Insurance Expense*			(d) 2 64 0 00	
27					
28					
29					

COMPLETING A WORK SHEET

CarLand follows the same procedures for completing a work sheet as described for Rugcare in Chapter 8 with the exception of the income summary account. Rugcare sells a service, not merchandise. Therefore, Rugcare has no amount recorded in the income summary account, a related account used to adjust Merchandise Inventory. CarLand sells merchandise. Therefore, the income summary account is used as the related account to adjust Merchandise Inventory. The merchandise inventory adjustment reflects the increases and decreases in the amount of goods on hand resulting from sales and purchases. Therefore, the amount recorded in Income Summary is extended to the work sheet's Income Statement Debit or Credit column. An Income Summary debit amount is extended to the Income Statement Debit column. An Income Summary credit amount is extended to the Income Statement Credit column. CarLand's completed work sheet is shown in Illustration 16-6 on pages 400 and 401.

Illustration 16-7 on page 402 summarizes the steps followed in completing an 8-column work sheet for a merchandising business.

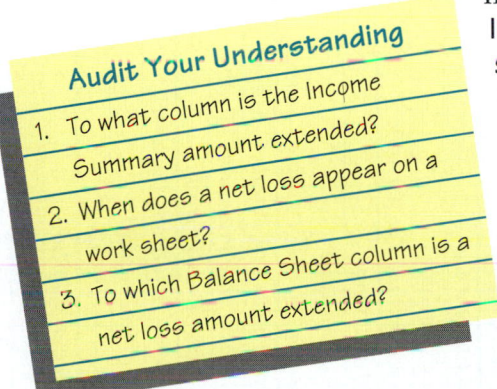

Audit Your Understanding

1. To what column is the Income Summary amount extended?

2. When does a net loss appear on a work sheet?

3. To which Balance Sheet column is a net loss amount extended?

ILLUSTRATION 16-6

Completed work sheet for a merchandising business

CarLand
Work Sheet
For Year Ended December 31, 19--

	TRIAL BALANCE		ADJUSTMENTS		INCOME STATEMENT		BALANCE SHEET	
ACCOUNT TITLE	DEBIT	CREDIT	DEBIT	CREDIT	DEBIT	CREDIT	DEBIT	CREDIT
1 Cash	2423357						2423357	
2 Petty Cash	50000						50000	
3 Accounts Receivable	933200						933200	
4 Merchandise Inventory	22540000			(a)13200000			21220000	
5 Supplies—Office	540000			(b) 394000			146000	
6 Supplies—Store	578000			(c) 326000			252000	
7 Prepaid Insurance	484000			(d) 264000			220000	
8 Accounts Payable		1045190						1045190
9 Employee Income Tax Payable		40200						40200
10 FICA Tax Payable		83216						83216
11 Sales Tax Payable		176000						176000
12 Unemployment Tax Payable—Federal		5915						5915
13 Unemployment Tax Payable—State		39926						39926
14 Health Insurance Premiums Payable		84000						84000
15 U.S. Savings Bonds Payable		4000						4000
16 United Way Donations Payable		6000						6000
17 Amy Kramer, Capital		10111800						10111800
18 Amy Kramer, Drawing	1820000						1820000	
19 Dario Mesa, Capital		10122800						10122800
20 Dario Mesa, Drawing	1860000						1860000	

Work Sheet (partial) — amount columns: Trial Balance (Debit/Credit), Adjustments (Debit/Credit), Income Statement (Debit/Credit), Balance Sheet (Debit/Credit)

#	Account Title	Trial Balance Debit	Trial Balance Credit	Adjustments Debit	Adjustments Credit	Income Statement Debit	Income Statement Credit	Balance Sheet Debit	Balance Sheet Credit
21	*Income Summary*			(a)1320000		1320000			
22	*Sales*		35260000				35260000		
23	Purchases	15830000				15830000			
24	Advertising Expense	550000				550000			
25	Credit Card Fee Expense	289000				289000			
26	Insurance Expense			(a) 264000		264000			
27	Miscellaneous Expense	218215				218215			
28	Payroll Taxes Expense	729975				729975			
29	Rent Expense	1800000				1800000			
30	Salary Expense	6015300				6015300			
31	Supplies Expense—Office			(b) 394000		394000			
32	Supplies Expense—Store			(c) 326000		326000			
33	Utilities Expense	318000				318000			
34		56979047	56979047	2304000	2304000	28054490	35260000	28924557	21719047
35	Net Income					7205510			7205510
36						35260000	35260000	28924557	28924557
37									
38									
39									
40									
41									
42									
43									
44									
45									
46									

SUMMARY ILLUSTRATION 16-7

Summary of an 8-column work sheet for a merchandising business

1 Prepare a trial balance in the Trial Balance columns.

2 Analyze and record adjustments in the Adjustments columns.

3 Extend balance sheet items to the work sheet's Balance Sheet columns.

4 Extend income statement items, including Income Summary, to the work sheet's Income Statement columns.

5 Total the Income Statement and Balance Sheet columns.

6 Calculate the net income or net loss. If the Income Statement Credit column total (revenue) is larger than the Debit column total (costs and expenses), a net income has occurred. If the Income Statement Debit column total (costs and expenses) is larger than the Credit column total (revenue), a net loss has occurred. CarLand's net income is calculated as shown below.

Income Statement Credit Column Total	−	Income Statement Debit Column Total	=	Net Income
$352,600.00	−	$280,544.90	=	$72,055.10

7 Extend the amount of net income or net loss to the Balance Sheet Debit or Credit column. When a net income occurs, the net income amount is extended to the Balance Sheet Credit amount column, as shown on line 35. When a net loss occurs, the net loss amount is extended to the Balance Sheet Debit amount column.

8 Total the four Income Statement and Balance Sheet amount columns.

9 Check that the totals for each pair of columns are in balance. As shown on line 36, the totals for the Income Statement columns, $352,600.00, are the same. The totals for the Balance Sheet columns, $289,245.57, are also the same. CarLand's work sheet is in balance.

	ACCOUNT TITLE	TRIAL BALANCE DEBIT	TRIAL BALANCE CREDIT	ADJUSTMENTS DEBIT	ADJUSTMENTS CREDIT	INCOME STATEMENT DEBIT	INCOME STATEMENT CREDIT	BALANCE SHEET DEBIT	BALANCE SHEET CREDIT	
1	Cash	24 233 57						24 233 57		1
2	Petty Cash	500 00						500 00		2
4	Merchandise Inventory	225 400 00			(a)13 200 00			212 200 00		4
5	Supplies—Office	5 400 00			(b) 3 940 00			1 460 00		5
8	Accounts Payable		10 451 90						10 451 90	8
19	Dario Mesa, Capital		101 228 00						101 228 00	19
20	Dario Mesa, Drawing	18 600 00						18 600 00		20
21	Income Summary			(a)13 200 00		13 200 00				21
22	Sales		352 600 00				352 600 00			22
23	Purchases	158 300 00				158 300 00				23
32	Supplies Expense—Store			(c) 3 260 00		3 260 00				32
33	Utilities Expense	3 180 00				3 180 00				33
34		569 790 47	569 790 47	23 040 00	23 040 00	280 544 90	352 600 00	289 245 57	217 190 47	34
35	Net Income					72 055 10			72 055 10	35
36						352 600 00	352 600 00	289 245 57	289 245 57	36
37										37

A 10-COLUMN WORK SHEET FOR A MERCHANDISING BUSINESS

Some large merchandising businesses *with many accounts to be adjusted* at the end of a fiscal period may use a 10-column work sheet. A 10-column work sheet includes an additional pair of amount columns titled *Adjusted Trial Balance,* as shown in the 10-column work sheet in Illustration 16-8, pages 404 and 405.

After adjustments have been recorded, the balance for each account listed in the Trial Balance columns is extended to the Adjusted Trial Balance columns. The Adjusted Trial Balance columns are then totaled to prove equality of debits and credits after adjustments. Following proof of debits and credits, amounts in the Adjusted Trial Balance columns are extended to the Balance Sheet and Income Statement columns. The Income Statement and Balance Sheet columns are totaled and ruled the same way as on an 8-column work sheet.

■ Bryan Choi ■
ARCHITECTS ASSOCIATED, DAYTON OHIO

Bryan Choi has been an architect all of his professional life. Bryan Choi is also a planner; he sets goals and works toward them. Before he started his own architectural firm, he planned for fifteen years. He started working in a large company, then went to a medium-sized company, and then to a small company, to learn everything there was to know about going into business for yourself.

Choi also knew for a long time that he would eventually start his own business. Therefore he saved diligently for that day. Choi says, "I started small and took very few risks. That's why I succeeded where others had failed." Because he planned for so long, there were none of the surprises that first-time entrepreneurs often encounter, such as underestimating the need for beginning capital.

Students who ask Choi what they need to do to succeed hear, "Learn to manage your time wisely. Set goals, establish good working habits, and continue to work at whatever it is you want to do until you master it."

Choi went to high school and also received his Bachelor's degree in his native Korea. He also earned a Master's degree in the United States, and was for a while an accounting major. He says that the hardest thing about American business that he had to learn was the culture, which was so different from Korea's. He says, "I learned early on to shut my mouth and open my ears. Listen and learn. In fact, that could be another rule for succeeding in business: Listen and learn."

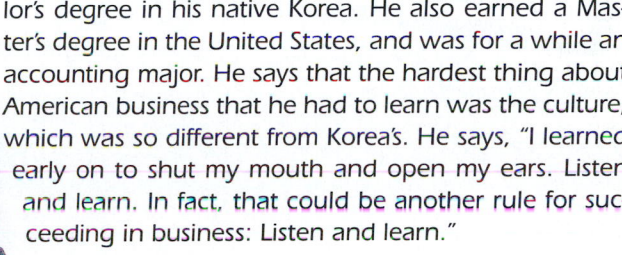

Personal Visions in Business

ILLUSTRATION 16-8   Ten-column work sheet (left page)

CarLand

Work Sheet

For Year Ended December 31, 19--

	ACCOUNT TITLE	TRIAL BALANCE DEBIT	TRIAL BALANCE CREDIT	ADJUSTMENTS DEBIT	ADJUSTMENTS CREDIT	
1	Cash	24 23 3 57				1
2	Petty Cash	5 00 00				2
3	Accounts Receivable	9 33 2 00				3
4	Merchandise Inventory	225 40 0 00			(a)13 20 0 00	4
5	Supplies—Office	5 40 0 00			(b) 3 94 0 00	5
6	Supplies—Store	5 78 0 00			(c) 3 26 0 00	6
7	Prepaid Insurance	4 84 0 00			(d) 2 64 0 00	7
8	Accounts Payable		10 45 1 90			8
9	Employee Income Tax Payable		4 02 00			9
10	FICA Tax Payable		8 32 16			10
11	Sales Tax Payable		1 76 0 00			11
29	Rent Expense	18 00 0 00				29
30	Salary Expense	60 15 3 00				30
31	Supplies Expense—Office			(b) 3 94 0 00		31
32	Supplies Expense—Store			(c) 3 26 0 00		32
33	Utilities Expense	3 18 0 00				33
34		569 79 0 47	569 79 0 47	23 04 0 00	23 04 0 00	34
35	Net Income					35
36						36

Audit Your Understanding

1. List the column heads for a 10-column work sheet.

2. What extra step is required when a 10-column work sheet is prepared instead of an 8-column work sheet?

Any business with adjustments to make at the end of a fiscal period could use either an 8-column or a 10-column work sheet. However, completing two extra amount columns when most of the account balances *are not* adjusted requires extra time and work. Account balances not adjusted must be extended from the Trial Balance columns to the Adjusted Trial Balance columns. Whereas, with an 8-column work sheet, account balances *not* adjusted are extended directly to the Balance Sheet or Income Statement columns. CarLand prefers to use an 8-column work sheet because only four adjustments are needed at the end of each fiscal period.

ILLUSTRATION 16-8 Ten-column work sheet (right page)

	5 ADJUSTED TRIAL BALANCE DEBIT	6 CREDIT	7 INCOME STATEMENT DEBIT	8 CREDIT	9 BALANCE SHEET DEBIT	10 CREDIT	
1	24 233 57				24 233 57		1
2	500 00				500 00		2
3	9 332 00				9 332 00		3
4	212 200 00				212 200 00		4
5	1 460 00				1 460 00		5
6	2 520 00				2 520 00		6
7	2 200 00				2 200 00		7
8		10 451 90				10 451 90	8
9		402 00				402 00	9
10		832 16				832 16	10
11		1 760 00				1 760 00	11
29	18 000 00		18 000 00				29
30	60 153 00		60 153 00				30
31	3 940 00		3 940 00				31
32	3 260 00		3 260 00				32
33	3 180 00		3 180 00				33
34	592 830 47	592 830 47	280 544 90	352 600 00	289 245 57	217 190 47	34
35			72 055 10			72 055 10	35
36			352 600 00	352 600 00	289 245 57	289 245 57	36

What is the meaning of each of the following?

1. **inventory**
2. **merchandise inventory**

1. Why do some general ledger accounts not have any entries posted and, therefore, zero balances at the end of a fiscal period?
2. Why is a work sheet used at the end of a fiscal period?
3. Which accounting concept is being applied when a work sheet is prepared at the end of each fiscal period?
4. Why are all general ledger accounts listed on the Trial Balance columns of a work sheet?
5. Which of CarLand's general ledger accounts need to be brought up to date at the end of a fiscal period?
6. What type of account is Merchandise Inventory, and what is its normal balance?
7. Why are the beginning and ending balances of the merchandise inventory account before adjustments the same?
8. What accounts are affected, and how, by the adjustment for merchandise inventory?
9. What does the amount of supplies not used during a fiscal period represent to a business?
10. Which accounting concept is being applied when expenses are recorded in the same accounting period in which the expenses contribute to earning revenue?
11. What two items are included in CarLand's office supplies account balance before adjustment?
12. What accounts are affected, and how, by the adjustment for office supplies inventory?
13. What two items are included in CarLand's prepaid insurance account balance before adjustment?
14. What accounts are affected, and how, by a prepaid insurance adjustment?
15. What type of merchandising business might use a 10-column work sheet?
16. What two additional amount columns are found on a 10-column work sheet?

CASE 1 After completing a work sheet, Kramer Merchandising Outlet finds that through an oversight, paper bags still in boxes were overlooked in calculating the supplies inventory. The value of the paper bags overlooked is $50.00. Joseph Kramer suggests that the accountant not worry about such a small amount because the oversight does not have any effect on balancing the Income Statement and Balance Sheet columns of the work sheet. Mr. Kramer further indicates that the oversight will be corrected anyway when the store supplies are counted at the end of the next fiscal period. The accountant recommends that the work sheet be re- done to reflect the recalculated supplies inventory. Do you agree with Mr. Kramer or the accountant? Explain your answer.

CASE 2 Quality Shoes paid $1,440.00 for a one-year fire insurance policy. The company prepares an income statement and balance sheet every three months. However, the accountant prepares a prepaid insurance adjustment only at the end of the year. Rachel Delfield, one of the partners in the business, thinks the prepaid insurance should be adjusted every three months. Who is correct? Why?

DRILL 16-D1 Analyzing adjusting entries

TUTORIAL

The following chart contains adjustment information related to the preparation of work sheets for three businesses.

Business	Account Title and Balance		End-of-Fiscal-Period Information	
A	1. Merchandise Inventory.......	$148,000.00	Merchandise inventory.......	$134,000.00
	2. Supplies—Office	5,750.00	Office supplies inventory	4,200.00
	3. Supplies—Store	4,920.00	Store supplies inventory......	3,840.00
	4. Prepaid Insurance..........	1,860.00	Value of prepaid insurance	1,240.00
B	1. Merchandise Inventory.......	$182,000.00	Merchandise inventory.......	$166,000.00
	2. Supplies—Office	4,680.00	Office supplies inventory	3,460.00
	3. Supplies—Store	5,930.00	Store supplies inventory......	4,320.00
	4. Prepaid Insurance..........	2,520.00	Value of prepaid insurance	1,260.00
C	1. Merchandise Inventory.......	$166,500.00	Merchandise inventory.......	$178,000.00
	2. Supplies—Office	5,460.00	Office supplies inventory	4,520.00
	3. Supplies—Store	6,480.00	Store supplies inventory......	4,960.00
	4. Prepaid Insurance..........	2,160.00	Value of prepaid insurance	1,080.00

A form for analyzing transactions is given in the working papers accompanying this textbook.

INSTRUCTIONS:

For each business, analyze the adjustments for merchandise inventory adjustment, office supplies inventory adjustment, store supplies inventory adjustment, and prepaid insurance adjustment. List the accounts affected and the amounts for each of the adjustments. List the account titles in Column 3 and the amounts in either Column 4 or 5. Adjustment 1 for Business A is given as an example in the working papers.

DRILL 16-D2 Extending balance sheet and income statement items

MATHEMATICS

Madison Enterprise's partially completed work sheet is given in the working papers accompanying this textbook.

INSTRUCTIONS:

1. Extend the balance sheet items to the Balance Sheet columns of the work sheet.
2. Extend the income statement items to the Income Statement columns of the work sheet.
3. Complete the work sheet.
   a. Total the Income Statement and Balance Sheet columns.
   b. Calculate and record the net income or net loss.
   c. Total and rule the Income Statement and Balance Sheet columns.

PROBLEM 16-1 Completing a work sheet

Eastside Supply's trial balance as of December 31 of the current year is recorded on a work sheet in the working papers accompanying this textbook.

INSTRUCTIONS:

1. Analyze the following adjustment information, and record the adjustments on the work sheet.

Adjustment Information, December 31

Merchandise inventory...............	$196,610.00
Office supplies inventory............	1,410.00
Store supplies inventory............	2,450.00
Value of prepaid insurance...........	1,935.00

2. Calculate and record the net income or net loss.

3. Complete the work sheet.

PROBLEM 16-2 Completing a work sheet

Jomar's trial balance as of December 31 of the current year is recorded on a work sheet in the working papers accompanying this textbook.

INSTRUCTIONS:

1. Analyze the following adjustment information, and record the adjustments on the work sheet.

Adjustment Information, December 31

Merchandise inventory...............	$246,600.00
Office supplies inventory............	1,790.00
Store supplies inventory............	1,510.00
Value of prepaid insurance...........	2,300.00

2. Calculate and record the net income or net loss.

3. Complete the work sheet.

ENRICHMENT PROBLEMS   EPT(c,d)

MASTERY PROBLEM 16-M Completing a work sheet

APPLICATION

Marine Supply's trial balance as of December 31 of the current year is recorded on a work sheet in the working papers accompanying this textbook.

INSTRUCTIONS:

Use the following adjustment information. Complete the work sheet.

Adjustment Information, December 31

Merchandise inventory...............	$208,600.00
Office supplies inventory............	1,855.00
Store supplies inventory............	2,355.00
Value of prepaid insurance...........	1,575.00

CHALLENGE PROBLEM 16-C Completing a 10-column work sheet

Ultimate Fashion's trial balance as of December 31 of the current year is recorded on a work sheet in the working papers accompanying this textbook.

INSTRUCTIONS:

Use the adjustment information given on the next page. Complete the 10-column work sheet.

Adjustment Information, December 31

Merchandise inventory	$205,370.00
Office supplies inventory	2,160.00
Store supplies inventory	2,195.00
Value of prepaid insurance	1,320.00

Financial Statements for a Partnership

ENABLING PERFORMANCE TASKS

After studying Chapter 17, you will be able to:

a Define accounting terms related to financial statements for a merchandising business organized as a partnership.

b Identify accounting concepts and practices related to financial statements for a merchandising business organized as a partnership.

c Prepare an income statement for a merchandising business organized as a partnership.

d Analyze an income statement using component percentages for a merchandising business organized as a partnership.

e Prepare a distribution of net income statement for a merchandising business organized as a partnership.

f Prepare an owners' equity statement for a merchandising business organized as a partnership.

g Prepare a balance sheet for a merchandising business organized as a partnership.

TERMS PREVIEW

cost of merchandise sold • gross profit on sales • distribution of net income statement • owners' equity statement • supporting schedule

410

The financial activities of a business are recorded in journals and ledgers during a fiscal period. At the end of a fiscal period, a work sheet is prepared to organize and summarize this financial information. The completed work sheet is used to prepare financial statements. Financial statements provide the primary source of information needed by owners and managers to make decisions on the future activity of a business.

All financial information must be reported in order to make sound business decisions. The financial statements should provide information about a business' financial condition, changes in this financial condition, and the progress of operations. *(CONCEPT: Adequate Disclosure)*

Comparing financial condition and progress for more than one fiscal period also helps owners and managers make sound business decisions. Therefore, financial information must be reported the same way from one fiscal period to the next. *(CONCEPT: Consistent Reporting)*

FINANCIAL STATEMENTS FOR A PARTNERSHIP

A business organized as a partnership prepares four financial statements to report financial progress and condition. A partnership prepares an income statement and a balance sheet similar to those used by a proprietorship. A partnership also prepares two additional financial statements. One statement reports the distribution of net income or net loss for each partner. The other statement reports the changes in owners' equity for the fiscal period.

INCOME STATEMENT

An income statement is used to report a business' financial progress. Merchandising businesses report revenue, cost of merchandise sold, gross profit on sales, expenses, and net income or loss. Current and previous income statements can be compared to determine the reasons for increases or decreases in net income. This comparison is helpful in making management decisions about future operations.

Preparing an Income Statement

Information from a completed work sheet is used to prepare an income statement. CarLand's income statement information on a work sheet for the year ended December 31 is shown in Illustration 17-1 on page 412.

The income statement of a merchandising business has three main sections. (1) Revenue section. (2) Cost of merchandise sold section. (3) Expenses section. The total original price of all merchandise sold during a fiscal period is called the **cost of merchandise sold.** *(CONCEPT: Historical Cost)* Cost of merchandise sold is

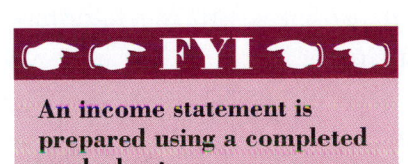

FYI

An income statement is prepared using a completed work sheet.

ILLUSTRATION 17-1 Income statement information on a work sheet

	TRIAL BALANCE		ADJUSTMENTS		INCOME STATEMENT		BALANCE SHEET	
ACCOUNT TITLE	DEBIT	CREDIT	DEBIT	CREDIT	DEBIT	CREDIT	DEBIT	CREDIT
4 Merchandise Inventory	225 400 00			(a)13 200 00			212 200 00	
22 Sales		352 600 00				352 600 00		
23 Purchases	158 300 00				158 300 00			
24 Advertising Expense	5 500 00				5 500 00			
25 Credit Card Fee Expense	2 890 00				2 890 00			
26 Insurance Expense			(d)2 640 00		2 640 00			
27 Miscellaneous Expense	2 182 15				2 182 15			
28 Payroll Taxes Expense	7 299 75				7 299 75			
29 Rent Expense	18 000 00				18 000 00			
30 Salary Expense	60 153 00				60 153 00			
31 Supplies Expense—Office			(b)3 940 00		3 940 00			
32 Supplies Expense—Store			(c)3 260 00		3 260 00			
33 Utilities Expense	3 180 00				3 180 00			
34	569 790 47	569 790 47	23 040 00	23 040 00	280 544 90	352 600 00	289 245 57	217 190 47
35 Net Income					72 055 10			72 055 10
36					352 600 00	352 600 00	289 245 57	289 245 57

sometimes known as cost of goods sold or cost of sales. CarLand's completed income statement is shown in Illustration 17-2.

CarLand uses seven steps in preparing an income statement.

1 Write the income statement heading on three lines.

2 Prepare the revenue section. Use the information from the Income Statement Credit column of the work sheet.

- Write the name of this section, *Revenue:*, at the extreme left of the wide column on the first line.
- Write the title of the revenue account, Sales, on the next line, indented about one centimeter.
- Write the balance of the sales account, *$352,600.00,* in the second amount column. For CarLand, this amount is also the total of the revenue section.

  For businesses with more than one source of revenue, each revenue account title is listed in the wide column. Each account balance is written in the first amount column. The words *Total Revenue* are written in the wide column on the next line below the last revenue account title. The total amount of revenue is written in the second amount column.

3 Prepare the cost of merchandise sold section.

- Write the name of this section, *Cost of Merchandise Sold:*, at the extreme left of the wide column.

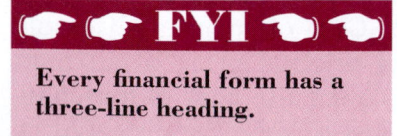

FYI

Every financial form has a three-line heading.

ILLUSTRATION 17-2 Income statement for a merchandising business

CarLand					
Income Statement					
For Year Ended December 31, 19--					

			% OF SALES
Revenue:			
Sales		352 600 00	100.0
Cost of Merchandise Sold:			
Merchandise Inventory, January 1, 19--	225 400 00		
Purchases	158 300 00		
Total Cost of Mdse. Available for Sale	383 700 00		
Less Mdse. Inventory, December 31, 19--	212 200 00		
Cost of Merchandise Sold		171 500 00	48.6
Gross Profit on Sales		181 100 00	51.4
Expenses:			
Advertising Expense	5 500 00		
Credit Card Fee Expense	2 890 00		
Insurance Expense	2 640 00		
Miscellaneous Expense	2 182 15		
Payroll Taxes Expense	7 299 75		
Rent Expense	18 000 00		
Salary Expense	60 153 00		
Supplies Expense—Office	3 940 00		
Supplies Expense—Store	3 260 00		
Utilities Expense	3 180 00		
Total Expenses		109 044 90	30.9
Net Income		72 055 10	20.4

• Indent about one centimeter on the next line, and write the items needed to calculate cost of merchandise sold. Write the amount of each item in the first amount column.

Beginning merchandise inventory, January 1. . . . . . $ 225,400.00
   (This amount is the debit balance of Merchandise Inventory in the Trial Balance Debit column of the work sheet.)

Plus purchases made during the fiscal period. . . . . .   +158,300.00
   (This amount is the debit balance of Purchases in the Income Statement Debit column of the work sheet.)

Equals total cost of merchandise available for sale during the fiscal period. . . . . $ 383,700.00

Less ending merchandise inventory, December 31. .   −212,200.00
   (This amount is the debit balance of Merchandise Inventory in the Balance Sheet Debit column of the work sheet.)

Equals cost of merchandise sold during the fiscal period. . . . . $ 171,500.00

- Indent about one centimeter on the next line, and write the words *Cost of Merchandise Sold.* Write the cost of merchandise sold amount, *$171,500.00*, in the second amount column.

4 Calculate the gross profit on sales. The revenue remaining after cost of merchandise sold has been deducted is called **gross profit on sales.**

- Write the words *Gross Profit on Sales* on the next line at the extreme left of the wide column.
- Write the gross profit on sales amount, *$181,100.00*, in the second amount column. (Total revenue, $352,600.00, *less* cost of merchandise sold, $171,500.00, *equals* gross profit on sales, $181,100.00.)

5 Prepare the expenses section. Use the information from the Income Statement Debit column of the work sheet.

- Write the name of this section, *Expenses:*, at the extreme left of the wide column.
- Indent about one centimeter on the next line, and list the expense account titles in the order in which they appear on the work sheet. Write the amount of each expense account balance in the first amount column.
- Indent about one centimeter, and write the words *Total Expenses* on the next line in the wide column below the last expense account title. Total the individual expense amounts and write the total, *$109,044.90*, in the second amount column on the total line.

6 Calculate the net income.

- Write the words *Net Income* on the next line at the extreme left of the wide column.
- Write the net income amount, *$72,055.10*, in the second amount column on the net income line. (Gross profit on sales, $181,100.00, *less* total expenses, $109,044.90, *equals* net income, $72,055.10.)

    Verify accuracy by comparing the amount of net income calculated on the income statement, $72,055.10, with the amount on the work sheet, $72,055.10. The two amounts must be the same.

7 Rule double lines across both amount columns to show that the income statement has been verified as correct.

Analyzing an Income Statement Showing a Net Income

For a merchandising business, every sales dollar reported on the income statement includes four components. (1) Cost of merchandise sold. (2) Gross profit on sales. (3) Total expenses. (4) Net income. To help make decisions about future operations, CarLand analyzes relationships between these four income statement com-

FYI

Amounts are listed in the first amount column of the financial statement and totaled in the second column. These are amount columns, not debit and credit columns.

INTERNATIONAL TELEPHONE COMMUNICATION

When placing direct telephone or fax calls to the United States and Canada, a simple system is followed. Each telephone number is preceded by a "1," which allows direct dialing without the assistance of an operator. The number is then followed by a three-digit area code and a 7-digit telephone number as shown below:

1	XXX	XXX-XXXX
Direct Dial	Area Code	Telephone Number

However, when calling other countries, the procedure is somewhat more involved. It is necessary to first dial the International Access Code, which is "011." This International Access Code allows you to dial a foreign country direct without the assistance of an operator.

The next set of digits that follows is the country code. Every country in the world has a country code. The country code can be one or more digits.

The country code is then followed by a city code. The city code can also be one or more digits. This is then followed by the telephone number of the receiving party as follows:

011	XX	XX	XXX-XXXX
International Access Code	Country Code	City Code	Local Number

Not all countries have direct dialing. So before making international phone calls, you should check with your local telephone company for information.

The chart below illustrates selected country codes and city codes.

CITY	COUNTRY CODE	CITY CODE
London, England (inner city)	44	71
Frankfurt, Germany	49	69
Keelung, Taiwan	886	32
Barcelona, Spain	34	3
Innsbruck, Austria	43	5222
Helsinki, Finland	358	0
Athens, Greece	30	1
Canberra, Australia	61	62
Cape Town, South Africa	27	21
Oslo, Norway	47	2

ponents and sales. The percentage relationship between one financial statement item and the total that includes that item is known as a component percentage. On an income statement, component percentages are calculated by dividing the amount of each component by the amount of sales. CarLand calculates a component percentage for cost of merchandise sold, gross profit on sales, total expenses, and net income. The relationship between each component and sales is shown in a separate column on the income statement.

Acceptable Component Percentages

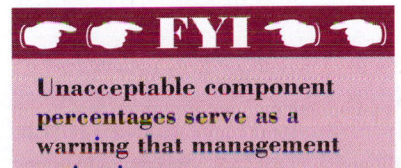

Unacceptable component percentages serve as a warning that management action is necessary.

For a component percentage to be useful, a business must know acceptable percentages. This information is determined by making comparisons with prior fiscal periods as well as with industry standards that are published by industry organizations. Based on these sources, CarLand determines the acceptable component percentages shown in the following table.

Income Statement Items	Acceptable Component Percentages	Actual Component Percentages
Sales	100.0%	100.0%
Cost of merchandise sold	not more than 50.0%	48.6%
Gross profit on sales	not less than 50.0%	51.4%
Total expenses	not more than 32.0%	30.9%
Net income	not less than 18.0%	20.4%

Each percentage represents the amount of each sales dollar that is considered acceptable. For example, CarLand determines that no more than 50 cents, or 50.0%, of each sales dollar should be devoted to cost of merchandise sold.

Cost of Merchandise Sold Component Percentage. The cost of merchandise sold is a major cost. Therefore, this cost must be kept as low as possible. Analysis of CarLand's income statement, Illustration 17-2, shows that the cost of merchandise sold is 48.6% of sales. This component percentage is calculated as shown below.

	Cost of Merchandise Sold	÷	Sales	=	Cost of Merchandise Sold Component Percentage
	$171,500.00	÷	$352,600.00	=	48.6%

The component percentage for cost of merchandise sold, 48.6%, is *less than* the maximum acceptable percentage, 50.0%. Therefore, CarLand's component percentage for cost of merchandise sold is considered acceptable.

Gross Profit on Sales Component Percentage. Gross profit must be large enough to cover total expenses and the desired amount of net income. CarLand determines that at least 50 cents, or 50.0%, of each sales dollar should result in gross profit. Analysis of Car-Land's income statement shows that the component percentage for gross profit on sales is 51.4%. This component percentage is calculated as shown below.

	Gross Profit on Sales	÷	Sales	=	Gross Profit on Sales Component Percentage
	$181,100.00	÷	$352,600.00	=	51.4%

The component percentage for gross profit on sales, 51.4%, is *not less than* the minimum acceptable percentage, 50.0%. Therefore, CarLand's component percentage for gross profit on sales is considered acceptable.

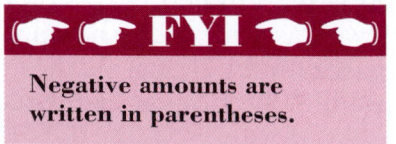

Negative amounts are written in parentheses.

Total Expenses Component Percentage. Total expenses must be less than gross profit on sales to provide a desirable net income. CarLand determines that no more than 32 cents, or 32.0%, of each sales dollar should be devoted to total expenses. Analysis of Car-

Land's income statement shows that the component percentage for total expenses is 30.9%. This component percentage is calculated as shown below.

	Total Expenses	÷	Sales	=	Total Expenses Component Percentage
	$109,044.90	÷	$352,600.00	=	30.9%

The component percentage for total expenses, 30.9%, is *not more than* the maximum acceptable percentage, 32.0%. Therefore, CarLand's component percentage for total expenses is considered acceptable.

Net Income Component Percentage. The component percentage for net income shows the progress being made by a business. CarLand determines that at least 18 cents, or 18.0%, of each sales dollar should result in net income. Analysis of CarLand's income statement shows that the component percentage for net income is 20.4%. This component percentage is calculated as shown below.

	Net Income	÷	Sales	=	Net Income Component Percentage
	$72,055.10	÷	$352,600.00	=	20.4%

The component percentage for net income, 20.4%, is *not less than* the minimum acceptable percentage, 18.0%. Therefore, CarLand's component percentage for net income is considered acceptable.

Analyzing an Income Statement Showing a Net Loss

When a business' total expenses are greater than the gross profit on sales, the difference is known as a net loss. For example, the income statement shown in Illustration 17-3 on page 418 shows a net loss of $3,770.00 for the fiscal period.

Total expenses, $109,120.00, *less* gross profit on sales, $105,350.00, *equals* net loss, $3,770.00. The net loss amount, *$3,770.00*, is written in parentheses in the second amount column on the line with the words *Net Loss*. An amount written in parentheses on a financial statement indicates a negative amount.

Autoworks uses the same acceptable component percentages as CarLand. Analysis of the income statement, Illustration 17-3, indicates unacceptable component percentages. (1) The component percentage for cost of merchandise sold, 53.3%, is *more than* the maximum acceptable component percentage, 50.0%. (2) The component percentage for gross profit on sales, 46.7%, is *less than* the minimum acceptable component percentage, 50.0%. (3) The component percentage for total expenses, 48.4%, is *more than* the maximum acceptable component percentage, 32.0%. (4) Because a net

FYI

The Uniform Partnership Act is a law that governs partnerships in most states.

loss occurred, the component percentage for net income, (1.67%), means that Autoworks lost 1.67 cents on each sales dollar. The net loss amount, $3,770.00, is considered unacceptable.

ILLUSTRATION 17-3   Income statement showing a net loss

Autoworks Income Statement For Year Ended December 31, 19--			% OF SALES
Revenue:			
Sales		225 400 00	100.0
Cost of Merchandise Sold:			
Merchandise Inventory, January 1, 19--	243 200 00		
Purchases	138 900 00		
Total Cost of Mdse. Available for Sale	382 100 00		
Less Mdse. Inventory, December 31, 19--	262 050 00		
Cost of Merchandise Sold		120 050 00	53.3
Gross Profit on Sales		105 350 00	46.7
Expenses:			
Advertising Expense	5 200 00		
Credit Card Fee Expense	3 120 00		
Insurance Expense	1 050 00		
Miscellaneous Expense	2 390 00		
Payroll Taxes Expense	8 340 00		
Rent Expense	14 400 00		
Salary Expense	62 310 00		
Supplies Expense—Office	4 620 00		
Supplies Expense—Store	4 280 00		
Utilities Expense	3 410 00		
Total Expenses		109 120 00	48.4
Net Loss		(3 770 00)	(1.67)

Actions to Correct Unacceptable Component Percentages

The goal of any business is to earn an acceptable net income. When component percentages are not acceptable, regardless of whether a net income or net loss occurred, management action is necessary.

Unacceptable Component Percentage for Gross Profit on Sales. The component percentage for gross profit on sales is directly related to sales revenue and cost of merchandise sold. An unacceptable component percentage for gross profit on sales requires one of three actions. (1) Increase sales revenue. (2) Decrease cost of merchandise sold. (3) Increase sales revenue and also decrease cost of merchandise sold.

Increasing sales revenue while keeping the cost of merchandise sold the same will increase gross profit on sales. To increase sales

revenue, management may consider increasing the markup on merchandise purchased for sale. However, a business must be cautious on the amount of the markup increase. If the increase in markup is too large, a decrease in sales revenue could occur for two reasons. (1) The sales price is beyond what customers are willing to pay. (2) The sales price is higher than what competing businesses charge for the same merchandise.

Decreasing the cost of merchandise sold while keeping the sales revenue the same will also increase gross profit on sales. To decrease cost of merchandise sold, management should review purchasing practices. For example, would purchasing merchandise in larger quantities or from other vendors result in a lower cost?

Combining a small increase in sales revenue and a small decrease in the cost of merchandise sold may also result in an acceptable component percentage for gross profit on sales.

Unacceptable Component Percentage for Total Expenses. Each expense account balance must be reviewed to determine if major increases have occurred. This review should include comparisons with prior fiscal periods as well as with industry standards. Actions must then be taken to reduce any expenses for which major increases have occurred or that are beyond industry standards.

Unacceptable Component Percentage for Net Income. If the component percentages for cost of merchandise sold, gross profit on sales, and total expenses are brought within acceptable ranges, net income will also be acceptable.

DISTRIBUTION OF NET INCOME STATEMENT

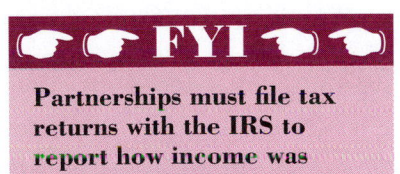

A partnership's net income or net loss may be divided in any way agreed upon by the partners. Amy Kramer and Dario Mesa, partners in CarLand, agreed to share net income or net loss equally.

A partnership distribution of net income or net loss is usually shown on a separate financial statement. A partnership financial statement showing net income or loss distribution to partners is called a **distribution of net income statement.**

Preparing a Distribution of Net Income Statement

The net income, $72,055.10, from the income statement shown in Illustration 17-2 is used to prepare the distribution of net income statement. CarLand's distribution of net income statement is shown in Illustration 17-4 on page 420.

CarLand uses seven steps in preparing a distribution of net income statement.

1 Write the heading of the distribution of net income statement on three lines.

ILLUSTRATION 17-4   Distribution of net income statement for a partnership

CarLand		
Distribution of Net Income Statement		
For Year Ended December 31, 19--		
Amy Kramer		
50.0% of Net Income		36 027 55
Dario Mesa		
50.0% of Net Income		36 027 55
Net Income		72 055 10

2 Write one partner's name, *Amy Kramer,* on the first line at the extreme left of the wide column.

3 Indent about one centimeter on the next line, and write Amy Kramer's share of net income as a percentage, *50.0% of Net Income.* Write Miss Kramer's share of net income, *$36,027.55* (50.0% × $72,055.10), in the amount column on the same line.

4 Write the other partner's name, *Dario Mesa,* on the next line at the extreme left of the wide column.

5 Indent about one centimeter on the next line, and write Dario Mesa's share of net income as a percentage, *50.0% of Net Income.* Write Mr. Mesa's share of net income, *$36,027.55* (50.0% × $72,055.10), in the amount column on the same line.

6 Write the words *Net Income* on the next line at the extreme left of the wide column. Add the distribution of net income for Amy Kramer, $36,027.55, and for Dario Mesa, $36,027.55. Write the total amount, *$72,055.10,* in the amount column. Verify accuracy by comparing the total amount, $72,055.10, with the net income reported on the income statement, $72,055.10. The two amounts must be the same.

7 Rule double lines across the amount column to show that the distribution of net income statement has been verified as correct.

Distribution of Net Income Statement with Unequal Distribution of Earnings

Regardless of how earnings are shared, the steps in preparing a distribution of net income statement are the same. The only difference is the description of how

Audit Your Understanding

1. What is the major difference between the income statement for a merchandising business and a service business?

2. How is the cost of merchandise sold calculated?

3. How can the amount of net income calculated on the income statement be verified?

4. What is the result if total expenses are greater than gross profit on sales?

the earnings are to be shared by the partners. A distribution of net income statement with unequal shares of earnings is shown in Illustration 17-5.

ILLUSTRATION 17-5

Distribution of net income statement with unequal distribution of earnings

Central Sporting Goods		
Distribution of Net Income Statement		
For Year Ended December 31, 19--		
Dolores Demski		
60.0% of Net Income	40 8 0 0 00	
Linda Kemp		
40.0% of Net Income	27 2 0 0 00	
Net Income	68 0 0 0 00	

Dolores Demski and Linda Kemp are partners in a business. Because Mrs. Demski spends more time in the business than Ms. Kemp, the partners agree to share net income or loss unequally. Mrs. Demski gets 60.0% of net income or loss. Ms. Kemp gets 40.0% of net income or loss. With a net income of $68,000.00, Mrs. Demski receives 60.0%, or $40,800.00. Ms. Kemp receives 40.0%, or $27,200.00.

OWNERS' EQUITY STATEMENT

The amount of net income earned is important to business owners. Owners are also interested in changes that occur in owners' equity during a fiscal period. A financial statement that summarizes the changes in owners' equity during a fiscal period is called an **owners' equity statement**. Business owners can review an owners' equity statement to determine if owners' equity is increasing or decreasing and what is causing the change. Three factors can change owners' equity. (1) Additional investments. (2) Withdrawals. (3) Net income or net loss.

Preparing an Owners' Equity Statement

An owners' equity statement shows information about changes during a fiscal period in each partner's capital. Information needed to prepare an owners' equity statement is obtained from the distribution of net income statement and the general ledger capital and drawing accounts. The distribution of net income statement shows each partner's share of net income or net loss. Three kinds of information are obtained from each partner's capital and drawing account. (1) Beginning capital amount. (2) Any additional investments made during the fiscal period. (3) Each partner's withdrawal of assets during the fiscal period.

The general ledger capital and drawing accounts of Amy Kramer and Dario Mesa, partners, are shown in Illustration 17-6 on page 422.

ILLUSTRATION 17-6   Partners' capital and drawing accounts

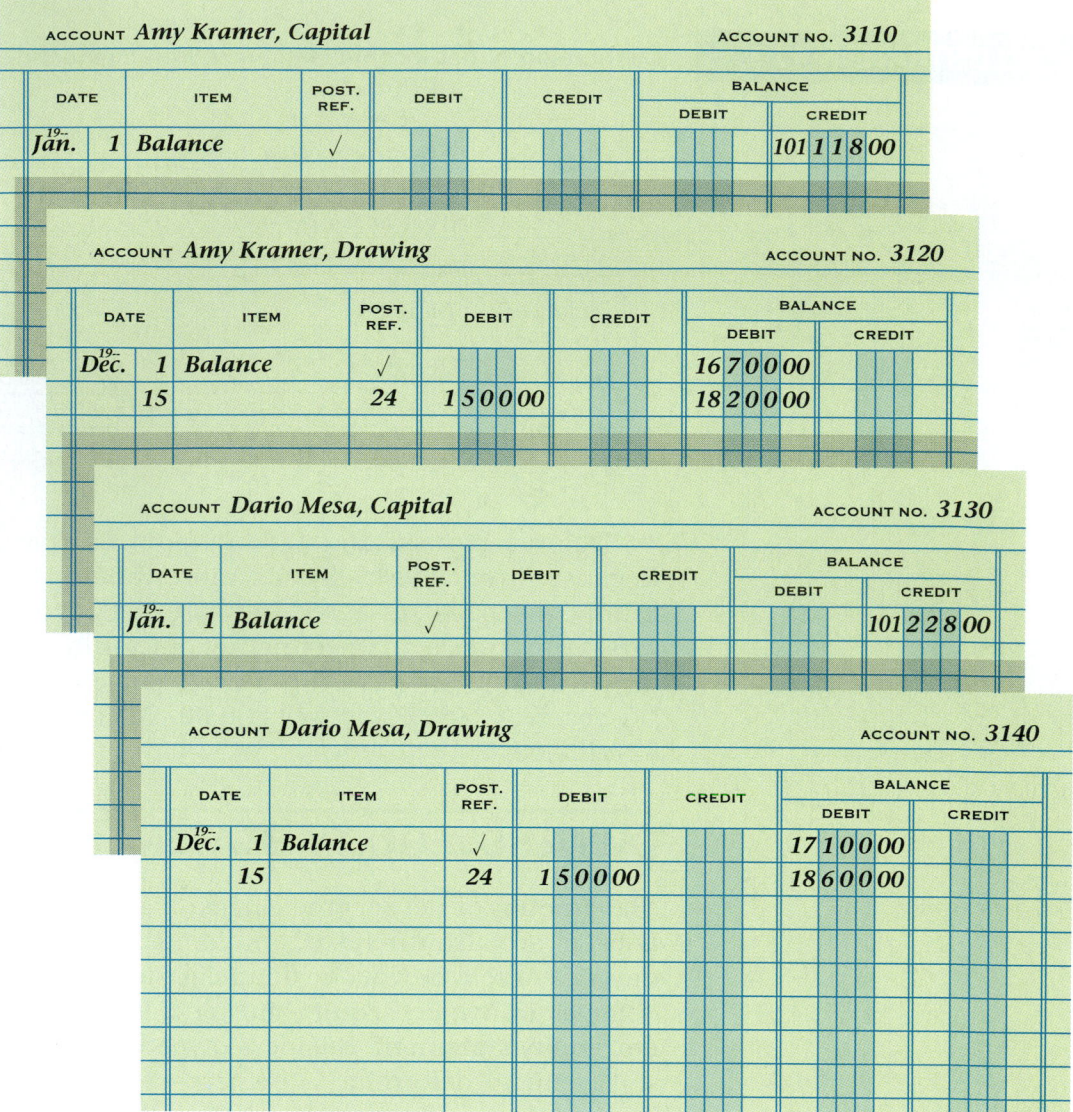

ACCOUNT *Amy Kramer, Capital*   **ACCOUNT NO.** *3110*

DATE	ITEM	POST. REF.	DEBIT	CREDIT	BALANCE DEBIT	BALANCE CREDIT
Jan. 1	Balance	✓				101 1 1 8 00

ACCOUNT *Amy Kramer, Drawing*   **ACCOUNT NO.** *3120*

DATE	ITEM	POST. REF.	DEBIT	CREDIT	BALANCE DEBIT	BALANCE CREDIT
Dec. 1	Balance	✓			16 7 0 0 00	
15		24	1 5 0 0 00		18 2 0 0 00	

ACCOUNT *Dario Mesa, Capital*   **ACCOUNT NO.** *3130*

DATE	ITEM	POST. REF.	DEBIT	CREDIT	BALANCE DEBIT	BALANCE CREDIT
Jan. 1	Balance	✓				101 2 2 8 00

ACCOUNT *Dario Mesa, Drawing*   **ACCOUNT NO.** *3140*

DATE	ITEM	POST. REF.	DEBIT	CREDIT	BALANCE DEBIT	BALANCE CREDIT
Dec. 1	Balance	✓			17 1 0 0 00	
15		24	1 5 0 0 00		18 6 0 0 00	

Neither Amy Kramer nor Dario Mesa invested any additional capital during the year ended December 31. The beginning and ending capital balances, therefore, are the same as recorded in the accounts on January 1. Both partners withdrew cash and merchandise during the year ended December 31.

CarLand's owners' equity statement, prepared for the year ended December 31, is shown in Illustration 17-7.

CarLand uses seven steps in preparing an owners' equity statement.

1 Write the heading of the owners' equity statement on three lines.

2 Write the name, *Amy Kramer*, on the first line at the extreme left of the wide column.

3 Calculate the net increase in capital for Amy Kramer.

ILLUSTRATION 17-7 Owners' equity statement

CarLand Owners' Equity Statement For Year Ended December 31, 19--						
Amy Kramer						
Capital, January 1, 19--				101 1 1 8 00		
Share of Net Income	36 0 2 7 55					
Less Withdrawals	18 2 0 0 00					
Net Increase in Capital			17 8 2 7 55			
Capital, December 31, 19--					118 9 4 5 55	
Dario Mesa						
Capital, January 1, 19--				101 2 2 8 00		
Share of Net Income	36 0 2 7 55					
Less Withdrawals	18 6 0 0 00					
Net Increase in Capital			17 4 2 7 55			
Capital, December 31, 19--					118 6 5 5 55	
Total Owners' Equity, December 31, 19--					237 6 0 1 10	

- Indent about one centimeter on the next line, and write the words *Capital, January 1, 19--*. Write the beginning capital amount, *$101,118.00*, in the second amount column on the same line. (This amount is obtained from Miss Kramer's capital account in the general ledger.)

- Indent about one centimeter on the next line, and write the words *Share of Net Income*. On the same line, write Miss Kramer's share of net income amount, *$36,027.55*, in the first amount column. (This amount is obtained from the distribution of net income statement.)

- Indent about one centimeter on the next line, and write the words *Less Withdrawals*. On the same line, write the withdrawals amount, *$18,200.00*, in the first amount column. (This amount is obtained from Miss Kramer's drawing account in the general ledger.)

- Indent about one centimeter on the next line, and write the words *Net Increase in Capital*. Write the net increase in capital amount, *$17,827.55*, on the same line in the second amount column. (The share of net income, $36,027.55, *less* withdrawals, $18,200.00, *equals* the net increase in capital, $17,827.55.)

- Indent about one centimeter on the next line, and write the words *Capital, December 31, 19--*. Write the December 31 capital amount, *$118,945.55*, on the same line in the third amount column. (The January 1 capital, $101,118.00, *plus* the net increase in capital, $17,827.55, *equals* the December 31 capital, $118,945.55.)

4 Write the name, *Dario Mesa*, on the next line at the extreme left of the wide column.

5 Calculate the net increase in capital for Dario Mesa.

- Indent about one centimeter on the next line, and write the words *Capital, January 1, 19--*. On the same line, write the beginning capital amount, *$101,228.00*, in the second amount column.

- Indent about one centimeter on the next line, and write the words *Share of Net Income*. On the same line, write Mr. Dario's share of net income amount, *$36,027.55*, in the first amount column.

- Indent about one centimeter on the next line, and write the words *Less Withdrawals*. On the same line, write the withdrawals amount, *$18,600.00*, in the first amount column.

- Indent about one centimeter on the next line, and write the words *Net Increase in Capital*. On the same line, write the difference, *$17,427.55*, in the second amount column.

- Indent about one centimeter on the next line, and write the words *Capital, December 31, 19--*. On the same line, write the December 31 capital amount, *$118,655.55*, in the third amount column.

6 Write the words *Total Owners' Equity, December 31, 19--* on the next line at the extreme left of the wide column. On the same line, write the total amount, *$237,601.10*, in the third amount column.

7 Rule double lines across the three amount columns to show that the totals have been verified as correct.

Some businesses include the owners' equity statement information as part of the balance sheet. An example of this method of reporting changes in owner's equity is shown in Illustration 9-13, Chapter 9.

Owners' Equity Statement with an Additional Investment and a Net Loss

On December 31 the capital accounts of Kevin Blaine and David Lamont showed additional investments of $10,000.00 each. Also, the income statement, Illustration 17-3, showed a net loss of $3,770.00. The partners agreed to share net income or net loss equally. The owners' equity statement for Autoworks is shown in Illustration 17-8.

BALANCE SHEET

Some management decisions can best be made after owners have determined the amount of assets, liabilities, and owners' equity. Owners could obtain some of the information needed by inspect-

Autoworks				
Owners' Equity Statement				
For Year Ended December 31, 19--				
Kevin Blaine				
Capital, January 1, 19--	104 3 0 0 00			
Plus Additional Investment	10 0 0 0 00			
Total		114 3 0 0 00		
Share of Net Loss	1 8 8 5 00			
Plus Withdrawals	14 8 0 0 00			
Net Decrease in Capital		16 6 8 5 00		
Capital, December 31, 19--			97 6 1 5 00	
David Lamont				
Capital, January 1, 19--	102 8 0 0 00			
Plus Additional Investment	10 0 0 0 00			
Total		112 8 0 0 00		
Share of Net Loss	1 8 8 5 00			
Plus Withdrawals	15 1 0 0 00			
Net Decrease in Capital		16 9 8 5 00		
Capital, December 31, 19--			95 8 1 5 00	
Total Owners' Equity, December 31, 19--			193 4 3 0 00	

A balance sheet reports a business' financial condition on a specific date.

ing general ledger accounts. The information needed might also be found on a work sheet. However, the information is easier to use when organized and reported on a balance sheet. A balance sheet reports a business' financial condition on a specific date. A balance sheet may be prepared in account form or report form. Rugcare, described in Chapter 9, uses the account form. CarLand uses the report form.

Preparing a Balance Sheet

The information used to prepare a balance sheet is obtained from two sources. (1) The Balance Sheet columns of a work sheet, as shown in Illustration 17-9 on page 426. (2) The owners' equity statement, as shown in Illustration 17-7.

CarLand's completed balance sheet on December 31, the last day of the fiscal year, is shown in Illustration 17-10 on page 427.

CarLand uses six steps in preparing a balance sheet.

1 Write the balance sheet heading on three lines.

2 Prepare the assets section of the balance sheet. Use information from the work sheet given in Illustration 17-9.

- Write the section title, *Assets*, on the first line in the middle of the wide column.

- Beginning on the next line, at the extreme left of the wide column, write the asset account titles in the order in which

| ILLUSTRATION 17-9 | Balance sheet information on a work sheet |

	1	2	3	4	5	6	7	8	
ACCOUNT TITLE	**TRIAL BALANCE**		**ADJUSTMENTS**		**INCOME STATEMENT**		**BALANCE SHEET**		
	DEBIT	CREDIT	DEBIT	CREDIT	DEBIT	CREDIT	DEBIT	CREDIT	
1 Cash	24 233 57						24 233 57		1
2 Petty Cash	500 00						500 00		2
3 Accounts Receivable	9 332 00						9 332 00		3
4 Merchandise Inventory	225 400 00			(a)13 200 00			212 200 00		4
5 Supplies—Office	5 400 00			(b) 3 940 00			1 460 00		5
6 Supplies—Store	5 780 00			(c) 3 260 00			2 520 00		6
7 Prepaid Insurance	4 840 00			(d) 2 640 00			2 200 00		7
8 Accounts Payable		10 451 90						10 451 90	8
9 Employee Income Tax Pay.		402 00						402 00	9
10 FICA Tax Payable		832 16						832 16	10
11 Sales Tax Payable		1 760 00						1 760 00	11
12 Unemploy. Tax Pay.—Fed.		59 15						59 15	12
13 Unemploy. Tax Pay.—State		399 26						399 26	13
14 Health Ins. Premiums Pay.		840 00						840 00	14
15 U.S. Savings Bonds Pay.		40 00						40 00	15
16 United Way Donations Pay.		60 00						60 00	16
17									17
18									18

they appear on the work sheet. Write the balance of each asset account in the first amount column.

- Write the words *Total Assets* on the next line below the last asset account title. Total the individual asset amounts, and write the total assets, *$252,445.57,* on the same line in the second amount column.

3 Prepare the liabilities section of the balance sheet. Use information from the work sheet given in Illustration 17-9.

- Write the section title, *Liabilities,* on the next line in the middle of the wide column.

- Beginning on the next line, at the extreme left of the wide column, write the liability account titles in the order in which they appear on the work sheet. Write the balance of each liability account in the first amount column.

- Write the words *Total Liabilities* on the next line below the last liability account title. Total the individual liability amounts, and write the total liabilities, *$14,844.47,* on the same line in the second amount column.

4 Prepare the owners' equity section of the balance sheet. Use information from the owners' equity statement given in Illustration 17-7.

- Write the section title, *Owners' Equity,* on the next line in the middle of the wide column.

- Write the account title, Amy Kramer, Capital, on the next line at the extreme left of the wide column. On the same line,

ILLUSTRATION 17-10   Balance sheet for a partnership

CarLand		
Balance Sheet		
December 31, 19--		
Assets		
Cash	24 2 33 57	
Petty Cash	5 00 00	
Accounts Receivable	9 33 2 00	
Merchandise Inventory	212 2 0 0 00	
Supplies—Office	1 4 6 0 00	
Supplies—Store	2 5 2 0 00	
Prepaid Insurance	2 2 0 0 00	
Total Assets		252 4 4 5 57
Liabilities		
Accounts Payable	10 4 5 1 90	
Employee Income Tax Payable	4 0 2 00	
FICA Tax Payable	8 3 2 16	
Sales Tax Payable	1 7 6 0 00	
Unemployment Tax Payable—Federal	5 9 15	
Unemployment Tax Payable—State	3 9 9 26	
Health Insurance Premiums Payable	8 4 0 00	
U.S. Savings Bonds Payable	4 0 00	
United Way Donations Payable	6 0 00	
Total Liabilities		14 8 4 4 47
Owners' Equity		
Amy Kramer, Capital	118 9 4 5 55	
Dario Mesa, Capital	118 6 5 5 55	
Total Owners' Equity		237 6 0 1 10
Total Liabilities and Owners' Equity		252 4 4 5 57

write the amount of Amy Kramer's current capital, *$118,945.55*, in the first amount column.

- Write the account title, Dario Mesa, Capital, on the next line at the extreme left of the wide column. On the same line, write the amount of Dario Mesa's current capital, *$118,655.55*, in the first amount column.

- Write the words *Total Owners' Equity* on the next line at the extreme left of the wide column. Add the two capital amounts, and write the total, *$237,601.10*, on the same line in the second amount column.

5 Total the liabilities and owners' equity sections of the balance sheet.

- Write the words *Total Liabilities and Owners' Equity* on the next line at the extreme left of the wide column. Total the

FYI

Verify accuracy of the balance sheet by comparing the total amount of assets and the total amount of liabilities and owner's equity. The two amounts must be the same.

liabilities and owners' equity, and write the total, $252,445.57, on the same line in the second amount column.

Verify accuracy by comparing the total amount of assets and the total amount of liabilities and owners' equity. These two amounts must be the same. The two amounts, $252,445.57, are the same. The balance sheet is assumed to be correct.

6 Rule double lines across both amount columns below Total Assets and below Total Liabilities and Owners' Equity. These two sets of double lines show that the amounts have been verified as correct.

Supporting Schedules for a Balance Sheet

A report prepared to give details about an item on a principal financial statement is called a **supporting schedule**. A supporting schedule is sometimes referred to as a supplementary report or an exhibit.

CarLand prepares two supporting schedules to accompany the balance sheet. The supporting schedules are a schedule of accounts payable and a schedule of accounts receivable. A balance sheet shows only the accounts payable total amount. The account balance for each vendor is not shown. When detailed information is needed, a supporting schedule of accounts payable is prepared showing the balance for each vendor. A balance sheet also shows only the accounts receivable total amount. When information about the account balance for each customer is needed, a supporting schedule of accounts receivable is prepared. CarLand's supporting schedules on December 31 are similar to the supporting schedules for November 30 shown in Chapter 13.

The chart shown in Illustration 17-11 summarizes the financial statements for a partnership.

Summary of financial statements for a partnership

1 Information from the completed work sheet is used to prepare the income statement.

2 Information from the income statement is used to prepare the distribution of net income statement.

3 Information from the distribution of net income statement and the general ledger capital and drawing accounts is used to prepare the owners' equity statement.

4 Information from the completed work sheet and the owners' equity statement is used to prepare the balance sheet.

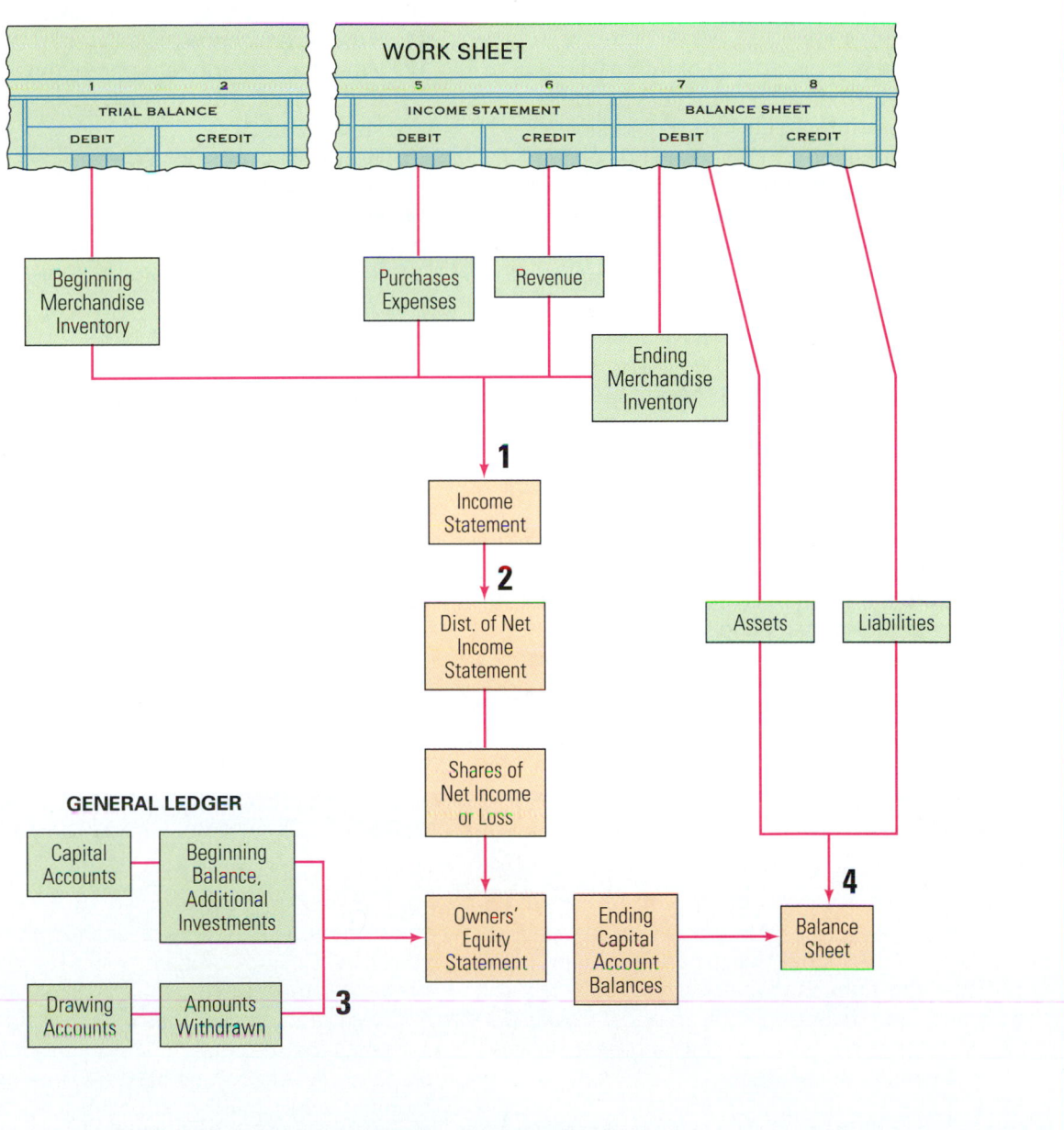

ACCOUNTING TERMS

What is the meaning of each of the following?

1. **cost of merchandise sold**
2. **gross profit on sales**
3. **distribution of net income statement**
4. **owners' equity statement**
5. **supporting schedule**

QUESTIONS FOR INDIVIDUAL STUDY

1. Why is a work sheet prepared at the end of a fiscal period?
2. What is the primary source of information needed by owners and managers to make decisions on future activities of a business?
3. Which accounting concept is being applied when financial statements contain all information necessary for a reader to understand a business' financial condition and progress?
4. Which accounting concept is being applied when accounting principles are applied the same way in preparing financial statements from one fiscal period to the next?
5. Which financial statement reports the financial progress of a business?
6. How may income statements be used to determine reasons for increases or decreases in net income?
7. Where does a business find the information needed to prepare an income statement?
8. What are the three main sections of an income statement for a merchandising business?
9. How is the cost of merchandise sold calculated?
10. How is the gross profit on sales calculated?
11. How is net income calculated?
12. What four component percentages does CarLand calculate to analyze its income statement?
13. How does a business determine acceptable component percentages?
14. How is net loss calculated?
15. What are two reasons why an increase in markup could result in a decrease in sales revenue?
16. Why does a partnership prepare a distribution of net income statement?
17. Why do businesses prepare an owners' equity statement?
18. What three factors can cause changes in owners' equity to occur?
19. Where does a business find the information needed to prepare an owners' equity statement?
20. Which financial statement reports the financial condition of a business?

CASES FOR CRITICAL THINKING

CASE 1 Jun Mori and Victoria Leben, partners, compared their current income statement with their income statement of a year ago. They noted that sales were 15.0% higher than a year ago. They also noted that the total expenses were 20.0% higher than a year ago. What type of analysis should be done to determine whether the increase in expenses is justified?

CASE 2 Rhoda Chalupa and Jonathan Fulton are partners in a paint and decorating store. The store operates on a yearly fiscal period. At the end of each year, an accountant is hired to prepare financial statements. At the end of each month during the year, Mrs. Chalupa prepares a work sheet. The work sheet is prepared to determine if the business made or lost money that month. The accountant suggests that monthly financial statements also be prepared. Mrs. Chalupa believes, however, that the monthly work sheet is sufficient to determine how the business is doing. Do you agree with Mrs. Chalupa or the accountant? Why?

A long written report should contain numerous headings. A heading enables the reader to focus on the primary idea of the next section. An outline is a special document that lists only the headings of a report. By reviewing an outline before and after reading a report, the reader can gain a better understanding of the relationship among the topics being presented.

Each chapter of this textbook is similar to a long report. Headings are used to separate and emphasize major concepts.

INSTRUCTIONS:

Prepare an outline of this chapter.

DRILLS FOR UNDERSTANDING   EPT(c,d,e)

DRILL 17-D1   Calculating the cost of merchandise sold

Information from the work sheets of three businesses is given in the working papers accompanying this textbook.

INSTRUCTIONS:

Calculate the cost of merchandise sold for each business.

DRILL 17-D2   Calculating net income or loss

Information from the work sheets of three businesses is given in the working papers accompanying this textbook.

INSTRUCTIONS:

Calculate the net income or loss for each business.

DRILL 17-D3   Calculating component percentages

Information from the income statements of three businesses is given in the working papers accompanying this textbook.

INSTRUCTIONS:

Calculate component percentages for cost of merchandise sold, gross profit on sales, total expenses, and net income for each business. Round percentage calculations to the nearest 0.1%.

DRILL 17-D4   Calculating the distribution of net income or loss

Information concerning net income or loss distribution for three businesses is given in the working papers accompanying this textbook.

INSTRUCTIONS:

1. Assume that each business earned a net income of $64,000.00. What is the amount of income to be distributed to each partner in each business?
2. Assume that each business had a net loss of $8,000.00. What is the amount of loss to be distributed to each partner in each business?

APPLICATION PROBLEMS   EPT(c,d,e,f,g)

PROBLEM 17-1   Preparing financial statements

The work sheet for Midwest Supply for the year ended December 31 of the current year is provided in the working papers accompanying this textbook.

INSTRUCTIONS:

1. Prepare an income statement. Calculate and record the following component percentages: (a) cost of merchandise sold, (b) gross profit on sales, (c) total expenses, and (d) net income or loss. Round percentage calculations to the nearest 0.1%.
2. Prepare a distribution of net income statement. Net income or loss is to be shared equally.
3. Prepare an owners' equity statement. No additional investments were made.
4. Prepare a balance sheet in report form.

PROBLEM 17-2 Preparing a distribution of net income statement and an owners' equity statement (net income)

Louise Cova and Diane Landon are partners in a merchandising business. The following information was taken from the records on December 31 of the current year.

Partner	Balance of Capital Account January 1	Balance of Drawing Account	Distribution of Net Income
Cova	$138,000.00	$15,260.00	60.0%
Landon	$124,000.00	$16,340.00	40.0%

INSTRUCTIONS:

1. On December 31 the partnership had a net income of $72,400.00. Prepare a distribution of net income statement for the partnership of C.L. Sales.
2. Prepare an owners' equity statement. No additional investments were made.

PROBLEM 17-3 Preparing an owners' equity statement (net loss)

Paul Chapman and Lawrence Jaffa are partners in a merchandising business. The following information was taken from the records on December 31 of the current year.

Partner	Balance of Capital Account	Balance of Drawing Account	Distribution of Net Loss
Chapman	$113,000.00	$12,680.00	$3,400.00
Jaffa	$107,000.00	$13,540.00	$3,400.00

INSTRUCTIONS:

Prepare an owners' equity statement for Riverside Supply. Additional investments made during the year: Paul Chapman, $11,000.00; Lawrence Jaffa, $9,000.00.

ENRICHMENT PROBLEMS   EPT(c,d,e,f,g)

MASTERY PROBLEM 17-M Preparing financial statements

Gallery Furniture prepared the work sheet on the following page for the year ended December 31 of the current year.

INSTRUCTIONS:

1. Prepare an income statement. Calculate and record the following component percentages: (a) cost of merchandise sold, (b) gross profit on sales, (c) total expenses, and (d) net income or loss. Round percentage calculations to the nearest 0.1%.

	Gallery Furniture							

Work Sheet

For Year Ended December 31, 19--

	ACCOUNT TITLE	TRIAL BALANCE		ADJUSTMENTS		INCOME STATEMENT		BALANCE SHEET	
		DEBIT	CREDIT	DEBIT	CREDIT	DEBIT	CREDIT	DEBIT	CREDIT
1	Cash	28792 00						28792 00	
2	Petty Cash	500 00						500 00	
3	Accounts Receivable	12835 00						12835 00	
4	Merchandise Inventory	290600 00			(a)14510 00			276090 00	
5	Supplies—Office	5375 00			(b) 3360 00			2015 00	
6	Supplies—Store	5840 00			(c) 3720 00			2120 00	
7	Prepaid Insurance	5145 00			(d) 2940 00			2205 00	
8	Accounts Payable		9130 00						9130 00
9	Sales Tax Payable		1072 00						1072 00
10	Jennifer Faust, Capital		142960 00						142960 00
11	Jennifer Faust, Drawing	18910 00						18910 00	
12	David Mason, Capital		137450 00						137450 00
13	David Mason, Drawing	18360 00						18360 00	
14	Income Summary			(a)14510 00		14510 00			
15	Sales		257300 00				257300 00		
16	Purchases	129280 00				129280 00			
17	Advertising Expense	5585 00				5585 00			
18	Credit Card Fee Expense	2360 00				2360 00			
19	Insurance Expense			(d) 2940 00		2940 00			
20	Miscellaneous Expense	2640 00				2640 00			
21	Rent Expense	19200 00				19200 00			
22	Supplies Expense—Office			(b) 3360 00		3360 00			
23	Supplies Expense—Store			(c) 3720 00		3720 00			
24	Utilities Expense	2490 00				2490 00			
25		547912 00	547912 00	24530 00	24530 00	186085 00	257300 00	361827 00	290612 00
26	Net Income					71215 00			71215 00
27						257300 00	257300 00	361827 00	361827 00
28									

2. Prepare a distribution of net income statement. Net income or loss is to be shared equally.

3. Prepare an owners' equity statement. No additional investments were made.

4. Prepare a balance sheet in report form.

CHALLENGE PROBLEM 17-C Preparing financial statements (unequal distribution of net income; additional investment)

Gallery Furniture's work sheet is shown in Mastery Problem 17-M.

INSTRUCTIONS:

1. Prepare a distribution of net income statement. The net income is to be shared as follows: Jennifer Faust, 75.0%; David Mason, 25.0%.

2. Prepare an owners' equity statement. Mr. Mason made an additional investment of $15,000.00 during the year. He had a beginning capital of $122,450.00.

18

Recording Adjusting and Closing Entries for a Partnership

ENABLING PERFORMANCE TASKS

After studying Chapter 18, you will be able to:

a Identify accounting concepts and practices related to adjusting and closing entries for a merchandising business organized as a partnership.

b Record adjusting entries for a merchandising business organized as a partnership.

c Record closing entries for a merchandising business organized as a partnership.

d Prepare a post-closing trial balance for a merchandising business organized as a partnership.

General ledger account balances are changed only by posting journal entries. Two types of journal entries change general ledger account balances at the end of a fiscal period. (1) Adjusting entries bring general ledger account balances up to date. (2) Closing entries prepare temporary accounts for the next fiscal period. *(CONCEPT: Matching Expenses with Revenue)* Information needed for journalizing adjusting entries is taken from the Adjustments columns of a work sheet. Information needed for journalizing closing entries is taken from the Income Statement and Balance Sheet columns of a work sheet and a distribution of net income statement.

RECORDING ADJUSTING ENTRIES

Four adjustments in the partial work sheet's Adjustments columns are shown in Illustration 18-1.

ILLUSTRATION 18-1   Partial work sheet showing adjustments

		1	2	3	4
	ACCOUNT TITLE	TRIAL BALANCE		ADJUSTMENTS	
		DEBIT	CREDIT	DEBIT	CREDIT
4	Merchandise Inventory	225 4 0 0 00			(a)13 2 0 0 00
5	Supplies—Office	5 4 0 0 00			(b) 3 9 4 0 00
6	Supplies—Store	5 7 8 0 00			(c) 3 2 6 0 00
7	Prepaid Insurance	4 8 4 0 00			(d) 2 6 4 0 00
21	Income Summary			(a)13 2 0 0 00	
26	Insurance Expense			(d) 2 6 4 0 00	
31	Supplies Expense—Office			(b) 3 9 4 0 00	
32	Supplies Expense—Store			(c) 3 2 6 0 00	
33					

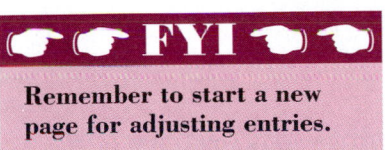

FYI

Remember to start a new page for adjusting entries.

Adjusting entries are recorded on the next journal page following the page on which the last daily transaction for the month is recorded. The adjusting entries are entered in the General Debit and Credit columns of a journal. CarLand's four adjusting entries are recorded in a journal as shown in Illustration 18-2 on page 436.

The heading, *Adjusting Entries*, is written in the middle of the journal's Account Title column. This heading explains all of the adjusting entries that follow. Therefore, indicating a source document is unnecessary. The first adjusting entry is recorded on the first two lines below the heading.

Adjusting Entry for Merchandise Inventory

The debit and credit parts of the merchandise inventory adjustment are identified on the work sheet by the letter (a), Illustration 18-1.

ILLUSTRATION 18-2   Adjusting entries recorded in a journal

PAGE 26

JOURNAL

	DATE		ACCOUNT TITLE	DOC. NO.	POST. REF.	GENERAL DEBIT	GENERAL CREDIT	ACCOUNTS RECEIVABLE DEBIT	ACCOUNTS RECEIVABLE CREDIT	
1			*Adjusting Entries*							1
2	Dec.	31	Income Summary			13 2 0 0 00				2
3			Merchandise Inventory				13 2 0 0 00			3
4		31	Supplies Expense—Office			3 9 4 0 00				4
5			Supplies—Office				3 9 4 0 00			5
6		31	Supplies Expense—Store			3 2 6 0 00				6
7			Supplies—Store				3 2 6 0 00			7
8		31	Insurance Expense			2 6 4 0 00				8
9			Prepaid Insurance				2 6 4 0 00			9

Income Summary

Adj. (a) 13,200.00	

Merchandise Inventory

Bal. 225,400.00	Adj. (a) 13,200.00
(New Bal. 212,200.00)	

The merchandise inventory adjustment includes a debit to Income Summary and a credit to Merchandise Inventory of $13,200.00.

CarLand's adjusting entry for merchandise inventory is shown on lines 2 and 3 of the journal, Illustration 18-2.

The effect of posting the adjusting entry for merchandise inventory is shown in the T accounts.

Adjusting Entry for Office Supplies Inventory

Supplies Expense—Office

Adj. (b) 3,940.00	

Supplies—Office

Bal. 5,400.00	Adj. (b) 3,940.00
(New Bal. 1,460.00)	

The debit and credit parts of the office supplies adjustment are identified on the work sheet by the letter (b), Illustration 18-1. The office supplies inventory adjustment includes a debit to Supplies Expense—Office and a credit to Supplies—Office of $3,940.00.

CarLand's adjusting entry for office supplies inventory is shown on lines 4 and 5 of the journal, Illustration 18-2.

The effect of posting the adjusting entry for office supplies inventory is shown in the T accounts.

Adjusting Entry for Store Supplies Inventory

Supplies Expense—Store

Adj. (c) 3,260.00	

Supplies—Store

Bal. 5,780.00	Adj. (c) 3,260.00
(New Bal. 2,520.00)	

The debit and credit parts of the store supplies adjustment are identified on the work sheet by the letter (c), Illustration 18-1. The store supplies inventory adjustment includes a debit to Supplies Expense—Store and a credit to Supplies—Store of $3,260.00.

CarLand's adjusting entry for store supplies inventory is shown on lines 6 and 7 of the journal, Illustration 18-2.

The effect of posting the adjusting entry for store supplies inventory is shown in the T accounts.

Adjusting Entry for Prepaid Insurance

The debit and credit parts of the prepaid insurance adjustment are identified on the work sheet by the letter (d), Illustration 18-1. The prepaid insurance adjustment includes a debit to Insurance Expense and a credit to Prepaid Insurance of $2,640.00.

CarLand's adjusting entry for prepaid insurance is shown on lines 8 and 9 of the journal, Illustration 18-2.

The effect of posting the adjusting entry for prepaid insurance is shown in the T accounts.

The four adjusting entries for a merchandising business organized as a partnership are summarized in Illustration 18-3.

Audit Your Understanding

1. What accounts are increased from zero balances after adjusting entries for prepaid insurance and merchandise inventory are journalized and posted?

2. When adjusting entries are journalized, why is no source document recorded?

3. What adjusting entry is recorded for a merchandising business that is not recorded for a service business?

Insurance Expense

Adj. (d)	2,640.00

Prepaid Insurance

Bal.	4,840.00	Adj. (d)	2,640.00
(New Bal.	2,200.00)		

SUMMARY ILLUSTRATION 18-3

Summary of adjusting entries for a merchandising business organized as a partnership

Adjusting Entry	JOURNAL		
	Account Title	General	
		Debit	Credit
1. Adjust merchandise inventory (increase in inventory)	Merchandise Inventory	X	
	Income Summary		X
(decrease in inventory)	Income Summary	X	
	Merchandise Inventory		X
2. Adjust office supplies inventory	Supplies Expense—Office	X	
	Supplies—Office		X
3. Adjust store supplies inventory	Supplies Expense—Store	X	
	Supplies—Store		X
4. Adjust prepaid insurance	Insurance Expense	X	
	Prepaid Insurance		X

RECORDING CLOSING ENTRIES

At the end of a fiscal period, the temporary accounts are closed to prepare the general ledger for the next fiscal period. *(CONCEPT: Matching Expenses with Revenue)* To close a temporary account, an amount equal to its balance is recorded on the side opposite the balance. CarLand records four kinds of closing entries.

1 An entry to close income statement accounts with credit balances.

2 An entry to close income statement accounts with debit balances.

3 An entry to record net income or loss and close the income summary account.

4 Entries to close the partners' drawing accounts.

The Income Summary Account

A temporary account is used to summarize the closing entries for revenue, cost, and expenses. The account is titled Income Summary because it is used to summarize information about net income. Income Summary is used only at the end of a fiscal period to help prepare other accounts for a new fiscal period. The income summary account is a unique account because it does not have a normal balance side.

Amounts needed for the closing entries are obtained from the Income Statement and Balance Sheet columns of the work sheet and from the distribution of net income statement.

Closing entries are recorded in the General Debit and Credit columns of a journal. The heading, *Closing Entries*, is written in the middle of the journal's Account Title column on the next line following the last adjusting entry. This heading explains all of the closing entries that follow. Therefore, indicating a source document is unnecessary. The first closing entry is recorded on the first two lines below the heading.

Closing Entry for an Income Statement Account with a Credit Balance

CarLand's work sheet has one income statement account with a credit balance, Sales, as shown in Illustration 18-4. This revenue account has a normal credit balance at the end of a fiscal period. This credit balance must be reduced to zero to prepare the account for the next fiscal period. *(CONCEPT: Matching Expenses with Revenue)* The closing entry for Sales is journalized as shown in Illustration 18-4.

To reduce the balance to zero, Sales is debited for the amount of the balance, $352,600.00. Income Summary is credited for $352,600.00 so that debits equal credits in this entry.

Sales			
Closing	352,600.00	Bal.	352,600.00
		(New Bal. zero)	

Income Summary			
Adj. (mdse. inv.)	13,200.00	Closing	
		(revenue)	352,600.00

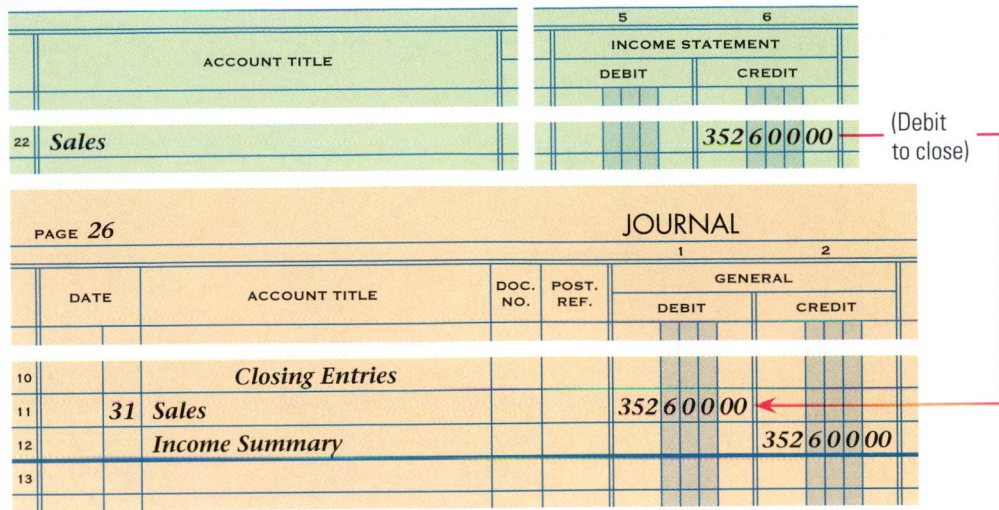

The effect of this closing entry on the general ledger accounts is shown in the T accounts.

The balance of Sales is now zero, and the account is ready for the next fiscal period.

Closing Entry for Income Statement Accounts with Debit Balances

CarLand's work sheet has eleven income statement accounts with debit balances, as shown in Illustration 18-5 on page 440. These eleven accounts are the cost account, Purchases, and the ten expense accounts. The cost and expense accounts have normal debit balances at the end of a fiscal period. These debit balances must be reduced to zero to prepare the accounts for the next fiscal period. (CONCEPT: Matching Expenses with Revenue) To reduce the balances to zero, the cost and expense accounts are credited for the amount of their balances. The account used for the debit of this closing entry is Income Summary. The closing entry for the cost and expense accounts is journalized as shown in Illustration 18-5.

The income summary amount shown on the work sheet, $13,200.00, is the amount of the adjustment for merchandise inventory. Income Summary is used to summarize the amounts that contribute to net income. The adjustment for merchandise inventory contributes to net income. However, Income Summary is not closed as part of this closing entry. Instead, the account is closed with the third closing entry when net income is recorded.

The debit to Income Summary is not entered in the amount column until all cost and expense balances have been journalized and the total amount calculated. The account title and balance of each cost and expense account is written in the Account Title and General Credit columns. After all cost and expense accounts and their

	ACCOUNT TITLE	INCOME STATEMENT	
		5 DEBIT	**6** CREDIT
21	*Income Summary*	13 2 0 0 00	
22	*Sales*		352 6 0 0 00
23	Purchases	158 3 0 0 00	
24	Advertising Expense	5 5 0 0 00	
25	Credit Card Fee Expense	2 8 9 0 00	
26	Insurance Expense	2 6 4 0 00	
27	Miscellaneous Expense	2 1 8 2 15	
28	Payroll Taxes Expense	7 2 9 9 75	
29	Rent Expense	18 0 0 0 00	
30	Salary Expense	60 1 5 3 00	
31	Supplies Expense—Office	3 9 4 0 00	
32	Supplies Expense—Store	3 2 6 0 00	
33	Utilities Expense	3 1 8 0 00	

(Credit to close)

PAGE *26* JOURNAL

	DATE	ACCOUNT TITLE	DOC. NO.	POST. REF.	**1** GENERAL DEBIT	**2** GENERAL CREDIT
13	31	*Income Summary*			267 3 4 4 90	
14		Purchases				158 3 0 0 00
15		Advertising Expense				5 5 0 0 00
16		Credit Card Fee Expense				2 8 9 0 00
17		Insurance Expense				2 6 4 0 00
18		Miscellaneous Expense				2 1 8 2 15
19		Payroll Taxes Expense				7 2 9 9 75
20		Rent Expense				18 0 0 0 00
21		Salary Expense				60 1 5 3 00
22		Supplies Expense—Office				3 9 4 0 00
23		Supplies Expense—Store				3 2 6 0 00
24		Utilities Expense				3 1 8 0 00

balances have been written in the journal, add the credit amounts for this entry. Write the total of the cost and expense accounts, *$267,344.90*, in the General Debit column on the same line as the account title Income Summary.

The effect of this closing entry on the general ledger accounts is shown in the T accounts on the following page.

The cost account, Purchases, and the expense accounts are now closed and have zero balances. Income Summary has three amounts. (1) A debit of $13,200.00, the amount of the merchandise inventory adjustment. (2) A credit of $352,600.00, the amount of the entry to close the revenue account. (3) A debit of $267,344.90, the total amount of the entry to close the cost and expense accounts. The balance of Income Summary is the net income for the fiscal period, $72,055.10.

FYI

When creating a partnership, the partners should write a business plan to outline the purposes and goals of the business.

Income Summary

Adj. (mdse. inv.)	13,200.00	Closing	
Closing (cost and		(revenue)	352,600.00
expenses)	267,344.90	(New Bal.	72,055.10)

Purchases					Rent Expense			
Bal.	158,300.00	Closing	158,300.00		Bal.	18,000.00	Closing	18,000.00
(New Bal. zero)					(New Bal. zero)			

Advertising Expense					Salary Expense			
Bal.	5,500.00	Closing	5,500.00		Bal.	60,153.00	Closing	60,153.00
(New Bal. zero)					(New Bal. zero)			

Credit Card Fee Expense					Supplies Expense—Office			
Bal.	2,890.00	Closing	2,890.00		Bal.	3,940.00	Closing	3,940.00
(New Bal. zero)					(New Bal. zero)			

Insurance Expense					Supplies Expense—Store			
Bal.	2,640.00	Closing	2,640.00		Bal.	3,260.00	Closing	3,260.00
(New Bal. zero)					(New Bal. zero)			

Miscellaneous Expense					Utilities Expense			
Bal.	2,182.15	Closing	2,182.15		Bal.	3,180.00	Closing	3,180.00
(New Bal. zero)					(New Bal. zero)			

Payroll Taxes Expense			
Bal.	7,299.75	Closing	7,299.75
(New Bal. zero)			

Closing Entry to Record Net Income or Loss and Close the Income Summary Account

Net income increases the partners' equity and, therefore, must be credited to the partners' capital accounts. The share of the net income to be recorded for each partner is shown on the distribution of net income statement. The balance of the temporary account Income Summary must be reduced to zero to prepare the account for the next fiscal period. The distribution of net income statement and the closing entry to record net income and close Income Summary are shown in Illustration 18-6 on page 442.

The effect of this closing entry on the general ledger accounts is shown in the T accounts.

The credits to the two partners' capital accounts, $36,027.55, record the partners' share of the net income. The debit to the income summary account, $72,055.10, reduces the account balance to zero and prepares the account for the next fiscal period.

If the business has a net loss, the partners' capital accounts are debited for their share of the net loss. Income Summary is credited for the total net loss.

Income Summary

Adj. (mdse. inv.)	13,200.00	Closing	
Closing (cost and		(revenue)	352,600.00
expenses)	267,344.90		
Closing			
(net income)	72,055.10	(New Bal. zero)	

Amy Kramer, Capital

		Bal.	101,118.00
		Closing	
		(net income)	36,027.55

Dario Mesa, Capital

		Bal.	101,228.00
		Closing	
		(net income)	36,027.55

CarLand
Distribution of Net Income Statement
For Year Ended December 31, 19--

Amy Kramer	
50% share of net income	36 0 2 7 55
Dario Mesa	
50% share of net income	36 0 2 7 55
Net Income	72 0 5 5 10

(Record net income in capital accounts)

(Close Income Summary)

PAGE 26 — JOURNAL

	DATE	ACCOUNT TITLE	DOC. NO.	POST. REF.	GENERAL DEBIT	GENERAL CREDIT
25	31	*Income Summary*			72 0 5 5 10	
26		*Amy Kramer, Capital*				36 0 2 7 55
27		*Dario Mesa, Capital*				36 0 2 7 55
28						
29						
30						

Closing Entries for the Partners' Drawing Accounts

Amy Kramer, Capital

Closing (drawing)	18,200.00	Bal.	101,118.00
		Closing (net income)	36,027.55
		(New Bal.	*118,945.55)*

Amy Kramer, Drawing

Bal.	18,200.00	Closing	18,200.00
(New Bal. zero)			

Dario Mesa, Capital

Closing (drawing)	18,600.00	Bal.	101,228.00
		Closing (net income)	36,027.55
		(New Bal.	*118,655.55)*

Dario Mesa, Drawing

Bal.	18,600.00	Closing	18,600.00
(New Bal. zero)			

The partners' drawing accounts are temporary accounts and must begin each fiscal period with zero balances. Because withdrawals are neither a revenue, cost, nor expense, the drawing accounts are not closed through Income Summary. The drawing account balances are closed directly to the partners' capital accounts.

A partial work sheet and the closing entries for the partners' drawing accounts are shown in Illustration 18-7. The closing entry is on lines 28-31 of the journal.

The credits to Amy Kramer, Drawing and Dario Mesa, Drawing reduce the account balances to zero. The accounts are prepared for the next fiscal period. The debits to Amy Kramer, Capital and Dario Mesa, Capital reduce the balances of these accounts by the amount of the partners' withdrawals during the fiscal period.

The effect of these closing entries on the general ledger accounts is shown in the T accounts.

After the closing entry for the partners' drawing accounts, the balances of the partners' capital accounts are the same as reported in the owners' equity section of the balance sheet, Illustration 18-8 on page 444.

ILLUSTRATION 18-7   Closing entries for the partners' drawing accounts

	ACCOUNT TITLE		7	8
			BALANCE SHEET	
			DEBIT	CREDIT
17	Amy Kramer, Capital			101 1 1 8 00
18	Amy Kramer, Drawing		18 2 0 0 00	
19	Dario Mesa, Capital			101 2 2 8 00
20	Dario Mesa, Drawing		18 6 0 0 00	

(Credit to close)

PAGE 26 — **JOURNAL**

	DATE	ACCOUNT TITLE	DOC. NO.	POST. REF.	1 GENERAL DEBIT	2 GENERAL CREDIT
28	31	Amy Kramer, Capital			18 2 0 0 00	
29		Amy Kramer, Drawing				18 2 0 0 00
30	31	Dario Mesa, Capital			18 6 0 0 00	
31		Dario Mesa, Drawing				18 6 0 0 00
32						
33						

■ Judy Sims ■
SOFTWARE SPECTRUM, GARLAND, TEXAS

Judy Sims chairs the Board of Directors and is Chief Executive Officer of Software Spectrum Inc., a company she co-founded in 1983. Software Spectrum is a leading national reseller of microcomputer software and a provider of technical services to large corporations.

Sims majored in accounting at Texas Tech University and worked as a C.P.A. for eleven years for national accounting firms. She advanced to the position of Audit Partner, and provided small and larger corporations with audit services. In 1983, she and two partners pooled $40,000 of personal funds and started Software Spectrum.

"The biggest lesson we learned early was to listen to the customer and quickly make changes in response to their needs," says Sims. "We started as a retail store selling education and entertainment software. But in the first six weeks, the cash register hardly ever rang. We then decided to focus on selling business software to corporations. These corporate customers wanted their software delivered and they wanted to buy it on account. So we changed our policies immediately."

Sims's advice to students is to set goals. She says that you should not just think about goals but actually write them down on paper and review them frequently. "The great thing about our country," says Sims, "is that there are only self-imposed limitations. Don't limit yourself—set high goals."

Sims reports that when the company's focus changed from retail to corporate software sales, they gave up their retail location in a shopping center. That store is now occupied by a business named "Positively Magic." Sims says that that is appropriate because "that initial location was positively magic for us—it was the launching pad for what has grown into a $219 million company."

Personal Visions in Business

ILLUSTRATION 18-8 Owner's equity section of a balance sheet

CarLand
Balance Sheet
December 31, 19--

Owners' Equity		
Amy Kramer, Capital	118 945 55	
Dario Mesa, Capital	118 655 55	
Total Owners' Equity		237 601 10
Total Liabilities and Owners' Equity		252 445 57

CarLand's closing entries recorded in a journal are shown in Illustration 18-9.

ILLUSTRATION 18-9 Closing entries for a partnership recorded in a journal

PAGE 26

JOURNAL

	DATE	ACCOUNT TITLE	DOC. NO.	POST. REF.	GENERAL DEBIT	GENERAL CREDIT	ACCOUNTS RECEIVABLE DEBIT	ACCOUNTS RECEIVABLE CREDIT	
10		*Closing Entries*							10
11	31	Sales			352 600 00				11
12		Income Summary				352 600 00			12
13	31	Income Summary			267 344 90				13
14		Purchases				158 300 00			14
15		Advertising Expense				5 500 00			15
16		Credit Card Fee Expense				2 890 00			16
17		Insurance Expense				2 640 00			17
18		Miscellaneous Expense				2 182 15			18
19		Payroll Taxes Expense				7 299 75			19
20		Rent Expense				18 000 00			20
21		Salary Expense				60 153 00			21
22		Supplies Expense—Office				3 940 00			22
23		Supplies Expense—Store				3 260 00			23
24		Utilities Expense				3 180 00			24
25	31	Income Summary			72 055 10				25
26		Amy Kramer, Capital				36 027 55			26
27		Dario Mesa, Capital				36 027 55			27
28	31	Amy Kramer, Capital			18 200 00				28
29		Amy Kramer, Drawing				18 200 00			29
30	31	Dario Mesa, Capital			18 600 00				30
31		Dario Mesa, Drawing				18 600 00			31

The closing entries for a merchandising business organized as a partnership are summarized in Illustration 18-10.

Summary of closing entries

Closing Entry	JOURNAL		
	Account Title	General	
		Debit	Credit
1. Transfers income statement accounts with credit balances to Income Summary	Revenue account Income Summary	X	X
2. Transfers income statement accounts with debit balances to Income Summary	Income Summary Cost and expense accounts	X	X
3. Transfers net income or loss to partners' capital accounts and closes Income Summary	Income Summary Partners' capital accounts (net income)	X	X
	Partners' capital accounts Income Summary (net loss)	X	X
4. Transfers partners' drawing account balances to partners' capital accounts	Partners' capital accounts Partners' drawing accounts	X	X

CHECKING A GENERAL LEDGER'S ACCURACY AFTER POSTING ADJUSTING AND CLOSING ENTRIES

CarLand's 4-column general ledger account form has separate Balance Debit and Balance Credit columns. Each time an entry is posted to a general ledger account, the account balance is calculated. The balance is then recorded in the appropriate balance column. Each general ledger account shows its current balance at all times. When an account is closed, a short line is drawn in both the Balance Debit and Credit columns. The ending balance for one fiscal period is the beginning balance for the next fiscal period.

Completed General Ledger

CarLand's completed general ledger after adjusting and closing entries are posted is shown in Illustration 18-11 on pages 446 through 451.

Balance sheet accounts (asset, liability, and capital accounts) have up-to-date balances to begin the new fiscal period. Balances in the balance sheet accounts agree with the amounts on the balance sheet, Illustration 17-10, Chapter 17. General ledger account balances on

December 31 of one year are the beginning balances for January 1 of the next year.

Income statement accounts (revenue, cost, and expense accounts) have zero balances to begin the new fiscal period. *(CONCEPT: Matching Expenses with Revenue)*

ILLUSTRATION 18-11   General ledger after adjusting and closing entries are posted

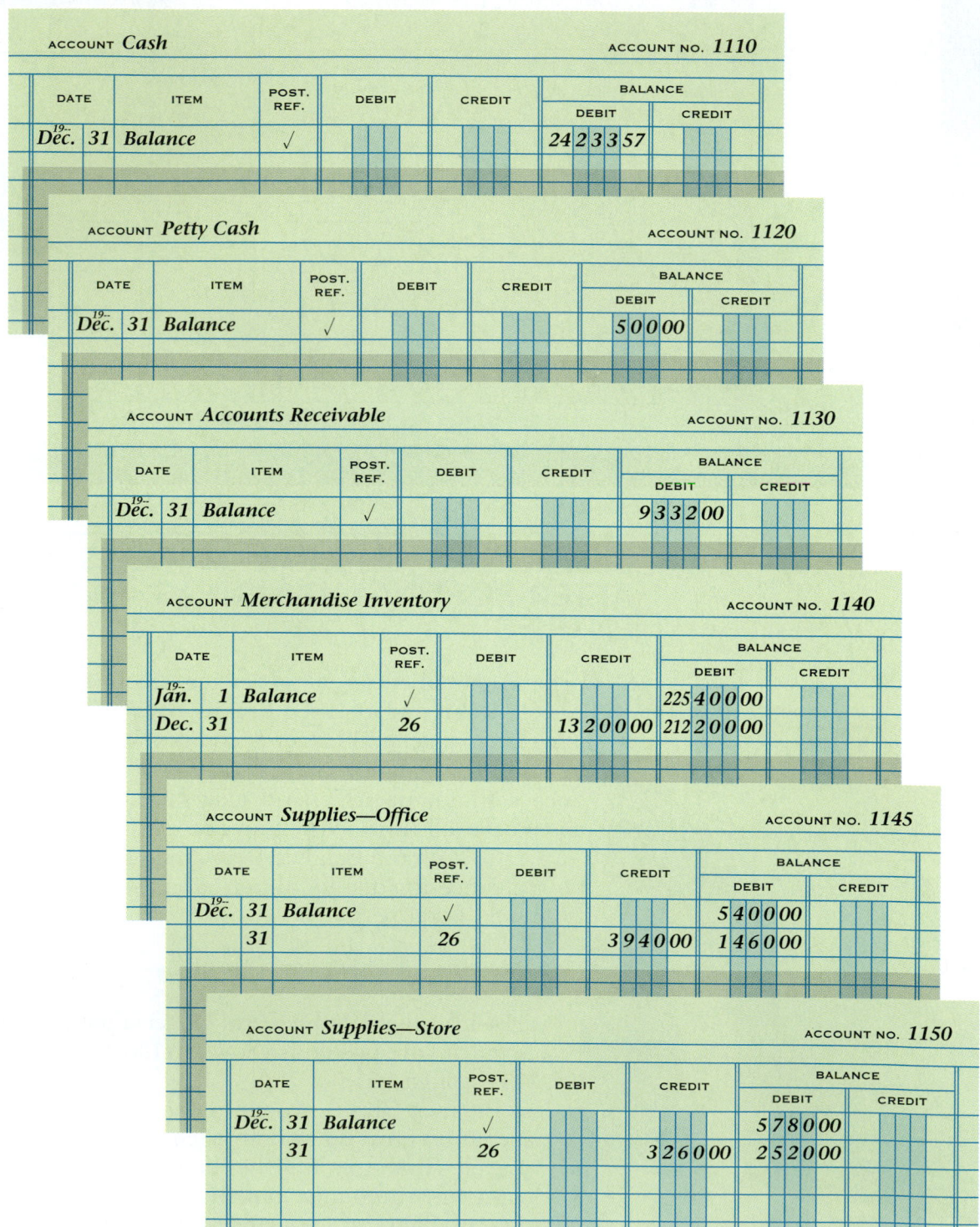

ACCOUNT **Cash**   ACCOUNT NO. **1110**

DATE	ITEM	POST. REF.	DEBIT	CREDIT	BALANCE DEBIT	BALANCE CREDIT
Dec. 31	Balance	✓			24 2 3 3 57	

ACCOUNT **Petty Cash**   ACCOUNT NO. **1120**

DATE	ITEM	POST. REF.	DEBIT	CREDIT	BALANCE DEBIT	BALANCE CREDIT
Dec. 31	Balance	✓			5 0 0 00	

ACCOUNT **Accounts Receivable**   ACCOUNT NO. **1130**

DATE	ITEM	POST. REF.	DEBIT	CREDIT	BALANCE DEBIT	BALANCE CREDIT
Dec. 31	Balance	✓			9 3 3 2 00	

ACCOUNT **Merchandise Inventory**   ACCOUNT NO. **1140**

DATE	ITEM	POST. REF.	DEBIT	CREDIT	BALANCE DEBIT	BALANCE CREDIT
Jan. 1	Balance	✓			225 4 0 0 00	
Dec. 31		26		13 2 0 0 00	212 2 0 0 00	

ACCOUNT **Supplies—Office**   ACCOUNT NO. **1145**

DATE	ITEM	POST. REF.	DEBIT	CREDIT	BALANCE DEBIT	BALANCE CREDIT
Dec. 31	Balance	✓			5 4 0 0 00	
31		26		3 9 4 0 00	1 4 6 0 00	

ACCOUNT **Supplies—Store**   ACCOUNT NO. **1150**

DATE	ITEM	POST. REF.	DEBIT	CREDIT	BALANCE DEBIT	BALANCE CREDIT
Dec. 31	Balance	✓			5 7 8 0 00	
31		26		3 2 6 0 00	2 5 2 0 00	

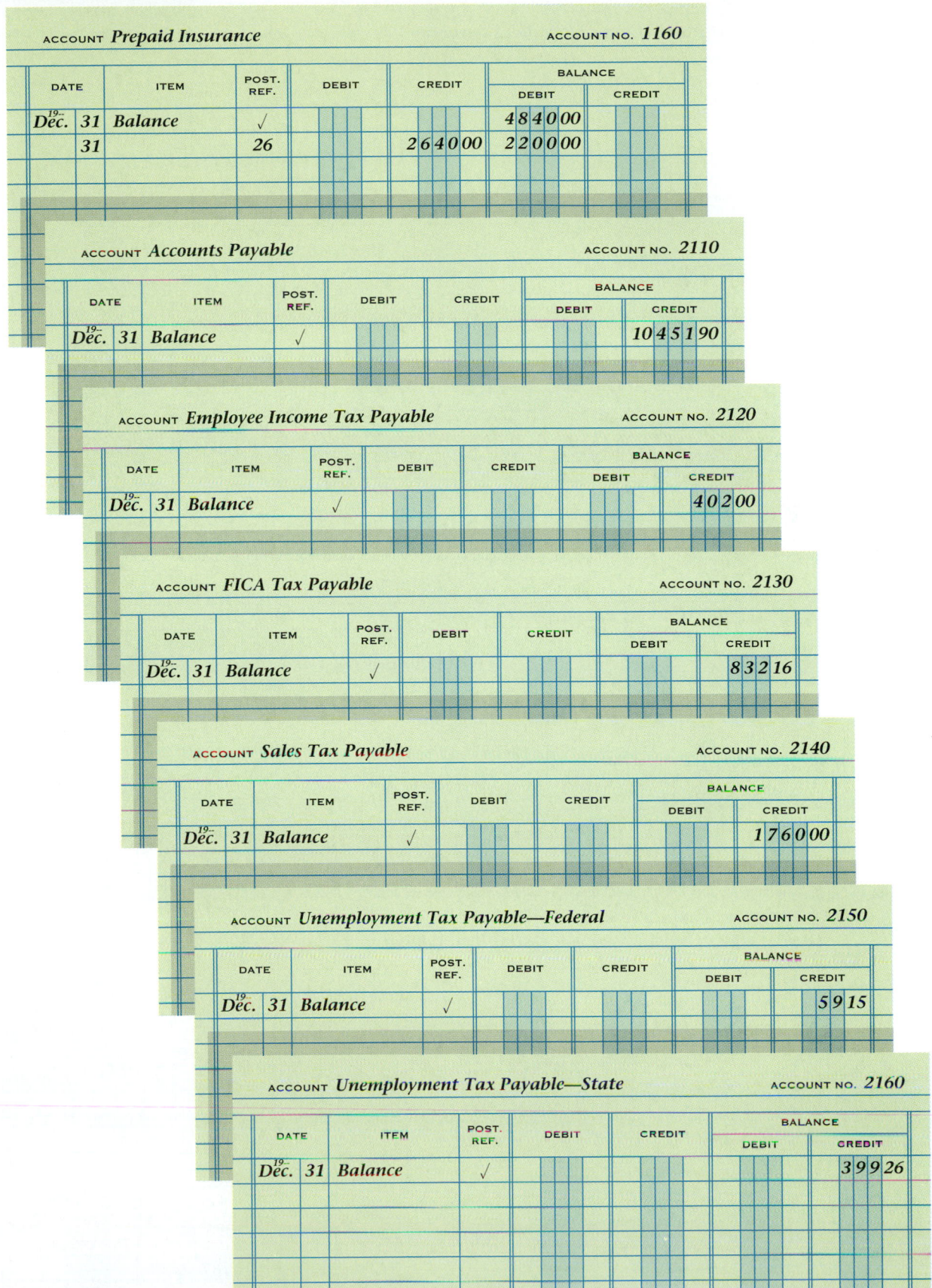

ACCOUNT *Prepaid Insurance*   ACCOUNT NO. *1160*

DATE		ITEM	POST. REF.	DEBIT	CREDIT	BALANCE DEBIT	BALANCE CREDIT
Dec.¹⁹⁻	31	Balance	✓			4 8 4 0 00	
	31		26		2 6 4 0 00	2 2 0 0 00	

ACCOUNT *Accounts Payable*   ACCOUNT NO. *2110*

DATE		ITEM	POST. REF.	DEBIT	CREDIT	BALANCE DEBIT	BALANCE CREDIT
Dec.¹⁹⁻	31	Balance	✓				10 4 5 1 90

ACCOUNT *Employee Income Tax Payable*   ACCOUNT NO. *2120*

DATE		ITEM	POST. REF.	DEBIT	CREDIT	BALANCE DEBIT	BALANCE CREDIT
Dec.¹⁹⁻	31	Balance	✓				4 0 2 00

ACCOUNT *FICA Tax Payable*   ACCOUNT NO. *2130*

DATE		ITEM	POST. REF.	DEBIT	CREDIT	BALANCE DEBIT	BALANCE CREDIT
Dec.¹⁹⁻	31	Balance	✓				8 3 2 16

ACCOUNT *Sales Tax Payable*   ACCOUNT NO. *2140*

DATE		ITEM	POST. REF.	DEBIT	CREDIT	BALANCE DEBIT	BALANCE CREDIT
Dec.¹⁹⁻	31	Balance	✓				1 7 6 0 00

ACCOUNT *Unemployment Tax Payable—Federal*   ACCOUNT NO. *2150*

DATE		ITEM	POST. REF.	DEBIT	CREDIT	BALANCE DEBIT	BALANCE CREDIT
Dec.¹⁹⁻	31	Balance	✓				5 9 15

ACCOUNT *Unemployment Tax Payable—State*   ACCOUNT NO. *2160*

DATE		ITEM	POST. REF.	DEBIT	CREDIT	BALANCE DEBIT	BALANCE CREDIT
Dec.¹⁹⁻	31	Balance	✓				3 9 9 26

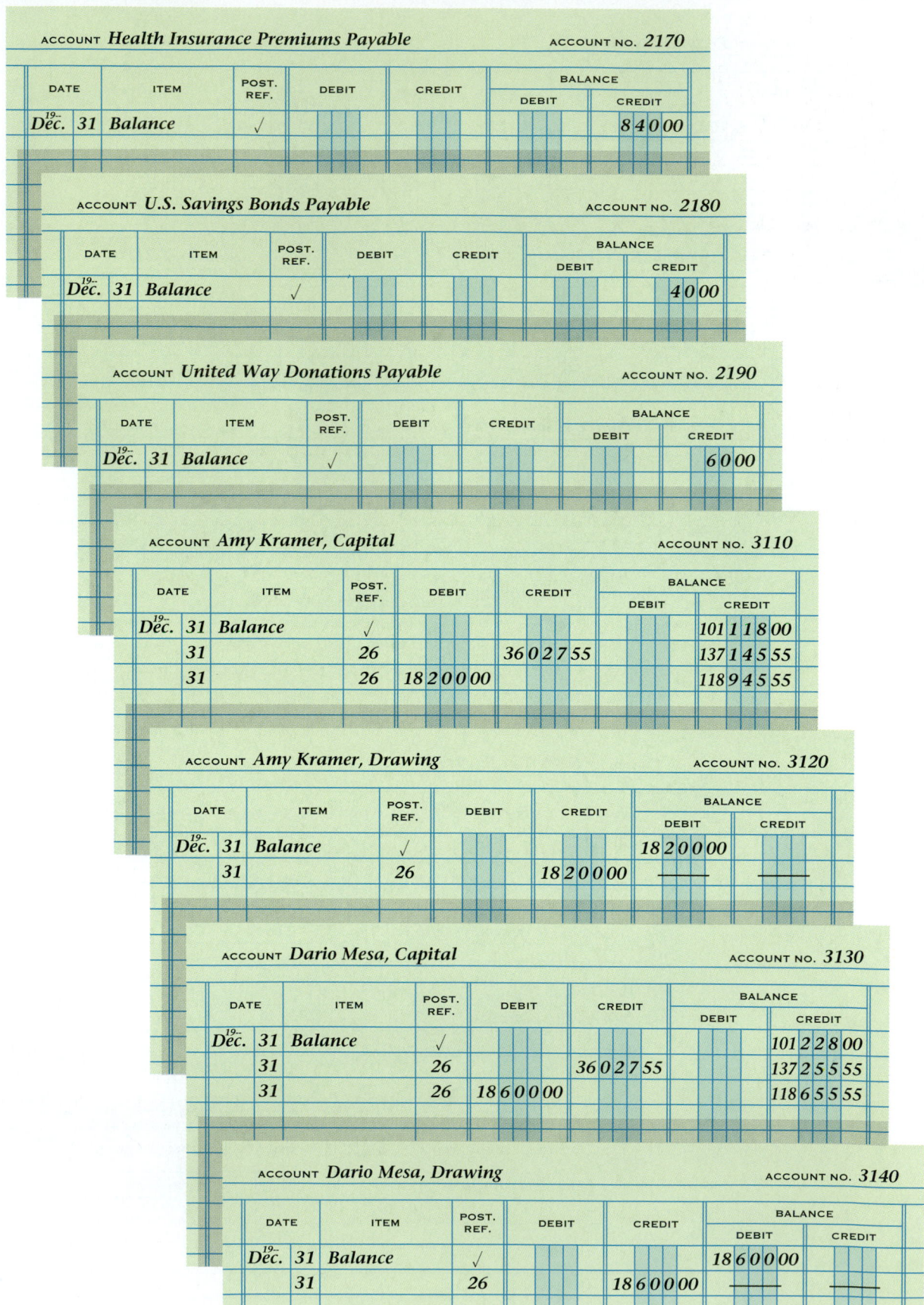

ACCOUNT **Health Insurance Premiums Payable** ACCOUNT NO. 2170

DATE	ITEM	POST. REF.	DEBIT	CREDIT	BALANCE DEBIT	BALANCE CREDIT
Dec. 31	Balance	✓				8 4 0 00

ACCOUNT **U.S. Savings Bonds Payable** ACCOUNT NO. 2180

DATE	ITEM	POST. REF.	DEBIT	CREDIT	BALANCE DEBIT	BALANCE CREDIT
Dec. 31	Balance	✓				4 0 00

ACCOUNT **United Way Donations Payable** ACCOUNT NO. 2190

DATE	ITEM	POST. REF.	DEBIT	CREDIT	BALANCE DEBIT	BALANCE CREDIT
Dec. 31	Balance	✓				6 0 00

ACCOUNT **Amy Kramer, Capital** ACCOUNT NO. 3110

DATE	ITEM	POST. REF.	DEBIT	CREDIT	BALANCE DEBIT	BALANCE CREDIT
Dec. 31	Balance	✓				101 1 1 8 00
31		26		36 0 2 7 55		137 1 4 5 55
31		26	18 2 0 0 00			118 9 4 5 55

ACCOUNT **Amy Kramer, Drawing** ACCOUNT NO. 3120

DATE	ITEM	POST. REF.	DEBIT	CREDIT	BALANCE DEBIT	BALANCE CREDIT
Dec. 31	Balance	✓			18 2 0 0 00	
31		26		18 2 0 0 00	——	——

ACCOUNT **Dario Mesa, Capital** ACCOUNT NO. 3130

DATE	ITEM	POST. REF.	DEBIT	CREDIT	BALANCE DEBIT	BALANCE CREDIT
Dec. 31	Balance	✓				101 2 2 8 00
31		26		36 0 2 7 55		137 2 5 5 55
31		26	18 6 0 0 00			118 6 5 5 55

ACCOUNT **Dario Mesa, Drawing** ACCOUNT NO. 3140

DATE	ITEM	POST. REF.	DEBIT	CREDIT	BALANCE DEBIT	BALANCE CREDIT
Dec. 31	Balance	✓			18 6 0 0 00	
31		26		18 6 0 0 00	——	——

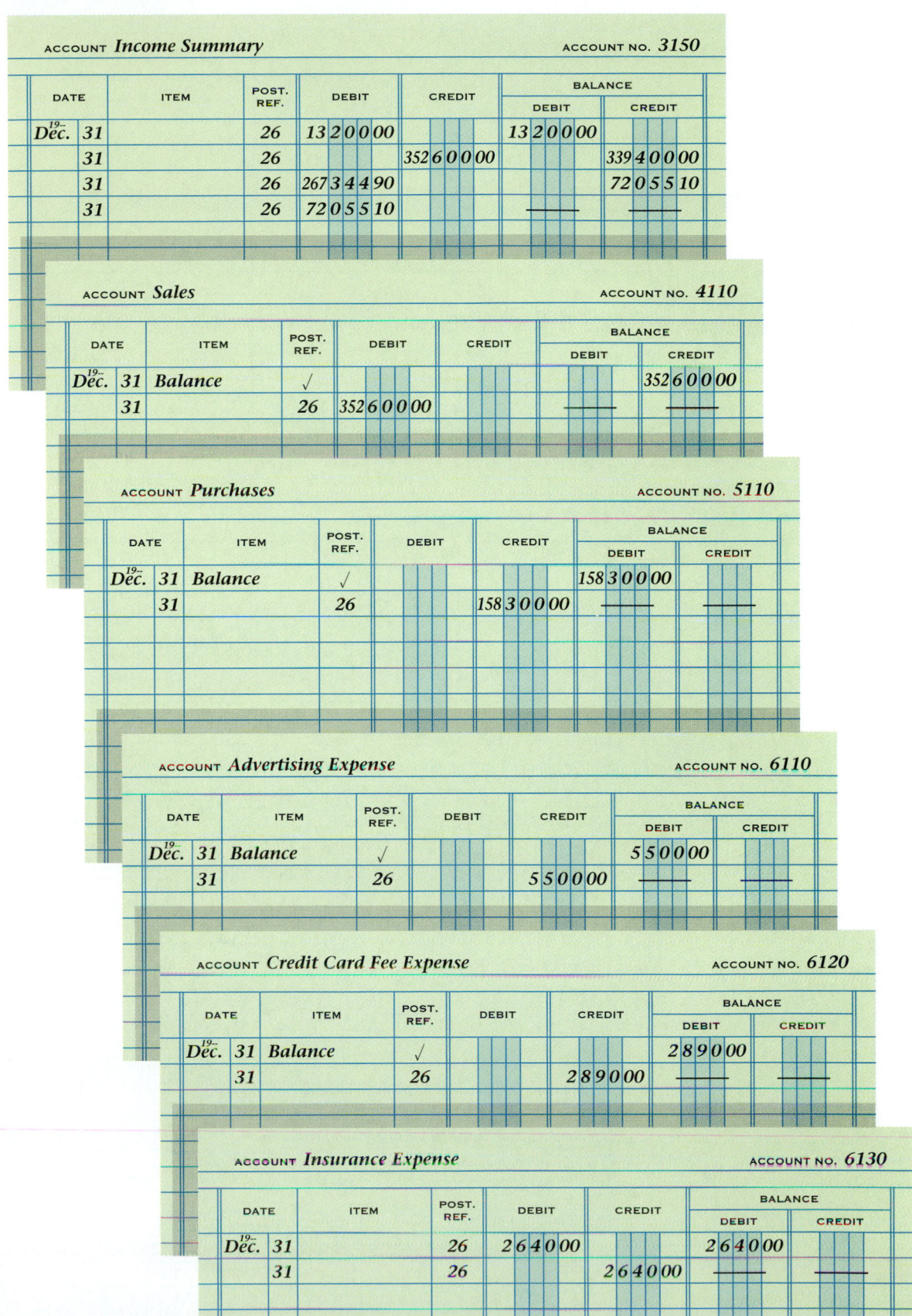

ACCOUNT **Income Summary**   ACCOUNT NO. *3150*

DATE		ITEM	POST. REF.	DEBIT	CREDIT	BALANCE DEBIT	BALANCE CREDIT
Dec.¹⁹⁻	31		26	13 2 0 0 00		13 2 0 0 00	
	31		26		352 6 0 0 00		339 4 0 0 00
	31		26	267 3 4 4 90			72 0 5 5 10
	31		26	72 0 5 5 10			

ACCOUNT **Sales**   ACCOUNT NO. *4110*

DATE		ITEM	POST. REF.	DEBIT	CREDIT	BALANCE DEBIT	BALANCE CREDIT
Dec.¹⁹⁻	31	Balance	✓				352 6 0 0 00
	31		26	352 6 0 0 00			

ACCOUNT **Purchases**   ACCOUNT NO. *5110*

DATE		ITEM	POST. REF.	DEBIT	CREDIT	BALANCE DEBIT	BALANCE CREDIT
Dec.¹⁹⁻	31	Balance	✓			158 3 0 0 00	
	31		26		158 3 0 0 00		

ACCOUNT **Advertising Expense**   ACCOUNT NO. *6110*

DATE		ITEM	POST. REF.	DEBIT	CREDIT	BALANCE DEBIT	BALANCE CREDIT
Dec.¹⁹⁻	31	Balance	✓			5 5 0 0 00	
	31		26		5 5 0 0 00		

ACCOUNT **Credit Card Fee Expense**   ACCOUNT NO. *6120*

DATE		ITEM	POST. REF.	DEBIT	CREDIT	BALANCE DEBIT	BALANCE CREDIT
Dec.¹⁹⁻	31	Balance	✓			2 8 9 0 00	
	31		26		2 8 9 0 00		

ACCOUNT **Insurance Expense**   ACCOUNT NO. *6130*

DATE		ITEM	POST. REF.	DEBIT	CREDIT	BALANCE DEBIT	BALANCE CREDIT
Dec.¹⁹⁻	31		26	2 6 4 0 00		2 6 4 0 00	
	31		26		2 6 4 0 00		

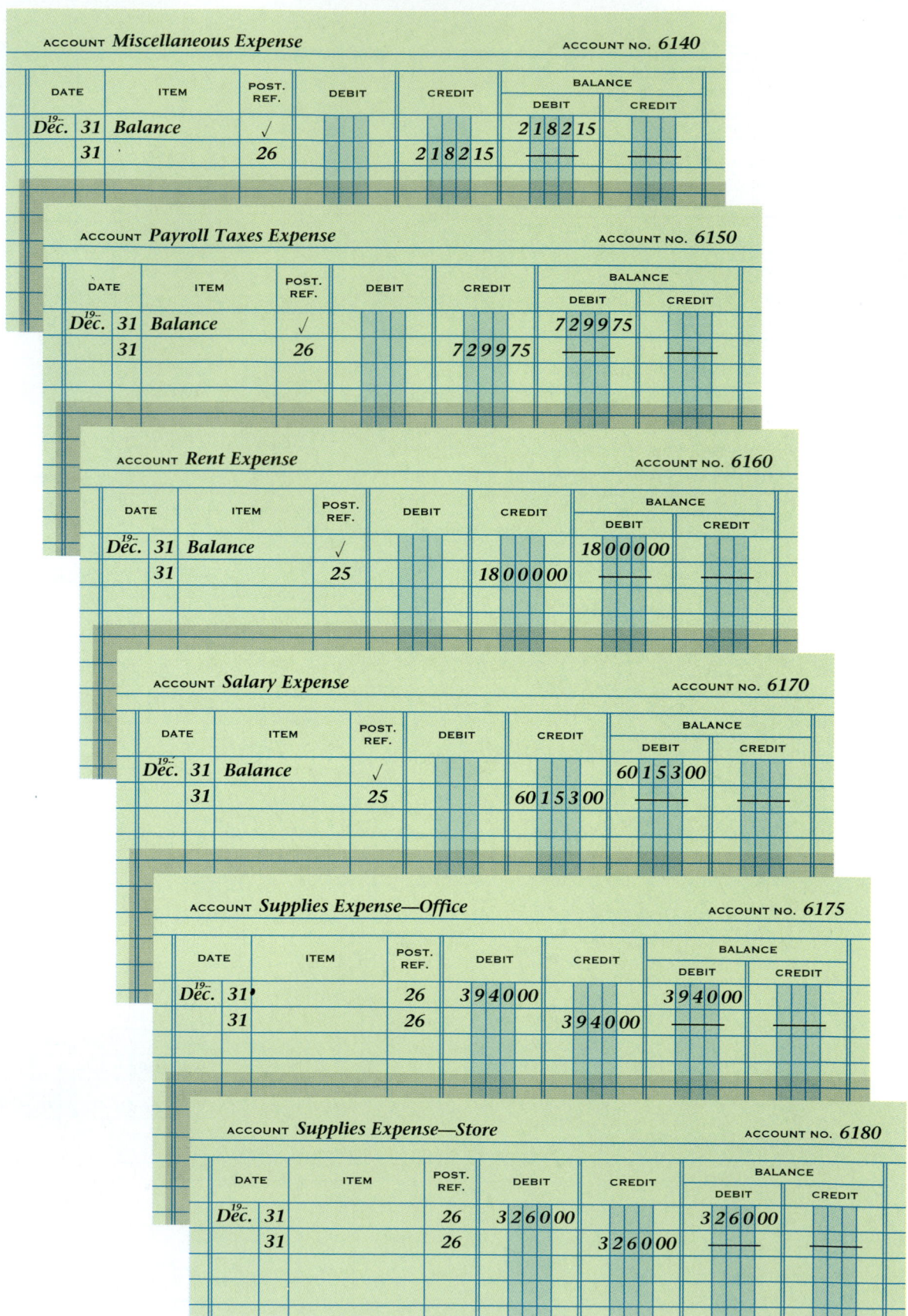

ACCOUNT *Miscellaneous Expense*　　ACCOUNT NO. *6140*

DATE	ITEM	POST. REF.	DEBIT	CREDIT	BALANCE DEBIT	BALANCE CREDIT
Dec. 31	Balance	✓			2 1 8 2 15	
31		26		2 1 8 2 15		

ACCOUNT *Payroll Taxes Expense*　　ACCOUNT NO. *6150*

DATE	ITEM	POST. REF.	DEBIT	CREDIT	BALANCE DEBIT	BALANCE CREDIT
Dec. 31	Balance	✓			7 2 9 9 75	
31		26		7 2 9 9 75		

ACCOUNT *Rent Expense*　　ACCOUNT NO. *6160*

DATE	ITEM	POST. REF.	DEBIT	CREDIT	BALANCE DEBIT	BALANCE CREDIT
Dec. 31	Balance	✓			18 0 0 0 00	
31		25		18 0 0 0 00		

ACCOUNT *Salary Expense*　　ACCOUNT NO. *6170*

DATE	ITEM	POST. REF.	DEBIT	CREDIT	BALANCE DEBIT	BALANCE CREDIT
Dec. 31	Balance	✓			60 1 5 3 00	
31		25		60 1 5 3 00		

ACCOUNT *Supplies Expense—Office*　　ACCOUNT NO. *6175*

DATE	ITEM	POST. REF.	DEBIT	CREDIT	BALANCE DEBIT	BALANCE CREDIT
Dec. 31		26	3 9 4 0 00		3 9 4 0 00	
31		26		3 9 4 0 00		

ACCOUNT *Supplies Expense—Store*　　ACCOUNT NO. *6180*

DATE	ITEM	POST. REF.	DEBIT	CREDIT	BALANCE DEBIT	BALANCE CREDIT
Dec. 31		26	3 2 6 0 00		3 2 6 0 00	
31		26		3 2 6 0 00		

ILLUSTRATION 18-11 General ledger after adjusting and closing entries are posted (concluded)

ACCOUNT Utilities Expense							ACCOUNT NO. 6190
DATE	ITEM	POST. REF.	DEBIT	CREDIT	BALANCE DEBIT	BALANCE CREDIT	
Dec. 31	Balance	✓			3 1 8 0 00		
31		26		3 1 8 0 00	—	—	

Post-Closing Trial Balance

The post-closing trial balance is prepared to prove the equality of debits and credits in the general ledger. Only accounts with balances are listed.

After adjusting and closing entries have been posted, a post-closing trial balance is prepared. The post-closing trial balance is prepared to prove the equality of debits and credits in the general ledger. CarLand's post-closing trial balance prepared on December 31 is shown in Illustration 18-12.

All general ledger accounts that have balances are listed on a post-closing trial balance. Accounts are listed in the same order as they appear in the general ledger. Accounts with zero balances are not listed on a post-closing trial balance.

ILLUSTRATION 18-12   Post-closing trial balance

CarLand		
Post-Closing Trial Balance		
December 31, 19--		
ACCOUNT TITLE	DEBIT	CREDIT
Cash	24 2 3 3 57	
Petty Cash	5 0 0 00	
Accounts Receivable	9 3 3 2 00	
Merchandise Inventory	212 2 0 0 00	
Supplies—Office	1 4 6 0 00	
Supplies—Store	2 5 2 0 00	
Prepaid Insurance	2 2 0 0 00	
Accounts Payable		10 4 5 1 90
Employee Income Tax Payable		4 0 2 00
FICA Tax Payable		8 3 2 16
Sales Tax Payable		1 7 6 0 00
Unemployment Tax Payable—Federal		5 9 15
Unemployment Tax Payable—State		3 9 9 26
Health Insurance Premiums Payable		8 4 0 00
U.S. Savings Bonds Payable		4 0 00
United Way Donations Payable		6 0 00
Amy Kramer, Capital		118 9 4 5 55
Dario Mesa, Capital		118 6 5 5 55
Totals	252 4 4 5 57	252 4 4 5 57

Account balances on the post-closing trial balance, Illustration 18-12, agree with the balances on the balance sheet, Illustration 17-10, Chapter 17. Also, because the post-closing trial balance debit and credit balance totals are the same, $252,445.57, the equality of debits and credits in the general ledger is proved. The general ledger is ready for the next fiscal period. *(CONCEPT: Accounting Period Cycle)*

SUMMARY OF AN ACCOUNTING CYCLE FOR A MERCHANDISING BUSINESS

Service and merchandising businesses use a similar accounting cycle. The accounting cycles are also similar for a proprietorship and a partnership. Variations occur when subsidiary ledgers are used. Variations also occur in preparing financial statements. Car-Land's accounting cycle for a merchandising business is summarized in Illustration 18-13.

QUESTIONS FOR INDIVIDUAL STUDY   EPT(a)

1. What two types of journal entries change general ledger account balances at the end of a fiscal period?

2. Where is the information obtained for journalizing adjusting entries?

3. Where is the information obtained for journalizing closing entries?

4. Where is the explanation for adjusting entries written in a journal?

5. Which accounting concept is being applied when temporary accounts are closed at the end of a fiscal period?

6. What four kinds of closing entries are recorded at the end of a fiscal period?

7. What is the title of the temporary account used to summarize information about net income at the end of a fiscal period?

8. Why is the income summary account considered a unique account?

9. Where is the explanation for closing entries written in a journal?

10. What are the three amounts recorded in the income summary account after closing the revenue, cost, and expense accounts?

11. Why are partners' withdrawals not closed to the income summary account?

12. What is recorded in the Balance Debit and Credit columns of a general ledger account when an account is closed?

13. Which accounting concept is being applied when revenue, cost, and expense accounts begin a new fiscal period with zero balances?

14. What accounts are listed on a post-closing trial balance?

SUMMARY ILLUSTRATION 18-13

Summary of an accounting cycle for a merchandising business

1 Source documents are checked for accuracy and transactions are analyzed into debit and credit parts.

2 Transactions, from information on source documents, are recorded in a journal.

3 Journal entries are posted to the accounts receivable ledger, the accounts payable ledger, and the general ledger.

4 Schedules of accounts receivable and accounts payable are prepared from the subsidiary ledgers.

5 Work sheet, including a trial balance, is prepared from the general ledger.

6 Financial statements are prepared from the work sheet.

7 Adjusting and closing entries are journalized from the work sheet.

8 Adjusting and closing entries are posted to the general ledger.

9 Post-closing trial balance of the general ledger is prepared.

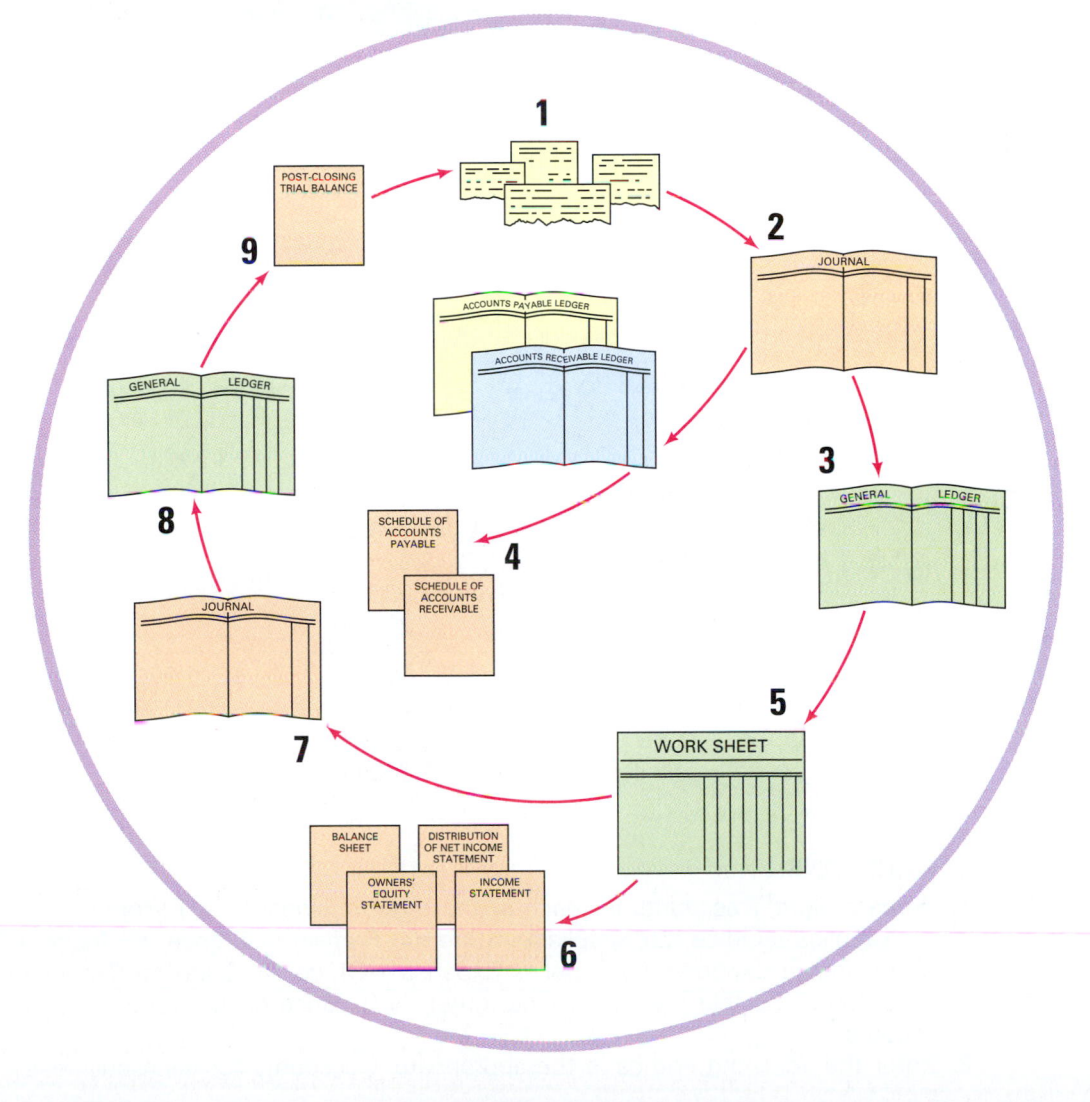

CASE 1 Household Furniture's Trial Balance Debit column of the work sheet shows a debit balance of $2,400.00 for the office supplies account. The ending office supplies inventory is determined to be $1,800.00. The accounting clerk journalized the following adjusting entry: debit Supplies Expense—Office, $1,800.00; credit Supplies—Office, $1,800.00. Susan Gray, partner, discussed the entry with the accounting clerk and suggested that the adjusting entry should have been for $600.00 instead of $1,800.00. The clerk indicated that there is no problem because the amounts will be adjusted again at the end of the next fiscal period. Do you agree with Miss Gray or the accounting clerk? Explain your answer.

CASE 2 Two businesses have been using different accounting practices. One business first closes the income summary account to record the net income in the capital accounts and then closes the drawing accounts. The other business first closes the drawing accounts and then closes the income summary account to record the net income in the capital accounts. Which practice is correct? Explain.

DRILLS FOR UNDERSTANDING
EPT(b,c)

DRILL 18-D1 Analyzing adjusting entries

TUTORIAL

The following information is related to adjustments needed at the end of a fiscal period for three businesses.

Business	Account Title	Account Balance in General Ledger	Adjustment Information	
			Ending Inventories	Ending Value
1	Merchandise Inventory	$388,000.00	$365,000.00	
	Supplies—Office	4,730.00	2,910.00	
	Supplies—Store	5,230.00	3,470.00	
	Prepaid Insurance	3,360.00		$840.00
2	Merchandise Inventory	$274,000.00	$286,000.00	
	Supplies—Office	3,620.00	1,840.00	
	Supplies—Store	3,950.00	2,110.00	
	Prepaid Insurance	2,850.00		$570.00
3	Merchandise Inventory	$292,000.00	$278,000.00	
	Supplies—Office	4,480.00	2,250.00	
	Supplies—Store	4,130.00	2,320.00	
	Prepaid Insurance	3,200.00		$800.00

INSTRUCTIONS:

1. Prepare eight T accounts for each of the three businesses. (1) Merchandise Inventory. (2) Supplies—Office. (3) Supplies—Store. (4) Prepaid Insurance. (5) Income Summary. (6) Insurance Expense. (7) Supplies Expense—Office. (8) Supplies Expense—Store. For those accounts that have a balance, enter the balance on the proper side of the T account.
2. Enter the adjusting entries in the appropriate T accounts for each business.

DRILL 18-D2 Analyzing closing entries

The following information is from the work sheet of Novak's Sport Center.

ACCOUNT TITLE	INCOME STATEMENT DEBIT	INCOME STATEMENT CREDIT
21 Income Summary	1200000	
22 Sales		23600000
23 Purchases	9440000	
24 Advertising Expense	325000	
25 Credit Card Fee Expense	213000	
26 Insurance Expense	252000	
27 Miscellaneous Expense	138000	
28 Rent Expense	1440000	
29 Supplies Expense—Office	298000	
30 Supplies Expense—Store	312000	

INSTRUCTIONS:

1. Prepare a T account for each account. In each T account, enter the amount that is shown in the Income Statement columns.
2. Enter the debit and credit amounts to close the income statement credit balance account. Enter the debit and credit amounts to close the income statement debit balance accounts.

APPLICATION PROBLEM   EPT(b,c,d)

PROBLEM 18-1   Journalizing and posting adjusting and closing entries; preparing a post-closing trial balance

AUTOMATED

Use the following partial work sheet of Jewel Box Company for the year ended December 31 of the current year. The general ledger accounts and their balances are in the working papers accompanying this textbook.

ACCOUNT TITLE	ADJUSTMENTS DEBIT	ADJUSTMENTS CREDIT	INCOME STATEMENT DEBIT	INCOME STATEMENT CREDIT
4 Merchandise Inventory		(a)1300000		
5 Supplies—Office		(b) 214000		
6 Supplies—Store		(c) 245000		
7 Prepaid Insurance		(d) 264000		
21 Income Summary	(a)1300000		1300000	
22 Sales				31600000
23 Purchases			12645000	
24 Advertising Expense			472000	
25 Credit Card Fee Expense			326000	
26 Insurance Expense	(d) 264000		264000	
27 Miscellaneous Expense			193000	
28 Payroll Taxes Expense			677300	
29 Rent Expense			1560000	
30 Salary Expense			5678700	
31 Supplies Expense—Office	(b) 214000		214000	
32 Supplies Expense—Store	(c) 245000		245000	
33 Utilities Expense			294000	
34	2023000	2023000	23869000	31600000
35 Net Income			7731000	
36			31600000	31600000

INSTRUCTIONS:

1. Use page 25 of a journal. Journalize the adjusting entries using information from the partial work sheet.
2. Post the adjusting entries.
3. Continue using page 25 of the journal. Journalize the closing entries using information from the work sheet. The distribution of net income statement shows equal distribution of earnings. The partners' drawing accounts show the following debit balances in the work sheet's Balance Sheet Debit column: Paula Chaney, Drawing, $14,580.00; Scott Chaney, Drawing, $14,720.00.
4. Post the closing entries.
5. Prepare a post-closing trial balance.

ENRICHMENT PROBLEMS   EPT(b,c,d)

MASTERY PROBLEM 18-M Journalizing and posting adjusting and closing entries; preparing a post-closing trial balance

Use the following partial work sheet of Robco Toys for the year ended December 31 of the current year. The general ledger accounts and their balances are in the working papers accompanying this textbook.

AUTOMATED

APPLICATION

	ACCOUNT TITLE	ADJUSTMENTS DEBIT (3)	ADJUSTMENTS CREDIT (4)	INCOME STATEMENT DEBIT (5)	INCOME STATEMENT CREDIT (6)
4	Merchandise Inventory		(a)12 500 00		
5	Supplies—Office		(b) 2 430 00		
6	Supplies—Store		(c) 2 270 00		
7	Prepaid Insurance		(d) 2 280 00		
21	Income Summary	(a)12 500 00		12 500 00	
22	Sales				325 630 00
23	Purchases			130 450 00	
24	Advertising Expense			5 180 00	
25	Credit Card Fee Expense			3 420 00	
26	Insurance Expense	(d) 2 280 00		2 280 00	
27	Miscellaneous Expense			2 060 00	
28	Payroll Taxes Expense			7 124 00	
29	Rent Expense			15 600 00	
30	Salary Expense			59 360 00	
31	Supplies Expense—Office	(b) 2 430 00		2 430 00	
32	Supplies Expense—Store	(c) 2 270 00		2 270 00	
33	Utilities Expense			2 880 00	
34		19 480 00	19 480 00	245 554 00	325 630 00
35	Net Income			80 076 00	
36				325 630 00	325 630 00
37					

INSTRUCTIONS:

1. Use page 25 of a journal. Journalize the adjusting entries using information from the partial work sheet.
2. Post the adjusting entries.

3. Continue using page 25 of the journal. Journalize the closing entries using information from the work sheet. The distribution of net income statement shows equal distribution of earnings. The partners' drawing accounts show the following debit balances in the work sheet's Balance Sheet Debit column: Marcus Florie, Drawing, $18,230.00; Karen Rader, Drawing, $18,710.00.

4. Post the closing entries.

5. Prepare a post-closing trial balance.

CHALLENGE PROBLEM 18-C   Completing end-of-fiscal-period work

AUTOMATED

Plaza Book Center's trial balance is recorded on a 10-column work sheet in the working papers accompanying this textbook. The general ledger accounts and their balances are also given.

INSTRUCTIONS:

1. Use the following adjustment information. Complete the 10-column work sheet.

Adjustment Information, December 31

Merchandise inventory	$204,680.00
Office supplies inventory	2,635.00
Store supplies inventory	2,310.00
Value of prepaid insurance	2,200.00

2. Prepare an income statement from the information on the work sheet. Calculate and record the following component percentages: (a) cost of merchandise sold, (b) gross profit on sales, (c) total expenses, and (d) net income or loss. Round percentage calculations to the nearest 0.1%.

3. Prepare a distribution of net income statement. Net income or loss is to be shared equally.

4. Prepare an owners' equity statement. No additional investments were made.

5. Prepare a balance sheet in report form.

6. Use page 25 of a journal. Journalize the adjusting entries.

7. Post the adjusting entries.

8. Continue using page 25 of the journal. Journalize the closing entries.

9. Post the closing entries.

10. Prepare a post-closing trial balance.

End-of-Fiscal-Period Work for a Partnership

Chapters 16 through 18 describe CarLand's manual accounting procedures for completing end-of-fiscal-period work. Integrating Automated Accounting Topic 6 describes procedures for using automated accounting software to complete CarLand's end-of-fiscal-period work. The Automated Accounting Problems contain instructions for using automated accounting software to solve Application Problem 18-1, Mastery Problem 18-M, and Challenge Problem 18-C, Chapter 18.

COMPLETING END-OF-FISCAL-PERIOD WORK

In automated accounting, end-of-fiscal-period reports are prepared by a computer based on instructions in the computer software. The run date used for all end-of-fiscal-period reports is the ending date of the accounting period. Before printing financial statements, the software is directed to prepare a trial balance. The trial balance is prepared to prove equality of general ledger debits and credits and to plan adjustments to general ledger accounts.

Preparing a Trial Balance

To prepare a trial balance the general ledger data base is retrieved. The Reports menu is selected from the menu bar. The Ledgers command is chosen from the Reports window. Trial Balance is selected from the Report Selection window to display the trial balance. The trial balance is printed as shown in Illustration T6-1.

FYI

A trial balance proves the equality of the debits and credits in the general ledger. A trial balance taken after closing entries are performed is a post-closing trial balance. The Trial Balance command must be chosen to display a post-closing trial balance.

ILLUSTRATION T6-1   Trial balance

```
                          CarLand
                       Trial Balance
                         12/31/--
-----------------------------------------------------------
Acct.   Account
Number  Title                       Debit            Credit
-----------------------------------------------------------
1110    Cash                       24233.57
1120    Petty Cash                   500.00
1130    Accounts Receivable         9332.00
1140    Merchandise Inventory     225400.00
1145    Supplies--Office            5400.00
1150    Supplies--Store             5780.00
1160    Prepaid Insurance           4840.00
2110    Accounts Payable                           10451.90
2120    Employee Income Tax Pay.                     402.00
2130    FICA Tax Payable                             832.16
2140    Sales Tax Payable                           1760.00
2150    Unemployment Tax Pay--Fed                     59.15
2160    Unemployment Tax Pay--St.                    399.26
2170    Health Ins. Premiums Pay.                    840.00
2180    U.S. Savings Bonds Pay.                       40.00
2190    United Way Donations Pay.                     60.00
3110    Amy Kramer, Capital                        101118.00
3120    Amy Kramer, Drawing        18200.00
3130    Dario Mesa, Capital                        101228.00
3140    Dario Mesa, Drawing        18600.00
4110    Sales                                      352600.00
5110    Purchases                 158300.00
6110    Advertising Expense         5500.00
6120    Credit Card Fee Expense     2890.00
6140    Miscellaneous Expense       2182.15
6150    Payroll Taxes Expense       7299.75
6160    Rent Expense               18000.00
6170    Salary Expense             60153.00
6190    Utilities Expense           3180.00
                                 ----------        ----------
        Totals                   569790.47         569790.47
                                 ==========        ==========
```

Recording Adjusting Entries

Adjusting entries are batched and recorded on a general journal input form. CarLand's completed general journal input form for the adjusting entries is shown in Illustration T6-2.

ILLUSTRATION T6-2   General journal input form with adjustments recorded

	DATE MM/DD	REFERENCE	ACCOUNT NO.	CUSTOMER/ VENDOR NO.	DEBIT	CREDIT	
1	12,31	Adj.Ent.	3150		13200 00		1
2	/		1140			13200 00	2
3	31	Adj.Ent.	6175		3940 00		3
4	/		1145			3940 00	4
5	31	Adj.Ent.	6180		3260 00		5
6	/		1150			3260 00	6
7	31	Adj.Ent.	6130		2640 00		7
8	/		1160			2640 00	8
25	/						25
				PAGE TOTALS	23040 00	23040 00	
				FINAL TOTALS	23040 00	23040 00	

RUN DATE 12,31,-- MM DD YY   GENERAL JOURNAL Input Form

CarLand has the following adjustment data on December 31.

Adjustment Information, December 31

Merchandise inventory	$212,200.00
Office supplies inventory	1,460.00
Store supplies inventory	2,520.00
Value of prepaid insurance	2,200.00

The information needed to journalize the adjusting entries is obtained from the trial balance. Income Summary is debited and Merchandise Inventory is credited for $13,200.00, the decrease in merchandise inventory. The journal entry to record this adjustment is on lines 1 and 2 of the general journal input form shown in Illustration T6-2. The abbreviation for adjusting entries, *Adj.Ent.*, is written in the Reference column for each entry.

Supplies Expense—Office is debited and Supplies—Office is credited for $3,940.00, the value of office supplies used. The journal entry to record this adjustment is on lines 3 and 4 of Illustration T6-2.

Supplies Expense—Store is debited and Supplies—Store is credited for $3,260.00, the value of store supplies used. The journal entry to record this adjustment is on lines 5 and 6 of Illustration T6-2.

Insurance Expense is debited and Prepaid Insurance is credited for $2,640.00, the value of insurance used. The journal entry to record this adjustment is on lines 7 and 8 of Illustration T6-2.

After all adjusting entries have been recorded, the Debit and Credit columns are totaled. The totals are entered on the Page Totals and Final Totals lines provided at the bottom of the input form. The totals are compared to assure that debits equal credits. As the totals are the same, $23,040.00, the adjusting entries on the general journal input form are assumed to be correct.

Processing Adjusting Entries

Dollar and cent signs are not entered on input forms.

The Journals menu is selected from the menu bar. The General Journal command is chosen from the Journals menu to display the data entry window for keying data.

After all lines on the input form have been keyed and posted, the Reports menu is selected from the menu bar. The Journals command is selected to display the Report Selection window. General Journal is selected from the Report Selection window. As CarLand wants to print only the adjusting entries, the abbreviation *Adj.Ent.* is keyed as a Reference restriction. The *Ok* button is pushed to display the general journal report. The report is checked for accuracy by comparing the report totals, $23,040.00, with the totals on the general journal input form. Because the totals are the same, the general journal report is assumed to be correct. The general journal report is printed, as shown in Illustration T6-3, and filed for future reference.

ILLUSTRATION T6-3   General journal report for adjusting entries

```
                          CarLand
                      General Journal
                         12/31/--
-------------------------------------------------------------------------
Date   Refer.    V/C Acct.  Title                        Debit      Credit
-------------------------------------------------------------------------
12/31  Adj.Ent.      3150   Income Summary             13200.00
12/31  Adj.Ent.      1140   Merchandise Inventory                  13200.00

12/31  Adj.Ent.      6175   Supplies Expense--Office    3940.00
12/31  Adj.Ent.      1145   Supplies--Office                        3940.00

12/31  Adj.Ent.      6180   Supplies Expense--Store     3260.00
12/31  Adj.Ent.      1150   Supplies--Store                         3260.00

12/31  Adj.Ent.      6130   Insurance Expense           2640.00
12/31  Adj.Ent.      1160   Prepaid Insurance                       2640.00
                                                       ---------- ----------
                            Totals                     23040.00   23040.00
                                                       ========== ==========
```

PROCESSING FINANCIAL STATEMENTS

To prepare the income statement, the Reports menu is selected from the menu bar. The Financial Statements command is chosen to display the Report Selection window. Income Statement is selected from the Report Selection window. The income statement is printed, as shown in Illustration T6-4 on page 462, and filed for future reference.

To prepare the balance sheet, the same steps are followed as to prepare an income statement. However, Balance Sheet is selected

```
                              CarLand
                          Income Statement
                      For Period Ended 12/31/--
---------------------------------------------------------------------
                          *****Monthly*****    *****Yearly******
                          Amount    Percent     Amount    Percent
---------------------------------------------------------------------
O p e r a t i n g   R e v e n u e
------------------------------------
Sales                     352600.00  100.00   352600.00   100.00

Total Operating Revenue   352600.00  100.00   352600.00   100.00

C o s t   o f   M e r c h a n d i s e   S o l d
----------------------------------------------------
Beginning Inventory       225400.00   63.93   225400.00    63.93
Purchases                 158300.00   44.90   158300.00    44.90

Merchandise Available for Sale 383700.00 108.82 383700.00  108.82
Less Ending Inventory    -212200.00  -60.18  -212200.00   -60.18

Cost of Merchandise Sold  171500.00   48.64   171500.00    48.64

Gross Profit              181100.00   51.36   181100.00    51.36

O p e r a t i n g   E x p e n s e s
------------------------------------
Advertising Expense          5500.00    1.56    5500.00     1.56
Credit Card Fee Expense      2890.00     .82    2890.00      .82
Insurance Expense            2640.00     .75    2640.00      .75
Miscellaneous Expense        2182.15     .62    2182.15      .62
Payroll Taxes Expense        7299.75    2.07    7299.75     2.07
Rent Expense                18000.00    5.10   18000.00     5.10
Salary Expense              60153.00   17.06   60153.00    17.06
Supplies Expense--Office     3940.00    1.12    3940.00     1.12
Supplies Expense--Store      3260.00     .92    3260.00      .92
Utilities Expense            3180.00     .90    3180.00      .90

Total Operating Expenses   109044.90   30.93  109044.90    30.93

Net Income                  72055.10   20.44   72055.10    20.44
                          ========== ========== ========== ==========
```

from the Report Selection window. The balance sheet is printed, as shown in Illustration T6-5, and filed for future reference.

CLOSING TEMPORARY ACCOUNTS

In automated accounting the software contains instructions for closing temporary accounts. After the balance sheet has been prepared, The Options menu is selected from the menu bar. The Period-End Closing command is chosen from the Options menu to close all temporary accounts.

PROCESSING A POST-CLOSING TRIAL BALANCE

After the financial statements have been prepared and period-end closing has been performed, a post-closing trial balance is

```
                        CarLand
                     Balance Sheet
                       12/31/--

A s s e t s
-----------
Cash                           24233.57
Petty Cash                       500.00
Accounts Receivable             9332.00
Merchandise Inventory         212200.00
Supplies--Office                1460.00
Supplies--Store                 2520.00
Prepaid Insurance               2200.00
                              ----------
Total Assets                             252445.57
                                         ==========
L i a b i l i t i e s
---------------------
Accounts Payable               10451.90
Employee Income Tax Pay.         402.00
FICA Tax Payable                 832.16
Sales Tax Payable               1760.00
Unemployment Tax Pay--Fed         59.15
Unemployment Tax Pay--St.        399.26
Health Ins. Premiums Pay.        840.00
U.S. Savings Bonds Pay.           40.00
United Way Donations Pay.         60.00
                              ----------
Total Liabilities                         14844.47

O w n e r ' s   E q u i t y
---------------------------
Amy Kramer, Capital           101118.00
Amy Kramer, Drawing           -18200.00
Dario Mesa, Capital           101228.00
Dario Mesa, Drawing           -18600.00
Net Income                     72055.10
                              ----------
Total Owner's Equity                     237601.10
                                         ----------
Total Liabilities & Equity               252445.57
                                         ==========
```

processed. The Reports menu is selected from the menu bar. The Ledgers command is chosen to display the Reports Selection window. Trial Balance is selected from the Report Selection window. The trial balance is printed, as shown in Illustration T6-6 on page 464, and filed for future reference.

OPTIONAL PROBLEM DB-6A

CarLand's general ledger data base is on the accounting textbook template. If you wish to complete Rugcare's end-of-fiscal-period work using automated accounting software, load the *Automated Accounting 6.0* or higher software. Select Data Base 6A (DB-6A) from the template disk. Read the Problem Instructions screen. Follow the procedures described to process CarLand's end-of-fiscal-period work.

```
                            CarLand
                          Trial Balance
                           12/31/--
----------------------------------------------------------------------
Acct.    Account
Number   Title                           Debit          Credit
----------------------------------------------------------------------
1110     Cash                          24233.57
1120     Petty Cash                      500.00
1130     Accounts Receivable            9332.00
1140     Merchandise Inventory        212200.00
1145     Supplies--Office               1460.00
1150     Supplies--Store                2520.00
1160     Prepaid Insurance              2200.00
2110     Accounts Payable                             10451.90
2120     Employee Income Tax Pay.                       402.00
2130     FICA Tax Payable                              832.16
2140     Sales Tax Payable                            1760.00
2150     Unemployment Tax Pay--Fed                      59.15
2160     Unemployment Tax Pay--St.                     399.26
2170     Health Ins. Premiums Pay.                     840.00
2180     U.S. Savings Bonds Pay.                        40.00
2190     United Way Donations Pay.                      60.00
3110     Amy Kramer, Capital                        118945.55
3130     Dario Mesa, Capital                        118655.55
                                      ----------     ----------
         Totals                       252445.57      252445.57
                                      ==========     ==========
```

AUTOMATED ACCOUNTING PROBLEMS

AUTOMATED

AUTOMATING APPLICATION PROBLEM 18-1 Journalizing and posting adjusting and closing entries; preparing a post-closing trial balance.

INSTRUCTIONS:

1. Use the end-of-fiscal-period work for Problem 18-1, Chapter 18. Use December 31 of the current year as the run date.

2. Load the *Automated Accounting 6.0* or higher software. Select data base F18-1 (First-Year Course Problem 18-1) from the accounting textbook template. Read the Problem Instructions Screen.

3. Select File from the menu bar and choose the Save As menu command. Key the path to the drive and directory that contains your data files. Save the data base with a file name of XXX181 (where XXX are your initials).

4. Display/print a trial balance.

5. Record the adjusting entries on a general ledger input form using the following information. Use the account numbers from the trial balance prepared in Instruction 4.

Adjustment Information, December 31

Merchandise inventory	$283,830.00
Office supplies inventory	2,570.00
Store supplies inventory	2,130.00
Value of prepaid insurance	1,100.00

6. Key the adjusting entries from the general journal input form.

7. Display/print the general journal report.

8. Display/print the income statement and balance sheet.

9. Perform period-end closing.

10. Display/print the post-closing trial balance.

AUTOMATING MASTERY PROBLEM 18-M Journalizing and posting adjusting and closing entries; preparing a post-closing trial balance

INSTRUCTIONS:

1. Use the end-of-fiscal-period work for Mastery Problem 18-M, Chapter 18. Use December 31 of the current year as the run date.
2. Load the *Automated Accounting 6.0* or higher software. Select data base F18-M (First-Year Course Mastery Problem 18-M) from the accounting textbook template. Read the Problem Instructions screen.
3. Select File from the menu bar and choose the Save As menu command. Key the path to the drive and directory that contains your data files. Save the data base with a file name of XXX18M (where XXX are your initials).
4. Display/print a trial balance.
5. Record the adjusting entries on a general journal input form using the following information. Use the account numbers from the trial balance prepared in Instruction 4.

Adjustment Information, December 31

Merchandise inventory	$276,140.00
Office supplies inventory	2,400.00
Store supplies inventory	2,010.00
Value of prepaid insurance	750.00

6. Key the adjusting entries from the general journal input form.
7. Display/print the general journal report.
8. Display/print the income statement.
9. Display/print the balance sheet.
10. Perform period-end closing.
11. Display/print the post-closing trial balance.

AUTOMATING CHALLENGE PROBLEM 18-C Completing end-of-fiscal-period work

INSTRUCTIONS:

1. Use the end-of-fiscal-period work for Challenge Problem 18-C, Chapter 18. Use December 31 of the current year as the run date.
2. Load the *Automated Accounting 6.0* or higher software. Select data base F18-C from the accounting textbook template. Read the Problem Instructions screen.
3. Select File from the menu bar and choose the Save As menu command. Key the path to the drive and directory that contains your data files. Save the data base with a file name of XXX18C (where XXX are your initials).
4. Display/print a trial balance.
5. Record the adjusting entries on a general journal input form using the following information. Use the account numbers from the trial balance prepared in Instruction 4.

Adjustment Information, December 31

Merchandise inventory	$204,680.00
Office supplies inventory	2,635.00
Store supplies inventory	2,310.00
Value of prepaid insurance	2,200.00

6. Key the adjusting entries from the general journal input form.
7. Display/print the general journal report.
8. Display/print the income statement and balance sheet.
9. Perform period-end closing.
10. Display/print the post-closing trial balance.

An Accounting Cycle for a Partnership: End-of-Fiscal-Period Work

AUTOMATED

The ledgers used in Reinforcement Activity 2, Part A, are needed to complete Reinforcement Activity 2, Part B.

Reinforcement Activity 2, Part B, includes those accounting activities needed to complete the accounting cycle of ClearView Optical.

END-OF-FISCAL-PERIOD WORK

INSTRUCTIONS:

10. Prepare a trial balance on a work sheet. Use December 31 of the current year as the date.

11. Complete the work sheet using the following adjustment information.

Adjustment Information, December 31

Merchandise inventory...............................	$203,200.00
Office supplies inventory.............................	2,370.00
Store supplies inventory	3,240.00
Value of prepaid insurance	260.00

12. Prepare an income statement. Figure and record the following component percentages: (a) cost of merchandise sold, (b) gross profit on sales, (c) total expenses, and (d) net income or loss. Round percentage calculations to the nearest 0.1%.

13. Prepare a distribution of net income statement. Net income or loss is to be shared equally.

14. Prepare an owners' equity statement. No additional investments were made.

15. Prepare a balance sheet in report form.

16. Use page 25 of a journal. Journalize and post the adjusting entries.

17. Continue using page 25 of the journal. Journalize and post the closing entries.

18. Prepare a post-closing trial balance.

Viking Marine is a merchandising business organized as a partnership. This business simulation covers the realistic transactions completed by Viking Marine, which sells personal watercraft and water sports items. Transactions are recorded in a journal similar to the one used by CarLand in Part 3. The following activities are included in the accounting cycle for Viking Marine. This business simulation is available from the publisher in either manual or automated versions.

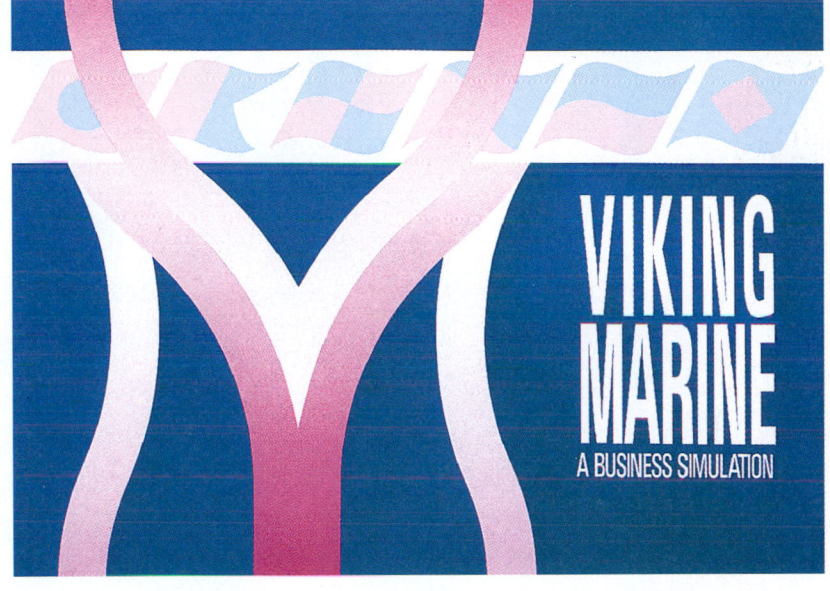

Activities in Viking Marine:

1. Recording transactions in a journal from source documents.

2. Posting items to be posted individually to a general ledger and subsidiary ledger.

3. Recording a payroll in a payroll register. Updating the employee earnings record. Recording payroll journal entries.

4. Posting column totals to a general ledger.

5. Preparing schedules of accounts receivable and accounts payable from subsidiary ledgers.

6. Preparing a trial balance on a work sheet.

7. Planning adjustments and completing a work sheet.

8. Preparing financial statements.

9. Journalizing and posting adjusting entries.

10. Journalizing and posting closing entries.

11. Preparing a post-closing trial balance.

Accounting for a Merchandising Business Organized as a Corporation

GENERAL GOALS

1. Know accounting terminology related to an accounting system for a merchandising business organized as a corporation.

2. Understand accounting concepts and practices related to an accounting system for a merchandising business organized as a corporation.

3. Demonstrate accounting procedures used in an accounting system for a merchandising business organized as a corporation.

Celluphone, Inc.

CHART OF ACCOUNTS

Balance Sheet Accounts

(1000) ASSETS

1100 Current Assets

1105 Cash
1110 Petty Cash
1115 Notes Receivable
1120 Interest Receivable
1125 Accounts Receivable
1130 Allowance for Uncollectible Accounts
1135 Merchandise Inventory
1140 Supplies
1145 Prepaid Insurance

1200 Plant Assets

1205 Office Equipment
1210 Accumulated Depreciation— Office Equipment
1215 Store Equipment
1220 Accumulated Depreciation— Store Equipment

(2000) LIABILITIES

2100 Current Liabilities

2105 Notes Payable
2110 Interest Payable
2115 Accounts Payable
2120 Employee Income Tax Payable
2125 Federal Income Tax Payable
2130 FICA Tax Payable
2135 Sales Tax Payable
2140 Unemployment Tax Payable—Federal
2145 Unemployment Tax Payable—State
2150 Health Insurance Premiums Payable
2155 Dividends Payable

(3000) STOCKHOLDERS' EQUITY

3105 Capital Stock
3110 Retained Earnings
3115 Dividends
3120 Income Summary

Income Statement Accounts

(4000) OPERATING REVENUE

4105 Sales
4110 Sales Discount
4115 Sales Returns and Allowances

(5000) COST OF MERCHANDISE

5105 Purchases
5110 Purchases Discount
5115 Purchases Returns and Allowances

(6000) OPERATING EXPENSES

6105 Advertising Expense
6110 Credit Card Fee Expense
6115 Depreciation Expense— Office Equipment
6120 Depreciation Expense— Store Equipment
6125 Insurance Expense
6130 Miscellaneous Expense
6135 Payroll Taxes Expense
6140 Rent Expense
6145 Salary Expense
6150 Supplies Expense
6155 Uncollectible Accounts Expense
6160 Utilities Expense

(7000) OTHER REVENUE

7105 Gain on Plant Assets
7110 Interest Income

(8000) OTHER EXPENSES

8105 Cash Short and Over
8110 Interest Expense
8115 Loss on Plant Assets

(9000) INCOME TAX EXPENSE

9105 Federal Income Tax Expense

The chart of accounts for Celluphone, Inc. is illustrated above for ready reference as you study Part 4 of this textbook.

19

Recording Purchases and Cash Payments Using Special Journals

ENABLING PERFORMANCE TASKS

After studying Chapter 19, you will be able to:

a Define accounting terms related to purchases and cash payments.

b Identify accounting concepts and practices related to purchases and cash payments.

c Analyze transactions affecting purchases and cash payments.

d Journalize and post transactions related to purchases and cash payments.

TERMS PREVIEW

corporation • share of stock • capital stock • special journal • purchases journal • cash payments journal • list price • trade discount • cash discount • purchases discount • cash short • cash over • general journal • purchases return • purchases allowance • debit memorandum

Reliable financial information is important for the successful operation of a business. However, the amount of information a business needs and can afford varies with the business' size and complexity. Several types of accounting systems may be used to record, summarize, and report a business' financial information. An accounting system may vary from a small manual system operated by one accounting clerk to a large computerized system that requires hundreds of accountants and clerks. A business should use an accounting system that provides the desired financial information with the least amount of effort and cost. Regardless of the accounting system used, financial information is reported for a specified period of time. *(CONCEPT: Accounting Period Cycle)*

CORPORATIONS

Many businesses need amounts of capital that cannot be easily provided by a proprietorship or a partnership. An organization with the legal rights of a person and which may be owned by many persons is called a **corporation**. Many businesses are organized as corporations. A corporation is formed by receiving approval from a state or federal agency. A corporation can own property, incur liabilities, and enter into contracts in its own name. A corporation may also sell ownership in itself. Each unit of ownership in a corporation is called a **share of stock**. Total shares of ownership in a corporation are called **capital stock**.

Celluphone, Inc. is organized as a corporation. Celluphone, Inc. sells cellular phones to corporate customers for use in their company cars and trucks. Celluphone was formed as a corporation because several owners can provide larger amounts of capital than one owner. The principal difference among the accounting records of proprietorships, partnerships, and corporations is in the capital accounts. Proprietorships and partnerships have a single capital and drawing account for each owner. A corporation has separate capital accounts for the stock issued and for the earnings kept in the business. The use of the different capital accounts is explained in more detail in Chapter 26. As in proprietorships and partnerships, information in a corporation's accounting system is kept separate from the personal records of the owners. *(CONCEPT: Business Entity)*

SPECIAL JOURNALS

A business with few transactions may need only one bookkeeper or accounting clerk to record transactions. When one person records transactions, a business may record all entries in one journal. In Part 2, Rugcare used a 5-column journal to record all transactions. In Part 3, CarLand used an 11-column expanded journal to record all transactions. However, a business with many daily transactions may use several different journals. A journal used to record only one kind of transaction is called a **special journal**. Using special journals allows the work of journalizing to be divided among several accounting clerks. The accounting clerks then specialize in the kind of transactions recorded. This specialization helps improve the efficiency of recording transactions.

Whether a single journal or several special journals are used, all business transactions are recorded in a common unit of measurement—the dollar. Recording all transactions in dollar values permits more meaningful comparisons with previous accounting periods and with other businesses. (CONCEPT: *Unit of Measurement*)

Celluphone uses four special journals along with a general journal to record its transactions.

1. Purchases journal—for all purchases on account
2. Cash payments journal—for all cash payments
3. Sales journal—for all sales on account
4. Cash receipts journal—for all cash receipts

A general journal is used for all other transactions.

RECORDING PURCHASES ON ACCOUNT USING A PURCHASES JOURNAL

A special journal used to record *only* purchase on account transactions is called a **purchases journal**. The relationship between Celluphone's purchases journal and the expanded journal described in Chapter 11 is shown in Illustration 19-1.

ILLUSTRATION 19-1 Purchases journal

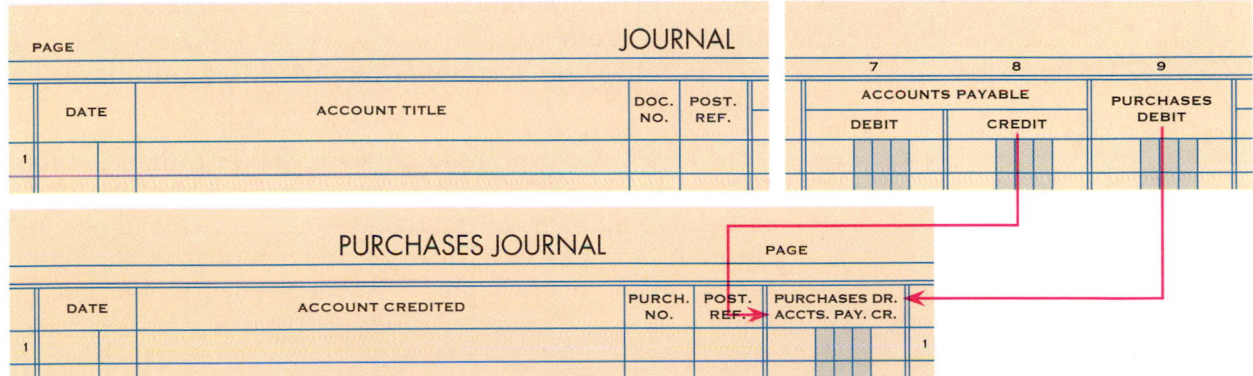

A purchase on account transaction can be recorded on one line of Celluphone's purchases journal. Each entry in the single amount column is both a debit to Purchases and a credit to Accounts Payable. The titles of both general ledger accounts are listed in the single amount column heading. Since the debit and credit entries always affect the same two accounts, recording time is reduced by using only one amount column.

Journalizing Purchases on Account

The source document for recording a purchase on account is a purchase invoice received from a vendor. *(CONCEPT: Objective Evidence)* Celluphone dates, numbers, and verifies each purchase invoice.

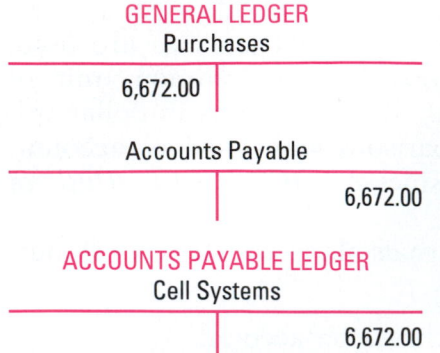

GENERAL LEDGER
Purchases

| 6,672.00 | |

Accounts Payable

| | 6,672.00 |

ACCOUNTS PAYABLE LEDGER
Cell Systems

| | 6,672.00 |

> *March 1, 19--. Purchased merchandise on account from Cell Systems, $6,672.00. Purchase Invoice No. 39.*

The balance of the purchases account is increased by this transaction. Thus, Purchases is debited for $6,672.00. The amount owed to a vendor is increased by this transaction. Therefore, Accounts Payable is credited for $6,672.00. The same amount is also credited to the account of Cell Systems in the accounts payable ledger.

Purchases are recorded at their cost. *(CONCEPT: Historical Cost)* The purchases journal entry to record this purchase on account transaction is shown in Illustration 19-2.

ILLUSTRATION 19-2

Purchases journal entry to record a purchase on account

	DATE		ACCOUNT CREDITED	PURCH. NO.	POST. REF.	PURCHASES DR. ACCTS. PAY. CR.	
1	Mar. 19--	1	Cell Systems	39		6 6 7 2 00	1
2							2
3							3
4							4

PURCHASES JOURNAL — PAGE 3

FYI

The purchases account is used to record only merchandise that will be sold to customers.

The date, *19--, Mar. 1,* is written in the Date column. The vendor name, *Cell Systems,* is written in the Account Credited column. The number stamped on the invoice, *39,* is entered in the Purch. No. column. The amount of the invoice, *$6,672.00,* is recorded in the amount column.

Each purchase on account is recorded in a purchases journal in the same way.

In Part 3, CarLand used an abbreviation to indicate the type of source document in the Post. Ref. column of the expanded journal because all kinds of transactions are recorded in one journal. However, only purchase invoices are recorded in the purchases journal so the abbreviation *P* is not needed in the Purch. No. column.

Posting from a Purchases Journal to an Accounts Payable Ledger

The amount on each line of a purchases journal is posted as a credit to the named vendor account in the accounts payable ledger.

Celluphone posts frequently to the accounts payable ledger. By posting frequently, each vendor account always shows an up-to-date balance. Posting from line 1 of a purchases journal to a vendor account in the accounts payable ledger is shown in Illustration 19-3.

ILLUSTRATION 19-3

Posting from a purchases journal to an accounts payable ledger

| | PURCHASES JOURNAL | | | | PAGE 3 | |

PURCHASES JOURNAL — PAGE 3

	DATE	ACCOUNT CREDITED	PURCH. NO.	POST. REF.	PURCHASES DR. ACCTS. PAY. CR.	
1	Mar. 1	Cell Systems	39	220	6 6 7 2 00	1
2						2

VENDOR *Cell Systems*   VENDOR NO. 220

DATE	ITEM	POST. REF.	DEBIT	CREDIT	CREDIT BALANCE
Mar. 1	Balance	✓			2 0 7 9 00
1		P3		6 6 7 2 00	8 7 5 1 00

The date, *1*, is recorded in the Date column of the vendor account. The abbreviation for the purchases journal and the page number of the journal, *P3*, is written in the Post. Ref. column of the account. The amount, *$6,672.00*, is entered in the Credit column of the vendor account. The amount in the Credit column is added to the previous balance in the Credit Balance column ($2,079.00 + $6,672.00 = $8,751.00). The new balance, *$8,751.00*, is recorded in the Credit Balance column. The vendor number for Cell Systems, *220*, is written in the Post. Ref. column of the purchases journal to show that posting has been completed for this line.

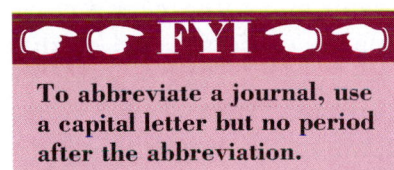

FYI

To abbreviate a journal, use a capital letter but no period after the abbreviation.

When several journals are used, an abbreviation is used to show the journal from which the posting is made. The abbreviation *P* is used for the purchases journal. The abbreviation *P3* means page 3 of the purchases journal.

Posting from a purchases journal to an accounts payable ledger is the same as posting from an expanded journal's Accounts Payable Credit column, as described in Chapter 13.

Posting from a Purchases Journal to a General Ledger

At the end of each month, a purchases journal is totaled and ruled, as shown in Illustration 19-4 on page 476.

A single line is ruled across the amount column of the purchases journal under the last amount recorded. The date of the last day of the month, *31*, is entered in the Date column. The word *Total* is written in the Account Credited column. The amount column is added, and the total is written directly below the single line. Double lines are ruled across the amount column under the total amount.

ILLUSTRATION 19-4   Posting from a purchases journal to a general ledger

	DATE	ACCOUNT CREDITED	PURCH. NO.	POST. REF.	PURCHASES DR. ACCTS. PAY. CR.	
23	31	Hopkins Company	61	250	2 1 1 0 00	23
24	31	Total			108 0 4 6 00	24
25					(5105) (2115)	25

PURCHASES JOURNAL   PAGE *3*

ACCOUNT *Purchases*   ACCOUNT NO. *5105*

DATE	ITEM	POST. REF.	DEBIT	CREDIT	BALANCE DEBIT	BALANCE CREDIT
16		CP6	2 0 0 00		3 3 7 0 00	
31		P3	108 0 4 6 00		111 4 1 6 00	

ACCOUNT *Accounts Payable*   ACCOUNT NO. *2115*

DATE	ITEM	POST. REF.	DEBIT	CREDIT	BALANCE DEBIT	BALANCE CREDIT
29		G4		1 2 0 00		12 4 6 6 00
31		P3		108 0 4 6 00		120 5 1 2 00

Illustration 19-4 also shows the posting of a purchases journal to a general ledger. The total amount of the purchases journal is posted to two general ledger accounts. The total amount, $108,046.00, is posted to Purchases as a debit and to Accounts Payable as a credit. This maintains the equality of debits and credits in the general ledger.

After the total is posted to Purchases, the account number, *5105*, is written under the total in the purchases journal. After this total is posted to Accounts Payable, the account number, *2115*, is written under the purchases journal total. Both account numbers are written in parentheses. This procedure is the same as posting totals of special amount columns in any journal.

Illustration 19-5 shows a summary of the procedure for journalizing and posting using a purchases journal.

Audit Your Understanding

1. What is a corporation?
2. Why are special journals used?
3. What is the source document for recording a purchase on account?

RECORDING CASH PAYMENTS USING A CASH PAYMENTS JOURNAL

Celluphone uses another special journal for recording *only* cash payments. A special journal used to record only cash payment transactions is called a **cash payments journal**. The relationship

1 Celluphone records a purchase on account transaction on a single line of a one-column purchases journal.

2 Items in the purchases journal's amount column are posted separately to vendor accounts in the accounts payable ledger.

3 At the end of the month, the purchases journal amount column total is posted to two general ledger accounts. **Purchases** is debited; **Accounts Payable** is credited.

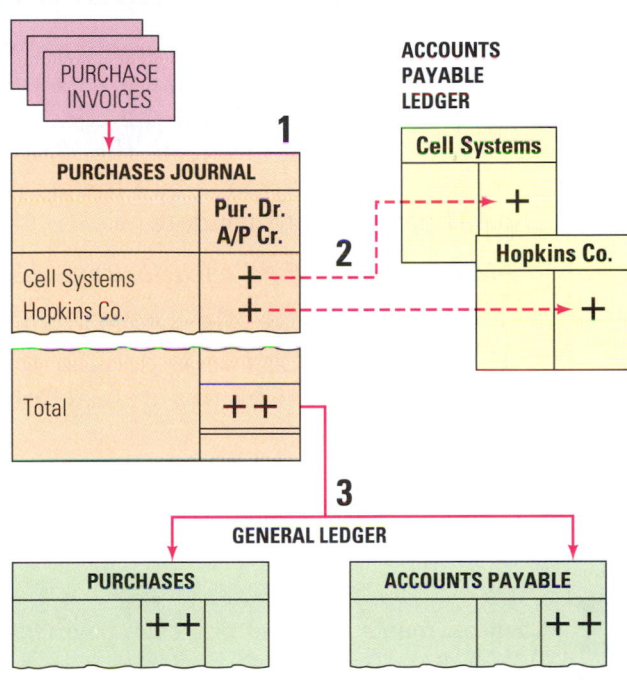

between Celluphone's cash payments journal and the expanded journal described in Chapter 11 is shown in Illustration 19-6.

ILLUSTRATION 19-6   Cash payments journal

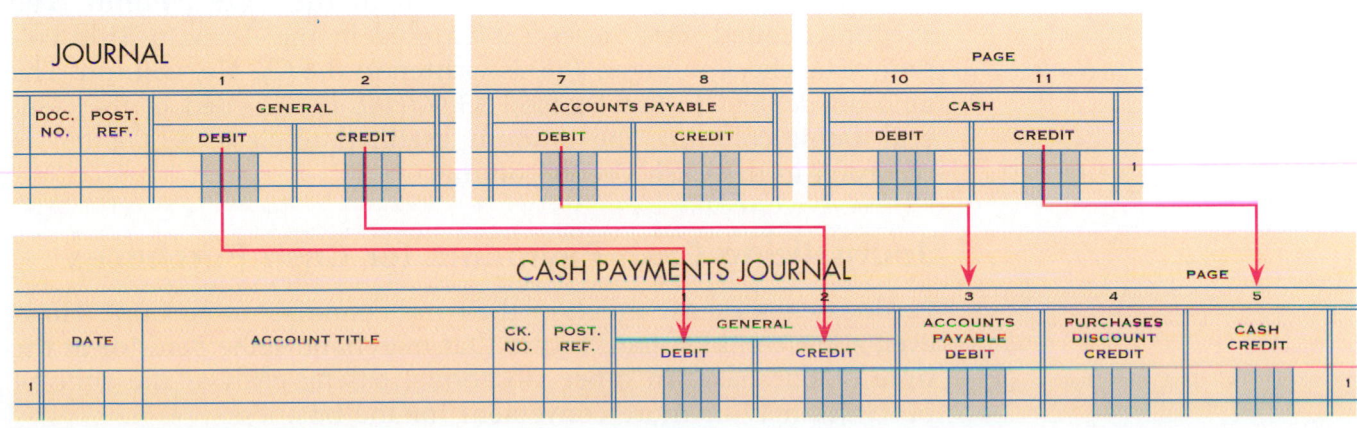

Those columns of an expanded journal needed to record only cash payments are included in Celluphone's cash payments journal. In addition, Celluphone has many cash payment transactions that include a discount on the purchases. Therefore, a special amount column is provided in the cash payments journal to record this discount. Transactions that do not occur often, such as monthly rent, are recorded in the General columns.

Journalizing Cash Payments for Expenses

All of Celluphone's cash payments are recorded in a cash payments journal. A few payments, such as bank service charges, are made as direct withdrawals from the company's bank account. For these payments not using a check, the source document is a memorandum. Most cash payments are for (1) expenses, (2) cash purchases, and (3) payments to vendors.

March 1, 19--. Paid cash for rent, $3,000.00. Check No. 148.

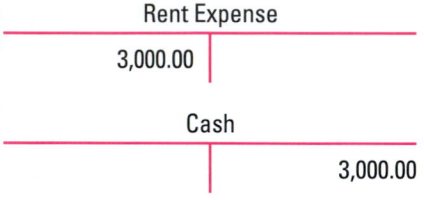

The amount of rent expense is increased by this transaction. Therefore, Rent Expense is debited for $3,000.00. The amount of cash is decreased by this transaction. Therefore, Cash is credited for $3,000.00.

The cash payments journal entry to record this cash payment for an expense is shown on line 1, Illustration 19-7.

ILLUSTRATION 19-7   Cash payments recorded in a cash payments journal

CASH PAYMENTS JOURNAL   PAGE 6

	DATE		ACCOUNT TITLE	CK. NO.	POST. REF.	GENERAL DEBIT	GENERAL CREDIT	ACCOUNTS PAYABLE DEBIT	PURCHASES DISCOUNT CREDIT	CASH CREDIT	
1	Mar.	1	Rent Expense	148		3 0 0 0 00				3 0 0 0 00	1
2		1	Purchases	149		4 8 0 00				4 8 0 00	2

The date, *19--, Mar. 1*, is written in the Date column. The account debited, Rent Expense, is entered in the Account Title column. The check number, *148*, is written in the Ck. No. column. The amount debited to Rent Expense, *$3,000.00*, is recorded in the General Debit column. The amount credited to Cash, *$3,000.00*, is recorded in the Cash Credit column.

Journalizing Cash Payments for Cash Purchases

Businesses purchase much of their merchandise on account. However, some vendors may require that merchandise be paid for at the time of purchase. In other situations, paying cash at the time of purchase may be more convenient for the business.

Trade Discount. Many manufacturers and wholesalers print price lists and catalogs to describe their products. Generally, prices listed in catalogs are the manufacturers' suggested retail prices. A business' printed or catalog price is called a **list price**. When a merchandising business purchases a number of products from a manufacturer, the price frequently is quoted as "list price less trade discount." A reduction in the list price granted to customers is called a **trade discount**. Trade discounts are used to quote different prices for different quantities purchased without changing catalog or list prices.

When a trade discount is granted, the seller's invoice shows the actual amount charged. This amount after the trade discount has been deducted from the list price is referred to as the invoice amount. Only the invoice amount is used in a journal entry. *(CONCEPT: Historical Cost)* The invoice is recorded by both the seller and buyer at the same amount. No journal entry is made to show the amount of a trade discount.

Cash Purchases. Celluphone wishes to buy 80 cellular phone carrying cases for cash. The price quoted to Celluphone was $10.00 list price per case less 40% trade discount. The total invoice amount is calculated in three steps.

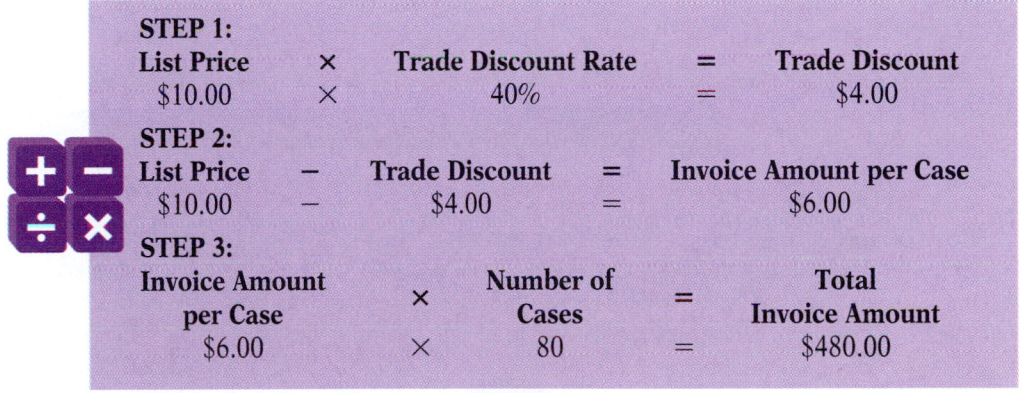

STEP 1:

List Price	×	Trade Discount Rate	=	Trade Discount
$10.00	×	40%	=	$4.00

STEP 2:

List Price	−	Trade Discount	=	Invoice Amount per Case
$10.00	−	$4.00	=	$6.00

STEP 3:

Invoice Amount per Case	×	Number of Cases	=	Total Invoice Amount
$6.00	×	80	=	$480.00

Celluphone's purchase price for the 80 carrying cases will be $480.00, the list price less the trade discount.

March 1, 19--. Purchased merchandise for cash, $480.00. Check No. 149.

The amount of purchases is increased by this transaction. Thus, Purchases is debited for $480.00. The amount of cash is decreased by this transaction. Therefore, Cash is credited for $480.00.

The entry to record this cash purchase of merchandise is shown on line 2 of the cash payments journal, Illustration 19-7.

The date, *1*, is written in the Date column. The account debited, Purchases, is entered in the Account Title column. The check number, *149*, is written in the Ck. No. column. The amount debited to

Purchases	
480.00	

Cash	
	480.00

Purchases, *$480.00*, is recorded in the General Debit column. The amount credited to Cash, $480.00, is recorded in the Cash Credit column.

Journalizing Cash Payments for Purchases on Account

Normally, the total amount shown on a purchase invoice is the amount that a customer is expected to pay by an agreed due date. However, some vendors offer their customers an incentive to pay before the due date.

A cash discount is given for early payment of an invoice.

Cash Discount. To encourage early payment, a vendor may allow a deduction from the invoice amount. A deduction that a vendor allows on the invoice amount to encourage prompt payment is called a **cash discount**. A cash discount is usually stated as a percentage that can be deducted from the invoice amount.

The terms of sale on an invoice may be written as *2/10, n/30*. These terms are commonly read *two ten, net thirty*. *Two ten* means 2% of the invoice amount may be deducted if the invoice is paid within 10 days of the invoice date. *Net thirty* means that the total invoice amount must be paid within 30 days. A business may also indicate the date for full payment of an invoice as *EOM*. Payment specified as *EOM* means that full payment is expected not later than the end of the month.

■ Philip Showalter ■

PHILIP SHOWALTER, D.D.S., GERMANTOWN, OHIO

Most people don't think of their dentist as a businessperson in the community. They don't stop to think that a dentist has to pay for office space, buy office and dental equipment, hire employees, and pay taxes just like any other businessperson.

Philip Showalter does know what kind of businessperson a dentist needs to be. Showalter is a dentist with his own practice. He says that people would be surprised—as he was—at the amount of time a dentist has to spend on the business side of the practice.

Showalter took a year of college accounting, figuring it would be useful no matter what business he went into.

When he started his own dental practice, he found that the accounting background helped him analyze the business side of the practice. Knowing the language of accounting along with having to analyze financial information helped him understand what his accountant was telling him and helped him make sound financial decisions.

Showalter was a dentist in the military and also worked as a dentist in the public health area. He saved just enough money to start his own practice. He says, however, "I had to work long, hard hours to make ends meet in the beginning, but eventually my persistence paid off and I was able to succeed."

When asked for advice to students, Showalter is very direct. He believes that students should stay in school and take their schoolwork seriously, just as they would a job. Persistence and determination are also key components of success.

Personal Visions in Business

Purchases

Debit side Normal balance Increase	Credit side Decrease

Purchases Discount

Debit side Decrease	Credit side Normal balance Increase

Purchases Discount. A cash discount on purchases taken by a customer is called a **purchases discount**. When a purchases discount is taken, the customer pays less cash than the invoice amount previously recorded in the purchases account. Therefore, purchases discounts are deducted from purchases. Purchases discounts are recorded in a general ledger account titled Purchases Discount.

In Celluphone's general ledger, the account Purchases Discount is numbered 5110. The purchases discount account is in the cost of merchandise division of Celluphone's general ledger. An account that offsets a related account is known as a contra account. Thus, on an income statement, the contra account, Purchases Discount, is deducted from the balance of its related account, Purchases.

Since contra accounts are deductions from their related accounts, contra account normal balances are opposite the normal balances of their related accounts. The normal balance for a purchases account is a debit. Therefore, the normal balance for Purchases Discount, a contra account to Purchases, is a credit.

Cash Payments on Account with Purchases Discounts. Celluphone's policy is to pay all vendors on or before the date for taking the purchases discount. This policy reduces the cost of merchandise purchased by Celluphone.

March 8, 19--. Paid cash on account to Cell Systems, $6,538.56, covering Purchase Invoice No. 39 for $6,672.00, less 2% discount, $133.44. Check No. 168.

The cash amount paid after the purchases discount is calculated in two steps.

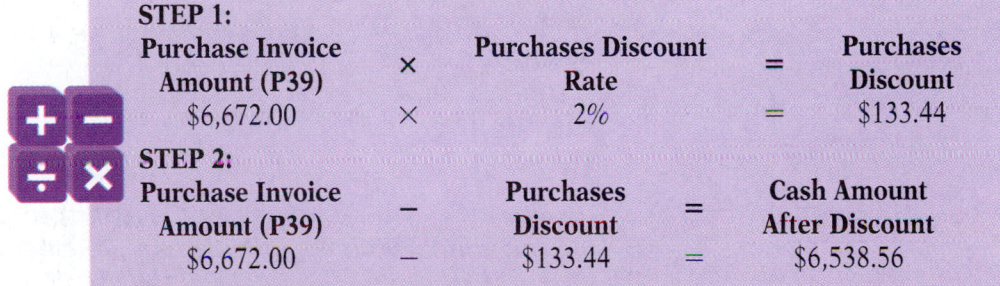

STEP 1:

Purchase Invoice Amount (P39)	×	Purchases Discount Rate	=	Purchases Discount
$6,672.00	×	2%	=	$133.44

STEP 2:

Purchase Invoice Amount (P39)	−	Purchases Discount	=	Cash Amount After Discount
$6,672.00	−	$133.44	=	$6,538.56

Accounts Payable is debited for the amount of the purchase invoice, $6,672.00. This debit decreases the amount owed to vendors. This same amount, $6,672.00, is also debited to the account of Cell Systems in the accounts payable ledger.

Cash is credited for the amount of the check, $6,538.56. Purchases Discount is credited for the amount of the purchases discount, $133.44.

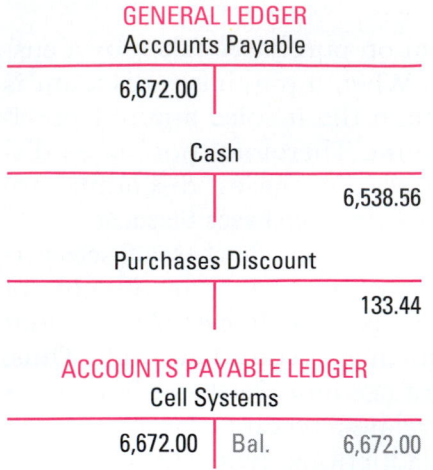

GENERAL LEDGER
Accounts Payable

| 6,672.00 | |

Cash

| | 6,538.56 |

Purchases Discount

| | 133.44 |

ACCOUNTS PAYABLE LEDGER
Cell Systems

| 6,672.00 | Bal. | 6,672.00 |

The cash payments journal entry to record this payment on account with a purchases discount is shown in Illustration 19-8.

The date, *8*, is written in the Date column. The vendor name, *Cell Systems*, is recorded in the Account Title column. The check number, *168*, is written in the Ck. No. column. The purchase invoice amount, *$6,672.00*, is entered in the Accounts Payable Debit column. The purchases discount amount, *$133.44*, is recorded in the Purchases Discount Credit column. The invoice amount less the purchases discount, *$6,538.56*, is entered in the Cash Credit column. The total of the two credits ($133.44 + $6,538.56) is $6,672.00, which is equal to the one debit of $6,672.00.

Purchases discounts are recorded frequently by Celluphone. Therefore, a special amount column, Purchases Discount Credit, is provided in the cash payments journal.

| **ILLUSTRATION 19-8** | Cash payments journal entry to record a cash payment on account with a purchases discount |

CASH PAYMENTS JOURNAL

PAGE 6

| | DATE | ACCOUNT TITLE | CK. NO. | POST. REF. | GENERAL | | ACCOUNTS PAYABLE DEBIT | PURCHASES DISCOUNT CREDIT | CASH CREDIT | |
					DEBIT	CREDIT				
21	8	Cell Systems	168				6 672 00	1 33 44	6 538 56	21
22										22
23										23

Cash Payments on Account without Purchases Discounts. Some vendors do not provide purchases discounts. In this case the full invoice amount is paid. Celluphone purchased merchandise on account from Electro Sound on February 2. Electro Sound's credit terms are n/30. Therefore, Celluphone will pay the full amount of the purchase invoice, $1,740.00, within 30 days of the invoice date, February 2.

March 2, 19--. Paid cash on account to Electro Sound, $1,740.00, covering Purchase Invoice No. 21. Check No. 150.

Accounts Payable is debited for the amount of the pur-chase invoice, $1,740.00. This debit decreases the amount owed to vendors. This same amount, $1,740.00, is also debited to the account of Electro Sound in the accounts payable ledger. Cash is decreased by this transaction. Therefore, Cash is credited for the amount of the check, $1,740.00, which is also the full amount of the purchase invoice.

The cash payments journal entry to record this payment on account without a purchases discount is shown in Illustration 19-9.

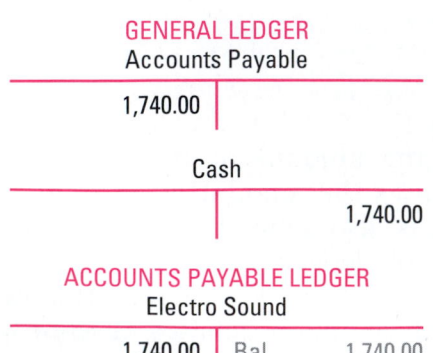

GENERAL LEDGER
Accounts Payable

| 1,740.00 | |

Cash

| | 1,740.00 |

ACCOUNTS PAYABLE LEDGER
Electro Sound

| 1,740.00 | Bal. | 1,740.00 |

CASH PAYMENTS JOURNAL   PAGE 6

					1	2	3	4	5
DATE	ACCOUNT TITLE	CK. NO.	POST. REF.	GENERAL DEBIT	GENERAL CREDIT	ACCOUNTS PAYABLE DEBIT	PURCHASES DISCOUNT CREDIT	CASH CREDIT	
2	Electro Sound	150				1 740 00		1 740 00	

The date, *2*, is written in the Date column. The vendor name, *Electro Sound*, is recorded in the Account Title column. The check number, *150*, is written in the Ck. No. column. The purchase invoice amount, *$1,740.00*, is entered in the Accounts Payable Debit column. The same amount, *$1,740.00*, is entered in the Cash Credit column.

Journalizing Cash Payments to Replenish a Petty Cash Fund

Establishing and replenishing a petty cash fund is described for Rugcare in Chapter 7. Celluphone follows procedures similar to those used by Rugcare to account for and safeguard its petty cash fund.

Regardless of how careful a petty cash custodian may be, errors may be made when making payments from a petty cash fund. These errors cause a difference between actual cash on hand and the custodian's record of the amount of cash that should be on hand. The amount of petty cash that should be on hand is the established amount of the petty cash fund less the amount of petty cash payments for the period. To keep the petty cash fund at a constant amount, differences are recorded at the end of a fiscal period as well as at other times when the petty cash fund is replenished. Differences are determined by comparing the amount that should be on hand with the amount of cash in the petty cash box.

Cash Short and Over Account.   Cash in the petty cash box may be less than what the cash balance should be according to the custodian's records. A petty cash on hand amount that is less than a recorded amount is called **cash short**. Cash in the petty cash box may also be more than the cash balance should be according to the custodian's records. A petty cash on hand amount that is more than a recorded amount is called **cash over**. Amounts of petty cash short and petty cash over are recorded in an account titled Cash Short and Over.

A cash short and over account is a temporary account. The account is used to record shortages and overages, if any, each time the petty cash fund is replenished throughout the year. At the end of the fiscal year, the cash short and over account is closed to Income

FYI

Petty cash is an amount of cash on hand and used for small payments.

Summary. The cash short and over account is unique because it may have the characteristics of an expense account or the characteristics of a revenue account. If the balance of the account is a debit, similar to expense accounts, the account balance is an expense. If the balance of the account is a credit, similar to revenue accounts, the account balance is revenue. Therefore, the balance side of a cash short and over account determines whether it is an expense or revenue.

Cash Short and Over	
Debit side Increase cash short	Credit side Increase cash over

Cash short is an expense and, therefore, is debited to the account Cash Short and Over. Cash over is revenue and, therefore, is credited to Cash Short and Over.

Petty Cash Short. A petty cash on hand amount that is less than a recorded amount is known as cash short. Celluphone has an established petty cash fund of $300.00. Prior to replenishment of the petty cash fund on March 31, the custodian had receipts for the following total payments: supplies, $87.80; advertising, $43.75; and miscellaneous, $97.90. A cash count shows $66.55 in the petty cash box. A comparison is made between the cash that should be on hand and the amount actually on hand in the petty cash box. From the information above, Celluphone's petty cash custodian prepares a petty cash report, as shown in Illustration 19-10.

ILLUSTRATION 19-10   Petty cash report for replenishment of a petty cash fund with cash short

PETTY CASH REPORT	Date: March 31, 19--		
Explanation	Amounts		
Fund total			300 00
Payments:			
Supplies	87	80	
Advertising	43	75	
Miscellaneous	97	90	
Less total payments			229 45
Equals recorded amount on hand			70 55
Less actual amount on hand			66 55
Equals cash short			4 00
Total payments			229 45
Plus cash short			4 00
Equals amount to replenish			233 45

The petty cash report in Illustration 19-10 shows that the actual cash on hand ($66.55) is $4.00 less than the amount the records show should be on hand ($70.55). Therefore, the petty cash fund is short.

The petty cash fund is replenished for the amount paid out, $229.45, plus cash short, $4.00. This total amount, $233.45, restores the fund's cash balance to its original amount, $300.00 ($229.45 + $4.00 + $66.55 cash on hand).

Supplies
| 87.80 | |

Advertising Expense
| 43.75 | |

Miscellaneous Expense
| 97.90 | |

Cash Short and Over
| 4.00 | |

Cash
| | 233.45 |

March 31, 19--. Paid cash to replenish the petty cash fund, $233.45: supplies, $87.80; advertising, $43.75; miscellaneous, $97.90; cash short, $4.00. Check No. 209.

Debit entries include the accounts for which cash payments have been made plus Cash Short and Over. Cash is decreased by this transaction. Therefore, Cash is credited for the amount of the check to replenish the petty cash fund, $233.45, which is also the sum of the debit entries.

The cash payments journal entry to record this replenishment of the petty cash fund with cash short is shown in Illustration 19-11.

Petty Cash Over. A petty cash on hand amount that is more than a recorded amount is known as cash over.

ILLUSTRATION 19-11 Cash payments journal entry to record replenishment of a petty cash fund with cash short

CASH PAYMENTS JOURNAL   PAGE 8

						1 GENERAL DEBIT	2 GENERAL CREDIT	3 ACCOUNTS PAYABLE DEBIT	4 PURCHASES DISCOUNT CREDIT	5 CASH CREDIT	
	DATE	ACCOUNT TITLE	CK. NO.	POST. REF.							
19	31	Supplies	209			87 80				233 45	19
20		Advertising Expense				43 75					20
21		Miscellaneous Expense				97 90					21
22		Cash Short and Over				4 00					22
23											23

Prior to Celluphone's replenishment of the petty cash fund on April 30, the custodian had receipts for the following total payments: supplies, $107.45; advertising, $57.00; and miscellaneous, $121.90. A cash count shows $16.20 in the petty cash box. A comparison is made between the cash that should be on hand and the amount actually on hand in the petty cash box. From the information above, Celluphone's petty cash custodian prepares a petty cash report, as shown in Illustration 19-12 on page 486.

The petty cash report in Illustration 19-12 shows that cash on hand ($16.20) is $2.55 more than what the records show should be on hand ($13.65). Therefore, the petty cash fund is over.

The petty cash fund will be replenished for the amount paid out, $286.35, less cash over, $2.55. This net amount, $283.80, will restore the fund's cash balance to its original amount, $300.00 ($286.35 − $2.55 + $16.20 cash on hand).

April 30, 19--. Paid cash to replenish the petty cash fund, $283.80: supplies, $107.45; advertising, $57.00; miscellaneous, $121.90; cash over, $2.55. Check No. 267.

ILLUSTRATION 19-12

Petty cash report for replenishment of a petty cash fund with cash over

PETTY CASH REPORT		Date: April 30, 19--	
Explanation		Amounts	
Fund total		300	00
Payments:			
Supplies	107 45		
Advertising	57 00		
Miscellaneous	121 90		
Less total payments		286	35
Equals recorded amount on hand		13	65
Less actual amount on hand		16	20
Equals cash over		2	55
Total payments		286	35
Less cash over		2	55
Equals amount to replenish		283	80

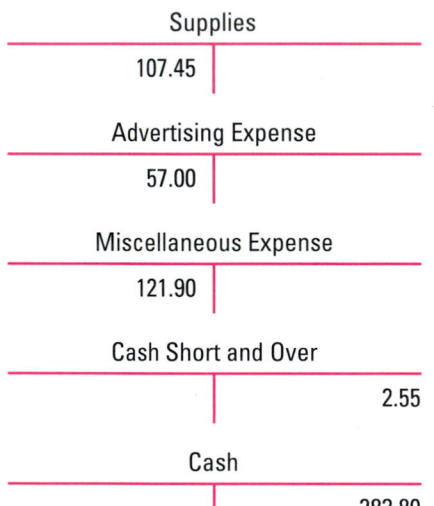

Supplies
107.45

Advertising Expense
57.00

Miscellaneous Expense
121.90

Cash Short and Over
2.55

Cash
283.80

Debit entries include the accounts for which cash payments have been made. Credit entries are Cash, $283.80, and Cash Short and Over, $2.55, since cash on hand was over this period. The sum of the debit entries equals the sum of the credit entries to Cash and Cash Short and Over.

The cash payments journal entry to record this replenishment of the petty cash fund with cash over is shown in Illustration 19-13.

Cash short is not an operating expense, nor is cash over operating revenue. Therefore, Cash Short and Over is not listed under operating expenses or operating revenue in a chart of accounts. Cash Short and Over is listed in the other expense division in a chart of accounts if the balance is a debit. If the account balance is a credit, the balance is listed in the other revenue division.

In Celluphone's general ledger, the account Cash Short and Over is numbered 8105. The cash short and over account may be an expense or a revenue, depending on whether it has a debit or credit

ILLUSTRATION 19-13

Cash payments journal entry to record replenishment of a petty cash fund with cash over

	DATE	ACCOUNT TITLE	CK. NO.	POST. REF.	GENERAL DEBIT	GENERAL CREDIT	ACCOUNTS PAYABLE DEBIT	PURCHASES DISCOUNT CREDIT	CASH CREDIT	
					1	2	3	4	5	
18	30	Supplies	267		107 45				283 80	18
19		Advertising Expense			57 00					19
20		Miscellaneous Expense			121 90					20
21		Cash Short and Over				2 55				21
22										22

balance. Celluphone lists the account in the other expense division of its general ledger, however, because the balance at year end normally is a debit, making the balance of the account an expense.

Posting from a Cash Payments Journal to an Accounts Payable Ledger

Illustration 19-14 shows the posting of a cash payments journal entry to a vendor account. Each entry in the Accounts Payable Debit column of a cash payments journal affects the vendor named in the Account Title column. Each amount listed in this column is posted separately to the proper vendor account in the accounts payable ledger. In this way, each vendor account shows an up-to-date balance.

| ILLUSTRATION 19-14 | Posting from a cash payments journal to an accounts payable ledger |

CASH PAYMENTS JOURNAL PAGE 6

					1 GENERAL DEBIT	2 GENERAL CREDIT	3 ACCOUNTS PAYABLE DEBIT	4 PURCHASES DISCOUNT CREDIT	5 CASH CREDIT	
DATE		ACCOUNT TITLE	CK. NO.	POST. REF.						
3	2	Electro Sound	150	240			1 7 4 0 00		1 7 4 0 00	3
4										4

VENDOR *Electro Sound*   VENDOR NO. **240**

DATE	ITEM	POST. REF.	DEBIT	CREDIT	CREDIT BALANCE
Mar. 1	Balance	✓			2 4 6 0 00
2		CP6	1 7 4 0 00		7 2 0 00

The date, *2*, is written in the Date column of the vendor account. *CP6* is entered in the Post. Ref. column. The abbreviation *CP6* means page 6 of the cash payments journal. The amount in the Accounts Payable Debit column, *$1,740.00*, is posted to the Debit column of the vendor account. The amount in the Debit column of the vendor account is subtracted from the previous balance in the Credit Balance column ($2,460.00 ms $1,740.00 = $720.00). The new balance, *$720.00*, is recorded in the Credit Balance column. The vendor number for Electro Sound, *240*, is written in the Post. Ref. column of the cash payments journal. This last step shows completion of posting of this line.

FYI

By the year 2000, the International Franchise Association (IFA) projects that almost half of all retail stores will be franchises.

Posting from a Cash Payments Journal to a General Ledger

Each amount in the General columns of a cash payments journal is posted separately to a general ledger account. Therefore, the totals of the general amount columns are not posted. However, the monthly total of each special amount column is posted to a general ledger account.

Posting from the General Columns of a Cash Payments Journal. Separate amounts in the General columns are posted individually to the general ledger account named in the Account Title column. Illustration 19-15 shows the posting from a General column of a cash payments journal to a general ledger account.

| ILLUSTRATION 19-15 | Posting from the general columns of a cash payments journal to a general ledger |

The date, *Mar. 1*, is written in the Date column of the account Rent Expense. *CP6* is recorded in the Post. Ref. column to show that the amount is from page 6 of the cash payments journal. The amount in the General Debit column, *$3,000.00*, is posted to the Debit column of the general ledger account **Rent Expense**. The existing amount in the Balance Debit column, *$6,000.00*, is added to the March 1 debit entry, *$3,000.00*. The new balance, *$9,000.00*, is written in the Balance Debit column. The number of the rent expense account, *6140*, is entered in the Post. Ref. column of the cash payments journal. This account number shows that posting of the general amount on this line in the journal is complete.

Posting Totals from the Special Columns of a Cash Payments Journal. At the end of each month, equality of debits and credits is proved for a cash payments journal. The cash payments journal is ruled as shown in Illustration 19-16. The total of each special column is then posted to the account named in the journal's column headings. The date and CP8 are recorded in the Date and Post. Ref. columns of the account. The total is entered in the appropriate amount column, and the new account balance is recorded. As a last step, the account number is written in parentheses below the journal column total. This procedure is followed until all special amount column totals are posted.

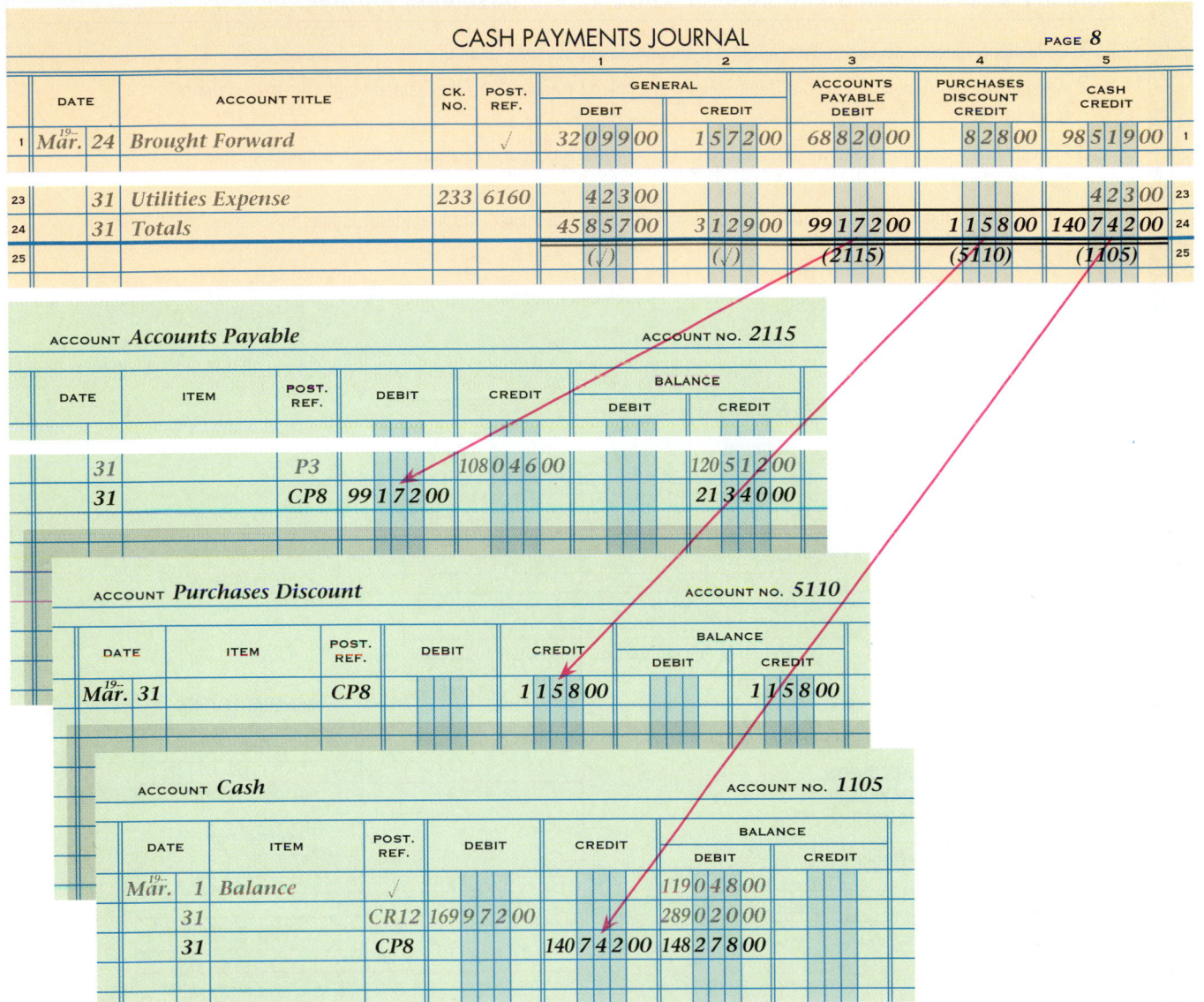

Posting totals from the special columns of a cash payments journal to a general ledger

Posting from a cash receipts journal to the cash account, shown on line 2 of the cash account, Illustration 19-16, is described in Chapter 20.

The totals of the General columns are not posted. Each amount in these columns was posted separately to a general ledger account. To indicate that these totals are not to be posted, a check mark is placed in parentheses below each column total.

Illustration 19-17 on page 490 shows a summary of the procedure for journalizing and posting cash payments using a cash payments journal.

Summary of journalizing and posting using a cash payments journal

1 Celluphone records all cash payments in a 5-column cash payments journal.

2 Amounts in the Accounts Payable Debit column are posted frequently to the named vendor in the accounts payable ledger.

3 Individual items in the General Debit and Credit columns are posted frequently during the month to the general ledger.

4 At the end of the month, the totals of the special columns are posted to the general ledger.

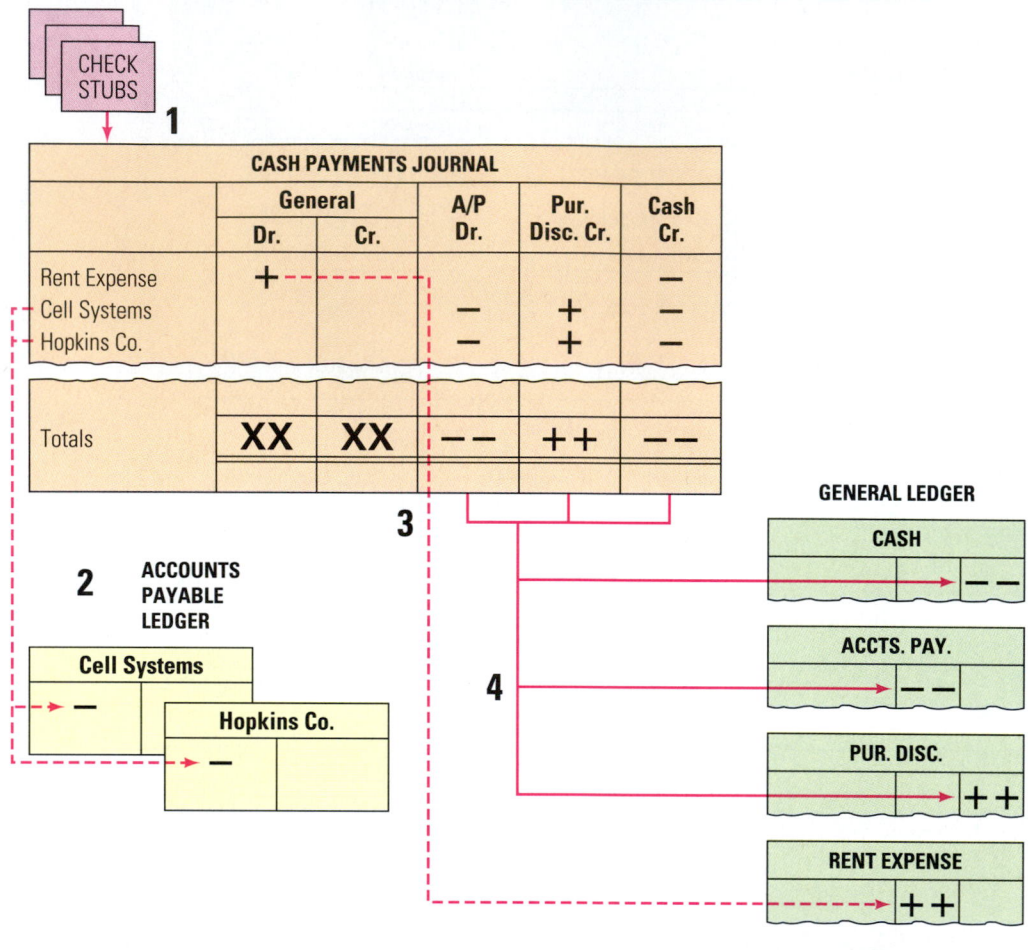

RECORDING TRANSACTIONS USING A GENERAL JOURNAL

General journals are used to record transactions that cannot be recorded in a special journal.

Not all transactions are recorded in Celluphone's special journals. For example, when Celluphone buys supplies on account, the transaction is not recorded in any of the special journals. The transaction is not a cash payment transaction, so it is not recorded in the cash payments journal. The transaction is not a purchase of merchandise on account, so it is not recorded in the purchases journal.

A journal with two amount columns in which all kinds of entries can be recorded is called a **general journal.** A general journal has only two amount columns: a Debit amount column and a Credit amount column. Any journal entry can be recorded in a general journal by writing the account title and amount for each account affected. Celluphone uses a general journal for recording journal entries that cannot be recorded in any of the special journals. Celluphone records transactions for purchases returns and allowances and for buying supplies on account in its general journal. The relationship between Celluphone's general journal and the expanded journal described in Chapter 11 is shown in Illustration 19-18.

ILLUSTRATION 19-18   General journal

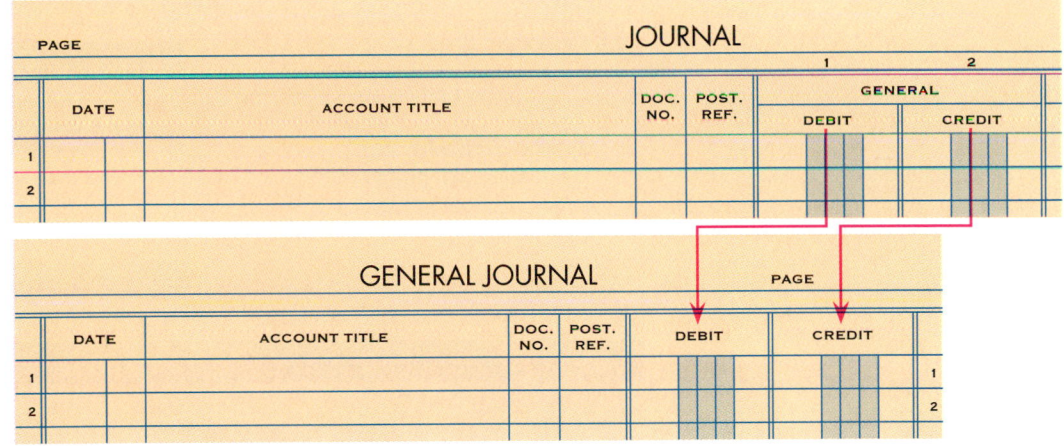

Purchases Returns and Allowances

A purchases return is made when a customer returns part or all of the merchandise purchased.

A customer may not want to keep merchandise that is inferior in quality or is damaged when received. A customer may be allowed to return part or all of the merchandise purchased. Credit allowed for the purchase price of returned merchandise, resulting in a decrease in the customer's accounts payable, is called a **purchases return.** When merchandise is damaged but still usable or is of a different quality than that ordered, the vendor may let the customer keep the merchandise at a reduced price. Credit allowed for part of the purchase price of merchandise that is not returned, resulting in a decrease in the customer's accounts payable, is called a **purchases allowance.**

A purchases return or allowance should be confirmed in writing. The details may be stated in a letter or on a form. A form prepared by the customer showing the price deduction taken by the customer for returns and allowances is called a **debit memorandum.** The form is called a debit memorandum because the customer records the amount as a debit (deduction) to the vendor account to show the decrease in the amount owed.

The customer may use a copy of the debit memorandum as the source document for journalizing purchases returns and allowances. However, the customer may wait for written confirmation from the vendor and use that confirmation as the source document. Celluphone issues a debit memorandum for each purchases return or allowance. This debit memorandum is used as the source document for purchases returns and allowances transactions. *(CONCEPT: Objective Evidence)* The transaction can be recorded immediately without waiting for written confirmation from the vendor. The original of the debit memorandum is sent to the vendor. The carbon copy is kept by Celluphone. The debit memorandum form used by Celluphone is shown in Illustration 19-19.

ILLUSTRATION 19-19 Debit memorandum for purchases returns and allowances

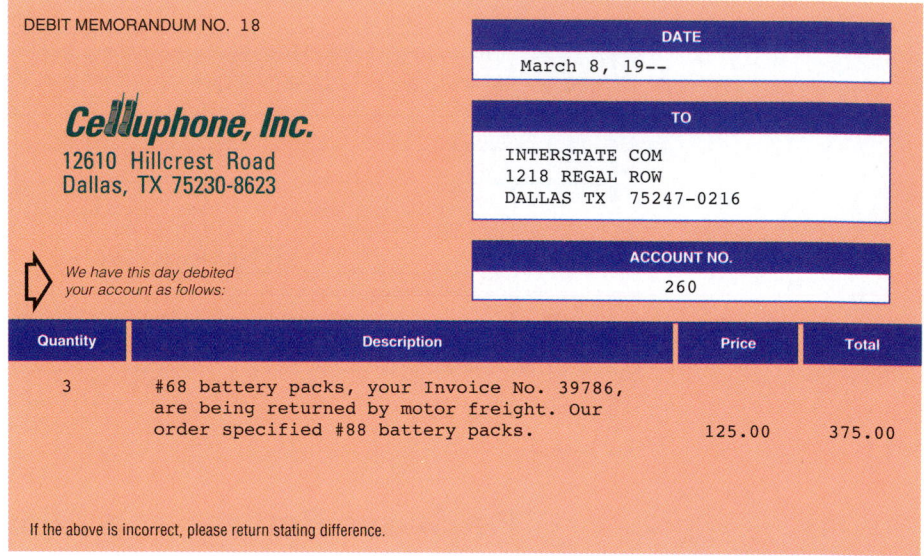

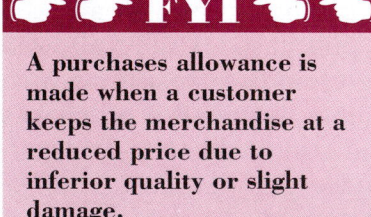

FYI

A purchases allowance is made when a customer keeps the merchandise at a reduced price due to inferior quality or slight damage.

Purchases	
Debit side Normal balance Increase	Credit side Decrease

Purchases Returns and Allowances	
Debit side Decrease	Credit side Normal balance Increase

Some businesses credit the purchases account for the amount of the purchases return or allowance. However, better information is provided if these amounts are credited to a separate account titled *Purchases Returns and Allowances*. A business can see how large its purchases returns and allowances are. Also, a business can see if purchases returns and allowances are increasing or decreasing from year to year. If the amounts are large, one account may be kept for purchases returns and another account for purchases allowances. Usually a single purchases returns and allowances account is satisfactory.

Purchases returns and allowances decrease the amount of purchases. Therefore, the account Purchases Returns and Allowances is a contra account to Purchases. Thus, the normal account balance of Purchases Returns and Allowances is a credit, the opposite of the normal account balance of Purchases, a debit.

Journalizing Purchases Returns and Allowances

Celluphone uses a single account, Purchases Returns and Allowances. The account is in the cost of merchandise division of Celluphone's chart of accounts.

GENERAL LEDGER
Accounts Payable

375.00	

Purchases Returns and Allowances

	375.00

ACCOUNTS PAYABLE LEDGER
Interstate Com

375.00	Bal.	740.00
	(New Bal.	365.00)

March 8, 19--. Returned merchandise to Interstate Com, $375.00, covering Purchase Invoice No. 30. Debit Memorandum No. 18.

The amount owed to a vendor is decreased by this transaction. Therefore, Accounts Payable is debited for the amount of the return, $375.00. The same amount is also debited to the account of Interstate Com in the accounts payable ledger. This transaction increases the contra account, Purchases Returns and Allowances with a $375.00 credit.

The general journal entry to record this purchases returns and allowances transaction is shown in Illustration 19-20.

ILLUSTRATION 19-20   General journal entry to record purchases returns and allowances

	DATE	ACCOUNT TITLE	DOC. NO.	POST. REF.	DEBIT	CREDIT	
1	Mar. 8	Accounts Payable/Interstate Com	DM18	/	3 7 5 00		1
2		Purchases Ret. and Allow.				3 7 5 00	2
3							3

GENERAL JOURNAL   PAGE 3

The date, *19--, Mar. 8,* is written in the Date column. The single debit amount is posted both to the general ledger account and the accounts payable ledger account. Therefore, the accounts to be debited, *Accounts Payable/Interstate Com,* are entered in the Account Title column. A diagonal line is placed between the two account titles to separate them clearly. A diagonal line is also placed in the Post. Ref. column to show that the debit amount is to be posted to two accounts. The source document for the entry, *DM18,* is entered in the Doc. No. column. The amount of the debit, *$375.00,* is recorded in the Debit column. The account to be credited, *Purchases Returns and Allowances,* is written on the next line in the Account Title column. This account title is indented about one centimeter. The amount of the credit, *$375.00,* is recorded in the Credit column.

FYI

The supplies account is used to record items that are bought for company use and are not to be sold to customers.

Journalizing Buying Supplies on Account

Celluphone generally buys supplies on account. Supplies are not merchandise. Only merchandise purchased on account is recorded in the purchases journal. Therefore, when any item that is not merchandise is bought on account, the transaction is recorded in the general journal.

March 9, 19--. Bought supplies on account from Kryger Supplies, $228.00. Memorandum No. 38.

GENERAL LEDGER
Supplies

| 228.00 | |

Accounts Payable

| | 228.00 |

ACCOUNTS PAYABLE LEDGER
Kryger Supplies

| | 228.00 |

A memorandum is used as the source document so that the supplies will not be recorded unintentionally as merchandise. The invoice received from Kryger Supplies is attached to the memorandum to confirm the price paid.

This transaction increases the balance of the supplies account. Therefore, Supplies is debited for $228.00. The amount owed to a vendor is also increased by this transaction. Therefore, Accounts Payable is credited for $228.00. The same amount is also credited to the account of Kryger Supplies in the accounts payable ledger.

The general journal entry to record this buying supplies on account transaction is shown in Illustration 19-21.

ILLUSTRATION 19-21   General journal entry to record buying supplies on account

	DATE	ACCOUNT TITLE	DOC. NO.	POST. REF.	DEBIT	CREDIT	
3	9	Supplies	M38		228 00		3
4		Accounts Payable/Kryger Supplies		/		228 00	4
5							5

GENERAL JOURNAL   PAGE 3

The date, *9*, is written in the Date column. The account to be debited, Supplies, is recorded in the Account Title column. The source document, *M38*, is entered in the Doc. No. column. The amount of the debit, *$228.00*, is entered in the Debit column. The accounts to be credited, *Accounts Payable/Kryger Supplies*, are written on the next line in the Account Title column. These accounts are indented about one centimeter. A diagonal line is placed between the two account titles. A diagonal line is also placed in the Post. Ref. column to show that the credit is to be posted to two accounts. The amount of the credit, *$228.00*, is entered in the Credit column.

Posting from a General Journal

Each amount in the general journal Debit and Credit columns is posted separately to a general ledger account. The posting of an entry for supplies bought on account from a general journal is shown in Illustration 19-22.

The debit amount is posted first. The date, *9*, is written in the Date column of the general ledger account Supplies. The abbreviation for the general journal, *G3*, is entered in the Post. Ref. column of the supplies account. The amount from the general journal Debit column, *$228.00*, is recorded in the Debit column of the supplies account. The amount in the Debit column is added to the previous balance in the Balance Debit column ($870.00 + $228.00 = $1,098.00). The new balance, *$1,098.00*, is recorded in the Balance

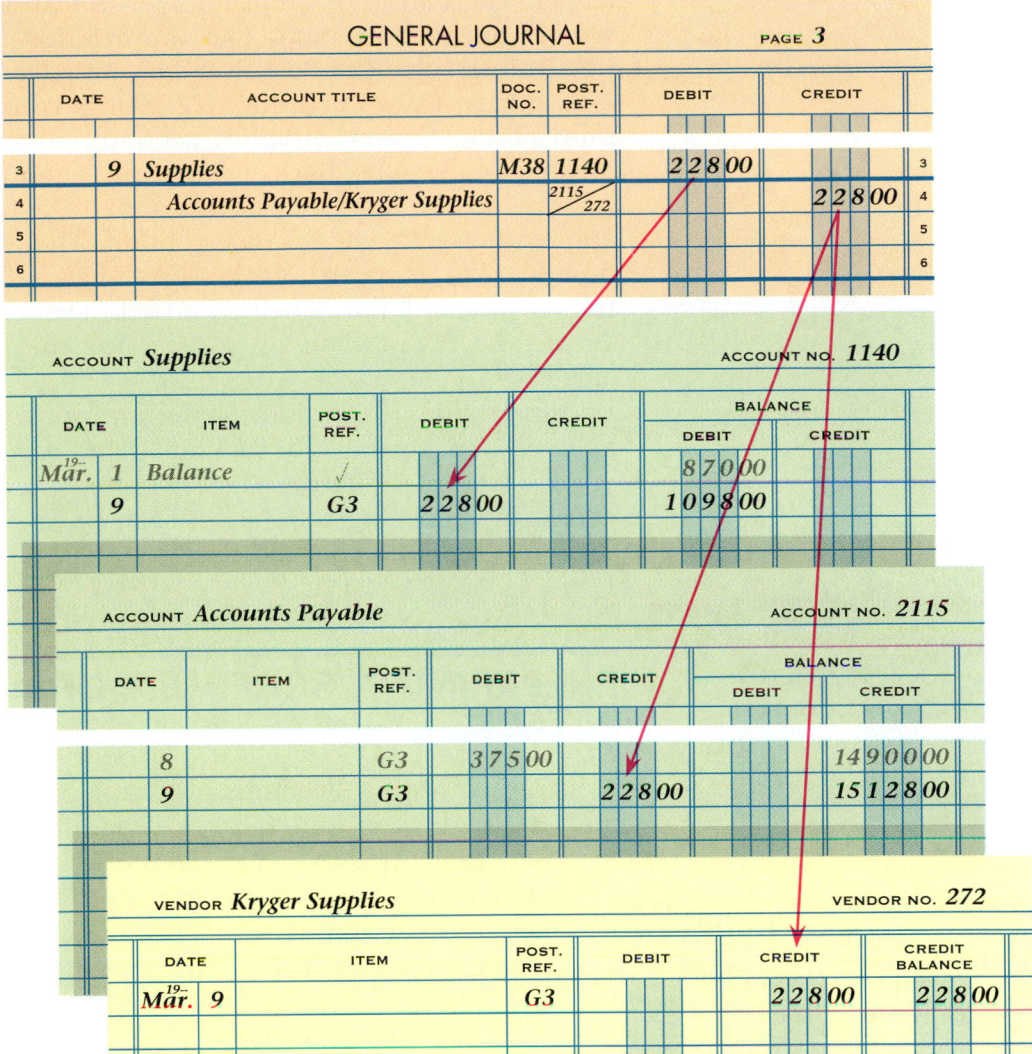

Debit column. The supplies account number, *1140*, is written in the Post. Ref. column of the general journal to show the completion of posting for this line.

Next the credit amount is posted. The date, *9*, is written in the Date column of the general ledger account Accounts Payable. The abbreviation for the general journal, *G3*, is entered in the Post. Ref. column of the accounts payable account. The amount from the general journal Credit column, *$228.00*, is recorded in the Credit column of the accounts payable account. The amount in the Credit column is added to the previous balance in the Balance Credit column ($14,900.00 + $228.00 = $15,128.00). The new balance, *$15,128.00*, is recorded in the Balance Credit column. The accounts payable account number, *2115*, is written at the left of the diagonal line in the Post. Ref. column of the general journal. The account number shows the completion of posting for this line to the general ledger.

After posting to the general ledger accounts is complete, the credit amount is also posted to the accounts payable subsidiary ledger. The date, *19--, Mar. 9*, is written in the Date column of the Kryger Supplies account. The abbreviation for the general journal, *G3*, is entered in the Post. Ref. column. The amount from the general journal Credit column, *$228.00*, is recorded in the Credit column of the Kryger Supplies account. Since there is no previous balance in the subsidiary account, the amount in the Credit column is also the balance of the account. Therefore, *$228.00*, is also entered in the Credit Balance column. The Kryger Supplies account number, *272*, is written at the right of the diagonal line in the Post. Ref. column of the general journal. The vendor account number shows the completion of posting for this line to the subsidiary ledger.

Illustration 19-23 shows a summary of the procedure for journalizing and posting transactions using a general journal.

Illustration 19-24 on page 498 shows a summary of the procedures for recording purchases, cash payments, and other transactions in special journals and a general journal.

Audit Your Understanding

1. What is the source document for purchases returns and allowances?

2. Why isn't the purchase of supplies on account recorded in the purchases journal?

3. What is a schedule of accounts payable?

PREPARING A SCHEDULE OF ACCOUNTS PAYABLE

A listing of vendor accounts, account balances, and total amount due all vendors is known as a schedule of accounts payable. A schedule of accounts payable is prepared before financial statements are prepared to prove the accounts payable ledger. If the total amount due on the schedule of accounts payable equals the accounts payable controlling account balance in the general ledger, the accounts payable ledger is proved. Preparation of a schedule of accounts payable is described in Chapter 13.

ACCOUNTING TERMS   EPT(a)

What is the meaning of each of the following?

1. corporation
2. share of stock
3. capital stock
4. special journal
5. purchases journal
6. cash payments journal

7. list price
8. trade discount
9. cash discount
10. purchases discount
11. cash short
12. cash over

13. general journal
14. purchases return
15. purchases allowance
16. debit memorandum

Summary of journalizing and posting using a general journal

1 Celluphone records in a general journal all transactions that cannot be recorded in any of the special journals.

2 Amounts in the Debit column are posted to the general ledger.

3 Amounts in the Credit column are posted to the genera ledger.

4 Amounts debited or credited to **Accounts Payable** are posted to the named vendor account in the accounts payable subsidiary ledger.

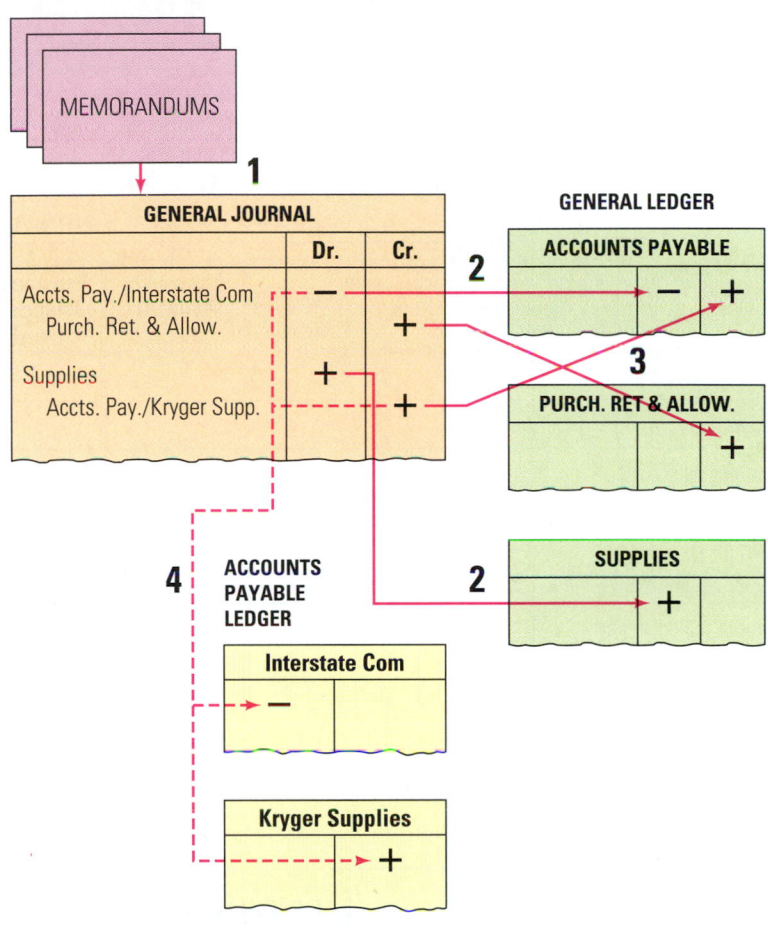

Summary of recording purchases and cash payments using special journals

Transaction	PURCHASES JOURNAL
	Purchases Debit Accts. Pay. Cr.
Purchases on account	X

Transactions	CASH PAYMENTS JOURNAL				
	1	2	3	4	5
	General		Accounts Payable Debit	Purchases Discount Credit	Cash Credit
	Debit	Credit			
Cash payment for expenses	X				X
Cash purchases	X				X
Cash payment for purchases on account with purchases discount			X	X	X
Cash payment for purchases on account without purchases discount			X		X
Cash payment to replenish petty cash with cash short	X				X
Cash payment to replenish petty cash with cash over	X	X			X

Transactions	GENERAL JOURNAL	
	Debit	Credit
Purchases returns and allowances	X	X
Buying supplies on account	X	X

1. What kind of accounting system should a business use?

2. Which accounting concept is being applied when a business reports financial information for a specified period of time?

3. What are some business transactions a corporation can conduct in its own name?

4. What is the principal difference between the accounting records of a corporation and those of a proprietorship or partnership?

5. Which accounting concept is being applied when a corporation keeps only information in its accounting system that relates to the corporation?

6. What is the major purpose for applying the Unit of Measurement concept by recording all business transactions in a common unit of measurement—the dollar?

7. What is the source document for recording a purchase on account?

8. Which accounting concept is being applied when a business records purchases at cost?

9. What accounts are affected, and how, when the total amount of the purchases journal is posted?

10. What is the last step in posting a purchases journal to a general ledger to show that posting is complete?

11. Why would a vendor grant a cash discount to a customer?

12. What is meant by terms of sale 2/10, n/30?

13. What kind of account offsets a related account?

14. What accounts are affected, and how, when a check is issued as payment on account for a purchase with a purchases discount?

15. How is a balance in the cash short and over account treated at the end of a fiscal period?

16. If cash is short when a petty cash fund is replenished, what entry is made to Cash Short and Over to record the shortage?

17. If cash is over when a petty cash fund is replenished, what entry is made to Cash Short and Over to record the overage?

18. Why are the totals for the General Debit and Credit columns of a cash payments journal not posted?

19. If purchases returns and allowances are a decrease in purchases, why are returns and allowances credited to a separate account?

20. When supplies are bought on account, why is the entry made in a general journal instead of a purchases journal?

CASES FOR CRITICAL THINKING — EPT(b)

CASE 1 McLain Florists, Inc. has employed an accounting firm to install a new accounting system using special journals. You and two other accountants are designing the special journals. Alisa Matthews, one of the accountants, recommends a cash payments journal with one special column—Cash Credit. Jose Ramundo, the other accountant, recommends a cash payments journal with three special columns—Accounts Payable Debit, Purchases Discount Credit, and Cash Credit. You have been asked to decide which cash payments journal should be used. Give your decision and the reason for that decision.

CASE 2 Gemini Company has established a $300.00 petty cash fund. During a routine review of the petty cash records, you discover that small shortages totaling $20.00 have occurred over the past four months. The fund custodian, Elaine Hilton, has not listed cash short or over on any of the reports prepared for replenishment. When asked about this practice, Miss Hilton said that she always waits until the amount of the shortage is significant—approximately $50.00. Then she requests replenishment for the amount of the shortage. What is your opinion of this practice? What action do you recommend?

The common stock of many corporations is traded on national stock exchanges. These corporations are required by the government to publish their financial statements in an annual report. The annual report also includes management's analysis of the year's operations and its projection of future financial activity. Annual reports are used by bankers, stockholders, and investment advisers for making business decisions.

INSTRUCTIONS:

Write a letter to a corporation requesting a copy of its annual report. Your letter should include your return address, inside address, and request for the report.

DRILLS FOR UNDERSTANDING   EPT(c,d)

DRILL 19-D1 Calculating trade and purchases discounts

The list price, trade discount rate, and purchases discount rate for four different purchases are given below.

Purchase Invoice No.	List Price	Trade Discount Rate	Purchases Discount Rate
1	$1,000.00	40%	2%
2	400.00	30%	3%
3	600.00	25%	1%
4	250.00	50%	2%

INSTRUCTIONS:

For each purchase, calculate the (a) trade discount, (b) invoice amount, (c) purchases discount, and (d) cash amount after discounts.

DRILL 19-D2 Calculating petty cash short and petty cash over

Four different companies have the following information related to petty cash transactions.

Company	Beginning Balance	Petty Cash Record			Amount of Cash in Cash Box
		Distribution of Payments			
		Supplies	Advertising Expense	Miscellaneous Expense	
A	$300.00	$46.25	$76.32	$91.87	$ 85.56
B	250.00	24.76	82.35	18.21	120.68
C	150.00	12.43	51.45	14.15	78.97
D	200.00	53.98	25.34	34.25	84.43

INSTRUCTIONS:

For each company, determine the amount, if any, of petty cash short or petty cash over.

DRILL 19-D3 Analyzing replenishing a petty cash fund

Petty cash is replenished for the amounts and on the dates shown in the following table.

Date on Which Replenished	Monthly Totals of Petty Cash Payment Records				
	Supplies	Advertising Expense	Miscellaneous Expense	Cash Short	Cash Over
May 31	$54.50	$15.30	$31.30	$4.01	
June 30	25.60	45.90	16.70	2.54	
July 31	14.20	64.00	42.20		$6.39
August 31	66.00	45.50	22.30	1.51	

INSTRUCTIONS:

For each date, prepare T accounts for the accounts affected by the cash payments journal entry to replenish petty cash. Record the amounts on the debit or credit side of each T account to show how the accounts are affected.

DRILL 19-D4 Analyzing the journalizing of purchases and cash payments transactions

A form for analyzing the journalizing of purchases and cash payments transactions is given in the working papers that accompany this textbook.

INSTRUCTIONS:

Complete the form for each of the following transactions. In Column A, write the title of the account(s) debited. In Column B, write the title of the account(s) credited. In Column C, write the name of the journal in which the transaction is recorded. In Columns D and E, write the names of the journal amount column(s) in which debit and credit amounts are recorded. Transaction 1 is given as an example in the working papers.

1. Paid cash on account to Hubburd Co.; no discount.
2. Purchased merchandise on account from Westward Company.
3. Bought supplies for cash.
4. Paid cash for rent.
5. Paid cash on account to Westward Company; no discount.
6. Purchased merchandise on account from Sadler, Inc.
7. Paid cash for advertising.
8. Returned merchandise to Westward Company.
9. Purchased merchandise for cash.
10. Returned merchandise to Sadler, Inc.
11. Paid cash on account to Olympus Gauge Company for a purchase invoice less discount.

The solution to Drill 19-D4 is needed to complete Drill 19-D5.

DRILL 19-D5 Analyzing the posting of purchases and cash payments transactions

The solution to Drill 19-D4 is needed to complete Drill 19-D5.

A form for analyzing the posting of purchases and cash payments is given in the working papers that accompany this textbook.

INSTRUCTIONS:

1. In Column A, write the titles of the accounts affected by each transaction in Drill 19-D4. These account titles are taken from Columns A and B of completed Drill 19-D4.
2. Place a check mark in Column B if the amount is posted individually to the general ledger. Place a check mark in Column C if the amount is posted individually to the accounts payable ledger. Place a check mark in Column D if the amount is not posted individually to any ledger. Transaction 1 is given as an example in the working papers.

PROBLEM 19-1 Journalizing and posting purchase on account transactions

The general ledger and accounts payable ledger accounts for Wholesale Office Supply Company are given in the working papers accompanying this textbook. The balances are recorded as of May 1 of the current year.

INSTRUCTIONS:

1. Journalize the following purchases on account completed during May of the current year. Use page 5 of a purchases journal. The abbreviation for purchase invoice is P.

May 2. Purchased merchandise on account from PXR, Inc., $1,500.00. P25.
      5. Purchased merchandise on account from Preston Office Supply, $154.00. P26.
      8. Purchased merchandise on account from Reznik Paper Company, $642.00. P27.
     11. Purchased merchandise on account from PXR, Inc., $414.00. P28.
     14. Purchased merchandise on account from Bird Enterprises, $2,268.00. P29.
     18. Purchased merchandise on account from Johnston Company, $1,849.00. P30.
     20. Purchased merchandise on account from PXR, Inc., $602.00. P31.
     24. Purchased merchandise on account from Preston Office Supply, $314.00. P32.
     26. Purchased merchandise on account from Reznik Paper Company, $1,988.00. P33.
     29. Purchased merchandise on account from Bird Enterprises, $735.00. P34.

2. Post each amount in the purchases journal to the accounts payable ledger.
3. Total and rule the purchases journal. Post the total.

PROBLEM 19-2 Journalizing and posting cash payment transactions

The general ledger and accounts payable ledger accounts for Jenson Company are given in the working papers that accompany this textbook. The balances are recorded as of July 1 of the current year.

INSTRUCTIONS:

1. Journalize the following cash payments completed during July of the current year. Use page 7 of a cash payments journal. The abbreviation for check is C.

July 1. Paid cash for rent, $600.00. C216.
      5. Paid cash on account to Gray's Decorum, $1,203.84, covering P127 for $1,216.00, less 1% discount, $12.16. C217.
      7. Paid cash for supplies, $128.00. C218.
      8. Paid cash on account to Lipson Company, $2,092.86, covering P128 for $2,114.00, less 1% discount, $21.14. C219.
      9. Paid cash for miscellaneous expense, $140.00. C220.
     12. Purchased merchandise for cash, $263.00. C221.
     14. Paid cash on account to Varsity Co., $1,410.22, covering P124 for $1,439.00, less 2% discount, $28.78. C222.
     19. Paid cash for supplies, $93.00. C223.
     23. Paid cash on account to Briggs Steel Company, $804.00, covering P126; no discount. C224.
     28. Paid cash for miscellaneous expense, $124.00. C225.
     30. Paid cash to replenish the petty cash fund, $105.00: advertising, $61.50; miscellaneous, $38.45; cash short, $5.05. C226.

2. Post accounts payable amounts to the appropriate accounts in the accounts payable ledger.
3. Post the amounts in the general columns to the appropriate general ledger accounts.
4. Prove and rule the cash payments journal. Post the totals of the special columns to the appropriate general ledger accounts.

PROBLEM 19-3 Journalizing and posting purchases and cash payment transactions

AUTOMATED

The general ledger and accounts payable ledger accounts for Sandy's Sewing Company are given in the working papers accompanying this textbook. The balances are recorded as of April 1 of the current year. Use the following account titles.

PARTIAL GENERAL LEDGER		ACCOUNTS PAYABLE LEDGER	
Account Number	**Account Title**	**Vendor Number**	**Vendor Name**
1105	Cash	210	Kelmans Supply
1110	Petty Cash	220	Office Emporium
1140	Supplies	230	Potters Equipment
2115	Accounts Payable	240	Threads, Inc.
5105	Purchases	250	York Company
5110	Purchases Discount		
5115	Purchases Returns and Allowances		
6105	Advertising Expense		
6130	Miscellaneous Expense		
6140	Rent Expense		
8105	Cash Short and Over		

INSTRUCTIONS:

1. Journalize the following transactions affecting purchases and cash payments completed during April of the current year. Use page 4 of a purchases journal, a general journal, and a cash payments journal. Source documents are abbreviated as follows: check, C; debit memorandum, DM; memorandum, M; purchase invoice, P.

April 1. Paid cash for rent, $1,450.00. C57.
  2. Purchased merchandise on account from Threads, Inc., $2,565.00. P65.
  2. Bought supplies on account from Office Emporium, $536.00. M15.
  Posting. Post the items that are to be posted individually. Post from the journals in this order: purchases journal, general journal, and cash payments journal.
  5. Purchased merchandise on account from York Company, $2,995.00. P66.
  7. Paid cash on account to Potters Equipment, $5,197.50, covering P64 for $5,250.00, less 1% discount, $52.50. C58.
  8. Returned merchandise to York Company, $188.00, from P66. DM7.
  10. Paid cash on account to Kelmans Supply, $1,644.44 covering P63 for $1,678.00, less 2% discount, $33.56. C59.
  Posting. Post the items that are to be posted individually.
  12. Purchased merchandise on account from Kelmans Supply, $4,683.00. P67.
  12. Paid cash on account to Threads, Inc., $597.96, covering P62 for $604.00, less 1% discount, $6.04. C60.
  15. Paid cash to replenish the petty cash fund, $96.20: supplies, $21.40; advertising, $43.20; miscellaneous, $35.00; cash over, $3.40. C61.
  16. Purchased merchandise for cash, $706.00. C62.
  16. Purchased merchandise on account from Threads, Inc., $4,243.00. P68.
  Posting. Post the items that are to be posted individually.
  19. Paid cash for miscellaneous expense, $114.00. C63.
  22. Paid cash on account to Kelmans Supply, $4,589.34, covering P67 for $4,683.00, less 2% discount, $93.66. C64.
  22. Purchased merchandise on account from Kelmans Supply, $1,976.00. P69.
  23. Purchased merchandise on account from Potters Equipment, $3,204.00. P70.
  23. Purchased merchandise on account from Threads, Inc., $1,020.00. P71.
  Posting. Post the items that are to be posted individually.
  26. Returned merchandise to Threads, Inc., $340.00, from P71. DM8.
  26. Paid cash on account to Office Emporium, $536.00, covering M15; no discount. C65.

April 28. Paid cash for miscellaneous expense, $214.00. C66.
   28. Purchased merchandise on account from York Company, $1,768.00. P72.
   30. Paid cash on account to York Company, $2,807.00, covering P66 for $2,995.00, less DM7, $188.00; no discount. C67.
   30. Paid cash on account to Threads, Inc., $4,200.57, covering P68 for $4,243.00, less 1% discount, $42.43. C68.
   30. Paid cash to replenish the petty cash fund, $75.00: supplies, $32.50; advertising, $16.40; miscellaneous, $23.25; cash short, $2.85. C69.
      Posting. Post the items that are to be posted individually.

2. Total and rule the purchases journal. Post the total.
3. Prove and rule the cash payments journal. Post the totals of the special columns.
4. Prepare a schedule of accounts payable similar to the one described in Chapter 13. Compare the schedule total with the balance of the accounts payable account in the general ledger. The total and balance should be the same.

ENRICHMENT PROBLEMS   EPT(b,c,d)

MASTERY PROBLEM 19-M Journalizing and posting purchases and cash payment transactions

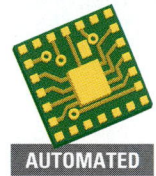

AUTOMATED

APPLICATION

The general ledger and accounts payable ledger accounts of City Plumbing Supply Company are given in the working papers that accompany this textbook. The balances are recorded as of August 1 of the current year. Use the following account titles.

PARTIAL GENERAL LEDGER		ACCOUNTS PAYABLE LEDGER	
Account Number	Account Title	Vendor Number	Vendor Name
1105	Cash	210	Barker Pipe Co.
1110	Petty Cash	220	Edson Tools, Inc.
1140	Supplies	230	Fullers Tape Company
2115	Accounts Payable	240	Renson Supplies
5105	Purchases	250	TenCorp Tubing
5110	Purchases Discount		
5115	Purchases Returns and Allowances		
6105	Advertising Expense		
6130	Miscellaneous Expense		
6140	Rent Expense		
8105	Cash Short and Over		

INSTRUCTIONS:

1. Journalize the following transactions affecting purchases and cash payments completed during August of the current year. Use page 8 of a purchases journal, a cash payments journal, and a general journal.

Aug. 2. Returned merchandise to Fullers Tape Company, $152.00, from P72. DM17.
   2. Paid cash for rent, $690.00. C504.
   4. Paid cash on account to Barker Pipe Co., $361.35, covering P74 for $365.00, less 1% discount, $3.65. C505.
   6. Purchased merchandise on account from TenCorp Tubing, $602.00. P75.
   6. Paid cash on account to Renson Supplies, $942.00, covering M14; no discount. C506.
      Posting. Post the items that are to be posted individually. Post from the journals in this order: purchases journal, general journal, and cash payments journal.

Aug. 9. Purchased merchandise on account from Edson Tools, Inc., $446.00. P76.
10. Paid cash on account to Fullers Tape Company, $556.00, covering P72 for $708.00, less DM17, $152.00; no discount. C507.
13. Paid cash for miscellaneous expense, $147.00. C508.
13. Bought supplies on account from Renson Supplies, $206.00. M15.
16. Paid cash to replenish the petty cash fund, $165.35: supplies, $22.50; advertising, $34.00; miscellaneous, $114.00; cash over, $5.15. C509.
16. Purchased merchandise on account from Fullers Tape Company, $687.00. P77.
16. Paid cash on account to TenCorp Tubing, $589.96, covering P75 for $602.00, less 2% discount, $12.04. C510.
18. Paid cash on account to Edson Tools, Inc., $441.54, covering P76 for $446.00, less 1% discount, $4.46. C511.
        Posting. Post the items that are to be posted individually.
19. Returned merchandise to Fullers Tape Company, $88.00, from P77. DM18.
20. Purchased merchandise on account from TenCorp Tubing, $315.00. P78.
23. Purchased merchandise on account from Barker Pipe Co., $1,463.00. P79.
25. Paid cash on account to Renson Supplies, $206.00, covering M15; no discount. C512.
26. Bought supplies on account from Renson Supplies, $341.00. M16.
27. Paid cash for miscellaneous expense, $76.00. C513.
30. Purchased merchandise on account from Edson Tools, Inc., $1,161.00. P80.
30. Paid cash on account to TenCorp Tubing, $308.70, covering P78 for $315.00, less 2% discount, $6.30. C514.
31. Paid cash on account to Barker Pipe Co., $1,448.37, covering P79 for $1,463.00, less 1% discount, $14.63. C515.
31. Paid cash to replenish the petty cash fund, $201.75: supplies, $45.45; advertising, $80.40; miscellaneous, $72.40; cash short, $3.50. C516.
        Posting. Post the items that are to be posted individually.

2. Total and rule the purchases journal. Post the total.

3. Prove and rule the cash payments journal. Post the totals of the special columns.

4. Prepare a schedule of accounts payable. Compare the schedule total with the balance of the accounts payable account in the general ledger. The total and balance should be the same.

CHALLENGE PROBLEM 19-C Journalizing transactions in a combined purchases-cash payments journal

The accountant for City Plumbing Supply Company has suggested that time could be saved if the purchases journal and the cash payments journal were combined into one journal. The accountant suggests using a journal such as the following.

				Purchases—Cash Payments Journal						
				1	2	3	4	5	6	7
Date	Account Title	Doc. No.	Post. Ref.	General		Purchases Debit	Accounts Payable		Purchases Discount Credit	Cash Credit
				Debit	Credit		Debit	Credit		

Christopher Howard, manager, has asked the accountant to show him how the journal would appear after transactions have been recorded.

INSTRUCTIONS:

1. Use page 8 of a purchases-cash payments journal and a general journal. Journalize the transactions given in Mastery Problem 19-M.

2. Prove and rule the combined purchases-cash payments journal.

3. Do you agree with the accountant that the combined purchases-cash payments journal used in this problem saves time in journalizing and posting? Why?

Recording Purchases and Cash Payments for a Corporation

Celluphone, the merchandising business described in Part 4, uses a manual accounting system. Celluphone's manual journalizing and posting procedures for purchases and cash payments are described in Chapter 19. Integrating Automated Accounting Topic 7 describes procedures for using automated accounting software to journalize and post Celluphone's purchases and cash payments transactions. The Automated Accounting Problems contain instructions for using automated accounting software to solve Application Problem 19-3 and Mastery Problem 19-M, Chapter 19.

AUTOMATED ACCOUNTING PROCEDURES FOR CELLUPHONE

Celluphone uses three input forms to arrange purchases, cash payments, and other transaction data for automated accounting.

1. Purchases journal input form for purchases on account.
2. Cash payments journal input form for all cash payments.
3. General journal input form for all other transactions.

FILE MAINTENANCE

Celluphone's general ledger chart of accounts is on page 470. Celluphone uses the same procedures as described for Rugcare in Part 2 and Celluphone in Part 3 to maintain its general ledger chart of accounts. The subsidiary ledgers are also a part of the general ledger data base stored on the template disk. Procedures for adding or changing a subsidiary account are the same as for a general ledger account. (1) An input form is prepared. (2) The data base is retrieved. (3) Data from the input form are keyed. (4) A revised chart of accounts, vendor list, or customer list is prepared to verify the accuracy of the data keyed. (5) The revised chart of accounts or subsidiary ledger lists are stored as part of the general ledger data base on the template disk.

FYI

File maintenance includes deleting accounts no longer needed and adding new accounts.

RECORDING PURCHASES ON ACCOUNT

Celluphone batches purchases on account transactions and records them on a purchases journal input form.

> *March 1, 19--. Purchased merchandise on account from Cell Systems, $6,672.00. Purchase Invoice No. 39.*

The journal entry to record this transaction is on line 1 of the purchases journal input form shown in Illustration T7-1.

The run date, *03/31/--*, is written in the space provided at the top of the input form.

On line 1, the date of the transaction, *03/01*, is recorded in the Date column. The vendor number, *220*, is entered in the Vendor No. column. The source document number, *P39*, is written in the Invoice No. column. The invoice amount, *$6,672.00*, is recorded in the Invoice Amount column. The general ledger account number for Purchases, *5105*, is entered in the Account No. column. The debit amount, *$6,672.00*, is written in the Debit column. The Credit column is left blank. The software automatically records the credit to Accounts Payable on a purchases on account transaction.

RECORDING CASH PAYMENTS

Celluphone batches cash payments and records them on a cash payments journal input form. Celluphone has two types of cash payments. (1) Direct payments. (2) Payments on account. A direct

Purchases journal input form with a purchase on account transaction recorded

RUN DATE 03,31,-- MM DD YY					PURCHASES JOURNAL Input Form		
	DATE MM/DD	VENDOR NO.	INVOICE NO.	INVOICE AMOUNT	ACCOUNT NO.	DEBIT	CREDIT	
1	03 01	220	P39	6672 00	5105	6672 00		1
2	05	210	P40	2000 00	5105	2000 00		2
3	10	250	P41	39456 00	5105	39456 00		3
4	16	240	P42	1864 00	5105	1864 00		4
5	18	230	P50	17584 00	5105	17584 00		5
6	21	210	P51	16930 00	5105	16930 00		6
7	23	260	P59	21430 00	5105	21430 00		7
8	31	250	P61	2110 00	5105	2110 00		8
25								25

NOTE: A credit to Accounts Payable is made automatically by the software.

payment transaction does not affect accounts payable, whereas a payment on account transaction does affect accounts payable.

Cash Payment of an Expense

A cash payment of an expense transaction is a direct cash payment not affecting accounts payable.

March 1, 19--. Paid cash for rent, $3,000.00. Check No. 148.

The journal entry to record this transaction is on line 1 of Illustration T7-2 on page 510.

The run date, *03/31/--*, is written in the space provided at the top of the form.

On line 1, the date of the transaction, *03/01*, is entered in the Date column. The Vendor No. column is left blank because a cash payment of an expense transaction does not involve a vendor. The source document number, *C148*, is recorded in the Check No. column. The Accounts Pay. Debit column is left blank. The general ledger account number for Rent Expense, *6140*, is written in the Account No. column. The amount of the expense, *$3,000.00*, is entered in the Debit column. The software automatically makes the credit to Cash, *$3,000.00*. Therefore, the Credit column is left blank.

Purchase of Merchandise for Cash

A purchase of merchandise for cash transaction is a direct payment not affecting accounts payable.

March 1, 19--. Purchased merchandise for cash, $480.00. Check No. 149.

FYI

For illustration purposes, some source document numbers have been omitted from input forms.

The journal entry to record this transaction is on line 2 of the cash payments journal input form shown in Illustration T7-2. The entry is similar to other direct payment transactions.

Cash payments journal input form with transactions recorded

RUN DATE 03,31,-- MM DD YY			CASH PAYMENTS JOURNAL Input Form					
DATE MM/DD	VENDOR NO.	CHECK NO.	ACCOUNTS PAY. DEBIT	ACCOUNT NO.	DEBIT	CREDIT	
1	03,01		C148		6140	3000 00		1
2	,01		C149		5105	480 00		2
3	,02	240	C150	1740 00				3
4	,05	220	C151	2437 00	5110		48 74	4
5	,07	210	C152	5921 00	5110		123 82	5
6	,08	220	C168	6672 00	5110		133 44	6
7	,08	260	C169	42600 00	5110		852 00	7
8	,12	272	C170	346 00				8
9	,16		C171		5105	200 00		9
10	,20	250	C172	39456 00				10
11	,28	230	C173	17584 00				11
12	,29	210	C208	16930 00				12
13	,31		C209		1140	87 80		13
14	,				6105	43 75		14
15	,				6130	97 90		15
16	,				8105	4 00		16
17	,31		C233		6160	423 00		17
25	,							25

NOTE: A credit to Cash is made automatically by the software.

Cash Payment on Account Without Purchases Discounts

A cash payment on account transaction affects both the controlling account Accounts Payable and a vendor account in an accounts payable subsidiary ledger.

March 2, 19--. Paid cash on account to Electro Sound, $1,740.00, covering Purchase Invoice No. 21. Check No. 150.

The journal entry to record this transaction is on line 3 of Illustration T7-2.

The date of the transaction, *02*, is written in the Date column. The vendor number, *240*, is entered in the Vendor No. column. The amount, *$1,740.00*, is recorded in the Accounts Pay. Debit column. The Account No., Debit, and Credit columns are left blank.

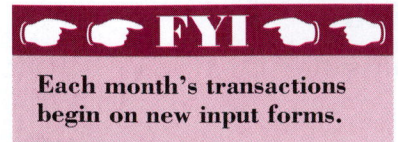

Each month's transactions begin on new input forms.

Cash Payment on Account with a Purchases Discount

Celluphone's policy is to pay all vendors on or before the date for taking the purchases discount. This procedure reduces the cost of merchandise purchased by Celluphone.

> *March 8, 19--. Paid cash on account to Cell Systems, $6,538.56, covering Purchase Invoice No. 39 for $6,672.00, less 2% discount, $133.44. Check No. 168.*

The journal entry to record this transaction is on line 6 of Illustration T7-2.

The date of the transaction, *08*, is written in the Date column. The vendor number, *220*, is entered in the Vendor No. column. The amount of the debit to Accounts Payable, *$6,672.00*, is recorded in the Accounts Pay. Debit column. The general ledger account number for *Purchases Discount*, *5110*, is written in the Account No. column. The Debit column is left blank. The purchases discount amount, *$133.44*, is entered in the Credit column.

Cash Payment to Replenish Petty Cash

A cash payment to replenish petty cash transaction is a direct payment not affecting accounts payable. Establishing and replenishing a petty cash fund is described for Rugcare in Chapter 7. Celluphone follows procedures similar to those used by Rugcare.

Cash in the petty cash box may be less than what the petty cash balance should be. A petty cash on hand amount that is less than a recorded amount is cash short.

> *March 31, 19--. Paid cash to replenish the petty cash fund, $233.45: supplies, $87.80; advertising, $43.75; miscellaneous, $97.90; cash short, $4.00. Check No. 209.*

The journal entry to record this transaction is on lines 13 through 16 of Illustration T7-2. This journal entry is similar to other direct payments.

A petty cash on hand amount that is more than a recorded amount is cash over. Amounts of petty cash short and petty cash over are recorded in an account titled *Cash Short and Over*. An amount of petty cash short is debited and an amount of petty cash over is credited to *Cash Short and Over*.

FYI

The account title Petty Cash is only used when establishing the petty cash fund.

RECORDING OTHER TRANSACTIONS

Celluphone uses a general journal input form to journalize transactions other than purchases on account and cash payments.

Purchases Returns and Allowances

> *March 8, 19--. Returned merchandise to Interstate Com, $375.00, covering Purchase Invoice No. 30. Debit Memorandum No. 18.*

The journal entry to record this transaction is on lines 1 and 2 of the general journal input form shown in Illustration T7-3.

The run date, *03/31/--*, is written in the space provided at the top of the form.

On line 1, the date of the transaction, *03/08*, is entered in the Date column. The source document number, *DM18*, is recorded in the Reference column. The general ledger account number for Accounts Payable, *2115*, is recorded in the Account No. column. The vendor number, *260*, is written in the Customer/Vendor No. column. The amount of the debit to the accounts payable subsidiary account, *$375.00*, is written in the Debit column.

ILLUSTRATION T7-3   General journal input form with transactions recorded

	DATE MM/DD	REFERENCE	ACCOUNT NO.	CUSTOMER/ VENDOR NO.	DEBIT	CREDIT	
1	03 08	DM18	2115	260	375 00		1
2	/		5115			375 00	2
3	09	M38	1140		228 00		3
4	/		2115	272		228 00	4
5	22	DM19	2115	240	580 00		5
6	/		5115			580 00	6
7	24	M39	1140		375 00		7
8	/		2115	272		375 00	8
9	27	DM20	2115	260	6552 00		9
10	/		5115			6552 00	10
11	29	M40	1140		120 00		11
12	/		2115	272		120 00	12
25	/						25

RUN DATE 03,31,-- MM DD YY

GENERAL JOURNAL Input Form

	DEBIT	CREDIT
PAGE TOTALS	8230 00	8230 00
FINAL TOTALS	8230 00	8230 00

On line 2, the general ledger account number for Purchases Returns and Allowances, *5115*, is entered in the Account No. column. The amount of the credit to the general ledger account, *$375.00*, is recorded in the Credit column.

Buying Supplies on Account

March 9, 19--. Bought supplies on account from Kryger Supplies, $228.00. Memorandum No. 38.

The journal entry to record this transaction is on lines 3 and 4 of Illustration T7-3.

On line 3, the date of the transaction, *09*, is written in the Date column. The source document number, *M38*, is recorded in the Reference column. The account number for Supplies, *1140*, is entered in the Account No. column. The amount, *$228.00*, is written in the Debit column.

On line 4, the account number for Accounts Payable, *2115*, is recorded in the Account No. column. The account number for Kryger Supplies, *272*, is entered in the Customer/Vendor No. column. The amount, *$228.00*, is written in the Credit column.

PROCESSING PURCHASES, CASH PAYMENTS, AND OTHER TRANSACTIONS

After all data from the input forms have been keyed and posted, three reports are displayed and printed. (1) A purchases journal report as shown in Illustration T7-4. (2) A cash payments journal report as shown in Illustration T7-5 on page 514. (3) A general journal report as shown in Illustration T7-6 on page 515. Each journal report is checked for accuracy by comparing the report with the appropriate journal input form.

After all journal reports have been verified and printed, the accounts payable account from the general ledger and the schedule of accounts payable are then printed as shown in Illustration T7-7

| **ILLUSTRATION T7-4** | Purchases journal report |

```
                        Celluphone, Inc.
                        Purchases Journal
                           03/31/--
    ------------------------------------------------------------------------
    Date    Refer.    V/C  Acct.  Title                      Debit      Credit
    ------------------------------------------------------------------------
    03/01   P39             5105  Purchases                6672.00
    03/01   P39       220   2115  AP/Cell Systems                       6672.00

    03/05   P40             5105  Purchases                2000.00
    03/05   P40       210   2115  AP/Action Phone Co.                   2000.00

    03/10   P41             5105  Purchases               39456.00
    03/10   P41       250   2115  AP/Hopkins Company                   39456.00

    03/16   P42             5105  Purchases                1864.00
    03/16   P42       240   2115  AP/Electro Sound                      1864.00

    03/18   P50             5105  Purchases               17584.00
    03/18   P50       230   2115  AP/Dafoe Communications              17584.00

    03/21   P51             5105  Purchases               16930.00
    03/21   P51       210   2115  AP/Action Phone Co.                  16930.00

    03/23   P59             5105  Purchases               21430.00
    03/23   P59       260   2115  AP/Interstate Com                    21430.00

    03/31   P61             5105  Purchases                2110.00
    03/31   P61       250   2115  AP/Hopkins Company                    2110.00
                                                        ----------  ----------
                                Totals                 108046.00   108046.00
                                                        ==========  ==========
```

on page 515 and Illustration T7-8 on page 516. The accounts payable balance in the general ledger is compared to the total of the schedule of accounts payable. These two amounts must be the same. The schedule and all journal reports are filed for future reference.

ILLUSTRATION T7-5 Cash payments journal report

```
                          Celluphone, Inc.
                        Cash Payments Journal
                             03/31/--
--------------------------------------------------------------------
Date   Refer.   V/C Acct.  Title                    Debit      Credit
--------------------------------------------------------------------
03/01  C148         6140   Rent Expense             3000.00
03/01  C148         1105   Cash                                3000.00

03/01  C149         5105   Purchases                 480.00
03/01  C149         1105   Cash                                 480.00

03/02  C150    240  2115   AP/Electro Sound         1740.00
03/02  C150         1105   Cash                                1740.00

03/05  C151    220  2115   AP/Cell Systems          2437.00
03/05  C151         5110   Purchases Discount                    48.74
03/05  C151         1105   Cash                                2388.26

03/07  C152    210  2115   AP/Action Phone Co.      5921.00
03/07  C152         5110   Purchases Discount                   123.82
03/07  C152         1105   Cash                                5797.18

03/08  C168    220  2115   AP/Cell Systems          6672.00
03/08  C168         5110   Purchases Discount                   133.44
03/08  C168         1105   Cash                                6538.56

03/08  C169    260  2115   AP/Interstate Com       42600.00
03/08  C169         5110   Purchases Discount                   852.00
03/08  C169         1105   Cash                               41748.00

03/12  C170    272  2115   AP/Kryger Supplies        346.00
03/12  C170         1105   Cash                                 346.00

03/16  C171         5105   Purchases                 200.00
03/16  C171         1105   Cash                                 200.00

03/20  C172    250  2115   AP/Hopkins Company      39456.00
03/20  C172         1105   Cash                               39456.00

03/28  C173    230  2115   AP/Dafoe Communications 17584.00
03/28  C173         1105   Cash                               17584.00

03/29  C208    210  2115   AP/Action Phone Co.     16930.00
03/29  C208         1105   Cash                               16930.00

03/31  C209         1140   Supplies                   87.80
03/31  C209         6105   Advertising Expense        43.75
03/31  C209         6130   Miscellaneous Expense      97.90
03/31  C209         8105   Cash Short and Over         4.00
03/31  C209         1105   Cash                                 233.45

03/31  C233         6160   Utilities Expense         423.00
03/31  C233         1105   Cash                                 423.00
                                                   ---------- ----------
                           Totals                  138022.45  138022.45
                                                   ========== ==========
```

General journal report

```
                        Celluphone, Inc.
                        General Journal
                           03/31/--
---------------------------------------------------------------------------
Date    Refer.   V/C Acct.  Title                          Debit     Credit
---------------------------------------------------------------------------
03/03   DM18     260 2115   AP/Interstate Com             375.00
03/03   DM18         5115   Purchases Ret. and Allow.                375.00

03/09   M38          1140   Supplies                      228.00
03/09   M38      272 2115   AP/Kryger Supplies                       228.00

03/22   DM19     240 2115   AP/Electro Sound              580.00
03/22   DM19         5115   Purchases Ret. and Allow.                580.00

03/24   M39          1140   Supplies                      375.00
03/24   M39      272 2115   AP/Kryger Supplies                       375.00

03/27   DM20     260 2115   AP/Interstate Com            6552.00
03/27   DM20         5115   Purchases Ret. and Allow.               6552.00

03/29   M40          1140   Supplies                      120.00
03/29   M40      272 2115   AP/Kryger Supplies                       120.00

                                                        ----------  ----------
                            Totals                      8230.00     8230.00
                                                        ==========  ==========
```

General ledger report

```
                        Celluphone, Inc.
                        General Ledger
                           03/31/--
---------------------------------------------------------------------------
Account          Journal   Date   Refer.      Debit     Credit    Balance
---------------------------------------------------------------------------
2115-Accounts Payable
                 Op. Bal.  03/01  Balances              5921.00    5921.00
                 Op. Bal.  03/01  Balances              2437.00    8358.00
                 Op. Bal.  03/01  Balances              2460.00   10818.00
                 Op. Bal.  03/01  Balances             42600.00   53418.00
                 Op. Bal.  03/01  Balances               346.00   53764.00
                 Purchases 03/01  P39                   6672.00   60436.00
                 Cash Pymt 03/02  C150       1740.00              58696.00
                 General   03/03  DM18        375.00              58321.00
                 Purchases 03/05  P40                   2000.00   60321.00
                 Cash Pymt 03/05  C151       2437.00              57884.00
                 Cash Pymt 03/07  C152       5921.00              51963.00
                 Cash Pymt 03/08  C168       6672.00              45291.00
                 Cash Pymt 03/08  C169      42600.00               2691.00
                 General   03/09  M38                    228.00    2919.00
                 Purchases 03/10  P41                  39456.00   42375.00
                 Cash Pymt 03/12  C170        346.00              42029.00
                 Purchases 03/16  P42                   1864.00   43893.00
                 Purchases 03/18  P50                  17584.00   61477.00
                 Cash Pymt 03/20  C172      39456.00              22021.00
                 Purchases 03/21  P51                  16930.00   38951.00
                 General   03/22  DM19        580.00              38371.00
                 Purchases 03/23  P59                  21430.00   59801.00
                 General   03/24  M39                    375.00   60176.00
                 General   03/27  DM20       6552.00              53624.00
                 Cash Pymt 03/28  C173      17584.00              36040.00
                 General   03/29  M40                    120.00   36160.00
                 Cash Pymt 03/29  C208      16930.00              19230.00
                 Purchases 03/31  P61                   2110.00   21340.00
```

Schedule of accounts payable report

```
                    Celluphone, Inc.
                Schedule of Accounts Payable
                        03/31/--
-----------------------------------------------------
Account
Number       Name                          Balance
-----------------------------------------------------
210          Action Phone Co.              2000.00
240          Electro Sound                 2004.00
250          Hopkins Company               2110.00
260          Interstate Com               14503.00
272          Kryger Supplies                723.00
                                          ----------
             Total                        21340.00
                                          ==========
```

OPTIONAL PROBLEM DB-7A

Celluphone's general ledger data base is on the accounting textbook template. If you wish to process Celluphone's purchases, cash payments, and other transactions using automated accounting software, load the *Automated Accounting 6.0* or higher software. Select Data Base 7A (DB-7A) from the template disk. Read the Problem Instructions screen. Use the completed purchases, cash payments, and general journal input forms, Illustrations T7-1, T7-2, and T7-3, and follow the procedures described to process Celluphone's purchases, cash payments, and other transactions.

AUTOMATED ACCOUNTING PROBLEMS

AUTOMATING APPLICATION PROBLEM 19-3   Recording purchases and cash payment transactions

INSTRUCTIONS:

1. Journalize transactions from Problem 19-3, Chapter 19, on the appropriate forms. Use April 30 of the current year as the run date.

2. Load the *Automated Accounting 6.0* or higher software. Select data base F19-3 (First-Year Course Problem 19-3) from the accounting textbook template. Read the Problem Instructions screen.

3. Select File from the menu bar and choose the Save As menu command. Key the path to the drive and directory that contains your data files. Save the data base with a file name of XXX193 (where XXX are your initials).

4. Key the data from each of the completed input forms.

5. Display/print the general journal report, purchases journal report, and the cash payments journal report.

6. Display/print the accounts payable account from the general ledger.

7. Display/print the schedule of accounts payable.

AUTOMATING MASTERY PROBLEM 19-M   Recording purchases and cash payment transactions

INSTRUCTIONS:

1. Journalize transactions from Mastery Problem 19-M, Chapter 19, on the appropriate input forms. Use August 31 of the current year as the run date.

2. Load the *Automated Accounting 6.0* or higher software. Select data base F19-M (First-Year Course Mastery Problem 19-M) from the accounting textbook template. Read the Problem Instructions screen.

3. Select File from the menu bar and choose the Save As menu command. Key the path to the drive and directory that contains your data files. Save the data base with a file name of XXX19M (where XXX are your initials).

4. Key the data from the completed input forms.

5. Display/print the general journal report, purchases journal report, and the cash payments journal report.

6. Display/print the accounts payable account from the general ledger.

7. Display/print the schedule of accounts payable.

20

Recording Sales and Cash Receipts Using Special Journals

ENABLING PERFORMANCE TASKS

After studying Chapter 20, you will be able to:

a Define accounting terms related to sales and cash receipts.

b Identify accounting concepts and practices related to sales and cash receipts.

c Analyze transactions affecting sales and cash receipts.

d Journalize and post transactions related to sales and cash receipts.

TERMS PREVIEW

sales journal • cash receipts journal • sales discount • sales return • sales allowance • credit memorandum • exports • imports • contract of sale • letter of credit • bill of lading • commercial invoice • draft • sight draft • time draft • trade acceptance

As the volume of business and the number of transactions increase for a business, efficiency of operation becomes more important in completing work accurately and on time. Celluphone has sales of about $2,000,000.00 annually and has numerous transactions to record each day. Because of the size and the numerous transactions of the business, Celluphone uses a system of special journals. Using special journals improves the efficiency of recording transactions and permits more than one accounting clerk to record transactions at the same time. Celluphone uses four special journals and a general journal. A sales journal, a cash receipts journal, and selected uses of a general journal are described in this chapter. A purchases journal, a cash payments journal, and selected uses of a general journal are described in Chapter 19.

RECORDING SALES ON ACCOUNT USING A SALES JOURNAL

Celluphone sells much of its merchandise for cash. However, to encourage additional sales, Celluphone sells on account to customers with approved credit. Regardless of when cash is received, revenue should be recorded when merchandise is sold. *(CONCEPT: Realization of Revenue)* Since many sales are made on account, Celluphone uses a special journal to record *only* sales on account transactions. A special journal used to record only sales on account transactions is called a **sales journal**. The relationship between Celluphone's sales journal and the expanded journal described in Chapter 11 is shown in Illustration 20-1.

Those columns used in an expanded journal and needed to record *only* sales on account are included in Celluphone's sales journal. These amount columns are Accounts Receivable Debit, Sales Credit, and Sales Tax Payable Credit. With these special amount columns, each sale on account transaction can be recorded on one line in Celluphone's sales journal.

ILLUSTRATION 20-1   Sales journal

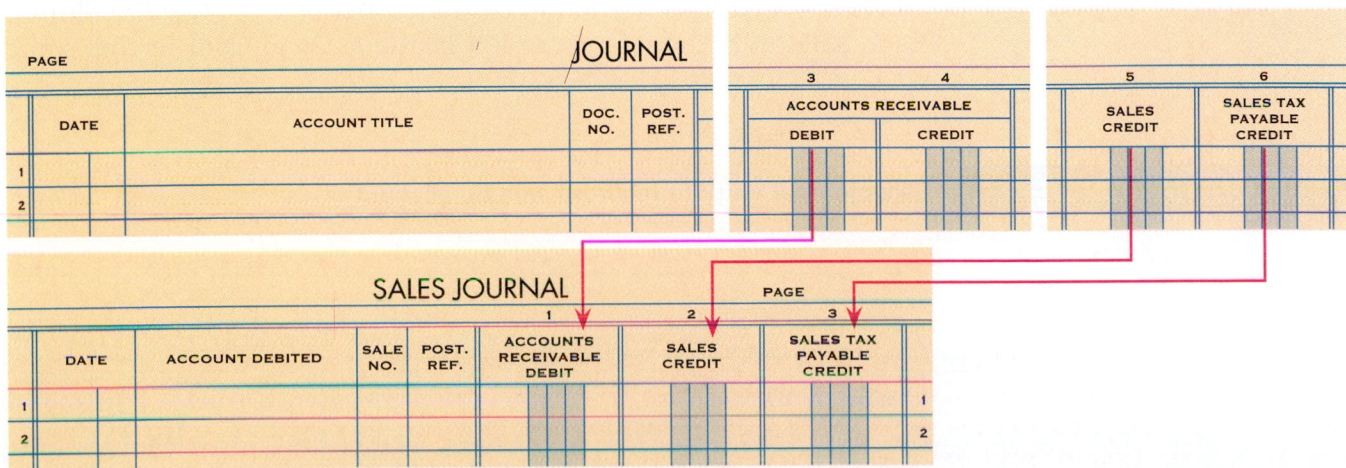

Sales tax rates vary from state to state and may even vary within a state. An 8% sales tax is collected on items sold at retail in the city in which Celluphone is located. A retail business must collect the sales tax from customers and periodically send the sales tax collected to the state. Therefore, Celluphone uses a sales journal with a Sales Tax Payable Credit column to keep a separate record of sales tax.

Journalizing Sales on Account

Celluphone prepares a sales invoice in duplicate for each sale on account. The original copy is given to the customer. The carbon copy of the sales invoice is the source document for journalizing a sales on account transaction. *(CONCEPT: Objective Evidence)* Celluphone's sales invoice is similar to the one described in Chapter 12.

March 1, 19--. Sold merchandise on account to DTex Imports, $1,600.00, plus sales tax, $128.00; total, $1,728.00. Sales Invoice No. 148.

GENERAL LEDGER
Accounts Receivable

| 1,728.00 | |

Sales

| | 1,600.00 |

Sales Tax Payable

| | 128.00 |

ACCOUNTS RECEIVABLE LEDGER
DTex Imports

| 1,728.00 | |

Accounts Receivable is debited for $1,728.00, the amount of the sale plus the sales tax. Sales is credited for $1,600.00, the amount of the sale. Sales Tax Payable is credited for $128.00, the amount of sales tax on this sale. Celluphone owes the tax to the state government. Therefore, the amount of sales tax charged each customer is a liability. DTex Imports' account in the accounts receivable ledger is also debited for $1,728.00.

The sales journal entry to record this sales on account transaction is shown in Illustration 20-2.

The date, *19--, Mar. 1,* is written in the Date column. The customer name, *DTex Imports,* is recorded in the Account Debited column. The sales invoice number, *148,* is entered in the Sale No. column. The sale amount plus the sales tax, *$1,728.00,* is written in the Accounts Receivable Debit column. The sale amount, *$1,600.00,* is entered in the Sales Credit column. The sales tax amount, *$128.00,* is written in the Sales Tax Payable Credit column. Each sale on account is recorded in the sales journal in this same way.

| ILLUSTRATION 20-2 | Sales journal entry to record a sale on account |

SALES JOURNAL   PAGE 8

	DATE		ACCOUNT DEBITED	SALE NO.	POST. REF.	ACCOUNTS RECEIVABLE DEBIT (1)	SALES CREDIT (2)	SALES TAX PAYABLE CREDIT (3)	
1	Mar.	1	DTex Imports	148		1728 00	1600 00	128 00	1
2									2

Since the source document for all entries in the sales journal is a sales invoice, it is not necessary to use an *S* with the document number.

Posting from a Sales Journal to an Accounts Receivable Ledger

Each amount in a sales journal's Accounts Receivable Debit column is posted individually to the customer account in the accounts receivable ledger. Each amount is posted as a debit to the customer account listed in the Account Debited column. Celluphone posts frequently to the accounts receivable ledger so that each customer account will show an up-to-date balance. Illustration 20-3 shows the posting of this entry on line 1 of the sales journal.

ILLUSTRATION 20-3

Posting from a sales journal to an accounts receivable ledger

SALES JOURNAL — PAGE 8

	DATE	ACCOUNT DEBITED	SALE NO.	POST. REF.	ACCOUNTS RECEIVABLE DEBIT (1)	SALES CREDIT (2)	SALES TAX PAYABLE CREDIT (3)	
1	Mar. 1	DTex Imports	148	120	1 7 2 8 00	1 6 0 0 00	1 2 8 00	1
2								2

CUSTOMER *DTex Imports* — CUSTOMER NO. 120

DATE	ITEM	POST. REF.	DEBIT	CREDIT	DEBIT BALANCE
Mar. 1	Balance	✓			4 8 6 00
1		S8	1 7 2 8 00		2 2 1 4 00

The date, *1*, is written in the Date column of the account. The abbreviation for the sales journal and the page number, *S8*, are recorded in the Post. Ref. column. The amount, *$1,728.00*, is entered in the Debit column of the customer account. The amount in the Debit column is added to the previous balance in the Debit Balance column ($486.00 + $1,728.00 = $2,214.00). The new balance, *$2,214.00*, is written in the Debit Balance column. The customer number for DTex Imports, *120*, is recorded in the Post. Ref. column of the sales journal to show that posting has been completed for this line.

Posting from a Sales Journal to a General Ledger

Equality of debits and credits is proved for a sales journal at the end of each month. The sales journal is then ruled, and the totals of special columns are posted, as shown in Illustration 20-4 on page 522.

ILLUSTRATION 20-4   Posting from a sales journal to a general ledger

	DATE	ACCOUNT DEBITED	SALE NO.	POST. REF.	ACCOUNTS RECEIVABLE DEBIT	SALES CREDIT	SALES TAX PAYABLE CREDIT	
					1	2	3	
23	31	Kirby's	221	130	1 4 0 4 00	1 3 0 0 00	1 0 4 00	23
24	31	Totals			88 6 1 4 00	82 0 5 0 00	6 5 6 4 00	24
25					(1125)	(4105)	(2135)	25
26								26

SALES JOURNAL   PAGE 11

ACCOUNT Accounts Receivable   ACCOUNT NO. 1125

DATE	ITEM	POST. REF.	DEBIT	CREDIT	BALANCE DEBIT	BALANCE CREDIT
30		G5		2 5 5 00	33 1 8 2 00	
31		S11	88 6 1 4 00		121 7 9 6 00	

ACCOUNT Sales   ACCOUNT NO. 4105

DATE	ITEM	POST. REF.	DEBIT	CREDIT	BALANCE DEBIT	BALANCE CREDIT
Mar. 31		S11		82 0 5 0 00		82 0 5 0 00

ACCOUNT Sales Tax Payable   ACCOUNT NO. 2135

DATE	ITEM	POST. REF.	DEBIT	CREDIT	BALANCE DEBIT	BALANCE CREDIT
31		CP8	10 6 5 6 00			
31		S11		6 5 6 4 00		6 5 6 4 00

A single line is ruled across the amount columns of the sales journal under the last amounts recorded. The date of the last day of the month, *31,* is written in the Date column. The word *Totals* is written in the Account Debited column. The column totals are written below the single line. Double lines are ruled across the amount columns under the totals. Next, each amount column total is posted to the general ledger account named in the sales journal column headings.

When each sales journal amount column total is posted, *S11* is written in the Post. Ref. column of the account. The account number is written in parentheses under the amount column total in the sales journal. The accounts receivable account number, *1125,* is written under the Accounts Receivable Debit column total in the sales journal. The sales account number, *4105,* is written under the Sales Credit column total. The sales tax payable account number,

FYI

Account numbers in parentheses under the totals of special amount columns in a journal show the general ledger accounts to which the totals have been posted. This cross-reference provides an audit trail.

2135, is written under the Sales Tax Payable Credit column total.

A summary of the procedure for journalizing and posting using a sales journal is shown in Illustration 20-5.

RECORDING CASH RECEIPTS USING A CASH RECEIPTS JOURNAL

Celluphone has many transactions involving the receipt of cash. Because of the numerous transactions involving sizable amounts of cash, Celluphone has two objectives. (1) To avoid the loss of any cash. (2) To efficiently account for the cash. To help meet these objectives, Celluphone uses a special journal to record *only* cash receipt transactions. A special journal used to record only cash receipt transactions is called a **cash receipts journal.**

SUMMARY ILLUSTRATION 20-5

Summary of journalizing and posting using a sales journal

1 All sales on account are recorded in a 3-column sales journal.

2 Individual items in the sales journal are posted frequently to the customer accounts in the accounts receivable ledger.

3 At the end of each month, each amount column total is posted. The Accounts Receivable Debit column total is posted to **Accounts Receivable** as a debit. The Sales Credit column total is posted to **Sales** as a credit. The Sales Tax Payable Credit column total is posted to **Sales Tax Payable** as a credit.

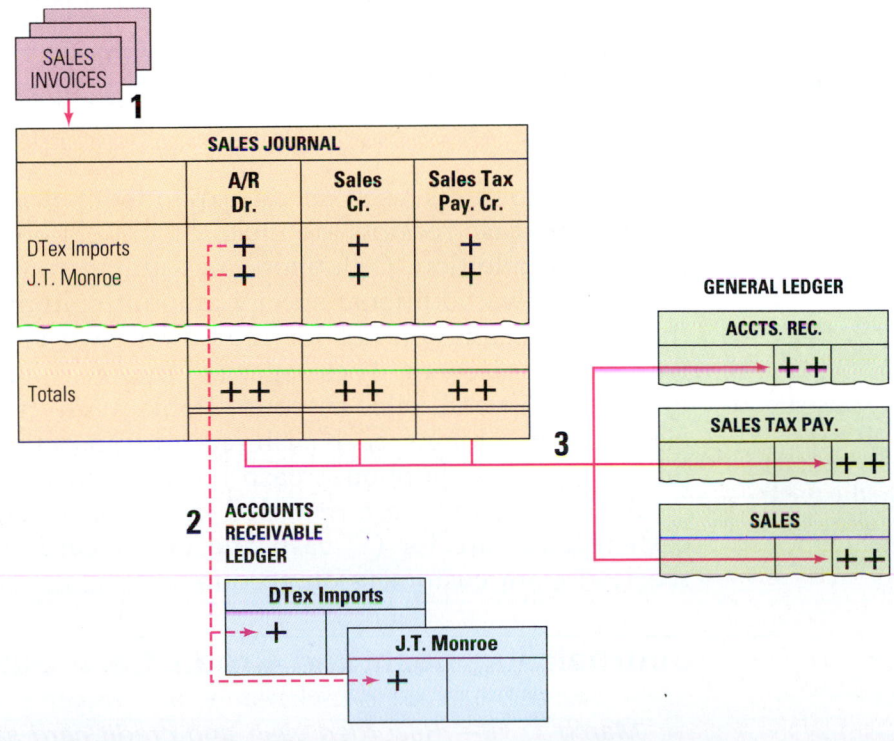

Using a cash receipts journal permits Celluphone to record all cash receipts in one location—the cash receipts journal. Thus the amount of cash received can be determined much more quickly and easily.

The relationship between Celluphone's cash receipts journal and the expanded journal described in Chapter 11 is shown in Illustration 20-6.

Cash receipts journal

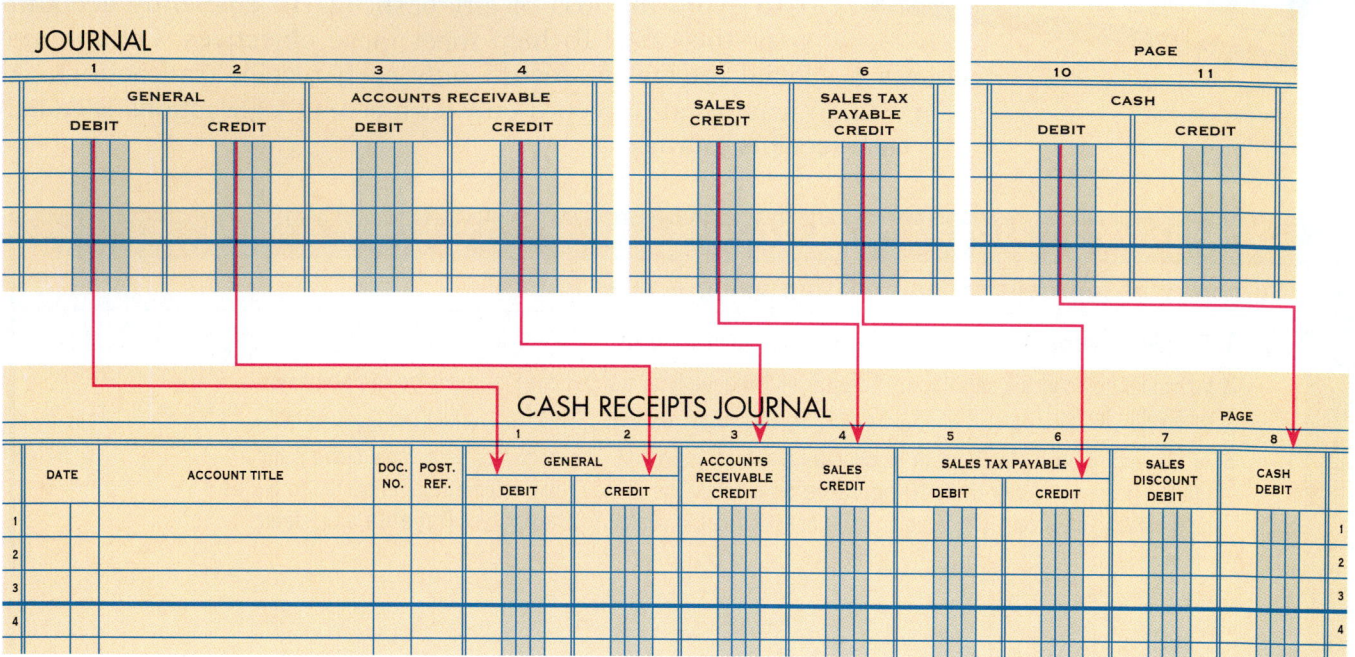

Those columns used in an expanded journal and needed to record *only* cash receipts are included in Celluphone's cash receipts journal. In addition, Celluphone has many transactions with cash discounts. Two additional special amount columns are provided in the cash receipts journal for recording cash received on account with a cash discount. These special amount columns are Sales Tax Payable Debit and Sales Discount Debit. With these additional special amount columns, each cash receipt transaction can be recorded on one line in Celluphone's cash receipts journal.

All cash receipts are recorded in a cash receipts journal. Most cash receipts are for (1) cash and credit card sales and (2) cash received from customers on account.

Journalizing Cash and Credit Card Sales

March 1, 19--. Recorded cash and credit card sales, $2,870.00, plus sales tax, $229.60; total, $3,099.60. Cash Register Tape No. 1.

Not all national credit cards are accepted by all businesses. Some cards are not accepted because the fee is too large a percentage of the sale for some businesses.

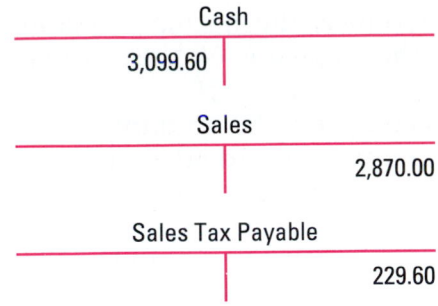

Cash

| 3,099.60 | |

Sales

| | 2,870.00 |

Sales Tax Payable

| | 229.60 |

Cash is debited for $3,099.60. Sales is credited for $2,870.00, and Sales Tax Payable is credited for $229.60.

The cash receipts journal entry to record this cash receipt transaction is shown in Illustration 20-7.

The date, 19--, Mar. 1, is written in the Date column. A check mark is recorded in the Account Title column to show that no account title needs to be written. The cash register tape number, T1, is entered in the Doc. No. column. A check mark is also recorded in the Post. Ref. column to show that separate amounts on this line are not posted individually. The amount credited to Sales, $2,870.00, is written in the Sales Credit column. The amount credited to Sales Tax Payable, $229.60, is recorded in the Sales Tax Payable Credit column. The amount of cash received, $3,099.60, is written in the Cash Debit column.

ILLUSTRATION 20-7   Cash receipts journal entry to record cash and credit card sales

CASH RECEIPTS JOURNAL   PAGE 9

				1	2	3	4	5	6	7	8	
				GENERAL		ACCOUNTS RECEIVABLE CREDIT	SALES CREDIT	SALES TAX PAYABLE		SALES DISCOUNT DEBIT	CASH DEBIT	
DATE	ACCOUNT TITLE	DOC. NO.	POST. REF.	DEBIT	CREDIT			DEBIT	CREDIT			
1	Mar. 1	√	T1	√				2 870 00		229 60		3 099 60	1
2												2

Sales Discounts

Selling merchandise on account usually helps a business increase the volume of its sales by providing more convenience to the customer. The sales transaction can be made by telephone or mail. The merchandise can be shipped to a customer when a sales agreement is reached. A customer can then pay for the merchandise after it is received. Because of this convenience, many sales are made on account. A customer is expected to pay the amount due within the credit period agreed upon.

To encourage early payment for a sale on account, a deduction on the invoice amount may be allowed. A deduction on the invoice amount to encourage prompt payment is known as a cash discount. A cash discount on sales is called a **sales discount**. When a sales discount is taken, a customer pays less cash than the invoice amount previously recorded in the sales account. Therefore, the amount of a sales discount is deducted from sales. Sales discounts are recorded in a general ledger account titled *Sales Discount*. The contra account Sales Discount follows the account to which it is related, Sales, in Cellphone's general ledger operating revenue division. The account is numbered 4110. Since sales discounts decrease sales, the account Sales Dis-

Sales

Debit side	Credit side
	Normal balance
Decrease	Increase

Sales Discount

Debit side	Credit side
Normal balance	
Increase	Decrease

count is a contra account to Sales. Therefore, the normal account balance of Sales Discount is a debit, the opposite of the normal account balance of Sales, a credit.

Some businesses debit the sales account for the amount of the sales discount. However, better information is provided if these amounts are debited to a separate account, Sales Discount. A separate account shows the amount being given as a sales discount. The amount of sales, sales discounts, and time of collections can be analyzed to determine whether sales discounts are effective and worth the cost.

Calculating and Journalizing Cash Receipts on Account with Sales Discounts

To encourage prompt payment, Celluphone gives credit terms of 1/10, n/30. When a customer pays the amount owed within 10 days, the sales invoice amount is reduced 1%.

On March 1, as shown in Illustration 20-2, Celluphone sold merchandise on account to DTex Imports for $1,600.00 plus 8% sales tax, $128.00, for a total invoice amount of $1,728.00. On March 11 Celluphone received payment for this sale on account within the discount period.

In the state where Celluphone is located, state regulations require that sales taxes be paid only on actual sales realized. When Celluphone prepares an invoice for a sale on account, the company does not know whether the customer will pay within the sales discount period. Therefore, the customer is invoiced for the full sales amount plus sales tax on that amount. Thus, on March 1, DTex Imports was invoiced for the full amount of the sale, $1,600.00, plus sales tax on that amount, $128.00, for a total invoice amount of $1,728.00. If payment for a sale on account is received within the discount period, the sales amount is reduced by the amount of the sales discount. The amount of sales tax is also reduced because the amount of the sale is reduced.

In some states sales taxes must be paid on the original invoice amount of sale. In these states a sales discount would not result in a reduction in the sales tax liability.

Three amounts must be calculated to prepare the journal entry and verify that the customer paid the correct amount. (1) The amount of the sales discount, which is a percentage of the amount originally credited to Sales. (2) The amount the sales tax liability is reduced, which is the amount of sales tax on the sales discount. (3) The amount of cash received, which is the original total invoice amount (the Accounts Receivable Debit amount at the time of the sale) less the sales discount and the reduction in sales tax liability. These three amounts are calculated as shown on page 527 for cash received on account within the discount period for Sales Invoice No. 148 to DTex Imports.

(1) Sales Discount:

Sales Invoice Amount	×	Sales Discount Rate	=	Sales Discount
$1,600.00	×	1%	=	$16.00

(2) Sales Tax Liability Reduction:

Sales Discount	×	Sales Tax Rate	=	Reduction in Sales Tax Payable
$16.00	×	8%	=	$1.28

(3) Cash Received:

Total Invoiced Amount	−	Sales Discount	−	Sales Tax Reduction	=	Cash Received
$1,728.00	−	$16.00	−	$1.28	=	$1,710.72

GENERAL LEDGER

Cash

Mar. 11	1,710.72	

Sales Discount

Mar. 11	16.00	

Sales Tax Payable

Mar. 11	1.28	Mar. 1	128.00

Accounts Receivable

Mar. 1	1,728.00	Mar. 11	1,728.00

ACCOUNTS RECEIVABLE LEDGER

DTex Imports

Mar. 1	1,728.00	Mar. 11	1,728.00

March 11, 19--. Received cash on account from DTex Imports, $1,710.72, covering Sales Invoice No. 148 for $1,728.00 ($1,600.00 plus sales tax, $128.00), less 1% discount, $16.00, and less sales tax, $1.28. Receipt No. 232.

Cash is debited for the total amount received, $1,710.72. Sales Discount is debited for the sales discount amount, $16.00. Sales Tax Payable is debited for $1.28, the amount of the reduction in sales tax liability. The sales tax payable on this discounted sale is now $126.72 ($128.00 less $1.28). Accounts Receivable is credited for $1,728.00, the amount debited to Accounts Receivable at the time of the sale on account. DTex Imports' account is also credited for the same amount as Accounts Receivable, $1,728.00.

The amounts for this transaction can be proved by making the calculations shown below.

Sales invoice amount.............................	$1,600.00
Less sales discount...............................	− 16.00
($1,600.00 × 1%)	
Equals reduced invoice amount....................	$1,584.00
Plus sales tax on reduced invoice amount............	+ 126.72
($1,584.00 × 8%)	
Equals cash received	$1,710.72

The cash receipts journal entry to record this cash receipt on account with a sales discount is shown in Illustration 20-8 on page 528.

The date, *11*, is written in the Date column. The customer name, *DTex Imports*, is entered in the Account Title column. The receipt number, *R232*, is written in the Doc. No. column. The amount credited to Accounts Receivable, *$1,728.00*, is recorded in the Accounts Receivable Credit column. The reduction in Sales Tax Payable, *$1.28*, is written in the Sales Tax Payable Debit column. The debit to Sales Discount, *$16.00*, is entered in the Sales Discount Debit column. The debit to Cash, *$1,710.72*, is written in the Cash Debit column. The

FYI

Most states exempt certain classifications of goods from sales tax. Food is frequently exempt from sales tax because it is considered a necessity.

ILLUSTRATION 20-8

Cash receipts journal entry to record a cash receipt on account with sales discount

CASH RECEIPTS JOURNAL — PAGE 9

					1	2	3	4	5	6	7	8
	DATE	ACCOUNT TITLE	DOC. NO.	POST. REF.	GENERAL DEBIT	GENERAL CREDIT	ACCOUNTS RECEIVABLE CREDIT	SALES CREDIT	SALES TAX PAYABLE DEBIT	SALES TAX PAYABLE CREDIT	SALES DISCOUNT DEBIT	CASH DEBIT
20	11	DTex Imports	R232				1728 00		1 28		16 00	1710 72

total of the three debits ($1.28 + $16.00 + $1,710.72) is $1,728.00 and is equal to the one credit of $1,728.00.

If a customer does not pay the amount owed within the sales discount period, the full invoice amount is due. If DTex Imports had not taken the sales discount, the journal entry would be a debit to Cash, $1,728.00, and a credit to Accounts Receivable, $1,728.00. The same amount, $1,728.00, would also be credited to the account of DTex Imports in the accounts receivable ledger.

Posting from a Cash Receipts Journal to an Accounts Receivable Ledger

Each entry in the Accounts Receivable Credit column affects the account of the customer named in the Account Title column. Each amount listed in the Accounts Receivable Credit column is posted individually to the proper customer account in the accounts receivable ledger. Illustration 20-9 shows the posting of a cash receipts journal entry to a customer account.

ILLUSTRATION 20-9

Posting from a cash receipts journal to an accounts receivable ledger

CASH RECEIPTS JOURNAL — PAGE 9

					1	2	3	4	5	6	7	8
	DATE	ACCOUNT TITLE	DOC. NO.	POST. REF.	GENERAL DEBIT	GENERAL CREDIT	ACCOUNTS RECEIVABLE CREDIT	SALES CREDIT	SALES TAX PAYABLE DEBIT	SALES TAX PAYABLE CREDIT	SALES DISCOUNT DEBIT	CASH DEBIT
20	11	DTex Imports	R232	120			1728 00		1 28		16 00	1710 72

CUSTOMER DTex Imports — CUSTOMER NO. 120

DATE	ITEM	POST. REF.	DEBIT	CREDIT	DEBIT BALANCE
1		S8	1728 00		2214 00
4		CR9		486 00	1728 00
11		CR9		1728 00	———

The date, *11*, is written in the Date column of the customer account. The abbreviation and page number of the cash receipts journal, *CR9*, is recorded in the Post. Ref. column. The amount in the Accounts Receivable Credit column, *$1,728.00*, is written in the Credit column of the customer account. The amount in the Credit column of the customer account is subtracted from the previous balance in the Debit Balance column ($1,728.00 − $1,728.00 = 0). A horizontal line is drawn in the Debit Balance column to indicate a new balance of zero. The customer number for DTex Imports, *120*, is recorded in the Post. Ref. column of the cash receipts journal to show that posting has been completed for this line.

Posting from a Cash Receipts Journal to a General Ledger

Each amount in the General amount columns of a cash receipts journal is posted individually to a general ledger account named in the Account Title column. However, only the total of each special amount column is posted to the general ledger account given in the column heading. Posting the special amount column totals of Celluphone's cash receipts journal is shown in Illustration 20-10 on page 530.

Posting from the General Columns of a Cash Receipts Journal. Each amount in the General columns is posted individually to the general ledger account named in the Account Title column. Entries that are recorded in the General columns are described in Chapter 24.

Posting Totals from the Special Columns of a Cash Receipts Journal. At the end of each month, equality of debits and credits is proved for a cash receipts journal. Cash is then proved as shown below.

Cash on hand at the beginning of the month . . . . (March 1, 19--, balance of cash account in general ledger)	$119,048.00
Plus total cash received during the month . . . . (Cash Debit column total, cash receipts journal, Illustration 20-10)	+169,972.00
Total	$289,020.00
Less total cash paid during the month . . . . (Cash Credit column total, cash payments journal, Illustration 19-16, Chapter 19)	−140,742.00
Equals cash on hand at the end of the month	$148,278.00
Checkbook balance on the next unused check stub. . .	$148,278.00

After cash is proved, the cash receipts journal is ruled as shown in Illustration 20-10 on page 530. Each special amount column total is posted to the account named in the cash receipts journal column heading.

Posting from a cash payments journal to the cash account is described in Chapter 19.

ILLUSTRATION 20-10

Posting totals of the special amount columns in a cash receipts journal to a general ledger

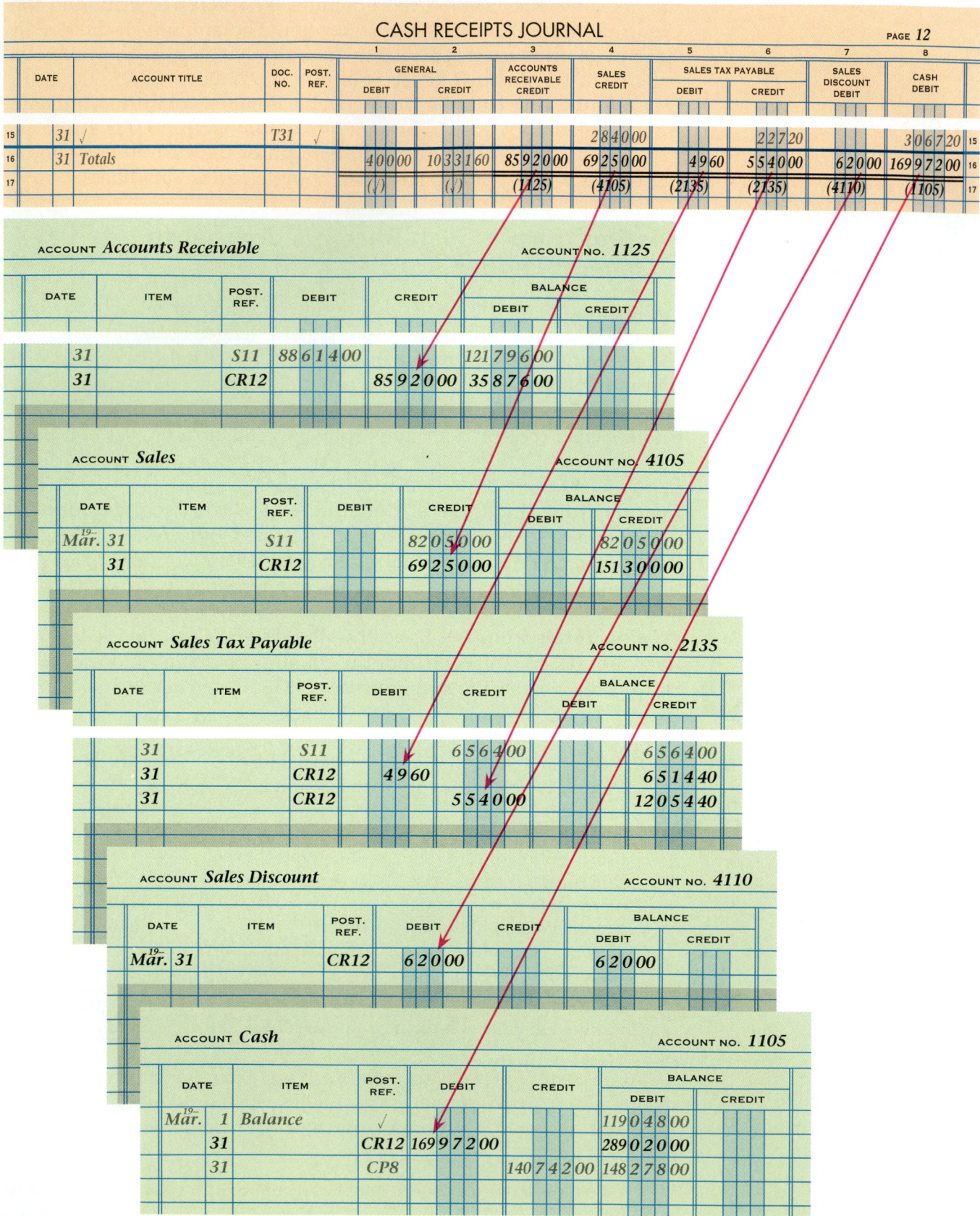

When each special amount column total is posted, *CR12* is written in the Post. Ref. column of the account. The general ledger account number is written below the related cash receipts journal column total. The account number, written in parentheses, shows that posting of a column total is complete.

The totals of the General amount columns are not posted. Each amount in these columns was posted individually to a general ledger account. To indicate that these totals are not posted, a check mark is placed in parentheses below each column total.

A summary of the procedure for journalizing and posting using a cash receipts journal is shown in Illustration 20-11 on page 532.

Audit Your Understanding

1. Why are cash and credit card sales recorded in a cash receipts journal instead of a sales journal?

2. How is a sales discount calculated?

3. How is the cash receipt amount for a sale on account with sales tax and sales discount calculated?

4. Why does the cash receipts journal have both Debit and Credit columns for Sales Tax Payable?

RECORDING TRANSACTIONS USING A GENERAL JOURNAL

Purchases related transactions recorded in a general journal are described in Chapter 19. Celluphone also records two sales related transactions in a general journal. These two transactions are not sales on account or cash receipts. Thus, they are not appropriate for either the sales journal or the cash receipts journal. These two transactions are (1) sales returns and allowances and (2) correcting entries that affect customer accounts but not the controlling account.

Sales Returns and Allowances

FYI

A credit memorandum is prepared by the vendor and sent to the customer. In the vendor's records, the credit memorandum authorizes a credit to the customer's account in the accounts receivable ledger.

Most merchandising businesses expect to have some merchandise returned because a customer decides not to keep the merchandise. A customer may have received the wrong style, the wrong size, or damaged goods. A customer may return merchandise and ask for a credit on account or a cash refund. Credit allowed a customer for the sales price of returned merchandise, resulting in a decrease in the vendor's accounts receivable, is called a **sales return**.

Credit may be granted to a customer without asking for the return of damaged or imperfect merchandise. Credit also may be given because of a shortage in a shipment. Credit allowed a customer for part of the sales price of merchandise that is not returned, resulting in a decrease in the vendor's accounts receivable, is called a **sales allowance.**

A vendor usually informs a customer in writing when a sales return or a sales allowance is granted. A form prepared by the vendor showing the amount deducted for returns and allowances is called a **credit memorandum.** The form is called a credit memorandum because the vendor records the amount as a credit to the customer account to show the decrease in Accounts Receivable.

Summary of journalizing and posting using a cash receipts journal

1 All cash receipts are recorded in an 8-column cash receipts journal.

2 Amounts in the Accounts Receivable Credit column are posted frequently to the customer accounts in the accounts receivable ledger.

3 At the end of the month, the totals of the special columns are posted to the general ledger.

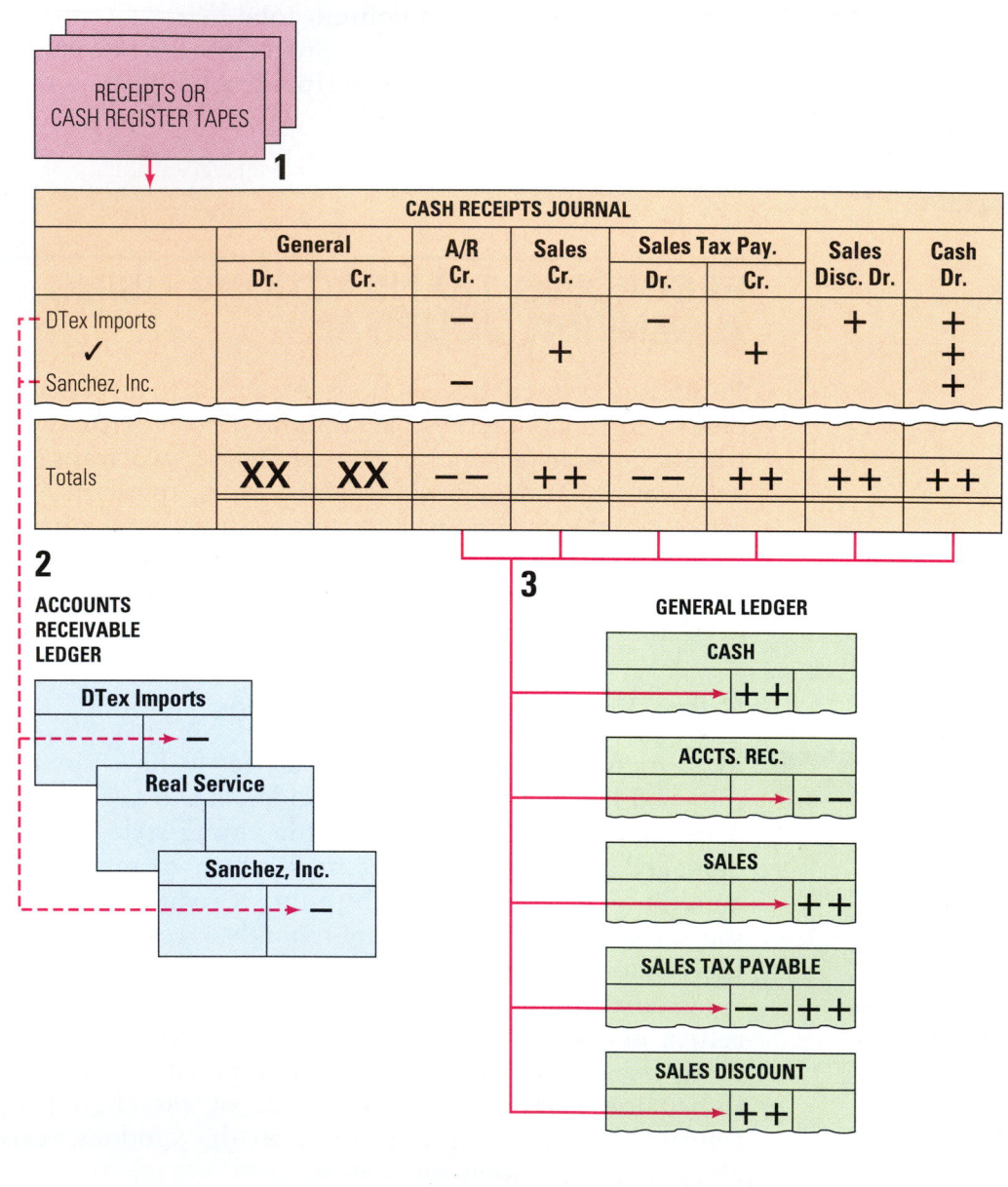

Celluphone issues a credit memorandum in duplicate for each sales return or sales allowance. The original copy is given to the customer. The second copy is used as the source document for sales returns and allowances. *(CONCEPT: Objective Evidence)* The credit memorandum form used by Celluphone is shown in Illustration 20-12.

ILLUSTRATION 20-12

Credit memorandum

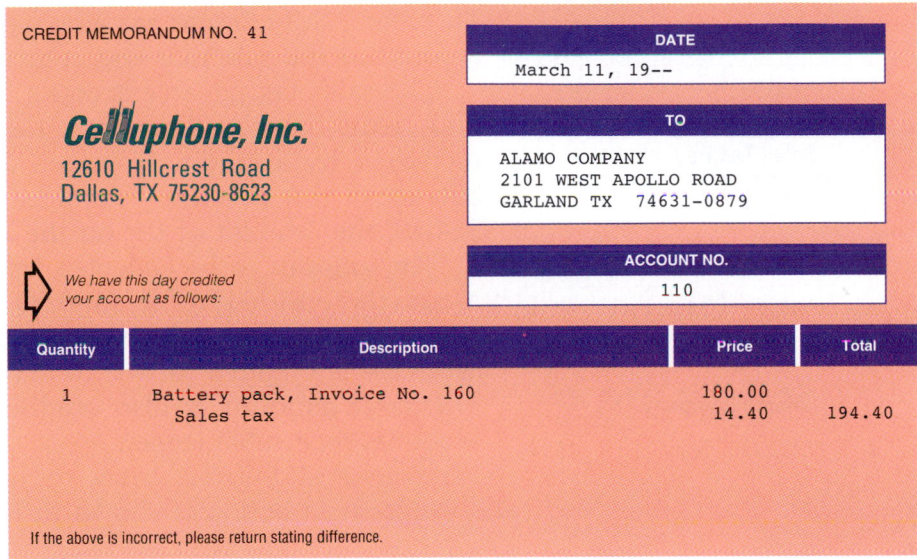

Sales returns and sales allowances decrease the amount of sales. Therefore, the account Sales Returns and Allowances is a contra account to the revenue account Sales. Thus, the normal account balance of Sales Returns and Allowances is a debit, the opposite of the normal balance of Sales, a credit.

Some businesses debit the sales account for the amount of a return or allowance. However, better information is provided if these amounts are debited to a separate account, Sales Returns and Allowances. A separate account shows how large the sales returns and allowances are. Also, a business can see if returns and allowances are increasing or decreasing from year to year. If the amounts are large, separate accounts may be kept for sales returns and for sales allowances. Usually a single, combined account is sufficient.

Celluphone uses a single contra revenue account, Sales Returns and Allowances. The account is in the general ledger's operating revenue division.

Sales	
Debit side	Credit side
	Normal balance
Decrease	Increase

Sales Returns and Allowances	
Debit side	Credit side
Normal balance	
Increase	Decrease

Journalizing Sales Returns and Allowances

On March 8 Celluphone sold merchandise on account to Alamo Company for $360.00. Alamo's account was debited for $388.80 ($360.00 sales and $28.80 sales tax). Later, Alamo returned part of the merchandise. A customer is entitled to credit for the amount of a sales return or allowance. The credit must include the sales tax on the return or allowance.

March 11, 19--. Granted credit to Alamo Company for merchandise returned, $180.00, plus sales tax, $14.40, from S160; total, $194.40. Credit Memorandum No. 41.

Because Sales has a normal credit balance, the contra revenue account, Sales Returns and Allowances, has a normal debit balance. Therefore, the sales returns and allowances account is increased by a debit. This transaction increases the balance of the account. Therefore, Sales Returns and Allowances is debited for $180.00, the amount of the sale that was returned.

The sales tax payable account, a liability account, has a normal credit balance. Therefore, the sales tax payable account is increased by a credit. However, this transaction decreases the balance of this account. Therefore, Sales Tax Payable is debited for $14.40, the amount of tax on the returned merchandise.

The amount to be collected from the customer is decreased. Alamo is entitled to a $180.00 credit for the merchandise returned and a $14.40 credit for sales tax. Therefore, Accounts Receivable is credited for the total amount of the return, $194.40. The same amount is also credited to Alamo's account in the accounts receivable ledger.

The general journal entry to record this sales returns and allowances transaction is shown in Illustration 20-13.

GENERAL LEDGER
Sales Returns and Allowances

Mar. 11	180.00		

Sales Tax Payable

Mar. 11	14.40	Mar. 8	28.80

Accounts Receivable

Mar. 8	388.80	Mar. 11	194.40

ACCOUNTS RECEIVABLE LEDGER
Alamo Company

Mar. 8	388.80	Mar. 11	194.40

ILLUSTRATION 20-13   General journal entry to record sales returns and allowances

	DATE	ACCOUNT TITLE	DOC. NO.	POST. REF.	DEBIT	CREDIT	
12	11	Sales Returns and Allowances	CM41		180 00		12
13		Sales Tax Payable			14 40		13
14		Accounts Receivable/Alamo Co.		/		194 40	14
15							15
16							16
17							17

GENERAL JOURNAL   PAGE *3*

The date, *11*, is written in the Date column. *Sales Returns and Allowances* is recorded in the Account Title column. The source document, *CM41*, is entered in the Doc. No. column. The amount of the debit, *$180.00*, is entered in the Debit column. *Sales Tax Payable* is written on the next line in the Account Title column. The amount of the debit, *$14.40*, is recorded in the Debit column. The accounts credited, *Accounts Receivable/Alamo Company*, are written on the next line in the Account Title column. These account titles are indented about one centimeter. A diagonal line is placed between the two account titles. A diagonal line also is placed in the Post. Ref. column to show that the credit is posted to two accounts. The amount of the credit, *$194.40*, is entered in the Credit column.

Journalizing Correcting Entries Affecting Customer Accounts

Errors may be made in recording amounts in subsidiary ledgers that do not affect the general ledger controlling account. For example, a sale on account may be recorded to the wrong customer in the sales journal. The column total posted from the sales journal to the general ledger is correct. The accounts receivable account shows the correct balance. However, two of the customer accounts in the accounts receivable ledger show incorrect balances. To correct this error, only the subsidiary ledger accounts need to be corrected.

ACCOUNTS RECEIVABLE LEDGER

Ridgecrest Co.

Mar. 12	297.00

Ridgepoint Co.

Feb. 26	297.00	Mar. 12	297.00

March 12, 19--. Discovered that a sale on account to Ridgecrest Co. on February 26, S133, was incorrectly charged to the account of Ridgepoint Co., $297.00. Memorandum No. 40.

On February 28 the total of the Accounts Receivable Debit column in the sales journal was posted correctly. Accounts Receivable was debited for the amount of the column total which included the $297.00 involved in this transaction. No correction is needed for this amount.

The account of Ridgepoint Co. was debited for $297.00 when the account of Ridgecrest Co. should have been debited. The correcting entry involves only subsidiary ledger accounts. Ridgecrest Co.'s account is debited for $297.00 to record the charge sale in the correct account. Ridgepoint Co.'s account is credited for $297.00 to cancel the incorrect entry. The general journal entry to record this correcting entry is shown in Illustration 20-14.

ILLUSTRATION 20-14

General journal entry to record a correcting entry affecting customer accounts

	DATE	ACCOUNT TITLE	DOC. NO.	POST. REF.	DEBIT	CREDIT	
15	12	Ridgecrest Co.	M40		297 00		15
16		Ridgepoint Co.				297 00	16
17							17
18							18

GENERAL JOURNAL   PAGE *3*

The date, *12*, is written in the Date column. The name of the correct customer, *Ridgecrest Co.*, is entered in the Account Title column. The source document, *M40*, is entered in the Doc. No. column. The debit amount, *$297.00*, is recorded in the Debit column.

On the next line, the name of the incorrectly charged customer, *Ridgepoint Co.*, is entered in the Account Title column. This account name is indented about one centimeter. The credit amount, *$297.00*, is recorded in the Credit column.

Posting from a General Journal

Each amount in the Debit and Credit columns of a general journal is posted to the account or accounts named in the Account Title column. The two general journal entries discussed in this chapter are posted in the same way as described in Chapter 19.

A summary of the procedure for journalizing and posting transactions using a general journal is shown in Summary Illustration 20-15.

PREPARING A SCHEDULE OF ACCOUNTS RECEIVABLE

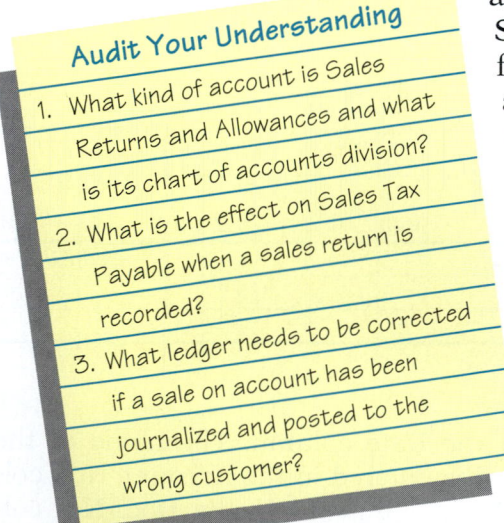

A listing of customer accounts, account balances, and total amount due from all customers is known as a schedule of accounts receivable. A schedule of accounts receivable is prepared before financial statements are prepared to prove the accounts receivable ledger. If the total amount shown on a schedule of accounts receivable equals the accounts receivable controlling account balance in the general ledger, the accounts receivable ledger is proved. Preparation of a schedule of accounts receivable is described in Chapter 13.

ORDER OF POSTING FROM SPECIAL JOURNALS

Items affecting customer or vendor accounts are posted often during the month. Some businesses post daily so that the balances of the subsidiary ledger accounts will be up to date. Since general ledger account balances are needed only when financial statements are prepared, the general ledger accounts may be posted less often during the month. All items, including the totals of special columns, must be posted before a trial balance is prepared.

The best order in which to post the journals is listed below.

1. Sales journal.
2. Purchases journal.
3. General journal.
4. Cash receipts journal.
5. Cash payments journal.

This order of posting usually puts the debits and credits in the accounts in the order the transactions occurred.

Audit Your Understanding

1. What kind of account is Sales Returns and Allowances and what is its chart of accounts division?

2. What is the effect on Sales Tax Payable when a sales return is recorded?

3. What ledger needs to be corrected if a sale on account has been journalized and posted to the wrong customer?

Summary of journalizing and posting using a general journal

1 All transactions that cannot be recorded in any of the special journals are recorded in the general journal.

2 Amounts in the Debit column are posted frequently to the general ledger.

3 Amounts in the Credit column are posted frequently to the general ledger.

4 Amounts debited or credited to **Accounts Receivable** are posted to the named customer account in the accounts receivable ledger.

5 Correcting entries involving only subsidiary ledger accounts are posted only to the appropriate subsidiary ledger.

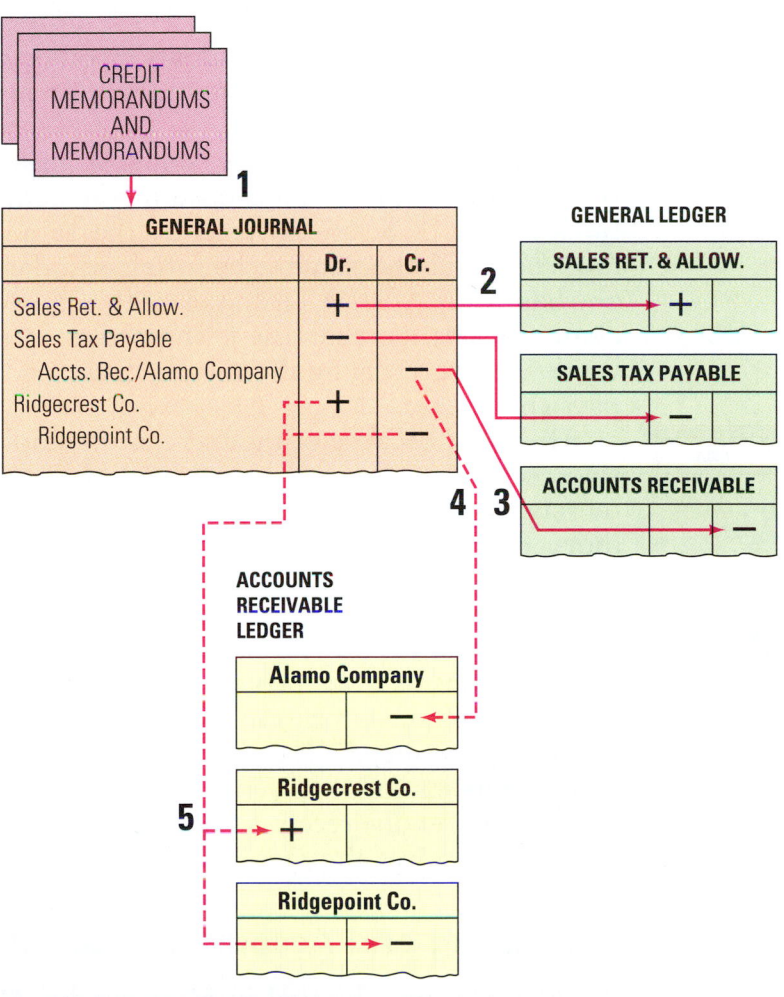

INTERNATIONAL SALES

With the improvement in communications and transportation, international trade has increased. Businesses throughout the world are finding it necessary to buy and sell products and services to and from businesses in foreign countries.

Goods or services shipped out of a seller's home country to a foreign country are called **exports**. Businesses may increase their volume of sales by expanding into the export markets.

Goods or services bought from a foreign country and brought into a buyer's home country are called **imports**. Businesses may be able to import materials or services that are not available or are less expensive than within their own country. Thus, many companies have entered into the export and import markets to maintain their competitiveness and provide the products and services to meet customer demand.

International Sales

Selling merchandise to individuals or other businesses within one's own country, generally referred to as domestic sales, is much simpler than international sales.

Most domestic sales are sold for cash or on account after reviewing and approving a customer's credit. Because all transactions in the U. S. are covered by the same universal commercial law code and the same accounting standards, many transactions are based on trust. A customer with approved credit orders merchandise. The merchandise is shipped and an invoice is sent by the vendor. After receiving the merchandise and invoice, the customer pays the vendor.

However, because of the increased complexities of international sales, several issues must be considered. The lack of a uniform commercial law code among countries makes settlement of disputes more difficult. Greater distances and sometimes more complex transportation methods increase the time to complete the transaction. The reduced ability to determine a customer's financial condition and ability to take legal action if a customer does not pay increases the risk of uncollected amounts. Unstable political conditions in some countries may affect the ability to receive payments from those countries. Therefore, most businesses dealing in exports and/or imports follow a general process in international trade that insures the vendor receives payment for merchandise sold and the customer receives the merchandise ordered.

Processing and Accounting for International Sales

World Wide, Inc., located in Minneapolis, Minnesota, contracts to sell $20,000.00 of merchandise to Gonzalez Compañía in Mexico City, D. F., Mexico. World Wide and Gonzalez follow a procedure for their transaction that is used frequently for international sales. The summary of general procedures for international sales is shown in Illustration 20-16.

A document that details all the terms agreed to by seller and buyer for a sales transaction is called a **contract of sale**. World Wide and Gonzalez agreed to the terms of a contract of sale. The contract includes a description and quantity of merchandise, price, point of delivery, packing and marking instructions, shipping information, insurance provisions, and method of payment. The contract

General procedures for international sales

1 Seller and buyer prepare a contract of sale.

2 Buyer applies for letter of credit to buyer's bank. Buyer's bank approves application and sends letter of credit to seller's bank. Seller's bank delivers letter of credit to seller.

3 Seller verifies letter of credit and ships merchandise.

4 Seller submits documents to seller's bank including (a) bill of lading, (b) commercial invoice, and (c) draft. Seller's bank forwards documents to buyer's bank.

5 Buyer's bank deducts amount of draft from buyer's account and sends amount to seller's bank.

6 Buyer's bank forwards documents to buyer. Buyer presents bill of lading and approved letter of credit to transportation company and receives merchandise.

7 Seller's bank receives payment from buyer's bank and deposits receipts in seller's account.

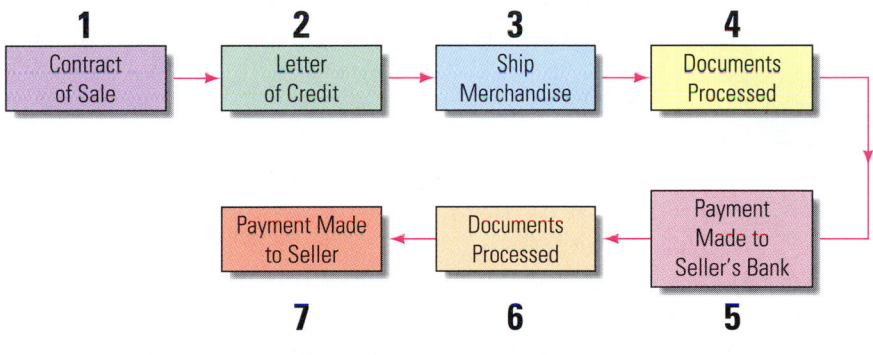

price is $20,000.00 in U.S. dollars, and merchandise is to be delivered to Mexico City, D. F. The Gonzalez Compañía is to pay transportation charges. A letter issued by a bank guaranteeing that a named individual or business will be paid a specified amount provided stated conditions are met is called a **letter of credit**. The contract of sale specified a letter of credit as the method of payment.

Gonzalez prepared an application with its bank, Banco Nacional de Mexico, to issue a letter of credit. Banco Nacional de Mexico approved Gonzalez's application and issued the letter of credit. Banco Nacional de Mexico forwarded the letter of credit to a bank in the vicinity of the seller, First Bank in Minneapolis, Minnesota.

First Bank delivered the letter of credit to World Wide. World Wide reviewed the letter of credit to insure that the provisions in the letter agreed with the contract of sale. World Wide then shipped the merchandise.

In order for World Wide to collect payment, three documents specified in the letter of credit must be submitted to First Bank: (1) bill of lading, (2) commercial invoice, and (3) draft. A receipt signed by the authorized agent of a transportation company for merchandise received that also serves as a contract for the delivery of the merchandise is called a **bill of lading**. The transportation company

FYI

The United States federal government does not collect a sales tax. However, many countries of the world do collect what is referred to as a "value added tax" or VAT. A value added tax is basically a national sales tax.

sends the bill of lading to World Wide when the merchandise is shipped. World Wide then prepares the other two documents. A statement prepared by the seller of merchandise addressed to the buyer showing a detailed listing and description of merchandise sold, including prices and terms, is called a **commercial invoice**. A written, signed, and dated order from one party ordering another party, usually a bank, to pay money to a third party is called a **draft**. A draft is sometimes referred to as a bill of exchange. A draft payable on sight, when the holder presents it for payment is called a **sight draft**.

First Bank examines the documents submitted by World Wide to insure that all terms of sale are in compliance with the letter of credit. First Bank then forwards the documents to Gonzalez Compañía's bank, Banco Nacional de Mexico. Banco Nacional de Mexico examines the documents to insure they are in compliance with the terms and conditions of the letter of credit. When Banco Nacional de Mexico determines all documents are in compliance, it deducts the amount of the sight draft from Gonzalez's account and sends that amount, $20,000.00, to World Wide's bank, First Bank.

Banco Nacional de Mexico then forwards the documents to Gonzalez Compañía. By presenting the bill of lading and letter of credit to the transportation company, Gonzalez can receive the merchandise.

After receiving payment from Banco Nacional de Mexico, First Bank deposits the payment for the sale in World Wide's account and sends World Wide a deposit slip for the amount deposited. After receiving the deposit slip from First Bank, World Wide prepares a memorandum as a source document for the cash received. The sale is then recorded as a cash sale.

April 1, 19--. Recorded international cash sale, $20,000.00. Memorandum 482.

Cash is debited to show the increase in the balance of this asset account. Sales is credited to show the increase in this revenue account.

The cash receipts journal entry to journalize this sales transaction is shown in Illustration 20-17.

Journalizing a cash sales transaction is described in more detail in Chapter 12.

GENERAL LEDGER

Cash

Apr. 1 20,000.00	

Sales

	Apr. 1 20,000.00

ILLUSTRATION 20-17   Cash receipts journal entry to record a sight draft for an international sales transaction

CASH RECEIPTS JOURNAL   PAGE 48

				GENERAL		ACCOUNTS RECEIVABLE CREDIT	SALES CREDIT	SALES TAX PAYABLE		SALES DISCOUNT DEBIT	CASH DEBIT
	DATE	ACCOUNT TITLE	DOC. NO.	POST. REF.	DEBIT	CREDIT			DEBIT	CREDIT		
1	Apr. 1 √		M482	√				20000 00				20000 00
2												

Sales taxes are normally paid only on sales to a consumer. World Wide's sale is to Gonzalez Compañía, another business. Therefore, sales tax is not collected.

The sales and collection process World Wide followed assured World Wide of receiving payment for its sale and Gonzalez Compañía of receiving the merchandise it ordered.

Time Drafts

World Wide, Inc. sold $10,000.00 of merchandise to Alvarez Hermanos, located in Merida, Yucatan, Mexico. The contract of sale with Alvarez was similar to the contract with Gonzalez Compañía, with one exception. World Wide agreed to delay receipt of payment 60 days. A draft that is payable at a fixed or determinable future time after it is accepted is called a **time draft**.

> A time draft is similar to a promissory note. Promissory notes are described in Chapter 24.

The sales process with Alvarez is the same as with Gonzalez except World Wide submits with the documentation a time draft due 60 days from the date the draft is accepted. On April 10, all documentation for the Alvarez sale is verified to be correct by the seller's and buyer's banks, and World Wide's time draft is accepted.

After verifying the documentation, Alvarez's bank, Banco Nacional de Mexico, returns the accepted time draft to World Wide and forwards the other documents to Alvarez Hermanos. Alvarez can receive the merchandise by presenting the bill of lading and letter of credit to the transportation company.

April 10, 19--. Received a 60-day, time draft from Alvarez Hermanos for international sale of merchandise, $10,000.00. Time Draft No. 8.

Time Drafts Receivable is debited for $10,000.00 to show the increase in this asset account. Sales is credited to show the increase in this revenue account.

The general journal entry to record this transaction is shown in Illustration 20-18.

When Alvarez Hermanos' time draft is due and presented to Alvarez's bank, Banco Nacional de Mexico, the bank pays the draft. The payment process is the same as the payment of Gonzalez Compañía's sight draft.

GENERAL LEDGER

Time Drafts Receivable

| Apr. 10 | 10,000.00 | |

Sales

| | | Apr. 10 | 10,000.00 |

ILLUSTRATION 20-18 General journal entry to record a time draft receivable for a sale of merchandise

	DATE		ACCOUNT TITLE	DOC. NO.	POST. REF.	DEBIT	CREDIT	
6	Apr. 19--	10	Time Draft Receivable	TD8		10000 00		6
7			Sales				10000 00	7

GENERAL JOURNAL   PAGE 3

GENERAL LEDGER
Cash

June 9	10,000.00	

Time Drafts Receivable

	June 9	10,000.00

June 9, 19--. Received cash for the value of Time Draft No. 8, $10,000.00. Receipt No. 962.

Cash is debited for $10,000.00 to show the increase in the balance of this asset account. Time Drafts Receivable is credited for $10,000.00 to show the decrease in the balance of this asset account.

The cash receipts journal entry to record this transaction is shown in Illustration 20-19.

ILLUSTRATION 20-19 Cash receipts journal entry to record receipt of cash for a time draft receivable

CASH RECEIPTS JOURNAL PAGE 61

	DATE	ACCOUNT TITLE	DOC. NO.	POST. REF.	GENERAL DEBIT	GENERAL CREDIT	ACCOUNTS RECEIVABLE CREDIT	SALES CREDIT	SALES TAX PAYABLE DEBIT	SALES TAX PAYABLE CREDIT	SALES DISCOUNT DEBIT	CASH DEBIT	
9	19-- June 9	Time Draft Receivable	R962			10000 00						10000 00	9
10													10
11													11

The process used by World Wide, Inc. for international sales relies upon letters of credit from banks to assure receipt of payment for those sales. Occasionally, World Wide grants an extension of time for payment to long-time international customers by submitting a time draft.

Trade Acceptances

A form signed by a buyer at the time of a sale of merchandise in which the buyer promises to pay the seller a specified sum of money usually at a stated time in the future is called a **trade acceptance**.

A trade acceptance is similar to a draft except a draft is generally paid by a bank and a trade acceptance by the buyer. A seller generally has much more assurance of receiving payment from a bank than from a buyer. Because of the many complexities, few businesses use trade acceptances in international sales. Some businesses, however, use trade acceptances for domestic sales to very reliable customers.

Audit Your Understanding

1. What kind of receipt can also serve as a contract for the delivery of merchandise?

2. In international sales, what is the main concern of the business that is selling merchandise?

3. In international sales, what is the main concern of the business that is purchasing merchandise?

SUMMARY OF RECORDING SALES AND CASH RECEIPTS USING SPECIAL JOURNALS

The charts shown in Summary Illustration 20-20 on page 543 summarize the entries for sales, cash receipts, and other transactions in special journals and a general journal.

Transaction	SALES JOURNAL		
	1	2	3
	Accounts Receivable Debit	Sales Credit	Sales Tax Payable Credit
Sales on account	X	X	X

Transactions	CASH RECEIPTS JOURNAL							
	1	2	3	4	5	6	7	8
	General		Accounts Receivable Credit	Sales Credit	Sales Tax Payable		Sales Discount Debit	Cash Debit
	Debit	Credit			Debit	Credit		
Cash receipts from sales				X		X		X
Cash receipts on account with sales discount			X		X		X	X
Cash receipts from sight drafts for international sales				X				X
Cash receipts from time draft receivables		X						X

Transactions	GENERAL JOURNAL	
	Debit	Credit
Sales returns and allowances	X	X
Correcting entry	X	X
International sale with a time draft receivable	X	X

What is the meaning of each of the following?

1. sales journal
2. cash receipts journal
3. sales discount
4. sales return
5. sales allowance
6. credit memorandum
7. exports
8. imports
9. contract of sale
10. letter of credit
11. bill of lading
12. commercial invoice
13. draft
14. sight draft
15. time draft
16. trade acceptance

QUESTIONS FOR INDIVIDUAL STUDY

EPT(b)

1. Why do some companies sell merchandise on account?
2. Which accounting concept is being applied when revenue is recorded as merchandise is sold regardless of when cash is received?
3. Why does Celluphone post frequently to customer accounts?
4. What objectives do companies with numerous transactions involving sizable amounts of cash frequently have?
5. Why do companies offer sales discounts?
6. What is the normal account balance of the sales discount account?
7. Are businesses that offer sales discounts required to use a sales discount account?
8. When cash is received on account within the discount period and sales tax is charged on the amount less the discount, what amounts must be calculated to prepare the journal entry for receipt of cash?
9. What general ledger accounts are affected, and how, by a cash receipt from a customer on account when there is a sales discount and sales tax?
10. Which amounts in a cash receipts journal are posted separately to general ledger accounts?
11. What general ledger accounts are affected, and how, by a sales returns and allowances transaction?
12. How can an error involving posting a debit amount to the wrong customer account be corrected?
13. Why have many businesses entered into the export and import business?
14. What are some of the issues that must be considered before making international sales?
15. What two purposes does a bill of lading serve?
16. How does a sight draft differ from a time draft?
17. Why do many companies dealing in international sales rely upon letters of credit from banks?
18. How does a trade acceptance differ from a draft?

CASES FOR CRITICAL THINKING

EPT(b)

CASE 1 Latson Company uses a 3-column sales journal with special amount columns similar to the one in this chapter. The company records sales tax payable at the time a sale on account is made. Christopher Chenault, the office manager, questions this practice. He suggests that sales tax payable not be recorded until cash is actually collected for a sale. Which procedure is preferable? Why?

CASE 2 Regents Office Supply sells office supplies to many local firms. Most of the store's sales are made on account. In order to encourage prompt payment, Regents offers a sales discount for those who pay within the discount period. Regents is considering changing its payroll policy for sales personnel from a salary plan to a commission-on-sales plan in order to encourage sales personnel to increase their sales efforts. Commissions would be 5% of sales. Various sales personnel have asked you, the manager, whether commissions would be based on gross sales or on sales after sales discounts and returns and allowances. What should your response be? Explain.

DRILL 20-D1 Analyzing the journalizing of sales and cash receipts transactions

A form for analyzing transactions is given in the working papers that accompany this textbook.

INSTRUCTIONS:

Complete the form for each of the following transactions. In Column A, write the title of the account(s) debited. In Column B, write the title of the account(s) credited. In Column C, write the name of the journal in which the transaction is recorded. In Columns D and E, write the names of the journal amount column(s) in which debit and credit amounts are recorded. Transaction 1 is given as an example.

1. Sold merchandise on account to James Harding plus sales tax.
2. Recorded cash and credit card sales plus sales tax.
3. Received cash on account from Accent Company; no sales discount.
4. Granted credit to Richco for merchandise returned plus sales tax.
5. Sold merchandise on account to Kennel Co. plus sales tax.
6. Granted credit to Silver Star for damaged merchandise plus sales tax.
7. Discovered that a sale on account to Rebecca Hind was incorrectly charged to Rebecca Hindle.
8. Received cash on account from Forms Co. less sales discount and sales tax.

The solution to Drill 20-D1 is needed to complete Drill 20-D2.

DRILL 20-D2 Analyzing the posting of sales and cash receipts transactions

The solution to Drill 20-D1 is needed to complete Drill 20-D2.

A form for analyzing transactions is given in the working papers that accompany this textbook.

INSTRUCTIONS:

1. In Column A, write the titles of the accounts affected by each transaction in Drill 20-D1.

2. Place a check mark in Column B if the amount is posted individually to the general ledger. Place a check mark in Column C if the amount is posted individually to the accounts receivable ledger. Place a check mark in Column D if the amount is not posted individually to any ledger. Transaction 1 is given as an example.

DRILL 20-D3 Calculating sales discounts and cash receipts

A form for recording the answers to this drill is given in the working papers that accompany this textbook.

INSTRUCTIONS:

1. Information about six sales invoices is given at the top of the next page. Use a sales tax rate of 6% and a cash discount rate of 2%. For Sales No. S1, S2, S3, and S4, calculate the sales discount amount, sales tax reduction, and amount of the cash receipt after the discount is taken.

2. For Sales No. S5 and S6, calculate the sales tax on the credit memorandum amount. Also calculate the sales discount amount, sales tax reduction, and amount of the cash receipt for the invoices less the credit memorandums.

Sale No.	Sale Amount	Sales Tax Amount	Invoice Amount	Credit Memo. Amount
S1	1,750.00	105.00	1,855.00	—
S2	955.00	57.30	1,012.30	—
S3	2,566.20	153.97	2,720.17	—
S4	3,621.00	217.26	3,838.26	—
S5	1,625.00	97.50	1,722.50	150.00
S6	2,892.00	173.52	3,065.52	225.00

APPLICATION PROBLEMS

EPT(c,d)

PROBLEM 20-1   Journalizing and posting sales on account transactions

The general ledger and accounts receivable ledger accounts for Capitol Sales Company are given in the working papers accompanying this textbook. The balances are recorded as of March 1 of the current year.

INSTRUCTIONS:

1. Journalize the following sales on account transactions completed during March of the current year. Use page 3 of a sales journal. The sales tax rate is 8%. The abbreviation for sales invoice is S.

Mar. 1. Sold merchandise on account to Daniel Noble, $204.00, plus sales tax, $16.32; total, $220.32. S58.

3. Sold merchandise on account to Austin Equipment Co., $330.65, plus sales tax, $26.45; total, $357.10. S59.

5. Sold merchandise on account to Crawford Company, $145.25, plus sales tax, $11.62; total, $156.87. S60.

8. Sold merchandise on account to Theresa Briggs, $215.90, plus sales tax, $17.27; total, $233.17. S61.

10. Sold merchandise on account to Tensil Company, $154.00, plus sales tax, $12.32; total, $166.32. S62.

12. Sold merchandise on account to Crawford Company, $198.55, plus sales tax, $15.88; total, $214.43. S63.

15. Sold merchandise on account to Midori Saga, $114.00, plus sales tax, $9.12; total, $123.12. S64.

20. Sold merchandise on account to Austin Equipment Co., $234.90, plus sales tax, $18.79; total, $253.69. S65.

26. Sold merchandise on account to Midori Saga, $233.00, plus sales tax, $18.64; total, $251.64. S66.

31. Sold merchandise on account to Daniel Noble, $164.25, plus sales tax, $13.14; total, $177.39. S67.

2. Post each amount in the Accounts Receivable Debit column of the sales journal to the accounts receivable ledger.

3. Prove and rule the sales journal. Post the totals of the special columns.

PROBLEM 20-2 Journalizing and posting cash receipts transactions

The general ledger and accounts receivable ledger accounts for The General Store are given in the working papers accompanying this textbook. The balances are recorded as of May 1 of the current year.

INSTRUCTIONS:

1. Journalize the following cash receipts transactions completed during May of the current year. Use page 5 of a cash receipts journal. The General Store offers terms of 1/10, n/30. The sales tax rate is 8%. Source documents are abbreviated as follows: receipt, R; sales invoice, S; cash register tape, T.

May 2. Received cash on account from Brandon Company, $641.52, covering S219 for $648.00 ($600.00 plus sales tax, $48.00), less discount, $6.00, and less sales tax, $0.48. R65.

5. Received cash on account from Kitchen Kettle, $157.00, covering S223; no discount. R66.

7. Received cash on account from Jason Denison, $213.84, covering S218 for $216.00 ($200.00 plus sales tax, $16.00), less discount, $2.00, and less sales tax, $0.16. R67.

8. Received cash on account from Cynthia Anson, $320.76, covering S217 for $324.00 ($300.00 plus sales tax, $24.00), less discount, $3.00, and less sales tax, $0.24. R68.

14. Recorded cash and credit card sales, $7,177.00, plus sales tax, $574.16; total, $7,751.16. T14.

21. Received cash on account from Stan's Eatery, $463.00, covering S220; no discount. R69.

31. Recorded cash and credit card sales, $6,947.00, plus sales tax, $555.76; total, $7,502.76. T31.

2. Post each amount in the Accounts Receivable Credit column of the cash receipts journal to the accounts receivable ledger.

3. Prove the equality of debits and credits for the cash receipts journal.

4. Prove cash. The cash balance on hand on May 1 was $10,233.00. The total of the Cash Credit column of the cash payments journal for The General Store is $14,003.83. The balance on the next unused check stub on May 31 is $13,279.21.

5. Rule the cash receipts journal. Post the totals of the special columns.

PROBLEM 20-3 Journalizing and posting sales and cash receipts transactions

The general ledger and accounts receivable ledger accounts for Pierce Imports are given in the working papers accompanying this textbook. The balances are recorded as of June 1 of the current year.

INSTRUCTIONS:

1. Journalize the following transactions affecting sales and cash receipts completed during June of the current year. Use page 6 of a sales journal, a general journal, and a cash receipts journal. Pierce Imports offers terms of 1/10, n/30. The sales tax rate is 8%. Source documents are abbreviated as follows: credit memorandum, CM; memorandum, M; receipt, R; sales invoice, S; cash register tape, T.

June 3. Received cash on account from Beverly's Gift Shop, $300.22, covering S136 for $303.25 ($280.79 plus sales tax, $22.46), less discount, $2.81, and less sales tax, $0.22. R83.

4. Sold merchandise on account to Geno's, $416.25, plus sales tax, $33.30; total, $449.55. S152.

June 4. Recorded cash and credit card sales, $3,556.00, plus sales tax, $284.48; total, $3,840.48. T4.

7. Received cash on account from Geno's, $342.54, covering S147 for $346.00 ($320.37 plus sales tax, $25.63), less discount, $3.20, and less sales tax, $0.26. R84.

9. Received cash on account from Hana Victor, $614.79, covering S149 for $621.00 ($575.00 plus sales tax, $46.00), less discount, $5.75, and less sales tax, $0.46. R85.

9. Discovered that a sale on account to Nan and Jenkins Decorators on May 26, S145, was incorrectly charged to the account of Frank Finnely, $415.00 ($384.26 plus sales tax, $30.74). M27.

10. Received cash on account from Frank Finnely, $273.72, covering S150 for $276.48 ($256.00 plus sales tax, $20.48), less discount, $2.56, and less sales tax, $0.20. R86.

11. Sold merchandise on account to Hana Victor, $604.15, plus sales tax, $48.33; total, $652.48. S153.

11. Recorded cash and credit card sales, $4,122.00, plus sales tax, $329.76; total, $4,451.76. T11.

Posting. Post the items that are to be posted individually. Post from the journals in this order: sales journal, general journal, and cash receipts journal.

14. Granted credit to The Import Shop for merchandise returned, $67.00, plus sales tax, $5.36, from S151; total, $72.36. CM31.

15. Sold merchandise on account to Beverly's Gift Shop, $414.00, plus sales tax, $33.12; total, $447.12. S154.

15. Sold merchandise on account to Susan Malta, $305.80, plus sales tax, $24.46; total, $330.26. S155.

17. Received cash on account from Nan and Jenkins Decorators, $415.00, covering M27; no discount. R87.

18. Recorded cash and credit card sales, $2,997.00, plus sales tax, $239.76; total, $3,236.76. T18.

Posting. Post the items that are to be posted individually.

21. Sold merchandise on account to Frank Finnely, $348.00, plus sales tax, $27.84; total, $375.84. S156.

21. Received cash on account from The Import Shop, $851.64 (covering S151 less CM31), no discount. R88.

21. Received cash on account from Hana Victor, $645.96, covering S153 for $652.48 ($604.15 plus sales tax, $48.33), less discount, $6.04, and less sales tax, $0.48. R89.

22. Received cash on account from Geno's, $449.55, covering S152; no discount. R90.

24. Sold merchandise on account to Frank Finnely, $149.80, plus sales tax, $11.98; total, $161.78. S157.

25. Sold merchandise on account to The Import Shop, $415.50, plus sales tax, $33.24; total, $448.74. S158.

27. Sold merchandise on account to Nan and Jenkins Decorators, $637.00, plus sales tax, $50.96; total, $687.96. S159.

30. Received cash on account from Susan Malta, $475.75, covering S146; no discount. R91.

30. Recorded cash and credit card sales, $1,582.00, plus sales tax, $126.56; total, $1,708.56. T30.

Posting. Post the items that are to be posted individually.

2. Prove and rule the sales journal. Post the totals of the special columns.

3. Prove the equality of debits and credits for the cash receipts journal.

4. Prove cash. The cash balance on hand on June 1 was $9,211.00. The total of the Cash Credit column of the cash payments journal for Pierce Imports is $15,672.58. The balance on the next unused check stub on June 30 is $11,145.15.

5. Rule the cash receipts journal. Post the totals of the special columns.

6. Prepare a schedule of accounts receivable similar to the one described in Chapter 13. Compare the schedule total with the balance of the accounts receivable account in the general ledger. The total and balance should be the same.

PROBLEM 20-4 Journalizing international sales transactions

INSTRUCTIONS:

1. Journalize the following international sales completed by Exports, Ltd. during April of the current year. Use page 8 of a cash receipts journal and a general journal. Sales tax is not charged on these sales. Source documents are abbreviated as follows: memorandum, M; time draft, TD, and receipt, R.

April 1. Recorded international cash sale, $25,000.00. M123.
      5. Received a 30-day time draft from Lih Fen Hwang for international sale of merchandise, $18,000.00. TD12.
      9. Received cash for the value of Time Draft No. 10, $23,000.00. R421.
    12. Recorded domestic cash sale, $17,500.00. M124.
    13. Received cash for the value of Time Draft No. 11, $15,000.00. R422.
    16. Recorded international cash sale, $32,800.00. M125.
    19. Received a 60-day time draft from Kittika Kamarsu for international sale of merchandise, $10,000.00. TD13.
    27. Recorded international cash sale, $41,200.00. M126.

2. Prove and rule the cash receipts journal.

ENRICHMENT PROBLEMS

EPT(c,d)

MASTERY PROBLEM 20-M Journalizing and posting sales and cash receipts transactions

AUTOMATED

APPLICATION

The general ledger and accounts receivable accounts for Founders Corporation are given in the working papers accompanying this textbook. The balances are recorded as of February 1 of the current year. Use the following account titles.

PARTIAL GENERAL LEDGER		ACCOUNTS RECEIVABLE LEDGER	
Account No.	**Account Title**	**Customer No.**	**Customer Name**
1105	Cash	110	Andrew Anderson
1125	Accounts Receivable	120	Brady and Co.
2135	Sales Tax Payable	130	Jessica Howe
4105	Sales	140	Kindercraft
4110	Sales Discount	150	Alford Lein
4115	Sales Returns and Allowances	160	Mandon, Inc.
		170	Platter Company
		180	Glenda Stevens

INSTRUCTIONS:

1. Journalize the following transactions affecting sales and cash receipts completed during February of the current year. Use page 2 of a sales journal, a general journal, and a cash receipts journal. Founders Corporation offers terms of 2/10, n/30. The sales tax rate is 8%. Source documents are abbreviated as follows: credit memorandum, CM; memorandum, M; receipt, R; sales invoice, S; cash register tape, T.

Feb. 1. Sold merchandise on account to Jessica Howe, $330.00, plus sales tax, $26.40; total, $356.40. S96.

1. Granted credit to Mandon, Inc., for merchandise returned, $48.00, plus sales tax, $3.84, from S90; total, $51.84. CM27.

5. Received cash on account from Platter Company, $423.36, covering S92 for $432.00 ($400.00 plus sales tax, $32.00), less discount, $8.00, and less sales tax, $0.64. R42.

8. Received cash on account from Glenda Stevens, $383.67, covering S95 for $391.50 ($362.50 plus sales tax, $29.00), less discount, $7.25, and less sales tax, $0.58. R43.

8. Recorded cash and credit card sales, $1,420.00, plus sales tax, $113.60; total, $1,533.60. T8.

   Posting. Post the items that are to be posted individually. Post from the journals in this order: sales journal, general journal, and cash receipts journal.

9. Sold merchandise on account to Mandon, Inc., $214.00, plus sales tax, $17.12; total, $231.12. S97.

11. Received cash on account from Jessica Howe, $367.20, covering S88; no discount. R44.

11. Granted credit to Andrew Anderson for merchandise returned, $112.50, plus sales tax, $9.00, from S91; total $121.50. CM28.

12. Received cash on account from Kindercraft, $150.00, covering S87; no discount. R45.

12. Received cash on account from Mandon, Inc., $326.16 (covering S90 less CM27), no discount. R46.

12. Recorded cash and credit card sales, $2,215.00, plus sales tax, $177.20; total, $2,392.20. T12.

   Posting. Post the items that are to be posted individually.

15. Received cash on account from Brady and Co., $404.56, covering S94; no discount. R47.

18. Sold merchandise on account to Platter Company, $205.00, plus sales tax, $16.40; total, $221.40. S98.

18. Received cash on account from Mandon, Inc., $226.50, covering S97 for $231.12 ($214.00 plus sales tax, $17.12), less discount, $4.28, and less sales tax, $0.34. R48.

19. Sold merchandise on account to Brady and Co., $420.00, plus sales tax, $33.60; total, $453.60. S99.

19. Recorded cash and credit card sales, $1,897.00, plus sales tax, $151.76; total, $2,048.76. T19.

   Posting. Post the items that are to be posted individually.

22. Received cash on account from Jessica Howe, $356.40, covering S96; no discount. R49.

22. Discovered that a sale on account to Platter Company on January 15, S93, was incorrectly charged to the account of Alford Lein, $216.00 ($200.00 plus sales tax, $16.00). M52.

23. Sold merchandise on account to Kindercraft, $296.00, plus sales tax, $23.68; total, $319.68. S100.

23. Received cash on account from Andrew Anderson, $108.00 (covering S91 less CM28), no discount. R50.

Feb. 23. Received cash on account from Brady and Co., $444.53, covering S99 for $453.60 ($420.00 plus sales tax, $33.60), less discount, $8.40, and less sales tax, $0.67. R51.

   25. Sold merchandise on account to Andrew Anderson, $356.00, plus sales tax, $28.48; total, $384.48. S101.

   28. Received cash on account from Kindercraft, $313.29, covering S100 for $319.68 ($296.00 plus sales tax, $23.68), less discount, $5.92, and less sales tax, $0.47. R52.

   28. Recorded cash and credit card sales, $2,197.00, plus sales tax, $175.76; total, $2,372.76. T28.

   Posting. Post the items that are to be posted individually.

2. Prove and rule the sales journal. Post the totals of the special columns.

3. Prove the equality of debits and credits for the cash receipts journal.

4. Prove cash. The cash balance on hand on February 1 was $6,354.00. The total of the Cash Credit column of the cash payments journal for Founders Corporation is $11,234.00. The balance on the next unused check stub on February 28 is $6,970.99.

5. Rule the cash receipts journal. Post the totals of the special columns.

6. Prepare a schedule of accounts receivable similar to the one described in Chapter 13. Compare the schedule total with the balance of the accounts receivable account in the general ledger. The total and balance should be the same.

CHALLENGE PROBLEM 20-C Journalizing and posting sales, purchases, cash receipts, and cash payments transactions

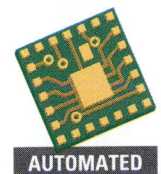

AUTOMATED

MATHEMATICS

The general ledger, accounts receivable ledger, and accounts payable ledger accounts for Princess Company are given in the working papers accompanying this textbook. The balances are recorded as of April 1 of the current year.

PARTIAL GENERAL LEDGER

Account No.	Account Title
1105	Cash
1110	Petty Cash
1125	Accounts Receivable
1140	Supplies
2115	Accounts Payable
2135	Sales Tax Payable
4105	Sales
4110	Sales Discount
4115	Sales Returns and Allowances
5105	Purchases
5110	Purchases Discount
5115	Purchases Returns and Allowances
6105	Advertising Expense
6130	Miscellaneous Expense
6140	Rent Expense
8105	Cash Short and Over

ACCOUNTS RECEIVABLE LEDGER

Customer No.	Customer Name
110	Barbra Almon
120	Bland Company
130	James Hart
140	Jefferson Co.
150	Linda Ponder

ACCOUNTS PAYABLE LEDGER

Vendor No.	Vendor Name
210	Dunn Supplies
220	Gibson Electric Co.
230	Roland and Barnes
240	Webb Co.

INSTRUCTIONS:

1. Journalize the following transactions affecting sales, purchases, cash receipts, and cash payments completed during April of the current year. Calculate and record sales tax on all sales and sales returns and allowances as described in this chapter. Use page 4 of a sales journal, a purchases journal, a general journal, a cash receipts journal, and a cash

payments journal. Princess Company offers its customers terms of 2/10, n/30. The sales tax rate is 8%. Source documents are abbreviated as follows: check, C; credit memorandum, CM; debit memorandum, DM; memorandum, M; purchase invoice, P; receipt, R; sales invoice, S; cash register tape, T.

Apr. 1. Wrote a check for April rent, $850.00. C84.
　　 1. Wrote a check to pay on account to Roland and Barnes, covering P74 for $366.00, less 1% discount. C85.
　　 2. Cash was received on account from Jefferson Co., $545.08, covering S53 for $556.20 ($515.00 plus sales tax, $41.20), less discount and less sales tax on discount. R26.
　　 2. Cash and credit card sales, $1,926.00, plus sales tax. T2.
　　　　 Posting. Post the items that are to be posted individually. Post the journals in this order: sales journal, purchases journal, general journal, cash receipts journal, and cash payments journal.
　　 5. Merchandise was returned to Webb Co., $468.32, from P75. DM9.
　　 6. Bland Company bought merchandise on account, $247.00, plus sales tax. S55.
　　 6. Wrote a check for money owed to Gibson Electric Co., $1,945.00, covering P64; no discount. C86.
　　 6. Received payment on account from Linda Ponder, $417.01, covering S54 for $425.52 ($394.00 plus sales tax, $31.52), less discount and less sales tax on discount. R27.
　　 7. Bought supplies on credit from Dunn Supplies, $537.00. M15.
　　 9. Cash was received on account from Barbra Almon, $330.48, covering S51; no discount. R28.
　　 9. Recorded cash and credit card sales, $1,820.00, plus sales tax. T9.
　　　　 Posting. Post the items that are to be posted individually.
　　 12. Merchandise was purchased on account from Gibson Electric Co., $1,675.00. P77.
　　 13. Wrote a check for money owed to Webb Co., covering P75 for $3,010.00, less DM9, $468.32, and less 2% discount. C87.
　　 14. Jefferson Co. bought merchandise on credit, $746.00, plus sales tax. S56.
　　 14. Paid for advertising, $450.00. C88.
　　 14. Issued a check on account to Dunn Supplies, $1,413.00, covering M14; no discount. C89.
　　 15. Bland Company returned merchandise for credit, $126.00, plus sales tax, from S55. CM18.
　　 16. Sold merchandise on account to Barbra Almon, $742.00, plus sales tax. S57.
　　 16. Received a check on account from Bland Company, $128.07, covering S55 for $266.76 ($247.00 plus sales tax, $19.76), less CM18 ($126.00 plus sales tax), less discount and less sales tax on discount. R29.
　　 16. Recorded cash and credit card sales, $2,246.00, plus sales tax. T16.
　　　　 Posting. Post the items that are to be posted individually.
　　 19. Cash was received on account from James Hart, $167.40, covering S50; no discount. R30.
　　 20. Merchandise was purchased on account from Roland and Barnes, $216.00. P78.
　　 21. Sold merchandise on credit to Linda Ponder, $623.00, plus sales tax. S58.
　　 23. Wrote a check for miscellaneous expense, $205.00. C90.
　　 23. Received on account from Jefferson Co., $789.57, covering S56 for $805.68 ($746.00 plus sales tax, $59.68), less discount and less sales tax on discount. R31.
　　 23. Cash and credit card sales, $2,152.00, plus sales tax. T23.
　　　　 Posting. Post the items that are to be posted individually.
　　 26. Sold merchandise on account to Bland Company, $915.00, plus sales tax. S59.
　　 26. Merchandise was purchased on account from Gibson Electric Co., $1,975.00. P79.
　　 29. Paid cash on account to Roland and Barnes, covering P78 for $216.00, less 1% discount. C91.
　　 29. Purchased merchandise on account from Webb Co., $985.00. P80.
　　 30. Recorded cash and credit card sales, $1,847.00, plus sales tax. T30.

Apr. 30. Issued a check to replenish the petty cash fund, $130.25: supplies, $45.15; advertising, $60.00; miscellaneous, $22.50; cash short, $2.60. C92.

Posting. Post the items that are to be posted individually.

2. Prove and rule the sales journal. Post the totals of the special columns.
3. Total and rule the purchases journal. Post the total.
4. Prove the equality of debits and credits for the cash receipts and cash payments journals.
5. Prove cash. The cash balance on hand on April 1 was $7,690.00. The balance on the next unused check stub on April 30 is $12,797.61.
6. Rule the cash receipts journal. Post the totals of the special columns.
7. Rule the cash payments journal. Post the totals of the special columns.
8. Prepare a schedule of accounts receivable and a schedule of accounts payable similar to the ones described in Chapter 13. Compare each schedule total with the balance of the controlling account in the general ledger. The total and balance should be the same.

Recording Sales and Cash Receipts for a Corporation

Celluphone's manual journalizing and posting procedures for sales and cash receipts are described in Chapter 20. Integrating Automated Accounting Topic 8 describes procedures for using automated accounting software to journalize and post Celluphone's transactions. The Automated Accounting Problems contain instructions for using automated accounting software to solve Mastery Problem 20-M and Challenge Problem 20-C, Chapter 20.

AUTOMATED ACCOUNTING PROCEDURES FOR CELLUPHONE

Celluphone uses three input forms to batch sales and cash receipts transaction data for automated accounting.
1. Sales journal input form for sales on account.
2. Cash receipts journal input form for all cash receipts.
3. General journal input form for all other transactions.

RECORDING SALES ON ACCOUNT

Celluphone batches sales on account transactions and records them on a sales journal input form.

> *March 1, 19--. Sold merchandise on account to DTex Imports, $1,600.00, plus sales tax, $128.00; total, $1,728.00. Sales Invoice No. 148.*

The journal entry to record this transaction is on lines 1 and 2 of the sales journal input form shown in Illustration T8-1.

The run date, *03/31/--*, is written in the space provided at the top of the form.

On line 1, the date of the transaction, *03/01*, is entered in the Date column. The customer number, *120*, is recorded in the Customer No. column. The source document number, *S148*, is written in the Invoice No. column. The general ledger account number for Sales, *4105*, is entered in the Account No. column. The Debit column is left blank. The automated accounting software automatically makes the debit to Accounts Receivable. The sale on account amount, *$1,600.00*, is recorded in the Credit column.

On line 2 for a sales on account transaction, the Date, Customer No., and Invoice Amount columns are left blank. The general ledger account number for Sales Tax Payable, *2135*, is written in the Account No. column. The sales tax amount, *$128.80*, is entered in the Credit column.

ILLUSTRATION T8-1   Sales journal input form with a sale on account transaction entered

	DATE MM/DD	CUSTOMER NO.	INVOICE NO.	INVOICE AMOUNT	ACCOUNT NO.	DEBIT	CREDIT	
RUN DATE 03/31/-- MM DD YY			SALES JOURNAL Input Form					
1	03/01	120	S148	1728 00	4105		1600 00	1
2	/				2135		128 00	2
3	/02	150	S149	11546 80	4105		10691 48	3
4	/				2135		855 32	4
5	/03	140	S150	39463 20	4105		36540 00	5
6	/				2135		2923 20	6
7	/05	110	S160	10368 00	4105		9600 00	7
8	/				2135		768 00	8
9	/22	140	S161	18360 00	4105		17000 00	9
10	/				2135		1360 00	10
11	/25	150	S162	4453 50	4105		4123 61	11
12	/				2135		329 89	12
13	/27	120	S163	1484 90	4105		1374 91	13
14	/				2135		109 99	14
15	/31	130	S221	1404 00	4105		1300 00	15
16	/				2135		104 00	16
25	/							25

NOTE: A debit to Accounts Receivable is made automatically by the software.

RECORDING CASH RECEIPTS

Celluphone batches cash receipts and records them on a cash receipts journal input form. Two types of cash receipts are recorded. (1) Direct receipts. (2) Receipts on account. A direct receipt transaction does not affect Accounts Receivable, whereas a receipt on account transaction does affect Accounts Receivable.

Cash and Credit Card Sales

A cash or credit card sales transaction is a direct receipt not affecting Accounts Receivable.

> *March 1, 19--. Recorded cash and credit card sales, $2,870.00, plus sales tax, $229.60; total, $3,099.60. Cash Register Tape No. 1.*

The journal entry to record this transaction is on lines 1 and 2 of Illustration T8-2.

The run date, *03/31/--*, is written in the space provided at the top of the form.

On line 1, the date of the transaction, *03/01*, is written in the Date column. The source document number, *T1*, is entered in the

FYI

Each month's transactions begin on new input forms.

ILLUSTRATION T8-2

Cash receipts journal input form with transactions entered

RUN DATE _03/31/--_
MM DD YY

CASH RECEIPTS JOURNAL
Input Form

	DATE MM/DD	CUSTOMER NO.	REFERENCE	ACCOUNTS REC. CREDIT	ACCOUNT NO.	DEBIT	CREDIT	
1	03/01		T1		4105		2870 00	1
2	/				2135		229 60	2
3	/02	150	R227	297 00				3
4	/03	130	R228	14525 35	4110	134 49		4
5					2135	10 76		5
6	/04	120	R229	486 00				6
7	/05	150	R230	7462 45				7
8	/06	110	R231	10411 20	4110	104 11		8
9	/				2135	8 33		9
10	/11	120	R232	1728 00	4110	16 00		10
11	/				2135	1 28		11
12	/12	150	R233	11546 80				12
13	/13	140	R234	39463 20	4110	365 40		13
14	/				2135	29 23		14
15	/15		T15		4105		63540 00	15
16	/				2135		5083 20	16
17	/31		T31		4105		2840 00	17
18	/				2135		227 20	18
25	/							25

NOTE: A debit to Cash is made automatically by the software.

Reference column. The general ledger account number for Sales, *4105*, is recorded in the Account No. column. The automated accounting software automatically makes the debit to Cash. Therefore, the Debit column is left blank. The amount of the sale, *$2,870.00*, is written in the Credit column.

On line 2, the general ledger account number for Sales Tax Payable, *2135*, is entered in the Account No. column. The sales tax payable amount, *$229.60*, is recorded in the Credit column.

Cash Receipt on Account

March 11, 19--. Received cash on account from DTex Imports, $1,710.72, covering Sales Invoice No. 148 for $1,728.00 ($1,600.00 plus sales tax, $128.00), less 1% discount, $16.00, and less sales tax, $1.28. Receipt No. 232.

The journal entry to record this transaction is on lines 10 and 11 of the cash receipts journal input form shown in Illustration T8-2.

On line 10, the date of the transaction, *11*, is entered in the Date column. The customer number, *120*, is recorded in the Customer No. column. The source document number, *R232*, is written in the Reference column. The amount of the cash receipt on account, *$1,728.00*, is entered in the Accounts Rec. Credit column. The account number for Sales Discount, *4110*, is recorded in the Account No. column. The sales discount amount, *$16.00*, is written in the Debit column. The software automatically makes the debit to *Cash*.

On line 11, the account number for Sales Tax Payable, *2135*, is entered in the Account No. column. The sales tax payable amount, *$1.28*, is recorded in the Debit column.

FYI

The run date is usually the date of the last transaction or the last day of a fiscal period.

RECORDING OTHER TRANSACTIONS

Celluphone uses a general journal input form to journalize transactions other than sales and cash receipts.

Sales Returns and Allowances

March 11, 19--. Granted credit to Alamo Company for merchandise returned, $180.00, plus sales tax, $14.40 from S160; total, $194.40. Credit Memorandum No. 41.

The run date, *03/31/--*, is written in the space provided at the top of the form.

The journal entry to record this transaction is on lines 1 through 3 of the general journal input form shown in Illustration T8-3.

Correcting Entries Affecting Customer Accounts

March 12, 19--. Discovered that a sale on account to Ridgecrest Co. on February 26 was incorrectly charged to the account of Ridgepoint Co., $297.00. Memorandum No. 40.

	DATE MM/DD	REFERENCE	ACCOUNT NO.	CUSTOMER/ VENDOR NO.	DEBIT	CREDIT	
1	03,11	CM41	4115		180 00		1
2	/		2135		14 40		2
3	/		1125	110		194 40	3
4	,12	M40	1125	140	297 00		4
5	/		1125	150		297 00	5
6	/						6
25	/						25
				PAGE TOTALS	491 40	491 40	
				FINAL TOTALS	491 40	491 40	

RUN DATE 03,31,-- MM DD YY

GENERAL JOURNAL
Input Form

The journal entry to record this transaction is on lines 4 and 5 of Illustration T8-3.

PROCESSING SALES, CASH RECEIPTS, AND OTHER TRANSACTIONS

FYI

When the cents are zero (.00), key only the dollar amount. For example, if the amount is 15.00, key 15. The software automatically assigns the .00.

After all data from the input forms have been keyed and posted, three reports are displayed and printed. (1) A sales journal report as shown in Illustration T8-4. (2) A cash receipts journal report as shown in Illustration T8-5. (3) A general journal report as shown in Illustration T8-6. Each report is checked for accuracy by comparing the report with the appropriate journal input form.

After all journal reports have been verified and printed, the accounts receivable account from the general ledger and the schedule of accounts receivable is displayed and printed as shown in Illustrations T8-7 and T8-8. The accounts receivable balance in the general ledger is compared to the total of the schedule of accounts receivable. These two amounts must be the same. The schedule and all journal reports are filed for future reference.

OPTIONAL PROBLEM DB-8A

AUTOMATED

Celluphone's general ledger data base is on the accounting textbook template. If you wish to process Celluphone's sales, cash receipts, and other transactions using automated accounting software, load the *Automated Accounting 6.0* or higher software. Select Data Base 8A (DB-8A) from the template disk. Read the Problem Instructions Screen. Use the completed sales, cash receipts, and general journal input forms, Illustrations T8-1, T8-2, and T8-3, and follow the procedures described to process Celluphone's sales, cash receipts, and other transactions.

```
                          Celluphone, Inc.
                           Sales Journal
                             03/31/--
------------------------------------------------------------------------------
Date   Refer.   V/C Acct.   Title                          Debit        Credit
------------------------------------------------------------------------------
03/01  S148    120  1125    AR/DTex Imports             1728.00
03/01  S148         4105    Sales                                      1600.00
03/01  S148         2135    Sales Tax Payable                           128.00

03/02  S149    150  1125    AR/Ridgepoint Co.          11546.80
03/02  S149         4105    Sales                                     10691.48
03/02  S149         2135    Sales Tax Payable                          855.32

03/03  S150    140  1125    AR/Ridgecrest Co.          39463.20
03/03  S150         4105    Sales                                     36540.00
03/03  S150         2135    Sales Tax Payable                         2923.20

03/05  S160    110  1125    AR/Alamo Company           10368.00
03/05  S160         4105    Sales                                      9600.00
03/05  S160         2135    Sales Tax Payable                          768.00

03/22  S161    140  1125    AR/Ridgecrest Co.          18360.00
03/22  S161         4105    Sales                                     17000.00
03/22  S161         2135    Sales Tax Payable                         1360.00

03/25  S162    150  1125    AR/Ridgepoint Co.           4453.50
03/25  S162         4105    Sales                                      4123.61
03/25  S162         2135    Sales Tax Payable                          329.89

03/27  S163    120  1125    AR/DTex Imports             1484.90
03/27  S163         4105    Sales                                      1374.91
03/27  S163         2135    Sales Tax Payable                          109.99

03/31  S221    130  1125    AR/Kirby's                  1404.00
03/31  S221         4105    Sales                                      1300.00
03/31  S221         2135    Sales Tax Payable                          104.00
                                                       ----------   ----------
                            Totals                     88808.40      88808.40
                                                       ==========   ==========
```

AUTOMATED ACCOUNTING PROBLEMS

AUTOMATING MASTERY PROBLEM 20-M Recording sales and cash receipts transactions

INSTRUCTIONS:

1. Journalize transactions from Mastery Problem 20-M, Chapter 20 on the appropriate input forms. Use February 28 of the current year as the run date.
2. Load the *Automated Accounting 6.0* or higher software. Select data base F20-M (First-Year Course Mastery Problem 20-M) from the accounting textbook template. Read the Problem Instructions screen.
3. Select File from the menu bar and choose the Save As menu command. Key the path to the drive and directory that contains your data files. Save the data base with a file name of XXX20M (where XXX are your initials).
4. Key the data from each of the completed input forms.
5. Display/print the general journal report, sales journal report, and the cash receipts journal report.

```
                          Celluphone, Inc.
                        Cash Receipts Journal
                            03/31/--
--------------------------------------------------------------------------
Date    Refer.   V/C  Acct.  Title                      Debit      Credit
--------------------------------------------------------------------------
03/01   T1            1105   Cash                      3099.60
03/01   T1            4105   Sales                                 2870.00
03/01   T1            2135   Sales Tax Payable                      229.60

03/02   R227          1105   Cash                       297.00
03/02   R227     150  1125   AR/Ridgepoint Co.                      297.00

03/03   R228          1105   Cash                     14380.10
03/03   R228          4110   Sales Discount             134.49
03/03   R228          2135   Sales Tax Payable           10.76
03/03   R228     130  1125   AR/Kirby's                           14525.35

03/04   R229          1105   Cash                       486.00
03/04   R229     120  1125   AR/DTex Imports                        486.00

03/05   R230          1105   Cash                      7462.45
03/05   R230     150  1125   AR/Ridgepoint Co.                     7462.45

03/06   R231          1105   Cash                     10298.76
03/06   R231          4110   Sales Discount             104.11
03/06   R231          2135   Sales Tax Payable            8.33
03/06   R231     110  1125   AR/Alamo Company                     10411.20

03/11   R232          1105   Cash                      1710.72
03/11   R232          4110   Sales Discount              16.00
03/11   R232          2135   Sales Tax Payable            1.28
03/11   R232     120  1125   AR/DTex Imports                       1728.00

03/12   R233          1105   Cash                     11546.80
03/12   R233     150  1125   AR/Ridgepoint Co.                    11546.80

03/13   R234          1105   Cash                     39068.57
03/13   R234          4110   Sales Discount             365.40
03/13   R234          2135   Sales Tax Payable           29.23
03/13   R234     140  1125   AR/Ridgecrest Co.                    39463.20

03/15   T15           1105   Cash                     68623.20
03/15   T15           4105   Sales                                63540.00
03/15   T15           2135   Sales Tax Payable                     5083.20

03/31   T31           1105   Cash                      3067.20
03/31   T31           4105   Sales                                 2840.00
03/31   T31           2135   Sales Tax Payable                      227.20

                                                      ----------  ----------
                             Totals                   160710.00   160710.00
                                                      ==========  ==========
```

6. Display/print the accounts receivable account from the general ledger.
7. Display/print the schedule of accounts receivable.

AUTOMATING CHALLENGE PROBLEM 20-C Recording sales, purchases, cash receipts, and cash payment transactions

INSTRUCTIONS:

1. Journalize transactions from Challenge Problem 20-C, Chapter 20 on the appropriate forms. Use April 30 of the current year as the run date.

```
                        Celluphone, Inc.
                        General Journal
                           03/31/--
-------------------------------------------------------------------
Date    Refer.   V/C Acct.  Title                    Debit     Credit
-------------------------------------------------------------------
03/11 CM41         4115    Sales Returns and Allow.   180.00
03/11 CM41         2135    Sales Tax Payable           14.40
03/11 CM41     110 1125    AR/Alamo Company                      194.40

03/12 M40      140 1125    AR/Ridgecrest Co.          297.00
03/12 M40      150 1125    AR/Ridgepoint Co.                     297.00

                                                    ----------  ----------
                           Totals                     491.40      491.40
                                                    ==========  ==========
```

2. Load the *Automated Accounting 6.0* or higher software. Select data base F20-C (First-Year Course Challenge Problem 20-C) from the accounting textbook template. Read the Problem Instructions screen.

3. Select File from the menu bar and choose the Save As menu command. Key the path to the drive and directory that contains your data files. Save the data base with a file name of XXX20C (where XXX are your initials).

4. Key the data from each of the completed input forms.

```
                        Celluphone, Inc.
                        General Ledger
                           03/31/--
-----------------------------------------------------------------------------
Account            Journal   Date   Refer.      Debit      Credit     Balance
-----------------------------------------------------------------------------
1125-Accounts Receivable
                   Op. Bal.  03/01  Balances   10411.20               10411.20
                   Op. Bal.  03/01  Balances     486.00               10897.20
                   Op. Bal.  03/01  Balances   14525.35               25422.55
                   Op. Bal.  03/01  Balances    7759.45               33182.00
                   Sales     03/01  S148        1728.00               34910.00
                   Sales     03/02  S149       11546.80               46456.80
                   Cash Rcpt 03/02  R227                    297.00    46159.80
                   Sales     03/03  S150       39463.20               85623.00
                   Cash Rcpt 03/03  R228                  14525.35    71097.65
                   Cash Rcpt 03/04  R229                    486.00    70611.65
                   Sales     03/05  S160       10368.00               80979.65
                   Cash Rcpt 03/05  R230                   7462.45    73517.20
                   Cash Rcpt 03/06  R231                  10411.20    63106.00
                   Cash Rcpt 03/11  R232                   1728.00    61378.00
                   General   03/11  CM41                    194.40    61183.60
                   Cash Rcpt 03/12  R233                  11546.80    49636.80
                   General   03/12  M40          297.00              49933.80
                   General   03/12  M40                     297.00    49636.80
                   Cash Rcpt 03/13  R234                  39463.20    10173.60
                   Sales     03/22  S161       18360.00               28533.60
                   Sales     03/25  S162        4453.50               32987.10
                   Sales     03/27  S163        1484.90               34472.00
                   Sales     03/31  S221        1404.00               35876.00
```

```
                        Celluphone, Inc.
                  Schedule of Accounts Receivable
                            03/31/--
--------------------------------------------------------------
Account
Number        Name                                    Balance
--------------------------------------------------------------
110           Alamo Company                          10173.60
120           DTex Imports                            1484.90
130           Kirby's                                 1404.00
140           Ridgecrest Co.                         18657.00
150           Ridgepoint Co.                          4156.50
                                                   ----------
              Total                                  35876.00
                                                   ==========
```

5. Display/print the general journal report, cash payments journal report, sales journal report, and the cash receipts journal report.
6. Display/print the accounts payable account from the general ledger.
7. Display/print the schedule of accounts payable.
8. Display/print the accounts receivable account from the general ledger.
9. Display print the schedule of accounts receivable.

An Accounting Cycle for a Corporation: Journalizing and Posting Transactions

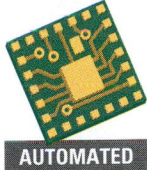

AUTOMATED

Reinforcement Activity 3 reinforces learnings from Part 4, Chapters 19 through 27, and covers a complete accounting cycle for a merchandising business organized as a corporation. Part A reinforces learnings from Chapters 19 and 20. Part B reinforces learnings from Chapters 21 through 27.

The general ledger account balances summarize transactions for the first eleven months of a fiscal year. The transactions given for December of the current year are for the last month of the fiscal year.

HARDWARE MART

Reinforcement Activity 3 includes accounting records for Hardware Mart. Hardware Mart sells home repair materials, electrical supplies, and small hand and power tools. The business, which is located in a shopping center, is open Monday through Saturday. Space for the business is rented. However, the corporation owns the office and store equipment.

CHART OF ACCOUNTS

Hardware Mart uses the chart of accounts shown on the next page.

JOURNALS AND LEDGERS

Hardware Mart uses the following journals and ledgers. Models of journals and ledgers are shown in the textbook illustrations given in the following chart.

Journals and Ledgers	Chapter	Illustration Number
Sales journal	20	20-4
Purchases journal	19	19-4
General journal	19	19-22
Cash receipts journal	20	20-10
Cash payments journal	19	19-16
Accounts receivable ledger	20	20-9
Accounts payable ledger	19	19-14
General ledger	19	19-4

RECORDING TRANSACTIONS

The account balances for the general and subsidiary ledgers are given in the working papers accompanying this textbook.

HARDWARE MART
CHART OF ACCOUNTS

Balance Sheet Accounts

(1000) ASSETS
1100 Current Assets

1105	Cash
1110	Petty Cash
1115	Notes Receivable
1120	Interest Receivable
1125	Accounts Receivable
1130	Allowance for Uncollectible Accounts
1135	Merchandise Inventory
1140	Supplies
1145	Prepaid Insurance

1200 Plant Assets

1205	Office Equipment
1210	Accumulated Depreciation—Office Equipment
1215	Store Equipment
1220	Accumulated Depreciation—Store Equipment

(2000) LIABILITIES
2100 Current Liabilities

2105	Notes Payable
2110	Interest Payable
2115	Accounts Payable
2120	Employee Income Tax Payable
2125	Federal Income Tax Payable
2130	FICA Tax Payable
2135	Sales Tax Payable
2140	Unemployment Tax Payable—Federal
2145	Unemployment Tax Payable—State
2150	Health Insurance Premiums Payable
2155	Dividends Payable

(3000) STOCKHOLDERS' EQUITY

3105	Capital Stock
3110	Retained Earnings
3115	Dividends
3120	Income Summary

Income Statement Accounts

(4000) OPERATING REVENUE

4105	Sales
4110	Sales Discount
4115	Sales Returns and Allowances

(5000) COST OF MERCHANDISE

5105	Purchases
5110	Purchases Discount
5115	Purchases Returns and Allowances

(6000) OPERATING EXPENSES

6105	Advertising Expense
6110	Credit Card Fee Expense
6115	Depreciation Expense—Office Equipment
6120	Depreciation Expense—Store Equipment
6125	Insurance Expense
6130	Miscellaneous Expense
6135	Payroll Taxes Expense
6140	Rent Expense
6145	Salary Expense
6150	Supplies Expense
6155	Uncollectible Accounts Expense
6160	Utilities Expense

(7000) OTHER REVENUE

7105	Gain on Plant Assets
7110	Interest Income

(8000) OTHER EXPENSES

8105	Cash Short and Over
8110	Interest Expense
8115	Loss on Plant Assets

(9000) INCOME TAX EXPENSE

9105	Federal Income Tax Expense

INSTRUCTIONS:

1. Journalize the following transactions completed during December of the current year. Use page 12 of a sales journal, a purchases journal, a general journal, and a cash receipts journal. Use pages 23 and 24 of a cash payments journal. Hardware Mart offers its customers terms of 1/10, n/30. The sales tax rate is 8%. Source documents are abbreviated as follows: check, C; credit memorandum, CM; debit memorandum, DM; memorandum, M; purchase invoice, P; receipt, R; sales invoice, S; cash register tape, T.

Dec. 1. Paid cash for rent, $1,750.00. C310.
   1. Received cash on account from Gerald Bell, $3,143.45, covering S180 for $3,175.20 ($2,940.00 plus sales tax, $235.20), less 1% discount, $29.40, and less sales tax, $2.35. R169.
   1. Purchased merchandise on account from Granger Company, $11,728.00. P95.
   2. Granted credit to Linda Franz for merchandise returned, $555.00, plus sales tax, $44.40, from S170; total, $599.40. CM23.
   2. Received cash on account from Linda Franz, $2,975.40 (covering S170 less CM23), no discount. R170.
   3. Sold merchandise on account to Paul Rodriguez, $2,130.00, plus sales tax, $170.40; total, $2,300.40. S188.
   3. Paid cash on account to Beta Hardware Supplies, $4,176.37, covering P92 for $4,261.60, less 2% discount, $85.23. C311.
   3. Recorded cash and credit card sales, $7,755.80, plus sales tax, $620.46; total, $8,376.26. T3.

   Posting. Post the items that are to be posted individually. Post the journals in this order: sales journal, purchases journal, general journal, cash receipts journal, and cash payments journal.

   5. Returned merchandise to Granger Company, $1,620.00, from P90. DM25.
   6. Paid cash on account to Sunbelt Corp., $3,132.86, covering P93 for $3,196.80, less 2% discount, $63.94. C312.
   7. Received cash on account from Paul Rodriguez, $5,116.12, covering S185 for $5,167.80 ($4,785.00 plus sales tax, $382.80), less 1% discount, $47.85, and less sales tax, $3.83. R171.
   7. Purchased merchandise on account from Western Tools, $5,730.00. P96.
   8. Sold merchandise on account to Roy Heflin, $2,481.00, plus sales tax, $198.48; total, $2,679.48. S189.
   8. Paid cash on account to Western Tools, $2,637.76, covering P94 for $2,664.40, less 1% discount, $26.64. C313.
   9. Received cash on account from Roy Heflin, $4,374.00, covering S183; no discount. R172.
   10. Paid cash for liability for November health insurance premiums, $625.00. C314.
   10. Recorded cash and credit card sales, $14,542.20, plus sales tax, $1,163.38; total, $15,705.58. T10.

   Posting. Post the items that are to be posted individually.

   12. Purchased merchandise on account from Sunbelt Corp., $11,652.00. P97.
   13. Paid cash for miscellaneous expense, $227.50. C315.
   13. Paid cash for supplies, $176.10. C316.
   13. Received cash on account from Paul Rodriguez, $2,277.40, covering S188 for $2,300.40 ($2,130.00 plus sales tax, $170.40), less 1% discount, $21.30, and less sales tax, $1.70. R173.
   14. Sold merchandise on account to Patricia Nielsen, $750.00, plus sales tax, $60.00; total, $810.00. S190.
   14. Paid cash for advertising, $579.50. C317.
   15. Paid cash for semimonthly payroll, $3,247.50 (total payroll, $4,450.00, less deductions: employee income tax, $534.00; FICA tax, $356.00; health insurance premiums, $312.50). C318.
   15. Recorded employer payroll taxes expense, $405.60 (FICA tax, $356.00; federal unemployment tax, $6.40; state unemployment tax, $43.20). M31.

Dec. 15. Paid cash for liability for employee income tax, $1,075.00, and for FICA tax, $1,360.00; total, $2,435.00. C319.

15. Paid cash for quarterly estimated federal income tax, $3,500.00. C320. (Debit **Federal Income Tax Expense**; credit **Cash**.)

15. Paid cash to replenish the petty cash fund, $178.50: supplies, $26.75; advertising, $44.00; miscellaneous, $109.75; cash over, $2.00. C321.

16. Paid cash on account to Western Tools, $5,672.70, covering P96 for $5,730.00, less 1% discount, $57.30. C322.

16. Received cash on account from Patricia Nielsen, $2,381.40, covering S186; no discount. R174.

17. Received cash on account from Roy Heflin, $2,652.69, covering S189 for $2,679.48 ($2,481.00 plus sales tax, $198.48), less 1% discount, $24.81, and less sales tax, $1.98. R175.

17. Purchased merchandise for cash, $470.00. C323.

17. Recorded cash and credit card sales, $18,096.00, plus sales tax, $1,447.68; total, $19,543.68. T17.

   Posting. Post the items that are to be posted individually.

19. Paid cash for miscellaneous expense, $124.60. C324.

19. Sold merchandise on account to Linda Franz, $2,675.00, plus sales tax, $214.00; total, $2,889.00. S191.

20. Paid cash on account to Granger Company, $2,464.70, covering P90 for $4,084.70, less DM25, $1,620.00; no discount. C325.

21. Paid cash on account to Decorator Systems, $3,552.50, covering P91; no discount. C326.

2. Prove and rule page 23 of the cash payments journal.

3. Forward the totals from page 23 to page 24 of the cash payments journal.

4. Continue recording the following transactions.

Dec. 21. Paid cash for miscellaneous expense, $288.00. C327.

22. Purchased merchandise on account from Beta Hardware Supplies, $7,165.00. P98.

22. Paid cash on account to Sunbelt Corp., $11,418.96, covering P97 for $11,652.00, less 2% discount, $233.04. C328.

23. Purchased merchandise for cash, $617.50. C329.

24. Sold merchandise on account to Roy Heflin, $650.00, plus sales tax, $52.00; total, $702.00. S192.

24. Recorded cash and credit card sales, $14,003.60, plus sales tax, $1,120.29; total, $15,123.89. T24.

   Posting. Post the items that are to be posted individually.

26. Bought supplies on account from HiValue Electrical Co., $339.00. M32.

27. Sold merchandise on account to Gerald Bell, $1,854.00, plus sales tax, $148.32; total, $2,002.32. S193.

27. Paid cash for advertising, $441.30. C330.

28. Purchased merchandise on account from Western Tools, $11,474.00. P99.

29. Received cash on account from Linda Franz, $2,860.11, covering S191 for $2,889.00 ($2,675.00 plus sales tax, $214.00), less 1% discount, $26.75, and less sales tax, $2.14. R176.

29. Paid cash on account to Granger Company, $11,728.00, covering P95; no discount. C331.

30. Sold merchandise on account to Paul Rodriguez, $875.00, plus sales tax, $70.00; total, $945.00. S194.

30. Paid cash for liability for sales tax, $4,932.60. C332. (Debit **Sales Tax Payable**; credit **Cash**.)

31. Paid cash for semimonthly payroll, $3,170.50 (total payroll, $4,300.00, less deductions: employee income tax, $473.00; FICA tax, $344.00; health insurance premiums, $312.50). C333.

31. Recorded employer payroll taxes expense, $368.80 (FICA tax, $344.00; federal unemployment tax, $3.20; state unemployment tax, $21.60). M33.

Dec. 31. Recorded credit card fee expense for December, $776.60. M34. (Debit **Credit Card Fee Expense**; credit **Cash**.)

31. Paid cash to replenish the petty cash fund, $171.20: supplies, $21.80; advertising, $52.00; miscellaneous, $96.40; cash short, $1.00. C334.

31. Recorded cash and credit card sales, $4,524.00, plus sales tax, $361.92; total, $4,885.92. T31.

Posting. Post the items that are to be posted individually.

5. Prove and rule the sales journal. Post the totals of the special columns.
6. Total and rule the purchases journal. Post the total.
7. Prove the equality of debits and credits for the cash receipts and cash payments journals.
8. Prove cash. The balance on the next unused check stub on December 31 is $54,777.45.
9. Rule the cash receipts journal. Post the totals of the special columns.
10. Rule the cash payments journal. Post the totals of the special columns.
11. Prepare a schedule of accounts receivable and a schedule of accounts payable. Compare each schedule total with the balance of the controlling account in the general ledger. The total and balance should be the same.

The general ledger used in Reinforcement Activity 3, Part A, is needed to complete Reinforcement Activity 3, Part B.

21

Accounting for Uncollectible Accounts Receivable

ENABLING PERFORMANCE TASKS

After studying Chapter 21, you will be able to:

a Define accounting terms related to uncollectible accounts.

b Identify accounting concepts and practices related to uncollectible accounts.

c Calculate estimated uncollectible accounts expense.

d Journalize and post entries related to uncollectible accounts.

TERMS PREVIEW

uncollectible accounts • allowance method of recording losses from uncollectible accounts • book value of accounts receivable • writing off an account

A business generally sells on account to encourage sales. If sales on account are offered, customers may buy merchandise today even though they will not have the cash needed until later. Also, when sales on account are offered, sales can be made over the telephone or by mail more easily without requiring immediate cash payment.

Although many businesses sell on account, they do expect full payment within the terms of sale. Most businesses thoroughly investigate customers before selling to them on credit. Even with a thorough credit investigation, however, some accounts receivable will be uncollectible. Accounts receivable that cannot be collected are called **uncollectible accounts**. Uncollectible accounts are also referred to as bad debts.

If a business fails to collect from a customer, the business loses part of the asset *Accounts Receivable*. The amount of the accounts receivable not collected is recorded as an expense. Celluphone records the expense caused by uncollectible accounts in an account titled *Uncollectible Accounts Expense*. Uncollectible Accounts Expense is also referred to as bad debts expense. An uncollectible amount does not decrease revenue. Instead, the loss is considered a regular expense of doing business. Revenue was earned when the sale was made. *(CONCEPT: Realization of Revenue)* Failing to collect an account does not cancel the sale. Therefore the loss is treated as an expense.

ESTIMATING AND RECORDING UNCOLLECTIBLE ACCOUNTS EXPENSE

Risk of loss occurs when a business sells on account. This potential loss is present even though several months may pass before the actual loss becomes known. Accurate financial reporting requires that expenses be recorded in the fiscal period in which the expenses contribute to earning revenue. *(CONCEPT: Matching Expenses with Revenue)* The balance of Accounts Receivable, a controlling account, must equal the sum of the customer accounts in the subsidiary ledger. A business does not know at the time sales are made which customer accounts will become uncollectible. If a business knew exactly which accounts would become uncollectible in the future, it could credit Accounts Receivable and each customer account for the uncollectible amounts. Uncollectible Accounts Expense could then be debited for the same amount. However, businesses do not know which customers will not pay their accounts in the future. Therefore, specific customer accounts cannot be credited for uncollectible amounts. The accounts receivable general ledger account also cannot be credited for these amounts. However, at the end of each fiscal period, a business can calculate and record an *estimated* amount of uncollectible accounts expense.

Estimating and recording uncollectible accounts expense at the end of a fiscal period accomplishes two objectives. (1) An up-to-date value of uncollectible accounts prevents an overstatement of the

Uncollectible Accounts Expense	
Debit side Normal balance Increase	Credit side Decrease

Accounts Receivable	
Debit side Normal balance Increase	Credit side Decrease

Allowance for Uncollectible Accounts	
Debit side Decrease	Credit side Normal balance Increase

FYI

Some companies use a predetermined number of past-due days to determine when an account is uncollectible. For example, all accounts more than 90 days overdue may be considered uncollectible.

FYI

Corporations that have important operations in more than one country are known as multinational corporations. Sometimes they are referred to simply as multinationals.

value of accounts receivable on the balance sheet. (2) Recording the estimated uncollectible accounts expense prevents an understatement of expenses on the income statement.

To record estimated uncollectible accounts, an adjusting entry is made affecting two accounts: Uncollectible Accounts Expense and Allowance for Uncollectible Accounts. The estimated value of uncollectible accounts is debited to Uncollectible Accounts Expense. An expense account has a normal debit balance. Therefore, the uncollectible accounts expense account is increased by a debit and decreased by a credit.

The estimated value of uncollectible accounts is also credited to an account titled Allowance for Uncollectible Accounts. An account that reduces a related account is known as a contra account. Allowance for Uncollectible Accounts is a contra account to its related asset account, Accounts Receivable. A contra asset account has a normal credit balance because it reduces the balance of an asset account. Therefore, Allowance for Uncollectible Accounts is increased by a credit and decreased by a debit.

Allowance for Bad Debts and Allowance for Doubtful Accounts are account titles sometimes used instead of Allowance for Uncollectible Accounts.

Crediting the estimated value of uncollectible accounts to a contra account is called the **allowance method of recording losses from uncollectible accounts.** The difference between the balance of Accounts Receivable and its contra account, Allowance for Uncollectible Accounts, is called the **book value of accounts receivable.** The book value of accounts receivable is reported on a balance sheet as shown in Chapter 27.

A contra account is usually assigned the next number of the account number sequence after its related account in the chart of accounts. Celluphone numbers its accounts in sequences of five. Celluphone's accounts receivable account is numbered 1125. Therefore Allowance for Uncollectible Accounts is numbered 1130.

Estimating Uncollectible Accounts Expense

Many businesses use a percentage of total sales on account to estimate uncollectible accounts expense. Each sale on account represents a risk of loss from an uncollectible account. Therefore, if the estimated percentage of loss is accurate, the amount of uncollectible accounts expense will be accurate regardless of when the actual losses occur. Since a sale on account creates a risk of loss, estimating the percentage of uncollectible accounts expense for the same period matches sales revenue with the related uncollectible accounts expense. *(CONCEPT: Matching Expenses with Revenue)*

Celluphone estimates uncollectible accounts expense by calculating a percentage of total sales on account. A review of Celluphone's previous experience in collecting sales on account shows that actual uncollectible accounts expense has been about 1% of total sales on account. The company's total sales on account for the year is $922,700.00. Thus, Celluphone's uncollectible accounts expense is calculated as shown on the next page.

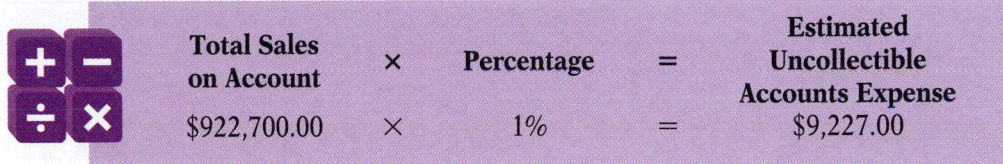

Total Sales on Account	×	Percentage	=	Estimated Uncollectible Accounts Expense
$922,700.00	×	1%	=	$9,227.00

Celluphone estimates that of the $922,700.00 sales on account during the year, $9,227.00 will eventually be uncollectible.

Analyzing an Adjustment for Uncollectible Accounts Expense

An adjustment is made to record estimated uncollectible accounts expense for a fiscal year. The effect of Celluphone's uncollectible accounts expense adjustment is shown in the T accounts.

Uncollectible Accounts Expense is debited for $9,227.00 to show the increase in the balance of this expense account. The balance of this account, $9,227.00, is the uncollectible accounts expense for the fiscal period.

Allowance for Uncollectible Accounts is credited for $9,227.00 to show the increase in the balance of this contra asset account. The previous balance, $265.00, plus the fiscal year increase, $9,227.00, equals the December 31 balance, $9,492.00. After the adjustment, Celluphone estimates that $9,492.00 of accounts receivable will be uncollectible.

Uncollectible Accounts Expense	
Dec. 31 Adj. 9,227.00	

Allowance for Uncollectible Accounts	
	Bal. 265.00
	Dec. 31 Adj. 9,227.00
	(New Bal. 9,492.00)

Entering an Adjustment for Uncollectible Accounts Expense on a Work Sheet

At the end of a fiscal period, an adjustment for uncollectible accounts expense is planned on a work sheet. Celluphone's adjustment for uncollectible accounts expense is shown in the Adjustments columns of the partial work sheet in Illustration 21-1.

ILLUSTRATION 21-1   Uncollectible accounts expense adjustment on a work sheet

	ACCOUNT TITLE	TRIAL BALANCE		ADJUSTMENTS	
		DEBIT	CREDIT	DEBIT	CREDIT
6	*Allowance for Uncollectible Accounts*		265 00		(b) 9227 00
45	*Uncollectible Accounts Expense*			(b) 9227 00	

On line 45 of the work sheet, Uncollectible Accounts Expense is debited for $9,227.00 in the Adjustments Debit column. On line 6 Allowance for Uncollectible Accounts is credited for $9,227.00 in the Adjustments Credit column.

FYI

Uncollectible accounts are also known as "bad debts" or "doubtful accounts."

The percentage of total sales on account method of estimating uncollectible accounts expense assumes that a portion of every sale on account dollar will become uncollectible. An Allowance for Uncollectible Accounts balance in the Trial Balance Credit column means that previous fiscal period estimates have not yet been identified as uncollectible. When the allowance account has a previous credit balance, the amount of the adjustment is added to the previous balance. The new balance is then extended to the Balance Sheet Credit column. This new balance of the allowance account is the estimated amount of accounts receivable that will eventually become uncollectible.

Journalizing an Adjusting Entry for Uncollectible Accounts Expense

Information used to journalize an uncollectible accounts expense adjusting entry is obtained from a work sheet's Adjustments columns. The adjusting entry for uncollectible accounts expense is shown in the general journal in Illustration 21-2.

ILLUSTRATION 21-2   Adjusting entry for uncollectible accounts expense

GENERAL JOURNAL   PAGE 15

	DATE	ACCOUNT TITLE	DOC. NO.	POST. REF.	DEBIT	CREDIT	
1		*Adjusting Entries*					1
4	31	*Uncollectible Accounts Expense*			9 2 2 7 00		4
5		*Allow. for Uncollectible Accts.*				9 2 2 7 00	5

Posting an Adjusting Entry for Uncollectible Accounts Expense

After the adjusting entry is posted, Accounts Receivable, Allowance for Uncollectible Accounts, and Uncollectible Accounts Expense appear as shown in Illustration 21-3.

ILLUSTRATION 21-3 General ledger accounts after adjusting entry for uncollectible accounts expense is posted

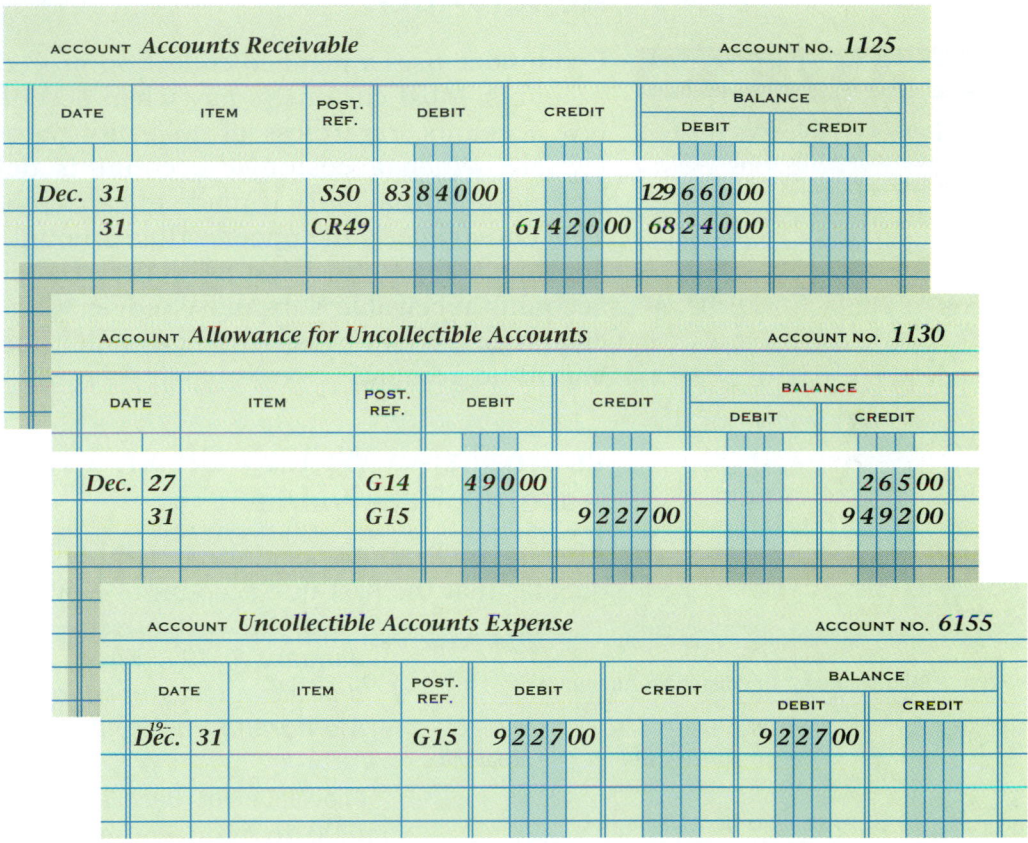

ACCOUNT **Accounts Receivable** ACCOUNT NO. *1125*

DATE	ITEM	POST. REF.	DEBIT	CREDIT	BALANCE DEBIT	BALANCE CREDIT
Dec. 31		S50	83 84 0 00		129 66 0 00	
31		CR49		61 42 0 00	68 24 0 00	

ACCOUNT **Allowance for Uncollectible Accounts** ACCOUNT NO. *1130*

DATE	ITEM	POST. REF.	DEBIT	CREDIT	BALANCE DEBIT	BALANCE CREDIT
Dec. 27		G14	49 0 00			2 65 00
31		G15		9 22 7 00		9 49 2 00

ACCOUNT **Uncollectible Accounts Expense** ACCOUNT NO. *6155*

DATE	ITEM	POST. REF.	DEBIT	CREDIT	BALANCE DEBIT	BALANCE CREDIT
Dec. 31		G15	9 22 7 00		9 22 7 00	

Accounts Receivable has a debit balance of $68,240.00, the total amount due from customers on December 31. Allowance for Uncollectible Accounts has a credit balance of $9,492.00 on December 31. The balance of this contra account is to be subtracted from the balance of its related account, Accounts Receivable, on the balance sheet. The debit balance of Uncollectible Accounts Expense is $9,227.00. This amount is the estimated uncollectible accounts expense for the current fiscal year ended December 31.

The December 27 Allowance for Uncollectible Accounts entry, $490.00, is the amount of an account that was determined to be uncollectible. Canceling uncollectible accounts is described in the next section of this chapter.

The book value of accounts receivable on December 31 is calculated as shown on the next page.

	Accounts Receivable	−	Balance of Allowance for Uncollectible Accounts	=	Book Value of Accounts Receivable
	$68,240.00	−	$9,492.00	=	$58,748.00

CANCELING UNCOLLECTIBLE ACCOUNTS RECEIVABLE

Celluphone uses a planned collection procedure to collect customer accounts. Most customers pay when accounts are due. However, a few accounts, regardless of collection efforts, prove to be uncollectible. When a customer account is determined to be uncollectible, a journal entry is made to cancel the uncollectible account. This entry cancels the uncollectible amount from the general ledger account Accounts Receivable as well as the customer account in the accounts receivable subsidiary ledger. Canceling the balance of a customer account because the customer does not pay is called **writing off an account.**

Journalizing Writing Off an Uncollectible Account Receivable

After several months of unsuccessful collection efforts, Celluphone decides that the past-due account of North Star Co. is uncollectible.

GENERAL LEDGER

Allowance for Uncollectible Accounts

Jan. 3	556.00	Bal. *(New Bal.*	9,492.00 *8,936.00)*

Accounts Receivable

Bal. *(New Bal.*	68,240.00 *67,684.00)*	Jan. 3	556.00

ACCOUNTS RECEIVABLE LEDGER

North Star Co.

Bal.	556.00	Jan. 3	556.00

January 3, 19--. Wrote off North Star Co.'s past-due account as uncollectible, $556.00. Memorandum No. 2.

Allowance for Uncollectible Accounts is debited for $556.00 to reduce the balance of this contra asset account. This specific amount, $556.00, is no longer an estimate because the account of North Star Co. has been determined to be uncollectible. Therefore, the amount of the uncollectible account is deducted from the allowance account. The new balance of the allowance account is $8,936.00 ($9,492.00 less $556.00).

Accounts Receivable is credited for $556.00 to reduce the balance due from customers. The new balance of the accounts receivable account is $67,684.00 ($68,240.00 less $556.00).

North Star's account in the accounts receivable ledger is also credited for $556.00. This entry cancels the debit balance of the account. North Star's account is written off.

The book value of accounts receivable is the same both before and after writing off an uncollectible account. The book value of accounts receivable before writing off North Star's account is calculated as shown on the next page.

	Accounts Receivable	−	Balance of Allowance for Uncollectible Accounts	=	Book Value of Accounts Receivable
	$68,240.00	−	$9,492.00	=	$58,748.00

The book value of accounts receivable after writing off North Star's account is calculated as shown below.

	Accounts Receivable	−	Balance of Allowance for Uncollectible Accounts	=	Book Value of Accounts Receivable
	$67,684.00	−	$8,936.00	=	$58,748.00

The book value remains the same because the same amount is deducted from both the accounts receivable account and the allowance account.

The general journal entry to write off North Star's account is shown in Illustration 21-4.

ILLUSTRATION 21-4

General journal entry to write off an uncollectible account

GENERAL JOURNAL   PAGE *18*

	DATE	ACCOUNT TITLE	DOC. NO.	POST. REF.	DEBIT	CREDIT	
8	3	Allow. for Uncollectible Accts.	M2		5 5 6 00		8
9		Accts. Rec./North Star Co.				5 5 6 00	9
10							10
11							11
12							12
13							13
14							14

Allowance for Uncollectible Accounts is debited for $556.00. Accounts Receivable and North Star's account are both credited for $556.00.

Posting an Entry to Write Off an Uncollectible Account Receivable

After the journal entry to write off an uncollectible account is posted, the two general ledger accounts, Accounts Receivable and Allowance for Uncollectible Accounts, and the customer account appear as shown in Illustration 21-5 on page 576. The words *Written off* are written in the Item column of the customer account to show the full credit history for the customer.

ILLUSTRATION 21-5 General ledger and customer accounts after entry for writing off an uncollectible account is posted

ACCOUNT	Accounts Receivable						ACCOUNT NO.	1125

DATE		ITEM	POST. REF.	DEBIT	CREDIT	BALANCE	
						DEBIT	CREDIT
	31		CR49		6142000	6824000	
Jan. 19X2	3		G18		55600	6768400	

ACCOUNT	Allowance for Uncollectible Accounts						ACCOUNT NO.	1130

DATE		ITEM	POST. REF.	DEBIT	CREDIT	BALANCE	
						DEBIT	CREDIT
	31		G15		922700		949200
Jan. 19X2	3		G18	55600			893600

CUSTOMER	North Star Co.					CUSTOMER NO.	150

DATE		ITEM	POST. REF.	DEBIT	CREDIT	DEBIT BALANCE
Apr. 19X1	6		S12	55600		55600
Jan. 19X2	3	Written off	G18		55600	———

COLLECTING WRITTEN-OFF ACCOUNTS RECEIVABLE

A business writes off a specific account receivable after determining that the account probably will not be collected. Occasionally, after an account has been written off, the customer pays the delinquent account. Several accounts must be changed to recognize payment of a written-off account receivable.

Journalizing Collecting a Written-Off Account Receivable

January 7, 19--. Received cash in full payment of North Star Co.'s account, previously written off as uncollectible, $556.00. Memorandum No. 3 and Receipt No. 4.

The accounts must be changed to show that North Star did pay its account. The accounts also should be changed to show a complete credit history of North Star's dealings with Celluphone. Two journal entries are recorded for the collection of a written-off account

GENERAL LEDGER
Accounts Receivable

Bal.	68,240.00	Jan. 3	556.00
Jan. 7	556.00		

Allowance for Uncollectible Accounts

Jan. 3	556.00	Bal.	9,492.00
		Jan. 7	556.00

ACCOUNTS RECEIVABLE LEDGER
North Star Co.

Bal.	556.00	Jan. 3	556.00
Jan. 7	556.00		
(New Bal.	556.00)		

receivable. (1) A general journal entry to reopen the customer account. (2) A cash receipts journal entry to record the cash received on account.

General Journal Entry to Reopen the Customer Account. To show an accurate credit history, North Star's account is reopened.

Accounts Receivable is debited for $556.00. This debit entry replaces the amount previously written off in the general ledger account Accounts Receivable. Allowance for Uncollectible Accounts is credited for $556.00. This credit entry replaces the amount in the allowance account that was removed when North Star's account was previously written off. Also, North Star's account in the accounts receivable ledger is debited for $556.00. This entry to reopen the account is the exact reverse of the entry to write off North Star's account.

The general journal entry to reopen North Star's account in the accounts receivable ledger is shown in Illustration 21-6.

ILLUSTRATION 21-6	General journal entry to reopen customer account previously written off

	DATE	ACCOUNT TITLE	DOC. NO.	POST. REF.	DEBIT	CREDIT	
16	7	Accts. Receivable/North Star Co.	M3	✓	556 00		16
17		Allow. for Uncollectible Accts.				556 00	17
18							18
19							19
20							20
21							21
22							22

GENERAL JOURNAL — PAGE 18

GENERAL LEDGER
Cash

Jan. 7	556.00		

Accounts Receivable

Bal.	68,240.00	Jan. 3	556.00
Jan. 7	556.00	Jan. 7	556.00

ACCOUNTS RECEIVABLE LEDGER
North Star Co.

Bal.	556.00	Jan. 3	556.00
Jan. 7	556.00	Jan. 7	556.00
		(New Bal.	zero)

Cash Receipts Journal Entry to Record Cash Received for an Account Previously Written Off. After the entry to reopen North Star's account is recorded, an entry is made to record the cash received on North Star's account.

Cash is debited for $556.00. Accounts Receivable is credited for $556.00. North Star's account in the accounts receivable ledger is also credited for $556.00.

The cash receipts journal entry to record the receipt of cash on account from North Star Co. is shown in Illustration 21-7.

ILLUSTRATION 21-7

Cash receipts journal entry to record cash received for an account previously written off

	DATE	ACCOUNT TITLE	DOC. NO.	POST. REF.	GENERAL DEBIT	GENERAL CREDIT	ACCOUNTS RECEIVABLE CREDIT	SALES CREDIT	SALES TAX PAYABLE DEBIT	SALES TAX PAYABLE CREDIT	SALES DISCOUNT DEBIT	CASH DEBIT	
					1	2	3	4	5	6	7	8	
1	Jan. ¹⁹ˣ² 7	North Star Co.	R4				556 00					556 00	1
2													2

CASH RECEIPTS JOURNAL — PAGE 51

Posting an Entry for Collecting a Written-Off Account Receivable

After posting the two entries to reopen North Star's account and to record collection of the account, the accounts affected appear as shown in Illustration 21-8.

ILLUSTRATION 21-8

General ledger and customer accounts after collection of a previously written-off account

ACCOUNT Accounts Receivable ACCOUNT NO. 1125

DATE	ITEM	POST. REF.	DEBIT	CREDIT	BALANCE DEBIT	BALANCE CREDIT
31		CR49		61420 00	68240 00	
Jan. ¹⁹ˣ² 3		G18		556 00	67684 00	
7		G18	556 00		68240 00	

ACCOUNT Allowance for Uncollectible Accounts ACCOUNT NO. 1130

DATE	ITEM	POST. REF.	DEBIT	CREDIT	BALANCE DEBIT	BALANCE CREDIT
31		G15		9227 00		9492 00
Jan. ¹⁹ˣ² 3		G18	556 00			8936 00
7		G18		556 00		9492 00

CUSTOMER North Star Co. CUSTOMER NO. 150

DATE	ITEM	POST. REF.	DEBIT	CREDIT	DEBIT BALANCE
Apr. ¹⁹ˣ¹ 6		S12	556 00		556 00
Jan. ¹⁹ˣ² 3	Written off	G18		556 00	—
7	Reopen account	G18	556 00		556 00
7		CR51		556 00	—

Audit Your Understanding

1. What ledgers are affected when an account receivable is written off?

2. What notation is made in the customer account when the account is written off? Why?

3. What are the steps for recording a receipt of cash from a customer whose account was previously written off?

North Star's account balance is zero. The entries in North Star's account show a complete history of North Star's credit dealings with Celluphone. The account shows the April 6 balance, $556.00, and the balance written off on January 3. On January 7 the account is debited for the same amount, $556.00, to reopen North Star's account. The words *Reopen account* are written in the Item column to describe this entry. Also, on January 7 the account is credited for $556.00 to record payment of the account.

Entries resulting from cash received for a previously written-off account are recorded in a cash receipts journal's special amount columns. These amounts are posted to the general ledger accounts at the end of the month as part of the column totals.

SUMMARY OF ACCOUNTING FOR UNCOLLECTIBLE ACCOUNTS RECEIVABLE

Summary Illustration 21-9 on page 580 shows four entries that affect Accounts Receivable and its related expense and contra accounts when there are uncollectible accounts.

1. *Adjusting entry for uncollectible accounts expense.* The expense account, Uncollectible Accounts Expense, is debited for the amount of estimated uncollectible accounts expense for the fiscal period. The contra asset account, Allowance for Uncollectible Accounts, is credited for the estimated amount of uncollectible accounts expense.

2. *Writing off an uncollectible account receivable.* When a specific account is determined to be uncollectible, the balance of the account must be removed. The specific account in the accounts receivable ledger has a debit balance; therefore, it is credited for the uncollectible amount. In the general ledger, the controlling account, Accounts Receivable, is also credited. The contra asset account, Allowance for Uncollectible Accounts, is debited.

3. *Collecting a previously written off account receivable (first entry).* When a previously written off account is collected, it is first reinstated. Accounts Receivable is debited to restore the amount, and the customer's account in the accounts receivable ledger is also debited. The contra asset account, Allowance for Uncollectible Accounts, is credited for the same amount. This amount was debited to the account when the customer's account was written off.

4. *Collecting a previously written off account receivable (second entry).* Once the customer's account is reinstated, the cash receipt on account is recorded using the usual procedures. Cash is debited for the amount of the cash receipt and Accounts Receivable and the customer's account in the accounts receivable ledger are credited.

By using two entries to record collection of a previously written off account, the accounts receivable ledger shows a complete history of the customer's account.

SUMMARY ILLUSTRATION 21-9

Summary of entries for uncollectible accounts receivable

Transactions		Cash Debit	Cash Credit	Accts. Rec. Debit	Accts. Rec. Credit	Allow. for Uncoll. Accts. Debit	Allow. for Uncoll. Accts. Credit	Uncoll. Accts. Expense Debit	Uncoll. Accts. Expense Credit	Customer Account Debit	Customer Account Credit
Adjusting entry for uncollectible accounts expense							X	X			
Write off uncollectible account receivable					X	X					X
Collect previously written off account receivable	Entry 1			X			X			X	
	2	X			X						X

What is the meaning of each of the following?

1. **uncollectible accounts**
2. **allowance method of recording losses from uncollectible accounts**
3. **book value of accounts receivable**
4. **writing off an account**

QUESTIONS FOR INDIVIDUAL STUDY   EPT(b)

1. Why might a business sell merchandise on account?
2. Why is an uncollectible account recorded as an expense rather than a reduction in revenue?
3. When does the risk of loss from a sale on account occur?
4. Which accounting concept is being applied when uncollectible accounts expense is recorded in the same fiscal period in which the expense contributes to earning revenue?
5. When do businesses normally estimate the amount of their uncollectible accounts expense?
6. What two objectives will be accomplished by recording an estimated amount of uncollectible accounts expense?
7. Why is Allowance for Uncollectible Accounts called a contra account?
8. Why would a business use a percentage of total sales on account to estimate uncollectible accounts expense?
9. What is the procedure for estimating uncollectible accounts expense based on total sales on account?

10. What accounts are affected, and how, when an adjusting entry is made to record uncollectible accounts expense?
11. What kind of situation would cause Allowance for Uncollectible Accounts to have a balance in the work sheet's Trial Balance Credit column?
12. How is the book value of accounts receivable calculated?
13. What accounts are affected, and how, when an uncollectible account is written off?
14. Why is Allowance for Uncollectible Accounts debited when a customer account is written off?
15. Does the book value of accounts receivable differ before and after writing off an account? Explain.
16. Why is a customer account reopened when the account is paid after being previously written off?
17. What accounts are affected, and how, when a written-off account receivable is collected?
18. How does the journal entry for reopening an account previously written off differ from an entry for writing off an account?

CASES FOR CRITICAL THINKING   EPT(b)

CASE 1 CompuCraft Corporation has always assumed that an account receivable is good until the account is proven to be uncollectible. When an account proves to be uncollectible, the credit manager notifies the accounting clerk to write off the account. The accounting clerk then debits Uncollectible Accounts Expense and credits Accounts Receivable. Recently the company's new accountant, Diane Wilson, suggested that the method be changed for recording uncollectible accounts expense. Mrs. Wilson recommended that the company estimate uncollectible accounts expense based on a percentage of total sales on account. Mrs. Wilson stated that the change would provide more accurate information on the income statement and balance sheet. Do you agree with Mrs. Wilson that her recommended method would provide more accurate information? Explain.

CASE 2 Ulrick Corporation credits Accounts Receivable for the amount of estimated uncollectible accounts expense at the end of each fiscal period. Lindsey Company credits Allowance for Uncollectible Accounts for the amount of estimated uncollectible accounts expense at the end of each fiscal period. Which company is using the better method? Why?

DRILL 21-D1 Calculating estimated uncollectible accounts expense

TUTORIAL

MATHEMATICS

The accounting records of six stores show the following summary information for the fiscal period ended December 31 of the current year.

Store	Total Sales on Account	Estimated Uncollectible Accounts as Percentage of Sales on Account	Balance of Allowance for Uncollectible Accounts Before Adjustment
1	$48,700.00	0.6%	$32.00 Credit
2	73,900.00	0.5%	63.00 Credit
3	95,200.00	1.0%	24.00 Debit
4	61,400.00	0.7%	79.00 Credit
5	54,800.00	0.4%	Zero
6	89,600.00	0.8%	57.00 Debit

INSTRUCTIONS:

For each of the six stores, calculate the following:

a. Uncollectible accounts expense.

b. Balance of Allowance for Uncollectible Accounts after adjustment.

c. Book value of accounts receivable after adjustment. Use a balance of $25,000.00 for accounts receivable for each store.

DRILL 21-D2 Analyzing entries for uncollectible accounts

INSTRUCTIONS:

Use a form similar to the following. Analyze each entry. For each entry, indicate how each account is affected by writing one of the following: *DR* if debited, *CR* if credited, or *NE* if no entry is made.

Transaction	General Ledger				Accounts Receivable Ledger Customer Account
	Cash	Accounts Receivable	Allowance for Uncollectible Accounts	Uncollectible Accounts Expense	
A. Adjusting entry for uncollectible accounts expense at end of fiscal period					
B. Wrote off an uncollectible account					
C. Collected account previously written off 1) Entry 1:					
2) Entry 2:					

PROBLEM 21-1 Estimating and journalizing entries for uncollectible accounts expense

Use the following information from the records of Caraway Company for three successive years.

Year	Total Sales on Account	Balance of Allowance for Uncollectible Accounts Before Adjustment
19X1	$473,221.00	$171.00 Credit
19X2	495,074.00	279.00 Credit
19X3	516,978.00	392.80 Credit

Caraway Company estimates uncollectible accounts expense as 1.0% of its total sales on account.

INSTRUCTIONS:

1. For each year record the uncollectible accounts expense adjustment on a work sheet.
2. For each year journalize the adjusting entry on page 13 of a general journal.

PROBLEM 21-2 Recording entries to write off uncollectible accounts receivable

During June of the current year, Alphacom Corporation determined that three accounts were uncollectible.

INSTRUCTIONS:

1. Journalize the entries to write off the following accounts. Use page 6 of a general journal.

June 4. Wrote off Davidson Corporation's past-due account as uncollectible, $347.00. M13.
     15. Wrote off Jordan Equipment Co.'s past-due account as uncollectible, $521.00. M20.
     30. Wrote off Porter, Inc.'s past-due account as uncollectible, $179.00, M27.

2. Post each entry to the customer accounts in the accounts receivable ledger.

PROBLEM 21-3 Recording transactions for collection of written-off accounts receivable

Abbott Electronics received payment for accounts that had previously been written off.

INSTRUCTIONS:

1. Journalize the following transactions completed during August of the current year. Use page 8 of a general journal and page 15 of a cash receipts journal.

Aug. 6. Received cash in full payment of Hargrove Inc.'s account, previously written off as uncollectible, $715.00. M4 and R34.
     20. Received cash in full payment of Andrews Corp.'s account, previously written off as uncollectible, $384.00. M27 and R92.
     27. Received cash in full payment of Tyler Co.'s account, previously written off as uncollectible, $443.00. M38 and R121.

2. Post each entry to the customer accounts in the accounts receivable ledger.

MASTERY PROBLEM 21-M Recording entries for uncollectible accounts

The accounts receivable ledger accounts for Travis Industries are given in the working papers accompanying this textbook.

INSTRUCTIONS:

1. Journalize transactions on page 584 completed during October, November, and December of the current year. Use pages 10, 11, and 12 of a general journal and pages 11 and 12 of a cash receipts journal.

Oct. 7. Wrote off Kingston Corporation's past-due account as uncollectible, $247.60. M202.

18. Wrote off Gentry Corporation's past-due account as uncollectible, $482.50. M206.
Posting. Post each entry to the customer accounts in the accounts receivable ledger.

Nov. 8. Wrote off Burrell Company's past-due account as uncollectible, $714.15. M219.

17. Received cash in full payment of Kingston Corporation's account, previously written off as uncollectible, $247.60. M223 and R461.
Posting. Post each entry to the customer accounts in the accounts receivable ledger.

Dec. 3. Wrote off Fiber-Tech's past-due account as uncollectible, $829.35. M226.

9. Received cash in full payment of Burrell Company's account, previously written off as uncollectible, $714.15. M229 and R514.

28. Received cash in full payment of Gentry Corporation's account, previously written off as uncollectible, $482.50. M235 and R547.
Posting. Post each entry to the customer accounts in the accounts receivable ledger.

2. Journalize the December 31 adjusting entry for estimated uncollectible accounts expense for the year. Use page 13 of the general journal. Uncollectible accounts expense is estimated as 1.0% of total sales on account. Total sales on account for the year were $1,051,080.00.

CHALLENGE PROBLEM 21-C Recording entries for uncollectible accounts

Sunrise Nursery has general ledger accounts for account number 1130, Allowance for Uncollectible Accounts, and account number 6165, Uncollectible Accounts Expense. At the beginning of the current year, the credit balance of Allowance for Uncollectible Accounts was $1,573.25. Uncollectible accounts expense is estimated as 0.75% of the total sales on account each quarter.

INSTRUCTIONS:

1. Journalize entries for the following transactions and adjusting entries completed during the current year. Use page 1 of a general journal and a cash receipts journal. (Usually a new journal page is started each month and adjusting entries are also recorded on a new journal page. To conserve space in the working papers, record all of the year's entries on the same page of the appropriate journal.)

Jan. 11. Received a check in full payment of Taylor Corporation's account, previously written off as uncollectible, $317.40. M2 and R4.

Mar. 3. Gibson Company's past-due account was written off as uncollectible, $629.80. M7.

31. Record the adjusting entry for estimated uncollectible accounts expense for the end of the first quarterly fiscal period. Total sales on account for the first quarterly fiscal period were $174,920.00.
Posting. Post entries to Allowance for Uncollectible Accounts and Uncollectible Accounts Expense.

May 5. Bowman, Inc.'s account, previously written off as uncollectible, was paid in full, $62.15. M13 and R39.

18. Wrote off Kirkwood Corporation's past-due account as uncollectible, $281.75. M16.

June 14. Liberty Landscapes' past-due account was written off as uncollectible, $753.40. M19.

30. End of second quarterly fiscal period. Record the adjusting entry for estimated uncollectible accounts expense. Sales on account for the second quarterly fiscal period totaled $195,800.00.
Posting. Post entries to Allowance for Uncollectible Accounts and Uncollectible Accounts Expense.

July 6. Wrote off Plant Dimension Co.'s past-due account as uncollectible, $594.30. M20.

28. The past-due account of Parker Fertilizer Company was written off as uncollectible, $256.10. M24.

Sept. 28. Jacobsen Corporation's past-due account was written off as uncollectible, $74.80. M37.

30. Record the adjusting entry for estimated uncollectible accounts expense for the end of the third quarterly fiscal period. Total sales on account for the third quarterly fiscal period were $201,760.00.

Posting. Post entries to Allowance for Uncollectible Accounts and Uncollectible Accounts Expense.

Nov. 1. The past-due account of Superior Design was written off as uncollectible, $789.20. M38.

23. Cash was received in full payment of Parker Fertilizer Company's account, previously written off as uncollectible, $256.10. M41 and R114.

Dec. 31. End of fourth quarterly fiscal period. Record the adjusting entry for estimated uncollectible accounts expense. Total sales on account for the fourth quarterly fiscal period were $219,860.00.

Posting. Post entries to Allowance for Uncollectible Accounts and Uncollectible Accounts Expense.

2. Assume that you are the accountant for Sunrise Nursery. You have determined that all possible procedures are now being used to reduce uncollectible accounts. Examine the year's activity in the account Allowance for Uncollectible Accounts. Are the accounting procedures for uncollectible accounts adequate and accurate? Should any changes in procedure be recommended? If so, what? Explain the reason for your response.

22

Accounting for Plant Assets and Depreciation

ENABLING PERFORMANCE TASKS

After studying Chapter 22, you will be able to:

a Define accounting terms related to plant assets, depreciation, and property tax expense.

b Identify accounting concepts and practices related to accounting for plant assets, depreciation, and property tax expense.

c Calculate depreciation expense and book value of a plant asset.

d Record plant asset information in a plant asset record.

e Record entries related to accounting for plant assets, depreciation, and property tax expense.

TERMS PREVIEW

current assets • plant assets • depreciation expense • estimated salvage value • straight-line method of depreciation • plant asset record • accumulated depreciation • book value of a plant asset • gain on plant assets • loss on plant assets • declining-balance method of depreciation • real property • personal property • assessed value

FYI

To classify assets as either current assets or plant assets, first determine the way the asset is used in the business.

Most businesses use two broad categories of assets in the operations of their businesses. Cash and other assets expected to be exchanged for cash or consumed within a year are called **current assets**. Assets which will be used for a number of years in the operation of a business are called **plant assets**. Some of the more significant current assets used by Celluphone are cash, accounts receivable, merchandise inventory, supplies, and prepaid insurance. Celluphone also has plant assets that will be used for a number of years in the operation of its business. Some of Celluphone's plant assets are computers, cash registers, sales display cases, and furniture. These assets are used in the business and are not intended for sale to its customers. Celluphone's complete list of current and plant assets is in the chart of accounts, page 470.

The telephones Celluphone uses in operating the business are classified as plant assets. The telephones Celluphone buys and resells to its customers are merchandise inventory and classified as current assets. The difference in classification is determined by the way the asset is used. Assets purchased to be resold are merchandise inventory and classified as current assets. Assets bought to be used in operating the business are classified as plant assets.

Businesses may have three major types of plant assets—equipment, buildings, and land. Celluphone owns equipment, such as computers, cash registers, and sales display cases, that it uses to operate the business. However, the company rents the building and the land where the business is located. Therefore, Celluphone has accounts for equipment, which is the only type of plant asset it owns.

To provide more detailed financial information, Celluphone records its equipment in two different equipment accounts—Office Equipment and Store Equipment. *(CONCEPT: Adequate Disclosure)*

BUYING AND RECORDING PLANT ASSETS

Procedures for recording the buying of a plant asset are similar to procedures for recording the buying of current assets such as supplies. The amount paid for a plant asset is debited to a plant asset account with a title such as Office Equipment. *(CONCEPT: Historical Cost)* A plant asset account has a normal debit balance. Therefore, a plant asset account such as Office Equipment is increased by a debit and decreased by a credit.

January 2, 19X1. Paid cash for a new printer, $820.00. Check No. 4.

Celluphone has a separate plant asset account for office equipment. Therefore, Office Equipment is increased by an $820.00 debit. Cash is decreased by an $820.00 credit.

The cash payments journal entry to record this transaction is shown in Illustration 22-1 on page 588.

Office Equipment	
Debit Side	Credit Side
Normal Balance	
Increase	Decrease

Office Equipment	
820.00	

Cash	
	820.00

ILLUSTRATION 22-1

Cash payments journal entry to record the buying of a plant asset

	DATE	ACCOUNT TITLE	CK. NO.	POST. REF.	GENERAL DEBIT	GENERAL CREDIT	ACCOUNTS PAYABLE DEBIT	PURCHASES DISCOUNT CREDIT	CASH CREDIT	
					1	2	3	4	5	
4	2	Office Equipment	4		8 2 0 00				8 2 0 00	4
5										5

CASH PAYMENTS JOURNAL — PAGE 1

After the entry for buying a printer is posted, the office equipment account in the general ledger appears as shown in Illustration 22-2.

ILLUSTRATION 22-2

A plant asset account in the general ledger

ACCOUNT Office Equipment   ACCOUNT NO. 1205

DATE	ITEM	POST. REF.	DEBIT	CREDIT	BALANCE DEBIT	BALANCE CREDIT
Jan. 1 19X1	Balance	✓			12 8 3 0 00	
2		CP1	8 2 0 00		13 6 5 0 00	

The $12,830.00 balance of Office Equipment is the original cost of office equipment owned on January 1. The $13,650.00 balance of Office Equipment is the original cost of office equipment owned on January 2. The debit balance of Office Equipment always shows the original cost of all office equipment owned. *(CONCEPT: Historical Cost)*

EFFECTS OF DEPRECIATION ON PLANT ASSETS

A business buys plant assets to use in earning revenue. Celluphone bought a new printer to use for preparing invoices and other correspondence for the business. Celluphone plans to use the printer for its entire useful life. However, plant assets such as Celluphone's printer decrease in value because of use. Plant assets also decrease in value with the passage of time as they become older and newer models become available. All plant assets, with the exception of land, have a limited useful life. However, plant assets generally have a useful life of several years.

In order to match revenue with the expenses used to earn the revenue, the cost of a plant asset should be allocated to an expense over the plant asset's useful life. Therefore, a portion of a plant asset's cost is transferred to an expense account in each fiscal period that a plant asset is used to earn revenue. *(CONCEPT: Matching Expenses with Revenue)* The portion of a plant asset's cost that is transferred to an expense account in each fiscal period during a plant asset's useful life is called **depreciation expense.**

Depreciation expense differs from many other business expenses in one significant way. For many business expenses, cash is paid out in the same fiscal period in which the expense is recorded. For example, cash is generally paid for salaries during the same fiscal period in which salary expense is recorded for those salaries. However, cash is generally paid out when a plant asset is bought, but depreciation expense is recorded over several years. Celluphone paid $820.00 for a new printer in 19X1, but a portion of the new printer's cost will be recorded as depreciation expense each year during the estimated useful life of the printer.

Two factors affect the useful life of a plant asset: (1) physical depreciation and (2) functional depreciation. Physical depreciation is caused by wear from use and deterioration from aging and weathering. Functional depreciation occurs when a plant asset becomes inadequate or obsolete. An asset is inadequate when it can no longer satisfactorily perform needed service. An asset is obsolete when a newer machine can operate more efficiently or produce better service.

Land, because of its permanent nature, generally is not subject to depreciation. Buildings, after years of use, eventually become unusable to a business. However, the building may be torn down and a new building constructed on the same land. Since land can be used indefinitely, it is considered permanent and is not depreciated.

Deterioration causes physical depreciation. Obsolescence causes functional depreciation.

CALCULATING DEPRECIATION EXPENSE

Depreciation expense is recorded for each fiscal period a plant asset is used. *(CONCEPT: Accounting Period Cycle)* Several factors are considered in calculating depreciation expense.

Factors Affecting Depreciation Expense

Three factors affect the amount of depreciation expense for a plant asset.

1. The original cost of a plant asset.
2. The estimated salvage value of a plant asset.
3. The estimated useful life of a plant asset.

Original Cost. The original cost of a plant asset includes all costs paid to make the asset usable to a business. These costs include the price of the asset, delivery costs, and any necessary installation costs. The original cost of the new printer bought by Celluphone is $820.00.

Estimated Salvage Value. Generally, a business removes a plant asset from use and disposes of it when the asset is no longer usable. The amount that will be received for an asset at the time of its

Depreciation does not represent the actual decline in value of an asset. Instead, it is an allocation of the asset's cost over several fiscal periods.

disposal is not known when the asset is bought. Thus, the amount that may be received at disposal must be estimated. The amount an owner expects to receive when a plant asset is removed from use is called **estimated salvage value**. Estimated salvage value may also be referred to as residual value or scrap value.

Celluphone estimates a salvage value of $100.00 for the new printer at the end of its useful life.

Estimated Useful Life.
The total amount of depreciation expense is distributed over the estimated useful life of a plant asset. When a plant asset is bought, the exact length of useful life is impossible to predict. Therefore, the number of years of useful life must be estimated.

Celluphone estimates that the useful life of a printer is five years. An estimate of useful life should be based on prior experience with similar assets and on available guidelines. Trade associations frequently publish guidelines for specialized plant assets. For tax purposes the Internal Revenue Service also publishes depreciation guidelines for plant assets.

Calculating Depreciation Expense for a Fiscal Year

The total cost of a plant asset that should be allocated to an expense over the asset's useful life is the amount paid for the asset (original cost) less the estimated salvage value. This difference, original cost less estimated salvage value, is the estimated total depreciation expense for the asset's entire useful life.

The total amount of estimated depreciation expense for the printer bought on January 2 is calculated as shown below.

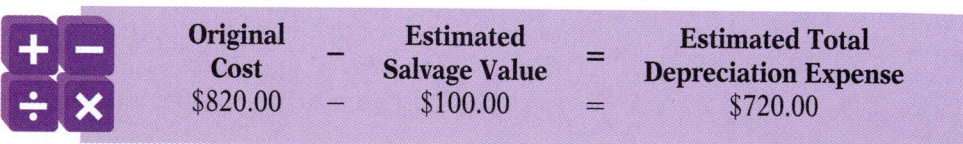

	Original Cost	−	Estimated Salvage Value	=	Estimated Total Depreciation Expense
	$820.00	−	$100.00	=	$720.00

Charging an equal amount of depreciation expense for a plant asset in each year of useful life is called the **straight-line method of depreciation**. Celluphone uses the straight-line method to calculate depreciation.

Depreciation expense for a fiscal year is calculated by dividing a plant asset's estimated total depreciation expense by the estimated useful life in years.

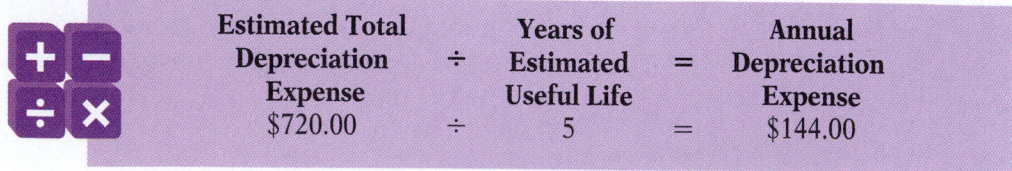

	Estimated Total Depreciation Expense	÷	Years of Estimated Useful Life	=	Annual Depreciation Expense
	$720.00	÷	5	=	$144.00

The depreciation expense for Celluphone's printer is $144.00 each year of use. Since Celluphone used the printer for all of the

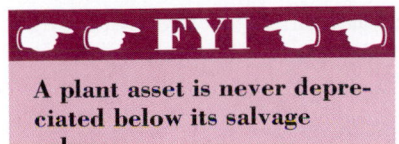
year it was bought, January 2 to December 31, one year's depreciation expense, $144.00, is charged as an expense for the year.

There are other methods of calculating depreciation expense. However, the straight-line method is widely used because it allocates a plant asset's original cost equally to each accounting period and is simple to calculate.

Calculating Depreciation Expense for Part of a Fiscal Year

Depreciation expense is calculated for a fiscal year for those plant assets used throughout the entire fiscal year. However, if a plant asset is bought during the year, the asset will be used only part of that fiscal year. Thus, depreciation expense should be calculated for only the part of the year the asset is used. To calculate depreciation expense for part of a year, the annual depreciation expense is divided by 12 to determine the depreciation expense for a month. The monthly depreciation expense is then multiplied by the number of months the plant asset is used that year.

Celluphone bought a new computer on July 1, 19X1. The original cost is $4,600.00, the estimated salvage value is $1,000.00, and the estimated useful life is four years. Celluphone calculated the computer depreciation expense for 19X1 by following four steps. The first two steps are similar to those illustrated previously for Celluphone's printer. The third and fourth steps are used to calculate depreciation expense for part of a year.

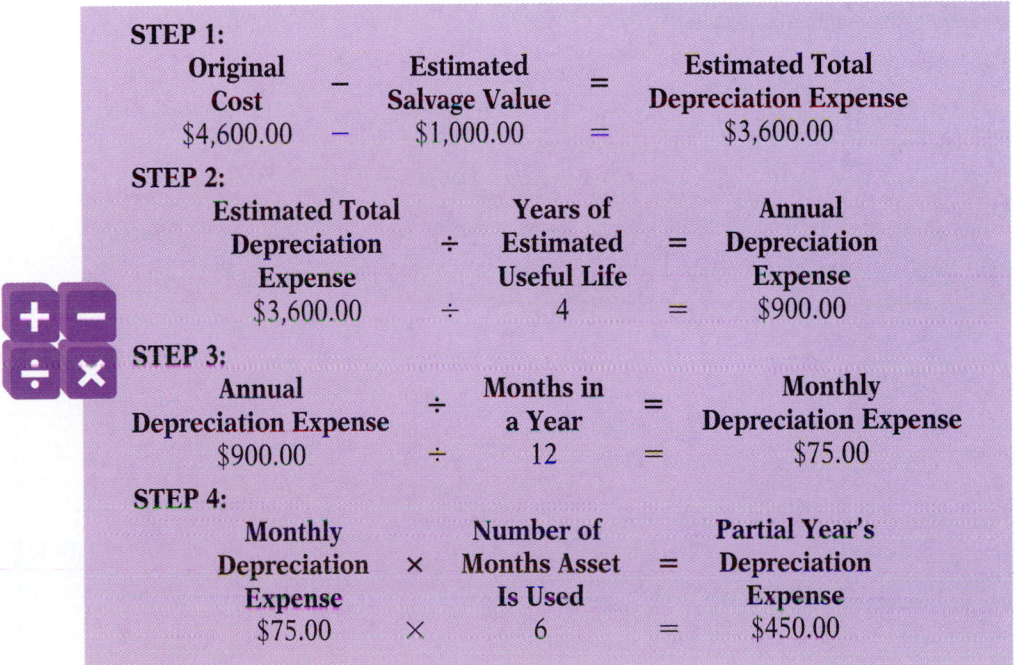

STEP 1:

Original Cost	–	Estimated Salvage Value	=	Estimated Total Depreciation Expense
$4,600.00	–	$1,000.00	=	$3,600.00

STEP 2:

Estimated Total Depreciation Expense	÷	Years of Estimated Useful Life	=	Annual Depreciation Expense
$3,600.00	÷	4	=	$900.00

STEP 3:

Annual Depreciation Expense	÷	Months in a Year	=	Monthly Depreciation Expense
$900.00	÷	12	=	$75.00

STEP 4:

Monthly Depreciation Expense	×	Number of Months Asset Is Used	=	Partial Year's Depreciation Expense
$75.00	×	6	=	$450.00

The depreciation expense for the part of the year Celluphone used the new computer is $450.00.

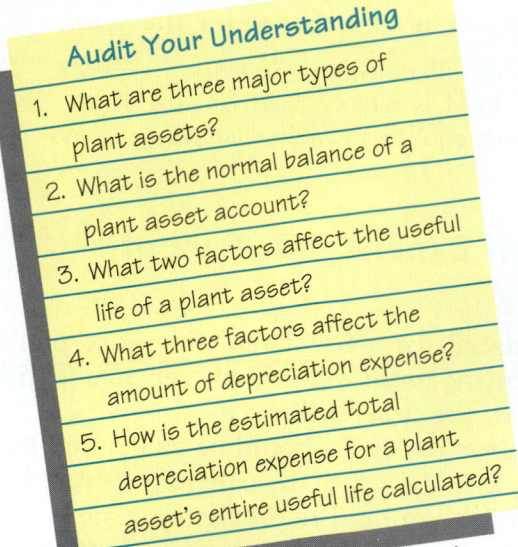

Audit Your Understanding

1. What are three major types of plant assets?

2. What is the normal balance of a plant asset account?

3. What two factors affect the useful life of a plant asset?

4. What three factors affect the amount of depreciation expense?

5. How is the estimated total depreciation expense for a plant asset's entire useful life calculated?

When determining the number of months to use in calculating depreciation for part of a year, most businesses round to the nearest whole month. For example, if an asset is bought on July 7, the asset is used for more than half the month. Thus, depreciation expense would be calculated for all of July. If an asset is bought on July 19, the asset is used for less than half the month. Thus, depreciation expense is not calculated for any of July.

PREPARING PLANT ASSET RECORDS

A separate record is kept for each plant asset. An accounting form on which a business records information about each plant asset is called a **plant asset record.**

Plant asset records may vary in arrangement for different businesses, but most records contain similar information. Celluphone's plant asset record, shown in Illustration 22-3, has three sections. Section 1 is prepared when a plant asset is bought. Information in this section shows the description, general ledger account title and number, date bought, serial number, and information needed to calculate annual depreciation expense for the plant asset. Section 2 provides space for recording disposition of the plant asset. This information will be filled in when the asset is disposed of. Section 3 provides space for recording annual depreciation expense and the changing book value of the asset each year it is used.

ILLUSTRATION 22-3   Plant asset record

PLANT ASSET RECORD

General Ledger Account No.	1205
Description	Computer
General Ledger Account	Office Equipment
Date Bought	July 1, 19X1
Serial Number	19X5-24867
Original Cost	$4,600.00
Estimated Useful Life	4 years
Estimated Salvage Value	$1,000.00
Annual Depreciation	$900.00

1

Disposed of: Discarded _____   Sold _____   Traded _____
Date _____   Disposal Amount _____

2

YEAR	ANNUAL DEPRECIATION EXPENSE	ACCUMULATED DEPRECIATION	ENDING BOOK VALUE
19X1	450.00	450.00	4,150.00
19X2	900.00	1,350.00	3,250.00
19X3	900.00	2,250.00	2,350.00
19X4	900.00	3,150.00	1,450.00
19X5	450.00	3,600.00	1,000.00

Continue record on back of card

3

At the end of each fiscal period, Celluphone brings each plant asset record up to date by calculating and recording three amounts:

(1) annual depreciation expense, (2) accumulated depreciation, and (3) ending book value.

The amount recorded in the Annual Depreciation Expense column is always the amount recorded for the fiscal year. The annual depreciation expense for the computer bought July 1, 19X1, is $900.00. However, the amount recorded for the year 19X1 in the Annual Depreciation Expense column is $450.00, the amount of depreciation expense for the part of the year Celluphone actually used the computer.

Depreciation is the portion of a plant asset's cost that is transferred to an expense account at the end of each fiscal period during the plant asset's useful life. Therefore, as the amount of depreciation expense increases, the remaining value of the plant asset decreases. However, important information would be lost if the plant asset account is reduced each time depreciation expense is recorded. Thus, information about the original cost of a plant asset and the total amount of depreciation expense recorded over the life of a plant asset should be retained. Therefore, the cumulative total of depreciation expense is recorded. The total amount of depreciation expense that has been recorded since the purchase of a plant asset is called **accumulated depreciation.**

At the end of the fiscal year 19X1, Celluphone has used its computer six months, or half a year. Since the computer had no previous depreciation expense in 19X1, the accumulated depreciation for 19X1 is the same amount as the depreciation expense, $450.00, as shown in Illustration 22-3.

A plant asset's accumulated depreciation each fiscal period is calculated as shown below for the first two years of life for Celluphone's computer.

	Year	Previous Year's Balance of Accumulated Depreciation	+	Current Year's Depreciation Expense	=	Current Year's Balance of Accumulated Depreciation
	19X1	0	+	$450.00	=	$ 450.00
	19X2	$450.00	+	$900.00	=	$1,350.00

For 19X1, $450.00 is recorded and for 19X2, $1,350.00 is recorded in the plant asset record's Accumulated Depreciation column.

The original cost of a plant asset minus accumulated depreciation is called the **book value of a plant asset.** To complete the end-of-fiscal-period updating of a plant asset record, the ending book value is calculated. The ending book value for Celluphone's computer is calculated as shown below.

FYI

Note that the word "accumulated" is spelled with two *c*s and one *m*.

	Year	Original Cost	–	Accumulated Depreciation	=	Ending Book Value
	19X1	$4,600.00	–	$ 450.00	=	$4,150.00
	19X2	$4,600.00	–	$1,350.00	=	$3,250.00

The book value is recorded each year in the plant asset record's Ending Book Value column, as shown in Illustration 22-3.

A plant asset is never depreciated below its estimated salvage value. Therefore, when a plant asset's book value equals its estimated salvage value, no further depreciation expense is recorded. The book value of Celluphone's computer at the end of 19X4, as shown in Illustration 22-3, is $1,450.00. Only $450.00 depreciation expense is needed to reduce the book value to the estimated salvage value, $1,000.00. Therefore, on December 31, 19X5, only $450.00 depreciation expense is recorded for Celluphone's computer. Thus, at the end of 19X5, and thereafter, the book value for the computer will remain at $1,000.00.

FYI

Book value is what the asset is worth in the "books" of the business. It is the difference between original cost (an actual amount) and accumulated depreciation (an estimated amount).

ACCOUNTS AFFECTING THE VALUATION OF PLANT ASSETS

Three general ledger accounts are used to record information about each kind of plant asset. (1) An asset account is used to record the original cost of the asset. (2) An expense account is used to record the amount of depreciation expense. (3) A contra asset account is used to record the accumulated depreciation.

Plant Asset Accounts

Celluphone uses two plant asset accounts: Office Equipment and Store Equipment. The appropriate plant asset account is debited for the an hourly fee. Ms. Iverson keys the papers during regular office hours only when she has no other company work.

Situation 3. Lorenzo Crowley, a sales representative, has been provided with a company car to enable him to make sales calls. Mr. Crowley uses the car during weekends for personal trips and always replaces the gas used.

Situation 4. Faye Powell, the chief executive officer, recently instructed the groundskeeper to construct a baseball field on vacant land owned by the company. The baseball field will be used by little league teams coached by employees of the company, including Ms. Powell. The company does not directly support any other civic activities.

INSTRUCTIONS:

1. Use the three-step checklist to determine whether each of these items demonstrates ethical behavior.

2. Assume each of these actions was taken without the written approval required by company policy. Should the board of directors approve each action? Use step three of the checklist to assist you in making your decision.

original cost when equipment is bought. The account is credited for the original cost when equipment is disposed of. Therefore, the balance of a plant asset account always shows the original cost of all equipment in current use.

Depreciation Expense Accounts

Depreciation is an expense to a business. To record depreciation expense for a fiscal period, an adjusting entry is made to two accounts. The amount of depreciation for a fiscal period is debited to an expense account titled Depreciation Expense.

Celluphone uses two depreciation expense accounts: Depreciation Expense—Office Equipment and Depreciation Expense—Store Equipment. The location of these expense accounts is shown in Celluphone's chart of accounts.

Accumulated Depreciation Accounts

Accumulated Depreciation	
Debit side	Credit side
	Normal balance
Decrease	Increase

The adjusting entry for the amount of depreciation for a fiscal period also has a credit to a contra asset account titled Accumulated Depreciation. A contra asset account has a normal credit balance. Therefore, the accumulated depreciation account is increased by a credit and decreased by a debit.

The account title Allowance for Depreciation is sometimes used instead of Accumulated Depreciation.

Celluphone uses two accumulated depreciation accounts: Accumulated Depreciation—Office Equipment and Accumulated Depreciation—

Store Equipment. The location of these contra asset accounts is shown in Celluphone's chart of accounts.

RECORDING DEPRECIATION EXPENSE

At the end of the fiscal year, Celluphone calculates the depreciation expense for each plant asset. Next, the total depreciation expense is calculated for all plant assets of the same kind. For example, in 19X1 the depreciation expense for the new printer is $144.00. The depreciation expense for other office equipment is $1,606.00. Thus, the total office equipment depreciation expense for the year is $1,750.00. Celluphone's accumulated depreciation for each kind of plant asset on December 31, 19X1, is calculated as shown below.

Kind of Equipment	Previous Year's Balance of Accumulated Depreciation	+	Current Year's Depreciation Expense	=	Current Year's Balance of Accumulated Depreciation
Office equipment	$3,625.00	+	$1,750.00	=	$ 5,375.00
Store equipment	$9,125.00	+	$6,325.00	=	$15,450.00

Analyzing an Adjustment for Depreciation Expense

An adjusting entry is made to record depreciation expense for a fiscal period. The T accounts show the office equipment account, depreciation expense account, and accumulated depreciation account before and after the adjustment for depreciation expense is made.

Depreciation Expense—Office Equipment is debited for $1,750.00 to show the increase in the balance of this expense account. The balance of this account, $1,750.00, is the estimated depreciation expense for the accounting period.

Accumulated Depreciation—Office Equipment is credited for $1,750.00 to show the increase in the balance of this contra asset account. The January 1 balance, $3,625.00, plus the annual increase, $1,750.00, equals the December 31 balance, $5,375.00. The office equipment account balance, $18,250.00, *minus* the accumulated depreciation account balance, $5,375.00, *equals* the office equipment book value, $12,875.00.

A similar adjusting entry is made to record depreciation expense for store equipment. The book value of each kind of plant asset after the adjustments on December 31, 19X1, is calculated as shown on the next page.

BEFORE ADJUSTMENT

Office Equipment

Jan. 1 Bal.	12,830.00	
Jan. 2	820.00	
July 1	4,600.00	
Dec. 31 Bal.	18,250.00	

Depreciation Expense—Office Equipment

Accumulated Depreciation—Office Equipment

| | | Jan. 1 Bal. | 3,625.00 |

AFTER ADJUSTMENT

Office Equipment

Jan. 1 Bal.	12,830.00	
Jan. 2	820.00	
July 1	4,600.00	
Dec. 31 Bal.	18,250.00	

Depreciation Expense—Office Equipment

| Dec. 31 Adj. | 1,750.00 | |

Accumulated Depreciation—Office Equipment

		Jan. 1 Bal.	3,625.00
		Dec. 31 Adj.	1,750.00
		Dec. 31 Bal.	5,375.00

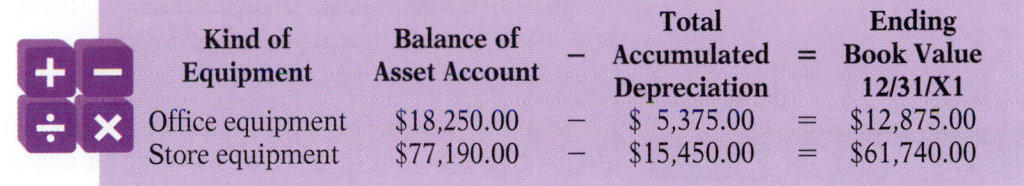

Kind of Equipment	Balance of Asset Account	−	Total Accumulated Depreciation	=	Ending Book Value 12/31/X1
Office equipment	$18,250.00	−	$ 5,375.00	=	$12,875.00
Store equipment	$77,190.00	−	$15,450.00	=	$61,740.00

Planning Depreciation Expense Adjustments on a Work Sheet

Celluphone plans the adjustments for depreciation expense in the Adjustments columns of a work sheet. The adjustments for depreciation expense are on the partial work sheet shown in Illustration 22-4.

ILLUSTRATION 22-4   Adjustments for depreciation expense on a work sheet

Celluphone, Inc.

Work Sheet

For Year Ended December 31, 19X1

		1	2	3	4
	ACCOUNT TITLE	TRIAL BALANCE		ADJUSTMENTS	
		DEBIT	CREDIT	DEBIT	CREDIT
10	Office Equipment	18 25 0 00			
11	Accum. Depr.—Office Equipment		3 62 5 00		(f) 1 75 0 00
12	Store Equipment	77 19 0 00			
13	Accum. Depr.—Store Equipment		9 12 5 00		(g) 6 32 5 00
37	Depr. Exp.—Office Equipment			(f) 1 75 0 00	
38	Depr. Exp.—Store Equipment			(g) 6 32 5 00	
39					

Adjustment for Depreciation of Office Equipment.   On line 37 the increase in Depreciation Expense—Office Equipment, *$1,750.00*, is entered in the Adjustments Debit column. On line 11 the increase in Accumulated Depreciation—Office Equipment, *$1,750.00*, is entered in the Adjustments Credit column.

Adjustment for Depreciation of Store Equipment.   On line 38 the increase in Depreciation Expense—Store Equipment, *$6,325.00*, is entered in the Adjustments Debit column. On line 13 the increase in Accumulated Depreciation—Store Equipment, *$6,325.00*, is entered in the Adjustments Credit column.

Journalizing Adjusting Entries for Depreciation Expense

Information needed to journalize adjustments for depreciation expense is obtained from the work sheet's Adjustments columns.

Celluphone's two adjusting entries to record depreciation expense are shown in Illustration 22-5.

ILLUSTRATION 22-5

Adjusting entries to journalize depreciation expense

	DATE	ACCOUNT TITLE	DOC. NO.	POST. REF.	DEBIT	CREDIT	
GENERAL JOURNAL						PAGE 15	
12	31	Depr. Exp.—Office Equipment			1 7 5 0 00		12
13		Accum. Depr.—Office Equipment				1 7 5 0 00	13
14	31	Depr. Exp.—Store Equipment			6 3 2 5 00		14
15		Accum. Depr.—Store Equipment				6 3 2 5 00	15
16							16
17							17

Posting Adjusting Entries for Depreciation Expense

After adjusting entries for depreciation expense are posted, the accounts appear as shown in Illustration 22-6.

Office Equipment and Store Equipment have debit balances showing the original cost of equipment. The two contra accounts for the equipment accounts have credit balances showing the accumulated depreciation recorded to date. The two depreciation expense accounts have debit balances showing depreciation expense for the current fiscal period.

DISPOSING OF A PLANT ASSET

A business uses a plant asset for its useful life. A plant asset may no longer be useful to a business for a number of reasons. The asset may not be needed. The asset may be worn out or more productive new assets may be available. Whatever the reason, when a plant asset is no longer useful to a business, the asset may be disposed of. The old plant asset may be sold, traded for a new asset, or discarded.

When a plant asset is disposed of, a journal entry is recorded that achieves the following three effects in the accounts.

1. Removes the original cost of the plant asset and its related accumulated depreciation.
2. Recognizes any cash or other asset received for the old plant asset.
3. Recognizes the gain or loss on the disposal, if any.

Audit Your Understanding

1. What three amounts are calculated at the end of each fiscal period to bring each plant asset record up to date?
2. How much depreciation expense is recorded after a plant asset's book value equals its estimated salvage value?
3. What is the normal balance of an accumulated depreciation account?
4. How is a plant asset account affected by the adjustment for depreciation expense?
5. What is the adjusting entry to record depreciation expense for the period?

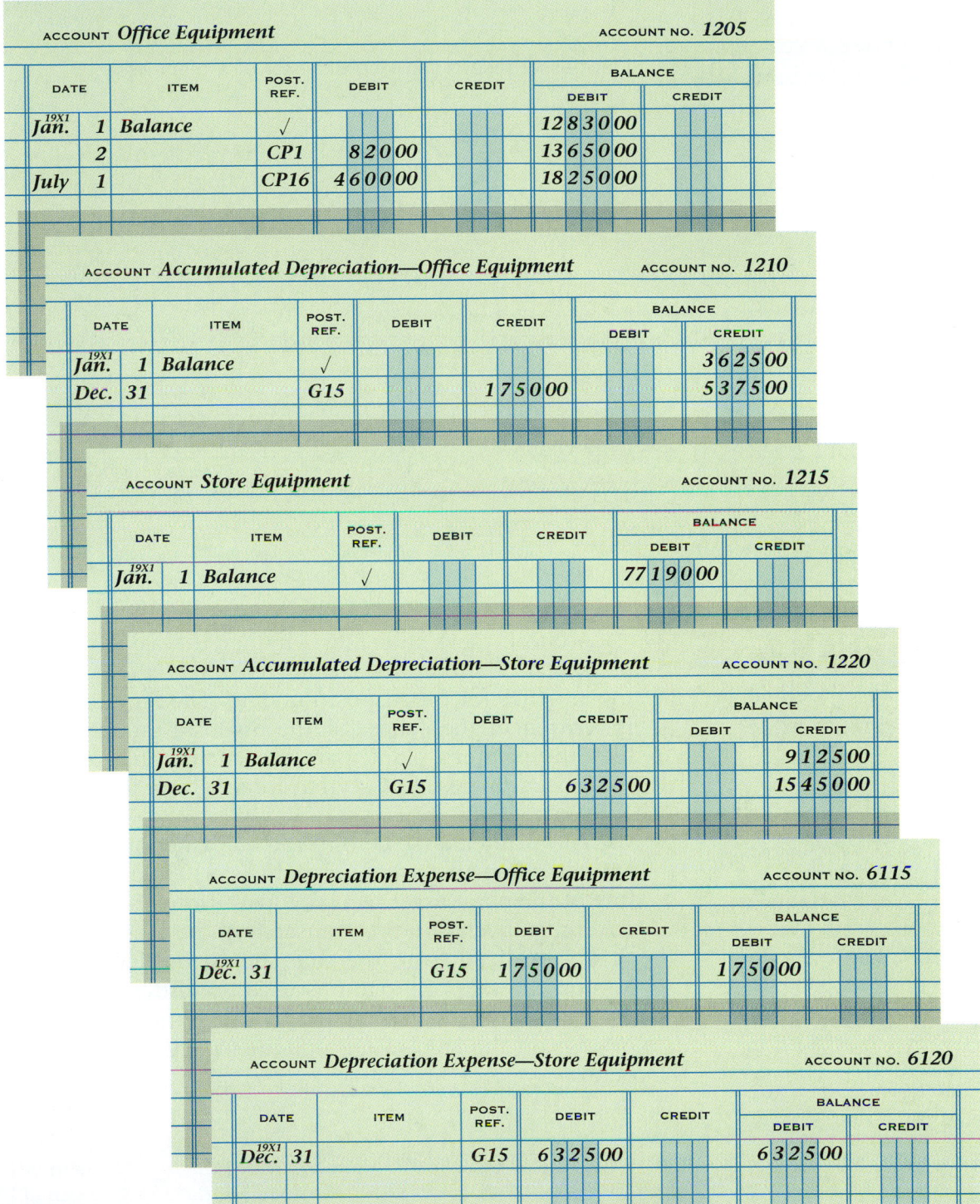

ACCOUNT *Office Equipment*					ACCOUNT NO. *1205*	
DATE	ITEM	POST. REF.	DEBIT	CREDIT	BALANCE DEBIT	BALANCE CREDIT
Jan. ^19X1 1	Balance	✓			12 830 00	
2		CP1	820 00		13 650 00	
July 1		CP16	4 600 00		18 250 00	

ACCOUNT *Accumulated Depreciation—Office Equipment*					ACCOUNT NO. *1210*	
DATE	ITEM	POST. REF.	DEBIT	CREDIT	BALANCE DEBIT	BALANCE CREDIT
Jan. ^19X1 1	Balance	✓				3 625 00
Dec. 31		G15		1 750 00		5 375 00

ACCOUNT *Store Equipment*					ACCOUNT NO. *1215*	
DATE	ITEM	POST. REF.	DEBIT	CREDIT	BALANCE DEBIT	BALANCE CREDIT
Jan. ^19X1 1	Balance	✓			77 190 00	

ACCOUNT *Accumulated Depreciation—Store Equipment*					ACCOUNT NO. *1220*	
DATE	ITEM	POST. REF.	DEBIT	CREDIT	BALANCE DEBIT	BALANCE CREDIT
Jan. ^19X1 1	Balance	✓				9 125 00
Dec. 31		G15		6 325 00		15 450 00

ACCOUNT *Depreciation Expense—Office Equipment*					ACCOUNT NO. *6115*	
DATE	ITEM	POST. REF.	DEBIT	CREDIT	BALANCE DEBIT	BALANCE CREDIT
Dec. ^19X1 31		G15	1 750 00		1 750 00	

ACCOUNT *Depreciation Expense—Store Equipment*					ACCOUNT NO. *6120*	
DATE	ITEM	POST. REF.	DEBIT	CREDIT	BALANCE DEBIT	BALANCE CREDIT
Dec. ^19X1 31		G15	6 325 00		6 325 00	

Sale of a Plant Asset for Book Value

After five years of use, Celluphone sold a printer.

> January 3, 19X6. Received cash from sale of the printer bought on January 2, 19X1, $100.00: original cost, $820.00; total accumulated depreciation through December 31, 19X5, $720.00. Receipt No. 4.

A notation is made in the second section of the plant asset record for this printer, as shown in Illustration 22-7.

ILLUSTRATION 22-7

Plant asset record showing disposal of a plant asset

PLANT ASSET RECORD

Description	_Printer_	General Ledger Account No. _1205_
		General Ledger Account _Office Equipment_

Date Bought	_January 2, 19X1_	Serial Number	_48C79623_	Original Cost	_$820.00_
Estimated Useful Life	_5 years_	Estimated Salvage Value	_$100.00_	Annual Depreciation	_$144.00_

Disposed of: Discarded _____   Sold _✓_   Traded _____

Date _January 3, 19X6_   Disposal Amount _$100.00_

YEAR	ANNUAL DEPRECIATION EXPENSE	ACCUMULATED DEPRECIATION	ENDING BOOK VALUE
_19X1_	_144.00_	_144.00_	_676.00_
_19X2_	_144.00_	_288.00_	_532.00_
_19X3_	_144.00_	_432.00_	_388.00_
_19X4_	_144.00_	_576.00_	_244.00_
_19X5_	_144.00_	_720.00_	_100.00_

FYI

When an asset is sold for book value, no gain or loss results.

A check mark indicates whether the asset was discarded, sold, or traded. The date the printer is sold, *January 3, 19X6*, is written in the space for the disposition date. The amount received, *$100.00*, is written in the space for the disposal amount. Celluphone then files the printer's plant asset record in a file for plant assets that have been disposed of so that information about the asset is available if needed.

The printer is sold for $100.00. The ending book value of the printer when the printer is sold is $100.00, as shown on the last line of the plant asset record, Illustration 22-7. Before analyzing the accounts affected in this transaction, the amount of any gain or loss that is realized from the sale should be determined. The gain or loss on the sale of a plant asset is the difference between the book value of the asset sold and the value of the asset received. The gain or loss on the sale of Celluphone's printer is calculated as shown below.

Value of Asset Received	−	Book Value of Asset Sold	=	Gain or Loss on Disposal of Plant Asset
		Cost $820.00		
		Accum. Dep. −720.00		
Cash $100.00	−	Book Value $100.00	=	0

Celluphone sold its printer for the printer's book value. Therefore, no gain or loss exists. The journal entry for the sale of a plant asset for book value must achieve the following two effects in the accounts.

1. Remove the original cost of the plant asset and its related accumulated depreciation.
2. Recognize the cash received.

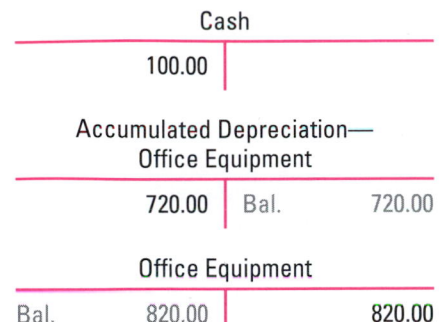

Cash is debited for $100.00 to show the increase in the balance of this asset account.

The accumulated depreciation account should show only the depreciation for plant assets still in use. Therefore, Accumulated Depreciation—Office Equipment is debited for $720.00 to show the decrease in this contra asset account's balance. The amount, $720.00, is the total depreciation recorded during the printer's entire life.

Office Equipment is credited for $820.00 to show the decrease in the balance of this plant asset account. This entry cancels the original cost, $820.00, that was debited to the office equipment account when the printer was bought.

The cash receipts journal entry to record the sale of the printer is shown in Illustration 22-8.

| **ILLUSTRATION 22-8** | Cash receipts journal entry to record the sale of a plant asset for book value |

					GENERAL		ACCOUNTS RECEIVABLE CREDIT	SALES CREDIT	SALES TAX PAYABLE		SALES DISCOUNT DEBIT	CASH DEBIT	
	DATE	ACCOUNT TITLE	DOC. NO.	POST. REF.	DEBIT	CREDIT			DEBIT	CREDIT			
8	3	*Accum. Depr.—Office Equipment*	R4		720 00							100 00	8
9		*Office Equipment*				820 00							9
10													10

CASH RECEIPTS JOURNAL — PAGE *1*

Sale of a Plant Asset for More than Book Value

Revenue that results when a plant asset is sold for more than book value is called **gain on plant assets.** After five years of use, Celluphone sold a cash register for $150.00.

April 1, 19X7. Received cash from sale of the cash register bought on April 1, 19X2, $150.00: original cost, $470.00; total accumulated depreciation through December 31, 19X6, $399.00; additional depreciation to be recorded through April 1, 19X7, $21.00. Memorandum No. 14 and Receipt No. 38.

The source documents for this transaction are a memorandum, detailing the need for an additional three months' depreciation, and a receipt. *(CONCEPT: Objective Evidence)*

Journalizing Depreciation for Part of a Year. A plant asset may be disposed of at any time during the asset's useful life. When a plant asset is disposed of, its depreciation from the beginning of the current fiscal year to the date of disposal is recorded. For example, Celluphone last recorded adjusting entries for depreciation expense on December 31, 19X6. The cash register is sold on April 1, 19X7. Before entries are made for the sale of the cash register, three months' depreciation must be recorded for the period January 1 through April 1. The additional depreciation for the cash register is calculated as shown below.

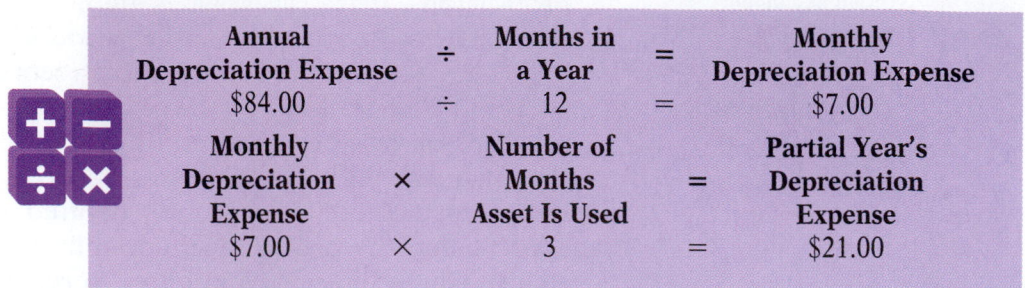

	Annual Depreciation Expense	÷	Months in a Year	=	Monthly Depreciation Expense
	$84.00	÷	12	=	$7.00
	Monthly Depreciation Expense	×	Number of Months Asset Is Used	=	Partial Year's Depreciation Expense
	$7.00	×	3	=	$21.00

Depreciation Expense—Store Equipment

Add. Depr.   21.00

Accumulated Depreciation— Store Equipment

Bal.	399.00
Add. Depr.	21.00
(New Bal.	420.00)

Depreciation Expense—Store Equipment is debited for $21.00 to show the increase in the balance of this expense account. Accumulated Depreciation—Store Equipment is credited for $21.00 to show the increase in this contra asset account.

The general journal entry to record the three months' depreciation is shown in Illustration 22-9.

ILLUSTRATION 22-9   General journal entry to record depreciation for part of a year

		GENERAL JOURNAL			PAGE 4	
	DATE	ACCOUNT TITLE	DOC. NO.	POST. REF.	DEBIT	CREDIT
1	19X7 Apr. 1	Depr. Exp.—Store Equipment	M14		21 00	
2		Accum. Depr.—Store Equipment				21 00
3						

Journalizing the Sale of a Plant Asset.   After the partial year's depreciation is recorded, a journal entry is made to record the sale of the cash register. The cash register is sold for $150.00. The ending book value when the cash register is sold is $50.00. The gain on the sale of Celluphone's cash register is calculated as shown below.

	Value of Asset Received	–	Book Value of Asset Sold	=	Gain on Disposal
			Cost $470.00		
			Accum. Dep. –420.00		
	Cash $150.00	–	Book Value $ 50.00	=	$100.00 Gain

Celluphone sold its cash register for $100.00 more than its book value. Since the asset received has greater value than the book value of the plant asset disposed of, the difference is recognized as a gain on plant assets. The gain is calculated as $150.00 cash received, *less* $50.00 book value of plant asset, *equals* $100.00 gain on plant asset.

The amount of gain realized on the disposal of a plant asset is credited to a revenue account titled *Gain on Plant Assets*. A revenue account has a normal credit balance. Therefore, the gain on plant assets account is increased by a credit and decreased by a debit.

A gain from the sale of plant assets is not an operating revenue. Therefore, Gain on Plant Assets is not listed under Operating Revenue in a chart of accounts. Gain on Plant Assets is listed in a classification titled *Other Revenue* in a chart of accounts.

The journal entry for the sale of a plant asset for more than book value must achieve the following three effects in the accounts.

1. Remove the original cost of the plant asset and its related accumulated depreciation.
2. Recognize the cash received.
3. Recognize the gain on disposal of the asset.

Cash is debited for $150.00 to show the increase in the balance of this asset account. Accumulated Depreciation—Store Equipment is debited for $420.00 to show the decrease in this contra asset account. This amount, $420.00, is the sum of all depreciation expense recorded during the entire time Celluphone has used this cash register. Store Equipment is credited for $470.00 to show the decrease in the balance of this plant asset account. This entry removes the original cost, $470.00, that was debited to the store equipment account when the cash register was bought. Gain on Plant Assets is credited for $100.00 to show the increase in this other revenue account.

The cash receipts journal entry to record the sale of the cash register is shown in Illustration 22-10.

Notations are made on the plant asset record to record the partial year's depreciation and disposal information.

Gain on Plant Assets

Debit side	Credit side
Decrease	Normal balance
	Increase

Cash

150.00	

Accumulated Depreciation—Store Equipment

420.00	Bal.	420.00

Store Equipment

Bal. 470.00		470.00

Gain on Plant Assets

	100.00

ILLUSTRATION 22-10   Cash receipts journal entry to record the sale of a plant asset for more than book value

CASH RECEIPTS JOURNAL — PAGE 10

	DATE		ACCOUNT TITLE	DOC. NO.	POST. REF.	GENERAL DEBIT	GENERAL CREDIT	ACCOUNTS RECEIVABLE CREDIT	SALES CREDIT	SALES TAX PAYABLE DEBIT	SALES TAX PAYABLE CREDIT	SALES DISCOUNT DEBIT	CASH DEBIT	
1	*Apr.*	1	*Accum. Depr.—Store Equipment*	R38		420 00							150 00	1
2			*Store Equipment*				470 00							2
3			*Gain on Plant Assets*				100 00							3

Sale of a Plant Asset for Less than Book Value

Loss that results when a plant asset is sold for less than book value is called **loss on plant assets.** Celluphone sold a computer for $800.00 after four years of use.

September 1, 19X5. Received cash from sale of the computer bought on September 1, 19X1, $800.00: original cost, $4,000.00; total accumulated depreciation through December 31, 19X4, $2,000.00; additional depreciation to be recorded through September 1, 19X5, $400.00. Memorandum No. 82 and Receipt No. 281.

Journalizing Depreciation for Part of a Year. Celluphone last recorded adjusting entries for depreciation expense on December 31, 19X4. Celluphone sold its computer on September 1, 19X5. Before entries are made for the sale of the computer, eight months' depreciation must be recorded. The eight months' depreciation is for the period January 1 through September 1. The additional depreciation for the computer is calculated as shown below.

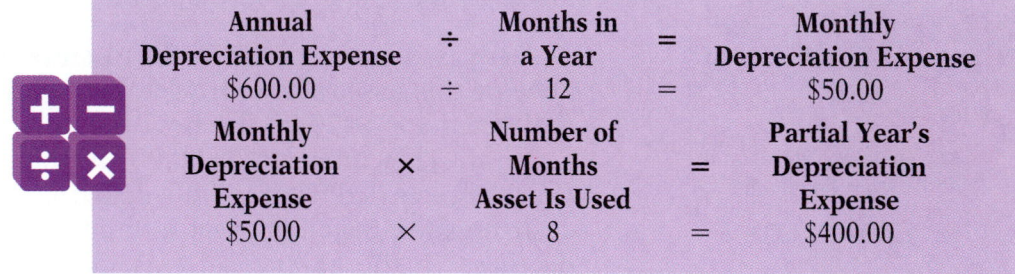

Annual Depreciation Expense	÷	Months in a Year	=	Monthly Depreciation Expense
$600.00	÷	12	=	$50.00

Monthly Depreciation Expense	×	Number of Months Asset Is Used	=	Partial Year's Depreciation Expense
$50.00	×	8	=	$400.00

Depreciation Expense—Office Equipment is debited for $400.00 to show the increase in the balance of this expense account. Accumulated Depreciation—Office Equipment is credited for $400.00 to show the increase in this contra asset account.

The general journal entry to record the eight months' depreciation is shown in Illustration 22-11.

Journalizing the Sale of a Plant Asset. After the partial year's depreciation is recorded, a journal entry is made to record the

Depreciation Expense—Office Equipment	
Add. Depr. 400.00	

Accumulated Depreciation— Office Equipment	
	Bal. 2,000.00
	Add. Depr. 400.00
	(New Bal. 2,400.00)

ILLUSTRATION 22-11   General journal entry to record depreciation for part of a year

GENERAL JOURNAL   PAGE 9

	DATE		ACCOUNT TITLE	DOC. NO.	POST. REF.	DEBIT	CREDIT	
1	19X5 Sept.	1	Depr. Exp.—Office Equipment	M82		4 0 0 00		1
2			Accum. Depr.—Office Equip.				4 0 0 00	2
3								3

sale of the computer. The computer is sold for $800.00. The ending book value when the computer is sold is $1,600.00. The loss on the sale of Celluphone's computer is calculated as shown below.

	Book Value of Asset Sold		−	Value of Asset Received	=	Loss on Disposal
Cost	$4,000.00					
Accum. Dep.	−2,400.00					
Book Value	$1,600.00		−	Cash $800.00	=	$800.00 Loss

Celluphone sold its computer for $800.00 less than its book value. Since the asset received has less value than the book value of the plant asset disposed of, the difference is recognized as a loss on plant assets. The loss is calculated as $1,600.00 book value of plant asset, *less* $800.00 cash received, *equals* $800.00 loss on plant asset.

The amount of loss realized on the disposal of a plant asset is debited to an expense account titled *Loss on Plant Assets*. An expense account has a normal debit balance. Therefore, Loss on Plant Assets is increased by a debit and decreased by a credit, as shown in the T account.

Loss on Plant Assets

Debit side Normal balance Increase	Credit side Decrease

A loss from the sale of plant assets is not an operating expense. Therefore, Loss on Plant Assets is listed in a classification titled *Other Expenses* in a chart of accounts.

The journal entry for the sale of a plant asset for less than book value must achieve the following three effects in the accounts.

1. Remove the original cost of the plant asset and its related accumulated depreciation.
2. Recognize the cash received.
3. Recognize the loss on disposal of the asset.

Cash

800.00	

Accumulated Depreciation— Office Equipment

2,400.00	Bal. 2,400.00

Loss on Plant Assets

800.00	

Office Equipment

Bal. 4,000.00	4,000.00

Cash is debited for $800.00 to show the increase in the balance of this asset account. Accumulated Depreciation—Office Equipment is debited for $2,400.00 to show the decrease in this contra asset account. This amount, $2,400.00, is the sum of all depreciation expense recorded during the entire period Celluphone has used this computer. Loss on Plant Assets is debited for $800.00 to show the increase in this expense account. Office Equipment is credited for $4,000.00 to show the decrease in the balance of this plant asset account. This entry removes the original cost, $4,000.00, which was debited to the office equipment account when the computer was bought.

The cash receipts journal entry to record the sale of Celluphone's computer is shown in Illustration 22-12.

Notations are made on the plant asset record to record the partial year's depreciation and disposal information.

CASH RECEIPTS JOURNAL PAGE 19

					GENERAL		ACCOUNTS RECEIVABLE CREDIT	SALES CREDIT	SALES TAX PAYABLE		SALES DISCOUNT DEBIT	CASH DEBIT	
	DATE	ACCOUNT TITLE	DOC. NO.	POST. REF.	DEBIT	CREDIT			DEBIT	CREDIT			
1	*Sept.* 1 (19X5)	*Accum. Depr.—Office Equipment*	R281		2 4 0 0 00							8 0 0 00	1
2		*Loss on Plant Assets*			8 0 0 00								2
3		*Office Equipment*				4 0 0 0 00							3

DECLINING-BALANCE METHOD OF CALCULATING DEPRECIATION

Celluphone uses the straight-line method of depreciation. An equal amount of depreciation expense is recorded each year during the useful life of a plant asset. However, not all assets depreciate the same amount each year. Many plant assets depreciate more in the early years of useful life than in later years. For example, a truck's value will decrease more the first year of service than in later years. Therefore, charging more depreciation expense in the early years of a plant asset may be more accurate than charging the same amount each year. *(CONCEPT: Matching Expenses with Revenue)*

Multiplying the book value at the end of each fiscal period by a constant depreciation rate is called the **declining-balance method of depreciation**. Although the rate is the same each year, the book value declines from one year to the next because of the increasing accumulated depreciation. The greatest book value exists during the first year. Therefore, the greatest depreciation expense is recorded in the first year. Because the smallest book value exists during the last year, the least depreciation expense is recorded in the last year.

The declining-balance depreciation rate, or percentage, is a multiple of the straight-line rate. Because of the ease in calculating, many businesses use a declining-balance rate that is two times the straight-line rate. For example, if a plant asset has an estimated useful life of five years, then the declining-balance rate is calculated as shown below.

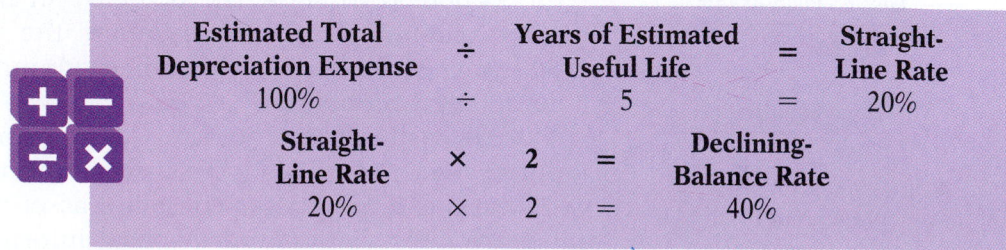

Estimated Total Depreciation Expense	÷	Years of Estimated Useful Life	=	Straight-Line Rate
100%	÷	5	=	20%

Straight-Line Rate	×	2	=	Declining-Balance Rate
20%	×	2	=	40%

The straight-line rate is generally stated when identifying the declining-balance method rate. Thus, if the rate is to be twice the straight-line rate, the rate would be stated as *double declining-balance*. Depreciation expense calculated using both the straight-line and the declining-balance methods is shown in Illustration 22-13.

ILLUSTRATION 22-13

Comparison of the straight-line and declining-balance methods of calculating annual depreciation expense for the same plant asset

	Plant asset: Truck Original cost: $20,000.00 Estimated salvage value: $2,000.00 Estimated useful life: 5 years					
Year	**Straight-Line Method**			**Declining-Balance Method**		
	Beg. Book Value	**Annual Depr.**	**End. Book Value**	**Beg. Book Value**	**Annual Depr.**	**End. Book Value**
1	$20,000.00	$3,600.00	$16,400.00	$20,000.00	$8,000.00	$12,000.00
2	16,400.00	3,600.00	12,800.00	12,000.00	4,800.00	7,200.00
3	12,800.00	3,600.00	9,200.00	7,200.00	2,880.00	4,320.00
4	9,200.00	3,600.00	5,600.00	4,320.00	1,728.00	2,592.00
5	5,600.00	3,600.00	2,000.00	2,592.00	592.00	2,000.00
Total Depr.	—	$18,000.00	—	—	$18,000.00	—

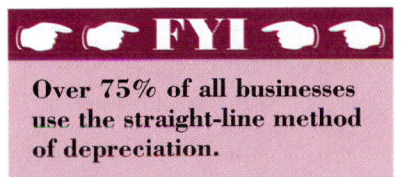

FYI

Over 75% of all businesses use the straight-line method of depreciation.

When using the declining-balance method, the annual depreciation expense is calculated using the beginning book value for each year. The beginning book value is the same as the ending book value from the previous year. More depreciation expense is recorded in the earlier years of a plant asset. The annual depreciation expense and ending book value for the first year using the declining-balance method are calculated as shown below.

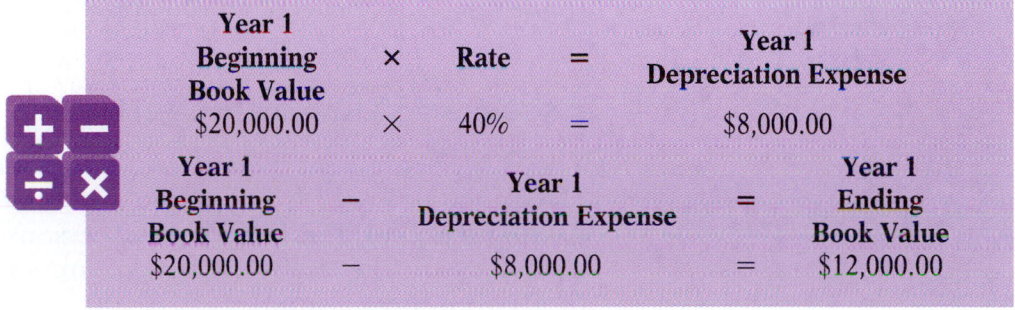

Year 1 Beginning Book Value	×	Rate	=	Year 1 Depreciation Expense
$20,000.00	×	40%	=	$8,000.00

Year 1 Beginning Book Value	−	Year 1 Depreciation Expense	=	Year 1 Ending Book Value
$20,000.00	−	$8,000.00	=	$12,000.00

The annual depreciation expense and ending book value for the second year using the declining-balance method are calculated as shown on the next page.

Year 2 Beginning Book Value	×	Rate	=	Year 2 Depreciation Expense
$12,000.00	×	40%	=	$4,800.00

Year 2 Beginning Book Value	−	Year 2 Depreciation Expense	=	Year 2 Ending Book Value
$12,000.00	−	$4,800.00	=	$7,200.00

When using the declining-balance method, a different amount of depreciation expense is recorded each year. Special care must be taken in calculating depreciation expense for the last year of useful life. A plant asset is never depreciated below its estimated salvage value. Therefore, in the last year, only enough depreciation expense is recorded to reduce the book value of the plant asset to its salvage value. For example, in Illustration 22-13, depreciation expense in the fifth year is only $592.00, the amount that will reduce the ending book value to $2,000.00, the estimated salvage value of the plant asset.

Regardless of the method used to calculate the amount of depreciation expense, the general ledger accounts affected are the same. The appropriate depreciation expense account is debited and the related accumulated depreciation account is credited for the amount of depreciation for the period.

CALCULATING AND PAYING PROPERTY TAX

Property taxes are a major source of funds for education in many states.

For tax purposes, state and federal governments define two kinds of property—real and personal. Land and anything attached to the land is called **real property.** Real property is sometimes referred to as real estate. All property not classified as real property is called **personal property.** For tax purposes, these definitions apply whether the property is owned by a business or an individual.

Assessed Value of Property

The value of an asset determined by tax authorities for the purpose of calculating taxes is called the **assessed value.** Assessed value is usually based on the judgment of persons referred to as assessors. Assessors are elected by citizens or are specially trained employees of a governmental unit.

The assessed value of an asset may not be the same as the book value on the business' or individual's records. The assessed value is assigned to an asset for tax purposes only. Often the assessed value is only a part of the true value of the asset.

Calculating Property Tax on Plant Assets

Most governmental units with taxing power have a tax based on the value of real property. The real property tax is used on buildings and land. Some governmental units also tax personal property such as cars, boats, trailers, and airplanes.

A governmental taxing unit determines a tax rate to use in calculating taxes. The tax rate is multiplied by an asset's *assessed value*, not the book value recorded on a business' records.

PhoneLand's buildings and land have been assessed for a total of $250,000.00. The city tax rate is 1.5%. PhoneLand's annual property tax is calculated as shown below.

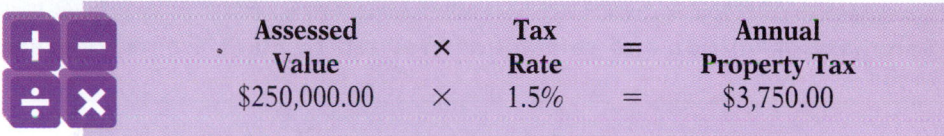

	Assessed Value	×	Tax Rate	=	Annual Property Tax
	$250,000.00	×	1.5%	=	$3,750.00

PhoneLand is required to pay current year property taxes not later than December 31.

Paying Property Tax on Plant Assets

On December 30, PhoneLand paid its property tax.

December 30, 19--. Paid cash for property tax, $3,750.00. Check No. 487.

Property Tax Expense

3,750.00	

Cash

	3,750.00

Property Tax Expense is increased by a $3,750.00 debit. Cash is decreased by a $3,750.00 credit.

The journal entry to record payment of property tax is shown in Illustration 22-14 on page 610.

Payment of all assessed taxes is necessary if a firm is to continue in business. Therefore, PhoneLand classifies property tax as an operating expense.

The first chart in Summary Illustration 22-15 on pages 610 and 611 analyzes the entries for transactions related to plant assets, depreciation, and property taxes. The second chart summarizes the calculations for amounts related to depreciation and sale of plant assets.

Audit Your Understanding

1. When is the most depreciation expense recorded when the declining-balance method is used?

2. When the declining-balance method of depreciation is used, how much depreciation is recorded in the last year of the plant asset's useful life?

3. Who usually determines the assessed value of property for tax purposes?

ILLUSTRATION 22-14   Journal entry to record payment of property tax

					GENERAL		ACCOUNTS PAYABLE DEBIT	PURCHASES DISCOUNT CREDIT	CASH CREDIT	
	DATE	ACCOUNT TITLE	CK. NO.	POST. REF.	DEBIT	CREDIT				
1	Dec. 30	Property Tax Expense	487		3 7 5 0 00				3 7 5 0 00	1
2										2

CASH PAYMENTS JOURNAL — PAGE 24

SUMMARY ILLUSTRATION 22-15

Summary of entries and calculations related to plant assets, depreciation, and property taxes

Transactions	GENERAL LEDGER													
	Cash		Equipment		Accumulated Depreciation		Depreciation Expense		Property Tax Expense		Gain on Plant Assets		Loss on Plant Assets	
	Debit	Credit	Debit	Credit	Debit	Credit	Debit	Credit	Debit	Credit	Debit	Credit	Debit	Credit
Buying a plant asset		X	X											
Recording depreciation expense for a fiscal period						X	X							
Sale of plant asset for book value	X			X	X									
Sale of plant asset for more than book value	X			X	X							X		
Sale of plant asset for less than book value	X			X	X								X	
Paying property tax on plant assets		X							X					

AMOUNTS	CALCULATIONS				
Annual Depreciation Expense	Original Cost − Estimated Salvage Value = Estimated Total Depreciation Expense ÷ Years of Estimated Useful Life = Annual Depreciation Expense
Partial Year's Depreciation Expense	Annual Depreciation Expense ÷ Months in a Year = Monthly Depreciation Expense × Number of Months Asset Is Used = Partial Year's Depreciation Expense
Current Year's Balance of Accumulated Depreciation	Previous Year's Balance of Accumulated Depreciation + Current Year's Depreciation Expense = Current Year's Balance of Accumulated Depreciation
Book Value of a Plant Asset	Original Cost − Accumulated Depreciation = Ending Book Value
Gain on Sale of a Plant Asset	Value of Asset Received − Book Value of Asset Sold = Gain on Disposal
Loss on Sale of a Plant Asset	Book Value of Asset Sold − Value of Asset Received = Loss on Disposal

What is the meaning of each of the following?

1. **current assets**
2. **plant assets**
3. **depreciation expense**
4. **estimated salvage value**
5. **straight-line method of depreciation**
6. **plant asset record**
7. **accumulated depreciation**
8. **book value of a plant asset**
9. **gain on plant assets**
10. **loss on plant assets**
11. **declining-balance method of depreciation**
12. **real property**
13. **personal property**
14. **assessed value**

QUESTIONS FOR INDIVIDUAL STUDY
EPT(b)

1. What are the two broad categories of assets used by most businesses in the operations of their businesses?

2. What is the reason for recording depreciation expense?

3. Which accounting concept is being applied when depreciation is recorded?

4. In what significant way does depreciation expense differ from many other business expenses?

5. Why is land generally not subject to depreciation?

6. What three factors affect the amount of depreciation expense for a plant asset?

7. What is included in the original cost of a plant asset?

8. Why is the estimated salvage value used in determining depreciation expense rather than the actual salvage value?

9. If, when purchased, the useful life of an asset cannot be reasonably estimated from past experience, where might this information be obtained?

10. How is the annual depreciation expense calculated for a plant asset using the straight-line method of depreciation?

11. When a plant asset record is brought up to date, what three amounts are generally recorded on the record?

12. How is the book value of a plant asset calculated?

13. When a plant asset's book value equals its estimated salvage value, how is the depreciation expense for the succeeding periods recorded?

14. On a work sheet, what accounts are affected, and how, in planning adjustments for depreciation of a plant asset?

15. What accounts are affected, and how, when a plant asset is sold for more than book value?

16. What accounts are affected, and how, when a plant asset is sold for less than book value?

17. What method of depreciation would be more accurate, straight-line or declining-balance, if a plant asset's value decreases more in the first year of service than in later years?

18. How does real property differ from personal property?

19. Who determines the assessed value of property?

20. What accounts are affected, and how, by an entry to pay property tax?

CASES FOR CRITICAL THINKING

CASE 1 Carol Ebener, owner of a small business, does not record depreciation expense for the business' plant assets. Ms. Ebener says that she does not make actual cash payments for depreciation. Therefore, she records an expense for the use of plant assets only when cash is paid for a plant asset. Do you agree with Ms. Ebener's method? Explain.

CASE 2 TriState Company sold a printer for $100.00 after using it for five years. TriState paid $800.00 for the printer and at that time estimated the useful life to be five years with an estimated salvage value of $50.00. When the printer was sold, a total of $750.00 accumulated depreciation had been recorded in its plant asset record. Jonathan Yancey, a new accounting clerk, recorded the sale as a $100.00 debit to **Cash** and a $100.00 credit to **Gain on Plant Assets**. When asked why he made that entry, Mr. Yancey said that since the printer had been used for its full estimated useful life, he thought any amount realized from its sale should be recorded as a gain. Is Mr. Yancey correct? Explain.

APPLIED COMMUNICATIONS

Financing expensive plant assets can be a complicated process for both individuals and businesses. Buying a car, for example, requires the buyer to evaluate numerous combinations of rebates, loan interest rates, and loan payment terms. Car dealers often offer the buyer either a cash rebate or a low interest loan.

INSTRUCTIONS:
1. For the car of your choice, identify two available financing options. Obtain financing information from a local bank or a car dealer. Using their estimated monthly payment, calculate the total money paid using each alternative.
2. Prepare a table summarizing your analysis. The table should include: purchase price, cash rebate, amount to be financed, financing terms (interest rate and payment term), estimated monthly payment, and total payments. Write a paragraph describing which alternative you would select, and support your answer.

DRILLS FOR UNDERSTANDING

DRILL 22-D1 Calculating depreciation expense

INSTRUCTIONS:

Use the straight-line method of calculating depreciation described in this chapter. Calculate the amount of annual depreciation expense for each of the following plant assets.

Plant Asset	Original Cost	Estimated Salvage Value	Estimated Useful Life
1	$ 730.00	$ 50.00	4 years
2	5,200.00	1,400.00	5 years
3	2,170.00	250.00	3 years
4	1,610.00	170.00	6 years
5	8,950.00	2,350.00	8 years
6	17,480.00	950.00	10 years
7	12,600.00	3,150.00	9 years
8	57,200.00	5,500.00	25 years
9	9,220.00	480.00	4 years
10	26,500.00	5,950.00	15 years

DRILL 22-D2 Calculating book value of plant assets

INSTRUCTIONS:

Calculate two amounts for each of the following plant assets.

a. Using the straight-line method of depreciation, calculate the amount of total accumulated depreciation that should be recorded through December 31, 19X6. Calculate the time of depreciation to the nearest number of months. Round amounts to the nearest cent.

b. Calculate the ending book value as of December 31, 19X6.

Plant Asset	Date Bought	Original Cost	Estimated Salvage Value	Estimated Useful Life
1	Jan. 1, 19X1	$ 1,050.00	$ 150.00	6 years
2	July 1, 19X1	4,700.00	400.00	10 years
3	Apr. 1, 19X2	25,500.00	1,500.00	15 years
4	Sept. 1, 19X2	12,800.00	1,250.00	7 years
5	Mar. 1, 19X3	10,700.00	1,100.00	8 years
6	Aug. 1, 19X4	6,200.00	500.00	5 years
7	Dec. 31, 19X4	930.00	110.00	4 years
8	Oct. 1, 19X5	2,700.00	300.00	3 years
9	May 1, 19X6	15,600.00	3,600.00	8 years
10	Nov. 1, 19X6	7,800.00	240.00	9 years

APPLICATION PROBLEMS   EPT(c,d,e)

PROBLEM 22-1 Journalizing the buying of plant assets

Holloway Company records plant assets in two accounts: **Office Equipment** and **Store Equipment**.

INSTRUCTIONS:

Journalize the following transactions completed during the current year. Use page 12 of a cash payments journal. (Usually a new journal page is started each month. However, to conserve space in the working papers, record all of the year's entries on the same page of the cash payments journal.) The abbreviation for check is C.

Jan. 1. Paid cash for office equipment, $9,270.00. C127.

Feb. 1. Paid cash for store equipment, $12,850.00. C159.

May 1. Paid cash for office equipment, $313.00. C228.

June 1. Paid cash for office equipment, $1,740.00. C263.

Nov. 1. Paid cash for store equipment, $3,684.00. C401.

Dec. 1. Paid cash for office equipment, $920.00. C442.

PROBLEM 22-2 Calculating depreciation expense

Creative Concepts, Inc. owns the following plant assets.

Plant Asset	Date Bought	Original Cost	Estimated Salvage Value	Estimated Useful Life
1	July 1, 19X1	$ 5,600.00	$ 800.00	12 years
2	Nov. 1, 19X1	5,000.00	380.00	7 years

Plant Asset	Date Bought	Original Cost	Estimated Salvage Value	Estimated Useful Life
3	May 1, 19X2	21,600.00	2,250.00	15 years
4	Feb. 1, 19X3	10,750.00	1,750.00	9 years
5	Apr. 1, 19X3	3,820.00	220.00	6 years
6	Aug. 1, 19X3	1,440.00	200.00	2 years

INSTRUCTIONS:

For each plant asset, calculate the depreciation expense to be recorded for the year ended December 31, 19X3. Use the straight-line method of calculating depreciation.

PROBLEM 22-3 Preparing a plant asset record

PhotoCraft bought a new high-speed photocopying machine on July 1 of the current year. Use the following additional information pertaining to the copier.

Account number: 1225

General ledger account: Store Equipment

Serial number of copier: KP3044987

Cost: $12,500.00

Estimated useful life: 7 years

Estimated salvage value: $2,000.00

INSTRUCTIONS:

Prepare a plant asset record. For each year of the plant asset's life, record year-end date, annual depreciation expense, accumulated depreciation, and ending book value. Use the straight-line method of calculating depreciation.

PROBLEM 22-4 Recording work sheet adjustments and journal entries for depreciation expense

Landmark Contractors' general ledger has the following accounts and balances on December 31 of the current year.

PARTIAL GENERAL LEDGER

Account Title	Balance Debit	Balance Credit
Office Equipment	$ 8,740.00	—
Accumulated Depreciation—Office Equipment	—	$2,130.00
Store Equipment	37,820.00	—
Accumulated Depreciation—Store Equipment	—	7,564.00
Depreciation Expense—Office Equipment	—	—
Depreciation Expense—Store Equipment	—	—

INSTRUCTIONS:

1. Record the account titles and balances in a work sheet's Account Title and Trial Balance columns for the current year ended December 31.

2. Record on the work sheet the adjustments for estimated depreciation for the year. Annual depreciation expenses are office equipment, $1,150.00, and store equipment, $1,890.00.

3. Journalize the adjusting entries on page 13 of a general journal.

PROBLEM 22-5 Journalizing the disposing of plant assets

Horizon Company records plant assets in two accounts: **Office Equipment** and **Store Equipment**.

INSTRUCTIONS:

Journalize the following transactions completed during 19X2. Use page 12 of a general journal and a cash receipts journal. Source documents are abbreviated as follows: memorandum, M; receipt, R.

Feb. 1. Received cash from sale of office equipment, $1,400.00: original cost, $10,700.00; total accumulated depreciation through December 31, 19X1, $9,000.00; additional depreciation to be recorded through February 1, 19X2, $300.00. M25 and R43.

Apr. 1. Received cash from sale of store equipment, $500.00: original cost, $5,200.00; total accumulated depreciation through December 31, 19X1, $4,500.00; additional depreciation to be recorded through April 1, 19X2, $200.00. M52 and R74.

June 1. Received cash from sale of office equipment, $200.00: original cost, $3,800.00; total accumulated depreciation through December 31, 19X1, $3,500.00; additional depreciation to be recorded through June 1, 19X2, $100.00. M97 and R133.

Aug. 1. Received cash from sale of office equipment, $1,200.00: original cost, $8,100.00; total accumulated depreciation through December 31, 19X1, $6,120.00; additional depreciation to be recorded through August 1, 19X2, $400.00. M132 and R206.

Oct. 1. Received cash from sale of store equipment, $600.00: original cost, $1,450.00; total accumulated depreciation through December 31, 19X1, $1,050.00; additional depreciation to be recorded through October 1, 19X2, $50.00. M197 and R289.

PROBLEM 22-6 Calculating depreciation expense using the straight-line and declining-balance methods

The following data, relating to a drill press, are obtained from the accounting records of Machine Works, Inc.

Original cost	$4,000.00
Estimated salvage value	300.00
Estimated useful life	4 years

INSTRUCTIONS:

Prepare a depreciation table similar to Illustration 22-13 showing annual depreciation expense, beginning book value, and ending book value. Calculate these amounts using the straight-line and the declining-balance methods. Use twice the straight-line rate for the declining-balance method.

PROBLEM 22-7 Calculating and journalizing property tax

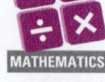

Excel Graphics has real property with an assessed value of $450,000. The tax rate in the city where the property is located is 2.5% of assessed value.

INSTRUCTIONS:

1. Calculate Excel Graphics' total annual property tax for the current year.
2. Journalize the payment of the property tax on March 1. Use page 4 of a cash payments journal. Check No. 187.

 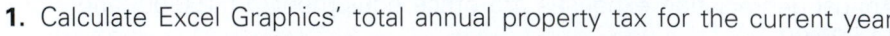

MASTERY PROBLEM 22-M Calculating depreciation expense and book value of plant assets; journalizing entries affecting plant assets

Taylor Lumber records plant assets in two accounts: Office Equipment and Store Equipment. Taylor Lumber owns the following plant assets.

Plant Asset	Asset Account	Date Bought	Original Cost	Estimated Salvage Value	Estimated Useful Life
1	Office Equipment	Apr. 1, 19X1	$ 7,300.00	$ 700.00	6 years
2	Store Equipment	July 1, 19X1	6,900.00	600.00	9 years
3	Store Equipment	Oct. 1, 19X1	5,700.00	840.00	3 years
4	Store Equipment	Aug. 1, 19X2	2,600.00	500.00	5 years
5	Store Equipment	Sept. 1, 19X2	3,100.00	700.00	4 years
6	Office Equipment	Nov. 1, 19X3	10,800.00	1,800.00	10 years
7	Office Equipment	May 1, 19X4	1,400.00	200.00	4 years
8	Office Equipment	July 1, 19X4	22,500.00	1,500.00	14 years

INSTRUCTIONS:

1. Calculate each plant asset's depreciation expense for the year ended December 31, 19X4. Use the straight-line method of calculating depreciation. Round amounts to the nearest cent.
2. Calculate each plant asset's ending book value as of December 31, 19X4.
3. Journalize the two adjusting entries for depreciation expense for the year ended December 31, 19X4. Use page 13 of a general journal.
4. Journalize the following transaction. Use page 4 of a cash receipts journal. Source documents are abbreviated as follows: memorandum, M; receipt, R.

19X5
Apr. 2. Received cash from sale of plant asset number 2, $4,200.00: original cost, $6,900.00; total accumulated depreciation through December 31, 19X4, $2,450.00; additional depreciation to be recorded through April 2, 19X5, $175.00. M125 and R193.

CHALLENGE PROBLEM 22-C Calculating depreciation expense and book value of plant assets; journalizing entries affecting plant assets

Candlewick Company records plant assets in two accounts: Office Equipment and Store Equipment. Candlewick Company owns the following plant assets.

Plant Asset	Asset Account	Date Bought	Original Cost	Estimated Salvage Value	Estimated Useful Life
1	Office Equipment	Jan. 1, 19X1	$ 1,750.00	$ 250.00	5 years
2	Store Equipment	Jan. 1, 19X2	7,250.00	1,000.00	5 years
3	Store Equipment	Apr. 1, 19X2	12,500.00	1,500.00	10 years
4	Office Equipment	July 1, 19X2	3,500.00	300.00	4 years
5	Office Equipment	Apr. 1, 19X3	4,400.00	500.00	6 years
6	Store Equipment	July 1, 19X3	1,400.00	200.00	3 years
7	Store Equipment	July 1, 19X5	6,050.00	800.00	7 years
8	Office Equipment	Oct. 1, 19X5	3,000.00	600.00	8 years

INSTRUCTIONS:

1. Calculate each plant asset's depreciation expense for the year ended December 31, 19X5. Use the straight-line method of calculating depreciation. Round amounts to the nearest cent.

2. Calculate each plant asset's total accumulated depreciation as of December 31, 19X5.

3. Calculate each plant asset's ending book value as of December 31, 19X5.

4. Journalize the two adjusting entries for depreciation expense for the year ended December 31, 19X5. Use page 13 of a general journal.

5. Journalize the following transactions completed during 19X6. Use page 25 of a cash receipts journal. Continue using page 13 of the general journal. Source documents are abbreviated as follows: memorandum, M; receipt, R.

19X6

Mar. 15. Sold plant asset number 1, $250.00. R72.

Apr. 30. Received cash from sale of plant asset number 2, $2,000.00. M97 and R115.

Aug. 1. Sold plant asset number 4, $850.00. M173 and R209.

Automated Accounting for Depreciation

Celluphone's manual methods for calculating depreciation and preparing depreciation schedules are described in Chapter 22. Integrating Automated Accounting Topic 9 describes procedures for using automated accounting software to calculate depreciation and prepare depreciation schedules for the straight-line and double declining-balance methods. The Automated Accounting Problems contain instructions for using automated accounting software to solve Application Problem 22-6, Mastery Problem 22-M, and Challenge Problem 22-C, Chapter 22.

PREPARING DEPRECIATION SCHEDULES

A separate record is kept for each plant asset when using either a manual or an automated accounting system. The arrangement of a plant asset record may vary for different businesses. Celluphone bought two plant assets during the current year.

Plant Asset	Description	Date Bought	Original Cost	Estimated Salvage Value	Estimated Useful Life
1	Printer	01/02/X1	$ 820.00	$ 100.00	5 Years
2	Computer	07/01/X1	4,600.00	1,000.00	4 Years

Straight-Line Depreciation Method

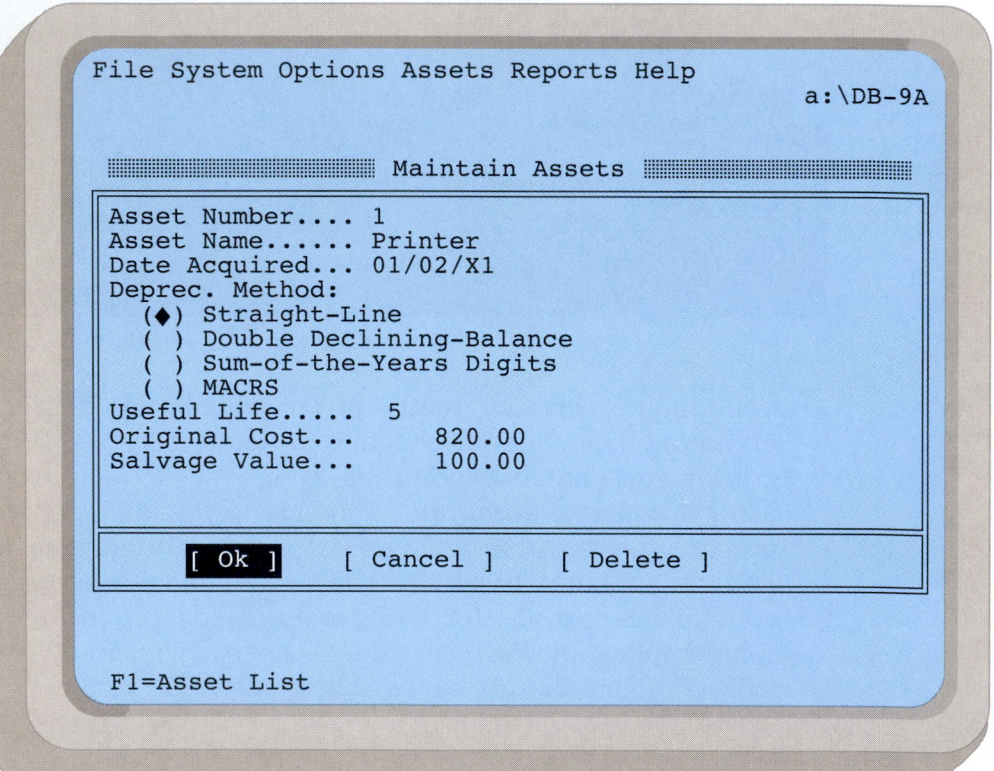
To prepare a plant asset record for each of Celluphone's plant assets using automated accounting software, the second module, Payroll/Assets/Bank Rec., must be loaded. The Payroll/Assets/Bank Rec. command is selected from the File menu. File is again selected from the menu bar. The Open Data File command is then chosen to retrieve the plant assets data base from the template disk.

The Assets menu command is selected from the menu bar. The Maintain Assets command is then chosen to display the data entry window for keying plant asset data. The information is keyed and the straight-line method is selected. Illustration T9-1 shows a completed data entry window for Celluphone's printer. The second plant asset information is entered in the same way.

ILLUSTRATION T9-1

A completed data entry for a plant asset

```
File System Options Assets Reports Help
                                              a:\DB-9A

▒▒▒▒▒▒▒▒▒▒▒▒▒▒▒▒▒▒▒  Maintain Assets  ▒▒▒▒▒▒▒▒▒▒▒▒▒▒▒▒▒▒▒

Asset Number.... 1
Asset Name...... Printer
Date Acquired... 01/02/X1
Deprec. Method:
  (♦) Straight-Line
  ( ) Double Declining-Balance
  ( ) Sum-of-the-Years Digits
  ( ) MACRS
Useful Life.....  5
Original Cost...      820.00
Salvage Value...      100.00


      [ Ok ]        [ Cancel ]       [ Delete ]


F1=Asset List
```

After all plant asset data have been keyed, the Reports menu is selected from the menu bar. The Plant Assets Report command is then chosen and printed, as shown in Illustration T9-2, and filed for future reference.

To prepare the straight-line depreciation schedule, the Reports menu is selected from the menu bar. The Depreciation Schedule is chosen from the Reports menu. As Celluphone wants depreciation schedules prepared for both plant assets, the *OK* check box is

Plant Asset Report for straight-line depreciation method

```
                    Celluphone, Inc.
                   Plant Assets Report
                      12/31/X1
------------------------------------------------------------------------------
Asset        Asset              Date   Depr. Useful  Original      Salvage
Number       Name           Acquired   Meth.  Life      Cost         Value
------------------------------------------------------------------------------
  1          Printer        01/02/X1    SL     5       820.00        100.00
  2          Computer       07/01/X1    SL     4      4600.00       1000.00
                                                      ----------
             Total                                    5420.00
                                                      ==========
```

selected from the Reports Selection Options menu to display the depreciation schedules. The schedules are printed and filed for future reference. The schedules for both plant assets are shown in Illustration T9-3.

Depreciation Schedules for straight-line depreciation method

```
                 Celluphone, Inc.
               Depreciation Schedule
                   12/31/X1

Asset Number..........1
Asset Name...........Printer
Date Acquired........01/02/X1
Depreciation Method...Straight-Line
Useful Life...........5
Original Cost........    820.00
Salvage Value........    100.00
```

Year	Annual Depreciation	Accumulated Depreciation	Book Value
19X1	144.00	144.00	676.00
19X2	144.00	288.00	532.00
19X3	144.00	432.00	388.00
19X4	144.00	576.00	244.00
19X5	144.00	720.00	100.00

```
Asset Number..........2
Asset Name...........Computer
Date Acquired........07/01/X1
Depreciation Method...Straight-Line
Useful Life...........4
Original Cost........   4600.00
Salvage Value........   1000.00
```

Year	Annual Depreciation	Accumulated Depreciation	Book Value
19X1	450.00	450.00	4150.00
19X2	900.00	1350.00	3250.00
19X3	900.00	2250.00	2350.00
19X4	900.00	3150.00	1450.00
19X5	450.00	3600.00	1000.00

Other Depreciation Methods

To prepare Celluphone's plant asset records using other depreciation methods, follow the same steps as those for straight-line depreciation. However, push the appropriate depreciation button in the data entry window for keying plant asset data.

OPTIONAL PROBLEM DB-9A

Celluphone's plant asset data base is on the accounting textbook template. If you wish to prepare Celluphone's depreciation schedules using automated accounting software, load the *Automated Accounting 6.0* or higher software and select the second module, Payroll/Assets/Bank Rec. Select Data Base 9A (DB-9A) from the template disk. Read the Problem Instructions screen. Follow the procedures described to prepare Celluphone's depreciation schedules.

AUTOMATED ACCOUNTING PROBLEMS

AUTOMATING APPLICATION PROBLEM 22-6 Preparing depreciation schedules

The following data, relating to a drill press bought on January 3 of the current year, are obtained from the accounting records of Machine Works, Inc. (This information is found in Application Problem 22-6, Chapter 22.)

Plant Asset	Description	Date Bought	Original Cost	Estimated Salvage Value	Estimated Useful Life
1	Drill Press	01/03/--	$4,000.00	$300.00	4 Years

INSTRUCTIONS:

1. Load the *Automated Accounting 6.0* or higher software. Bring up the Payroll/Assets/Bank Rec. module.
2. Select data base F22-6 (First-Year Course Application Problem 22-6) from the accounting textbook template. Read the Problem Instructions screen.
3. Pull down the File menu and choose the Save As menu command. Key the path to the drive and directory that contains your data files. Save the data base with a file name of XXX226 (where XXX are your initials).
4. Key the data for the plant asset for the straight-line depreciation method.
5. Display/Print a plant asset report for the straight-line depreciation method.
6. Display/Print a depreciation schedule.

AUTOMATING MASTERY PROBLEM 22-M Preparing depreciation schedules

INSTRUCTIONS:

1. Load the *Automated Accounting 6.0* or higher software. Bring up the Payroll/Assets/Bank Rec. module.
2. Select data base F22-M from the accounting textbook template. Read the Problem Instructions screen.
3. Pull down the File menu and choose the Save As menu command. Key the path to the drive and directory that contains your data files. Save the data base with a file name of XXX22M (where XXX are your initials).
4. Use the plant asset data given in Mastery Problem 22-M, Chapter 22. Key the data for the plant assets for the straight-line depreciation method.
5. Display/Print a plant asset report for the straight-line depreciation method.
6. Display/Print a depreciation schedule.

AUTOMATED

AUTOMATING CHALLENGE PROBLEM 22-C Preparing depreciation schedules

INSTRUCTIONS:

1. Load the *Automated Accounting 6.0* or higher software. Bring up the Payroll/Assets/Bank Rec. module.

2. Select data base F22-C from the accounting textbook template. Read the Problem Instructions screen.

3. Pull down the File menu and choose the Save As menu command. Key the path to the drive and directory that contains your data files. Save the data base with a file name of XXX22C (where XXX are your initials).

4. Use the plant asset data given in Challenge Problem 22-C, Chapter 22. Key the data for the plant assets for the straight-line depreciation method.

5. Display/Print a plant asset report for the straight-line depreciation method.

6. Display/Print a depreciation schedule.

23

Accounting for Inventory

ENABLING PERFORMANCE TASKS

After studying Chapter 23, you will be able to:

a Define accounting terms related to inventory.

b Identify accounting concepts and practices related to inventory.

c Determine the cost of merchandise inventory using the fifo, lifo, and weighted-average inventory costing methods.

d Estimate the cost of merchandise inventory using the gross profit method of estimating inventory.

TERMS PREVIEW

periodic inventory • perpetual inventory • inventory record • stock record • stock ledger • first-in, first-out inventory costing method • last-in, first-out inventory costing method • weighted-average inventory costing method • gross profit method of estimating inventory

Merchandise inventory on hand is typically the largest asset of a merchandising business. Successful businesses must have merchandise available for sale that customers want. A business, therefore, needs controls that assist managers in maintaining a merchandise inventory of sufficient quantity, variety, and price.

The cost of merchandise inventory is reported on both the balance sheet and the income statement. An accurate cost of merchandise inventory is required to correctly report current assets and retained earnings on the balance sheet. The accuracy of the inventory cost will also assure that gross profit and net income are reported correctly on the income statement. (CONCEPT: *Adequate Disclosure*)

CONTROLLING THE QUANTITY OF MERCHANDISE INVENTORY

To determine the most efficient size of inventory, a business makes frequent analysis of purchases, sales, and inventory records. Many businesses fail because too much or too little merchandise inventory is kept on hand. A business that stocks merchandise that does not satisfy the demand of its customers is also likely to fail.

A merchandise inventory that is larger than needed may decrease the net income of a business for several reasons.

1. Excess inventory requires that a business spend money for expensive store and warehouse space.
2. Excess inventory uses capital that could be invested in other assets to earn a profit for the business.
3. Excess inventory requires that a business spend money for expenses, such as taxes and insurance premiums, that increase with the cost of the merchandise inventory.
4. Excess inventory may become obsolete and unsaleable.

Merchandise inventory that is smaller than needed may also decrease the net income of a business for several reasons.

1. Sales may be lost to competitors if items wanted by customers are not on hand.
2. Sales may be lost to competitors if there is an insufficient variety of merchandise to satisfy customers.
3. When a business frequently orders small quantities of an item, the price paid is often more per unit than when merchandise is ordered in large quantities.

DETERMINING THE QUANTITY OF MERCHANDISE INVENTORY

The quantity of items in inventory at the end of a fiscal period must be determined in order to calculate the cost of merchandise sold.

Two principal methods are used to determine the quantity of each item of merchandise on hand.

1. A merchandise inventory determined by counting, weighing, or measuring items of merchandise on hand is called a **periodic inventory.** A periodic inventory is also referred to as a physical inventory.
2. A merchandise inventory determined by keeping a continuous record of increases, decreases, and balance on hand is called a **perpetual inventory.** A perpetual inventory is also referred to as a book inventory.

Periodic Inventory

Counting, weighing, or measuring merchandise on hand for a periodic inventory is commonly referred to as "taking an inventory." Employees count each item of inventory and record the quantities on special forms. To assure an accurate and complete count, a business will typically be closed during the periodic inventory. Taking an inventory is often a large and expensive task. Therefore, a periodic inventory usually is taken only at the end of a fiscal period.

Businesses frequently establish their fiscal period to end when inventory is at a minimum because it takes less time to count a smaller inventory. For example, a department store may take an inventory at the end of December. The amount of merchandise on hand is smaller because of holiday sales. Few purchases of additional merchandise are made in December after the holiday sales. All of these activities make the merchandise inventory smaller at the end of December.

Celluphone has found from past experience that relatively few sales are made after the holiday season. Thus, the quantity of merchandise on hand is relatively small at the end of December. Therefore, Celluphone ends its annual fiscal period on December 31. Celluphone takes its periodic inventory during the last week of December.

A form used during a periodic inventory to record information about each item of merchandise on hand is called an **inventory record.** The inventory record has space to record the stock number, unit description, number of units on hand, unit price, and total cost of each item. The inventory record used by Celluphone is shown in Illustration 23-1 on page 627.

Information is typed in the Stock Number column and Description column before the periodic inventory begins. Employees taking the inventory write the actual count in the No. of Units on Hand column. Inventory records are then sent to the accounting department where the Unit Price and Total Cost columns are completed.

Perpetual Inventory

Some businesses keep inventory records that show continuously the quantity on hand for each kind of merchandise. A form used to show the kind of merchandise, quantity received, quantity sold, and

FYI

Businesses often take inventory when stock levels are at a minimum because it takes less time to count a smaller inventory.

MULTICULTURAL AWARENESS

Ancient China

By approximately 1,000 B.C. the Chinese had developed one of the most sophisticated accounting systems in the world. The Chao Dynasty ruled China from 1122 to 256 B.C. and oversaw a period of expansion of territory and a Golden Age in literature and philosophy. The famous philosopher **Confucius**, who lived during this dynasty, was said to have been a government recordkeeper. During this period the Chinese used a system of currency and had a central bank. The Office of the Superintendent of Records furnished compilations of receipts and payments, maps, tabulations of the number of workers in each occupation, kinds and quantities of production tools, and estimates of natural resources. Similar kinds of records are kept by governments today.

ILLUSTRATION 23-1   Inventory record

INVENTORY RECORD

DATE _December 31, 19--_   ITEM _Antennas_

1	2	3	4	5
STOCK NUMBER	DESCRIPTION	NO. OF UNITS ON HAND	UNIT PRICE	TOTAL COST
3410	Standard	32	9.80	313.60
3420	Deluxe	28	10@12.20	
			18@12.50	347.00
3600	Retractable	13	21.40	278.20
	Total			938.80

balance on hand is called a **stock record**. A separate stock record is prepared for each kind of merchandise on hand. A file of stock records for all merchandise on hand is called a **stock ledger.** A stock record for Celluphone is shown in Illustration 23-2.

ILLUSTRATION 23-2   Stock record

STOCK RECORD

Description _Hand Sets_   Stock No. _4516B_
Reorder _40_   Minimum _10_   Location _Aisle F_

1	2	3	4	5	6	7
	INCREASES			DECREASES		BALANCE
DATE	PURCHASE INVOICE NO.	QUANTITY	DATE	SALES INVOICE NO.	QUANTITY	QUANTITY
Jan. 1						23
			Jan. 12	3269	15	8
Feb. 1	9281	40				48
			Feb. 4	3461	5	43
			Feb. 12	3489	10	33
			Feb. 20	3511	8	25

A perpetual inventory system provides day-to-day information about the quantity of merchandise on hand. The minimum balance allowed before a reorder must be placed is also shown on each stock record. The minimum balance is the quantity of merchandise that will typically last until the ordered merchandise can be received from the vendors. When the quantity falls below the minimum, additional merchandise is ordered in the quantity shown on the reorder line of the stock record. A stock record shows the quantity but usually not the cost of the merchandise.

When a perpetual inventory of merchandise is kept, entries are made on the stock records to show the following information.

1. Increases in the quantity on hand when additional merchandise is received.
2. Decreases in the quantity on hand when merchandise is sold.
3. The balance on hand after each increase or decrease is recorded. The quantity of merchandise on hand is the last amount in the Balance column of a stock record.

When a perpetual inventory is kept, errors may be made in recording or calculating amounts. Also, some stock records may be incorrect because merchandise is taken from stock and not recorded on stock records. A customary practice is to take a periodic inventory at least once a fiscal period. The periodic inventory is then compared with the perpetual inventory records. The perpetual records are corrected to reflect the actual quantity on hand as determined by the periodic inventory.

Perpetual Inventory Using a Computer

Many merchandising businesses use a computer to keep perpetual inventory records. Special cash registers and checkout counters are used. The checkout counters have devices to read the Universal Product Codes (UPC codes) marked on products. An example of a UPC code is shown in Illustration 23-3.

ILLUSTRATION 23-3

Universal Product Code (UPC code)

9 780538 123457   90000

A stock ledger for all merchandise on hand is stored in the computer. Each time a UPC code is read at the checkout counter, the computer checks the stock ledger to obtain the product description and the sales price. The product description and price are then displayed on the cash register. At the same time, the computer reduces the units on hand to reflect the item sold. In complex inventory systems the computer is programmed to periodically check the quantities in the stock ledger and print a list of the items that need to be reordered.

Audit Your Understanding

1. What are the two principal methods used to determine the quantity of each item of merchandise on hand?
2. When are periodic inventories usually taken?
3. What does UPC represent?

DETERMINING THE COST OF MERCHANDISE INVENTORY

Costs are not recorded on inventory records at the time a periodic inventory is taken. After the quantities of merchandise on hand are counted, purchase invoices are used to find merchandise unit prices. The total costs are then calculated using the quantities and unit prices recorded on the inventory records. Most businesses use one of three inventory costing methods to calculate the cost of merchandise inventory: (1) first-in, first-out, (2) last-in, first-out, or (3) weighted-average.

First-In, First-Out Inventory Costing Method

The account Merchandise Inventory is shown on both the balance sheet and the income statement. Therefore, an accurate value is important to financial reporting.

The term fifo is an acronym. An acronym is a word formed by using the first letter or letters of a longer group of words.

Celluphone takes a periodic inventory at the end of each fiscal period. The quantity of each item on hand is recorded on an inventory record. The inventory records are sent to the accounting department to determine the unit price and total cost of each item on hand. Celluphone uses the most recent invoices for purchases to determine the unit price of an item. The earliest invoices for purchases, therefore, are used to determine the cost of merchandise sold.

Using the price of merchandise purchased first to calculate the cost of merchandise sold first is called the **first-in, first-out inventory costing method.** The cost of the ending inventory, therefore, consists of the most recent cost of merchandise purchased. The first-in, first-out method is frequently abbreviated as *fifo* (the first letter of each of the four words). On December 31 a periodic inventory of Model 88 cellular phone batteries, Stock No. MS130, showed 16 batteries on hand. Purchase information for this item during the fiscal period is shown below.

Purchase Dates	Units	Unit Price	Total Cost
January 1, beginning inventory..........	4	$40.00	$ 160.00
April 14, purchases....................	10	42.00	420.00
June 22, purchases....................	8	44.00	352.00
September 6, purchases...............	16	45.00	720.00
November 28, purchases	12	48.00	576.00
Totals............................	50		$2,228.00

During the fiscal period, 34 batteries were sold. Using the fifo method, the cost of the 16 inventory units on hand on December 31 is determined using the most recent unit prices. The most recent unit prices are $48.00 and $45.00. The inventory cost using the fifo method is calculated as shown below.

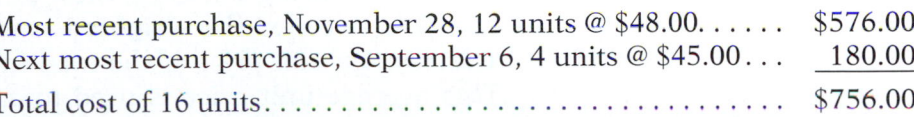

Most recent purchase, November 28, 12 units @ $48.00......	$576.00
Next most recent purchase, September 6, 4 units @ $45.00...	180.00
Total cost of 16 units................................	$756.00

The most recent purchase, November 28, is used to cost 12 of the 16 units in ending inventory. The remaining 4 units in ending inventory are costed using the next most recent purchase, September 6.

On the inventory record, the 16 batteries are shown as having a total cost of $756.00. The cost of the 34 batteries sold is calculated as shown on the following page.

	Total Purchases	−	Cost of Ending Inventory	=	Cost of Merchandise Sold
	$2,228.00	−	$756.00	=	$1,472.00

Last-In, First-Out Inventory Costing Method

FYI

Acronyms are often pronounced as words. The acronyms "fifo" and "lifo" are pronounced as words using a long "i" sound and a long "o" sound.

Using the price of merchandise purchased last to calculate the cost of merchandise sold first is called the **last-in, first-out inventory costing method.** The last-in, first-out method is frequently abbreviated as *lifo.* This method is based on the idea that the most recent costs of merchandise should be charged against current revenue. *(CONCEPT: Matching Expenses with Revenue)*

Using the lifo method, each item on the inventory records is recorded at the earliest prices paid for the merchandise. The lifo inventory cost for the 16 batteries previously described is calculated as shown below.

Beginning inventory, January 1, 4 units @ $40.00	$160.00
Next earliest purchase, April 14, 10 units @ $42.00	420.00
Next earliest purchase, June 22, 2 units @ $44.00	88.00
Total cost of 16 units.	$668.00

The earliest prices consist of the 4 units in the January 1 beginning inventory. The next earliest purchase, April 14, of 10 units is then used to cost 10 units in ending inventory. The remaining 2 units in ending inventory are costed using the next earliest purchase, June 22.

On the inventory record, the 16 batteries would show a total cost of $668.00. The cost of merchandise sold for the 34 batteries sold would be recorded as $1,560.00, the difference between total purchases, $2,228.00, and the cost of ending inventory, $668.00.

Weighted-Average Inventory Costing Method

Using the average cost of beginning inventory plus merchandise purchased during a fiscal period to calculate the cost of merchandise sold is called the **weighted-average inventory costing method.** The average unit price of the total inventory available is calculated. This average unit price is used to calculate both ending inventory and cost of merchandise sold. The average cost of merchandise is then charged against current revenue. *(CONCEPT: Matching Expenses with Revenue)*

Using the weighted-average method, the inventory is costed at the average price per unit of the beginning inventory plus the cost of all purchases during the fiscal year. The weighted-average inventory cost for the 16 batteries previously described is calculated as shown on the following page.

Weighted-Average Inventory Costing Method Quantity on Hand, 16 Units			
Purchase			
Date	Units	Unit Price	Total Cost
January 1, beginning inventory........	4	$40.00	$160.00
April 14, purchases..................	10	42.00	420.00
June 22, purchases	8	44.00	352.00
September 6, purchases	16	45.00	720.00
November 28, purchases.............	12	48.00	576.00
Totals......................	50		$2,228.00

Total of Beginning Inventory and Purchases	÷	Total Units	=	Weighted-Average Price per Unit
$2,228.00	÷	50	=	$44.56

Units in Ending Inventory	×	Weighted-Average Price per Unit	=	Cost of Ending Inventory
16	×	$44.56	=	$712.96

On the inventory record, the 16 batteries would show a total cost of $712.96. The cost of merchandise sold for the 34 units sold would be recorded as $1,515.04, the difference between total purchases, $2,228.00, and the cost of ending inventory, $712.96. Since the weighted-average method uses an average unit price, the same unit price may be used to calculate the cost of both ending inventory and cost of merchandise sold. Thus, the cost of merchandise sold could also be calculated as shown below.

Units Sold	×	Weighted-Average Price per Unit	=	Cost of Merchandise Sold
34	×	$44.56	=	$1,515.04

A business usually determines the order in which products are sold based on the type of inventory. A grocery store, for example, must sell its earliest purchases first. A hardware store, however, could sell its most recent purchases first. The inventory costing method used to calculate the cost of merchandise sold should not, however, be determined by the order in which items are sold. A business should choose the inventory costing method that provides its managers with the best accounting information.

A comparison of the three inventory methods used in determining the cost of merchandise sold is shown in Illustration 23-4 on page 632.

The fifo method gives the highest possible ending inventory cost and the lowest cost of merchandise sold. The lifo method gives the lowest possible ending inventory cost and the highest cost of merchandise sold. The weighted-average method gives ending inventory cost and cost of merchandise sold between fifo and lifo. As the cost of merchandise sold increases, gross profit and net income decrease.

ILLUSTRATION 23-4   Comparison of inventory costing methods

	Fifo	Lifo	Weighted Average
Cost of Merchandise Sold:			
Merchandise Inventory, Jan. 1	$ 160.00	$ 160.00	$ 160.00
Net Purchases	2,068.00	2,068.00	2,068.00
Merchandise Available for Sale	$2,228.00	$2,228.00	$2,228.00
Less Ending Inventory, Dec. 31	756.00	668.00	712.96
Cost of Merchandise Sold.	$1,472.00	$1,560.00	$1,515.04
Relative Cost of Ending Inventory	highest	lowest	intermediate
Relative Cost of Merchandise Sold	lowest	highest	intermediate

Thus, net income is highest under the fifo method, lowest under the lifo method, and intermediate under the weighted-average method.

All three inventory costing methods are acceptable accounting practices. However, a business should select one method and use

■ Bert N. Mitchell ■
MITCHELL, TITUS & CO.

Bert N. Mitchell is the co-founder and CEO of Mitchell, Titus & Co., the nation's largest minority-controlled CPA firm. Mitchell and his partner, Robert P. Titus, founded the firm in 1974 and built it to become a national leader among domestic CPA firms. Not only is it the largest minority-controlled CPA firm, but it also ranks among the top 40 out of 50,000 CPA firms in the U.S. The firm has more than 200 employees in offices in New York, Washington, D.C., and Philadelphia.

Mitchell is a native of Jamaica who came to America in 1958. While working full-time as a clerk, he went to school at the Bernard M. Baruch School of Business of the City University of New York. Although he originally wanted to become an engineer, he did so well in business courses that he turned to accounting instead.

Mitchell worked as a bookkeeper for a union and later as an accountant at Lucas, Tucker & Co., the oldest black accounting firm in the nation. Eventually he and Robert Titus joined to form their own firm.

In the firm's first years, Mitchell found that he could not always convince the people he wanted to come work for him. In fact, he

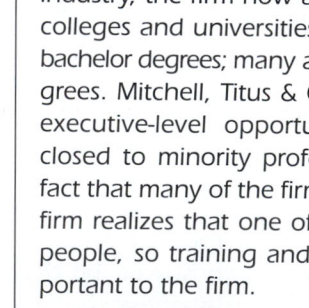

sometimes found it difficult to attract good people to the firm. He was also surprised that some clients would not pay on time. He said, "I always paid my bills on time and I expected my customers to do the same. I was surprised to find that that's not always the case."

Mitchell and Titus still manage the firm, but they recruit young talent to be sure the firm will grow and prosper. With its excellent record of growth and position in the industry, the firm now attracts top candidates from top colleges and universities. All the professional staff have bachelor degrees; many are CPAs and hold advanced degrees. Mitchell, Titus & Co. has provided a fast track to executive-level opportunities that were traditionally closed to minority professionals, as evidenced by the fact that many of the firm's partners are in their 30s. The firm realizes that one of its most important assets is its people, so training and personal development are important to the firm.

The firm has a very international feel. About 30% of the partnership's employees are not native-born Americans.

Mitchell advises young people to set high standards for themselves and then live up to those standards. He said, "Some people will tell you that you won't or can't make it. But you have to put your faith in yourself and your abilities."

Personal Visions in Business

that same method continuously for each fiscal period. Using the same inventory costing method for all fiscal periods provides financial statements that can be compared with other fiscal period statements. If a business changes inventory costing methods, part of the difference in gross profit and net income may be caused by the change in methods. Therefore, to provide financial statements that can be analyzed and compared with statements of other fiscal periods, the same inventory costing method should be used each fiscal period. *(CONCEPT: Consistent Reporting)*

ESTIMATING THE COST OF MERCHANDISE INVENTORY

Estimating inventory by using the previous years' percentage of gross profit on operations is called the **gross profit method of estimating inventory.** The gross profit method of estimating inventory is often used to estimate the cost of the monthly ending inventory. The ending inventory cost is used to prepare monthly financial statements. The gross profit method of estimating inventory provides a business with a method of calculating inventory costs that is less expensive than taking a periodic inventory or maintaining a perpetual inventory system.

Celluphone prepares an income statement at the end of each month. *(CONCEPT: Accounting Period Cycle)* To estimate the ending merchandise inventory on January 31, the following information is obtained.

Beginning inventory, January 1	$205,160.00
Net purchases for the period, January 1 to 31 . .	119,900.00
Net sales for the period, January 1 to 31	168,400.00
Gross profit on operations (percentage based on records of previous year's operations)	30.0%

Celluphone's fiscal year ends on December 31. A periodic inventory was taken on December 31 to provide an accurate cost of ending inventory for annual financial statements. The ending inventory on December 31 of the prior fiscal period, $205,160.00, is also the beginning inventory on January 1 for the next fiscal period. Therefore, the January 1 inventory cost, which has been verified by taking a periodic inventory, is used as the basis for estimating monthly ending inventory.

In the prior fiscal period, Celluphone's gross profit was 30.0% of its net sales. Celluphone can use this percentage in the current fiscal period to estimate the cost of merchandise sold and gross profit.

Four steps are followed to estimate the ending merchandise inventory for Celluphone on January 31.

1 Determine the cost of merchandise available for sale.

Beginning inventory, January 1	$205,160.00
Plus net purchases, January 1 to 31	+119,900.00
Equals cost of merchandise available for sale . . .	$325,060.00

2 Estimate the gross profit on operations.

Net sales for January 1 to 31	$168,400.00
Times previous year's gross profit percentage. . . .	× 30.0%
Equals estimated gross profit on operations	$ 50,520.00

3 Estimate the cost of merchandise sold.

Net sales for January 1 to 31	$168,400.00
Less estimated gross profit on operations (from Step 2)	−50,520.00
Equals estimated cost of merchandise sold	$117,880.00

4 Estimate the cost of ending merchandise inventory.

Cost of merchandise available for sale (from Step 1)	$325,060.00
Less estimated cost of merchandise sold (from Step 3)	−117,880.00
Equals estimated ending merchandise inventory	$207,180.00

The estimated ending merchandise inventory for Celluphone on January 31, $207,180.00, is used to prepare the January income statement. Celluphone's income statement prepared on January 31 is shown in Illustration 23-5.

ILLUSTRATION 23-5   Income statement with estimated inventory

Celluphone, Inc.
Income Statement
For Month Ended January 31, 19--

			% of Net Sales
Operating Revenue:			
Net Sales		$168,400.00	100.0
Cost of Merchandise Sold:			
Beginning Inventory, January 1.	$205,160.00		
Net Purchases.	119,900.00		
Merchandise Available for Sale	$325,060.00		
Less Est. Ending Inv., January 31 . . .	207,180.00		
Cost of Merchandise Sold.		117,880.00	70.0
Gross Profit on Operations		$ 50,520.00	30.0
Operating Expenses.		37,385.00	22.2
Net Income		$ 13,135.00	7.8

The beginning inventory on January 1, $205,160.00, is the ending inventory from the income statement on December 31 of the prior year. The amount of merchandise inventory purchased in January, $119,900.00, is obtained from the general ledger. By using the $207,180.00 estimate of ending merchandise inventory, Celluphone calculated its estimated cost of merchandise sold to be $117,880.00.

An estimated inventory is not completely accurate. The actual rate of gross profit on operations may not be exactly the percentage used in the estimate. Also, some merchandise may have been stolen or damaged. However, an estimated ending inventory is accurate enough for management to prepare a monthly income statement without taking the time to count the inventory. Businesses using a monthly estimate of the merchandise inventory usually take an annual periodic inventory. This is necessary in order to have accurate information for the end-of-year financial statements and tax reports.

Audit Your Understanding

1. Which inventory costing method uses the price of merchandise purchased first to calculate cost of merchandise sold?

2. Which inventory costing method uses the cost of merchandise purchased last to calculate cost of merchandise sold?

3. Which inventory costing method uses the average cost of beginning inventory plus merchandise purchased to calculate cost of merchandise sold?

4. How can a cost be assigned to merchandise inventory when it is too expensive to take a periodic inventory?

SUMMARY OF AN INVENTORY SYSTEM

At the end of the fiscal year, a merchandising business will usually determine the actual quantity of each item by taking a periodic inventory. The cost of merchandise inventory can be calculated using the fifo, lifo, or weighted-average inventory costing method, as shown in Illustration 23-6 on page 636.

A merchandising business can control its merchandise inventory by maintaining a continuous record of item quantities known as a perpetual inventory. At any time a business can determine the quantity of any inventory item on hand by examining the stock record in the stock ledger.

A merchandising business can also estimate monthly ending merchandise inventory costs by using the gross profit method of estimating inventory. The previous years' percentage of gross profit on operations is used to estimate the cost of merchandise inventory sold during the period. This estimate is subtracted from the merchandise available for sale to calculate the estimated ending merchandise inventory.

INVENTORY COSTS FOR DECEMBER 31
ENDING INVENTORY OF 16 UNITS

	Units	Unit Price	Total Cost
January 1, beginning inventory.........	4	$16.00	$ 64.00
March 3, purchases................	10	18.00	180.00
April 15, purchases................	10	20.00	200.00
June 17, purchases................	12	22.00	264.00
November 29, purchases.............	12	24.00	288.00
Totals	48		$996.00

Lifo Inventory
4 units @ $16.00 = $ 64.00
10 units @ $18.00 =   180.00
2 units @ $20.00 =   40.00

Total.........$284.00

Fifo Inventory
12 units @ $24.00 = $288.00
4 units @ $22.00 =   88.00

Total.........$376.00

Weighted-Average Inventory
Weighted-average price per unit:
$996.00 ÷ 48 = $20.75

Cost of ending inventory:
16 units × $20.75 = $332.00

ACCOUNTING TERMS

What is the meaning of each of the following?

1. **periodic inventory**
2. **perpetual inventory**
3. **inventory record**
4. **stock record**
5. **stock ledger**
6. **first-in, first-out inventory costing method**
7. **last-in, first-out inventory costing method**
8. **weighted-average inventory costing method**
9. **gross profit method of estimating inventory**

QUESTIONS FOR INDIVIDUAL STUDY

1. What item is typically the largest asset of a merchandising business?
2. Why do successful businesses need an effective inventory system?
3. Identify four reasons why a merchandise inventory that is larger than needed may decrease the net income of a business.
4. What two methods can be used to determine the quantity of each item of merchandise on hand?
5. When are periodic inventories normally taken?
6. How do inventory levels affect the period a business selects for its fiscal year? Why?
7. What action should a business take when the minimum balance is reached on a stock record?
8. When a perpetual inventory of merchandise is kept, entries are made on a stock record to show what information?
9. How is the accuracy of a perpetual inventory checked?
10. When the fifo method is used, how is the price of each kind of merchandise determined?
11. On what idea is the lifo method based?
12. When the weighted-average method is used, how is the cost of each kind of merchandise determined?
13. Which inventory costing method gives the highest cost of merchandise sold?
14. Why should a business select one inventory costing method and use that same method continuously for each fiscal period?
15. When neither a perpetual system is maintained nor a periodic inventory is taken, how can an ending merchandise inventory be determined that is accurate enough for a monthly income statement?

CASES FOR CRITICAL THINKING

CASE 1 Marshall Company uses the fifo method of costing its merchandise inventory. The manager is considering a change to the lifo method. Costs have increased steadily over the past three years. What effect will the change have on the following items? (1) The amount of net income on the income statement. (2) The amount of income taxes to be paid. (3) The quantity of each item of merchandise that must be kept in stock. Why?

CASE 2 The Craft Shop stocks many kinds of merchandise. The store has always taken a periodic inventory at the end of a fiscal year. The store has not kept a perpetual inventory because of the cost. However, the manager wants a reasonably accurate cost of merchandise inventory at the end of each month. The manager needs the amount to prepare monthly income statements and to help in making decisions about the business. What would you recommend?

DRILLS FOR UNDERSTANDING

DRILL 23-D1 Determining quantities of merchandise on hand using a perpetual inventory

Accounting records at Blette Company show the following inventory increases and decreases for one item of merchandise. Beginning inventory on July 1 was 68 units.

Increases		Decreases	
Date	**Quantity**	**Date**	**Quantity**
		July 5	34
		July 7	25
July 8	50		
		July 12	15
July 15	125		
		July 16	108
		July 23	52
July 28	100		

INSTRUCTIONS:

1. Use a stock record similar to the one in the chapter. Record the increases and decreases.
2. Calculate and record the balance of units on hand for each date a transaction occurred.

DRILL 23-D2 Calculating cost of ending inventory using fifo, lifo, and weighted-average methods

Accounting records at Zapata Company show the following beginning inventory and purchases for Inventory Item No. 87.

Purchase Dates	Units	Unit Price	Total Cost
January 1, beginning inventory	5	$20.00	$100.00
March 20, purchases	7	22.00	154.00
May 12, purchases	8	24.00	192.00
September 24, purchases	12	25.00	300.00
November 16, purchases	8	27.00	216.00
Total available	40		$962.00
Units sold	26		
Units in inventory, December 31	14		

INSTRUCTIONS:

Calculate the total cost of ending inventory on December 31 using the fifo, lifo, and weighted-average methods.

APPLICATION PROBLEMS   EPT(c,d)

PROBLEM 23-1 Determining cost of ending inventory using the fifo, lifo, and weighted-average methods

Accounting records at Wimberly Company show the following purchases and periodic inventory counts.

Model No.	Beginning Inventory January 1	First Purchase	Second Purchase	Third Purchase	Periodic Inventory Count December 31
A48	15 @ $12.00	24 @ $14.00	20 @ $15.00	16 @ $18.00	29
G56	6 @ $40.00	8 @ $42.00	4 @ $44.00	9 @ $45.00	12
Q392	24 @ $ 7.00	18 @ $ 6.00	30 @ $ 6.00	26 @ $ 5.00	42
S49	6 @ $40.00	8 @ $45.00	10 @ $45.00	5 @ $48.00	16
P32	14 @ $12.00	12 @ $10.00	22 @ $ 9.00	10 @ $ 8.00	30
K235	4 @ $30.00	16 @ $35.00	8 @ $35.00	10 @ $38.00	19

SPREADSHEET

INSTRUCTIONS:

1. Calculate the total cost of ending inventory on December 31 using the fifo method. The inventory cost for Model No. A48 is given as an example in the working papers that accompany this textbook. Use the following procedure to complete the form.

    a. Record the model number and number of units of each model on hand on December 31.

    b. Record the unit price of each model. When more than one unit price is used, list the units and unit prices on separate lines as shown in the example.

    c. Calculate the cost of ending inventory of each model, and write the amount in the Cost of Ending Inventory column.

    d. Add the amounts in the Cost of Ending Inventory column to calculate the total cost of ending inventory.

2. On another form in the working papers, calculate the total cost of ending inventory using the lifo method. Follow the steps given in Instruction 1.

3. On another form in the working papers, calculate the total cost of ending inventory using the weighted-average method. Use the following procedure.

    a. Record the model number and number of units of each model on hand on December 31.

    b. Calculate the weighted-average price per unit for each model. Round the amount per unit to the nearest cent. Write the amount in the Unit Price column.

    c. Calculate the cost of ending inventory of each model, and write the amount in the Cost of Ending Inventory column.

    d. Add the amounts in the Cost of Ending Inventory column to calculate the total cost of ending inventory.

4. Compare the total cost of ending inventory obtained in Instructions 1, 2, and 3. Which method, fifo, lifo, or weighted-average, resulted in the lowest cost of ending inventory?

PROBLEM 23-2 Estimating ending inventory using the gross profit method of estimating inventory

SPREADSHEET

MATHEMATICS

The following information is from the accounting records of two different companies for July of the current year.

	Companies	
	Daniel	Pearson
Beginning inventory, July 1	$12,900.00	$32,900.00
Net purchases for July	32,300.00	63,200.00
Net sales for July	76,500.00	98,500.00
Gross profit on operations as a percent of sales . . .	60.0%	45.0%
Operating expenses for July	25,400.00	37,600.00

INSTRUCTIONS:

1. For each company, estimate the ending inventory for July of the current year using the gross profit method of estimating inventory.

2. For each company, prepare an income statement for the month ended July 31 of the current year similar to the one shown in Illustration 23-5.

ENRICHMENT PROBLEMS   EPT(c,d)

MASTERY PROBLEM 23-M Determining cost of ending inventory using the fifo, lifo, and weighted-average methods

Accounting records at SummerSport Company show the following purchases and periodic inventory counts.

Model No.	Beginning Inventory January 1	First Purchase	Second Purchase	Third Purchase	Periodic Inventory Count December 31
23B2	4 @ $4.50	12 @ $4.75	8 @ $4.90	15 @ $5.20	22
13M2	3 @ $3.50	6 @ $3.30	2 @ $3.20	5 @ $3.10	8
45V23	23 @ $1.20	45 @ $1.25	35 @ $1.30	40 @ $1.40	35
90F2	12 @ $7.40	15 @ $7.50	16 @ $7.80	20 @ $7.90	30
10K3	32 @ $5.40	38 @ $5.10	19 @ $4.90	26 @ $4.80	40
34P2	2 @ $2.50	5 @ $2.70	4 @ $2.80	3 @ $3.00	4

INSTRUCTIONS:

1. Calculate the total cost of ending inventory on December 31 using the fifo method. The inventory cost for Model No. 23B2 is given as an example in the working papers that accompany this textbook. Use the following procedure to complete the form.

   a. Record the model number and number of units of each model on hand on December 31.

   b. Record the unit price of each model. When more than one unit price is used, list the units and unit prices on separate lines as shown in the example.

   c. Calculate the cost of ending inventory of each model, and write the amount in the Cost of Ending Inventory column.

   d. Add the amounts in the Cost of Ending Inventory column to calculate the total cost of ending inventory.

2. On another form in the working papers, calculate the total cost of ending inventory using the lifo method. Follow the steps given in Instruction 1.

3. On another form in the working papers, calculate the total cost of ending inventory using the weighted-average method. Use the following procedure.

   a. Record the model number and number of units of each model on hand on December 31.

   b. Calculate the weighted-average price per unit for each model. Round the amount per unit to the nearest cent. Write the amount in the Unit Price column.

   c. Calculate the cost of ending inventory of each model, and write the amount in the Cost of Ending Inventory column.

   d. Add the amounts in the Cost of Ending Inventory column to calculate the total cost of ending inventory.

4. Compare the total cost of ending inventory obtained in Instructions 1, 2, and 3. Which method, fifo, lifo, or weighted-average, resulted in the lowest cost of ending inventory?

CHALLENGE PROBLEM 23-C Determining the cost of merchandise inventory destroyed in a fire

A fire completely destroyed the warehouse of Fleming Lighting Company on the night of October 12. The accounting records of the company and $6,500 of merchandise inventory remained safe in the company's showroom. The company does not maintain a perpetual inventory system. The insurance company, therefore, has requested an estimate of the merchandise inventory destroyed in the fire.

The following income statement is for the previous fiscal year.

Fleming Lighting Company
Income Statement
For Year Ended July 31, 19--

Operating Revenue:		
Net Sales		$746,900.00
Cost of Merchandise Sold:		
Beginning Merchandise Inventory, Aug. 1	$ 72,430.00	
Net Purchases	291,300.00	
Merchandise Available for Sale	$363,730.00	
Less Ending Inventory, July 31	79,610.00	
Cost of Merchandise Sold		284,120.00
Gross Profit on Operations.		$462,780.00
Operating Expenses.		416,900.00
Net Income.		$ 45,880.00

The following additional financial information is obtained from the current year's accounting records.

Net purchases, August 1 to October 12	$ 70,190.00
Net sales, August 1 to October 12	162,790.00
Operating expenses, August 1 to October 12	87,280.00

INSTRUCTIONS:

1. Calculate the prior year's gross profit on operations as a percentage of net sales. Round the percentage calculation to the nearest whole percent.

2. Use the percentage calculated in Instruction 1 and the current year's financial information to calculate an estimate of the total merchandise inventory as of October 12.

3. To calculate the cost of the inventory destroyed in the fire, subtract the cost of the merchandise inventory from the estimate of the total merchandise inventory as of October 12.

4. Prepare an income statement for the period August 1 to October 12.

24

Accounting for Notes and Interest

ENABLING PERFORMANCE TASKS

After studying Chapter 24, you will be able to:

a Define accounting terms related to notes and interest.

b Identify accounting concepts and practices related to notes and interest.

c Calculate interest and maturity dates for notes.

d Analyze and record transactions for notes payable and notes receivable.

TERMS PREVIEW

promissory note • date of a note • time of a note • payee of a note • principal of a note • interest rate of a note • maturity date of a note • maker of a note • number of a note • interest • interest-bearing note • non-interest-bearing note • maturity value • creditor • notes payable • current liabilities • interest expense • bank discount • discounted note • proceeds • notes receivable • interest income • dishonored note

Cash is the primary medium of exchange for business transactions. *(CONCEPT: Unit of Measurement)* Cash is used to purchase merchandise and to pay salaries and other expenses. In turn, businesses receive cash when they sell their products or services and collect payment. The cash received for products or services can be used to purchase more merchandise and continue to pay salaries and other expenses. Thus, the business cycle continues.

Sometimes a business receives more cash from sales than is needed to pay for purchases and expenses. When this occurs, a business may deposit the extra cash in a bank or other financial institution for a short period. At other times, the receipt of cash from sales does not occur at the same time and in sufficient amounts to pay for needed purchases and expenses. When this occurs, a business needs to borrow additional cash or make arrangements with its vendors to delay payment for a period of time. Generally, when a bank or other business lends money to another business, the loan agreement is made in writing.

PROMISSORY NOTES

A written and signed promise to pay a sum of money at a specified time is called a **promissory note**. A promissory note frequently is referred to as a note.

FYI

Notes are usually issued either to borrow money or to gain an extension of time on an account.

Promissory notes are used when money is borrowed for a period of time from a bank or other lending agency. Sometimes a business requests a note from a customer who wants credit beyond the usual time given for sales on account. Notes have an advantage over oral promises and accounts receivable or payable. A note, like a check, can be endorsed and transferred to a bank in return for cash. Thus, the business can get its money before the note is due. Notes can also be useful in a court of law as written evidence of a debt. One form of a promissory note is shown in Illustration 24-1.

| **ILLUSTRATION 24-1** | A promissory note |

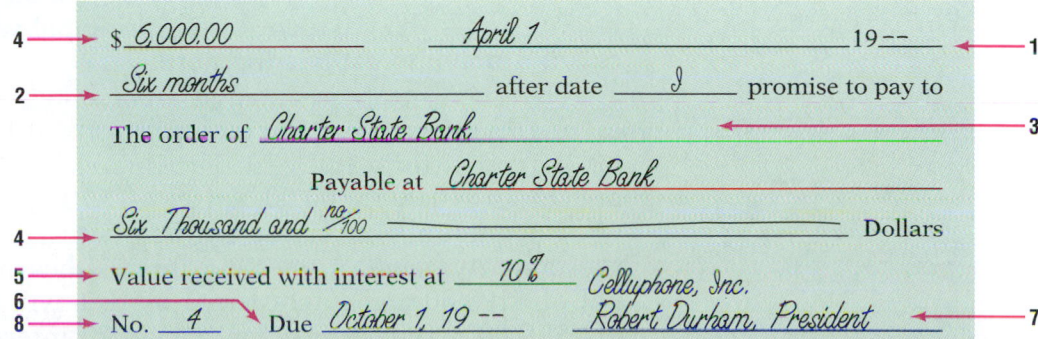

The terms defined below apply to the promissory note shown in Illustration 24-1.

	Term	Definition	Illustration
1	**Date of a note**	The day a note is issued.	April 1, 19--
2	**Time of a note**	The days, months, or years from the date of issue until a note is to be paid.	Six months
3	**Payee of a note**	The person or business to whom the amount of a note is payable.	Charter State Bank
4	**Principal of a note**	The original amount of a note. Sometimes referred to as face amount of a note.	$6,000.00
5	**Interest rate of a note**	The percentage of the principal that is paid for use of the money.	10%
6	**Maturity date of a note**	The date a note is due.	October 1, 19--
7	**Maker of a note**	The person or business who signs a note and thus promises to make payment.	Celluphone, Inc. Robert Durham, President
8	**Number of a note**	The number assigned by the maker to identify a specific note.	4

INTEREST ON PROMISSORY NOTES

An amount paid for the use of money for a period of time is called **interest**. Banks and other lending institutions generally charge interest on money loaned to their customers.

When businesses borrow money from banks, other lending institutions, or other businesses, promissory notes generally are prepared to provide written evidence of the transaction. Most promissory notes require the payment of interest. A promissory note that requires the payment of principal plus interest when the note is due is called an **interest-bearing note**. A promissory note that requires only the payment of the principal when the note is due is called a **non-interest-bearing note.**

The interest rate is stated as a percentage of the principal. *Interest at 10%* means that 10 cents will be paid for the use of each dollar borrowed for a full year. The interest on $100.00 for a full year at 10% is $10.00 ($100.00 × 10% = $10.00).

The amount that is due on the maturity date of a note is called the **maturity value.** A one-year interest-bearing note with a principal of $100.00 and interest rate of 10% will have a maturity value of $110.00 ($100.00 principal + $10.00 interest).

Sometimes partial payments on a note are made each month. This arrangement is particularly true when an individual buys a car and signs a note for the amount owed. The monthly payment includes part of the principal and part of the interest to be paid.

Calculating Interest

To calculate interest for one year, the principal is multiplied by the interest rate. The interest on a $1,000.00, 12% interest-bearing note for one year is calculated as shown below.

Principal	×	Interest Rate	×	Time in Years	=	Interest for One Year
$1,000.00	×	12%	×	1	=	$120.00

When the time of a note is expressed in months, the time used in calculating interest is stated as a fraction of 12 months. The interest on a $1,000.00, 12% interest-bearing note for three months (3/12 of a year) is calculated as shown below.

Principal	×	Interest Rate	×	Time as Fraction of Year	=	Interest for Fraction of Year
$1,000.00	×	12%	×	$\frac{3}{12}$	=	$\frac{\$360.00}{12} = \$30.00$

The time of a note is often stated as a number of days, such as 30 days, 60 days, or 90 days. When the time of a note is stated in days, the time used in calculating interest is stated as a fraction of 360 days. The interest on a $1,000.00, 12% interest-bearing note for 60 days (60/360 of a year) is calculated as shown below.

Principal	×	Interest Rate	×	Time as Fraction of Year	=	Interest for Fraction of Year
$1,000.00	×	12%	×	$\frac{60}{360}$	=	$\frac{\$7,200.00}{360} = \$20.00$

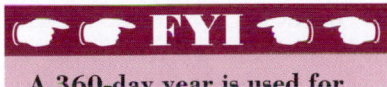
Agencies of the federal government generally use a 365-day year when calculating interest. Consumer interest is also generally calculated on a 365-day year. However, many banks use a 360-day year when calculating interest. Therefore, the interest calculations in this textbook use a 360-day year.

Calculating Maturity Date

The time between the date a note is issued and the date a note is due may be expressed in either years, months, or days. When the time of a note is stated in months, the maturity date is calculated by counting the number of months from the date of issuance. For example, a six-month note dated April 11 would be due on October 11.

When the time of a note is expressed in days, the maturity date is calculated by counting the exact number of days. The date the note is written is not counted, but the maturity date is counted. To calculate this maturity date, find the number of days remaining in the month the note was written. Then add the days in the following months until the total equals the required number of days. For example, a 60-day note dated March 3 is due on May 2. The maturity date is calculated as shown below.

March 3 through 31	28 days	(31 − 3 = 28)
April 1 through 30	30 days	
May 1 through 2	2 days	(Maturity date: May 2)
	60 days	

Audit Your Understanding

1. What is the difference between the maturity value of an interest-bearing note and a non-interest-bearing note?

2. What is the interest on $500 at 10% for a full year?

3. What is the maturity value of a $400 6-month note at 8%?

4. What is the maturity date of a 3-month note dated November 22?

5. What is the maturity date of a 60-day note dated March 23?

NOTES PAYABLE

A person or organization to whom a liability is owed is called a **creditor**. Promissory notes that a business issues to creditors are called **notes payable**. Liabilities due within a short time, usually within a year, are called **current liabilities**. Since notes payable generally are paid within one year, they are classified as current liabilities.

⟨☞ FYI ☞⟩

To calculate a maturity date, remember that April, June, September, and November have 30 days; all other months, except February, have 31 days.

Issuing a Note Payable to Borrow Money from a Bank

When a business issues a note payable, the principal or face amount of the note is credited to a liability account titled *Notes Payable*. A liability account has a normal credit balance. Therefore, the notes payable account is increased by a credit and decreased by a debit, as shown in the T account.

On April 1 Celluphone arranges to borrow money from its bank. A note payable is issued to the bank as evidence of the debt. The bank deposits the principal amount of the note in Celluphone's checking account.

Notes Payable	
Debit side	Credit side
	Normal balance
Decrease	Increase

April 1, 19--. Issued a 6-month, 10% note, $6,000.00. Note Payable No. 4.

```
            Cash
Apr. 1    6,000.00  |


       Notes Payable
                    |  Apr. 1    6,000.00
```

The bank retains the original of the note until Celluphone pays the maturity value. A copy of the note payable is the source document used by Celluphone to record this transaction. *(CONCEPT: Objective Evidence)*

Cash is debited for $6,000.00 to show the increase in the balance of this asset account. Notes Payable is credited for $6,000.00 to show the increase in the balance of this liability account. No entry is made for interest until a later date when the interest is paid.

The cash receipts journal entry to record this transaction is shown in Illustration 24-2.

ILLUSTRATION 24-2   Cash receipts journal entry to record cash received for the issuance of a note payable

					GENERAL		ACCOUNTS RECEIVABLE CREDIT	SALES CREDIT	SALES TAX PAYABLE		SALES DISCOUNT DEBIT	CASH DEBIT	
	DATE	ACCOUNT TITLE	DOC. NO.	POST. REF.	DEBIT	CREDIT			DEBIT	CREDIT			
6	1	Notes Payable	NP4			6 000 00						6 000 00	6
7													7
8													8
9													9

CASH RECEIPTS JOURNAL — PAGE *13*

```
      Interest Expense
Debit side        |  Credit side
Normal balance    |
Increase          |  Decrease
```

Paying Principal and Interest on a Note Payable at Maturity

When a note payable reaches its maturity date, the maker of the note pays the maturity value to the payee. The maturity value of a note is the principal (original amount borrowed) plus the interest that has accrued during the time of the note. The interest accrued on money borrowed is called **interest expense.**

The interest accrued on a note payable is debited to an expense account titled *Interest Expense.* An expense account has a normal debit balance. Therefore, the interest expense account is increased by a debit and decreased by a credit, as shown in the T account.

Interest expense is a financial expense rather than an expense of the business' normal operations. Therefore, Interest Expense is listed in a classification titled *Other Expenses* in a chart of accounts.

Celluphone paid the six-month note payable it had issued on April 1.

October 1, 19--. Paid cash for the maturity value of Note Payable No. 4: principal, $6,000.00, plus interest, $300.00; total, $6,300.00. Check No. 573.

Notes Payable

Oct. 1	6,000.00	Apr. 1	6,000.00

Interest Expense

Oct. 1	300.00

Cash

	Oct. 1	6,300.00

Notes Payable is debited for $6,000.00 to show the decrease in the balance of this liability account. Interest Expense is debited for $300.00 to show the increase in the balance of this other expense account. Cash is paid for the maturity value of the note. Thus, Cash is credited for $6,300.00 ($6,000.00 principal + $300.00 interest) to show the decrease in the balance of this asset account.

The cash payments journal entry to record this transaction is shown in Illustration 24-3.

ILLUSTRATION 24-3	Cash payments journal entry to record payment of maturity value of a note payable

CASH PAYMENTS JOURNAL

PAGE 28

	DATE	ACCOUNT TITLE	CK. NO.	POST. REF.	GENERAL DEBIT	GENERAL CREDIT	ACCOUNTS PAYABLE DEBIT	PURCHASES DISCOUNT CREDIT	CASH CREDIT	
1	Oct. 1	Notes Payable	573		6 000 00				6 300 00	1
2		Interest Expense			300 00					2
3										3
4										4
5										5
6										6
7										7

Issuing and Paying a Note Payable for an Extension of Time

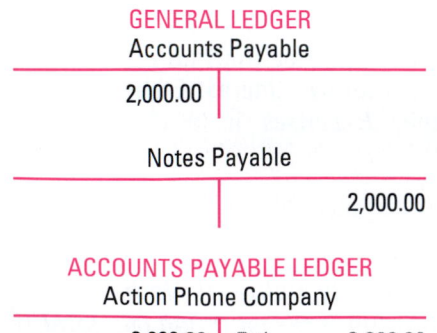

FYI

A promissory note given to a vendor changes an account payable to a note payable.

A business may ask for an extension of time if it is unable to pay an account when due. When a request for more time is made, sometimes the business is asked to issue a note payable. The note payable does not pay the amount owed to the vendor. However, the form of the liability is changed from an account payable to a note payable.

April 5, 19--. Issued a 60-day, 12% note to Action Phone Company for an extension of time on this account payable, $2,000.00. Note Payable No. 5.

Accounts Payable is debited for $2,000.00 to show the decrease in the balance of this liability account. Notes Payable is credited for $2,000.00 to show the increase in the balance of this liability account. The vendor account, Action Phone Company, is debited for $2,000.00 to show the decrease in the balance of this accounts payable ledger account. Whenever Accounts Payable is decreased, the vendor account in the accounts payable ledger is also decreased by the same amount. No entry is made for interest expense until a later date when interest is paid.

The general journal entry to record this transaction is shown in Illustration 24-4.

GENERAL LEDGER
Accounts Payable

2,000.00	

Notes Payable

	2,000.00

ACCOUNTS PAYABLE LEDGER
Action Phone Company

2,000.00	Bal.	2,000.00

ILLUSTRATION 24-4

General journal entry to record issuing a note payable for an extension of time on an account payable

DATE		ACCOUNT TITLE	DOC. NO.	POST. REF.	DEBIT	CREDIT	
17	5	Accounts Payable/Action Phone Co.	NP5	/	2 000 00		17
18		Notes Payable				2 000 00	18

GENERAL JOURNAL   PAGE 5

When this entry is posted, the balance of the accounts payable account for Action Phone Company will be zero. One liability, Accounts Payable, is replaced by another liability, Notes Payable.

Note Payable No. 5 is due on June 4. The maturity date for Note Payable No. 5 is calculated as shown below.

April 5 through 30	25 days (30 − 5 = 25)
May 1 through 31	31 days
June 1 through 4	4 days (Maturity date: June 4)
	60 days

June 4, 19--. Paid cash for the maturity value of Note Payable No. 5: principal, $2,000.00, plus interest, $40.00; total, $2,040.00. Check No. 328.

The interest expense is calculated as shown below.

Principal	×	Interest Rate	×	Time as Fraction of Year	=	Interest for Fraction of Year
$2,000.00	×	12%	×	$\frac{60}{360}$	=	$\frac{\$14,400.00}{360} = \$40.00$

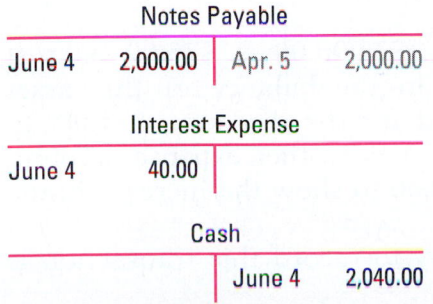

Notes Payable

| June 4 | 2,000.00 | Apr. 5 | 2,000.00 |

Interest Expense

| June 4 | 40.00 | |

Cash

| | | June 4 | 2,040.00 |

Notes Payable is debited for $2,000.00 to show the decrease in the balance of this liability account. Interest Expense is debited for $40.00 to show the increase in the balance of this other expense account. Cash is credited for the principal of the note plus the interest, $2,040.00, to show the decrease in the balance of this asset account.

The cash payments journal entry to record this transaction is shown in Illustration 24-5.

CASH PAYMENTS JOURNAL — PAGE 15

	DATE	ACCOUNT TITLE	CK. NO.	POST. REF.	GENERAL DEBIT	GENERAL CREDIT	ACCOUNTS PAYABLE DEBIT	PURCHASES DISCOUNT CREDIT	CASH CREDIT	
1	June 4	Notes Payable	328		2 0 0 0 00				2 0 4 0 00	1
2		Interest Expense			4 0 00					2
3										3
4										4
5										5
6										6

Issuing and Paying a Discounted Note Payable

Some banks require that the interest be paid at the time a note is issued. Interest collected in advance on a note is called **bank discount**. A note on which interest is paid in advance is called a **discounted note**. The amount received for a note after the bank discount has been deducted is called **proceeds**.

> *May 3, 19--. Discounted at 10% a 3-month non-interest-bearing note, $3,000.00; proceeds, $2,925.00, interest, $75.00. Note Payable No. 6.*

The bank deposited the proceeds, $2,925.00, in Celluphone's checking account. The amount of the discount and the proceeds are calculated as shown below.

Maturity Value	×	Discount Rate	×	Time as Fraction of Year	=	Bank Discount
$3,000.00	×	10%	×	$\frac{3}{12}$	=	$\frac{\$900.00}{12} = \$75.00$

Maturity Value	−	Bank Discount	=	Proceeds
$3,000.00	−	$75.00	=	$2,925.00

Cash

May 3 2,925.00	

Interest Expense

May 3 75.00	

Notes Payable

	May 3 3,000.00

Cash is debited for $2,925.00 ($3,000.00 − $75.00 interest expense) to show the increase in the balance of this asset account. Interest Expense is debited for the discount, $75.00, to show the increase in the balance of this other expense account. Notes Payable is credited for $3,000.00 to show the increase in the balance of this liability account.

The cash receipts journal entry to record this transaction is shown in Illustration 24-6.

ILLUSTRATION 24-6

Cash receipts journal entry to record cash received for a discounted note payable

	DATE	ACCOUNT TITLE	DOC. NO.	POST. REF.	GENERAL DEBIT	GENERAL CREDIT	ACCOUNTS RECEIVABLE CREDIT	SALES CREDIT	SALES TAX PAYABLE DEBIT	SALES TAX PAYABLE CREDIT	SALES DISCOUNT DEBIT	CASH DEBIT	
					1	2	3	4	5	6	7	8	
6	3	*Interest Expense*	NP6		75 00							2925 00	6
7		*Notes Payable*				3000 00							7
8													8
9													9
10													10

CASH RECEIPTS JOURNAL — PAGE *17*

When Note Payable No. 6 is paid on August 3, Check No. 450 is issued to the bank. This check is in payment of the principal. No payment of interest expense is necessary at this time because the bank collected the interest in advance when the note was discounted. Therefore, the maturity value of a discounted note is the principal of the note. Because no interest is paid on the maturity date, a discounted note is considered a non-interest-bearing note.

August 3, 19--. Paid cash for the maturity value of non-interest-bearing Note Payable No. 6, $3,000.00. Check No. 450.

Notes Payable is debited for $3,000.00 to show the decrease in the balance of this liability account. Cash is credited for the amount paid, $3,000.00, to show the decrease in the balance of this asset account.

The cash payments journal entry to record this transaction is shown in Illustration 24-7.

```
              Notes Payable
Aug. 3    3,000.00  |  May 3    3,000.00

                 Cash
                    |  Aug. 3    3,000.00
```

ILLUSTRATION 24-7

Cash payments journal entry to record payment of a discounted note payable

	DATE	ACCOUNT TITLE	CK. NO.	POST. REF.	GENERAL DEBIT	GENERAL CREDIT	ACCOUNTS PAYABLE DEBIT	PURCHASES DISCOUNT CREDIT	CASH CREDIT	
					1	2	3	4	5	
3	3	*Notes Payable*	450		3000 00				3000 00	3
4										4
5										5
6										6
7										7

CASH PAYMENTS JOURNAL — PAGE *20*

NOTES RECEIVABLE

Promissory notes that a business accepts from customers are called **notes receivable**. Notes receivable generally are paid within one year. Therefore, they are classified as current assets.

Accepting a Note Receivable from a Customer

A promissory note signed by a customer changes an account receivable to a note receivable.

A customer who is unable to pay an account on the due date may request additional time. When a request for more time is made, a business may agree to accept a note receivable. A note receivable does not pay the amount the customer owes. However, the form of the asset is changed from an account receivable to a note receivable.

If a customer needs extra time to pay, most businesses prefer a note receivable over an account receivable for several reasons. A note receivable usually earns interest whereas an account receivable does not. By signing the promissory note, the customer provides a written confirmation of the amount owed, which provides evidence of the debt in case legal action is required to collect.

When a business accepts a note receivable, the principal or face amount of the note is debited to an asset account titled *Notes Receivable*. An asset account has a normal debit balance. Therefore, the notes receivable account is increased by a debit and decreased by a credit, as shown in the T account.

Celluphone agrees to accept a promissory note from Ann Nance. Celluphone accepts the note because Ms. Nance is unable to pay the account receivable when due. The note Ms. Nance issues, which will be payable to Celluphone, is an interest-bearing note. Although Celluphone has not yet collected the cash Ms. Nance owes, the promissory note does provide a written promise to pay the amount owed plus interest.

	Notes Receivable	
Debit side		Credit side
Normal balance		
Increase		Decrease

As defined earlier, a promissory note is a written and signed promise to pay a sum of money at a specified time. A note is recorded as a note receivable by the person or business to whom the amount of the note is payable. A note is recorded as a note payable by the maker of the note, the person or business who signs the note and thus promises to make payment. Therefore, the note issued by Ms. Nance to Celluphone is recorded by Celluphone as a note receivable. This same note is recorded by Ms. Nance as a note payable.

GENERAL LEDGER
Notes Receivable

Apr. 22	800.00	

Accounts Receivable

		Apr. 22	800.00

ACCOUNTS RECEIVABLE LEDGER
Ann Nance

Bal.	800.00	Apr. 22	800.00

April 22, 19--. Received a 2-month, 12% note from Ann Nance for an extension of time on her account, $800.00. Note Receivable No. 10.

Notes Receivable is debited for $800.00 to show the increase in the balance of this asset account. Accounts Receivable is credited for $800.00 to show the decrease in the balance of this asset account. The customer account, Ann Nance, is also credited for $800.00 to show the decrease in the balance of this accounts receivable ledger account. Whenever Accounts Receivable is decreased, the customer account in the accounts receivable ledger is also decreased by the same amount.

The general journal entry to record this transaction is shown in Illustration 24-8.

ILLUSTRATION 24-8

General journal entry to record a note receivable for an extension of time on an account

	DATE	ACCOUNT TITLE	DOC. NO.	POST. REF.	DEBIT	CREDIT	
		GENERAL JOURNAL				PAGE 6	
6	22	Notes Receivable	NR10		800 00		6
7		Accounts Receivable/Ann Nance		/		800 00	7
8							8
9							9
10							10
11							11

FYI

For a non-interest-bearing note, the interest is paid when the note is issued; therefore, the maturity value equals the principal.

When this entry is posted, the balance of the accounts receivable account for Ms. Nance will be zero. One asset, Accounts Receivable, is replaced by another asset, Notes Receivable.

Collecting Principal and Interest on a Note Receivable at Maturity

When a note receivable reaches its maturity date, the payee of the note receives the maturity value from the maker of the note. The maturity value of a note is the principal (original amount of the note) plus the interest earned during the time of the note. The interest earned on money loaned is called **interest income.**

The interest earned on a note receivable is credited to a revenue account titled *Interest Income.* A revenue account has a normal credit balance. Therefore, the interest income account is increased by a credit and decreased by a debit, as shown in the T account.

Interest Income	
Debit side	Credit side
	Normal balance
Decrease	Increase

Interest income is investment revenue rather than revenue from the business' normal operations. Therefore, Interest Income is listed in a classification titled *Other Revenue* in a chart of accounts.

Celluphone received cash from Ann Nance for the principal and interest of the note accepted from Ms. Nance on April 22.

June 22, 19--. Received cash for the maturity value of Note Receivable No. 10: principal, $800.00, plus interest, $16.00; total, $816.00. Receipt No. 497.

Cash

June 22	816.00	

Notes Receivable

Apr. 22	800.00	June 22	800.00

Interest Income

		June 22	16.00

Cash is debited for $816.00 ($800.00 principal + $16.00 interest income) to show the increase in the balance of this asset account. Notes Receivable is credited for $800.00 to show the decrease in the balance of this asset account. Interest Income is credited for $16.00 ($800.00 × 12% × 2/12 = $16.00) to show the increase in the balance of this other revenue account.

The cash receipts journal entry to record this transaction is shown in Illustration 24-9.

After the entry is recorded, the original copy of Note Receivable No. 10 is marked *Paid* and returned to Ann Nance, the maker.

ILLUSTRATION 24-9 Cash receipts journal entry to record receipt of maturity value of a note receivable

CASH RECEIPTS JOURNAL PAGE 22

	DATE	ACCOUNT TITLE	DOC. NO.	POST. REF.	GENERAL DEBIT	GENERAL CREDIT	ACCOUNTS RECEIVABLE CREDIT	SALES CREDIT	SALES TAX PAYABLE DEBIT	SALES TAX PAYABLE CREDIT	SALES DISCOUNT DEBIT	CASH DEBIT	
18	22	Notes Receivable	R497			800 00						816 00	18
19		Interest Income				16 00							19
20													20
21													21
22													22
23													23

Recording a Dishonored Note Receivable

A note that is not paid when due is called a **dishonored note**. The balance of the notes receivable account should show only the total amount of notes that probably will be collected. The amount of a dishonored note receivable should therefore be removed from the notes receivable account. The amount of the note plus interest income earned on the note is still owed by the customer. Therefore, the total amount owed should be debited to the accounts receivable account in the general ledger. The amount owed should also be debited to the customer account in the accounts receivable ledger. The customer account will then show the total amount owed by the customer, including the amount of the dishonored note and interest earned. This information may be important if the customer requests credit in the future or if collection is achieved later.

FYI

Interest income is recorded even for a dishonored note because the interest has been earned even if it will not be collected.

May 12, 19--. Keith Leising dishonored Note Receivable No. 9, a 1-month, 12% note, maturity value due today: principal, $200.00; interest, $2.00; total, $202.00. Memorandum No. 65.

Accounts Receivable is debited for $202.00 ($200.00 principal + $2.00 interest income) to show the increase in the balance of this

Accounts Receivable

May 12	202.00

Notes Receivable

Apr. 12	200.00	May 12	200.00

Interest Income

	May 12 2.00

ACCOUNTS RECEIVABLE LEDGER

Keith Leising

May 12	202.00

asset account. Notes Receivable is credited for $200.00 to show the decrease in the balance of this asset account. Interest Income is credited for $2.00 ($200.00 × 12% × 1/12 = $2.00) to show the increase in the balance of this other revenue account. The customer account, Keith Leising, is also debited for $202.00 ($200.00 principal + $2.00 interest) to show the increase in the balance of this accounts receivable ledger account.

The interest income has been earned even though it has not been paid. Keith Leising owes the principal amount of the note plus the interest earned. Therefore, the total of principal plus interest ($200.00 + $2.00 = $202.00) is debited to Accounts Receivable and to the customer account.

The general journal entry to record this transaction is shown in Illustration 24-10.

ILLUSTRATION 24-10   General journal entry to record a dishonored note receivable

GENERAL JOURNAL						PAGE 8
	DATE	ACCOUNT TITLE	DOC. NO.	POST. REF.	DEBIT	CREDIT
9	12	Accounts Receivable/Keith Leising	M65		202 00		9
10		Notes Receivable				200 00	10
11		Interest Income				2 00	11
12							12
13							13
14							14

Audit Your Understanding

1. What is the normal balance side of Notes Receivable?

2. What is the balance of a customer account after a business accepts a note receivable from a customer for an extension of time on account?

3. Why isn't Interest Income considered operating revenue?

4. Should a company always write off an account on the date a note receivable is dishonored?

Celluphone does not write off Mr. Leising's account when the note is dishonored. Instead, the company continues to try to collect the account.

Later Celluphone may decide that the account cannot be collected from Mr. Leising. At that time the balance of the account will be written off as an uncollectible account. Allowance for Uncollectible Accounts will be debited, and Accounts Receivable and Keith Leising's account will be credited.

The chart shown in Illustration 24-11 on pages 656 and 657 summarizes the journal entries for recording notes payable and notes receivable transactions and the calculations for interest and discounted notes.

Summary of accounting for notes and interest

Transactions	GENERAL LEDGER														SUBSIDIARY LEDGERS			
	Cash		Notes Rec.		Accts. Rec.		Notes Pay.		Accts. Pay.		Interest Income		Interest Expense		Accts. Rec.		Accts. Pay.	
	Dr.	Cr.	Dr.	Cr.	Dr.	Cr.	Dr.	Cr.	Dr.	Cr.	Dr.	Cr.	Dr.	Cr.	Dr.	Cr.	Dr.	Cr.
Issuing a note payable to borrow money from a bank	X							X										
Paying principal and interest on a note payable at maturity		X					X						X					
Issuing a note payable for an extension of time							X	X									X	
Paying principal and interest on a note for an extension of time		X					X						X					
Issuing a discounted note payable for cash	X							X					X					
Paying a discounted note payable		X					X											
Accepting a note receivable from a customer			X			X										X		
Collecting principal and interest on a note receivable at maturity	X			X								X						
Recording a dishonored note receivable				X	X							X			X			

AMOUNTS	CALCULATIONS							
Interest for Years	Principal	×	Interest Rate	×	Time in Years	=	Interest for Years	
Interest for Fraction of Year	Principal	×	Interest Rate	×	Time as Fraction of Year	=	Interest for Fraction of Year	
Bank Discount	Maturity Value	×	Discount Rate	×	Time as Fraction of Year	=	Bank Discount	
Proceeds	Maturity Value		−		Bank Discount	=	Proceeds	

ACCOUNTING TERMS

EPT(a)

What is the meaning of each of the following?

1. promissory note
2. date of a note
3. time of a note
4. payee of a note
5. principal of a note
6. interest rate of a note
7. maturity date of a note
8. maker of a note

9. number of a note
10. interest
11. interest-bearing note
12. non-interest-bearing note
13. maturity value
14. creditor
15. notes payable
16. current liabilities

17. interest expense
18. bank discount
19. discounted note
20. proceeds
21. notes receivable
22. interest income
23. dishonored note

QUESTIONS FOR INDIVIDUAL STUDY

EPT(b)

1. What conditions would cause a business to have extra cash to deposit in a bank, yet at another time of year, need to borrow extra cash from a bank?
2. Why does a business sometimes request a promissory note from a credit customer?
3. What is the advantage of a promissory note over an account receivable?
4. What is the difference between the payee and the maker of a note?
5. What does interest at 10% mean?
6. How is interest calculated for a fraction of a year?
7. Why are notes payable generally classified as current liabilities?

8. Which accounting concept is being applied when a copy of a note payable is used as the source document for recording the issuance of a note payable?
9. What accounts are affected, and how, when a business issues a note payable to borrow money from a bank?
10. When an interest-bearing note is paid, why is the credit to Cash greater than the debit to Notes Payable?
11. What accounts are affected, and how, when a business issues an interest-bearing note payable for an extension of time on its account payable?

12. What accounts are affected, and how, when a business pays an interest-bearing note payable that had been issued for an extension of time on its account payable?

13. How much will the maker receive from a one-year non-interest-bearing note with a face value of $1,000.00, discounted at 10%?

14. What accounts are affected, and how, when a non-interest-bearing note payable is discounted at a bank?

15. What accounts are affected, and how, when a discounted note payable is paid at maturity?

16. When a business accepts a note receivable from a credit customer for an extension of time on the customer's account receivable, how does the amount and form of the business asset change?

17. What accounts are affected, and how, when a business receives the principal and interest on a note receivable at maturity?

18. What accounts are affected, and how, when a customer dishonors an interest-bearing note receivable?

19. Why is interest income recorded at the time a note is dishonored even though cash has not been received?

CASES FOR CRITICAL THINKING

EPT(b,c)

CASE 1   Because of a temporary cash shortage, Jupiter Company requested an extension of time on its purchases on account. Jupiter's regular vendor, Custom Suppliers, requires that a 12% interest-bearing note be issued to them for any extension of time over one month. Jupiter usually needs 3 months from time of purchase to time of payment. Because of the extra costs for interest expense, Jupiter has been exploring other vendor options. Another vendor, Page Supplies, has been located that will sell merchandise on account with credit terms of net due in 3 months. For the same quantity and brand of merchandise, Custom Suppliers' cost is $10,000.00; for Page Supplies, $10,250.00. Since Page Supplies offers 3 months credit terms without any interest charges and the merchandise is only 2.5% higher than that from Custom Suppliers, Jupiter's purchasing manager, Robert Jimerson, has decided to buy the merchandise from Page. When asked why he is buying from the company with costs 2.5% higher, he said, "A 2.5% higher price is better than the 12% interest we would have to pay Custom Suppliers." Do you agree with Mr. Jimerson? Explain.

CASE 2   Alexandra Davis requested a $1,000.00 bank loan for one year. The loan officer agreed to the loan and offered Miss Davis her choice of a 10% interest-bearing note or a note discounted at 10%. Which choice should Miss Davis accept?

APPLIED COMMUNICATIONS

As a bookkeeper for a corporation, you have been asked to assist the president in making a presentation to the board of directors. The president wants to report the 4-year growth in sales of four major products. The following table presents product sales (in thousands of dollars) from 19X1 to 19X4.

	19X1	19X2	19X3	19X4
Stereo Receivers	$235	$312	$322	$284
Speakers	197	211	187	205
CD-Players	62	156	199	276
Telephones	155	143	135	132

INSTRUCTIONS:

Prepare a graph depicting the data presented in the table.

DRILL 24-D1 Calculating interest on notes

TUTORIAL

MATHEMATICS   SPREADSHEET

INSTRUCTIONS:

Calculate the interest for each of the following notes.

No. of Note	Principal of Note	Interest Rate	Time of Note
1	$ 700.00	8%	1 year
2	1,200.00	12%	6 months
3	500.00	15%	30 days
4	800.00	9%	4 months
5	600.00	10%	60 days

DRILL 24-D2 Calculating maturity dates of notes

MATHEMATICS

INSTRUCTIONS:

Calculate the maturity date for each of the following notes.

No. of Note	Date of Note	Time of Note
1	Jan. 11	90 days
2	Feb. 5	1 year
3	May 17	30 days
4	July 1	3 months
5	Oct. 20	6 months

DRILL 24-D3 Calculating maturity dates and interest on notes

SPREADSHEET

INSTRUCTIONS:

For each of the following notes, calculate (1) the maturity date and (2) the interest.

No. of Note	Date of Note	Principal of Note	Interest Rate	Time of Note
1	Jan. 4	$ 400	9%	30 days
2	Mar. 21	800	11%	1 year
3	May 8	1,200	13%	60 days
4	July 15	1,700	12%	6 months
5	Sept. 1	2,000	10%	90 days

DRILL 24-D4 Analyzing recording notes payable transactions

INSTRUCTIONS:

A form for analyzing recording notes payable transactions is given in the working papers that accompany this text. For each transaction, write the title of the accounts affected in the Account Title column. For each account title, place a check mark in the Debit or Credit column to show whether the account is debited or credited. The abbreviation for note payable is NP. Transaction 1 is given as an example in the working papers.

1. Discounted at 14% a 60-day non-interest-bearing note. NP135.
2. Issued a 1-year, 12% note. NP136.
3. Issued a 6-month, 10% note. NP137.
4. Discounted at 11% a 90-day non-interest-bearing note. NP138.
5. Discounted at 13% a 2-month non-interest-bearing note. NP139.
6. Issued a 30-day, 15% note for an extension of time on an account payable. NP140.
7. Paid cash for the maturity value of non-interest-bearing NP135.
8. Paid cash for the maturity value of NP136.

DRILL 24-D5   Analyzing recording notes receivable transactions

INSTRUCTIONS:

A form for analyzing notes receivable transactions is given in the working papers that accompany the text. For each transaction, write the title of the accounts affected in the Account Title column. For each account title, place a check mark in the Debit or Credit column to show whether the account is debited or credited. The abbreviation for note receivable is NR. Transaction 1 is given as an example.

1. Received a 60-day, 14% note for an extension of time on an account. NR26.
2. Received a 1-year, 10% note for an extension of time on an account. NR27.
3. Received a 3-month, 12% note for an extension of time on an account. NR28.
4. Received a 90-day, 11% note for an extension of time on an account. NR29.
5. Received a 6-month, 13% note for an extension of time on an account. NR30.
6. Received cash for the maturity value of NR26.
7. Received cash for the maturity value of NR27.
8. Maker dishonored NR28, a 3-month, 12% note, maturity value due today.

APPLICATION PROBLEMS   EPT(d)

PROBLEM 24-1   Journalizing notes payable transactions

The following transactions were completed by Coastal Construction during the current year.

INSTRUCTIONS:

1. Journalize the following transactions. Use page 10 of a general journal, page 20 of a cash receipts journal, and page 18 of a cash payments journal. (Usually a new journal page is started each month. However, to conserve space in the working papers, record all of the year's entries on the same page of each journal.) Source documents are abbreviated as follows: check, C; note payable, NP.

Mar. 3. Issued a 90-day, 13% note, $6,000.00. NP179.
　　 12. Paid cash for the maturity value of NP169: principal, $3,500.00, plus interest, $35.00; total, $3,535.00. C2117.
　　 31. Issued a 30-day, 12% note to Santa Fe Company for an extension of time on this account payable, $1,500.00. NP180.
Apr. 8. Paid cash for the maturity value of NP158: principal, $12,500.00, plus interest, $375.00; total, $12,875.00. C2189.
　　 30. Paid cash for the maturity value of NP180: principal, $1,500.00, plus interest, $15.00; total, $1,515.00. C2234.
May 13. Issued a 60-day, 12% note, $5,500.00. NP181.
June 1. Paid cash for the maturity value of NP179: principal, $6,000.00, plus interest, $195.00; total, $6,195.00. C2415.
　　 17. Issued a 30-day, 11% note to Universal Lumber for an extension of time on this account payable, $8,000.00. NP182.
July 12. Paid cash for the maturity value of NP181: principal, $5,500.00, plus interest, $110.00; total, $5,610.00. C2543.
　　 17. Paid cash for the maturity value of NP182: principal, $8,000.00, plus interest, $73.33; total, $8,073.33. C2561.

2. Prove the cash receipts and cash payments journals.

PROBLEM 24-2   Journalizing notes payable transactions

The following transactions were completed by Manhattan Concepts, Inc., during the current year.

INSTRUCTIONS:

1. Journalize the following transactions. Use page 16 of a general journal, page 23 of a cash receipts journal, and page 20 of a cash payments journal.

Jan. 17. Issued a 90-day, 12% note, $9,000.00. NP134.

29. Paid cash for the maturity value of NP112: principal, $2,000.00, plus interest, $18.33; total, $2,018.33. C1073.

Feb. 2. Discounted at 13% a 60-day non-interest-bearing note, $7,000.00; proceeds, $6,848.33, interest, $151.67. NP135.

9. Paid cash for the maturity value of NP120: principal, $3,000.00, plus interest, $30.00; total, $3,030.00. C1103.

21. Issued a 30-day, 11% note to Newport Company for an extension of time on this account payable, $5,000.00. NP136.

Mar. 8. Discounted at 12% a 45-day non-interest-bearing note, $4,500.00; proceeds, $4,432.50, interest, $67.50. NP137.

23. Paid cash for the maturity value of NP136: principal, $5,000.00, plus interest, $45.83; total, $5,045.83. C1234.

Apr. 3. Paid cash for the maturity value of non-interest-bearing NP135, $7,000.00. C1279.

17. Paid cash for the maturity value of NP134: principal, $9,000.00, plus interest, $270.00; total, $9,270.00. C1312.

22. Paid cash for the maturity value of non-interest-bearing NP137, $4,500.00. C1335.

2. Prove the cash receipts and cash payments journals.

PROBLEM 24-3   Journalizing notes receivable transactions

The following transactions were completed by Westport Company during the current year.

INSTRUCTIONS:

1. Journalize the following transactions. Use page 19 of a general journal and page 22 of a cash receipts journal.

Jan. 10. Received a 90-day, 11% note from Gary Shelton for an extension of time on his account, $1,500.00. NR67.

18. Received cash for the maturity value of NR49: principal, $500.00, plus interest, $25.00; total, $525.00. R37.

Feb. 3. Received a 30-day, 10% note from Joanne Davis for an extension of time on her account, $800.00. NR68.

12. Received cash for the maturity value of NR53: principal, $4,000.00, plus interest, $80.00; total, $4,080.00. R83.

27. Received a 60-day, 12% note from Andrew McCormick for an extension of time on his account, $2,400.00. NR69.

Mar. 5. Received cash for the maturity value of NR68: principal, $800.00, plus interest, $6.67; total, $806.67. R99.

Apr. 10. Gary Shelton dishonored NR67, a 90-day, 11% note, maturity value due today: principal, $1,500.00; interest, $41.25; total, $1,541.25. M251.

28. Received cash for the maturity value of NR69: principal, $2,400.00, plus interest, $48.00; total, $2,448.00. R154.

2. Prove the cash receipts journal.

ENRICHMENT PROBLEMS   EPT(c,d)

MASTERY PROBLEM 24-M   Journalizing notes payable and notes receivable transactions

The following transactions were completed by Peterson Sporting Goods during the current year.

INSTRUCTIONS:

1. Journalize the following transactions. Use page 14 of a general journal, page 20 of a cash receipts journal, and page 16 of a cash payments journal.

Apr. 2. Issued a 30-day, 12% note to Devco Supply Company for an extension of time on this account payable, $6,500.00. NP120.

7. Received a 90-day, 13% note from Jill Bankston for an extension of time on her account, $700.00. NR154.

14. Discounted at 11% a 90-day non-interest-bearing note, $12,000.00; proceeds, $11,670.00, interest, $330.00. NP121.

26. Issued a 30-day, 13% note to Dayton Corporation for an extension of time on this account payable, $4,000.00. NP122.

30. Received a 60-day, 12% note from Jeremy Hicks for an extension of time on his account, $300.00. NR155.

May 2. Paid cash for the maturity value of NP120: principal, $6,500.00, plus interest, $65.00; total, $6,565.00. C175.

5. Received a 30-day, 11% note from Suzanne Johnson for an extension of time on her account, $550.00. NR156.

11. Issued a 60-day, 10% note, $7,000.00. NP123.

26. Paid cash for the maturity value of NP122: principal, $4,000.00, plus interest, $43.33; total, $4,043.33. C189.

June 4. Received cash for the maturity value of NR156: principal, $550.00, plus interest, $5.04; total, $555.04. R225.

8. Issued a 30-day, 12% note to Winston Company for an extension of time on this account payable, $2,500.00. NP124.

17. Received a 60-day, 10% note from Melissa Albertson for an extension of time on her account, $600.00. NR157.

29. Jeremy Hicks dishonored NR155, a 60-day, 12% note, maturity value due today: principal, $300.00; interest, $6.00; total $306.00. M310.

July 6. Received cash for the maturity value of NR154: principal, $700.00, plus interest, $22.75; total, $722.75. R253.

8. Paid cash for the maturity value of NP124: principal, $2,500.00, plus interest, $25.00; total, $2,525.00. C251.

10. Paid cash for the maturity value of NP123: principal, $7,000.00, plus interest, $116.67; total, $7,116.67. C262.

13. Paid cash for the maturity value of non-interest-bearing NP121, $12,000.00. C274.

Aug. 16. Received cash for the maturity value of NR157: principal, $600.00, plus interest, $10.00; total, $610.00. R278.

2. Prove the cash receipts and cash payments journals.

CHALLENGE PROBLEM 24-C Journalizing notes payable and notes receivable transactions

The following transactions were completed by Briarcraft Apparel Company during the current year.

INSTRUCTIONS:

1. Journalize the following transactions. Use page 20 of a general journal, page 27 of a cash receipts journal, and page 31 of a cash payments journal.

Feb. 3. A 90-day, 13% note was issued to Rainbow Manufacturing. This is for an extension of time on this account payable, $7,550.00. NP158.

7. We discounted a 10%, 6-month non-interest-bearing note, $15,000.00. NP159.

9. We received a note dated February 6 from William Andrews. This note is a 30-day, 12% note for an extension of time on his account, $985.00. NR84.

24. A note dated February 23 was received from Elizabeth Townsend. This is a 2-month, 13% note for an extension of time on her account, $1,275.00. NR85.

Mar. 1. A 3-month, 12% note was issued to Livingston Company for an extension of time on this account payable, $6,995.00. NP160.

Mar. 8. A check was received for the maturity value of NR84. R273.

15. Store equipment was bought from Warner Company, $2,875.00. Paid cash, $1,200.00, and issued a 4-month, 11% note for the balance, $1,675.00. C124 and NP161. Journalize the transaction in the cash payments journal in one combined entry. Record the check number in the Ck. No. column. Write *NP161* in parentheses after the account title for notes payable to complete the audit trail.

Apr. 24. Elizabeth Townsend dishonored NR85, maturity value due today. M64.

May 4. Issued a check for the maturity value of NP158. C172.

June 1. Paid cash for the maturity value of NP160. C183.

July 15. The maturity value of NP161 is due today. Issued a check. C197.

21. Elizabeth Townsend sent a check for $600.00 for part of the balance charged to her account on April 24. R325. Wrote off the remainder of this account receivable as uncollectible. M99. Journalize the check in the cash receipts journal. Journalize the write-off of the customer account in the general journal.

Aug. 7. Wrote a check for the maturity value of non-interest-bearing NP159. C215.

2. Prove the cash receipts and cash payments journals.

25

Accounting for Accrued Revenue and Expenses

ENABLING PERFORMANCE TASKS

After studying Chapter 25, you will be able to:

a Define accounting terms related to accrued revenue and accrued expenses.

b Identify accounting concepts and practices related to accrued revenue and accrued expenses.

c Record adjusting, closing, and reversing entries for accrued revenue.

d Record adjusting, closing, and reversing entries for accrued expenses.

TERMS PREVIEW

accrued revenue • accrued interest income • reversing entry • accrued expenses • accrued interest expense

Generally accepted accounting procedures require that revenue and expenses be recorded in the accounting period in which revenue is earned and expenses are incurred. *(CONCEPT: Matching Expenses with Revenue)* Some revenues, however, are earned each day but are usually recorded only when cash is actually received. For example, interest is earned for each day an interest-bearing note receivable is held. However, the interest may not be received until the maturity date of the note. Likewise, some expenses may be incurred before they are actually paid. An interest-bearing note payable incurs interest expense each day the note is outstanding. Yet, the interest generally is not paid until the note's maturity date. At the end of the fiscal period, adjusting entries are recorded for these revenues and expenses.

ACCRUED REVENUE

Revenue earned in one fiscal period but not received until a later fiscal period is called **accrued revenue.** At the end of a fiscal period, accrued revenue is recorded by an adjusting entry. *(CONCEPT: Realization of Revenue)* The adjusting entry for accrued revenue increases the accrued revenue account, an other revenue account. The adjusting entry also increases the accrued revenue receivable account, an asset account. The income statement will then report all revenue earned for the period even though some of the revenue has not yet been received. The balance sheet will report all the assets, including the accrued revenue receivable. *(CONCEPT: Adequate Disclosure)*

Adjusting Entry for Accrued Interest Income

At the end of each fiscal period, Celluphone examines the notes receivable on hand. The amount of interest income earned but not yet collected is calculated. Interest earned but not yet received is called **accrued interest income.** On December 31 Celluphone has one note receivable on hand, Note Receivable No. 15. Note Receivable No. 15 is a 3-month, $550.00, 12% note from J. T. Monroe, dated October 31. The accounting records should show all the interest income for the fiscal period. *(CONCEPT: Adequate Disclosure)* Therefore, an adjusting entry must be made to record the amount of interest earned to date on this note.

The time period from October 31 to December 31 is two months. Therefore, the time stated as a fraction of a year is $\frac{2}{12}$. Accrued interest on this note to the end of the fiscal year is calculated as shown below.

	Principal	×	Interest Rate	×	Time as Fraction of Year	=	Accrued Interest Income
	$550.00	×	12%	×	$\frac{2}{12}$	=	$11.00

```
                Interest Receivable
Dec. 31 Adj.          11.00  │

                Interest Income
                             │  Dec. 31 Bal.   203.00
                             │  Dec. 31 Adj.    11.00
                             │ (New Bal.       214.00)
```

Interest Receivable is debited for $11.00 to show the increase in the balance of this asset account. The interest receivable account balance is the amount of interest income that has accrued at the end of the fiscal period. However, this revenue will not be collected until the next fiscal period.

Interest Income is credited for $11.00 to show the increase in the balance of this other revenue account. The new interest income account balance, $214.00, is the total amount of interest income earned during the fiscal period.

The adjustment for accrued interest income is planned on a work sheet. Celluphone's accrued interest income adjustment for the year ended December 31 is shown in Illustration 25-1.

ILLUSTRATION 25-1	Accrued interest income adjustment on a work sheet

Celluphone, Inc.
Work Sheet
For Year Ended December 31, --

	ACCOUNT TITLE	TRIAL BALANCE		ADJUSTMENTS		INCOME STATEMENT		BALANCE SHEET		
		1 DEBIT	2 CREDIT	3 DEBIT	4 CREDIT	5 DEBIT	6 CREDIT	7 DEBIT	8 CREDIT	
4	Interest Receivable			(a) 11 00				11 00		4
48	Interest Income		203 00		(a) 11 00		214 00			48

FYI

The interest receivable balance will appear on the balance sheet as an asset.

FYI

The interest income balance will appear on the income statement as other revenue.

On line 4 of the work sheet, Interest Receivable is debited for $11.00 in the Adjustments Debit column. This amount, $11.00, is extended to the Balance Sheet Debit column. On line 48 Interest Income is credited for $11.00 in the Adjustments Credit column. The interest income adjustment, $11.00, is added to the previous balance in the Trial Balance Credit column, $203.00. The new balance, $214.00 ($11.00 + $203.00), is extended to the Income Statement Credit column.

Information used to journalize an adjustment for accrued interest income is obtained from the Adjustments columns of a work sheet. The adjusting entry is shown in Illustration 25-2.

After the adjusting entry is posted, the interest receivable and interest income accounts appear as shown in Illustration 25-3.

The interest receivable account has a debit balance of $11.00 and will appear on the balance sheet as a current asset. This debit balance is the accrued interest income earned but not yet collected at the end of the year. The interest income account has a credit balance of $214.00 and will appear on the income statement as other revenue. This amount is the total interest income for the year.

ILLUSTRATION 25-2   Adjusting entry for accrued interest income

	DATE		ACCOUNT TITLE	DOC. NO.	POST. REF.	DEBIT	CREDIT	
1			*Adjusting Entries*					1
2	*Dec.*¹⁹⁻⁻	*31*	*Interest Receivable*			11 00		2
3			*Interest Income*				11 00	3
4								4
5								5

GENERAL JOURNAL   PAGE *15*

Closing Entry for Interest Income

Interest Income

Dec. 31 Closing	214.00	Dec. 31 Bal.	203.00
		Dec. 31 Adj.	11.00
		(New Bal. zero)	

Income Summary

	Dec. 31 Closing	214.00

Information needed to record closing entries is obtained from the Income Statement columns of a work sheet. Interest Income is closed to the income summary account.

Interest Income is closed as part of the regular closing entry for income statement accounts with credit balances. Interest Income is debited for $214.00 to reduce the account balance to zero. The $214.00 is also credited to Income Summary as part of the entry to close all income statement accounts with credit balances. After the closing entry is posted, the interest income account is closed. Closing entries for all revenue and expense accounts are described in Chapter 27.

ILLUSTRATION 25-3   General ledger accounts after adjusting entry for accrued interest income is posted

ACCOUNT *Interest Receivable*   ACCOUNT NO. *1120*

DATE	ITEM	POST. REF.	DEBIT	CREDIT	BALANCE DEBIT	BALANCE CREDIT
*Dec.*¹⁹⁻⁻ *31*		G15	11 00		11 00	

ACCOUNT *Interest Income*   ACCOUNT NO. *7110*

DATE	ITEM	POST. REF.	DEBIT	CREDIT	BALANCE DEBIT	BALANCE CREDIT
Dec. *29*		CR49		23 00		203 00
31		G15		11 00		214 00

Reversing Entry for Accrued Interest Income

Adjusting entries for accrued revenues have an effect on transactions to be recorded in the following fiscal period. For example, on the maturity date of Note Receivable No. 15, January 31, Celluphone will receive cash for the note's principal and interest. Total interest earned for the 3-month note is $16.50, calculated as shown below.

	Principal	×	Interest Rate	×	Time as Fraction of Year	=	Interest
	$550.00	×	12%	×	$\frac{3}{12}$	=	$16.50

However, an adjusting entry was made to record the amount of interest earned last year, $11.00, by debiting Interest Receivable and crediting Interest Income. Thus, $11.00 of the $16.50 total interest income has already been recorded as revenue. The remaining $5.50 of the $16.50 total interest was earned during the current year. Determining how much of the cash received is for interest income earned and accrued during the previous year and how much is earned during the current year is inconvenient. To avoid this inconvenience, a reversing entry is made at the beginning of the new fiscal period. An entry made at the beginning of one fiscal period to reverse an adjusting entry made in the previous fiscal period is called a **reversing entry**.

 **FYI**

A reversing entry is the opposite of an adjusting entry.

The reversing entry results in a debit balance of $11.00 in Interest Income. A debit balance is the opposite of the normal balance of the interest income account. When the full amount of interest is received, $16.50, this amount will be credited to Interest Income. The account will then have a credit balance of $5.50 ($16.50 credit − $11.00 debit), the amount earned in the new year.

The reversing entry to Interest Receivable reduces that account to a zero balance. Thus, when the interest is received, no credit entry will be required to recognize collection of the balance of Interest Receivable. The total amount of interest received will be credited to Interest Income. Celluphone's reversing entry for accrued interest income is shown in Illustration 25-4.

The reversing entry is the opposite of the adjusting entry shown in Illustration 25-2.

Celluphone uses the following rule of thumb to determine whether or not reversing entries are made. If an adjusting entry creates a balance in an asset or liability account that initially had a zero balance, the adjusting entry is reversed. The adjusting entry for accrued interest income creates a balance in the asset account, Interest Receivable. Therefore, Celluphone uses reversing entries for all accrued interest income adjusting entries.

Interest Income

Dec. 31 Closing	214.00	Dec. 31 Bal.	203.00
Jan. 1. Rev.	11.00	Dec. 31 Adj.	11.00
(New Bal.	*11.00)*	*(New Bal. zero)*	

Interest Receivable

Dec. 31 Adj.	11.00	Jan. 1 Rev.	11.00
(New Bal. zero)			

FYI

A reversing entry is made if an adjusting entry creates a balance in an asset or liability account.

A balance is "created" in an account when the account balance is changed from a zero balance to an amount.

ILLUSTRATION 25-4   Reversing entry for accrued interest income

	DATE		ACCOUNT TITLE	DOC. NO.	POST. REF.	DEBIT	CREDIT	
1			*Reversing Entries*					1
2	*Jan.* 19--	1	*Interest Income*			11 00		2
3			*Interest Receivable*				11 00	3
4								4

GENERAL JOURNAL   PAGE *17*

Collecting a Note Receivable Issued in a Previous Fiscal Period

On January 31 Celluphone received the maturity value (principal plus interest) of the only note receivable on hand December 31, the end of the previous fiscal year. The maturity value for Note Receivable No. 15 is calculated as shown below.

Principal	×	Interest Rate	×	Time as Fraction of Year	=	Interest
$550.00	×	12%	×	$\frac{3}{12}$	=	$16.50

Principal	+	Interest	=	Maturity Value
$550.00	+	$16.50	=	$566.50

January 31, 19--. Received cash for the maturity value of Note Receivable No. 15: principal, $550.00, plus interest, $16.50; total, $566.50. Receipt No. 38.

The total interest, $16.50, was earned during two fiscal periods, $11.00 during the previous fiscal period and $5.50 during the current fiscal period. Since Celluphone uses reversing entries, the entry to record the collection of this note receivable and interest is the same as the entry to record a note accepted and collected in a single fiscal year.

When Note Receivable No. 15 is collected on January 31, Cash is debited for the total amount received, $566.50, to record the increase in this asset account. Notes Receivable is credited for the principal of the note, $550.00, to record the decrease in the balance of this asset account. Interest Income is credited

Cash

Jan. 31 Rec'd	566.50	

Notes Receivable

Oct. 31 NR15	550.00	Jan. 3 Rec'd	550.00

Interest Income

Dec. 31 Closing	214.00	Dec. 31 Bal.	203.00
Jan. 1 Rev.	11.00	Dec. 31 Adj.	11.00
		(New Bal. zero)	
		Jan. 31 Rec'd	16.50
		(New Bal.	*5.50)*

for the total amount of interest, $16.50, to record the increase in this other revenue account. The interest income account now has a credit balance of $5.50 ($16.50 credit − $11.00 debit), the amount of interest earned during the current fiscal period.

The cash receipts journal entry to record this receipt of cash for a note receivable when reversing entries are used is shown in Illustration 25-5.

ILLUSTRATION 25-5   Cash receipts journal entry to record note receivable accepted in previous fiscal period when reversing entries are used

CASH RECEIPTS JOURNAL   PAGE 53

	DATE	ACCOUNT TITLE	DOC. NO.	POST. REF.	GENERAL DEBIT	GENERAL CREDIT	ACCOUNTS RECEIVABLE CREDIT	SALES CREDIT	SALES TAX PAYABLE DEBIT	SALES TAX PAYABLE CREDIT	SALES DISCOUNT DEBIT	CASH DEBIT	
12	31	Notes Receivable	R38			5 5 0 00						5 6 6 50	12
13		Interest Income				1 6 50							13
14													14

Audit Your Understanding

1. What is the adjusting entry to record interest earned but not yet collected?

2. What is the closing entry for interest income?

3. What is an entry called that is made at the beginning of one fiscal period to reverse an adjusting entry made in the previous fiscal period?

4. What is the formula for maturity value?

After the cash receipts journal entry is posted, the notes receivable, interest receivable, and interest income accounts appear as shown in Illustration 25-6.

Notes Receivable has a zero balance. This account will be used again when additional notes receivable are accepted. After the reversing entry is recorded, Interest Receivable has a zero balance. Interest Receivable will not be used again until it is needed for an adjusting entry at the end of the current fiscal year. Interest Income has a credit balance of $5.50, the amount of interest earned on Note Receivable No. 15 in the current year.

ACCRUED EXPENSES

Expenses incurred in one fiscal period but not paid until a later fiscal period are called **accrued expenses**. At the end of a fiscal period, accrued expense is recorded by an adjusting entry. *(CONCEPT: Matching Expenses with*

ILLUSTRATION 25-6   General ledger accounts after posting cash receipt for note receivable accepted in previous fiscal period when reversing entries are used

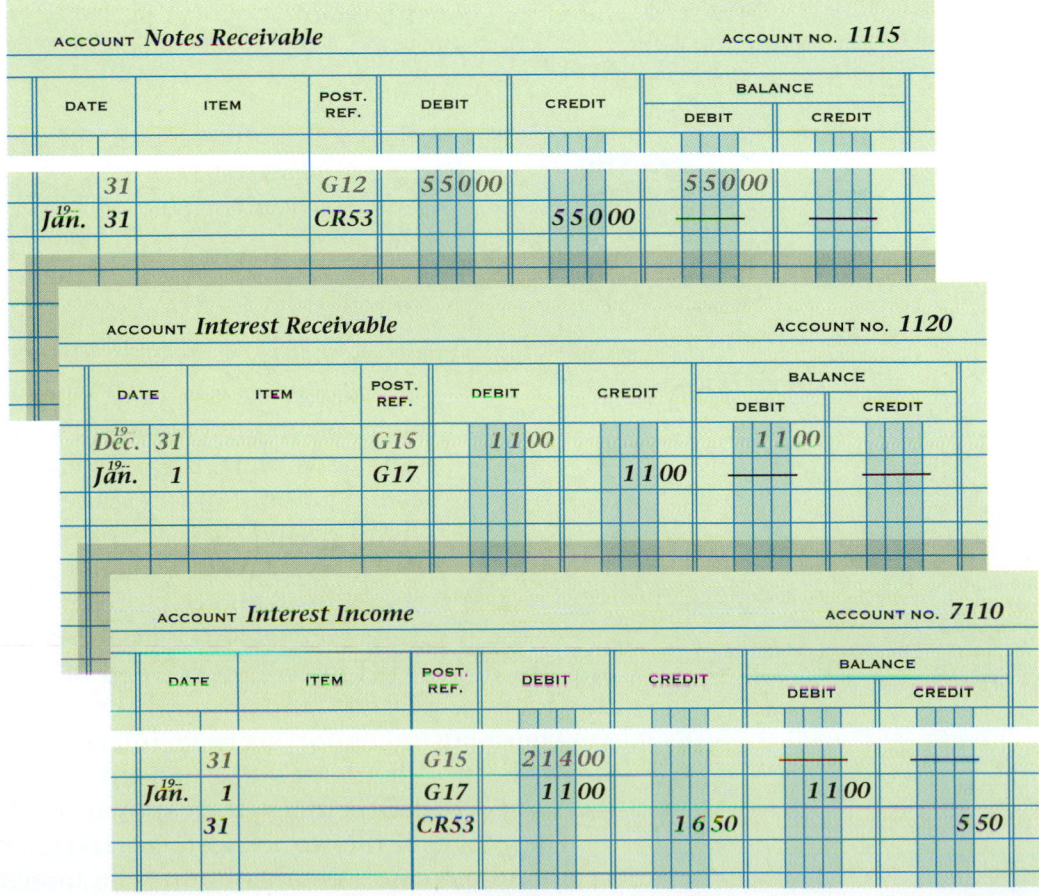

Revenue) The adjusting entry for accrued expense increases the accrued expense account, an other expense account. The adjusting entry also increases the accrued expense payable account, a liability account. The income statement will then report all expenses for the period even though some of the expenses have not yet been paid. The balance sheet will report all liabilities, including the accrued expenses payable. *(CONCEPT: Adequate Disclosure)*

Adjusting Entry for Accrued Interest Expense

Interest incurred but not yet paid is called **accrued interest expense**. At the end of each fiscal period, Celluphone examines the notes payable outstanding and calculates the accrued interest expense. On December 31, Celluphone has one note payable outstanding, Note Payable No. 10. Note Payable No. 10 is a 9-month, 10% note for $2,800.00 issued to First National Bank on September 30. The accounting records should show all the interest expense for the fiscal period. *(CONCEPT: Adequate Disclosure)* Therefore, an adjusting entry is made to record the amount of accrued interest expense to date on this note.

The time period from September 30 to December 31 is three months. Therefore, the time stated as a fraction of a year is $\frac{3}{12}$. Accrued interest on this note at the end of the fiscal year is calculated as shown below.

	Principal	×	Interest Rate	×	Time as Fraction of Year	=	Accrued Interest Expense
	$2,800.00	×	10%	×	$\frac{3}{12}$	=	$70.00

Interest Expense

Dec. 31 Bal.	1,375.00	
Dec. 31 Adj.	70.00	
(New Bal.	1,445.00)	

Interest Payable

| | | Dec. 31 Adj. | 70.00 |

Interest Expense is debited for $70.00 to show the increase in the balance of this other expense account. The new interest expense account balance, $1,445.00, is the amount of interest expense incurred during the fiscal period.

Interest Payable is credited for $70.00 to show the increase in the balance of this liability account. The interest payable account balance, $70.00, is the amount of accrued interest at the end of the fiscal period. However, this interest will not be paid until the next fiscal period.

The adjustment for accrued interest expense is planned on a work sheet. Celluphone's accrued interest expense adjustment for the year ended December 31 is shown in Illustration 25-7.

On line 50 of the work sheet, Interest Expense is debited for $70.00 in the Adjustments Debit column. The interest expense adjustment,

ILLUSTRATION 25-7

Accrued interest expense adjustment on a work sheet

Celluphone, Inc.
Work Sheet
For Year Ended December 31, 19--

		1	2	3	4	5	6	7	8	
	ACCOUNT TITLE	TRIAL BALANCE		ADJUSTMENTS		INCOME STATEMENT		BALANCE SHEET		
		DEBIT	CREDIT	DEBIT	CREDIT	DEBIT	CREDIT	DEBIT	CREDIT	
15	Interest Payable				(h) 70 00				70 00	15
50	Interest Expense	1 3 7 5 00		(h) 70 00		1 4 4 5 00				50

$70.00, is added to the previous balance in the Trial Balance Debit column, $1,375.00. The new balance, $1,445.00 ($70.00 + $1,375.00), is extended to the Income Statement Debit column. On line 15 Interest Payable is credited for $70.00 in the Adjustments Credit column. This amount, $70.00, is extended to the Balance Sheet Credit column.

Information used to journalize an adjustment for accrued interest expense is obtained from the Adjustments columns of a work sheet. The adjusting entry is shown in Illustration 25-8.

ILLUSTRATION 25-8

Adjusting entry for accrued interest expense

	DATE	ACCOUNT TITLE	DOC. NO.	POST. REF.	DEBIT	CREDIT	
		GENERAL JOURNAL		PAGE **15**			
1		*Adjusting Entries*					1
16	31	Interest Expense			70 00		16
17		Interest Payable				70 00	17
18							18
19							19
20							20

After the adjusting entry is posted, the interest payable and interest expense accounts appear as shown in Illustration 25-9.

The interest payable account has a credit balance of $70.00 and will appear on the December 31 balance sheet as a current liability. This credit balance is the accrued interest expense incurred but not yet paid at the end of the year. The interest expense account has a debit balance of $1,445.00 and will appear on the income statement for the year ended December 31 as an other expense. This amount is the total interest expense for the year.

The interest payable balance will appear on the balance sheet as a liability.

ILLUSTRATION 25-9 General ledger accounts after adjusting entry for accrued interest expense is posted

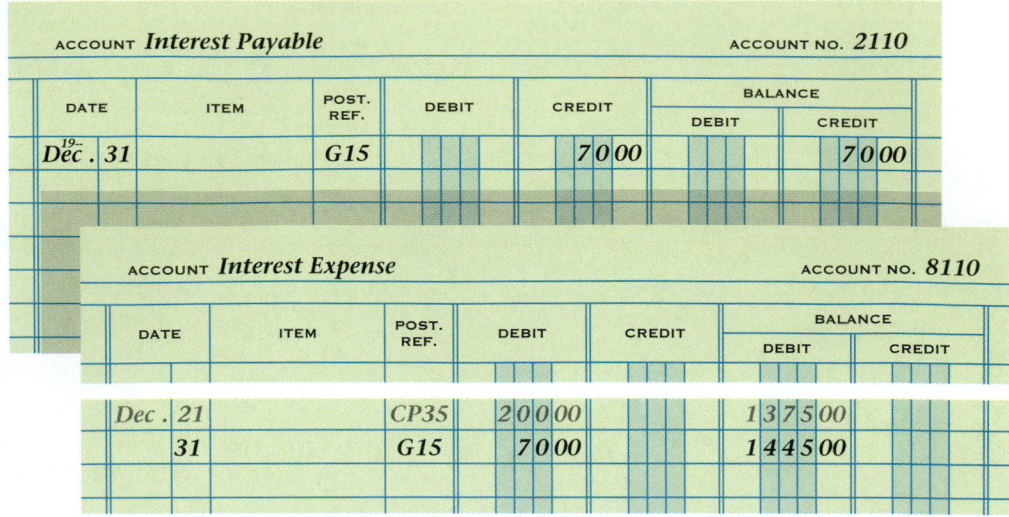

ACCOUNT Interest Payable					ACCOUNT NO. 2110	
DATE	ITEM	POST. REF.	DEBIT	CREDIT	BALANCE DEBIT	CREDIT
Dec. 31		G15		70 00		70 00

ACCOUNT Interest Expense					ACCOUNT NO. 8110	
DATE	ITEM	POST. REF.	DEBIT	CREDIT	BALANCE DEBIT	CREDIT
Dec. 21		CP35	200 00		1375 00	
31		G15	70 00		1445 00	

Closing Entry for Interest Expense

Income Summary	
Dec. 31 Closing	1,445.00

Interest Expense			
Dec. 31 Bal.	1,375.00	Dec. 31 Closing	1,445.00
Dec. 31 Adj.	70.00		
(New Bal. zero)			

Information needed to record closing entries is obtained from the Income Statement columns of a work sheet. Interest Expense is closed to the income summary account.

Interest Expense is closed as part of the regular closing entries. The $1,445.00 will also be a part of the debit entry to Income Summary to close all income statement accounts with debit balances. Interest Expense is credited for $1,445.00 to reduce the account balance to zero. After the closing entry is posted, the interest expense account is closed.

Reversing Entry for Accrued Interest Expense

On the maturity date of Note Payable No. 10, June 30, Celluphone will pay the note's maturity value (principal and interest). Total interest incurred for the 9-month note is $210.00, calculated as shown below.

	Principal	×	Interest Rate	×	Time as Fraction of Year	=	Interest
	$2,800.00	×	10%	×	$\frac{9}{12}$	=	$210.00

However, an adjusting entry was made to record the amount of accrued interest expense last year, $70.00, by debiting Interest Expense and crediting Interest Payable. Thus, $70.00 of the $210.00 total interest expense was incurred and recorded in the previous year. The remaining $140.00 of the $210.00 total interest expense was incurred during the current year. Determining how much of the cash paid is for accrued interest expense and how much applies to the current year is an inconvenience. To avoid this inconvenience, a reversing entry is made at the beginning of the new fiscal period.

The adjusting entry for accrued interest expense creates a balance in the liability account Interest Payable. Therefore, Celluphone uses reversing entries for all accrued interest expense adjusting entries.

The reversing entry results in a credit balance of $70.00 in Interest Expense. A credit balance is the opposite of the normal balance of the interest expense account. When the full amount of interest is paid, $210.00, this amount will be debited to Interest Expense. The account will then have a debit balance of $140.00 ($210.00 debit − $70.00 credit), the amount of interest expense incurred in the new year.

The reversing entry to Interest Payable reduces that account to a zero balance. Thus, when the interest is received, no debit entry will be required to recognize payment of the balance of Interest Payable. The total amount of interest paid will be debited to Interest Expense. Celluphone's reversing entry for accrued interest expense is shown in Illustration 25-10.

The reversing entry is the opposite of the adjusting entry shown in Illustration 25-8.

Interest Payable

| Jan. 1 Rev. | 70.00 | Dec. 31 Adj. | 70.00 |
| | | *(New Bal. zero)* | |

Interest Expense

Dec. 31 Bal.	1,375.00	Dec. 31 Closing	1,445.00
Dec. 31 Adj.	70.00	Jan. 1 Rev.	70.00
(New Bal.	*70.00)*		

FYI

Reversing entries are always optional; however, many businesses record them because they make recording the following year's entries easier.

ILLUSTRATION 25-10   Reversing entry for accrued interest expense

	DATE		ACCOUNT TITLE	DOC. NO.	POST. REF.	DEBIT	CREDIT	
1			*Reversing Entries*					1
4		1	*Interest Payable*			70 00		4
5			*Interest Expense*				70 00	5
6								6
7								7
8								8
9								9
10								10

GENERAL JOURNAL   PAGE 17

Paying a Note Payable Issued in a Previous Fiscal Period

On June 30 Celluphone paid the maturity value (principal plus interest) of the only note payable on hand December 31, the end of the previous fiscal year. The maturity value for Note Payable No. 10 is calculated as shown below.

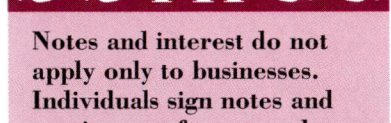

	Principal	×	Interest Rate	×	Time as Fraction of Year	=	Interest
	$2,800.00	×	10%	×	$\frac{9}{12}$	=	$210.00

	Principal	+	Interest	=	Maturity Value
	$2,800.00	+	$210.00	=	$3,010.00

Notes Payable

June 30 Paid	2,800.00	Sept. 30 NP10	2,800.00

Interest Expense

Dec. 31 Bal.	1,375.00	Dec. 31 Closing	1,445.00
Dec. 31 Adj.	70.00	Jan. 1 Rev.	70.00
(New Bal. zero)			
June 30 Paid	210.00		
(New Bal.	140.00)		

Cash

		June 30 Paid	3,010.00

June 30, 19--. Paid cash for the maturity value of Note Payable No. 10: principal, $2,800.00, plus interest, $210.00; total, $3,010.00. Check No. 982.

The total interest, $210.00, was incurred during two fiscal periods, $70.00 during the previous fiscal period and $140.00 during the current fiscal period. Since Celluphone uses reversing entries, the entry to record the payment of this note payable and interest is the same as the entry to record a note issued and paid in a single fiscal year.

Notes Payable is debited for the principal of the note, $2,800.00, to record the decrease in the balance of this current liability account. Interest Expense is debited for the total amount of interest, $210.00, to record the increase in this other expense account. The interest expense account now has a debit balance of $140.00, the amount of interest expense incurred during the current fiscal period. Cash is credited for the total amount paid, $3,010.00, to record the decrease in this asset account.

The cash payments journal entry to record this payment of a note payable when reversing entries are used is shown in Illustration 25-11.

ILLUSTRATION 25-11 Cash payments journal entry to record note payable issued in previous fiscal period when reversing entries are used

CASH PAYMENTS JOURNAL   PAGE 55

					1 GENERAL DEBIT	2 GENERAL CREDIT	3 ACCOUNTS PAYABLE DEBIT	4 PURCHASES DISCOUNT CREDIT	5 CASH CREDIT	
	DATE	ACCOUNT TITLE	CK. NO.	POST. REF.						
21	30	Notes Payable	982		2800 00				3010 00	21
22		Interest Expense			210 00					22
23										23
24										24
25										25

After the cash payments journal entry is posted, the notes payable, interest payable, and interest expense accounts appear as shown in Illustration 25-12.

Notes Payable has a zero balance. This account will be used again when additional notes payable are issued. After the reversing entry is recorded, Interest Payable has a zero balance. Interest Payable will not be used again until it is needed for an adjusting entry at the end of the current fiscal year. Interest Expense has a debit balance of $140.00, the amount of interest incurred on Note Payable No. 10 in the current year.

The chart shown in Summary Illustration 25-13 on the next page summarizes the journal entries for recording accrued revenue and expenses.

ILLUSTRATION 25-12   General ledger accounts after posting cash payment for note payable issued in previous fiscal period when reversing entries are used

ACCOUNT *Notes Payable*   ACCOUNT NO. *2105*

DATE	ITEM	POST. REF.	DEBIT	CREDIT	BALANCE DEBIT	BALANCE CREDIT
30		CR26		2800 00		2800 00
June 30		CP55	2800 00		———	———

ACCOUNT *Interest Payable*   ACCOUNT NO. *2110*

DATE	ITEM	POST. REF.	DEBIT	CREDIT	BALANCE DEBIT	BALANCE CREDIT
Dec. 31		G15		70 00		70 00
Jan. 1		G17	70 00		———	———

ACCOUNT *Interest Expense*   ACCOUNT NO. *8110*

DATE	ITEM	POST. REF.	DEBIT	CREDIT	BALANCE DEBIT	BALANCE CREDIT
31		G16		1445 00	———	———
Jan. 1		G17		70 00		70 00
June 30		CP55	210 00		140 00	

Summary of journal entries for recording accrued revenue and expenses

Journal Entries	GENERAL LEDGER															
	Cash		Notes Receivable		Interest Receivable		Notes Payable		Interest Payable		Income Summary		Interest Income		Interest Expense	
	DR	CR	DR	CR	DR	CR	DR	CR	DR	CR	DR	CR	DR	CR	DR	CR
Adjusting entry for accrued interest income on note receivable					X									X		
Entry to close interest income account												X	X			
Reversing entry for accrued interest income						X							X			
Received cash for note receivable accepted in previous fiscal period when reversing entries are used	X			X										X		
Adjusting entry for accrued interest expense on note payable										X					X	
Entry to close interest expense account											X					X
Reversing entry for accrued interest expense									X							X
Paid cash for note payable issued in previous fiscal period when reversing entries are used		X					X								X	

What is the meaning of each of the following?

1. **accrued revenue**
2. **accrued interest income**
3. **reversing entry**
4. **accrued expenses**
5. **accrued interest expense**

1. When do generally accepted accounting procedures require that revenue and expenses be recorded?
2. Which accounting concept is being applied when an adjusting entry is made at the end of the fiscal period to record accrued revenue?
3. Why should accrued revenue be recorded by an adjusting entry before financial statements are prepared at the end of a fiscal period?
4. What accounts are affected, and how, by the adjusting entry for accrued interest income?
5. Where is the information obtained that is needed to journalize an adjustment for accrued interest income?
6. After closing entries are posted, what is the balance of the interest income account?
7. Why does a business use reversing entries as part of its procedures for accounting for accrued interest income?
8. What accounts are affected, and how, by the reversing entry for accrued interest income?

9. Interest of $15.00 on a note receivable is earned and accrued on December 31 and an additional $25.00 interest is earned by the note's maturity date. What entry will be made to **Interest Income** when the maturity value of the note is received? (The business uses reversing entries for all accrual adjusting entries.)
10. Why should accrued expenses be recorded by an adjusting entry before financial statements are prepared at the end of a fiscal period?
11. What accounts are affected, and how, by the adjusting entry for accrued interest expense?
12. What accounts are affected, and how, by the reversing entry for accrued interest expense?
13. Immediately after a reversing entry for accrued interest expense is recorded, what is the balance of the interest payable account?

CASE 1 As a new accounting clerk at The Print Shop, you discover that $80.00 accrued interest income on notes receivable was not recorded at the end of the current fiscal period. When you consult with the manager, the manager says, "Don't worry about recording the interest income. It will be recorded when we collect the note and interest." Is the manager's approach acceptable? Explain your answer. What effect will the omission of accrued interest income have on the current fiscal year's (a) income statement and (b) balance sheet?

CASE 2 At the end of each fiscal period, Jet-Air prepares adjusting entries to record accrued interest expense. However, the company does not record reversing entries for the accrued interest expense. At the end of the current fiscal year, Jet-Air had Note Payable No. 12 outstanding, a $3,000.00, 3-month, 10% note issued October 31. Jet-Air made the following journal entries related to Note Payable No. 12.

Issued Oct. 31			Winifred Harwick, a newly employed accounting
Cash	$3,000.00		supervisor, says that generally accepted accounting
Notes Payable		$3,000.00	principles require that reversing entries be used in
Adj. Entry Dec. 31			conjunction with adjusting entries for accrued ex-
Interest Expense	50.00		penses. Thus, Ms. Harwick says Jet-Air must begin
Interest Payable		50.00	using reversing entries for all accrued expenses. Is
Clos. Entry Dec. 31			Ms. Harwick correct? Do the procedures Jet-Air has
Income Summary	50.00		been using result in incorrect financial statements?
Interest Expense		50.00	Explain your answer.
Paid Note Jan. 31			
Notes Payable	3,000.00		
Interest Payable	50.00		
Interest Expense	25.00		
Cash		3,075.00	

DRILL 25-D1   Analyzing entries for notes receivable and accrued revenue

TUTORIAL

A form for analyzing transactions is given in the working papers that accompany this textbook.

INSTRUCTIONS:

For each of the following entries, indicate by a check mark which account(s) should be debited and which account(s) should be credited.

1. Received a note receivable from a customer for an extension of time on account.
2. Recorded an adjusting entry at the end of the fiscal period for interest earned but not yet received.
3. Closed interest income account.
4. Recorded reversing entry for accrued interest income.
5. Received cash for maturity value of a note receivable accepted in previous fiscal period for a business that uses reversing entries.

DRILL 25-D2   Analyzing entries for notes payable and accrued expenses

A form for analyzing transactions is given in the working papers that accompany this textbook.

INSTRUCTIONS:

For each of the following entries, indicate by a check mark which account(s) should be debited and which account(s) should be credited.

1. Issued a note payable to a vendor for an extension of time on an account payable.
2. Recorded an adjusting entry at the end of the fiscal period for interest incurred but not yet paid.
3. Closed interest expense account.
4. Recorded reversing entry for accrued interest expense.
5. Paid cash for maturity value of a note payable issued in previous fiscal period for a business that uses reversing entries.

PROBLEM 25-1   Journalizing and posting entries for accrued revenue

MATHEMATICS

The general ledger accounts for Citation Corporation are given in the working papers accompanying this textbook. The balances are recorded as of December 31 of the current year before adjusting entries.

Citation Corporation completed the following transactions related to notes receivable during the current year and the following year. The first transaction has already been journalized and posted. Note Receivable No. 11 is the only note receivable on hand at the end of the fiscal period. Source documents are abbreviated as follows: note receivable, NR; receipt, R.

19X1
Nov. 1.   Received a 3-month, 12% note from Peter Mendoza for an extension of time on his account, $800.00. NR11.

19X2
Feb. 1.   Received cash for the maturity value of NR11: principal, $800.00, plus interest, $24.00; total, $824.00. R110.

INSTRUCTIONS:

1. Use page 14 of a general journal. Journalize the adjusting entry for accrued interest income on December 31. Post this entry.

2. Continue to use page 14 of a general journal. Journalize the closing entry for interest income. Post this entry.

3. Use page 15 of a general journal. Journalize the reversing entry for accrued interest income. Post this entry.

4. Use page 18 of a cash receipts journal. Journalize the receipt of cash for the maturity value of NR11. Post this entry.

PROBLEM 25-2   Journalizing and posting entries for accrued expenses

MATHEMATICS

The general ledger accounts for Charter Corporation are given in the working papers accompanying this textbook. The balances are recorded as of December 31 of the current year before adjusting entries.

Charter Corporation completed the following transactions related to notes payable during the current year and the following year. The first transaction has already been journalized and posted. Note Payable No. 5 is the only note payable on hand at the end of the fiscal period. Source documents are abbreviated as follows: check, C; note payable, NP.

19X1
Sept. 1.   Issued a 6-month, 12% note, $4,000.00. NP5.

19X2
Mar. 1.   Paid cash for the maturity value of NP5: principal, $4,000.00, plus interest, $240.00; total, $4,240.00. C189.

INSTRUCTIONS:

1. Use page 15 of a general journal. Journalize the adjusting entry for accrued interest expense on December 31. Post this entry.

2. Continue to use page 15 of a general journal. Journalize the closing entry for interest expense. Post this entry.

3. Use page 16 of a general journal. Journalize the reversing entry for accrued interest expense. Post this entry.

4. Use page 20 of a cash payments journal. Journalize the cash payment for the maturity value of NP5. Post this entry.

MASTERY PROBLEM 25-M   Journalizing and posting entries for accrued revenue and expenses

The general ledger accounts for Hahn Company are given in the working papers accompanying this textbook. The balances are recorded as of December 31 of the current year before adjusting entries.

Hahn Company completed the following transactions related to notes receivable and notes payable during the current year and the following year. The first two transactions have already been journalized and posted. Note Receivable No. 8 and Note Payable No. 4 are the only notes on hand at the end of the fiscal period.

19X1
Oct. 31. Received a 3-month, 12% note from Donald Ritter for an extension of time on his account, $600.00. NR8.
　　 31. Issued a 4-month, 14% note, $2,400.00. NP4.

19X2
Jan. 31. Received cash for the maturity value of NR8: principal, $600.00, plus interest, $18.00; total, $618.00. R207.
Feb. 28. Paid cash for the maturity value of NP4: principal, $2,400.00, plus interest, $112.00; total, $2,512.00. C423.

INSTRUCTIONS:

1. Use page 15 of a general journal. Journalize the adjusting entries for accrued interest income and accrued interest expense on December 31. Post these entries.
2. Continue to use page 15 of a general journal. Journalize the closing entries for interest income and interest expense. Post these entries.
3. Use page 16 of a general journal. Journalize the reversing entries for accrued interest income and accrued interest expense. Post these entries.
4. Use page 19 of a cash receipts journal. Journalize the receipt of cash for the maturity value of NR8. Post this entry.
5. Use page 25 of a cash payments journal. Journalize the cash payment for the maturity value of NP4. Post this entry.

CHALLENGE PROBLEM 25-C   Journalizing and posting entries for accrued revenue and expenses

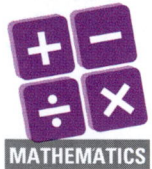

The general ledger accounts for Castoldo Corporation are given in the working papers accompanying this textbook. The balances are recorded as of December 31 of the current year before adjusting entries.

Castoldo Corporation completed the following transactions related to notes receivable and notes payable during the current year and the following year. The first two transactions have already been journalized and posted. Note Receivable No. 6 and Note Payable No. 11 are the only notes on hand at the end of the fiscal period.

19X1
Nov. 30. We received a note from Margaret Snider. This note is a 4-month, 12% note for an extension of time on her account, $400.00. NR6.
Dec. 15. A 5-month, 12% note was issued, $2,500.00. NP11.

19X2
Mar. 31. Margaret Snider dishonored NR6, maturity value due today. M83.
May 15. Paid cash for the maturity value of NP11. C465.

INSTRUCTIONS:

1. Use page 13 of a general journal. Journalize the adjusting entries for accrued interest income and accrued interest expense on December 31. Post these entries.

2. Continue to use page 13 of a general journal. Journalize the closing entries for interest income and interest expense. Post these entries.
3. Use page 14 of a general journal. Journalize the reversing entries for accrued interest income and accrued interest expense. Post these entries.
4. Use page 16 of a general journal. Journalize the dishonored note, NR6. Post this entry to the general ledger accounts.
5. Use page 33 of a cash payments journal. Journalize the cash payment for the maturity value of NP11. Post this entry.

26

Distributing Dividends and Preparing a Work Sheet for a Corporation

ENABLING PERFORMANCE TASKS

After studying Chapter 26, you will be able to:

a Define accounting terms related to distributing dividends and preparing a work sheet for a merchandising business organized as a corporation.

b Identify accounting concepts and practices related to distributing dividends and preparing a work sheet for a merchandising business organized as a corporation.

c Journalize the declaration and payment of a dividend for a merchandising business organized as a corporation.

d Plan end-of-fiscal-period adjustments for a merchandising business organized as a corporation.

e Complete a work sheet for a merchandising business organized as a corporation.

TERMS PREVIEW

stockholder • retained earnings • dividends • board of directors • declaring a dividend

Many accounting procedures used for a corporation are similar to the procedures used for a proprietorship or a partnership. Consequently, preparing a work sheet for a corporation is similar to preparing a work sheet for a proprietorship or a partnership.

There are, however, three principal differences between accounting for a proprietorship or partnership and accounting for a corporation. (1) Different accounts are used to record owners' equity. (2) Different procedures are used to distribute income to owners. (3) Corporations calculate and pay federal income tax. Corporations must pay income tax on their net income. Proprietorship and partnership net income is treated as part of each owner's personal income for income tax purposes. Thus, income tax is not calculated for a proprietorship or partnership business.

STOCKHOLDERS' EQUITY ACCOUNTS USED BY A CORPORATION

A corporation's ownership is divided into units. Each unit of ownership in a corporation is known as a share of stock. An owner of one or more shares of a corporation is called a **stockholder**. Each stockholder is an owner of a corporation.

Separate general ledger owners' equity accounts are maintained for each owner of a proprietorship or a partnership. However, a corporation may have many stockholders. Therefore, a separate owners' equity account is not maintained for each owner of a corporation. Instead, a single owners' equity account, titled Capital Stock, is used for the investment of all owners.

Owners' equity accounts for a corporation normally are listed under a major chart of accounts division titled *Stockholders' Equity*. The stockholders' equity section of Celluphone's chart of accounts is shown in Illustration 26-1.

ILLUSTRATION 26-1

Stockholders' equity section of a corporation chart of accounts

(3000) STOCKHOLDERS' EQUITY
3105 Capital Stock
3110 Retained Earnings
3115 Dividends
3120 Income Summary

A second stockholders' equity account is used to record a corporation's earnings. An amount earned by a corporation and not yet distributed to stockholders is called **retained earnings.** Retained Earnings is the title of the account used to record a corporation's earnings.

A third stockholders' equity account is used to record the distribution of a corporation's earnings to stockholders. Earnings distributed to stockholders are called **dividends.** A corporation's

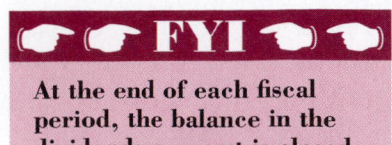
dividend account is a temporary account similar to a proprietorship's or partnership's drawing account. Each time a dividend is declared, an account titled Dividends is debited. At the end of each fiscal period, the balance in the dividends account is closed to Retained Earnings. Dividends could be recorded as debits to a corporation's retained earnings account. However, many corporations record dividends in a separate account so that the total amounts are easily determined for each fiscal period.

DISTRIBUTING CORPORATE DIVIDENDS TO STOCKHOLDERS

Net income increases a corporation's total stockholders' equity. Some income may be retained by a corporation for business expansion. Also, some income may be given to stockholders as a return on their investments. Dividends can be distributed to stockholders *ONLY* by formal action of a corporation's board of directors. *(CONCEPT: Business Entity)* A group of persons elected by the stockholders to manage a corporation is called a **board of directors**.

Declaring a Dividend

Action by a board of directors to distribute corporate earnings to stockholders is called **declaring a dividend.** Dividends normally are declared on one date and paid on a later date. A corporation's board of directors is not required to declare a dividend. In fact, dividends cannot be declared that would exceed the balance of the retained earnings account. However, when a board of directors does declare a dividend, the corporation is then obligated to pay the dividend. The dividend is a liability that must be recorded in the corporation's accounts.

Celluphone's board of directors declares a dividend every three months so that stockholders can share the corporation's earnings throughout the year. Celluphone declares dividends each March 15, June 15, September 15, and December 15. The dividends are then paid on the 15th of the month following the declaration.

December 15, 19--. Celluphone's board of directors declared a quarterly dividend of $2.00 per share; capital stock issued is 10,000 shares; total dividend, $20,000.00. Date of payment is January 15, 19--. Memorandum No. 195.

A dividend declaration increases the balance of the dividends account. The stockholders' equity account, Dividends, has a normal debit balance and is increased by a debit. Dividends, therefore, is debited for $20,000.00 (10,000 shares × $2.00 per share). Dividends Payable is credited for $20,000.00 to show the increase in this liability account.

Dividends		
3/15 Decl.	20,000.00	
6/15 Decl.	20,000.00	
9/15 Decl.	20,000.00	
12/15 Decl.	20,000.00	

Dividends Payable			
4/15 Paid	20,000.00	3/15 Decl.	20,000.00
7/15 Paid	20,000.00	6/15 Decl.	20,000.00
10/15 Paid	20,000.00	9/15 Decl.	20,000.00
		12/15 Decl.	20,000.00

INTERNATIONAL TRAVEL

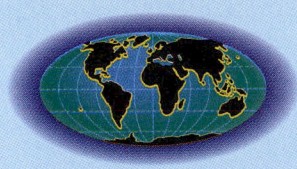

When traveling internationally, a passport is usually required. A passport is a formal document that allows exit from and reentry into the country. It proves citizenship and provides identity for the traveler.

For the first-time passport applicant to receive a passport, a passport application must be completed. The application may be obtained from the United States Postal Service office and submitted with the following.

1. Proof of U.S. citizenship. Proof of U.S. citizenship is usually a certified birth certificate.
2. Proof of identity. Proof of identity is a document such as a driver's license.
3. Two photographs. Two photographs must be submitted that are identical and 2″ × 2″ in size. These photos cannot be snapshots as they must meet certain criteria. There are many local photo studios that advertise passport photos service.
4. Fee. The applicable fee when this textbook was written was $65. The passport is valid for ten years.

This information must be sent to a designated postal service employee at a selected post office; a clerk of a Federal or State court of record or a judge or clerk of a probate court who accepts applications; a U.S. consular official; or an agent at a Passport Agency in Boston, Chicago, Honolulu, Houston, Los Angeles, Miami, New Orleans, New York, Philadelphia, San Francisco, Seattle, Stamford, or Washington D.C.

Some countries require an additional endorsement or stamp by foreign country officials to be placed on the U.S. passport that allows entrance into that country. This stamp is known as a visa. Visas may be obtained from the appropriate embassy of the country being visited.

Immunizations are sometimes required by countries under the International Health Regulations adopted by the World Health Organization. Be sure to check with the Center for Disease Control to see if vaccinations such as those to prevent yellow fever or cholera are necessary before entering a particular country.

FYI

The general journal is used to record declaration of a dividend.

A transaction for a declaration of a dividend is not appropriately journalized in any of the special journals. Therefore, the entry is journalized in a general journal. The general journal entry to record Celluphone's quarterly declaration of a dividend is shown in Illustration 26-2.

ILLUSTRATION 26-2

General journal entry to record the declaration of a dividend by a corporation

GENERAL JOURNAL — PAGE 14

	DATE		ACCOUNT TITLE	DOC. NO.	POST. REF.	DEBIT	CREDIT	
1	Dec.	15	Dividends	M195		20 00 0 00		1
2			Dividends Payable				20 00 0 00	2
3								3
4								4
5								5
6								6

Dividends is debited for the dividend declared, $20,000.00. Dividends Payable is credited for the liability incurred by the dividend declaration, $20,000.00.

Paying a Dividend

Celluphone issues one check for the amount of the total dividend to be paid. This check is deposited in a special dividend checking account. A separate check for each stockholder is drawn on this special account. The special account avoids a large number of cash payments journal entries and also reserves cash specifically for paying dividends.

A check is often made payable to an agent, such as a bank. The agent then handles the details of sending dividend checks to individual stockholders.

January 15, 19--. Paid cash for quarterly dividend declared December 15, 19--, $20,000.00. Check No. 794.

In this transaction the balance of the liability account, Dividends Payable, is decreased. The balance of the asset account, Cash, is also decreased. Therefore, Dividends Payable is debited for $20,000.00 and Cash is credited for $20,000.00.

The cash payments journal entry to record Celluphone's quarterly dividend payment of $20,000.00 is shown in Illustration 26-3.

Dividends Payable is debited for the amount of dividends paid, $20,000.00. Cash is credited for the total amount of cash paid, $20,000.00. When this entry is posted, the dividends payable account has a zero balance.

Dividends Payable			
4/15 Paid	20,000.00	3/15 Decl.	20,000.00
7/15 Paid	20,000.00	6/15 Decl.	20,000.00
10/15 Paid	20,000.00	9/15 Decl.	20,000.00
1/15 Paid	20,000.00	12/15 Decl.	20,000.00

Cash			
		1/15 Paid	20,000.00

Audit Your Understanding

1. Who is responsible for declaring dividends?
2. What is the entry to record declaration of a dividend?
3. What is the entry to record payment of a dividend?

ILLUSTRATION 26-3   Cash payments journal entry to record the payment of a dividend

CASH PAYMENTS JOURNAL   PAGE 37

	DATE	ACCOUNT TITLE	CK. NO.	POST. REF.	GENERAL DEBIT	GENERAL CREDIT	ACCOUNTS PAYABLE DEBIT	PURCHASES DISCOUNT CREDIT	CASH CREDIT	
1	Jan. 15	Dividends Payable	794		20 00 00 0				20 00 00 0	1
2										2
3										3
4										4
5										5
6										6
7										7
8										8

PREPARING A WORK SHEET FOR A CORPORATION

Work sheets for proprietorships, partnerships, and corporations are similar. Businesses use work sheets to plan adjustments and provide information needed to prepare financial statements. Celluphone may prepare a work sheet at any time financial statements are needed. However, Celluphone always prepares a work sheet and financial statements at the end of a fiscal year. (CONCEPT: *Accounting Period Cycle*)

Entering a Trial Balance on a Work Sheet

To prepare a work sheet, a trial balance is first entered in the Trial Balance columns. All general ledger accounts are listed in the same order as they appear in the general ledger. Trial Balance columns are totaled to prove equality of debits and credits.

Celluphone's trial balance on December 31 is shown on the work sheet, Illustration 26-4 on pages 690 and 691. A corporation's accounts are similar to those of a proprietorship or partnership except for the capital stock, retained earnings, dividends, and federal income tax accounts.

Planning Adjustments on a Work Sheet

Some general ledger accounts need to be brought up to date before financial statements are prepared. Accounts are brought up to date by planning and entering adjustments on a work sheet. Most adjustments on a corporation's work sheet are similar to those for proprietorships and partnerships.

The adjustments for merchandise inventory, supplies, and prepaid insurance are described in earlier chapters. Celluphone also makes six other adjustments. (1) Interest Income. (2) Uncollectible Accounts Expense. (3) Depreciation Expense—Office Equipment. (4) Depreciation Expense—Store Equipment. (5) Interest Expense. (6) Federal Income Tax Expense.

Adjustments for depreciation expense, uncollectible accounts expense, interest income, and interest expense could also be made by proprietorships and partnerships. However, the adjustment for federal income tax is unique to corporations. This adjustment is not made for proprietorships and partnerships because taxes are paid by the owners, not the business. Adjustments generally are made in the order that accounts are listed on a work sheet.

Interest Income Adjustment. Interest income earned during the current fiscal period but not yet received needs to be recorded. Two accounts are used for the adjustment for accrued interest income: Interest Receivable and Interest Income. An analysis of Celluphone's adjustment for accrued interest income is described in Chapter 25. Celluphone's accrued interest income adjustment is labeled *(a)* on

ILLUSTRATION 26-4

Completed work sheet for a corporation

Celluphone, Inc.
Work Sheet
For Year Ended December 31, 19--

	ACCOUNT TITLE	TRIAL BALANCE DEBIT	TRIAL BALANCE CREDIT	ADJUSTMENTS DEBIT	ADJUSTMENTS CREDIT	INCOME STATEMENT DEBIT	INCOME STATEMENT CREDIT	BALANCE SHEET DEBIT	BALANCE SHEET CREDIT
1	Cash	4096800						4096800	
2	Petty Cash	30000						30000	
3	Notes Receivable	55000						55000	
4	Interest Receivable			(a) 1100				1100	
5	Accounts Receivable	6824000						6824000	
6	Allowance for Uncollectible Accounts		26500		(b) 922700				949200
7	Merchandise Inventory	20516000		(c) 701800				21217800	
8	Supplies	1545500			(d) 1169000			376500	
9	Prepaid Insurance	1355000			(e) 859800			495200	
10	Office Equipment	1825000						1825000	
11	Accumulated Depreciation—Office Equip.		362500		(f) 175000				537500
12	Store Equipment	7719000						7719000	
13	Accumulated Depreciation—Store Equip.		912500		(g) 632500				1545000
14	Notes Payable		2800000						2800000
15	Interest Payable				(h) 7000				7000
16	Accounts Payable		8396575						8396575
17	Employee Income Tax Payable		234000						234000
18	Federal Income Tax Payable				(i) 221923				221923
19	FICA Tax Payable		269500						269500
20	Sales Tax Payable		1098200						1098200
21	Unemployment Tax Payable—Federal		4700						4700
22	Unemployment Tax Payable—State		31725						31725
23	Health Insurance Premiums Payable		99500						99500
24	Dividends Payable		2000000						2000000
25	Capital Stock		10000000						10000000

Account Title	Trial Balance Debit	Trial Balance Credit	Adjustments Debit	Adjustments Credit	Income Statement Debit	Income Statement Credit	Balance Sheet Debit	Balance Sheet Credit
26 Retained Earnings		14911800						14911800
27 Dividends	8000000						8000000	
28 Income Summary				(c) 701800		701800		
29 Sales		205044000				205044000		
30 Sales Discount	564200				564200			
31 Sales Returns and Allowances	2431800				2431800			
32 Purchases	145479800				145479800			
33 Purchases Discount		1076600				1076600		
34 Purchases Returns and Allowances		531000				531000		
35 Advertising Expense	3260000				3260000			
36 Credit Card Fee Expense	2046800				2046800			
37 Depr. Expense—Office Equipment			(f) 175000		175000			
38 Depr. Expense—Store Equipment			(g) 632500		632500			
39 Insurance Expense			(e) 859800		859800			
40 Miscellaneous Expense	2235000				2235000			
41 Payroll Taxes Expense	2372000				2372000			
42 Rent Expense	5640000				5640000			
43 Salary Expense	25193200				25193200			
44 Supplies Expense			(d) 1169000		1169000			
45 Uncollectible Accounts Expense			(b) 922700		922700			
46 Utilities Expense	489000				489000			
47 Gain on Plant Assets		22500				22500		
48 Interest Income		20300		(a) 1100		21400		
49 Cash Short and Over	300				300			
50 Interest Expense	137500		(h) 7000		144500			
51 Loss on Plant Assets	46000				46000			
52 Federal Income Tax Expense	3460000		(i) 221923		3681923			
53	245321900	245321900	4690823	4690823	197343523	207397300	50640400	40586623
54 Net Income after Federal Income Tax					10053777			10053777
55					207397300	207397300	50640400	50640400

lines 4 and 48 in the work sheet Adjustments columns, Illustration 26-4, pages 690 and 691.

Interest Receivable is debited for the amount of accrued interest income, $11.00. Interest Income is credited for the same amount.

Uncollectible Accounts Expense Adjustment. The estimated amount of uncollectible accounts expense for a fiscal period needs to be brought up to date. Two accounts are used for the adjustment for uncollectible accounts expense: Uncollectible Accounts Expense and Allowance for Uncollectible Accounts. An analysis of Celluphone's uncollectible accounts expense adjustment is described in Chapter 21. The uncollectible accounts expense adjustment is labeled *(b)* on lines 6 and 45 in the work sheet Adjustments columns, Illustration 26-4. Uncollectible Accounts Expense is debited for the amount of estimated uncollectible accounts expense, $9,227.00. Allowance for Uncollectible Accounts is credited for the same amount.

Merchandise Inventory Adjustment. The merchandise inventory account balance in a trial balance is the beginning inventory for a fiscal period. The amount of the ending inventory is determined by counting the merchandise on hand at the end of the fiscal period. An adjusting entry is made to bring merchandise inventory up to date so that the end-of-fiscal-period balance will be shown in the merchandise inventory account. The merchandise inventory adjustment is labeled *(c)* on lines 7 and 28 in the work sheet Adjustments columns, Illustration 26-4.

The process used to adjust Celluphone's merchandise inventory account is the same as that described for a partnership business in Chapter 16.

Celluphone's beginning merchandise inventory, $205,160.00, is shown on line 7 in the Trial Balance Debit column on the work sheet. Celluphone's ending merchandise inventory on December 31 is counted and determined to be $212,178.00. To bring Celluphone's merchandise inventory account up to date, the balance of Merchandise Inventory needs to be increased by $7,018.00 ($212,178.00 ending inventory less $205,160.00 beginning inventory). Merchandise Inventory is debited for the amount of the increase, $7,018.00. Income Summary is credited for the same amount.

If the ending merchandise inventory is less than the beginning merchandise inventory, the difference (decrease) is debited to Income Summary and credited to Merchandise Inventory.

Supplies Adjustment. Two accounts are used for the adjustment for supplies: Supplies and Supplies Expense. The supplies adjustment is labeled *(d)* on lines 8 and 44 in the work sheet Adjustments columns, Illustration 26-4. Supplies Expense is debited for the value of supplies used, $11,690.00. Supplies is credited for the same amount.

Prepaid Insurance Adjustment. Insurance premiums are debited to a prepaid insurance account when paid. Insurance expense, however, must be recorded for the fiscal period in which the insurance is used. (CONCEPT: *Matching Expenses with Revenue*) Therefore, Prepaid Insurance and Insurance Expense are adjusted at the end of the fiscal period. The prepaid insurance adjustment is labeled *(e)* on lines 9 and 39 in the work sheet Adjustments columns, Illustration 26-4. Insurance Expense is debited for the value of insurance used, $8,598.00. Prepaid Insurance is credited for the same amount.

Depreciation Expense Adjustments. An analysis of Celluphone's depreciation expense adjustments is described in Chapter 22. The depreciation expense adjustments are labeled *(f)* and *(g)* on lines 11, 13, 37, and 38 in the work sheet Adjustments columns, Illustration 26-4.

Depreciation Expense—Office Equipment is debited for the amount of office equipment depreciation expense, $1,750.00. Accumulated Depreciation—Office Equipment is credited for the same amount. Depreciation Expense—Store Equipment is debited for the amount of store equipment depreciation expense, $6,325.00. Accumulated Depreciation—Store Equipment is credited for the same amount.

Interest Expense Adjustment. Interest expense incurred during the current fiscal period but not yet paid needs to be recorded. Two accounts are used for the adjustment for accrued interest expense: Interest Payable and Interest Expense. An analysis of Celluphone's adjustment for accrued interest expense is described in Chapter 25. The interest expense adjustment is labeled *(h)* on lines 15 and 50 in the work sheet Adjustments columns, Illustration 26-4.

Interest Expense is debited for the amount of accrued interest expense, $70.00. Interest Payable is credited for the same amount.

Federal Income Tax Expense Adjustment

Corporations anticipating annual federal income taxes of $500.00 or more are required to pay their estimated taxes each quarter. Estimated income tax is paid in quarterly installments in April, June, September, and December. However, the actual income tax owed is calculated at the end of a fiscal year. Based on the actual tax owed for a year, a corporation must file an annual return. Any additional tax owed that was not paid in quarterly installments must be paid when the final return is sent.

Early in the current year, Celluphone estimated $34,600.00 federal income tax for the year. Celluphone paid $8,650.00 in each quarterly installment for a total of $34,600.00. Each tax payment is recorded as a debit to Federal Income Tax Expense and a credit to Cash.

Federal income tax is an expense of a corporation. However, the amount of tax depends on net income before the tax is recorded. Five steps are used to calculate the total amount of federal income tax expense and the amount of the adjustment needed on a work sheet.

1 Complete all adjustments on a work sheet except the federal income tax expense adjustment.

FYI

After paying quarterly taxes, a corporation must still file an annual tax return and send any additional tax owed with the return.

2 Extend all amounts except the federal income tax expense account balance to the appropriate Income Statement or Balance Sheet columns.

3 On a separate sheet of paper, total the work sheet's Income Statement columns. Calculate the difference between the two totals. This difference is the net income before federal income tax expense. Celluphone's net income before federal income tax is calculated from the Income Statement columns of the work sheet, Illustration 26-4.

Total of Income Statement Credit column	$2,073,973.00
Less total of Income Statement Debit column before federal income tax	−1,936,616.00
Equals net income before federal income tax	$ 137,357.00

4 Calculate the amount of federal income tax expense using a tax rate table furnished by the Internal Revenue Service. Celluphone's federal income tax for the current year is $36,819.23.

> Tax rate tables showing income tax rates for corporations are distributed by the Internal Revenue Service. Each corporation should check a current table to find the applicable rates. Corporation tax rates in effect when this text was written were used to calculate Celluphone's federal income tax expense.

5 Calculate the amount of the federal income tax expense adjustment.

> The difference between the total federal income tax expense and the estimated tax already paid is the amount of the adjustment, $2,219.23 ($36,819.23 − $34,600.00 = $2,219.23).

Celluphone's federal income tax expense adjustment is shown in the T accounts. Celluphone paid quarterly federal income tax installments of $8,650.00 each. Federal Income Tax Expense has a debit balance of $34,600.00 at the end of the fiscal period before the adjustment is made.

Federal Income Tax Expense

4/15	8,650.00
6/15	8,650.00
9/15	8,650.00
12/15	8,650.00
(12/15 Bal.	34,600.00
12/31 Adj. (i)	2,219.23
(New Bal.	36,819.23)

Federal Income Tax Payable

12/31 Adj. (i)	2,219.23

To enter the adjustment for income tax expense, Celluphone debits Federal Income Tax Expense for $2,219.23 to show the increase in the balance of this expense account. The new balance of this account, $36,819.23, is the total federal income tax expense for the fiscal period. Federal Income Tax Payable is credited for $2,219.23 to show the increase in this liability account. Celluphone's federal income tax payable account balance, $2,219.23, is the amount of income tax expense still unpaid at year end. Celluphone's federal income tax expense adjustment is labeled *(i)* on lines 18 and 52 in the work sheet Adjustments columns, Illustration 26-4.

Federal Income Tax Expense is debited for the amount of the increase, $2,219.23. Federal Income Tax Payable is credited for the same amount.

Federal Income Tax Expense is an expense account. The account appears under a major division titled *Income Tax Expense* as the last item in Celluphone's chart of accounts. **Federal Income Tax Payable**, a liability account, appears under the heading *Current Liabilities*.

After the federal income tax expense adjustment is recorded, the Adjustments columns are totaled and ruled. Next, the balances of the income tax accounts are extended to the appropriate work sheet columns. The federal income tax expense account balance is extended to the Income Statement Debit column. The federal income tax payable account balance is extended to the Balance Sheet Credit column.

Completing a Work Sheet

The Income Statement and Balance Sheet columns are totaled. Totals are written as shown on line 53 of Celluphone's work sheet, Illustration 26-4. The Income Statement Credit column total for Celluphone is $2,073,973.00, which is more than the Income Statement Debit column total of $1,973,435.23. (The Credit column total, $2,073,973.00, *less* the Debit column total, $1,973,435.23, *equals* the difference, $100,537.77.) This amount, *$100,537.77*, is written in the Income Statement Debit column on line 54 of the work sheet. *Net Income after Federal Income Tax* is written in the Account Title column on the same line. Income Statement columns are then totaled as shown on line 55 of the work sheet.

The net income after federal income tax amount, $100,537.77, is written in the Balance Sheet Credit column, line 54. Balance Sheet columns are totaled as shown on line 55. The totals of both the Balance Sheet Debit and Balance Sheet Credit columns are the same and assumed to be correct. Double lines are ruled across the Income Statement and Balance Sheet columns on line 55 to show that the totals have been verified as correct.

The chart shown in Summary Illustration 26-5 on pages 696 and 697 summarizes the steps followed in preparing an 8-column work sheet for a corporation.

Audit Your Understanding

1. What type of adjusting entry is unique to corporations?

2. If a physical inventory shows that ending inventory is greater than beginning inventory, what is the entry to record the adjustment?

3. How is the amount of the federal income tax expense adjustment calculated?

Summary of preparing a work sheet for a corporation

1 Prepare a trial balance in the Trial Balance columns.

2 Analyze and record all adjustments except the federal income tax expense adjustment in the Adjustments columns.

3 Extend all amounts except the federal income tax expense account balance to the appropriate Income Statement or Balance Sheet columns.

4 On a separate sheet of paper, total the work sheet's Income Statement columns. Calculate the difference between the two totals. This difference is the net income before federal income tax.

Income Statement Credit column	$2,073,973.00
Less total of Income Statement Debit column	−1,936,616.00
Equals net income before federal income tax	$ 137,357.00

5 Calculate the amount of federal income tax expense.

6 Calculate and enter the federal income tax expense adjustment in the Adjustments columns.

Total federal income tax expense	$36,819.23
Less balance of Federal Income Tax Expense	−34,600.00
Equals federal income tax expense adjustment	$ 2,219.23

7 Total and rule the Adjustments columns.

8 Extend the federal income tax expense account balance to the Income Statement Debit column. Extend the federal income tax payable account balance to the Balance Sheet Credit column.

9 Total the Income Statement and Balance Sheet columns.

10 Calculate the net income or net loss.

11 Enter the amount of net income in the Income Statement Debit column and in the Balance Sheet Credit column. If there is a net loss, enter the amount of net loss in the Income Statement Credit column and in the Balance Sheet Debit column.

12 Total the four Income Statement and Balance Sheet amount columns.

13 Check that both totals of the Income Statement columns are the same and that both totals of the Balance Sheet columns are the same.

14 Rule double lines across the Income Statement and Balance Sheet column totals to show that the totals have been verified as correct.

		1	2	3

	ACCOUNT TITLE	TRIAL BALANCE		ADJUSTMENTS		INCOME STATEMENT		BALANCE SHEET	
		DEBIT	CREDIT	DEBIT	CREDIT	DEBIT	CREDIT	DEBIT	CREDIT
1	Cash	40 96 8 00						40 96 8 00	
6	Allowance for Uncollectible Accounts		2 6 5 00		(b) 9 2 2 7 00				9 4 9 2 00
7	Merchandise Inventory	205 1 6 0 00		(c) 7 0 1 8 00				212 1 7 8 00	
18	Federal Income Tax Payable				(i) 2 2 1 9 23				2 2 1 9 23
52	Federal Income Tax Expense	34 6 0 0 00		(i) 2 2 1 9 23		36 8 1 9 23			
53		2453 2 1 9 00	2453 2 1 9 00	46 9 0 8 23	46 9 0 8 23	1973 4 3 5 23	2073 9 7 3 00	506 4 0 4 00	405 8 6 6 23
54	Net Income after Federal Income Tax					100 5 3 7 77			100 5 3 7 77
55						2073 9 7 3 00	2073 9 7 3 00	506 4 0 4 00	506 4 0 4 00
56									
57									

6 **8** **9** **10, 11** **7** **12, 13, 14**

What is the meaning of each of the following?

1. **stockholder**
2. **retained earnings**
3. **dividends**
4. **board of directors**
5. **declaring a dividend**

1. How does accounting for a corporation differ from accounting for a proprietorship or partnership?
2. Why don't partnerships and proprietorships pay federal income tax?
3. How many accounts are kept for the investment of all owners of a corporation?
4. In which chart of accounts division is the capital stock account listed?
5. What account does a corporation use to record earnings not yet distributed to stockholders?
6. Why do many corporations record dividends declared in a separate dividends account?
7. What action is required before a corporation can distribute income to its stockholders?
8. When is a dividend recorded as a liability in a corporation's general ledger accounts?
9. What accounts are affected, and how, when a dividend is declared?
10. What accounts are affected, and how, when a dividend is paid?
11. In what order are general ledger accounts listed on a corporation work sheet?
12. What circumstances would require an adjustment that debits **Merchandise Inventory**?
13. What circumstances would require an adjustment that credits **Merchandise Inventory**?
14. What accounts are affected, and how, by the adjustment for accrued interest expense?
15. Why is federal income tax expense not calculated until all other adjustments have been planned on a work sheet?
16. What accounts are affected, and how, by the adjustment for federal income tax expense?

CASE 1 Fahle Company's net income has been fluctuating between a small net income and a small net loss during the first four years of the corporation's existence. The company is hoping to earn $12.00 per share during its fifth year. Janet Riley, newly appointed president of Fahle Company, believes the corporation needs to take some positive action to regain the confidence of the stockholders. She suggests the corporation declare a $10.00 per share dividend December 15 to be paid February 1. By February 1 financial statements for Fahle's fifth year ending December 31 will be completed so the net income earned for the year will be known. Mrs. Riley also suggests that if the net income is not as high as expected, the board of directors can cancel the declared dividend before it is paid. Do you agree with Mrs. Riley's proposal? Explain.

CASE 2 At the beginning of the current year, Bower Company changed its organization from a partnership to a corporation. The president suggested that since the same six individuals owned the corporation as had owned the partnership, the same procedures should be used for paying income tax on the earnings of the business. The net income of the corporation would be treated as part of each corporation owner's personal income for income tax purposes. "If this procedure is followed," said the president, "the corporation will not need to pay any income tax." Do you agree with the president's suggestion? Explain.

DRILL 26-D1 Analyzing adjustments on a work sheet

TUTORIAL

A form for analyzing adjustments is given in the working papers that accompany this textbook.

INSTRUCTIONS:

For each of the following adjustments, write the title of the account debited and the title of the account credited.

1. Supplies
2. Accrued interest income
3. Merchandise inventory (increased)
4. Merchandise inventory (decreased)
5. Uncollectible accounts expense
6. Prepaid insurance
7. Depreciation expense—store equipment
8. Accrued interest expense
9. Additional federal income tax owed

DRILL 26-D2 Extending account balances on a work sheet

A form for analyzing extending account balances on a work sheet is given in the working papers that accompany this textbook.

INSTRUCTIONS:

For each of the following accounts, place a check mark in the work sheet column to which the account balance should be extended.

1. Allowance for Uncollectible Accounts
2. Sales Returns and Allowances
3. Notes Payable
4. Retained Earnings
5. Accounts Receivable
6. Purchases Discount
7. Merchandise Inventory
8. Dividends
9. Federal Income Tax Expense
10. Accumulated Depreciation—Store Equipment

PROBLEM 26-1 Journalizing dividends

Century Center Corporation completed the following transactions during December of the current year and January of the next year.

Dec. 15. The board of directors declared a dividend of $10.00 per share; capital stock issued is 1,500 shares; total dividend, $15,000.00. Date of payment is January 15. M126.
Jan. 15. Paid cash for dividend declared December 15, $15,000.00. C432.

INSTRUCTIONS:

1. Use page 12 of a general journal. Journalize the dividend declared on December 15.
2. Use page 15 of a cash payments journal. Journalize payment of the dividend.

PROBLEM 26-2 Preparing a work sheet for a corporation

Eagle System Corporation's general ledger accounts and balances are recorded on a work sheet in the working papers.

INSTRUCTIONS:

Complete the work sheet for the current year ended December 31. Record the adjustments on the work sheet using the following information.

Adjustment Information, December 31

Accrued interest income....................................	$ 277.20
Uncollectible accounts expense estimated as 1.5% of sales on account.	
Sales on account for year, $499,000.00.	
Merchandise inventory	90,066.26
Supplies inventory	327.88
Value of prepaid insurance	3,023.60
Annual depreciation expense—office equipment	2,690.00
Annual depreciation expense—store equipment................	1,607.60
Accrued interest expense.................................	545.16
Federal income tax expense for the year......................	21,446.41

ENRICHMENT PROBLEMS   EPT(c,d,e)

MASTERY PROBLEM 26-M Journalizing dividends and preparing a work sheet for a corporation

Universal Corporation's general ledger accounts and balances are recorded on a work sheet in the working papers.

INSTRUCTIONS:

1. Complete the work sheet for the current year ended December 31. Record the adjustments on the work sheet using the following information.

Adjustment Information, December 31

Accrued interest income....................................	$ 118.00
Uncollectible accounts expense estimated as 1.0% of sales on account.	
Sales on account for year, $407,800.00.	
Merchandise inventory	123,952.00
Supplies inventory	1,592.10
Value of prepaid insurance	5,906.00
Annual depreciation expense—office equipment	1,386.00
Annual depreciation expense—store equipment................	9,800.00
Accrued interest expense.................................	94.00
Federal income tax expense for the year......................	12,950.28

2. Use page 36 of a cash payments journal. Journalize the following transaction completed during the next year. The abbreviation for check is C.

Jan. 15. Paid cash for quarterly dividend declared December 15, $10,500.00. C604.

CHALLENGE PROBLEM 26-C Preparing a 10-column work sheet for a corporation

Austin Sports Center's general ledger accounts and balances are recorded on a 10-column work sheet in the working papers.

INSTRUCTIONS:

Complete the 10-column work sheet for the current year ended December 31. Record the adjustments on the work sheet using the following information.

Adjustment Information, December 31

Accrued interest income...	$ 119.25
Uncollectible accounts expense estimated as 1.5% of sales on account.	
Sales on account for year, $306,933.33.	
Merchandise inventory	81,356.00
Supplies inventory	1,872.00
Value of prepaid insurance	4,440.00
Annual depreciation expense—office equipment	1,360.00
Annual depreciation expense—store equipment...................	15,304.00
Accrued interest expense..	57.00

Federal income tax for the year is calculated at the following rates:
- 15% of net income before taxes, zero to $50,000.00.
- Plus 25% of net income before taxes, $50,000.00 to $75,000.00.
- Plus 34% of net income before taxes, $75,000.00 to $100,000.00.
- Plus 39% of net income before taxes, $100,000.00 to $335,000.00.
- Plus 34% of net income before taxes over $335,000.00.

27

Financial Statements and End-of-Fiscal-Period Entries for a Corporation

ENABLING PERFORMANCE TASKS

After studying Chapter 27, you will be able to:

a Define accounting terms related to financial statements for a merchandising business organized as a corporation.

b Identify accounting concepts and practices related to financial statements and end-of-fiscal-period entries for a merchandising business organized as a corporation.

c Prepare and analyze an income statement for a merchandising business organized as a corporation.

d Prepare a statement of stockholders' equity for a merchandising business organized as a corporation.

e Prepare and analyze a balance sheet for a merchandising business organized as a corporation.

f Record adjusting and closing entries for a merchandising business organized as a corporation.

g Record reversing entries for a merchandising business organized as a corporation.

Corporations prepare financial statements that report financial information similar to the information reported by proprietorships and partnerships. To provide the corporation's managers and stockholders with information on how well the corporation is progressing, financial statements are prepared annually and sometimes monthly or quarterly. *(CONCEPT: Accounting Period Cycle)*

FINANCIAL STATEMENTS FOR A CORPORATION

Financial statements are used to report a business' financial progress and condition as well as changes in the owners' equity. To report this information, Celluphone prepares three financial statements. (1) Income statement. (2) Statement of stockholders' equity. (3) Balance sheet.

A corporation prepares an income statement and a balance sheet similar to those used by proprietorships and partnerships. However, a corporation reports changes in owners' equity differently. First, owners' equity for all owners is reported as a single amount rather than for each owner. Second, owners' equity is reported in two categories. (1) Capital contributed by the owners. (2) Capital earned by the corporation.

Income Statement

An income statement reports financial progress of a business during a fiscal period. *(CONCEPT: Accounting Period Cycle)* Revenue, cost of merchandise sold, gross profit on operations, operating expenses, and net income or net loss are reported on an income statement. *(CONCEPT: Adequate Disclosure)* To help make decisions about current and future operations, Celluphone also analyzes relationships between revenue and expense items. Based on this analysis, Celluphone reports component percentages for all major income statement items.

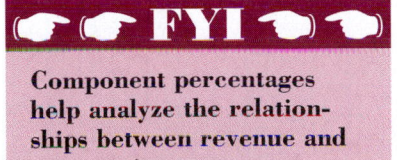

FYI

Component percentages help analyze the relationships between revenue and expense items.

Preparing an Income Statement.
Celluphone's income statement is prepared from information found in the Trial Balance, Income Statement, and Balance Sheet columns of the work sheet, Illustration 27-1, shown on pages 704–705.

Procedures for preparing Celluphone's income statement are similar to those used by any merchandising business. Celluphone's income statement for the current year ended December 31 is shown in Illustration 27-2 on page 706.

ILLUSTRATION 27-1   Work sheet for a corporation

Celluphone, Inc.
Work Sheet
For Year Ended December 31, 19--

| | TRIAL BALANCE | | ADJUSTMENTS | | INCOME STATEMENT | | BALANCE SHEET | |
| | 1 | 2 | 3 | 4 | 5 | 6 | 7 | 8 |
ACCOUNT TITLE	DEBIT	CREDIT	DEBIT	CREDIT	DEBIT	CREDIT	DEBIT	CREDIT
1 Cash	4096800						4096800	
2 Petty Cash	30000						30000	
3 Notes Receivable	55000						55000	
4 Interest Receivable			(a)1100				1100	
5 Accounts Receivable	6824000						6824000	
6 Allowance for Uncollectible Accounts		26500		(b)922700				949200
7 Merchandise Inventory	20516000			(c)7018000			21217800	
8 Supplies	1545500			(d)1169000			376500	
9 Prepaid Insurance	1355000			(e)859800			495200	
10 Office Equipment	1825000						1825000	
11 Accumulated Depreciation—Office Equip.		362500		(f)175000				537500
12 Store Equipment	7719000						7719000	
13 Accumulated Depreciation—Store Equip.		912500		(g)632500				1545000
14 Notes Payable		2800000						2800000
15 Interest Payable				(h)7000				7000
16 Accounts Payable		8396575						8396575
17 Employee Income Tax Payable		234000						234000
18 Federal Income Tax Payable				(i)221923				221923
19 FICA Tax Payable		269500						269500
20 Sales Tax Payable		1098200						1098200
21 Unemployment Tax Payable—Federal		4700						4700
22 Unemployment Tax Payable—State		31725						31725
23 Health Insurance Premiums Payable		99500						99500
24 Dividends Payable		200000						200000
25 Capital Stock		10000000						10000000

#	Account Title	Trial Balance Debit	Trial Balance Credit	Adjustments Debit	Adjustments Credit	Income Statement Debit	Income Statement Credit	Balance Sheet Debit	Balance Sheet Credit
26	Retained Earnings		14911800						14911800
27	Dividends	8000000						8000000	
28	Income Summary				(c) 701800	701800			
29	Sales		205044000				205044000		
30	Sales Discount	564200				564200			
31	Sales Returns and Allowances	2431800				2431800			
32	Purchases	145479800				145479800			
33	Purchases Discount		1076600				1076600		
34	Purchases Returns and Allowances		531000				531000		
35	Advertising Expense	3260000				3260000			
36	Credit Card Fee Expense	2046800				2046800			
37	Depr. Expense—Office Equipment			(f) 175000		175000			
38	Depr. Expense—Store Equipment			(g) 632500		632500			
39	Insurance Expense			(e) 859800		859800			
40	Miscellaneous Expense	2235000				2235000			
41	Payroll Taxes Expense	2372000				2372000			
42	Rent Expense	5640000				5640000			
43	Salary Expense	25193200				25193200			
44	Supplies Expense			(d) 1169000		1169000			
45	Uncollectible Accounts Expense			(b) 922700		922700			
46	Utilities Expense	489000				489000			
47	Gain on Plant Assets		22500				22500		
48	Interest Income		20300		(a) 1100		21400		
49	Cash Short and Over	300				300			
50	Interest Expense	137500		(h) 7000		144500			
51	Loss on Plant Assets	46000				46000			
52	Federal Income Tax Expense	34600000		(i) 221923		34821923			
53		245321900	245321900	4690823	4690823	197343523	207397300	506404000	405866623
54	Net Income after Federal Income Tax					10053777			10053777
55						207397300	207397300	506404000	506404000
56									

ILLUSTRATION 27-2   Income statement for a corporation

Celluphone, Inc.
Income Statement
For Year Ended December 31, 19--

				% of Net Sales
Operating Revenue:				
Sales			$2,050,440.00	
Less: Sales Discount		$ 5,642.00		
Sales Ret. and Allow.		24,318.00	29,960.00	
Net Sales			$2,020,480.00	100.0
Cost of Merchandise Sold:				
Merchandise Inv., Jan. 1, 19--			$ 205,160.00	
Purchases		$1,454,798.00		
Less: Purchases Discount	$10,766.00			
Purch. Ret. and Allow.	5,310.00	16,076.00		
Net Purchases			1,438,722.00	
Total Cost of Mdse. Avail. for Sale			$1,643,882.00	
Less Mdse. Inventory, Dec. 31, 19--			212,178.00	
Cost of Merchandise Sold			1,431,704.00	70.9
Gross Profit on Operations			$ 588,776.00	29.1
Operating Expenses:				
Advertising Expense		$ 32,600.00		
Credit Card Fee Expense		20,468.00		
Depreciation Exp.—Office Equip.		1,750.00		
Depreciation Exp.—Store Equip.		6,325.00		
Insurance Expense		8,598.00		
Miscellaneous Expense		22,350.00		
Payroll Taxes Expense		23,720.00		
Rent Expense		56,400.00		
Salary Expense		251,932.00		
Supplies Expense		11,690.00		
Uncollectible Accounts Expense		9,227.00		
Utilities Expense		4,890.00		
Total Operating Expenses			449,950.00	22.3
Income from Operations			$ 138,826.00	6.9
Other Revenue:				
Gain on Plant Assets		$ 225.00		
Interest Income		214.00		
Total Other Revenue			$ 439.00	
Other Expenses:				
Cash Short and Over		$ 3.00		
Interest Expense		1,445.00		
Loss on Plant Assets		460.00		
Total Other Expenses			1,908.00	
Net Deduction			1,469.00	0.1
Net Income before Fed. Inc. Tax			$ 137,357.00	6.8
Less Federal Income Tax Exp.			36,819.23	1.8
Net Income after Fed. Inc. Tax			$ 100,537.77	5.0

Celluphone's income statement differs in four ways from Car-Land's income statement shown in Part 3.

1. Net sales is listed in the Operating Revenue section. Total sales less sales discount and sales returns and allowances is called **net sales.** Net sales is reported in the Operating Revenue section of Celluphone's income statement, as shown in Illustration 27-3.

ILLUSTRATION 27-3

Net sales reported on an income statement

				% of Net Sales
Operating Revenue:				
Sales			$2,050,440.00	
Less: Sales Discount	$ 5,642.00			
Sales Ret. and Allow.	24,318.00	29,960.00		
Net Sales			$2,020,480.00	100.0

2. Net purchases is reported in the Cost of Merchandise Sold section. Total purchases less purchases discount and purchases returns and allowances is called **net purchases.** Net purchases is reported in the Cost of Merchandise Sold section of Celluphone's income statement, as shown in Illustration 27-4.

ILLUSTRATION 27-4

Net purchases reported on an income statement

Cost of Merchandise Sold:			
Merchandise Inv., Jan. 1, 19--			$ 205,160.00
Purchases		$1,454,798.00	
Less: Purchases Discount	$10,766.00		
Purch. Ret. and Allow.	5,310.00	16,076.00	
Net Purchases			1,438,722.00

3. Income from operations is reported separately from net income. Income from operations is the income earned only from normal business activities. Celluphone's normal business activities are selling cellular phones to corporate customers. Other revenue and expenses, such as interest income, interest expense, and gains or losses on plant assets, are not normal business activities. Other revenue and expenses are not included in calculating income from operations.

4. Net income before and net income after federal income tax are reported separately. Reporting net income before and after federal income tax is unique to corporation income statements. Corporations pay federal income tax on their net income. However, federal income taxes are not paid by proprietorships and

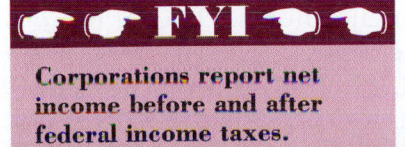

FYI

Corporations report net income before and after federal income taxes.

partnerships because they are paid by the owners. Thus, proprietorships and partnerships do not report federal income tax on their income statements. Net income is reported in the Net Income section of Celluphone's income statement as shown in Illustration 27-5.

ILLUSTRATION 27-5	Federal income tax reported on an income statement

Net Income before Fed. Inc. Tax	$ 137,357.00	6.8
Less Federal Income Tax Exp.	36,819.23	1.8
Net Income after Fed. Inc. Tax.	$ 100,537.77	5.0

Analyzing an Income Statement. For a business to determine whether it is progressing satisfactorily, results of operations are compared with industry standards and/or previous fiscal periods. To provide meaningful comparisons, the same accounting concepts must be followed for preparing the income statements for each fiscal period. *(CONCEPT: Consistent Reporting)*

To help management improve future fiscal periods, items contributing to net income should be analyzed. By analyzing items of revenue, cost, and expense, items that should be improved can be identified.

The percentage relationship between one financial statement item and the total that includes that item is known as a component percentage. Celluphone prepares component percentages for six major items on its income statement. Celluphone uses net sales as the base for calculating component percentages. The amount of each item on the income statement is divided by the amount of net sales. Thus, each component percentage shows the percentage that item is of net sales. For example, Celluphone's cost of merchandise sold component percentage is calculated as shown below.

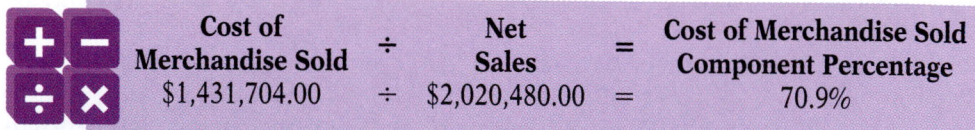

Cost of Merchandise Sold	÷	Net Sales	=	Cost of Merchandise Sold Component Percentage
$1,431,704.00	÷	$2,020,480.00	=	70.9%

A limited liability company (LLC) provides the limited protection of a corporation.

This component percentage indicates that during the current fiscal year, Celluphone spent 70.9 cents out of each $1.00 of sales for the merchandise sold. Component percentages for each major item on Celluphone's income statement are listed in a separate column in Illustration 27-2.

When analyzing an income statement, Celluphone first reviews the component percentages for the six major items. (1) Cost of merchandise sold. (2) Gross profit on operations. (3) Total operating expenses. (4) Income from operations. (5) Net addition or deduction from other revenue and expenses. (6) Net income before federal income tax. The last two items on the income statement, federal income tax expense and net income after federal income tax, are important. Celluphone does not have much control over these two items because the tax rate, set by the Internal Revenue Service, determines these amounts. However, the company is interested in what portion of each sales dollar is paid to the federal government for income taxes. Therefore, the component percentage for federal income tax is calculated. Celluphone also calculates the component percentage for net income after federal income tax.

Acceptable Component Percentages. Based on comparisons with industry standards as well as previous accounting periods, Celluphone has determined acceptable component percentages for each major item of cost and expense on its income statement. For comparative purposes, Celluphone's acceptable and actual component percentages are shown in Illustration 27-6.

ILLUSTRATION 27-6   Income statement acceptable component percentages

Income Statement Items	Acceptable Component Percentages	Actual Component Percentages
Net sales	100.0%	100.0%
Cost of merchandise sold	not more than 71.0%	70.9%
Gross profit on operations	not less than 29.0%	29.1%
Total operating expenses	not more than 22.4%	22.3%
Income from operations	not less than 6.6%	6.9%
Net deduction	not more than 0.1%	0.1%
Net income before federal income tax	not less than 6.5%	6.8%

If the component percentage of any cost or expense item for a fiscal period exceeds the acceptable percentage, that cost or expense is reviewed further to determine the reason. After determining the reason why a cost or expense exceeded the acceptable percentage, ways are sought to bring the expense within acceptable limits.

Achieving acceptable component percentages for the six major income statement items indicates that the business is keeping costs and expenses at an acceptable level compared with revenue. For the current year ended December 31, Celluphone has achieved acceptable percentages for all six major items. Component percentages for cost of merchandise sold, 70.9%, total operating expenses, 22.3%, and deductions for other revenue and expenses, 0.1%, are all equal to or less than the maximum acceptable level for each item, a positive result. The component percentages for gross profit on operations, 29.1%, income from operations, 6.9%, and net income before federal income tax, 6.8%, are all more than the minimum acceptable percentage for each item, a positive result.

However, if a major item shows a negative result, further analysis should be made of each item to determine and correct any negative results of individual income statement items. For example, in the previous fiscal period, the component percentage for Celluphone's total operating expenses was more than the acceptable level, a negative result. A further review of each expense item showed that component percentages for salary expense and payroll taxes expense were higher than the acceptable percentages, a negative result. Further investigation revealed that Celluphone had employed additional temporary employees during the company's busy season. However, during the year, Celluphone retained these temporary employees two months longer than needed because of a lack of coordination between managers. Since the cause of the excessive salary expense was identified, Celluphone took action to more carefully control these expenses in the future.

Statement of Stockholders' Equity

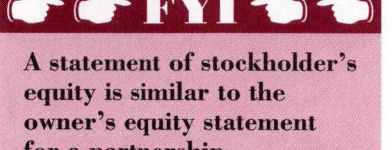

A statement of stockholder's equity is similar to the owner's equity statement for a partnership.

A financial statement that shows changes in a corporation's ownership for a fiscal period is called a **statement of stockholders' equity.** A statement of stockholders' equity is similar to the owners' equity statement for a partnership.

A statement of stockholders' equity contains two major sections. (1) Capital stock. (2) Retained earnings. Celluphone's statement of stockholders' equity for the current year ended December 31 is shown in Illustration 27-7.

ILLUSTRATION 27-7   Statement of stockholders' equity for a corporation

Celluphone, Inc. Statement of Stockholders' Equity For Year Ended December 31, 19--			
Capital Stock:			
$100.00 Per Share			
January 1, 19--, 1,000 Shares Issued		$100,000.00	
Issued during Current Year, None		0	
Balance, December 31, 19--, 1,000 Shares Issued			$100,000.00
Retained Earnings:			
Balance, January 1, 19--		$149,118.00	
Net Income after Federal Income Tax for 19--	$100,537.77		
Less Dividends Declared during 19--	80,000.00		
Net Increase during 19--		20,537.77	
Balance, December 31, 19--			169,655.77
Total Stockholders' Equity, December 31, 19--			$269,655.77

The first section of Celluphone's statement of stockholders' equity shows that the corporation started the current fiscal year on January 1 with $100,000.00 in capital stock. This capital stock consisted of 1,000 shares of stock issued in previous years at $100.00 per share. During the current fiscal year, no additional capital stock was issued. Thus, at the end of the current fiscal year, Celluphone still has $100,000.00 capital stock issued. This information is obtained from the previous year's statement and the capital stock account.

The second section of Celluphone's statement of stockholders' equity shows that Celluphone started the current fiscal year on January 1 with $149,118.00 retained earnings. This amount represents previous years' earnings that have been kept in the business and not distributed to stockholders. For the current fiscal year ended December 31, Celluphone earned net income after federal income tax of $100,537.77. This amount is obtained from line 54 of the work sheet, Illustration 27-1.

Net income increases a corporation's total capital. Some income may be retained by a corporation for business expansion. Some income may be distributed to stockholders as a return on their investments.

During the year, Celluphone's board of directors declared $80,000.00 in dividends. The amount of dividends declared is obtained from line 27 of the work sheet's Balance Sheet Debit column. Changes in Celluphone's retained earnings during the current fiscal year are calculated as shown below.

Retained earnings balance, January 1, 19--		$149,118.00
Net income after federal income tax for 19--	$100,537.77	
Less dividends declared during 19--	− 80,000.00	
Net increase during 19--		+ 20,537.77
Retained earnings balance, December 31, 19--		$169,655.77

Celluphone's capital stock, $100,000.00, plus retained earnings, $169,655.77, equals total stockholders' equity on December 31, $269,655.77.

Balance Sheet

A corporation balance sheet reports assets, liabilities, and stockholders' equity on a specific date. (CONCEPT: *Accounting Period Cycle*)

Celluphone's balance sheet, shown in Illustration 27-8 on page 712, is prepared from information found in the Balance Sheet columns of the work sheet, Illustration 27-1, and the statement of stockholders' equity, Illustration 27-7.

Classifying Assets. Celluphone classifies its assets into two categories. (1) Current assets. (2) Plant assets. These categories are based on the length of time the assets will be in use. A business owning both current assets and plant assets usually lists them under separate headings on a balance sheet.

Cash and other assets expected to be exchanged for cash or consumed within a year are known as current assets. Current assets

ILLUSTRATION 27-8 Balance sheet for a corporation

Celluphone, Inc.
Balance Sheet
December 31, 19--

ASSETS

Current Assets:		
Cash		$ 40,968.00
Petty Cash		300.00
Notes Receivable		550.00
Interest Receivable		11.00
Accounts Receivable	$68,240.00	
Less Allowance for Uncollectible Accounts	9,492.00	58,748.00
Merchandise Inventory		212,178.00
Supplies		3,765.00
Prepaid Insurance		4,952.00
Total Current Assets		$321,472.00
Plant Assets:		
Office Equipment	$18,250.00	
Less Accumulated Depreciation—Office Equipment	5,375.00	$ 12,875.00
Store Equipment	$77,190.00	
Less Accumulated Depreciation—Store Equipment	15,450.00	61,740.00
Total Plant Assets		74,615.00
Total Assets		$396,087.00

LIABILITIES

Current Liabilities:		
Notes Payable		$ 2,800.00
Interest Payable		70.00
Accounts Payable		83,965.75
Employee Income Tax Payable		2,340.00
Federal Income Tax Payable		2,219.23
FICA Tax Payable		2,695.00
Sales Tax Payable		10,982.00
Unemployment Tax Payable—Federal		47.00
Unemployment Tax Payable—State		317.25
Health Insurance Premiums Payable		995.00
Dividends Payable		20,000.00
Total Liabilities		$126,431.23

STOCKHOLDERS' EQUITY

Capital Stock	$100,000.00	
Retained Earnings	169,655.77	
Total Stockholders' Equity		269,655.77
Total Liabilities and Stockholders' Equity		$396,087.00

include such items as cash, accounts receivable, merchandise inventory, supplies, and prepaid insurance. Assets that will be used for a number of years in the operation of a business are known as plant assets. Plant assets include such items as cash registers, computers, and display cases.

Reporting Book Value of Assets. An account that reduces a related account on financial statements is known as a contra account. Celluphone reports three contra accounts on its balance sheet. (1) Allowance for Uncollectible Accounts. (2) Accumulated Depreciation—Office Equipment. (3) Accumulated Depreciation—Store Equipment. The difference between an asset's account balance and its related contra account balance is called **book value.** Celluphone reports the book value for Accounts Receivable and the two equipment accounts on its balance sheet. An asset's book value is reported on a balance sheet by listing three amounts. (1) The balance of the asset account. (2) The balance of the asset's contra account. (3) Book value. Book value of Celluphone's accounts receivable and plant asset accounts is reported as shown on the partial balance sheet, Illustration 27-9.

| ILLUSTRATION 27-9 | Book value of asset accounts reported on a balance sheet |

Celluphone, Inc. Balance Sheet December 31, 19--			
ASSETS			
Current Assets:			
Accounts Receivable.......................................	$68,240.00		
Less Allowance for Uncollectible Accounts.................	9,492.00	58,748.00	
Plant Assets:			
Office Equipment	$18,250.00		
Less Accumulated Depreciation—Office Equipment	5,375.00	$ 12,875.00	
Store Equipment...	$77,190.00		
Less Accumulated Depreciation—Store Equipment..........	15,450.00	61,740.00	
Total Plant Assets.......................................			74,615.00

Celluphone uses the following procedure to report the book value of accounts receivable on the balance sheet. The total amount of accounts receivable, *$68,240.00,* is written in the first amount column of the balance sheet. *Less Allowance for Uncollectible Accounts* is written on the next line, indented about one centimeter. The amount, *$9,492.00,* is written below the $68,240.00. The difference between the two amounts, *$58,748.00,* is written in the second amount column on the same line. The amount of the difference, $58,748.00, is the book value of accounts receivable on December 31. Similar procedures are followed to report book values of the plant asset accounts. The total of the two individual book values, *$74,615.00,* is written in the third amount column of the balance sheet.

Classifying Liabilities. Liabilities are classified according to the length of time until they are due. Liabilities due within a short time, usually within a year, are known as current liabilities. All of Celluphone's liabilities are listed on the balance sheet in Illustration 27-8 as current liabilities because they come due within a year.

Liabilities owed for more than a year are called **long-term liabilities.** An example of a long-term liability is Mortgage Payable. On

FYI

A limited liability company (LLC) provides the flexibility of a partnership by allowing earnings to flow through its partners as personal income. This eliminates the double taxation feature of corporations.

December 31 of the current year, Celluphone does not have any long-term liabilities.

Electro Company has both current liabilities and long-term liabilities. A portion of Electro's balance sheet is shown in Illustration 27-10.

ILLUSTRATION 27-10 Liabilities section of a balance sheet showing current and long-term liabilities

LIABILITIES		
Current Liabilities:		
Notes Payable.	$ 12,560.00	
Dividends Payable.	25,000.00	
Total Current Liabilities		$ 48,369.00
Long-term Liabilities:		
Mortgage Payable		86,000.00
Total Liabilities.		$134,369.00

Reporting a Corporation's Stockholders' Equity. A major difference between corporation balance sheets and proprietorship or partnership balance sheets is the owners' equity section. The owners' equity section of Celluphone's balance sheet, Illustration 27-8, is labeled *Stockholders' Equity.* Some corporations use the same label, Owners' Equity, as proprietorships and partnerships. Either label is acceptable.

The Stockholders' Equity section contains accounts related to capital stock and earnings kept in the business. For Celluphone, these accounts are Capital Stock and Retained Earnings. Total stockholders' equity on Celluphone's balance sheet, Illustration 27-8, is $269,655.77, the same as on Celluphone's statement of stockholders' equity, Illustration 27-7.

Analyzing a Balance Sheet. To continue operating successfully, a business must have adequate financial resources. A business must be able to buy additional merchandise, pay employee salaries, and pay for other operating expenses. Financial strength analysis measures the ability of a business to pay its debts. The balance sheet is the primary source of data to determine the financial strength of a business.

Celluphone analyzes its financial strength to assist the company in planning for future periods and to insure that adequate resources are available to operate the business. Creditors and investors also use financial strength analysis to determine if the company is a good credit and investment risk. Before a creditor sells merchandise to a company on account, the creditor must believe that the company will later pay for the merchandise. A company that is considered to be a poor credit risk is usually a bad investment for an investor.

Celluphone uses two analyses to evaluate financial strength. (1) Working capital. (2) Current ratio.

SPREADSHEET OPTIONS

GRAPHICS ENHANCE FINANCIAL STATEMENT ANALYSIS

The electronic spreadsheet is an effective tool for preparing financial statements. The income statement of Celluphone, Inc. in Illustration 27-2 is keyed on a spreadsheet. The printed spreadsheet would closely resemble the income statement in Illustration 27-2. In future fiscal periods, Celluphone's accountants can quickly prepare income statements by inputting new values. Formulas use these values to calculate other income statement values, such as net sales and cost of merchandise sold, and all the component percentages.

The electronic spreadsheet provides management with an additional valuable feature—the ability to view financial information in graphic form. **Graphs** are an effective way to communicate summary information such as component percentages.

A variety of graph styles is available to display different types of financial information. A **pie graph** is an appropriate graph style to illustrate how several values together comprise another value. In this graph, the total pie represents the net sales component percentage. Each slice represents the component percentage for an income statement item. The component percentages together equal the net sales component percentage.

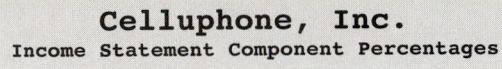

Celluphone, Inc.
Income Statement Component Percentages

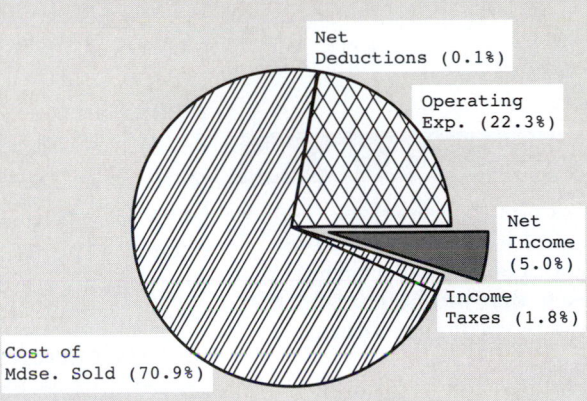

- Net Deductions (0.1%)
- Operating Exp. (22.3%)
- Net Income (5.0%)
- Income Taxes (1.8%)
- Cost of Mdse. Sold (70.9%)

The software automatically determines the size of each slice using the component percentages. To emphasize the net income component percentage, the accountant preparing this graph instructed the software to "explode" the net income value. The graph can be displayed on the computer monitor or printed. The graph can also be inserted into reports created using other software such as a word processor.

FYI

Current financial reporting requirements include a statement of cash flows. A similar statement, no longer required, is the statement of changes in financial position.

Current assets less current liabilities is the amount of financial resources a company has available to conduct its daily operations. Current assets include cash, notes receivable, interest receivable, accounts receivable, merchandise inventory, supplies, and prepaid insurance. Current liabilities include notes payable, interest payable, accounts payable, taxes payable, health insurance premiums payable, and dividends payable. For a company to operate efficiently, an adequate supply of resources must be available after current liabilities are paid.

The amount of total current assets less total current liabilities is called **working capital**. Working capital is the amount of current assets available for use in the business after current liabilities are paid. The amount is stated in dollars. Celluphone's working capital for December 31 of the current year is calculated as shown below.

	Total Current Assets	−	Total Current Liabilities	=	Working Capital
	$321,472.00	−	$126,431.23	=	$195,040.77

Working capital should not be confused with cash. Celluphone does not have $195,040.77 of excess cash. However, Celluphone does have $195,040.77 of assets that will be converted to cash and will be available for use in daily operations during the next fiscal year.

Working capital is a measure of the amount of financial resources available for the daily operations of the business. Although working capital is a useful measure, working capital does not permit a business to compare itself to its industry or to provide a convenient relative measurement from year to year.

A more useful measure results from comparing the amount of total current assets to total current liabilities. A comparison between two numbers showing how many times one number exceeds the other is called a **ratio**. A ratio that shows the numeric relationship of current assets to current liabilities is called the **current ratio**. The current ratio is a measure of a company's ability to pay its current liabilities. Creditors use the ratio to determine if merchandise should be sold to a company on account.

Based on the balance sheet information, Celluphone's current ratio is calculated as shown below.

	Total Current Assets	÷	Total Current Liabilities	=	Current Ratio
	$321,472.00	÷	$126,431.23	=	2.5 to 1

Celluphone's current ratio is stated as 2.5 to 1, which means that total current assets are 2.5 times total current liabilities.

Based on previous experience and industry guidelines, Celluphone has established a minimum acceptable current ratio of 2.0 to 1. On December 31 of the current year, Celluphone's current ratio, 2.5 to 1, exceeds the minimum acceptable ratio. This year's current ratio indicates a favorable condition of financial strength.

The chart shown in Summary Illustration 27-11 summarizes the financial statements for a corporation.

ADJUSTING, CLOSING, AND REVERSING ENTRIES FOR A CORPORATION

The end-of-fiscal-period work of corporations is similar to the work of proprietorships and partnerships except for differences in the equity accounts. After corporate financial statements are prepared,

Summary of financial statements for a corporation

```
                    ┌─────────────────────────────────────┐
                    │                                      │
                    │              Work Sheet              │
                    │                                      │
                    └─────────────────────────────────────┘
                         │              │              │
              ┌──────────────────┐ ┌──────────────────┐ ┌──────────────┐
              │ Revenue, Costs,  │ │ Beginning Balance│ │   Assets,    │
              │  and Expenses    │ │ of Retained      │ │  Liabilities │
              │                  │ │ Earnings,        │ │              │
              │                  │ │ Dividends        │ │              │
              └──────────────────┘ └──────────────────┘ └──────────────┘
                       │1
```

Information from the completed work sheet is used to prepare the income statement.

1 → Income Statement

Net Income

Information from the previous year's statement of stockholders' equity, the general ledger capital stock account, and the work sheet are used to prepare the statement of stockholders' equity.

2

Previous Year's Statement of Stockholders' Equity

Capital Stock Account

2 → Statement of Stockholders' Equity

Information from the work sheet and statement of stockholders' equity are used to prepare the balance sheet.

3 → Balance Sheet

adjusting and closing entries are journalized and posted. A post-closing trial balance is then prepared. Finally, reversing entries are journalized and posted.

Adjusting Entries

A corporation's adjusting entries are made from the Adjustments columns of a work sheet. Each adjustment is journalized and posted to general ledger accounts. With the exception of federal income tax, adjustments are similar to those for proprietorships and partnerships. Celluphone's adjusting entries for December 31 are shown in Illustration 27-12.

Procedures for journalizing Celluphone's adjusting entries are similar to those previously described for other businesses.

ILLUSTRATION 27-12   Adjusting entries for a corporation

GENERAL JOURNAL
PAGE 15

	DATE		ACCOUNT TITLE	DOC. NO.	POST. REF.	DEBIT	CREDIT	
1			*Adjusting Entries*					1
2	Dec.	31	Interest Receivable			1 1 00		2
3			Interest Income				1 1 00	3
4		31	Uncollectible Accounts Expense			9 2 2 7 00		4
5			Allowance for Uncoll. Accts.				9 2 2 7 00	5
6		31	Merchandise Inventory			7 0 1 8 00		6
7			Income Summary				7 0 1 8 00	7
8		31	Supplies Expense			11 6 9 0 00		8
9			Supplies				11 6 9 0 00	9
10		31	Insurance Expense			8 5 9 8 00		10
11			Prepaid Insurance				8 5 9 8 00	11
12		31	Depreciation Exp.—Office Equip.			1 7 5 0 00		12
13			Accum. Depr.—Office Equip.				1 7 5 0 00	13
14		31	Depreciation Exp.—Store Equip.			6 3 2 5 00		14
15			Accum. Depr.—Store Equip.				6 3 2 5 00	15
16		31	Interest Expense			7 0 00		16
17			Interest Payable				7 0 00	17
18		31	Federal Income Tax Expense			2 2 1 9 23		18
19			Federal Income Tax Payable				2 2 1 9 23	19
20								20

Closing Entries

Closing entries for a corporation are made from information in a work sheet. Closing entries for revenue and expense accounts are similar to those for proprietorships or partnerships. A corporation's last two closing entries are similar to those previously studied but affect different accounts. A corporation records the following four closing entries.

1. Closing entry for income statement accounts with credit balances (revenue and contra cost accounts).
2. Closing entry for income statement accounts with debit balances (cost, contra revenue, and expense accounts).
3. Closing entry to record net income or net loss in the retained earnings account and close the income summary account.
4. Closing entry for the dividends account.

Closing Entry for Income Statement Accounts with Credit Balances. The closing entry for Celluphone's income statement credit balance accounts on December 31 is shown in Illustration 27-13, page 720. Income statement credit balance accounts are revenue (Sales, Gain on Plant Assets, and Interest Income) and the contra cost accounts (Purchases Discount and Purchases Returns and Allowances). Information needed for closing income statement credit balance accounts is obtained from the work sheet's Income Statement Credit column as shown in Illustration 27-13.

Celluphone begins its closing entries on a new page of the general journal. Thus, all the closing entries are together on one page.

Closing Entry for Income Statement Accounts with Debit Balances. The closing entry for Celluphone's income statement debit balance accounts on December 31 is shown in Illustration 27-14 on page 721. Income statement debit balance accounts are the contra revenue accounts (Sales Discount and Sales Returns and Allowances) and the cost (Purchases) and expense accounts. Information needed for closing income statement debit balance accounts is obtained from the work sheet's Income Statement Debit column, as shown in Illustration 27-14, page 721.

If Cash Short and Over has a credit balance, the account balance amount is closed to Income Summary with the credit balance accounts.

After closing entries for the income statement debit balance accounts are posted, Income Summary has a credit balance of $100,537.77. This credit balance is the amount of net income. This amount is the same as on line 54 of Celluphone's work sheet.

Closing Entry to Record Net Income or Net Loss in the Retained Earnings Account and Close the Income Summary Account. A corporation's net income is recorded in the retained earnings account. The closing entry to record Celluphone's net income and close Income Summary is shown in Illustration 27-15. Information needed for this entry is obtained from line 54 of Celluphone's work sheet, as shown in Illustration 27-15 on page 722.

After the entry to record net income is posted, Income Summary has a zero balance. The net income, $100,537.77, has been recorded as a credit to Retained Earnings.

ILLUSTRATION 27-13

Closing entry for a corporation's income statement accounts with credit balances

Celluphone, Inc.
Work Sheet
For Year Ended December 31, 19--

	ACCOUNT TITLE	INCOME STATEMENT DEBIT	INCOME STATEMENT CREDIT
28	Income Summary		7 0 18 00
29	Sales		2050 4 4 0 00
30	Sales Discount	5 6 4 2 00	
31	Sales Returns and Allowances	24 3 1 8 00	
32	Purchases	1454 7 9 8 00	
33	Purchases Discount		10 7 6 6 00
34	Purchases Returns and Allowances		5 3 1 0 00
35	Advertising Expense	32 6 0 0 00	
36	Credit Card Fee Expense	20 4 6 8 00	
37	Depr. Expense—Office Equipment	1 7 5 0 00	
38	Depr. Expense—Store Equipment	6 3 2 5 00	
39	Insurance Expense	8 5 9 8 00	
40	Miscellaneous Expense	22 3 5 0 00	
41	Payroll Taxes Expense	23 7 2 0 00	
42	Rent Expense	56 4 0 0 00	
43	Salary Expense	251 9 3 2 00	
44	Supplies Expense	11 6 9 0 00	
45	Uncollectible Accounts Expense	9 2 2 7 00	
46	Utilities Expense	4 8 9 0 00	
47	Gain on Plant Assets		2 2 5 00
48	Interest Income		2 1 4 00
49	Cash Short and Over	3 00	
50	Interest Expense	1 4 4 5 00	
51	Loss on Plant Assets	4 6 0 00	
52	Federal Income Tax Expense	36 8 1 9 23	
53		1973 4 3 5 23	2073 9 7 3 00
54	Net Income after Fed. Inc. Tax	100 5 3 7 77	
55		2073 9 7 3 00	2073 9 7 3 00
56			
57			

GENERAL JOURNAL PAGE 16

	DATE		ACCOUNT TITLE	DOC. NO.	POST. REF.	DEBIT	CREDIT	
1			Closing Entries					1
2	Dec.	31	Sales			2050 4 4 0 00		2
3			Purchases Discount			10 7 6 6 00		3
4			Purchases Returns and Allowances			5 3 1 0 00		4
5			Gain on Plant Assets			2 2 5 00		5
6			Interest Income			2 1 4 00		6
7			Income Summary				2066 9 5 5 00	7
8								8
9								9

ILLUSTRATION 27-14

Closing entry for a corporation's income statement accounts with debit balances

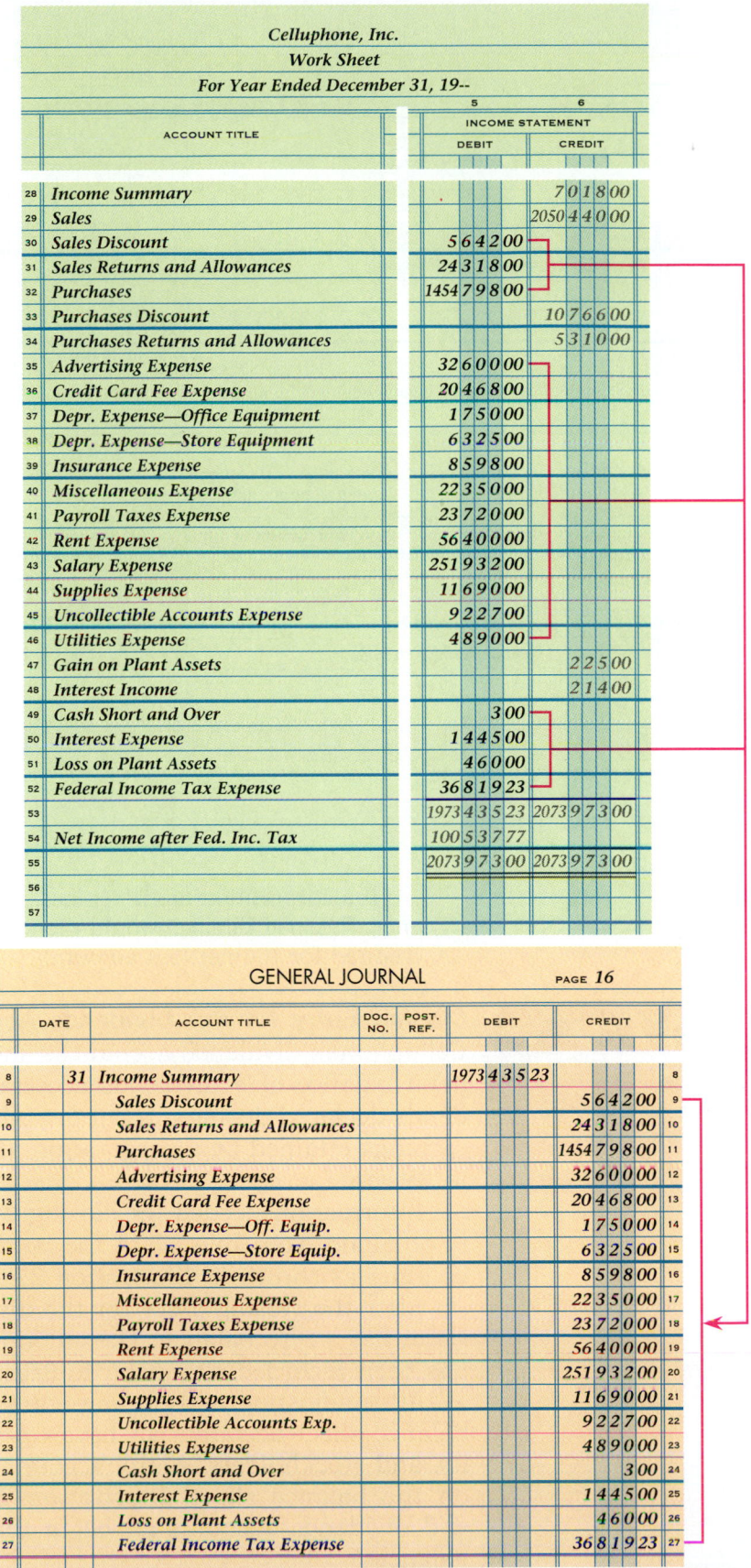

Celluphone, Inc.

Work Sheet

For Year Ended December 31, 19--

	ACCOUNT TITLE	INCOME STATEMENT	
		DEBIT	CREDIT
28	Income Summary		7 0 1 8 00
29	Sales		2050 4 4 0 00
30	Sales Discount	5 6 4 2 00	
31	Sales Returns and Allowances	24 3 1 8 00	
32	Purchases	1454 7 9 8 00	
33	Purchases Discount		10 7 6 6 00
34	Purchases Returns and Allowances		5 3 1 0 00
35	Advertising Expense	32 6 0 0 00	
36	Credit Card Fee Expense	20 4 6 8 00	
37	Depr. Expense—Office Equipment	1 7 5 0 00	
38	Depr. Expense—Store Equipment	6 3 2 5 00	
39	Insurance Expense	8 5 9 8 00	
40	Miscellaneous Expense	22 3 5 0 00	
41	Payroll Taxes Expense	23 7 2 0 00	
42	Rent Expense	56 4 0 0 00	
43	Salary Expense	251 9 3 2 00	
44	Supplies Expense	11 6 9 0 00	
45	Uncollectible Accounts Expense	9 2 2 7 00	
46	Utilities Expense	4 8 9 0 00	
47	Gain on Plant Assets		2 2 5 00
48	Interest Income		2 1 4 00
49	Cash Short and Over	3 00	
50	Interest Expense	1 4 4 5 00	
51	Loss on Plant Assets	4 6 0 00	
52	Federal Income Tax Expense	36 8 1 9 23	
53		1973 4 3 5 23	2073 9 7 3 00
54	Net Income after Fed. Inc. Tax	100 5 3 7 77	
55		2073 9 7 3 00	2073 9 7 3 00
56			
57			

GENERAL JOURNAL   PAGE 16

	DATE	ACCOUNT TITLE	DOC. NO.	POST. REF.	DEBIT	CREDIT	
8	31	Income Summary			1973 4 3 5 23		8
9		Sales Discount				5 6 4 2 00	9
10		Sales Returns and Allowances				24 3 1 8 00	10
11		Purchases				1454 7 9 8 00	11
12		Advertising Expense				32 6 0 0 00	12
13		Credit Card Fee Expense				20 4 6 8 00	13
14		Depr. Expense—Off. Equip.				1 7 5 0 00	14
15		Depr. Expense—Store Equip.				6 3 2 5 00	15
16		Insurance Expense				8 5 9 8 00	16
17		Miscellaneous Expense				22 3 5 0 00	17
18		Payroll Taxes Expense				23 7 2 0 00	18
19		Rent Expense				56 4 0 0 00	19
20		Salary Expense				251 9 3 2 00	20
21		Supplies Expense				11 6 9 0 00	21
22		Uncollectible Accounts Exp.				9 2 2 7 00	22
23		Utilities Expense				4 8 9 0 00	23
24		Cash Short and Over				3 00	24
25		Interest Expense				1 4 4 5 00	25
26		Loss on Plant Assets				4 6 0 00	26
27		Federal Income Tax Expense				36 8 1 9 23	27

Celluphone, Inc.
Work Sheet
For Year Ended December 31, 19--

		5 INCOME STATEMENT	6	7 BALANCE SHEET	8	
	ACCOUNT TITLE	DEBIT	CREDIT	DEBIT	CREDIT	
51	Loss on Plant Assets	4 6 0 00				51
52	Federal Income Tax Expense	36 8 1 9 23				52
53		1973 4 3 5 23	2073 9 7 3 00	506 4 0 4 00	405 8 6 6 23	53
54	Net Income after Fed. Inc. Tax	100 5 3 7 77			100 5 3 7 77	54
55		2073 9 7 3 00	2073 9 7 3 00	506 4 0 4 00	506 4 0 4 00	55
56						56
57						57

GENERAL JOURNAL   PAGE **16**

	DATE	ACCOUNT TITLE	DOC. NO.	POST. REF.	DEBIT	CREDIT	
28	31	Income Summary			100 5 3 7 77		28
29		Retained Earnings				100 5 3 7 77	29
30							30
31							31
32							32

If a corporation has a net loss, Income Summary has a debit balance. Retained Earnings would then be debited and Income Summary credited for the net loss amount.

FYI

The last closing entry for a corporation is to close the dividends account into retained earnings.

Closing Entry for the Dividends Account.   The closing entry for Celluphone's dividends account is shown in Illustration 27-16. The debit balance of a dividends account is the total amount of dividends declared during a fiscal period. Since dividends decrease the earnings retained by a corporation, the dividends account is closed to Retained Earnings.

Information needed for closing Celluphone's dividends account is obtained from line 27 of the work sheet's Balance Sheet Debit column, as shown in Illustration 27-16.

After the closing entry for the dividends account is posted, Dividends has a zero balance. The amount of the dividends, $80,000.00, has been recorded as a debit to Retained Earnings.

After adjusting and closing entries are journalized and posted, balance sheet accounts all have up-to-date balances. Asset, liability, and stockholders' equity account balances agree with amounts on the balance sheet, Illustration 27-8. Revenue, cost, expense, and dividends accounts all begin the new fiscal period with zero balances.

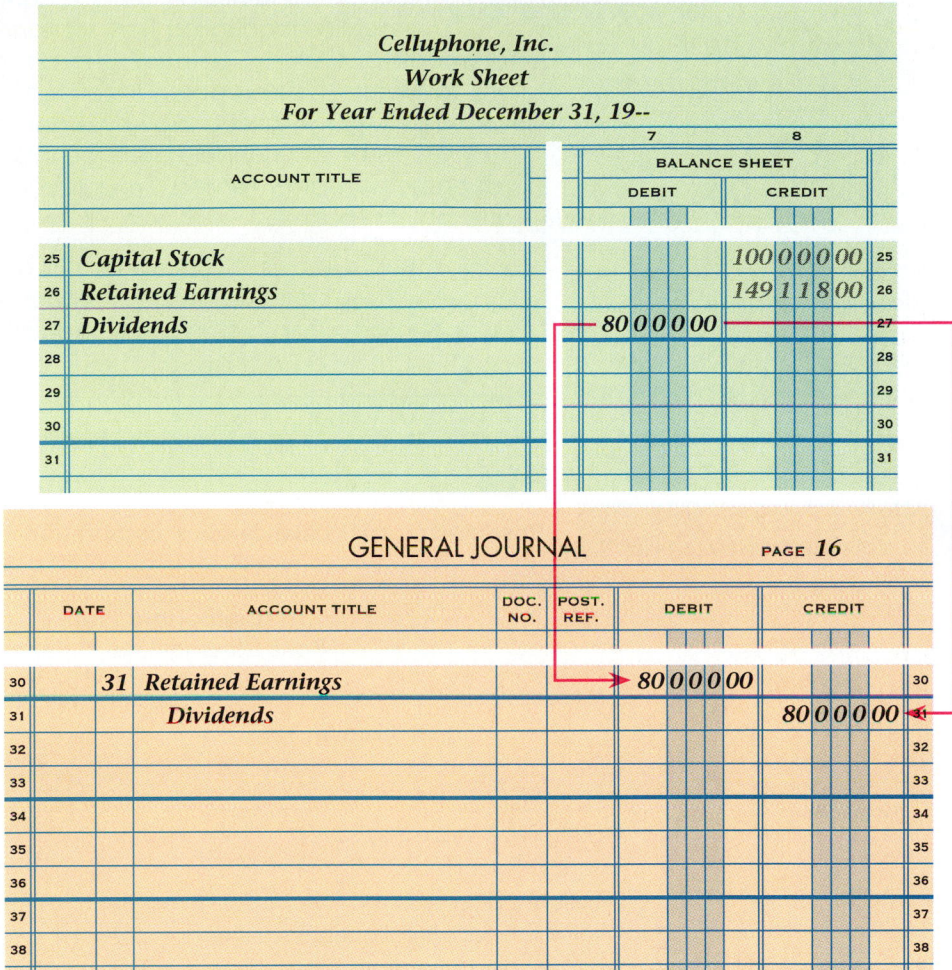

Post-Closing Trial Balance

A post-closing trial balance is prepared to prove the equality of debits and credits in the general ledger after adjusting and closing entries have been posted. Celluphone's December 31 post-closing trial balance is shown in Illustration 27-17 on page 724. Celluphone's general ledger is ready for the next fiscal period. *(CONCEPT: Accounting Period Cycle)*

Reversing Entries

If an adjusting entry creates a balance in an asset or liability account, Celluphone reverses the adjusting entry. A review of Celluphone's adjusting entries shows that the adjusting entry for accrued interest income created a balance in the interest receivable account. The adjusting entry for accrued interest expense created a balance in the interest payable account. Therefore, reversing entries are recorded for these two adjusting entries, as shown in Illustration 27-18 on page 725.

Should Tax Fraud Be Reported?

Rhonda Bender, CPA, is an accountant for Sutton and Associates, a public accounting firm. While reviewing the quarterly financial statements of Walker Company, she discovers that the company's prior year tax return was prepared incorrectly. The accounting records show that sales were $946,000. However, the tax return shows sales of only $746,000. When Ms. Bender asked the chief financial officer about the discrepancy, he sternly replied "Your firm doesn't do our tax return, so it's none of your business!"

Ms. Bender knows that accountants are not required to notify the government if they become aware of fraudulent tax returns. In addition, professional accounting standards require accountants to keep client

ILLUSTRATION 27-17   Post-closing trial balance for a corporation

Celluphone, Inc.
Post-Closing Trial Balance
December 31, 19--

Account Title	Debit	Credit
Cash	$ 40,968.00	
Petty Cash	300.00	
Notes Receivable	550.00	
Interest Receivable	11.00	
Accounts Receivable	68,240.00	
Allowance for Uncollectible Accounts		$ 9,492.00
Merchandise Inventory	212,178.00	
Supplies	3,765.00	
Prepaid Insurance	4,952.00	
Office Equipment	18,250.00	
Accumulated Depreciation—Office Equipment		5,375.00
Store Equipment	77,190.00	
Accumulated Depreciation—Store Equipment		15,450.00
Notes Payable		2,800.00
Interest Payable		70.00
Accounts Payable		83,965.75
Employee Income Tax Payable		2,340.00
Federal Income Tax Payable		2,219.23
FICA Tax Payable		2,695.00
Sales Tax Payable		10,982.00
Unemployment Tax Payable—Federal		47.00
Unemployment Tax Payable—State		317.25
Health Insurance Premiums Payable		995.00
Dividends Payable		20,000.00
Capital Stock		100,000.00
Retained Earnings		169,655.77
Totals	$426,404.00	$426,404.00

information confidential. Therefore, Ms. Bender decides to write a letter to Walker's board of directors reporting the error and relaying the chief financial officer's response to her inquiry. The letter states that Sutton and Associates will be forced to resign unless the company reports and corrects the tax return.

Upon learning that the board of directors has decided not to correct the tax return, Ms. Bender informs the company that Sutton and Associates has resigned as its accountants.

INSTRUCTIONS Use the three-step checklist to determine whether Sutton and Associates' resignation as Walker Company's accountants demonstrates ethical behavior.

ILLUSTRATION 27-18	Reversing entries

GENERAL JOURNAL PAGE *17*

	DATE		ACCOUNT TITLE	DOC. NO.	POST. REF.	DEBIT	CREDIT	
1			*Reversing Entries*					1
2	Jan.	1	*Interest Income*			1 1 00		2
3			*Interest Receivable*				1 1 00	3
4		1	*Interest Payable*			7 0 00		4
5			*Interest Expense*				7 0 00	5
6								6
7								7
8								8
9								9
10								10
11								11

Audit Your Understanding

1. Where is information needed for closing income statement credit balance accounts obtained from?

2. In what account is a corporation's net income recorded?

3. Why is a post-closing trial balance prepared after adjusting and closing entries have been posted?

Celluphone's adjusting entry for federal income tax expense does create a balance in the federal income tax payable account. During the new year, cash will be paid for accrued income tax expense for the previous year plus periodic payments for the current year's income tax expense. To avoid confusing the amount of income tax expense recorded for each of these years and to provide year-to-date income tax expense information for each year, Celluphone does not reverse this adjusting entry. For similar reasons many corporations do not reverse accrued income tax adjusting entries.

The chart shown in Summary Illustration 27-19, page 726, summarizes the end-of-fiscal-period entries for a corporation.

Work Sheet

1

Record adjusting entries from information in the Adjustments columns of the work sheet.

1

GENERAL JOURNAL
Adjusting Entries

2

GENERAL JOURNAL
Closing Entries

1. Closing entry for income statement accounts with credit balances (revenue and contra cost accounts).

2. Closing entry for income statement accounts with debit balances (cost, contra revenue, and expense accounts).

3. Closing entry to record net income or net loss in the retained earnings account and close the income summary account.

4. Closing entry for the dividends account.

2

Record the closing entries from information on the work sheet.

4

4

GENERAL LEDGER

4

GENERAL JOURNAL
Reversing Entries

3

POST-CLOSING
TRIAL BALANCE

4

At the beginning of the next fiscal year, record the reversing entries.

3

After all adjusting and closing entries are journalized and posted, prepare a post-closing trial balance to prove the equality of debits and credits.

What is the meaning of each of the following?

1. **net sales**

2. **net purchases**

3. **statement of stockholders' equity**

4. **book value**

5. **long-term liabilities**

6. **working capital**

7. **ratio**

8. **current ratio**

1. Which accounting concept is being applied when a corporation prepares financial statements annually and sometimes monthly or quarterly?

2. In what two ways does a corporation report changes in owners' equity differently from a proprietorship or partnership?

3. What financial information does an income statement report?

4. Where is the information found to prepare a corporation income statement?

5. What is the difference between sales and net sales reported on an income statement?

6. Why are other revenue and other expenses reported separately on the income statement from sales, cost of merchandise sold, and operating expenses?

7. How may the information on an income statement be used to determine whether the business is progressing satisfactorily?

8. Which accounting concept is being applied when the same accounting concepts are used for preparing income statements for each fiscal period?

9. What information is shown by component percentages on an income statement?

10. What financial information does a statement of stockholders' equity report?

11. Where is the information found to prepare a statement of stockholders' equity?

12. What financial information does a corporation balance sheet report?

13. Where is the information found to prepare a balance sheet?

14. What three amounts are reported on a balance sheet to show book value of a plant asset?

15. What determines whether a liability on a balance sheet is classified as current or long term?

16. For what purposes is the financial strength of a business analyzed?

17. What is working capital?

18. What kind of balances do income statement accounts have immediately after adjusting and closing entries are journalized and posted?

19. Why is a post-closing trial balance prepared?

CASE 1 The president of Kalikow Company asked the accounting department to provide as much information as possible to help management improve the company's net income. Paul Jayroe, a senior accountant, suggests that an income statement showing all the revenue and expense amounts should provide all the information management needs to analyze the company's results of operations. Do you agree with the accountant's suggestion? If not, what additional information do you recommend? Explain your answer.

CASE 2 Riverside Company recently organized as a corporation with five stockholders. Tamara Connell, the bookkeeper, is developing the accounting system. She suggested that although there are five stockholders, only one equity account be used. The account would be titled **Corporation Capital**. The president of Riverside questions the bookkeeper's recommendation. Is the bookkeeper's recommendation acceptable? If not, how should capital be recorded and reported? Explain your answer.

DRILLS FOR UNDERSTANDING · EPT(b)

DRILL 27-D1   Classifying a corporation's revenue, cost, and expense accounts

TUTORIAL

A form for classifying a corporation's revenue, cost, and expense accounts is given in the working papers that accompany this textbook.

INSTRUCTIONS:

For each of the following accounts, place a check mark in the column that correctly classifies the account.

1. Advertising Expense
2. Sales
3. Interest Income
4. Salary Expense
5. Sales Returns and Allowances
6. Purchases
7. Depreciation Expense
8. Purchases Discount
9. Interest Expense
10. Sales Discount
11. Uncollectible Accounts Expense
12. Purchases Returns and Allowances
13. Gain on Plant Assets
14. Utilities Expense
15. Cash Short and Over (cash short)

DRILL 27-D2   Classifying a corporation's assets, liabilities, and stockholders' equity accounts

A form for classifying a corporation's assets, liabilities, and stockholders' equity accounts is given in the working papers that accompany this textbook.

INSTRUCTIONS:

For each of the following accounts, place a check mark in the column that correctly classifies the account.

1. Cash
2. Accumulated Depreciation—Office Equipment
3. Federal Income Tax Payable
4. Prepaid Insurance

5. Notes Payable
6. Interest Receivable
7. Accounts Payable
8. Notes Receivable
9. Office Equipment
10. Interest Payable
11. Capital Stock
12. Mortgage Payable
13. Employee Income Tax Payable
14. Dividends Payable
15. Retained Earnings
16. Petty Cash
17. Accumulated Depreciation—Store Equipment
18. FICA Tax Payable
19. Merchandise Inventory
20. Allowance for Uncollectible Accounts

APPLICATION PROBLEMS   EPT(c,d,e,f,g)

PROBLEM 27-1 Preparing financial statements for a corporation

MATHEMATICS

AmTech Company completed the work sheet shown on pages 730–731 for the current year ended December 31.

INSTRUCTIONS:

1. Prepare an income statement. Calculate and record the following component percentages. (a) Cost of merchandise sold. (b) Gross profit on operations. (c) Total operating expenses. (d) Income from operations. (e) Net addition or deduction resulting from other revenue and expenses. (f) Net income before federal income tax. Round percentage calculations to the nearest 0.1%.

2. Analyze AmTech's income statement by determining if component percentages are within acceptable levels. If any component percentage is not within an acceptable level, suggest steps that the company should take. AmTech considers the following component percentages acceptable.

Cost of merchandise sold	Not more than 73.0%
Gross profit on operations	Not less than 27.0%
Total operating expenses	Not more than 24.9%
Income from operations	Not less than 2.1%
Net deduction from other revenue and expenses	Not more than 0.1%
Net income before federal income tax	Not less than 2.0%

3. Prepare a statement of stockholders' equity. Use the following additional information.

January 1 balance of capital stock account	$100,000.00
(1,000 shares issued for $100.00 per share)	
January 1 balance of retained earnings account	68,085.20

4. Prepare a balance sheet.

5. Calculate AmTech's (a) working capital and (b) current ratio. Determine if these items are within acceptable levels. AmTech considers the following levels acceptable.

Working capital	Not less than $100,000.00
Current ratio	Between 2.2 to 1 and 2.8 to 1

AmTech Company
Work Sheet
For Year Ended December 31, 19--

| | TRIAL BALANCE | | ADJUSTMENTS | | INCOME STATEMENT | | BALANCE SHEET | |
ACCOUNT TITLE	DEBIT	CREDIT	DEBIT	CREDIT	DEBIT	CREDIT	DEBIT	CREDIT
Cash	85399 00						85399 00	
Petty Cash	250 00						250 00	
Notes Receivable	3500 00						3500 00	
Interest Receivable			(a) 131 00				131 00	
Accounts Receivable	55618 00						55618 00	
Allowance for Uncollectible Accounts		378 00		(b) 5064 00				5442 00
Merchandise Inventory	40537 00		(c) 2954 60				43491 60	
Supplies	7726 40			(d) 5667 20			2059 20	
Prepaid Insurance	14652 00			(e) 9768 00			4884 00	
Office Equipment	12821 60						12821 60	
Accumulated Depr.—Office Equipment		2574 00		(f) 1496 00				4070 00
Store Equipment	77880 00						77880 00	
Accumulated Depr.—Store Equipment		14949 00		(g) 16834 40				31783 40
Notes Payable		1650 00						1650 00
Interest Payable				(h) 62 70				62 70
Accounts Payable		56953 50						56953 50
Employee Income Tax Payable		1535 00						1535 00
Federal Income Tax Payable				(i) 415 51				415 51
FICA Tax Payable		8060 00						8060 00
Sales Tax Payable		6256 00						6256 00
Unemployment Tax Payable—Federal		38 00						38 00
Unemployment Tax Payable—State		256 50						256 50
Health Insurance Premiums Payable		526 00						526 00
Dividends Payable		6000 00						6000 00
Capital Stock		100000 00						100000 00

731

#	Account Title	Trial Balance Debit	Trial Balance Credit	Adjustments Debit	Adjustments Credit	Income Statement Debit	Income Statement Credit	Balance Sheet Debit	Balance Sheet Credit
26	Retained Earnings		6 808 5 20						6 808 5 20
27	Dividends	24 000 00						24 000 00	
28	Income Summary			(c) 2 954 60		2 954 60			
29	Sales		1443 961 20				1443 961 20		
30	Sales Discount	4 431 90				4 431 90			
31	Sales Returns and Allowances	17 517 00				17 517 00			
32	Purchases	1056 290 00				1056 290 00			
33	Purchases Discount		7 824 30				7 824 30		
34	Purchases Returns and Allowances		3 850 00				3 850 00		
35	Advertising Expense	23 355 20				23 355 20			
36	Credit Card Fee Expense	13 035 00				13 035 00			
37	Depr. Expense—Office Equipment			(f) 1 496 00		1 496 00			
38	Depr. Expense—Store Equipment			(g) 16 834 40		16 834 40			
39	Insurance Expense			(e) 9 768 00		9 768 00			
40	Miscellaneous Expense	27 735 40				27 735 40			
41	Payroll Taxes Expense	16 292 10				16 292 10			
42	Rent Expense	46 200 00				46 200 00			
43	Salary Expense	181 031 00				181 031 00			
44	Supplies Expense			(d) 5 667 20		5 667 20			
45	Uncollectible Accounts Expense			(b) 5 064 00		5 064 00			
46	Utilities Expense	3 465 00				3 465 00			
47	Gain on Plant Assets		264 00				264 00		
48	Interest Income		394 00		(a) 131 00		525 00		
49	Cash Short and Over	8 80				8 80			
50	Interest Expense	184 80		(h) 62 70		247 50			
51	Loss on Plant Assets	170 50				170 50			
52	Federal Income Tax Expense	4 200 00		(i) 415 51		4 615 51			
53		1716 300 70	1716 300 70	42 393 41	42 393 41	1433 224 51	1459 379 10	310 034 40	283 879 81
54	Net Income after Federal Income Tax					26 154 59			26 154 59
55						1459 379 10	1459 379 10	310 034 40	310 034 40
56									
57									

PROBLEM 27-2 Journalizing adjusting, closing, and reversing entries for a corporation

Use the completed work sheet shown in Problem 27-1 to complete Problem 27-2.

INSTRUCTIONS:

1. Use page 18 of a general journal. Journalize the adjusting entries.

2. Use page 19 of a general journal. Journalize the closing entries.

3. Use page 20 of a general journal. Journalize the reversing entries for the accrued interest income and accrued interest expense.

ENRICHMENT PROBLEMS   EPT(c,d,e,f,g)

MASTERY PROBLEM 27-M Preparing financial statements and end-of-fiscal-period entries for a corporation

SPREADSHEET

Accent, Inc., completed the work sheet shown on pages 734–735 for the current year ended December 31.

INSTRUCTIONS:

1. Prepare an income statement. Calculate and record the following component percentages. (a) Cost of merchandise sold. (b) Gross profit on operations. (c) Total operating expenses. (d) Income from operations. (e) Net addition or deduction resulting from other revenue and expenses. (f) Net income before federal income tax. Round percentage calculations to the nearest 0.1%.

2. Analyze Accent's income statement by determining if component percentages are within acceptable levels. If any component percentage is not within an acceptable level, suggest steps that the company should take. Accent considers the following component percentages acceptable.

Cost of merchandise sold	Not more than 72.0%
Gross profit on operations	Not less than 28.0%
Total operating expenses	Not more than 22.0%
Income from operations	Not less than 6.0%
Net deduction from other revenue and expenses	Not more than 0.1%
Net income before federal income tax	Not less than 5.9%

3. Prepare a statement of stockholders' equity. Use the following additional information.

January 1 balance of capital stock account	$150,000.00
(15,000 shares issued for $10.00 per share)	
January 1 balance of retained earnings account	42,387.20

4. Prepare a balance sheet.

5. Calculate Accent's (a) working capital and (b) current ratio. Determine if these items are within acceptable levels. Accent considers the following levels acceptable.

Working capital	Not less than $125,000.00
Current ratio	Between 2.0 to 1 and 2.6 to 1

6. Use page 20 of a general journal. Journalize the adjusting entries.

7. Use page 21 of a general journal. Journalize the closing entries.

8. Use page 22 of a general journal. Journalize the reversing entries for the accrued interest income and accrued interest expense.

CHALLENGE PROBLEM 27-C Preparing financial statements and end-of-fiscal-period entries for a corporation

AUTOMATED

Glass Design Corporation's general ledger accounts and balances are recorded on a 10-column work sheet in the working papers.

INSTRUCTIONS:

1. Complete a 10-column work sheet for the current year ended December 31. Record the adjustments on the work sheet using the following information.

Adjustment Information, December 31

Accrued interest income.	$ 250.00
Uncollectible accounts expense estimated as 1.2% of sales on account.	
Sales on account for year, $561,375.00.	
Merchandise inventory	85,059.56
Supplies inventory	295.12
Value of prepaid insurance	2,720.80
Annual depreciation expense—office equipment	2,421.00
Annual depreciation expense—store equipment.	1,446.84
Accrued interest expense.	490.64

Federal income tax for the year is calculated at the following rates:
15% of net income before taxes, zero to $50,000.00.
Plus 25% of net income before taxes, $50,000.00 to $75,000.00.
Plus 34% of net income before taxes, $75,000.00 to $100,000.00.
Plus 39% of net income before taxes, $100,000.00 to $335,000.00.
Plus 34% of net income before taxes over $335,000.00.

2. Prepare an income statement. Calculate and record the following component percentages. (a) Cost of merchandise sold. (b) Gross profit on operations. (c) Total operating expenses. (d) Income from operations. (e) Net addition or deduction resulting from other revenue and expenses. (f) Net income before federal income tax. Round percentage calculations to the nearest 0.1%.

3. Analyze Glass Design's income statement by determining if component percentages are within acceptable levels. If any component percentage is not within an acceptable level, suggest steps that the company should take. Glass Design considers the following component percentages acceptable.

Cost of merchandise sold	Not more than 70.0%
Gross profit on operations.	Not less than 30.0%
Total operating expenses	Not more than 24.0%
Income from operations.	Not less than 6.0%
Net deduction from other	
revenue and expenses	Not more than 0.1%
Net income before federal	
income tax	Not less than 5.9%

4. Prepare a statement of stockholders' equity. Use the following additional information.

January 1 balance of capital stock account	$100,000.00
(10,000 shares issued for $10.00 per share)	
January 1 balance of retained earnings account. .	33,028.87

Accent, Inc.
Work Sheet
For Year Ended December 31, 19--

	ACCOUNT TITLE	TRIAL BALANCE DEBIT	TRIAL BALANCE CREDIT	ADJUSTMENTS DEBIT	ADJUSTMENTS CREDIT	INCOME STATEMENT DEBIT	INCOME STATEMENT CREDIT	BALANCE SHEET DEBIT	BALANCE SHEET CREDIT
1	Cash	5228300						5228300	
2	Petty Cash	30000						30000	
3	Notes Receivable	440000						440000	
4	Interest Receivable			(a) 12980				12980	
5	Accounts Receivable	5909640						5909640	
6	Allowance for Uncollectible Accounts		38610		(b) 448580				487190
7	Merchandise Inventory	10556410		(c) 1278310				11834720	
8	Supplies	823240			(d) 648109			175131	
9	Prepaid Insurance	1559250			(e) 909590			649660	
10	Office Equipment	1362130						1362130	
11	Accumulated Depr.—Office Equipment		273460		(f) 152460				425920
12	Store Equipment	8274640						8274640	
13	Accumulated Depr.—Store Equipment		1588290		(g) 1078000				2666290
14	Notes Payable		274340						274340
15	Interest Payable				(h) 10340				10340
16	Accounts Payable		6826500						6826500
17	Employee Income Tax Payable		162910						162910
18	Federal Income Tax Payable				(i) 150560				150560
19	FICA Tax Payable		197780						197780
20	Sales Tax Payable		664730						664730
21	Unemployment Tax Payable—Federal		3400						3400
22	Unemployment Tax Payable—State		22950						22950
23	Health Insurance Premiums Payable		55660						55660
24	Dividends Payable		1200000						1200000
25	Capital Stock		15000000						15000000

#	Account Title	Trial Balance Debit	Trial Balance Credit	Adjustments Debit	Adjustments Credit	Income Statement Debit	Income Statement Credit	Balance Sheet Debit	Balance Sheet Credit
26	Retained Earnings		42 387 20						42 387 20
27	Dividends	48 000 00						48 000 00	
28	Income Summary				(c) 12 783 10		12 783 10		
29	Sales		1 506 985 70				1 506 985 70		
30	Sales Discount	7 593 30				7 593 30			
31	Sales Returns and Allowances	17 867 30				17 867 30			
32	Purchases	1 077 414 80				1 077 414 80			
33	Purchases Discount		5 890 50				5 890 50		
34	Purchases Returns and Allowances		3 927 00				3 927 00		
35	Advertising Expense	20 742 70				20 742 70			
36	Credit Card Fee Expense	13 555 30				13 555 30			
37	Depr. Expense—Office Equipment			(f) 1 524 60		1 524 60			
38	Depr. Expense—Store Equipment			(g) 10 780 00		10 780 00			
39	Insurance Expense			(e) 9 095 90		9 095 90			
40	Miscellaneous Expense	28 289 80				28 289 80			
41	Payroll Taxes Expense	17 355 80				17 355 80			
42	Rent Expense	48 000 00				48 000 00			
43	Salary Expense	184 650 40				184 650 40			
44	Supplies Expense			(d) 6 481 09		6 481 09			
45	Uncollectible Accounts Expense			(b) 4 485 80		4 485 80			
46	Utilities Expense	3 619 00				3 619 00			
47	Gain on Plant Assets		2 25 00				2 25 00		
48	Interest Income		3 90 50		(a) 1 29 80		5 20 30		
49	Cash Short and Over	1 2 10				1 2 10			
50	Interest Expense	3 09 10		(h) 1 03 40		4 12 50			
51	Loss on Plant Assets	3 46 50				3 46 50			
52	Federal Income Tax Expense	13 300 00		(i) 1 505 60		14 805 60			
53		1 822 892 20	1 822 892 20	46 889 29	46 889 29	1 467 032 49	1 530 331 60	387 172 01	323 872 90
54	Net Income after Federal Income Tax					63 299 11			63 299 11
55						1 530 331 60	1 530 331 60	387 172 01	387 172 01
56									
57									

5. Prepare a balance sheet.

6. Calculate Glass Design's (a) working capital and (b) current ratio. Determine if these items are within acceptable levels. Glass Design considers the following levels acceptable.

Working capital . . . .   Not less than $125,000.00
Current ratio . . . .   Between 2.0 to 1 and 2.5 to 1

7. Use page 13 of a general journal. Journalize the adjusting entries.

8. Use page 14 of a general journal. Journalize the closing entries.

9. Use page 15 of a general journal. Journalize the reversing entries for the accrued interest income and accrued interest expense.

End-of-Fiscal-Period Work for a Corporation

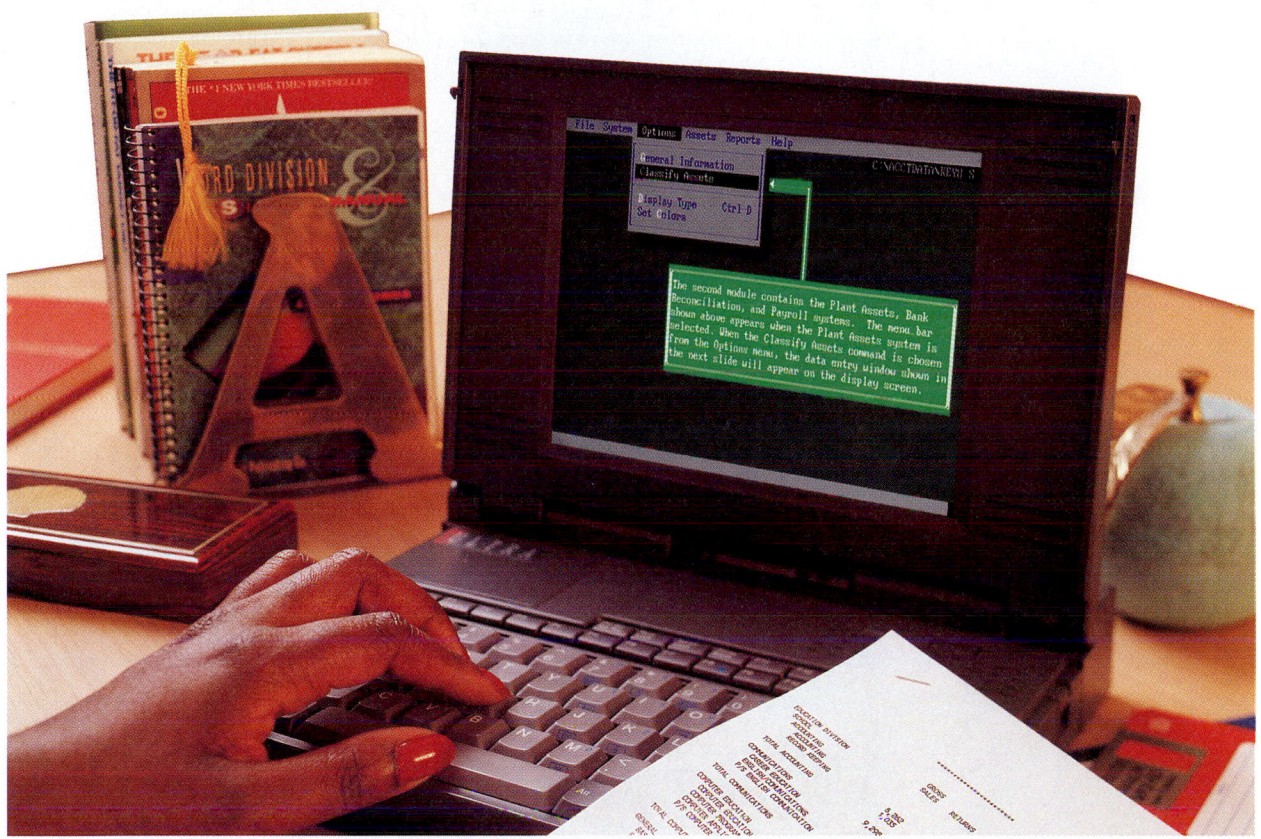

Celluphone's manual accounting procedures for completing a corporation's end-of-fiscal-period work are described in Chapter 27. Integrating Automated Accounting Topic 10 describes procedures for using automated accounting software to complete Celluphone's end-of-fiscal-period work. The Automated Accounting Problem contains instructions for using automated accounting software to solve Challenge Problem 27-C, Chapter 27.

PLANNING ADJUSTMENTS

A trial balance is prepared by the software to check the equality of debits and credits in the general ledger. Celluphone's trial balance is shown in Illustration T10-1 on page 738.

The trial balance also serves as the basis for planning adjusting entries. Adjusting entries are batched and recorded on a general journal input form. Celluphone's December 31 adjustment data is shown at the bottom of the next page.

Trial balance prepared by automated accounting software

```
                         Celluphone, Inc.
                          Trial Balance
                            12/31/--
----------------------------------------------------------------
Acct.   Account
Number  Title                          Debit          Credit
----------------------------------------------------------------
1105    Cash                         40968.00
1110    Petty Cash                     300.00
1115    Notes Receivable               550.00
1125    Accounts Receivable          68240.00
1130    Allow. for Uncoll. Accts.                      265.00
1135    Merchandise Inventory       205160.00
1140    Supplies                     15455.00
1145    Prepaid Insurance            13550.00
1205    Office Equipment             18250.00
1210    Acc. Depr.--Office Equip.                     3625.00
1215    Store Equipment              77190.00
1220    Acc. Depr.--Store Equip.                      9125.00
2105    Notes Payable                                 2800.00
2115    Accounts Payable                             83965.75
2120    Employee Income Tax Pay.                      2340.00
2130    FICA Tax Payable                              2695.00
2135    Sales Tax Payable                            10982.00
2140    Unemployment Tax Pay--Fed                       47.00
2145    Unemployment Tax Pay--St.                      317.25
2150    Health Ins. Premiums Pay.                      995.00
2155    Dividends Payable                            20000.00
3105    Capital Stock                               100000.00
3110    Retained Earnings                           149118.00
3115    Dividends                    80000.00
4105    Sales                                      2050440.00
4110    Sales Discount                5642.00
4115    Sales Ret. and Allowances    24318.00
5105    Purchases                  1454798.00
5110    Purchases Discount                           10766.00
5115    Purchases Ret. and Allow.                     5310.00
6105    Advertising Expense          32600.00
6110    Credit Card Fee Expense      20468.00
6130    Miscellaneous Expense        22350.00
6135    Payroll Taxes Expense        23720.00
6140    Rent Expense                 56400.00
6145    Salary Expense              251932.00
6160    Utilities Expense             4890.00
7105    Gain on Plant Assets                           225.00
7110    Interest Income                                203.00
8105    Cash Short and Over              3.00
8110    Interest Expense              1375.00
8115    Loss on Plant Assets           460.00
9105    Federal Income Tax Exp.      34600.00
                                    ----------     ----------
        Totals                     2453219.00     2453219.00
                                    ==========     ==========
```

Adjustment Information, December 31

Accrued interest income.............................	$ 11.00
Uncollectible accounts expense......................	9,227.00
Merchandise inventory...............................	212,178.00
Supplies inventory..................................	3,765.00
Value of prepaid insurance	4,952.00
Annual depreciation expense—office equipment	1,750.00
Annual depreciation expense—store equipment........	6,325.00
Accrued interest expense	70.00
Federal income tax expense for the year	36,819.23

After all adjusting entries have been recorded on the general journal input form, the Debit and Credit columns are totaled. The totals are entered on the Page Totals and Final Totals lines provided at the bottom of the input form. The totals are compared to assure that debits and credits are equal. As the totals are the same, $46,908.23, the adjusting entries on the general journal input form are assumed to be correct. Celluphone's completed general journal input form for the adjusting entries is shown in Illustration T10-2.

| ILLUSTRATION T10-2 | General journal input form with adjusting entries recorded |

RUN DATE 12/31/-- MM DD YY

GENERAL JOURNAL
Input Form

	DATE MM/DD	REFERENCE	ACCOUNT NO.	CUSTOMER/ VENDOR NO.	DEBIT	CREDIT	
1	12/31	Adj.Ent.	1120		11 00		1
2	/		7110			11 00	2
3	/31	Adj.Ent.	6155		9227 00		3
4	/		1130			9227 00	4
5	/31	Adj.Ent.	1135		7018 00		5
6	/		3120			7018 00	6
7	/31	Adj.Ent.	6150		11690 00		7
8	/		1140			11690 00	8
9	/31	Adj.Ent.	6125		8598 00		9
10	/		1145			8598 00	10
11	/31	Adj.Ent.	6115		1750 00		11
12	/		1210			1750 00	12
13	/31	Adj.Ent.	6120		6325 00		13
14	/		1220			6325 00	14
15	/31	Adj.Ent.	8110		70 00		15
16	/		2110			70 00	16
17	/31	Adj.Ent.	9105		2219 23		17
18	/		2125			2219 23	18
19	/						19
25	/						25
	PAGE TOTALS				46908 23	46908 23	
	FINAL TOTALS				46908 23	46908 23	

After all lines on the input form have been keyed and posted, a general journal report is prepared. Celluphone's general journal report is shown in Illustration T10-3 on page 740.

PREPARING END-OF-FISCAL-PERIOD REPORTS

After the general journal report for adjusting entries has been prepared, an income statement is displayed and printed. Celluphone's income statement is shown in Illustration T10-4 on page 741.

In Celluphone's manual accounting system, a statement of stockholders' equity is prepared to show changes in stockholders'

```
                         Celluphone, Inc.
                         General Journal
                            12/31/--
-----------------------------------------------------------------------
Date   Refer.    V/C Acct.   Title                       Debit    Credit
-----------------------------------------------------------------------
12/31  Adj.Ent.      1120    Interest Receivable         11.00
12/31  Adj.Ent.      7110    Interest Income                       11.00

12/31  Adj.Ent.      6155    Uncoll. Accounts Expense  9227.00
12/31  Adj.Ent.      1130    Allow. for Uncoll. Accts.            9227.00

12/31  Adj.Ent.      1135    Merchandise Inventory     7018.00
12/31  Adj.Ent.      3120    Income Summary                       7018.00

12/31  Adj.Ent.      6150    Supplies Expense         11690.00
12/31  Adj.Ent.      1140    Supplies                            11690.00

12/31  Adj.Ent.      6125    Insurance Expense         8598.00
12/31  Adj.Ent.      1145    Prepaid Insurance                    8598.00

12/31  Adj.Ent.      6115    Depr. Exp.--Office Equip. 1750.00
12/31  Adj.Ent.      1210    Acc. Depr.--Office Equip.            1750.00

12/31  Adj.Ent.      6120    Depr. Exp.--Store Equip.  6325.00
12/31  Adj.Ent.      1220    Acc. Depr.--Store Equip.             6325.00

12/31  Adj.Ent.      8110    Interest Expense            70.00
12/31  Adj.Ent.      2110    Interest Payable                       70.00

12/31  Adj.Ent.      9105    Federal Income Tax Exp.   2219.23
12/31  Adj.Ent.      2125    Federal Income Tax Pay.              2219.23

                                                       ----------  ----------
                             Totals                    46908.23    46908.23
                                                       ==========  ==========
```

equity during the fiscal period. In Celluphone's automated accounting system, changes in stockholders' equity are shown on the balance sheet. Celluphone's balance sheet is shown in Illustration T10-5 on page 742.

After the balance sheet has been prepared, the software is directed to perform period-end closing.

After the financial statements have been prepared and period-end closing has been performed, a post-closing trial balance is prepared. Celluphone's post-closing trial balance is shown in Illustration T10-6 on page 743.

RECORDING REVERSING ENTRIES

Celluphone records two reversing entries after the post-closing trial balance is prepared. (1) An entry to reverse the adjusting entry for accrued interest income. (2) An entry to reverse the adjusting entry for accrued interest expense. The reversing entries are batched and recorded on a general journal input form. Celluphone's reversing entries are on the general journal input form shown in Illustration T10-7 on page 743.

FYI

Reversing entries are completed at the beginning of the next fiscal period.

```
                        Celluphone, Inc.
                        Income Statement
                    For Period Ended 12/31/--
---------------------------------------------------------------
                     *****Monthly*****    *****Yearly******
                     Amount    Percent    Amount     Percent
---------------------------------------------------------------
Operating Revenue
---------------------------------------------
Sales                2050440.00  101.48 2050440.00   101.48
Sales Discount         -5642.00    -.28   -5642.00     -.28
Sales Ret. and Allowances -24318.00 -1.20 -24318.00    -1.20
                      ----------  ------ ----------   ------
Total Operating Revenue 2020480.00 100.00 2020480.00  100.00

Cost of Merchandise Sold
---------------------------------------------
Beginning Inventory    205160.00   10.15  205160.00    10.15
Purchases             1454798.00   72.00 1454798.00    72.00
Purchases Discount     -10766.00    -.53  -10766.00     -.53
Purchases Ret. and Allow. -5310.00  -.26   -5310.00     -.26
                      ----------  ------ ----------   ------
Merchandise Available for Sale 1643882.00 81.36 1643882.00 81.36
Less Ending Inventory -212178.00  -10.50 -212178.00   -10.50
                      ----------  ------ ----------   ------
Cost of Merchandise Sold 1431704.00 70.86 1431704.00  70.86
                      ----------  ------ ----------   ------
Gross Profit           588776.00   29.14  588776.00    29.14

Operating Expenses
---------------------------------------------
Advertising Expense     32600.00    1.61   32600.00     1.61
Credit Card Fee Expense 20468.00    1.01   20468.00     1.01
Depr. Exp.--Office Equip. 1750.00    .09    1750.00      .09
Depr. Exp.--Store Equip.  6325.00    .31    6325.00      .31
Insurance Expense        8598.00    .43    8598.00      .43
Miscellaneous Expense   22350.00    1.11   22350.00     1.11
Payroll Taxes Expense   23720.00    1.17   23720.00     1.17
Rent Expense            56400.00    2.79   56400.00     2.79
Salary Expense         251932.00   12.47  251932.00    12.47
Supplies Expense        11690.00    .58    11690.00      .58
Uncoll. Accounts Expense 9227.00    .46    9227.00      .46
Utilities Expense        4890.00    .24    4890.00      .24
                      ----------  ------ ----------   ------
Total Operating Expenses 449950.00 22.27  449950.00    22.27
                      ----------  ------ ----------   ------
Net Income from Operations 138826.00 6.87 138826.00     6.87

Other Revenue
---------------------------------------------
Gain on Plant Assets      225.00    .01     225.00      .01
Interest Income           214.00    .01     214.00      .01

Other Expense
---------------------------------------------
Cash Short and Over         3.00              3.00
Interest Expense         1445.00    .07     1445.00      .07
Loss on Plant Assets      460.00    .02      460.00      .02
                      ----------  ------ ----------   ------
Net Income before Income Tax 137357.00 6.80 137357.00   6.80

Income Tax
---------------------------------------------
Federal Income Tax Exp.  36819.23   1.82   36819.23     1.82
                      ----------  ------ ----------   ------
Net Income after Income Tax 100537.77 4.98 100537.77    4.98
                      ==========  ====== ==========   ======
```

```
                      Celluphone, Inc.
                       Balance Sheet
                         12/31/--

A s s e t s
-----------
Cash                                   40968.00
Petty Cash                               300.00
Notes Receivable                         550.00
Interest Receivable                       11.00
Accounts Receivable                    68240.00
Allow. for Uncoll. Accts.              -9492.00
Merchandise Inventory                 212178.00
Supplies                                3765.00
Prepaid Insurance                       4952.00
                                      ----------
Total Current Assets                  321472.00

Office Equipment                       18250.00
Acc. Depr.--Office Equip.              -5375.00
Store Equipment                        77190.00
Acc. Depr.--Store Equip.              -15450.00
                                      ----------
Total Plant Assets                     74615.00
                                      ----------
Total Assets                                      396087.00
                                                  ==========
L i a b i l i t i e s
---------------------
Notes Payable                           2800.00
Interest Payable                          70.00
Accounts Payable                       83965.75
Employee Income Tax Pay.                2340.00
Federal Income Tax Pay.                 2219.23
FICA Tax Payable                        2695.00
Sales Tax Payable                      10982.00
Unemployment Tax Pay--Fed                 47.00
Unemployment Tax Pay--St.                317.25
Health Ins. Premiums Pay.                995.00
Dividends Payable                      20000.00
                                      ----------
Total Liabilities                                 126431.23

S t o c k h o l d e r s '   E q u i t y
----------------------------------------
Capital Stock                         100000.00
Retained Earnings                     149118.00
Dividends                             -80000.00
Net Income                            100537.77
                                      ----------
Total Stockholders' Equity                        269655.77
                                                  ----------
Total Liabilities & Equity                        396087.00
                                                  ==========
```

After all lines on the input form have been keyed and posted, a general journal report is prepared. Celluphone's general journal report for reversing entries is shown in Illustration T10-8 on page 744.

OPTIONAL PROBLEM DB-10A

Celluphone's general ledger data base is on the accounting textbook template. If you wish to process Celluphone's end-of-fiscal-period work using automated accounting software, load the

Post-closing trial balance prepared by automated accounting software

```
                         Celluphone, Inc.
                          Trial Balance
                            12/31/--
--------------------------------------------------------------------
Acct.   Account
Number  Title                              Debit            Credit
--------------------------------------------------------------------
1105    Cash                             40968.00
1110    Petty Cash                         300.00
1115    Notes Receivable                   550.00
1120    Interest Receivable                 11.00
1125    Accounts Receivable              68240.00
1130    Allow. for Uncoll. Accts.                           9492.00
1135    Merchandise Inventory           212178.00
1140    Supplies                          3765.00
1145    Prepaid Insurance                 4952.00
1205    Office Equipment                 18250.00
1210    Acc. Depr.--Office Equip.                           5375.00
1215    Store Equipment                  77190.00
1220    Acc. Depr.--Store Equip.                           15450.00
2105    Notes Payable                                       2800.00
2110    Interest Payable                                      70.00
2115    Accounts Payable                                   83965.75
2120    Employee Income Tax Pay.                            2340.00
2125    Federal Income Tax Pay.                             2219.23
2130    FICA Tax Payable                                    2695.00
2135    Sales Tax Payable                                  10982.00
2140    Unemployment Tax Pay--Fed                             47.00
2145    Unemployment Tax Pay--St.                            317.25
2150    Health Ins. Premiums Pay.                            995.00
2155    Dividends Payable                                  20000.00
3105    Capital Stock                                     100000.00
3110    Retained Earnings                                 169655.77
                                         ----------        ----------
        Totals                          426404.00         426404.00
                                         ==========        ==========
```

Automated Accounting 6.0 or higher software. Select Data Base 10A (DB-10A) from the template disk. Read the Problem Instructions screen. Using the completed general journal input forms, Illustrations T10-2 and T10-7, follow the procedures described to process Celluphone's end-of-fiscal-period work.

General journal input form with reversing entries recorded

RUN DATE 01/01/-- MM DD YY

GENERAL JOURNAL
Input Form

	DATE MM/DD	REFERENCE	ACCOUNT NO.	CUSTOMER/ VENDOR NO.	DEBIT	CREDIT	
1	01/01	Rev.Ent.	7110		11 00		1
2	/		1120			11 00	2
3	/01	Rev.Ent.	2110		70 00		3
4	/		8110			70 00	4
5	/						5
25	/						25
				PAGE TOTALS	81 00	81 00	
				FINAL TOTALS	81 00	81 00	

```
                          Celluphone, Inc.
                          General Journal
                            01/01/--
-----------------------------------------------------------------------
Date   Refer.   V/C  Acct.  Title                    Debit      Credit
-----------------------------------------------------------------------
01/01  Rev.Ent.       7110  Interest Income          11.00
01/01  Rev.Ent.       1120  Interest Receivable                  11.00

01/01  Rev.Ent.       2110  Interest Payable         70.00
01/01  Rev.Ent.       8110  Interest Expense                     70.00

                                                   ---------- ----------
                            Totals                   81.00      81.00
                                                   ========== ==========
```

AUTOMATED ACCOUNTING PROBLEM

AUTOMATING CHALLENGE PROBLEM 27-C **Preparing financial statements and end-of-fiscal-period entries for a corporation**

INSTRUCTIONS:

1. Load the *Automated Accounting 6.0* or higher software. Select data base F27-C (First-Year Course Challenge Problem 27-C) from the accounting textbook template. Read the Problem Instructions screen.
2. Select File from the menu bar and choose the Save As menu command. Key the path to the drive and directory that contains your data files. Save the data base with a file name of XXX27C (where XXX are your initials).
3. Display/print a trial balance.
4. Display/print the chart of accounts.
5. Record the adjusting entries on a general journal input form using the information given below. Net income before federal income tax for the year is $87,030.57. Use December 31 of the current year as the run date.

Adjustment Information, December 31

Accrued interest income.	$ 250.00
Uncollectible accounts expense estimated at 1.2% of sales on account. Sales on account for the year, $561,375.00.	
Merchandise inventory	85,059.56
Supplies inventory	295.12
Value of prepaid insurance	2,720.80
Annual depreciation expense—office equipment	2,421.00
Annual depreciation expense—store equipment.	1,446.84
Accrued interest expense.	490.64
Federal income tax expense for the year.	17,840.39

6. Key the adjusting entries from the completed general journal input form.
7. Display/print the general journal report.
8. Display/print the income statement and balance sheet.
9. Perform period-end closing.
10. Display/print the post-closing trial balance.
11. Record the reversing entries on a general journal input form. Use January 1 of the following year as the run date.
12. Key the reversing entries from the completed general journal input form.
13. Display/print the general journal report.

An Accounting Cycle for a Corporation: End-of-Fiscal-Period Work

AUTOMATED

The general ledger used in Reinforcement Activity 3, Part A, is needed to complete Reinforcement Activity 3, Part B.

Reinforcement Activity 3, Part B, includes those accounting activities needed to complete an accounting cycle for a corporation. In Part A Hardware Mart's transactions were recorded for the last month of a fiscal year. In Part B end-of-fiscal-period work is completed.

END-OF-FISCAL-PERIOD WORK

INSTRUCTIONS:

12. Prepare a work sheet for the fiscal year ended December 31 of the current year. Use the following adjustment information.

Adjustment Information, December 31

Accrued interest income..	$ 84.00
Uncollectible accounts expense is estimated as 1.5% of sales on account.	
Sales on account for the year, $120,800.00.	
Merchandise inventory	65,661.20
Supplies inventory	242.50
Value of prepaid insurance	2,160.00
Annual depreciation expense—office equipment	2,130.00
Annual depreciation expense—store equipment..............	3,410.00
Accrued interest expense...................................	500.00
Federal income tax for the year..............................	14,579.41

13. Prepare an income statement. Calculate and record the following component percentages as a percent of net sales: (a) cost of merchandise sold; (b) gross profit on operations; (c) total operating expenses; (d) income from operations; (e) net additions/deductions from other revenue and expenses; and (f) net income before federal income tax. Round percentage calculations to the nearest 0.1%.

14. Analyze Hardware Mart's income statement by determining if component percentages are within acceptable levels. If any component percentage is not within an acceptable level, suggest steps that the company should take. Hardware Mart considers the following percentages acceptable.

Cost of merchandise sold	Not more than 66.0%
Gross profit on operations	Not less than 34.0%
Total operating expenses	Not more than 25.0%
Income from operations	Not less than 9.0%
Net deductions from other revenue and expenses	Not more than 0.5%
Net income before federal income tax	Not less than 8.5%

15. Prepare a statement of stockholders' equity. Use the following additional information.

January 1 balance of capital stock account...................	$40,000.00
(4,000 shares issued for $10.00 per share)	
January 1 balance of retained earnings account..............	34,894.40

16. Prepare a balance sheet.

17. Calculate Hardware Mart's (a) working capital and (b) current ratio. Determine if these items are within acceptable levels. Hardware Mart considers the following amounts acceptable.

Working capital	Not less than $50,000.00
Current ratio	Between 2.0 to 1 and 2.5 to 1

18. Journalize the adjusting entries on page 13 of a general journal. Post the adjusting entries.

19. Journalize the closing entries on page 14 of a general journal. Post the closing entries.

20. Prepare a post-closing trial balance.

21. Journalize the reversing entries on page 15 of a general journal for the accrued interest income and accrued interest expense adjusting entries. Post the reversing entries.

Western Rider, Inc. is a merchandising business organized as a corporation. This business simulation covers the realistic transactions completed by Western Rider, Inc., which sells clothing, tack, and other items to those who own and show horses or who simply ride horses for pleasure. Transactions are recorded in special journals and a general journal similar to the ones used by Celluphone, Inc. in Part 4. The following activities are included in the accounting cycle for Western Rider, Inc. This business simulation is available from the publisher in either manual or automated versions.

Activities in Western Rider, Inc.:

1. Recording transactions in special journals from source documents.

2. Posting items to be posted individually to a general ledger and subsidiary ledger

3. Posting column totals to a general ledger.

4. Preparing schedules of accounts receivable and accounts payable from subsidiary ledgers.

5. Preparing a trial balance on a work sheet.

6. Planning adjustments and completing a work sheet.

7. Preparing financial statements.

8. Journalizing and posting adjusting entries.

9. Journalizing and posting closing entries.

10. Preparing a post-closing trial balance.

11. Journalizing and posting reversing entries.

PART 5

The Legal Environment of Business

28

Forming and Dissolving Business Organizations

ENABLING PERFORMANCE TASKS

After studying Chapter 28, you will be able to:

a Define accounting terms related to forming and liquidating business organizations.

b Identify the legal requirements for forming and dissolving various forms of business organizations.

c Journalize entries for initial investment for a proprietorship, partnership, and corporation.

d Journalize entries for liquidation of a proprietorship and a partnership.

TERMS PREVIEW

dissolution • liquidation • partnership agreement • articles of incorporation • par value • par-value stock

When starting a business, one of three basic forms of ownership can be chosen. A business can be organized as a proprietorship, partnership, or corporation. Each form of business ownership has legal and accounting implications that the owners must consider when making a choice.

A business organization may stop operations at any time for a variety of reasons. The process of stopping the operation of a business is called **dissolution**. The process of paying all liabilities of a business and distributing remaining cash to the owner(s) is called **liquidation**.

FORMING A PROPRIETORSHIP

A business owned by one person is known as a proprietorship. Roger Moher is starting a sporting goods business called Sports-Lure. Because Mr. Moher is the only owner, SportsLure is a proprietorship. Mr. Moher will have total control over the business and will be able to make all decisions for SportsLure. The advantages of a proprietorship include:

1. Ease of formation. A proprietorship is relatively easy to form.
2. Total control. Mr. Moher has total control of the proprietorship.
3. Unshared profits. Mr. Moher gets all profits made by SportsLure.

Mr. Moher has also considered the disadvantages of a proprietorship. The disadvantages include:

1. Limited resources. Since Mr. Moher is the only owner, he is the only person who can invest cash and other assets in the business.
2. Unlimited liability. Mr. Moher is totally responsible for the liabilities of SportsLure. Mr. Moher's personal assets, such as his house and car, can be claimed by creditors to pay SportsLure's liabilities.
3. Limited time, energy, and experience. The amount of time, energy, and experience that Mr. Moher will be able to put into the business is limited.
4. Limited life. A proprietorship must be dissolved when the owner dies or decides to stop doing business.

When Mr. Moher started SportsLure, he was required to follow the laws of the federal government as well as the laws of the state and city in which the business was formed.

Legal Requirements for Forming a Proprietorship

A proprietorship is the simplest form of business to organize. The legal requirements for organizing a proprietorship vary from state to state. However, most cities and states have few, if any, legal procedures to follow. In some states, if the name of the business is different from the name of the owner, the name of the business must be registered with the Secretary of State. In addition, some cities

CHAPTER 28   Forming and Dissolving Business Organizations   **751** require a proprietorship to obtain an operating license to run a business in that locality. Once these legal requirements have been met, the proprietorship can officially begin business. To begin operation of SportsLure, the owner, Mr. Moher, filed the name of the business with the state and obtained the required city operating license.

Accounting Transaction for Forming a Proprietorship

Once SportsLure was legally established, Mr. Moher invested $10,000.00 of his own money in the business.

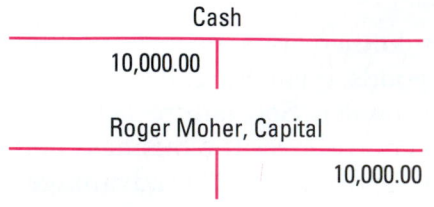

April 1, 19--. Received cash from owner as an investment, $10,000.00. Receipt No. 1.

Cash is debited for $10,000.00. Roger Moher, Capital is credited for $10,000.00.

The journal entry to record this transaction is shown in Illustration 28-1.

ILLUSTRATION 28-1	Journal entry to record receiving cash from owner as an investment

CASH RECEIPTS JOURNAL   PAGE 1

					GENERAL		ACCOUNTS RECEIVABLE CREDIT	SALES CREDIT	SALES TAX PAYABLE		SALES DISCOUNT DEBIT	CASH DEBIT	
	DATE	ACCOUNT TITLE	DOC. NO.	POST. REF.	DEBIT	CREDIT			DEBIT	CREDIT			
1	Apr. 1	Roger Moher, Capital	R1			10 0 0 0 00						10 0 0 0 00	1
2													2
3													3

DISSOLVING A PROPRIETORSHIP

A proprietor may choose to dissolve the proprietorship at any time. Legal requirements must be completed and correct accounting procedures must be followed when a proprietorship is dissolved.

Legal Requirements for Dissolving a Proprietorship

To dissolve a business, the proprietor merely stops doing business and settles all the affairs of the business. If the business has employees, the owner must notify the appropriate federal and state tax authorities that the business has terminated operations.

Liquidation of a Proprietorship

Once a proprietorship is legally dissolved, the liquidation process can begin. When a proprietorship is liquidated, noncash assets are

Bankruptcy is a legal procedure in which a company that cannot meet its financial obligations is relieved of its debts. The assets are distributed to the creditors.

usually sold and the cash is used to pay creditors. Any remaining cash is distributed to the owner.

After many years of business, Mr. Moher decided to terminate SportsLure. Necessary legal documents were filed, and on June 30 financial statements were prepared and adjusting and closing entries were journalized and posted. After the end-of-fiscal-period work was completed, the business had account balances as shown in the T accounts.

Cash			Accounts Payable	
21,000.00				9,000.00

Supplies			Roger Moher, Capital	
5,000.00				17,000.00

Selling Noncash Assets for Less than Book Value.   Noncash assets are sometimes sold for less than the recorded book value.

July 1, 19--. Received cash from sale of supplies, $3,500.00; book value of supplies, $5,000.00. Receipt No. 744.

Cash			Supplies	
Bal.	21,000.00		Bal.	5,000.00		5,000.00
	3,500.00		(New Bal. zero)	
(New Bal.	24,500.00)			

Roger Moher, Capital		
1,500.00	Bal.	17,000.00
	(New Bal.	15,500.00)

The loss on the sale of the supplies is calculated as shown below.

	Book Value of Asset Sold	−	Value of Asset Received	=	Loss on Sale
	Supplies $5,000.00	−	Cash $3,500.00	=	$1,500.00

Because the business is in the process of liquidation, the loss on sale is recorded directly in the owner's capital account.

Cash is debited for the amount received, $3,500.00. Roger Moher, Capital is debited for $1,500.00, the loss on the sale of the supplies. Supplies is credited for the recorded book value of the supplies sold, $5,000.00.

The journal entry to record this transaction is shown in Illustration 28-2 on page 754.

The loss on sale could be recorded in an expense account. Recording the loss in an expense account would provide management with better information regarding the effect of the transaction on owner's equity. However, when a business is being liquidated, this additional information is unnecessary. Therefore, the loss on sale is recorded directly in the owner's capital account.

ILLUSTRATION 28-2   Journal entry to record loss on liquidation of noncash assets

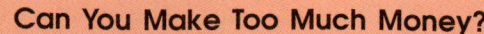

CASH RECEIPTS JOURNAL   PAGE 13

	DATE	ACCOUNT TITLE	DOC. NO.	POST. REF.	GENERAL DEBIT	GENERAL CREDIT	ACCOUNTS RECEIVABLE CREDIT	SALES CREDIT	SALES TAX PAYABLE DEBIT	SALES TAX PAYABLE CREDIT	SALES DISCOUNT DEBIT	CASH DEBIT	
1	July 1	Roger Moher, Capital	R744		1500 00							3500 00	1
2		Supplies				500 00							2
3													3

GENERAL LEDGER
Accounts Payable

9,000.00	Bal.	9,000.00
	(New Bal. zero)	

Cash

Bal.	24,500.00	9,000.00
(New Bal.	15,500.00)	

ACCOUNTS PAYABLE LEDGER
Sampe Sports

5,000.00	Bal.	5,000.00
	(New Bal. zero)	

Sports Supply Co.

4,000.00	Bal.	4,000.00
	(New Bal. zero)	

Distributing Cash to Creditors. Once all noncash assets have been sold, cash is used to pay all creditors.

July 2, 19--. Paid cash to all creditors: Sampe Sports, $5,000.00; Sports Supply Co., $4,000.00. Check Numbers 711-712.

Accounts Payable is debited for $9,000.00. Each subsidiary ledger account is debited for the account balance. Cash is credited for $9,000.00.

The journal entry to record this transaction is shown on lines 1 and 2 of Illustration 28-3.

				GENERAL		ACCOUNTS PAYABLE DEBIT	PURCHASES DISCOUNT CREDIT	CASH CREDIT	
	DATE	ACCOUNT TITLE	CK. NO.	POST. REF.	DEBIT	CREDIT				
1	19-- July 2	Sampe Sports	711				5 0 0 00		5 0 0 00	1
2		Sports Supply Co.	712				4 0 0 00		4 0 0 00	2
3	3	Roger Moher, Capital	713		15 5 0 0 00				15 5 0 0 00	3

CASH PAYMENTS JOURNAL   PAGE 13

Distributing Remaining Cash to Owner. The last step in the liquidation of a proprietorship is to distribute the remaining cash to the owner.

July 3, 19--. Recorded final distribution of remaining cash to Roger Moher, $15,500.00. Check No. 713.

Roger Moher, Capital is debited for $15,500.00. Cash is credited for $15,500.00.

Roger Moher, Capital

| 15,500.00 | Bal. 15,500.00 |
| | (New Bal. zero) |

Cash

| Bal. 15,500.00 | 15,500.00 |
| (New Bal. zero) | |

The journal entry to record this transaction is shown on line 3 of Illustration 28-3.

After this journal entry is posted, all general ledger accounts will have zero balances. The proprietorship is now liquidated.

Audit Your Understanding

1. Which form of business is the simplest to organize?
2. What is the entry to record investing money to start a proprietorship?
3. What is the last step in liquidating a proprietorship?
4. When a proprietorship is being liquidated, and an asset is sold for less than book value, what is the effect on the proprietor's capital account?

FORMING A PARTNERSHIP

A business in which two or more persons combine their assets and skills is known as a partnership. Michelle Marier and Ron Morgan started a partnership called Rosebud Nursery. The partners chose to form the business as a partnership because of the advantages a partnership has as compared to a proprietorship. The advantages include:

1. More resources. Both Ms. Marier and Mr. Morgan will be investing cash and other assets in the business.
2. More time, energy, and experience. Rosebud Nursery will benefit by having two owners who can invest time and energy in the business. Also, both partners will bring experience and skill to the new partnership.

3. Transfer of ownership. If a partnership wants to admit a new partner or if a partner dies or a partner wants to leave the business, the partnership must be dissolved and a new partnership formed. However, the assets of the partnership can be transferred to the new partnership. The assets do not have to be liquidated.

Michelle Marier and Ron Morgan also considered the disadvantages of a partnership. The disadvantages include:

1. Shared decision making. Business decisions must be discussed and agreement reached by both partners.
2. Unlimited liability. *Each* partner is totally responsible for the liabilities of Rosebud Nursery, even those liabilities incurred by the other partner. Therefore, either partner's personal assets may be claimed by creditors to pay all of the partnership's liabilities.
3. Shared profits. Any profits earned by Rosebud Nursery must be divided between the partners based on the agreement between the partners. Losses must also be shared.

When Ms. Marier and Mr. Morgan started Rosebud Nursery, they were required to follow the laws of the state in which the business was formed.

Legal Requirements for Forming a Partnership

In most states, the minimum legal requirement to form a partnership is to file a document to register the name of the partnership with the state in which it is located. An additional document should be created by the partners. A written agreement setting forth the conditions under which a partnership is to operate is called a **partnership agreement**. Although not required by law, it is in the best interest of the partners to sign a partnership agreement. The partnership agreement includes the name and description of the business, capital investments of each partner, distribution of profits and losses, duties and responsibilities of each partner, and provisions for dissolving the partnership. If a partnership agreement is not signed, the laws of the state will determine the conditions under which the partnership is to operate.

Partnership agreements are not required by law but are in the best interests of both partners.

Accounting Transactions for Forming a Partnership

Michelle Marier and Ron Morgan completed the legal requirements to form a partnership named Rosebud Nursery. The partnership agreement called for each partner to invest $5,000.00 in the business.

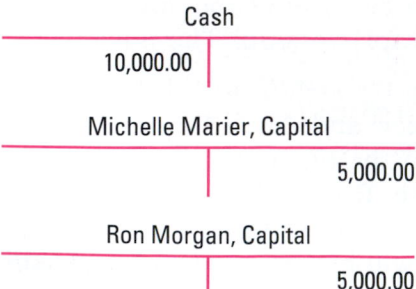

May 2, 19--. Received cash from partners as initial investment: from Michelle Marier, $5,000.00; from Ron Morgan, $5,000.00. Receipt Nos. 1 and 2.

In a partnership, a capital account is established for each partner. Cash is debited for the total investment, $10,000.00. Michelle Marier, Capital is credited for $5,000.00. Ron Morgan, Capital is credited for $5,000.00.

The journal entry to record this transaction is shown in Illustration 28-4.

ILLUSTRATION 28-4   Journal entry to record partners' initial investment

| | CASH RECEIPTS JOURNAL | | | | | | | | | | PAGE 1 |
| | | | | 1 | 2 | 3 | 4 | 5 | 6 | 7 | 8 |
DATE	ACCOUNT TITLE	DOC. NO.	POST. REF.	GENERAL DEBIT	GENERAL CREDIT	ACCOUNTS RECEIVABLE CREDIT	SALES CREDIT	SALES TAX PAYABLE DEBIT	SALES TAX PAYABLE CREDIT	SALES DISCOUNT DEBIT	CASH DEBIT
May 2	Michelle Marier, Capital	R1			500000						500000
2	Ron Morgan, Capital	R2			500000						500000

DISSOLVING A PARTNERSHIP

A partnership may be dissolved for any of several reasons. One or more of the partners may want to discontinue doing business. The partners may need more capital and agree to admit an additional partner. The partners may disagree on how to operate the business. The partnership agreement may call for the partnership to be dissolved on a specific date. When a partnership is dissolved, legal requirements must be met and correct accounting procedures must be followed.

FYI

In some bankruptcies, a company may continue to exist, satisfying its creditors by a plan for paying part of the debts and writing off the rest.

Legal Requirements for Dissolving a Partnership

The terms of the dissolution may be set forth in the partnership agreement if one was created when the partnership was formed. Any terms of dissolution set forth in the partnership agreement must be followed when the partnership is dissolved. If no partnership agreement was created for the business, the laws of the state will govern the dissolution of the partnership.

Whenever a partnership has a change in partners—bringing in additional partners or current partners leaving—the partnership must be legally dissolved and a new partnership established. However, a change in partners does not require the partnership to be liquidated.

Two basic legal actions are usually taken to dissolve a partnership. First, if the name of the partnership was registered with the state when formed, a document should be filed notifying the state that the partnership is being dissolved. If the business has employees, the partners must notify the appropriate federal and state tax authorities that the business has terminated operations.

Liquidation of a Partnership

Once a partnership is dissolved, the liquidation process can begin. When a partnership is liquidated, noncash assets are usually sold and the available cash is used to pay creditors. Any remaining cash is distributed to the partners.

After many years of business, Ms. Marier and Mr. Morgan agreed to dissolve and liquidate Rosebud Nursery. Necessary legal documents were filed, and on August 31 financial statements were prepared and adjusting and closing entries were journalized and posted. After the end-of-fiscal-period work was completed, the partnership had account balances as shown in the T accounts.

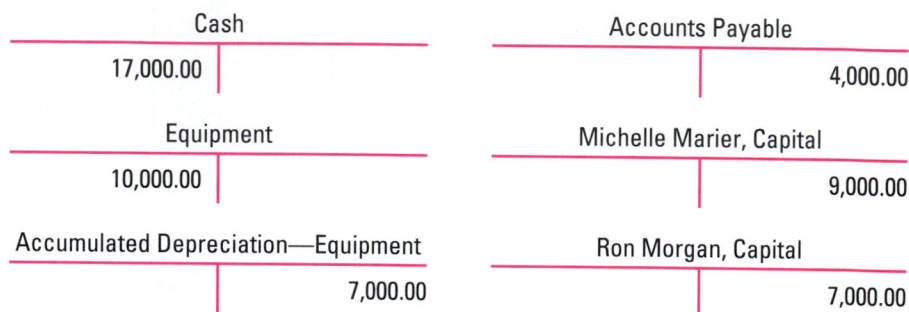

Cash		Accounts Payable	
17,000.00			4,000.00

Equipment		Michelle Marier, Capital	
10,000.00			9,000.00

Accumulated Depreciation—Equipment		Ron Morgan, Capital	
	7,000.00		7,000.00

Selling Noncash Assets for More than Book Value. Noncash assets are sometimes sold for more than the recorded book value. When this occurs, the amount received in excess of the book value is added to the partners' capital accounts.

September 1, 19--. Received cash from sale of equipment, $5,000.00; original cost, $10,000.00; total accumulated depreciation recorded to date, $7,000.00. Receipt No. 512.

The gain on the sale of the equipment is calculated as shown below.

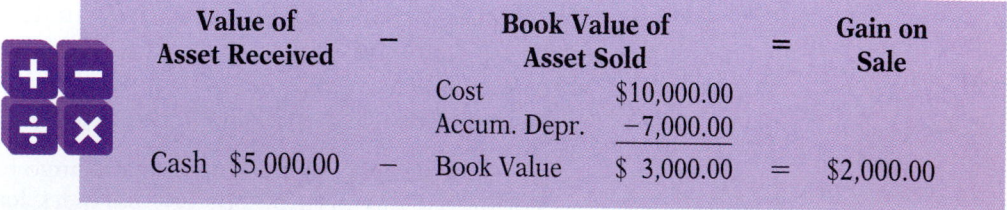

	Value of Asset Received	−	Book Value of Asset Sold		=	Gain on Sale
			Cost	$10,000.00		
			Accum. Depr.	−7,000.00		
	Cash $5,000.00	−	Book Value	$ 3,000.00	=	$2,000.00

Because the partnership is in the process of liquidation, the gain on sale is recorded directly in the partners' capital accounts. The partnership agreement for Rosebud Nursery calls for the partners to share equally in any liquidation gains or losses. Therefore, the $2,000.00 gain is divided equally between the two partners.

Cash is debited for the amount received, $5,000.00. Accumulated Depreciation—Equipment is debited for the total depreciation recorded to date, $7,000.00. Equipment is credited for the cost of the equipment, $10,000.00. Michelle Marier, Capital is credited for $1,000.00, her share of the gain. Ron Morgan, Capital is credited for $1,000.00, his share of the gain.

Cash				Equipment		
Bal.	17,000.00			Bal.	10,000.00	10,000.00
	5,000.00			(New Bal. zero)		
(New Bal.	22,000.00)					

Accumulated Depreciation—Equipment				Michelle Marier, Capital		
7,000.00	Bal.	7,000.00			Bal.	9,000.00
	(New Bal. zero)					1,000.00
					(New Bal.	10,000.00)

Ron Morgan, Capital	
Bal.	7,000.00
	1,000.00
(New Bal.	8,000.00)

The journal entry to record this transaction is shown in Illustration 28-5.

ILLUSTRATION 28-5   Journal entry to record gain on liquidation of noncash assets

	DATE	ACCOUNT TITLE	DOC. NO.	POST. REF.	GENERAL DEBIT	GENERAL CREDIT	ACCOUNTS RECEIVABLE CREDIT	SALES CREDIT	SALES TAX PAYABLE DEBIT	SALES TAX PAYABLE CREDIT	SALES DISCOUNT DEBIT	CASH DEBIT	
1	Sept. 1	Accum. Depr.—Equipment	R512		7000 00							5000 00	1
2		Equipment				10000 00							2
3		Michelle Marier, Capital				1000 00							3
4		Ron Morgan, Capital				1000 00							4
5													5

CASH RECEIPTS JOURNAL   PAGE 17

The gain on sale could be recorded in an other revenue account. Recording the gain in an other revenue account would provide management with better information regarding the effect of the transaction on partners' equity. However, when a business is being liquidated, this additional information is unnecessary. Therefore, the gain on sale is recorded in the partners' capital accounts.

Distributing Cash to Creditors.   Once all noncash assets have been sold, cash is used to pay all creditors.

GENERAL LEDGER

Accounts Payable

4,000.00	Bal.	4,000.00
	(New Bal. zero)	

Cash

Bal.	22,000.00		4,000.00
(New Bal.	18,000.00)		

ACCOUNTS PAYABLE LEDGER

American Tree Company

2,300.00	Bal.	2,300.00
	(New Bal. zero)	

Waltham Sod Farm

1,700.00	Bal.	1,700.00
	(New Bal. zero)	

September 3, 19--. Paid cash to all creditors: American Tree Company, $2,300.00; Waltham Sod Farm, $1,700.00. Check Numbers 589-590.

Accounts Payable is debited for $4,000.00. Each subsidiary ledger account is debited for the account balance. Cash is credited for $4,000.00.

The journal entry to record this transaction is shown on lines 1 and 2 of Illustration 28-6.

Distributing Remaining Cash to Partners.

The last step in the liquidation of a partnership is to distribute the remaining cash to the partners. The balance in each partner's capital account is distributed to each partner.

ILLUSTRATION 28-6	Journal entries to record liquidation of liabilities and distribution of remaining cash to partners

CASH PAYMENTS JOURNAL   PAGE **17**

	DATE		ACCOUNT TITLE	CK. NO.	POST. REF.	GENERAL DEBIT	GENERAL CREDIT	ACCOUNTS PAYABLE DEBIT	PURCHASES DISCOUNT CREDIT	CASH CREDIT	
1	Sept.	3	American Tree Company	589				2 3 0 0 00		2 3 0 0 00	1
2			Waltham Sod Farm	590				1 7 0 0 00		1 7 0 0 00	2
3		4	Michelle Marier, Capital	591		10 0 0 0 00				10 0 0 0 00	3
4			Ron Morgan, Capital	592		8 0 0 0 00				8 0 0 0 00	4

September 4, 19--. Recorded final distribution of remaining cash to partners: to Michelle Marier, $10,000.00; to Ron Morgan, $8,000.00. Check Numbers 591 and 592.

Michelle Marier, Capital

10,000.00	Bal.	10,000.00
	(New Bal. zero)	

Ron Morgan, Capital

8,000.00	Bal.	8,000.00
	(New Bal. zero)	

Cash

Bal.	18,000.00		18,000.00
(New Bal. zero)			

Michelle Marier, Capital is debited for $10,000.00. Ron Morgan, Capital is debited for $8,000.00. Cash is credited for $18,000.00.

The journal entry to record this transaction is shown on lines 3 and 4 of Illustration 28-6.

After this journal entry is posted, all general ledger accounts will have zero balances. The partnership is now liquidated.

FORMING A CORPORATION

An organization with the legal rights of a person and which may be owned by many persons is known as a corporation. Each unit of ownership in a corporation is known as a share of stock. An owner of one or more shares of a corporation is known as a stockholder.

A group of owners is starting a corporation called LakeShore, Inc. The owners considered the advantages and disadvantages of a corporate form of business.

The advantages of a corporation include:

One advantage of a corporation is limited liability.

1. Expanded resources. Corporations such as LakeShore, Inc. raise funds by selling stock. The sale of stock means that LakeShore, Inc. may be able to acquire more capital than would be possible as a proprietorship or partnership.
2. Limited liability. Stockholders of LakeShore, Inc. are not usually personally responsible for the liabilities of the corporation.
3. Ease of transfer of ownership. Ownership is transferred when a share of stock is sold. The process of selling stock does not affect the continuation of the corporation.
4. Legal rights. Since a corporation has the legal rights of a person, the corporation may buy, own, and sell property in its corporate name.

The disadvantages of a corporation include:

1. High organization cost. A corporation is the most complex and expensive form of business to establish.
2. Extensive government regulation. Corporations must comply with numerous government regulations, which often require the completion of extensive reports.
3. Double taxation. As a separate legal entity, corporations are subject to taxation. In addition, the profits distributed to a stockholder are subject to taxation as personal income for the stockholder.

When LakeShore, Inc. was formed, the owners were required to follow the laws of the state in which the business was formed and the states in which it intended to operate.

Legal Requirements for Forming a Corporation

A merger occurs when two or more companies combine to form one new company.

A corporation is the most complex kind of business to form. Many laws must be followed to legally form a corporation. Several legal documents must be created and filed. A written application requesting permission to form a corporation is called the **articles of incorporation.** The articles of incorporation are filed with the Secretary of State where the corporation is formed. The articles of incorporation contain the name and nature of the business, the number of shares of stock authorized, the names of incorporators and officers, and other conditions about the new corporation. The articles of incorporation is just one of many legal documents necessary for incorporating a business. Failure to comply with these laws can result in loss of corporate status for the business. Since the forming of a corporation is complex, the incorporators should seek legal advice.

Accounting Transactions for Forming a Corporation

Once a corporation is legally established, the corporation may begin selling shares of stock. Shares of stock are frequently assigned a value as part of the articles of incorporation. A value assigned to a share of stock and printed on the stock certificate is called **par value**. A share of stock that has an authorized value printed on the stock certificate is called **par-value stock**.

The incorporators of Lakeshore, Inc. completed the legal requirements for a corporation. The corporation received $100,000.00 in cash for which 100,000 shares of common stock are to be issued.

> *March 1, 19--. Received cash for 100,000 shares of $1.00 par-value common stock, $100,000.00. Receipt Nos. 1–7.*

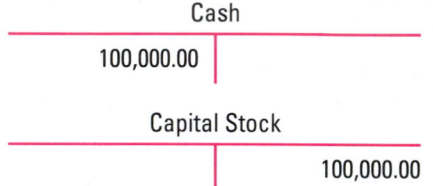

In a corporation, a capital account is *not* established for each owner. Instead, one summary general ledger capital account titled Capital Stock is used for all stock issued. Cash is debited for $100,000.00. Capital Stock is credited for $100,000.00.

The journal entry to record this transaction is shown in Illustration 28-7.

| | ILLUSTRATION 28-7 | Journal entry to record sale of stock at par value |

CASH RECEIPTS JOURNAL — PAGE 1

	DATE		ACCOUNT TITLE	DOC. NO.	POST. REF.	GENERAL DEBIT	GENERAL CREDIT	ACCOUNTS RECEIVABLE CREDIT	SALES CREDIT	SALES TAX PAYABLE DEBIT	SALES TAX PAYABLE CREDIT	SALES DISCOUNT DEBIT	CASH DEBIT	
1	Mar.	1	Capital Stock	R1–7			100000 00						100000 00	1
2														2
3														3

DISSOLVING A CORPORATION

When a corporation is dissolved, legal requirements must be met and correct accounting procedures must be followed. Legal and accounting procedures have been established for the dissolution of a corporation. However, it is rare that a corporation is dissolved. The proprietorship and partnership forms of business are both tied very closely to the owner(s). When the owner(s) die or decide to stop doing business, the business is legally dissolved. A corporate form of ownership, however, is based on the idea of a perpetual life *(CONCEPT: Going Concern)*. When an owner (stockholder) decides not to participate in the corporation, the stockholder merely sells all shares of stock owned. The corporation is not dissolved.

Legal Requirements for Dissolving a Corporation

The corporation is also the most complex form of business to dissolve. The dissolution of a corporation involves many legal procedures and documents. Documents that must be filed include a notice to the state in which the business was incorporated and a notice to all creditors of the corporation. Since the dissolution of a corporation is complex, the board of directors should seek legal advice.

Liquidation of a Corporation

Once a corporation is dissolved, the liquidation process can begin. When a corporation is liquidated, noncash assets are usually sold and the available cash is used to pay creditors. The procedure for selling noncash assets is similar to that for proprietorships and partnerships. However, since a corporation is a taxable entity, the gains and losses on the sale of noncash assets are subject to taxation. Therefore, additional tax reports for the corporation must be filed.

The accounting aspects of actually liquidating a corporation are extremely complex. Therefore, obtaining professional accounting services to assist in the liquidation of a corporation is recommended.

The chart shown in Summary Illustration 28-8 on page 764 summarizes the processes of forming and liquidating business organizations.

Audit Your Understanding

1. What is each unit of ownership in a corporation called?

2. What is a written application requesting permission to form a corporation called?

3. What is meant by "double taxation" for corporations?

4. What is the entry to record the issuance of stock for a corporation?

5. Why are corporations rarely dissolved?

Summary of forming and liquidating business organizations

	Proprietorship	Partnership	Corporation
Ownership	1 person	2 or more partners	All stockholders
Legal Requirements to Establish	Simple	Moderate	Complex
Investment Account	1 capital account	1 capital account for each partner	1 capital stock account
Entry for Cash Investment	Debit: Cash Credit: Owner's Capital Account	Debit: Cash Credit: Each Partner's Capital Account	Debit: Cash Credit: Capital Stock
Steps for Liquidation	1. Sell noncash assets 2. Pay creditors 3. Distribute remaining cash to owner	1. Sell noncash assets 2. Pay creditors 3. Distribute remaining cash to partners	Complex process requiring the help of legal and accounting professionals

ACCOUNTING TERMS   EPT(a)

What is the meaning of each of the following?

1. **dissolution**
2. **liquidation**
3. **partnership agreement**
4. **articles of incorporation**
5. **par value**
6. **par-value stock**

1. What are the advantages of the proprietorship form of business?

2. What are the disadvantages of the proprietorship form of business?

3. What is the simplest form of business to organize?

4. What accounts are affected, and how, when an owner invests in a proprietorship?

5. What is the formula for calculating a loss on sale?

6. In the liquidation of a proprietorship, what accounts are affected, and how, when supplies are sold for less than the recorded book value?

7. In a liquidation, what general ledger accounts are affected, and how, when cash is distributed to creditors?

8. What is the last step in the liquidation of a proprietorship?

9. In the liquidation of a proprietorship, what accounts are affected, and how, when the remaining cash is distributed to the owner?

10. What are the advantages of the partnership form of business as compared to a proprietorship?

11. What are the disadvantages of the partnership form of business as compared to a proprietorship?

12. What is the formula for calculating a gain on sale?

13. In the liquidation of a partnership, what accounts are affected, and how, when equipment is sold for more than the recorded book value?

14. How are liquidation gains or losses divided between partners?

15. In the liquidation of a partnership, what accounts are affected, and how, when the remaining cash is distributed to the partners?

16. What is the owner of one or more shares of a corporation called?

17. What are the advantages of the corporate form of business?

18. What are the disadvantages of the corporate form of business?

19. What accounts are affected, and how, when stock is sold?

20. Why is it recommended that professional accounting services be employed to assist in the liquidation of a corporation?

CASE FOR CRITICAL THINKING EPT(b)

CASE 1 Barbara Sather wants to open a hair salon. She also knows several people who would like to go into the business with her. What should Ms. Sather consider when deciding the form of ownership that is most appropriate for her?

APPLIED COMMUNICATIONS

Public speakers are judged by the ability of their audience to remember important points of their presentation. Effective public speakers use a variety of techniques to encourage the audience to listen to their message.

INSTRUCTIONS:

Contact an instructor in your school or a local businessperson you have heard speak at school or community functions. Ask the person to describe the techniques used to help the audience listen and retain the message. Write a short report summarizing these techniques. Be prepared to present your report orally in class.

DRILL 28-D1 Calculating loss on sale

INSTRUCTIONS:

Calculate the amount of loss on sale for each transaction listed below.

Transaction 1. Received cash from sale of supplies, $1,000.00; book value of supplies, $1,600.00.

Transaction 2. Received cash from sale of equipment, $1,500.00; original cost, $4,000.00; total accumulated depreciation recorded to date, $2,200.00.

Transaction 3. Received cash from sale of truck, $5,000.00; original cost, $12,000.00; total accumulated depreciation recorded to date, $4,000.00.

DRILL 28-D2 Calculating gain on sale

INSTRUCTIONS:

Calculate the amount of gain on sale for each transaction listed below.

Transaction 1. Received cash from sale of supplies, $1,200.00; book value of supplies, $1,100.00.

Transaction 2. Received cash from sale of equipment, $2,100.00; original cost, $6,000.00; total accumulated depreciation recorded to date, $4,500.00.

Transaction 3. Received cash from sale of truck, $8,000.00; original cost, $15,000.00; total accumulated depreciation recorded to date, $9,000.00.

APPLICATION PROBLEMS
EPT(c,d)

PROBLEM 28-1 Journalizing entries to form and liquidate a proprietorship

INSTRUCTIONS:

Journalize the following transactions completed during the first and last years of operation. Use page 1 of a cash receipts journal for the first transaction. Use page 17 of a cash receipts journal and a cash payments journal for all remaining transactions.

Mar. 1, 19X1. Received cash from James McKimmy as an investment, $3,000.00. R1.

Sept. 1, 19X9. Received cash from sale of supplies, $1,250.00; book value of supplies, $1,400.00. R258.

Sept. 1, 19X9. Paid cash to all creditors: Cline Carpet, $1,250.00; Carpet Wholesalers, $2,450.00. C541-542.

Sept. 2, 19X9. Recorded final distribution of remaining cash to James McKimmy, $6,500.00. C543.

PROBLEM 28-2 Journalizing entries to form and liquidate a partnership

INSTRUCTIONS:

Journalize the following transactions completed during the first and last years of operation. Use page 1 of a cash receipts journal for the first transaction. Use page 5 of a cash receipts journal and a cash payments journal for all remaining transactions. The partnership agreement states that all losses or gains on sale are to be divided equally between the partners.

Nov. 1, 19X1. Received cash from partners as initial investment: from Laura Erickson, $4,000.00; from Kent Dodge, $6,000.00. R1-2.

Mar. 1, 19X8. Received cash from sale of equipment, $11,000.00; original cost, $20,000.00; total accumulated depreciation recorded to date, $12,000.00. R329.

Mar. 1, 19X8. Paid cash to all creditors: Precision Supplies, $4,100.00; Wacher Florist, $1,100.00. C492-493.
Mar. 2, 19X8. Recorded final distribution of remaining cash to partners: to Laura Erickson, $5,000.00; to Kent Dodge, $9,500.00. C494-495.

PROBLEM 28-3 Journalizing entries to form a corporation

INSTRUCTIONS:

Journalize the following transaction completed during the current year. Use page 1 of a cash receipts journal. Source documents are abbreviated as follows: receipt, R.

June 1. Received cash for 120,000 shares of $1.00 par-value common stock, $120,000.00. R1-6.

ENRICHMENT PROBLEMS   EPT(c,d)

MASTERY PROBLEM 28-M Journalizing entries to form and liquidate business organizations

INSTRUCTIONS:

1. Journalize the following transaction. Use page 1 of a cash receipts journal.

Jan. 1, 19X1. Received cash from Dennis Moen as an investment, $4,000.00. R1.

Dennis Moen has decided to liquidate his business and start a partnership with his sister.

2. Journalize the following transactions. Use page 7 of a cash receipts journal and a cash payments journal.

April 1, 19X3. Received cash from sale of supplies, $1,000.00; book value of supplies, $1,200.00. R175.
April 1, 19X3. Paid cash to all creditors: Industrial Cleaners, $550.00; Neiman Interiors, $650.00. C233-234.
April 2, 19X3. Recorded final distribution of remaining cash to Dennis Moen, $1,500.00. C235.

Dennis Moen and Dorothy Moen agree to form a partnership called Moen Music Company.

3. Journalize the following transaction. Use page 1 of a cash receipts journal.

April 15, 19X3. Received cash from partners as initial investment: from Dennis Moen, $1,500.00; from Dorothy Moen, $2,000.00. R1-2.

Dennis and Dorothy Moen have agreed to liquidate their business and form a corporation with other business associates.

4. Journalize the following transactions. Use page 9 of a cash receipts journal and a cash payments journal. The partnership agreement states that all losses or gains on sale are to be divided equally between the partners.

May 1, 19X7. Received cash from sale of equipment, $8,000.00; original cost, $22,000.00; total accumulated depreciation recorded to date, $15,000.00. R222.
May 1, 19X7. Paid cash to all creditors: Burke Piano Movers, $250.00; Thomas Musical Instruments, $2,950.00. C256-257.
May 2, 19X7. Recorded final distribution of remaining cash to partners: to Dennis Moen, $6,000.00; to Dorothy Moen, $8,000.00. C258-259.

Dennis Moen and four other business associates agree to form a corporation called Moen, Inc.

5. Journalize the following transaction. Use page 1 of a cash receipts journal.

June 1, 19X7. Received cash for 75,000 shares of $1.00 par-value common stock, $75,000.00. R1-6.

CHALLENGE PROBLEM 28-C Journalizing entries to liquidate a partnership

INSTRUCTIONS:

1. Journalize the following transactions completed during June of the current year. Use page 11 of a cash receipts journal and a cash payments journal. The partnership agreement states that all losses or gains on sale are to be divided 60% to Vivian Stone and 40% to Carol Vance.

June 15. Received cash from sale of equipment, $2,000.00; original cost, $12,000.00; total accumulated depreciation recorded to date, $11,000.00. R321.

June 16. Paid cash to all creditors: Hunter Company, $1,320.00; Twain Inc., $3,880.00. C765-766.

June 16. Recorded final distribution of remaining cash to partners: to Vivian Stone, $2,000.00; to Carol Vance, $3,500.00. C767-768.

Accounting Concepts

The following accounting concepts and their definitions are provided in this appendix for ready reference.

ACCOUNTING CONCEPTS

Accounting personnel are guided in their work by generally accepted accounting concepts. Ten commonly accepted accounting concepts are described in this appendix. Each concept is fully explained in the text the first time an application of the concept is described. Throughout the textbook, each time a concept application occurs, a concept reference is given, such as *(CONCEPT: Business Entity)*.

1. ACCOUNTING PERIOD CYCLE. [Chapter 8]
   Changes in financial information are reported for a specific period of time in the form of financial statements.

2. ADEQUATE DISCLOSURE. [Chapter 9]
   Financial statements contain all information necessary to understand a business' financial condition.

3. BUSINESS ENTITY. [Chapter 2]
   Financial information is recorded and reported separately from the owner's personal financial information.

4. CONSISTENT REPORTING. [Chapter 8]
   The same accounting procedures are followed in the same way in each accounting period.

5. GOING CONCERN. [Chapter 2]
   Financial statements are prepared with the expectation that a business will remain in operation indefinitely.

6. HISTORICAL COST. [Chapter 11]
   The actual amount paid for merchandise or other items bought is recorded.

7. MATCHING EXPENSES WITH REVENUE. [Chapter 8]
   Revenue from business activities and expenses associated with earning that revenue are recorded in the same accounting period.

8. OBJECTIVE EVIDENCE. [Chapter 5]
   A source document is prepared for each transaction.

9. REALIZATION OF REVENUE. [Chapter 12]
   Revenue is recorded at the time goods or services are sold.

10. UNIT OF MEASUREMENT. [Chapter 2]
    Business transactions are stated in numbers that have common values, that is, using a common unit of measurement.

Using a Calculator and Computer Keypad

KINDS OF CALCULATORS

Many different models of calculators, both desktop and hand held, are available. All calculators have their own features and particular placement of operating keys. Therefore, it is necessary to refer to the operator's manual for specific instructions and locations of the operating keys for the calculator being used. A typical keyboard of a desktop calculator is shown in Illustration B-1.

ILLUSTRATION B-1   Typical desktop calculator keyboard

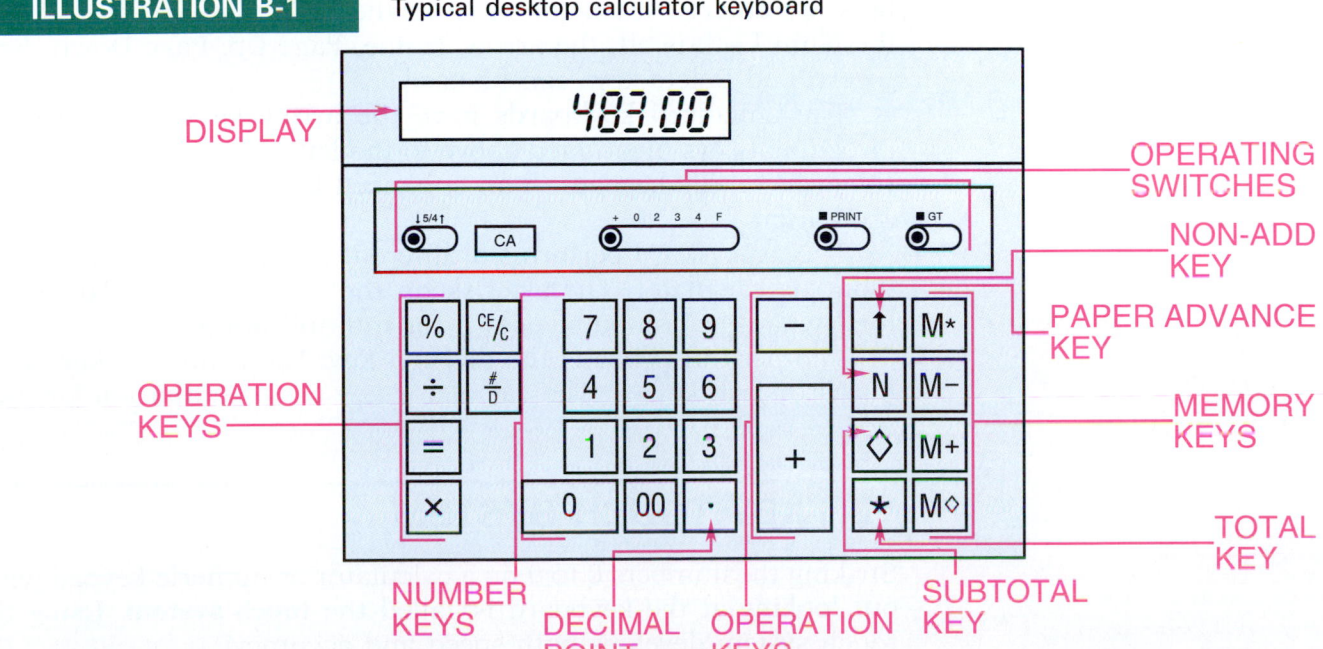

DESKTOP CALCULATOR SETTINGS

Several operating switches on a desktop calculator must be engaged before the calculator will produce the desired results.

The *decimal selector* sets the appropriate decimal places necessary for the numbers that will be entered. For example, if the decimal selector is set at 2, both the numbers entered and the answer will have two decimal places. If the decimal selector is set at F, the calculator automatically sets the decimal places. The F setting allows the answer to be unrounded and carried out to the maximum number of decimal places possible.

The *decimal rounding selector* rounds the answers. The down arrow position will drop any digits beyond the last digit desired. The up arrow position will drop any digits beyond the last digit desired and round the last digit up. In the 5/4 position, the calculator rounds the last desired digit up only when the following digit is 5 or greater. If the following digit is less than 5, the last desired digit remains unchanged.

The *GT* or *grand total switch* in the on position accumulates totals.

KINDS OF COMPUTER KEYBOARDS

The computer has a keypad on the right side of the keyboard called the **numeric keypad.** Even though several styles of keyboards for the IBM® and compatible computers are found, there are two basic layouts for the numeric keypad. The standard layout and enhanced layout are shown in Illustration B-2 on page B-3. On the standard keyboard the directional arrow keys are found on the number keys. To use the numbers, press the key called **Num Lock.** (This key is found above the "7" key.) When the Num Lock is turned on, numbers are entered when the keys on the keypad are pressed. When the Num Lock is off, the arrow, Home, Page Up, Page Down, End, Insert, and Delete keys can be used.

The enhanced keyboards have the arrow keys and the other directional keys mentioned above to the left of the numeric keypad. When using the keypad on an enhanced keyboard, Num Lock can remain on.

The asterisk (*) performs a different function on the computer than the calculator. The asterisk on the calculator is used for the total while the computer uses it for multiplication.

Another difference is the division key. The computer key is the forward slash key (/). The calculator key uses the division key (÷).

TEN-KEY TOUCH SYSTEM

Striking the numbers 0 to 9 on a calculator or numeric keypad without looking at the keyboard is called the **touch system.** Using the touch system develops both speed and accuracy.

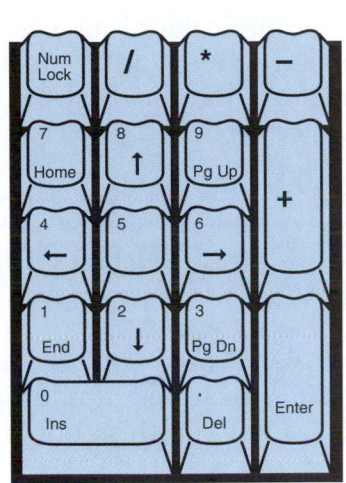

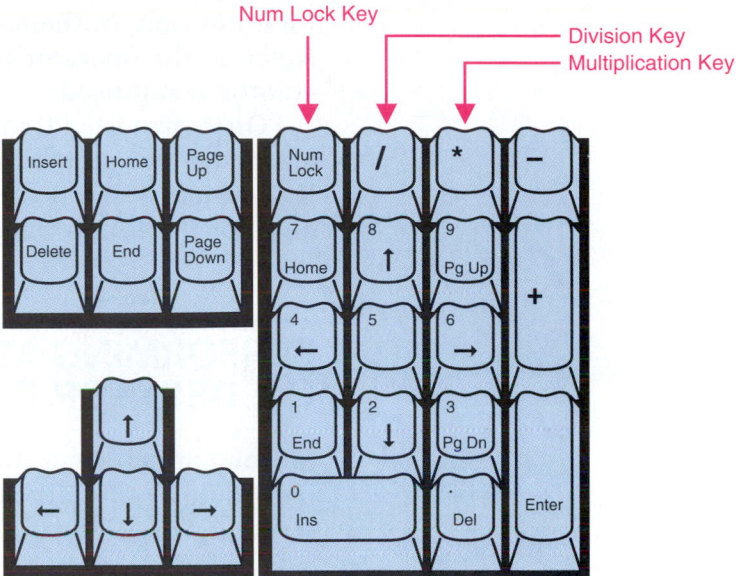

Standard
Keyboard Layout

Enhanced
Keyboard Layout

The 4, 5, and 6 keys are called the **home row.** If the right hand is used for the keyboard, the index finger is placed on the 4 key, the middle finger on the 5 key, and the ring finger on the 6 key. If the left hand is used, the ring finger is placed on the 4 key, the middle finger on the 5 key, and the index finger on the 6 key.

Place the fingers on the home row keys. Curve the fingers and keep the wrist straight. These keys may feel slightly concaved or the 5 key may have a raised dot. The differences in the home row allow the operator to recognize the home row by touch rather than by sight.

Maintain the position of the fingers on the home row. The finger used to strike the 4 key will also strike the 7 key and the 1 key. Stretch the finger up to reach the 7; then stretch the finger down to reach the 1 key. Visualize the position of these keys.

Again, place the fingers on the home row. Stretch the finger that strikes the 5 key up to reach the 8 key, then down to reach the 2 key. Likewise, stretch the finger that strikes the 6 key up to strike the 9 and down to strike the 3 key. This same finger will stretch down again to hit the decimal point.

If the right hand is used, the thumb will be used to strike the 0 and 00 keys and the little finger to strike the addition key. If the left hand is used, the little finger will be used to strike the 0 and 00 keys and the thumb to strike the addition key.

HAND-HELD CALCULATORS

Hand-held calculators are slightly different from desktop calculators, not only in their size and features but also in their operation. Refer to the operator's manual for specific instructions for the calculator being used.

On a hand-held calculator, the numeric keys are usually very close together. In addition, the keys do not respond to touch as easily as on a desktop calculator. Therefore, the touch system is usually not used on a hand-held calculator.

PERFORMING MATHEMATICAL OPERATIONS ON DESKTOP CALCULATORS

Mathematical operations can be performed on a calculator both quickly and efficiently. The basic operations of addition, subtraction, multiplication, and division are used frequently on a calculator.

Addition

Each number to be added is called an **addend.** The answer to an addition problem is called the **sum.**

Addition is performed by entering an addend and striking the addition key (+). All numbers are entered on a calculator in the exact order they are given. To enter the number 4,455.65, strike the 4, 4, 5, 5, decimal, 6, and 5 keys in that order, and then strike the addition key. Commas are not entered. Continue in this manner until all addends have been entered. To obtain the sum, strike the total key on the calculator.

Subtraction

The top number or first number of a subtraction problem is called the **minuend.** The number to be subtracted from the minuend is called the **subtrahend.** The answer to a subtraction problem is called the **difference.**

Subtraction is performed by first entering the minuend and striking the addition key (+). The subtrahend is then entered, followed by the minus key (−), followed by the total key.

Multiplication

The number to be multiplied is called the **multiplicand.** The number of times the multiplicand will be multiplied is called the **multiplier.** The answer to a multiplication problem is called the **product.**

Multiplication is performed by entering the multiplicand and striking the multiplication key (×). The multiplier is then entered, followed by the equals key (=). The calculator will automatically multiply and give the product.

Division

The number to be divided is called the **dividend**. The number the dividend will be divided by is called the **divisor**. The answer to a division problem is called the **quotient**.

Division is performed by entering the dividend and striking the division key (÷). The divisor is then entered, followed by the equals key (=). The calculator will automatically divide and give the quotient.

Correcting Errors

If an error is made while using a calculator, several methods of correction may be used. If an incorrect number has been entered and the addition key or equals key has not yet been struck, strike the clear entry (CE) key one time. This key will clear only the last number that was entered. However, if the clear entry key is depressed more than one time, the entire problem will be cleared on some calculators. If an incorrect number has been entered and the addition key has been struck, strike the minus key one time only. This will automatically subtract the last number added, thus removing it from the total.

PERFORMING MATHEMATICAL OPERATIONS ON COMPUTERS AND HAND-HELD CALCULATORS

On a computer keypad or a hand-held calculator, addition is performed in much the same way as on a desktop calculator. However, after the + key is depressed, the display usually shows the accumulated total. Therefore, the total key is not found. Some computer programs will not calculate the total until Enter is pressed.

Subtraction is performed differently on many computer keypads and hand-held calculators. The minuend is usually entered, followed by the minus (−) key. Then the subtrahend is entered. Pressing either the + key or the = key will display the difference. Some computer programs will not calculate the difference until Enter is pressed.

Multiplication and division are performed the same way on a computer keypad and hand-held calculator as on a desktop calculator. Keep in mind that computers use the * for multiplication and / for division.

SAFETY CONCERNS

Whenever electrical equipment such as a calculator or computer is being operated in a classroom or office, several safety rules apply. These rules protect the operator of the equipment, other persons in the environment, and the equipment itself.

1. Do not unplug equipment by pulling on the electrical cord. Instead, grasp the plug at the outlet and remove it.

2. Do not stretch electrical cords across an aisle where someone might trip over them.

3. Avoid food and beverages near the equipment where a spill might result in an electrical short.

4. Do not attempt to remove the cover of a calculator, computer, or keyboard for any reason while the power is turned on.

5. Do not attempt to repair equipment while it is plugged in.

6. Always turn the power off or unplug equipment when finished using it.

CALCULATION DRILLS

INSTRUCTIONS FOR DESKTOP CALCULATORS

Complete each drill using the touch method. Set the decimal selector at the setting indicated in each drill. Compare the answer on the calculator to the answer in the book. If the two are the same, progress to the next problem. It is not necessary to enter 00 in the cents column if the decimal selector is set at 0-F. However, digits other than zeros in the cents column must be entered preceded by a decimal point.

INSTRUCTIONS FOR COMPUTER KEYPADS

Complete each drill using the touch method. There is no decimal selector on computer keypads. Set the number of decimal places as directed in the instructions for the computer program. In spreadsheets, for example, use the formatting options to set the number of decimal places. When the drill indicates "F" for floating, leave the computer application in its default format. Compare the answer on the computer monitor to the answer in the book. If the two are the same, progress to the next problem. It is not necessary to enter 00 in the cents column. However, digits other than zeros in the cents column must be entered preceded by a decimal point.

DRILL D-1   **Performing addition using the home row keys**
Decimal Selector—2

4.00	44.00	444.00	4,444.00	44,444.00
5.00	55.00	555.00	5,555.00	55,555.00
6.00	66.00	666.00	6,666.00	66,666.00
5.00	45.00	455.00	4,455.00	44,556.00
4.00	46.00	466.00	4,466.00	44,565.00
5.00	54.00	544.00	5,544.00	55,446.00
6.00	56.00	566.00	5,566.00	55,664.00
5.00	65.00	655.00	6,655.00	66,554.00
4.00	64.00	644.00	6,644.00	66,555.00
5.00	66.00	654.00	6,545.00	65,465.00
49.00	561.00	5,649.00	56,540.00	565,470.00

DRILL D-2 **Performing addition using the 0, 1, 4, and 7 keys**
Decimal Selector—2

4.00	11.00	444.00	4,440.00	44,000.00
7.00	44.00	777.00	7,770.00	77,000.00
4.00	74.00	111.00	1,110.00	11,000.00
1.00	71.00	741.00	4,400.00	41,000.00
4.00	70.00	740.00	1,100.00	71,000.00
7.00	10.00	101.00	4,007.00	10,000.00
4.00	14.00	140.00	7,001.00	10,100.00
1.00	17.00	701.00	1,007.00	40,100.00
4.00	40.00	700.00	1,004.00	70,100.00
7.00	77.00	407.00	7,700.00	74,100.00
43.00	428.00	4,862.00	39,539.00	448,400.00

DRILL D-3 **Performing addition using the 2, 5, and 8 keys**
Decimal Selector—2

5.00	58.00	588.00	8,888.00	88,855.00
8.00	52.00	522.00	5,555.00	88,822.00
5.00	85.00	888.00	2,222.00	88,852.00
2.00	52.00	222.00	8,525.00	88,222.00
5.00	25.00	258.00	2,585.00	85,258.00
8.00	58.00	852.00	8,258.00	22,255.00
5.00	82.00	225.00	8,585.00	22,288.00
2.00	28.00	885.00	5,258.00	22,258.00
5.00	88.00	882.00	2,852.00	22,888.00
8.00	22.00	228.00	2,288.00	25,852.00
53.00	550.00	5,550.00	55,016.00	555,550.00

DRILL D-4 **Performing addition using the 3, 6, 9, and decimal point keys**
Decimal Selector—2

6.00	66.66	666.66	6,666.99	66,699.33
9.00	99.99	999.99	9,999.66	99,966.66
6.00	33.33	333.33	3,333.99	33,366.33
3.00	33.66	666.99	3,366.99	36,963.36
6.36	33.99	999.66	6,699.33	69,636.36
3.36	99.66	333.66	9,966.33	33,333.66
9.36	99.33	696.36	9,636.69	66,666.99
9.63	33.36	369.63	3,696.36	99,999.33
6.33	33.69	336.69	6,963.99	96,369.63
9.93	69.63	963.36	6,699.33	36,963.36
68.97	603.30	6,366.33	67,029.66	639,965.01

DRILL D-5 **Performing subtraction using all number keys**
Decimal Selector—F

456.73	789.01	741.00	852.55	987.98
−123.21	−456.00	−258.10	−369.88	−102.55
333.52	333.01	482.90	482.67	885.43

DRILL D-6 Performing multiplication using all number keys
Decimal Selector—F

654.05	975.01	487.10	123.56	803.75
× 12.66	× 27.19	× 30.21	× 50.09	× 1.45
8,280.273	26,510.5219	14,715.291	6,189.1204	1,165.4375

DRILL D-7 Performing division using all number keys
Decimal Selector—F

900.56	÷	450.28	=	2.
500.25	÷	100.05	=	5.
135.66	÷	6.65	=	20.4
269.155	÷	105.55	=	2.550023685*
985.66	÷	22.66	=	43.49779346*

Number of decimal places may vary due to machine capacity.

APPENDIX C

Recycling Problems

NOTE: No recycling problems are provided for Chapter 1.

RECYCLING PROBLEM 2-R Determining how transactions change an accounting equation and preparing a balance sheet

Kim Suomi is starting Suomi Service Center, a telephone-answering business. Suomi Service Center uses the accounts shown in the following accounting equation. Use a form similar to the following to complete this problem.

Trans. No.	Assets			=	Liabilities	+	Owner's Equity
	Cash +	Supplies +	Prepaid Insurance	=	Olson Office Supply	+	Kim Suomi, Capital
Beg. Bal.	0	0	0		0		0
1.	+700						+700 (investment)
New Bal.	700	0	0		0		700
2.							

Transactions
1. Received cash from owner as an investment, $700.00.
2. Bought supplies on account from Olson Office Supply, $100.00.
3. Paid cash for insurance, $150.00.
4. Paid cash for supplies, $50.00.
5. Paid cash on account to Olson Office Supply, $50.00.

INSTRUCTIONS:

1. For each transaction, complete the following. Transaction 1 is given as an example.
   a. Analyze the transaction to determine which accounts in the accounting equation are affected.
   b. Write the amount in the appropriate columns, using a plus (+) if the account increases or a minus (−) if the account decreases.
   c. For transactions that change owner's equity, write in parentheses a description of the transaction to the right of the amount.
   d. Calculate the new balance for each account in the accounting equation.
   e. Before going on to the next transaction, determine that the accounting equation is still in balance.
2. Using the final balances in the accounting equation, prepare a balance sheet. Use February 7 of the current year as the date of the balance sheet.

RECYCLING PROBLEM 3-R Determining how transactions change an accounting equation and preparing a balance sheet

Steve Bird operates a service business called Office Plants Company. Office Plants Company uses the accounts shown in the following accounting equation. Use a form similar to the following to complete the problem.

Trans. No.	Assets			=	Liabilities	+	Owner's Equity
	Cash +	Supplies +	Prepaid Insurance	=	Stanton Company	+	Steve Bird, Capital
Beg. Bal.	1,600	200	400		500		1,700
1.	−90						−90 (expense)
New Bal.	1,510	200	400		500		1,610
2.							

Transactions

1. Paid cash for telephone bill, $90.00.
2. Received cash from sales, $230.00.
3. Paid cash for equipment repair, $25.00.
4. Received cash from owner as an investment, $300.00.
5. Paid cash for rent, $400.00.
6. Received cash from sales, $250.00.
7. Paid cash for advertising, $100.00.
8. Paid cash on account to Stanton Company, $500.00.
9. Paid cash for water bill, $60.00.
10. Paid cash for miscellaneous expense, $10.00.
11. Bought supplies on account from Stanton Company, $300.00.
12. Paid cash for supplies, $200.00.
13. Received cash from sales, $270.00.
14. Paid cash to owner for personal use, $600.00.
15. Paid cash for insurance, $150.00.

INSTRUCTIONS:

1. For each transaction, complete the following. Transaction 1 is given as an example.
   a. Analyze the transaction to determine which accounts in the accounting equation are affected.
   b. Write the amount in the appropriate columns, using a plus (+) if the account increases or a minus (−) if the account decreases.

c. For transactions that change owner's equity, write in parentheses a description of the transaction to the right of the amount.

d. Calculate the new balance for each account in the accounting equation.

e. Before going on to the next transaction, determine that the accounting equation is still in balance.

2. Using the final balances in the accounting equation, prepare a balance sheet. Use the date November 15 of the current year.

RECYCLING PROBLEM 4-R Analyzing transactions into debit and credit parts

Alicia Valdez owns a business called QuickWash. QuickWash uses the following accounts.

Cash	Sales
Supplies	Advertising Expense
Prepaid Insurance	Miscellaneous Expense
Kishler Office Supplies	Rent Expense
Travis Office Supplies	Repair Expense
Alicia Valdez, Capital	Utilities Expense
Alicia Valdez, Drawing	

Transactions
Mar. 1. Received cash from owner as an investment, $3,000.00.
   2. Paid cash for supplies, $60.00.
   5. Paid cash for rent, $200.00.
   5. Received cash from sales, $350.00.
   6. Bought supplies on account from Travis Office Supplies, $500.00.
   9. Paid cash for repairs, $10.00.
   12. Received cash from sales, $200.00.
   13. Paid cash for insurance, $100.00.
   17. Bought supplies on account from Kishler Office Supplies, $50.00.
   19. Paid cash for miscellaneous expense, $5.00.
   19. Received cash from owner as an investment, $800.00.
   19. Received cash from sales, $300.00.
   20. Paid cash on account to Travis Office Supplies, $50.00.
   24. Paid cash for telephone bill (utilities expense), $25.00.
   25. Paid cash for advertising, $35.00.
   26. Received cash from sales, $320.00.
   30. Paid cash to owner for personal use, $500.00.
   31. Received cash from sales, $100.00.

INSTRUCTIONS:

1. Prepare a T account for each account.

2. Analyze each transaction into its debit and credit parts. Write the debit and credit amounts in the proper T accounts to show how each transaction changes account balances. Write the date of the transaction in parentheses before each amount.

RECYCLING PROBLEM 5-R Journalizing transactions

Mary Ching owns a service business called Ching's Accounting. Ching's Accounting uses the following accounts.

Cash	Sales
Supplies	Advertising Expense
Prepaid Insurance	Miscellaneous Expense
West Supplies	Rent Expense
Wilson's Office Supplies	Repair Expense
Mary Ching, Capital	Utilities Expense
Mary Ching, Drawing	

INSTRUCTIONS:

1. Journalize the following transactions completed during October of the current year. Use page 1 of a journal similar to the one described in Chapter 5 for Rugcare. Source documents are abbreviated as follows: check, C; memorandum, M; receipt, R; calculator tape, T.

Oct. 1. Received cash from owner as an investment, $14,000.00. R1.
    2. Paid cash for rent, $700.00. C1.
    5. Paid cash for supplies, $500.00. C2.
    6. Paid cash for insurance, $1,500.00. C3.
    7. Bought supplies on account from West Supplies, $2,000.00. M1.
    9. Paid cash for miscellaneous expense, $5.00. C4.
   12. Paid cash on account to West Supplies, $1,000.00. C5.
   12. Received cash from sales, $450.00. T12.
   13. Received cash from sales, $400.00. T13.
   14. Paid cash for telephone bill, $60.00. C6.
   14. Received cash from sales, $480.00. T14.
   15. Paid cash for repairs, $80.00. C7.
   15. Paid cash to owner for personal use, $400.00. C8.
   15. Received cash from sales, $550.00. T15.
   16. Received cash from sales, $480.00. T16.
   19. Received cash from sales, $380.00. T19.
   20. Received cash from sales, $520.00. T20.
   21. Bought supplies on account from Wilson's Office Supplies, $600.00. M2.
   21. Received cash from sales, $400.00. T21.
   22. Paid cash for supplies, $1,200.00. C9.
   22. Received cash from sales, $550.00. T22.
   23. Received cash from sales, $450.00. T23.

2. Prove and rule page 1 of the journal. Carry the column totals forward to page 2 of the journal.

3. Use page 2 of the journal. Journalize the following transactions completed during October of the current year.

Oct. 26. Paid cash for advertising, $100.00. C10.
    26. Bought supplies on account from West Supplies, $60.00. M3.
    26. Received cash from sales, $460.00. T26.
    27. Received cash from sales, $370.00. T27.
    28. Paid cash for electric bill, $40.00. C11.
    28. Received cash from sales, $400.00. T28.
    29. Paid cash on account to West Supplies, $60.00. C12.
    29. Received cash from sales, $330.00. T29.
    30. Paid cash for supplies, $50.00. C13.
    30. Received cash from sales, $550.00. T30.
    31. Paid cash to owner for personal use, $400.00. C14.

4. Prove page 2 of the journal.
5. Prove cash. The beginning cash balance on October 1 is zero. The balance on the next unused check stub is $14,675.00.
6. Rule page 2 of the journal.

RECYCLING PROBLEM 6-R Journalizing and posting to a general ledger

Al Burns owns a service business called Burns Cleaning. Burns Cleaning uses the same journal used by Rugcare in Chapter 6.

INSTRUCTIONS:

1. Open a general ledger account for each of the following accounts.

Assets

110 Cash
120 Supplies
130 Prepaid Insurance

Liabilities

210 Mitchell Office Supplies

Owner's Equity

310 Al Burns, Capital
320 Al Burns, Drawing

Revenue

410 Sales

Expenses

510 Advertising Expense
520 Miscellaneous Expense
530 Rent Expense
540 Utilities Expense

2. Journalize the following transactions completed during November of the current year. Use page 1 of a journal. Source documents are abbreviated as follows: check, C; memorandum, M; receipt, R; calculator tape, T.

Nov. 1. Received cash from owner as an investment, $7,000.00. R1.
3. Paid cash for insurance, $250.00. C1.
5. Paid cash for miscellaneous expense, $5.00. C2.
6. Received cash from sales, $410.00. T6.
9. Paid cash for rent, $400.00. C3.
11. Paid cash for supplies, $550.00. C4.
13. Bought supplies on account from Mitchell Office Supplies, $700.00. M1.
13. Received cash from sales, $380.00. T13.
16. Paid cash for electric bill, $50.00. C5.
18. Paid cash on account to Mitchell Office Supplies, $350.00. C6.
20. Paid cash for advertising, $35.00. C7.
20. Received cash from sales, $1,020.00. T20.
25. Paid cash for supplies, $100.00. C8.
27. Paid cash for supplies, $120.00. C9.
27. Received cash from sales, $1,660.00. T27.
30. Paid cash to owner for personal use, $500.00. C10.
30. Received cash from sales, $450.00. T30.

3. Prove the journal.
4. Prove cash. The beginning cash balance on November 1 is zero. The balance on the next unused check stub is $8,560.00.
5. Rule the journal.
6. Post from the journal to the general ledger.

RECYCLING PROBLEM 7-R Reconciling a bank statement; journalizing a bank service charge, a dishonored check, and petty cash transactions

Sarah Getz owns a business called Quick Service. Quick Service completed the following transactions during August of the current year.

INSTRUCTIONS:

1. Journalize the following transactions completed during August of the current year. Use page 8 of a journal. Source documents are abbreviated as follows: check, C; memorandum, M.

Aug. 24. Paid cash to establish a petty cash fund, $200.00. C81.
25. Received notice from the bank of a dishonored check, $50.00, plus $5.00 fee; total, $55.00. M28.
26. Paid cash for miscellaneous expense, $18.00. C82.
27. Paid cash for supplies, $60.00. C83.
28. Paid cash for repairs, $35.00. C84.
31. Paid cash to owner for personal use, $500.00. C85.
31. Paid cash to replenish the petty cash fund, $105.00: supplies, $65.00; miscellaneous expense, $40.00. C86.

2. On August 31 of the current year, Quick Service received a bank statement dated August 30. Prepare a bank statement reconciliation. Use August 31 of the current year as the

date. The following information is obtained from the August 30 bank statement and from the records of the business.

Bank statement balance	$1,970.00
Bank service charge	6.00
Outstanding deposit, August 31	520.00
Outstanding checks, Nos. 85 and 86	
Checkbook balance on Check Stub No. 87	1,891.00

3. Continue using the journal and journalize the following transaction.

Aug. 31. Received bank statement showing August bank service charge, $6.00. M29.

RECYCLING PROBLEM 8-R Completing a work sheet

On May 31 of the current year, ServiceAll has the following general ledger accounts and balances. The business uses a monthly fiscal period.

Account Title	Account Balances Debit	Credit
Cash	$3,900.00	
Petty Cash	100.00	
Supplies	3,400.00	
Prepaid Insurance	850.00	
Gordon Supplies		$ 170.00
Weil Company		90.00
James McCurdy, Capital		6,000.00
James McCurdy, Drawing	340.00	
Income Summary	—	—
Sales		3,500.00
Advertising Expense	270.00	
Insurance Expense	—	
Miscellaneous Expense	120.00	
Rent Expense	400.00	
Supplies Expense	—	
Utilities Expense	380.00	

INSTRUCTIONS:

1. Prepare the heading and trial balance on a work sheet.
2. Analyze the following adjustment information into debit and credit parts. Record the adjustments on the work sheet.

Adjustment Information, May 31

Supplies on hand	$2,000.00
Value of prepaid insurance	350.00

3. Extend the up-to-date account balances to the Balance Sheet or Income Statement columns.
4. Complete the work sheet.

RECYCLING PROBLEM 9-R Preparing financial statements

See the following page for information obtained from the work sheet of Best Delivery Service for the month ended December 31 of the current year.

INSTRUCTIONS:

1. Prepare an income statement for the month ended December 31 of the current year. Calculate and record the component percentages for total expenses and net income. Round percentage calculations to the nearest 0.1%.
2. Prepare a balance sheet for December 31 of the current year.

	ACCOUNT TITLE	INCOME STATEMENT DEBIT	INCOME STATEMENT CREDIT	BALANCE SHEET DEBIT	BALANCE SHEET CREDIT	
		5	6	7	8	
1	Cash			6 0 7 5 00		1
2	Petty Cash			2 0 0 00		2
3	Supplies			6 3 0 0 00		3
4	Prepaid Insurance			2 1 0 0 00		4
5	Dale Supplies				3 8 0 0 00	5
6	Niles Office Supplies				9 7 0 00	6
7	Evert Pole, Capital				9 7 0 0 00	7
8	Evert Pole, Drawing			1 0 0 0 00		8
9	Income Summary					9
10	Sales		4 5 6 0 00			10
11	Advertising Expense	3 0 0 00				11
12	Insurance Expense	1 5 0 00				12
13	Miscellaneous Expense	1 2 0 00				13
14	Rent Expense	2 5 0 0 00				14
15	Supplies Expense	1 6 5 00				15
16	Utilities Expense	1 2 0 00				16
17		3 3 5 5 00	4 5 6 0 00	15 6 7 5 00	14 4 7 0 00	17
18	Net Income	1 2 0 5 00			1 2 0 5 00	18
19		4 5 6 0 00	4 5 6 0 00	15 6 7 5 00	15 6 7 5 00	19
20						20
21						21
22						22
23						23

RECYCLING PROBLEM 10-R Journalizing adjusting and closing entries

The following information is obtained from the partial work sheet of Lawn Services for the month ended September 30 of the current year.

	ACCOUNT TITLE	ADJUSTMENTS DEBIT	ADJUSTMENTS CREDIT	INCOME STATEMENT DEBIT	INCOME STATEMENT CREDIT	BALANCE SHEET DEBIT	BALANCE SHEET CREDIT	
		3	4	5	6	7	8	
1	Cash					3 1 5 0 00		1
2	Supplies		(a) 1 7 5 00			6 7 5 00		2
3	Prepaid Insurance		(b) 2 3 0 00			2 5 0 00		3
4	Lodge Supplies						4 5 0 00	4
5	Verner Supplies						1 0 0 00	5
6	Norman Eli, Capital						3 1 3 0 00	6
7	Norman Eli, Drawing					3 1 5 00		7
8	Income Summary							8
9	Sales				1 6 1 5 00			9
10	Insurance Expense	(b) 2 3 0 00		2 3 0 00				10
11	Miscellaneous Expense			7 5 00				11
12	Rent Expense			4 2 5 00				12
13	Supplies Expense	(a) 1 7 5 00		1 7 5 00				13
14		4 0 5 00	4 0 5 00	9 0 5 00	1 6 1 5 00	4 3 9 0 00	3 6 8 0 00	14
15	Net Income			7 1 0 00			7 1 0 00	15
16				1 6 1 5 00	1 6 1 5 00	4 3 9 0 00	4 3 9 0 00	16
17								17
18								18

INSTRUCTIONS:

1. Use page 3 of a journal. Journalize the adjusting entries.

2. Continue to use page 3 of the journal. Journalize the closing entries.

RECYCLING PROBLEM 11-R Journalizing purchases, cash payments, and other transactions

Eva Akemi and Daniel Marino, partners, own a furniture store.

INSTRUCTIONS:

Journalize the following transactions completed during November of the current year. Use page 11 of a journal similar to the one described in Chapter 11. Source documents are abbreviated as follows: check, C; memorandum, M; purchase invoice, P.

Nov. 2. Paid cash for rent, $1,200.00. C251.
2. Purchased merchandise on account from Baines Furniture Co., $2,335.00. P88.
3. Paid cash for office supplies, $66.00. C252.
5. Paid cash on account to Decor-Concepts, $985.00, covering P85. C253.
7. Purchased merchandise for cash, $130.00. C254.
9. Purchased merchandise on account from Metaline Co., $950.00. P89.
9. Bought store supplies on account from Gateway Supply, $140.00. M40.
10. Purchased merchandise for cash, $83.00. C255.
12. Paid cash on account to Furniture Industries, $1,400.00, covering P86. C256.
12. Bought office supplies on account from Scott Supply, $95.00. M41.
14. Discovered that a transaction for store supplies bought in October was journalized and posted in error as a debit to Purchases instead of Supplies—Store, $74.00. M42.
16. Eva Akemi, partner, withdrew cash for personal use, $1,000.00. C257.
17. Daniel Marino, partner, withdrew cash for personal use, $1,000.00. C258.
17. Paid cash for advertising, $75.00. C259.
19. Paid cash on account to Classic Furniture, $1,345.00, covering P87. C260.
19. Purchased merchandise on account from Metaline Co., $1,250.00. P90.
20. Daniel Marino, partner, withdrew merchandise for personal use, $152.00. M43.
22. Purchased merchandise for cash, $60.00. C261.
24. Paid cash on account to Baines Furniture Co., $2,335.00, covering P88. C262.
25. Eva Akemi, partner, withdrew merchandise for personal use, $225.00. M44.
27. Paid cash for store supplies, $78.00. C263.
30. Paid cash to replenish the petty cash fund, $301.00: office supplies, $78.00; store supplies, $52.00; advertising, $125.00; miscellaneous, $46.00. C264.
30. Paid cash on account to Metaline Co., $950.00, covering P89. C265.

RECYCLING PROBLEM 12-R Journalizing sales and cash receipts

Ana Lamas and Alex Keyser, partners, own an office supply store.

INSTRUCTIONS:

1. Journalize the following transactions completed during September of the current year. Use page 9 of a journal similar to the one described in Chapter 12. A 4% sales tax has been added to each sale. Source documents are abbreviated as follows: receipt, R; sales invoice, S; cash register tape, T.

Sept. 1. Sold merchandise on account to Samuel Quist, $75.00, plus sales tax, $3.00; total, $78.00. S53.
1. Received cash on account from David Plouff, $85.28, covering S49. R85.
2. Sold merchandise on account to Carmen Estevez, $125.00, plus sales tax, $5.00; total, $130.00. S54.

Sept. 5. Sold merchandise on account to Keith Aldrich, $265.00, plus sales tax, $10.60; total, $275.60. S55.

5. Recorded cash and credit card sales, $1,940.00, plus sales tax, $77.60; total, $2,017.60. T5.

7. Received cash on account from Edward Jarmen, $249.60, covering S50. R86.

9. Sold merchandise on account to Perez Accounting Co., $345.00, plus sales tax, $13.80; total, $358.80. S56.

10. Sold merchandise on account to Nancy Cain, $85.00, plus sales tax, $3.40; total, $88.40. S57.

11. Received cash on account from Bonner Secretarial Service, $249.60, covering S51. R87.

12. Recorded cash and credit card sales, $2,350.00, plus sales tax, $94.00; total, $2,444.00. T12.

14. Received cash on account from David Doran, $187.20, covering S52. R88.

15. Sold merchandise on account to Hazel Ervin, $65.00, plus sales tax, $2.60; total, $67.60. S58.

18. Received cash on account from Samuel Quist, $78.00, covering S53. R89.

19. Recorded cash and credit card sales, $2,450.00, plus sales tax, $98.00; total, $2,548.00. T19.

21. Received cash on account from Carmen Estevez, $130.00, covering S54. R90.

25. Received cash on account from Keith Aldrich, $275.60, covering S55. R91.

26. Recorded cash and credit card sales, $2,140.00, plus sales tax, $85.60; total, $2,225.60. T26.

29. Sold merchandise on account to Susan Gates, $145.00, plus sales tax, $5.80; total, $150.80. S59.

30. Recorded cash and credit card sales, $1,285.00, plus sales tax, $51.40; total, $1,336.40. T30.

2. Total the journal. Prove the equality of debits and credits.

3. Rule the journal.

RECYCLING PROBLEM 13-R Opening accounts and journalizing and posting business transactions

INSTRUCTIONS:

1. Open the following accounts in the general ledger of Catalina Shoes. Record the balances as of September 1 of the current year.

Account No.	Account Title	Account Balance
1110	Cash	$ 13,200.00
1130	Accounts Receivable	441.00
1140	Supplies—Office	1,830.00
1150	Supplies—Store	1,560.00
2110	Accounts Payable	3,820.00
2120	Sales Tax Payable	937.50
3120	Sophia Kizer, Drawing	9,820.00
3140	Brian Rankin, Drawing	9,600.00
4110	Sales	150,000.00
5110	Purchases	88,000.00
6110	Advertising Expense	2,310.00
6140	Miscellaneous Expense	1,260.00
6160	Rent Expense	7,600.00
6190	Utilities Expense	1,620.00

2. Open the following vendor accounts in the accounts payable ledger. Record the balances as of September 1 of the current year.

Vendor No.	Vendor Name	Purchase Invoice No.	Account Balance
210	A & J Shoes	P66	$1,480.00
220	Colormate Shoes	—	—
230	Sanz Supply	—	—
240	Suave Shoe Co.	P65	2,340.00

3. Open the following customer accounts in the accounts receivable ledger. Record the balances as of September 1 of the current year.

Customer No.	Customer Name	Sales Invoice No.	Account Balance
110	Joyce Abler	S53	$178.50
120	Helen Gorthy	—	—
130	Joshua Lentz	—	—
140	Earl Ward	S52	262.50

4. Journalize the following transactions completed during September of the current year. Use page 9 of a journal similar to the one described in Chapter 13. A 5% sales tax has been added to each sale. Source documents are abbreviated as follows: check, C; memorandum, M; purchase invoice, P; receipt, R; sales invoice, S; cash register tape, T.

Sept. 1. Paid cash for rent, $950.00. C225.
2. Purchased merchandise on account from Colormate Shoes, $1,650.00. P67.
4. Received cash on account from Earl Ward, $262.50, covering S52. R33.
5. Recorded cash and credit card sales, $3,350.00, plus sales tax, $167.50; total, $3,517.50. T5.
   Posting. Post the items that are to be posted individually.
7. Paid cash for electric bill, $158.10. C226.
9. Bought office supplies on account from Sanz Supply, $135.00. M32.
10. Paid cash on account to Suave Shoe Co., $2,340.00, covering P65. C227.
12. Recorded cash and credit card sales, $4,140.00, plus sales tax, $207.00; total, $4,347.00. T12.
   Posting. Post the items that are to be posted individually.
14. Sold merchandise on account to Helen Gorthy, $260.00, plus sales tax, $13.00; total, $273.00. S54.
15. Sold merchandise on account to Joshua Lentz, $125.00, plus sales tax, $6.25; total, $131.25. S55.
15. Sophia Kizer, partner, withdrew cash for personal use, $1,200.00. C228.
15. Brian Rankin, partner, withdrew cash for personal use, $1,200.00. C229.
18. Purchased merchandise on account from A & J Shoes, $940.00. P68.
19. Recorded cash and credit card sales, $4,080.00, plus sales tax, $204.00; total, $4,284.00. T19.
   Posting. Post the items that are to be posted individually.
21. Discovered that a transaction for office supplies bought for cash was journalized and posted in error as a debit to Supplies—Store instead of Supplies—Office, $118.00. M33.
22. Sophia Kizer, partner, withdrew merchandise for personal use, $125.00. M34.
24. Sold merchandise on account to Earl Ward, $135.00, plus sales tax, $6.75; total, $141.75. S56.
25. Sold merchandise on account to Joyce Abler, $95.00, plus sales tax, $4.75; total, $99.75. S57.
26. Recorded cash and credit card sales, $4,530.00, plus sales tax, $226.50; total, $4,756.50. T26.
   Posting. Post the items that are to be posted individually.
28. Received cash on account from Joyce Abler, $178.50, covering S53. R34.
28. Paid cash on account to A & J Shoes, $1,480.00, covering P66. C230.
30. Paid cash to replenish the petty cash fund, $201.50: office supplies, $42.00; store supplies, $57.50; advertising, $64.00; miscellaneous, $38.00. C231.

Sept. 30. Purchased merchandise on account from Suave Shoe Co., $860.00. P69.

30. Recorded cash and credit card sales, $1,970.00, plus sales tax, $98.50; total, $2,068.50. T30.

Posting. Post the items that are to be posted individually.

5. Total the journal. Prove the equality of debits and credits.
6. Prove cash. The balance on the next unused check stub is $25,084.90.
7. Rule the journal.
8. Post the totals of the special columns of the journal.
9. Prepare a schedule of accounts payable and a schedule of accounts receivable. Prove the accuracy of the subsidiary ledgers by comparing the schedule totals with the balances of the controlling accounts in the general ledger. If the totals are not the same, find and correct the errors.

RECYCLING PROBLEM 14-R Preparing a semimonthly payroll

The following information is for the semimonthly pay period June 1–15 of the current year.

Employee		Marital Status	No. of Allow- ances	Earnings		Deductions
No.	Name			Regular	Overtime	Health Insurance
3	Cahill, Bryan M.	S	2	$598.40	$40.00	$25.00
4	Dykes, Eleanor S.	M	3	525.60		30.00
7	Holcomb, David K.	S	1	624.00		
1	Kirby, Sharon A.	S	1	552.00	9.30	
5	Mendez, Thomas T.	M	2	545.60		25.00
6	Salassi, Carol W.	M	3	576.00		30.00
8	Tsang, Elaine C.	M	2	651.20	44.40	25.00

INSTRUCTIONS:

1. Prepare a payroll register. The date of payment is June 16. Use the federal income tax withholding tables in Illustration 14-4 to find the income tax withholding for each employee. Calculate FICA tax withholding using an 8% tax rate. None of the employee accumulated earnings has exceeded the FICA tax base.
2. Prepare a check for the total amount of the net pay. Make the check payable to Payroll Account, and sign your name as a partner of Riddley Company. The beginning check stub balance is $7,687.89.
3. Prepare payroll checks for David Holcomb, Check No. 332, and Carol Salassi, Check No. 335. Sign your name as a partner of Riddley Company. Record the two payroll check numbers in the payroll register.

RECYCLING PROBLEM 15-R Journalizing payroll taxes

Johnson Manufacturing completed payroll transactions during the period February 28 to April 30 of the current year. Payroll tax rates are as follows: FICA, 8%; federal unemployment, 0.8%; and state unemployment, 5.4%. No total earnings have exceeded the tax base for calculating unemployment taxes.

INSTRUCTIONS:

1. Journalize the following transactions on page 4 of a journal. Source documents are abbreviated as follows: check, C, and memorandum, M.

Feb. 28. Paid cash for monthly payroll, $3,312.16 (total payroll, $4,298.00, less deductions: employee income tax, $642.00; FICA tax, $343.84). C167.

28. Recorded employer payroll taxes expense. M34.

Mar. 15. Paid cash for liability for employee income tax, $642.00, and for FICA tax, $687.68; total, $1,329.68. C192.
   31. Paid cash for monthly payroll, $3,328.84 (total payroll, $4,327.00, less deductions: employee income tax, $652.00; FICA tax, $346.16). C235.
   31. Recorded employer payroll taxes expense. M39.
Apr. 15. Paid cash for liability for employee income tax, $652.00, and for FICA tax, $692.32; total, $1,344.32. C251.
   30. Paid cash for federal unemployment tax liability for quarter ended March 31, $103.62. C272.
   30. Paid cash for state unemployment tax liability for quarter ended March 31, $699.41. C273.

2. Prove and rule the journal.

RECYCLING PROBLEM 16-R Completing a work sheet

On December 31 of the current year, Klimer has the following general ledger accounts and balances.

Account Title	Balance
Cash	$ 19,865.00
Petty Cash	500.00
Accounts Receivable	9,260.00
Merchandise Inventory	226,320.00
Supplies—Office	5,085.00
Supplies—Store	5,420.00
Prepaid Insurance	4,300.00
Accounts Payable	9,720.00
Sales Tax Payable	950.00
Dorothy Klimer, Capital	107,365.00
Dorothy Klimer, Drawing	15,880.00
Howard Klimer, Capital	106,190.00
Howard Klimer, Drawing	15,730.00
Income Summary	—
Sales	189,540.00
Purchases	85,250.00
Advertising Expense	4,735.00
Credit Card Fee Expense	1,930.00
Insurance Expense	—
Miscellaneous Expense	2,360.00
Rent Expense	14,400.00
Supplies Expense—Office	—
Supplies Expense—Store	—
Utilities Expense	2,730.00

INSTRUCTIONS:

Prepare Klimer's work sheet for the fiscal period ended December 31 of the current year.

Adjustment Information, December 31

Merchandise inventory	$218,770.00
Office supplies inventory	2,195.00
Store supplies inventory	2,205.00
Value of prepaid insurance	1,720.00

RECYCLING PROBLEM 17-R Preparing financial statements

Discount Footwear prepared the work sheet on page C-13 for the year ended December 31 of the current year.

Discount Footwear
Work Sheet
For Year Ended December 31, 19--

	TRIAL BALANCE		ADJUSTMENTS		INCOME STATEMENT		BALANCE SHEET	
ACCOUNT TITLE	DEBIT	CREDIT	DEBIT	CREDIT	DEBIT	CREDIT	DEBIT	CREDIT
1 Cash	1939500						1939500	
2 Petty Cash	30000						30000	
3 Accounts Receivable	893000						893000	
4 Merchandise Inventory	25720000			(a) 975000			24745000	
5 Supplies—Office	512000			(b) 298000			214000	
6 Supplies—Store	487500			(c) 314000			173500	
7 Prepaid Insurance	483000			(d) 276000			207000	
8 Accounts Payable		836000						836000
9 Sales Tax Payable		98000						98000
10 Joseph Kane, Capital		11164000						11164000
11 Joseph Kane, Drawing	1584000						1584000	
12 Gail Miles, Capital		11036000						11036000
13 Gail Miles, Drawing	1593000						1593000	
14 Income Summary			(a) 975000		975000			
15 Sales		23545000				23545000		
16 Purchases	10595000				10595000			
17 Advertising Expense	496500				496500			
18 Credit Card Fee Expense	213000				213000			
19 Insurance Expense			(d) 276000		276000			
20 Miscellaneous Expense	228500				228500			
21 Rent Expense	1680000				1680000			
22 Supplies Expense—Office			(b) 298000		298000			
23 Supplies Expense—Store			(c) 314000		314000			
24 Utilities Expense	224000				224000			
25	46679000	46679000	1863000	1863000	15300000	23545000	31379000	23134000
26 Net Income					8245000			8245000
27					23545000	23545000	31379000	31379000
28								

INSTRUCTIONS:

1. Prepare an income statement. Calculate and record the following component percentages: (a) cost of merchandise sold, (b) gross profit on sales, (c) total expenses, and (d) net income or loss. Round percentage calculations to the nearest 0.1%.
2. Prepare a distribution of net income statement. Net income or loss is to be shared equally.
3. Prepare an owners' equity statement. No additional investments were made.
4. Prepare a balance sheet in report form.

RECYCLING PROBLEM 18-R Journalizing adjusting and closing entries

Use the following partial work sheet of Cook & Latzco Paints for the year ended December 31 of the current year.

	ACCOUNT TITLE	3 ADJUSTMENTS DEBIT	4 ADJUSTMENTS CREDIT	5 INCOME STATEMENT DEBIT	6 INCOME STATEMENT CREDIT
4	Merchandise Inventory		(a) 9 8 4 0 00		
5	Supplies—Office		(b) 2 5 1 0 00		
6	Supplies—Store		(c) 2 6 3 0 00		
7	Prepaid Insurance		(d) 2 5 8 0 00		
21	Income Summary	(a) 9 8 4 0 00		9 8 4 0 00	
22	Sales				310 9 2 0 00
23	Purchases			124 3 5 0 00	
24	Advertising Expense			4 7 8 0 00	
25	Credit Card Fee Expense			3 9 8 0 00	
26	Insurance Expense	(d) 2 5 8 0 00		2 5 8 0 00	
27	Miscellaneous Expense			2 1 4 0 00	
28	Payroll Taxes Expense			7 0 7 0 00	
29	Rent Expense			13 2 0 0 00	
30	Salary Expense			58 9 2 0 00	
31	Supplies Expense—Office	(b) 2 5 1 0 00		2 5 1 0 00	
32	Supplies Expense—Store	(c) 2 6 3 0 00		2 6 3 0 00	
33	Utilities Expense			2 7 6 0 00	
34		17 5 6 0 00	17 5 6 0 00	234 7 6 0 00	310 9 2 0 00
35	Net Income			76 1 6 0 00	
36				310 9 2 0 00	310 9 2 0 00
37					
38					
39					
40					
41					

INSTRUCTIONS:

1. Use page 25 of a journal. Journalize the adjusting entries using information from the partial work sheet.
2. Continue using page 25 of the journal. Journalize the closing entries using information from the work sheet. The distribution of net income statement shows equal distribution of earnings. The partners' drawing accounts show the following debit balances in the work sheet's Balance Sheet Debit column: Angela Cook, Drawing, $14,780.00; Alan Latzco, Drawing, $15,120.00.

Journalizing and posting purchases and cash payment transactions

INSTRUCTIONS:

1. Open the following accounts in the general ledger of Dunhill Corporation. Record the balances as of October 1 of the current year.

PARTIAL GENERAL LEDGER

Account No.	Account Title	Account Balance
1105	Cash..	$23,410.00
1110	Petty Cash	250.00
1140	Supplies......................................	957.00
2115	Accounts Payable............................	1,382.00
5105	Purchases	—
5110	Purchases Discounts	—
5115	Purchases Returns and Allowances	—
6105	Advertising Expense	—
6130	Miscellaneous Expense.......................	—
6140	Rent Expense.................................	—
8105	Cash Short and Over.........................	—

2. Open the following vendor accounts in the accounts payable ledger. Record the balances as of October 1 of the current year.

ACCOUNTS PAYABLE LEDGER

Vendor No.	Vendor Name	Terms	Purchase Invoice Number	Account Balance
210	Adkin Supplies	n/15	—	—
220	Blair Company	n/30	—	—
230	Friedmans Company	n/30	P92	$625.00
240	Hargrove, Inc	1/10, n/30	P100	757.00
250	Stovall Company	2/10, n/30	—	—
260	Winston Company	1/10, n/30	—	—

3. Journalize the following transactions affecting purchases and cash payments completed during October of the current year. Use page 10 of a purchases journal, a general journal, and a cash payments journal. Source documents are abbreviated as follows: check, C; debit memorandum, DM; memorandum, M; purchase invoice, P.

Oct. 1. Paid cash for rent, $1,500.00. C163.
　　 1. Purchased merchandise on account from Blair Company, $1,482.00. P101.
　　 5. Purchased merchandise on account from Winston Company, $225.00. P102.
　　 5. Returned merchandise to Friedmans Company, $70.00, from P92. DM61.
　　　　Posting. Post the items that are to be posted individually. Post from the journals in this order: purchases journal, general journal, and cash payments journal.
　　 8. Paid cash on account to Friedmans Company, $555.00, covering P92 for $625.00, less DM61, $70.00; no discount. C164.
　　 8. Paid cash on account to Hargrove, Inc., $749.43, covering P100 for $757.00, less 1% discount, $7.57. C165.
　　 12. Purchased merchandise for cash, $720.00. C166.
　　 14. Purchased merchandise on account from Winston Company, $1,296.00. P103.
　　 15. Paid cash on account to Winston Company, $222.75, covering P102 for $225.00, less 1% discount, $2.25. C167.
　　 15. Paid cash to replenish the petty cash fund, $158.80: supplies, $47.50; advertising, $53.60; miscellaneous, $61.75; cash over, $4.05. C168.
　　 15. Bought supplies on account from Adkin Supplies, $304.00. M17.
　　　　Posting. Post the items that are to be posted individually.
　　 18. Paid cash for miscellaneous expense, $218.00. C169.

Oct. 20. Purchased merchandise on account from Friedmans Company, $350.00. P104.

20. Returned merchandise to Blair Company, $177.00, from P101. DM62.

21. Paid cash on account to Winston Company, $1,283.04, covering P103 for $1,296.00, less 1% discount, $12.96. C170.

22. Paid cash for advertising, $345.00. C171.

25. Purchased merchandise on account from Winston Company, $817.00. P105.

27. Paid cash on account to Blair Company, $1,305.00, covering P101 for $1,482.00, less DM62, $177.00; no discount. C172.

28. Returned merchandise to Winston Company, $34.00, from P105. DM63.

29. Paid cash on account to Adkin Supplies, $304.00, covering M17; no discount. C173.

29. Purchased merchandise on account from Stovall Company, $925.00. P106.

29. Paid cash to replenish the petty cash fund, $187.80: supplies, $14.30; advertising, $78.60; miscellaneous, $90.00; cash short, $4.90. C174.

   Posting. Post the items that are to be posted individually.

4. Total and rule the purchases journal. Post the total.

5. Prove and rule the cash payments journal. Post the totals of the special columns.

6. Prepare a schedule of accounts payable. Compare the schedule total with the balance of the accounts payable account in the general ledger. The total and balance should be the same.

RECYCLING PROBLEM 20-R Journalizing and posting sales and cash receipts transactions

INSTRUCTIONS:

1. Open the following accounts in the general ledger of Thompson Company. Record the balances as of June 1 of the current year.

PARTIAL GENERAL LEDGER

Account No.	Account Title	Account Balance
1105	Cash	$9,216.00
1125	Accounts Receivable	3,024.01
2135	Sales Tax Payable	—
4105	Sales	—
4110	Sales Discount	—
4115	Sales Returns and Allowances	—

2. Open the following customer accounts in the accounts receivable ledger. Record the balances as of June 1 of the current year.

ACCOUNTS RECEIVABLE LEDGER

Customer No.	Customer Name	Sale No.	Account Balance
110	Bolero Company	S84	$616.45
120	Franklin, Inc.	S88	448.20
130	Mooney and Associates	S85	398.76
140	Powers Company	S89	702.00
150	David Reed	S90	858.60

3. Journalize the following transactions affecting sales and cash receipts completed during June of the current year. Use page 6 of a sales journal, a general journal, and a cash receipts journal. Thompson Company offers its customers terms of 2/10, n/30. The sales tax rate is 8%. Source documents are abbreviated as follows: credit memorandum, CM; receipt, R; sales invoice, S; cash register tape, T.

June 1. Received cash on account from Franklin, Inc., $439.24, covering S88 for $448.20 ($415.00 plus sales tax, $33.20), less discount, $8.30, and less sales tax, $0.66. R21.

June 4. Granted credit to David Reed for merchandise returned, $126.00, plus sales tax, $10.08, from S90; total, $136.08. CM8.

7. Received cash on account from Powers Company, $687.96, covering S89 for $702.00 ($650.00 plus sales tax, $52.00), less discount, $13.00, and less sales tax, $1.04. R22.

7. Recorded cash and credit card sales, $1,980.00, plus sales tax, $158.40; total, $2,138.40. T7.

Posting. Post the items that are to be posted individually. Post from the journals in this order: sales journal, general journal, and cash receipts journal.

9. Received cash on account from David Reed, $722.52 (covering S90 less CM8), no discount. R23.

9. Received cash on account from Mooney and Associates, $398.76, covering S85; no discount. R24.

11. Recorded cash and credit card sales, $2,358.00, plus sales tax, $188.64; total, $2,546.64. T11.

Posting. Post the items that are to be posted individually.

13. Sold merchandise on account to Franklin, Inc., $1,236.00, plus sales tax, $98.88; total, $1,334.88. S91.

15. Granted credit to Franklin, Inc., for merchandise returned, $36.40, plus sales tax, $2.91, from S91; total, $39.31. CM9.

15. Received cash on account from Bolero Company, $616.45, covering S84; no discount. R25.

18. Recorded cash and credit card sales, $2,678.00, plus sales tax, $214.24; total, $2,892.24. T18.

Posting. Post the items that are to be posted individually.

21. Sold merchandise on account to David Reed, $540.00, plus sales tax, $43.20; total, $583.20. S92.

22. Sold merchandise on account to Bolero Company, $415.00, plus sales tax, $33.20; total, $448.20. S93.

22. Sold merchandise on account to Powers Company, $643.00, plus sales tax, $51.44; total, $694.44. S94.

25. Recorded cash and credit card sales, $1,916.00, plus sales tax, $153.28; total, $2,069.28. T25.

Posting. Post the items that are to be posted individually.

28. Sold merchandise on account to Bolero Company, $756.00, plus sales tax, $60.48; total, $816.48. S95.

29. Received cash on account from Franklin, Inc., $1,295.57 (covering S91 less CM9), no discount. R26.

29. Received cash on account from David Reed, $571.54, covering S92 for $583.20 ($540.00 plus sales tax, $43.20), less discount, $10.80, and less sales tax, $0.86. R27.

30. Sold merchandise on account to Franklin, Inc., $772.50, plus sales tax, $61.80; total, $834.30. S96.

30. Recorded cash and credit card sales, $1,606.00, plus sales tax, $128.48; total, $1,734.48. T30.

Posting. Post the items that are to be posted individually.

4. Prove and rule the sales journal. Post the totals of the special columns.

5. Prove the equality of debits and credits for the cash receipts journal.

6. Prove cash. The cash balance on hand on June 1 was $9,216.00. The total of the Cash Credit column of the cash payments journal for Thompson Company is $14,753.00. The balance on the next unused check stub on June 30 is $10,576.08.

7. Rule the cash receipts journal. Post the totals of the special columns.

8. Prepare a schedule of accounts receivable similar to the one described in Chapter 13. Compare the schedule total with the balance of the accounts receivable account in the general ledger. The total and the balance should be the same.

RECYCLING PROBLEM 21-R Recording entries for uncollectible accounts

Colonial Plastics has the following accounts in its accounts receivable ledger.

PARTIAL ACCOUNTS RECEIVABLE LEDGER

Account No. and Title	Date	Post. Ref.	Debit	Debit Balance
125 Dixon Company	May 19	S5	$ 621.00	$ 621.00
135 Fire Star Co.	Mar. 25	S3	1,295.00	1,295.00
140 Haber Corporation	Jan. 26	S1	916.00	916.00
190 Tri-State Corporation	Feb. 1	S2	384.00	384.00

INSTRUCTIONS:

1. Journalize the following transactions completed during October, November, and December of the current year. Use pages 10, 11, and 12 of a general journal and pages 11 and 12 of a cash receipts journal. Source documents are abbreviated as follows: memorandum, M; receipt, R.

Oct. 2. Wrote off Tri-State Corporation's past-due account as uncollectible, $384.00. M332.
   14. Wrote off Haber Corporation's past-due account as uncollectible, $916.00. M336.
      Posting. Post each entry to the customer accounts in the accounts receivable ledger.

Nov. 17. Wrote off Dixon Company's past-due account as uncollectible, $621.00. M342.
   22. Received cash in full payment of Tri-State Corporation's account, previously written off as uncollectible, $384.00. M347 and R409.
      Posting. Post each entry to the customer accounts in the accounts receivable ledger.

Dec. 13. Wrote off Fire Star Co.'s past-due account as uncollectible, $1,295.00. M355.
   21. Received cash in full payment of Dixon Company's account, previously written off as uncollectible, $621.00. M362 and R476.
   26. Received cash in full payment of Haber Corporation's account, previously written off as uncollectible, $916.00. M368 and R482.
      Posting. Post each entry to the customer accounts in the accounts receivable ledger.

2. Journalize the December 31 adjusting entry for estimated uncollectible accounts expense for the year. Use page 13 of the general journal. Uncollectible accounts expense is estimated as 1.0% of total sales on account. Total sales on account for the year were $1,206,470.00.

RECYCLING PROBLEM 22-R Calculating depreciation expense and book value of plant assets; journalizing entries affecting plant assets

Magnolia Company records plant assets in two accounts: **Office Equipment** and **Store Equipment**. Magnolia Company owns the following plant assets.

Plant Asset	Asset Account	Date Bought	Original Cost	Estimated Salvage Value	Estimated Useful Life
1	Office Equipment	Apr. 1, 19X1	$ 7,500.00	$ 500.00	7 years
2	Store Equipment	Sept. 1, 19X1	18,900.00	2,400.00	10 years
3	Office Equipment	Oct. 1, 19X1	6,300.00	300.00	5 years
4	Store Equipment	Mar. 1, 19X2	5,200.00	1,240.00	6 years
5	Store Equipment	July 1, 19X2	13,700.00	1,100.00	12 years
6	Store Equipment	June 1, 19X3	9,600.00	2,040.00	9 years
7	Office Equipment	Nov. 1, 19X4	1,250.00	350.00	3 years
8	Office Equipment	July 1, 19X5	2,800.00	800.00	4 years

INSTRUCTIONS:

1. Calculate each plant asset's depreciation expense for the year ended December 31, 19X5. Use the straight-line method of calculating depreciation. Round amounts to the nearest cent.

2. Calculate each plant asset's ending book value as of December 31, 19X5.
3. Journalize the two adjusting entries for depreciation expense for the year ended December 31, 19X5. Use page 13 of a general journal.
4. Journalize the following transaction. Use page 4 of a cash receipts journal. Source documents are abbreviated as follows: memorandum, M; receipt, R.

19X6
Apr. 2. Received cash from sale of plant asset number 2, $12,200.00: original cost, $18,900.00; total accumulated depreciation through December 31, 19X5, $7,150.00; additional depreciation to be recorded through April 2, 19X6, $412.50. M125 and R193.

RECYCLING PROBLEM 23-R Determining cost of ending inventory using the fifo, lifo, and weighted-average methods

Accounting records at Northland Company show the following purchases and periodic inventory counts.

Model No.	Beginning Inventory January 1	First Purchase	Second Purchase	Third Purchase	Periodic Inventory Count December 31
C23	10 @ $15.00	8 @ $16.00	12 @ $18.00	16 @ $20.00	20
R79	15 @ $ 9.00	18 @ $10.00	20 @ $12.00	12 @ $14.00	25
C152	8 @ $ 6.25	12 @ $ 6.00	15 @ $ 5.90	10 @ $ 5.75	14
D34	42 @ $23.00	35 @ $22.00	40 @ $20.00	40 @ $18.00	67
R493	8 @ $ 5.20	9 @ $ 5.80	5 @ $ 6.30	7 @ $ 6.50	15
G549	20 @ $10.00	15 @ $11.00	15 @ $12.00	25 @ $12.00	35

INSTRUCTIONS:

1. Calculate the total cost of ending inventory on December 31 using the fifo method. Use a form similar to the following. The inventory cost for Model No. C23 is given as an example.

Model No.	No. of Units on Hand	Unit Price	Cost of Ending Inventory
C23	20	16 @ $20.00 4 @ 18.00	$392.00

Use the following procedure to complete the form.
(a) Record the model number and number of units of each model on hand on December 31.
(b) Record the unit price of each model. When more than one unit price is used, list the units and unit prices on separate lines as shown in the example.
(c) Calculate the cost of ending inventory of each model, and write the amount in the Cost of Ending Inventory column.
(d) Add the amounts in the Cost of Ending Inventory column to calculate the total cost of ending inventory.
2. On another form, calculate the total cost of ending inventory using the lifo method. Follow the steps given in Instruction 1.

3. On another form, calculate the total cost of ending inventory using the weighted-average method. Use the following procedure.
   (a) Record the model number and number of units of each model on hand on December 31.
   (b) Calculate the weighted-average price per unit for each model. Round the amount per unit to the nearest cent. Write the amount in the Unit Price column.
   (c) Calculate the cost of ending inventory of each model, and write the amount in the Cost of Ending Inventory column.
   (d) Add the amounts in the Cost of Ending Inventory column to calculate the total cost of ending inventory.
4. Compare the total cost of ending inventory obtained in Instructions 1, 2, and 3. Which method, fifo, lifo, or weighted-average, resulted in the lowest cost of ending inventory?

RECYCLING PROBLEM 24-R Journalizing notes payable and notes receivable transactions

The following transactions were completed by Arrowhead Manufacturing during July of the current year.

INSTRUCTIONS:

1. Journalize the following transactions. Use page 7 of a general journal, page 14 of a cash receipts journal, and page 18 of a cash payments journal. Source documents are abbreviated as follows: check, C; memorandum, M; note payable, NP; note receivable, NR; receipt, R.

July 2. Received cash for the maturity value of NR95: principal, $1,100.00, plus interest, $11.00; total, $1,111.00. R132.
   5. Issued a 60-day, 10% note, $3,000.00. NP155.
   6. Paid cash for the maturity value of NP149: principal, $7,000.00, plus interest, $140.00; total, $7,140.00. C1043.
   8. Discounted at 11% a 30-day non-interest-bearing note, $2,500.00; proceeds, $2,477.08, interest, $22.92. NP156.
   11. Received cash for the maturity value of NR92: principal, $600.00, plus interest, $12.00; total, $612.00. R147.
   13. Received cash for the maturity value of NR94: principal, $575.00, plus interest, $5.75; total, $580.75. R152.
   17. Paid cash for the maturity value of NP151: principal, $4,500.00, plus interest, $90.00; total, $4,590.00. C1212.
   18. Issued a 3-month, 12% note to McKinney Company for an extension of time on this account payable, $1,700.00. NP157.
   21. Melinda Blair dishonored NR80, a 6-month, 12% note, maturity value due today: principal, $500.00; interest, $30.00; total, $530.00. M113.
   25. Discounted at 11% a 6-month non-interest-bearing note, $12,500.00; proceeds, $11,812.50, interest, $687.50. NP158.
   27. Received a 30-day, 13% note from Miles Browning for an extension of time on his account, $1,500.00. NR96.
   29. Paid cash for the maturity value of NP131: principal, $3,500.00, plus interest, $192.50; total, $3,692.50. C1235.

2. Prove the cash receipts and cash payments journals.

RECYCLING PROBLEM 25-R Journalizing and posting entries for accrued revenue and expenses

The following accounts are from Willem Corporation's general ledger. The balances are recorded as of December 31 of the current year before adjusting entries.

PARTIAL GENERAL LEDGER

Account No.	Account Title	Account Balance
1115	Notes Receivable	$ 720.00
1120	Interest Receivable	—
2105	Notes Payable	4,000.00
2110	Interest Payable	—
3120	Income Summary	—
7110	Interest Income	132.00
8110	Interest Expense	575.00

Willem Corporation completed the following transactions related to notes receivable and notes payable during the current year and the following year. The first two transactions have already been journalized and posted. Note Receivable No. 7 and Note Payable No. 10 are the only notes on hand at the end of the fiscal period. Source documents are abbreviated as follows: check, C; note payable, NP; note receivable, NR; receipt, R.

19X1
Oct. 1. Received a 4-month, 15% note from Joseph Dowd for an extension of time on his account, $720.00. NR7.
Nov. 1. Issued a 6-month, 14% note, $4,000.00. NP10.

19X2
Feb. 1. Received cash for the maturity value of NR7: principal, $720.00, plus interest, $36.00; total, $756.00. R194.
May 1. Paid cash for the maturity value of NP10: principal, $4,000.00, plus interest, $280.00; total, $4,280.00. C426.

INSTRUCTIONS:

1. Open the seven general ledger accounts and record the balances.
2. Use page 14 of a general journal. Journalize the adjusting entries for accrued interest income and accrued interest expense on December 31. Post these entries.
3. Continue to use page 14 of a general journal. Journalize the closing entries for interest income and interest expense. Post these entries.
4. Use page 15 of a general journal. Journalize the reversing entries for accrued interest income and accrued interest expense. Post these entries.
5. Use page 21 of a cash receipts journal. Journalize the receipt of cash for the maturity value of NR7. Post this entry.
6. Use page 22 of a cash payments journal. Journalize the cash payment for the maturity value of NP10. Post this entry.

RECYCLING PROBLEM 26-R Journalizing dividends and preparing a work sheet for a corporation

On December 31 of the current year, Specialty Design Corporation has the following general ledger accounts and balances.

Account Title	Account Balance
Cash	$ 67,277.00
Petty Cash	300.00
Notes Receivable	5,937.00
Interest Receivable	—
Accounts Receivable	26,115.00
Allowance for Uncollectible Accounts	36.00
Merchandise Inventory	142,806.00
Supplies	3,450.00
Prepaid Insurance	12,300.00
Office Equipment	8,787.50

Account Title	Account Balance
Accumulated Depreciation—Office Equipment	1,175.00
Store Equipment	27,125.00
Accumulated Depreciation—Store Equipment	6,251.00
Notes Payable	12,500.00
Interest Payable	—
Accounts Payable	38,945.00
Employee Income Tax Payable	1,732.00
Federal Income Tax Payable	—
FICA Tax Payable	2,000.00
Sales Tax Payable	4,980.00
Unemployment Tax Payable—Federal	35.00
Unemployment Tax Payable—State	236.25
Health Insurance Premiums Payable	1,487.00
Dividends Payable	7,000.00
Capital Stock	100,000.00
Retained Earnings	60,487.25
Dividends	28,000.00
Income Summary	—
Sales	1,340,500.00
Sales Discount	3,361.00
Sales Returns and Allowances	3,415.00
Purchases	982,935.00
Purchases Discount	4,807.00
Purchases Returns and Allowances	3,678.00
Advertising Expense	4,039.00
Credit Card Fee Expense	13,446.00
Depreciation Expense—Office Equipment	—
Depreciation Expense—Store Equipment	—
Insurance Expense	—
Miscellaneous Expense	2,225.00
Payroll Taxes Expense	16,910.00
Rent Expense	42,600.00
Salary Expense	179,890.00
Supplies Expense	—
Uncollectible Accounts Expense	—
Utilities Expense	3,227.00
Gain on Plant Assets	75.00
Interest Income	690.00
Cash Short and Over (cash short)	14.00
Interest Expense	1,460.00
Loss on Plant Assets	95.00
Federal Income Tax Expense	10,900.00

INSTRUCTIONS:

1. Complete a work sheet for the current year ended December 31. Record the adjustments on the work sheet using the following information.

Adjustment Information, December 31

Accrued interest income	$ 140.00
Uncollectible accounts expense estimated as 2.0% of sales on account. Sales on account for year, $453,800.00.	
Merchandise inventory	140,700.00
Supplies inventory	450.00
Value of prepaid insurance	4,100.00
Annual depreciation expense—office equipment	950.00

Adjustment Information, December 31

Annual depreciation expense—store equipment...............	4,065.00
Accrued interest expense..............................	290.00
Federal income tax for the year.......................	12,146.50

2. Use page 1 of a cash payments journal. Journalize the following transaction completed during the next year. The abbreviation for check is C.

Jan. 20. Paid cash for quarterly dividend declared December 20, $7,000.00. C568.

RECYCLING PROBLEM 27-R Preparing financial statements and end-of-fiscal-period entries for a corporation

Just-In-Time Supplies completed the work sheet on pages C-24 and C-25 for the current year ended December 31.

INSTRUCTIONS:

1. Prepare an income statement. Calculate and record the following component percentages. (a) Cost of merchandise sold. (b) Gross profit on operations. (c) Total operating expenses. (d) Income from operations. (e) Net addition or deduction resulting from other revenue and expenses. (f) Net income before federal income tax. Round percentage calculations to the nearest 0.1%.

2. Analyze Just-In-Time's income statement by determining if component percentages are within acceptable levels. If any component percentage is not within an acceptable level, suggest steps that the company should take. Just-In-Time considers the following component percentages acceptable.

Cost of merchandise sold	Not more than 73.0%
Gross profit on operations...........................	Not less than 27.0%
Total operating expenses.............................	Not more than 20.0%
Income from operations...............................	Not less than 7.0%
Net deduction from other revenue and expenses	Not more than 0.5%
Net income before federal income tax	Not less than 6.5%

3. Prepare a statement of stockholders' equity. Use the following additional information.

January 1 balance of capital stock account	$80,000.00
(16,000 shares issued for $5.00 per share)	
January 1 balance of retained earnings account	25,928.60

4. Prepare a balance sheet.

5. Calculate Just-In-Time's (a) working capital and (b) current ratio. Determine if these items are within acceptable levels. Just-In-Time considers the following levels acceptable.

Working capital	Not less than $90,000.00
Current ratio................................	Between 2.0 to 1 and 2.5 to 1

6. Use page 13 of a general journal. Journalize the adjusting entries.

7. Use page 14 of a general journal. Journalize the closing entries.

8. Use page 1 of a general journal. Journalize the reversing entries for the accrued interest income and accrued interest expense.

RECYCLING PROBLEM 28-R Journalizing entries to form and liquidate business organizations

INSTRUCTIONS:

1. Journalize the following transaction. Use page 1 of a cash receipts journal. Source documents are abbreviated as follows: receipt, R.

Feb. 1, 19x1. Received cash from Paul Edwall as an investment, $2,500.00. R1.

Paul Edwall has decided to terminate his business and start a partnership with a friend.

2. Journalize the following transactions. Use page 7 of a cash receipts journal and a cash payments journal. Source documents are abbreviated as follows: check, C; receipt, R. (Continued on page C-26.)

Just-In-Time Supplies
Work Sheet
For Year Ended December 31, 19--

	TRIAL BALANCE		ADJUSTMENTS		INCOME STATEMENT		BALANCE SHEET	
ACCOUNT TITLE	DEBIT	CREDIT	DEBIT	CREDIT	DEBIT	CREDIT	DEBIT	CREDIT
1 Cash	3081700						3081700	
2 Petty Cash	30000						30000	
3 Notes Receivable	540000						540000	
4 Interest Receivable			(a) 10800				10800	
5 Accounts Receivable	2350300						2350300	
6 Allowance for Uncollectible Accts.		3200		(b) 484056				487256
7 Merchandise Inventory	8852540		(c) 791400				9643940	
8 Supplies	310000			(d) 270000			40000	
9 Prepaid Insurance	1107000			(e) 738000			369000	
10 Office Equipment	791000						791000	
11 Accum. Depr.—Office Equipment		1057000		(f) 85500				1142500
12 Store Equipment	4441200						4441200	
13 Accum. Depr.—Store Equipment		5625590		(g) 365850				5991440
14 Notes Payable		1125000						1125000
15 Interest Payable				(h) 28125				28125
16 Accounts Payable		3444590						3444590
17 Employee Income Tax Payable		155800						155800
18 Federal Income Tax Payable				(i) 100710				100710
19 FICA Tax Payable		180000						180000
20 Sales Tax Payable		448200						448200
21 Unemployment Tax Payable—Federal		3200						3200
22 Unemployment Tax Payable—State		21600						21600
23 Health Insurance Premiums Payable		133830						133830
24 Dividends Payable		600000						600000
25 Capital Stock		8000000						8000000

Account Title	Trial Balance Debit	Trial Balance Credit	Adjustments Debit	Adjustments Credit	Income Statement Debit	Income Statement Credit	Balance Sheet Debit	Balance Sheet Credit
Retained Earnings		2592860						2592860
Dividends	2400000						2400000	
Income Summary				(c) 791400		791400		
Sales		119764000				119764000		
Sales Discount	302490				302490			
Sales Returns and Allowances	307350				307350			
Purchases	88464150				88464150			
Purchases Discount		432630				432630		
Purchases Returns and Allowances		331020				331020		
Advertising Expense	363500				363500			
Credit Card Fee Expense	1210140				1210140			
Depr. Expense—Office Equipment			(f) 855500		855500			
Depr. Expense—Store Equipment			(g) 3658850		3658850			
Insurance Expense			(e) 738000		738000			
Miscellaneous Expense	200250				200250			
Payroll Taxes Expense	1521900				1521900			
Rent Expense	3840000				3840000			
Salary Expense	16190100				16190100			
Supplies Expense			(d) 270000		270000			
Uncollectible Accounts Expense			(b) 484056		484056			
Utilities Expense	290400				290400			
Gain on Plant Assets		7000				7000		
Interest Income		60000		(a) 10800		70800		
Cash Short and Over	750				750			
Interest Expense	382950		(h) 28125		411075			
Loss on Plant Assets	8500				8500			
Federal Income Tax Expense	985000		(i) 100710		1085710			
	137971220	137971220	2874441	2874441	116139721	121396850	18440811	23697940
Net Income after Federal Inc. Tax					5257129			5257129
					121396850	121396850	23697940	23697940

April 1, 19x3. Received cash from sale of supplies, $1,500.00; book value of supplies, $1,850.00. R145.

April 1, 19x3. Paid cash to all creditors: Addams Supply, $900.00; Burnstein and Associates, $1,000.00. C322-323.

April 2, 19x3. Recorded final distribution of remaining cash to Paul Edwall, $3,500.00. C324.

Paul Edwall and Leonard Simm agree to form a partnership called OfficeMart.

3. Journalize the following transaction. Use page 1 of a cash receipts journal. Source documents are abbreviated as follows: receipt, R.

April 15, 19x3. Received cash from partners as initial investment: from Paul Edwall, $4,500.00; from Leonard Simm, $2,500.00. R1-2.

Mr. Edwall and Mr. Simm agreed to terminate their business and form a corporation with other business associates.

4. Journalize the following transactions. Use page 9 of a cash receipts journal and a cash payments journal. The partnership agreement states that all losses or gains on sale are to be divided equally between the partners. Source documents are abbreviated as follows: check, C; receipt, R.

May 1, 19x7. Received cash from sale of equipment, $4,000.00; original cost, $10,000.00; total accumulated depreciation recorded to date, $7,000.00. R122.

May 1, 19x7. Paid cash to all creditors: Douglas Distributors, $2,200.00; Irwin Supply Company, $500.00. C187-188.

May 2, 19x7. Recorded final distribution of remaining cash to partners: to Paul Edwall, $5,600.00; to Leonard Simm, $8,000.00. C189-190.

Paul Edwall and five associates agree to form a corporation, Office Supplies, Inc.

5. Journalize the following transaction. Use page 1 of a cash receipts journal. Source documents are abbreviated as follows: receipt, R.

June 1, 19x7. Received cash for 125,000 shares of $1.00 par-value common stock, $125,000.00. R1-6.

Answers to
Audit Your Understanding

CHAPTER 1, PAGE 11

1. The language of business.
2. Accountants, bookkeepers, accounting clerks, and other general office workers.
3. The American Institute of Certified Public Accountants (AICPA).

CHAPTER 1, PAGE 13

1. Communication is the transfer of information between two or more individuals.
2. When an individual disregards his or her principles of right and wrong by choosing the wrong action.
3. **(1)** Is the action illegal? **(2)** Does the action violate company or professional standards? **(3)** Who is affected, and how, by the action?

CHAPTER 2, PAGE 21

1. A business owned by one person.
2. Assets = Liabilities + Owner's Equity.
3. Assets.
4. Liabilities and Owner's Equity.

CHAPTER 2, PAGE 26

1. The left side equals the right side.
2. The right side must be increased.
3. An account is increased by the same amount another account on the same side is decreased.

CHAPTER 2, PAGE 29

1. Assets, liabilities, and owner's equity.
2. Assets.
3. Liabilities and owner's equity.
4. Find the errors before completing any more work.

CHAPTER 3, PAGE 41

1. Increased.
2. Decreased.
3. Decreased.

CHAPTER 3, PAGE 43

1. Assets.
2. Liabilities and owner's equity.
3. Total assets.
4. Total liabilities and owner's equity.

CHAPTER 4, PAGE 55

1. Assets = Liabilities + Owner's Equity

2. **(1)** Account balances increase on the normal balance side of an account. **(2)** Account balances decrease on the side opposite the normal balance side of an account.

CHAPTER 4, PAGE 64

1. **(1)** What accounts are affected? **(2)** How is each account classified? **(3)** How is each account balance changed? **(4)** How is each amount entered in the accounts?
2. Debit.
3. Credit.
4. Debit.
5. Credit.
6. Debit.

CHAPTER 5, PAGE 76

1. General Debit, General Credit, Sales Credit, Cash Debit, and Cash Credit.
2. By date.
3. Checks, calculator tapes, receipts, memorandums.
4. Source documents are one way to verify the accuracy of a specific journal entry.

CHAPTER 5, PAGE 83

1. Date, debit, credit, source document.

CHAPTER 5, PAGE 87

1. Cash on hand at the beginning of the month, plus total cash received, less total cash paid.

2. (1) Rule a single line across all amount columns directly below the last entry to indicate that the columns are to be added. **(2)** On the next line, write the date in the Date column. **(3)** Write the word, *Totals*, in the Account Title column. **(4)** Write each column total below the single line. **(5)** Rule double lines below the column totals across all amount columns. The double lines mean that the totals have been verified as correct.

CHAPTER 6, PAGE 103

1. The first digit indicates in which general ledger division the account is located. The second and third digits indicate the location of the account within that division.
2. (1) Write the account title in the heading. **(2)** Write the account number in the heading.

CHAPTER 6, PAGE 112

1. (1) Write the date in the Date column of the account. **(2)** Write the journal page number in the Post. Ref. column of the account. **(3)** Write the amount in the Debit or Credit column. **(4)** Calculate and write the new account balance in the Balance Debit or Balance Credit column. **(5)** Write the account number in the Post. Ref. column of the journal.

CHAPTER 7, PAGE 140

1. Blank endorsement, special endorsement, and restrictive endorsement.
2. (1) Write the amount of the check in the space after the dollar sign at the top of the stub. **(2)** Write the date of the check on the Date line at the top of the stub. **(3)** Write to whom the check is to be paid on the To line at the top of the stub. **(4)** Record the purpose of the check on the For line. **(5)** Write the amount of the check in the amount column at the bottom of the stub on the line with the words "Amt. this Check." **(6)** Calculate the new checking account balance and record the new balance in the amount column on the last line of the stub.

CHAPTER 7, PAGE 147

1. (1) Calculate the adjusted check stub balance. **(2)** Calculate the adjusted bank balance. **(3)** Compare adjusted balances.

2.

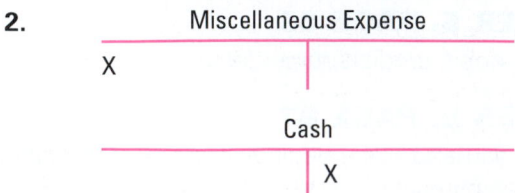

CHAPTER 7, PAGE 153

1.

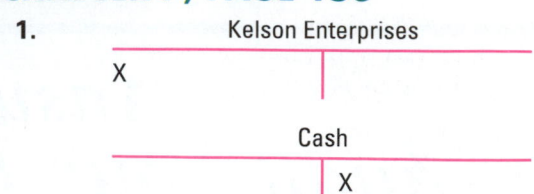

2.

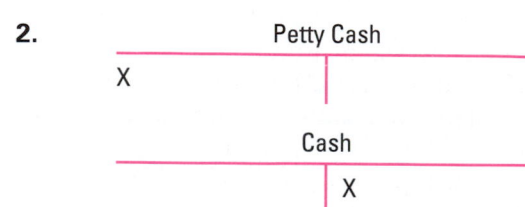

3.

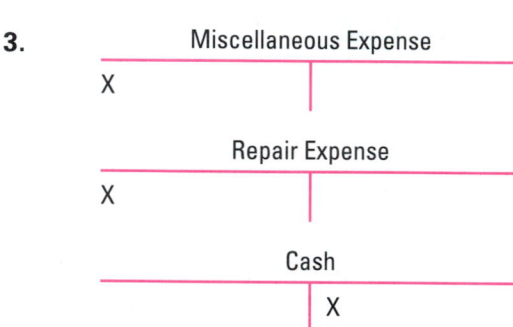

CHAPTER 8, PAGE 183

1. One year.
2. Name of business, name of report, and date of report.
3. (1) What is the balance of the account? **(2)** What should the balance be for this account? **(3)** What must be done to correct the account balance? **(4)** What adjustment is made?
4. Assets, liabilities, and owner's equity accounts.
5. Revenue and expense accounts.

CHAPTER 8, PAGE 187

1. Subtract the smaller total from the larger total to find the difference.
2. The difference between two column totals can be divided evenly by 9.
3. A slide.

CHAPTER 9, PAGE 199

1. Heading, revenue, expenses, and net income or net loss.
2. Total Expenses ÷ Total Sales = Total Expenses Component Percentage.
3. Net Income ÷ Total Sales = Net Income Component Percentage.

CHAPTER 9, PAGE 204

1. Heading, assets, liabilities, and owner's equity.
2. Capital Account Balance + Net Income − Drawing Account Balance = Current Capital.

CHAPTER 10, PAGE 213

1. To update general ledger accounts.
2. Adjustments column of the work sheet.
3. Insurance Expense and Supplies Expense.

CHAPTER 10, PAGE 223

1. Beginning balances.
2. Changes in the owner's capital account for a single fiscal period.
3. **(1)** An entry to close income statement accounts with credit balances. **(2)** An entry to close income statement accounts with debit balances. **(3)** An entry to record net income or net loss and close the income summary account. **(4)** An entry to close the drawing account.

CHAPTER 10, PAGE 227

1. To assure a reader that a balance has not been omitted.
2. Only those with balances (permanent accounts).
3. Because they are closed and have zero balances.

CHAPTER 11, PAGE 253

1. To save time and space in journalizing transactions.
2.

Purchases	
dr.	cr.
+	−

Accounts Payable	
dr.	cr.
−	+

3. To show that no account title needs to be written.
4. To show that amounts on that line are not to be posted individually.
5. A business purchases merchandise to sell but buys supplies for use in the business. Supplies are not intended for sale.

CHAPTER 11, PAGE 259

1. Cash is decreased by a credit.
2. Cash and merchandise.
3. A journal entry made to correct an error in the ledger.

CHAPTER 12, PAGE 273

1. Price of Goods × Sales Tax Rate = Sales Tax
2.

Sales Tax Payable	
dr.	cr.
−	+

Accounts Receivable	
dr.	cr.
+	−

3. Cash is increased; Accounts Receivable and the customer's account are decreased.

CHAPTER 12, PAGE 277

1. The columns are totaled and the equality of debits and credits is verified.
2. **(1)** Write the page number at the top of the journal. **(2)** Write the date in the Date column. **(3)** Write the words, Brought Forward, in the Account Title column. A check mark is also placed in the Post. Ref. column to show that nothing on this line needs to be posted. **(4)** Record the column totals brought forward from page 21 of the journal.
3. Cash on hand at the beginning of the month, *plus* total cash received during the month, *less* total cash paid during the month, *equals* cash balance on hand at end of the month. Cash is proved if the balance on the next unused check stub is the same as the cash proof.

CHAPTER 13, PAGE 290

1. An account in a general ledger that summarizes all accounts in a subsidiary ledger.
2. The balance of a controlling account equals the total of all account balances in its related subsidiary ledger.
3. Debit, Credit, Debit Balance, and Credit Balance.
4. Accounts for vendors from whom items are purchased or bought on account.
5. Accounts for charge customers.

CHAPTER 13, PAGE 298

1. Credit Balance. Because accounts payable are liabilities and liabilities have normal credit balances.
2. By writing the vendor name and vendor number on the heading of the ledger account.
3. **(1)** Write the date in the Date column of the account. **(2)** Write the journal page number in the Post. Ref. column of the account. **(3)** Write the credit amount in the Credit amount column of the account. **(4)** Add the amount in the Credit amount column to the previous balance in the Credit Balance column. Write the new account balance in the Credit Balance column. **(5)** Write the vendor number in the Post. Ref. column of the journal. The vendor number shows that the posting for this entry is completed.
4. Debit Balance. Because accounts receivable are assets and assets have normal debit balances.

CHAPTER 13, PAGE 302

1. By preparing a schedule of accounts receivable and schedule of accounts payable.
2. All vendor accounts that have balances.
3. When the total of the schedule of accounts receivable equals the balance of the accounts receivable general ledger account.

CHAPTER 14, PAGE 330

1. The total amount earned by all employees for a pay period.
2. Overtime hours X overtime rate (time and one half).
3. 3½.
4. $400.00.

CHAPTER 14, PAGE 334

1. Marital status and withholding allowance.
2. Both the employer and employee.
3. Employer.
4. Employer.

CHAPTER 14, PAGE 341

1. The total earnings and payroll withholdings of all employees.
2. By using tax tables provided by the federal government.
3. By subtracting total deductions from total earnings.

CHAPTER 14, PAGE 344

1. To enable the company to complete required tax forms at the end of the year.
2. Recording information on several forms with one writing.

CHAPTER 15, PAGE 359

1. Salary Expense.
2. Employee Income Tax Payable.
3. FICA Tax Payable.

CHAPTER 15, PAGE 363

1. Employers must pay 8% of each employee's total earnings up to the tax base.
2. Employers must pay 0.8% of total earnings of each employee up to a base of $7,000.00.

CHAPTER 15, PAGE 367

1. Federal income tax and FICA taxes.
2. By January 31.
3. Federal income tax and FICA employee and employer taxes.

CHAPTER 16, PAGE 398

1. A columnar form on which the financial information needed to prepare financial statements is summarized.
2. To prove the equality of debits and credits in the general ledger.
3. Merchandise Inventory.
4. Merchandise Inventory and Income Summary.

CHAPTER 16, PAGE 399

1. Income Statement Debit or Credit column.
2. When the Income Statement Debit column total (costs and expenses) is larger than the Credit column total (revenue).

3. Balance Sheet Debit.

CHAPTER 16, PAGE 404

1. Trial Balance Debit and Credit columns; Adjustments Debit and Credit columns; Adjusted Trial Balance Debit and Credit columns; Income Statement Debit and Credit columns; and Balance Sheet Debit and Credit columns.
2. Trial balance amounts after adjustments are extended to the Adjusted Trial Balance columns and the Adjusted Trial Balance columns are proved before extending amounts to the Income Statement and Balance Sheet columns.

CHAPTER 17, PAGE 420

1. The cost of merchandise sold section.
2. Beginning merchandise inventory, *plus* purchases, *equals* total cost of merchandise available for sale, *less* ending merchandise inventory, *equals* cost of merchandise sold.
3. By comparing it with the amount calculated on the work sheet.
4. Net loss.

CHAPTER 17, PAGE 428

1. Each partner's share of net income or net loss.
2. Beginning capital, additional investments, and withdrawal of assets.
3. Schedules of accounts receivable and schedule of accounts payable.

CHAPTER 18, PAGE 437

1. Insurance Expense and Income Summary.
2. Because the explanation "Adjusting Entries" is recorded in the Account Title column to explain all of the adjusting entries that follow.
3. Adjusting entry for merchandise inventory.

CHAPTER 18, PAGE 452

1. Income Statement and Balance Sheet columns of the work sheet and a distribution of net income statement.
2. Income Summary.
3. An amount equal to its balance is recorded on the side opposite the balance.
4. General ledger accounts with balances.

CHAPTER 19, PAGE 476

1. An organization with the legal rights of a person and which may be owned by many persons.
2. To allow accounting clerks to specialize in recording one kind of transaction to improve efficiency.
3. The purchase invoice received from a vendor.

CHAPTER 19, PAGE 489

1. To quote different prices for different quantities purchased without changing catalog or list prices.
2. To encourage prompt payment.

3. Cash, Cash Short and Over.
4. Writing the account number in parentheses below the journal column total.

CHAPTER 19, PAGE 496

1. A debit memorandum.
2. Only merchandise purchased on account is recorded in the purchases journal. Supplies are not merchandise.
3. A listing of vendor accounts, account balances, and total amount due all vendors.

CHAPTER 20, PAGE 523

1. Accounts Receivable is debited; Sales Tax Payable and Sales are credited.
2. Posted individually to the customer account in the accounts receivable ledger.
3. Individual items should be posted frequently to the customer accounts in the accounts receivable ledger. Column totals are posted to the general ledger at the end of each month.

CHAPTER 20, PAGE 531

1. Because the sales journal is used only for sales on account and because they are receipts of cash.
2. Sales invoice amount times sales discount rate.
3. Total invoiced amount, *less* sales discount, *less* sales tax reduction *equals* cash received.
4. The Debit column is used for cash receipts on account with sales discounts and the Credit column is used for cash and credit card sales.

CHAPTER 20, PAGE 536

1. Contra revenue account in the operating revenue division.
2. Sales Tax Payable is debited (decreased).
3. Accounts receivable ledger.

CHAPTER 20, PAGE 542

1. Bill of lading.
2. Receiving payment for the sale.
3. Receiving the merchandise.

CHAPTER 21, PAGE 573

1. To record the expense in the same fiscal period in which the sales were made. This is an application of the Matching Expenses with Revenue accounting concept.
2. At the time the expense is recorded, the actual amount is not known because the accounts have not yet become uncollectible. Therefore, an estimate is needed.
3. Credit.
4. Debit.

CHAPTER 21, PAGE 579

1. General ledger and accounts receivable ledger.

2. The words "Written off" are written in the Item column. To show the full credit history for the customer.
3. Record an entry for reopening the customer account. Record an entry for the cash receipt.

CHAPTER 22, PAGE 592

1. Equipment, buildings, and land.
2. Debit.
3. Physical depreciation and functional depreciation.
4. Original cost, estimated salvage value, and estimated useful life.
5. Original cost less estimated salvage value.

CHAPTER 22, PAGE 598

1. (1) Annual depreciation expense, (2) accumulated depreciation, and (3) ending book value.
2. None.
3. Credit.
4. No effect on the plant asset account; the amount is recorded in the accumulated depreciation account.
5. Debit Depreciation Expense, credit Accumulated Depreciation.

CHAPTER 22, PAGE 606

1. (1) Original cost and accumulated depreciation are removed from the accounts. (2) Cash or other asset received is recognized. (3) Gain or loss on the disposal is recognized.
2. By calculating the difference between the book value of the asset disposed of and the value of the asset received.
3. When additional depreciation expense should be recorded for the time from the last adjustment for depreciation expense and the date of disposal.
4. Annual depreciation expense divided by 12 equals monthly depreciation expense. Monthly depreciation expense is multiplied by the number of the months in the partial year.

CHAPTER 22, PAGE 609

1. In the earlier years of the plant asset's life.
2. Only enough depreciation expense to reduce the book value to the salvage value.
3. Assessors who are elected by citizens or trained by the government.

CHAPTER 23, PAGE 628

1. Periodic inventory, perpetual inventory.
2. At the end of a fiscal period.
3. Universal Product Code.

CHAPTER 23, PAGE 635

1. Fifo.
2. Lifo.
3. Weighted-average.

4. By estimating inventory using the gross profit method of estimating inventory.

CHAPTER 24, PAGE 646

1. The maturity value of an interest-bearing note is the principal plus the interest; the maturity value of a non-interest-bearing note is the principal only.
2. $50 ($500 $\times$ 10% $\times$ 1).
3. $416 ($400 $\times$ 8% $\times$ $\frac{6}{12}$).
4. February 22.
5. May 22 (March 23–31, 8 days; April 1–30, 30 days; May 1–22, 22 days).

CHAPTER 24, PAGE 651

1. Credit.
2. Because it is a financial expense rather than an expense of normal operations.
3. When the note is discounted; it is a non-interest-bearing note.

CHAPTER 24, PAGE 655

1. Debit.
2. Zero.
3. Because it is revenue from investment rather than normal operations.
4. Not necessarily; they may continue to try to collect the account before writing it off.

CHAPTER 25, PAGE 671

1. Debit Interest Receivable, credit Interest Income.
2. Debit Interest Income, credit Income Summary.
3. A reversing entry.
4. Principal + Interest = Maturity Value.

CHAPTER 25, PAGE 677

1. Debit Interest Expense, credit Interest Payable.
2. Debit Income Summary, credit Interest Expense.
3. A reversing entry.

CHAPTER 26, PAGE 688

1. The board of directors.
2. Debit Dividends, credit Dividends Payable.
3. Debit Dividends Payable, credit Cash.

CHAPTER 26, PAGE 695

1. The adjustment for federal income tax expense.
2. Debit Merchandise Inventory, credit Income Summary.
3. Total federal income tax expense minus estimated taxes already paid in quarterly installments.

CHAPTER 27, PAGE 716

1. A component percentage.
2. A statement of stockholders' equity.
3. Cash, accounts receivable, merchandise inventory, supplies, and prepaid insurance.

4. Working capital and current ratio.

CHAPTER 27, PAGE 725

1. The work sheet's Income Statement Credit column.
2. Retained Earnings.
3. To prove the equality of debits and credits in the general ledger.

CHAPTER 28, PAGE 755

1. A proprietorship.
2. Debit Cash, Credit Capital.
3. Distributing remaining cash to the owner.
4. Capital is decreased with a debit for the amount of loss.

CHAPTER 28, PAGE 760

1. A partnership agreement.
2. The partnership must be legally dissolved and a new partnership established.
3. The balance of the cash account which includes cash received from buyers of the noncash assets.
4. The partnership's creditors are paid first and any remaining cash is distributed to the partners.

CHAPTER 28, PAGE 763

1. A share of stock.
2. The articles of incorporation.
3. Corporations pay federal income tax on their net income and stockholders pay an additional personal income tax on profits distributed to them as dividends.
4. Debit Cash, credit Capital Stock.
5. Because they are based on the idea of perpetual life.

Glossary

Account: a record summarizing all the information pertaining to a single item in the accounting equation. (p. 22)

Accountant: a person who plans, summarizes, analyzes, and interprets accounting information. (p. 6)

Account balance: the amount in an account. (p. 22)

Accounting: planning, recording, analyzing, and interpreting financial information. (p. 5)

Accounting clerk: a person who records, sorts, and files accounting information. (p. 7)

Accounting cycle: the series of accounting activities included in recording financial information for a fiscal period. (p. 227)

Accounting equation: an equation showing the relationship among assets, liabilities, and owner's equity. (p. 21)

Accounting period: see *fiscal period*.

Accounting records: organized summaries of a business' financial activities. (p. 5)

Accounting system: a planned process for providing financial information that will be useful to management. (p. 5)

Account number: the number assigned to an account. (p. 100)

Accounts payable ledger: a subsidiary ledger containing only accounts for vendors from whom items are purchased or bought on account. (p. 285)

Accounts receivable ledger: a subsidiary ledger containing only accounts for charge customers. (p. 285)

Account title: the name given to an account. (p. 22)

Accrued expenses: expenses incurred in one fiscal period but not paid until a later fiscal period. (p. 671)

Accrued interest expense: interest incurred but not yet paid. (p. 672)

Accrued interest income: interest earned but not yet received. (p. 665)

Accrued revenue: revenue earned in one fiscal period but not received until a later fiscal period. (p. 665)

Accumulated depreciation: the total amount of depreciation expense that has been recorded since the purchase of a plant asset. (p. 593)

Addend: each number to be added. (p. B-4)

Adjusting entries: journal entries recorded to update general ledger accounts at the end of a fiscal period. (p. 211)

Adjustments: changes recorded on a work sheet to update general ledger accounts at the end of a fiscal period. (p. 175)

Allowance method of recording losses from uncollectible accounts: crediting the estimated value of uncollectible accounts to a contra account. (p. 570)

Articles of incorporation: a written application requesting permission to form a corporation. (p. 761)

Assessed value: the value of an asset determined by tax authorities for the purpose of calculating taxes. (p. 608)

Asset: anything of value that is owned. (p. 20)

Automated accounting: an accounting system in which data are recorded and reported mostly by using automated machines. (p. 123)

Automated accounting system: a collection of computer programs designed to computerize accounting procedures. (p. 124)

Automatic check deposit: depositing payroll checks directly to an employee's checking or savings account in a specific bank. (p. 340)

Bad debts: see *uncollectible accounts*.

Balance ruled account: see *account*.

Balance sheet: a financial statement that reports assets, liabilities, and owner's equity on a specific date. (p. 26)

Bank discount: interest collected in advance on a note. (p. 650)

Bank statement: a report of deposits, withdrawals, and bank balance sent to a depositor by a bank. (p. 140)

Batch: a group of journal entries. (p. 309)

Bill of exchange: see *draft*.

Bill of lading: a receipt signed by the authorized agent of a transportation company for merchandise received that also serves as a contract for the delivery of merchandise. (p. 593)

Blank endorsement: an endorsement consisting of only the endorser's signature. (p. 137)

Board of directors: a group of persons elected by the stockholders to manage a corporation. (p. 686)

Book inventory: see *perpetual inventory*.

Bookkeeper: a person who does general accounting work plus some summarizing and analyzing of accounting information. (p. 7)

Book value: the difference between an asset's account balance and its related contra account balance. (p. 713)

Book value of accounts receivable: the difference between the balance of Accounts Receivable and its contra account, Allowance for Uncollectible Accounts. (p. 574)

Book value of a plant asset: the original cost of a plant asset minus accumulated depreciation. (p. 593)

Business ethics: the use of personal ethics in making business decisions. (p. 12)

Capital: the account used to summarize the owner's equity in the business. (p. 22)

Capital stock: total shares of ownership in a corporation. (p. 472)

Cash discount: a deduction that a vendor allows on the invoice amount to encourage prompt payment. (p. 480)

Cash over: a petty cash on hand amount that is more than a recorded amount. (p. 485)

Cash payments journal: a special journal used to record only cash payment transactions. (p. 476)

Cash receipts journal: a special journal used to record only cash receipt transactions. (p. 523)

Cash sale: a sale in which cash is received for the total amount of the sale at the time of the transaction. (p. 268)

Cash short: a petty cash on hand amount that is less than a recorded amount. (p. 483)

Cell: the space on an electronic spreadsheet where a column intersects with a row. (p. 145)

Cell address: the column letter and row number of a cell. (p. 145)

Charge sale: see *sale on account*.

Chart of accounts: a list of accounts used by a business. (p. 55)

Check: a business form ordering a bank to pay cash from a bank account. (p. 74)

Checking account: a bank account from which payments can be ordered by a depositor. (p. 135)

Closing entries: journal entries used to prepare temporary accounts for a new fiscal period. (p. 215)

Commercial invoice: a statement prepared by the seller of merchandise addressed to the buyer showing a detailed listing and description of merchandise sold, including prices and terms. (p. 540)

Component percentage: the percentage relationship between one financial statement item and the total that includes that item. (p. 197)

Computer program: a set of instructions followed by a computer to process data. (p. 124)

Contra account: an account that reduces a related account on a financial statement. (p. 63)

Contract of sale: a document that details all the terms agreed to by seller and buyer for a sales transaction. (p. 538)

Controlling account: an account in a general ledger that summarizes all accounts in a subsidiary ledger. (p. 285)

Corporation: an organization with the legal rights of a person and which may be owned by many persons. (p. 472)

Correcting entry: a journal entry made to correct an error in the ledger. (p. 258)

Cost of goods sold: see *cost of merchandise sold*.

Cost of merchandise: the price a business pays for goods it purchases to sell. (p. 247)

Cost of merchandise sold: the total original price of all merchandise sold during a fiscal period. (pp. 411–412)

Credit: an amount recorded on the right side of a T account. (p. 54)

Credit card sale: a sale in which a credit card is used for the total amount of the sale at the time of the transaction. (p. 268)

Credit memorandum: a form prepared by the vendor showing the amount deducted for returns and allowances. (p. 531)

Creditor: a person or organization to whom a liability is owed. (p. 646)

Current assets: cash and other assets expected to be exchanged for cash or consumed within a year. (p. 587)

Current liabilities: liabilities due within a short time, usually within a year. (p. 646)

Current ratio: a ratio that shows the numeric relationship of current assets to current liabilities. (p. 716)

Customer: a person or business to whom merchandise or services are sold. (p. 267)

Data base: a prearranged file in which data can be entered and retrieved. (p. 124)

Date of a note: the day a note is issued. (p. 644)

Debit: an amount recorded on the left side of a T account. (p. 54)

Debit memorandum: a form prepared by the customer showing the price deduction taken by the customer for returns and allowances. (p. 491)

Declaring a dividend: action by a board of directors to distribute corporate earnings to stockholders. (p. 686)

Declining-balance method of depreciation: multiplying the book value at the end of each fiscal period by a constant depreciation rate. (p. 606)

Depreciation expense: the portion of a plant asset's cost that is transferred to an expense account in each fiscal period during a plant asset's useful life. (p. 589)

Difference: the answer to a subtraction problem. (p. B-4)

Discounted note: a note on which interest is paid in advance. (p. 650)

Dishonored check: a check that a bank refuses to pay. (p. 146)

Dishonored note: a note that is not paid when due. (p. 654)

Dissolution: the process of stopping the operation of a business. (p. 751)

Distribution of net income statement: a partnership financial statement showing distribution of net income or net loss to partners. (p. 419)

Dividend: the number to be divided. (p. B-5)

Dividends: earnings distributed to stockholders. (p. 685)

Divisor: the number the dividend will be divided by. (p. B-5)

Double-entry accounting: the recording of debit and credit parts of a transaction. (p. 74)

Draft: a written, signed, and dated order from one party ordering another party, usually a bank, to pay money to a third party. (p. 540)

Electronic funds transfer: a computerized cash payment system that uses electronic impulses to transfer funds. (p. 148)

Electronic spreadsheet: a group of rows and columns displayed on a computer monitor. (p. 145)

Employee earnings record: a business form used to record details affecting payments made to an employee. (p. 341)

Endorsement: a signature or stamp on the back of a check transferring ownership. (p. 137)

Endorsement in full: see *special endorsement.*

Entry: information for each transaction recorded in a journal. (p. 74)

Equities: financial rights to the assets of a business. (p. 21)

Estimated salvage value: the amount an owner expects to receive when a plant asset is removed from use. (p. 590)

Ethics: the principles of right and wrong that guide an individual in making decisions. (p. 12)

Exhibit: see *supporting schedule.*

Expense: a decrease in owner's equity resulting from the operation of a business. (p. 38)

Exports: goods or services shipped out of a seller's home country to a foreign country. (p. 538)

Face amount: see *principal of a note.*

Federal Insurance Contributions Act: see *FICA tax.*

Federal unemployment tax: a federal tax used for state and federal administrative expenses of the unemployment program. (pp. 333–334)

FICA tax: a federal tax paid by employees and employers for old-age, survivors, disability, and hospitalization insurance. (p. 333)

Fifo: see *first-in, first-out inventory costing method.*

File maintenance: the procedure for arranging accounts in a general ledger, assigning account numbers, and keeping records current. (pp. 101–104)

First-in, first-out inventory costing method: using the price of merchandise purchased first to calculate the cost of merchandise sold first. (p. 629)

Fiscal period: the length of time for which a business summarizes and reports financial information. (p. 171)

Gain on plant assets: revenue that results when a plant asset is sold for more than book value. (p. 601)

General amount column: a journal amount column that is not headed with an account title. (p. 73)

General journal: a journal with two amount columns in which all kinds of entries can be recorded. (p. 491)

General ledger: a ledger that contains all accounts needed to prepare financial statements. (p. 100)

General office clerk: a person who does general kinds of office tasks, including some accounting tasks. (p. 8)

Gross earnings: see *total earnings*.

Gross pay: see *total earnings*.

Gross profit method of estimating an inventory: estimating inventory by using the previous years' percentage of gross profit on operations. (p. 633)

Gross profit on sales: the revenue remaining after cost of merchandise sold has been deducted. (p. 414)

Imports: goods or services bought from a foreign country and brought into a buyer's home country. (p. 538)

Income statement: a financial statement showing the revenue and expenses for a fiscal period. (p. 178)

Interest: an amount paid for the use of money for a period of time. (p. 644)

Interest-bearing note: a promissory note that requires the payment of principal plus interest when the note is due. (p. 644)

Interest expense: the interest accrued on money borrowed. (p. 746)

Interest income: the interest earned on money loaned. (p. 653)

Interest rate of a note: the percentage of the principal that is paid for use of the money. (p. 644)

Internal Revenue Service (IRS): the branch of the U.S. Treasury Department concerned with enforcement and collection of income taxes. (pp. 171, 635, 694)

Inventory: the amount of goods on hand. (p. 393)

Inventory card: see *stock record*.

Inventory record: a form used during a periodic inventory to record information about each item of merchandise on hand. (p. 626)

Invoice: a form describing the goods sold, the quantity, and the price. (p. 249)

Journal: a form for recording transactions in chronological order. (p. 73)

Journal entry: see *entry*.

Journalizing: recording transactions in a journal. (p. 73)

Last-in, first-out inventory costing method: using the price of merchandise purchased last to calculate the cost of merchandise sold first. (p. 630)

Ledger: a group of accounts. (p. 100)

Letter of credit: a letter issued by a bank guaranteeing that a named individual or business will be paid a specified amount provided stated conditions are met. (p. 539)

Liability: an amount owed by a business. (p. 21)

Lifo: see *last-in, first-out inventory costing method*.

Liquidation: the process of paying all liabilities of a business and distributing remaining cash to the owner(s). (p. 751)

List price: a business' printed or catalog price. (p. 479)

Long-term liabilities: liabilities owed for more than a year. (p. 713)

Loss on plant assets: loss that results when a plant asset is sold for less than book value. (p. 604)

Maker of a note: the person or business who signs a note and thus promises to make payment. (p. 644)

Management accountant: see *private accountant*.

Manual accounting: an accounting system in which data are recorded and reported mostly by hand. (p. 123)

Markup: the amount added to the cost of merchandise to establish the selling price. (p. 247)

Maturity date of a note: the date a note is due. (p. 644)

Maturity value: the amount that is due on the maturity date of a note. (p. 644)

Medicare: the federal health insurance program for people who have reached retirement age. (p. 332)

Memorandum: a form on which a brief message is written describing a transaction. (p. 76)

Menu: a list of options from which an activity may be selected. (p. 126)

Merchandise: goods that a merchandising business purchases to sell. (p. 246)

Merchandise inventory: the amount of goods on hand for sale to customers. (p. 393)

Merchandising business: a business that purchases and sells goods. (p. 246)

Minuend: the top number or first number of a subtraction problem. (p. B-4)

Multiplicand: the number to be multiplied. (p. B-4)

Multiplier: the number of times the multiplicand will be multiplied. (p. B-4)

Net income: the difference between total revenue and total expenses when total revenue is greater. (p. 180)

Net loss: the difference between total revenue and total expenses when total expenses is greater. (p. 182)

Net pay: the total earnings paid to an employee after payroll taxes and other deductions. (p. 337)

Net purchases: total purchases less purchases discount and purchases returns and allowances. (p. 707)

Net sales: total sales less sales discount and sales returns and allowances. (p. 707)

Nominal account: see *temporary accounts.*

Non-interest-bearing note: a promissory note that requires only the payment of the principal when the note is due. (p. 644)

Note: see *promissory note.*

Notes payable: promissory notes that a business issues to creditors. (p. 646)

Notes receivable: promissory notes that a business accepts from customers. (p. 652)

Number of a note: the number assigned by the maker to identify a specific note. (p. 644)

Opening an account: Writing an account title and number on the heading of an account. (p. 102)

Owner's equity: the amount remaining after the value of all liabilities is subtracted from the value of all assets. (p. 21)

Owners' equity statement: a financial statement that summarizes the changes in owners' equity during a fiscal period. (p. 421)

Partner: each member of a partnership. (p. 246)

Partnership: a business in which two or more persons combine their assets and skills. (p. 246)

Partnership agreement: a written agreement setting forth the conditions under which a partnership is to operate. (p. 756)

Par value: a value assigned to a share of stock and printed on the stock certificate. (p. 762)

Par-value stock: a share of stock that has an authorized value printed on the stock certificate. (p. 762)

Payee of a note: the person or business to whom the amount of a note is payable. (p. 644)

Pay period: the period covered by a salary payment. (p. 327)

Payroll: the total amount earned by all employees for a pay period. (p. 327)

Payroll register: a business form used to record payroll information. (p. 334)

Payroll taxes: taxes based on the payroll of a business. (p. 330)

Pegboard: a special device used to write the same information at one time on several forms. (p. 343)

Periodic inventory: a merchandise inventory determined by counting, weighing, or measuring items of merchandise on hand. (p. 626)

Permanent accounts: accounts used to accumulate information from one fiscal period to the next. (p. 214)

Perpetual inventory: a merchandise inventory determined by keeping a continuous record of increases, decreases, and balance on hand. (p. 626)

Personal property: all property not classified as real property. (p. 608)

Petty cash: an amount of cash kept on hand and used for making small payments. (p. 149)

Petty cash slip: a form showing proof of a petty cash payment. (p. 151)

Physical inventory: see *periodic inventory.*

Plant asset record: an accounting form on which a business records information about each plant asset. (p. 592)

Plant assets: assets which will be used for a number of years in the operation of a business. (p. 587)

Post-closing trial balance: a trial balance prepared after the closing entries are posted. (pp. 226, 237)

Postdated check: a check with a future date on it. (p. 139)

Posting: transferring information from a journal entry to a ledger account. (p. 103)

Principal of a note: the original amount of a note. (p. 644)

Private accountant: an accountant who is employed by a single business. (p. 7)

Proceeds: the amount received for a note after the bank discount has been deducted. (p. 650)

Product: the answer to a multiplication problem. (p. B-4)

Profit: see *net income.*

Promissory note: a written and signed promise to pay a sum of money at a specified time. (p. 643)

Proprietorship: a business owned by one person. (p. 20)

Proving cash: determining that the amount of cash agrees with the accounting records. (p. 86)

Public accounting firm: a business selling accounting services to the general public. (p. 6)

Purchase invoice: an invoice used as a source document for recording a purchase on account transaction. (p. 249)

Purchase on account: a transaction in which the merchandise purchased is to be paid for later. (p. 249)

Purchases allowance: credit allowed for part of the purchase price of merchandise that is not returned, resulting in a decrease in the customer's accounts payable. (p. 491)

Purchases discount: a cash discount on purchases taken by a customer. (p. 481)

Purchases journal: a special journal used to record only purchase on account transactions. (p. 473)

Purchases return: credit allowed for the purchase price of returned merchandise, resulting in a decrease in the customer's accounts payable. (p. 491)

Quotient: the answer to a division problem. (p. B-5)

Ratio: a comparison between two numbers showing how many times one number exceeds the other. (p. 716)

Real accounts: see *permanent accounts*.

Real estate: see *real property*.

Real property: land and anything attached to the land. (p. 608)

Receipt: a business form giving written acknowledgement for cash received. (p. 75)

Residual value: see *estimated salvage value*.

Restrictive endorsement: an endorsement restricting further transfer of a check's ownership. (p. 138)

Retained earnings: an amount earned by a corporation and not yet distributed to stockholders. (p. 685)

Revenue: an increase in owner's equity resulting from the operation of a business. (p. 37)

Reversing entry: an entry made at the beginning of one fiscal period to reverse an adjusting entry made in the previous fiscal period. (p. 668)

Run date: the date to be printed on reports prepared by a computer. (p. 125)

Salary: the money paid for employee services. (p. 327)

Sale on account: a sale for which cash will be received at a later date. (p. 269)

Sales allowance: credit allowed a customer for part of the sales price of merchandise that is not returned, resulting in a decrease in the vendor's accounts receivable. (p. 531)

Sales discount: a cash discount on sales. (p. 525)

Sales invoice: an invoice used as a source document for recording a sale on account. (p. 269)

Sales journal: a special journal used to record only sales on account transactions. (p. 519)

Sales return: credit allowed a customer for the sales price of returned merchandise, resulting in a decrease in the vendor's accounts receivable. (p. 531)

Sales slip: see *sales invoice*.

Sales tax: a tax on a sale of merchandise or services. (p. 267)

Salvage value: see *estimated salvage value*.

Schedule of accounts payable: a listing of vendor accounts, account balances, and total amount due all vendors. (p. 301)

Schedule of accounts receivable: a listing of customer accounts, account balances, and total amount due from all customers. (p. 301)

Scrap value: see *estimated salvage value*.

Service business: a business that performs an activity for a fee. (p. 20)

Share of stock: each unit of ownership in a corporation. (p. 472)

Sight draft: a draft payable on sight when the holder presents it for payment. (p. 540)

Social security taxes: see *FICA tax*.

Software: programs used to direct the operations of a computer. (p. 124)

Sole proprietorship: see *proprietorship*.

Source document: a business paper from which information is obtained for a journal entry. (p. 74)

Special amount column: a journal amount column headed with an account title. (p. 73)

Special endorsement: an endorsement indicating a new owner of a check. (p. 137)

Special journal: a journal used to record only one kind of transaction. (p. 473)

State unemployment tax: a state tax used to pay benefits to unemployed workers. (p. 334)

Statement of stockholders' equity: a financial statement that shows changes in a corporation's ownership for a fiscal period. (p. 710)

Stockholder: an owner of one or more shares of a corporation. (p. 685)

Stock ledger: a file of stock records for all merchandise on hand. (p. 627)

Stock record: a form used to show the kind of merchandise, quantity received, quantity sold, and balance on hand. (p. 627)

Straight-line method of depreciation: charging an equal amount of depreciation expense for a plant asset in each year of useful life. (p. 590)

Subsidiary ledger: a ledger that is summarized in a single general ledger account. (p. 285)

Subtrahend: the number to be subtracted from the minuend. (p. B-4)

Sum: the answer to an addition problem. (p. B-4)

Supplementary report: see *supporting schedule.*

Supporting schedule: a report prepared to give details about an item on a principal financial statement. (p. 428)

T account: an accounting device used to analyze transactions. (p. 53)

Taking an inventory: see *periodic inventory.*

Tax base: the maximum amount of earnings on which a tax is calculated. (p. 336)

Template: a model of a computer application stored on a computer disk for repeated use. (p. 124)

Temporary accounts: accounts used to accumulate information until it is transferred to the owner's capital account. (p. 215)

Terms of sale: an agreement between a buyer and a seller about payment for merchandise. (p. 250)

Time draft: a draft that is payable at a fixed or determined future time after it is accepted. (p. 541)

Time of a note: the days, months, or years from the date of issue until a note is to be paid. (p. 644)

Total earnings: the total pay due for a pay period before deductions. (p. 329)

Trade acceptance: a form signed by a buyer at the time of a sale of merchandise in which the buyer promises to pay the seller a specified sum of money usually at a stated time in the future. (p. 542)

Trade discount: a reduction in the list price granted to customers. (p. 479)

Trade-in value: see *estimated salvage value.*

Transaction: a business activity that changes assets, liabilities, or owner's equity. (p. 21)

Trial balance: a proof of the equality of debits and credits in a general ledger. (p. 172)

Uncollectible accounts: accounts receivable that cannot be collected. (p. 569)

Vendor: a business from which merchandise is purchased or supplies or other assets are bought. (p. 248)

Vertical analysis: see *component percentage.*

Weighted-average inventory costing method: using the average cost of beginning inventory plus merchandise purchased during a fiscal period to calculate the cost of merchandise sold. (p. 630)

Withdrawal: asset taken out of a business for the owner's personal use. (p. 40)

Withholding allowance: a deduction from total earnings for each person legally supported by a taxpayer. (p. 332)

Working capital: the amount of total current assets less total current liabilities. (p. 715)

Work sheet: a columnar accounting form used to summarize the general ledger information needed to prepare financial statements. (p. 172)

Writing off an account: canceling the balance of a customer account because the customer does not pay. (p. 574)

Index

Bold page numbers indicate illustrations.

prepared by automated accounting software, **741**
preparing, 411–414, 703–708
revenue section of, 195, **195**
showing net income, analyzing, 414–415
showing net loss, **418**
analyzing, 417–418
with two sources of revenue, 198–199, **198**
Income statement account
with credit balance, closing entry for, 216–217, **216**, 719, **720**
with debit balance, closing entry for, 217–219, **218**, 719, **721**
Income statement account balances, extending on work sheet, 179–180, **180**
Income Statement column, checking for errors in, 185
Income Statement option, 235
Income summary account, 215–216, 438, 439
closing entries for, 441, **442**, 719–722, **722**
closing entries to close, 219–220, **219**, 441, **442**
Income tax. *See also* Federal income tax
employee, 331–332
paying liability for, 365–366
recording payment of, 378
Income tax expense adjustment, federal, 693–695
Income tax withholding table, **336**, **337**
Incorporation, articles of, defined, 761
Incoterms, 538
India, professional accounting associations of, 88
Inflation, 279
Institute of Chartered Accountants in Australia, 88
Institute of Chartered Accountants of Bangladesh, 88
Institute of Chartered Accountants of India, 88
Institute of Chartered Accountants of Nigeria, 88
Institute of Chartered Accountants of Pakistan, 88
Institute of Management Accountants, 11
Insurance. *See also* Prepaid insurance
paying cash for, 23–24, **24**, 57–58, **58**, 79, **79**, 129
Insurance adjustment, prepaid, 398–399
analyzing, 398–399
recording on work sheet, 399, **399**
Interest
calculating, 645
defined, 644
summary of accounting for, **656–657**
Interest-bearing note, defined, 644
Interest expense
accrued
adjusting entry for, 672–673, **673**
defined, 672
reversing entry for, 674–675, **675**
closing entry for, 674
defined, 746
Interest expense adjustment, 693
Interest income
accrued
adjusting entry for, 665–666, **667**
defined, 665
reversing entry for, 668–669, **669**
closing entry for, 667
defined, 653
Interest income adjustment, 689–692
Interest rate of a note, defined, 644
Internal control, 575, 576
Internal Revenue Service (IRS), 171, 635, 694

Internal Revenue Service Form 8109, **365**, **366**
Internal Revenue Service Form W-2, 362–363, **363**
Internal Revenue Service Form W-3, 363–364, **364**
Internal Revenue Service Form W-4, **331**, 337
International Access Code, 415
International Chamber of Commerce, 538
International Federation of Accountants, 11
International Franchise Association (IFA), 487
International sales, 537–542
procedures for, **539**
processing and accounting for, 538–541
International travel, 687
International weights and measures, 572
Inventory. *See also* Merchandise inventory
defined, 393
periodic, 626
defined, 626
perpetual, 626–628
defined, 626
using computer, 628
Inventory card. *See* Stock record
Inventory costing method
comparison of, **632**
first-in, first-out, defined, 629
last-in, first-out, defined, 630
summary of, **636**
weighted-average, 630–633
defined, 630
Inventory record, **627**
defined, 626
Inventory system, summary of, 635, **636**
Inventory tax, 628
Invoice
commercial, defined, 540
defined, 249
purchase, **249**
defined, 249
sales, 269–270, **270**, 521
defined, 269
IRS. *See* Internal Revenue Service

J.C. Penney, 60
Jamaica, 632
Japan, 541
computer power, 603
professional accounting associations of, 88
Japanese Institute of Certified Public Accountants, 88
Job description, 359
Journal, 73–74. *See also specific type*
accuracy, 73–74
adjusting entries recorded in, **436**
chronological record, 74
completing at end of month, 86–88
defined, 73
double-entry accounting, 74
five-column, **73**
recording transactions in, 77–83
form, 73
posting to accounts payable ledger, 292–294
posting to accounts receivable ledger, 297–298
posting to general ledger, 103–116
summary of, **116**
ruling at end of month, **86**, 87–88
special, 472–473
defined, 473
Journal entry
checking for errors in, 187
posting payment of payroll, 353–354
processing, 130–131

recording accrued revenue and expenses, **678**
recording cash and credit card sales, **269**
recording cash payment on account, **254**
recording cash payment of expense, **255**
recording cash payment to replenish petty cash, **256**
recording cash receipt on account, **272**
recording cash withdrawal by partner, **257**
recording correcting entry, **259**
recording dishonored check, **148**
recording distribution of remaining cash to owner, **755**
recording distribution of remaining cash to partners, **760**
recording employer payroll taxes, **357**
recording establishing petty cash fund, **150**
recording gain on liquidation of noncash assets, **759**
recording liquidation of liabilities, **755**, **760**
recording loss on liquidation of noncash assets, **754**
recording merchandise withdrawal by partner, **257**
recording partners' initial investment, **757**
recording payment of liability for employee income and FICA tax, **366**
recording payment of liability for federal unemployment tax, **367**
recording payment of liability for state unemployment tax, **367**
recording payment of property tax, **610**
recording a payroll, **353**
recording receiving cash from owner as investment, **752**
recording replenishing of petty cash fund, **153**
recording sale on account, **271**
recording sale of stock at par value, **762**
recording supplies bought on account, **253**
recording supplies bought for cash, **252**
Journalizing
adjusting entry for depreciation expense, 597–598, **598**
adjusting entry for uncollectible account expense, 572, **572**
bank service charge, 144–145, **144**
buying supplies, 251–253
on account, 493–494
cash and credit card sales, 524–525
cash payments, 253–256
for cash purchases, 478–480
for expenses, 478
for purchases on account, 480–483
to replenish petty cash fund, 483–487
cash receipts on account with sales discounts, 526–528
collecting written-off account receivable, 576–577
correcting entries affecting customer accounts, 535–536
defined, 73
depreciation for part of year, 601–602, 604
dishonored check, 147, **148**
employer payroll tax, 357–358
payment of payroll, 352–353
purchases on account, 474, **474**
purchases returns and allowances, 493
sale of plant asset, 602–605
sales on account, 520–521
sales and cash receipts for sales, 267–273
sales returns and allowances, 533–535
summary of, **90**
using cash payments journal, **490**
using cash receipts journal, **532**

Number of a note, defined, 644
Numerals, Arabic, 332

Objective evidence concept, 74
Obsolescence, 589
Office supplies inventory, adjusting entry for, 436
Office supplies inventory adjustment, analyzing, 397
Open Accounting File command, 164
Open Data File command, 161, 620
Opening an account, 102–103, **103**, 292
　defined, 102
Operating license, 751
Options menu, 237
Oral communication, 11
Organizations, professional, 11, 20
Original cost, depreciation expense and, 589
Outlining, 431
Owner's equity, 27, 28
　on balance sheet, 201–204, **204**
　defined, 21
　how transactions change, 37–42
　section of balance sheet, **444**
　summary of changes in, 40–42
　summary of transactions affecting, 43
Owners' equity statement, 421–424, **423**
　with additional investment and net loss, 424, **425**
　defined, 421
　preparing, 421–424

Pakistan, professional accounting associations of, 88
Papyrus, 526
Parentheses, negative amounts in, 416
Parsons School of Design, 109
Partner
　defined, 246
　withdrawal by
　　journalizing, 256–258, **257**
　　merchandise, 313–314
Partnership
　balance sheet for, **427**
　closing entries in journal, **444**
　defined, 246
　dissolving, 757–760
　　legal requirements for, 757–758
　financial statements for, 411
　forming, 755–757
　　accounting transactions for, 756–757
　　legal requirements for, 756
　liquidation of, 758–760
　summary of financial statements for, **429**
Partnership agreement, defined, 756
Par value, defined, 762
Par-value stock, defined, 762
Passport, 687
Payee of a note, defined, 644
Pay period
　biweekly, 327, 351
　defined, 327
　semimonthly, 327, 351
Payroll
　analyzing payment of, 351–352
　defined, 327
　journal entry to record, **353**
　journalizing payment of, 352–353
　posting journal entry for payment of, 353–354
　processing with pegboard, 343–344
　recording, 351–354
　recording payment of, 375–376
Payroll accounting, automated, 375–377

Payroll bank account, 340
Payroll check, 339–341, **339**
　with detachable stub, **340**
Payroll clerk, 351
Payroll deductions, 352
Payroll payment, processing, 376–377
Payroll record, summary of preparing, **344**
Payroll register, 334–339, **334**, **352**, 368
　calculating net pay in, 337
　completing, 338
　defined, 334
　electronic spreadsheet and, 333
　recording deductions in, 335–338
　recording earnings in, 335
Payroll tax, 330–334
　defined, 330
　employer
　　annual reporting of, 363–364
　　journal entry recording, **357**
　　journalizing, 357–358
　　posting, 358–359
　　processing, 376–377
　　recording, 354–360, 376
　paying, 364–368, 377–379
　processing payment of, 379
　reporting, 360–364
Payroll time card, 327–330, **327**
　analyzing, 328
Payroll transactions, recording, 374–379
Pegboard, **343**
　defined, 343
　processing payroll using, 343–344
People's Republic of China, work week in, 271
Period-End Closing command, 237
Periodic inventory, 626
　defined, 626
Permanent account, defined, 214
Perpetual inventory, 626–628
　defined, 626
　using computer, 628
Personal property, defined, 608
Personal visions in business feature
　AMKOR Cleaners, 670
　Architects Associated, 403
　Arriola, Joe, 60
　Avanti Press, 60
　Boo-Boo-Baby, Inc., 109
　Choi, Bryan, 403
　Holder, McCall, and Richardson, LLP, 212
　Hughes, Belinda, 109
　Mitchell, Bert N., 632
　Mitchell, Titus & Co., 632
　NAS, Inc., 287
　Richardson, Tom, 212
　Robbins, Jan, 287
　Showalter, Philip, 480
　Sims, Judy, 443
　Software Spectrum, 443
　VanHorn, Jean Myong, 670
　Peru, 393, 751
　currency of, 28
Petty cash, 149–153, 483
　cash payment to replenish, 255–256, **256**, 312–313, 511
　defined, 149
Petty cash custodian, 483
Petty cash fund
　establishing, 150, **150**, 162
　journalizing cash payments to replenish, 483–487
　making payments from, 151
　replenishing, 151–153, **153**, 163–164
　summary of procedures, **154**
Petty cash over, 485–487
Petty cash report, **152**

for replenishment of petty cash fund with cash over, **486**
for replenishment of petty cash fund with cash short, **484**
Petty cash short, 484–485
Petty cash slip, **151**
　defined, 151
Physical depreciation, 589
Physical inventory. *See* Periodic inventory
Pie graph, 715
Plant asset
　accounts affecting valuation of, 594–596
　book value of, defined, 593
　buying and recording, 587–588
　calculating property tax on, 609
　completed data entry for, **620**
　defined, 587
　disposing of, 598–605
　effects of depreciation on, 588–589
　entries and calculations related to, **610–611**
　journalizing sale of, 602–605
　paying property tax on, 609
　sale for less than book value, 604–605
　sale for more than book value, 601–603
Plant asset account, 594–595
Plant asset data base, 620
Plant asset record, **592**
　defined, 592
　preparing, 592–594
　showing disposal of plant asset, **600**
Plant asset report, for straight-line depreciation method, **621**
Plant Assets Report command, 620
Point-of-sale (POS), 625
Policy manual, 594–595
POS. *See* Point-of-sale
Post-closing trial balance, 226–227, **226**, **237**, 451–452, **451**, 723
　for corporation, **724**
　defined, 226, 237
　prepared by automated accounting software, **743**
　processing, 237
Postdated check, defined, 139
Posting
　to accounts payable ledger, 290–294
　to accounts receivable ledger, 295–299
　adjusting entries, 445, **446–451**
　　for depreciation expense, 598
　　for uncollectible account expense, 573
　Cash Credit column, 110–111, **111**, **288**
　Cash Debit column, 110, **110**
　from cash payments journal to accounts payable ledger, 487, **487**
　from cash payments journal to general ledger, 487–489, **488**
　from cash receipts journal to accounts receivable ledger, 528–529, **528**
　from cash receipts journal to general ledger, 529–531, **530**
　checking for errors in, 186–187
　closing entries, 445, **446–451**
　credit to accounts payable ledger, 292–293, **292**
　credit to accounts receivable ledger, 298, **299**
　debit to accounts payable ledger, 293–294, **293**
　debit to accounts receivable ledger, 297–298, **298**
　defined, 103
　employer payroll taxes entry, 358–359
　entry for collecting written-off account receivable, 578–579
　entry to write off uncollectible account receivable, 575, **576**